Forensic Psychiatry

Forensic Psychiatry
Clinical, Legal and Ethical Issues

Edited by
John Gunn
Professor of Forensic Psychiatry, Institute of Psychiatry,
London

and

Pamela J. Taylor
Professor of Special Hospital Psychiatry, Broadmoor Hospital
and the Institute of Psychiatry, London; formerly Head of
Medical Services, Special Hospital Service Authority,
London.

BUTTERWORTH
HEINEMANN

Butterworth-Heinemann Ltd
Linacre House, Jordan Hill, Oxford OX2 8DP

A member of the Reed Elsevier plc group

OXFORD LONDON BOSTON
MUNICH NEW DELHI SINGAPORE SYDNEY
TOKYO TORONTO WELLINGTON

First published 1993
Paperback edition 1995

© John Gunn and Pamela J. Taylor 1993

British Library Cataloguing in Publication Data
Forensic Psychiatry:Clinical, Legal and
  Ethical Issues
  I. Gunn, John   II. Taylor, Pamela
  616.89

ISBN 0 7506 2317 9

Library of Congress Cataloguing in Publication Data
Forensic psychiatry: clinical, legal, and ethical issues/edited by
  John Gunn and Pamela Taylor.
     p.   cm.
  Includes bibliographical references and index.
  ISBN 0 7506 2317 9
  1. Forensic psychiatry—England.   2. Forensic psychiatry—Wales.
  I. Gunn, John Charles.   II. Taylor, Pamela (Pamela Jane)
  [DNLM: 1. Crime   2. Criminal Psychology.   3. Forensic Psychiatry.
  4. Mental Disorders—Great Britain—legislation.   5. Substance
  Abuse.   6. Substance Dependence.   W 740 F7149]
  RA1151.F658   1993
  614'.1–dc20
                                                           92–48948
                                                                CIP

Printed and bound in Great Britain by
Harnolls Ltd, Bodmin, Cornwall

Contents

Contributors

Addresses are in Great Britain unless otherwise indicated

Hans Adserballe, MD DMSc
Chief Physician, Associate Professor of Psychiatry, University Psychiatric Hospital of Aarhus, Risskov, Denmark

Ann Barker, MRCPsych, MPhil
Consultant Forensic Psychiatrist, Broadmoor Hospital, Crowthorne, Berks

Maureen Barry, Dip Soc S
Chief Probation Officer, SW London Probation Service, Surrey

John V Basson, FRCPsych
Principal Medical Officer, Scottish Office, Psychiatric Adviser, Secretary of State for Scotland, St Andrews House, Edinburgh

Wolfgang Berner, MD
Associate Professor, Head of Psychiatry and Psychotherapy, Department of JA Mittersteig, Vienna, Austria

Ronald Blackburn, MA(Cantab), MSc, PhD, CPsychol, FBPsS
Professor of Clinical and Forensic Psychological Studies,Liverpool University and Ashworth Hospital, Liverpool

Oliver V Briscoe, FRCP FRCPsych
Woldingham, Surrey

Frederick W A Browne, BSc, MB, BCh, MRCPsych
Consultant Forensic Psychiatry, Purdysburn Hospital, Belfast, N Ireland

David Carson, LLB
Senior Lecturer in Law, Faculty of Law, University of Southampton, Southampton

Derek Chiswick, MB,MPhil, FRCPsych
Consultant Forensic Psychiatrist, Royal Edinburgh Hospital, Honorary Senior Lecturer in Psychiatry, University of Edinburgh, Edinburgh

Petko Dontschev, MD, MDsc
Professor of Psychiatry and Forensic Psychiatry, Head of Forensic Psychiatry Department, Institute of Neurology and Psychiatry, Sofia, Bulgaria

Enda M Dooley, MB, BCR, BAO, MRCPsych
Director of Prison Medical Services, Department of Justice, Dublin, Eire

Paul T d'Orbán, MB, ChB, FRCPsych, DPM
Honorary Consultant in Forensic Psychiatry, Department of Psychiatry, Royal Free Hospital, London

Nigel L G Eastman, BSc(Econ), MB, ChB, MRCPsych, Barrister at Law
Senior Lecturer in Forensic Psychiatry, Section of Forensic Psychiatry, St George's Hospital Medical School, London

David P Farrington, MP, PhD(Cambridge)
Professor of Psychological Criminology, Cambridge University, President of British Society of Criminology, Institute of Criminology, Cambridge

David M Forshaw, MB, ChB, MRCPsych, DHMSA, DPMSA
Senior Registrar in General Psychiatry, Maudsley Hospital, London

Loraine R Gelsthorpe, BA(Hons), MPhil, PhD (Cantab)
Lecturer in the Sociology of Crime and Deviance, Institute of Criminology, University of Cambridge, Cambridge

Adrian Grounds, DM, MRCPsych
University Lecturer in Forensic Psychiatry, Institute of Criminology and Department of Psychiatry, University of Cambridge, Cambridge

Don Grubin, MA, BS, MRCPsych, MD
Lecturer in Forensic Psychiatry, Institute of Psychiatry, London

Gisli H Gudjonsson, BSc, MSc, PhD, CPsychol
Senior Lecturer in Clinical Psychology, Institute of Psychiatry, London

John Gunn, MD, FRCPsych
Professor of Forensic Psychiatry, Institute of Psychiatry, London

David Hall, BA(Hons), CQSW, FRSH
Assistant Area Manager, Gloucester Social Services Department, Cheltenham

John Hamilton, MD, FRCPsych (Deceased)
Formerly Medical Director, Broadmoor Hospital, Crowthorne, Berks

Timothy Harding, MB, BS, MRCPsych, Privat Docent (Geneva)
Professor of Forensic Medicine & Director of the University Institute of Legal Medicine, Geneva, Switzerland

Jonathan Hill, BA, MRCP, MRCPsych
Professor of Child & Adolescent Psychiatry, University of Liverpool, Royal Liverpool Children's Hospital, Liverpool

Anthony Holland, Bsc, MB, BS, MRCP, MRCPsych, MPhil
Lecturer, Academic Department of Psychiatry, Cambridge University, Addenbrooks Hospital, Cambridge

Stephen J Hucker, MB, BS, FRCP(C), FRCPsych
Head of Forensic Division, Clarke Institute of Psychiatry, Associate professor, Department of Psychiatry, University of Toronto, Canada

Martin Humphreys, BDS, MB, BS, MRCPsych
Lecturer in Forensic Psychiatry, Edinburgh University Department of Psychiatry, Royal Edinburgh Hospital, Edinburgh

S Assen Jablensky, MD, DMSc, FRCPsych
Professor of Psychiatry, University of Western Australia, Perth, Australia

Andrew Johns, BSc, MRCPsych
Senior Lecturer in Psychiatry of Addictive Behaviour, Department of Addictive Behaviour, St George's Hospital Medical School, London

Michael D Kopelman, PhD, FBPsC, MRCPsych
Senior Lecturer in Neuropsychiatry and Honorary Consultant Psychiatrist, Academic Unit of Psychiatry, St Thomas' Hospital, London

Anthony Maden, MRCPsych, MD
Senior Lecturer in Forensic Psychiatry, Department of Forensic Psychiatry, Institute of Psychiatry, London

David Mawson, DPM, FRCPsych
Consultant Forensic Psychiatrist, Broadmoor Hospital, Crowthorne, Berks

Jeffrey S McPherson, LRCP, MRCS, MRCPsych, DRCOG
Consultant Psychiatrist, Southern Derbyshire Health Authority, Pastures Hospital, Derby

Gillian C Mezey, MB, BS, MRCPsych
Consultant & Honorary Senior Lecturer in Forensic Psychiatry, St George's Hospital & Medical School, London

John Monahan, PhD
Doherty Professor of Law, Professor of Psychology and Legal Medicine, School of Law, University of Virginia, Charlottesville, Virginia, USA.

Allison Morris, LLB, PhD, Dip Crim
Lecturer in Criminology, University of Cambridge, Institute of Criminology, Cambridge

Paul E Mullen, MB, BS, MRCPsych, MPhil, FRANZCP
Professor of Forensic Psychiatry, Monash University, Director of Forensic Psychiatry Services, Rosanna Forensic Psychiatry Centre, Victoria, Australia

Peter Noble, MA, MD, DPM, FRCP, FRCPsych
Consultant Psychiatrist, Maudsley and Bethlem Royal Hospital, London

Gary Rix, RMM, BSc, DMS
Senior Nurse, South Glamorgan Health Authority, Temple of Peace and Health, Cardiff

Graham Robertson, PhD
Lecturer in Forensic Psychiatry, Department of Forensic Psychiatry, Institute of Psychiatry, London

Robert Sharrock, BSc, CPsychol
Formerly Lecturer in Psychology, Institute of Psychiatry, London

Pete Snowden, MB, ChB, BSc, MRCPsych
Consultant Forensic Psychiatrist, Northwestern Regional Health Authority and to the Home Office. Clinical Lecturer, University of Manchester, Edenfield Centre, Prestwich Hospital, Manchester

Leslie Sohn, MBChB, DPM, FRCPsych
Consultant Psychotherapist, Denis Hill Unit, Bethlem Royal Hospital, Supervising Psycho-analyst, British Psycho-analytic Institute, London

Stephen Stanley, MB, MSc
Intelligence Officer, Inner London Probation Service, London

John Strang, MD, BS, MRCPsych
Consultant Psychiatrist in Drug Dependence, Joint Bethlem Maudsley Hospital, London

Pamela J Taylor, MB,BS, MRCP, FRCPsych
Head of Medical Services, Special Hospitals Service Authority, Charles House, Kensington, London, Senior Lecturer, Institute of Psychiatry, London

Simon Wessely, MA, MSc, MRCP, MRCPsych
Senior Lecturer in Psychological Medicine, Kings College Hospital & Institute of Psychiatry, London

Donald J West, MD, LittD, FRCPsych
Emeritus Professor of Clinical Criminology, Cambridge

Bruce Westmore, MB, BS, FRANZCP
The Northside Clinic, Greenwich, NSW Australia

Robert M. Wettstein, MD
Law and Psychiatry Programme, Western Psychiatric Institute & Clinic, Department of Psychiatry, University of Pittsburgh, School of Medicine, Pittsburgh, USA

Preface

This textbook is intended to be a practical guide to the psychiatry of mentally abnormal offenders and other victims. It is not a comprehensive encyclopaedia, and is certainly not the last word on our subject, but it does try to draw extensively on the growing body of knowledge which is available. Inevitably it is biased. Its first bias is that it is a medical book, largely written by doctors. Other professionals have contributed, and we are very attached to a multidisciplinary perspective, but it would be disingenuous and unfair to other disciplines to pretend that the prevailing view is anything other than a medical one. The second bias is that it is written from the United Kingdom and heavily emphasizes the law of England and Wales. In some ways it is even more parochial than that, for it reflects to a considerable extent practice and opinion at the Institute of Psychiatry (the Maudsley) in London. It draws on our clinical experience and gives some idea of what we teach. A further bias is that it gives much greater emphasis to adult than to child and adolescent psychiatry. That, unfortunately, reflects the current position in the UK, yet conduct disorder and personality development are central to both adolescent and adult forensic psychiatry.

We have given a good deal of emphasis to victims. We see them at the heart of forensic psychiatry. The prevention of harm to others is one aim of forensic psychiatry. Victims not only pose medico-legal problems, but many of them turn their fears and their anger back on to society in antisocial reactions. Some adults have a complete personality change as a result of trauma. Victimization during childhood seriously affects the development of the growing personality. Most offender patients are themselves victims in one way or another.

A problem with any modern textbook is that it is out of date before the ink is dry, because changes in knowledge, changes in law, and changes in practice are rapid and common. Our difficulties in this respect have been compounded by the slow progress in writing which is made when the authors are busy practitioners. Our hope is that the usefulness of the stable information will outweigh the other disadvantages. Our long-suffering publishers have been sorely tried by our slow progress, but, we like to believe, have been persuaded to endure it because our irritating busyness represents practical experience. The authors between them have worked with all the types of patient described, in all the British facilities discussed, and have tested all the justice and treatment approaches mentioned at first hand. We have also had a lot of contact with overseas colleagues.

Although this text has a medical perspective, it is not written exclusively for medical practitioners. We aim to inform not only psychiatrists but nurses, psychologists, social workers, lawyers and police officers among others. A tall order, but we believe that, for example, it is useful for a social worker to have ready access to a medical perspective. We urge our students to read into other disciplines. We hope that, for example, lawyers will urge their students to read this type of book (or even this book! *eds*). We hope, too, that professionals who are dealing with a healthier population than we usually do will find some assistance from a closer understanding of psychopathology, its development and management. We hope that forensic psychiatry will begin to contribute to the prevention of disease, and to the prevention of a part of the spectrum of antisocial behaviour. This could not even be an aspiration without effective multidisciplinary communication, mutual understanding and cooperation. In brief, we hope that non-medical readers will learn something of the medical approach so that they can know how to respond to that approach.

A further hope is that the essential Englishness of this book does not prevent it being of value elsewhere. We would like readers from other countries to set our approach alongside their own. Chapter 3 gives an excellent overview of how this might be done. We intend that trainee forensic psychiatrists in all common law countries will find the book of value in their training. At the very least, it can be used as a source of references, as an entrance to a rich and fascinating literature. The clinical material, which forms the bulk of the book, is less susceptible to national boundaries than the administrative and legal matters.

A comment is needed on two minutiae of style which have considerably exercised authors and editors alike. First, attribution; it has been impossible to acknowledge everybody who has contributed ideas and inspiration to this book. However, we have tried to attribute correctly and fairly everyone who has written something original for the book. Some people have done much more than others, all have been subject to heavy editing, many have been asked to compromise their views in order to accommodate other views in the same chapter. All have been scholarly and understanding about this process, which we believe has contributed to a better balanced book than we would otherwise have had. The attributions at the heads of the chapters are intended to reflect this process. It has not, however, been possible to introduce every subtle nuance of contribution into our system. The attributions should not be read as implying significance and importance beyond the bald statements given. Most of them are given in alphabetical order to avoid invidious rankings. The second stylistic issue reflects a political matter of the end of the twentieth century; sex! The English language does not have a collective for 'him or her', or 'she and he'. We had to decide whether or not to use the older convention of allowing masculine words to stand for both sexes, as is done in British legislation, and as is growing in popularity in occupational nouns such as 'actor' and 'manager'. Inevitably, opinion among our authors and authoresses divided and, at times, divided strongly, although it is of interest that opinion could not be predicted from sex alone. After a lot of consultation, the editors (he and she!) decided that masculine words should be taken in their generic sense and assumed to include men and women unless the sense dictates otherwise. We hope that those who are thus offended will forgive.

We have based our references on the Harvard system and included (we hope) a complete list at the end of the book giving full journal titles and publishers' names where appropriate. Readers should also be able to use this list as an author/article index. 'Cases cited' have given us much more trouble. Each case is referred to in the text by an identifying name. This name may have no meaning or significance beyond this textbook, but it will lead to the alphabetical list at the end of the book, where the legal references will be found. The cases are listed alphabetically, irrespective of country. We have tried to adopt the conventions used in legal textbooks for these references and hope they are comprehensible and accurate, but readily admit we encountered difficulties with a discipline which is not our own. The 'cases cited' list, like the references, can also be used as an index. Abbreviations have been obsessionally listed and defined to suit non-medical readers and non-British readers, as well as British medical readers. Abbreviations are often indicated in the text as well.

We will welcome any feedback on the text from readers, especially constructive criticisms. We apologise, in advance, for the factual errors which readers will surely find, and we want to know what those errors are. Please write to us at the Institute of Psychiatry, Camberwell, London SE5 8AF, England. Every letter will be carefully considered and kept for future reference.

Our references give a reasonably comprehensive entrance into the literature of forensic psychiatry. They omit, however, that wider literature which could be read for other insights: plays, novels and poetry. Perhaps we should have had a list of relevant works, but our courage failed. We would have to include everything from Shakespeare's *Othello*, to Pushkin's *Queen of Spades*, from Ibsen's *Hedda Gabler* to Fowles's *The Collector*. Perhaps we can tempt any doubter about this ancillary field of study by some extracts from a remarkable early nineteenth-century English poem *Peter Grimes* by George Crabbe (e.g. Opie & Opie, 1983).

> His father's love he scorned, his power defied,
> But being drunk, wept sorely when he died . . .
> He knew not justice, and he laughed at law.
> On all he marked, he stretched his ready hand;
> He fished by water and he filched by land; . . .
> But no success could please his cruel soul,
> He wished for one to trouble and control,
> He wanted some obedient boy to stand
> And bear the blow of his outrageous hand,
> And hoped to find in some propitious hour
> A feeling creature subject to his power . . .
> Some few in town observed in Peter's trap
> A boy, with jacket blue and woollen cap; . . .
> Pinned, beaten, cold, pinched, threatened and abused—
> His efforts punished and his food refused— . . .
> The savage master grinned in horrid glee . . .

For three sad years the boy his tortures bore,
And then his pains and trials were no more . . .
Another boy with equal ease was found,
The money granted and the victim bound
And what his fate?—One night it chanced he fell
From the boat's mast and perished in her well, . . .
Then came a boy, of manners soft and mild— . . .
His liquor failed and Peter's wrath arose—
No more is known—the rest we must suppose, . . .
The mayor himself with tone severe replied—
'Henceforth with thee shall never boy abide,' . . .
The sailors' wives would stop him in the street,
And say, 'Now, Peter, thou'st no boy to beat' . . .
He growled an oath, and in an angry tone
Cursed the whole place and wished to be alone . . .
Cold nervous tremblings shook his sturdy frame,
And strange disease—he couldn't say the name,
Wild were his dreams, and oft he rose in fright, . . .
Furious he grew, and up the country ran,
And there they seized him—a distempered man.
Him we received, and to a parish-bed,
Followed and cursed, the groaning man was led . . .
The priest attending, found he spoke at times
As one alluding to his fears and crimes; . . .
'But, gazing on the spirits, there was I.
They bade me leap to death, but I was loth to die:
And every day, as sure as day arose,
Would these three spirits meet me ere the close,
To hear and mark them daily was my doom, . . .
"All days alike! for ever" did they say,
"And unremitted torments every day—"
Yes, so they said'—But here he ceased and gazed
On all around, affrightened and amazed; . . .
Then dropped exhausted and appeared at rest,
Till the strong foe the vital powers possessed!
Then with an inward, broken voice he cried,
'Again they come' and muttered as he died.

Thus is set out the career of one who might now be referred for a special hospital bed. Clearly, it was based on an astute real life observation; a man who had an abnormal relationship with his father, became a young delinquent, found a way of acquiring young boys and sadistically controlling and then killing them and, when reviled, became increasingly isolated, and ended his life in an institution in a psychosis. Not for Crabbe the constraints of twentieth-century jargon; the terms psychosis, psychopath, personality disorder, survivor, treatability are not mentioned (although victim and disease are); yet, as the brief extracts we quote indicate, he managed to convey the full horror of a common-place human tragedy.

December, 1992

John Gunn
Pamela J. Taylor

Acknowledgements

It is quite impossible to thank all the many people who have contributed to this textbook, for example many of our contributors have given assistance far beyond the individual pieces of text which are attributed to them within the book. In some ways the whole of the Institute of Psychiatry, which has fostered and developed the Department of Forensic Psychiatry there and made the whole enterprise possible, deserves special mention. The work of the book has made significant inroads into other departmental activities, but successive deans and many members of the Department of Forensic Psychiatry have been not only tolerant of the enterprise, but positively encouraging. The burden of typing, proof reading, compiling endless reference lists, assisting with the index, and other thankless repetitive tasks has fallen on the shoulders of the Department secretarial staff. Maureen Bartholomew and her assistants Carole Double and Geraldine Gane, have given of themselves far beyond their normal call of duty. Their relaxed, cheerful, helpful approach to a daunting task has been an invigorating experience. The library at the Institute of Psychiatry has been a further essential component in the development of this book and we want to pay tribute to Martin Guha, Clare Martin, and their staff. Within the University of London further library assistance was also obtained from Paul Norman, who is the senior assistant librarian at the Institute of Advanced Legal Studies. The second understanding employer who has assisted and encouraged this work has been the Special Hospitals Service Authority and our special thanks go to David Edmond and Charles Kaye who have recognised the central importance of academic work in the functions of the Authority and thus encouraged the production of the textbook.

The usual slightly dismissive, 'thanks to our publishers for being so understanding' will certainly not do on this occasion. One of us has good reason to understand the difference which publishing skills can make to a seemingly straightforward textbook. Heinemann, later Butterworth-Heinemann, have provided the structure, support, professional know-how, and the sheer tolerance which has been required to get this book finished. We are particularly grateful to Richard Barling who recruited the text at a particularly depressing low point in the career of this book. He helped us re-establish our self esteem and sketched the multi-author strategy which proved so resilient in the end. After he left Heinemann, Susan Devlin took his place as Senior Medical Editor and has nursed and nurtured not only the text but also the editors, giving them the distinct impression that this was the most important book on her list, perhaps even the only one! So silent and efficient is the publishing operation that we are not aware of all those who have been involved, but we want to make special mention of Elizabeth

Lamplugh, Susan Devlin's assistant, and Alison Duncan who has master-minded the proof reading and, of course, Chris Jarvis whose superb knowledge of printing and production ensured that we had a book at all. We also have a special word of thanks for Ann Kirk, who had the unenviable task of copy-editing a long text produced by obsessional, but not entirely accurate, writers. Last, but by no means least, the index has been compiled with the assistance of John Gibson.

Many of the authors have contributed by advice and criticism of texts beyond the pieces attributed to them. We acknowledge our debt as should be clear from the Preface. There were also other potential authors and helpful colleagues who gave advice and criticism who are not otherwise mentioned at all. For help of this kind we are particularly grateful to Susan Bailey, Murray Cox, Frans Derks, Julie Feldbrugge, Philip Joseph, Harry Kennedy and David Tidmarsh. German Berrios gave us particular help with Chapter 22 (ethics)

The last two years' work on the book coincided with the work of the Reed Committee (Department of Health, Home Office, 1992) in which both senior editors and several authors participated. The discussion and thinking of that Committee will therefore have played some part in shaping our ideas even though, because of the virtual simultaneous production of the two texts, we have given only scant formal reference to the Reed Report.

We are grateful to Her Majesty's Stationery Office for permission to publish extracts from the Mental Health Acts of the United Kingdom, and the Code of Practice to the Mental Health Act 1983 for England and Wales; to the American Psychiatric Press for permission to reproduce the Principles of Medical Ethics with Annotations especially applicable to Psychiatry 1989; to the American Medical Association for permission to reprint the AMA Principles of Medical Ethics; to the *British Journal of Psychiatry* for per-mission to reproduce Table 7.1 on p.292; to *Behavioural Sciences and the Law* for permission to reproduce Table 7.3 on p.294; to Alwyn Lishman for permission to reproduce the table on p.299; to H Hafner, W Boker, and Springer Verlag, Heidleberg, for permission to reproduce Table 12.3, on p.514; to Roy Walmsley of the Home Office Research and Planning Unit for permission to use his classification of personal violence (p.500); to Derek Eaves for giving permission to reproduce his table on the new Canadian Criminal Code (Appendix 6); to Little Brown & Co. for permission to reproduce Table 12.1 on p.499; to Robin White, Professor of Law, University of Leicester; and to Basil Blackwell Ltd for permission to use Table 4.1 on p.170.

JG
PJT

Table of Statutes and Statutory Instruments

United Kingdom
(excluding Acts now operational in the Republic of Ireland)

Abbreviations

This list does not include the abbreviations of law lists and journals which are given at the beginning of the list of cases cited p. 1028

AA	Alcoholics Anonymous
ABH	actual bodily harm
ABWOR	assistance by way of representation (under English legal aid scheme)
ADSS	Association of Directors of Social Services
AIDS	auto-immune deficiency syndrome
AL	Alabama
ALI	American Law Institute
AMA	American Medical Association
AMP	adenosine 3',5'-monophosphate
APA	American Psychiatric Association
ASW	approved social worker (for MHA 1983 purposes)
AUTP	Association of University Teachers of Psychiatry (UK)
BMA	British Medical Association
BNF	British National Formulary (British Medical Association and Royal Pharmaceutical Society of Great Britain, continuous)
BPD	borderline personality disorder
CA	California
Ch. and ch.	chapter
CH	Cane Hill hospital
CICB	Criminal Injuries Compensation Board (England and Wales)
CID	Criminal Investigations Department (detective agency, England and Wales)
Cm.	Numbering system used by HMSO
CMH	Central Mental Hospital (Dundrum, Dublin, Republic of Ireland)
Cmnd.	Numbering system used by HMSO
CNS	Central nervous system
cols	columns
cont.	continued
CP(I)A	Criminal Procedure (Insanity) Act 1964
CPS	Crown Prosecution Service (England and Wales)
CP(S)A	Criminal Procedure (Scotland) Act 1975
CSF	Cerebro-spinal fluid
CSP	Counseil de Surveillance Psychiatrique (Geneva, Switzerland)

CT	Connecticut *or* computerised tomography (computerised three-dimensional x-ray examination of soft tissues)
CVS	coroner's verdict of suicide
DC	District of Columbia (location of US capital)
dept	department
DHA	district health authority (England)
DIS	Diagnostic Inverview Schedule (Robins et al., 1979)
DHSS	Department of Health and Social Security (England) (subsequently replaced by DOH and DSS) *also* Department of Health and Social Services (Northern Ireland) (according to content)
DOH	Department of Health (England) (previously part of DHSS)
Dmd	Numbering system used by HMSO
DMS	Director of Medical Services (SHSA)
DNS	Director of Nursing Services (SHSA)
DPP	Director of Public Prosecutions (England and Wales)
DPS	Directorate of Psychological Services (HM Prisons, England and Wales)
Dr/dr	doctor (i.e. medical practitioner)
DSM–III	Diagnostic and Statistical Manual of Mental Disorders (Third Edition) (American Psychiatric Association 1980)
DSM–III R	Diagnostic and Statistical Manual of Mental Disorders (Third Edition–Revised) (American Psychiatric Association 1987)
DSS	Department of Social Security (England) (previously part of DHSS)
E	extroversion (Eysenck's theory)
EAS	emotionality, activity, sociability
ECT	electroconvulsive therapy
Ed(s)	Editor(s)
Edn	edition
EDR	earliest date of release (from prison)
EE	expressed emotion
EEC	European Economic Community
EEG	electroencephalogram (examination of electrical activity of the brain)
e.g.	*exempli gratia* (for example)
EMIT	Enzyme Multiplied Immunoassay Techniques
EPI	Eysenck Personality Inventory (Eysenck & Eysenck, 1964)
et al.	(*et alii*) and others (authors)
etc.	*et cetera* (and so on)
f	females *and* following pages (in index)

FBI	Federal Bureau of Investigation (detective agency—USA)
FD	Financial Director (SHSA)
fig.	figure
g.	gramme(s)
GAMMA GT	gamma glutamyl transpeptidase
GBH	grievous bodily harm
GBMI	guilty but mentally ill
GC	gas chromatography
GHQ	General Health Questionnaire (Goldberg, 1972)
GMC	General Medical Council (UK)
GP	general practitioner (family doctor, primary care, physician)
GPI	general paralysis of the insane (tertiary syphilis)
h.	hour
HAS	Health Advisory Service (an NHS inspectorate)
HC	House of Commons (used as numbering system in Hansard which is the official report of UK parliamentary proceedings)
HCl	hydrochloride
HH	Hellingly hospital
HIA	hyperactivity impulsivity attention deficit
HIV	human immunodeficiency virus (causes AIDS)
HM	Her Majesty's (government, prison,etc.—indicates UK Crown ownership)
HMP	Her Majesty's prison(s) (UK prison(s))
HMSO	Her Majesty's Stationery Office (UK government publisher)
HPLC	high pressure liquid chromatography
ICD–8	International Classification of Diseases 8th Revision
ICD–9	International Classification of Diseases 9th Revision. Mental Disorder Glossary (World Health Organisation 1978)
ICD–10	International Classification of Diseases 10th Revision. Mental and Behavioural Disorders (World Health Organisation 1992)
i.e.	*id est* (that is)
ILL	Illinois
ILPS	Inner London Probation Service
IQ	intelligence quotient (as measured by a standard test)
IRA	Irish Republican Army
ISU	interim security unit (prior to developing an RSU)
J	Justice or Judge
JCHPT	Joint Committee on Higher Psychiatric Training (UK)
JP	justice of the peace (magistrate)
LAC	local authority circular (from UK government)

LGBR	Lieutenant-Governor's Board of Review (Canada)
LRC	local review committee (of English Parole Board)
LSD	lysergic acid diethylamide (an hallucinogenic drug)
m	males
MA	Massachusetts
MADS	Maudsley Assessment of Delusions Schedule (Taylor et al., in press)
MAIOs	monoamine oxidase inhibitors (a special group of antidepressant drugs)
MASS	Massachusetts
MD	Maryland
MENCAP	Royal Society for Mentally Handicapped Children and Adults
METFORS	Metropolitan Toronto Forensic Service (Canada)
mg(s)	milligram(s) (unit of weight)
mg/dl	milligrams per decilitre (a weight/volume ratio used in measuring the concentration of substances e.g. in blood)
mg/ml	milligrams per millilitre (a weight/volume ratio as above)
MHA 1959	Mental Health Act 1959 (for England and Wales)
MHA 1983	Mental Health Act 1983 (for England and Wales)
MHAs	MHA 1983 + MH(S)A 1984 + MH(NI)O 1986
MHAC	Mental Health Act Commission (England and Wales)
MHC	Mental Health Commission (Northern Ireland)
MH(NI)O 1986	Mental Health (Northern Ireland) Order 1986
MHO	Mental Health Offices (Scotland)
MHRT	Mental Health Review Tribunal
MH(S)A 1984	Mental Health (Scotland) Act 1984
MHT	Mental Health Tribunal (Queensland, Australia)
MI	Michigan
MIND	The National Association for Mental Health (UK)
MLC	Medico-Legal Council (Denmark)
mm³	cubic millimetre (unit of volume)
MMPI	Minnesota Multiphasic Personality Inventory (Buros, 1970, Dahlstom & Welsh, 1960, Hathaway & McKinley, 1940)
MORI	Market and Opinion Research International (opinions survey company)
MWC	Mental Welfare Commission (Scotland)
N	neuroticism (Eysenck's theory)
NACRO	National Association for the Care and Resettlement of Offenders (England and Wales)
NB	*nota bene* (please note)
NE	north east
NGRI	not guilty by reason of insanity
NHS	National Health Service (UK)

NI	Northern Ireland
NIACRO	Northern Ireland Association for the Care and Resettlement of Offenders
NIO	Northern Ireland Office
NIMH	National Institute of Mental Health (USA)
NJ	New Jersey
NMS	neuroleptic malignant syndrome
No.	Number
NSPCC	National Society for the Prevention of Cruelty to Children
NSW	New South Wales (Australia)
NW	north west
NY	New York
p.	page number (pp. in plural)
P	psychoticism (Eysenck's theory)
PACE	Police and Criminal Evidence Act 1984
pd	property damage
PET	positron emission tomography (technique for visualizing brain structures and metabolic activities)
PCP	phencyclidine (Angel Dust—an hallucinogenic drug)
PMS	Prison Medical Service (England and Wales)
P & O	Peninsular & Oriental Steam Navigation Company
POW	prisoner of war
pp.	pages
PRES	pre-release employment scheme (English prisons)
PRT	Patient Review Tribunal (Queensland, Australia)
PTA	post traumatic amnesia
PTSD	post-traumatic stress disorder
QC	Queen's counsel (leading barrister in British legal system)
RAG	Research and Advisory Group (to English Home Office)
RCP	Royal College of Physicians
RCPsych	Royal College of Psychiatrists
RDC	Research Diagnostic Criteria (Spitzer & Endicott, 1978)
REM	rapid eye movements (found in sleep)
REM sleep	rapid eye movement sleep (the dreaming phase)
RHA	regional health authority (in England)
RMO	responsible medical officer (a consultant with a technical medical role in MHAs)
RSU	regional security unit
S.	section (it is followed by the appropriate number and refers to a clause in a statute)
SADS	Schedule for Affective Disorders and Schizophrenia
SE	south east
SETRHA	South East Thames Regional Health Authority
SHA	special health authority
SHSA	Special Hospitals Service Authority (England and Wales)

SODQ	Severity of Alcohol Dependence Questionnaire
SOVA	Society for Voluntary Associates
Suppl.	Supplement
SW	south west
TBS	Ter Beschikkingstelling (Dutch secure treatment clinics)
TLC	thin layer chromatography
Trans.	translated by
TUC	Trades Union Congress (UK)
TV	television
UCLA	University of California at Los Angeles
UK	United Kingdom of Great Britain (England, Wales, Scotland) and Northern Ireland
Univ.	University
US and USA	United States of America
USSR	Union of Soviet Socialist Republics
VIR	viral infectivity restrictions (in England and Wales—mainly for AIDS)
vol(s)	volume(s)
VT	Vermont
WAIS	Wechsler Adult Intelligence Scale (for measuring IQ)
WISC	Wechsler Intelligence Scale for Children
WHO	World Health Organisation
WLG	Warrant of the Lieutenant Governor (Canada)
WMA	World Medical Association
WW1	World War 1
WW2	World War 2
XO	Turner's syndrome (sex chromosomal abnormality in females producing short stature, webbed neck, wide carrying angle of arms, amenorrhoea) (Cowie, 1977)
XXY	Kleinfelter's syndrome (sex chromosomal abnormality in males producing gynaecomastia, small testis, low IQ, emotional immaturity)
XYY	sex chromosomal abnormality in males producing excessive height and infertility

1
Introduction

Written by
John Gunn
Pamela J. Taylor

'Who in the rainbow can draw the line where the violet tint ends and the orange tint begins? Distinctly we see the difference of the colors, but where exactly does the one first blendingly enter into the other? So with sanity and insanity. In pronounced cases there is no question about them. But in some supposed cases, in various degrees supposedly less pronounced, to draw the exact line of demarcation few will undertake, though for a fee becoming considerate some professional experts will. There is nothing nameable, but that some men will, or undertake to, do it for pay.'

H. Melville (1924) *Billy Budd, Sailor*

Forensic Psychiatry

Forensic psychiatry is not just a way of getting paid for trying to answer unanswerable legal questions, although it does have a germ of that danger within it. The detection of the shades of pathology, the boundaries between diseases, between normality and mental disease and the contribution of mental diseases to socially proscribed acts is, however, very much the art of forensic psychiatry.

At its simplest, forensic psychiatry can be defined as that part of psychiatry which deals with patients and problems at the interface of the legal and psychiatric systems. In many parts of the world it is a growth area of medicine. There are a number of factors which may have contributed to this growth. These include social pressures to reject the chronically sick, the handicapped, the disruptive and the aggressive, the development of new assessment and treatment skills for the behaviourally disordered, an increasing interest in institutions and what happens in them, and a rising concern with the problem of 'dangerousness'.

In England and Wales the Butler Report (Home Office, DHSS 1974, 1975) resulted in ear-marked government funding for forensic psychiatry and the development of medium security units in most health regions. These regional security units have become the focus of forensic psychiatry developments in England.

Table 1.1
Forensic Psychiatry Skills

1. The assessment of behavioural abnormalities
2. The writing of reports for courts and lawyers
3. The giving of evidence in court
4. Understanding and using security as a means of treatment
5. The treatment of chronic disorders, especially those which exhibit behavioural problems such as severe psychoses and personality disorders
6. A knowledge of mental health law
7. Skill in the psychological treatments (particularly psychotherapy) of behaviour disorders

A list of the skills which form the basis of the expertise in forensic psychiatry has previously been suggested. (Table 1.1) (Gunn 1982, 1986a). These skills should be developed from and be additional to the skills of general psychiatry, supplemented by basic knowledge of child and adolescent psychiatry and the psychiatry of mental handicap. Diagnostic skills, understanding of basic psychiatric nursing, of psychopharmacology and community care are also essential, as is an integration of the fundamental academic skills of training others and evaluation of the work.

Forensic psychiatry has developed further since then, and now we put an additional emphasis on the problems of victims. Most patients who come to forensic psychiatrists are victims of one sort or another. A few present soon after a traumatic event. They may suffer from anxiety states such as post-traumatic stress disorder, from depressive reactions or less typical responses. Many find that their previously healthy and stable lives are disrupted not only by the new and devastating experience of mental ill-health, but also by legal processes and other adverse social problems. Some develop behavioural problems; these patients have often suffered multiple victimization in the sense that they have suffered earlier psychological trauma, usually in childhood. Many of these do not present until these behavioural problems are well established and the early traumas hardly remarked. These deleterious experiences include poverty, social deprivation, inconsistent discipline, violence or sexual abuse, or, as adolescents or adults, inadequate or harsh treatment for primary problems (such as schizophrenia and behaviour disorders). Treatment of such patients makes a contribution to prevention of behavioural problems and thus further victimization.

We offer, therefore, a definition of forensic psychiatry which seems to us to be more fundamental and which we hope will lead to more and better therapeutics in this field. **Forensic psychiatry is the prevention, amelioration and treatment of victimization which is associated with mental disease.**

A Victim Centred Approach

The victim centred approach to this book is indicated by, among other things, a substantial chapter (23) on victims. In some centres, particularly outside the UK, forensic psychiatrists and psychologists put a lot of emphasis on their work in civil law suits for compensation following accidents. Whilst not wishing to underplay the value of that work, we are emphasizing here the service provision for victims of all sorts. It is a curious anomaly in service provision that very little special attention is given to victims, whether children or adults, whether from domestic or public circumstances. In the criminal court, the victim might understandably think that he ought to play a central role in the drama of the trial. This is not the case. The criminal court in the UK still views the primary victim as the Sovereign, i.e. the State. Victims of assault, or rape, or burglary, may be accorded the privilege of being called as witnesses. They then have no right of legal representation, nor do they necessarily enjoy any protection of their antecedent history. While these are not strictly matters of primary concern to the medical professions, they do give an indication of the context in which research into and the treatment of victims has to be set.

The principal interest for forensic psychiatry in victims is in the identification and treatment of disorder as a form of preventive medicine. The limitation of acute distress and prevention of acute disorder has been seen as a potentially important issue for many years. The prevention of major mental disease and chronic disability is only now emerging as an important prospect. Physical and emotional abuse in childhood can now be construed as a precursor of serious adult disorder in a significant proportion of traumatized individuals (e.g. Mullen, 1990) (Ch. 23). Few professionals working with mentally abnormal offenders have failed to observe that many were, prior to their offending, also victims, often of similar offences to those they have subsequently perpetrated. An equally striking observation is the extent to which many assume, or are maintained in, the victim role by the services which seek to limit their unwanted behaviour. Assisting victims towards becoming survivors is thus central to work with mentally abnormal offenders. The understanding of the consequences of victimization in its many guises may shed light on the genesis of personality disorders.

Academic Developments

The healthy growth of forensic psychiatry is dependent upon complementary academic developments. Specialist higher training schemes for would-be forensic psychiatrists have developed throughout Great Britain. A national body, the Joint Committee on Higher Psychiatric Training (JCHPT), inspects these training schemes. The schemes train full specialists in forensic psychiatry, or general psychiatrists who wish to take a special interest or responsibility in the subject. Other disciplines are also developing specialist training. Nurses in the special hospitals, for example, have developed a 9-month course recognized by the English National Board.

Lewis drew attention to the distinction between training and education. As he put it: 'psychiatrists are neither athletes nor circus elephants' (Lewis, 1947), meaning that proficiency in practical skills is not enough. To this end, the student of forensic psychiatry needs to study other basic disciplines such as criminology, law, philosophy (*see also* Gunn, 1986a). Pickering (1962) elaborated:

> Education demands the active participation of the student's mind. The student learns not by being told, but by doing. What he does is then subject to discussion, appraisal, correction, approval or discord.

Ultimately, neither training nor clinical services can progress without research and peer review. The Forensic Psychiatry Specialist Advisory Committee of JCHPT has now added research as the eighth required skill for forensic psychiatry (JCHPT 1990). The Department of Health is fostering the development of medical audit. Nevertheless, the training of academic forensic psychiatrists is embryonic in the UK, and indeed in most countries.

Medical Terminology

Work with people who have problems both in health and at law is not the province of any one group of professionals. Effective help in these areas requires collaboration and cooperation between those trained in a range of disciplines. The very advantages of such multidisciplinary working, however, also create traps for the unwary, traps which are to the disadvantage of the patient. Differences in expertise mean differences in expectations, philosophy, concepts, and even language. Even within disciplines, terms can be used differently and misunderstood. It is appropriate, therefore, to try and define some of the confusing medical terms encountered.

Words, phrases, terms are of great importance in psychiatry which is largely concerned with the way that people think, feel and act. On a particular term may hang an important clinical or legal decision. Indeed, it is probably no exaggeration to say that particular terms are chosen to have particular effects. In Britain, for example, it is not rare to find that an individual may be labelled as suffering from, say, 'schizophrenia' until he is arrested for an offence or series of offences, whereupon the diagnosis changes to, say, 'personality disorder', and his legal classification to 'psychopathic disorder'. One reason for this is that most people, including psychiatrists, think that schizophrenia is a medical problem and merits hospital care whereas, regrettably, there is less consensus about this for personality disorder. It is easier to argue that such disorders are untreatable and do not merit hospital care, but either some non-medical social support, or maybe punishment.

Doctors, psychiatrists, develop many technical terms, and they also give technical (largely private) meanings to words of the vernacular. Lawyers do the same, sometimes using the same words with different meaning. Yet the vernacular is important. Medicine, psychiatry and the law are rooted in it, and such disciplines are invented by the needs of ordinary people. Psychiatrists did not invent mental disorder. Mental disorder is a common experience, and psychiatrists were invented to treat it.

In the *Shorter Oxford Dictionary* there are definitions for most of the contentious words of psychiatry, e.g.

Disease. An absence of ease. A condition of the body or some part or organ of the body in which its functions are disturbed or deranged. A morbid condition of the mind or disposition. An ailment.

Disorder. An absence or undoing of order. Confusion. Irregularity. Disturbance. Commotion. Disturbance of mind. An ailment. Disease.

Disturb. To agitate and destroy. To agitate mentally, discompose the peace of mind. To trouble, perplex.

Illness. Badness, unpleasantness. Bad or unhealthy conditions of the body. Disease, ailment, sickness.

Several points emerge from this list. Firstly, the terms in the vernacular are almost interchangeable; secondly, they refer equally to body and mind, and, thirdly, several of the definitions include moral aspects, this is especially true for 'illness'.

Does all this matter when psychiatry can develop its own technical meanings? It does, for the very good reason that psychiatrists have to communicate with laymen. If a distraught family brings a malfunctioning relative to a clinic, it is confusing, even hostile, to tell them to take him away again because he is not 'ill'. It is confusing because all the lay people around have probably come to the considered view that he is ill, and it is hostile because it means that the plea for help is being rejected. It might even be regarded as a betrayal of professional obligations if a distressed person volunteers himself for treatment and the assessing doctor makes no arrangement to help him. These are illustrations of a political aspect of terminology. There is an underlying, perhaps ill-formed policy in the doctor's mind about how he will or will not deal with different kinds of case. This policy is then expressed in apparently technical language which either prevents arguments or shifts them on to obscure ground. It is important to recognize this tendency, because of the way in which psychiatrists make diagnoses. Usually, they decide on the diagnosis in the first few minutes of an interview, and spend the rest of the interview confirming this impression (Kendell, 1973).

It soon became clear in the construction of this book that terminological differences were just as prominent amongst our small group of similarly trained authors as anywhere else. Yet in a textbook it is important to have some consistency in the use of language, and to have definitions or explanations which the reader can understand, even if only to disagree with.

We have not entirely achieved this, we doubt whether a multi-author book ever could. We shall set out here the editors' thoughts on a few common words used in psychiatry.

Mental Illness

Mental illness is a term which is so widely used and so little agreed upon that we have kept its use in this textbook to a minimum. Illness is an evaluative term. It is something undesirable. It is a term which we confine to animals and it is mainly reserved for human beings. There the consensus ends. It is not even clear whether physical illness and mental illness are both subcategories of the same broad category (Fulford, 1989), but for the purposes of this book that is how we shall regard them. In the UK, 'mental illness' is also a legal term, because it is an important subcategory of mental disorder in the various mental health acts. It is the key to important provisions and actions in those acts, yet unlike other subcategories, it remains undefined and is largely what the admitting/treating psychiatrist says it is. For Szasz (1962), it is a *'myth'*:

> Psychiatrists are not concerned with mental illnesses and their treatments. In actual practice they deal with personal, social, and ethical problems in living. . . . Human behaviour is fundamentally moral behaviour.

We largely reject the view of mental illness espoused in Szasz's book, yet we agree with him thus far. Human behaviour can be viewed in moral terms and mental illness is not a tangible thing. Moral language is the language of the vernacular and it is very powerful. This does not, however, as Szasz believes, invalidate a medical view of human behaviour. The two views run in parallel. All illnesses are abstract concepts; this does not apply exclusively to those that are the province of the psychiatrist. Pneumonia, for example, is not a thing. The *pneumococcus* organism is a thing, but the term 'pneumonia' is a way of describing its effect in an afflicted person. The terminology helps us to understand something of the individual's problems, and how they might be helped, by reference to a body of technical knowledge, but 'illness' cannot be touched and seen like Mrs Brown, who suffers it, or the organisms that have invaded her can be touched and seen.

Another confusion about the term 'illness' is that it is 'not merely a "condition", but also a social role' (Parsons, 1951; *see* pp. 414–15). Someone who is 'ill' is excused duties, and is treated differently from the healthy person. Furthermore, this social role is not defined by scientific and clinical criteria. 'I am ill doctor' is usually sufficient to effect the social role, at least initially. Problems may arise if medical examinations and tests are negative and the status of illness is removed. Just occasionally, the reverse may occur and others will say 'you are ill' and, despite protests from the sufferer, normal social responsibilities may be removed and the new role instated instead. It is this social aspect of the term 'illness' with its removal of ordinary duties and responsibilities and the substitution of new ones—including that of submission to medical care—which makes the term so central to psychiatry, and so objectionable to some—including Szasz. He who is mentally diseased or disordered can, in some circumstances, be forced into the ill or sick role under the powers of mental health legislation. It is for these complex social reasons that we have tried to minimize the use of the term 'mental illness' in this book. We believe that it is more meaningful to use the term 'disease' or the less explicit, but more widespread term 'disorder'.

Before leaving concepts of illness, though, the strange expression 'formal mental illness' which has crept into modern British psychiatry requires comment. It is difficult enough to determine what is meant by a mental illness let alone a 'formal' one. What, further, is an informal mental illness? One possibility is that the term derives from a misunderstanding of the word 'formal' in the term 'formal thought disorder' which means a disorder of the form of thoughts, but Scadding (1990) advanced a more likely explanation. He referred to a study of the use of psychiatric terms in general practice (Jenkins et al., 1988) and said (of general practitioners):

> Faced with a patient in whom mood changes accompanied various social and economic stresses and recognised physical diseases, they preferred to describe the situation in informal terms, rather than commit themselves to a formal diagnosis which would imply that the changed mood should be regarded as due to a postulated 'mental disorder'.

Perhaps the psychiatrists who say their patients have 'no formal mental illness' are indicating, like the general practitioners, that they recognize the features of mental disease, but are not prepared to make a diagnosis. Given the context in which this jargon arises, it may further mean that the doctor is not prepared to offer the social status of illness, is not prepared to allow any excuses for the patient's behaviour, and is not prepared to provide or recommend treatment. In other words, he would be using the jargon as a political statement. It seems to us that the correct response to the assessment of 'no formal mental illness' should be, 'but what medical problems *does* he have?' and if he does have any, 'what management, what help, should be offered?'

Disease

Introducing the term 'disease' raises the most vexed question of all, the relationship between illness and disease. Boorse (1975, 1976) argued that disease is a value free term and that illness is a subcategory of it with value attached. Thus everyone may have minor diseases, but only severe ones make us ill. Diseases can be identified objectively, but illnesses are subjective and have social consequences. Fulford (1989) disagreed and said that, on the contrary, both disease and illness are evaluative terms and disease is a subcategory of illness or malady. Fulford preferred to think of several types of malady such as wounds, disabilities and diseases. The controversy is complicated and unresolved. We believe, however, that the term 'disease' can be defined more objectively than illness, and are inclined to the Boorse view that it is also less value laden.

Disease is a term that is not very commonly used in psychiatry. Although psychiatrists regularly refer to the 'International Classification of Diseases', they then refer to the individual diseases as 'disorders' or 'diagnoses'. The third, revised edition of the American Diagnostic and Statistical Manual (DSM-III R) does not use the term at all, but 'disorder' is carefully defined as:

> A clinically significant behavioral or psychological syndrome or pattern that occurs in a person and is associated with present distress . . . or disability . . . or with a significantly increased risk of suffering, death, pain, disability, or an important loss of freedom (American Psychiatric Association, 1987a).

No assumption is made 'that each mental disorder is a discrete entity with sharp boundaries', which may be why the term 'disorder' is preferred to that of disease, which is otherwise defined in similar terms (Spitzer and Williams, 1987).

Spitzer and Williams also pointed out that DSM-III R is a classification of mental disorders, not of people. It thus avoids terms such as 'a schizophrenic' or 'an epileptic' and uses instead 'a person with schizophrenia/epilepsy', which not only indicates a more robust, Hippocratic theoretical position (*see* below), but is also less pejorative. It may also be more therapeutic. Rogers (1961), whose work included extensive experience with problem and delinquent children and adolescents, observed of his professional (and personal) relationships:

> If, in my encounter with him, I am dealing with him as an immature child, an ignorant student, a neurotic personality, or a psychopath, each of these concepts of mine limits what he can be in the relationship.

In a brief, but masterly, review of the disease concept in psychiatry, Clare (1986) pointed out that two views of disease have existed since ancient Greece. Hippocrates saw disease as a cluster of signs and symptoms occurring together so frequently as to constitute a recognizable and typical picture. In other words, this is a syndrome view of disease. It begs no questions about aetiology and can be viewed as a 'present state'. Plato, by contrast, envisaged diseases as separate entities, as having an existence of their own separate from the people afflicted by them, and thus a recognizable history/aetiology and future/prognosis. At the end of his review, Clare concluded:

> Psychiatry lacks an accepted nomenclature or list of approved terms for describing and recording clinical observations. It also lacks a reliable system of classification. Nevertheless, the broad consensus within psychiatry at the present time is that the advantages of the disease approach, the diagnostic exercise, and the present rudimentary classification systems outweigh the disadvantages and that the early results of attempts to improve the situation are encouraging.

Schwartz and Schwartz (1976) asked 'Are personality disorders diseases?' They bemoaned the fact that 'mental illness has come to mean almost any type of maladaptive or socially unacceptable behaviour' and went on to explain why, in their view, personality disorders should not be classified as diseases, suggesting that they be dropped from official classifications of diseases. They argued that if this were to happen then psychiatry could reject what they regard as excessive demands for it to perform non-medical functions such as psychotherapy, custodial and rehabilitative care for long-term patients and social therapy! These functions, it is argued, could be carried out by psychologists, social workers and correctional officers, leaving the psychiatrist to perform the medical functions of pharmacotherapy and the giving of ECT. They went on to accept that patients with, for example, chronic schizophrenia, are, in some ways, equivalent to patients with personality disorder and therefore should be handed over to the non-medical professionals along with the personality disordered people. In the world of Schwartz and Schwartz the psychiatrist would concentrate on treating 'anxiety states, affective disorders, and psychoses' but not on—

> patients who have recovered from an acute psychotic illness in the past, but are unable to return to the community because of multiple personality inadequacies which render them incapable of functioning independently.

Holistic medicine does not appear to be on their agenda.

One function of the disease concept in medicine is to avoid the political use of terminology. Can we escape from it? Not entirely, but one of the best expositions of how to try is given by Wing (1978).

> Putting forward a diagnosis is like putting forward a theory. It can be tested. Is it useful or not? . . . The first requirement of a disease theory is the recognition of a cluster of undesirable traits or characteristics that tend to occur together. . . . The second essential element in any disease theory is the hypothesis that the cluster of traits is 'symptomatic' of some underlying biological disturbance.

Scadding (1990) argued that the abstract concepts which are useful to physicians and therefore appropriately called diseases are those that infer biological disadvantages. His own definition of disease is:

> The sum of the abnormal phenomena displayed by a group of living organisms in association with a specified common characteristic, or set of characteristics, by which they differ from the norm for their species in such a way as to place them at a biological disadvantage (Scadding, 1967).

He argued that if the criterion of biological disadvantage applies to a given cluster of phenomena then 'there should be no doubt about the propriety of medical intervention', a far cry from the rejection on grounds of 'untreatability' applied to some patients by some doctors. He recognized that short-term distress (e.g. bereavement) may be biologically adaptive, but still deserves some medical assistance, and he recognized a grey area where doctors will disagree about the degree of biological disadvantage. Here he had good advice which can be taken straight into the heart of forensic psychiatry for he pointed out that it matters not whether a patient's symptoms are conceived of as part of a disease or merely as a response to social circumstances, the symptoms still merit medical attention. Of course, all this becomes much more complicated when matters of *compulsory* treatment are to be considered.

A somewhat different view has been put by a psychologist, Ausubel (1961). Like many authors he made no distinction between 'illness' and 'disease', but he firmly tackled the Szasz (1962) view which was just emerging at that time. In particular, he challenged the view that only physical lesions constitute disease, and he noted the subjectivity of all disease assessments, whether physical or mental. Ausubel accepted Szasz's view that neurotic and personality disorders may be in some way regarded as expressions of problems in living, but suggested that it is perfectly possible to construe a syndrome in these social terms and simultaneously construe it in medical terms also. Manifestions of impaired functioning, adaptive compensation, and defensive over-reaction also occur in physical disease.

> The concept of mental illness has never been advanced as a demonological cause of human disharmony, but only as a co-manifestation with it of certain inescapable difficulties and hazards in personal and social adjustment.

Szasz's notion that mental illness is merely misbehaviour is dismissed as unhelpful because, whilst it is perfectly possible to construe behavioural problems in moral terms or in social terms, this does not conflict with a medical construction of behaviour. These different perspectives are not mutually incompatible, they rest on different precepts.

The Schwartz and Schwartz perspective on these problems has no place in this volume. The view of the psychiatrist as merely a prescriber of medicines and ECT belies good medical training, and certainly does not fulfil the practical reality of consumer expectations, and consumers should have some say in this matter. Further, doctors are, or should be, more than simple mechanistic operators. The psychotherapies, as among the most powerful, direct routes to the evaluation and modification of some aspects of brain function, cannot be ignored as a medical tool.

Other professionals, such as psychologists or social workers, are likely to develop specific skills in psychotherapy or sociotherapy and perhaps become more proficient in them than most doctors, and doubtless they will fill any vacuum left by psychiatrists if the latter do retreat from work with the behaviourally disordered. The most fundamental attribute of a well-trained doctor, however, is the capacity to see not only a diseased organ and a specific prescription, but also the whole organism that is the patient and the context of its existence. Only such a holistic approach would ensure a comprehensive service for patients.

In this book we are attempting to use the term 'disease' in the sense indicated by Wing and by Scadding, and in preference to the term 'disorder', which has been adopted in DSM-III R, for two reasons: first the term 'mental disorder' has acquired a legal meaning in Britain because of the various

British mental health acts, and secondly in order to keep psychiatric terminology in step with other medical terminology. We are content that personality disorders are classified as headings in the major classifications of diseases, even though this is mixed terminology, because the term personality disorder is now universal. We have to confess that not all our authors share the editors' enthusiasm for this perspective and some have been strict, according to their own tenets, in, for example, refusing to call personality disorders, diseases. We have done our best to arrive at a consensus, but respect these nosological differences. Readers should, therefore, not be surprised to find the terms used slightly differently in different chapters.

Disturbed

We have not used the term 'disturbed' very much, because we respect the vernacular definition and regard agitation as a central component of a disturbed mental state. Disturbed mental states may, therefore, be either the product of a mental disease, or of severe external stress in the absence of mental disease. We have not used the term 'disturbed' to mean 'neurotic' as is sometimes the case, nor as a generic term to avoid the term 'mentally disordered' with its legal connotations.

Insight

Lewis (1934) complained 'Little has been written about insight as a psychiatric problem'. He defined complete insight 'as a correct attitude towards a morbid change in oneself', but then went on to point out that it is very difficult to define what is meant by 'a correct attitude' and that in these terms insight may be as limited among those with physical disease as among those with mental disease. He also disliked the neurotic/psychotic dichotomy with the implication that loss of insight is necessarily confined to patients with psychosis, and he showed distaste for those who ask whether something is not 'really psychotic' or 'only a neurosis' and argued:

> It is I think correct to say that gross disorders of insight are often found in neuroses. . . . The obsessional's attitude towards his illness or to any special symptoms is vastly different from that of his wife, or his friend, or his doctor. . . . As for the hysteric—who would suppose that a girl with *dermatitis artefacta* has a healthy or normal attitude towards her symptom?

In modern texts Gelder et al. (1989) are among those who have tackled this issue. They defined insight for those with mental disease as 'awareness of one's own mental condition' but also stressed that it is not simply absent or present, it is a matter of degree. They urged that the concept be unpacked into four components:

1. Is the patient aware of the phenomena noticed by others?
2. If so, does he recognize that these phenomena are abnormal?
3. If so, does he consider that they are caused by mental illness?
4. If so, does he think he needs treatment?

In a review David (1990) carried this idea forward and developed an assessment schedule for what he regarded as the three dimensions of insight:

1. awareness of illness;
2. the capacity to relabel psychiatric experiences as abnormal; and
3. treatment compliance.

The measurement of insight is a fundamental part of the Maudsley Evaluation of Delusions Schedule (MADS; Taylor et al., in press). This extends the range of enquiry not only in relation to a patient's self-selected most important delusion, in which such independent variables as the patient's capacity to expose his belief to others are rated, but also in relation to the patient's resultant antisocial action(s) when these occur. Separate enquiry is made about his understanding of the moral, legal, risk engendering and provocative implications of his act. In the evaluation of the schedule with actively psychotic patients these items did not co-vary. Lewis (1934) earlier had pointed out that successful treatment and acquisition of insight might even be negatively correlated in a particular patient, poor insight being an advantage in some cases, because it leads the patient to repudiate the disease.

There is a further problem which is only partly addressed by some of these authors. Insight necessitates a subjective judgement made by one person about a subjective state in another. Such a judgement will depend on the skill of the observer in diagnosing mental disease, as well as the patient's attitudes to that disease. It will also depend to some extent on the observer's own attitudes and beliefs. For established rating schedules reliability has been addressed and confirmed, but this is generally a state that can only be attained between those of comparable training and experience, at best on more than one occasion. The concept of validity of the experience of a delusion, or insight is far more elusive, given that these are, in any case, subjective experiences. Nevertheless, it is in part the introduction of such standardized techniques of evaluation that have highlighted diagnostic and evaluative discrepancies at some levels of decision between US and UK psychiatrists (Cooper et al., 1972) and more recently, and at perhaps more serious levels, between psychiatrists in the West and in the former USSR.

It would be naive to suggest that all of those Russian psychiatrists who labelled political dissidents as mentally ill were lying; at least some of them will have genuinely assessed the prisoners brought before them as suffering from psychopathology and reduced insight. A further test, therefore, might be to try and rate the degree of integration or dissonance of three primary mental functions, spoken thoughts, actions, and apparent emotions. One of us has a patient with schizophrenia whose delusions remit nicely with depot phenothiazines, but he continues to be agitated. Whilst denying this, he drinks heavily and claims that each drink is the last and now he is reformed, all just a few hours before getting drunk again. He claims that he is now fit for work, or that he is studying, yet he spends most of his day doing nothing, or drinking, in spite of prompts by nurses. The patient is charming and casual observers quickly agree with him that he has 'recovered' and no longer requires treatment. We say he has little insight, not just because of scores on a rating scale, but also because of the dissonance between his words, his actions and his affect. Even this approach, however, is fraught with difficulty. It assumes that patients will speak frankly and that their actions will be overt. Wessely et al. (in press) found that there was little overall correlation between patient accounts of beliefs and action on them and informant accounts, given independently to researchers. This was largely accounted for by the fact that many beliefs were not volunteered and many 'actions' had gone unobserved, mostly because of their emphasis on avoidance, but occasionally because of their apparent ordinariness. For one patient, for example, the wearing of a green tie was a deliberate act of immense personal significance in the context of his delusion, but it was an act that had gone unobserved and had not been placed in a clinical context.

When discharge decisions are being considered for offender patients, a common question to arise is 'does the patient show remorse?' This may seem an inappropriate question, almost tantamount to 'does he show evidence of having suffered?' but it is related to very important wider questions of insight. It is better construed as an evaluation of the patient's understanding of the effect of his offence on other people, those directly involved and society as a whole. It is not enough simply to ask the patient about his guilt feelings. Thorough discussion is necessary of the patient's understanding of the factors surrounding the offence, including the steps he could have taken to prevent it happening, his views of what it would have been like to be on the receiving end are important, as are his views on the public reaction to his offence, including the reaction of the judge and jury at his trial. A full appraisal of these issues, as outlined in the MADS (mentioned above), is likely to go a long way towards giving guidance about the possibility of a recurrence of the behaviour.

Treatability

In Great Britain certain categories of patients cannot be admitted for treatment against their wishes unless 'such treatment is likely to alleviate or prevent a deterioration' of the condition. They are those defined in jthe Mental Health Act 1983 as psychopathically disordered, mentally impaired, or in the Mental Health (Scotland) Act 1984 as those with a mental disorder manifested only by abnormally aggressive or seriously irresponsible conduct. The adoption, in this way, in law, of another quasi-medical concept may have resulted in more disadvantage than advantage to mentally diseased people. The regulation was intended to safeguard people of uncertain psychiatric diagnosis from unjustified compulsory detention, in other words, imprisonment in hospital. There was particular concern about potentially dangerous patients, because experience suggested that they were more likely to spend exceptionally long periods in such detention.

Unfortunately, the provision tends to be interpreted in a way that protects existing services at least as much as the prospective patients, and remarkably little effort has been expended in developing testable methods of predicting response to treatment in the patient groups concerned. Worse, patients can be turned away as untreatable simply because the assessing service does not itself provide the means to treat the patient rather than because the patient is unresponsive to all known appropriate treatments.

Another problem is that clinicians may confuse treatability with curability. Hundreds of, perhaps most, diseases are incurable, but they can, nevertheless, usually be treated with great benefit to the patient. Specific treatments may be effective, but only partially so, or only for a finite period of time. In addition, the patients may be treated with nursing, palliatives, support and environmental adjustment. Accepting a role more limited than that of curer is difficult for some doctors, who may have been given inappropriate notions of medical omnipotence at medical school.

The issue of compulsion creates its own difficulties. Doctors are sometimes reluctant to offer patients with personality disorders the same judicious mixture of informal and compulsory care that they are willing to offer other patients. It is difficult to know why this should be, but it may be related to the questions of disease and illness mentioned above, personality disordered patients being deemed 'not ill' and therefore not morally eligible for compulsory treatment, the treatability criterion being used as a device to escape what might otherwise be a legal obligation which conflicts with this moral construction. It may follow from recognition that one of the key characteristics of people who acquire the label of psychopathic disorder is established recidivism, and given the populist view that nothing predicts reoffending as well as previous offending, fear of the responsibilities entailed in attempting to help is overwhelming. It is a sad fact that if such a patient commits a serious offence after leaving psychiatric care, then it seems that the psychiatrist and psychiatric services are as likely to be as vociferously condemned in the national media as the offender himself. It is perhaps unsurprising that some psychiatrists would try to avoid 'guilt by association'. Another important issue, advanced by a number of psychiatrists, particularly relates to those personality disordered people who have also committed very serious offences. The belief that if admitted to hospital these people would, in effect, be subject to indefinite custodial detention, whereas if dealt with outside the NHS they would receive determinate sentences and that this would somehow be fairer or more just, is an important factor in deterring them from making a hospital recommendation. Comparative studies of the long-term careers of such people following different pathways through the system have not been done.

Treatability should be assessed in the full awareness of the therapist's own attitudes and fears. These can then be relegated to a minor place in the assessment which should turn on the patient's diagnosis, his needs, his insight and his expressed treatment preferences. If the non-treatment option is seriously considered, then the consequences of such a decision for the patient should also be thoroughly considered. It could be, for example, that he is almost certain to go to prison where he may be affected adversely and thus deteriorate. Such a conclusion should swing the decision in favour of admission to hospital, because it would 'prevent a deterioration' as allowed for within the Act.

Evil

'Evil is doing things that hurt people when you know they wouldn't want you to do them'. So said a behaviourally disordered patient of limited intelligence. He has certainly captured one of the common views of evil—an intended harmful action.

Textbooks of psychiatry do not usually mention the subject of evil. That is interesting in itself considering that it is such a widespread human concept, but we do not believe that a textbook of forensic psychiatry can escape entirely from touching on this topic. The Sutcliffe trial is dealt with in Ch. 2, its central feature was the question of whether the defendant was mad or bad. The correspondent from the *Observer*, Piers Paul Read, wrote on Sunday, 24 May 1981:

> If one believes in the Devil, not as an abstract idea, but as a real being with the power of Satan in the Book of Job to 'roam about the earth' then it is possible to postulate demonic possession of a murderer like Sutcliffe. . . . It seemed plausible that some other being had entered into him—not the spirit of God as he claimed, but some demon with an ironic sense of humour. . . . If this was true then the contentions of both prosecution and defence would have been right. Peter Sutcliffe might have been both evil and mad.

This debate between madness and evil permeates much of forensic psychiatry, and the practitioner has to be aware of it. It is the language of the layman and the politician. It is even on occasions the language of prison governors. The governor of Strangeways prison blamed the 1990 riot on the work of the devil!

Wickedness is the subject of a book by Midgley (1984). A review in the *Spectator* printed on the fly leaf said:

> This topic raises so many problems that social scientists have lately tended to sweep it right under the carpet, reducing wrong-doing to mental illness, social

conditioning, or a figment of the punitive imagination, while philosophers have concealed it behind a decent veil of general scepticism.

Note the *'reducing* of wrong-doing to mental illness' (italics added), it could never be 'elevating', even though, after struggling with her daunting task, Midgley concluded that evil is actually a negative, the absence of good. 'Evil, in spite of its magnificent pretentions, turns out to be mostly a vacuum'. This just side-steps the question, because it leaves the problem of understanding good. Midgley argued against the view of evil as an outside agency; 'it seems necessary' she wrote 'to locate some of its sources in the unevenness of (the) original equipment' (i.e. our bodies and minds). She commended Freud's notion of a destructive force within us, a death wish (Freud, 1920), but also noted that it is an idea akin to demonic possession. She highlighted Darwin's profound view that—

> any animal whatever, endowed with well marked social instincts . . . would inevitably acquire a moral sense or conscience as soon as its intellectual powers had become as well, or as nearly as well developed, as in man (Darwin, 1883),

but she went on virtually to equate evil with Fromm's concept of necrophilia (*see* p. 392) 'the attraction to what is dead, decaying, lifeless and purely mechanical' (Fromm, 1974). Finally, Midgley concluded that, in evolution, increasing intelligence brings to consciousness conflicts which in other animals seem to pass unnoticed:

> Human beings are forced on pain of disintegration, to form some kind of policies for reconciling their contrary impulses. This makes some kind of morality necessary.

The problem with Midgley's book is that it makes two assumptions which are unlikely. The first is that there really is a thing called evil, and the second seems to be that the language of morality is legitimately amalgamated with the language of medicine and science. Midgley opened by asking 'is wickedness mythical' and, answering in the negative, urged her readers to make their notion of wickedness more realistic. This is the error of reification which was discussed in relation to the disease concept above. It leads directly to the conclusion which Midgley tried to avoid, that of evil as a 'force' or a 'possession'. That, as figures from a 1983 *Observer* survey quoted in her book show, is what the average European thinks. Some writers make no bones about it. Hampshire (1989), for example, said:

> The notion of evil is the idea of a force, or forces, which are not merely contrary to all that is more praiseworthy and admirable and desirable in human life, but a force which is actively working against all that is praiseworthy and admirable.

This seems to have much in common with Mackay's (1869) account of 'witch mania', just one of a range of 'extraordinary popular delusions' that he cited as afflicting western societies at various stages of their development. He described not only accusers, but also the accused as being reluctant to take human behaviour at face value:

Depraved persons, who in ordinary times would have been thieves or murderers, added the desire of sorcery to their depravity, sometimes with the hope of acquiring power over their fellows. . . .

This introduction of an additional quality, of power over others is interesting. It is close to Fromm's (1974) view of sadism (*see* p. 390). After an account of an investigation of allegations of devil worship and witchcraft involving children in a remote Swedish village, resulting in 70 executions, as well as numerous lesser punishments, Mackay observed:

When men wish to construct or support a theory, how they torture facts into their service! . . . if, instead of commissioners as deeply sunk in the slough of ignorance as the people they were sent amongst, there had been deputed a few men firm in courage and clear in understanding, how different would have been the result!

This accords essentially with our view that the languages of morality and of science, or medicine, should not be confused, *but*, and it is a very big but, that does not mean that doctors do not have moral views, being people they clearly do, nor that they do not use those moral views in their work. Neither does it mean that doctors do not apply moral values to scientific concepts, they do. Diseases are 'bad', leucocytes are 'good' even 'laudable'.

In this book, we try to take a Darwinian view about the moral sense. That means we regard it as the inevitable consequence of evolution. It is universal, powerful and very unlikely to die out. Darwin (1883) argued that human sociability makes men want to please one another and enables them to sympathize with others, their intellect gives them memories of things that have happened to them, and intellect also enables them to communicate, so that common opinions about what is good and bad can develop and group pressures can emphasize those things that are for 'the public good'. People also develop habits of obedience, and conformity to the wishes of the community. Darwin further argued that if—

men were reared under precisely the same conditions as hive-bees there can hardly be any doubt that our unmarried females, like the worker-bees, would think it a sacred duty to kill their brothers, and mothers would strive to kill their fertile daughters.

He saw a moral sense as a regulator of behaviour, a facilitator of actions that are biologically advantageous. It is easy to understand how man has nurtured, made sacred and studied this vital aspect of social living. It is easy, too, to see how man wants to inject reality into morality and find causes for it.

Morality is, however, just one way of construing human behaviour. Medicine and psychology have developed another which is based on empirical observation and laboratory science, and which proves especially useful in understanding certain abnormalities, malfunctions and aberrations. They provide possibilities for limiting or changing such abnormalities, and so they too are powerful. Neither medicine nor psychology are, however, necessarily in conflict with a moral perspective unless there is insistence on reification of the syndromes or diseases of medicine, or the constructs of psychologists, and the evils of morality.

In that case, why all the fuss? Mainly because few can accept that more than one view of a phenomenon can legitimately coexist. That is partly because if each view leads to action, then one view must prevail, as usually only one action can be taken at a time. This type of conflict can be particularly evident in court. To return to the Sutcliffe trial, the moral argument that his behaviour was wicked led inevitably to condemnation and imprisonment, whilst the view that he suffered from a disease led to hospital care (albeit secure care for a long period, even indefinitely) and an attempt to treat and change him. In practice, such conflicts are unusual, and courts have a knack of having a little bit of the moral view and a little bit of the medical view. The depressed shoplifter may be found guilty, given a moral lecture and then handed over to doctors for treatment.

Society construes individuals as having moral responsibility, guilt, blame in terms of their goodness and badness. Admittedly, in court, 'insanity' and other forms of mental ill health, concepts borrowed from a different language, are allowed as partial or complete 'excuses', but the very word excuse indicates that this too is done on moral grounds. Responsibility, then, a topic of much interest to lawyers and one where they frequently consult the psychiatrist, is a question of morality. This is why some of us advocate that when debates about responsibility occur in court, those debates should be conducted by lawyers and laymen alone, the physician is likely to talk at cross-purposes and, in any case, is no expert in morality, even if the excuse which is being imputed is mental disorder. All the doctor can do is to give an objective medical view, suggest a medical remedy and see whether the moral arguments will accommodate this in the case at issue. (*see* Gunn, 1991a for further discussion).

We have emphasized the different perspectives of medicine and the law because we are doctors. In dealings with offenders who are not mentally disordered, or whose mental disorder is largely irrelevant to their offending, many of the same principles apply to sociological constructs and social work interventions that may be advanced. This will remain so while society itself continues to place multiple constructions on its non-conforming or damaging members. Its greatest conflict perhaps lies between the moral and the pragmatic—and the sometimes dissonant resultant interests in punishment or excuse on the one hand, and the pragmatics of working towards real prevention of harm on the other.

The Psychiatrist and the Law

It is inevitable that large sections of this book cover matters which are specifically medico-legal. One or two points are thus worth emphasizing. It is extremely important, in spite of the evident overlap of interests, for psychiatrists to avoid playing amateur lawyers and *vice versa*. It is even more important for psychiatrists to recognize and listen to sound legal advice. This is a central skill in forensic psychiatry. There is much legal advice, only a proportion of which is sound. How can the sound be distinguished from the unsound? Sound legal advice will usually come from someone who is well read or experienced in the field concerned. Lawyers, like doctors, specialize. Sound legal advice will usually follow a coherent pattern of argument and make sense in a broader context, it will only rarely be dogmatic and/or partisan. Unsound legal advice will come from enthusiasts and zealots, it will frequently be dogmatic and difficult to follow to a logical conclusion.

On the whole, British law is very supportive of good professional practice. The doctor who works well within the limits of medical ethics, who puts patients before personal interests, and who practises to the best of his ability will rarely, if ever, be in conflict with the law. The first prerequisite for lawful practice, therefore, is good medicine. The law intrudes into medical practice in only a limited number of ways. Specific laws dealing with medical problems are enacted by Parliament, and should always be available for reference. Some sections of the British mental health acts are appended to this book. Patients may sue doctors after a poor outcome to a course of treatment. Here the best defence is high professional standards, tested with an informed peer or peer group. In psychiatry, because of the psychiatrists' special powers of detention, there is a complex set of laws, regulations and institutions to deal with these powers. Knowledge of the local arrangements is as essential to the practice of psychiatry as is knowledge of the pharmaco-poeia. Any psychiatrist should see this knowledge therefore, or access to this knowledge, as part of good professional practice.

Beyond a basic knowledge of the legal framework of psychiatry and good practice, the best way of avoiding legal difficulties is to engage in peer review quite frequently. This can be done through informal consultations, formal one-to-one consultations, seminars and medical audit.

Court Work

Court work can have a significant impact on the work of a psychiatrist, especially a forensic psychiatrist. Such work can be mystifying, intimidating, time-consuming and frustrating. Guidance is given in subsequent chapters about techniques for avoiding these negative factors. As a preliminary to those chapters, it is worth noting that court work should never, for the psychiatrist, become an end in itself. It should always be possible to explain easily and openly why a particular piece of court work is of benefit to a patient or to patients as a group. Court work should be strictly limited and, if the benefits are not obvious, avoided. Court work should always be justifiable in terms of efficiency, that is the time invested should be in proportion to the benefits obtained. If matters, such as responsibility, can be argued just as well without a psychiatric perspective, then the temptation to provide such a perspective should be resisted.

In court, no quarter should be given to the view that 'our side must win', and doctors will sometimes have quite different considerations from the lawyers with whom they work. A doctor should take an objective view of the issues before him, and only be as partisan as medical ethics require. In law, the doctor, like any other expert, is supposed to have 'no other desire than to assist the court' (*Nowell*). That implies that everything, including all clinical duties, should be suspended for this high purpose. In practice, it can be taken to indicate that the doctor is expected to give a balanced view, not dependent on which 'side' employed him, but professional judgements will have to be made in each case as to how far the court's desires should interfere with medical standards. In England this doctrine has been taken to the point where it seems perfectly proper for a doctor to provide the court with information which the employing solicitor would prefer to suppress (*Edgell*).

2

The Law, Adult Mental Disorder, and the Psychiatrist in England and Wales

(With comments from the rest of the United Kingdom and the Republic of Ireland)

Edited by
John Gunn

Written by
Oliver Briscoe
David Carson
Paul d'Orbán
Don Grubin
John Gunn
Paul Mullen
Stephen Stanley
Pamela J. Taylor

With contributions from

Fred Browne (*N. Ireland*); Derek Chiswick and Martin Humphreys (*Scotland*); Enda Dooley (*Republic of Ireland*); Jeff McPherson (Military Law); Peter Noble (part of Civil Law)

This chapter is parochial, for law is parochial, although some core concepts such as *mens rea* are universal in the common law world. The discussion rarely extends beyond the United Kingdom and only occasionally beyond England and Wales, but many of the principles are of wider application.

The Common Law

Legal systems arise from diverse local customs, and become formalized as a society's development requires uniformity and predictability in the control of crime, the regulation of interpersonal relations, and the ordering of commercial transactions. The two most influential legal systems are Roman law and systems derived from it, and English common law with its developments overseas. Countries in continental Europe have legal systems derived from Roman law, as does Scotland. In many of the countries of the Commonwealth, and in North America, the English common law has been transplanted. In many developing Commonwealth countries, there is an admixture of traditional law, both systems being administered by the courts. Religion has also had a formative influence on the Law. Islamic law is important in countries where that religion is dominant. The canon law of the Christian Church developed both by the Church and in the medieval universities, enriched the development of the English common law, particularly in the importance to be attached to the individual conscience in the determination of criminal responsibility and to the pledge in contracts. Mercantile law flowed into the common law in the 17th century with the growth of trade.

In England the postconquest seignorial courts gradually gave way to the unifying effect of a common law administered by the royal judges riding out on circuit from Westminster to hold assizes in major towns and, by the end of the 13th century, the supremacy of the King's courts was established. To ease the burden upon the royal judges of administering the criminal law nationwide, the forerunners of present-day magistrates were appointed by 1328. The King's Bench was one of the principal central courts set up at that time. The exercise of the early common law depended upon a limited number of particular writs issued by the King's Chancery and only certain wrongs were recognized as capable of being redressed. The embryonic centralized or common law was developed by the royal judges adapting customs and such principles as they knew. They were held to be the repository of the law and would declare what it was when confronted by a particular set of circumstances. Thus, we can see the origins of the present concept of precedent where an established principle decided in a specific case is applicable in subsequent cases, although superior courts can overrule a precedent.

The early writs were not sufficiently flexible for a developing society, and pleas for justice, where no writ was available, began to be made to the King. The Court of Chancery was established as the pleas addressed to the King were passed to the Lord Chancellor who tended to decide according to what he thought was equitable instead of following strict common law principles hammered out by the King's judges. So the common law grew by the experience of innumerable cases, leavened by the individualistic remedies of the Chancery. As more cases were heard in the Chancery courts, it too began to develop rules and principles as precise as those of common law. That system came to be known as equity. For many years the common law and equity developed side by side, practised in different courts by different judges. In 1873 the Judicature Act fused these two systems so that courts today employ both blended together. A contemporary example would be the legal mortgage and the equitable mortgage, both capable of being held in respect of the same property, but subject to different rules (*see* Walker, 1980 for definitions).

A strength of the common law was its roots in the country's history and social customs. It became an integral and growing part of society, adapted by the judges as they saw the need. This natural indigenous strength enabled it to withstand the otherwise probable introduction of Roman law at the time of the Renaissance. Roman law had the attraction of a logically coherent system, international, familiar to the Church and supported by the universities. The contrast was drawn by the celebrated American judge, Justice Holmes, who said 'the life of the (common) law is experience and not logic'. Thus, the common law grew by adaptation and response to actual circumstances and situations, instead of starting with a general theoretical formulation of legal principles which would then be applied to particular cases as in Roman law (*see* Pollock and Maitland, 1968 for further reading).

In England the adversarial system of justice is employed. When a criminal case is heard in the Crown Court the parties to the case are the accused or defendant, and the Crown or prosecution. The legal representatives of both sides present their view of the facts, examine and cross-examine witnesses, and make closing speeches to the jury. The judge sums up, and instructs the jury upon the law. The jury are the judges of fact, they consider the evidence, bring in a verdict, and the judge passes sentence. Only some cases are officially reported, but those that are add to the ever-growing body of reported decisions which influence the results in future cases on identical or similar relevant facts. There are many sets of printed reports. The All England Law Reports are an example. Databases, such as Lexis, are now recording all the decisions of the High Court and above.

The doctrine of precedent is very important to the practice of law in England. Judgments are said to be binding or persuasive. Thus a judgment in the Court of Appeal on a particular set of facts will bind judges in the Crown Court in a case on conceptually similar facts. A judgment in the House of Lords will bind the Court of Appeal. A judgment in the Crown Court will be only of persuasive authority if a similar case is heard in the Crown Court.

The common law used to describe English law has many meanings. It may mean all case law, as distinct from statutes. It may mean the original common law as distinct from equity. It may mean case law and statute together, as distinct from Roman law. Civil law is another confusing term. It may refer to the common law only, and be used to distinguish criminal cases from others. On the other hand, the civil law and 'civilians' (those who practise it), can also be used to mean Roman law as distinct from common law.

In modern English law, statute (i.e. Acts of Parliament) plays an increasingly important part. Sometimes statutes are used to codify parts of the law, where perhaps a myriad of individual case decisions have become what Cromwell called an 'ungodly jumble', and have made the law uncertain. The Theft Acts 1968 and 1978 are examples of codifying statutes. Sometimes, like the Mental Health Act 1983 (MHA 1983) statutes arise purely from

Parliamentary concern and debate. Statutes are often framed in general terms, and precise definition may not be given. Thus the term 'responsible medical officer' (RMO) in the Mental Health Act 1983 is not defined. If a particular case required the term to be defined, this would be a question of law for a judge in the particular circumstances of the case. Another example might be the meaning of 'treatment' in a particular statute.

Thus the common law in its broadest sense is a cycle of accumulating case decisions which may require clarification by statute, itself to be interpreted by further case law. How the cases concentrate and what statutes are required depend upon the issues in contemporary society, its philosophy, its politics, ethics, and its concept of rights. Since Britain joined the European Economic Community, the European Court has erected a further tier of binding authority above the House of Lords.

The significance of common law for the psychiatrist is that many ordinary medical procedures and actions are underpinned by this comprehensive and flexible legal system. It is an older system of law than modern statute law. It is gradually being codified by Parliamentary statutes, but it should not be thought that in situations where little or no statute law has been enacted there is no law. Usually there is well-developed common law. A case in point is the law of battery. This is the infliction of unlawful personal violence by one person on another. Violence in this sense includes all degrees of personal contact (e.g. touching) without consent or other lawful authority. Clearly, this is of great importance in medicine, for much that is done by a doctor could be called battery unless it is with the consent of the patient. Hence the importance of the law of consent. The MHA 1983 deals with consent in a few special circumstances, all other circumstances are covered by common law principles and cases. It is, therefore, quite fallacious to assume that physical contact with mentally disordered patients, which is not covered by the MHA 1983, is either forbidden, or covered by no law—it is, in fact, covered by common law principles. To carry the example one final step, sex-change operations, cosmetic surgery, and organ transplants in the mentally disordered are all legal in certain circumstances provided the patient is capable of giving proper consent, and consents. A second opinion would always be helpful in such cases.

Many other circumstances are covered by the common law. It is not possible to deal extensively with the common law authorities or cases in this book. Professionals in doubt about the legal position in a particular case should consult legal textbooks and, on occasions, legal advisers. However, and this is most important, they should not allow ignorance of the law, or absence of advice prevent them from acting in the patient's best interests. If a matter is urgent, then good medical care should be offered without looking backwards to law. The commonest civil suit that patients bring against clinicians is one of negligence, but the law of negligence emphasizes both contemporary standards of professional practice and what level of competence was to be reasonably expected. Acting in good faith with proper professional skill on behalf of the patient is usually a sound defence when negligence is alleged, particularly in an emergency (*see* for example S.62 MHA 1983). Indeed, inaction may itself be unlawful in some situations because, if the law construed that someone has a duty to take a particular action, then failure to take that action may give rise to a criminal charge or to a civil liability.

Mental Health Law (England and Wales)

The Mental Health Act 1983

The legislation which currently most affects the mentally disordered, in England and Wales, is the MHA 1983. It represents the consolidation of two earlier Acts—the Mental Health Act 1959 and the Mental Health (Amendment) Act 1982. The reforms which came to psychiatric practice in England and Wales were followed by similar measures for Scotland in 1984, and in Northern Ireland in 1986. Only the tiny island communities of the Channel Islands and the Isle of Man were essentially untouched by the changes. No attempt is made within this text to discuss the law in any detail. More detailed information can be found in Hoggett (1990a). We believe that the principles and some of the main elements should give the reader sufficient outline information for further study, especially if these are amplified by the extracts of the Act itself and the Code of Practice given in Appendices 1 and 2.

Scope

The Act is wide-ranging and deals separately with different mental capacities. Capacity to decide about becoming a hospital inpatient is one thing, capacity to decide about treatment once there quite another, capacity to manage personal affairs is again distinct, and so on. Mechanisms are laid down for the monitoring of general standards of care, principally through the Mental Health Act Commission (MHAC), an independent body introduced by the MHA 1983 (*see* Ch. 4 p. 194), and for the care of individuals who are compulsorily detained, through the managers of the detaining hospital, the MHAC and the mental health review tribunals (MHRTs) (*see* Ch. 4 p. 188).

Weaknesses of the MHA 1983 lie in its web of legalism and bureaucracy, and its depletion of the pool of treatment resources available for the mentally disordered because of its demand on resources without attendant new funding. Only when a court may wish to place an offender in a hospital bed are there explicit provisions for the courts to require the Regional Health Authority 'to furnish the court with such information as that Authority has . . . with respect to the hospital . . . at which arrangements could be made for the admission. . . .' (S.39). The Act stops short of requiring the Authority to provide a bed. The District Health Authorities and the local social services have a duty to provide aftercare (S.117) for those who have been detained under a civil treatment order (S.3), as well as those detained by a hospital order imposed by the courts (S.37), for as long as they believe it is necessary. The ordinary outpatient, the informal inpatient, even the patient compulsorily detained up to 28 days for assessment (S.2) has no such legally enshrined right to care.

Most of the Act is concerned with setting limits. Part I sets the limits of mental disorder for the purposes of the Act; Part II the limits for compulsory admission of ordinary patients; Part III for offender patients; Part IV sets the limits on the nature and extent of treatment allowed, while Part V deals with limits on continuing detention. The remaining five parts of the Act deal with such matters as the transport of patients, deportation, the management of patients' property, oversight of the system, offences against the Act and a miscellany of duties to inform patients' relatives, and power to bring the mentally disordered to a place of safety for assessment.

Legal definitions of mental disorder

'Mental disorder' in the MHA 1983 means:

1. mental illness, undefined: as the memorandum on the Act (Dept. Health & Social Security 1987) notes its usage is a matter for clinical judgement;
2. severe mental impairment: arrested or incomplete development of mind which includes severe impairment of intelligence *and* social functioning *and* is associated with abnormally aggressive or seriously irresponsible conduct;
3. mental impairment: as (2) above, substituting 'significant' for 'severe';
4. psychopathic disorder: a persistent disorder or disability of mind, irrespective of intelligence level, which also results in abnormally aggressive or seriously irresponsible conduct.

'Mental disorder' also includes 'any other disorder or disability of mind' which is vague and broad. It surely implies that every kind of mental disease is covered by the Act apart from the specific exceptions of section 1 which indicate that a person may not be dealt with under the Act as mentally disordered 'by reason *only* of promiscuity or other immoral conduct, sexual deviancy or dependence on alcohol or drugs' (our emphasis).

This clause is widely misinterpreted as a reason for not providing treatment for sex offenders. It should be noted, however, that it is *compulsory* treatment for promiscuity, immoral conduct and sexual deviancy which is in doubt. Further, if all mental disorder may be subject to compulsory care at times, then diseases such as paedophilia are included. Whether an individual patient should be subject to compulsory treatment, depends upon the range of variables (insight, motivation, treatability, dangerousness, and deterioration) which apply to any patient. Surely, the point of the clause is to prevent someone who does not have a recognized disease being subject to the Act simply because his behaviour is questionable or illegal. A rapist, for example, may have no mental disorder, i.e. no sexual deviation, no personality disorder, no mental illness. His rape may be related to insensitivity, misunderstanding, thoughtlessness or revenge. Such a man would not qualify for compulsory treatment under the Act.

The powers to detain under treatment and hospital orders are further limited in relation to mental impairment and psychopathic disorder by requiring that treatment in hospital 'is likely to alleviate or prevent deterioration of the condition' (S.3) and (S.37). While it is important that no-one, even the mentally ill or severely subnormal, is forced into hospital for treatment that will produce no benefit, the clause implies that some individuals although diseased, can legitimately be denied hospital care as untreatable. In practice, some psychiatrists use the clause as a convenient method of ensuring that difficult, troublesome, unpopular, or chronic patients are excluded from hospital, many ending up in prison instead. It is clear that this is not the intention of the Act, for in section 145 medical treatment is taken to include nursing, care, habilitation and rehabilitation, all of which are appropriate treatment for many cases of personality disorder. *Dillon* makes it clear that treatment as envisaged in S.145 is sufficient.

In our view, the only acceptable test of treatability is a consideration of what would happen if all treatment was withheld, i.e. nursing, occupational therapy, support and counselling. If this would be likely to produce a deterioration, then the patient is treatable within the meaning of the Act.

Compulsory admission to hospital

Section 131 of the MHA 1983 tells us that 'Nothing in this Act shall be construed as preventing a patient who requires treatment for mental disorder from being admitted . . . without any application, order or direction, rendering him liable to be detained under this Act . . .', thus emphasizing the pre-eminence of informality, of treating the mentally disordered patient as far as possible like any other patient.

The civil provisions for compulsory assessment and treatment.   The current emergency provisions are shown in Table 2.1. The preferred method of compulsory admission to hospital for assessment (under which the resultant treatment is also covered) is under S.2 of the Act for a maximum of 28 days (Table 2.2). Two registered medical practitioners must examine the patient, not more than 5 days apart, and recommend the detention. One of the doctors must be approved by the 'Secretary of State' (in practice, the local health authority) as having special experience in the diagnosis or

Table 2.1

Provisions for the Compulsory Care of Mentally Disordered Patients in an Emergency in England and Wales

Place of crisis in patient's care	Section MHA 1983	Necessary conditions	Rules for application	Maximum period of detention and action
New/renewed presentation to doctor	4 (2)	Suffering from mental disorder **and** Ought to be detained in hospital in interests of (a) own health/safety **or** (b) protection of others **and** Specify urgency	Application by an approved social worker or **nearest** relative **and** Recommendation by medical practitioner (doctor) **and** The applicants and doctor must have seen the patient in the previous 24 h	72 h from the time of admission to hospital
Public place	136	Appears to be suffering from mental disorder **and** In immediate need of care and control	Removal by constable to place of safety (incl. local authority accommodation, hospital or police station)	72 h from arrival at place of safety Assessment by doctor **and** approved social worker
In self seclusion/ private accommodation	135	Believed to be suffering from mental disorder **and** Being ill-treated, neglected or without control	Application by approved social worker **or** constable **or** other authorized by Act **and** Warrant issued by magistrate Resultant entry to premises by constable accompanied by doctor and approved social worker	72 h from arrival in place of safety
Already in hospital	5(2/3)	Appears to doctor in charge of patient **or** to nominated deputy that application should be made	Doctor provides written report for hospital managers	72 h from time of report
	5(4)	Appears to nurse that patient is suffering from mental disorder of a degree necessary for his health or safety **or**	Nurse provides written report to hospital managers	6 h from report or until arrival of doctor

	Protection of others that he be immediately restrained from leaving hospital **and** A doctor is not immediately available			
In prison on remand	48	Suffering from mental illness or severe mental impairment of a nature and degree that make hospital appropriate Urgency specified	Evidence from at least two doctors to Satisfy the Secretary of State who may Issue a warrant for transfer	Limited by recovery and/or report by RMO to Secretary of State or by trial
under sentence	47	*See* Table 1.3: no different for emergency		

Table 2.2
Provisions for Non-emergency Compulsory Care of Patients in England and Wales

Nature of provision	Section of MHA 1983	Necessary conditions	Rules for application	Maximum period
Assessment	2	Suffering from mental disorder— not further classified Ought to be detained in hospital in interests of (a) own health/safety **or** (b) protection of others	Application by approved social worker or nearest relative Recommendation by two doctors (one must be approved)	Up to 28 days
Treatment	3	Suffering from a named category of mental disorder In case of psychopathic disorder and mental impairment, treatment is likely to alleviate condition or prevent deterioration As S.2 above	Application by nearest relative or a social worker unless nearest relative objects Recommendation by two doctors (one must be approved)	Up to 6 months in the first instance, can be extended for further 6 months, then for further periods of one year at a time
Guardianship	7	Patient over 16 years old Suffering from specified mental disorder Necessary for welfare of patient or protection of others	Application by nearest relative or approved social worker Recommendations of two doctors (one must be approved) Guardian may be local authority or person acceptable to that authority	Up to 6 months in the first instance, can be extended for further 6 months, then for further periods of one year at a time

treatment of mental disorder (under S.12) and, unless that doctor has previously known the patient then, where possible, the other doctor should know him. The nearest relative or an approved social worker, having consulted with the nearest relative, must make an application for admission. The concept of the nearest relative (S.26–30) for these purposes is complicated, Table 2.3 sets out the order of precedence. In clinical practice, the Act itself should be consulted. The nearest relative may prevent an application for a treatment or guardianship order by a social worker by objecting to the social worker or the local authority.

Table 2.3
The Nearest Relative
Mental Health Act 1983 S.26–30
Mental Health (Scotland) Act 1984 S.53–56
Mental Health (Northern Ireland) Order Act 1986 S.32–38

For adults

1. The person living with or caring for the patient takes precedence, including in rank order:

   Spouse*
   Opposite sex cohabitee for 6 months
   Other person with whom patient has ordinarily lived for not less than 5 years
   Blood relative (*see 2*)

2. Blood relative in rank order
   (within each category older/oldest takes precedence):

   Child
   Legitimate parent
   Mother if illegitimate
   Sibling (whole blood takes precedence over half blood)
   Grandparent
   Grandchild
   Uncle or aunt
   Nephew or niece

3. Another person authorized by the nearest relative

4. Court appointed 'acting nearest relative' (where otherwise no-one, an incompetent, one who unreasonably objects to the admission, or one who recklessly discharges from hospital)

For minors

1. The guardian or local authority (for a child in care)

2. The High Court in wardship cases

* Problems can arise over whether spouses are actually separated

N.B. *This is a guidance only. The legislation itself must be consulted in cases of doubt. See also* pp. 952–3.

When the doctors are agreed that the patient is suffering from a mental disorder of a nature or degree that warrants detention in hospital, and that it would be in the interests of the patient, or for the protection of others, to admit, and doctors and applicant alike are satisfied that there is no alternative to compulsory admission, the papers must be received by or on behalf of the managers of the hospital where the patient is to be detained. Only then does the detention order take legal effect. The wording of these sections is given in Appendix 1 p. 945. **It is important to note that, in essence, the patient may be detained either for the safety of others *or* for the sake of his own health**. It is not necessary for a patient to be 'a danger' as seems to be believed on occasions (*see* Weleminsky and Birley, 1990).

The same fundamental principles apply to the compulsory admission to hospital for treatment (S.3) (Table 2.2) and to guardianship (S.7–10). The latter requires a patient to reside in a place specified by the guardian. The guardian may be a named person or the local authority. For these longer periods of detention or controlled residence respectively, extra stringencies are introduced. For compulsory admission for treatment (as opposed to assessment), it is not sufficient to designate the patient 'mentally disordered', the legal category of the disorder must be specified, as described above. For guardianship, the 'treatability' clauses for psychopathy and mental impairment may be omitted, but guardianship cannot apply to anyone under the age of 16 years.

Both the treatment order and the guardianship order last for up to 6 months in the first instance. Renewal, in both cases, requires examination and further reporting by the responsible doctor, enquiry by a social worker and scrutiny by the retaining/authorizing authority. The first period of renewal (i.e. after the first 6 months), similarly has a limit of 6 months but, thereafter, renewal may be for periods of up to 12 months. Occasionally, during the course of such detention, it may be found that the predominant mental disorder has changed. The illness may largely recover, for example, but the personality disorder may remain apparent, and be of a sufficient degree to merit continuing detention or guardianship. Section 16 makes provision for a reclassification, in legal terms, of the category of disorder of such patients. Patients detained under these powers have periodic rights of appeal to an MHRT (*see* pp. 188–94).

Whilst the use of treatment orders is common, guardianship orders are rare. This may be related to the fact that local authorities have some reluctance to take them on, because patients who would be suitable for such orders would make substantial demands on resources. Whatever the reasons, it is a pity that this important provision is so little used. If good collaboration is established between social worker (or relative) and doctor, it can be used to keep a patient functioning in the community and prevent relapses and repeated admissions (*see* Law Commission 1990).

Offender patients and compulsory detention (*see also* pp. 72–5). The MHA 1983 also provides for the compulsory detention in hospital of anyone suspected, charged or convicted of criminal offences. The majority of compulsorily detained offender patients are detained under Part III of the Act and the principal provisions are listed in Table 2.4.

A tiny minority is detained under the provisions of the Criminal Procedure (Insanity and Unfitness to Plead) Act 1991 described below (pp. 44–8, 72–5). A few people, in spite of being offenders, are detained under the civil provisions (Part II) of the MHA 1983. Considerable numbers of patients who have broken the law and who need psychiatric treatment are assessed or treated on a wholly voluntary basis. Some are constrained by other measures which, unlike the MHA 1983, do not confer holding powers on the hospital, but ensure sanctions if conditions are breached. Such arrangements include conditions of bail, probation, bind over and parole, and are discussed further below.

The 1983 Act introduced some innovative measures for detaining in hospital potential patients who are awaiting trial or sentence, but the experiment has not been entirely satisfactory. The remands to hospital for report (S.35) and treatment (S.36) are both time-limited to 12 weeks in all and not more than 28 days at a time. Those on a murder charge cannot be remanded to hospital for treatment (S.36), because they are ineligible for a hospital order. Compulsory treatment is not covered by a remand to hospital for a report (S.35), although compulsory treatment can be provided either under the common law in an emergency or by the addition of a treatment order (S.3) (*see* Code of Practice p. 1005). Remands for treatment (S.36) can be imposed only by the Crown Court. A transfer from custodial remand (S.48) offers slightly more flexibility in not excluding those people on murder charges and in being limited in length mainly by the responsible doctor, who may even defer the time of trial if he believes the patient to be too disordered to appear in court. Patients with psychopathic disorder or mental impairment alone cannot be transferred under this provision and urgency has to be specified (NB urgent is much broader than an emergency). Cumbersome and uncertain though it is, the combination of a bail remand and use of one of the civil powers of detention remains the only useful way forward for some patients. A remand on bail with condition of residence in a hospital is not in itself sufficient to empower hospital staff to detain patients. All these provisions are little used (Mental Health Act Commission, 1987). A recommendation to combine sections 35 and 36 into a single power (MHAC, 1987) is unlikely to change the picture much further because the likeliest reason for the poor implementation is lack of resources.

Once convicted of an imprisonable offence other than murder, detention in hospital for a trial of treatment, under an interim treatment order (S.38), or for treatment under a hospital order (S.37) becomes possible (*see below* p. 72–5).

Consent to treatment

In most circumstances, attempts to enforce any form of physical treatment on a patient without his explicit consent could result in a civil suit alleging battery. The nature of mental disorder, however, means that a number of patients will not be able to understand the nature of their illnesses or the implications of treatment and, thus, not be able to give valid consent to treatment. Further, they may refuse treatment as a result of their illness. Before the MHA 1983, common law was the chief source of protection for patients against wrongful treatment or its inappropriate withholding, or for medical and nursing staff against such allegations. The MHA 1983 introduced a new legal concept of consent to treatment. It is confusing that the same words are applied to the new legal construct as to a medical and lay

Table 2.4
The Powers of the Criminal System to Detain in Hospital

Nature of provision	Section of MHA 1983	Court/authority	Offender conditions	Psychiatric conditions	Effects of order
Remand to hospital for reports	35	Magistrates *or* Crown	Charged **or** Convicted Bail impractical (not applicable if *convicted* of an offence with a fixed penalty)	Written/oral evidence from *one* doctor recognized under S.12 of mental disorder **and** availability of bed within 7 days	Up to **28 days' detention** Renewable for 28 days on production of further psychiatric evidence **Maximum 12 weeks** **Absconding** means rearrest without warrant and return to court
Remand to hospital for treatment	36	Crown	Charged **or** Convicted Bail impractical	Written/oral evidence from *two* doctors, one recognized under S.12 of mental illness **or** severe mental impairment **and** availability of bed in 7 days	Up to **28 days' detention** Renewable for 28 days on written/oral psychiatric evidence **and** legal **representation** of patient in Court **Maximum 12 weeks** Absconding, as for S.35
Interim hospital order	38	Magistrates *or* Crown	Convicted **and** Hospital order (S.37) **may** be appropriate	Written/oral evidence of *two* doctors, one recognized under S.12, **and** one of whom must be employed by the hospital specified in the order mental disorder **and** availability of a bed within 28 days	Up to **12 weeks'** detention Renewable as S.36 but to maximum of 6 months Absconding as S.35 and 36

Order	Section	Authority	Status	Evidence	Effect
Hospital order *or* Guardianship order	37	Magistrates *or* Crown	Convicted	Written/oral evidence of two doctors one recognized under S.12 of: Mental illness or severe mental impairment **or** psychopathic disorder or mental impairment if treatment will alleviate or prevent deterioration **and** Minimum age 16 (for guardianship only) **and** Confirmation from doctor who will be in charge of treatment or representative of hospital managers of bed within 28 days	Up to 6 months' detention at doctor's discretion. Renewable on acceptance by hospital managers of report from doctor: for 6 months in the first instance and thereafter for periods of 12 months — Absconding means retaking by hospital staff or approved social worker or police and return to hospital within 28 days of absconding
Transfer to hospital of sentenced prisoners	47	Secretary of State (Home Office)	Convicted	Written evidence of two doctors, one recognized under S.12, of categories of mental disorder as in S.37 above	Detention in hospital as under S.37 unless, as is usual, restrictions on discharge have been applied (*see* 49 below)
Transfer to hospital of remanded prisoners	48	Secretary of State (Home Office)	Charged with **any offence and** subject to custodial remand; civil prisoners; detainees under Immigration Act 1971	Written evidence of two doctors of mental illness **or** severe mental impairment **and** urgency specified	Limited by recovery and/or report by RMO to Secretary of State **or** by trial
Restrictions on discharge	41	Crown Court	Subject to S.37 **and** dangerous i.e. order necessary for the protection of the public from serious harm	One of the two doctors giving evidence for S.37 gives **oral** evidence in court	Duration of order specified by court, commonly without limit of time — Leave outside hospital and discharge may be granted only by Secretary of State

Nature of provision	Section of MHA 1983	Court/authority	Offender conditions	Psychiatric conditions	Effects of order
Restrictions on discharge					Absconding: as S.37 but limit of period for retaking set by court limits (usually indefinite)
	49	Secretary of State	Subject to term of imprisonment		As S.41 with duration of restriction limited by length of imprisonment—expires at earliest release date taking earned remission into account

The Essential preconditions in all cases are that the offence may be punishable by imprisonment and except for S.47 and S.48, the sentence is not fixed by law, and for S.35 the accused has not been convicted of an offence where the sentence is fixed by law.

view of the concept. Thus, 'treatment not requiring consent' is not an invitation to ride roughshod over a patient's wishes, but simply an indication that the common law continues to apply to any treatment not specified in the Act or in its Code of Practice.

The special provisions of Part IV of the MHA 1983 apply only to the treatment of mental disorder. There is nothing in the Act to facilitate treatment of physical disorders, where a patient may be unable to consent to such treatment, or be refusing it, because of mental disorder. It seems reasonable to assume that doctors have a duty to treat actively where life is endangered, and a patient is mentally disordered (*see also* Ch. 22). It is not even clear whether epilepsy counts as a mental disorder. We believe it should be given the wide definition used in section 1 of the Act, but this is debatable.

The Act also provides for the denial of the rights of competent patients to determine their own destiny for specified treatments, albeit in only two, rather extreme, forms of treatment—psychosurgery, and hormonal *implants* for the control of male sexual drive, and thus few patients are affected. The MHAC (1987) reported that 92 patients nationally had been assessed for psychosurgery between September, 1983 and June, 1987 and that there were just three applications relating to the surgical implant of hormones. Nevertheless, some powers of self-determination have been removed from a small group of competent patients. Figure 2.1 illustrates the conditions which have to be met before treatments can proceed. Great emphasis is placed on consultation with a nurse, and another professional involved in the care of the patient, who is neither a nurse nor a doctor. In practice, it seems that the latter is usually a social worker (MHAC, 1987). The MHAC conceded that the process inevitably inflicts great stress on the patient.

The remaining limits are set for detained patients only and are essentially for the protection of staff. They enable treatment to be given legally to patients detained under any order which specifies treatment (emergency provisions and remand for assessment are not covered), not only when the patients cannot consent, but in some cases when they explicitly refuse. The procedures are set out in Fig. 2.2. Section 62 of the Act exempts treatments specified under S.57 and S.58 from such procedures when they are immediately necessary to save the patient's life, or, if reversible, are otherwise urgent. There are rarely substantial delays in getting an appointed doctor to visit and so, in practice, this means that a course of ECT may be started and hospital staff are generally covered to continue with medication even if a patient suddenly withdraws consent, until such time as an MHAC-appointed doctor can visit. Up to June, 1987, 5845 such second opinions had been given, disagreements between the MHAC doctor and medical officer occurring in only 4–6% of cases (MHAC, 1987). The MHAC seemed to justify the continuing high work load for such apparently low returns by arguing that in many cases a treatment plan is modified after comments have been made by the scrutinizing doctor. It may also be that the scrutiny ensures that a coherent treatment plan is drawn up and documented.

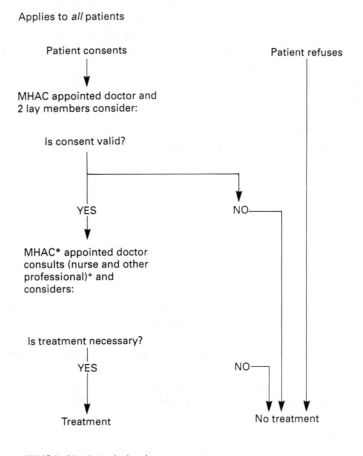

Applies to *all* patients

Patient consents   Patient refuses

MHAC appointed doctor and
2 lay members consider:

Is consent valid?

            YES   NO

MHAC* appointed doctor
consults (nurse and other
professional)⁺ and
considers:

Is treatment necessary?

            YES   NO

        Treatment   No treatment

*MHC in Northern Ireland
⁺Person (s) appearing principally
 concerned with patient's medical treatment
 in Northern Ireland

Fig. 2.1 Consent for psychosurgery or hormone implants for control of libido (S.57 MHA 1983; Article 63 MH (NI) O 1986).

The MHA 1983 provisions for compulsory treatment apply only to recognized hospitals. Prison hospitals are not covered and prison medical officers can enforce psychiatric treatment only under the common law in an emergency. There can be no question of continuing treatment against a prisoner's wishes and, if this appears necessary, a transfer to a recognized hospital is essential. Similarly, treatment cannot be enforced in the community in the long term. Until a treatment order expires, a patient can be kept on trial leave from hospital. If, during that period, medication is refused and deterioration sets in, then the patient's leave can be ended. It is not

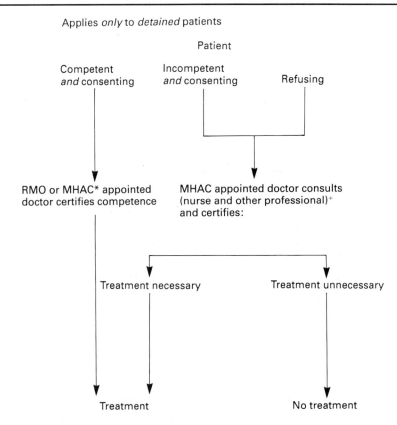

Applies *only* to *detained* patients

Fig. 2.2   Consent for ECT and for psychotropic drugs which have been given for longer than 3 months (S.58 MHA 1983; Article 64 MH (NI) O 1986).

permissible for patients to be readmitted briefly, solely for reassessment and renewal of the detention order (*Hallstrom & Gardiner*).

Treatment as a condition of discharge under Home Office restrictions (S.41, S.49) usually means a requirement to see a psychiatrist, but specific treatment cannot be enforced as an outpatient. Such restricted patients know, however, that a deterioration in their condition will result in a readmission to hospital, often a secure hospital, and so they usually comply with recommended treatments. Under a guardianship order, the patient can be brought to the psychiatrist but, again, there is no provision for enforcing treatment. Nevertheless, the guardianship order does provide structure and control, and may be sufficient to secure the cooperation of a patient and thus maintain his health. It deserves to be used more widely. The MHAC (1986), among others, has advanced arguments in favour of introducing some form of community treatment order, perhaps as an extension of guardianship, in special and tested circumstances. A probation order with a condition of treatment provides for sanctions against a patient who does not comply with treatment (*see* p. 70), but this does not amount to enforcement of treatment.

Remaining provisions of the Mental Health Act 1983

The role of hospital managers is central in safeguarding the rights of patients to appropriate and good treatment. Managers must accept applications and recommendations for compulsory detention before they become legal. They have a duty to ensure that detained patients (S.132) and their nearest relatives have adequate information and that the latter are informed of the discharge of their relative (S.133). They have the power to discharge unrestricted patients compulsorily held under the Act (S.23) and a duty to refer to an MHRT any patient under a treatment order (S.3) or hospital order (S.37) who has not applied for such a tribunal after the first 6 months or at least once during any subsequent 3-year period of detention. Managers may intercept and search the mail of any detained patient, except where this is addressed to Members of Parliament, legal advisers, a court or statutory body.

The 'managers' are the legal authority responsible for the hospital. In practice, they delegate their responsibilities to a group or subcommittee, sometimes, as at the Joint Bethlem Maudsley Hospital, this group consists entirely of 'lay' (i.e. non-medical, non-nursing) members of the Authority. This delegation to non-professionals is not necessary and a multidisciplinary group of 'managers' could be constituted, if professionals can be persuaded to give up the time.

Most of the other major provisions of the MHA 1983 are dealt with elsewhere in this book, in particular the nature and powers of the principal limiting bodies including MHRTs, the Court of Protection and the MHAC (Ch. 4). For further information see Bluglass (1984).

Under section 118 of the MHA 1983, the Secretary of State has a duty to produce a Code of Practice. After a long delay, initially because of disagreements between practising professionals and the MHAC, this Code was laid before Parliament in 1989. It gives detailed guidance about implementing the provisions of the Act. Edited extracts from it are reproduced in Appendix 2 p. 999.

Criminal Law in England and Wales

Background

The laws relating to someone accused of an offence are numerous. No textbook of psychiatry can deal with these completely. Here is simply an attempt to introduce the reader to those laws, and to simplify them to some extent by examining the process to which an accused person may be submitted.

It is a long-standing principle of English common law that to be guilty of a crime and subject to the full rigours of the appropriate punishment two elements should be proved (except in cases of strict liability, such as careless driving). First, it has to be shown that an illegal act or omission has occurred and been carried out by an identified person (*actus reus*). Further, it has to be shown that the act or omission caused the offending consequences. In *White*, quoted in Smith and Hogan (1988), Mr White put poison in his mother's drink in order to kill her; she drank some of the poison and died, but from a heart attack; thus no *actus reus* of murder took place and Mr White was convicted of attempted murder instead. Second, it has to be shown that the person had the state of mind (*mens rea*) proscribed in relation to that crime. There is plenty of room for debate on both of these issues in many cases; resolution of these is one important function of criminal courts. The second or 'mental' element is the one with the greater potential for debate and throughout this section is the one under discussion.

Mens rea means the mental state or quality of behaviour (such as 'recklessly') required for the offence being considered, and it is expressedly stated or implied in the definition of the particular offence. For example, in the Theft Act 1968, theft is defined in section 1 as 'dishonestly appropriating property belonging to another with the intention of permanently depriving the other of it'. Thus the *mens rea* for the offence of theft implies both dishonesty and an intention permanently to deprive the victim of the property. In other offences expressions such as 'knowingly' and 'maliciously' describe the required *mens rea*. Clearly 'mental state' is used here in a very restricted sense; it is concerned largely with the cognitive aspects of a person's mental state and not with the emotional aspects. *Mens rea* may include intentionality, recklessness, 'guilty knowledge' (i.e. knowing that one is doing wrong), competence and responsibility. Such concepts antedate psychiatry, and are *not* subservient to medical ideas.

The concept of responsiblity, for example, is fundamental to our view of man as a free, intentional being. Every society, every culture uses it. It is the basis of every criminal code and system of punishment. We understand that some people (e.g. the young, the mentally abnormal) are less responsible than others, and we sometimes excuse people of responsibility. Lawyers use a list of excuses which includes mistake, accident, provocation (to a charge of murder), duress and insanity (Hart, 1968). Psychiatrists are sometimes called upon to give evidence in support of these excuses. As we shall see below, they should, on the whole, resist the temptation except in very special circumstances or in the case of insanity. They should note too that they are called upon to give *evidence* rather than take the decision, even though courts press hard on occasions for medical opinions about these non-medical matters. The rules concerning expert testimony limit such witnesses to their expertise and psychiatrists should, in particular, avoid being drawn into discussions of moral or legal responsibility.

In considering the way a legal system handles these matters, it is as well to remember that 'the law' is neither logical nor consistent, nor does it satisfy everyone's notion of justice. It is human, pragmatic, and has developed by piecemeal legislation, by precedent and by tradition (*see* Smith, 1981 for a good account). In England, it is so pragmatic that it has produced the apparent paradox that all but a tiny handful of mentally abnormal people are found guilty of their antisocial/illegal acts even if they were clearly mentally abnormal at the time of the act, and matters of responsibility and culpability are dealt with as mitigation of sentence. This is probably true even in other legal systems which use the insanity defence more often.

For convenience, the criminal process including the court hearing will be divided into three phases: pretrial, trial, and sentence. These three phases can be detected in every criminal hearing even if they are very brief or amalgamated. Table 2.5 indicates the issues to be considered in each phase.

Table 2.5
Criminal Hearing

Pretrial	*Trial*	*Sentence*
Prosecution	Automatism	Psychiatric
Fitness to	Insanity	mitigation
plead	Diminished	
	responsibility	

Pretrial

For illustration let us take a mentally abnormal man who has been violent. The police are called and the criminal process begins. As soon as the facts are clear and a defendant is arrested, the police officer in charge of the case has decisions to make about *mens rea* and/or mitigation (although he does not call them that); he has to decide whether a prosecution should proceed at all. If the patient is already having psychiatric treatment, he may ask the doctor and/or hospital to deal with the matter as a medical one. Indeed, he is encouraged to give 'sympathetic' consideration to offenders 'suffering from some form of mental illness or impairment, especially when the strain of criminal proceedings would lead to a worsening of their condition' in Home

Office Circular (1985), No. 14, which gives guidelines on the cautioning of offenders. He is also told that prosecution may be 'inappropriate' where the person is showing signs of severe emotional distress. However, if the hospital or doctor declines to take the patient or the police officer believes that to fail to prosecute would be against the public interest because the matter of medical v penal disposal should be debated in a different, more public arena, then he will report the case to the Crown Prosecution Service. Once again, the question of going forward will be debated and here, too, it is possible for psychiatric advice to be sought and, if appropriate, for the case to be diverted from the penal system to the health care system.

Another option available to the policeman, if the arrest was made in a public place, is to move the offender directly into a mental hospital under the police powers (section 136) within the MHA 1983. This can be done irrespective of whether the offender is already a patient or not. If the offensive behaviour was in a public place and the policeman thinks that he is 'suffering from mental disorder and to be in immediate need of care or control' in the patient's own interests or for the protection of others, the constable should take the patient to 'a place of safety', which can be a hospital, to await a medical examination. The detention is for a maximum of 72 hours and the hospital has to agree to take the patient (it may refuse). The 'place of safety' may also be a police cell, but no one believes that this is an appropriate place to care for an acutely disturbed patient. Prosecution decisions are not necessarily affected by this process, although admission to hospital may make prosecution less likely and hospital rejection may make it more likely.

If it is decided to prosecute the offender, then he will have to appear in a magistrates' court. Here he will be remanded on bail or in custody according to the rules of the Bail Act 1976. The bail decision will be influenced by medical opinion about suitability for treatment and availability treatment facilities. The court may also wish to remand the offender to hospital, either as a voluntary patient, or under the powers of the MHA 1983 (*see* p. 33). As the criminal process moves on, the magistrates' court will have to decide whether there is a case to answer (the ancient grand jury function) and, if so, whether it should be tried in a lower court or moved up to the Crown Court. The rules which are applied are complicated but, briefly there are three categories of seriousness: the most serious or indictable which have to go to the higher court, the least serious or non-indictable which are always tried in a magistrates' court (summary trial), and a large middle group which is triable either way, and in which any of the parties—prosecution, defence, or court—can opt for trial by jury in the Crown Court.

Fitness to plead

If someone is so mentally disordered that it is thought unfair to proceed with his trial, then the trial can be postponed, often indefinitely. Magistrates may postpone or adjourn the case to await a more favourable time; if they adjourn the proceedings *sine die* (i.e. postpone the case without a date for a further hearing), this is tantamount to excusing the accused from a trial. The other options available to them are either to promote the case to the Crown Court, so that the question of fitness to plead can be tested by a jury, or to proceed with the trial in order to hear the facts against the accused and consider a hospital order without recording a conviction (*see below*). If a remanded prisoner is suffering from 'mental illness or severe mental impairment', it is also possible to transfer him to hospital under section 48 of the MHA 1983.

The concept of being unfit to plead emerged from the rituals of the medieval court of law where a trial had to begin with the taking of the plea. If an individual was mute and did not enter a plea, the court had to decide whether this was through malice or by visitation of God; by the 19th century, the court also made a further determination of whether the accused could conduct a 'defence with discretion' (*Dyson*, Whitlock 1963). An individual who was unfit to plead was said to be insane on arraignment and, subsequent to the Lunatics Act 1800, held at Her Majesty's Pleasure, usually in an asylum.

The criteria by which an individual is determined to be unfit to plead, and thereby insane, evolved through 19th century case law, mainly in relation to cases of deaf mutes who were unable to communicate; the most important case was that of *Pritchard*. In essence, an individual is unfit to plead if he is not of sufficient intellect to make a proper defence. Fitness has been interpreted as—

being able to plead with understanding to the indictment;
being able to comprehend the details of evidence;
being able to follow court proceedings;
knowing that a juror can be challenged;
being able to instruct legal advisers.

Clearly, these criteria are concerned with intellectual performance. This is one illustration of the difference between the legal category of insanity and the medical concept of mental illness, showing how much weight is put on understanding or cognition in the former. Although the Criminal Procedure (Insanity) Act 1964 (CP(I)A) codified the process whereby a person is found unfit to plead (known in it as 'disability in bar of trial') and integrated it into modern legal practice, it remained silent on the factors that actually render an accused unfit to plead. The criteria, therefore, remain those relating to 19th century legal concepts of insanity.

The question of fitness to plead can be raised by the defence, the prosecution or the judge. Although the judge can delay consideration of the question until after the prosecution has presented its case to ensure that there is, in fact, a case to answer, in practice, the issue is usually raised and decided pretrial. A special jury (that is, a jury different from the one hearing the facts of the substantive case) is empanelled to hear evidence and determine the accused's fitness to plead. This usually (but not always) involves evidence and testimony by a psychiatrist directed towards the criteria listed above.

The number of individuals found unfit to plead has been declining steadily since the late 1940s (Walker, 1968); since 1980 there have been on average about 20 cases a year in England and Wales (Grubin, 1991a). Individuals who are found unfit to plead, including those who are mentally impaired or deaf, are then sent to 'such hospital as may be specified by the Secretary of State'.* The bed has to be made available within 2 months. Little is known about the fate of those who have been found unfit to plead before 1976, but one of us has documented the course of all individuals found unfit to plead between 1976 and 1988 (Grubin, 1991a,b,c). Since 1976, most have been sent to local, catchment area hospitals, although about 30% have been sent to maximum security special hospitals. Once in hospital, the patient is treated as though detained on a hospital order with Home Office restrictions on discharge, unlimited in time, and comes under the jurisdiction of the MHA 1983. Thus, it would be possible for an individual found unfit to plead to be held in hospital for the remainder of his life without ever having been tried. Because of this risk of unlimited detention, it is often said that the issue of fitness to plead is only raised in cases where the charges are serious. In fact, however, only about one-quarter of cases between 1976 and 1988 involved charges of a severe nature; about one-third were related to cases of only mild severity, the most infamous of which involved Glen Pearson, accused of stealing £5 and three lightbulbs from a neighbour's house (the case is described by Emmins, 1986).

Until 1982, it was uncommon for an individual who was found unfit to plead to be remitted to court for trial. Since then, however, nearly half of those found unfit to plead have returned for their day in court. The Home Secretary can also discharge the patient from restrictions instead of remitting for trial. In addition, because the patient is detained under the MHA 1983, discharge via an MHRT is also possible. Patients who cannot convince doctors and civil servants that they are not mentally ill or mentally impaired, and not dangerous, are liable to long-term compulsory hospitalization with a status somewhere between patient and criminal. Of those found unfit to plead between 1976 and 1988, almost a quarter remained in hospital in 1990. Most were, in fact, quite unwell and needed to be in hospital in view of their mental health. However, because they were held on the grounds of being unfit to plead, rather than subsequent to a definitive court disposal, management was complicated, particularly in those cases which would not ordinarily have attracted a restriction order.

Following repeated criticism of the CP(I)A, the law relating to both fitness to plead and insanity was amended in the Criminal Procedure (Insanity and Unfitness to Plead) Act 1991. This new law made two important reforms.

* In practice the Home Secretary

First, it required a trial of the facts of the case against an individual found unfit to plead to be held to determine whether he is likely to have committed the offence in question; if the evidence against him is weak, the charges are dropped and the defendant discharged. Second, it introduced flexible sentencing for findings of unfitness to plead and verdicts of not guilty by reason of insanity, removing the inevitability of a hospital order with indefinite restrictions on discharge. This meant that a range of sentencing options became available to the court, including absolute discharge, a guardianship order, or a hospital order without restrictions. Though these reforms were long overdue, it will be interesting to see whether they will result in more individuals being found unfit to plead or insane.

One way of avoiding or illuminating these weighty matters in the case of an individual who meets the criteria for mental illness or severe mental impairment is for the court to remand the patient to hospital under S.36 MHA 1983. If the patient improves quickly, then the trial may proceed, if not, then there is more information available. Another way (*see below* p. 47) is to make a hospital order without recording a conviction.

Amnesia

From time to time, a good deal of attention has been given to the question of memory and fitness to plead. It is sometimes argued that if someone has a loss of memory for the time during which he is alleged to have committed an offence, then he cannot properly defend himself and so should be regarded as unfit to plead. All common law jurisdictions have ruled that amnesia does not affect fitness to plead. They could hardly rule otherwise if the courts are to continue to function. The most notable case concerning this issue was that of *Podola*.

Mr Podola was charged with the murder of a policeman by shooting. He submitted that he was unfit to plead because of amnesia for the events. He was found fit to plead and subsequently convicted. On appeal, the principle that the defence should only have to prove the unfitness on the balance of probabilities was clearly enunciated, and the jury's verdict that the hysterical amnesia from which Podola was alleged to have suffered was insufficient to amount to a disability in relation to the trial was confirmed. His counsel had submitted that he could not 'comprehend' the details of the evidence. The Appeal Court judges ruled that, nevertheless, he was of sufficient intellect to comprehend the course of the trial proceedings and that was what mattered. Further, a previous Scottish case had ruled that loss of memory on the part of a defendant did not render his trial unfair because the accused can tell the jury that he has no recollection of events. The Court of Appeal concurred and agreed that the jury should take the loss of memory into account, but of itself it should not render an accused unfit to plead.

Between one-half and one-third (O'Connell, 1960; Taylor and Kopelman, 1984; Kopelman, 1987a) of people charged with serious offences, especially homicide, have some degree of amnesia for their offence and cannot adequately recall what happened at the time. Few questions about this issue will be asked of the psychiatrist in the pretrial phase in England.

The Trial

A prominent myth concerning forensic psychiatry is that questions of insanity in the trial are an important part of the job. In reality, very few cases of insanity come to the courts each year in England and Wales and the average forensic psychiatrist can expect to deal with only two or three in a professional lifetime.

Hospital orders without a conviction

There is a special mechanism in the lower or magistrates' court for dealing with mentally ill and severely mentally impaired offenders.* Quite simply, the magistrates press on with the case if it is within their jurisdiction, hearing the evidence for and against conviction. If they are persuaded that the accused carried out the act as charged, they can then take psychiatric evidence about him. If a recommendation is forthcoming that the man should go to hospital rather than prison, and hospital order papers are signed, they can then accept that option *and* simultaneously decide, under section 37(3) of the MHA 1983 *not to convict him*. This neat device ensures a proper hearing, but allows a psychiatric disposal without the stigma of a criminal conviction in the tradition that the mentally ill should be excused the behavioural consequences of their illness (insanity). The disposal is not used very often, most such offenders are convicted and then given a psychiatric disposal. Perhaps it should be used more often. It should always be considered as a possibility by the examining psychiatrist and discussed with the patient's lawyer when the patient is to be recommended for a hospital order in the lower court. It is also helpful in cases where the accused is charged with a relatively trivial offence, but seems unfit to plead.

The special verdict

In England, legal insanity is a valid defence to any serious charge which can be tried in the Crown Court unless the offence concerned is of absolute liability. Under the CP(I)A 1964, any defendant found not guilty by reason of insanity (NGRI, the 'special verdict') was sent, like his 'unfit' counterpart, to hospital under the control of the Home Secretary. The court had no flexibility, as this was the only disposal available. For this reason, individuals

---

* It should be noted that the MHA 1983 does not extend this arrangement to patients classified as psychopathic or mentally impaired.

with psychiatric illness frequently eschewed the insanity defence in the hope of either a full acquittal or a finite sentence (such as is theoretically possible for almost every offence except murder). Occasionally, the defence struggled with the difficulties of the insanity defence, even for charges that might not attract a long prison sentence, on the basis that the verdict was worth having, in spite of its mandatory consequences, because it is an acquittal and thus did not have the same stigma nor the long-term social harm for the offender and his family. The Criminal Procedure (Insanity and Unfitness to Plead) Act 1991 brought in flexible sentencing following an insanity verdict, giving the court a range of disposal options. This may gradually increase the numbers of cases in which the special verdict is used.

The tests of insanity used in the trial are different from those used in the pretrial phase, although again they are focused on knowing and understanding. The tests for the trial are the 1843 *McNaughton* Rules (*see* West and Walk, 1977). In essence, the rules state:

> Every man is presumed to be sane, until the contrary be proved, and that to establish a defence on the ground of insanity it must be clearly proved that at the time of committing the act the accused party was labouring under such a defect of reason, from disease of the mind, as not to know the nature and quality of the act he was doing, or if he did know it, that he did not know that what he was doing was wrong.

A lesser-known rule says:

> If the accused labours under a partial delusion only, and is not in other respects insane, he should be considered in the same situation as to responsibility as if the facts with respect to which the delusion exists were real.

This latter rule relates to the defence of mistake, and is difficult for psychiatrists to understand because of the difficulty of knowing what is meant here by a partial delusion and, in practice, is rarely employed. A partial delusion is probably not simply an overvalued idea, but is more likely a monosymptomatic delusion. The rule seems to be saying that if, for example, the man accused held a single delusional belief that his ear surgeon had implanted a transmitting device in his head and the device was interfering with his brain or giving out messages, then an assault (let us say on the surgeon) should be judged by the jury as if that were really true.

Clearly the McNaughton Rules are strict rules. Most psychiatrists and lawyers would agree that few offenders would come within them, perhaps another reason for their current disuse. In fact, however, the pragmatism of the law has ensured that they have been used flexibly in the past. As Walker (1968) has pointed out, the introduction of the Rules in the middle of the 19th century made little difference to the steadily increasing number of murderers escaping the death penalty on the grounds of insanity.

Most jurisdictions using these Rules have found them unsatisfactory and tried various devices to circumvent them. For example in the USA there is the Durham Rule, the American Law Institute Rule, and there is even a verdict of guilty but mentally ill in some states. This last piece of legislation has been highly contentious because it is argued that an insane person cannot be guilty (*see* Blunt and Stock, 1985, and Weiner, 1985, for discussions). However, very few mentally abnormal offenders in any jurisdiction are protected against conviction by their mental status at the time of the offence. The special verdict was of much greater importance in Britain when the mandatory sentence for murder was capital punishment. Arguments about the McNaughton Rules became arguments about life and death, and were dichotomized between sane and insane. The 20th century has seen attempts to find a middle way between the extremes of sanity and insanity. British attempts to circumvent the mandatory outcome more completely and to give flexibility of sentencing to the judge have two roots, one in the consequences of childbirth, the other in Scottish law.

Infanticide

Special legislation concerning women who kill their children originated in an 'Act to Prevent the Murthering of Bastard Children' of 1624, which decreed that if an unmarried woman concealed a birth and the child was subsequently found dead, she was presumed to have killed it unless she could prove that the child was born dead. The Act was aimed as much at discouraging immorality as against the killing of children, and the penalty was death. In the 17th and 18th centuries most infanticide charges were under this statute; three-quarters of the accused were spinsters (Beattie, 1986). By the mid-18th century attitudes began to change and both judges and juries became reluctant to convict. An Act of 1803 changed the onus of proof, and infanticides were then treated like other kinds of murder. Concealment of birth became a separate offence in 1828 (Smith, 1981). The last woman executed for killing her child was Rebecca Smith in 1849; she had used poison (suggesting premeditation) and was suspected of poisoning several other children (Walker, 1968). Since the mid-19th century the death penalty has been invariably commuted, and by 1864–65, when the Royal Commission on Capital Punishment heard evidence, most witnesses were in favour of exculpatory legislation on infanticide. After a series of unsuccessful Bills the first Infanticide Act was passed in 1922. It was restricted to the killing of 'newly-born' children, but uncertainties of interpretation led to the enactment of the Infanticide Act 1938 which extended the age limit to 12 months.

The Act provides that if a woman kills her child under the age of 12 months in circumstances which would otherwise amount to murder, but at the time 'the balance of her mind was disturbed by reason of her not having fully recovered from the effect of giving birth to the child or by reason of the effect of lactation consequent upon the birth of the child' she will be convicted of infanticide, an offence punishable as if she had been guilty of manslaughter. In practice, it is dealt with leniently. In the decade 1976–85, an annual average of seven women were convicted of infanticide; the majority was put on probation and none was imprisoned (Home Office, 1985a).

The Infanticide Acts were thus a precursor of diminished responsibility. The medical concepts of puerperal and lactational insanity on which they were based are now somewhat outdated, for about half the women convicted of infanticide kill newborn children in the context of unwanted, concealed pregnancies, and about half are battering mothers. Mental illness is rarely a factor and social and psychological stresses are more relevant (d'Orbán, 1979), although puerperal psychosis must not be forgotten as a potentially lethal illness (*see* Ch. 15).

Infanticide can be charged in the first instance, but often the initial charge is murder, and infanticide is pleaded as a defence to the murder charge. Once evidence has been adduced to raise the defence, the burden of disproving it rests on the Crown; in this respect it differs from the defences of insanity or diminished responsibility, where the burden of proof is on the defence using the balance of probabilities standard. Further differences are that infanticide does not require proof that the killing resulted from the abnormal mental state, merely that, at the time, the mother's 'balance of mind' was disturbed. The jury do not have to weigh the question of responsibility. The degree of abnormality implied by the disturbance of 'balance of mind' is in practice much less than that required to substantiate 'abnormality of mind' in the diminished responsibility defence (d'Orbán, 1979).

Despite some anomalies, the Infanticide Act 1938 continues to serve a useful purpose. One anomaly is that it only applies to the killing of the last born child, although the mother's other children may also become victims. Another anomaly, the lack of provision for an offence of attempted infanticide, has been remedied by the Criminal Attempts Act 1981, so that a woman whose baby victim survives can now be charged with attempted infanticide rather than attempted murder (Wilkins, 1985).

Diminished responsibility

To understand the second, Scottish, root to diminished responsibility read Walker (1968). England embraced the concept for the same reason that it had embraced infanticide: growing abhorrence of the death penalty. All these concepts allow a killer to be convicted of a serious offence, one carrying life imprisonment if appropriate, but they all give discretion to the judge and in the days of hanging avoided the death penalty.

The Homicide Act 1957 states:

> Where a person is party to the killing of another, he shall not be convicted of murder if he was suffering from such abnormality of mind (whether arising from a condition of arrested or retarded development of mind or any inherent causes or induced by disease or injury) as substantially impaired his mental responsibility for his acts and omissions in doing or being a party to the killing.

He would be convicted of manslaughter instead. The defence is available *only* if the charge is murder.

It was not long before this curious Parliamentary wording was subject to a deal of legal wrangling. In *Byrne* a judge's direction was overturned by the Court of Appeal and Lord Chief Justice Parker ensured that, from 1960 onwards, the concept of abnormality used in the statute could be interpreted very widely. He ruled:

> Abnormality of mind . . . means a state of mind so different from that of ordinary human beings that the reasonable man would term it abnormal. It appears to us to be wide enough to cover the mind's activities in all its aspects, not only the perception of physical acts and matters and the ability to form a rational judgement whether an act is right or wrong, but also the ability to exercise will-power to control physical acts in accordance with that rational judgement.

This remarkable judgment made legal history. It introduced the long-disputed concept of the irresistible impulse into the law on homicide and allowed all forms of mental disorder—handicap, neurosis, personality disorder—to be considered for the verdict. Byrne was himself a dull, personality-disordered individual.

Presumably the intention was to allow the most disordered people to be excused as insane, other middle ground cases to be liable to conviction of manslaughter, leaving only the mentally normal to the full rigours of a conviction for murder. Presumably too, the Lord Chief Justice would have expected the proportion of people excused from murder on psychiatric grounds to increase, but this did not happen. As Walker (1968) showed, if the number of people avoiding a murder conviction on any psychiatric grounds (e.g. fitness to plead, insanity, dimished responsibility) are added together, the proportion is between 40 and 45% of those charged, and this proportion remains constant in spite of changing legislation. It is true that diminished responsibility has slowly made unfitness to plead and insanity almost redundant, but this is within the 40–45% of 'excused' cases.

The defence can only raise the question of diminished responsibility on medical grounds, and it has to be demonstrated on the balance of probabilities. Frequently, the prosecution and defence agree that there is such a probability (this is usually in cases where both the psychiatrist instructed by the defence and the one instructed by the Crown come to similar conclusions). If so, they can then put their agreement to the trial judge; if he accepts the position and the facts are clear, there is no trial, the accused is convicted of manslaughter and the sentencing can begin. If either the prosecution or the judge dispute the defence submission, then the matter is argued out in the usual way in front of a jury who make the final decision.

The problems with this defence are considerable. As Griew (1988) has indicated, the terms used in the Homicide Act 1957 are extremely odd. He pointed to the origins of the terms in long since disused legislation and their modern importation without proper attention to contemporary practicality.

As a result, he said, judges and psychiatrists have responded to the definitions in ways which range from the very generous to the very strict.

> Psychiatrists, rather more than lawyers, have agonized over the statutory expression, have looked unavailingly to the lawyers for enlightenment, and have contributed to the inconsistency in the use of the section by the differences in their own reading of it. . . . There can be little doubt that the fate of some people charged with murder since 1957 has turned on the qualities of robustness and sophistication shown by those professionally involved in their cases.

Curiously, however, in spite of all the difficulties the Homicide Act 1957 seems to work. In a study of its use Dell (1984) found that in only about 13% of cases was there disagreement in court about these potentially highly contentious matters. In half of the cases where there was disagreement, it arose because one of the doctors considered that there was no abnormality of mind. In the other half, there was disagreement as to whether the abnormality agreed upon substantially impaired the offender's mental responsibility— a legal or a moral question, certainly not a medical one, which has to be decided by the jury. Griew (1988) pointed out that psychiatrists are frequently asked such non-medical questions. As Dell said:

> That doctors routinely testify to matters that are not within their professional competence, and that judges accept and act upon that testimony, bears witness to the necessity, while the mandatory sentence for murder exists, of making the diminished responsibility defence work.

To Griew this is the ultimate paradox: 'section 2 is so badly worded that it can be made to work—and work better than its framers intended.' Dell (1984) has also shown that in spite of an increasing number of homicides in England and Wales between 1964 and 1979, the proportion of men who have their conviction reduced to manslaughter by reason of diminished responsibility has remained fairly constant at 20% (34% are convicted of murder and 46% of other types of manslaughter). However, the number of such convicted men going to hospital has also not changed (about 24 per annum) while the number of men going to prison has increased sharply (12 men in 1964, 48 in 1979). Dell analysed the possible reasons for this increasing proportion being sent to prison and found that the main factor seems to be a decreasing readiness of psychiatrists and prison doctors to recommend hospital places. In turn, this reluctance is based on a tightening up of the criteria for admission to special hospitals. The Department of Health has become more rigorous in ensuring that only those in need of maximum security get a bed in special hospitals with the hope that regional health authorities will provide a bed instead. In practice, reporting doctors increasingly fail to recommend this option and more and more men go off to prison. Over the years, the characteristics of the diminished responsibility group have hardly changed. They are still 36 years old on average, 20% diagnosed as schizophrenic, 37% as depressed, 27% as personality disordered, 8% as brain damaged or epileptic, 5% as mentally handicapped, and 7% as having no psychiatric abnormality (these categories are not mutually exclusive). Ninety per cent of the population killed one person, the multiple deaths were usually family homicides. Only 13% of the victims were strangers, 32% were wives, 6% paramours, the rest friends or relatives. Among the non-psychotic, amorous jealousy or possessiveness was the commonest motive. None of these features has varied significantly over the years.

Disputed actus *and mental disorder*

A small but important point to note about the murder trial is the peculiar difficulty in which a defendant finds himself if he both disputes the facts of the alleged killing and is also mentally disordered. In the case of any other charge up to and including attempted murder, the matter is straightforward, the defendant simply pleads not guilty using whatever evidence is available to him (e.g. an alibi). If that defence does not succeed, then at the sentencing stage psychiatric evidence can be adduced in mitigation. If, however, the victim dies and the charge is murder, the same defendant would be in a much more difficult situation. There is no mitigation possible against the life sentence for murder. Any psychiatric evidence would have to be adduced in the trial to either insanity or diminished responsibility, and this would have to be done at the same time as trying to convince the jury that the wrong person had been charged anyway. A difficult task indeed—the psychiatric case is almost bound to reduce the credibility of the factual one and the jury may become muddled as to their task. Occasionally, mentally ill people are convicted of murder after a not guilty plea. They automatically receive a life sentence and then the Prison Department has to sort out their problems (they should be transferred to a hospital under S.47 MHA 1983).

Psychiatrists and lawyers in conflict

In 1863 Charles Fooks was tried for a vicious murder (*Fooks*; Smith, 1981). There was considerable evidence that Mr Fooks had paranoid delusions, no less an alienist* than Dr Harrington Tuke coming from London to testify to that fact. The prison doctor said that the man was sane, and admitted his education in psychiatry was not from books but from 'common sense'. The judge directed the jury 'you are not to be deprived of the exercise of your common sense because a gentleman comes from London and tells you scientific sense'. Mr Fooks was found guilty and hanged. The *Journal of Mental Science (Fooks)* mused:

> A monomaniac with perverted emotions and homicidal tendencies cannot, says science, control his conduct, and cannot therefore be held responsible for his acts. The law says he can and shall be. The issue lies thus in a few words. If the theories of law are to continue to displace the patient study of disease, let the burden of the consequences rest with our lawgivers and judges.

* An early term for psychiatrist

A further difficulty for the psychiatrist is that in court he may be expected to give an opinion on the level of responsibility which the accused had for the killing and even whether the accused 'suffers from' diminished responsibility, as though it were a disease. The psychiatrist should resist, within the bounds of propriety, the temptation to give a medical view on the question of the level of responsibility. Instead, he should set out the medical evidence, give an account of the relationship of the killing (if admitted) to those medical facts (especially the mental state) and indicate how far, in his opinion, the medical features and/or diagnosis influenced the aggressive and other relevant behaviour. The reply to direct questioning about the diminution of responsibility should reiterate the nature of any mental disorder discovered and then the point should be made that only a layman's view about the ultimate question can be given. That view, is, however, frequently demanded from the psychiatrist (*see*, for example, Masters, 1985).

Why all these scruples? The main reason is to prevent, as far as possible, psychiatry being used to justify or explain decisions that are made on quite other grounds. The way in which the law used psychiatry in this way has been amply illustrated by the recent notorious 'Yorkshire Ripper' case. The publicity and perfectly understandable public emotion connected with this case were no doubt major factors in what happened. Mr Peter Sutcliffe was charged with the murder of 13 women. He pleaded guilty to their manslaughter trying to use the defence of diminished responsibility. The doctors who saw Mr Sutcliffe diagnosed classic and florid schizophrenia. He killed the women because a loud hallucination from God told him to do so. God had given him a mission to rid the world of prostitutes. At first he tried to resist the command, but later gave in because he realized he could not resist and because what God told him to do could not be wrong. The prosecution accepted the defence submission, but the trial judge ordered the prosecution to challenge the defence of diminished responsibility in front of a jury. As the *News of the World* put it (24 May 1981):

> Mr Justice Boreham must have known well that psychiatrists and do-gooders who sit on the paroles of the supposedly-mad are all too fallible.

There followed several extraordinary days. The facts were not disputed, but various psychiatrists were harangued in the witness box, mainly about the diagnosis of schizophrenia, and whether Mr Sutcliffe was making it all up to fool them. It was even suggested at one point that the accused man's wife was the mentally ill one and the accused had copied her illness. The jury found him guilty of murder in spite of the unanimous medical evidence. The doctors felt that they (or at least psychiatry) had been discredited.

On that occasion the medical view was not useful to the court, it got in the way of the public need to exact the maximum permissible revenge on a hated figure, mad or not. Within minutes of the verdict, however, the medical view became useful. One of the psychiatrists, rapidly rehabilitated as an 'expert', was put in the witness box. He said:

In the light of the present knowledge of the illness of schizophrenia, we believe that he (Sutcliffe) should be kept in custody for the rest of his natural life.

In spite of the fact that the verdict was tantamount to a repudiation of the idea that Sutcliffe suffered from schizophrenia, the judge must have thought the doctor had a point, for he sentenced Peter Sutcliffe to 20 concurrent terms of life imprisonment, with a recommendation to the Home Secretary that he should serve at least 30 years. (This account is distilled from newspapers published between 30 April and 24 May, 1981, mainly *The Times, Daily Mail, Sunday Telegraph, Observer*.)

The resemblance of this case to the *Fooks* case mentioned above and others quoted by Smith (1981) is striking. However, as a footnote, an important difference should be noted—Fooks was hanged. Sutcliffe languished inappropriately in gaol for about 2 years, but was then removed to a special hospital under the powers of the Mental Health Act 1983.

Psychiatrists should draw two conclusions: (1) insanity is a legal/lay concept not a medical one; (2) if a doctor appears to have power in court, it is on loan and it can readily be withdrawn; he has no inherent power in such a setting. It may seem odd to say that insanity is not a medical concept, but it has to be recognized that the concept goes back to the earliest written history and was thoroughly established by the time that medicine began to advance significantly. Indeed, a public concept of 'insanity' is probably one reason for the development of a profession of psychiatry. Contemporary psychiatry does not concern itself very much with 'insanity' which is an abstract, philosophical way of construing aberrant thinking and behaviour; psychiatry is more concerned with 'mental disorder' or disease, a concept which, although still abstract to some extent, uses a medical model. As the concepts are not totally congruent, it is theoretically possible for an individual to be sane and mentally disordered or insane and not mentally disordered. The tests are *lay* tests within a non-medical moral discourse. The essence of the test is responsibility which is a concept we all intuitively understand. We use the word 'responsibility' constantly in our everyday life; we cannot conceive of human life without using the concept. When we become jurors, we do not need a doctor to tell us about this matter. We are as informed as he is. This is especially true when the lives of heads of state are threatened.

We can only speculate about the thinking of jurors. For example, we might guess that in the case of Sutcliffe they were impressed that, psychotic or not, he planned all his killings which were, therefore, clearly intentional. It may also have been that the jury muddled their abhorrence of the crimes with their technical task—'we cannot say that anyone who does such terrible things is "not guilty", however mad he is.' Some support for these speculations comes from a recent study by Finkel and Handel (1989) who found that mock jurors used a variety of constructs to test insanity (all far removed from the McNaughton rules), which included impaired awareness, distorted thinking, loss of control, and 'evil' motive. As Smith (1981) has shown in an interesting analysis of 19th century trials, when public feelings run high, then legal matters become especially aberrant. If a study on legal decision-making could be done, it might show that the most powerful factor in determining outcome is public pressure as mediated through the press, radio and television. After all, to a large extent, a criminal trial is a resolution of conflict between 'us' as a collective (note it is not the victim!) and 'him' the defendant.

Non-insane automatism

The arbitrary way in which legal history has defined insanity has left a remarkable exclusion, which has escaped the insanity regulations from 1800 onwards simply because it is defined as 'non-insane'. This is partly because, in law, for an act to have been carried out at all (*actus reus*) it must be voluntary. Some 'acts' have been considered automatic and, therefore, involuntary. Automatism in law is:

> The state of a person who, though capable of action is not conscious of what he is doing. It means unconscious involuntary action and it is a defence because the mind does not go with what is being done. (Kilmuir LJ in *Bratty*).

A defence of non-insane automatism should establish:

1. The existence of a condition capable of compromising the consciousness of the accused, e.g. evidence of previous blow to the head from which concussion could repeatedly be inferred at the time of the offence, from an external cause rather than an internal condition (*Burgess*);
2. That the commission of the crime was compatible with the actions of a person in such a disordered state of consciousness that they lack voluntary control, e.g. an offence involving deliberate planning or extended purposeful activity is incompatible with significant disturbance of consciousness. Thus certain offences such as rape are ruled out, as are violent offences, which clearly involved well organized and well directed violence;
3. A lack of obvious motivation or provoking events which make the actions easily understandable as a response to the actual situation;
4. Behaviour subsequent to the offence which is appropriate to someone who is unaware of their actions. If they were not conscious of their actions at the time, then clearly attempting to hide the results, or establish an alibi, must raise doubts about how conscious the act had been.

Clouding of consciousness which does not amount to total loss of consciousness is not sufficient to substantiate automatism (*see Roberts*). Just like insanity, the term is a legal one, not a medical one, when used in court. In medicine, the term is largely reserved for epileptic mental states, but, as we shall see, these are now largely excluded from the legal definition. As Smith and Hogan (1988) put it:

Where the alleged automatism arises from a 'disease of the mind', the defence is one of insanity and the onus of proof is on the Crown. What is a disease of the mind is a question of law. So in *R v Kemp* [1956] where D alleged that he acted involuntarily because he suffered from arteriosclerosis which cut off the supply of blood to his brain, Devlin J held that he had set up the defence of insanity. But in *R v Charlson* Barry J treated an allegation of automatism arising from a cerebral tumour as a defence to be disproved beyond reasonable doubt by the Crown. The cases appear irreconcilable. . . .

So they do up to a point, but they clearly indicate the legal trend over the past 30–40 years. *Kemp* came after *Charlson* and the judge took the earlier judgment into account. The trend is illustrated by what has happened to epileptic automatism. At one time it was a fairly certain non-insane excuse. Lord Denning began to alter that. *Bratty* killed a girl by strangulation with one of her stockings. He said that a 'blackness' came over him and that he did not know what he was doing. He was said to suffer from psychomotor epilepsy. At the trial, the defences of insanity and automatism were both raised, but the trial judge refused to allow the defence of automatism. The jury found Bratty guilty. On appeal, the conviction was upheld in the House of Lords. In a long judgment (*see also* Smith and Hogan, 1986) Lord Denning said:

> It seems to me that any mental disorder which has manifested itself in violence and is prone to recur is a disease of the mind. At any rate, it is the sort of disease for which a person should be detained in hospital rather than be given an unqualified acquittal.

Thus was the concept of insanity enlarged and that of non-insane automatism diminished. A further step on the road was the case of *Sullivan*, also finally decided in the House of Lords. Mr Sullivan was described as a man of 'blameless reputation' who suffered from epilepsy and had been treated for several years as an outpatient. When he was visiting a neighbour, he had a seizure and attacked an elderly man who was talking to him by knocking him down and kicking him about the head and body. The elderly man had to be treated in hospital, and Mr Sullivan was charged with causing grievous bodily harm. His defence was to be one of automatism and evidence was given that he was almost certainly in an epileptic state at the time of the assault. Nevertheless, the judge ruled that the defence was really one of not guilty by reason of insanity. At this point, the defendant changed his plea to guilty and was given 3 years on probation with a condition of treatment. Lord Diplock dismissed an appeal against conviction on the grounds that epilepsy is properly defined as a 'disease of the mind'. This meant that, in future, epilepsy is to be regarded as insanity in the legal sense. We suspect this will only be true for serious charges in the Crown Court, but time will tell. To compound this decision, it has since been decided that in some circumstances diabetes can also be regarded as a disease of the mind (*Hennesy*) if complicated by hyperglycaemia (*sic*, hypoglycaemia?).

The Sullivan case sparked off letters to the medical journals and a symposium to discuss it all (*see* Fenwick and Fenwick, 1985). What had happened was the pragmatic reaffirmation that people who do violent things will be subject to legal controls whatever semantic contortions have to be endured. Like most offenders with diseases, mental or physical, Mr Sullivan was found guilty, and thus the mitigating factors in his case were taken into account at the sentencing stage. He received a sensible disposal and was not punished for his automatic behaviour. Even so, this is not entirely satisfactory, the law still has some further modernization to undergo. At the trial, the effect of all this on the patient was described:

> PS, like Rogozhin (Dostoevsky's character in *The Idiot*), never contradicted his clever counsel, although he clearly found his eloquence beyond his comprehension. . . . We told him that the judge was prepared to consider him not guilty by reason of insanity 'But I'm not insane' said PS. We advised him, because of the consequences of this, to plead guilty. 'But I'm not guilty' said PS. Even the eloquent counsel paused, then PS spoke again: 'But you're three intelligent, educated people—I'll do whatever you say' (Taylor, 1985a).

In *Burgess*, in a case of a serious assault which occurred during alleged sleepwalking, the Court of Appeal ruled as in *Sullivan*, a danger of recurrence of a mental disorder manifesting itself in violence may be a reason for categorising the condition as a disease of the mind, but the absence of such danger is not a reason for saying that it cannot be a disease of the mind. This meant that abnormalities or disorders, albeit transitory, due to internal factors, whether functional or organic which manifested themselves in violence and which might recur are to be regarded as diseases of the mind and falling within the terms of legal insanity. The court also drew attention to Lord Diplock's comment in *Sullivan* in which he said the label 'insanity' is inappropriate in some senses and a purely technical one.

As the door closes on epilepsy and sleep-walking in England, it is still left open for concussion and drug-induced states of altered consciousness. Two mental hospital nurses were charged with causing actual bodily harm to a patient by assaulting him. One of them was a diabetic and he said that, before the assault, he had taken his insulin, but had eaten too little and had no recollection of the incident. His medical evidence supported hypoglycaemia at the material time. The trial judge (Bridge J) ruled that the proper defence would be insanity, whereupon the defendant pleaded guilty. His appeal was, however, allowed on grounds that a disease of the mind within the meaning of the McNaughton Rules is a malfunction caused by disease as opposed to a transitory external agent (such as insulin). The Court concluded:

> In our judgment the fundamental concept is of a malfunctioning of the mind caused by disease. A malfunctioning of the mind of transitory effect caused by the application to the body of some external factor such as violence, drugs, including antibiotics, alcohol, and hypnotic influences, cannot fairly be said to be due to disease. Such malfunctioning, unlike that caused by a defect of reason from disease of the mind, will not always relieve an accused from criminal responsibility. A self-induced incapacity will not excuse, *see Lipman*, nor will one which could have been reasonably foreseen as a result of either doing, or omitting to do

something, as, for example, taking alcohol against medical advice after using prescribed drugs, or failing to have regular meals while taking insulin (*Quick and Paddison*).

Although the violent epileptic has been firmly put in the insanity category, this case opens the possibility (no more than that) that an epileptic fit caused by an external agent, for example a flickering light, could still successfully plead non-insane automatism. Some tentative support to this view has been given by an unreported case in Leeds (*Owen*)*. A man with a history of depression and social inadequacy was prescribed an antidepressant drug, maprotiline 75 mg three times a day. One evening he had a strange staring attack whilst watching the TV. His mother, with whom he was living and who doted upon him, ran next door and asked neighbours to assist her and to call the police. The defendant was found sitting on a settee staring at a disconnected TV screen—he did not answer his name. When the neighbour looked at him, he grabbed the neighbour's hand and said 'I'm going to get thee.' The neighbour went leaving the defendant and his mother together. There was a noise, the mother fell against the door, having been assaulted, and she died. When the police came, the defendant was calm and rational, but amnesic for the fatal events. An EEG showed a right-sided temporal lobe abnormality. He had no history of epileptic fits. However, the court accepted the submission from two psychiatrists that the defendant attacked his mother during a temporal lobe seizure induced by an antidepressant drug (one known to be liable to precipitate fits) and acquitted him by reason of non-insane automatism. He was admitted to hospital informally, treated with carbamazepine, and allowed to go home after 3 months having had no further attacks. White (1991) has described six cases in which a defence based upon epilepsy was put, or nearly put, in a magistrates court. None of these successfully bypassed the McNaughton Rules, but the paper raises the interesting point that magistrates courts should be able to acquit on grounds of insanity without the special verdict, and quotes some Home Office correspondence which seems to support that view. This grey area is less significant following the passage of the Criminal Procedure (Insanity & Unfitness to Plead) Act 1991 (p. 45).

Alcohol and drugs

Intoxicating substances require a special section because they raise legal and philosophical issues which are quite different from other issues dealt with in the trial.

Self-induced intoxication is generally no defence to a criminal charge. Traditionally, it has been regarded as an aggravating factor rather than an excuse. Thus Aristotle in the Nichomachean Ethics stated that penalties were doubled if the offender was drunk. He also formulated the modern

* We are indebted to Drs Kay and Milne for details of this case.

concept of recklessness: the drunken man is punished even if he did not know what he was doing because he is responsible for getting himself drunk (d'Orbán, 1986). Coke in the 17th century and Blackstone in the 18th both regarded drunkenness as exacerbating the offence (Whitlock, 1963; Walker, 1968). However, during the 19th century these rigid views were modified to allow for the partial exculpation of the intoxicated offender in the case of serious crimes which would otherwise attract harsh penalties (Fingarette and Hasse, 1979). There are now two circumstances in which drugs or alcohol may be relevant to criminal responsibility: first, if intoxication is of such a degree that the accused does not have the necessary intent to commit the offence; second, if they give rise to a mental disorder. In some cases either of these arguments could lead to a defence under the McNaughton Rules.

Intoxication and intent.   A distinction has developed between crimes that require a mental element of 'specific intent' and those that require only 'basic intent'. The objective was to allow some intoxicated offenders to be convicted of offences that carried less serious penalties (Fingarette and Hasse, 1979). Crimes of specific intent are those in which the intention can be negatived by intoxication; examples are murder, wounding with intent to cause grievous bodily harm, theft or burglary. Other crimes such as manslaughter, assault or unlawful wounding require only 'basic intent' which cannot be negatived by intoxication. The point of this artificial distinction is that intoxication may be a defence to crimes of 'specific intent' if it can be shown that the accused was so intoxicated that he did not form the intent required for the offence. The accused may still be convicted of a lesser offence for which only 'basic intent' is required. For example, he may have been too drunk to do the criminal damage, but that would not matter if he was reckless, because recklessness is sufficient to constitute the *mens rea* of criminal damage (see Ashworth 1991 for a discussion).

This doctrine was formulated by Lord Birkenhead in the case of Beard, who had suffocated a girl while raping her (*Beard*):

> Where a specific intent is an essential element in the offence, evidence of a state of drunkenness rendering the accused incapable of forming such an intent should be taken into consideration in order to determine whether he had in fact formed the intent necessary to constitute the particular crime. If he was so drunk that he was incapable of forming the intent required he could not be convicted of a crime which was committed only if the intent was proved. . . . In a charge of murder based upon intention to kill or to do grievous bodily harm, if the jury are satisfied that the accused was, by reason of his drunken condition, incapable of forming the intent to kill or to do grievous bodily harm . . . he cannot be convicted of murder. But nevertheless unlawful homicide has been committed by the accused . . . and that is manslaughter. . . . The law is plain beyond all question that in cases falling short of insanity a condition of drunkenness at the time of committing an offence causing death can only, when it is available at all, have the effect of reducing the crime from murder to manslaughter.

The question is whether or not the defendant, in fact, formed the intent (*see also Sheehan; Garlick*).

Although the law originally developed in relation to alcohol intoxication, drugs are treated in a similar fashion (*Lipman*). Lipman killed a girl while under the influence of LSD; he thought he was struggling with snakes and asphyxiated her by stuffing a sheet down her throat. He was acquitted of murder, as he lacked the required specific intent, but was convicted of manslaughter as he was deemed to have been reckless (*mens rea* for manslaughter).

For crimes that require only 'basic intent', intoxication is no defence. This was reaffirmed in *Majewski*. After taking barbiturates, amphetamines and alcohol Majewski assaulted a publican and three policemen; the following morning he had no recollection of the events. He was convicted of assault and his subsequent appeal was dismissed. The House of Lords were then asked to decide 'whether a defendant may be properly convicted of assault, notwithstanding that by reason of self-induced intoxication he did not intend to do the act alleged to constitute the assault'. The House of Lords answered the question in the affirmative. The Lord Chancellor said that in cases of manslaughter, assault and unlawful wounding, it was:

> No excuse in law that, because of drink or drugs which the accused himself had taken knowingly and willingly, he had deprived himself of the ability to exercise self-control, to realize the possible consequences of what he was doing, or even to be conscious that he was doing it.

Thus, if the intoxication is self-induced, the accused can be convicted of a crime of 'basic intent' even if he was in a state of automatism and lacked the *mens rea* normally required for the offence; his recklessness in getting himself into an intoxicated state may provide the necessary *mens rea*. The ruling was in part justified on the grounds of public policy, as there would otherwise be no sanction against those who inflict injury while under the influence of drugs or alcohol to the extent that they lack volition. The Butler Committee (Home Office, DHSS, 1975) had previously suggested the creation of a new offence of 'Dangerous Intoxication' to deal with this problem; it would have overcome the present confusing and illogical state of the law relating to different types of intent. Under the present law, the drunken shoplifter can be acquitted of theft, but may be convicted of assaulting the store detective who arrested him.

Alcohol, drugs and mental disorder

1. *The insanity defence (special verdict).*   If alcohol or drugs give rise to psychotic illness (for example delirium tremens or amphetamine psychosis) the McNaughton Rules, in theory, may be applicable, although, in practice, the insanity defence is now rarely used. In *Davies*, a man was charged with wounding with intent to murder during an attack of delirium tremens, Stephen J drew a clear distinction between simple intoxication and disease caused by alcohol:

> Drunkenness is one thing and the diseases to which drunkenness lead are different things: and if a man by drunkenness brings on a state of disease which causes such a degree of madness, even for a time, which would have relieved him of responsibility if it had been caused in any other way, then he would not be criminally responsible.

2. *Diminished responsibility.*   Under section 2 of the Homicide Act 1957, an 'abnormality of mind' must arise from one of the causes specified in the Act; those of possible relevance to drugs and alcohol are disease, injury or inherent causes. An abnormality of mind arising from intoxication is no defence (*Fenton*).

It is doubtful whether alcohol or drug dependence alone without any psychiatric complications or additional factors would qualify as a disease causing 'abnormality of mind'. The essence of the legal disease concept of dependence is the assumption that the conduct of the addict is involuntary, and this cannot be accepted as a general proposition (Fingarette and Hasse, 1979). In *Tandy*, it was explicitly stated that the very first drink of the day would have to be completely involuntary—a tough test indeed.

The question of alcohol dependence as an 'inherent cause' was discussed in *Fenton* where the defence argued that:

> Part of the appellant's mental make up is . . . an inability to resist the temptation to drink, and accordingly when he succumbs to this temptation he must be regarded as succumbing to an abnormality of mind due to inherent causes.

Dismissing the appeal, the court nevertheless left the door open, stating that:

> A case may arise where the defendant proves such a craving for drink or drugs as to produce in itself an abnormality of mind within the meaning of section 2 (of the Homicide Act).

In *Di Duca* the defendant who was convicted of murder in the furtherance of theft had pleaded an abnormality of mind arising from injury by alcohol, as he had been drinking beforehand. Dismissing the appeal, the Court found that whether or not alcohol caused 'injury', in Di Duca's case, there was no evidence that it had led to 'abnormality of mind'. This leaves open the possibility that demonstrable evidence of 'injury' by alcohol, if sufficiently severe, could substantiate diminished responsibility. Cortical atrophy on a CT scan combined with psychological deficits (Ron, 1983) would seem consistent with the concept of injury from the toxic effects of alcohol.

The status of pathological intoxication as a 'disease' within section 2 is less clear. Coid (1979) argued that pathological intoxication is an ill-defined diagnostic category and that 'pathological drunkenness' (ICD-9, 291.4) should be omitted from the International Classification of Diseases; many states of supposed pathological intoxication may be attributable to alcohol-induced hypoglycaemia, organic brain damage or psychopathy. However, there are still some authors who retain the concept of pathological intoxication as a specific syndrome, with alteration of mood correlating with slowing of the EEG and subsequent amnesia (Maletsky, 1976; Wolf, 1980). This could lead to arguments in court. An unreported case in England where EEG abnormality was demonstrated resulted in a manslaughter verdict on the grounds of lack of intent, although the defence could also have been based on insanity or diminished responsibility (d'Orbán, 1986).

Alcoholic amnesia is a common clinical problem, but the issue of diminished responsibility is unlikely to arise unless there is some abnormality additional to intoxication and subsequent amnesia. If the amnesia is accepted as genuine, the problem is to decide whether the accused was able to form intent at the material time (Glatt, 1982). The same consideration applies to other drugs which may cause amnesia, particularly benzodiazepines (Subhan, 1984).

In most cases where diminished responsibility becomes an issue, drugs or alcohol interact with other factors such as depression, personality disorder or organic brain damage. Although it is an artificial exercise, for legal purposes the effects of intoxication have to be discounted. In order to establish diminished responsibility the associated condition (such as depression) must in itself be of sufficient severity to constitute an 'abnormality of mind'. Thus in *Fenton*, five psychiatrists agreed that the accused had a psychopathic personality disorder, that he suffered from reactive depression and that he was disinhibited and possibly confused by drink. The jury were directed to convict him of murder if they were satisfied that the combined effect of the factors *other* than alcohol was insufficient to substantially impair responsibility, and this direction was upheld on appeal. The ruling was confirmed by *Gittens*. A man suffering from depression who took drink and prescribed drugs was taunted by his wife about the paternity of their sons; he clubbed her to death and then raped and strangled his stepdaughter. Three doctors said he had diminished responsibility due to depression, while a fourth said his abnormality of mind was brought on by drink and drugs and was not due to illness. The jury were invited to decide what was the substantial cause of his behaviour, and convicted him of murder. On appeal it was held that the judge's direction was improper: the jury must be instructed to disregard the effects of drugs or alcohol and then to consider whether the other matters which fall within section 2 amounted to an abnormality of mind which would substantially impair his responsibility; a verdict of manslaughter was substituted.

The defence of involuntary intoxication is applicable both to cases where a person's drink is 'laced' without his knowledge, and to intoxication by drugs prescribed in the course of medical treatment. If successful, the defence of involuntary intoxication results in acquittal but, in practice, it is extremely rare. d'Orbán (1989) reported the case of a man who developed a severe psychotic illness from dexamethasone administered for a maxillary operation. Suffering from messianic delusions, he attacked his fiancée believing that he had to kill her to save the world. He was charged with her attempted murder, but was acquitted on the grounds of involuntary intoxication. The Court made no distinction in this case between drug intoxication and a drug-induced mental illness.

Recently, the courts have distinguished unforeseen intoxication or unexpected side-effects produced by 'therapeutic drugs' from intoxication caused by alcohol or 'dangerous drugs' (Brahams, 1987; *Bailey*; *Hardie*). In the case of therapeutic drugs, the defendant may be considered reckless if he appreciates that the drug 'may lead to aggressive, unpredictable, and uncontrollable conduct, yet deliberately runs the risk or otherwise disregards it' (*Bailey*). Therapeutic drugs do not necessarily refer to those prescribed for the patient; they may include diazepam taken in good faith from another person's medicine cabinet (*Hardie*). The distinction between the two classes of drug is not entirely clear, but dangerous drugs seem to be those that are commonly known to cause aggressive or unpredictable behaviour (*Bailey*).

Other 'mental' excuses

So far in the trial phase we have been concerned with the two defences of insanity (which may be used for any charge) and diminished responsibility (which is specific to the murder charge). What about lesser degrees of mental abnormality that do not amount to insanity in respect of other charges? We have noted the way in which magistrates either disregard such questions altogether and simply convict an otherwise acknowledged offender or send him to hospital without conviction. In the High Court the second option does not apply and mentally ill offenders, not charged with murder, are simply found guilty, even if their illness is severe.

Theoretically, there is no reason to prevent psychiatric evidence being called to support the other 'excuses' (as Hart, 1968 calls them) i.e. mistake, accident, provocation, and duress. For example, it could be argued in the case of a man who stabs his wife that he was not McNaughton insane but, nevertheless, was so depressed and as a result so absent-minded that, during an argument with his victim, he did not realize he was wielding a knife and hence the stabbing was accidental. Such a defence is highly unlikely to succeed and in the Crown Court the judge is likely to rule that all psychiatric matters should be dealt with under the McNaughton Rules, i.e. as insanity *v* sanity, and so these defences are rare in English courts and seem to be confined to property offences such as shoplifting (theft). In the *Clarke* case, the defendant pleaded not guilty to stealing from a shop on the grounds that she was absent-minded as a result of a depressive illness. The assistant recorder directed that her defence was actually the insanity defence and the McNaughton Rules applied, so she changed her plea to guilty. However, the Court of Appeal said the judge was wrong in his interpretation and the conviction was quashed; absent-mindedness did not amount to insanity.

So, psychiatric evidence in the trial is virtually limited to insanity, infanticide or diminished responsibility (for a charge of murder), or non-insane automatism. A Court of Appeal case (*Chard*) indicates why. Peter Chard was convicted of murder. He had been examined by a prison doctor who pronounced 'mental illness, substantially diminished responsibility, the McNaughton Rules, subnormality and psychopathic disorder, do not appear to me to be relevant to the issue', but the doctor went on to add, 'what does seem clear to me in the light of this man's personality was there was no intent or *mens rea* on his part to commit murder at any time that evening'. Defence counsel believed that opinion should have been admitted at the trial, even although he could find no precedent for so doing. Roskill LJ was not surprised that no precedent could be found:

> It seems to this Court that his submission, if accepted, would involve the Court admitting medical evidence in other cases not where there was an issue, for example, of insanity or diminished responsibility, but where the sole issue which the jury had to consider, as happens in scores of different kinds of cases, was the question of intent.

Concurring, Lane LJ said:

> One purpose of jury trials is to bring into the jury box a body of men and women who are able to judge ordinary day-to-day questions by their own standards . . . where, as in the present case, they are dealing with someone who by concession was on the medical evidence entirely normal, it seems to this Court abundantly plain . . . that it is not permissible to call a witness, whatever his personal experience, merely to tell the jury how he thinks an accused man's mind—assumedly a normal mind—operated at the time of the alleged crime with reference to the crucial question of what the man's intention was (*Chard*).

If, of course, the mind is not normal, then the medical evidence can be admitted, but not in such a way as to frustrate the intentions of the various Acts that have since 1800 decreed that the 'insane' offender shall be detained in hospital (*see* for example the discussion in Williams, 1965). In other words, there shall be no loopholes for the mentally abnormal offender (other than the loophole of automatism) to evade being considered for and perhaps compelled to have psychiatric care and/or social control.

To illustrate just how far fetched some legal philosophy can be, the concept of multiple personality is worth noting as a final legal oddity (*see* p. 427 for a clinical account). Multiple personality has been claimed to equate with the sleep-walker and, it is argued, should benefit from a similar defence. Abrams (1983) quotes the case of one Milligan accused in Ohio of multiple rapes who was found not guilty by reason of insanity because he was diagnosed as having a multiple personality. It was stated that at the time of the rapes he could neither distinguish right from wrong nor control his actions. Presumably, these disabilities were thought to arise because he was in the grips of an alter personality which dominated his normal and presumably 'real', non-offending, non-raping self!

A similar argument of 'unconsciousness' has been advanced for cases of multiple personality (French and Schechmeister, 1983) again resting on the analogy between the somnambulist and the multiple personality when in a state dominated by one of their subsidiary personalities. These contentions appear to be based on assumptions that—

1. there is only one real or primary personality and that the other personalities are excrescences created by disease or disorder, for which the sufferer cannot be held responsible;
2. the primary personality is incapable of controlling the actions of the secondary personality; and
3. when an amnesic barrier exists between the innocent primary personality and the guilty secondary one, this is tantamount to the primary personality being unconscious at the time of the offending.

The unconsciousness and uncontrollability are connected. In this context, the frequently made analogy to sleep-walking is worth pursuing. Even if the analogy is correct, the issues of culpability and sleep-walking are not straightforward. Complex motor behaviours can occur in subjects who are unequivocally asleep (usually stage IV sleep) or who are in a state of transition between sleep and waking (stage I sleep). In the sleep-walker's wandering, habitual tasks can be carried out and in those awoken suddenly, particularly from vivid frightening dreams, brief episodes of poorly coordinated and occasional violent activity may occur. What does not occur is extended periods of purposeful, novel activity which is complex and goal directed. You may, whilst asleep, wander into another bedroom or out into a neighbour's garden. You do not force entry, selectively remove valuables, make good your escape and return with the stolen goods nor, on entering the wrong bedroom, do you pause to commit rape before continuing your somnambulistic peregrinations. In cases where the defence of multiple personality is advanced, the motivation is usually clear. The activities leading up to it are complex, extended over time and are goal directed. Frequently, no documented history exists prior to the offending of the multiple personality disorder which comes to light only after being charged with the offence.

The other argument advanced by advocates of defences based on multiple personality disorder is that because the defendant is amnesic with respect to the offence, then he cannot assist counsel or prepare his own evidence (French and Schechmeister, 1983). The issue of amnesia for both responsibility and fitness to plead is raised by a number of states including intoxication and head injury. Further, in many serious crimes there can be an inability or unwillingness to recall the actual offence. In homicide, for example, nearly half of offenders are reported to have either no memory or the haziest recollection of the crime (*see* pp. 291–5). In fact, in both English and American jurisdictions, amnesia has been held not to affect fitness to plead, nor of itself to nullify responsibility. In practice, the ruling can hardly be otherwise.

A story, probably apocryphal, is told of an Old Bailey judge called upon to sentence a man whose defence claimed he suffered from multiple personality. The judge admitted to the sadness he felt that the model citizen and blameless character who stood before him should have to share his body with the villainous perpetrator of the offences and, moreover, would have to be confined together with this criminal in a prison cell for the period of the sentence which he was about to impose. Although such an approach might be considered a crude attempt to hold the body responsible for its actions irrespective of the mental element, it does appeal to those who respect a sceptical approach both to the all too human attempts to avoid the consequences of our actions, and to the pretensions of experts (*see also* Ch. 10).

Sentence

The length and complexity of the discussion of the role of psychiatry in the trial phase of a hearing does not signify especial importance. It is more a reflection of the detailed complexity which legal philosophy leads to and which can be so disconcerting to the medical practitioner. In practice, it is in the sentencing phase where the psychiatrist is most needed, can do most good for his patients, and is most comfortable, for the philosophical issues are simpler, the legal jargon is minimal, the adversarial process is over and a genuine clinical discussion can be held. One word of warning at the outset may, nevertheless, be appropriate. At the sentencing stage, a great deal of power and authority is, on occasions, loaned to the psychiatrist who should realize that this may be happening. It is not part of a doctor's function to recommend that his patients are punished, e.g. recommendations for imprisonment, or for particular lengths of imprisonment should always be eschewed. Punishments may be inevitable, but those recommendations will come from elsewhere and the doctor's role is the provision of realistic mitigation. Realistic mitigation means the provision of explanation and meaning to the crime being considered; it means sensible offers of treatment and disposal. Both rejection and/or condemnation on the one hand and wildly overoptimistic proposals on the other are bad practice, as is any encouragement of the belief that the offender will get adequate treatment in prison.

Sentencing theory

Before the question of psychiatric disposal is examined, it is as well to note briefly some of the principles of sentencing to which the judge will attend. In recent times, textbooks of sentencing theory and practice have emerged in Britain (*see* for example Thomas, 1979; Walker, 1985). The psychiatrist does not need to be an expert in this field, but it is important for him to understand what is happening in this crucial phase of the hearing, as it is the phase in which psychiatry and the law have the greatest impact on each other.

Thomas (1979) reminds us that in legal terms current sentencing practice is a modern development beginning in the latter half of the 19th century. Originally, the common law allowed the sentencer no discretion in cases of felony other than recommendations of royal clemency and/or transportation to the colonies for the many capital offences then extant. By 1840, however, the number of capital offences was considerably reduced and, later, transportation gave way to penal servitude. In this century, Parliament began to give to courts powers to deal with offenders as individuals. Perhaps the most notable milestone in this respect is the Probation of Offenders Act 1907 which gave courts the power to make probation orders in any case they chose except where the penalty is fixed by law. In Thomas's view the effect of the British legal history of sentencing has been to create two distinct systems of sentencing, reflecting different penal objectives and governed by different principles. The sentencer may choose either a sentence to reflect culpability, or he may subject the offender to an appropriate measure of supervision, treatment or confinement.

Underlying the first type of sentencing, which is usually done in the name of general deterrence, is the tariff. This 'represents a complex of penal theories—general deterrence, denunciation, occasionally expiation', with an overriding principle of proportionality between the offence and the sentence (Thomas, 1979). This means that the sentence is chosen more by reference to the offence than to the offender.

Individualization, on the other hand, looks primarily to the offender, although everyone would concede that the offence is always taken into account to some extent. Individualizing measures are more likely for four grades of offenders: those under 21, those in need of psychiatric treatment, recidivists who have reached a critical point in their life, and persistent recidivists who are in danger of becoming completely institutionalized. The court will generally rely heavily on psychiatric advice in respect of those requiring psychiatric treatment provided such people are clearly identified, the nature of their problem is explained comprehensively, and a practical plan of management is outlined which is compatible with the judge's view of public safety.

It should be noted at once that individualization does not always produce a lesser sentence (although it may). For example, a man who attacks with a knife may not cause much injury, and on the tariff system his offence might be 'worth' 3–5 years, say but, because he has a mental disorder, he might be sent to a hospital with a restriction order and stay there 10 years or more. He may even be given a life sentence on psychiatric grounds which could result in his spending many more years actually in prison than the 2–3 years he would otherwise have expected.

In 1961, the important Streatfeild Report on the business of the criminal courts was published (Home Office, Lord Chancellor's Office 1961). The report considers the role of the medical report in the sentencing process and concludes that it is relevant in three ways:

1. it helps the court to assess an offender's culpability (by indicating facts which affect his culpability or responsibility);
2. it helps the court to pass a sentence designed to stop him from offending again (by indicating treatment which could usefully be given, whether in custody or not);
3. it helps the court to pass a sentence to protect society from him.

The report urges the doctors to state their opinions frankly and give reasons for them, and to express their views on the effects that particular sentences may have on the offender except, that in this regard, both doctors and probation officers are requested to refrain from speculation and to confine themselves to reporting established facts or actual experience. The doctor—

> should feel free to indicate treatment which in his view could usefully be given to the offender, whether in custody or on probation, although, like the probation officer, he should take care not to give his report in a form which suggests that the proper treatment of the offender will be the only consideration in the court's mind.

The Streatfeild Report also considers some administrative matters in relation to psychiatric reports which are of some importance. Where the defendant is in custody, the prison medical officer has the primary responsibility for providing the sentencing court with any medical report. Furthermore, prison doctors have been instructed to supply courts with *pretrial* reports in writing whenever they think it is desirable to draw attention to some abnormality in the prisoner. This, of course, means that prison doctors are being asked, by and large, to comment on psychiatric abnormality in an untried prisoner, but the court can ignore the report if the prisoner is found not guilty. If this happens, ideally, the defendant should be given appropriate medical advice anyway. The Streatfeild Committee urged probation officers to look for psychiatric disturbances and report these to prison doctors. Under section 26(4) of the Magistrates' Court Act 1952, magistrates have the power to make it a condition of bail that the defendant undergoes a medical examination. Probation officers are usually asked to find an appropriate clinic for the accused. This procedure frequently operates pretrial even though the medical evidence is required for sentencing, but it can also be used after a conviction.

If the defence believes that a psychiatric report will assist a defendant then, providing funds are available (usually through legal aid), defending solicitors will employ doctors, on a private basis, to visit their clients in prison, or examine them on bail with a view to providing another medical opinion to the court.

One important recommendation made right at the end of the Streatfeild Report is that 'a copy of any written report submitted to the court should, on conviction, be given to the offender or his counsel'. They also indicate that 'it should remain the responsibility of the court to decide, in the interests of the proper administration of justice, what parts, if any, of a written report (of whatever kind) should be read aloud in open court'. Courts are usually very discreet in this respect, especially if a medical report is marked as: 'Preferably not to be used as oral evidence'. Defence solicitors, however, very often show the medical report to their clients and then discuss it with them (*see* Ch. 22 for details about the preparation of psychiatric reports).

Below are listed the main sentencing decisions which particularly affect the mentally abnormal offender. The court does, of course, have all the usual punitive options available as well, such as fixed term imprisonment, and financial penalties. For a full account of such sentences the reader is referred to Thomas (1979). Compensation orders are briefly mentioned on p. 105 and p. 225.

Discharges

Discharges conditional or absolute are used, maybe on the recommendation of a psychiatrist, when a mentally disordered individual needs the opportunity to undertake psychiatric treatment, either inpatient or outpatient, is willing to have such treatment but, in the circumstances of the case, a probation order with a condition of medical treatment would be inappropriate (perhaps too severe). An example in this category is the first-time shoplifter who is depressed. The discharge is usually a conditional discharge which is made on condition that the offender does not reoffend within a specified period of time, usually one year.

Psychiatric probation orders

Probation is an important topic and is dealt with elsewhere (pp. 769 & 783). Here all that is noted is that under the Powers of the Criminal Courts Act 1973 a probation order can be made, for periods up to a maximum of 3 years, and this can include a condition of psychiatric treatment. This is to be 'under the direction of a duly qualified medical practitioner' (i.e., a psychiatrist approved under S.12 of the MHA 1983) 'with a view to the improvement of the offender's mental condition'. Like other probation orders, it is a voluntary arrangement, which means that the offender, the probation service, and the named doctor all have to agree to it before the court can award it. Once established, however, the offender has to remember that serious challenges to the authority of the medical and probation supervisors may be dealt with as a breach of probation and lead the offender back to court for a different type of sentence and maybe an extra sentence for breach of probation. Leaving hospital against medical advice, or failing to attend an outpatient clinic, are examples of matters which can be regarded as a breach of probation. This Act is careful to specify, however (S.6(7)), that no breach shall be implied simply on the ground that the probationer has refused to undergo any particular treatment such as surgical or electrical treatment if 'in the opinion of the court, his refusal was reasonable having regard to all the circumstances'.

Only one 'duly qualified' medical practitioner (i.e. approved under S.12(2) of the MHA 1983) is required to testify to the mental condition of an offender: the mental condition is defined as that which requires and may be susceptible to treatment, but does not warrant detention under the Mental Health Act 1983.

The treatment to be offered has to be specified as—

1. treatment as a resident in a hospital or a nursing home (but not a special hospital); or
2. treatment as a non-resident (outpatient) at a hospital; or
3. treatment under the direction of a named psychiatrist.

More detailed specification is not required and the specifications can be changed as the order proceeds by agreement between the doctor, the probationer and the probation officer. These rules give a great deal of flexibility and make the psychiatric probation order an extremely useful tool in forensic psychiatry. The possibility of supervised outpatient care with a trained social worker added to the team is particularly helpful.

Such probation orders may be given for a wide variety of offences ranging from very serious ones such as manslaughter, wounding, blackmail, arson, and indecent assault down to trivial ones. Inevitably, theft is the commonest offence (Lewis, 1980). As the disposal is available for cases which do not warrant a Mental Health Act hospital order, some consider it especially suitable for drug addicts and alcoholics although, in practice, it is used in a wide variety of psychiatric conditions (*see* again Lewis, 1980). No data are available about the 'success' of such orders (an extremely complex issue in any case), but clinical experience would suggest that the more serious the offence, the more seriously all the participants take the order, and detailed groundwork thrashing out the terms and conditions of the order *before* it is made leads to better cooperation, and a more effective order.

If the patient is in breach of the treatment condition, the probation officer may bring a breach action before the supervising court, who, if the breach is proved, has the options of imposing a small fine, making a community service order, or imposing any other sentence appropriate to the original offence. The court may also decide to take no action. There is little a court can do, however, to enforce a treatment condition.

The Criminal Justice Act 1991, adds a specific condition of treatment for drug and alcohol addiction. This can be ordered without the need for a medical practitioner to be involved in the treatment, but otherwise follows the form of the psychiatric condition, which is re-enacted. The 1991 Act makes probation a sentence in its own right and generally treats conditions in probation orders as restrictions on liberty commensurate with the serious-ness of the offence(s) for which the order has been made. Treatment conditions do not always fit this justice model of sentencing.

Binding-over with a condition of treatment

One problem with the psychiatric probation order is that it can only last for 3 years whilst psychiatric disorder may last much longer. In an attempt to provide something akin to the psychiatric probation order but for longer, courts have occasionally had recourse to the ancient common law technique of binding-over to be of good behaviour and adding in the condition that psychiatric treatment must also be undertaken. A bind-over can last up to 5 years. The authors know of two unreported cases in which this arrangement was applied with considerable success. The first patient was a recidivist paedophile who, under the arrangements, submitted himself to oestrogen treatment; the second man was a severe alcoholic who set fire to a public house with people in it. He responded moderately well to psychotherapy for 5 years. The authors also know of a third case which was a complete failure—he was a paranoid man who could not cope with psychotherapy and who severely reoffended and received a life sentence.

Hospital orders

Hospital orders are available to both the Crown Courts and magistrates' courts (including youth courts) for individuals who have been convicted of an offence for which they could suffer imprisonment, provided two doctors (one of whom is approved under S.12 of the MHA 1983) are prepared to sign forms stating that the offender suffers from mental disorder (any of the four categories) and the managers of a hospital agree to have the patient. The doctors also have to state that admission is 'appropriate' and, in the case of mental impairment or psychopathic disorder, that 'such treatment is likely to alleviate or prevent a deterioration of his condition'.

This gives very wide powers to commit offenders to hospital, including offenders with personality disorders and mental impairment, provided (and it is a very big proviso) that a hospital is willing to accept them. The practical effect is to hand the offender over to medical care which is almost identical to the care provided for civilly committed people under S.3 of the MHA 1983 (*see* pp. 27–32). However, unlike patients on treatment orders, those on hospital orders cannot apply to the MHRT for discharge within the first 6 months, and relatives never gain any powers of discharge.* The powers

---

* It is a curious anomaly, however, that such patients can apply to the managers immediately after admission, just like all S.3 patients (*see* p. 1007).

given to magistrates to impose a hospital order without recording a conviction have already been mentioned (p. 47).

The issue of finding a bed is crucial, especially as available NHS resources decline. If, after an order is made, the hospital changes its mind, then the order lapses 28 days after it was imposed. This does not prevent a new order being made. If the patient is not transferred within 21 days, the Home Office tries to bring pressure on the hospital concerned. The MHA 1983 introduced the *interim hospital order* (under S.38). This is an arrangement whereby, if the court is in a position to make a hospital order, it can arrange for a trial period first. The arrangement is for 12 weeks in the first instance, renewable for further periods of 4 weeks (28 days) by the court (on the advice of the RMO) up to a maximum of 6 months. Some of the conditions are slightly different to a full hospital order. One of the doctors signing the forms has to work at the receiving hospital. The patient is not entirely handed over to the hospital; his final sentence is yet to be determined so if, during the period of the order, he runs away, he can be brought back to court. The grounds for making the interim order are slightly less rigorous in that the doctors only have to state that there is 'reason to suppose' that a hospital order is appropriate rather than it 'is' appropriate. An important difference between interim and full hospital orders is that patients on interim orders do not have the right to apply to the hospital managers or to an MHRT at all. Magistrates' courts do not have the power to impose an interim hospital order without recording a conviction. The point of all this is that if there is any doubt about the suitability of a particular patient for a hospital order, then a trial period can be undertaken before (or instead of) a full commitment. It was perhaps primarily intended to test the treatability of those with mental impairment or psychopathic disorder, but it is little used in this way.

Another way of carrying out a trial period of treatment before the hospital order decision is finally made is for the Crown Court to remand the offender to hospital (under S.36 MHA 1983) for treatment. Magistrates' courts cannot make an order under S.36, it can only be done for patients suffering from mental illness or severe mental impairment, and is only possible for periods of 28 days at a time and 12 weeks in all.

Restriction orders

The effect of a restriction order is to give the powers of leave, transfer and discharge, which are normally held by the RMO, to the Home Secretary. Such orders are made after a hospital order has been made (they are not available for civilly committed cases) or in respect of transferred prisoners. They are made under S.41 of the MHA 1983 only when—

> it appears to the court, having regard to the nature of the offence, the antecedents of the offender and the risk of his committing further offences if set at large, that it is necessary for the protection of the public from serious harm.

One of the reporting (form filling) doctors in respect of the hospital order has to give oral evidence in court before the order can be made, and the order can only be made in the Crown Court. If magistrates believe that a restriction order might be appropriate, then they have to promote the case to the Crown Court.

In his oral evidence, the doctor will be asked for his views on the appropriateness of a restriction order. He will have to think about questions of dangerousness bearing in mind that the restriction order provides, as a rule, compulsory aftercare with both medical and social work supervision. Whatever the doctor thinks, however, the judge has the last word (once the hospital order is in place) and will impose a restriction order if he believes that the criteria have been fulfilled and the public need to be protected.

The whole question of dangerousness is a vexed one, to be dealt with in Chap. 16. Here it should be noted that a restriction order may be imposed when the current offence, perhaps a burglary or a petty theft, would not seem to warrant it, because other factors such as the antecedents of the offender and the content of any medical reports are taken into account. Another trap for the unwary psychiatrist! Second, although the legislation allows a time limit to be put to a restriction order, this is only rarely done, and almost all restriction orders are 'without limit of time'. This seems to be for two reasons. The Lord Chief Justice in *Gardiner* said that a time limit should be specified 'only where the doctors are able to assert confidently that recovery will take place in a fixed period'. For their part, many forensic psychiatrists believe that the time limit is wrong because they want indefinite control of indefinite disorders such as schizophrenia and personality disorder. Patients, on the other hand, often see restriction orders without limit of time as punitive, akin to life imprisonment, because such an order is just as uncertain as a sentence of life imprisonment, and it is equally controlled by the Home Secretary. Since 1983, there has been the opportunity to appeal to a special MHRT chaired by a judge, but release by such tribunals is rare. If justice arguments were to be paramount, then it would seem reasonable for the courts to view the hospital order as a medical disposal and the restriction order as a penal addition which could be timed according to the usual principles of sentencing. This would mean that if the offence would have otherwise merited life imprisonment, then the restriction order would be unlimited in time but, if the offence would have merited 5 years, then the restriction order would run out at the end of 5 years. Of course, the hospital order would not be timed, but at the end of the restriction order full control of the case would revert to the RMO who could then decide whether to continue the hospital order, and for how long on ordinary civil criteria. Doctors are, however, unlikely to be in favour of this arrangement unless they have some kind of community care order which would substitute for the supervisory powers provided under the restriction order.

Guardianship orders

A court may impose a guardianship order instead of a hospital order in suitable cases. Such orders are, however, rare. The usual effect of such an order is to hand over the care of the offender to the local authority, thus giving a social worker limited powers over the patient. It is also possible for someone else to become the guardian. The patients who are most likely to benefit are those who are mentally handicapped or socially impaired, provided they fulfil one of the Mental Health Act categories of mental disorder. Like a probation order, there may be a stipulation about where the patient is to reside; unlike a probation order the patient's consent is not required before the order is imposed. One problem with the order is that little can be done if the patient refuses to cooperate, but some patients respond to the knowledge that there is a formal order imposed upon them. Other patients cooperate completely and are relieved to have a social worker advise them on most of the important decisions in their life. The conditions of the order are identical to those imposed under the civil arrangements and give to the guardian (1) the power to decide where the patient is to reside, (2) the power to require the patient to attend for medical treatment, occupation, education, or training, (3) the power to require access to the patient by a doctor, social worker, or other specified person. Such guardianship orders are underused partly because local authorities are reluctant to supervise them, and partly because psychiatrists do not have much experience with them.

Life imprisonment

A sentence of life imprisonment means that the offender will remain liable to imprisonment for the rest of his life. It rarely means that the prisoner will stay in prison for all his life—the average length of stay in prison in 1989 was 10½ years. It does, however, mean that he will be subject to supervision and to other conditions of his life licence if he is released. The Home Office may issue a warrant for recall not only in the event of a further offence, but also if the 'lifer' is giving the supervising probation officer 'cause for concern'. In practice, lifers who progress well are subject to supervision for about 5 years, but a minority will remain on indefinite supervision.

A good summary of the High Court's attitude towards the use of life imprisonment for mentally abnormal offenders is given by Thomas (1979):

> The sentence is reserved for persons who have committed offences of substantial gravity and who appear to be suffering from some disorder of personality or instability of character which makes them likely to commit grave offences in the future if left at large or released from a fixed term of imprisonment. The sentence is not normally used as a tariff sentence to deal with offenders of normal mentality who have committed offences of great gravity.

Approximately 50 or 60 such life sentences are imposed each year (*see* Walker, 1985).

In practice, it is difficult for the observer to understand precisely what criteria are being used by the courts. In the case of *Blackburn* the Court of Appeal said that a life sentence should not be imposed—

> unless there is clear evidence of mental instability as opposed to mental disorder which would indicate that the person is likely to be a danger to the public.

As Walker (1985) pointed out, it seems clear from other cases (e.g. *Bryant & Mead*) that this distinction between mental instability and mental disorder was not meant to exclude mental disorder, merely to indicate that the condition need not amount to mental disorder (which, of course, could be dealt with under the MHA 1983).

Thomas (1979) has indicated that a sentence of life imprisonment should not be passed without a full psychiatric investigation of the offender, but as Walker (1985) reminded us, 'the offender's mental condition need not necessarily be one which psychiatrists can name or treat'. Further, even if the condition satisfies the requirements of a hospital order the court may either be prevented from making one (by the lack of a bed), or it may prefer a life sentence.

In these circumstances, the burden falling on the examining psychiatrist can be very heavy, perhaps too heavy. Certainly reports to courts at the sentencing stage must be considered extremely carefully. It is all too easy to be tacitly or implicitly recommending life imprisonment (the gravest punishment available in Britain) and being persuasive enough to convince the judge who would otherwise have imposed a fixed sentence. Sometimes this can happen by careless medical talk, forgetting that a court is not a clinical seminar room and a place for a clinical debate or playing the Devil's advocate. Sometimes refusal to admit to a particular ward or hospital can lead to needless over emphasis of unsuitability. A couple of cases may illustrate the awesome responsibility of the psychiatrist in these circumstances.

Ashdown was given life imprisonment for a robbery of £2 from a man held up in the street with an air pistol. He had many previous convictions, but the crucial evidence leading to this sentence seems to have been that one psychiatrist described him as schizoid with an abnormally high sex drive and potentially very dangerous, requiring a prolonged period of custodial treatment in a secure situation, suitable for an indeterminate sentence with treatment in prison and possible transfer under the MHA 1983 to hospital if his condition deteriorated. Another doctor recommended a hospital order with restrictions but, at the time of the appeal, no longer considered that course appropriate. The judge imposed life imprisonment on the basis that A would receive treatment. However, he did not go to Grendon prison because of his low IQ, nor did he receive any other sort of psychiatric treatment. He had to be segregated from other prisoners because of their hostility. He had taken tablets to reduce his libido and a hormone implant was to be offered on release. At appeal a third doctor urged retention of the life sentence because of the potential danger A represented to young children. The sentence was upheld. The court expressed the view that but for the mental element the appropriate sentence would have been 5 years' imprisonment.

A man set fire to some curtains in a hospital causing minor damage. A doctor described him as suffering from psychopathic disorder, unsuitable for treatment in a local hospital and unsuitable for a place in a special hospital because the hospital role would be custodial rather than therapeutic. Again, the life sentence was upheld on appeal (*Thornton*).

Before such significant recommendations are made to the court, there should be some kind of ethical debate (a clinical conference would do nicely) with as many peers as possible. It is also probably true that in some cases a clearer understanding of the concept of dangerousness and/or a clearer understanding of the treatment available for personality disorder would lead to sounder conclusions and recommendations.

It seems difficult to escape the view that, as in the trial stage of the hearing, psychiatric evidence is liable to be used in the sentencing stage by the courts against the interests of some patients. It must be the job of the psychiatrist to try to prevent this happening. He can only do so by constant vigilance, constant peer review, and above all by ensuring that psychiatric facilities are maximized and offered.

A recent analysis by Dell (1984) has shown that a life sentence is dealt with quite differently from a hospital order restricted without limit of time. Even though both are ultimately under the control of the Home Secretary, they are dealt with by entirely different divisions of the Home Office, only one of which develops an expertise in mental disorder. Dell showed that currently about half of all killers found not guilty of murder, but guilty of manslaughter by reason of diminished responsibility are sent to prison. When she compared those given life imprisonment with those receiving a hospital order restricted without limit of time, there were very few differences between the groups at the time of sentence except the medical recommendation, but the life sentence men were much slower in being released from prison on licence than were the hospital order men in getting away from maximum security. She argued:

> This situation seems to make a mockery of the judicial concept, upheld by the Court of Appeal, of life imprisonment as a sentence that will ensure that people who have shown some mental abnormality will be detained as long as is necessary in the interests of public safety, but no longer.

Fixed-term sentences

Many mentally abnormal people are sentenced to fixed-term imprisonment. This may be because their disorder has not been recognized, or it has been ignored, or because no one is offering the court a sensible alternative disposal. When a psychiatrist has no offer to make, he can sometimes assist his patient by indicating any damage which could occur to the individual if sent to prison. A patient with severe epilepsy, for example, lived on a knife-edge of fit control; previous prison sentences had produced either paranoid psychotic states or status epilepticus, or both. He persisted in being a lorry thief. The court was told of the dangers to his health of imprisonment, but no suitable hospital accommodation could be found, and he was sentenced to 3 years' imprisonment. He died in prison in unrecognized status epilepticus.

Another potential trap for the unwary psychiatrist lies in making statements about the length of treatment required in prison should an offender receive it. On such statements some judges will base a sentencing decision. Psychiatric resources are very scarce in prison and courts have no control over activities within a prison. They have, for example, no power to send a man to a particular prison, such as Grendon. A court can make recommendations about these matters, but that is all. Further, it is no part of the medical role to recommend punishment. Sometimes, the use of custody has to be advised to hold a patient until treatment can be arranged, but this is different from recommending imprisonment itself.

Mentally Disordered Prisoners

Sentenced prisoners may be mentally disordered—either no hospital placement was available for them at the time of sentencing or they have become ill in prison. In these circumstances, the Secretary of State may sanction transfer to hospital under S.47, MHA 1983, but only rarely is S.47 alone employed. Usually, restrictions on discharge are added (S.49) such that not only is discharge absolutely restricted until the offender's earliest date of release (EDR) from prison, calculated with allowance for remission, but also leave from the hospital is usually absolutely proscribed until within a month or two of the EDR. An important problem arises for fixed-term prisoners in that they have to give up their rights to apply for a parole hearing while they remain in hospital, but they cannot, ordinarily, be discharged by an MHRT, except, where this is an issue, back to prison. The MHRT can only recommend discharge to the Home Secretary, who may then refer the case to the parole board. The situation for those under life sentence has been improved, allowing discharge directly from hospital for rehabilitation purposes, but, unless special arrangements have been made in advance of transfer, release must be negotiated through the parole board, who must consult with the judiciary.

The Rest of the UK and The Republic of Ireland

So far, this chapter has dealt with matters of English law (which also covers Wales). Within the British Isles, there are no less than four legal systems, three of them determined by the British parliament in London. Psychiatrists from the three non-English/Welsh jurisdictions have been asked to add brief notes to this chapter to highlight some of the special mental health legal features of their own countries. Space does not allow us to encompass the rest of the world, but Ch. 3 is a further attempt to show both general principles and differences in a selection of other western countries.

Scotland

Civil matters

The status of the common law in the care of the mentally disordered in Scotland came under recent scrutiny by the House of Lords (*Forsey*) which confirmed that the laws of compulsory detention and treatment are those, and only those, contained in the Mental Health (Scotland) Act 1984, see Appendix 1). This legislation, although broadly similar to its English counterpart, contains some important differences of principle and detail. Applications for compulsory admission, other than for short-term detention, require the approval of a sheriff, a legally qualified judge. In considering the application, the sheriff must give the patient, and any objecting nearest relative, an opportunity to be heard. The categories of mental disorder are similar to those in England except that the term 'psychopathic disorder' does not appear by name in the Scottish Act; instead, a phase nearly identical to the English definition of the disorder is included within the category of mental illness. Treatability clauses for that disorder and for mental impairment are the same as in the English Act. In applications for guardianship orders, mental handicap (not mental impairment or severe mental impairment) and mental illness are the two medical criteria (Tables 2.6; 2.7).

Appeals against detention and guardianship are heard by a sheriff; there are no mental health review tribunals in Scotland. The Mental Welfare Commission for Scotland has authority to discharge compulsory patients except those with restrictions on discharge. Provision for consent to treatment for mental disorder is similar to that of England with one exception: the mandatory procedures for determining consent to psychosurgery or to the implantation of libido-reducing hormones apply only to detained patients (Fig. 2.3). However psychosurgery is not at present available in Scotland (Fig. 2.4).

Mentally disordered offenders

Discretion in respect of the arrest and prosecution of mentally abnormal offenders in Scotland is wide and subject to geographical variation (Chiswick et al., 1984). A small number of people arrested by the police are, following medical examination, immediately admitted to a psychiatric hospital; this

Table 2.6

Provisions for Emergency Compulsory Care of Patients in Scotland

Mental Health (Scotland) Act 1984

Place of crisis in patient's care	Section of MH(S)A 1984	Necessary conditions	Rules for application	Maximum period of detention and action
New/renewed presentation to doctor	24	Suffering from mental disorder **and** Ought to be detained in hospital in interests of own health/safety **or** protection of others	Emergency recommendation by medical practitioner (doctor) on day of examination. Where practicable, consent by relative or mental health officer (MHO). If not, statement of reason for failure to obtain consent	Removal to hospital within 3 days of recommendation; 72 h from time of admission to hospital
Public place	118	Appears to be suffering from mental disorder **and** In immediate need of care or control	Removal by constable to place of safety (hospital, residential home, but not a police station, unless no other place available). Inform responsible person residing with patient and nearest relative of removal	72 h from arrival Examination by doctor Make arrangements for treatment and care
In self-seclusion/ private accommodation	117	Believed to be suffering from mental disorder **and** Being ill treated or neglected or without control **or** Unable to care for self, living alone, or uncared for in any place	MHO/Medical Commissioner of Mental Welfare Commission have reasonable cause to believe conditions fulfilled. Magistrates' warrant to allow constable and doctor entry if entry refused or refusal anticipated	72 h from arrival in place of safety
Already in hospital	25(1)	As in section 24 above	As in section 24 above	72 h

Already in hospital	25(2/3)	Appears to nurse that: Patient is suffering from mental disorder of a degree necessary for his own health or safety **or** protection of others that he be immediately restrained from leaving hospital **and** It is not practicable to secure immediate attendance of a doctor	Nurse makes written report to hospital managers, including the facts of the necessity, fact of detention and time of detention	2 h from time first detained or until arrival of doctor
Expiry of section 24 or 25 with continued need for short-term detention	26	Suffering from mental disorder of nature or degree which makes it appropriate for him to be detained in hospital for at least a limited period **and** Ought to be detained in the interests of his own health or safety **or** protection of others	Report by approved doctor of reasons for detention, consent of relative or MHO **or** if not, a statement of reasons for failure to obtain consent	28 days from time of expiry of 72 h period of section 24 or 25(1)

Table 2.7

Provisions for Non-emergency Compulsory Care of Patients in Scotland
Mental Health (Scotland) Act 1984

Place of crisis in patients care	Section of MH(S)A 1984	Necessary conditions	Rules for application	Maximum period of detention and action
Community or hospital	17/18	Suffering from mental disorder of a nature or degree which makes it appropriate for him to receive medical treatment in a hospital, and that if (a) the mental disorder is one manifested only by abnormally aggressive or seriously irresponsible conduct; **or** (b) mental handicap, comprising mental impairment, such treatment is likely to alleviate **or** prevent a deterioration of his condition Necessary for own health/safety; **or** protection of others, and treatment cannot be provided unless he is so detained	Application for admission by nearest relative or mental health officer (MHO), founded on and accompanied by two medical recommendations with agreement between the two about the form of mental disorder. One recommendation must be by Section 20-approved doctor. Application submitted to sheriff for approval	No period specified Reviewed at 28 days, 6 months, 6 months and then annually
In prison on remand	70	Same grounds as S.17	Satisfy Secretary of State of grounds; he may apply to sheriff who may make a transfer order after receipt of two doctors' reports	Same effect as hospital order with restriction order without limit of time
Under sentence	71/72	Same grounds as S.17	Reports from two doctors which satisfy Secretary of State who may make a transfer order	Same effect as hospital order with discretionary restriction order

| Need for civil guardianship | 36 | Suffering from mental disorder of a nature or degree which warrants his reception into guardianship
Necessary in the interests of the welfare of the patient that he be so received | Two doctors' recommendations with agreement as to form of mental disorder, plus MHO recommendation
Application submitted to sheriff for approval | Confers following powers to guardian:
1. to require patient to reside at specified place
2. to require patient to attend at specified places and times for purpose of medical treatment, occupation, education or training
3. to require access to the patient to be given to patient's residence to doctor, MHO or other person. If patient absent without leave he may be taken into custody and returned to designated place of residence. If absent for longer than 28 days, patient ceases to be subject to guardianship |

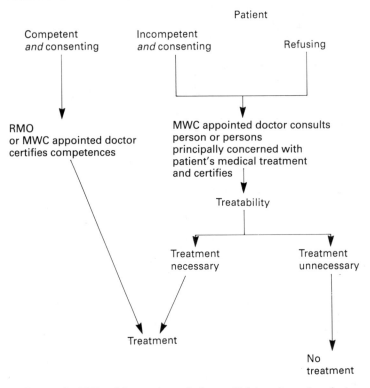

Applies *only* to *detained* patients

Fig. 2.3 Consent for ECT and for psychotropic drugs which have been given for longer than 3 months (Mental Health (Scotland) Act 1984, section 98).

may remove them from the criminal justice system. Where prosecution follows, the psychiatrist may be asked to give advice at various stages in the prosecution-trial-sentence procedure. The psychiatric questions at issue are broadly similar to those described for England, but the procedure, criteria and the nature of the court disposals show important differences. Procedural matters are governed by the Criminal Procedure (Scotland) Act 1975, but criteria for the psychiatric defences are derived from common law (Table 2.8).

Criminal proceedings may be under summary or solemn procedure. In the former, a judge (usually a sheriff, but sometimes a lay justice of the peace or stipendiary magistrate) sits without a jury and decides questions of both law and fact. Under solemn procedure the judge (High Court judge or sheriff) determines the questions of law, and the jury (15 laymen) decides, by simple majority, questions of fact. Most psychiatric issues and disposals may be determined under both summary and solemn procedures. Pretrial remand of a defendant to hospital can be ordered by a court on the basis of one doctor's

Applies *only* to *detained* patients

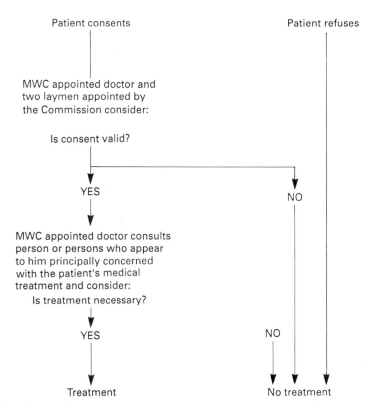

Fig. 2.4 Consent for psychosurgery or hormone implants for control of libido (Mental Health (Scotland) Act 1984, section 97).

oral or written recommendation; the court must be satisfied that a place is available in a suitable hospital.

In former years, most psychiatric disposals were effected by way of a finding of insanity in bar of trial (unfitness to plead); this is returnable under summary and solemn procedure. Criteria for the finding (*Brown*) are broader than in England and relate to the legal concept of insanity (Chiswick, 1978). A hospital disposal is automatic, but a mandatory restriction order only applies under solemn procedure.

The insanity defence provides a complete defence and results in a verdict of acquittal on the ground of insanity; disposal is by way of an indeterminate restriction order to the State Hospital. The criteria are not the McNaughton Rules, but the judge's charge to the jury in *Kidd*. There must be an alienation of reason by virtue of a mental defect. The defence is not available under summary procedure.

Table 2.8

The Powers of the Criminal System to Detain in Hospital – Scotland

Criminal Procedure (Scotland) Act 1975

Nature of provision	Section		Offender conditions	Psychiatric conditions	Effects of order
	Summary procedure	Solemn procedure			
Remand to hospital (untried)	330	25	Remanded or committed for trial	Mental disorder / Written/oral evidence of doctor / Hospital available and suitable	Detained for period of remand or committal unless liberated earlier in due course of law
Remand to hospital (convicted)	381	180	Convicted	In need of enquiry into mental or physical condition	Remand in custody or bail at institution or place / No single period exceeding three weeks
Interim hospital order	375A	174A	Convicted of any charge other than murder. Prior to sentence being passed	Mental disorder such that it may be appropriate for hospital order to be made to the State Hospital	Initially 12 weeks (normally to State Hospital) / Renewable every 28 days to maximum of 6 months
Hospital order or guardianship order	376	175	Convicted	Written/oral evidence from two doctors (one recognized under section 20, Mental Health (Scotland) Act 1984 of mental disorder with agreement about its nature. / Hospital available within 28 days	At RMO's discretion reviewed at 28 days, 6 months, 6 months, then annually
Restrictions on discharge	379	178	Convicted	Subject to S.376/175 and 'dangerous' / Order necessary for the protection of the public from serious harm	Duration specified by court; either without limit of time or limit for specified period / Leave and discharge may only be granted by Secretary of State

Admission to the State Hospital	376(7)	175(4)	Subject to hospital order under section 175 or 376 CP(S)A 1975	Subject to S.175/376 and of dangerous, violent or criminal propensities, and requires treatment under conditions of special security	Detentions under hospital order at the State Hospital
Psychiatric probabion order	385	184	Convicted	Mental disorder requires and is susceptible to treatment but does not warrant detention under MH(S)A 1984 Evidence from approved doctor	Treatment as inpatient or outpatient under direction of a registered doctor Maximum period of treatment 12 months

Since 1867, the defence of diminished responsibility has been available in Scotland; it reduces a charge of murder to one of culpable homicide and gives the judge complete flexibility in sentencing. It was introduced and continues to be governed by case law (currently *Savage*) and not by statute as in England. Contested cases are unusual; many pleas are accepted pretrial by the Crown. In practice, interpretation is narrower than in England; psychopathic disorder has been excluded from its ambit. An absence of intent to murder due to voluntary intoxication was rejected by the Scottish court of criminal appeal (*Brennan*). Infanticide, the English forerunner of diminished responsibility, does not exist in Scotland. Most cases of infant-killing are indicted by the Crown as culpable homicide.

Scotland was the home of one of the earliest sleep-walking trials (*Fraser*), but automatism, due to any cause other than insanity, virtually ceased to exist as a defence with the case of *Cunningham*. In a recent sleep-walking case (Oswald and Evans, 1985) the Crown dropped the prosecution, thus losing an opportunity for the contemporary examination of non-insane automatism. The Scottish Court of Criminal Appeal has ruled that where involuntary ingestion of drugs causes an absence of *mens rea*, the defendent is entitled to an acquital (*Ross*).

At the sentencing stage, courts have available to them a wide range of psychiatric disposals which mirror those in England (Nicholson, 1981). These include the psychiatric probation order, interim hospital order, hospital or guardianship orders and restriction order. There are no regional secure units in Scotland. The only facility other than an ordinary psychiatric hospital is the State Hospital at Carstairs; this provides treatment under conditions of special or maximum security. Judges have power to defer a case for sentence with almost unlimited conditions; voluntary psychiatric treatment may be one such condition.

Mentally disordered prisoners can be transferred to hospital from prison during the course of a sentence; an order restricting discharge is automatic unless there is only a short period of sentence remaining. Transferred prisoners have the right to appeal (to a sheriff) against transfer, and to apply in the normal way for early release on parole. The interested reader is referred for further material to Gordon (1978).

Northern Ireland

Northern Ireland law is complex—a reflection of the rich and varied history of the province. Dickson (1989) gives a very useful overview. English law was introduced with the arrival of the Normans in 1169, but the ancient Brehon law still held some influence until the early 17th century. Thereafter, English and Irish law, although the product of different administrative systems, were based on the same principles and, in practice, were similar. In

1920, Ireland was partitioned, and the North developed a different legal system from the Republic in the South. In 1932, the Northern Ireland local parliament was located in Stormont in Belfast and the Stormont Parliament kept in step with England over most local legislation until it was suspended in 1972. Since then, attempts to establish a local elected Assembly have failed and Northern Ireland remains under direct rule. The province is effectively controlled by the Northern Ireland Office headed by the Secretary of State for Northern Ireland who, in turn, is a cabinet member of the United Kingdom government.

Mental health legislation in Northern Ireland has shadowed that in England and Wales. The current legislation is the Mental Health (Northern Ireland) Order 1986 (henceforth referred to as 'the Order'). It is possible only to draw attention to some of the more important differences between the MHA 1983 ('the Act') and the Order. For further details, the reader is referred to the Order itself (*see* pp. 983–98) and the accompanying Guide published by the Northern Ireland DHSS. The Order is a wide-ranging piece of legislation encompassing issues which are not dealt with under the Act, such as registration of private hospitals, the procedure in cases of unfitness to be tried, and the insanity defence. The Order also reflects the different structure of the health service in Northern Ireland, for example, the powers which are vested in hospital managers in England and Wales tend to reside with the four Health and Social Services Boards in Northern Ireland. So after admission, a compulsory patient can theoretically write to his local Board to appeal against admission, but this rarely, if ever, happens and most appeals go to the Northern Ireland MHRT. The Guide to the Order points out that:

> The Board will rarely exercise the right to discharge since the medical opinion to enable it to do so would normally come from the responsible medical officer who has this power.

Part I of the Order defines mental disorder, mental illness, mental handicap, severe mental handicap and severe mental impairment. It is the first piece of UK legislation to define mental illness:

> A state of mind which affects a person's thinking, perceiving, emotion or judgment to the extent that he requires care or medical treatment in his own interests or the interests of other persons.

This definition is clearly circular (and in this respect reminiscent of the MHA 1983 definition of psychopathic disorder). The Order's definition of severe mental impairment is the same as in the 1983 Act, but a distinction is drawn between mental *impairment* and mental *handicap*, the latter term having no connotations of 'abnormally aggressive or seriously irresponsible conduct'. The Order provides no definition of psychopathic disorder and indeed Article 3(2) states:

> No person shall be treated under this Order as suffering from mental disorder, or from any form of mental disorder by reason only of personality disorder. . . .

Table 2.9

Provisions for the Compulsory Care of Mentally Disordered Patients in an Emergency (Northern Ireland)

Place of crisis in patient's care	Article of MH(NI)O 1986	Necessary conditions	Rules for application	Maximum period of detention and action
New/renewed presentation to doctor	4	Suffering from mental disorder of a nature or degree which warrants detention in hospital **and** failure to detain him would create a substantial likelihood of serious or physical harm to himself or other persons	Application by (a) nearest relative or (b) approved social worker **and** Recommendation by doctor **and** The applicant and doctor must have seen the patient in the previous 2 days	Admit to hospital within 2 days Immediate medical examination on admission Detention up to 7 days initially
Public place	130	Appears to be suffering from mental disorder In immediate need of care or control	Removal by constable to place of safety	Detention up to 48 h in place of safety Examination by doctor and approved social worker
In self seclusion/ private accommodation	129	Believed to be suffering from mental disorder **and** Has been, or is being ill-treated, neglected, or kept otherwise than in proper control **or** Being unable to care for himself is living alone	Application by officer of a Board or constable **and** Warrant issued by magistrate Resultant entry to premises by constable accompanied by doctor	Detention up to 48 h in place of safety
Already in hospital	7(1)	It appears to a doctor on the staff of the hospital that an application for assessment ought to be made	Report furnished to the Board on the prescribed form (form 5)	Detention in hospital up to 48 h

7(3)	It appears to a nurse of the prescribed class that an application for assessment ought to be made **and** It is not practicable to secure the immediate attendance of a doctor	Nurse records opinion on the prescribed form (form 6)	Detention up to 6 h or until arrival of doctor
54 In prison on remand, civil prisoners or detainees under the Immigration Act 1971	Suffering from mental illness or severe impairment **and** Of a nature and degree that make hospital appropriate **and** Treatment is urgently needed	Two written medical reports (one by a Part II doctor) Satisfy the Secretary of State who may Issue a transfer direction	Limited by recovery and/or report by RMO to Secretary of State or by trial
53 Under sentence	See Table 2.11	No differences for emergency	

Table 2.10
Provisions for Non-emergency Compulsory Care of Patients in Northern Ireland

Nature of provision	Article of MH(NI)O 1986	Necessary conditions	Rules for application	Maximum period
Admission for assessment	4	Suffering from mental disorder Failure to detain would create substantial likelihood of serious physical harm to self or others	Application by nearest relative or approved social worker Recommendation by one doctor	Up to 48 h or up to 7 days (renewable) depending on who sees the patient after admission
Detention for treatment	12	Detained under article 4 Suffering from mental illness or severe mental impairment Failure to detain would create a substantial likelihood of serious physical harm to self or others	Doctor appointed by Commission (not same doctor as signed assessment recommendation)	Up to 6 months in first instance, renewable for further 6 months, then for further periods of a year at a time
Guardianship	18	Suffering from mental illness or severe mental handicap Necessary in interests of welfare of patient	Application by nearest relative or approved social worker Recommendations from two doctors Recommendation of an approved social worker	Up to 6 months in first instance, renewable for further 6 months, then for further periods of a year at a time

It is a matter for debate whether this exclusion of personality disorder is a coup for civil libertarians or an abdication of responsibility by psychiatrists. In practice, it probably simplifies the position of the psychiatrist making recommendations to the criminal courts; it places an onus on the Northern Ireland prisons to cater for psychopathic people of every kind and it no longer allows for the detention beyond his release date of a psychopathic person serving a finite prison sentence—no matter how dangerous he is perceived to be, he cannot be detained under mental health legislation. Other issues in clinical practice, which may be affected by this exclusion of personality disordered patients, include the management of persistent self-injurers, who attract a diagnosis of personality disorder and who might otherwise benefit from a period of stability as a detained patient. There is also a greater onus on the clinician to ensure he does not incorrectly diagnose the early onset of a psychotic illness as a disorder of personality.

The criteria for detention under the civil part of the Order are stricter than under the English Act (Tables 2.9; 2.10). Not only must the patient be suffering from mental disorder of the appropriate type, but also failure to detain the patient must create a substantial likelihood of serious physical harm to himself or other persons. To fulfil this latter criterion there must be evidence:

1. that the patient has inflicted, or threatened or attempted to inflict serious physical harm on himself; or
2. that the patient's judgment is so affected that he is, or would soon be, unable to protect himself against serious physical harm and that reasonable provision for this protection is not available in the community, or
3. that the patient has behaved violently towards other persons or
4. that the patient has so behaved himself that other persons were placed in reasonable fear of serious physical harm to themselves.

While this move towards using explicit observed behaviour as a criterion for admission may be laudable, in practice fears have been expressed that mentally ill patients who are in the early stages of relapse may have to be allowed to remain undetained until their condition has deteriorated further so that their behaviour then meets these specific admission criteria.

There is no separate procedure for emergency admissions from the community. The medical recommendation for admission to hospital is usually made by the patient's general practitioner and supported by an application for admission which is completed either by the nearest relative or an approved social worker. Initially the patient is detained for a period of 7 days. He must be seen by the responsible medical officer or a Part II approved doctor (in practice, a consultant psychiatrist) within the first 48 hours of admission, and by the same doctor or a doctor of similar standing before admission can be extended for a further period of 7 days. Article 10 is innovative in that it allows this initial period of admission for assessment to be disregarded for many purposes, for example, when giving information about one's health to an employer. If, at the end of the 14 days' admission for assessment, the patient still needs to be detained in hospital, he can be detained for treatment for a period of up to 6 months in the first instance. Throughout the process of admission and detention in hospital, the safeguards for patients are generally at least as strict and often stricter under the Order compared with the English Act. The legislation on consent to treatment is similar to the English Act (pp. 33, 38) and there is provision for MHRTs and the Mental Health Commission (*see* p. 207).

For patients concerned in criminal proceedings or under sentence, the Order provides the same range of remands to hospital, hospital guardianship and restriction orders as the English Act (Table 2.11). There are a few differences in procedure, for example, the approved psychiatrist must give

Table 2.11

The Powers of the Criminal System to Detain in Hospital (Northern Ireland)

Nature of provision	Article of MH(NI)O 1986	Court/authority	Offender conditions	Psychiatric conditions	Effects of order
Remand to hospital for report	42	Magistrate or Crown	Crown court—arraigned or awaiting trial Magistrates court—convicted or court satisfied he committed the charge Bail impracticable	Oral evidence from one part II doctor Accused suspected of suffering from mental illness or severe mental impairment Department given opportunity to make representation to court	Up to 28 days' detention Renewable for 28 days on written/oral evidence of RMO. Patient need not attend court if legally represented Maximum 12 weeks Absconding means rearrest without warrant and return to court
Remand to hospital for treatment	43	Crown	Awaiting trial Pre-sentence	Oral evidence from one part II doctor Accused suffers from mental illness or severe impairment Department given opportunity to make representation to the Court	Up to 28 days' detention Renewable for 28 days on written/or evidence of RMO Patient need not attend court if legally represented Maximum 12 weeks Absconding means re-arrest without warrant and return to court
Interim hospital order	45	Magistrates or Crown	Convicted and hospital order may be appropriate	Oral evidence from a part II doctor and written/oral evidence from another doctor Mental illness or severe mental impairment Department given an opportunity to make representation to the court	Up to 12 weeks' detention Renewable as articles 42 and 43 but to a maximum of 6 months Absconding as articles 42 and 43

Article	Type	Order made by	Conditions	Medical evidence	Effect / Duration
44	Hospital order or Guardianship order	Magistrates *or* Crown	Convicted or court satisfied accused committed the charge	Oral evidence from a part II doctor and written/oral evidence from another doctor (hospital order) **or** Written/oral evidence from approved social worker (guardianship order) Mental illness or severe mental impairment **and** Minimum age 16 (guardianship order only) Department given an opportunity to make representation to the court	Up to 6 months' detention at RMO's discretion renewable on further reports from RMO, initially for 6 months and thereafter at 12-monthly intervals Absconding means retaking by hospital staff or approved social worker or police and return to hospital within 28 days of absconding
53	Transfer to hospital of sentenced prisoners	Secretary of State (Northern Ireland Office)	Convicted	Written evidence of two doctors, one recognized under part II Mental illness or severe mental impairment Bed available within 14 days	Detention in hospital as under article 44 unless, as is usual, restriction on discharge have been applied (*see* article 55 below)
54	Transfer to hospital of remanded prisoners	Secretary of State (Northern Ireland Office)	Charged with any offence and subject to custodial remand, civil prisoners, detainees under Immigration Act 1971	Written evidence of two doctors, one recognized under part II Mental illness or severe mental impairment and urgent treatment required	Limited by recovery and/or report by RMO to Secretary of State or by trial

Table 2.11 (cont.)

The Powers of the Criminal System to Detain in Hospital (Northern Ireland)

Nature of provision	Article of MH(NI)O 1986	Court/authority	Offender conditions	Psychiatric conditions	Effects of order
Restrictions on discharge	47	Magistrates *or* Crown	Subject to article 44 and order for the protection of the public from serious harm	One of the two doctors giving evidence for the article 44 gives oral evidence to the court	Duration of the Order specified by court, commonly without limit of time Leave outside hospital and discharge may be granted only by Secretary of State (NIO) Absconding as article 44 but limit of retaking set by court limits (usually indefinite)
	55	Secretary of State (Northern Ireland) Office	Subject to term of imprisonment		As article 47 with duration of imprisonment limited by length of imprisonment—expires at earliest release date taking remission into account
Unfitness to be tried	49	Crown		Unfit to be tried	As hospital order together with a restriction order without limit of time
Not guilty by reason of insanity	50	Crown		Insanity (defined in Criminal Justice Act (Northern Ireland) 1966)	As hospital order together with a restriction order without limit of time
Detention during Her Majesty's pleasure	52	Secretary of State and Court Martial	Serviceman	Not guilty by reason of insanity or unfit to stand trial by a court martial	As hospital order together with a restriction order without limit of time

The *essential precondition* in all cases is that the offence may be punishable by imprisonment, but that, except under Articles 53 and 54, the sentence is not fixed by law.

oral evidence to the court, and an opportunity to make representation (about designating the receiving hospital) to the court must be given to the Department of Health and Social Services (in practice, this latter function is delegated to the four Health and Social Services Boards).

Psychiatric defences in Northern Ireland

The procedure covering the issues of unfitness to plead and unfitness to be tried is contained in the Order (Article 49). The potential outcome is a restriction order without limit of time.

Northern Ireland also has a different insanity defence from England and Wales—the McNaughton Rules were superceded by the Criminal Justice Act (NI) 1966. A defendant who is found to have been at the time of the alleged offence 'an insane person within the meaning of the Act' shall not be convicted. 'Insane persons' means 'a person who suffers from mental abnormality which prevents him—

1. from appreciating what he is doing; or
2. from appreciating that what he is doing is either wrong or contrary to law; or
3. from controlling his own conduct.'

'Mental abnormality' is defined as 'an abnormality of mind which arises from a condition of arrested or retarded development of mind or any inherent causes or is induced by disease or injury'. Clearly this insanity defence is based on the McNaughton Rules, but is wider in its application. Again, however, the potential outcome is a restriction order without limit of time (Article 50 of the Order).

The Criminal Justice (NI) Act 1966 also defines the defence of 'impaired mental responsibility':

> Where a party charged with murder has killed or was party to the killing of another, and it appears to the jury that he was suffering from mental abnormality which substantially impaired his mental responsibility for his acts and omissions in doing or being a party to the killing, the jury shall find him not guilty of murder but shall find him guilty (whether as principal or accessory) of manslaughter.

The same definition of 'mental abnormality' is applicable to both defences. Although the diminished responsibility defences in Northern Ireland and England and Wales share similar definitions, in practice, in Northern Ireland a diagnosis of psychopathy or personality disorder without evidence of mental illness or organic impairment would be most unlikely to lead to a successful defence, whereas, in England, it would have a better prospect. Further details of Northern Ireland criminal law are given in Stannard (1984) and sentencing law and practice are covered by Boyle and Allen (1983).

The Republic of Ireland (Table 2.12)

Civil matters

Under the Mental Treatment Act 1945 civil treatment can be provided either:

1. on a voluntary basis where the person is willing to go to hospital or actually requests admission; or
2. by means of temporary certification where the patient is detained in hospital involuntarily and known as a 'temporary' patient. This is used where a person is considered to be in need of treatment and is unwilling to accept this or unable to make the decision.

If somebody living at home is considered by the family to be ill and possibly a risk to themselves or others, the procedure is that (if the patient is unwilling to be admitted voluntarily) the family GP would see the patient and, following an initial application by the closest relative (or social worker if no family member is available or willing), the GP would recommend admission. If the form is brought to the local hospital, steps can be taken to remove the patient to hospital, against his/her will if necessary. Once in hospital, the patient must be examined by a consultant psychiatrist within 12 hours and the temporary form completed if this is considered appropriate. In other words, there needs to be an application and two medical recommendations.

If a person is found in a public place and considered a potential risk, then the police can either arrest and charge or informally bring the person to the local psychiatric hospital where the temporary procedure can be initiated. The application would be made by a social worker and the initial medical recommendation by a doctor who has *no* interest in the hospital into which the person is to be admitted. Under S.165 of the 1945 Act a policeman may remove a person, believed to be of unsound mind, to a police station for further assessment.

Once detained on a temporary basis, the initial detention may last up to 6 months, renewable for 6 months, and then at yearly intervals. There is no appeal procedure except by recourse to the courts. Discharge is at the discretion of the RMO. The patient may be granted 'leave', in which case the power of detention lapses at the end of the 6-month period. If the patient absconds, he can be returned to hospital forcibly (if necessary by the police), but the order lapses if the patient remains at liberty for over 28 days. Treatment can be administered to a temporary patient against his will. There is no means of statutory review.

The courts have no part to play in any of these procedures, except in the rare case where someone who is detained for treatment appeals to the courts against his detention (habeas corpus).

Table 2.12
Provisions for Admission to Hospital under the Mental Treatment Act 1945
Republic of Ireland

Section	Type of Admission	Conditions	Duration
190–192	Voluntary	Application by the patient (or parent/guardian if under 16 years of age) Application supported by a medical recommendation received within 7 days prior to admission	
184–189	Temporary (Compulsory)	Person mentally ill (including addiction) Requires hospital treatment Is unfit to be treated as a voluntary patient *Application by* 1. Nearest relative or involved Social Worker supported by 2. Medical recommendation (GP)—patient seen within 7 days prior to admission 3. Consultant in receiving hospital	6/12 months initially
165	Removal from a public place	A policeman can take an individual into custody if he believes that a mentally ill person requires such for the public or his own safety	Until assessed by a doctor at a police station
207	Transfer to Central Mental Hospital	Detained patient charged with indictable offence District Court believes that patient has committed an offence and would be unfit to plead Patient assessed by Inspector of Mental Hospitals who reports to the Minister of Health Ministerial order effects transfer	Until considered well enough for transfer or discharge
		Provisions for Mentally Disordered in Prison	
17 (Criminal Justice Administration Act 1914)	Transfer of a remanded or sentenced prisoner to Central Mental Hospital for psychiatric assessment or treatment	Ministerial order	Patient must be released or admission to district hospital arranged at earliest date of release

Criminal matters

Until recent years, people who offended in a minor way and who were obviously mentally ill tended not to be charged, but to be brought to their local psychiatric hospital by the police. Latterly, however, due to the needs of police administration (clear-up rates), mentally ill people have tended to come before the courts more often.

In Ireland, a person generally appears in a district court (magistrates' court) on the morning after being charged. If there is any question of mental disorder at this stage, the accused is generally remanded in custody for a week so that a psychiatric report may be obtained. The report is usually requested by the judge or defence solicitor. Arrangements are then made by the prison authorities for the accused to be seen by a psychiatrist (usually from the Central Mental Hospital, Dundrum) for the purposes of preparing a report. If it is considered by the examining psychiatrist that a week will be insufficient to prepare a report, arrangements can be made for transfer of the accused to the Central Mental Hospital for inpatient assessment. This transfer is effected by means of a Department of Justice hospital order which can be arranged at short notice. This method of transfer is also used in the case of sentenced prisoners requiring inpatient psychiatric care. If a remanded prisoner is transferred to Dundrum, a doctor from Dundrum has to give written or oral evidence to the court to the effect that the accused 'is not well enough to attend the court by reason of mental illness'. The doctor can then state what length of remand he feels would be adequate to prepare a report or treat the accused. Usually the court would require statements at 4-weekly intervals, although at least one patient in Dundrum charged with murder, who was chronically unfit to plead, received 6 month remands.

Irish courts have no power to impose any form of hospital order similar to section 37 of the English MHA 1983, except where a verdict of 'guilty but insane' is reached, and indefinite detention in the Central Mental Hospital, Dundrum, is ordered. On occasions, if the charge is petty, the doctor from Dundrum will make informal arrangements with the charging policeman to drop the charge on the condition that the accused is admitted to his local hospital for psychiatric treatment (arrangements having previously been made by the doctor with the admitting hospital). This arrangement is only feasible in the Dublin area, as hospital staff from Dundrum have to accompany the accused to court and escort him on to hospital. In the absence of any available medical disposal, a court may apply the Probation Act or impose a prison sentence on a mentally ill person. In sentencing, the judge usually adds an instruction that the person receive psychiatric care in prison.

At present, the psychiatric facilities available within the Irish Prison Service are inadequate. The prisons in the Dublin area are serviced by sessions provided by the psychiatric staff from Dundrum. The role of the visiting psychiatrist within the prison system has been the subject of much discussion and dispute. The prisons outside Dublin (Cork, Limerick,

Portlaoise) have their psychiatric services provided by local general psychiatrists on a sessional basis.

If mentally ill or disordered persons are seen in prison and are considered to require treatment, arrangements are made for their transfer to the Central Mental Hospital. This transfer is by means of the hospital order mentioned above. Prisoners from outside Dublin have to be transferred to the Central Mental Hospital for treatment. When considered well enough, arrangements are made with the prison for return of the prisoner with follow-up provided by the visiting psychiatrist. In the event that a patient remains ill and in need of treatment at the end of his sentence, a problem arises in that the Central Mental Hospital is not legally empowered to keep patients after their earliest date of release. Ideally, the patient should return to the local district hospital, but this is largely dependent on the willingness of the patient, as he must be released either from Dundrum or, more usually, from prison at his EDR. In the case of somebody who is floridly psychotic, steps have to be taken to arrange civil certification at the time of release so that he may be transferred to his local hospital.

Patients in local psychiatric facilities who are violent and considered a danger to others are dealt with under section 207 of the Mental Treatment Act 1945. This is a cumbersome mechanism whereby the patient is charged (usually with some form of assault) before a special sitting of the district court convened in the hospital. Evidence is given that the patient committed the offence and, if placed on trial, would be unfit to plead. An order is then made for the transfer of the patient to the Central Mental Hospital. Ideally, when well enough, the patient should be returned to his local district hospital. In practice, this has proved very difficult in view of the stigma of the special hospital label and various administrative and staff resistances. A further problem is the distance between some centres and Dublin, which obviously poses difficulties of liaison between the professionals and the patient's family.

The third category of patients in the Central Mental Hospital is those found guilty of a major offence (usually murder) who are detained under a High Court order. The McNaughton Rules are still used as a criteria of insanity. There is currently no verdict of 'diminished responsibility' available in Irish law until further order of the government. The alternatives, therefore, are to be found guilty of murder and receive a mandatory life sentence, or to be found guilty but insane, and to be detained at the Central Mental Hospital until further order of the High Court. The guilty but insane verdict is, in effect, a form of 'restriction order' where any application for parole or discharge has to be approved by the Government (Minister for Justice). This is generally a very lengthy and cumbersome procedure and people found guilty but insane in Ireland generally will be detained much longer than those found guilty of murder, where a life sentenced prisoner may be reviewed for parole in 8–10 years.

Civil Law in England and Wales

Compensation (including a note on compensation for victims of crime)

Since 1974 in the USA (*Prince et al.*) and in 1982 in the UK (*McLoughlin*), it has been possible for someone suffering psychological injury following trauma to claim compensation in the courts for that injury, providing the legal conditions are fulfilled. In the USA, following the Buffalo Creek disaster, it was held that—

> all survivors—even those who were outside the valley at the time of the disaster—could collect for mental injury if we could convince the jury that the coal company's conduct was reckless (i.e. more than merely negligent), and that this reckless conduct caused the survivors' mental suffering (Stern, 1976).

Psychic impairment was the American term coined for these injuries.

To receive compensation for personal injury under English common law, the plaintiff must prove fault or blame. The hearing takes place in the civil court, both the verdict and the damages being decided by a judge. This is unlike damages for libel which are determined by a jury. The judge decides the issues on the balance of probabilities. Most civil cases relate to accidents at work or road traffic accidents. Compensation is also available to the victim of crime either through an order from the court or from the publicly-funded Criminal Injuries Compensation Board. Compensation is payable for both psychiatric and physical injury. Psychiatric damage is often referred to by lawyers as *nervous shock*. This was defined in *McLoughlin* by Lord Bridge:

> The common law gives no damages for the emotional distress which any normal person experiences when someone he loves is killed or injured. Anxiety and depression are normal human emotions. Yet an anxiety neurosis or a reactive depression may be recognizable psychiatric illnesses, with or without psychosomatic symptoms. So the first hurdle which a plaintiff claiming damages of the kind in question must surmount is to establish that he is suffering, not merely grief, distress, or other normal emotion, but a positive psychiatric illness.

Lord Bridge suggested that there are three criteria for nervous shock in English law:

1. The plaintiff must be suffering from a 'positive psychiatric illness';
2. A chain of causation between the negligent act and the psychiatric illness must be clearly established;
3. The chain of causation was 'reasonably foreseeable' by the reasonable man.

Clearly, it is correct for a psychiatrist to express a view on the first point and incorrect to express a view on the third point. It is debatable as to whether he should express a view on the second point, but most authorities, including Lord Bridge think not.

The term 'positive psychiatric illness' can embrace the whole range of morbid emotional responses as well as the ordinary form of neurotic and psychotic disorders. The doctor thus must attempt to determine the existence of any psychiatric disorder and its relation to the incident. The court is more concerned with the existence of disorder in itself, its attribution, and its consequences than with the niceties of diagnosis and classification. Diagnostic terms should be used simply and conventionally, but it is unnecessary to follow slavishly definitions from textbooks and glossaries such as the DSM-III R or ICD-9.

Trivial physical injuries may have considerable emotional implications. Psychiatric disorder may occur in the absence of any direct physical injury. Examples include the victims of crime or the uninjured survivors from frightening and life-threatening accidents. Recently, attention has focused on the psychological problems that may occur in survivors from major disasters such as the King's Cross fire or the sinking of the P & O ferry *The Herald of Free Enterprise*. The term 'post-traumatic stress disorder' (PTSD) is now being used increasingly commonly as a catch-all phrase to describe the psychological sequelae of such accidents. It is discussed in more detail in Ch. 23, but here it should be noted that PTSD is simply one rather special kind of anxiety state. Serious trauma and threats to life can precipitate many other kinds of psychiatric disorder instead or as well.

Bereavement is a common and well recognized cause of psychiatric disorder including depression and abnormal grief reactions. It is more difficult to accept and adjust to a death which is sudden and due to human error rather than some natural process. It is of importance to note that pathological grief has been specifically allowed as a category of positive psychiatric illness by the arbitrators in the *Herald of Free Enterprise* claims (*see below*). 'Nervous shock' may also be caused by witnessing fatal or serious injury particularly to a close relative. The plaintiff need not necessarily have witnessed the actual incident to make a claim. In a series of 'aftermath cases', the courts have allowed claims where the plaintiff has come to the scene of the accident, or has seen the victims shortly afterwards. In *McLoughlin*, compensation for psychiatric damage was awarded to a woman who saw her injured family shortly after their arrival in hospital. Claims are now also being pursued in respect of other secondary victims, such as those who have suffered psychiatric disease as a result of a bereavement caused by a serious accident.

Procedural considerations are very important in compensation cases because such cases can become protracted, wearisome and highly expensive. It also seems likely that the legal process with its uncertainty, its constant rehearsal of painful events and its sheer laboriousness are important extra stressors for the damaged individual. To offset some of these difficulties in disaster cases in which a large number of cases are dealt with simultaneously, English solicitors have devised a new procedural method. This has perhaps been best exemplified by the claims following the capsize of the *Herald of Free Enterprise*. On 6 March 1987, the *Herald* with approximately 600 passengers capsized just outside Zeebrugge harbour in Belgium; 188 people died. This meant that compensation claims were lodged for the 400 survivors and an unknown number of bereaved relatives. Most of the solicitors agreed to form a consortium which, in turn, formed a steering committee, led by one large firm of solicitors which specializes in compensation work. The steering committee developed broad policies, hired barristers, psychiatrists and psychologists, and conducted much of the negotiation with the solicitors of the shipping company. Among other things, these negotiations produced agreement that there would be test case arbitration between the plaintiffs and the shipping line. This was done by employing three distinguished arbitrators and agreeing in advance to accept their ruling on points of principle and levels of compensation for ten exemplary cases and for all other cases to be settled out of court using the established principles and levels. The model arbitration took place in February 1989, just less than two years after the accident, which is quite fast by legal standards. The arbitration took the form of a semiformal hearing at which barristers for the two sides put their cases, presented medical evidence, and cross-examined witnesses. The results of the arbitration were important because they are likely to have a significant (persuasive) effect on future compensation claims. One or two quotes will highlight points of medical interest:

> Post-traumatic stress disorder (PTSD) is now a recognized psychiatric illness.
>
> Some of the claimants lost one or more relatives in the disaster and suffered from what is termed 'pathological grief' or 'pathological mourning'. This, too, is a recognized psychiatric illness.
>
> Unhappily, some of the claimants continue to suffer to a significant extent. However in all cases improvement is possible and in most complete recovery is probable. This is not to say the victim will ever forget the experience or that painful intrusive thoughts will cease, plainly that is impossible. However in such cases the improvement will reach a point at which it can be said that, in spite of remaining intrusive thoughts, etc, the victim is no longer suffering from psychiatric illness. Since compensation for nervous shock is compensation for psychiatric illness, it is the period until illness ceases which is compensable. This has to be assessed, as is everything else, on the balance of probabilities. . . . Counsel for the claimants has urged us to bear in mind that, quite apart from the guarded nature of the prognosis, very understandably, some claimants are reluctant to undergo treatment, which involves recollecting the distressing circumstances of the disaster and may baulk at undergoing such treatment. We have no hesitation in accepting this argument.
>
> An injury to a limb leaves it vulnerable, for example, it is notorious that 'once a bad back, always a bad back' will cause trouble at the slightest cause. It is the same with psychiatric problems. . . . This is a factor which must be taken into account when assessing compensation.
>
> Sir Michael Ogden QC
Michael Wright QC
William Crowther QC
(1989)

Damages in the civil courts may be augmented or replaced by extra procedures when the injuries are caused by crime. These are noted below.

Compensation orders

An English criminal court may, after a finding of guilt, decide that the offender shall pay compensation to his victim and this will be in addition to any other penalties imposed. This can be compensation for personal injury or loss (particularly from theft), but it cannot be for losses associated with motor vehicles nor for losses arising from the death of a victim. The offender's means have to be taken into account. The order can be reduced subsequently if the property concerned (say) is returned. If damages are awarded in a civil action, the level given has to take into account the sum already awarded under any compensation order (*see* Thomas (1979) for details).

Restitution orders

In England, the Theft Act 1968 authorizes four types of restitution order after someone has been convicted of theft: (1) restoration of the stolen goods; (2) delivery of the proceeds of the stolen goods, e.g. the cash raised by their sale; (3) restitution out of money taken from the offender, of up to the value of the stolen goods; and (4) restitution in favour of an innocent third party, e.g. the unknowing buyer of stolen goods.

Criminal Injuries Compensation Board

Marjorie Fry (1951, 1959) took an important role in stimulating compensation for victims. A Home Office working party set up in 1959 focused particularly on the possibility of state compensation (Home Office, 1961). On the basis that the state had a duty to protect its citizens, arguments had arisen that where citizens were injured in criminal activity the duty had failed, and victims thus had a right to compensation from the state. The Home Office document refuted this, but provided for the possibility of furthering equity between victims such that 'deserving' victims of crime might expect provision for any needs in much the same way as victims of fate or illness. The Criminal Injuries Compensation Board (CICB) was set up in 1964. Awards were payable whether or not an offender had been brought to justice, although only providing the offence had been reported to the police. The victims of domestic violence were excluded from consideration initially, but this approach was modified following subsequent reviews of the Board's work and their consequent recommendations (e.g. Samuels, 1973; Home Office, 1978a; Miers, 1978). The principle of the compensation was largely of financial loss, hardship or anticipated loss of earnings, with assistance towards expenses, but no legal costs (unlike most American schemes (McGillis and Smith, 1983)), and no compensation for loss of peace of mind, or provision for exemplary or punitive damages. The award is, in effect, an *ex gratia* payment.

The scheme has been described as 'no more than a symbolic gesture' (Miers, 1980). Mawby and Gill (1987) cited the *Meah* case. Meah had been injured in a car accident and, in a civil action, received £45,750 damages against the driver. Following his injuries, however, he had raped two women who then took civil proceedings against him. The two women were awarded a total of £17,560. In the context of an outcry about the discrepancy in the awards, levels of compensation of rape cases generally being regarded as particularly low (e.g. Shapland et al., 1985), it was revealed that from the CICB the women had been awarded a mere £3600 and £1000 respectively.

Another criticism of the CICB is its relative inaccessibility. The onus is on victims to apply, but information about the process is not always available (Shapland et al., 1985) and applicants are not entitled to legal costs or legal aid. Newburn (1988) showed that despite efforts to publicize the CICB, magistrates and police had little knowledge of its practical workings. In a pilot survey of the Board, Newburn (1989) explained that the scheme operates in two stages. First the application is considered by a single member of the Board (there are 33 altogether); an award may be made at this stage. The applicant has also, however, a right to a 'hearing' in front of three members (the second stage) and the single member may refer the case to a 'hearing' anyway; such a hearing has the final decision. Just over one-quarter of all applicants receive no award. The level of compensation granted in Newburn's survey varied between £400 and £10 000 for general damages, the majority (64%) were for less than £1000. Only 1–2% of cases received awards of £5000 and over. Applicants may also receive an award for special damages in respect of loss of earnings and out of pocket expenses. These awards only added small sums to the award, 76% were for less than £100 and only 5% were for £500 and over. This has to be set in the context of only 92 out of 387 victims (24%) requiring hospital inpatient treatment and only 10 (3%) requiring more than 1 week in hospital.

Medical negligence

Medical negligence is an increasing source of claims for compensation and this has been reflected in recent increases in medical defence subscriptions (*see* for example Smith, 1988). Psychiatrists are placed in a low risk category, but substantial claims still occur. Many claims against psychiatrists are from relatives of patients who have committed suicide; others because of the negligent prescribing of various drugs including benzodiazepines, MAOIs, and neuroleptics; a few from the injured survivors of attempts at self-harm; and a few relate to the effects of inadequately monitored lithium carbonate. Drug side-effects have received wide publicity, particularly in respect of benzodiazepine dependence and tardive dyskinesia. Care and caution in the use of these medications cannot be overemphasized.

The psychiatrist is most likely to get involved in medical negligence matters as an expert witness in cases where the alleged injury is said to have caused psychological damage, such as drug dependence, depression, anxiety or brain disease. Such cases take years to settle and are very expensive in legal fees and the process itself may actually be a stressor making the injury itself worse (Rutherford and Fee, 1988). A large body of opinion, supported by the British Medical Association, has suggested that some form of no fault compensation should be introduced instead, rather along the lines of the schemes already in place in Sweden and New Zealand (Mann, 1989). This has the further support of the Royal College of Physicians (1990a).

The Royal College of Physicians (RCP) report is useful in dissecting out some of the legal issues. To have a successful claim, a plaintiff must establish two points: causation and negligence. *Causation* can be through an act of commission or omission but it is a legal test. On the balance of probabilities, would the loss have happened but for the allegedly negligent act? *Negligence* is a breach of the duty to use reasonable care. In practice, medical duty is determined by the standards doctors set themselves. A doctor's acts will be negligent if they would not be supported by a responsible body of co-professional opinion. Circumstances such as emergency are taken into account. There is no negligence if damage results from the normal risks associated with medical treatment, provided the appropriate warnings have been given, neither is there negligence if the event leading to the damage was unforeseeable.

The RCP working party looked at three other possible systems: *patient insurance* (the system used in Sweden), in which all patients are insured against damage; *accident compensation* (the system used in New Zealand), in which victims can claim for loss of earnings and lump-sum payments; and *general disability income*, a scheme giving support on the basis of severity of injury without having to prove either cause or negligence.

They did not favour any one of them, but recommended a no fault scheme, limited to compensating the adverse consequences of medical intervention with a number of safeguards, including the capping of damages recoverable and a disqualification of beneficiaries from further negligence claims.

Not everybody is so convinced that this route is the best one. Mr Justice Kennedy has argued that a no fault scheme would still make arbitrary distinctions between those who are compensated and those who are not, 'All we will succeed in doing is moving the goal posts.' He would prefer improvements in doctors' training, more openness in medical litigation, a reduction in doctors' working hours, and the introduction of medical audit (Dyer, D., 1988).

Mental Incapacity and Decision-making

In English law, mental capacity for decision-making is presumed until proved otherwise, and capacity has to be assessed in respect of a particular decision, not just decision-making in general. The psychiatrist is fairly familiar with this specificity for it is clear that a patient may be too disordered to decide for himself whether he should be admitted to hospital or not, yet capable of deciding whether to refuse or accept any medication offered. Two other important decisions with their own specific tests are consent to marriage and testamentary capacity. These are considered separately. Then there is brief consideration of the powers available in England and Wales to take over the decision-making of individuals who have lost their mental capacity in some important respect. For a fuller account of this topic *see* Hoggett (1990a), which forms the basis of the scheme used here.

Marriage and divorce

The Matrimonial Causes Act 1973 lists the following grounds for a marriage being void:

1. the marriage has not been consumated owing to the incapacity of either party to consumate it;
2. the marriage has not been consumated owing to the wilful refusal of either party;
3. either party to the marriage did not readily consent to it, whether in consequence of duress, mistake, or soundness of mind or otherwise;
4. at the time of the marriage either party though giving a valid consent, was suffering (whether continuously, or intermittently) from mental disorder within the meaning of the MHA 1983 of such a kind or to such an extent as to be unfitted for marriage.

Psychiatric disorder may be a cause of impotence and may distort emotion and lead to abhorrence or refusal of sex. In practice, psychiatric evidence is rarely called. It is the incapacity or refusal itself which is legally important, not its possible psychiatric origin.

Psychiatric disorder, dementia, and mental subnormality may all impair the ability to give a valid consent. The legal test is:

> Was the (person) capable of understanding the nature of the contract into which he was entering, or was his mental condition such that he was incapable of understanding it? To ascertain the nature of the contract of marriage a man must be mentally capable of appreciating that it involves the responsibilities attached to marriage (*Park*).

In clinical practice, the issues are not clear cut. Medical evidence for legal proceedings is rarely required, but requests for advice, particularly from the family of the mentally ill person, are quite common. Handicapped persons, including chronic psychotic patients, are encouraged to live in the community and understandably often wish to marry. Sometimes, these unions result in fulfilment and mutual support, but there are immense risks, particularly in the care of any resulting children. The acute phase of a psychotic illness, particularly a manic illness, may temporarily impair judgement and lead the patient to wish to contract a marriage quite alien to his own long-term inclinations and interests.

Intervention is difficult. Often the impairment does not satisfy the strict criteria for legal incapacity. Powers under the MHA 1983, guardianship orders, and the Court of Protection do not relate to marriage. Often nothing can be done unless the person is so severely ill that compulsory admission is appropriate and justified. Even then, the individual may be deemed competent to enter into a marriage contract. Long-term patients detained in hospital (for example special hospital) can and do marry, sometimes against medical advice (*see also* p. 822–4). The present law relating to mental incapacity is piecemeal and inefficient.

The doctor may also be involved in proceedings for divorce or an injunction or exclusion order stemming from domestic violence or other unacceptable behaviour. The test is an objective one. The court will consider the behaviour of the respondent and its likely effects on the other spouse. Mental illness in the respondent does not serve as an excuse or mitigation. In this difficult area, the doctor should be extremely cautious. Clear distinction must be made between direct observation and allegation or hearsay.

Testamentary capacity

The making of a valid will requires 'a sound disposing mind and memory' on the part of the testator. In practice, this means that the testator must understand the nature of the document, the extent of the property to be disposed of and the claims of other people upon it. Ordinarily this capacity is taken for granted, but it is particularly likely to be challenged if the testator is enfeebled, elderly or psychiatrically ill, or if the will itself is idiosyncratic.

The criteria for testamentary capacity are a legal not a medical matter. The doctor's role is merely to provide a report which will assist solicitors or the court to arrive at a correct decision. There should be some account of the subject's general demeanour and intellectual and emotional state, with particular reference to memory and orientation. Any positive phenomena such as marked abnormality of mood, hallucinations, delusions and misinterpretations should be recorded. It is often helpful to record verbatim replies to simple questions such as 'what do you have to leave?', 'who are your children and dependents?'. If decisions seem idiosyncratic, the subject's reasons for them should be patiently explored and given in the report. If no mental disorder is found, this should be clearly stated. An examination specially conducted for the purpose of determining testamentary capacity is usually straightforward. Difficult decisions most commonly occur in individuals who become increasingly idiosyncratic and eccentric, but do not display clear evidence of psychiatric illness or brain damage.

Often a medical report is not requested until the will is challenged some time after the death. The practitioner may then face the unenviable task of attempting to reconstruct a case history from imperfect memories and inadequate case notes. If relevant information is not recorded, it is dangerous to speculate and if there are no data say so without hesitation. Wherever possible, such a psychiatric postmortem should include interviews with a wide range of friends, relatives, and colleagues (remembering that some, especially relatives, may be interested parties), and the examination of as much of the dead person's written material (diaries, letters) as possible. Sometimes an outside psychiatrist who did not treat the dead person may be engaged to conduct such a psychiatric postmortem from scratch, a fascinating but time-consuming task.

Personal care

1. **Compulsory admission to hospital** has been dealt with above (pp. 27–33).

2. **Guardianship under the MHA 1983** has also already been covered briefly (p. 39). It is limited in its scope by the definitions of mental disorder used in the MHA 1983 and thus a lot of mentally handicapped people who could perhaps be assisted by guardianship, but who are not 'mentally ill' nor 'mentally impaired' are rendered ineligible. Indeed, the guardianship provisions of the MHA 1983 are notable for their rarity of use. Only 120 such orders were made in 1986 and 1987 (Mental Health Act Commission, 1987).

3. **Entry to effect an emergency removal from home** may be authorized by a magistrate under the MHA 1983 if an approved social worker testifies that there is reasonable suspicion that the individual is suffering from a mental disorder and that that person is either being ill-treated or neglected, or is unable to care for himself. The person is usually taken to a psychiatric hospital where he can remain for up to 72 hours for assessment. A community physician can also apply to a magistrate for an order to remove someone from their home, this time under S.47 of the National Assistance Act 1948 to 'secure the necessary care and attention' if the individual is suffering from grave chronic disease, or is living in insanitary conditions and unable to cope. Detention under the Act may last for 3 months and is renewable. As Hoggett (1990a) said, these powers are usually regarded as draconian and stigmatizing and are rarely used, perhaps 200 times per year.

4. **Parens patriae**, an expression more commonly used in the USA than in the UK, refers to the powers of the Crown to be paternalistic over its subjects, particularly 'lunatics, idiots and others of unsound mind'. These common law powers were codified in the *Court of Protection* (*see* p. 197) and modified by the MHAs of 1959 and 1983, so that there are few if any prerogative powers remaining with the Crown.

5. **Declarations** refer to the judgments given by the Family Division of the High Court when an adult is unable to give valid consent to medical

treatment. *Re F* which concerned the sterilization of a 36-year-old woman with the mental age of a small child, suggests that whilst a legal declaration is not a necessary preliminary to treatment it is strongly advised for 'sensitive' treatment, e.g. sterilization (Hoggett, 1990a).

Property

1. *The Court of Protection*

Described in Ch. 4, the Court of Protection is authorized to make orders in relation to the estates of those who cannot manage their own affairs by reason of mental disorder. The Court's powers are limited to 'property and affairs', usually property of at least moderate size and significance. Once subject to the powers of the Court of Protection, the patient loses legal capacity in respect of all other financial matters except making a will, but even this may also come under the Court in some cases. The test to be applied is that the individual is 'incapable by reason of mental disorder of managing and administering his property and affairs' (S.94(2) MHA 1983).

2. *Enduring powers of attorney*

Enduring powers of attorney are relatively new. Under the Powers of Attorney Act 1971, an individual (the donor) has the right to give to another (the attorney) the power to act on his behalf. When making such an arrangement, the donor must have the capacity to give the power, further-more such capacity must continue or else the power of attorney lapses. The Enduring Power of Attorney Act 1985 enables a power of attorney, however limited or extensive, to be continued beyond the failure of the donor's mental capacity. It is thus very useful for those who wish a family member to handle their affairs after they have become mentally disordered. Its obvious drawback is that it requires considerable foresight on the part of the potential patient. After mental incapacity in the donor has begun, the arrangements have to be registered with the Court of Protection. It is clear from these rules that the enduring power of attorney may not apply to the severely mentally handicapped, who have never had the capacity to appoint an attorney.

3. *Appointees*

Appointees are 'the poor man's Court of Protection'. Under regulation 26 of the Social Security (Claims and Payments) Regulations 1981, the Secretary of State for Social Security can appoint someone to exercise on behalf of a social security beneficiary any right that person has under the Social Security Act 1986, and to receive any sums payable on behalf of the beneficiary. It is widely used, e.g. 45 000 appointments in 1984 (Age Concern, quoted in

Hoggett, 1990b). The procedures are simple, the appointee applies in writing to the local social security office and the staff there then have to satisfy themselves about the beneficiary's capacity to handle his affairs. A medical report may be required, but not always. Its simplicity is an asset, but there is a greater likelihood than with other procedures of abuse. The Department of Social Security tries to appoint close relatives as appointees, but for the homeless it usually has to rely on a hostel warden, or maybe the proprietor of a private hotel. This may be ideal, but it may not, and it is often not welcomed by the beneficiary.

To augment these procedures and bring the UK into line with some other countries, a proposal has suggested that expanded guardianship powers should be available. The Court of Protection should have extended powers, special multidisciplinary tribunals should be established, the age of minority should be extended for mentally handicapped people, and the concept of living wills (as used in the USA) should be imported into Britain (*see* Hoggett, 1990b; Carson, 1990a).

Driving in England and Wales (*see also* pp. 438–9)

Safe driving requires alertness, concentration, perception, and the application of motor skills. It may be adversely affected by physical and psychiatric illness, by fatigue, and by sedatives including alcohol, even in healthy individuals.

It is a statutory requirement that an applicant for a driving licence should inform the Licensing Centre if he is suffering from a designated disease. These are prescribed or 'relevant' disabilities, prospective disabilities and limb disabilities. Relevant disabilities are epilepsy, severe abnormality (a wide term which includes severe mental deficiency), liability to sudden attacks of disabling giddiness or fainting, and inability to meet the prescribed eyesight requirements. Prospective disabilities are ones which might develop into a relevant disability. Limb disabilities are the absence of a limb or the deformity of a limb, or the loss of use of a limb. Licence holders are required to inform the Licensing Centre of the development of a relevant disability or a prospective disability, or the worsening of a previously notified disability. Temporary limb disabilities (lasting up to 3 months) do not need to be notified.

In this context, epilepsy refers to both major and minor seizures and also includes focal and myoclonic seizures. A single seizure, or seizures, following exceptional precipitants such as febrile convulsions, does not necessarily indicate that the person is 'suffering from epilepsy', which implies some tendency to recurrence. Much depends on the clinical picture and the results of investigations. Nevertheless, the Licensing Authority must be advised of these seizures. Current British regulations permit patients with epilepsy to drive in some circumstances which include two seizure-free years or, in the case of epilepsy during sleep, 3 years in which there has been no seizure when awake. An epilepsy sufferer who holds a driving licence and has his medication changed or withdrawn should inform the Authority. There are approximately 130 000 such people who are potential drivers. Many conceal their disability and continue to drive.

Similar safety considerations apply to any cerebral or vascular disorder including diabetes, which results in sudden loss or disturbance of consciousness.

The personality of the driver makes an important contribution to safety or dangerousness. Gibbens (1978) considered that people with personality disorders were responsible for more accidents than those with all other mental and physical disorders combined. A wide range of psychiatric conditions are associated with at least transitory impairment of attention, concentration and judgment. Disturbed personality may lead to overanxiety, anger, irritability, aggressiveness and indecisiveness. Depression of mood, particularly if there is suicidal intent, may lead to reckless or deliberately self-destructive behaviour. In mania, the associated irritability, aggressiveness and impulsiveness quite commonly result in road traffic accidents, and psychotic manic patients who attempt to drive almost always present a severe danger. Schizophrenia may affect the ability to drive in a number of ways. There is often an impairment of attention, concentration and volition which is associated with poor judgment and fecklessness. Interference may also occur from delusions and hallucinations. The motor car may be used as a weapon, or traffic signals and regulations may be deliberately flouted because of psychotic ideas.

Dementia impairs capacity to drive and may, particularly in the elderly, present as an accident or unwarranted series of accidents. The patient often lacks insight, and it is no kindness to allow an elderly and demented person to continue to drive until some tragedy occurs.

It is recommended that patients suffering from a psychotic disorder should not drive before treatment becomes effective and should notify the Licensing Authority if the condition is likely to last more than 3 months. Patients on medication should be advised of its likely side-effects, and the additional risks if even small quantities of alcohol are taken simultaneously. Capacity to drive may be affected by a wide range of psychiatric and emotional states and, if the doctor believes that there is impairment, the patient should be advised accordingly. He could be liable for negligence if he failed to do so. Unfortunately, the sort of personality traits which are associated with dangerousness are often not amenable to simple medical advice.

The above comments apply predominantly to the private driver. Similar but more strict considerations apply to the drivers of heavy goods vehicles, public service vehicles and taxis. Their licensing is also subject to a stricter statutory regulation. The statutory obligation to report a condition lies with the driver not with the doctor. Ordinarily, medical responsibility is discharged by advising the patient. This advice may not be followed, and the doctor may become aware that his patient is driving illegally and dangerously. There may then be a conflict between the doctor's duty to the safety of the patient and the public on the one hand, and medical confidentiality on the other. The obligation of confidentiality is never absolute and, on occasion, it would be appropriate to write and inform the medical adviser to the Licensing Authority. Indeed, the doctor might be held negligent if he colluded with a dangerous situation which ended in tragedy. In the case of the mentally disturbed or the elderly, relatives may often be helpful in dissuading the individual from driving or even preventing them by some simple practical measure such as removing the car or car keys. The medical adviser at the Licensing Centre will discuss any problematic cases or matter by letter or telephone.

Problems commonly arise from the side-effects of medication. All sedatives, antidepressants, antipsychotics and anticonvulsants impair concentration, alertness and coordination. The impairment varies greatly with the dosage and the susceptibility of the individual. Almost always some impairment will be detectable on careful testing, and sometimes the impairment is gross. The position is not straightforward. Many psychiatric patients are safer drivers if correctly maintained on a modest dose of medication than if left untreated. Each case must be judged on its merits. The patient should be warned of the potential side-effects. Ordinarily, patients should be advised not to drive within 24 hours of starting medication, or materially altering the dosage, and then only to drive if alert and coordinated. Many professional drivers (e.g. bus drivers, policemen) are not allowed by their employers to drive whilst taking any form of psychotropic or sedative medication.

It is now common practice for pharmacists to put automatically cautionary and advisory warnings on the labels of dispensed medicines in accordance with a code which is listed in the British National Formulary (British Medical Association and Royal Pharmaceutical Society of Great Britain, continuous). Most psychiatric and sedative medication carries the 'cautionary label wording 2' which states: 'Warning. May cause drowsiness. If affected do not drive or operate machinery. Avoid alcoholic drink'. Hypnotics also carry the additional warning that 'drowsiness may persist until the next day'.

Drinking and driving is dangerous, whether or not the indulgence is secondary to alcoholism or some other psychiatric disorder. One in three of all drivers killed has more than the legal limit of alcohol in the blood (80 mg/100 ml). Following the recommendations of the Blennerhassett Committee (Dept. of the Environment, 1976) offenders with two driving offences within the past 10 years, including one offence with a blood alcohol level above 200 mg/100 ml are subjected to a thorough investigation before they are reissued with a driving licence following the second conviction.

The Department of Transport recommend that doctors should advise patients known to be severe alcohol abusers not to drive and that if this advice is not heeded should consider notifying the Medical Advisory Branch of the Licensing Authority.

For further reading on these matters see Raffle (1985).

Military Law in the United Kingdom

The disciplinary powers of the armed services are contained in a distinct legal code known as military law. All servicemen and also members of their families, and civilians employed by the forces outside of the United Kingdom are subject to military law.

Since 1971 the disciplinary powers of the three services have been combined in the Armed Forces Act which is subject to annual review by both Houses of Parliament and is re-enacted each 5 years. The Acts serve to continue, and usually amend in various minor ways, the Army Act 1955, the Air Force Act 1955 and the Naval Discipline Act 1957. This review process allows military law to reflect change in conditions while acknowledging the special needs of the services.

The special provisions of military law are considered necessary to maintain good order and discipline and ensure the operational efficiency of an armed force. Most contraventions of civil law by a serviceman may be dealt with by the military authorities under military law and there are, in addition, a range of particular offences which are peculiar to military law.

In the United Kingdom, the offences which affect the person or property of a civilian are normally dealt with by a civil court, but offences which involve only service personnel or property are normally dealt with by the military authorities. The offences of treason, murder, manslaughter, felony or rape may not be dealt with under military law in the United Kingdom. In the majority of overseas countries where British forces are based, the jurisdiction of these civil powers are waived in favour of the military authorities in keeping with standing agreements or treaties.

Offences of a minor nature committed by junior ranking servicemen may be dealt with by commanding officers who have limited powers of summary jurisdiction. More serious cases will be tried by court martial and, in some instances, a judge advocate general will sit with the court to advise on legal matters. The same rules of evidence apply as in the criminal courts of England.

Punishment is considered to be one of the means available for the maintenance of discipline. In awarding a sentence, courts martial will always take into account the level of sentence a particular offence might have attracted in a civilian court. The award of a custodial sentence, which would be undertaken in a civil prison, necessarily entails dismissal from the service. Detention, on the other hand, is intended to provide a means of reform in rehabilitating an offender prior to returning to military service and is carried out in the Military Corrective Training Centre. The findings and sentences of courts martial are subject to successive reviews by higher military authorities and there is also a right of appeal to the Courts Martial Appeal

Court. The death penalty remains available to military courts and the arguments for retaining this were debated extensively by the last Select Committee on the Armed Forces Bill (House of Commons, 1986a).

Two interesting examples of the different way in which military law aproaches certain offences is provided in the way homosexuality and drug abuse are dealt with. Homosexual acts continue to be forbidden under military law and may be prosecuted as 'disgraceful conduct of an indecent kind'. When this somewhat anomalous situation was most recently examined by the Select Committee, they considered that the existence of sexual relationships between servicemen in closed male communities was likely to generate tension of a kind harmful to morale and military efficiency, and decided that it would not be wise to change military law. In recent years, a few cases have come to trial, but have usually been dealt with administratively by commanding officers. Most individuals who have indulged in homosexual behaviour are discharged from the services, whether they are predominantly homosexual or not. Psychiatric referral may be initiated when it is thought that a mental disorder may be involved, or when circumstances are of such an ambiguous nature that psychiatric opinion concerning the serviceman's personality may assist the commanding officer in deciding his course of action. In a somewhat similar way, possession or use of illicit drugs is always dealt with very severely by military authorities.

Mental Health Legislation

Service hospitals in the UK are not defined as either hospitals or nursing homes in terms of the MHA 1983, or any other enabling legislation, and it is not, therefore, possible to detain or treat any patient in a service hospital under the powers of the MHA 1983. In practice, when service patients require compulsory detention or treatment, they are transferred to a local NHS facility for this.

Limited powers to detain and treat patients in various hospitals overseas are provided in the Armed Forces Act 1981, section 13. These powers are enacted by the signing of a 'detention in hospital order' by an authorized officer, usually the individual's commanding officer, on the recommendation of one registered medical practitioner for a 5-day order, or of two registered medical practitioners, one of whom must have special experience in psychiatry, for a 28-day order. No longer form of treatment order is available under military law, but the available powers do provide for the removal of a patient to the UK, if this should be considered necessary, with provision that, on return to the UK, such a detained patient must become an informal patient within 24 hours, or be detained in a NHS hospital under the MHA 1983.

The Armed Forces Act 1981, section 14, also provides for the temporary removal to a place of safety of children of persons subject to military law overseas who are considered to be at risk. The Armed Forces Act 1986 set up the formal legal framework for the transfer of a child back to care in the UK when this was the recommendation of an executive case conference.

Psychiatric Advice in the Services

All three armed services have a small psychiatric department within their medical services, with in- and outpatient facilities, both in the UK and overseas. Most of the consultants and all the junior doctors are serving officers in their relevant service. Each service has regulations which outline a procedure whereby commanding officers, in consultation with the unit medical officer, may arrange for an accused to be examined by a service psychiatrist. The only situation in which psychiatric examination is mandatory is that of a serviceman remanded for trial by court martial overseas on a charge of murder, although reports are frequently requested in other situations. The service psychiatrist acts in an impartial way, providing a forensic opinion available to both prosecution and defence. The armed services also have honorary advisers in psychiatry and its subspecialties, including forensic psychiatry.

3
A Comparative Survey of Medico-Legal Systems

Edited and written by
Timothy Harding
(Switzerland)

With national descriptions from

Hans Adserballe (*Denmark*); Wolfgang Berner (*Austria*); P. Dontschev
(*Bulgaria*); Stephen J. Hucker (*Canada*); Assen Jablensky (*Bulgaria*);
Bruce Westmore (*Australia*); Robert M. Wettstein (*USA*)

The Scope and Limits of the Comparative Approach

Comparison is a powerful tool in medicine: a physician compares the size
and reaction of two pupils or the state of a patient before and after a
therapeutic intervention. By observing differences, we are able to construct
and test hypotheses about normalcy and also apply judgements about healthy
and unhealthy states. Comparison between groups of individuals forms the
basis of epidemiologic and clinical trials.

In making comparisons across national, geographical and cultural boundaries, we extend this approach, but interpreting differences becomes far
more complex. The incidence and prevalence of diseases vary widely between
geographical regions; differences depend on climatic factors, the presence of
vectors and, above all, on the level of socio-economic development. Comparative studies in forensic psychiatry are unlike most comparative approaches
in medicine, since legal provisions and procedures are an important determinant of forensic psychiatric practice, and they reflect national sovereignty.
Comparing forensic psychiatric assessment or the treatment of mentally
abnormal offenders is, therefore, fundamentally different from comparing
the incidence of diseases, or the way in which other forms of health care are
provided. Nevertheless, it should be recalled that legislative action can have
significant health-related effects in other fields, for example by influencing
the availability of alcohol, which will, in turn, effect the whole range of
alcohol-related disorders.

There is a danger that comparative forensic psychiatry is limited to a compilation of legal provisions covering key areas such as competency, criminal responsibility, management of mentally abnormal offenders and civil commitment. While such a 'stamp collecting' approach might appeal to our obsessional traits, it has little relevance in understanding and improving our respective practices.

This chapter provides a comparative framework with descriptions of legal provisions and forensic psychiatric practice in seven countries: three with a common legal heritage historically based on the English legal system: Australia, Canada and the USA; while four are in the legal tradition of continental Europe, where the Napoleonic code provided a model of criminal law whose influence is still widespread: Austria, Bulgaria, Denmark and Switzerland. Nevertheless, as will be seen, considerable divergence and differentiation has occurred among both groups of countries, while some striking similarities now exist between the two groups.

No example of developing countries has been included in this survey, despite the inclusion of developing countries (Egypt, Thailand, Brazil and Swaziland) in one comparative study which covered forensic psychiatric examinations (Soothill et al., 1983), dangerousness assessments (Montandon and Harding, 1984) and involuntary hospitalization (Soothill et al., 1981). In few developing countries has there been any legislative innovation concerning psychiatry (notable exceptions being Senegal, Trinidad and Tobago) and resources are too limited to permit significant development of services in such a specialized field. Indeed, the pressing needs of development of mental health care for priority conditions in the community (WHO Expert Committee on Mental Health, 1975) would seem to argue against the development of forensic psychiatry as a distinct entity early in the developmental process of mental health care. Collomb (1979) has warned forcefully of the dangers of scientific imperialism in the field of psychiatry, and of the imposition of alien values and judgements from one culture to another. The appropriateness of forensic psychiatry as described in this textbook to rural communities and urban centres in developing countries is far from obvious. The transplantation of the custodial mental hospital during the colonial period has been described as an inappropriate and insufficient response resulting in prison-like facilities (Collomb, 1972). Mental health legislation provides a fine example of the tenacity of inappropriate alien models in the neo-colonial period. In most Third World countries mental health laws are still those imposed by the colonial powers. The Indian Lunacy Act 1912, modelled on the English and Welsh Lunacy Act 1890, is still in force not only in India (despite a recent amendment act which, at the time of writing, has not yet been brought into force), but in Pakistan, Bangladesh and Burma, while virtually identical legislation is in force in democratic Yemen, Fiji and Tanzania.

This survey is, therefore, limited to forensic psychiatry as it has evolved in industrialized countries. Even between industrialized countries, there are striking differences between the conceptual and institutional bases of forensic psychiatry, as was shown clearly in the different points of view expressed by representatives from European countries (WHO, 1977). A key issue was the extent to which forensic psychiatrists should be limited to the role of assisting the courts in their work. In certain countries they have acquired an active therapeutic role in prisons, hospitals, special units and the community. We have, therefore, tried to describe the situation in a limited number of countries, not only describing legal provisions and the institutions, but also the way in which forensic psychiatry is practised, and what actually happens to mentally abnormal offenders and other people requiring forensic psychiatric intervention.

At the end of this chapter, we have described four cases of people involved in criminal proceedings with an account of how each case would be dealt with in each of the seven countries in our comparative survey as well as in the UK. The reader will have an opportunity to see how the legal provisions, court procedures and forensic services, described hereafter, function and what degree of diversity exists in practice.

National, Subnational and Supranational Legal Structures

The political structure of a country obviously influences its laws. Variations in political structure can introduce complexities in comparative descriptions. In three of the countries studied, Austria, Bulgaria and Denmark, criminal and mental health laws are both at national level while, in the other countries, there is a two-tiered legislative structure. In Australia, mental health legislation is enacted at state or territory level while, in the USA, criminal law exists both at state and federal levels, the latter being for crimes committed on federal property and certain other specified crimes. In Canada and Switzerland, criminal law is federal, while commitment laws are found at provincial or cantonal level. One advantage of a federal structure is that innovative legislation can often be introduced more easily and tried out, before being progressively applied to the rest of the country. A further element in legal complexity has been introduced for the 23 member states of the Council of Europe. The European Convention of Human Rights guarantees certain fundamental rights, including procedural guarantees for all individuals deprived of their liberty, and the freedom from torture and inhuman or degrading treatment. The Convention provides legal procedures for individuals who claim that these rights have not been respected. There is, therefore, a supranational legislative and judicial tier. A number of cases of mental patients have been heard by the Commission of Human Rights and three important judgments have been made by the European Court of Human Rights directly affecting psychiatric patients (Harding, 1989). Several of the cases heard or pending involve mentally abnormal offenders subject to hospital orders or other security measures (*see Luberti* v *Italy*; *X* v *United Kingdom*). These supranational judicial bodies are likely to play an important role in the future of European mental health legislation. This already existing mechanism should not be confused with the proposal to 'harmonize' mental health legislation in the 12 countries of the EEC.

Controversial Issues and Shifts in Public and Professional Opinions

The social and political climate of each country influences legislation as well as decisions taken by the courts and authorities. Forensic psychiatrists are often the object of public controversy and their work can be significantly modified by legislative action.

In the USA, while many forensic issues presented by the criminal law remain fundamentally unchanged for decades, American society has shifted somewhat to a more conservative posture which emphasizes increased criminal responsibility of defendants, longer criminal sentences, and the use of the death penalty. In the last decade, most state and federal jurisdictions have modified their statutes in the direction of increasing court supervision over mentally disordered offenders. Yet, in contrast to many other countries, the special verdict of insanity continues to be a viable criminal defence in the USA. At the same time, psychiatrists are becoming more sophisticated in their understanding of legal and forensic issues, as well as more sensitive to psychopathology in forensic populations. Mental health treatment programmes in many correctional facilities are being expanded in view of the rising number of inmates. Criminally committed patients and prisoners are increasingly afforded the legal right to refuse psychotropic medications; formal legal hearings are often necessary to adjudicate the patient's or prisoner's competency to consent or refuse such medication before it can be administered (Appelbaum, 1988).

The return of the capital sentence to US jurisprudence in 37 states in the last decade poses major problems for US forensic psychiatrists, which their colleagues elsewhere would be unwise to ignore. Some states have permitted the use of evidence of a defendant's mental condition at the time of the offence to determine whether a capital sentence will be ordered by a judge or jury following conviction. Here, at a capital sentencing proceeding, psychiatric testimony may be offered as a mitigating factor by the defence. Testimony can include evidence of the defendant's personality disorder or other mental disorders not otherwise exculpating through the insanity defence or *mens rea* rule. On the other hand, in some states, the state will attempt to establish through its own psychiatric testimony that the defendant is likely to repeat his antisocial and violent behaviour in the future unless executed (Dix, 1984). These long-term psychiatric predictions of dangerousness are troublesome in their potential overprediction of future violence (Monahan, 1981).

The number of death sentences in the last decade has outpaced the rate of executions. At the end of 1986, 1781 prisoners were on death row, yet there were just 18 executions in that year; the average time to execution since sentence was imposed for this group was 7 years and 2 months (Bureau of Justice Statistics, 1986). At the end of 1987, 1984 prisoners were on death row and there were 25 executions (Bureau of Justice Statistics, 1987). For the 11-year period of 1977–1987, there were 93 executions in 12 states, and none by the Federal Government (Bureau of Justice Statistics, 1987). Because of the lengthy delay prior to execution, it is not surprising that death row inmates develop severe mental disorders pending execution, and that the question whether a state could execute a severely mentally ill inmate would arise. In the *Soering* case, the European Court of Human Rights held that the extradition from the United Kingdom of a US citizen to the US where he faced charges carrying the death sentence would constitute inhuman and degrading treatment in view of the potential long period of detention awaiting execution. In *Ford* v *Wainwright*, the US Supreme Court held that it was a violation of an 'insane' inmate's federal constitutional rights for a state to execute him. With psychiatric treatment, however, the inmate can be restored to competency for execution, and then executed; the death sentence is not thereby changed to long-term imprisonment. This issue clearly presents serious ethical problems for mental health professionals who evaluate and treat death row inmates. Some have argued that mental health professionals should not participate in the evaluation or treatment of mentally incompetent death row prisoners, since treatment facilitates the execution (Appelbaum, 1986). There are also arguments that it would be improper not to provide treatment to such mentally ill inmates (Mossman, 1987). Both law and psychiatric practice are as yet unsettled in this new area (Radelet and Barnard, 1986; Ward, 1986; Heilbrun, 1987; Radelet and Barnard, 1988; *see also* pp. 882–3).

Other legal aspects of the death penalty involve mental health professionals. The US Supreme Court rejected the death penalty for a defendant who committed a first-degree murder at the age of 15 (*Thompson* v *Oklahoma*). On the other hand, it has affirmed the death sentences of teenagers who killed when they were 16 and 17 years old (*Stanford* v *Kentucky*). Some 26 states specify a minimum age (usually 18) at the time of the offence for which the death penalty has been imposed (Bureau of Justice Statistics, 1987). The Supreme Court has also ruled that a defendant's mild to moderate mental retardation does not prohibit a state from executing him (*Penry* v *Lynaugh*).

In other countries, current controversies are less dramatic, but nevertheless illustrate the same underlying conflicts between individual rights and collective security as well as between therapeutic, welfare-based reactions to antisocial behaviour and punitive, 'just desserts' values. In Bulgaria, such conflicting social expectations and attitudes are evident. On the one hand, there is evidence that there is at present better tolerance in the community towards the mentally ill, as illustrated by the fact that fewer than 5% of all psychiatric patients in Bulgaria are in hospitals at any given time. On the other hand, there is a growing tendency to set new administrative barriers to the social participation of the mentally ill. For example, an increasing number of employers request psychiatric examination as part of the pre-employment medical clearance of job applicants. Similar requirements now exist in relation to marriage, higher education and the acquisition of a driving licence. The result is an increasing demand for forensic psychiatric services.

In Denmark, there has been a move away from the treatment philosophy for 'criminal psychopaths' which reached its height in the fifties. In the seventies, mental health professionals manifested increasing opposition to this approach, and challenged the effectiveness and ethical basis of indeterminate sentences and obligatory treatment. These approaches have been progressively abandoned. Demands for admission to the only special institution for dangerous psychotic patients, the Security Detention Institute, associated with the mental hospital at Nykøbing, have increased because of the lower tolerance for such patients in ordinary mental hospitals. This institute deals exclusively with psychotic men considered dangerous and is within the mental health system.

In Austria, the Penal Code which came into force in 1975 is the subject of continuing debate, which illustrates in a particularly striking way the conflict between treatment and social control. Two conflicting viewpoints can be distinguished. On the one hand, there is a widespread opinion among the population that the enforcement system has become too liberal. This supposed liberalization meets heavy criticism whenever a spectacular crime is committed. The public are particularly resistant to the fact that prisoners are given the chance to prove their ability to live outside the prison prior to the end of their term of imprisonment; this is used by the sensational press to speak of 'holidays from prison' as a catchphrase, and thus to stir up emotions against such liberalization, at the same time raising the circulation figures of their newspaper. On the other hand, a better informed minority complains of the fact that, under the guise of 'liberalization', a much more comprehensive and intensive restriction of liberty is possible as a result of the 1975 legal provisions. This applies especially to the Penal Code provision, according to which a person may be further detained after the end of the prison term if a medical expert still regards him as dangerous. Such confinement could theoretically last for life. Psychiatrists and other members of the therapeutic team frequently complain of the lack of motivation among patients committed to an institution following a court report. Extreme difficulties as to motivation are encountered in cases where the confinement during a security measure exceeds the prison term.

A number of experts are also critical of the fact that the release of offenders from security measures is too closely linked to the prediction of dangerousness of the offenders, such predictions lacking a sound scientific basis. Judges, on the other hand, welcome the law on security measures as a new instrument of social control, including the possibility of control in cases which were previously excluded from the judicial system.

In Canada, public opinion over patients' rights has become sensitized. There has, for example, been a sharp revision of opinion over whether involuntary patients have the right to refuse treatment (*see* Gordon and Verdun-Jones, 1983). Recent changes in the legislation in one Canadian province, Ontario, have resulted in a situation where a certified patient who is mentally competent to make the decision may refuse treatment. For incompetent patients, the facility must approach a hierarchy of relatives for surrogate consent; in their absence, this task falls to the Public Trustee.

Changes such as these have anticipated the effects of the Canadian Charter of Rights and Freedoms (1982) under which some aspects of the mental health acts of the various provinces are likely to be challenged with increasing frequency in the future (*see* Savage and McKague, 1987, and note at the end of this chapter).

In Australia, there has been a remarkable degree of legislative activity in some states creating new procedures and judicial bodies bridging the mental health and penal systems. Despite innovative laws, concern is expressed about inadequate housing and treatment of forensic patients in old buildings of inappropriate design and structure. Concern is also felt about deinstitutionalization in some states, with seriously ill patients discharged without adequate provision for their continued care in the community.

In Switzerland, psychiatrists are seeking to redefine their role in criminal proceedings by giving up the notion of diminished responsibility, for which no objective or reliable evaluative criteria exist. The psychiatric expert could then provide a descriptive account of the accused's history and personality together with therapeutic proposals. The notion of total irresponsibility would be retained for cases of major mental disorder with symptomatic antisocial acts. Many jurists do not accept these proposals, preferring to see the psychiatrists in the traditional role of weighing up the artificial concept of criminal responsibility rather than describing clinical and social realities.

The tendencies and controversies in different countries suggest that the relationship between psychiatry and criminal justice will always be, and perhaps should be, uncomfortable. Societies, which have slowly and grudgingly accepted the reality of the suffering of mental patients, remain highly ambivalent towards the mentally abnormal offender, who risks becoming the scapegoat in visceral reactions to violence. This survey suggests that forensic psychiatrists should be sensitive to these issues, not only in their own countries, and that they should be prepared to intervene actively in public debate and political decision-making. Otherwise, they risk finding themselves in ethical dilemmas being expected to perform assessments and carrying out treatment under impossible conditions.

Forensic Psychiatric Interventions in Criminal Law

Fitness to Plead

The importance of this legal concept varies considerably. As will be seen, the USA has the most elaborate case law and judicial processes in relation to 'fitness' or 'competency' to stand trial.

Austria, Bulgaria, Denmark and Switzerland

The concept of fitness to plead in criminal proceedings hardly exists in Austria, Bulgaria, Denmark and Switzerland. All accused persons will appear before an examining magistrate. If the person's mental state prevents his or her understanding of the legal process, a psychiatric report will be requested. Even if the person does not appear in court, a decision will be taken on the basis of the psychiatric report. Typically in these countries, the 'incompetent' or 'unfit' defendant in Anglo-saxon jurisdiction would be regarded as 'irresponsible' and not subject to punishment. A security measure (hospitalization or internment in a special institution) would be proposed. The person would not be brought to trial, even if their mental state subsequently improves.

Australia

The concept of 'unfitness to plead' exists in Australian as in English law. In Queensland a finding by the jury of unfitness to plead in cases of indictable offences leads to admission to the Security Patient's Hospital as a restricted patient. Further decisions are always passed by the Patient Review Tribunal (*see below* for a description of this body). In New South Wales, provision exists to ensure that persons found unfit for trial will not be detained longer than they would have been if they had been found guilty of the offence with which they were charged and had been sentenced to an appropriate term of imprisonment. The Mental Health Review Tribunal determines if the person is likely to be fit to plead within 12 months. If not, a special hearing (trial with jury) is held. If the person is found guilty of the offence, a 'limiting term' is fixed, beyond which the offender may not be detained either in prison or hospital. In South Australia and Western Australia, a court finding of unfitness to plead results in hospitalization in a secure institution for an indeterminate period with the possibility of a trial once the patient has recovered sufficiently.

Canada (*see* note on p. 166)

The Canadian Criminal Code does not specify the criteria which are to be satisfied for a finding of fitness, but generally it is considered that the ability to understand the court proceedings and to instruct legal counsel are basic requirements (*see* Schiffer, 1978, and Savage and McKague, 1987). Evaluations for fitness to stand trial are most often carried out in the local jail where the accused is in custody. In some provinces where there is a centralized system of forensic services, such as British Columbia or Quebec, the examining psychiatrist may be employed by that system. Elsewhere, he may be on the staff of a mental health facility contracted to provide such services or be a private practitioner. In Toronto, a specialized assessment unit, the Metropolitan Toronto Forensic Service (METFORS), was established to provide brief assessments primarily of fitness to stand trial. Defendants are brought from the local jail for the day, during which period the evaluation takes place, and then returned to custody in the evening. Cases requiring more comprehensive evaluation may be admitted as in-patients. In-patient assessments may be ordered by the judge for periods up to 60 days. Individuals found 'unfit to stand trial' are detained at the pleasure of the Lieutenant-Governor for an indefinite period. They are held in the same institutions and subject to the same review procedure as individuals found 'not guilty by reason of insanity' (*see below*).

United States of America

In all federal and state jurisdictions of the USA, a defendant must be mentally competent to stand trial before the trial can proceed. This is designed to preserve the dignity of the criminal trial, achieve accuracy in the adjudication of the defendant's guilt, and protect the constitutional rights of the defendant (Brakel et al., 1985).

A finding of incompetency to stand trial has significant consequences for a defendant in that it delays the defendant's criminal trial, typically results in a period of involuntary psychiatric hospitalization, jeopardizes his release on bail, and potentially stigmatizes the defendant with a label of 'mental illness'.

Formulation of the legal standard of competency to stand trial vary somewhat across jurisdictions. The earlier *Dusky* v *United States* standard of the US Supreme Court asked whether the defendant has 'sufficient present ability to consult his lawyer with a reasonable degree of rational understanding and whether he has a rational as well as factual understanding of the proceedings against him'. This was superseded by the Comprehensive Crime Control Act of 1984, a federal statute which inquires whether 'the defendant is presently suffering from a mental disease or defect rendering him mentally incompetent to the extent that he is unable to understand the nature and consequences of the proceedings against him or to assist properly in his defense (US Code, title 18, section 4241). Although this statute applies only to federal crimes, analogous competency standards are prevalent throughout the state jurisdictions.

If a defendant is adjudicated incompetent to stand trial, he is ordinarily sent by the criminal court to a forensic psychiatric hospital to restore his fitness for trial. This may be a medium or maximum security facility, usually run by each state's department of mental health, although in rare cases some defendants are treated in private psychiatric hospitals or as outpatients. These hospitalizations are usually time-limited (e.g. 2–6 months), but the time can often be extended indefinitely when the charges are homicide. A US Supreme Court decision in 1972 held that a defendant could not be detained for more than the reasonable period of time necessary to determine if he will regain the capacity to stand trial; if it appears that this is not the case, then the state must institute civil commitment proceedings or release the defendant (*Jackson* v *Indiana*). After his competency to stand trial has been restored, the defendant is returned to jail or remains on bond, pending trial. If the defendant relapses waiting trial, the entire process could be repeated.

Because of its prevalence, competency to stand trial is the most significant pretrial forensic psychiatric issue. Other specific pretrial criminal competency issues include competency to provide a confession, waive rights to counsel, or plead guilty. Defendants are, however, rarely found incompetent in these areas.

Evaluation of a criminal defendant's competency to stand trial is preferentially performed when the defendant is outside of a psychiatric hospital. Many large cities or countries have fully staffed criminal court clinics which provide psychiatric evaluations and competency to stand trial evaluations of defendants while the defendant is in jail or in the community on bail. In smaller communities, such evaluations are provided by mental health professionals on a part-time or contractual basis with the jurisdiction. When a *bona fide* question of the defendant's competency to stand trial has been raised, he is entitled to an evaluation at public expense, if he cannot afford to obtain an evaluation at his own expense. Those who can privately afford to obtain such evaluations can procure more than a single report if one appears unfavourable to his case. In some cases, a defendant will be court-ordered for an in-hospital evaluation of his competency to stand trial, usually at a state forensic psychiatric hospital. In these cases, the hospitalization will usually last a few months. Adjudications of competency to stand trial are formal, adversarial court proceedings before a judge; each defendant will have an attorney. In some states defendants can request a jury determination of their competency. In most jurisdictions, psychiatrists and doctoral-level psychologists are entitled to perform these evaluations and testify in court. In some jurisdictions, psychiatric social workers with master's degrees and special training are also permitted to do this work.

Psychiatric Defences and Measures in Criminal Proceedings

All legal systems provide some limitations to the application of penal sanctions following an offence, for example in the case of young children acts normally considered as criminal are not subject to criminal proceeding. Children are exculpated by their age. There are also various forms of mitigating circumstances which can justify a less severe sanction, for example, in the case of provocation. Acts committed by mentally disordered persons may be covered by one or other of these concepts. The mad person may be considered as incapable of controlling his mind and his actions, and is consequently treated as a child, as far as exculpation is concerned. This concept has its origins in antiquity. A more recent and subtle approach is that which regards the mentally disordered person as guilty, but less so, than a healthy person committing the same act. If the mentally abnormal offender benefits from one or other form of exculpatory generosity, societal ambivalence is, nevertheless, reflected by the use of security measures (internment, hospitalization, compulsory treatment) which can result in deprivation of liberty at least as long as a prison sentence for an equivalent offence. This section shows how this ambivalence is given concrete form in the penal systems of the seven countries considered. Terminology is confusing in comparing the defences which can be used in the case of mentally abnormal offenders, particularly the different ways in which the word 'responsibility' is used.

In jurisdictions in the tradition of the French Penal Code, the term 'responsibility' is a unified concept covering the capacity to understand the unlawful nature of an act and the capacity to control one's behaviour. In the presence of mental disorder (*'demence'* in article 64 of the French Penal Code) and if one or both of these capacities is absent, the accused is then not considered guilty and is not subject to punishment. This concept of 'irresponsibility' exists in Austria, Bulgaria, Denmark and Switzerland.

In Austria and Bulgaria responsibility/irresponsibility is a dichotomous, all-in-one concept while, in Switzerland, diminished responsibility can be found in cases of less severe mental disorder, when the capacities mentioned above are impaired but not absent. The court may then attenuate the penal sanction, but the degree of attenuation is left to the court's discretion.

Although not included in our sample, it should be noted that two European countries have given up 'responsibility' as a central concept in criminal proceedings: Sweden, where the criterion used to decide on a mental health disposal is the person's need of treatment and Belgium, where, for all but minor offences, the Social Defence Law is applied to cases of offences committed by mentally disordered persons so that the provisions on criminal responsibility are no longer applied.

In two states of Australia (Queensland and New South Wales), the term 'diminished responsibility' has a much more limited application (as in England and Wales), of a special defence in cases of murder, whereby if the defence is successful the charge is reduced to manslaughter. In these two States, as in the rest of Australia and in Canada, the insanity defence in the McNaughton tradition, is available and is usually referred to as 'not guilty by reason of insanity'. This defence is also available in certain jurisdictions of the USA, where 'criminal responsibility' is now often used as an umbrella term to cover the three main psychiatric defences: not guilty by reason of insanity (NRGI), guilty but mentally ill (GBMI) and the *mens rea* form of diminished capacity.

Let us now consider in more detail the psychiatric defences available in each of the seven countries and the legal proceedings involved:

Australia

The State of Queensland has introduced legislation through part IV of the Mental Health Services Act (1978–1987) which is to be construed with the criminal code, so that terms used have the same meaning as in the criminal code. Two forms of defence are defined, neither of which is particularly innovative:

Diminished responsibility

When a person who unlawfully kills another, which under normal circumstances would constitute murder, is at the time of doing the act or making the omission which causes death in such a state of abnormality of mind as substantially to impair his capacity to understand what he is doing, or his capacity to control his actions, or his capacity to know that he ought not to do the act or make the omission, he is guilty of manslaughter only.

Unsoundness of mind

A person is not criminally responsible for an act or omission if at the time of doing the act or making the omission he is in such a state of mental disease or natural mental infirmity as to deprive him of capacity to understand what he is doing, or of capacity to control his action, or of capacity to know that he ought not to do the act or make the omission.

The innovation in Queensland's legislation resides in the function of the Mental Health Tribunal in criminal matters. This tribunal consists of a Judge of the Supreme Court who is advised by two psychiatrists (the psychiatrists are not a constituent part of the tribunal). The tribunal is divorced from the atmosphere of a criminal court and is unique in mental health legislation. Where there is reasonable cause to believe that a person alleged to have committed an indictable offence is mentally ill, or was mentally ill at the time that the alleged offence was committed, the matter of the person's mental condition may be referred to the Mental Health Tribunal. Referrals may be made by the patient concerned, his legal adviser or nearest relative, a crown law officer, or the Director of Psychiatric Services (a psychiatrist). Proceedings before the Tribunals are deemed to be judicial proceedings and, unless directed by the judge, are open to the public. Every person concerned in the proceedings before the tribunal is entitled to legal representation. The functions of the tribunal include determining questions of criminal responsibility, including diminished responsibility, fitness to plead and fitness to be tried, as well as the hearing of appeals from the Patient Review Tribunal. The Mental Health Tribunal may order psychiatric, medical or other examinations and, unless the tribunal otherwise orders, a copy of each report relating to the examinations made is available to all persons concerned in the reference.

Psychiatric reports before the tribunal address the following issues:

the patient's mental condition;
the relationship (if any) between the patient's mental illness and the alleged offence, in particular the mental capacity of the patient at the time of the alleged offence (having specific regard to the issue of unsoundness of mind);
the duration of the mental illness and the likely outcome of treatment;
any other matter likely to assist the Tribunal.

Regardless of the tribunal's findings, a person may elect to go to trial or may appeal (to the Court of Criminal Appeals) against the decisions of the tribunal.

Cases which do not go to trial after having been dealt with by the Mental Health Tribunal are referred to the Patient Review Tribunal for determination of certain management issues (e.g. placement). This system is free of political influence and replaces 'Queen's pleasure' detention.

Each Patient Review Tribunal consists of three to five members and is chaired by a district court judge. The other members of the tribunal must include a medical practitioner and a mental health professional. This independent tribunal has specific functions in relation to reviews of cases of civilly committed patients as well as patients involved in the criminal justice process (*see below* under Civil Commitment p. 145).

In New South Wales, the insanity defence (NGRI) and the plea of diminished responsibility are available as in Queensland—their application is decided by the criminal courts. The Mental Health Review Tribunal of New South Wales, established under the Mental Health Act 1983, operates in criminal matters under the Crimes (Mental Disorder) Amendment Act 1983, and deals with people who are found to be not guilty of a criminal offence on the grounds of mental ill health or were found unfit to be tried or who, whilst waiting trial or serving a sentence, had been transferred from a prison to a hospital. The tribunal consists of a lawyer (chairman), a psychiatrist and a third member (qualifications unspecified). Cases are reviewed each 6 months with the tribunal recommending discharge from detention if it is found that the safety of the patient or any member of the public will not be seriously endangered by the patient's release. The tribunal also makes recommendations about continuing care or treatment if the person's detention is to continue when prisoners are transferred to psychiatric hospital from prison, the Tribunal also conducts 6-monthly reviews to ensure that the patient is not detained in hospital any longer than is psychiatrically necessary.

The Mental Health Review Tribunal is an independent body, it is not a court nor a branch of the Department of Health. In law, it is regarded as a quasi-judicial tribunal. Proceedings of the tribunal are open to the public, a patient is entitled to legal or other representation and the patient may (unless otherwise directed) have access to his medical records.

Only Queensland and New South Wales offer the mentally ill offender the avenue of diminished responsibility, resulting in a verdict of manslaughter instead of murder where it applies.

In Victoria, there is, as a consequence, a strong reliance on the 'insanity defence'. Where a person has been found guilty of a criminal offence and the court is satisfied on the evidence and by a certificate of a psychiatrist that the convicted person is suffering from a mental illness, the court may issue a hospital order authorizing that the person be detained either in prison or hospital to enable diagnosis, assessment and treatment. Prison to hospital transfers are made on ministerial authorization, but only after psychiatric reports are available to indicate that the person is suffering from a mental illness and the receiving hospital agrees to admit and treat the patient.

Austria

The definition of criminal irresponsibility in Austria is rather narrow and is clearly defined by the Austrian Penal Code:

> The behaviour of a person is not culpable if performed at a time when, as a consequence of mental disease, imbecility, deep disturbance of consciousness, or other grave psychic disturbance equivalent to one of these conditions, he lacks the capacity either to appreciate the criminality of his behaviour or to conform his conduct to this appreciation.

Irresponsibility is appreciated by the judge or by the jury (in cases of assize court procedures), after hearing a psychiatric expert. The consequence of a finding of irresponsibility is that no punishment, as such, may be applied.

Since 1975, when the new Penal Code came into force as a result of a long-term reform movement, in which Willibald Sluga as a psychiatrist had taken an active part, provisions have existed to commit irresponsible insane offenders, provided that they are regarded as dangerous.

> Where a person who has committed an offence punishable by imprisonment of more than one year cannot be so punished, for the sole reason that he committed the offence while under the influence of a condition that precluded responsibility and was based on a high degree of mental or emotional abnormality, the court shall order him to be placed in an institution for mentally abnormal offenders, if his personality and condition and the nature of the offence give grounds for apprehension that under the influence of his mental or emotional abnormality he would otherwise commit a punishable offence of serious consequences.
> Where such grounds of apprehension exist, any person who, while under the influence of a high degree of mental or emotional abnormality without however lacking responsibility, has committed an offence punishable by imprisonment of more than one year shall likewise be ordered to be placed in an institution for

mentally abnormal offenders. In such a case the confinement shall be ordered at the time when the sentence is passed.

These provisions have a 'catch-all' characteristic, since commitment to a special institution is possible whether or not the person is irresponsible. The key criterion is 'dangerousness'.

The Austrian legal system has no provision for 'diminished responsibility'. A person is responsible or irresponsible (the latter finding being virtually restricted to cases of clearly diagnosed psychosis). Nevertheless, non-psychotic persons (mostly psychopathic persons with sexual deviancy or feeble minded persons, appearing as arsonists, for instance), can be committed to a special institution for treatment as well as receiving a custodial sentence. The end of the committal is decided by a committee of judges who take into account reports from the institution and external psychiatric experts. Psychiatric experts are not asked to decide whether or not the person is still ill, they have to assess only his/her dangerousness. There are, of course, many doubts expressed in the international and Austrian literature over psychiatrists' ability to assess dangerousness (Kozol et al., 1972; Montandon and Harding, 1984; Berner and Karlick-Bolten, 1986; Gratz, 1986).

The fact that these provisions are applicable only in cases of offences punishable by imprisonment of more than one year, means that the risk of further offences may be rather high. The regulations for an order for probation on discharge (lasting 5 years) are rather strict.

In the cases of treatment orders for drug-dependent and alcoholic offenders, the discharge criteria are less strict. Such measures can be discontinued if the treatment seems to be senseless or without any effect.

> Where a person who is addicted to the abuse of intoxicants or narcotics is convicted for having committed a criminal offence in a state of inebriety or otherwise in connection with these addictions, or is convicted for a punishable behaviour performed in a state of full intoxication, the court shall order him to be placed in an institution for addicted offenders in need of withdrawal if his personality and the nature of the offence give grounds for apprehension that in connection with his addiction to intoxicants or narcotics he would otherwise commit either a punishable offence of serious consequences or at least punishable offences entailing not merely light consequences. The court shall refrain from ordering such confinement if the offender has to serve more than two years in prison, if the requirements are satisfied for his confinement in an institution for mentally abnormal offenders, or if the endeavour to cure him appears to be hopeless from the outset.

Since the provisions of the new Penal Code came into force in 1975, several new institutions have developed, emptying the old psychiatric hospitals of their 'forensic cases'. Only women who are committed for 'forensic treatment' are still placed in traditional psychiatric hospitals.

For 'forensic cases', three institutions have been created. The special institution Göllersdorf is a modern high security hospital, the only one in Austria. It has 130 beds, run by psychiatric personnel (2 full-time and 6 half-time psychiatrists from the University Clinic of Vienna), psychiatric nurses and security officers. This psychiatric hospital belongs administratively to the Ministry of Justice. Patients are placed there by the same authorities responsible for the placement of prisoners. The institution was created especially for 'irresponsible' mentally abnormal offenders who are committed to treatment according to the new provisions of the Penal Code. The hospital is also used in cases of acute psychosis occurring during a regular sentence in prison, for brief admission followed by a return to prison. Psychiatric personnel working in the institution tend to be very sensitive to the important human rights issues for inmate patients in such a setting, and have a tendency to observe psychiatric symptoms rather than enforcing treatment against the patient's wishes.

The special prison Mittersteig has the task of treating patients committed according to the provisions of the Penal Code for non-psychotic persons with mental disorders who receive a prison sentence which is replaced by a treatment. Its 80 places serve 50 such referrals by the court and another 30 patients selected from prison, because they seem in need of treatment, wish to be treated, are serving a long-term sentence (more than ten years) and cannot be released without social training and rehabilitation.

In most cases these patients display either personality disorders, sexual deviancy or disorders of impulse control. The mixture of sociotherapy with possibilities of work and leisure activities outside the institution and individual and group psychotherapy is carried out by a therapeutic staff of 2 psychiatrists (part-time), 5 psychologists, and 5 social workers. Supervision is obligatory for the therapeutic staff and available for the security staff, whose training is generally inadequate.

Vienna-Favoriten special centre can accommodate approximately 80 patients, some being committed by the provisions of the Penal Code, others are referred from prison because of their need of treatment for addiction. Psychologists, social workers, probation officers and one part-time psychiatrist have developed special programmes, mainly based on group therapy to treat young male addicts, sometimes in close cooperation with other centres for non-forensic patients, who are willing to take them. The atmosphere in this institution is more liberal because withdrawal treatment cannot lead to a committal longer than the prison sentence, as is the case for inmates treated at Mittersteig.

Apart from the above-mentioned institutions, there exist special departments in prisons, which have the task of treating patients committed according to the Penal Code who cannot be allocated to Mittersteig or Favoriten, because of lack of places or other obstacles to treatment. Most of them are not willing to be treated psychologically, or are too dangerous for the liberal atmosphere at the therapeutic institutions. Altogether there are 40 such places. Patients are seen by a psychiatrist daily or every other day, but there are only limited possibilities for further treatment other than drugs.

Bulgaria

The Bulgarian Penal Code 1896, which was influenced by Russian and Austrian models and was drafted with the participation of the Bulgarian Medical Society, contained a well-developed formulation of exemption from criminal responsibility, which was based on three medical and two psychological criteria. Since the adoption of that law, the legal doctrine and forensic psychiatric theory in Bulgaria have been marked by a preference for a dual (biological and psychological) diagnostic approach and a dichotomous model for the concept of penal responsibility. Nevertheless, the concept of diminished responsibility has had some prominent advocates among forensic psychiatrists (Danadjiev, 1922, 1927; Tscholakov, 1947).

Psychiatric assessment of responsibility constitute the bulk of forensic psychiatric evaluations. Such assessments are commissioned by the prosecution or the court not only in cases of serious crimes, but also in relatively minor offences if an abnormal mental state is suspected in the offender. According to the current Penal Code the legal age of responsibility is 14. However, responsibility for offences committed between the ages of 14 and 18 can be contested in court without invoking mental disorder or abnormality. After the age of 18, criminal responsibility can be deemed absent only if at least one of the three medical criteria is present (i.e. 'underdevelopment of mind', 'persistent disorder of mind' or 'short-lived disorder of mind') and at the same time at least one of the two psychological criteria is satisfied (i.e. 'understanding the nature and significance of one's action' and 'capacity for guiding one's own actions').

When the judicial decision concerning criminal irresponsibility is reached, a penal sanction is not applied, being replaced by medical measures. Those legally found as lacking responsibility are liable to compulsory treatment in a psychiatric hospital; those declared responsible and sentenced while suffering from a non-incapacitating mental disorder are entitled to appropriate medical treatment and care within the penal institution.

The treatment of mentally disordered prisoners falls to forensic psychiatry, so forensic psychiatrists have prison attachments as consultants, and operate a special inpatient unit for prisoners with mental disorders. However, Bulgaria has no special 'therapeutic prisons'. Psychiatric rehabilitation programmes for prisoners do exist, but they are administered in the ordinary prison environment.

Canada (see note on p. 166)

The Criminal Code of Canada is a national or federal law, the administration of which is the responsibility of the individual provinces and there are, therefore, local variations in its application.

Each province has its own courts which may try almost any offence. In practice, however, serious criminal cases such as murder are typically heard in the provincial District or Supreme Court (or Court of Queen's Bench in some provinces). Appeals may be heard through the Appeal Division of the Supreme Court and from there, the final arbiter, the Supreme Court of Canada.

The Canadian law on insanity essentially consists of a modification of the McNaughton Rules (*see* Hucker et al., 1981). There are two main requirements: the presence of (1) 'natural imbecility' or a 'disease of the mind' of such severity as (2) to 'render him incapable of appreciating the nature and quality of an act or omission or know that it is wrong'. As in other jurisdictions, the meanings of the various key words in this legal definition of insanity have been subjected to a long line of judicial interpretations. Although the term 'disease of the mind' has been interpreted very broadly, recent rulings by the Supreme Court of Canada restrict the availability of an insanity defence for individuals with 'psychopathic' or similar personality disorders. Thus, in *Kjeldsen* it was reaffirmed that—

> to be capable of 'appreciating' the nature and quality of his acts, an accused person must have the capacity to know what he is doing . . . and in addition he must have the capacity to estimate and to understand the physical consequences which would flow from his act. . . .

While 'insanity' is usually raised as a defence to a charge, under Canadian law, evidence of insanity may, even against the wishes of the accused but at the discretion of the trial judge, be raised by the prosecution.

'Diminished responsibility' is not an available defence in Canada. However, mental illness falling short of insanity, as well as intoxication with drugs or alcohol, may mitigate if there is evidence that it negated the 'specific intent' required for the particular offence and result in a conviction for a lesser offence. This form of mitigation is closely similar to the *mens rea* rule, described in the section on the USA pp. 143–4.

The defence of automatism is also available in Canada. Automatism due to a 'disease of the mind' is subsumed under the insanity defence. Non-insane automatism, on the other hand, when not produced by voluntary intoxication by drugs and alcohol, may, if successful, provide a complete defence. Concussion, hypoglycemia, somnambulism and involuntary intoxication due to medically administered drugs have all been included in this category. However, it has often proved difficult to distinguish insane and non-insane automatism in cases caused by 'emotional shock'. Thus, in the Canadian case of *Rabey*, for example, the Supreme Court of Canada by a four to three majority held that a 'dissociative state' produced by a 'psychological blow' was a 'disease of the mind' and, therefore, considered the offence an insane automatism.

Psychiatric assessments may be ordered by the court either under the criminal code or under the mental health act of the province in which the court is based. Determination of criminal responsibility or sentencing recommendations are typically conducted in maximum security hospitals or specialized forensic units. In larger centres, such assessments are often carried out in the jails by psychiatrists in private practice.

Individuals found 'unfit to stand trial' or 'not guilty by reason of insanity' are detained at the pleasure of the Lieutenant Governor for an indefinite period.

Individuals held under Warrant of the Lieutenant Governor (WLG) are treated in either maximum security psychiatric facilities, medium secure units, open wards of regional psychiatric hospitals, or psychiatric units in general hospitals. In some provinces, a very small number of WLG cases are held in the penitentiary system.

WLG patients are reviewed by the Board of Review consisting of three to five members, of which two are psychiatrists, one a lawyer, one a lay person, and a chairman, usually a retired senior judge. These reviews are held within the first 6 months of the issue of the warrant and annually thereafter.

Under the influence of the new Canadian Charter of Rights and Freedoms (1982) a number of significant new proposals for amendments to the Criminal Code have been put forward. One of the main proposals includes a limitation on the length of time an individual can be held on a WLG to no longer than would have been the case if he had been convicted of the original charge. There is also a proposal for 'hospital orders' so that an offender, after conviction, can request to spend the first 60 days of his sentence in a suitable psychiatric facility.

The Criminal Code of Canada includes a special part on 'dangerous offenders' which allows for the preventive detention of an individual who has been convicted of a 'serious personal injury offence' involving violence or sexual behaviour likely to endanger life or inflict severe psychological damage. The court must be satisfied that the individual poses a threat to the life or safety, physical or mental, of others based on a pattern of (1) repetitive behaviour and likelihood of causing injury or severe psychological damage in the future; (2) persistent aggression (including the offence for which he has just been convicted) showing a substantial degree of indifference towards reasonably foreseeable consequences of the behaviour and that (3) the behaviour in the index offence was so brutal as to 'compel the conclusion that his behaviour in the future is unlikely to be inhibited by normal standards of behaviour or restraint' or, in the case of the sex offender, has shown 'a failure to control sexual impulses and likely to cause injury pain or other evil to other persons' in the future.

Denmark

The Danish Penal Code of 1930 provided for the establishment of: youth prisons, special institutions for alcoholics, labour camps, security detention institutions, prison for psychopaths, and special detention centres for criminal psychopaths (Svendsen, 1977). Treatment philosophy in criminology was at its height in the 'fifties. In the 'seventies there were increasing doubts about the effectiveness and the ethics of treatment of offenders under a system of indeterminate sentences. Penal reforms in 1973 and 1975 took away practically all the special arrangements of indeterminate duration, including the detention centre for criminal psychopaths at Herstedvester, where Sturup, treated 'the untreatable' (Sturup, 1968). The Herstedvester Institution is today a special prison. Non-psychotic offenders now usually receive ordinary sentences, and the number of mental reports to the courts has decreased considerably since the penal reform.

The possibility of indeterminate preventive detention of dangerous offenders remains, but it is used less than five times a year and only for reasons of security. If a detainee needs psychiatric treatment, he can be placed in the Herstedvester Institution for all or part of the determinate sentence. These developments indicate that the idea of universal treatment for offenders has been abandoned by lawyers and politicians—thus limiting the scope of forensic psychiatry to offender patients with severe mental illness.

The present Danish Penal Code states:

> Persons, who at the time of the act were irresponsible owing to mental illness or quite similar conditions or a pronounced mental deficiency are not punishable.

'Mental illness' corresponds to the psychiatric term 'psychosis'. In practice, all psychotic serious offenders are considered potentially irresponsible by the court, and will not be punished without regard to the possible connection between the criminal act and psychotic symptoms.

For psychotic offenders considered irresponsible, the court has to decide on a mental health management which is considered to be expedient for the prevention of further crimes. If less radical provisions such as supervision, psychiatric treatment and so on are considered insufficient, the court may decide that the person concerned shall be placed in a psychiatric hospital.

Non-psychotic offenders can also be sentenced to treatment or placement in a psychiatric hospital, but ordinarily only for up to one year, if it is found 'more suitable' to prevent relapse than a prison sentence. If the offender, at the time of the offence, was in a condition of defective development, or impairment or disturbance of his mental function, the court may decide instead of punishment to use the provisions for non-psychotic offenders. However, the courts have been reluctant to order psychiatric treatment within this group, especially for psychopaths—the great majority are sentenced to imprisonment.

The provisions of treatment or placement for irresponsible offenders are mainly dependent on an evaluation of the dangerousness of the offender. Following a serious crime and/or if the person is considered as dangerous, the usual sentence will be indeterminate placement in a psychiatric hospital. The most dangerous psychotic offenders can be interned in the Security Detention Institution.

The difference between the two sanctions—psychiatric treatment and internment—is a question of security. The hospital is not allowed to discharge an interned patient without a court decision. However, the psychiatrist can decide whether he should stay in a closed or an open ward. Psychiatric treatment does not necessarily include hospitalization. The patient can be discharged by the hospital when appropriate and, if necessary, be readmitted for treatment, due to aggravation of his mental disorder or following a new offence.

A cross-sectional study on 1 June, 1987 of all persons in Denmark sentenced to psychiatric treatment or internment showed that among a total of 573 persons, 11% were interned and 89% sentenced to psychiatric treatment. The geographic distribution was uneven with accumulation in the Copenhagen area. Schizophrenic patients amounted to 49% of the total, followed by character deviations (20%) (Lund, 1988).

Thus, today in Denmark, mentally ill and mentally retarded offenders with a 'psychiatric sentence' are treated within the ordinary mental health services, including the psychiatric hospitals. There has been no essential change in this system following the revision of the penal code. The fact that offenders are hospitalized without limitation of time has been the subject of criticism. The principle of normalization and the right to be sentenced to ordinary punishment have played an important part, in particular with regard to some mentally retarded offenders. Only for the most dangerous psychiatric patients or offenders has a special institution been preserved: The Security Detention Institution, associated with the mental hospital of Nykøbing. Patients and offenders from the whole country, as well as Greenland, can be admitted. The institution now has 30 beds.

In the Danish Penal Code, there is a range of options from non-custodial sentences and suspended sentences to custodial sentences: imprisonment 'for life' is rarely used. Ordinarily a prisoner is released on parole ('conditional release'), when two-thirds of the punishment is served.

A prisoner can be transferred to a hospital or to another suitable institution either temporarily or for the rest of the penalty, if it is found appropriate—a provision representing a link between the criminal justice system and the health system.

The institutions within the prison system, including four closed state prisons, have for some years had psychiatric consultants with a few hours' work weekly.

The Herstedvester Institution, which has a certain renown in the history of forensic psychiatry, now has the clearly defined aim of providing psychiatric care within the prison system. Persons, who are thought to have a particular need of psychiatric treatment will—possibly temporarily—be placed in or transferred to the Herstedvester Institution.

Herstedvester is a prison and a treatment institution. Since 1982 it has been run by a prison governor, who is a lawyer. Conflicts are well known between the personnel in uniform and the therapeutic staff. The institution has a maximum of 130 inmates. In total, the staff includes about 225 persons, a considerably higher staff/inmate ratio than other Danish prisons. There are 3 fully qualified psychiatrists. Offenders with personality disorders form the bulk of inmates. In principle, psychotic prisoners are transferred to a psychiatric hospital for treatment but, nevertheless, at any time there are some psychotic inmates in Herstedvester, such patients requiring a high level of security. The inmates represent all degrees of dangerousness from quite harmless to extremely dangerous persons. Sexual offenders are a special category. A new special ward for females was opened in 1987.

It is intended that psychiatric treatment should follow the same lines as in other psychiatric institutions outside the prison system—as far as possible. More than half of the inmates receive psychiatric/psychological treatment. The duration of stay varies widely; about 50% of the inmates are serving sentences exceeding 5 years. A released prisoner will be supported by a series of social measures and different kinds of treatment—among others, treatment of substance abuse.

According to the Administration of Justice Act 1989, a person charged with a crime must be subjected to a medico-legal assessment, when it is considered important for reaching the judicial decision. A circular indicates the criteria for carrying out medico-legal assessment: when there is reason to suppose that the charged person is psychotic, mentally retarded, psychologically deviant, an abuser of alcohol or drugs, or when the charge concerns serious and dangerous crime. Today about 7% of all accused persons with offences serious enough to merit sentences greater than a fine are examined. The medical observation is usually carried out at the pretrial stage by one psychiatrist, but some mental reports are still made by non-psychiatrists (public health officers). The examination can be performed during a hospital stay or as an outpatient, while the offender is under arrest.

Ordinarily, the mental reports on mentally disordered and dangerous persons are submitted to the Medico-Legal Council for review and possible modification.

Switzerland

The provisions of the Swiss Penal Code were strongly influenced by progressive psychiatrists at the turn of the century, notably August Forel, professor of psychiatry in Zurich (Bomio, 1990).

At that time, each canton had a separate penal code. Most included a conceptualization of irresponsibility closely modelled on the French penal code of 1810. Indeed, the canton of Geneva had been subject to the French code during the first years of its application (1810–15) when Geneva was part of the 'Department de Leman' integrated into Napoleonic France.

Forel and his colleagues wanted to break away from what they considered two overly simple, rigid and limited concepts: on the one hand the single diagnostic entity 'demence'—and, on the other hand, a binary distinction between responsibility and irresponsibility. Their view was strongly influenced by the intellectual climate of the day, notably the positivist school of criminology, a deterministic view of human behaviour (as demonstrated by experiments with hypnosis) and the emerging doctrine of social defence. They, therefore, argued for the inclusion of several psychopathological categories, some of which correspond to diagnostic concepts, while others are essentially symptomatic. They also pressed for a concept of diminished responsibility with attenuation of the sentence.

These ideas strongly influenced Carl Stoos who prepared the first draft of the unified Swiss Penal Code in 1893. The negotiations needed to arrive at a consensus on the penal code were long and arduous; the gestational period was ended by a federal referendum in 1938 and the Swiss penal code came into force in 1942. Nevertheless, the original proposals concerning criminal responsibility were essentially those proposed by Stoos and, therefore, represent the fruit of medico-legal collaboration in the 1890s. The Swiss system is, therefore, at a midpoint between the earliest formulations of criminal irresponsibility, influenced by Esquirol and his followers in France, and current thinking in forensic psychiatry. The ideas embodied in the Swiss system are essentially generous and therapeutic in nature, based on a deterministic view of human behaviour, inspired by a dimensional model of psychopathology, which is an expression of a biological concept with three axes (1) mental illness; (2) mental retardation; and (3) level of consciousness.

The notion of responsibility is treated early in the disposition of the Swiss penal code. In conceptual terms, therefore, the Swiss legislator places responsibility (articles 10–13) before the consideration of guilt (article 18), which is, in turn, based on the notions of intention and will. This conceptual hierarchy of responsibility before guilt raises difficult theoretical issues, since there is inevitably a degree of semantic interference between the two concepts.

A finding of irresponsibility or diminished responsibility is based on two separate evaluations. The first step is diagnostic according to three possible types of psychopathology. For irresponsibility, these are:

1. mental illness: this term is clearly used as a modern equivalent of 'alienation';
2. feeblemindedness: severe cognitive deficit either congenital or acquired;
3. severe alteration of the level of consciousness: i.e. acute delirium, intoxications, post-epileptic states.

Only if one or more of these states was present at the time of the offence is the second step of the evaluation carried out. This concerns the capacity to understand the illicit nature of the act and the capacity to control one's behaviour in the light of this appreciation. If the psychopathology was the origin of the absence of one of these capacities, the accused person should be considered irresponsible. If this conclusion is accepted by the judicial authorities, the criminal proceedings are interrupted and the person is not subject to punishment. In virtually every such case, a treatment and security measure is ordered and the majority of such mentally abnormal offenders are transferred to the mental health system.

The psychopathological typology for findings of irresponsibility is repeated in each case with a lesser degree of severity for the definition of diminished responsibility. 'Mental illness' becomes a 'disturbance of mental health'; 'feebleminded' becomes 'incomplete development of the mind'; and, 'severe alteration of the level of consciousness' becomes 'disturbance of the level of consciousness'. Should one of these lesser degrees of psychopathology have been present at the time of the offence, the psychiatrist can consider whether either the capacity to understand or the capacity of self control were diminished. Such an analysis leads to a conclusion of diminished responsibility. In this case, the offender will go to trial and a punitive sanction such as imprisonment can be inflicted. This punishment may, however, be attenuated on the grounds of diminished responsibility. The degree of attenuation is left to the discretion of the court.

Several points should be noted about the formal structure of this conceptual system:

1. In the absence of a psychopathology corresponding to the entities indicated above, the psychiatrist cannot proceed to an assessment of the capacities of understanding and control. In particular, this excludes consideration of pathology defined at the level of a couple or a family group.
2. Irresponsibility as a possible conclusion is limited to cases of major psychiatric pathology.
3. Punitive sanctions, which are not applied in the case of irresponsibility, are applicable in the case of diminished responsibility.

Attempts have been made to translate the terminology found in the Penal Code, in terms of modern psychopathological and nosological concepts. Thus, ICD-9 and the DSM-III R are both used to indicate the extent and limits of each term. The most important of these definitions are:

1. mental illness is interpreted as psychotic disorders (ICD-9 codes 290–299; DSM-III R: organic mental disorders, schizophrenia, delusional disorders and mood disorders, excluding cyclothymia and dysthymia);
2. incomplete mental development includes not only moderate forms of mental retardation, but also personality disorders; thus, psychiatric reports frequently indicate the presence of a DSM-III R Axis II diagnosis, most usually in cluster B.

In the Canton of Geneva, psychiatric assessments are requested in 3–5% of criminal cases. These assessments result most frequently in a finding of diminished responsibility (56%). However, a significant proportion of conclusions was of full criminal responsibility (39%). Only 5% of psychiatric assessments lead to a conclusion of irresponsibility. This means that in roughly 2 per thousand criminal cases, a penal sanction is not applied on psychiatric grounds; while in 24 per thousand the punishment may be of a lesser severity as a result of the psychiatrist's intervention.

The ideas which inspired the provisions on criminal responsibility in the Swiss penal code were generous and even idealistic. The practical application within the current realities of the criminal justice system is, however, disappointing. The demonstrable results either in terms of justice or in terms of treatment are meagre. Medico-legal dialogue is inevitably impoverished when based on a concept devoid of a solid theoretical foundation either in medical or in juridical terms.

The most problematic element in this system is the concept of diminished responsibility. Judges are aware of the lack of rigour in applying this concept. Not infrequently, there is a clear impression that a conclusion of diminished responsibility is accepted by the court, but had little or no effect on the practical outcome. There even appears to be a paradoxical effect of such conclusions in the case of some violent offences, where the impression left on jurors is that the accused is in some way 'half mad', still deserving punishment with no effective psychiatric management available. This may explain very heavy sentences imposed in such cases, despite a conclusion of diminished responsibility. Some Swiss forensic psychiatrists have advocated abandoning entirely the concept of responsibility and adopting provision based on the Swedish experience since 1965. Psychiatrists would then limit their evaluations to diagnosis, therapeutic proposals and a prognostic assessment (including risk of violent behaviour associated with psychopathology). However, the majority of Swiss psychiatrists favour the retention of the provisions concerning irresponsibility based on a psychiatric evaluation, but giving up the notion of diminished responsibility. The cases which currently are assigned to the category 'diminished responsibility' could still benefit from a psychiatric evaluation and the conclusions could be taken into account under the assessment of mitigating circumstances.

United States of America

The criminal code in each state and federal jurisdiction specifies the manner in which a defendant's mental condition is relevant to his criminal responsibility at trial. The code specifies the standards and procedures to exculpate him or reduce the criminal charges against him, as well as the subsequent disposition of the case.

The special verdict of insanity is available to a defendant in all states except Idaho, Montana, and Utah (Callahan et al., 1987), and in all federal jurisdictions. The McNaughton Rules are used in 26 of these 47 states while the remainder apply the American Law Institute (ALI) standard of the Model Penal Code.

> A person is not responsible for criminal conduct if at the time of such conduct as a result of mental disease or defect he lacks substantial capacity either to

appreciate the criminality of his conduct or to conform his conduct to the requirements of law (American Law Institute 1962).

The federal courts used several different rules defined by case law until the Congress, motivated by the federal trial court verdict in *Hinckley* enacted the Comprehensive Crime Control Act of 1984, which established a new rule for all federal courts.

> The defendant, as a result of a severe mental disease or defect, was unable to appreciate the nature and quality or the wrongfulness of his acts (US Code, title 18, section 20 (a)).

This formulation, which eliminates the volitional component of the ALI rule, adopted the proposal of the American Psychiatric Association (1983a), and rejected that of the American Medical Association (1984) to abolish the insanity verdict. This law also placed the burden of proving insanity on the defendant rather than the prosecution; this had not previously been uniform in the federal courts. After *Hinckley*, many states also shifted their burden of proof of insanity to the defendant.

Following an acquittal by reason of insanity, an acquittee is evaluated for commitment to a forensic psychiatric hospital, usually run by a state department of mental health, and testimony is presented at a commitment hearing. The acquittee can be involuntarily hospitalized on an indeterminate basis (*Jones*), or referred for mandatory outpatient psychiatric treatment (Bloom et al., 1986).

In 13 states, but not in the federal courts, an additional verdict of GBMI permits a jury or trial court alternatively to find the defendant guilty even though a severe mental illness was present at the time of the alleged offence. To qualify for a GBMI verdict, the defendant must not be considered to meet the criteria for legal insanity at the time of the offence. After such a verdict, available only since 1975, the defendant is confined to a regular prison, where treatment can be provided, or he may be sent on a temporary or permanent basis to a forensic mental health facility for treatment (Slobogin, 1985). This verdict usually offers little or no benefit to a defendant in terms of the outcome following conviction; in a recent case, for example, the Indiana Supreme Court held that a defendant found GBMI on charges of murder could still receive a death sentence (*Harris*; Petrella et al., 1985). Ostensibly designed to reduce the number of insanity acquittals by providing an opportunity for the jury to convict the defendant rather than acquit him, enactment of the GBMI verdict does not seem to have accomplished its goal (Blunt and Stock, 1985).

In addition to the special verdicts of NGRI and GBMI, evidence of mental disorder at the time of an alleged offence may also be admitted at trial in half of the states, as well as the federal courts, to negate the statutory mental element or specific intent of the offence required for conviction on that charge. This is referred to as the *mens rea* form of diminished capacity, and was promulgated by the American Medical Association (1984) in lieu of the insanity defence. It is the sole use of psychiatric testimony in criminal trials in the three states which have no insanity defence. In theory, it is a rule of evidence rather than an affirmative psychiatric defence, and is distinguishable from the diminished or partial responsibility doctrines used in Europe (Morse, 1984). In practice, the *mens rea* rule is used mostly in homicides when severe mental disorder or drug and alcohol intoxication is present at the time of the offence. The defendant can be found guilty of a lesser degree of criminal homicide which does not require the contested state of mind. Although there is no published data on the frequency of its use or success, it is uncommonly used in those states with prevalent NGRIs.

As in the case of examinations of competency to stand trial, defendants receive predominantly outpatient criminal responsibility evaluations, either at state expense or privately. It is common for the defence and prosecution each to identify expert witnesses willing to testify for their side, although many insanity verdicts are obtained without contest (Rogers *et al.*, 1984). Although the use of the insanity defence often attracts considerable public attention, it is infrequently used, and even less frequently successful (Pasewark and McGinley, 1985). Some states have virtually no insanity acquittees, while a few others have 50–100 each year (Rogers *et al.*, 1984; Blunt and Stock, 1985; Wettstein and Mulvey, 1988). Defendants are found NGRI on a variety of criminal charges, but charges of serious interpersonal violence are overrepresented among acquittees. At least half of insanity acquittees are psychotic at the time of the offence and are involuntarily hospitalized following acquittal; many remain in the hospital longer than if they had been convincted of the offence and imprisoned (Pasewark, 1981; Steadman, 1985; Wettstein and Mulvey, 1988).

Some states have the authority to order mandatory court-supervised outpatient psychiatric treatment for insanity acquittees immediately following acquittal or following discharge from the hospital (Bloom *et al.*, 1986). Acquittees must comply with the terms of the conditional release programme, including medication, psychotherapy, and substance abuse treatment, or be involuntarily returned to the hospital. This innovative process represents a substantial improvement in the state's ability to manage insanity acquittees in the community.

As noted earlier for criminal competency evaluations, psychiatrists and doctoral-level psychologists are permitted to perform criminal responsibility evaluations and testify at trial about this matter. Other mental health professionals have not yet been accorded this privilege.

Evidence of a defendant's mental disorder in the past, at the time of the offence, or at the time of the examination can also be considered in determining the appropriate sentence following conviction. Psychiatric treatment, often involuntary, can be ordered on an outpatient basis as a condition of probation to the community. This can include substance abuse treatment, abstention from substance abuse, restrictions on travel, and obtaining employment. In addition, a prison inmate who becomes mentally ill following incarceration can be transferred to a forensic mental health facility for treatment on a voluntary or involuntary basis; treatment for mentally ill prisoners is also provided within many prisons (Halleck, 1986).

A limited number of state jurisdictions have special statutes for securing those charged with or convicted of offenses involving deviant sexual activity. These sexually dangerous persons laws, or sex psychopath statutes, permit the indefinite confinement of such individuals, usually in a prison or forensic mental health facility, for voluntary or involuntary treatment. These laws are presently disfavoured, and have been repealed in some places (Brakel et al., 1985).

Civil Commitment

Civil commitment standards are virtually always based on the presence of mental disorder together with one or both of the following criteria: dangerousness and the need for treatment. 'Need for treatment' is based on a paternalistic approach (Chodoff, 1983) according to which involuntary hospitalization is a requisite for necessary treatment in the patient's interest: commitment is seen as a therapeutic measure carried out without consent for which the patient will thank the psychiatrist following recovery—hence the 'thank-you' theory or what French authors have elegantly, but perhaps confusingly, called 'anticipated consent'. The 'need for treatment' standard is typically associated with a welfare model of state intervention.

There has been a distinct move away from the paternalistic approach towards the dangerousness criterion for civil commitment, such that most recent legislation requires dangerousness with or without need for treatment (Harding and Curran, 1979). Associated with this tendency is the conceptualization of commitment as a form of deprivation of liberty, rather than a treatment intervention. This corresponds to the provisions of the European Convention of Human Rights which defines the exceptions to the right of liberty as including 'the lawful detention of . . . persons of unsound mind, alcoholics or drug addicts or vagrants' (article 5.1 e). If commitment is seen as a form of detention, albeit requiring procedural guarantees of due process before an independent court (article 5.4), then what Stromberg and Stone (1983) have called the 'cruel paradox' of psychiatric detention without treatment becomes possible for the committed patient who is considered competent to refuse treatment. Fortunately, the jurisprudence of the European Court of Human Rights has gone some way towards establishing a treatment model as implicitly necessary within psychiatric commitment: thus detention must take place in a hospital or an establishment conceived for the mentally ill and conditions must correspond to therapeutic standards. Another important principle established in the case of *Winterwerp* was the right to regular judicial review. Over 50 psychiatric cases have been the subject of published decisions of the European Commission of Human

Rights and 5 cases have been heard by the European Court (Harding, 1989a). An increasingly frequent aspect of modern legislation is the requirement that attempts to provide treatment in the community have been exhausted; this tendency is associated with interest in community treatment orders as an alternative form of involuntary intervention avoiding custodial treatment.

Perhaps more important than the difference between 'need for treatment' and 'dangerousness' standards are the broadness and the precision of the criteria as constraints on professional discretion. Segal (1989) has demonstrated in a comparative study between England and Wales, Italy and the United States that broader professional discretionary powers, derived from loosely defined 'need for treatment' criteria, as opposed to more narrowly defined dangerousness standards were each associated with very different hospitalized patient profiles. This finding may be due to other factors however, and Beigel et al. (1984) in a decision-making exercise were unable to demonstrate that a narrow definition of dangerousness led to more restricted patient selection.

International standards on civil commitment have been the subject of heated debate in recent years. The Draft Body of Principles, Guidelines and Guarantees for the Mentally Ill considered by the UN Sub-Commission on Prevention of Discrimination and Protection of Minorities on the initiative of its special rapporteur, Mrs Erica Daes, is regarded as impractical, over legalistic and badly drafted. Substantial revision of these principles was proposed by the World Health Organisation in 1988, and incorporated in a new draft set of guidelines (the so-called Palley report, United Nations Economic and Social Council, 1988). The modified guidelines were adopted by the UN General Assembly in December 1991. Meanwhile, Recommendation R(83) adopted by the Council of Europe's Committee of Ministers in 1983 has met with widespread approval.

Australia

Queensland legislation (Mental Health Services Act 1974) defines three forms of involuntary admission with inversely varying degrees of complexity and urgency. Thus, medical admission provides a complex interaction between medical examination, an 'authorized person' (mental health professional or patient's relative), a second medical practitioner, the psychiatrist and the Patient Review Tribunal. This system is represented in Fig. 3.1 and may be considered as a model of a complex form of protective mechanism. Patients may, in addition, appeal to the Patient Review Tribunal against their detention at any stage of their regulated admission.

Two much simpler forms of admission exist: one requires a warrant to be issued by a justice of the peace (JP) on receiving any information. The JP must be satisfied that a psychiatric emergency exists and that the interests of the person or the safety of others is at issue. The warrant is acted on by the

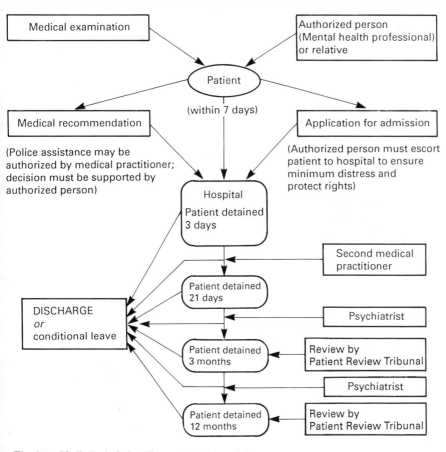

Fig. 3.1   Medical admission (Queensland, Australia).

police, a medical practitioner or a 'designated authorized person' to hospitalize the patient. In emergency situations creating an imminent danger for the person or others, the police may conduct the patient to hospital without a warrant.

The New South Wales Mental Health Act 1983 is characterized by an emphasis on patients' 'right to treatment', on community-based services and on stringent standards of proof for establishing the presence of mental illness and the criteria of behaviour of a dangerous nature for involuntary hospitalization.

In Victoria, the police have the authority to force entry into premises where they have reasonable ground for believing that a person is mentally ill (e.g. attempting suicide or threatening harm to others). The police or any other persons who believe that an individual is incapable of caring for themselves may seek a special warrant to have the person examined by a

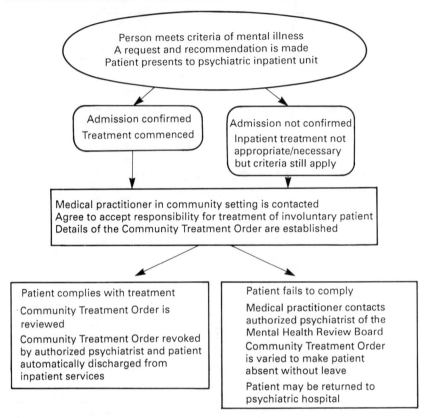

Fig. 3.2 Interaction between hospitalization and community treatment orders (New South Wales, Australia).

medical practitioner. An involuntary patient can be admitted to a psychiatric inpatient service by any registered medical practitioner and the patient must be examined within 24 hours of being admitted by an authorized psychiatrist. The psychiatrist must either discharge or confirm the admissions. A community treatment order is an alternative to involuntary hospitalization (Fig. 3.2). Discharge from involuntary detention may occur either by decision of an authorized psychiatrist or on appeal to or review by the Mental Health Board.

Austria

In Austria, there is no separate mental health legislation. A statute regulating the operation of hospitals includes the provisions under which the placement in such an institution may be enforced (involuntary commitment).

The control of the legality of such coercive measures is in the hands of the district courts, and the judges have to apply the relevant rules of a law about the placement of mentally ill (Bundesgesetz über die Unterbringung psychisch Kranker in frankenanstalten) which came into force in 1991.

In Austria, approximately one-third of hospitalized psychiatric patients are involuntary. They are hospitalized by order of a public health officer. But commitment is also possible if two psychiatrists of the hospital separately come to the conclusion that it is necessary to prevent danger to life and health of the patient himself or other persons and if treatment in the community has been exhausted. In that case a 'patient-solicitor' has to be nominated immediately. The patient-solicitor is a social worker belonging to an association independent from the court and hospital. A first hearing of the patient by the local judge is ordered within 4 days and within a fortnight a regular trial with participation of expert psychiatrists, patient-solicitor, relatives of the patient and staff of the hospital has to take place at the hospital. The court has to decide if detention is necessary and the first term should not exceed 3 months. In a follow-up procedure a second term of 6 months is possible. Longer commitments must be controlled by the court at least once a year and after hearing at least two independent psychiatrist's opinions. Involuntary treatment of the committed person needs separate consent by the court, if there is no special situation of immediately threatening danger for life or health of the patient.

Bulgaria

A major objective of forensic psychiatry in Bulgaria is the prevention of offences and dangerous behaviour in persons suffering from mental disorders. Although it makes use of knowledge accumulated through forensic work in preparing court reports, preventive forensic psychiatry is basically a public health activity which takes place in two different kinds of setting: the hospital and the community. Hospital-based preventive measures include the mandatory treatment of psychiatric patients at high risk of harming either themselves or others as defined by the Public Health Act 1975. Involuntary hospitalization under these provisions can be initiated by the health authorities either upon a petition by the patient's next of kin, or upon a request in writing by the head of the psychiatric service with which the patient is in contact. In either instance, imminent danger or risk must be demonstrable, and the decision about hospitalization must be confirmed by the court. Patients hospitalized on orders for compulsory or mandatory treatment are admitted to general psychiatric units, under the same conditions as voluntary patients. Bulgaria has only one small special security unit for dangerous patients.

Persons suffering from alcohol or drug dependence are subject to legal preventive measures only if imminent danger can be demonstrated, to themselves or to other persons in their environment. In such instances, compulsory treatment may be mandated by the court on the basis of relevant texts in the Criminal Code and the Public Health Act 1975. The length of compulsory hospital admissions may not exceed one year, and it is regarded as a prelude to long-term treatment on an outpatient basis, which is the responsibility of the local psychiatric dispensary.

Provisions of the Public Health Act 1975 relevant to psychiatry are:

> Obligatory treatment of persons with mental disorders, as defined in the Rules of Application, may only be mandated upon an expertise (i.e. an independent assessment) by a commission of specialists. . . . Involuntary admission to a psychiatric unit is decided by the district Court.
>
> If the state of the mentally disordered person requires immediate measures, the medical director of a treatment unit may inform the district prosecutor who informs the Court of any decisions. . . . Once a year the Court must examine the continuation or discontinuation of compulsory treatment.
>
> Persons suffering from alcohol disease, or any other drug-related disease, who refuse voluntary treatment or evade it, to the detriment of their own families, to public order, and the community at large, may be subject to involuntary treatment. If the Court is in agreement with the public prosecutor's proposal, the Court determines the specialized health service unit and the term of the compulsory treatment. The term must not exceed one year.
>
> Compulsory treatment may only take place in specialized health services approved by the Ministry of Public Health.
>
> *Rules of Application of the Public Health Act*: Subject to obligatory treatment in appropriate health care services are persons . . . who, owing to mental disorder, may commit offences of significant public danger, or themselves represent a hazard to their own health.

Canada (*see* note on p. 166)

Although there are local variations among the provincial mental health acts, there are also certain consistent features. In the process of civil commitment, the power lies with physicians, the judiciary playing only a limited role in the context of review of applications and appeals. In most provinces, the legislation provides for initial short-term confinement (usually 24–72 hours) for the purpose of evaluation. If the formal criteria for admission are satisfied, admission certificates can be completed which authorize the patient's continued involuntary hospitalization. The maximum duration of this confinement varies considerably from province to province (2 weeks–1 year), but in most, the period may be extended by means of renewal certificates. In all jurisdictions, the police may apprehend mentally disturbed persons without a warrant. Again, however, there are interprovincial differences in the exact scope of this power and the conditions which must be satisfied before it can be exercised.

The criteria for formal admission to a psychiatric facility are set out with varying degrees of precision within the provincial mental health acts. All the acts require that there be evidence of mental disorder. Some provinces define this in terms of specific diagnostic categories, others favour description of symptoms.

'Dangerousness', the second criterion for formal admission, is prominent in most of the provincial mental health acts, although few use it as the only criterion and the meaning of the term varies from reference to the 'safety' of the patient or others to a very narrow definition.

Most Canadian jurisdictions establish a special review board to which involuntary patients can apply for review of their detention. These boards are usually comprised of 3–5 members including a lawyer, a lay person and a psychiatrist; the latter must not usually be a member of the staff of the facility making the application. In some provinces, review applications are brought before a court rather than a review board, in others it can be either. Most provinces require the patient or his representative to take the initiative in requesting review. Other provinces, such as Saskatchewan and Ontario provide for automatic reviews. The patient may have given written consent in all provinces for release of information from his clinical records to designated third parties. However, the patient's right to see his or her own record varies between the provinces.

Denmark

The legal basis of the non-penal involuntary hospitalization is now the Act on Deprivation of Liberty and Use of Other Compulsion within Psychiatry, which by October 1989 replaced the old act on Hospitalization of the Mentally Ill 1938. There had been some criticism of the old act in public, among lawyers and politicians (Vestergaard, 1984). One objection was that several committed persons were later regarded as non-psychotic in spite of the primary criterion of psychosis. Others stressed that the safeguards and controls were inadequate.

The criteria of compulsory admission and detention are essentially preserved in the new Act. A patient may be committed involuntarily to a psychiatric hospital, if he is psychotic or in a quite similar condition, and furthermore dangerous to himself or others, or in urgent need of treatment. Discharge of a voluntary or involuntary patient can be refused by the chief physician, if the patient fulfils the same criteria. It is an important feature of the law that psychosis is the first and necessary condition of involuntary treatment in hospital. As a consequence non-psychotic substance abusers cannot be committed.

Several new provisions for the treatment and use of compulsion during hospital stay are now included. On the whole, the control and the safeguards are strengthened—with more bureaucracy. The new act includes 42 sections, the old one had only 14.

Complaints concerning deprivation of liberty are not submitted directly to the courts and the use of other kinds of coercion, i.e. medical restraint and compulsory medication are supervised by regional bodies of complaint.

The percentage of commitments decreased in the 1970s and 1980s to a low rate in 1990 of about 3–4% of all admissions per year, one of the lowest recorded rates according to international comparisons. Schizophrenia and manic-depressive psychosis are the most frequent diagnosis among committed patients. It is an important feature that the duration of hospitalization of the committed patients on an average is not longer than for voluntarily admitted patients.

Switzerland

Each canton has separate legislation on civil commitment. Thus separate laws are applied to jurisdictions with an average population of less than ¼ million. Such laws can be subjected to popular votes.

The provisions vary considerably, e.g. dangerousness is a necessary criterion in less than half of the cantons. The cantonal laws must, however, correspond to the Swiss Civil Code, which since 1981 includes provisions on 'deprivation of liberty on the grounds of assistance'. These provisions follow those of the European Convention of Human Rights. Commitment on the grounds of mental illness must be based on a medical report. Committed patients must have access to a judicial review. Recent interpretations by the Federal Court have provided that such appeals must allow the patient to appear before the whole review tribunal rather than a delegated representative.

United States of America

Civil commitment in the US is governed by the mental health codes of each state. These codes define the commitment criteria as well as the legal procedures which must be followed prior to and during commitment, both commitment criteria and commitment procedures vary somewhat from state to state. In some states, for example, a judge or jury decides whether the patient will be committed; in others, an attorney or hearing officer will do so, outside of a courtroom. There is also much litigation by the courts which interprets the statutes (e.g. definition of mental illness and dangerousness). Courts also become involved in psychiatric malpractice or civil rights cases when there are allegations of improper commitment, and they provide release of the patient from the hospital or monetary compensation for wrongful commitments. There is currently considerable controversy about the expansion of commitment criteria to include the non-dangerous mentally ill who need treatment, as well as commitment for minor forms of dangerousness, such as property damage (Durham and La Fond, 1985; Peters et al., 1987). Model commitment laws have been proposed by the American Psychiatric Association (1983a), and the National Center for State Courts (National Center, 1986). Not every psychiatric hospital accepts committed patients; many private hospitals do not do so.

Once patients have been civilly committed to a psychiatric hospital, they have a qualified right to refuse treatment and psychotropic medication. The states vary widely in their recognition of this right to refuse treatment (Appelbaum, 1988). In some states (California, Colorado, Indiana, Massachusetts, Minnesota, New Hampshire, New York, Oklahoma, and Wisconsin), patients can refuse medication until a court has declared them incompetent to refuse treatment and a legal guardian has been appointed (Wettstein, 1989). In other states, the treatment team may need to obtain an independent psychiatric opinion of the patient's need for treatment or petition an administrative personnel hearing to override the patient's refusal.

Forensic Psychiatric Services and Institutions

In international perspective, forensic psychiatry is an ill-defined specialty. Its historical origins are as the specialist in mental health who facilitates the work of a court just as a forensic pathologist carries out autopsies when the findings are likely to interest a court. This function remains an important element in forensic psychiatry, as is illustrated in the descriptions already given of psychiatric court clinics in the USA or the METFORS facility in Toronto, Canada. Otherwise, special institutes for pretrial assessments are not features of the services in the seven countries surveyed. This is perhaps surprising in view of the widespread admiration for the work of the Pieter Baan Centre in Holland which performs about 200 seven-week long multidisciplinary assessments each year. The quality of these assessments is certainly a factor which allows the Dutch TBS units to function effectively (Beyaert, 1980). Most forensic psychiatrists carry out pretrial assessments in remand prisons, in psychiatric hospitals or in outpatient clinics.

The increasing diversity of units and institutions in the grey area between the traditional prison setting and the general psychiatric unit provides another kind of professional identity for forensic psychiatrists. A good example is the development of regional psychiatric units in French prisons, which has stimulated some remarkable therapeutic experiences with offender patients (Balier, 1988), another example being the development of regional secure units in England and Wales (*see* Ch. 18).

The description of Austrian special institutions within or parallel to the prison system illustrates some of the ethical issues and therapeutic problems which can arise in settings where patient motivation and compliance are systematically compromised and the forensic psychiatrist risks becoming closely identified with the penal system. These problems are also illustrated in the evolution of the Danish Herstedvester Institution. The European Committee on the Prevention of Torture and Inhuman or Degrading Treatment has made critical comments following its visits to Herstedvester about the ambiguous states of inmates and the difficulty of treatment without consent in a prison setting. Similar comments were made about Brixton prison's F Wing in England (see *Lancet* 1991).

Bulgaria offers an example of forensic psychiatry integrated into a National Health Service. The beginnings of forensic psychiatry in Bulgaria are traceable to the 1890s, i.e. shortly after the nation regained its independence from the Ottoman Empire as a result of the Russo-Turkish war (1876–1878). The strong impulses of the new statehood, the rebuilding of a national administration, and the development of a modern legal system awakened an early interest in criminal anthropology (Pasmanik, 1899) and forensic psychiatry. The academic interest in the field was sustained by the leadership of Schipkowensky (1938, 1963, 1975). The concepts, methodology and practice of Bulgarian forensic psychiatry today are broadly determined by the structure and organization of psychiatric care which is part of the National Health Service (Donchev, 1983). The emphasis in the development of mental health care during the past decades has been placed on outpatient and community services. The role of the psychiatric hospital in Bulgaria has always been more limited than in Western Europe. A network of forensic psychiatry units has been in existence for the past 25 years, as part of the psychiatric 'dispensaries' (mental health centres). Each unit has a forensic psychiatrist on its staff, who works in a team with a community nurse and, in most instances, a social worker. Each forensic psychiatry unit serves two principal objectives: (1) prevention of dangerous behaviour of psychiatric patients in the community; (2) follow-up care for legally incapacitated patients. Central support is provided by the forensic psychiatry section of the Institute of the Neurology, Psychiatry and Neurosurgery of the Bulgarian Medical Academy. The section also operates as a postgraduate training course for psychiatrists and clinical psychologists, and collects and analyses statistical information. Forensic psychiatric research is carried out by academic departments of psychiatry attached to the medical schools. There are now over 200 psychiatrists who, apart from their day-to-day work, may be called as forensic experts on an *ad hoc* basis. In addition, 30 psychiatrists have forensic work as their principal professional activity. Forensic psychiatric evaluation in the context of criminal and civil law is the mainstream of forensic psychiatry in Bulgaria. Psychiatric expert opinion can only be requested by the court or by the examining magistrate (i.e. not by the parties involved in the legal action), and assessments must be carried out by the National Health Service. The overall management and regulation of forensic psychiatric work, and the training of specialists, are the responsibility of the Ministry of Health and Social Welfare. Forensic psychiatry opinion also plays an important role in Bulgarian civil law, e.g. in legal decision concerning competence.

Two types of organizational model exist in Canada (Phillips, 1983), a centralized system in which one institution coordinates forensic services for the entire province and a decentralized system with no coordination at all. In recent years, there has been a trend towards centralization. The Forensic Psychiatric Service Commission of British Columbia and the system in Quebec, based on the Institut Philippe Pinel in Montreal are examples of the centralized model. On the other hand, Ontario, a large province of nearly nine million, currently has no organizational structure. Most assessments for the courts in that province are conducted in university-based forensic units, such as the Royal Ottawa Hospital and the Clarke Institute of Psychiatry in Toronto. The latter incorporates METFORS referred to earlier (p. 126).

Provision of psychiatric services to convicted prisoners is complicated by the fact that there are two organizations responsible for them. In Canada, sentences of 2 years or less are served in reformatories which are the responsibility of Ministries of Corrections of the individual provinces. Some provinces provide services to reformatories through a centralized agency, others contract with psychiatrists from university centres or private practice. In some instances, mentally ill inmates are transferred to secure provincial psychiatric hospitals. Elsewhere, such individuals would be treated in the reformatories themselves, as the availability of secure hospital beds is very limited.

Longer sentences are served in federal penitentiaries which are the responsibility of Correctional Services of Canada. Within the federal penitentiary system, there is a more clearly identifiable system. The Chalke report (1973) recommended that each of the country's five penitentiary regions (Atlantic, Quebec, Ontario, Prairies and Pacific) develop regional psychiatric centres which would provide assessments for the courts and parole boards, treatment of convicted prisoners and also those detained on warrants of the Lieutenant Governor. Three such centres were opened (Abbotsford, British Columbia; Saskatoon, Saskatchewan; and Kingston, Ontario). Plans are currently being drawn up for a further centre for the Atlantic Region. In Quebec, the adopted system has been to contract with the Provincial Ministry of Health to provide services at the Institut Philippe Pinel in Montreal, a maximum security psychiatric hospital. The Chalke report, thus, recommended that all types of forensic services, whether they be for the courts, or for convicted prisoners or for those found not guilty by reason of insanity, be centralized in these regional facilities within the prison system. Those which already exist share costs to a varying degree with the appropriate provincial ministries.

In Denmark, forensic psychiatry has a limited number of executants. There are no academic chairs. Two departments of forensic psychiatry are connected with the psychiatric hospitals in Aarhus and at Nykøbing, and a clinic of forensic psychiatry is attached to the Ministry of Justice, Copenhagen.

The Medico-Legal Council plays an important part in Danish forensic psychiatry. It is an independent advisory body consisting of 11 ordinary members and a number of experts covering the whole field of medicine. Seven of the ordinary members are psychiatrists. Psychiatric cases are the largest group considered by the council—about 40% of all cases. All members and experts are paid by the Ministry of Justice and are independent of personal or economic interest in the cases. Only courts and other public authorities can ask for the opinion of the Council. The main group of psychiatric cases consists of mentally abnormal offenders. Involuntary hospitalizations constitute another significant category of cases brought to the Council's attention.

In the vast majority of cases, the opinion of the Council is given on the basis of written material. Typically, two or three members are involved in a case. The influence of the statements of the Council is considered; as a consequence, the appearance of doctors as expert witnesses in court is considered necessary only in a few cases. On rare occasions, the members of the Council are examined by the court—it is then considered as a college. The Council ensures uniform guidelines in the different regions and a satisfactory quality of psychiatric reports and opinions.

The Medico-Legal Council has been subject to some criticism. Thus, questions have been raised as to how disinterested a body of doctors could be when evaluating their colleagues. It has also been pointed out as a limitation that the work of the council is almost exclusively an assessment of documents, not of persons. Others have found it unsatisfactory that the members do not appear in court. More openness has been requested. However, many are satisfied that the Council, as an independent link between psychiatry and the legal system, has been of great value (Lund, 1985). A committee under the Ministry of Justice was set up in 1989 to examine the criticisms and the general function of the Council. Its report, published in 1990, confirmed several of the criticisms mentioned above, but no change has yet taken place.

In Switzerland, a small sociotherapeutic unit has been developed at the Geneva prison for the treatment of sentenced prisoners with severe personality disorders (see p. 753). Two small secure psychiatric units in the Cantons of Geneva and Zurich exist for the treatment of mentally ill prisoners. Most mentally abnormal offenders considered irresponsible are transferred to ordinary psychiatric hospitals. General psychiatrists have some practical experience in preparing court reports during their postgraduate training and some continue to do this work on a part-time basis. At the University of Geneva, forensic psychiatry is attached to forensic medicine to form a specialty termed 'legal medicine' which exists also in Genoa and Lyon (Franchini et al., 1984). Forensic psychiatric experience is included in the training of legal medicine specialists.

Treatment of the mentally disordered offender (incompetent to stand trial, NGRI, GBMI, transfers from prison) in the USA is provided in the state or federal jurisdiction in which the offence has occurred, and is typically ordered on an involuntary basis. In 1980, such individuals constituted 7% of all psychiatric admissions (Steadman *et al.*, 1988). A range of treatment facilities is available in most states, from a specialized, maximum security forensic hospital, to a medium security forensic hospital, to secure units of general psychiatric hospitals. The selection of a particular facility depends upon the patient or prisoner's mental disorder, history of violence, as well as political, social and economic factors. Most mentally disordered offenders in the USA are treated in public rather than private hospitals (Steadman *et al.*, 1988). Hospital admission and discharge of offenders (except for prisoners transferred to hospital for treatment) is accomplished through the criminal courts, which have become increasingly unwilling to release patients who are at risk of future violence. Outpatient treatment of the mentally disordered offender is available in public mental health clinics or privately, for those patients who can afford to obtain this care. Sexual offender treatment programmes have developed in many areas of the country to treat outpatients, both charged and uncharged with a criminal offence. Generally, there are few specialized treatment programmes for outpatient mentally ill offenders. The National Institute of Mental Health has published a directory of programmes and facilities for mentally disordered offenders in the USA (National Institute of Mental Health, 1986).

The USA has evolved an organized postgraduate training and certification system in forensic psychiatry, so that forensic psychiatry has a clearly defined identity. Recent years have witnessed significant growth in education and training programmes for psychiatrists and doctoral-level psychologists interested in criminal and civil law issues. Fellowship or postgraduate training programmes at many medical centres and university psychology departments now offer either full-time or part-time didactic and clinical experience in forensic mental health settings including court clinics, forensic hospitals, and correctional institutions. Specialist training in forensic psychiatry is certified through an examination sponsored by the American Board of Forensic Psychiatry. The corresponding organization for psychologists is the American Board of Forensic Psychology.

Illustrative Cases

In order to strengthen the comparative framework of this chapter, we have considered four cases of mentally disordered offenders described in brief vignettes. For each country, the most likely sequence of events in criminal procedure and management of these cases has been described in tabular form. Where one or more alternative sequences are of particular interest, these are indicated in parentheses. To link this chapter with the rest of the book, comments on the position in the UK are also included. The following abbreviations are used in the tables:

Review bodies:
  MLC = Medico-Legal Council (*Denmark*)
  MHT = Mental Health Tribunal (*Queensland, Australia*)
  PRT = Patient Review Tribunal (*Queensland, Australia*)
  CSP = Conseil de Surveillance Psychiatrique (*Geneva, Switzerland*)
  LGBR = Lieutenant Governor's Board of Review (*Canada*)

Court decisions:
  NGRI = not guilty by reason of insanity
  GBMI = guilty but mentally ill
  Irr.   = irresponsible (and not punishable)

Please note that the law in Canada has changed since this chapter was written. Please refer to pp. 1026–7.

Case 1

A 28-year-old single man, with a long criminal record and previous prison sentences, a history of intermittent opiate abuse and dependence over 10 years, in whom the DSM-III R criteria for antisocial personality disorder are amply met, charged with robbery with violence, an offence committed while under the influence of alcohol (Table 3.1).

This man would probably have a pretrial psychiatric assessment in only one or two countries. One reason for such an assessment would be to assess the degree of alcohol intoxication at the moment of the offence. In the USA and Canada, a *mens rea* defence (diminished capacity of intent) could be put forward. If successful, this defence could reduce the gravity of the charge substantially. Similarly, a high level of alcohol intoxication could lead to a conclusion of no criminal responsibility in Austria or diminished responsibility in Switzerland. However, the man would almost uniformly be expected to serve a prison sentence of several years' duration (the possibility of probation with treatment is mentioned in the USA). In England and Wales, there is a small chance of a restricted hospital order or a later transfer leading to treatment in a maximum security hospital (this would not happen in Scotland or Northern Ireland). Only in Austria is there a strong possibility that the man would be transferred to a special institution for treatment of drug and alcohol abuse problems. This transfer would be ordered by the court, probably for the duration of the prison sentence. Treatment programmes would be available on the man's request during the prison sentence in Canada, Bulgaria, Switzerland and the USA. In Canada, adherence to a treatment programme would probably be a prerequisite for early parole. In Denmark, treatment would be provided as part of after-care during parole after two-thirds of the sentence.

Table 3.1
Case 1

	Psychiatric assessment before court proceedings	*Legal decision*	*Management*	*Remarks*
Australia (Queensland)	Unlikely	Guilty: prison sentence	Normal prison regime	
Austria	Possible	Guilty, responsible; with substance abuse in need of treatment: prison sentence with concurrent treatment order	Sentence served in special institution for substance abusers	Severe alcohol intoxication at time of offence could lead to conclusion of 'irresponsibility'
Bulgaria	Possible	Guilty: prison sentence	Possible rehabilitation programme in prison	
Canada	Possible	Guilty: prison sentence	Offender could apply for treatment in prison—necessary for early parole	Diminished capacity plea might reduce gravity of charge
Denmark	Possible (with review by MLC)	Guilty: prison sentence	Normal prison regime--treatment during parole after ⅔ sentence	Possible transfer to special prison (Herstedvester) if psychiatric treatment indicated
Switzerland (Geneva)	Unlikely	Guilty: prison sentence	Could apply for transfer to treatment unit for personality disorder or substance abuse	
UK	Probable psychiatric report to court	Guilty: prison sentence	Normal prison regime	In England & Wales such a man could find his way to a special hospital under the psychopath arrangements in the MHA
USA	Unlikely	Guilty: prison sentence	Treatment available in prison	Diminished capacity plea might reduce gravity of charge

Case 2

A 30-year-old married woman with three children, with no previous convictions, has drowned her one-month-old son while in a state corresponding to a major depressive episode with psychotic (mood congruent) features in the context of a bipolar affective disorder (DSM-III R criteria) (Table 3.2).

This woman would certainly have a pretrial psychiatric assessment in all countries. In two countries the assessment would be performed in an inpatient setting. Occasionally, a hospital assessment would occur in the UK. In six countries the woman would almost certainly be considered either as without criminal responsibility and, therefore, not punishable, or not guilty by reason of insanity. In Canada, the USA, and the UK a prison sentence would be possible, after conviction for infanticide (Canada and UK) or following a *mens rea* defence (diminished capacity to form intent), leading to conviction on a lesser charge than murder (USA and UK). The possibility also exists in the USA and the UK that the jury would consider the psychiatric condition irrelevant. In the USA a further possibility is a NGRI verdict with an involuntary treatment order (hospital or outpatient).

In six countries, the woman would be transferred to a normal psychiatric hospital and the subsequent treatment programme would be reviewed by a special review body. Commitment to a secure forensic psychiatric facility is the most likely outcome in the USA, and is a definite possibility in the UK.

Table 3.2
Case 2

	Psychiatric assessment before court proceedings	Legal decision	Management	Remarks
Australia (Queensland)	Review by MHT (includes psychiatric examination)	NGRI	Hospitalization	Regular review by PRT
Austria	Psychiatric report to examining magistrate	No criminal responsibility	Hospitalization	Further review by court
Bulgaria	Psychiatric report to examining magistrate	No criminal responsibility	Hospitalization	6-monthly review
Canada	Psychiatric report to court	Infanticide: prison sentence 5 years	Prison with possible transfer to mental health system	NGRI defence might be raised
Denmark	Remand in psychiatric hospital for assessment and treatment Review by MLC	No criminal responsibility	Sentenced to compulsory treatment (in- or outpatient)	Court decision to cancel measure after review by MLC
Switzerland (Geneva)	Psychiatric report after transfer to hospital unit	No criminal responsibility	Hospitalization	Supervision by CSP
UK	Psychiatric report to court	Infanticide or diminished responsibility	Hospitalization	Wide variations are possible e.g. imprisonment and secure hospitalization with restriction
USA	Psychiatric report to court	NGRI (in 47/50 states) or GBMI (in 13/50 states) Diminished capacity with acquittal or lesser charge	Committed to secure forensic psychiatric facility Mandatory outpatient treatment	Judge or jury might consider psychiatric condition irrelevant and sentence to prison

Case 3

A 35-year-old divorced man suffering from schizophrenic disorder, paranoid type, chronic course with acute exacerbations (DSM-III R criteria), who had previously knifed his father 'because he (the father) was transformed into a rat', has on numerous occasions punched strangers in public places while under the influence of delusional beliefs and has recently fatally wounded a stranger in the street while a voice told him he would be 'walled alive unless he killed a man'. His violent behaviour has always been associated with active psychotic symptoms. Treatment including neuroleptics is usually effective in producing remission, but the man is non-compliant in treatment programmes (Table 3.3).

Pretrial psychiatric assessment would lead to a conclusion of not guilty by reason of insanity or lack of criminal responsibility in seven countries (with exception of three states in the USA where this defence is not available). In the UK this could happen but is unlikely, the usual outcome would be a conviction for manslaughter on grounds of diminished responsibility. The patient would be treated in an ordinary psychiatric hospital in two countries, while in six countries transfer to a special security hospital for a period of many years is likely.

Table 3.3
Case 3

	Psychiatric assessment before court proceedings	Legal decision	Management	Remarks
Australia (Queensland)	Review by MHT (includes psychiatric examination)	NGRI	Hospitalization in Security Patients' Hospital	Regular review by PRT
Austria	Psychiatric report to examining magistrate	No criminal responsibility	Treatment in psychiatric security unit for indefinite period	Court decision required for release
Bulgaria	Psychiatric report to examining magistrate	No criminal responsibility	Hospitalization	6-monthly review
Canada	Psychiatric examination in prison of forensic psychiatric facility	NGRI	Maximum security psychiatric hospital	Review by LGBR Possible transfer to less secure facility (Could refuse treatment in Ontario, if competent)
Denmark	Psychiatric assessment in Security Detention Institute Review by MLC	No criminal responsibility	Treatment in Security Detention Institute— possibly for years	Transfer to ordinary hospital and outpatient treatment: court decision, review by MLC
Switzerland (Geneva)	Psychiatric report to examining magistrate	No criminal responsibility	Hospitalization (security measure: prison and prison hospital unit if considered highly dangerous)	Review by CSP
UK	Psychiatric report to court	Manslaughter by reason of diminished responsibility	Secure hospitalization; later release on licence	Remains liable to recall for many years after release from hospital
USA	Psychiatric report to court	NGRI (in 47/50 states) *or* GBMI (in 13/50 states) (diminished capacity plea)	Committed to secure forensic psychiatric facility (prison with treatment)	

Case 4

A 30-year-old married man who is arrested for the first time admits a series of sexual offences against children involving threats, orogenital contacts and buggery. According to DSM-III R criteria he presents paedophilia and personality disorder (dependant type), but no other psychiatric disorder. He appears motivated to undertake treatment for his sexual deviation (Table 3.4).

A pretrial psychiatric assessment would be carried out in five or six countries. A prison sentence would be expected in all countries, although the possibility of treatment in a secure hospital or a restricted hospital order exists in the UK. Treatment could be provided in prison on the man's request in three countries, while in two other countries the man would be transferred to a special prison facility with a treatment programme. In the USA and Canada such a case would probably have been dealt with by probation with a treatment order until a few years ago.

The processing and management of these four criminal cases presenting various form of psychopathology is, therefore, broadly similar despite differences in legal provisions and procedures. In countries with well developed secure facilities, mentally abnormal offenders are less likely to be treated early after the offence in an ordinary psychiatric hospital.

Pretrial psychiatric assessments appear to be most likely in Denmark and Austria and least in Australia (Queensland), although in the case of offences clearly related to psychotic disorder such assessment would be carried out everywhere. The role in this respect of the Mental Health Tribunal in Queensland, Australia and the Medico-legal Council in Denmark is noteworthy. The latter body also intervenes in posttrial decisions and, therefore, occupies a key position in decision-making for individual cases and standard-setting and policy-formulation in general. The Austrian system is noteworthy in that treatment in a special institution was indicated for every case, while in five of the countries at least two of the cases would have served a sentence in a normal prison.

Conclusion

This chapter shows that forensic psychiatry is about fundamental issues in the relationship between society and the individual and not simply about interpreting mental health laws and criminal codes. Ideal legislation does not exist and international models of detailed provisions are probably undesirable. Some 'bottom-line' guarantees of human rights are useful, as in the European Convention. Forensic psychiatrists should seek a dialogue not only with lawyers and the judiciary, but also with politicians and the general public on underlying issues such as risk management and the degree of acceptable danger in the community. Psychiatrists have to accept that some issues are subject to irrational swings in public opinion, for example the move towards more punitive responses for sex offenders. The USA illustrates the major ethical problems that the forensic psychiatrist faces in relation to

Table 3.4
Case 4

	Psychiatric assessment before court proceedings	Legal decision	Management	Remarks
Australia (Queensland)	Unlikely	Guilty: prison sentence	Normal prison	
Austria	Psychiatric report to examining magistrate	Guilty: responsible, with mental abnormality needing treatment Treatment order	Compulsory treatment Indefinite period in special treatment centre in penal system	Court review
Bulgaria	Unlikely	Guilty: prison sentence	Normal prison	Treatment not available
Canada	Possible	Guilty: prison sentence	Normal prison (suspended sentence with compulsory treatment)	Psychotherapy or antihormonal treatment in prison and on parole
Denmark	Possible with review by MLC	Guilty: prison sentence	Transfer to special prison: Herstedvester	Release and treatment during after-care after ⅔ sentence
Switzerland (Geneva)	Psychiatric report to examining magistrate	Guilty: prison sentence	Treatment on request while in prison	Follow-up treatment available in outpatient clinic for ex-prisoners
UK	Probable court report	Guilty: prison sentence	Imprisonment Segregated for own security Slim possibility of group treatment	Slim possibility of treatment in secure hospital
USA	Possible	Guilty: prison sentence	Treatment on request	In some states, indeterminate commitment under Sexual Psychopath Statute possible

the death penalty. Its introduction in other countries could create an acute professional crisis and psychiatrists might consider taking pre-emptive action in order to clarify their position prior to such a change.

Abuses of psychiatry in a few countries have recently illustrated how badly things can go wrong in the relationship between the State and psychiatrists. These examples show, on the one hand, that professional autonomy from State organs is essential and, on the other hand, that legal supervision of non-voluntary forms of intervention must be accepted by the profession. In addition, we have shown that societies accept that certain antisocial behaviours which are the direct consequence of clearly defined serious mental illness can be dealt with by psychiatric treatment rather than by penal sanctions. Deciding how wide the definition of mental illness should be and how diverse the institutional treatment setting should be depends upon the generosity implicit in any medical treatment model, medical attitudes, medical knowledge and social attitudes about unacceptable behaviour.

The comparative approach, therefore, yields an impression that forensic psychiatry should be modest in its aspirations, should accept inevitable tensions and contradictions in its interactions with the judicial and penal systems and should beware of 'ideal' legal or institutional models. Practising forensic psychiatry means facing an irreducible degree of unjustness and unpredictability in the human condition, seeking a minimum level of observance of human rights for the most ostracized people in society, and applying proven therapeutic methods according to accepted diagnostic criteria and ethical standards of general psychiatry.

Note

Since this text went to press the Canadian criminal code has been radically amended. Details of these changes are given in Appendix 6, p. 1026.

4

The Courts and Bodies Overseeing and Administering the Laws in the United Kingdom (and Ireland)

Edited by	*Written by*
Ann Barker	Ann Barker
John Gunn	John Gunn
	John Hamilton
	Stephen Stanley

With additional material from:

Fred Browne (*N. Ireland*); Derek Chiswick (*Scotland*);
Enda Dooley (*Republic of Ireland*)

This chapter is largely concerned with those courts and bodies which oversee and administer the law in England and Wales. A few comments are added at the end in respect of the broad differences with other parts of the British Isles. Readers from other countries may, therefore, find this chapter of marginal interest except in so far as it illustrates principles of administration which should be understood for their own sake. It may also be helpful to the non-English reader as a cross-reference to terms and arrangements which are referred to in the more clinical chapters.

Traditionally, English courts of law are divided into the criminal and the civil courts. However, a significant development in this century has been a considerable increase in 'administrative justice' dispensed in special courts or quasi courts outside the ordinary system (*see* Smith and Keenan, 1982 for an account). Examples of such courts are the social security tribunals, adjudicating over claims for sickness or unemployment benefit. Mental health review tribunals (MHRTs) are another example, and are reviewed later in this chapter. Other institutions, such as the Home Office and the Probation Service, are also important in administering the law as it relates to the mentally disordered offender, and their role is similarly reviewed.

It is probably true to say that 'the reach of the law into everyday lives continues to increase, so that there are today few activities wholly unregulated by the law' (White, 1985). New laws are enacted with such rapidity that it is wise to recall that lawyers are paid to be familiar with the changes, and that lawyers are themselves as specialized as doctors. Similarly, the bodies which implement the laws change with the changing needs of society. Coroners' courts, for example, now have diminished powers; family courts are a possible innovation of the future. Nevertheless, it should be noted that the English legal system also makes widespread use of lay men and women in both criminal and civil cases: justices of the peace (magistrates) deal with the bulk of criminal cases in English courts; juries determine issues of fact in the Crown Court, and are used on rare occasions in civil cases. Expert lay members can be called upon to sit with High Court judges in Admiralty and commercial cases; and lay members sit alongside lawyer chairmen in tribunals. The contribution of lay people is regarded as important, providing 'an antidote to excessive technicality' and 'some guarantee that law does not diverge too far from reality' (Stein, 1984).

This chapter can only present very rudimentary information about the bodies which administer the law, and point to sources of more detailed information. For most work involving mentally abnormal offenders, however, all that is necessary is a grasp of the basic principles.

Criminal and Civil Proceedings in England and Wales

Civil law and civil proceedings aim to determine the rights and obligations of individuals as between each other. Examples are the determination of rights arising under a contract, of obligations to pay damages for torts, such as negligence, nuisance or defamation, or questions of status such as divorce, adoption and the custody of children. Psychiatrists may be asked to testify in some of these cases. Under criminal law, in contrast, the proceedings are concerned with wrongs regarded as committed by the individual against society (the people in the USA, the crown in the UK). So, whereas the objective of civil proceedings is to provide a remedy for the person wronged, usually in the form of damages, the objective of criminal proceedings is to determine the guilt or innocence of the accused person, and if that person is found to be guilty, to punish the wrongdoer and perhaps prevent further criminal activity.

This fundamental distinction in English law between civil and criminal proceedings can seem somewhat unhelpful on occasions. It can, for example, be a highly traumatic experience for the relative of someone who has died in a road traffic accident to find that the driver of the car, who has been charged only with 'driving without due care and attention', receives in the criminal court a penalty of only, say, £100 fine and has his licence endorsed. The redress for the relatives lies not in the criminal court, but in the civil court, for the loss of life.

The building itself in which proceedings occur is not an indication of the difference: many civil proceedings take place, for example, in magistrates' courts. The distinction between civil and criminal proceedings is marked by a difference in terminology.

In almost all British courts, proceedings are conducted on an adversarial system. In the criminal courts a prosecutor institutes a prosecution against a defendant or accused person. The outcome is the determination of guilt or innocence. The prosecution almost invariably has the burden of proof (i.e. must prove the facts on which the claim is based), which in criminal proceedings must be to a standard which is beyond all reasonable doubt. A finding that the accused person is not guilty is termed an acquittal. If the offence is proved, the court imposes a sentence.

In most civil proceedings the person beginning the proceedings is the plaintiff who sues or brings an action against a defendant, seeking a remedy, usually in the form of damages, but possibly also in the form of an injunction (an order prohibiting the defendant from committing or continuing to commit some wrongful act). Most civil proceedings are heard by a judge sitting alone; only very rarely, and usually in defamation cases, is there a jury in civil proceedings. In civil proceedings, the plaintiff usually has the burden of proof, to a lower standard than in a criminal court simply on the balance of probabilities. The judge hears the action and delivers a judgment.

Either type of case may go to appeal, when the terminology again changes. The party appealing is called the appellant and the other party who responds is called the respondent. Appeals to the House of Lords are by petition and the Law Lords give opinions rather than deliver judgments.

Civil and criminal courts are structured in a clear hierarchy in which the decisions of the superior courts are binding on inferior courts. The inferior courts are limited in their jurisdiction both geographically, by amounts of money involved and in other powers. The Crown Court is a hybrid. The higher courts fulfil an apellate function in that, on appeal, they may review the decisions of the lower courts, and a supervisory function, ensuring that inferior courts and tribunals do not act wrongly in law or in excess of their jurisdiction. The decisions of the superior courts are published regularly in legal proceedings such as the All England Law Reports and Criminal Appeal Reports. The Supreme Court of Judicature is the collective title given to the Court of Appeal, the High Court and the Crown Court. The structure of the court hierarchy is summarized in Table 4.1.

Criminal Courts

Classification of criminal offences

Such romantic terms from the past as felonies, misdemeanours, Assizes and Quarter Sessions disappeared from England following the Beeching report (Royal Commission on Assizes and Quarter Sessions, 1969), when one of the most comprehensive reforms in British judicial administration was

Table 4.1
The Hierarchy of the Courts

THE HOUSE OF LORDS

Type: superior court
Judges: law lords
Jurisdiction: appellate only; unlimited
Audience: barristers only

COURT OF APPEAL

Type: superior court, part of the Supreme Court of Judicature,
divided into:

Civil Division

Judges: Master of the Rolls lords justice of
appeal
Jurisdiction: appellate only, civil,
unlimited
Audience: barristers only

Criminal Division

Judges: Lord Chief Justice and lords
justice of appeal
Jurisdiction: appellate only, criminal,
unlimited
Audience: barristers only

HIGH COURT

Type: superior court, part of
Supreme Court of Judicature,
divided into: Chancery Division
Queen's Bench Division
Family Division
Judges: puisne judges
Jurisdiction: appellate supervisory and first
instance civil and criminal, unlimited
Audience: barristers only

CROWN COURT

Type: superior court *except* when
exercising appellate jurisdiction; part of
Supreme Court of Judicature
Judges: puisne judges, circuit judges,
recorders, lay justices
Jurisdiction: appellate, first instance,
almost always criminal, unlimited
Audience: barristers, and sometimes
solicitors

COUNTY COURTS

Type: inferior courts
Judges: circuit judges
Jurisdiction: first instance, civil and
limited geographically and by amount of
claims
Audience: barristers and solicitors

MAGISTRATES' COURTS

Type: inferior courts
Judges: justices of the peace, stipendiary
magistrates
Jurisdiction: first instance, civil and
criminal limited by function and
seriousness of offence
Audience: barristers and solicitors

(From White, 1985 reproduced with permission of the author and publisher, Basil Blackwell Ltd.)

implemented in the Courts Act 1971. There are now two tiers of courts of original or first instance jurisdiction in England and Wales: magistrates' courts, and the Crown Court.

In line with this new division of the courts, there are now only three classes of offences in England and Wales, which determine the mode of trial: indictable, summary, and either-way. It is the nature and seriousness of the offence which determines whether a case will be dealt with by a magistrates' court or the Crown Court. Indictable offences may be tried only in the Crown Court, summary offences only in the magistrates' court, and either-way offences may be tried in either. Accused persons or magistrates can ask for an either-way offence to be tried in the Crown Court. Offences are periodically reclassified under Acts of Parliament and over the years there has been a tendency to restrict the types of cases for which trial by jury is available. The detailed revisions of the law are published annually in, for example, *Stone's Justices' Manual*—in three volumes (Richman and Draycott, 1988).

The police

The central role of the police is sometimes overlooked in descriptions of the criminal justice system. Police functions were defined in the final report of the Royal Commission on the Police (1962); the range is broad, but includes 'detection of crime and interrogation of suspected persons', as well as 'befriending anyone who needs their help, and coping with emergencies both major and minor'.

In administering the law, the police are those who take the first policy decisions. When a policeman decides to take no action, the possibility of prosecution ends forthwith unless the victim decides to bring a private prosecution, but this is so difficult that it is a rare event. The police have considerable discretion in investigating and prosecuting criminal offences; chief constables, for example, have a discretion in how their force should in general be allocated to fulfil the various functions of the police; in individual cases, in the face of undoubted evidence, there is a discretion as to whether a prosecution should be brought. Further, the investigation of crimes by searching for offenders by 'stereotypes' may well be the fruitful product of experience; it may also, however, help to explain, for example, the discrepant numbers of ethnic minorities entering the criminal justice system (Smith, 1985).

For the mentally disordered offender in the UK, the police have the power not to charge, but to take the offender to a place of safety, for example under S.136 of the Mental Health Act 1983 (England and Wales). Too little is known about police activity in relation to the mentally disordered in their caring capacity (Teplin, 1985; Fahy and Dunn 1987; Fahy et al., 1987). Clearly, in an era of deinstitutionalization and community care for psychiatric patients, the role of the police is important.

Offenders reach the courts either by being charged at a police station, or having had a summons issued against them after information has been laid in court. Alternatively, the police have a discretionary power to caution. A police caution is a formal warning given to a person who admits to having committed a criminal offence, which could have led to a prosecution. Police cautioning was adopted in Liverpool in 1951 among juvenile first offenders.

The policy has been adopted among adults with varying degrees of enthusiasm in other parts of Britain, such that the rate of cautioning (defined as the number of persons cautioned as a percentage of those found guilty or cautioned) varies from 45 to 85% over England and Wales. The overall numbers are quite large; for example, 29% of all indictable offences notified by the police in 1988 received a caution only.

In the Codes of Practice issued under the Police and Criminal Evidence Act 1984, the police have an obligation to protect the mentally ill, the mentally handicapped and juveniles, by ensuring, for example, that there is an 'appropriate adult' present when they are being interviewed in a police station in connection with an offence. The police are dealt with more extensively in Ch. 19.

The Crown Prosecution Service

A Crown Prosecution Service for England and Wales was established under the Prosecution of Offences Act 1985. A prosecution service deploys the power of the state to put people on trial, acting on behalf of the Crown. Previously in England and Wales, the police service had prosecuted individuals in its capacity as a 'private' agency, a right shared by many agencies and every citizen. The transfer of police prosecutions to an independent body is therefore, in principle, immensely significant (Sanders, 1986).

The Crown Prosecution Service is headed by the Director of Public Prosecutions; England and Wales are divided into areas, each headed by a Chief Crown Prosecutor. All members of the Service are civil servants. Its chief function is to take over the conduct of virtually all criminal proceedings which are instituted on behalf of a police force at the stage of charge or issue of summons. It even has powers in magistrates' courts to discontinue proceedings (Sanders, 1986). The Crown Prosecution Service is directed by its Code of Practice to pay attention to mental disorder. It is advised to observe general humanitarian grounds for dropping a charge, such as the age or circumstances of the suspect. In particular, however, it—

> should have regard to any medical reports which have been made available by the defence solicitor, and may arrange through the defence solicitor for an independent medical examination where this is necessary.

The right of 'private' prosecution is seen by many as a fundamental constitutional right (*see* Samuels, 1986), and HM Government rejected the Philips' Commission's (Royal Commission on Criminal Procedure, 1981) recommendation to abolish the right of private prosecutions. Non-Crown prosecutions constitute one-fifth to one-quarter of all cases coming before the criminal courts, mostly involving relatively minor matters, the vast majority in the magistrates' courts (Samuels, 1986). About one-quarter of crime is thus prosecuted 'privately' as shown in Table 4.2. The agencies bringing these prosecutions are diverse and include, for example, local

Table 4.2
Percentage of Non-Crown Prosecutions

	%
Television licences	25
Vehicle excise licence	18
Transport	17
Local authority	11
Retail stores	10
Social security fraud	7
Customs & excise, VAT	3
Individuals	2

authorities (food and drugs, or false trade descriptions) and the Royal Society for the Prevention of Cruelty to Animals. They retain the power to conduct the prosecution in court, but they vary widely in practice. Some, for example, appear to be quick to prosecute (e.g. the Department of Social Security in social security fraud); yet others see prosecution as a very last resort (e.g. the Health and Safety at Work Inspectorate). Such a diversity of practice raises important questions of public interest and social justice. For example, tax frauds are often not prosecuted, thefts from shops frequently are. In the overwhelming majority of tax contraventions, prosecution is seen as the ultimate sanction and used infrequently (Samuels, 1986).

Legal aid

Fear of costs, often arising out of ignorance, is one of the major factors inhibiting clients from consulting lawyers. It is estimated, for example, that over 750 000 accidents occur each year in which the victim believes some other person was wholly or partly to blame; such accidents result in only 250 000 compensation claims (Royal Commission on Civil Liability and Compensation for Personal Injury, 1978). The legal aid scheme of England and Wales, first set up in 1949, is administered by the Law Society, under the general control of the Lord Chancellor; it is financed by the Treasury. Those administering the scheme give regular exhortations to be frugal in granting legal aid. Its impact has been greatest in personal injuries and matrimonial proceedings, and in the defence of those charged with serious criminal offences: almost all defendants appearing in the Crown Court are legally aided (White, 1985).

Under the so-called 'green form' scheme, any person is entitled to ask for advice on any question of English law. Provided the person is eligible, based on a simple means test, a solicitor can provide £50 worth of his services without any prior authority; he can give advice on any subject, draft letters or documents, although he may not take proceedings in court without the court's permission. If the costs are greater than £50, the solicitor can apply to the Law Society for authority to spend the additional sum. There is no limit to the number of different problems which can be taken to a solicitor under this scheme (for example, a check on welfare benefits, making a will, changing name, complaints against the police).

In criminal proceedings, application for legal aid is made either orally or in writing to the Clerk of the Court, and the defendant must submit a written statement of his means. Before getting it, however, the court must be satisfied that legal aid is necessary 'in the interests of justice', defined by the Widgery Criteria (Smith and Keenan, 1982). These criteria include defendants who are unable to follow the proceedings and state their own case because of 'inadequate knowledge of English, mental illness, or other mental or physical disability'. The court's refusal to grant legal aid can be reviewed only if the offence is indictable or triable either-way. Solicitors commonly give initial advice to defendants under the green form scheme when they are uncertain whether legal aid will be granted in the case.

Following the implementation of the Police and Criminal Evidence Act 1984, legal advice to a maximum of £90 totally free, without means testing, is available to those detained in police custody, under a 24-hour duty solicitor scheme (Richman, 1987). A parallel duty solicitor scheme in court was set up by the Law Society, and also offers free legal advice. It is aimed at defendants in custody, bail applications, straightforward guilty pleas and general advice, but not committals for trial, nor 'not guilty' pleas or continuing advice and representation, nor, generally, non-imprisonable offences.

The Legal Aid Act 1979 extended the green form scheme to include assistance by way of representation (ABWOR) in magistrates' courts in civil matters. Potentially, however, such assistance may be used for any proceedings. Currently its main uses are: applications to the domestic panel of the magistrates' courts for various kinds of matrimonial relief; representations of parents in care proceedings; and applications to MHRTs.

Magistrates' courts

No matter how grave, all crime has its first hearing in the magistrates' courts, where basic issues are addressed, such as whether there is sufficient evidence against the accused to constitute a 'case to answer' in a higher court, and whether he should be granted bail.

Magistrates' courts deal with about 98% of crime in England and Wales; a little under 100 000 cases annually are committed to the Crown Court for trial. In magistrates' courts, less than two out of ten defendants plead not guilty; in the Crown Court, only one in three pleads not guilty (White, 1985). Details of the history, composition and procedure of these courts may be found in various texts such as Walker (1985), White (1985) and Skyrme (1983). Such courts try offences occurring within their own catchment area or petty sessional division, of which there are some 600 in the country. The maximum penalty which may be imposed is 6 months' imprisonment for a single offence (and 1 year for two offences), in addition to fines, the upper limit of which is currently set at £2000. Apart from about 50 stipendiary magistrates who are legally qualified, paid for the work, and who sit alone, the function of judge (in sentencing) and jury (in deciding issues of innocence and guilt) is performed by two or three justices of the peace, who are unpaid lay members of the public who have had some training. The linchpin in the magistrates' court is the justices' clerk, who advises on points of law and procedure. The courts are of 'summary' jurisdiction, in which brevity is of the essence. Over 90% of cases are dealt with without a request for psychiatric opinion or intervention. Even so, magistrates' courts pass the bulk of the hospital orders which are made each year.

Remands

In many cases, it is not possible to deal with the case immediately, and the matter is thus adjourned. If remanded, the defendant is under an obligation to return to court. Under the Bail Act 1976, there is in general a presumption in favour of a defendant being granted bail before his case is heard or sentence is passed. The reasons for a remand in custody include a belief by the court that the defendant would fail to surrender to custody, or commit an offence while on bail, or interfere with witnesses or otherwise obstruct the course of justice. The court can also remand in custody if it believes that the defendant would be better protected or cared for there, or if it does not think it has 'been practicable to obtain sufficient information for the purpose of taking the decision'. The same clause enables courts to remand defendants in custody for a psychiatric report from the prison medical service, even though the offence with which they are charged does not carry a penalty of imprisonment and, therefore, there is no possibility of even making a hospital order! In spite of the general presumption in favour of bail, large numbers of defendants are still remanded in custody pretrial or presentence. Conditions may be applied to bail, so that, for example, the defendant should make himself available for a medical report, or that he should reside at a named address, which may be a hospital or a bail hostel. Prior to conviction, remands in custody are weekly; after conviction, the length of the remand until the next court hearing is 4 weeks on bail or 3 weeks in custody. Failure to answer to bail is in itself an offence, for which a warrant for arrest may be issued.

Committal is a stage in the trial of either-way or indictable offences at which the defendant is formally remanded to attend the Crown Court for his hearing, at a date that will later be announced by the Crown Court. The original charges are reformulated as a bill of indictment in which separate offences are listed as counts. Most commonly, committal is a brief formality; occasionally, however, the defence may choose an old style committal, in which the prosecution evidence is presented orally to the court, with the request that the court should consider whether sufficient evidence has been produced to provide a 'case to answer'. The length of time at present between committal proceedings and trial is unacceptably long; if the defendant is remanded to hospital to await trial, the effect of the impending court case may make therapeutic intervention very difficult (McGarry, 1965).

The plea

A guilty plea is tantamount to a conviction. In certain cases, e.g. driving offences, an accused may enter a plea of guilty by post. In the hearing, the prosecution advocate, usually the crown prosecutor, presents the brief facts in the case. The court is then told of the accused's past record, good or bad, which is obtained from the Criminal Records Office. At this point, the court may decide to adjourn the case for reports before sentencing. The vast majority of these reports are social enquiry reports made by the probation service; a psychiatric report may be requested in addition. Before sentence is passed, the defence solicitor (if there is one) will make a plea in mitigation, or the defendant is asked if he wishes to say anything. The court may, when passing sentence, take into consideration other offences the accused admits having committed, but with which he has not been charged. Defendants convicted of either-way offences may be committed to the Crown Court for sentence if the magistrates' court considers that its powers of sentencing are insufficient to deal with the offender.

If the defendant pleads not guilty, then the prosecution, on whom the burden of proof rests, is heard first. An opening statement may be made, before the evidence is called, to give a preview and help the court appreciate the evidence to come. Prosecution witnesses remain outside the court until called to give evidence, when they are examined in chief by the prosecution advocate, cross-examined by the defence to test the credibility of the evidence, and re-examined by either side. At the end of the prosecution evidence, the court decides whether a *prima facie* case has been established, that is, whether the defendant could properly be convicted if he made no answer to the prosecution case.

In the case for the defence, the accused may give evidence himself and call witnesses, or may call witnesses without himself giving evidence. He and his witnesses are asked questions in the same manner, but with the roles of the two sides now reversed. At the end of the evidence, both parties may sum up, but the defence has the last word.

In reaching a verdict, guilt has to be proved 'beyond reasonable doubt'. The decision is based on the facts presented in evidence—legal facts are not only actions, but also intentions in offences in which *mens rea* is an essential element. A feature of English adversarial proceedings as distinct from European inquisitorial proceedings is that there is no additional duty to 'seek out some independent truth' (Lord Wilberforce in *Air Canada*). It may be—

from the imperfection of evidence, or the withholding of it . . . that an adjudication has to be made which is not, and is known not to be, the whole truth of the matter; yet, if the decision has been in accordance with the available evidence and with the law, justice will have been fairly done.

It is useful to note this English legal view of justice, which is different from the use of the word 'justice' in the vernacular.

The Crown Court

The Crown Court tries serious criminal cases. It is a professional court, where the defendant is usually represented by solicitor and counsel, and the judge is a professional judge. For the purposes of administration, England and Wales are divided into six circuits, in which trials are presided over by judges of varying seniority, according to the gravity and complexity of the case.

In spite of its professionalism, the lay-man still has a central role in the Crown Court; it is the jury who determine the guilt or innocence of the accused. The process of jury decision-making is secret; research has never been allowed into the process (Baldwin and McConville, 1979) and is now specifically prohibited by law. The best that researchers can do is to study simulated trials.

In a not-guilty plea, the division of function between judge and jury is such that the judge deals with questions of law, and the jury with questions of fact, presented according to the rule of evidence and procedure. At the end of the trial the judge sums up the case, summarizing the legal issues in contention, and commenting on factors which may lend weight to, or cast doubt on, certain evidence.

Appeals

Acquittal by jury cannot be overturned; defendants, however, have a right of appeal against conviction and, or, sentence. Since 1989 the prosecution can also appeal against a sentence. It is important to note that, in English law, there is no inherent over-riding principle that the purpose of an appeal is to avoid a miscarriage of justice. An appeal against sentence is a disagreement with the penalty imposed by the lower court. An appeal against conviction, however, is a claim that the conviction was improper, in that, for example, there was a misdirection in the applicable law, or an error in the procedure.

As far as magistrates' courts are concerned, appeals against conviction or sentence lie in the Crown Court. Applications for judicial review (available to both prosecution and defence in order to cure some illegality of proceedings) go to the Queen's Bench Division of the High Court. A third type of appeal against a magistrate's decision is by way of case stated when either prosecution or defence believe that a decision is wrong in law or in excess of a court's jurisdiction. It is even possible for the prosecution to challenge an acquittal under this arrangement. Like judicial reviews, these also go to the High Court. Appeals against Crown Court decisions are much more difficult. Until the Criminal Appeal Act of 1907 which established the Court of Criminal Appeal, decisions following trial on indictment were final. The defendant has a right of appeal on a question which is solely of law, but this is rare. For all other appeals, he has to obtain leave to appeal from the Court of Appeal criminal division itself, as does the prosecution if it wishes to appeal against sentence. Leave is given (or not) by a single judge who just reads the papers.

The House of Lords may hear appeals which are either allowed by the Queen's Bench Division of the High Court (these cases come from the Crown Court in its function as an appeal court to a magistrates' court) or are allowed by the Court of Criminal Appeal. A certificate has to be granted that a point of law of general public importance is involved, and leave to appeal must be granted as well.

Outside the judicial system, the Home Secretary, through the 'Royal Prerogative of Mercy', has the power to grant pardons and remissions of sentence, and has a statutory power to refer cases to the Court of Appeal if there are grounds for believing that a miscarriage of justice has occurred (*see* White, 1985 for details).

Civil Courts

For an eminently readable description of the structure and practice of the civil courts, the reader is directed to Robin White's book *The Administration of Justice* (1985). Litigation involving contract or tort for major claims may be heard in the High Court (Queen's Bench Division) or in one of over 300 local county courts. The county courts process over 1.5 million cases as compared to about 150 000 cases in the High Court, and their jurisdiction is limited to claims under £5000 which have some local connection with that court. Any claim can be brought to the High Court.

One of the notable features of civil proceedings is that the majority are settled before the case reaches court; only about 3% come to trial, and only in 1% is there a real contest about liability. It might thus be thought that court cases have little impact on the operation of the system. However, one decision of the Court of Appeal may lead to the settling of many thousands of cases by insurance companies. The case law also gives important guidance on the matter of quantum of compensation for particular injuries (Atiyah, 1983).

One factor which accounts for the settlement of so many personal injury claims without resort to court is the presence of insurance. It is, for example, a requirement of law that motorists carry insurance for potential liability to accident victims. Where the injuries sustained are not too serious and the question of liability is reasonably arguable, many insurers seek to settle out of court, since, in the long term, this is far cheaper than fighting every claim.

The rules of civil procedures which govern the handling of cases are technical, complex and detailed. They can be found in the large volumes entitled *The Supreme Court Practice* (known as 'the White Book') and *The County Court Practice* (known as 'the Green Book') (White, 1985). The outlines of an action are given in Stevens (1981). The objectives of the rules are—

1. to ensure that the facts on which a claim is based are accurate and appropriately arranged, so that the issues between the parties can be identified;
2. to ensure that the correct and appropriate rule of law is found and applied; and
3. to ensure that the remedy or remedies prescribed by that rule of law can be adequately enforced.

A second notable feature of civil proceedings is the protracted nature of litigation; in the rare case that comes to trial, some three or more years may have elapsed since the original event. The trial itself proceeds on the basis of orality: almost every document and every piece of evidence, even though agreed by both parties, is read out. In the High Court each spoken word is recorded; in county courts the only record of proceedings are the judge's notes. The English system of civil procedure is based on the adversary principle: a series of statements of fact are put forward by one party, to be attacked by the opposing party. The judge acts principally as umpire or referee, and leaves it to the opposing parties to put the case before him. A jury is unusual, except in cases of defamation.

At the end of the presentation of the case for the plaintiff and for the defendant, the judge gives a reasoned judgment in which he will determine both liability and the quantum of damages, either immediately or at some later time (reserved judgment).

Appeals

Appeals in civil proceedings are to the Court of Appeal and the House of Lords. They have two main functions. The first, 'review', function is the process by which defects in the trial process are corrected. These may typically be errors of practice and procedure, incorrect conclusions on the facts, or an incorrect application of established legal principles.

The second function is 'supervision', which is the process of the laying down by the courts of guidelines for the development of legal principles. The process may involve a critical reconsideration of an area of law in the light of changing social conditions, or an authoritative interpretation of a statutory provision of law. The Court of Appeal exercises, in theory, the functions of 'review' and 'supervision'. It is, however, a busy court and its work appears predominantly to be concerned with determining appeals involving 'review'. It is also, in general, bound by its own previous decisions.

The House of Lords is no longer bound by its own previous decisions and enjoys a unique power to reshape legal principles, established by an accumulation of case law. The House of Lords is also the final appeal court for civil cases originating in Scotland and Northern Ireland, which have their own legal systems.

While permitting a degree of 'creativity', the doctrine of precedent (i.e. being bound by previous decisions), even in the House of Lords, operates to limit the changes in the law which the judges are willing to make. The judges can develop the law, but major exercises in 'judicial legislation' are not constitutional. Such changes in the law are reserved for full consideration by Parliament.

Coroners' Courts

Coroners' courts are an example of courts whose powers have waned in recent times; they are also a rare example of a court in England and Wales which conducts its proceedings on the inquisitorial rather than the adversarial basis. Readers are directed to four textbooks for detailed information on the subject (Burton et al., 1983; Kavanagh, 1985; Knapman and Powers, 1985; Matthews and Foreman, 1986).

The modern system is a 'fail-safe' procedure, which provides that the registration of every death shall be subject to scrutiny and investigation for possible criminal involvement. The law requires the registration of the death of every person; registration cannot be effected without two stringent conditions being fulfilled: first, that there is a valid certificate giving the cause of death, and second, that the cause of death must be entirely 'natural'. If death is shown to be 'violent or unnatural', the Coroner is required by law to conduct an inquest. The basis for the modern system stems from the recommendations of the Brodrick Report (Home Office 1971c), which have been much reflected in legislation: the Criminal Law Act 1977 and the Coroners Act 1980. In England and Wales about 170 000 cases are referred annually to coroners; 23 000 become the subject of inquests.

An inquest is an impartial inquiry, conducted by the Coroner on behalf of the Crown, for the purpose of establishing the truth concerning the events leading to, and the ultimate cause of, death—including the identification of the deceased person, the date and place where death occurred, and such other particulars as are required by law to be registered concerning the death. There are no opposing parties, no provision of legal aid, or any award of costs, and no enforceable judgment or order can be made (Burton et al., 1983).

At the inquest, a Coroner always has the discretion to summon a jury, but he has the statutory duty to summon one in prescribed situations, as, for example, where the death occurred in prison or in police custody. The presence of a jury at the inquest into the death of a patient detained for psychiatric treatment is not at present a statutory requirement, although it is usual.

Every inquest must be opened, adjourned and closed in a formal manner. Sometimes, the Coroner has a statutory duty to adjourn, where, for example, a person involved has criminal charges laid against him, in order to avoid prejudice. The procedure at an inquest is under the control of the Coroner. The Coroner must 'examine on oath, touching the death, all persons who tender their evidence respecting the facts, and all persons having knowledge of the facts whom he thinks it expedient to examine' (Burton et al., 1983). Any person having relevant evidence to give concerning a death has a duty to present himself to the Coroner for examination. Any person who has a 'proper interest' in the circumstances in which an unnatural death has occurred is entitled to attend in person or be represented at the inquest and question witnesses. Interested parties can ask questions of the witnesses (with permission of the Coroner), but may not address the court on the facts.

In announcing his verdict, the Coroner is strictly limited by the Coroner's rules: he does not produce any legally enforceable judgment or order; and no finding of negligence, blame, culpability or guilt will be recorded. He no longer has a duty to commit for trial persons to be charged with murder, manslaughter or infanticide, but must instead adjourn the case and send particulars of the evidence to the Director of Public Prosecutions. The verdict of the inquest is not subject to appeal; it may, however, be questioned in the Divisional Court by way of judicial review on grounds such as fraud, error of law, bias, excess of jurisdiction, or insufficiency of evidence.

The most likely source of contention is a verdict of 'suicide': successions of High Court judgments have made it clear that only on the clearest and most unequivocal evidence should such a finding be recorded. Aggrieved relatives may not understand, however, that the Coroner's court is not the place to apportion blame to doctors in cases where they consider that the death was due to the treatment rather than the disease. In publicly controversial inquests, for example inquests where the conduct of the police is called into question, there may be an expectation of a wide-ranging inquiry which, however, is not a function that Coroners are able to perform: an inquest is neither a trial nor a public enquiry.

The Home Office

In England and Wales, the Home Office has some of the functions which are performed in other countries by a Department of Justice. It manages the prison service centrally, it has a watching brief over the police forces of the UK and a particular role as the police authority for the metropolitan area of London. It coordinates and funds the probation services of England and Wales. It has special responsibilities in relation to the care and control of dangerous convicted offenders, including mentally abnormal offenders, and of those who have been charged with serious offences, but are so mentally ill that they are considered to be either unfit to plead or not guilty by reason of insanity (NGRI). The Home Office has no jurisdiction over the law courts, or the judiciary, which are the responsibility of the Lord Chancellor's Department. Within the prisons, there are many mentally abnormal people. These are the responsibility of the Prison Medical Service (PMS) which is entirely separate from the National Health Service (NHS), and is run by the Home Office under the control of the Director of Prison Medical Services. The PMS and the care of mentally abnormal offenders are dealt with in Ch. 9.

C3 Division

Within the Criminal Policy Department of the Home Office, one division, C3, exercises control over (1) the mentally abnormal offenders who have been convicted and sent to hospital by courts under a restriction order (section 41) of the MHA 1983; (2) those who are unfit to plead and (3) those who have been found to be NGRI. The latter two groups are small in number. Patients with restriction orders (see p. 73–4) may be sent to any psychiatric hospital, but the bulk of them are sent to special hospitals. The effect of this is to provide that control of the patient's movements and discharge may be exercised only with the consent of the Home Secretary. In practice, the powers are administered by a Minister of State or a Parliamentary Under Secretary and C3 division in the Home Office. The civil servants in C3 maintain a large dossier on each patient under their jurisdiction. This contains information about the original offence, copies of all official correspondence, and copies of medical, psychological and social work reports. At regular intervals, the hospital consultants have to send reports to the Home Office about the progress of their patients.

Discharge decisions are almost never initiated by Home Office officials. The procedure is that the responsible medical officer (RMO) consults C3 division about leave or discharge arrangements; he also consults the Special Hospitals Service Authority if the patient is in a special hospital. If the consultant wishes to send a patient on escorted or unescorted leave, or to prepare his or her discharge, then again correspondence will occur between the consultant and the Home Office. The civil servants who are involved in the decision may request further information from the hospital. Informal telephone and other oral communications between C3 division and the RMO are extremely useful in effective patient management. Indeed, one of the best ways of informing Home Office officials about the care and progress of a particular patient and his/her readiness for onward move is to invite the key civil servant involved to a case conference.

Questions which C3 division emphasize include the motivation for the index offence, evidence of persistent and/or preoccupying fantasies about violent, sexually abnormal or fire-raising behaviour, the response to medication (if any), the patient's ability/willingness to cooperate with medication, impulsivity, explosive behaviour, frustration tolerance, insight into disorder, and the role of alcohol and drugs in the patient's life and/or offending.

When all the appropriate information has been gathered, the key civil servant will put a recommendation to the minister concerned. If the minister is satisfied that the proposal is a good one, it is then authorized. If the minister disagrees with the proposal, he may give an indication to the local team about the kinds of steps which would make the case more persuasive. A further application for leave or discharge can then be made later, when there is evidence of further adjustment to the patient's condition and/or circumstances. The patient is entitled, under the MHA 1983, to appeal against Home Office refusal when the patient is next eligible for an MHRT (*see* p. 188). Patients under a restriction order can be absolutely or conditionally discharged, against the Home Secretary's wishes, by one of the special tribunals chaired by a judge.

C3 division also has responsibility for prisoners who have been transferred from prison to hospital under section 47 of the MHA 1983 and who are subject to a restriction order under section 49. However, their needs are slightly different as they may be serving fixed-terms of imprisonment. They may be given periods of rehabilitative leave with the consent of the Home Office after they have reached their parole eligibility date (usually after one-third of the sentence), but they may return to prison to complete their sentence if their mental disorder improves sufficiently and their RMO recommends this course. If they remain in hospital, the Home Secretary loses control over their movement at the time at which they would have been released from prison. Prisoners serving life imprisonment (i.e. an indefinite sentence) may also be rehabilitated direct from hospital if this is thought desirable on mental health grounds, but proposals for their discharge are normally dealt with by the Parole Board. In some cases, the judiciary and/or the Home Office agree that the case is better dealt with as a medical rather than a penal problem, and then such lifers fall to the ordinary C3 arrangements.

Supervision of Conditionally Discharged Restricted Patients

When a patient on a restricted hospital order is conditionally discharged from hospital, he will be subject usually to a combination of social work and medical supervision. Guidance notes on the arrangements for social and psychiatric supervisions have been issued by the Home Office and the Department of Health. Social supervision can be carried out by a local authority social worker or by a probation officer. In a study of releases from Broadmoor Hospital, Norris (1984) found that two-thirds of cases on restriction order licences were supervised by probation officers, one-third by local authorities. Norris further found an association between the patient's diagnosis and the nature of the supervising agency: probation officers were mainly responsible for 'psychopaths', and social workers responsible for schizophrenics.

The choice of which agency should provide the social supervision is discretionary, the Home Office stipulating only that it should be 'a responsible person' (Home Office Circular No.69/1983, Annex, para 20). It can be undertaken by a probation officer (by warrant of the Probation Rules) or by a local authority social worker (under S.117 of the MHA 1983). Obviously, contingent factors such as the extent of previous agency involvement with the patient and/or his family will play an important part in the decision, as will the quality of liaison between the hospital and the different agencies. The choice of social supervisor is also strongly influenced by the wishes and intentions of hospital staff. Where, however, the hospital staff have no clear view, it may be agreed between the local probation service and social services department. The general view is that social services have control over community resources, and a framework for health service liaison, whereas the probation service has experience of supervising clients with a background of offending. However, with reduced funding, social services departments seem less and less able to assist with mentally abnormal offenders and the balance of cases may swing strongly towards probation services.

Social supervision has several components. It involves monitoring the mental state of the patient and reporting any changes, rehabilitation, giving advice to a patient who is considering any change of circumstances, and regular reporting to the Home Office on the progress of supervision, so that the Home Office can form a view as to the appropriateness of continued community care or the need for recall to hospital. The responsibilities of probation officers in supervising mentally disordered offenders are thus in many ways similar to those they exercise in the supervision of parolees and of life-sentence prisoners released on licence. Officers have a responsibility to ease and enable their clients' transfers from institutions to the community *and* a duty to 'monitor' their behaviour and recommend a recall to the institution if that behaviour gives cause for concern.

The monitor role, the duty to report deterioration, both to the Home Secretary and the RMO has to take priority (Home Office circular 69/1983). However, the duty of care is also vital. *Jarvis's Probation Officers' Manual* (Weston, 1987) states that the responsibilities of the supervising officer are—

1. to provide support and guidance to the patient;
2. to provide an early warning of any relapse in the patient's mental condition or deterioration in behaviour, giving rise to danger to himself/herself or others.

The hope is that by close social supervision, including home visits and appropriate medical treatment in the community, 'such a relapse will be avoided'.

This description emphasizes the helping relationship, the resettlement of the ex-patient into the community being the main objective, with after-care supervision the method available to achieve it, and recall being a sanction available should it fail to do so. It is clear that social supervision and monitoring for the Home Office are intimately linked. Recall may be necessary to prevent harm to the patient or to others on occasions but, clearly, recall in those circumstances is also good clinical practice. Furthermore, recall does not have to be for a prolonged period.

Advisory Board on Restricted Patients

In 1971 Graham Young, a young man with known poisoning propensities, was conditionally discharged from Broadmoor Hospital. Only 9 months after his release he was rearrested on a charge of murder and the following year convicted of that murder, committed by poisoning. A public outcry concerning the case persuaded the, then, Home Secretary and the Secretary of State for Health and Social Services to set up a committee under the chairmanship of Sir Carl Aarvold to investigate the matter. Their report (Aarvold et al., 1973) recommended a special advisory board to review a small proportion of restricted patients who presented special anxieties and/or dangers. It was originally thought that sadists, sexual offenders and arsonists were likely to be in this category. It was recommended that the board be multiprofessional and consist of forensic psychiatrists, social workers (including probation officers) and lawyers, with a lawyer as the chairman. The Board was first established in 1973 under the chairmanship of Sir Carl Aarvold himself and is, therefore, sometimes known as the 'Aarvold Board', even though there have been three subsequent chairmen. In 1985, two additional 'lay' members with particular experience in the criminal justice system were added to the Board.

The arrangements for referring patients to the Board are straightforward. The key civil servant responsible for a particular case may identify that case as especially worrying and, therefore, advise the minister to seek the further assessment and opinion of the Board. In other cases, the minister himself may refer a case directly before he agrees to make a final decision one way or the other. Exceptionally the RMO, or the hospital managers, may suggest a reference to the Board.

The Advisory Board usually meets each month, and normally deals with six or seven cases at each meeting. Before each meeting, each member is provided with a copy of the Home Office dossier and one member is delegated to visit the patient in hospital, and a report from that visit is written for presentation at the forthcoming board meeting. The visits are non-professional in the sense that the psychiatrists do not undertake to write a psychiatric report, nor the social workers a social work report, and so on. The purpose of the visit is to check the hospital file to see that all the important and relevant information, especially psychology and social work reports is, in fact, in the Home Office dossier, to meet key members of staff, particularly the RMO and senior nurses, to discuss the case and proposals for discharge or leave, and to meet the patient to assess his understanding of the current situation and his realism in future planning. Some reassurance is also sought from the patient that there is understanding of the significance of the past offences and of the importance of future absence of such behaviour. Some members also look for 'remorse'. From the perspective of the staff and the patient, it gives an extra opportunity to transmit views which might be more difficult via the written word.

At the monthly meeting, each member of the Board expresses a view about each case. A collective view is accumulated and an advisory note written by the chairman of the Board which goes directly to the minister, together with the minutes of the meeting. The minister may or may not accept the Board's advice. All communications between the Board and the minister are confidential, but after a decision has been made, some information may be fed back to the hospital team about the reasons for a particular decision by the Home Office, especially if that decision was a negative one.

Parole Board

The Parole Board in England and Wales is an independent body appointed by the Home Secretary to advise him on the release of prisoners on parole under the Criminal Justice Act 1967. Parole is a form of early and conditional release on licence.

Each prison has a local review committee comprising the Governor, members of the Board of Visitors, senior members of the probation service, and persons who have no official connection with the prison. The committee reviews the cases of all prisoners who are eligible, and who do not decline to be considered, on the basis of as full a documentation as the prison can provide.

The local committee sends these papers to the Home Office for its views on whether the prisoner is or is not suitable for parole. The Home Secretary is empowered to release certain categories of prisoner directly on the favourable recommendation of the Committee without reference to the Parole Board—these are usually the less serious cases. All other cases which the local review committee consider suitable are referred to the Board, together with certain cases which have not secured a favourable local recommendation. If the Board does not recommend parole in a particular case, then the Home Secretary may not authorize release. If the Board does recommend release, however, the Home Secretary still has a power of veto. The Board is also responsible for advising on conditions to be included in the parole licence of cases referred to it, and their subsequent variation or cancellation.

The Board normally sits in panels to consider cases, each panel consisting of four members. The panel is chosen from one or more lay members and representatives of the category specified in the Act (i.e. judges, psychiatrists, social workers/probation officers, criminologists).

Life sentence prisoners are also referred to the Parole Board, as a person sentenced to imprisonment for life may be released at any time by the Home Secretary on the recommendation of the Board. This is not parole, but life licence. The Home Secretary usually consults the Lord Chief Justice and the trial judge before release. Under the November 1983 rules, murderers of police or prison officers, terrorist murderers, sexual sadistic murderers of children, and murderers by firearms in the course of robbery, can normally expect to serve at least 20 years in custody. When a life prisoner is released on licence, a set of conditions will have to be accepted by him/her, and these may include attendance at a psychiatric clinic in the case of those with a psychiatric history. After some years, the licence restrictions may be loosened or removed altogether, but it is worth noting that the life sentence prisoner is never free from the risk of recall if there is a serious breach of the conditions of release.

The Criminal Justice Act 1991 abolished parole and instituted a new set of arrangements for the early release of sentenced prisoners. All prisoners will serve at least half their sentence. Prisoners serving less than four years are eligible for release automatically (subject to good behaviour in prison) after half their sentence has been served. Prisoners serving 4 years or more are eligible for release, at the recommendation of the Parole Board, between the half-way and two-thirds points of their sentences. All prisoners serving a year or more are released on licence to probation service supervision up to the three-quarters point of their sentence. This system is the same for young offenders, except that the provision for a minimum of three months' supervision after release (and provided the offender does not reach the age of 22) is also retained for those serving less than twelve months. There are separate provisions for sexual offenders where the sentencing court may order the period of supervision on licence to extend up to the actual end of the sentence, if this is necessary to protect the public from serious harm from the offender. These provisions apply to offenders sentenced to custody after 30 September, 1992. For those sentenced before that date, the parole system will still apply. The local review committees will continue to meet until 1994, although their workloads will diminish over time. From 1994 the Parole Board will begin to consider cases for discretionary supervised release, as well as those referred from local review committees by the Home Secretary; the former will eventually become the dominant part of the Parole Board's workload. The emphasis in the 1991 Act on the just deserts approach to sentencing suggests that the criteria for discretionary supervised release may come to differ from those for parole, in that more emphasis may be placed on the offence and response to prison and less on criminal history and home circumstances.

The Probation Service

The principal roles of the probation service are twofold: to provide social work advice to the courts—criminal and civil—and to supervise offenders in the community. A smaller area of supervision lies in matrimonial and family work. All this means that, between professionals, there is perhaps the greatest overlap of all between the work of the probation service and the work of forensic psychiatrists. Greater detail about the origins and development of the probation service and much of its work is provided in Ch. 19, with additional material in relation to court reporting in Ch. 21, and the supervision of offender patients in Ch. 18.

Mental Health Review Tribunals

Mental health review tribunals (MHRTs) are the most important means detained patients in England and Wales have of appealing against their compulsory detention.

Constitution and Administration

MHRTs were established in 1960 with the implementation of the MHA 1959. Under section 65 of the MHA 1983, MHRTs are established for each health authority region. Under schedule 2 of the 1983 Act, the tribunal is appointed by the Lord Chancellor and consists of legal, medical and lay members. Lay members are those who have experience in administration, knowledge of social services or other qualifications or experience. Medical members are usually psychiatrists. The tribunal is chaired by the legal member. Where the tribunal is to hear the case of a restricted patient, the legal member is drawn from a panel of specially appointed lawyers who have had substantial judicial experience in the criminal courts and who are circuit judges, or recorders who are QCs.

Tribunals are administered by a Clerk to the Tribunal who receives and processes applications and who attends hearings. There are tribunal offices in London, Cardiff, Liverpool and Nottingham. There are no MHRTs in Scotland where the equivalent power of discharge is vested in the Mental Welfare Commission for Scotland and in sheriffs.

Representation and Legal Aid

Under section 2 of the Legal Aid Act 1974 patients with limited means are entitled to legal advice and assistance in engaging a solicitor to help them prepare their case (known as the 'green form scheme' see pp. 173–4). Furthermore, under the Legal Advice and Assistance (Amendment) Regulations 1982, patients may also be represented at the hearing under the assistance by way of representation scheme (known as ABWOR *see* p. 174). Hospital managers and social workers assist patients with these financial aspects and in finding a solicitor through one of the Law Society's legal aid area centres. Solicitors may obtain the services of a psychiatrist to prepare an independent psychiatric report. Such a doctor is entitled to interview the patient in private and to see his hospital case notes.

Applications and Reference

All patients detained for more than 72 hours (other than those on orders for remand to hospital for assessment or treatment, or on interim hospital orders) can apply to an MHRT within certain periods of eligibility. Only one application may be made in each eligibility period. If a patient does not make use of his opportunity to apply within a certain period, his case should be automatically referred to the tribunal by the hospital managers or, if he is a restricted patient, by the Secretary of State. A child under the age of 16 must have his case heard at least annually. The Secretary of State for Health or the Home Secretary can refer to a tribunal at any time the case of any unrestricted or restricted patient even when the patient is not eligible to apply himself. A patient may withdraw an application with the consent of the tribunal, in which case he does not lose his eligibility to apply again within the same eligibility period.

For unrestricted patients, the nearest relative may make an application to the tribunal if an RMO has issued a certificate barring the nearest relative from discharging the patient from hospital, and also when the patient has had the category of mental disorder under which he is detained reclassified. Other than in these circumstances, nearest relatives cannot in England and Wales make applications for patients detained under assessment orders or treatment orders. For patients on hospital orders without restrictions, the nearest relative may apply as often as can the patient. Nearest relatives cannot apply to tribunals in respect of patients on restriction orders.

The periods of eligibility for patients detained under the most common detention orders are shown in Table 4.3.

Procedure and Hearings

Following receipt of an application, the tribunal obtains from the hospital authority a statement including a medical report from the RMO, who usually represents the detaining authority at the hearing. The RMO's report will include the patient's medical history and a full report on the patient's mental condition. Where practicable an up-to-date social circumstances report is

Table 4.3
Periods of Eligibility for MHRTs (England and Wales)

Category of detention (Section of Mental Health Act 1983)	Application by patient	Automatic reference
(S.2) Assessment order	within 14 days of admission	None
(S.3) Treatment order	Within the first 6 months of admission, within the second 6 months and thereafter annually	After the first 6 months if no application made in first 6 months Once every 3 years
(S.7) Guardianship order	As for treatment order	None
(S.37) Hospital order	Between 6 and 12 months following admission and thereafter annually	Once every 3 years
(S.37+41) Restricted hospital order	As for hospital order to special tribunal	As for hospital order to special tribunal
(S.41(5)) Derestricted hospital order	As for hospital order from date of end of restriction order	Once every 3 years after end of restriction order
(S.42(2)) Licensed restricted patient	Between 1 and 2 years following conditional discharge and in each subsequent 2-year period	None
(S.42(3)) Recalled restricted patient	Between 6 and 12 months after recall and thereafter annually	Within 1 month of recall and thereafter once every 3 years
(S.47) Transfer to hospital of sentenced prisoners (transfer direction)	As for hospital order	As for hospital order
(S.48) Transfer to hospital of prisoner on remand (transfer direction)	As for hospital order	As for hospital order
(S.49) Restricted transfer direction (restriction direction)	As for restricted hospital order	As for restricted hospital order
(S.5) of Criminal Procedure (Insanity) Act 1964	As for restricted hospital order	As for restricted hospital order

also submitted by the detaining authority and, in the case of restricted patients, the Home Secretary must provide a further statement relevant to the application which will normally give the Home Office view on the patient's suitability for discharge.

Prior to the hearing, the medical member of the tribunal examines the patient and may interview others to assist him in forming an opinion as to the patient's mental condition. Social workers and nursing staff may be called to give evidence, and the tribunal has the power to subpoena witnesses. The hearings usually take place at the hospital where the patient is detained.

The procedure at hearings is governed by the Mental Health Review Tribunal Rules 1983. Under rule 6, the detaining authority and the Home Secretary can ask for any part of their statement, which would adversely affect the health or welfare of the patient or others, not to be disclosed to the patient. Specific reasons should be given. Every statement must, however, be disclosed to the patient's representative and any medical practitioner participating in the hearing.

Hearings may be in private or in public and the procedure adopted can be informal or formal. Usually tribunals are held in private. If the patient requests a public hearing, the tribunal will ask the RMO whether that would be against the patient's interests before coming to a decision. The proceedings in private hearings are normally conducted in an informal atmosphere with all interested parties present at the same time and able to ask each other questions. The tribunal may adjourn the hearing to obtain additional information relevant to the issues before them, but not in order to review the patient's progress at a later date.

Powers of Tribunals

Tribunals have a range of options open to them—their possible decisions will be considered separately for unrestricted and restricted patients.

Unrestricted patients

The tribunal *must* discharge a patient detained on an assessment order, if it is satisfied that he is not suffering from a mental disorder of a nature or degree which warrants his detention in hospital for assessment for at least a limited period, or if his detention is not considered necessary in the interests of his health or safety or for the protection of others.

For any other unrestricted patient, the tribunal *must* discharge him if it considers that he is not suffering from any of the four categories of mental disorder given in section 1 of the MHA 1983 (mental illness, psychopathic disorder, mental impairment, severe mental impairment) of a nature or degree which makes detention in hospital appropriate, or if his detention is not necessary in the interests of his health or safety or for the protection of others. In the case of a patient on a transfer direction who still has time on his prison sentence to serve, the discharge is back to prison. Where an RMO has barred the patient's discharge by his nearest relative, the tribunal must discharge the patient if it considers that the patient, if released, would not be likely to act in a manner dangerous to himself or others. A tribunal also must discharge a patient from guardianship if it is satisfied that he is not suffering from one of the four categories of mental disorder given in the Act, or if it is considered that it is not necessary in the interests of the welfare of the patient or for the protection of others that he should remain under guardianship.

Besides these obligations on the tribunal, it *may* discharge unrestricted patients in cases where the criteria given above are not met. In so doing, it must consider (other than for patients detained on an assessment order) the likelihood that medical treatment in hospital will alleviate or prevent a deterioration in the patient's condition and (for those detained within the category of mental illness or severe mental impairment), the likelihood that the patient, if discharged, would be able to care for himself, obtain the care he needs or to guard himself against serious exploitation.

For unrestricted patients, the tribunal may also recommend that he be granted leave of absence, be transferred to another hospital or be placed under guardianship if it believes that the patient should not be immediately discharged, but that such action would be appropriate with a view to facilitating his discharge at a future date. If such recommendations are not put into action, the tribunal may further consider the patient's case. Tribunals may also direct that a patient be discharged at a future date, thus leaving time for adequate after-care arrangements to be made. Tribunals may also direct that the category of mental disorder under which the patient is detained be reclassified to another category of mental disorder.

Restricted patients

Restricted patients are dealt with by a special tribunal chaired by a judge, or a recorder who is a QC. When hearing the cases of such patients, the tribunal has no obligation to consider the treatability of the patient's condition. The discretionary powers given to tribunals in respect of unrestricted patients do not apply to those subject to restriction orders.

The tribunal *must* order the *absolute* discharge of a patient subject to a restriction order if it is satisfied that:

1. he is not suffering from mental illness, psychopathic disorder, mental impairment or severe mental impairment or from any of those forms of mental disorder or a nature or degree which makes it appropriate for him to be liable to be detained in hospital for medical treatment;
2. it is not necessary for the health and safety of the patient or for the protection of others that he should receive such treatment; **and**
3. it is not appropriate for the patient to remain liable to be recalled to hospital for further medical treatment.

The tribunal must order the *conditional* discharge of a restricted patient if it is satisfied that the patient should remain liable to recall but that:

1. he is not suffering from one of the four categories of mental disorder or

from any of those forms of disorder of a nature or degree which makes it appropriate for him to be liable to be detained in hospital for medical treatment; *or*

2. it is not necessary for the health and safety of the patient or for the protection of others that he should receive such treatment.

A directive of conditional discharge may be deferred until the necessary arrangements, such as for medical care, social work or probation supervision, or for accommodation, have been made.

Patients who have been transferred from prison and who are subject to a restriction direction cannot be discharged by a tribunal. The tribunal may, however, inform the Home Secretary of its opinion that the patient could, if not subject to a prison sentence, be conditionally or absolutely discharged and may recommend that, if the patient cannot be discharged, he should continue to be detained in hospital rather than be returned to prison. Following receipt of the tribunal's recommendation, the Home Secretary may agree that the patient be discharged and thus allow the tribunal to discharge him, or he may return the prisoner to prison, or he can allow him to remain in hospital.

In hearing the cases of restricted patients, tribunals have no statutory authority to make recommendations or to reclassify the category of mental disorder, although they often do make recommendations, and reclassifications are recognized by the Home Office.

Research

Tribunals are one of the few courts or bodies overseeing and administering the law which have been subjected to any form of systematic research or scrutiny. Peay (1989) undertook a descriptive study of the workings of tribunals focusing primarily on patients detained in special hospitals. She interviewed patients in a special hospital and also talked to their RMOs and to the judicial members of the tribunal relating to that special hospital. She observed tribunals in different settings, and looked at the tribunal files in two regional offices. Although she had a number of harsh things to say about the tribunal system, she also conceded that—

from many perspectives the tribunals could be assessed to be working reasonably well. Decision making is approached judiciously, decisions to release may be characterized by the care, indeed caution, with which they are made. Full consideration is usually given to therapeutic considerations. Patients as the consumers of the system, by and large, do not express dissatisfaction.

Peay made a number of recommendations. Her final two, however, give the flavour of her useful book for the reader who needs more detailed information. She recommends improved training for tribunal members, especially the 'lay' members, and the urgent provision of real alternatives to compulsory hospital care, concluding that 'legal safeguards are only likely to be effective in the context of adequate resource provisions' for 'decisions to discharge are recourse-, and reality-oriented, not rule-, and law-oriented'.

The Mental Health Act Commission

The predecessors of the Mental Health Act Commission (MHAC) were the Commissioners in Lunacy who were established by the Lunatics Act 1845 and the Board of Control who replaced them in 1913. They, in turn, were disbanded in 1960 with the coming into force of the MHA 1959, leaving no independent body with a statutory duty to visit psychiatric hospitals and to safeguard the interests of patients. Subsequently, in the 1960s and 1970s, there were a succession of scandals over conditions in mental hospitals such as Ely, St Augustine's, Farleigh, Normansfield and Rampton. Allegations of ill-treatment, neglect, cruelty and inadequate medical and nursing care were substantiated (*see* Martin J. P., 1984 and Ch. 20). In 1969 the Hospital Advisory Service was set up to encourage and disseminate good practice and to advise the Secretary of State for Health and Social Services on standards of care and management practices in hospitals.

In setting up the MHAC, the government expressed its hope that it would exercise a general protective function, be a 'real safeguard' for detained patients and that it would build up a body of knowledge and experience which would throw light on the whole field of mental health.

The Commission has no responsibility for informal patients other than on rare occasions providing second opinions where it is proposed to carry out psychosurgery or to implant hormones to reduce sexual drive. The MHAC has no power to discharge patients, but is otherwise responsible for the welfare and interests of the 7000 detained patients that are in England and Wales at any one time.

The Commission was established in 1983 as a special health authority and as such is responsible to the Secretary of State for Health, but is an independent body with a chairman and 91 other part-time members from the fields of medicine, nursing, law, social work and psychology together with lay members and academics. The functions of the Commission are laid down in section 121 of the MHA 1983 and in the MHAC (Establishment and Constitution) Order 1983, which gives it six statutory functions.

Second Opinions

The first function of the Commission concerns the requirement under the MHA 1983 for consultant psychiatrists to obtain a concurring second opinion from a doctor appointed by the Commission before administering either medication for more than 3 months or routine electroconvulsive therapy at any time to a patient who is inacpable of consent or who refuses consent to treatment. In its first biennial report (Mental Health Act Commission, 1985) the MHAC says that the great majority of doctors have adopted this system without complaint and with increasing ease. It says there has been a high measure of agreement between appointed doctors and consultants, probably in the order of over 90%. There have, however, been some difficulties: there is no formal appeal mechanism for consultants against the refusal of an appointed doctor to provide an authorizing certificate; coherently written treatment plans supporting the proposal for treatment are sometimes lacking; and there has been difficulty in the availability of qualified professionals whom the appointed doctor is required to consult before issuing a certificate.

There is also some confusion about the legal responsibilities following the refusal of the appointed second opinion doctor to allow a plan of treatment to proceed. The legal responsibility for the patient's care remains with the RMO. However, it seems unlikely that the appointed second opinion doctor can escape the legal liabilities for his own quite powerful actions, for when giving a second opinion, he is acting as an independent medical practitioner, but this has never been tested in law.

The lack of possibility of appeal against a refusal to permit a plan of treatment causes great consternation sometimes. It is best dealt with by reviewing the case in the light of the remarks of the second opinion doctor, remarshalling the clinical arguments and, if it is thought appropriate, making a new request to the Commission for a second opinion; it is bound to provide such a second opinion and it may instruct a different doctor, although it does not have to do so.

Reports on Detention

The Commission receives reports from RMOs, where treatment has been given in the above circumstances, at the time when the detained patient's detention is renewed or at the time of the statutory annual report by the RMO concerning a patient subject to a restriction order. The Commission may also request a report from the RMO on the patient's treatment and condition at any time.

Visits and Complaints

The Commission has a duty to visit and interview detained patients in hospital and, in its first two years, it paid nearly 1000 visits to some 500 hospitals. The MHAC says it aims to be 'a catalyst of good practice, to observe and detect both the good and the bad policies and practices and to disseminate the good'. In the section in its report on the special hospitals, the Commission says that initial suspicion on behalf of staff has not been easily or totally overcome and there is 'much still left to do'.

Along with this duty to visit, the Commission has a duty to investigate a detained patient's complaints which the patient considers have not been satisfactorily dealt with by the hospital managers. Although the Commission says that this is the normal route which it initially recommends, a primary investigative function is not ruled out in some cases. The first biennial report (1985) gives details of the 1549 communications which could broadly be called complaints, of which 533 were judged as needing investigation. The Commission believes that its advent undoubtedly led to expectations by patients that it would be possible at last to cut through obstacles to a clear outcome.

> The Commission was thought to be endowed with teeth. In fact it does not bite very much, but it can exert pressure, and exert it in increasing degrees in the right quarters.

Code of Practice

The MHAC was given the task of drafting for the Secretary of State a Code of Practice for the guidance of doctors, managers and staff of hospitals and approved social workers in relation to the admission of patients to hospitals, and for the guidance of doctors and members of other professions in relation to the medical treatment of patients suffering from mental disorder. A draft of a proposed Code of Practice was issued for consultation to professional bodies by the Secretary of State in December 1985 and was received unfavourably by the medical profession (Hamilton, 1986). A revised Code has been published (DOH and Welsh Office 1990 *see* Appendix 2 for details).

Review of Mail of Special Hospital Patients

The fifth duty of the Commission is to review decisions made at special hospitals on the withholding of postal packets or their contents when this has been necessary in the interests of the safety of the patient or for the protection of others. Appeals to the MHAC against such decisions are rare.

Biennial Reports

The Commission has the duty to publish a report every two years which must be laid before Parliament. These reports deal with matters such as: community care; factors affecting black and ethnic minority groups; further development of multidisciplinary teamwork; the care and treatment of informal patients who are physically detained against their expressed wishes in a locked ward or room; consent to treatment of long-stay informal patients, and the mentally disordered in prison; overcrowding in Broadmoor; delays in transferring patients from special hospitals; escorted leave for special hospital patients; provision for difficult offender patients, patients with learning difficulties; and the investigation of complaints.

The Court of Protection

The Court of Protection exists to take responsibility for patients who are so mentally disordered that they are incapable of managing their property and affairs. Just being mentally disordered or being a detained patient does not of itself make a person incapable of handling his finances and only something in the order of 25 000 persons come under the Court of Protection's jurisdiction. Most are elderly mentally ill or mentally handicapped and are long-term patients in psychiatric and geriatric hospitals or in nursing homes.

The historical background of the Court of Protection has been described by Gostin (1983a). For many centuries, the Crown claimed a royal prerogative over the estates of the mentally disordered. This power (and duty) was exercised by the Lord Chancellor, later by judges. Part VII of the MHA 1983 deals with the management of property and affairs of patients and section 93(2) states:

> There shall continue to be an office of the Supreme Court, called the Court of Protection, for the protection and management, as provided by this part of the Act, of the property and affairs of persons under disability.

The Lord Chancellor nominates judges and other officers to carry out the work of the Court under the Master of the Court of Protection.

Functions and Powers

Under section 94 of the MHA 1983, the functions of a judge of the Court—

> shall be exercisable where, after considering medical evidence, he is satisfied that a person is incapable, by reason of mental disorder, of managing and administering his property and affairs.

The term 'mental disorder' has the meaning attached to it in the rest of the 1983 Act, namely mental illness, arrested or incomplete development of mind, psychopathic disorder and any other disorder or disability of mind. In other words, the term used is the broad one applicable for short-term detention orders rather than the narrower terms necessary for longer-term detention, thus including the mentally handicapped rather than only those who would meet the definition of mental illness or severe mental impairment.

The functions and powers of the Court are set out in sections 93–109 of the MHA 1983 and its procedures are governed by the Court of Protection Rules 1984. In general, the Court may—

> with respect to the property and affairs of a patient, do or secure the doing of all such things as appear necessary or expedient for the maintenance or other benefit of the patient, the patient's family or other persons for whom the patient might be expected to provide if he were not mentally disordered.

In doing so, the Court has as its priority the requirements of the patient, but it must also have regard to the interests of any creditors of the patient. The Court may, *inter alia*, sell the patient's property, acquire other property for the patient, make arrangements for the carrying on of his business, carry out legal proceedings on behalf of the patient, execute (write) a will for the patient, dissolve a partnership.

In cases where the patient's assets are limited, the Court may empower an officer of the Court to manage the patient's affairs without recourse to receivership. In an emergency, the Court has the power to make immediate provisions for handling the patient's property and affairs.

Receivership

One way in which the Court often carries out its functions is by appointing a receiver who, by virtue of section 99 of the MHA 1983, 'shall do all such things in relation to the property and affairs of the patient' as the judge authorizes. The receiver is usually a close relative of the patient, but he may be a solicitor, the director of the local social services authority or even the Official Solicitor.

The Enduring Powers of Attorney Act 1985 (Carson, 1987) enables individuals to prepare themselves for the possibility of their becoming both mentally disordered and incapable of managing their property and affairs, and they can specify who is to do what, and with what, whenever they become incapable. When such an individual later becomes mentally disordered, his attorney must apply to the Court of Protection to have the enduring power of attorney registered, whereupon the attorney can make binding decisions about the individual's property until he recovers. The role of the Court of Protection is to register such documents and to consider complaints about their administration relying on others, such as health and social services, to bring abuses to its attention.

Applications and Medical Evidence

Anyone, usually the nearest relative, may make an application to the Court of Protection, whereupon the applicant will be sent forms which after completion need to be sworn in front of a Commissioner of Oaths (most solicitors are Commissioners of Oaths). Medical evidence as to the patient's incapacity is required from a medical practitioner. This is normally from the doctor in charge of the patient's treatment and not necessarily a specialist in psychiatry. The medical report should not simply state a diagnosis (such as senile dementia or chronic schizophrenia), but should particularize the aspects of the patient's cognitive abilities which are affected, such as those of memory, reasoning and understanding. Tangible evidence of the patient's limited capacities based on a knowledge of the patient's behaviour is essential.

When the Court has received the sworn affidavits, it will notify the patient that a hearing will take place and the patient has an opportunity to object and contest the evidence. However, the patient may not be notified if it is considered that to do so would damage his health or if it is thought that the patient would be unable to understand the procedures.

The Royal College of Psychiatrists (1983) has published guidelines to assist doctors who may be involved in preparing medical certificates for the Court of Protection, and the Master of the Court (Macfarlane, 1985) has given further advice on what the Court looks for in terms of medical evidence and on the completion of the necessary forms.

Lord Chancellor's Visitors

Under section 102 of the MHA 1983, the Lord Chancellor appoints medical, legal and general visitors whose duties are to visit patients at the request of a judge of the Court. General visitors are lay officials of the Lord Chancellor's department, medical visitors are specialists in psychiatry and legal visitors are senior solicitors or barristers. Visitors may enquire into the ability of the patient to manage his affairs, such as when an application has been made for a receiver to be appointed, or to ascertain a patient's testamentary capacity. Medical visitors can see the patient in private and require the production of his medical records.

The Official Solicitor

The Official Solicitor has powers and duties arising from the Supreme Court Act 1981 and various common law directions. Central to his role is to act as next friend or guardian *ad litem* to mental patients involved in legal proceedings where there is no one else to take on that role. He is also involved on behalf of minors in wardship and adoption proceedings. He may represent the interests of a patient to the Court of Protection.

When a solicitor or a psychiatrist, or a hospital administrator, believes that an individual is a mental patient and there is no friend or relative willing to act as next friend or guardian *ad litem*, he should obtain medical evidence about the psychiatric health of that person. If a psychiatrist thinks that the client falls within the terms of section 94 MHA 1983 (i.e. he is 'a person incapable, by reason of mental disorder, of managing and administering his property and affairs') and is thus 'a patient' (*see also* p. 197—Court of Protection), then the Official Solicitor should be consulted, at Penderel House, 287 High Holborn, London WC1V 7HP (Nicholls, 1988).

General Medical Council

Professions are usually considered to be groups of workers who not only earn money for services rendered, but who also govern their own affairs including standards of conduct and licensing arrangements. The medical profession is such an organization in many countries. It may, therefore, be useful in this medical textbook to include a brief note on the way in which the British medical profession deals with those doctors who break the law.

Ultimately, the medical profession in Britain, like everybody else, is governed by Parliament. Under the Medical Act 1858, powers were delegated to the General Medical Council (GMC) which, in turn, was responsible to the Privy Council. It is curious that many members of the public believe that the profession is regulated by the British Medical Association (BMA) which is, of course, a trade union and one of the bodies which doctors may turn to for help if they find themselves at cross purposes with the GMC. In addition to regulating standards of practice, the GMC has education functions which also have a direct bearing on the granting of licences to practise, but they will not be dealt with here.

The Council currently conforms to the provisions of the Medical Act 1983 and is a body of just under 100 people, some appointed directly by universities, some elected by the profession, two appointed by the Government and eleven lay members, to represent the patients, appointed by the Privy Council. This is an important difference from other professional bodies, notably the BMA, which are entirely medical and, therefore, will be viewed as partisan. The GMC is concerned with all doctors in the United Kingdom.

The Committee on Standards of Professional Conduct and Medical Ethics within the Council formulates guidance on professional conduct and discipline, and the criteria for fitness to practise which are issued periodically to the profession as 'the blue book' (e.g. General Medical Council, 1987). This book has almost the force of a set of bye-laws and doctors know that they ignore its 'advice' at personal risk. It is concerned with the disciplinary processes of the Council, professional misconduct, standards of conduct and ethics, and fitness to practise. The remainder of this section on the GMC is based on the blue book. However, readers must consult the book for accuracy. New editions are produced and here only the briefest precis can be given.

Disciplinary Processes

The Medical Act 1983 provides that if any registered practitioner is found to have been convicted in the 'British Islands' of a criminal offence or is judged to have been guilty of serious professional misconduct, his name can be erased from the Medical Register, or his registration suspended for 12 months, or his registration be made provisional for 3 years, with specified requirements during that period.

'Convictions' are findings of guilt in any criminal court in the British islands and the Professional Conduct Committee is bound to accept the determination of the court—it is not open to a doctor to plead before the GMC that a mistake has been made. However, decisions of a medical service committee do not count as convictions.

'Serious professional misconduct' is determined by the Professional Conduct Committee and implies something which is reasonably regarded as disgraceful or dishonourable by his professional brethren. The Professional Conduct Committee is elected annually and consists of 20 members, only 10 of whom sit in any one case. Of the 20, 12 have to be elected members and 2 lay members. The Committee sits in public and its procedures are akin to those of a court of law. Witnesses may be subpoenaed and evidence is given on oath. Doctors may be legally represented. The Preliminary Proceedings Committee consists of 11 members. It sits in private and decides on the basis of written evidence who should be referred to the Professional Conduct Committee or the Health Committee.

Convictions are normally reported to the Council by the police. Other complaints come from a variety of sources, e.g. a medical service committee or a committee of enquiry. Complaints from other doctors or members of the public must be accompanied by sworn statements. If it is decided to proceed with the case, the doctor is informed and invited to submit a written explanation. All this then goes to the Preliminary Proceedings Committee. It may refer the matter to the Professional Conduct Committee, or to the Health Committee, or send the doctor a warning letter, or drop the case. If the case is referred to one of the higher committees, then the doctor may either be suspended on an interim basis or given interim conditional registration, either of these may last for up to 2 months.

If the case is thought serious enough to go to the Professional Conduct Committee then, in the case of convictions, there is an enquiry to establish the gravity of the offence and to take account of mitigating circumstances. In the case of misconduct allegations, the case against the doctor must either be admitted or proved by evidence.

If the case is proved, then the Committee can—

admonish the doctor; or
postpone its determination; or
continue registration on conditions, laid down in each

case, for up to 3 years, or
suspend registration for 12 months; or
erase the doctor's name from the register.

Appeals against the last three of these possibilities can be lodged with the Judicial Committee of the Privy Council. Pending appeal, the decision may not be implemented. If it is, then there is also a more rapid route of appeal to the High Court (or the Court of Session in Scotland) which is in addition to the appeal to the Privy Council.

Applications for restoration may be made after 10 months from the date of erasure.

Forms of Misconduct which may lead to Disciplinary Hearings

1. Neglect or disregard of personal responsibilities to patients for their care and treatment.
2. Abuse of professional privileges or skills. The privileges conferred by law, which may be abused, include the improper prescription of drugs, the improper signing of medical certificates, and the unlawful termination of pregnancy. The privileges conferred by custom, which may be abused, include the misuse of professional confidences, the use of undue influence, e.g. to obtain money or alter a will, and the misuse of personal doctor/patient relationships, e.g. to enter into an emotional or sexual relationship. Some of these matters, especially confidentiality are dealt with in Ch. 22.
3. Conduct derogatory to the reputation of the profession, especially the misuse of alcohol or other drugs, dishonesty, and indecent or violent behaviour.
4. Advertising, canvassing and related professional offences.

Fitness to Practise

Where the Council receives information suggesting that the fitness to practise of a doctor may be seriously impaired (e.g. by alcoholism, drug dependency, dementia, psychosis), the information is considered by the Preliminary Screener. If there is reasonable evidence, then the doctor is invited to submit to a medical examination by two doctors chosen from pre-established panels. The doctor himself may also get a further opinion for the Preliminary Screener. The examiners are asked to make recommendations which are given to the doctor under scrutiny. He is then asked to accept these recommendations, which may include limitations on his practice. If he does, then the Preliminary Screener will normally request a medical supervisor to monitor the doctor's progress.

It is only when the doctor refuses to be medically examined, or to accept the recommendations of the medical examiners or, if having accepted them, he subsequently fails to follow them, that the case may be referred to the Health Committee. Cases are also referred to the Health Committee by the Preliminary Proceedings Committee or Professional Conduct Committee.

The Health Committee is elected annually and comprises eleven doctors and one lay member. It meets in private and assesses medical evidence in a judicial manner. If it finds that the doctor's fitness to practise is seriously impaired, it may impose conditions on his registration for 3 years or suspend his registration for up to 12 months. There is no right of appeal to the Privy Council except on questions of law.

The Health Committee is a relatively new innovation (since 1980) and has prevented many sick doctors suffering the full rigours of the disciplinary procedures, as well as effectively bringing some of them into treatment, maybe for the first time. It is a good example of diversion from a disciplinary approach to a health care approach which could be emulated by the penal system.

Scotland

Criminal Matters

Law, procedures and institutions relating to the prosecution of crime in Scotland differ from those elsewhere in the UK. The first private prosecution in Scotland since 1909 took place in a *cause célèbre* in 1982 (*X v Sweeney*); a woman in Glasgow brought a successful prosecution for rape against three youths after the Crown had dropped proceedings. That apart, the Lord Advocate and the Solicitor-General for Scotland are responsible for the investigation and prosecution of serious crime. Much of the work is delegated to advocates-depute who, together with a staff of civil servants, constitute the Crown Office in Edinburgh. Less serious crime is investigated and prosecuted locally in the sheriff court by the procurator fiscal, a qualified lawyer.

There are no committal proceedings equivalent to those in England. An arrested person likely to face trial under solemn procedure may undergo judicial examination by a procurator fiscal before a sheriff. This gives the accused an opportunity to put forward any disincriminating explanation. He is legally represented and is not obliged to answer questions; his answers, or failure to answer, may be referred to subsequently at trial. If remanded in custody (prison or hospital), the accused must be brought to trial within 40 days (summary procedure) or 110 days (solemn procedure) or be liberated with immunity from further proceedings for that offence.

Under summary procedure before a sheriff, the maximum sentence of imprisonment is 3 months or, on reconviction for certain offences, 6 months.

Solemn procedure refers to trial by sheriff and jury in the sheriff court (maximum sentence 3 years), or by judge and jury in the High Court of Justiciary. The sheriff can remit a case to the High Court if he considers a sentence in excess of 3 years may be appropriate. No preliminary description of the case takes place; after the charge has been read in court, Crown counsel leads evidence from his first witness. Apart from the usual verdicts of 'guilty' and 'not guilty', a third verdict, 'not proven', is also recognized— it results in acquittal. A jury of 15 people reaches its decision by simple majority, but a guilty verdict can only be returned if at least 8 of the jury are in favour of it. Corroboration of evidence is essential; with few exceptions 2 witnesses are necessary to establish proof. Thus an accused cannot be convicted solely on the basis of his confession.

Appeals against conviction or sentence under summary procedure are made to the High Court, which may also hear an appeal by the Crown on a point of law. Under solemn procedure, appeals are made to at least three judges of the High Court sitting as a Court of Appeal. There is no appeal from the criminal courts in Scotland to the House of Lords.

The age of criminal responsibility in Scotland is 8 years. However, there are no juvenile courts; prosecution of children aged under 16 is rare and may only take place on the instruction of the Lord Advocate. Instead, since 1971, children who, for whatever reason, may be in need of compulsory measures of care are referred to three lay people (children's hearing) drawn from a list of such people (the children's panel) which each local authority is required to establish (*see also* pp. 236–8).

Civil Matters

Scotland is divided into six sheriffdoms, each presided over by a Sheriff Principal, and each divided into sheriff court districts. The great bulk of civil litigation is dealt with in the sheriff court e.g. debt, contract, damages, actions concerning the use of property, divorce and the custody of children. Appeals against the decision of a sheriff are to the Sheriff Principal, and thereafter to the Court of Session and ultimately to the House of Lords (as in *B v Forsey*). Sheriffs are also responsible for conducting formal inquiries into fatal accidents and sudden deaths; they do so without a jury. The office of Her Majesty's Coroner does not exist in Scotland.

The Court of Session sits at Parliament House, Edinburgh, and consists of the Lord President, the Lord Justice-Clerk and not more than 22 judges who are also the judges of the High Court of Justiciary. Decisions are made by judges sitting singly, but are subject to review by a plurality of judges. The Court is divided into an Inner House, which functions as a court of appeal, and an Outer House, which is a court of first instance.

Other Statutory Bodies

The Mental Welfare Commission for Scotland is the principal body charged with protecting the interests of psychiatric patients in Scotland (Mental Welfare Commission for Scotland, 1989). It has a duty to visit mental hospitals, interview long-stay, detained patients and order the discharge of patients whom it considers to be improperly detained. All patients, including those under restriction orders, have the right of appeal against detention to a sheriff. Discharge of restricted patients is determined by the Secretary of State for Scotland through the mental health branch of the Scottish Home and Health Department. A psychiatric adviser to the Secretary of State interviews all restricted patients at regular intervals. There is no Advisory Board for restricted patients in Scotland; on occasions, the psychiatric adviser may convene a panel of psychiatrists to consider difficult cases.

Management of the affairs and property of a mentally disordered person who is *incapax* may be placed in the hands of a *curator bonis* appointed by the sheriff court; his powers are broadly similar to those of a receiver appointed by the Court of Protection. The latter does not exist in Scotland, although some patients under its authority are domiciled in Scotland.

Release of prisoners on parole is at the discretion of the Secretary of State for Scotland, but can only take place with the agreement of the Parole Board for Scotland. Prisoners serving sentences of 18 months or less are not eligible for parole. The system of parole in Scotland differs from that in England and has recently undergone review (Scottish Home and Health Department, 1989).

Legal aid in Scotland is the responsibility of the Scottish Legal Aid Board established by the Legal Aid (Scotland) Act 1986; it includes advice, assistance and representation in civil and criminal court proceedings. Detained psychiatric patients, who are legally aided, receive legal representation in court when appealing against detention.

Northern Ireland

In Northern Ireland, the structure of the courts and their procedures are similar to those in England and Wales. However, the civil disturbances which have continued since 1969 have had a significant impact on both criminal and civil legislation. Emergency legislation has been introduced in an effort to combat terrorism. The Northern Ireland (Emergency Provisions) Act 1978 is the principal antiterrorist act. It consolidates earlier enactments dating back to 1973 and is itself extensively amended by the Northern Ireland (Emergency Provisions) Act 1987. In addition, most of the Prevention of Terrorism (Temporary Provisions) Act 1989, which applies to the rest of the UK, also applies to Northern Ireland. The emergency legislation is wide-ranging and affects *inter alia* powers of arrest and detention, photographing and finger-printing of suspects, bail applications, admissibility of confession evidence and court proceedings.

The Criminal Evidence (Northern Ireland) Order 1988, which came into operation at the end of 1988, applies to the general criminal law in Northern Ireland because of the Government's concern at the challenge to the rule of law posed by not only those involved in terrorism, but also those involved in racketeering for personal profit and in other serious crimes. The Order allows the courts to attach whatever weight they think proper to the fact that someone remained silent in certain specific circumstances, where an innocent person might reasonably have been expected to protest his innocence and draw attention to facts which serve to establish it. In a written parliamentary answer on 20 October 1988, the Home Secretary announced his intention of bringing forward legislation on this subject for England and Wales at the earliest opportunity.

Schedule 4 of the 1988 Act lists certain offences such as murder and causing an explosion, which are commonly committed by terrorists, and which are dealt with under the emergency procedures. The list of scheduled offences contains both hybrid offences (such as membership of a proscribed organization) and indictable offences, but it is in the latter category that court procedure is most affected—because of the fear of bias or intimidation of jurors, scheduled offences tried on indictment are heard before a single judge sitting without a jury (so-called Diplock Courts). Certain offences may be 'de-scheduled' by the Attorney-General if no element of terrorism is involved, for example, in the case of a domestic murder.

Victims of terrorist or non-terrorist crime may claim compensation for personal injury or for loss or damage to property under the Criminal Injuries (Compensation) (N.I.) Order 1988 and the Criminal Damage (Compensation) (N.I.) Order 1977 respectively. The provision for compensation for property damage is more extensive in Northern Ireland than in England. There is also a scheme for compensating those whose property is damaged under the Northern Ireland (Emergency Provisions) Act 1987.

The Northern Ireland Office

The Northern Ireland Office (NIO) is responsible for the operation and management of the prison system in Northern Ireland, but the Prison Medical Service is run by the Department of Health and Social Services (NI) and the psychiatric care of prisoners is provided by consultant psychiatrists working in the Health Service. The Criminal Justice Policy Branch of the NIO discharges the Secretary of State's responsibilities in relation to mentally abnormal offenders who are subject to either restriction orders made by the courts or restriction directions placed on prisoners who have to be transferred to hospital for psychiatric treatment. There is no Advisory Board for

Restricted Patients because the number of patients on restriction orders in the province is small, and there is no maximum security hospital in Northern Ireland, patients requiring such management being sent to England or, more usually, to Scotland.

Northern Ireland has no parole system for prisoners serving determinate sentences who may, however, gain up to one-half remission (cf remission of one-third in England and Wales, but with the possibility of release on parole from as early as one-third of sentence). The Prevention of Terrorism (Temporary Provisions) Act 1989 reduces the maximum rate of remission, however, to one-third in the case of a sentence of 5 years or more for a scheduled offence committed after the Act came into force (15 March 1989). This brought Northern Ireland more into line with the Home Office policy since 1983 that prisoners serving more than 5 years for offences of violence or drug trafficking cannot generally expect to receive a substantial period of parole.

Uniquely, Northern Ireland operates a conditional release scheme under which prisoners discharged with the benefit of remission may have the rest of their sentences reactivated if they commit a fresh offence on release. Under part II of the Treatment of Offenders (Northern Ireland) Order 1976, a prisoner released from a sentence of more than one year, who commits and is convicted of an imprisonable offence before his period of remission on the sentence has expired, may be returned to prison by the courts to serve what remains of this period. This is in addition to any fresh sentence which may be imposed. The Prevention of Terrorism (Temporary Provisions) Act 1989 made such a return mandatory in the case of a released prisoner who was given a prison sentence for a scheduled offence committed within his period of remission and, in these cases only, made the return period ineligible for further remission. As a result of the civil disturbances in Northern Ireland, many prisoners are serving indeterminate sentences—either life sentences or detention during Her Majesty's pleasure (the latter 'pleasure' cases having been under 18 years of age at the time of their offence). Their cases are reviewed regularly by the Life Sentence Review Board and the decision to release on licence is taken by the Secretary of State after consultation with the Lord Chief Justice and the trial judge, if he is available.

The Mental Health Tribunal and the Mental Health Commission

In Northern Ireland, the MHRT functions in a broadly similar fashion to those in England and Wales, but with a few variations in detail, e.g. patients detained for treatment are automatically referred to a tribunal every 2 years, if this period has elapsed since the tribunal last considered the case, and the only special requirement relating to the hearing of cases of patients on restriction orders is that they are presided over by either the chairman or the deputy chairman of the review tribunal. The Mental Health Commission for

Northern Ireland differs significantly from the English MHAC in that its protective role extends to anyone suffering or even appearing to suffer from mental disorder, including, for example, voluntary patients and patients in nursing homes, residential accommodation, prison, etc.

The Probation Board for Northern Ireland

The Probation Board for Northern Ireland was established in 1982. In Northern Ireland, a probation order may last up to 3 years, but a condition of it requiring psychiatric treatment may last no longer than 12 months. The Probation Board may enter into arrangements with voluntary bodies, such as the Extern Organisation and the Northern Ireland Association for the Care and Resettlement of Offenders (NIACRO), for the provision of certain services.

Republic of Ireland

Between 1800 and 1922 the parliament at Westminster was the sole legislature for all of Ireland. At the time of establishment of the Irish Free State in 1922 (subsequently to become the Republic of Ireland in 1948), the legal and judicial system was essentially that which existed in the rest of the UK. Although this inheritance from English rule has meant that the structure and terminology of the Irish courts is essentially similar to that existing in England, the years since the granting of independence have seen a number of changes in the structure and function of the Irish courts, and these will be outlined below. For a full description of Irish law, the reader should consult one of the standard texts (O'Siochain, 1981; Doolan, 1986; Grimes and Horgan, 1988).

The original Constitution of 1922 was replaced by that of 1937, and this is the fundamental legal document of the country. It outlines the structure of the State, Parliament and courts, and also outlines personal rights and social principles. Any law can be challenged in the courts on the basis that it is repugnant to the constitution. Amendments to the constitution can only be authorized by a majority of voters in a referendum.

As in Britain, the courts are divided into superior (the Supreme Court and the High Court) and inferior courts, with varying degrees of jurisdiction both in civil and criminal matters. Except in the composition of juries, the Irish legal system does not make use of lay people—all judges are legally qualified and are appointed by the President.

The district court is the lowest court in the Irish system. It handles by far the greatest number of cases (as do the magistrates' courts in England). The court is presided over by a district court justice who is a solicitor or barrister of at least ten years' experience. The district court hears summary offences and the maximum sentence it can impose is 6 months (or 12 months in the case of indictable offences where the accused has waived the right of trial by jury). In more serious cases, the district court conducts a preliminary hearing and, if satisfied that there is sufficient evidence, remands the accused for trial by jury in a higher court. In civil cases it can award damages of up to £2500.

The next court is the Circuit Court and it consists of a judge and jury. It hears indictable cases referred to it by the district court and also appellate cases from the lower court. In civil cases its jurisdiction is limited to £15 000. The country is divided into eight circuits and the judge assigned to that circuit sits in various towns on a number of occasions each year. There are permanent sittings in Dublin and Cork due to the volume of business in these centres.

The High Court has jurisdiction over the whole country. It generally sits in Dublin. In criminal cases, it is known as the Central Criminal Court. It hears very serious cases (murder, treason, etc.) and in civil cases can award unlimited damages. In addition, it has a number of consultative functions on points of law and the constitution, and possesses considerable supervisory jurisdiction. The Court of Criminal Appeal hears appeals from the Circuit and High courts on points of law.

As well as summary trial, trial by jury, and trial by military court, the constitution allows for trial by Special Court. These courts are established by statute when it is considered that the ordinary courts are inadequate to secure the effective administration of justice and the preservation of public peace and order. They are activated and de-activated by government order. The Special Court deals with scheduled offences, which are offences laid down by the government. The court consists of three members and the decision is that of the majority. The present Special Criminal Court was brought into operation in 1972 and deals mainly with terrorist offences.

At the apex of the Irish legal system is the Supreme Court. This consists of the Chief Justice and a number of high court judges. It has no original jurisdiction in civil or criminal cases. It hears appeals from the Central Criminal Court and the Court of Criminal Appeal. There is no automatic right of appeal and permission must be granted either by the lower court or by the Director of Public Prosecutions. In addition, the Supreme Court rules on points of law and the constitutionality of certain matters.

The constitution provides for the position of Attorney General who is the legal adviser to the government in matters of law and legal opinion. Though not a member of the government, the Attorney General is appointed by the President on the recommendation of the Taoiseach (Prime Minister). The Attorney General retires when the Taoiseach resigns. The office of the Director of Public Prosecutions (DPP) was established in 1974 and the DPP is responsible for prosecuting crime in the name of the people.

5

Juveniles—Laws and Facilities in the United Kingdom

Written by
Allison Morris and Loraine Gelsthorpe

Facilities and Laws Governing Juvenile Offenders in the UK

The policy and practice of juvenile justice in most jurisdictions reflects a marked social and legal ambivalence towards juveniles* who break the law (Children & Young Persons Review Group, 1979; Asquith, 1983; Adler, 1985; Klein, 1985). There is an underlying uncertainty about the extent to which they should be treated as legally or morally responsible for their conduct; how far they should be punished or treated; and whether the focus of attention should be their circumstances or their conduct. This has produced a tension between what has traditionally been called a social control orientation and a social welfare orientation (Morris and McIsaac, 1978). A social control orientation sees the delinquent as a law breaker who poses a threat to the community and who, therefore, requires punishment and firm discipline. A social welfare approach, on the other hand, has a rather different set of concerns: it refers to needs rather than guilt and to assistance rather than punishment; and it assesses the need for intervention on the basis of juveniles' problems rather than their conduct.

Although this has been a useful distinction in understanding juvenile justice policy and practice, it now appears somewhat crude and oversimplified. In many senses, control and welfare are not incompatible: welfare is itself a means of exerting control. Also, both approaches are concerned with inducing conformity and socially acceptable behaviour in the juvenile and both can lead to long-term incapacitatory strategies. Moreover, the control/welfare dichotomy ignores other emerging perspectives which have questioned and modified traditional approaches towards juvenile offending.

* English law distinguishes between children, that is those aged 10–13, and young persons, that is those aged 14–16. From October 1992 17-year-olds are also dealt with in youth courts. For ease of reading, the term 'juvenile' is used to apply to all three age groups post 1992 and those under 17 before that date.

First, in recent years there has been a growing emphasis upon the need for fairness and equality and a concern for juveniles' legal rights and due process protections (Morris, 1978a; Morris et al., 1980; Taylor et al., 1980; Morris and Giller, 1983). This is now described as the justice or just deserts model. It focuses on making the discretionary practices of those working in the system visible and reviewable and on limiting sanctions by reference to principles of proportionality, determinacy and the least restrictive alternative. Second, increasing attention has recently been paid to an approach called diversion. This emphasizes the potentially stigmatizing effects of formal processing in the courts and advocates that juveniles should be diverted from them whenever possible.

This chapter will deal primarily with English laws and systems and provides notes on Scotland and Northern Ireland at the end of both main sections.

Towards Welfare

The notion of a juvenile delinquent or juvenile offender is comparatively new. In the 19th century, half of those convicted of crimes were under 21 and both adults and juveniles were subject to the same laws and penalties. The age of criminal responsibility was 7 in common law. Juveniles between the ages of 7 and 14 were presumed incapable of committing crimes (*doli incapax*), but this presumption was usually rebutted by the mere commission of the offence. The reasoning was that the law sought not to reform offenders, but to punish them in order to expiate the crime and to deter potential offenders. Thus juveniles were executed, transported and imprisoned. It was only as the century progressed that they were considered other than miniature criminals.

Gradually, the dangers of holding juveniles and adults together in the same institutions was recognized and separate facilities for juveniles were developed: initially houses of refuge and, later in the century, industrial and reformatory schools. Similar thinking led to modifications in (or attempts to modify) procedures which influenced the trials of juveniles. For example, in 1847, the Juvenile Offenders Act was passed which allowed thefts committed by persons under 14 to be heard by magistrates in Petty Sessions. This was amended in 1850 to those under the age of 16 and in 1879 there was a further major change. Under the Summary Jurisdiction Act of that year, juveniles under 16 could be tried summarily for nearly all indictable (serious) offences.

Towards the end of the century, some towns began to operate separate juvenile courts and these were established throughout England and Wales after the Children Act 1908. It set out for the first time the principle that juvenile offenders should be heard separately from adults in special sittings of the magistrates' court. In essence, however, the new juvenile courts functioned as criminal courts and the mode of trial was much the same as it was for adults. The prevailing idea was that the juvenile was a wrongdoer and that the procedures for dealing with adult offenders were appropriate in most respects for dealing with juveniles. In addition, although the courts were given a wide and flexible range of dispositions—for example, admonition, fines, whipping, committal to a reformatory or industrial school and probation—decisions were governed by such considerations as the seriousness of the offence and the interest of the public. On the other hand, there was some concern for the welfare of the child. Herbert Samuel, in introducing the Bill, stated that one of its main principles was that juvenile offenders should receive at the hands of the law a treatment differentiated to suit their special needs.

The juvenile courts remained like this until 1933, when certain statutory changes were made: the appointment of magistrates with a special interest in juveniles, restrictions on reporting cases affecting juveniles in newspapers, the abolition of the terms 'conviction' and 'sentence' and the substitution of the terms 'finding of guilt' and 'order on such a finding', and the direction that magistrates should have regard to the welfare of the child. The reformatory and industrial schools were also merged into one type of institution—approved schools—and the age of criminal responsibility was raised to 8.

Two further changes were made in 1948. One of the concerns which had emerged from the Second World War years was the apparent increase in the number of juveniles who were from broken homes or who were illegitimate. Consequently, in 1945 the Government initiated an enquiry (the Curtis Committee) into the child care services to review means of providing substitute families for such juveniles (Home Office, 1946). The Children Act 1948 which followed the recommendations of this Committee enabled local authorities to take juveniles considered to be in need of care or protection into their care and to assume the powers and duties of their parents. That same year, however, the Criminal Justice Act 1948 increased the range of penalties available to magistrates for dealing with juvenile delinquents. It introduced detention centres and attendance centres as a substitute for whipping, which was abolished.

From the 1950s, juvenile crime was seen as increasing and it was widely believed that there were categories of juveniles with whom the juvenile justice system, particularly the approved schools, could not cope. These concerns about appropriate responses to juvenile offenders reflected concerns about the juvenile justice process itself. Thus, in 1956, the Home Office set up a Committee, chaired by Viscount Ingleby, to inquire into the operation of the juvenile court and to make recommendations for its improvement. The Committee was also invited to consider whether local authorities should be given new powers and duties to prevent or forestall the suffering of juveniles through neglect in their own homes. The Committee made no radical proposals for change (Home Office, 1960) and the subsequent Children and Young Persons Act 1963 merely raised the age of criminal responsibility from 8 to 10. Section 1 emphasized the need for preventive work with juveniles and their families, but few resources were committed to this.

Also in the early 1960s, the Labour Party began to rethink the role of the criminal law in relation to juveniles and, when it became the Government, it produced a series of white papers—*The Child, The Family and The Young Offender* in 1965 (Home Office, 1965) and *Children in Trouble* in 1968 (Home Office, 1968). Underlying the proposals was the belief that delinquency was often a normal part of growing up and that criminal proceedings were inappropriate where delinquency was trivial. The existing machinery of the law was said to be reserved for working-class juveniles; middle-class juveniles were believed to be dealt with without the intervention of the juvenile courts (for example, through schools or the psychiatric services). Serious delinquency, on the other hand, was seen as evidence of the need for help and guidance. Criminal proceedings in such cases were said to be indefensible; what was needed was the application of the necessary treatment without the stigma of a criminal court appearance. In these cases, the causes of juvenile delinquency, like child neglect, were traced to a primary source: inadequacy or breakdown in the family. Delinquency was viewed as evidence of the lack of care, guidance and opportunities which good parents should provide. The juvenile who offended was assumed to have needs which could be diagnosed, treated and eventually cured. Protecting society from delinquency and helping the juvenile delinquent's development were seen as complementary objectives. As a consequence, it was proposed that the juvenile court should perform a new role—enabling juveniles to receive the help they required. The exact form and content of that help was to be left to those with specialist skills, such as social workers, and the order providing such help was to be of sufficient length to enable the juvenile to be properly treated. When circumstances changed, different treatments were to be tried.

These principles were embodied in the Children and Young Persons Act 1969. Although the formal composition and constitution of the juvenile courts were left virtually unchanged, its jurisdiction was radically altered. Juveniles under the age of 14 were not to be referred to the juvenile court solely on the ground that they had committed offences. Rather, where it could be established that such juveniles were not receiving the care, protection and guidance a good parent might reasonably be expected to give, it was proposed that 'care and protection' proceedings should be brought. Criminal proceedings were to be possible against juveniles aged 14–17 who had committed offences, but only after mandatory consultation had taken place between the police and social service departments. The expectation was that these juveniles would also, in the main, be dealt with under care and protection proceedings.

Integral to these proposals was the creation of an enlarged and significant role for local authority social workers. In addition to mandatory consultations with social workers before taking proceedings in the juvenile court, and to increased social work with families and juveniles both on a voluntary and compulsory basis, considerable power was also placed in the hands of social workers to vary and implement the dispositions made by the courts. Magistrates were no longer to make detailed decisions about the kind of treatment appropriate for juveniles. Social workers, within the limits of the particular order, were to determine this. Thus approved school orders which had determined the placement of juveniles in approved schools were to be replaced by care orders which allowed social workers to place juveniles wherever they felt appropriate, including leaving them at home. Attendance centres and detention centres were also to be replaced by a new form of treatment—intermediate treatment—and the form which this would take was also to be determined by the social services. It was envisaged both as a component in a supervision order (which was to replace the probation order) and as a pre-court preventive measure. Borstals* were also not to be available for juveniles.

The general aims of the Act were to reduce the number of juveniles appearing before the juvenile court—that is, to divert them wherever possible—and to make the commission of an offence no longer a sufficient ground for intervention—that is, to 'decriminalize' the court's jurisdiction. The juvenile court was to become a welfare providing agency, but it was also to become an agency of last resort: referral to the juvenile court was to take place only where a voluntary and informal agreement could not be reached between social workers, juveniles and their parents.

The Failure of the Children and Young Persons Act 1969

The 1969 decriminalization model never came to fruition. Ideological differences between the political parties caused key sections of the Act to remain unimplemented. Criminal proceedings for offenders under 14 were not prohibited, nor were they restricted in the case of offenders aged 14–17. Similarly, the minimum age qualification for a borstal sentence was not increased from 15 to 17, and detention centres and attendance centres were not phased out. Thus parts of the new system were introduced—care orders and supervision orders—but the old one continued.

Broadly speaking, two opposing trends occurred in the 1970s which are worthy of comment: an increase in the use of penal measures in general, and of custodial institutions in particular, and an increase in the use of diversion.

Towards custody

Fines, attendance centre orders and custodial sentences were increasingly relied upon by magistrates for 14–16-year-old boys at the expense of

_____
* These were replaced by youth custody centres in 1982 and by young offender institutions in 1988.

middle-range, community-based alternatives and those dispositions, the precise operation of which was left in the hands of social workers. For example, in 1965, 1 in 800 of the 14–16-year-old boys referred to the juvenile court was sent to a detention centre or borstal. By 1979, the chances of that happening had substantially increased so that 1 in every 180 in this age group was given a custodial penalty. Only one-sixth of this increased use of custody could be explained on the basis of changes in juvenile crime (Department of Health and Social Security, 1981). About a third was attributable to the more frequent use of custodial sentences for theft and about a quarter to the more frequent use of custodial penalties for burglary. The DHSS report also showed that throughout the 1970s, those given custodial penalties had not necessarily experienced previously the full range of non-custodial options which the juvenile courts had available to them. This was particularly so for boys given detention centre orders. Thus, changes in the use of custody reflected changes in sentencing practice rather than changes in the nature of juvenile crime. The opposite effect to that intended by the 1969 Act had occurred—sentencing had become more penal rather than more welfare-orientated—and, paradoxically, the Act was blamed for this.

This rapid growth in the use of custodial penalties was undoubtedly the most notable feature of juvenile court sentencing in the 1970s. It was accompanied by a parallel growth in the number of secure places within the child care system.* Between the passing of the 1969 Act and the end of the 1970s, these increased from 60 to over 300. Researchers who investigated this expansion have clearly demonstrated that this was not simply a response to an increasing number of 'hard core' juvenile offenders with whom community resources could not cope. In comparison with juveniles, who were in these facilities prior to the implementation of the 1969 Act, the research suggests that they were, in fact, a less deviant group. Also, they were not found to be more serious offenders or more disordered than their counterparts in open institutions (Millham et al., 1978; Cawson and Martell, 1979). For Cawson and Martell, the hallmark of the system of secure accommodation was:

> The constant passing on of children to others considered more 'expert' or 'specialist', the perpetuation of myths about 'diagnosis' and 'treatment' or 'cure' at the expense of 'care' . . . and the use of therapeutic euphemisms which indicate unwillingness to face the reality that children were being locked up for extended periods occasionally in solitary confinement (1979).

---

* In addition to children's homes and penal establishments, juveniles may also be detained in hospitals for the mentally ill and mentally handicapped. Stewart and Tutt (1987) estimated that around 3000 juveniles are so detained and that 142 were compulsorily detained on the day on which they carried out a census. It is not known whether or not this represents an increase over past years.

Towards diversion

The second trend in the 1970s was the increased reliance on diversion. Diversion has been a dominant thrust in western juvenile justice policy for the past 25 years (Klein, 1985). Even prior to that, arguments in favour of diversion appear in embryo form in the debates in the 19th century which accompanied the establishment of separate institutions and separate courts for juvenile offenders. It was believed that these, in part, would protect juveniles from the contaminating influence of adult offenders.

Diversion is a concept with multiple meanings and, within any one juvenile justice system, not all forms of diversion will necessarily be pursued (Tutt and Giller, 1987). Broadly speaking, three forms of diversion are discussed in the literature.

1. *Diversion from crime.*   This is mainly associated with policies of crime prevention either directed at reducing opportunities for the commission of offences or targeted on particular crime-prone groups (such as juveniles) who participate in certain offences.
2. *Diversion from court.*   Here those who act as gatekeepers into the court system are given the opportunity to discontinue proceedings (entirely or conditionally) and either do nothing or substitute some kind of informal intervention.
3. *Diversion from institutions.*   In this, community-based programmes are promoted as an alternative to institutions (welfare or penal) for those who would otherwise be removed from the community because of their offending.

Proponents of diversion claim a number of advantages for such strategies. Diversion is believed to break the seeming inability of the juvenile court system to respond constructively to law-breaking and to avoid the negative consequences of traditional forms of intervention. Its major strength is claimed to be the avoidance of the labelling process associated with appearance in the juvenile court. Thus it is said to avoid stigmatizing offenders and to avert the development in the juvenile of a deviant self-image and a sustained criminal career. Diversion, it is argued, also avoids the contagion effect on naive and inexperienced offenders when exposed to their more experienced counterparts. Linked with each of these points is the argument that diversion is less costly than the formal processing of cases through the full juvenile justice system, and that resources can thereby be saved or reallocated.

An alternative body of opinion favouring diversion, and one which has proved far more influential elsewhere than here, is that diversion can be a means whereby deviant juveniles (not merely those who commit offences) can be identified at an early stage and worked with in a range of 'treatment' programmes. These programmes can involve counselling and giving advice, but they can also include behaviour modification, vocational training and reparation (Sarri, 1983; Klein, 1985). In England in the 1970s, this form of diversion took the form of preventive intermediate treatment (Thorpe et al., 1980). By the end of the 1970s, it was evident that this use of intermediate treatment far outweighed its role in providing juvenile courts with a range of programmes geared to diverting juveniles appearing in the juvenile courts from institutions.

There was without doubt a substantial expansion in the number of children and young persons cautioned by the police during the 1970s. In 1970, 35% of known juvenile offenders were cautioned by the police for indictable offences; in 1979, the proportion had reached 50%. In absolute terms, this meant that, in 1970, 53 000 children and young persons received a formal caution; in 1979, the number was 82 000.

However, it was acknowledged early in the 1970s that a paradox had developed in this area of juvenile justice practice: an increase in the use of a measure intended to divert juvenile offenders from the juvenile courts was not, in fact, having the effect of reducing the number of juveniles entering that system (a feature well documented in the USA; for a review, *see* Morris, 1978b). Rather than operating as real diversion, the cautioning procedure was said to be widening the net of officially labelled delinquents.

An early and influential report on this point was by Ditchfield (1976). He showed that those police force areas with the greatest increase in the number of cautions in the early 1970s were also the areas with the largest increase in the known offender population, but they also showed the largest increase in the proportion of juveniles to adults in the known offender population. These increases were much larger than could reasonably be accounted for by changes in the age structure of the population. Ditchfield (1976) concluded that this process of net-widening occurred—

> because changes in police practice brought about by the 1969 Act have resulted in a number of juveniles being officially cautioned, when previously they would have been dealt with by informal warning or no further action (*see also* Farrington and Bennett, 1981).

Diversion in the 1980s

Police cautioning has continued to increase throughout the 1980s and, nationally, for example in 1988, 86% of 10–13-year-old arrested boys and 60% of 14–16-year-old arrested boys were cautioned by the police for indictable offences.* A criticism of practice in the 1970s was that cautioning had had a net-widening effect. This appears not to be so now. The number of juveniles appearing in the juvenile courts and the total number of juveniles within the juvenile justice system have both decreased in the last 10 years. In 1978, for example, the number of juveniles found guilty or cautioned for indictable offences was around 177 000; in 1988 it was 119 300.

---

* The comparable figures for girls were 95% and 80%

In part, this may be explained by the fact that the eligible population of juvenile offenders is declining. But it may also be explained by the fact that in response to previous criticisms, the administration of cautions has changed so that diversion is now taking place. Certainly, in some areas it is becoming very rare for juveniles under the age of 14 to appear in the juvenile court. Generally, there is a presumption in favour of cautioning juveniles and a few areas (for example, Devon and Cornwall) even operate a five tier framework of cautions.

The Re-emergence of the Delinquent

A variety of reports were published in the 1970s which both criticized and responded to criticisms in the 1969 Act, for example, the Report of the House of Commons Expenditure Committee (1975a) and the Government's response to it (Home Office et al., 1976). These culminated in the publication in 1980 of the white paper *Young Offenders* (Home Office et al., 1980). It proposed giving the power to juvenile court magistrates to impose a residential care order on a juvenile offender already in the care of the local authority who was found guilty of a further imprisonable offence; to impose on offenders aged 15–16 a sentence of youth custody for a term of up to 12 months; to order a supervision order which would include a specific programme of activities; to impose community service orders on offenders aged 16 and to require parents to pay the fines imposed on their children. The white paper also proposed increasing the amount of financial recognizance which parents could be ordered to forfeit if they failed to exercise proper control over their child, and retaining attendance and detention centres for male offenders aged 14–16 (but with a new minimum period of 3 weeks' custody and a maximum of 4 months).

Basically, these proposals hit at the root of the social welfare philosophy underlying the 1969 Act. They represented a move towards notions of punishment and individual and parental responsibility. They also represented a move away from executive (social workers) to judicial decision-making and from the belief in 'the child in need' to the juvenile criminal, what Tutt (1981) calls the 'rediscovery of the delinquent'. Indeed, the white paper is noteworthy in that, throughout, it refers to juvenile and young adult offenders as young offenders. Overall, the proposals can be viewed as a toughening and tightening-up of the provisions of the 1969 Act.

The recommendations of this white paper formed the basis of the Criminal Justice Act 1982. Details of the current sentencing powers of the juvenile court are discussed in detail below. In brief, the 1982 Act made available to justices three new powers of disposal: youth custody, care orders with charge and control conditions (the equivalent of earlier proposals for residential care orders) and community service. Further, there were three major changes to existing powers: shorter periods in detention centres, restrictions on activities as part of supervision orders, and it was to become normal practice to fine parents rather than the juvenile.

The Criminal Justice Act 1982 was not, however, simply about toughening-up the 1969 Act. There was general agreement by the early 1980s that some kind of change was necessary: first, to reverse a number of the unintended consequences of the 1969 Act and, second, to take account of growing demands to introduce 'justice for children'.

The unintended consequences—primarily expansion of the use of custody—have already been discussed. By the end of the 1970s, the philosophy of welfare as an appropriate basis for responding to juveniles who commit offences was also increasingly being questioned (Morris et al., 1980; Taylor et al., 1980).

Critics have argued that the approach over-simplifies our understanding of the causes of juvenile crime. For example, research contradicts the assumption that delinquency has a pathological base akin to a medical condition (President's Commission, 1967). The search for unique aetiological factors has also produced inconclusive results (Rutter and Giller, 1983).

Given our weak theoretical understanding of the causes of crime, the assumption that we have a range of treatments or interventions which we can successfully use to affect delinquency is equally flawed (Rutter and Giller, 1983). In practice, the application of these interventions has led to stigmatizing the juveniles involved. Furthermore, the discretionary powers given to those who operate welfare interventions have frequently been used to 'widen the net' of the service. This brings into the system those 'at risk' as well as those adjudicated as 'delinquent'.

Much influenced by American writings (for example, by the volumes of standards produced by the American Bar Association/Institute of Judicial Administration, 1977), critics of a welfare approach have argued that the sole justification for the punishment of juvenile offenders should be the commission of a specifically defined offence; that there should be proportionality between the seriousness of the crime and the penalty; that penalties should be determinate in nature and of the least restrictive alternative and that the rights of juveniles (and their parents) should be protected by legal representation.

The proposals of the Black Committee (Children and Young Person's Review Group, 1979) in Northern Ireland, subsequently accepted by the Government, reflect this thinking (*see also* p. 239). It identified the premises which underlie both a welfare and a justice approach to juvenile delinquency and their respective weaknesses. From this, it developed principles which, it believed, would respond to both juveniles' needs and society's demand for protection, and it identified 'key considerations' which, it believed, should determine any policy for dealing with juveniles who offend. In essence, it recommended diversion of juveniles wherever possible and separation of the care and criminal jurisdiction of the juvenile court into two distinct tribunals. (These proposals have not yet been the subject of legislation but there have been some changes in practice, see below pp. 238–9.)

More directly relevant to developments in England was the publication in 1981 of a report on young offenders by the Parliamentary All-Party Penal Affairs Group (1981), chaired by Robert Kilroy-Silk. This group was particularly concerned about the increasing trend towards the use of custody for juveniles. Thus its main recommendations concerned attempts to reverse that trend, and to deal with juveniles in the community as far as possible. Overall, it argued that its proposals would lead to a 'more humane, more cost effective and more just response' to offending by juveniles. With respect to a 'more just response', the group argued for determinate residential and custodial orders, mandatory legal representation in certain situations, statutory criteria to guide the decisions of sentencers and local authorities, and the requirement to give reasons for some decisions.

Cumulatively, these publications had an impact on the content of the 1982 Act. For example, criteria were introduced into the Act which restricted the use of care and custodial orders and also of secure placements, and the Act specified certain situations in which the court had to obtain a social enquiry report and offer legal representation. Thus, the 1982 Act reflected not only elements of a tougher crime control strategy, but also of justice. This trend was taken further in the Criminal Justice Act 1988 which refined the criteria which restricted the use of custody. It was taken further still in the Criminal Justice Act 1991 which restructured the use of custody. These two changes to juvenile practice have occurred within the framework of criminal justice acts which deal primarily with adults, thus reflecting changing attitudes towards juvenile offenders.

Inside the Youth Court

Youth courts look now much as juvenile courts did at their inception in 1908. Few such courts are in buildings separate from the magistrates' court although changes in architecture, building materials and design have made courtrooms somewhat less austere than their Victorian counterparts. A panel of magistrates, drawn from the bench of each petty sessional division because of their experience or interest in juveniles, are appointed to the youth court. Youth court sittings usually form only a part of the magistrates' wider duties. In the Inner London area there is a distinct youth court bench.

Ordinarily, three magistrates sit in the youth court, at least one of whom must be a woman and one a man. It is not uncommon to find a preponderance of female magistrates on youth court panels. Similarly, younger magistrates are also encouraged to take on these responsibilities. Youth court magistrates can serve until they are 65 years of age, although they can continue to sit in the magistrates' court until their 70th birthday. While magistrates are lay people who are intended to represent the character of the local community, the selection process is such that they tend to be drawn disproportionately from the professional and higher social classes (Baldwin, 1976). The Lord Chancellor's Department has attempted to broaden their base, but little change has occurred.

Induction training is now provided to all those appointed to the Youth court, as are refresher courses for longer serving magistrates and special courses for chairmen. Such training includes summaries of the law, practice developments, sentencing exercises and recent policy initiatives from both central and local government. Contributions are usually made by justices' clerks, social workers, probation officers, police officers and, occasionally, academics.

Magistrates are assisted by the clerk to the court. The clerk, who is usually professionally trained in the law or undergoing such training, should have up-to-date information on the criminal law and on sentencing policy and practice. In addition to advising the magistrates on these matters, the clerk has a key role in ensuring the smooth administration of the court.

Integral to providing resources to the youth court are the probation service and local authority social services department. They both provide reports to the courts and supervise juveniles on behalf of the courts. Increasingly frequently, lawyers are present in courts, even in non-contested cases. For the prosecution, a lawyer from the Crown Prosecution Service will appear and an increasing number of defendants are legally represented. Whereas, in 1969, only 3% of juveniles appearing in a juvenile court were represented with legal aid support, by 1988 the figure had reached 57% (Home Office, 1989a). These figures do not include those cases in which representation has been privately financed and research suggests that, in some courts, over 70% of juvenile defendants are represented in delinquency cases (Parker et al., 1981).

Remands in the Youth Court

Most juveniles appear in the youth court on a summons. If the case is not ready to proceed, the magistrates can adjourn it to a future date. Where the juvenile is charged with a more serious offence and has been bailed to attend the court, then the youth court will remand the juvenile, either on bail, to be looked after by the local authority or in custody, if the case cannot proceed. The youth court may also adjourn for reports after a finding of guilt. Where the youth court is dealing with a mentally ill juvenile, it may remand the youth to a mental hospital for assessment or treatment or may make an interim hospital order (sections 35, 36 and 38 of the MHA 1983). All of these procedures operate in much the same way as for adults.

Normally, where juveniles cannot be bailed to their own homes, remands are to local authority accommodation.

In exceptional circumstances juveniles have been detained in penal establishments and provision for this remains although it is intended to end this completely. The Criminal Justice Act 1991 provides that a court may not remand a juvenile in custody unless 'the court is of the opinion that only remanding him to a remand centre or prison would be adequate to protect the public from serious harm from him'. The Act also gives new powers to courts which are remanding juveniles to local authority accommodation. Courts making such remands will be able to: impose conditions of the kind that they can already impose when granting bail; stipulate that the juvenile must not be placed by the local authority with a named person and require that a young person aged 15 or 16 be held in secure accommodation. These first two powers came into force in October 1992; the third will only come into force when remands of juveniles in custody are abolished and courts will only be able to impose this requirement when they consider it necessary to protect the public from serious harm.

Youth Court Dispositions

Most juveniles who appear in the youth court admit the offence and the main role of magistrates is to deal with or sentence (as it would be called in the adult court) juvenile offenders. The powers of disposition available have been substantially changed with the introduction of the Criminal Justice Act 1982 and further refined by the Criminal Justice Act 1988. Further changes were also introduced in the Children Act 1989. The following description of dispositions mentions these where appropriate. It starts with those involving the least intervention in the juvenile's life through to the custodial sanctions. Where it is possible to provide information about the effectiveness of particular measures, this is included. However, as Farrington (1984) notes, such information is often not available (*see also* Rutter and Giller, 1983, for a review of the difficulties involved in such research). Tables 5.1 and 5.2 provide information on the pattern of dispositions for boys and girls for 1978 and 1988.

Bind-over (Recognizance)

The youth court can order a juvenile to undertake to pay a fixed sum of money for subsequent misbehaviour over a period of up to 3 years. As such, a bind-over resembles a suspended fine. A bind-over can be made in addition to or instead of another disposition, and it is not limited to those against whom there has been a finding or guilt or admission. It can be imposed on any person involved in the offence including the complainant. A bind-over can also be made up to the sum of £1000 against parents or guardians, as a way of making them exercise proper control over the juvenile. The party must agree to the imposition of a bind-over. If later misbehaviour takes place, the juvenile court can order that all or part of the original sum be paid

Table 5.1

Percentage of Persons Aged 10 and under 14 Sentenced for Indictable Offences who Received Various Sentences by Sex and Type of Sentence or Order in England and Wales

Sex and year	Total	Absolute or conditional discharge	Supervision order	Fine	Attendance centre order	Care order	Otherwise dealt with
Males							
1978	100	32	21	23	14	10	–*
1988	100	47	15	13	21	3	1
Females							
1978	100	37	26	28	N/A	10	–*
1988	100	64	13	18	3	2	–*

Percentage of total persons sentenced

* less than 0.5 %

Table 5.2

Percentage of Persons Aged 14 or under 17 Sentenced for Indictable Offences who Received Various Sentences by Sex and Type of Sentence or Order in England and Wales

Sex and year	Total	Absolute or conditional discharge	Supervision order	Fine	Community service order	Attendance centre order	Care order	Young offender institution*	Otherwise dealt with
						Percentage of total persons sentenced			
Males									
1978	100	20	16	38	N/A	11	4	12	1
1988	100	25	18	22	5	16	1	11	2
Females									
1978	100	29	22	40	N/A	N/A	8	1	–**
1988	100	43	20	24	2	5	2	1	1

* Includes borstal training (abolished May 1983), detention centre orders and youth custody (both abolished October 1988)

** less than 0.5%

over. Bind-overs were not widely used in the juvenile court and were most frequently made in minor or public order offences. HM Government in a white paper (Home Office, 1990a) believe that more use could be made of this power against parents. Previously, this power could not be used when supervision orders or most other orders were imposed on juvenile offenders. The Government removed this restriction and courts *are required* to consider binding-over the parents of juveniles convicted of criminal offences *in every case*. The courts will also be given the power to fine parents who refuse to be bound-over where the court considers their refusal to be ill founded or unreasonable.

Absolute discharge

The most lenient action which the juvenile court can take is an absolute discharge, and it is usually imposed in situations in which the magistrates believe that no penalty is justified; for example, where the breach of the criminal law was technical. It is infrequently used and, in part, this is due to the willingness of the police to caution juveniles for minor offences. There are some indications that in areas with a low rate of cautioning absolute discharges are used more frequently than elsewhere (Somerville, 1969).

Conditional discharge

A conditional discharge means that the offender will be discharged if there is no further offence within a period of up to 3 years. If offenders are convicted of another offence within the period specified, then they may be sentenced for both the new offence and the original offence. Conditional discharges were a popular measure in juvenile courts and accounted for more than a quarter (28%) of all sentences in 1988 (Home Office, 1989a). In the main, they were imposed on those appearing in the juvenile court for the first time.

Compensation orders

Section 67 of the Criminal Justice Act 1982 changed the juvenile courts' powers to make compensation orders. Previously such orders could only be made in addition to some other penalty (usually a fine). Compensation orders are now penalties in their own right. Magistrates can award compensation of up to £2000 for any one offence. The magistrates can also make an order against the parent or guardian. This power is discussed further in the next section.

Fines

Fines were a frequently used penalty in the juvenile court and accounted for 20% of sentences in 1988 (Home Office, 1989). For children, the upper limit of a fine is £250 and, for young persons, it is £1000. While fines were often imposed upon those appearing in the juvenile court for the first time, they were also used for minor offences even where more severe dispositions (including custodial sentences) had been used previously. Failure to pay a financial penalty can lead to an attendance centre order being imposed on the juvenile. Fines are calculated in units. The size of the fine is determined by multiplying the number of units (representing the gravity of the offence) by the weekly disposable income of the offender.

Significant changes in the power to fine (and to award costs and compensation orders against) parents were introduced by sections 26–28 of the Criminal Justice Act 1982. The juvenile court had a *duty* to impose these financial orders against the parents or guardian of the juvenile rather than the offender unless the court is satisifed that—

> the parent or guardian cannot be found or it would be unreasonable to make an order for payment, having regard to the circumstances of the case.

In 1988, only 13% of fines and 21% of compensation orders imposed on juveniles were 'parents to pay' orders (Home Office, 1989a). The white paper, *Crime, Justice and Protecting the Public* (Home Office, 1990a) describes these figures as 'surprisingly low', since the statutory provision just described is a duty (subject to certain exceptions) rather than a discretionary power. The Government considers the imposition on parents of a formal requirement to pay has an important effect in bringing home to them the consequences of their children's behaviour. It reinforced the duty in the Criminal Justice Act 1991 and the unit fine system applies to financial penalties imposed on parents. The 1991 Act also enables courts to require local authorities to pay any compensation or fines when a juvenile in their care is convicted of an offence and the court is satisfied that the offence followed a failure by the local authority to carry out its duties. The courts in these circumstances will not be bound by the juvenile's means up to a maximum amount appropriate for an offender of that age.

The Criminal Justice Act 1991 specifically named the following sentences as 'community sentences': an attendance centre order, a supervision or probation order, a curfew order, a community service order and a combination order. The court cannot pass a community sentence (which can include one or other of the above sentences with certain exceptions) unless it is of the opinion that the offence, or a combination of the offence and one other associated with it, is serious enough to warrant the sentence. The order should be, in the opinion of the court, the most suitable for the offender and the restrictions on the offender's liberty must be commensurate with the seriousness of the offence and other offences associated with it. These requirements reflect in part the endorsement of a 'just deserts' approach and, in part, reflect a continued acceptance of 'welfare' considerations.

Attendance centre orders

Attendance centres were introduced by the Criminal Justice Act 1948 as a 'short, sharp, shock' to deprive offenders of their leisure time at weekends. The Children and Young Persons Act 1969 intended to replace attendance centres with schemes of intermediate treatment, but this policy has now been reversed. There are more than a hundred junior attendance centres in England and Wales (most are for boys, although a few are for girls and for both sexes). Orders currently last for up to 12 hours for 10–13-year-olds and for between 12 and 24 hours for 14–16-year-olds. HM Government has raised this to 36 hours for 16-year-olds. In 1988, 21% of male offenders aged 10–13 and 16% of male offenders aged 14–16 were made the subject of attendance orders (Home Office, 1989a). The comparable figures for girls were 3% and 5%. Nearly half of the attendance centre orders made are imposed on those who have no previous sentences and such orders are rarely made on those with three or more previous convictions (Dunlop, 1980; Gelsthorpe and Morris, 1983; Tutt, 1985; Gelsthorpe and Tutt, 1986). An offender who fails to attend when ordered or who breaks the rules of the centre can be returned to the court and sentenced for the original offence. According to Dunlop (1980), 29% of the boys in her sample offended while the order was in force and only 52% completed their orders without unauthorized absences.

The majority of attendance centres are run by the police (a few are run by social services departments, education departments or the probation service) and occupy schools or similar public buildings for 2–3 hours on a Saturday afternoon. Police officers working in the centres do so as civilians and are assisted by staff with particular skills—teachers or instructors. The activities at the centre usually combine physical exercise with some handicrafts training, but some attendance centres include social skills, remedial education and counselling.

Supervision orders

Supervision orders place the juvenile under the supervision of a supervising officer for a period of up to 3 years. Supervision is usually undertaken by a social worker in the local social services department, although it can be undertaken by the local probation service. The nature and content of supervision is at the discretion of the supervising officer. Frequently, it takes the form of weekly meetings during the first 3–6 months of the order and then tapers to monthly or less regular meetings. There has been a steady decline in the use of supervision. In 1970, 24% of juvenile court dispositions were supervision orders (Home Office, 1971a), while, in 1988, the corresponding figure was 18% (Home Office, 1989a).

In order to increase the use of supervision orders by magistrates, a number of conditions can be attached to the order. These are intermediate treatment, supervised activity, night restriction and refraining conditions. Breach of a condition in a supervision order can lead to the juvenile being returned to the youth court. The court then has the power to fine juveniles up to £100 or make an attendance centre order.

Intermediate treatment.   A requirement can be added to a supervision order which enables the supervisor to direct the supervised person to participate in specified activities for a period of up to 90 days. These provisions were intended to replace attendance centres, detention centres and borstal training for juvenile offenders. However, in practice, they were little used in the 1970s. Intermediate treatment was viewed then as lacking a coherent philosophy and strategy (Thorpe et al., 1980). Moreover, when intermediate treatment requirements were imposed, implementation was at the discretion of the supervisor and this could mean that little was, in fact, done (Webb and Harris, 1984).

A new financial initiative to develop intermediate treatment as a direct alternative to care and custody was launched in a circular by the DHSS in 1983. Research indicates that in some local juvenile justice systems this has reduced the number of juveniles being removed from the community (Social Information Systems, 1986). The term 'intermediate treatment', however, is often used by social workers and others to describe a wide range of programmes and projects directed at non-delinquent, disadvantaged juveniles or those said to be at risk of delinquency. Attempts have been made recently, on the other hand, to reserve intermediate treatment for those juveniles sentenced by the courts as an alternative to care or custody (Jones, 1986). These revisions have taken the form of confronting juveniles with their delinquent behaviour through individual and group-work exercises and developing with them alternative strategies for dealing with opportunities to offend (Denman, 1982). Such programmes can be linked to victim-offender or community-based reparation schemes, activity groups and discussion of social problems for example, youth unemployment or solvent and drug abuse (*see* Rutherford, 1986a for a fuller discussion).

Supervised activity requirements.   These requirements are the same in form as the intermediate treatment requirements except that it is for the juvenile court magistrates, rather than the supervisor, to determine the nature of the activity programme in which the juvenile must participate and the duration of the requirements (up to 90 days). Supervised activity requirements cannot be imposed in addition to intermediate treatment requirements. These requirements can be used specifically as an alternative to custody; consequently, if juveniles break them, they may be given custodial orders.

Night restriction requirements (curfew).   The youth court can attach to a supervision order a requirement which orders the juvenile to remain at home for 10 hours between 6 p.m. and 6 a.m. for a maximum period of 30 days within the first 3 months of a supervision order. Opposition by social work professionals to this condition and difficulties in its enforcement have meant that it is not widely used (Tildesley and Bullock, 1983). For example, in 1985, less than twenty requirements of night restriction and refraining conditions were recorded as having been imposed on juveniles (Home Office, 1986a). The Government in a white paper (Home Office, 1990a) expressed the view that courts should make greater use of this power than they currently do and has suggested combining it with the binding-over of the parents.

Refraining conditions. The youth court can also order a supervised person to refrain from participating in certain activities specified in the order for certain days or for the whole of the supervision order. This could presumably include requiring the juvenile to refrain from attending football matches, discos, and other such activities associated with the offending.

Residence requirement

This requirement was introduced in the Children Act 1989 and requires a juvenile to live in local authority accommodation for a specific period, up to 6 months. This can only be added if certain conditions are met:

1. a supervision order which imposed either specified activities or a residence requirement has previously been made on the juvenile; *and*
2. the juvenile has been found guilty of an offence which was committed while that order was in force, that the offence if committed by a person under 21 would have been punishable with imprisonment and in the opinion of the court the offence is serious; *and*
3. the Court is satisfied that the behaviour which constituted the offence was due to a significant extent to the circumstances in which the juvenile was living.

The court must obtain a social enquiry report to satisfy itself on the above conditions and the juvenile must have had the opportunity to be legally represented.

Community service orders

Community service is available for juveniles aged 16 and 17 years. Such schemes are organized and administered by the probation service and the orders can be for any period up to 240 hours. In 1988, it was used for about 1400 boys and 100 girls (Home Office, 1989a). The Government wishes to encourage the further use of community service.

In practice, distinctive schemes have not been developed for juveniles and community work is undertaken alongside young adult and adult offenders.

Failure to carry out work under a community service order can lead to the juvenile being returned to the youth court to be dealt with in any way in which he could have been dealt with by the court making the original order.

Probation Orders

The Criminal Justice Act 1991 made probation a sentence in its own right and available for 16-year-olds for the first time. Additional requirements such as attendance at a day centre or involvement in an intensive probation programme can be added as conditions to the order. Probation operates for juveniles in much the same way as it does for adults.

Curfew Order

This order, introduced in the Criminal Justice Act 1991, is available as a sentence for 16 and 17-year-olds. The maximum length of the order is 6 months and the curfew period is for between 2 and 12 hours in any one day. The curfew order may include requirements for securing the electronic monitoring of the offender's wherabouts during the curfew period specified in the order.

Combination order

The Criminal Justice Act 1991 introduced an order which combines probation and community service. It requires a person over 16 years of age to be under the supervision of a probation officer for a specified period of between 12 months and three years and to perform community service for a specified number of hours between 40 and 100.

Detention in a young offender institution

Until 1 October 1988, detention centre orders could be made on boys aged 14–16 and youth custody orders could be made on juvenile offenders (male and female) aged 15–16. Magistrates could impose these orders only if it was 'appropriate', and the Criminal Justice Act 1982 specified the situations in which it was:

1. the offender is unable or unwilling to respond to non-custodial penalties; or
2. the custodial sentence is necessary for the protection of the public; or
3. the offence is so serious that a non-custodial sentence cannot be justified.

These criteria were amended in the Criminal Justice Act 1988. The courts then had to be satisfied that the circumstances (including the nature and gravity of the offence) were such that, if the offender were aged 21 or over, the court would impose a sentence of imprisonment and that the offender qualifies for a custodial sentence. An offender qualified for a custodial sentence if:

1. there was a history of failure to respond to non-custodial penalties and the offender was unwilling or unable to respond to them; or
2. only a custodial sentence would be adequate to protect the public from serious harm; or
3. the offence was so serious that a non-custodial sentence could not be justified.

The Criminal Justice Act 1991 introduced a new framework for custodial sentencing. Section 1 of the Act states that a court shall not pass a custodial sentence on an offender unless it is of the opinion that a) 'the offence, or the combination of the offence and one other offence associated with it, was so serious that only such a sentence can be justified for the offence'; or b) 'where the offence is a violent or sexual offence, that only such a sentence would be adequate to protect the public from serious harm from him.' These conditions relate to the threshold for custody: the first refers to 'just deserts' criterion and the second to 'dangerousness'. Section 2 deals with the criteria for determining the length of a custodial sentence. For the first condition the criterion is 'commensurability' with the seriousness of the offence and others associated with it. With respect to the second condition the court can pass a sentence longer than justified on a tariff basis if it is in the court's opinion necessary to protect the public from serious harm from the offender. As a general rule courts should not have regard to the previous convictions of the offender in determining whether or not custody is warranted and in determining the length of custody. The Criminal Justice Act 1991 abolished the sentence of detention in a young offender institution for 14-year-old boys. The minimum length of a sentence of detention for both boys and girls is two months and the maximum is twelve months.

The youth court must also obtain a social inquiry report to assist it in determining these issues and legal representation must be offered to the juvenile.

Periods of remand in custody or in care on secure accommodation prior to the making of the order are deducted from the time to be served and the offender is released after serving one half of the sentence imposed. On release, supervision lasts for 3 months and can be undertaken by the probation service or the local social services department. Failure to comply with the conditions of supervision on release is punishable by way of a fine (up to £200) or by a further 30 days in custody.

In 1988, around 3200 boys and less than 50 girls were sentenced to detention in young offender institutions. This represented a marked decline in the use of custody over 10 years, in 1978 the comparable figures were 7300 and 100.

The proportionate use of custody, however, has declined only slightly for boys: from 12% in 1978 to 11% in 1988; and, for girls, it has increased slightly from 1% in 1978 to 2% in 1988 (Home Office, 1989a). Overall, since 1981, the number of juveniles under 17 given custodial sentences has fallen by more than 50%. Indeed, the Government recently questioned whether it was necessary to keep the sentence of detention in a young offender institution for girls under 18. It felt that most could be dealt with by intensive supervision in the community. For the more serious female offender aged under 18, section 53 detention would continue to be available. This is described later.

All the new institutions will have the same aim—that of preparing the offender for resettlement in the community. The main features of the regimes for juveniles are:

a brisk regime;
a full and structured daily routine;
a grade system;
emphasis on education and physical education with a minimum of 15
    hours schooling a week;
a personal officer scheme.

It is intended that male juvenile offenders will be kept separated from young adult offenders (the 17–21 group) either in separate centres or separate wings. Because of the small numbers, this is not currently feasible for female offenders.

Juveniles serving sentences who require medical care or who show signs of disturbance can go to one or two psychiatrically supported establishments. These have full-time medical staff and inpatient treatment units, although the majority of inmates within the institutions are not psychiatrically abnormal. Glen Parva has a 20-bed psychiatric hospital which takes remands and sentenced offenders. It admits offenders who are mentally ill, who may serve their sentences there, and offenders who present with disturbed behaviour, particularly self-harm. It also has a 14-place unit staffed by hospital officers under the direction of a psychiatrist. This runs a structured regime utilizing group therapy, individual counselling and social skills training. It has fairly wide admission criteria accepting trainees who are thought likely to benefit from this treatment and who want to come. A typical patient would have been admitted to the hospital after an episode of self-harm and would have subsequently been transferred. Trainees of below average intelligence and those near the end of their sentence are not excluded.

Feltham provides a similar hospital facility. It also has a wing for trainees who are unable to cope with their sentence (often those who are of low intelligence or socially inept). This unit aims to protect these trainees rather than provide therapy.

Although we cannot be certain, it seems likely that the practice of many of the former youth custody and detention centres redesignated as young offender institutions will continue much as before. Sixty-one per cent of boys released from detention centres in 1985 reoffended within 2 years; 81% of boys released from youth custody in 1985 had also reoffended within 2 years. The comparable figure for girls was 49%. There are as yet no figures on reoffending on release from young offender institutions.

Special powers for mentally ill juveniles

There are additional powers available for mentally ill juvenile offenders, namely hospital orders, guardianship orders and supervision orders with a condition of treatment by a specified medical practitioner. A hospital order (*see* p. 72) authorizes the juvenile's treatment in a hospital. Where the juvenile is a young person, and it appears to the juvenile court that the offence is so serious that there should be an order restricting the offender's discharge, the court can commit the juvenile to the Crown Court to be dealt with under the MHA 1983, section 43. A guardianship order which applies only to those who are 16 or over allows the juvenile to remain as an outpatient. Under sections 8 and 37 of the MHA 1983, the guardian has powers to—

1. require residence at a specified place;
2. require the patient to attend at specified places and times for treatment, education, training or occupation;
3. require access to the patient to be given to a doctor, social worker or other specified person.

Guardianship orders are intended essentially as a means of providing care or oversight in the community. Both hospital and guardianship orders are rarely used for juveniles. In 1986, for example, only six such orders were made (Home Office, 1987a).

A youth court may also, as with adults, make an order under the MHA 1983, section 37, without making a finding of guilt if, having heard all the evidence including medical evidence, it is satisfied that the offender committed the offence. However, the court may only make such an order in respect of a person suffering from mental illness or severe mental impairment. In addition, a juvenile's mental state may be grounds for bringing care proceedings where, for example, the parents refuse to provide treatment for a juvenile's mental illness.

Mental health legislation in England and Wales gives no special protection to juveniles. However, the formal detention in mental hospitals of patients who are juveniles is rare. Generally, they are placed there by parents or guardians. The Children's Legal Centre suggests that during 1980 there were only 34 juveniles out of 2674 persons compulsorily admitted under the MHA 1959 (quoted in Stewart and Tutt, 1987).

Deferment of sentence

The youth court has power to defer sentence for any period up to 6 months. Deferment should not be used as a test of treatment, for example, to test a young person's suitability for an intermediate treatment programme, but it can be used to see if the circumstances of the offender change within the designated period, for example, by making reparation to the victim. The court should make clear to defendants what the purposes of the deferment are and what is expected of them during the period of deferment.

A note on dispositions in the juvenile court

The information provided in Tables 5.1 and 5.2 shows that for boys and girls aged 10–13 and for girls aged 14–16 the most frequently used disposition is an absolute or conditional discharge. For girls of both age groups and for boys in older age groups the next most frequently used disposition is the fine; for younger boys it is an attendance centre order. It clearly emerges from this that, overall, the welfare oriented dispositions have made a limited impact on practices within the juvenile court. Indeed, the data show that their use has not increased between 1978 and 1988 despite the Government's intention in the Criminal Justice Act 1982 to make them more attractive to magistrates. The Criminal Justice Act 1991 is a further attempt to increase the number and the attractiveness of community sentences.

With respect to custody, although the number of juveniles made the subject of such orders has gone down significantly, the proportionate use of custody was only slightly less in 1988 than in 1978 for boys and increased from 1 to 2% for girls. This may indicate the failure of magistrates to have regard to the criteria in the 1982 Act and to the failure of lawyers to challenge such reasons (Burney, 1985). The Criminal Justice Act 1988 did not seem to change this, although there are signs that lawyers are taking a more active interest (National Association for the Care and Resettlement of Offenders, 1990a). These figures may also indicate, however, that 'alternative to custody' packages, which were intended to restrict the use of custody, have been used as alternatives to other non-custodial measures rather than to custody (Parker et al., 1987). It is, however, also clear that in some areas the existence of these packages has led to a reduction in the use of custody (National Association for the Care and Resettlement of Offenders, 1989a).

Circumventing the Youth Court

Most jurisdictions have arrangements to transfer juveniles from, or waive the jurisdiction of, the juvenile system when dealing with certain serious offences. In England and Wales, section 53 of the Children and Young Persons Act 1933 is the relevant legislation. Juveniles appearing before the Crown Courts on serious charges can be made the subject of section 53 sentences. This involves detention in a place which, and under such conditions as, the Home Secretary directs. The Home Secretary's powers include directing the detention to be undertaken in a community home controlled by a local authority. For those under 16 years of age at the time of the conviction, the case is usually referred to the Department of Health (DOH) for placement (for example, to one of the two youth treatment centres or to a community home with secure accommodation, Millham et al., 1978; Cawson and Martell 1979).

In recent years, the number of juveniles detained under this section has increased (Dunlop and Frankenburg, 1982): from 11 in 1970 to 63 in 1983 and to 177 in 1988. This increase is, in part, due to an extension of the number of crimes which make such orders possible. In its original form, section 53 was limited to offences of murder, manslaughter and wounding with intent to cause grievous bodily harm. In 1961, however, the Criminal Justice Act extended the range of offences to include all those for which an adult convicted on indictment could be sentenced to imprisonment for 14 years or more. This brought within the ambit of the section offences of robbery, arson, some sexual offences and burglary. The majority of those currently detained under section 53 have been convicted of property offences. In 1988, 84 juveniles convicted of robbery and 25 convicted of burglary were so detained. In part, however, the increase in the number of section 53 sentences also reflects the fact that sentences of youth custody for juveniles are limited to 12 months.

Youth Treatment Service

Two centres exist as a national resource within the Youth Treatment Service under an executive unit of the DOH. The first (St Charles in Essex) was opened in 1971 and the second (Glenthorne in Birmingham) was opened in 1978. Reid (1982) citing Barlow (1978) suggests that these were intended to cater for a heterogeneous group of juveniles.

> There was originally a small group of both boys and girls who could not be coped with by the existing approved school system. Special units offering secure accommodation had been set up to take boys out of the schools who were seen as a disruptive hard core, but amongst these were a few more who were regarded as highly disturbed and thought to need more specialised, long-term care than these units could offer. At that time there was a lack of any secure provision whatever (except prisons and remand centres) for the care of difficult girls. There was no equivalent to the boys' secure units which could take the disruptive or habitual absconders out of girls' approved schools. A number of cases began to appear before the courts involving children who had committed very serious offences . . . and which attracted considerable publicity and political interest. The lack of any suitable place for these children which was both secure in the interests of public safety and also more appropriate for the child than adult offender establishments, caused some embarrassment to the authorities.

Admission to the two centres is by a committee of professional advisers representing the DOH and the directors of the centres. Generally, they admit juveniles between the ages of 12 and 18, who have been committed to the care of the local authority and over whom the local authority has assumed parental rights, or whom the court has sentenced to a period of detention under section 53 of the Children and Young Persons Act 1933. Local authorities are also expected to show that there are no other appropriate placements. By far the majority of admissions are boys. In Glenthorne, for example, from the period since it opened to the end of 1984, 110 boys and 29 girls had been admitted.

The stated aims of the youth treatment centres, quoted by Reid (1982), are 'to provide long-term care and treatment first within conditions of total security, and then in increasingly open conditions.' The regime at Glenthorne was based on a token economy system, but now involves a wider range of social strategies, relaxation training and the teaching of self control skills. St Charles, on the other hand, adopted a psychodynamic model of delinquency and so its practices involve group and individual psychotherapy and family casework. However, there, too, behavioural techniques are used as day-to-day management tools.

Prevention of Juvenile Crime

The Children Act 1989 has placed a duty on local authorities to take such steps as are reasonable to reduce the need to bring criminal proceedings against juveniles, and to encourage juveniles in their area not to commit criminal offences. It is not clear what this will amount to in practice, and whether or not the Government will provide local authorities with additional funding.

Procedures in Scotland

The English system of juvenile justice is an amalgam of welfare, justice, crime control and diversion and so it inevitably reflects the tensions inherent in these diverse approaches. What other alternatives are there? Some continue to look with favour towards Scotland (The Association of County Councils, 1984; McCabe and Treitel, 1984; the Association of Directors of Social Services, 1985). Scotland managed to implement, at least in theory, a social welfare approach. An interesting question is how the Scots were able to achieve this, in 1971, given the considerable opposition to similar proposals in England and Wales. Indeed, the Scottish system may have been even more radical than the English, for it abolished the juvenile courts and replaced them with welfare tribunals staffed by lay people. Children's hearings, as these are called, are concerned only with disposition. There is a complete separation between the judicial and disposition functions. If the juvenile or parent denies the commission of the offence, the case is referred to the sheriff's court for the offence to be proved. If they object to the decision made by the children's hearing on the appropriate disposition, they can also appeal to the sheriff's court. In both these instances, the parents and the juvenile are entitled to legal aid. (This is not available before a children's hearing.) Key figures in the system are the reporters. It is their function to decide, on the basis of reports, whether the juvenile referred to them by the police, social worker or education department is 'in need of compulsory measures of care'. If the reporter believes that this is so, the juvenile is then referred to the children's hearing. The new system applies to juveniles under the age of 16, although where they enter the system before 16, they remain within it until the age of 18 unless the children's hearing terminates its jurisdiction. The children's hearing can discharge the referral or impose a supervision order—the latter may include residential conditions. The hearing has continuing jurisdiction; cases are reviewed annually. It has no power to fine, to send the juvenile to a detention centre or to remit him (or her) to the sheriff's court. It is important, however, to keep in mind that, strictly speaking, Scotland has a two-tier or bifurcated system: that is, some juvenile offenders are still dealt with in the sheriff's courts.

There is now a considerable amount of research on the day-to-day operation of the children's hearing system (Morris and McIsaac, 1978; Martin et al., 1981; Asquith, 1983; Adler, 1985) although it is possible that practice has changed since. This research has questioned the adequacy of the hearings' observance of procedural requirements. The findings suggest that panel members often depart from the statutory procedures which were designed to assist juveniles and their parents to participate in the proceedings and to protect their civil liberties. According to Martin et al. (1981), less than a third of the hearings attended by them came near to the desired procedural safeguards. Only 3% achieved the highest score. Furthermore, when panel members were asked to describe aspects of an ideal hearing, only 6% mentioned the observance of all procedural requirements. Also, while some commentators have referred to participation by the families in the hearing and communication between the parties as a positive feature of the system (Martin et al., 1981; Asquith, 1983; Bottoms, 1985), the research findings do not lead to such clear conclusions. Juveniles and their parents do appear to participate more in the children's hearings than in the juvenile courts. For example, in Asquith's (1983) research, only 16% of contributions to magistrates in the juvenile court were made by juveniles or their parents in contrast with 90% to panel members in children's hearings. However, Asquith goes on to note that on only 11 occasions did members of the hearings disagree with the recommendations made in the social inquiry reports submitted to them compared with 30 such occasions amongst the magistrates. He provides no information on the extent to which the juveniles or their parents agreed with these recommendations and so it is possible at least to raise the issue that, despite their contributions, juveniles and their parents had a limited impact on the final decision of the hearing.

Research has also questioned the nature of the communication taking place within the hearing. Martin et al. (1981) present a series of exchanges between panel members and parties to the hearing. These provide examples of sarcasm, denial of parents' and their children's accounts of or reasons for the offence, moralizing and threats. Moreover, Martin et al. document that the key issues believed to be the reasons for the juvenile's behaviour were avoided. For example, most panel members believed that parental inadequacy was the root of juvenile delinquency. This would have come as a surprise to the parents. Exchanges with parents, according to Martin et al., were characterized by the evasion of sensitive issues and a concentration on topics deemed safe.

Much has been made of the positive feelings that juveniles held of the children's hearings. For example, 78% of the children in Martin et al.'s sample thought the decision reached was fair. Martin et al. accordingly concluded that the hearings system had gone further than most courts in encouraging a sense of fairness. However, a small sample of parents and children interviewed by Morris and Giller (1977) reached a similar conclusion about the English juvenile courts. Thus Martin et al.'s inference is of doubtful validity. If it is wrong, how can we make sense of these surprisingly compatible assessments by English and Scottish parents and children? It is possible that relief that nothing worse happened determines the content of the interviewee's responses; the components of 'fairness' and what it means to parents and children remain relatively unexplored. There is some support for this suggestion in the finding that the children and parents in Martin et al.'s sample who experienced dispositions which involved a residential placement tended to have 'more negative reactions' to the hearings.

It seems unlikely that England will move in the direction of the Scottish hearings. There are two main reasons for this. First, many of the advantages claimed for the Scottish system—diversion, participation and communication between the parties—are not unique to a welfare approach; they can be part of systems based on quite different principles. Second, there is a belief that a welfare approach to juvenile offenders is fundamentally flawed; that it involves over-simplification of the causes of juvenile crime. Such a belief has already led to the rejection and demise of a welfare approach in other jurisdictions (for example, in the USA).

Procedures in Northern Ireland

The Children and Young Persons (Northern Ireland) Act 1968 provides the current legislative framework for dealing with juvenile offenders and children deemed to be in need of care, protection and control. This piece of legislation is very similar to that which pertained in the rest of the UK prior to the enactment of the Social Work (Scotland) Act 1968 and the Children and Young Persons Act (England and Wales) 1969.

The juvenile court remains the judicial forum in which any statutory intervention into the lives of children and young persons takes place. The court is presided over by a magistrate who has at least 6 years' experience as a practising lawyer, assisted by two members of a lay panel. Disposals available to the juvenile court under the 1968 Act are: committal to a training school; committal to the care of a fit person order; supervision order (for children only, that is, those between 10 and 13 years of age); an attendance centre order and committal to a remand home. Under other legislation, the court can order a period of probation including conditions or a period in a young offenders' centre or community service for juveniles who are 16 years or more. The court can also order fines and impose conditional discharges.

In 1976, a committee under the chairmanship of Sir Harold Black was established to review legislation and services relating to the care and treatment of children and young people under the Children and Young Persons Act. Its report was published at the end of 1979 (Children and Young Persons Review Group, 1979). Heavily influenced by the 'Justice for Children' lobby, the committee made several radical suggestions including the separation of the juvenile justice and child welfare systems. Within the juvenile justice system, it was suggested that disposal should be determined by the offence alone and not be affected by any 'welfare' considerations. Also, custodial disposals were to be reserved for the serious and persistent offender, determinate and served in a single secure unit replacing the existing training school system. Successive administrations accepted the Black report 'in principle', but the proposed changes have been repeatedly postponed. Moreover, the report has been considerably diluted. Black's proposals for determinate sentencing and for a fixed number of custodial places, for example, look as though they may not be implemented. However, the Children and Young Persons (Northern Ireland) Order 1989 dealing with the public law aspects of child care gives effect to at least some of the Black report recommendations.

The Children Act 1989, Legal Proceedings for Dealing with Children in Need of Care in the UK

The Children Act 1989, brought into force in October 1991, covers virtually all the law relating to children and has consolidated and simplified the many complex provisions of the old law into a single more consistent and practical code. The focus of this section is on the different ways local authorities and other public agencies can take action under statutory powers to acquire the exclusive right to care for a child, either temporarily or permanently. The intention is to describe the provisions and procedures and not to discuss them, although some issues clearly remain controversial. The interested reader may like to consult Allen (1990), Eekelaar and Dingwell (1990), White et al. (1990) or the Children's Legal Centre *Briefing Paper* on the Act (1990) for in depth analysis of some of these issues. In some instances, depending on the circumstances of a particular case, it may be necessary to consult the many Regulations and Rules of court which describe detailed policy and procedural matters. As with the first section, the procedures and facilities described are the English ones. Scotland and Northern Ireland are dealt with briefly at the end.

The Children Act 1989 was precipitated by the report of the Social Services Select Committee of the House of Commons (1984) which had conducted a series of hearings into the working of the law in disputes between public authorities and parents about the care or custody of children. One of the main recommendations of this Committee was that the Government should carry out a thorough review of legislation and practice in this area. The review itself was undertaken by an interdepartmental working party of civil servants in cooperation with the Law Commission (an independent, though publicly funded body responsible for monitoring the general development of the law). The fruit of their labours was the Consultative Document *Review of Child Care Law* (Department of Health and Social Security, 1985). The Government presented its response in a white paper, *The Law on Child Care and Family Services* (Department of Health and Social Security, 1987b).

The Law Commission had itself been carrying out a simultaneous review of this area because of the seemingly confused legal position of children (Law Commission, 1987, 1988). It is also important to note that the form of the legislation may have been influenced by public opinion and by reports from various inquiries into apparent failures of the child protection system. The most critical of these were the reports into the death of Jasmine Beckford (London Borough of Brent, 1985) and the report of the inquiry into the Cleveland affair (Butler-Sloss, 1988) regarding the handling of alleged child sexual abuse.

The Framework

There is now parallel jurisdiction with regard to all family proceedings and in relation to applications for care or supervision. The 1989 Act gives the Lord Chancellor power to make rules requiring cases to start in a specific tier of court and to be transferred between different tiers of court or latterly among courts of the same tier. One of the key principles in the Act is the belief that parents are responsible for looking after their children. The Act promotes the principle that children are generally best looked after within their own families, and that the State should not intervene unless it is necessary to do so to safeguard the child's welfare.

To ensure that the child's welfare is given paramount consideration when reaching any decision about its upbringing, the Act includes a checklist of seven features to which the court must address itself in interpreting the welfare principle in contested private proceedings and all proceedings which lead to a care or supervision order. The court has the discretion to apply the checklist in other circumstances too. The checklist dictates that the court should have regard to the following:

1. the ascertainable wishes and feelings of the child concerned (considered in the light of his age and understanding);

2. the child's physical, emotional and educational needs;
3. the likely effect on the child of any change in circumstances;
4. the child's age, sex, background and any characteristics of his which the court considers relevant;
5. any harm which the child has suffered or is at risk of suffering;
6. how capable the child's parents, and any other person in relation to whom the court considers the question to be relevant, is of meeting the child's needs;
7. the range of powers available to the Court under the Act in the proceedings in question.

It is also significant that the Act outlines that the court must observe the general principle that any delay in determining a question which relates to the upbringing of a child is likely to prejudice the child's welfare. To this end, the court is required to draw up a timetable for the case to avoid delay, and may give directions to ensure adherence to the timetable.

The Act also creates two major duties—the provision of services and the provision of accommodation to children in need. The general duty of local authorities is:

1. to safeguard and promote the welfare of children within their area who are in need; and
2. so far as is consistent with that duty, to promote the upbringing of such children by their families, by providing a range and level of services appropriate to those children's needs.

Much depends on resources, but the local authority may arrange for these services to be carried out on their behalf by voluntary organizations. Services include: means-tested financial assistance in exceptional circumstances; the identification and assessment of children in need in the area (including the keeping of a register of disabled children); prevention of neglect or ill-treatment through accommodation or cash support to those willing to remove a child from premises where there is suffering; and family support (counselling, home help, holiday assistance, family centre activities). Services also include day care for children under 5 considered to be in need, and care and activities for others in need outside school hours and in holidays.

The local authority has specific duties to provide accommodation for any child in need, but these children are not 'in care', they are to be described as being 'looked after' by the local authority. This is to emphasize the voluntary and flexible characteristics of arrangements made between parents, and carers and the local authority. One new duty is to provide accommodation for any 16 and 17-year-old young person they consider is likely to be seriously prejudiced if no accommodation is provided. With certain limiting conditions, any person with parental responsibility may remove a child from accommodation at any time.

The Act also extends the investigative duties of local authorities who are required to investigate the following five circumstances:

1. they have reasonable cause to suspect that a child who lives or is found in their area is suffering or is likely to suffer significant harm (S.47(1)(b));

2. they have obtained an emergency protection order (S.47(2));
3. they are informed that a child who lives or is found in their area is subject to an emergency protection order or is in police protection (S.47(1)(a));
4. a court in family proceedings directs them to investigate a child's circumstances (S.37(1));
5. a local education authority notifies them that a child is persistently failing to comply with directions given under an education supervision order (Schedule 3, para 19).

In circumstances (1) and (3), the local authority can make enquiries directly or through another agency—the object being to establish whether or not the authority should exercise any of its powers under the Act. The local authority must try to ensure that the child is seen, unless it already has sufficient information and can apply for a court order (either compulsory proceedings or child protection measures) in the case of refusal of access or refusal to disclose the child's whereabouts. An obligation to assist with enquiries is placed on other local authorities, the education, housing and health authority, unless it would be unreasonable for them to do so.

Remedies available to the Court

With some minor exceptions these fall into two major categories; section 8 orders and care and supervision orders. There are four section 8 orders in family proceedings (replacing custody, access and custodianship under the old law); (1) the *residence order* (which specifies with whom the child should live); (2) the *contact order* (which replaces access and includes contact such as by letter or telephone, contact is defined as the child's right); (3) the *prohibited steps order* (which limits an exercise of parental authority) and (4) the *specific issues order* (which allows direction regarding any aspect of parental authority, for example, education or medical treatment).

These latter two orders are modelled on the wardship jurisdiction. These orders may be applied for by parents and carers or made by the court of its own volition under the Act or in other specified family proceedings (such as Adoption Act 1976, or Domestic Violence and Matrimonial Proceedings Act 1976).

Compulsory Intervention

Prior to the Act, there were more than twenty legal provisions under which a child could be admitted to care. There are now five methods of compulsory intervention: the emergency protection order, the child assessment order, the police protection power, the supervision order and the care order. The aim of the Act here is to restate the rules relating to public agency intervention in clear and straightforward terms and to examine the precise legal position of the agency, the child and the child's family in order to give all parties a better deal.

Emergency protection orders (Ss. 44, 45, 48)

It is inevitable that there will be some occasions when immediate compulsory intervention is necessary to protect a child until a full court hearing can be held. Under the old law, this was achieved by obtaining a place of safety order. Emergency protection orders may be granted by a single magistrate who, in an emergency, is satisfied that there is reasonable cause to believe that the child is likely to suffer significant harm if—

1. the child is not removed to accommodation provided by or on behalf of the applicant; or
2. the child does not remain in the place in which he is then being accommodated.

In theory, anyone may apply for an emergency protection order but, in practice, this will normally be done by a social worker acting on behalf of a local authority.

A court (magistrate) may also make an emergency protection order if the local authority (represented by a social worker) or an 'authorized person' (the NSPCC) is investigating suspected abuse and finds that access to a child is being frustrated by unreasonable refusal to allow the child to be seen, provided that there is reasonable cause to believe that such access is urgently required (S.44(1)(b) and (e)). The applicant must provide a written statement to support evidence given on oath within 12 hours. The magistrate has to record the reasons for making the order or refusing it. The magistrate has a duty to appoint a guardian *ad litem* for the child, unless satisfied that this is not necessary.

Where an emergency protection order is in force, anyone in a position to do so must hand the child over to the applicant if asked. The applicant, normally the local authority, is then authorized to accommodate the child and prevent removal of that child from a place of safety, such as a hospital ward, although the applicant may allow a child to stay at home. Medical personnel may *advise* against the discharge of a child from hospital, but they have no legal authority to prevent it unless an emergency protection order is in force. In other words, the applicant acquires parental responsibility over the child (S.44(4)), but no one else loses responsibility.

The emergency protection order allows the applicant to take action to meet the parental responsibility of safeguarding or promoting the welfare of the child. In effect, this limits medical (or other) actions to those necessary for the child's immediate welfare. If additional diagnostic work is required, the applicant must state this when applying for the order. The court can then give appropriate directions regarding the medical or psychiatric examination or other assessment of the child (S.44(6)(b)). If this is overlooked, the applicant can go back to the court for an appropriate extension. The child's parents can also ask for the directions to be varied at any time. The court granting the emergency protection order can impose conditions that there should be *no* medical or psychiatric assessment. Furthermore, in accordance with the *Gillick* principle, a child of sufficient understanding can refuse to submit to examination or assessment (S.44(7)).

When a child is being held under an emergency protection order, the applicant must still allow or even encourage 'reasonable contact' with the parents (including an unmarried father who does not have parental responsibility); anyone who has parental responsibility for the child; anyone with whom the child was living immediately prior to the emergency protection order being made; anyone in whose favour a contact order is in force with respect to the child, and anyone acting on behalf of those persons (S.44(13)). Again, applicants must anticipate if there is reason to fear the consequences of such contacts in their applications, since the magistrate or court can direct which contacts should or should not be allowed between the child and any named person (S.44(6)(a)). Directions can also be sought (and challenged) after the imposition of an emergency protection order.

Emergency protection orders should last no longer than 8 days, although the period can be extended by 7 days if the magistrate has reasonable cause to believe that the child concerned is likely to suffer significant harm if the order is not extended (S.45(5)). There is no appeal against the making of, or refusal to make, an emergency protection order, or any directions in an order. However, after 72 hours, the child, the parents or anyone with 'parental responsibility' prior to the order being made may apply for it to be discharged. But they cannot do this if they were given notice of the hearing at which the emergency protection order was made and attended it. Nor can they appeal against an extension of the order.

Child assessment orders (S.43)

The court (again, a single magistrate) may make a child assessment order if satisfied that—

1. the applicant has reasonable cause to suspect that the child is suffering, or is likely to suffer, significant harm;
2. an assessment of the child's 'health or development, or of the way in which he has been treated' is necessary to establish if the suspicions are well founded; and
3. it is unlikely such an assessment can be satisfactorily made without a child assessment order (S.43(1)).

Only a local authority or an authorized person (the NSPCC) may apply for a child assessment order. A child assessment order can be made even if there are not reasonable grounds for believing that the child is likely to suffer significant harm if not moved or kept from the home environment.

A child assessment order can last only 7 days; it cannot be extended and a second application cannot be made before 6 months from the expiry of the order without leave of the court (S.91(15)(c)). Where assessment of certain conditions cannot be accomplished with this limited time span, particularly where psychiatric assessment is required, or where it is unclear whether or not a failure to thrive is due to neglect or disease, it will be necessary to apply for an interim care order. Indeed, DOH guidance suggests that comprehensive assessment will take about 3 months (Department of Health and Social Services 1989).

Whereas the emergency protection order can be obtained quickly, simply on application of a social worker or other such field worker, in the case of the child assessment order notice of application must be served on the child, the child's parents, anyone with whom the child is living and even someone in whose favour a contact order is in force. There is room for appeal in the case of the child assessment order. Furthermore, courts are empowered to make an emergency protection order even if the application is for a child assessment order.

Police protection powers (S.46)

Despite the introduction of the emergency protection order, the police continue to have power to remove children into suitable places or to prevent their removal from hospital if there is reasonable cause to believe that the children will suffer significant harm if this is not done (S.46(1)). But these powers do not mean that they can enter premises without a warrant except under their general powers to save life or limb under S.17 of the Police and Criminal Evidence Act 1984. They must inform the local authority and everyone with parental responsibility for the child, including those with whom the child has been living.

The police did not acquire 'parental responsibility', but they must do what they can to safeguard or promote the child's welfare (S.46(9)). Their powers last for up to 72 hours after which they can apply for an emergency protection order without necessarily informing the local authority. Access to the child is at the discretion of the police, if they think it 'both reasonable and in the child's best interests' (S.46(10)) but, as with the emergency protection order, there is a presumption of contact with parents, carers and others with contact orders in their favour.

Care and supervision orders (S.31, 35 and Schedule 3 Part II)

Under the old law there were many different routes into compulsory care or supervision with different criteria for admission. The 1989 Act provides one set of criteria for all applications. The court cannot make such orders of its own volition, although it can direct the local authority to investigate and report to the court whether or not an application should be made (S.37(1)).

Applications may be made on their own or in any other family proceedings (S.31(4)).

A care order or a supervision order may be made only if the court is satisfied that:

1. the child concerned has suffered significant harm or is likely to suffer such harm; and
2. the harm or likelihood of harm is attributable to:
   (a) the care given to the child or likely to be given to him if the Order were not made, not being what it would be reasonable to expect a parent to give to him; or
   (b) the child's being beyond parental control (S.31(2)).

Some of this requires elaboration. The child must be under 17 (or 16 if married). Conditions 1 and 2 are cumulative and both must be proved before an order can be made. 'Harm' is defined in the legislation as both ill-treatment (which includes sexual abuse and non-physical ill-treatment such as emotional abuse) and the impairment of health or development means physical, intellectual, emotional, social or behavioural development (S.31(9)). 'Significant' is not defined, but the legislation does offer some guidance as to how 'significance' might be assessed:

> Where the question of whether harm suffered by a child is significant, turns on the child's health or development, his health or development shall be compared with that which could reasonably be expected of a similar child (S.31(10)).

In practice, this means that there is comparison with a hypothetical similar child and with standard development criteria such as those prepared for the DHSS by Mary Sheridan (Sheridan, 1960). The second criterion regarding the grounds for a care or supervision order connects the harm with the quality of care given to the child by the parents. This remains controversial, since what has become known as the 'reasonable parent test' does not address what can be reasonably expected of the child's parents in their particular circumstances at a particular time. The 'beyond parental control' condition is also difficult to define and, therefore, remains controversial; some critics would argue that it is inappropriate to use child protection law to control the conduct of a child (Eekelaar and Dingwall, 1990).

Under care orders (S.33), parental responsibility is acquired by the local authority which has the power to limit the exercise of the parental responsibility retained by the parents provided that it is necessary to do so in order to safeguard and promote the child's welfare. Local authority duties towards children looked after by them are also specified in the Act. There are general welfare duties (S.22), a duty to consult with the parents or others with parental responsibilities as well as with the child, a duty to give consideration to the child's religious persuasion, racial origin and cultural and linguistic background in reaching a decision about the child, a duty to rehabilitate (and reunite the child with his parents or carers unless this is not consistent with his welfare), a duty to promote contact between the child and parents or carers and, finally, a duty to advise and befriend young people aged between 16 and 21 whom they have looked after if they consider that the young person is in need and they are able to provide the help requested. There are also detailed regulations regarding the treatment of the child in care.

A care order continues in force until the child reaches the age of 18, but there are a number of ways in which the care order can be brought to an end prior to the statutory expiry date, including discharging the order or adoption of the child.

A supervision order (S.35 and Schedule 3, Part II) is a form of compulsory intervention which is designed for cases with a child protection element where a range of supervisors' powers are needed over and above general social work support. Specifically, there are now obligations on the 'responsible person' (someone with parental responsbility or with whom the child is living) as well as the child to ensure that the child complies with any directions given by the supervisor. Such directions may include medical or psychiatric examination or treatment as ordered by the court and other activities. The 'responsible person' has to inform the supervisor of the child's address and allow him reasonable contact with the child. A search warrant may be obtained if this is refused (S.102). There is also a specific education supervision order (S.36 and Schedule 3, Part III) which outlines the duty of the supervisor to 'advise, assist and befriend and give directions to' the child and his parents 'in such a way as will . . . secure that he is properly educated'.

Interim orders (S.38)

An interim order or supervision order is, as its name suggests, a temporary or holding measure normally used to allow all participants to prepare their case, and the guardian *ad litem* to investigate the matter. To obtain it, the applicant must present evidence that there are reasonable grounds for believing that the conditions for making a care or supervision order exist. The advantage of having an interim care order is that it has the effect of conferring on the local authority full parental responsibility for the child for the period it is in force. This will allow the authority to make a full diagnostic assessment of the child if it is deemed necessary. The court has the power to make specific directions about this. An interim supervision order does not confer parental responsibility on the applicant, but may contain directions regarding medical or psychiatric examination of the child.

Interim orders can last up to 8 weeks, but the authority can apply for further interim orders as long as these do not delay the final hearing for more than 4 weeks beyond that original 8 weeks (S.38(4) and (5)).

Implications

The Children Act 1989 and its new framework for action regarding children in need has important implications for both public and private agencies involved in child care. Although local authorities have the leading role in this area, many children's problems will initially be identified by other agencies including health agencies. Any legal proceedings will normally follow extensive discussion between different agencies—usually through the case conference. In some cases where immediate action is required for an emergency protection order to be made, for example, there will be preliminary meetings between agencies prior to the case conference. But, ultimately, there may be a case conference, the purpose being to bring together information, evaluate it and advise the responsible authority (social services) on the appropriate action to take.

If the conference believes that further action is necessary they must consider:

1. the need to identify a key worker;
2. whether to place the child's name on the child protection register;
3. whether a specialist assessment team should be involved;
4. plans of future action for the case; and
5. the need to inform the parents (and child) of what is proposed.

It is at this stage, assuming that a decision has been taken to seek a care or supervision order (or interim order) as the appropriate intervention, that legal proceedings will be initiated. As indicated earlier, there is concurrent jurisdiction but, in practice, care proceedings are likely to begin in family proceedings courts. There will be a preliminary hearing to arrange a timetable for the course of proceedings and to resolve any difficulties regarding the preparation of the case. Presenting the case itself is enormously complex and prime consideration must be given to issues surrounding the translation of professional judgments into legally admissible evidence.

Administrative arrangements in respect of the Act are set out in the Department of Health's own Introduction to the Act (Department of Health and Social Services, 1989).

Legal Proceedings for dealing with Children in Need in Scotland

The Children Act 1989 has limited application in Scotland. The sections of the Act dealing with child minding and day care, and minor amendments relating to adoption and private fostering are being adopted, but Scottish child care law is generally organized rather differently. Indeed, it is based around the children's hearing system as for juvenile offenders, and children who are deemed to be in need can be dealt with in the same way—through compulsory measures of care (supervision, with optional conditions of residential care). Where a child has been detained (on a warrant) in a place of safety, and the reporter considers that the child needs compulsory measures of care, he or she will refer the case to a children's hearing.

However, it is important to note that Scotland has been conducting its own child care law review—

> to identify, in the light of developments since the implementation of the Social Work (Scotland) Act 1968, options for change and improvement in child care law which would simplify and improve arrangements for protecting children at risk and caring for children and families in need; to assess the resource implications of any proposals for amendment of the law, and to report to the Secretary of State.

The Review Committee was appointed in 1988 and published its final report *Review of Child Care Law in Scotland* in November 1990 (Child Care Law Review Group, 1990).

Among the Review Committee's recommendations are proposals to—

> foster liaison between health, education and social work authorities through a code of practice on procedures for the admission of children to long-term care in health and social work establishments, and for subsequent monitoring;
>
> increase positive planning with regard to 'voluntary receptions' into care (in England and Wales, of course, the concept of voluntary care is abolished by the Children Act 1989);
>
> develop more respite care services;
>
> empower children's hearing to attach access conditions to place of safety Orders;
>
> oblige the calling of a children's hearing to review supervision requirements where a 'significant' change in access arrangement is proposed;
>
> increase the number of reviews on children in care;
>
> make it easier for parents to challenge the loss of parental rights by developing a new 'parental rights order'; and
>
> clarify and extend the current grounds for referral (the Social Work (Scotland) Act 1968 currently lists eleven separate grounds on which a child may be referred to a children's hearing as being possibly in need of compulsory measure of care).

Interestingly, there are no plans to introduce a composite ground as introduced by the Children Act 1989 in England and Wales, based on the notion of a child suffering, or being likely to suffer significant harm.

The Review Committee have also addressed the issue of Emergency Protection (provided for in warrants and place of safety orders). Section 37 of the Social Work (Scotland) Act 1968 currently permits a police constable, or any person authorized by a court or a justice of the peace, to take a child to a place of safety in certain circumstances. The reporter is then obliged to call a hearing 'on the first lawful' day if practicable, but certainly within 7 days. Children's hearings can authorize further detention of the child for two periods of 21 days. A further two 21-day detention extensions may be obtained on application to the sheriff. Section 40 of the Act makes a parallel set of provisions for detention of the child up to 84 days on a warrant issued to ensure that the child is brought before the hearings. As a consequence of these two parallel sections, there is the possibility that a child might be detained for two consecutive 84-day periods. Here the Review Committee is concerned to rationalize the use of warrants, so that a child may only be subject to one 84-day series.

At the moment, children detained under place of safety orders and warrants are not officially 'in the care of' the local authority. Parents retain all rights, including rights of access and the right to consent or refuse to consent to medical examination or treatment. Needless to say, this does not reflect the reality of the situation, since such children often need protection, monitoring, and medical examination and treatment in the face of refusal of parental consent. The Review Committee has thus proposed that children detained in a place of safety should be 'in care' and subject to care reviews. Further, it has proposed that place of safety orders should empower the local authority to arrange medical examinations or treatment, for therapeutic or forensic purposes. Warrants should contain conditions relating to medical examination or treatment.

The recommendations of the Review Committee are far reaching. We have touched on only a few points here; further recommendations relate to operational aspects of the hearing system, long-term planning for children in care, rules regarding the transfer of children across jurisdictions and so on. (For details of proposals *see* Scottish Child Law Centre, 1990 and Child Care Law Review Group, 1990.) Scotland's child care law is clearly in a state of flux, but it is important to stress that the review has proceeded on the basis that the hearings system is working satisfactorily and that no radical review of the law is required.

Legal Proceedings for dealing with Children in Need in Northern Ireland

The current procedures for dealing with children in need are governed by the Children and Young Persons (Northern Ireland) Act 1968. The existing provisions for place of safety orders, care orders and so on thus correspond generally to those in operation in England and Wales prior to the Children Act 1989. However, as in the case of Scotland, Northern Ireland is proposing changes to some aspects of the law relating to children. Both private law relating to guardianship and custody of children, and to illegitimacy, and public law, which governs in the main the child care responsibilities of the Department of Health and Social Services, and Health and Social Services Boards are under scrutiny.

Perhaps the main point to note here is that Northern Ireland intends to introduce legislation which broadly corresponds with the Children Act 1989 (replacing place of safety provisions with emergency protection provisions and so on). Northern Ireland has produced several consultative documents (*see*, for example, the consultation paper on 'Proposed changes to some aspects of the law relating to children in Northern Ireland' published by the Office of Law Reform and the Department of Health and Social Services, 1989) and are currently preparing legislation in this sphere. Northern Ireland has also introduced revised guidelines on procedures for the prevention, detection and management of child abuse, including child sexual abuse. The interested reader should refer to *Co-operating To Protect Children*, which is a guide for Health and Social Services Boards on the management of child abuse (Department of Health and Social Services, 1989).

6
The Psychosocial Milieu of the Offender

Written by
David P. Farrington

The Scope of this Chapter

This chapter concentrates on the types of offences that dominate the official criminal statistics, principally theft, burglary, robbery, violence, vandalism and drug abuse. It is not concerned with more specialized offences such as white collar crime or sex crime. It focuses on offending in the UK and the USA, with some reference to other similar Western democracies, principally Canada, Australia, New Zealand and the Scandinavian countries. It also focuses on offending by males, since most criminological research has been conducted on males and since gender differences are discussed elsewhere in this book.

It is plausible to suggest that criminal behaviour results from the interaction between a person (with a certain degree of criminal potential or antisocial tendency) and the environment (which provides criminal opportunities). Given the same environment, some people will be more likely to commit offences than others and, conversely, the same person will be more likely to commit offences in some environments than in others.

Criminological research typically concentrates on either the development of criminal persons or the occurrence of criminal events, but rarely on both. The focus in this chapter is primarily on offenders rather than offences. An advantage of studying offenders is that they are predominantly versatile rather than specialized. The typical offender who commits violence, vandalism or drug abuse also tends to commit theft or burglary. For example, in a recent study only 7 out of 50 convicted violent offenders had no convictions for non-violent offences (Farrington, 1991). Hence, in studying offenders, it is unnecessary to develop a different theory for each different type of offence. In contrast, in trying to explain why offences occur, the situations are so diverse and specific to particular crimes that it probably is necessary to have different explanations for different types of offences. The most popular theory of offending events suggests that they occur in response to specific opportunities, when their expected benefits (e.g. stolen property, peer approval) outweigh their expected costs (e.g. legal punishment, parental disapproval). For example, Clarke and Cornish (1985) outlined a theory of residential burglary which included such influencing factors as whether a house was occupied, whether it looked affluent, whether there were bushes to hide behind, whether there were nosey neighbours, whether the house had a burglar alarm and whether it contained a dog.

The prevalence of offenders varies according to the definition of offending and the method of measurement (official records or self-reports usually). For example, 96% of a sample of inner-city London males admitted committing at least one of ten common offences (including theft, burglary, violence, vandalism, and drug abuse) at some time between ages 10 and 32, whereas only 33% of them had been convicted of at least one of these offences during this age range (Farrington, 1989b). Therefore, in order to compare offenders and non-offenders, it is important to set a sufficiently high criterion for 'offending' (e.g. in terms of frequency, seriousness, or duration, or in terms of arrests or convictions), so that the vast majority of the male population are not classified as offenders. When the high rate of admission of minor offences first became widely known in the 1960s, this led some sociologists to argue that there were no differences between offenders and non-offenders (since 'everybody does it'), and hence that the marked differences seen in the official statistics (especially in social class) reflected selection biases by the police or courts. However, more recent reviews (e.g. Hindelang et al., 1981) show that, with comparable criteria of seriousness of offending, official statistics and self-reports yield quite concordant results, and both demonstrate numerous significant differences between offenders and non-offenders. Generally, the worst offenders according to self-reports tend also to be the worst offenders according to official records (e.g. Farrington, 1973; Huizinga and Elliott, 1986).

For detailed reviews of the correlates of offending, *see* Rutter and Giller, 1983, and Wilson and Herrnstein, 1985. A few key studies of offending will be reviewed here, studies chosen in terms of their methodological adequacy. The better studies are defined here according to their possession of as many as possible of the following criteria:

1. a large sample size of at least several hundred;
2. a large number of different types of variables measured (which makes it possible to study the effect of one independently of others, or interactive effects);
3. a longitudinal design spanning at least 5 years (which makes it possible to establish causal order, to study the strength of effects at different ages, and to control extraneous variables better by investigating changes within individuals; *see* Farrington, 1988a);
4. a prospectively chosen, general population sample (as opposed to

Table 6.1
Key Studies of Offending

Principal investigators	Sample
Douglas and Wadsworth (UK)	5362 children selected from all legitimate single births in England, Scotland & Wales in 1 week of March 1966. Followed up in criminal records to age 21. Mainly medical and school data collected, but interviewed at ages 26 and 36. (Wadsworth, 1979)
Elliott and Huizinga (USA)	Nationally representative sample of 1725 adolescents 11–17 years old in 1976. Interviewed in 5 successive years and again in 1984 and 1987. Arrest records collected up to 1985. (Elliott et al., 1985; 1989)
S. Glueck and E. Glueck (USA)	500 delinquents in Massachusetts correctional schools in 1939–44, and 500 matched non-delinquents. Contacted at average ages of 14, 25 and 31. (Glueck and Glueck, 1950; 1968) Non-delinquents followed up to age 47 by Vaillant (1983)
Janson and Wikstrom (Sweden)	All 15 117 children born in 1953 and living in Stockholm in 1963. Tested in schools in 1966. Subsample of mothers interviewed in 1968. Followed up in police records to 1983. (Janson, 1984; Wikstrom, 1987)
LeBlanc and Frechette (Canada)	(1) Representative sample of 3070 French speaking Montreal adolescents. Completed self-report questionnaires in 1974 at age 12–16, and again in 1976. (2) 470 male delinquents seen at age 15 in 1974, and again at ages 17 and 22. All followed-up in criminal records to age 25. (Le Blanc and Frechette, 1989)
Magnusson (Sweden)	1027 children born in Orebro in 1955 and followed-up from 1965 to 1971. Followed up in criminal records to 1984. Two other cohorts born in 1950 and 1952 also followed-up. (Stattin et al., 1986)
J. McCord and W. McCord (USA)	650 boys (average age 10) nominated as difficult or average by Cambridge and Somerville (Massachusetts) schools in 1937–39. Followed-up in 1975–80 by mail questionnaires and interviews and in criminal records. (McCord 1978; 1988)
Mednick (Denmark)	(1) All 14 427 children born in Denmark in 1924–47 and adopted by someone outside their families. Conviction records obtained in 1976–78. (2) All 28 879 males born in Copenhagen in 1944–47 and still living in Denmark in 1974. Followed-up in police records to age 27–30. (Mednick and Christiansen, 1977)
Miller and Kolvin (UK)	All 1142 children born in Newcastle in May–June 1947. Children and families contacted at least once a year up to age 15 and finally at age 22. Children followed-up in criminal records to age 33. (Miller et al., 1974; 1985)

Pulkkinen (*Finland*)	369 children aged 8–9 in Jyvaskyla in 1968 completing peer, teacher and self-ratings. Followed-up to age 20 with interviews and to age 27 in criminal records. (Pulkkinen, 1988)
Robins (*USA*)	(1) 524 children treated in St Louis child guidance clinic in 1924–29 and 100 public school children. Interviewed more than 30 years later. (2) 235 black males born in St Louis in 1930–34 and located in elementary school records. Interviewed in 1965–66. (Robins, 1966; 1979)
Rutter and Quinton (*UK*)	(1) All 1689 10-year-old children in Inner London borough attending state schools in 1970. (2) All 1279 10-year-old children on the Isle of Wight attending state schools in 1964. Both samples retested at age 14. Inner London children followed-up to age 25 in criminal records. (Rutter, 1981b)
Silva and Moffitt (*New Zealand*)	1037 children born in 1972–73 in Dunedin, followed from birth to age 15. Biennial evaluations on health, psychological, educational and family factors. Self-reported delinquency measured at ages 13 and 15. Police records collected at 13. (Moffitt and Silva, 1988a, b, c)
Werner (*USA*)	698 children tracked from birth in Kauai, Hawaii in 1955. Interviewed at ages 10, 18 and 30–32. Health, education and police records collected. (Werner, 1987; Werner and Smith, 1982)
West and Farrington (*UK*)	All boys aged 8–9 in 1961–2; all those of that age in 6 London schools. Boys contacted about every 2–3 years up to age 32. Families contacted every year while boy at school. Boys and all relatives searched in criminal records up to 1987. (West and Farrington, 1973; 1977)
Wolfgang and Figlio (*USA*)	(1) 9945 boys born in Philadelphia in 1945 and living there at least between age 10 and 18, followed-up in arrest records to age 18. Ten per cent of sample interviewed at 26 and followed-up in records to 38. (2) 27 160 children born in Philadelphia in 1958 and living there at least between ages 10 and 18. Subsample interviewed in 1988–89. (Wolfgang et al., 1972; 1987)

retrospective comparisons between prisoners and controls, for example); and

5. self-reported and official measures of offending (since results replicated with both methods probably provide information about offending rather than about any measurement biases).

Very few projects fulfil all or nearly all of these criteria, and abbreviated details of the most important are listed in Table 6.1. (For a more extensive review of these kinds of projects, *see* Farrington, 1988a).

The Natural History of Offending

The prevalence of offending increases to a peak in the teenage years and then decreases in the twenties. This pattern is seen both cross-sectionally and longitudinally (Farrington, 1986a). For example, in England and Wales in 1987, the rate of findings of guilt or cautions of males for indictable offences increased from 0.9 per 100 at age 10 to a peak of 7.9 at age 15, then decreased to 6.0 at age 20 and 3.0 at age 25–29 (Home Office, 1988a). In the USA in 1986, the rate of arrests of males for index offences increased from 4.2 per 100 at age 13–14 to a peak of 7.4 at age 17, then decreased to 3.3 at age 24 and 2.0 at age 30–34 (Federal Bureau of Investigation, 1988). These figures do not exactly correspond to the prevalence of offending, since a minority of offenders are arrested or convicted more than once in a year. However, prevalence varies with age in much the same way as these rates vary. In the London longitudinal survey of 411 males (*see* Table 6.1), the prevalence of convictions increased to a peak at age 17 and then declined (Farrington and West, 1990). It was 1.5 per 100 males at age 10, 5.4 at age 13, 11.2 at age 17, 6.4 at age 22, and 3.2 at age 30. The median age for most types of offences (burglary, robbery, theft of and from vehicles, shoplifting) was 17, while it was 20 for violence and and 21 for fraud. In the Philadelphia cohort study of Wolfgang et al. (1987), the arrest rate increased to a peak at age 16 and then declined. Similarly, the peak age for the prevalence of official offending in a Swedish survey was at 15–17 (Magnusson, 1988).

Self-report studies also show that the most common types of offending decline from the teens to the twenties. In the London longitudinal survey, the prevalence of burglary, shoplifting, theft of and from vehicles, theft from slot machines and vandalism all decreased from the teens to the twenties, but the same decreases were not seen for theft from work, assault, drug abuse and fraud (Farrington, 1989b). For example, burglary (since the last interview) was admitted by 13.2% at age 14, 10.9% at age 18, 4.5% at age 21, and 2.2% at both ages 25 and 32. In their American National Youth Survey, Elliott et al. (1989) found that self-reports of the prevalence of offending increased from 11–13 to a peak at 15–17 and then decreased by 19–21.

Few researchers have investigated whether the relationship between the prevalence of offending and age holds independently of other variables. However, it clearly holds independently of (or at different levels of) sex and race, and the peak in the teenage years is generally seen in different countries in different time periods (Hirschi and Gottfredson, 1983).

Many theories have been proposed to explain why offending peaks in the teenage years (*see* Farrington, 1986a). For example, offending has been linked to testosterone levels in males, which increase during adolescence and early adulthood and decrease thereafter, and to changes in physical abilities or opportunities for crime. The most popular explanation focuses on social influence. From birth, children are under the influence of their parents, who generally discourage offending. However, during their teenage years, juveniles gradually break away from the control of their parents and become influenced by their peers, who may encourage offending in many cases. After age 20, offending declines again as peer influence gives way to a new set of family influences hostile to offending, originating in spouses and cohabitees.

While the absolute prevalence of offending varies with age, there is also considerable continuity in offending over time. In the London longitudinal survey, nearly three-quarters of those convicted as juveniles (age 10-16) were reconvicted between ages 17 and 24, and nearly half of the juvenile offenders were reconvicted between ages 25 and 32 (Farrington and West, 1990). The males first convicted at the earliest ages tended to become the most persistent offenders in committing large numbers of offences at high rates over long time periods. In the Philadelphia cohort study, Wolfgang (1980) reported that 39% of those arrested as juveniles (age 7–17) were also rearrested at adults (age 18–30) in comparison with only 9% of the remainder. Conversely, 69% of those arrested as adults had been arrested as juveniles, compared with only 25% of the remainder. The later book by Wolfgang et al. (1987) confirms the link between juvenile and adult offending.

This continuity over time does not merely reflect continuity in police reaction to crime. In London, for 10 specified offences, the significant continuity between offending in one age range and offending in a later age range held for both self-reports and official convictions (Farrington, 1989b). Therefore, it might be concluded that the relative ordering of individuals on some underlying construct such as criminal tendency stays fairly constant over time, even though the behavioural manifestations of this construct may change.

Genetic Factors

There are two major ways in which criminologists have investigated the hereditary transmission of criminal tendencies: by studying twins and adopted children.

In twin studies, the separate contributions of heredity and environment are estimated by comparing identical (monozygotic) twin pairs and same-sex fraternal (dizygotic) twin pairs. Monozygotic twins are identical genetically, whereas dizygotic twins share only about half of their genes. Where both types of twin pairs are brought up in the same environment, any greater similarity of monozygotic twins to each other is taken as evidence of a genetic influence.

Reviews of twin studies of the prevalence of official offending (e.g. Wilson and Herrnstein, 1985) clearly show that monozygotic twins are more concordant than dizygotic twins. In the most extensive study, Christiansen (1977) followed-up over 3500 twin pairs born in Denmark over a 30-year period. He found that the concordance in official offending was 52% for male monozygotic twin pairs (in other words, when one twin was criminal, the other twin was also criminal 52% of the time) and 22% for male dizygotic twin pairs. Similarly, Rowe and Osgood (1984), in a smaller study of 265 twin pairs in Ohio, showed that the concordance for self-reported offending was greater for monozygotic twins than for dizygotic twins.

The major problem of interpretation in twin studies centres on how far the greater similarity of monozygotic twins reflects their more similar environment: perhaps they are treated more alike because they look more alike. The best way to resolve this issue would be to compare monozygotic twins reared together with monozygotic twins reared apart. If the two kinds of twins were equally concordant in offending, this would be powerful evidence in favour of a genetic factor. Unfortunately, a large-scale study of separated and unseparated monozygotic twins, focusing on offending, has not yet been published, although smaller-scale studies indicate that separated and unseparated monozygotic twins are equally concordant in intelligence and personality (Shields 1962; Rowe 1987).

The basic method in an adoption study is to investigate children who were separated from their biological parents at birth and brought up by adoptive parents. The comparison between the offending of the biological parents and the offending of the children is taken as evidence of genetic influences (since they share about half of their genes, but none of their environment), while the comparison between the offending of the adoptive parents and the offending of the children is taken as evidence of environmental influences (since they share their environment, but not their genes).

The most extensive study of adopted children was based on all non-familial adoptions of children born in Denmark in 1924–47 (Mednick et al., 1983; see Table 6.1). This clearly shows more similarity in the prevalence of convictions between boys and their biological parents than between boys and their adoptive parents. These results held independently of the age of adoption (which was usually within the first year of life) and of any matching of adoptive and biological parents (in social class) by the major Danish adoption agency. Also, the results held regardless of whether the biological parents were convicted before or after the boy was born, thereby excluding the possibility that they were caused by the negative labelling of the sons of criminal biological parents. Furthermore, a large-scale adoption study of offending in over 850 Stockholm male adoptees born in 1930–49 also found important genetic effects (Cloninger et al., 1982).

It can be concluded that there must be some kind of genetic transmission of an underlying construct or tendency that is conducive to offending, such as aggressiveness, although the precise genetic mechanism is not known. This does not, of course, mean that a person's criminality is determined at birth and fixed for life, since heredity and environment always interact to produce observed behavioural outcomes. For example, height is to some extent genetically influenced. However, this influence sets a range of potential heights, and the actual height achieved depends crucially on environmental factors such as the level of nutrition in childhood. Similarly, any genetic factor in crime should only influence the potential for offending, and whether the potential became the actuality would depend crucially on exposure to such environmental factors as particular child-rearing methods or peer influence.

Intelligence

Loeber and Dishion (1983) and Loeber and Stouthamer-Loeber (1987) extensively reviewed the predictors of male offending. They concluded that poor parental child management techniques, offending by parents and siblings, low intelligence and educational attainment, separation from parents, and low socio-economic status were all important predictors. Longitudinal (and indeed cross-sectional) surveys have consistently demonstrated that children with low intelligence are disproportionally likely to become offenders.

In the London longitudinal survey it was found that one-third of the boys scoring 90 or less on a non-verbal intelligence test (Raven's Progressive Matrices) at age 8–10 were convicted as juveniles, twice as many as among the remainder (West and Farrington, 1973). Non-verbal intelligence was highly correlated with verbal intelligence (vocabulary, word comprehension, verbal reasoning) and with school attainment, and all of these measures predicted juvenile convictions to much the same extent. Low non-verbal intelligence was especially characteristic of the juvenile recidivists (who had an average IQ of 89) and those first convicted at the earliest ages (10–13). Furthermore, low non-verbal intelligence predicted juvenile self-reported offending to almost exactly the same degree as juvenile convictions, and measures of intelligence predicted measures of offending independently of other variables such as family income and family size.

Similar results have been obtained in other projects. (For a detailed review, see Wilson and Herrnstein, 1985.) In the Philadelphia cohort study, Wolfgang et al. (1972) found that measures of intelligence and attainment in the first six grades (age 6–11) were significantly related to juvenile arrests, and Jensen (1976) showed that these measures were more strongly related to offending than was race. Wolfgang and his colleagues demonstrated that their 'chronic' offenders (those with 5 or more arrests) had lower intelligence and attainment than their non-chronic offenders. For example, independently of race and socio-economic status, the chronic offenders had an IQ score on average 10 points below that of the one-time offenders.

Studies using the Wechsler intelligence scale for children (WISC) tests have often reported that offenders score lower on performance IQ scales (reflecting such skills as block design, object assembly, and picture arrangement) than on verbal IQ scales (reflecting such skills as reading, use of language and the ability to manipulate abstract concepts). For example, in the New Zealand Health and Development Study (*see* Table 6.1), Moffitt and Silva (1988a) found that arrested juveniles were significantly low on verbal IQ according to the WISC, but not significantly low on performance IQ. Overall, the full scale IQ was significantly low for arrested and self-reported delinquents.

While the link between low intelligence and offending is clear, its interpretation is not. It is not caused by any tendency for more stupid people to get caught by the police more often, since low intelligence predicts self-reported as well as official offending. It might have been expected that intelligence would be only weakly related to self-reported offending, since less intelligent people are more likely to be missing from survey samples and more likely to give invalid responses.

It is possible that moral reasoning is an intervening factor between intelligence and offending. Kohlberg (1976) described a series of stages of moral thinking, through which people progressed. At the youngest ages, people defined what was wrong in terms of what was punished. At older ages, they defined wrongness in terms of what threatened relationships or the social system, while the most advanced moral thinkers defined wrongness in terms of threats to social justice or basic human rights. According to this theory, offenders were essentially retarded in their moral development, and this has been confirmed in several empirical studies (e.g. Thornton, 1987; Lee and Prentice, 1988).

The key explanatory factor underlying the link between intelligence and offending is probably the ability to manipulate abstract concepts. People who are poor at this tend to do badly in intelligence tests such as the Matrices and in school attainment, and they also tend to commit offences, mainly because of their poor ability to foresee the consequences of their offending and to appreciate the feelings of victims (low empathy). Certain family backgrounds are less conducive than others to the development of abstract reasoning. For example, lower class, poorer parents tend to live for the present and to have little thought for the future, and tend to talk in terms of the concrete rather than the abstract. A lack of concern for the future is also linked to the concept of impulsivity.

While low intelligence is linked to offending, high intelligence may tend to protect high-risk children from becoming offenders. For example Kandel et al. (1988) studied the sons of imprisoned fathers in another Danish birth cohort of nearly 2000 males born in Copenhagen, and found that those sons who avoided imprisonment had significantly higher intelligence than those sons who were imprisoned. High intelligence may also be an important means of escape from a ghetto background.

Modern research is studying not just intelligence, but also detailed patterns of cognitive and neuropsychological deficit. For example, in the New Zealand longitudinal study, Moffitt and Silva (1988b) found that self-reported offending was related to verbal memory and visual-motor integration deficits, independently of low social class and family adversity. Neuropsychological research might lead to important advances in knowledge about the link between brain functioning and delinquency. For example, the 'executive functions' of the brain, located in the frontal lobes, include sustaining attention and concentration, abstract reasoning and concept formation, anticipation and planning, self-monitoring of behaviour, and the inhibition of inappropriate or impulsive behaviour (Moffitt, 1989). Deficits in these executive functions are conducive to low measured intelligence and to offending.

Personality and Impulsivity

There has been a good deal of research investigating the relationship between personality and offending. However, the personality scales that correlate more reliably with offending (the psychopathic deviate scale of the Minnesota Multiphasic Personality Inventory and the socialization scale of the California Psychological Inventory: see Tennenbaum, 1977) are probably measuring much the same antisociality construct that underlies offending itself. Hence, these personality constructs could not be regarded as separate causes of offending. One of the best-known theories linking personality and offending was proposed by Eysenck (1977). He viewed offending as essentially rational behaviour, and assumed that a person's criminal tendency varied inversely with the strength of his conscience. The conscience was essentially a conditioned anxiety response that was built up in a social learning process. Each time a child committed a disapproved act and was punished by his parents, the anxiety aroused in him tended to become associated with the act by a process of classical conditioning. After the child had been punished several times for the same act, he felt anxiety when he next contemplated it, and this anxiety tended to stop him committing the act.

Eysenck (1977) concluded that offenders tended to be those who had not built up strong consciences, because they were constitutionally poor at building up conditioned responses. He also linked conditionability to his dimensional theory of personality, predicting that those who were high on

Extraversion (E) and Neuroticism (N) would tend to have the weakest consciences and hence that they were the most likely to be offenders. (At a later stage, he also linked offending with his third dimension, curiously called Psychoticism (P). However, this dimension was not well integrated into the theory, had no clear biological basis, had low internal consistency, and its linkage with offending is probably tautological. Hence it will not be considered further.)

An earlier review of studies relating Eysenck's personality dimensions to official and self-reported offending concluded that N (but not E) was related to official offending, while E (but not N) was related to self-reported offending (Farrington et al., 1982). In the London longitudinal survey, those high on both E and N tended to be juvenile self-reported offenders, adult official offenders and adult self-reported offenders, but not juvenile official offenders. Furthermore, these relationships held independently of other variables such as low family income, low intelligence, and poor parental child-rearing behaviour. However, when individual items of the personality questionnaire were studied, it was clear that the significant relationships were caused by the items measuring impulsivity (e.g. doing things quickly without stopping to think). Hence, it was concluded that the major contribution of research inspired by the Eysenck theory was to identify a link between impulsivity and offending.

Many other investigators have reported a link between the constellation of personality factors variously termed 'hyperactivity-impulsivity-attention deficit' or HIA (Loeber, 1987) and offending. For example, Satterfield (1987) tracked 110 HIA and 88 matched control boys in Los Angeles between ages 9 and 17 and showed that six times as many of the HIA boys were arrested for serious offences. Gittelman et al. (1985) followed up 100 HIA boys and 100 controls in New York between ages 9 and 18, and found that 20% of the HIA boys were arrested, in comparison with 8% of the controls.

Many of the boys in these and other longitudinal studies of hyperactivity (e.g. Nylander, 1979; Huessy and Howell, 1985; Weiss and Hechtman, 1986) probably displayed not only HIA, but also conduct disorder as well, making it difficult to know how far the results might have reflected the well-known continuity between childhood antisocial behaviour and later offending (e.g. Craig and Glick, 1968; Robins and Ratcliff, 1980; Spivack 1983; Farrington 1986b). However, the London longitudinal survey showed that HIA at age 8–10 significantly predicted juvenile convictions independently of conduct disorder at age 8–10 (Farrington et al., 1990b). Therefore, it can be concluded that the linkage between impulsivity and offending holds independently of the continuity in antisocial behaviour. In this London survey, a rating of 'daring' at age 8–10 by parents and peers significantly predicted convictions up to age 32 independently of all other variables.

Family Influences

Loeber and Stouthamer-Loeber (1986) completed an exhaustive review of family factors as correlates and predictors of juvenile conduct problems and delinquency. They found that poor parental supervision or monitoring, erratic or harsh parental discipline, marital disharmony, parental rejection of the child, and low parental involvement with the child (as well as antisocial parents and large family size) were all important predictors of offending.

In the Cambridge-Somerville study (*see* Table 6.1), McCord (1979) reported that poor parental supervision was the best predictor of both violent and property crimes. Parental aggressiveness (which included harsh discipline, shading into child abuse at the extreme) and parental conflict were significant precursors of violent, but not property crimes, while the mother's attitude (passive or rejecting) was a significant precursor of property, but not violent crimes. Robins (1979), in her long-term follow-up studies, also found that poor supervision and discipline were consistently related to later offending.

Similar results were obtained in London (West and Farrington, 1973). Harsh or erratic parental discipline, cruel, passive or neglecting parental attitude, poor supervision, and parental conflict, all measured at age 8, all predicted later juvenile convictions. Furthermore, poor parental child-rearing behaviour (a combination of discipline, attitude and conflict) and poor parental supervision both predicted juvenile self-reported as well as official offending (Farrington, 1979) and poor parental child-rearing behaviour predicted offending independently of other factors such as low family income and low intelligence. Harsh parental discipline and attitude at age 8 also significantly predicted later violent as opposed to non-violent offenders (Farrington, 1978), although more recent research showed that it was equally predictive of violent and non-violent but frequent offenders (Farrington, 1991). Poor parental child-rearing behaviour was related to early rather than later offending (Farrington, 1986b), and was not characteristic of those first convicted as adults (West and Farrington, 1977).

Broken homes and early separations also predict offending. McCord (1982) carried out an interesting study of the relationship between homes broken by loss of the natural father and later serious offending. She found that the prevalence of offending was high for boys reared in broken homes without affectionate mothers (62%) and for those reared in united homes characterized by parental conflict (52%). The prevalence of offending was low for those reared in united homes without conflict (26%) or in broken homes with affectionate mothers (22%). These results suggest that is is not so much the broken home (or a one-parent female headed household) which is criminogenic as the parental conflict which causes it. However, teenage childbearing combined with a one-parent female-headed household is conducive to offending (Morash and Rucker, 1989). The importance of the cause of the broken home is also shown in the British national longitudinal survey of over 5000 children born in one week of 1946 (Wadsworth, 1979, *see* Table 6.1, p. 254). Boys from homes broken by divorce or separation had an increased likelihood of being convicted or officially cautioned up to age 21 (27%) in comparison with those from homes broken by death (16%) or from unbroken homes (14%). Remarriage (which happened more often after divorce or separation than after death) was also associated with an increased risk of offending.

The London longitudinal study showed that both permanent and temporary (more than 1 month) separations before age 10 predicted official offending, providing that they were not caused by death or hospitalization (West and Farrington, 1973). Furthermore, such separations were related to self-reported as well as to official offending (Farrington, 1979). However, homes broken at an early age were not unusually criminogenic. Separations predicted convictions up to age 32 independently of all other variables (Farrington, 1990).

Criminal, antisocial and alcoholic parents also tend to have criminal sons as Robins (1979) found. For example, in her follow-up of over 200 black men in St Louis (Robins et al., 1975), arrested parents (her subjects) tended to have arrested children, and the juvenile records of the parents and children showed similar rates and type of offences. McCord (1977), in her 30-year follow-up of about 250 treated boys in the Cambridge-Somerville study, also reported that convicted sons (her subjects) tended to have convicted fathers. Whether there is a specific relationship in her study between types of convictions of parents and children is not clear. McCord found that 29% of fathers convicted for violence had sons convicted for violence, in comparison with 12% of other fathers, but this may reflect the general tendency for convicted fathers to have convicted sons rather than any specific tendency for violent fathers to have violent sons. Craig and Glick (1968) in New York City also showed that the majority of boys who became serious or persistent delinquents (84%) had criminal parents or siblings, in comparison with 24% of the remainder.

In London, the concentration of offending in a small number of families was remarkable; less than 5% of the families were responsible for about half of the criminal convictions of all family members (fathers, mothers, sons and daughters) (West and Farrington, 1977). Further, having convicted mothers, fathers, or brothers by a boy's tenth birthday significantly predicted his own later convictions (West and Farrington, 1973), and convicted parents and delinquent siblings were related to self-reported as well as to official offending (Farrington, 1979). Unlike most early precursors, convicted parents were related less to offending of early onset (age 10–13) than to later offending (Farrington, 1986b). Also, convicted parents predicted which juvenile offenders went on to become adult criminals and which recidivists at age 19 continued offending (West and Farrington, 1977), and they predicted convictions up to age 32 independently of all other variables (Farrington, 1990a).

These results are concordant with the theory that offending occurs when the normal social learning process is disrupted by erratic discipline, poor supervision, parental disharmony and unsuitable (antisocial or criminal) parental models (e.g. Trasler, 1962). However, some part of the link between criminal parents and delinquent sons may reflect genetic influences.

Just as early family factors predict the early onset or prevalence of offending, later family factors may predict the later desistance from offending. For example, it is often believed that male offending decreases after marriage, and there is some evidence in favour of this (e.g. Bachman et al., 1978). In the London survey, there was a clear tendency for convicted men who got married at age 22 or earlier to be reconvicted less in the next two years than comparable convicted men who did not get married (West, 1982). However, in the case of both the men and their fathers, convicted men tended to marry convicted women, and convicted men who married convicted women continued to offend at the same rate after marriage as matched unmarried men. Offenders who married convicted women incurred more convictions after marriage than those who married unconvicted women, independently of their conviction records before marriage. Hence, it was concluded that the reformative effect of marriage was lessened by the tendency of male offenders to marry women who were also offenders.

Peer Influences

The reviews by Zimring (1981) and Reiss (1988) show that delinquent acts are committed in small groups (usually of two or three people) rather than alone. Generally, the frequency of co-offending decreases with age, although some researchers (Craig and Budd, 1967) have found that it is more common at age 14–16 than at younger ages. In the London longitudinal survey, most officially recorded juvenile and young adult offences were committed with others, but the incidence of co-offending declined steadily with age from 10 onwards. Burglary, robbery and theft from vehicles were particularly likely to involve co-offenders. Co-offenders tended to be similar in age and sex to the study males and lived close to the males' homes and to the locations of the offences. The study males were most likely to offend with brothers when they had brothers who were similar in age to them (Reiss and Farrington, 1991).

Most analyses are based on offenders rather than offences. The frequency of group offenders will always be greater than the frequency of group offences, because of the multiple counting of offenders. To take a Norwegian example from Sveri (1965, his Table 1), at age 13–14 only 17% of offenders were alone, 29% were in a group of two, 17% were in a group of three, and 37% were in a group of four or more. Assuming an average group size of 6 for those in a group of four or more, 39% of offences were committed by lone offenders, 33% by groups of two, 13% by groups of three, and only 15% by groups of four or more.

The above figures refer to official offenders. If people committing offences in groups are more likely to be apprehended than those acting alone, official figures could overestimate the true prevalence of co-offending. In agreement with this suggestion, Hindelang (1976) found that offenders in groups were more likely to be picked up by the police than those acting alone, even after controlling for the frequency and seriousness of offending. Self-reported offending surveys rarely provide detailed information about co-offending. If they enquire about this at all, they often ask whether each act was committed usually alone or usually with others (e.g. Shapland, 1978), rather than trying to obtain precise quantitative estimates of numbers of acts committed and numbers of persons involved. One of the most useful studies is the systematic comparison of group offending in official records and self-reports by Eynon and Reckless (1961) in Ohio. They found that both methods indicated that about three-quarters of institutionalized male delinquents had been with companions when they had committed their first delinquent act at an average age of about 13.

While co-offending is very common, delinquent gangs are not. Probably the major study of gangs was carried out in Chicago by Short and Strodtbeck (1965). They could not find any gangs whose primary activities were crimes of dishonesty or drug use, nor any middle-class gangs. They studied 16 gangs, totalling nearly 600 boys, which were the most notorious in Chicago in 1960 (using detached workers), and these were primarily black gangs oriented towards violence. Surprisingly, the gang members were little different from non-gang members or even from middle-class boys in their evaluation of middle-class values.

Later studies disagree about the extent to which gang membership is an important factor in the totality of offending. Miller (1975) carried out a national survey of several of the largest American cities, questioning police and other agencies. He reported that about one-third of all juveniles arrested for violence were gang members, and that gang members accounted for about a quarter of all juvenile homicides. O'Hagan (1976), in a small survey of 60 institutionalized Scottish delinquents, found that 80% claimed to be members of juvenile gangs which committed theft, vandalism or violence.

Morash (1983) in Boston found that there was a negligible association between being a member of a stereotypical gang and committing offences. In the London longitudinal survey, 85% of boys went around in a group of four or more males, but only 5% were members of a gang with a recognizable identity, a leadership structure, and some kind of uniform. These mostly centred round a particular club or cafe. While official convictions were greater among those who went round in a group, fewer of the gang boys were convicted than of the remainder (West and Farrington, 1977).

The major problem of interpretation is whether young people are more likely to commit offences while they are in groups than while they are alone, or whether the high prevalence of co-offending merely reflects the fact that, whenever young people go out, they tend to go out in groups. Do peers tend to encourage and facilitate offending, or is it just that most kinds of activities out of the home (both delinquent and non-delinquent) tend to be done in groups? Another possibility is that the commission of offences encourages association with other delinquents, perhaps because 'birds of a feather flock together' or because of the stigmatizing and isolating effects of court appearances and institutionalization. It is surprisingly difficult to decide among these various possibilities, although most researchers argue that peer influence is an important factor.

There is clearly a close relationship between the delinquent activities of a young person and those of his friends. Both in the USA (Hirschi, 1969) and in the UK (West and Farrington, 1973), it has been found that a boy's reports of his own offending are significantly correlated with his reports of his friends' delinquency. Similarly, Hardt and Peterson (1968) showed that the official delinquency records of a boy's friends were significantly related to his own official and self-reported offending. In the National Youth Survey of Elliott et al. (1985), having delinquent peers was the best independent predictor of self-reported offending in a multivariate analysis.

An important problem of interpretation follows from the fact that, since most delinquent acts are committed in groups, those who commit such acts will very likely tend to have delinquent friends with whom they commit their acts. In other words, self-reports of offending and of delinquent peers may be measuring the same underlying theoretical construct of offending. However, in the National Youth Survey, Elliott and Menard (1988) concluded that having delinquent peers increased a person's own offending and that a person's own offending also increased his likelihood of having delinquent peers. Hence, both effects were operating.

In the London survey, association with delinquent friends was not measured until age 14, and so this was not investigated as a precursor of offending (which began at age 10). However, it was a significant independent predictor of convictions at the young adult ages (Farrington, 1986b). Also, the recidivists at age 19 who ceased offending differed from those who persisted, in that the desisters were more likely to have stopped going round in a group of male friends. Furthermore, spontaneous comments by the youths indicated that withdrawal from the delinquent peer group was seen as an important influence on ceasing to offend (West and Farrington, 1977). Therefore, continuing to associate with delinquent friends may be an important factor in determining whether juvenile delinquents persist in offending as young adults or desist.

Delinquent peers are likely to be most influential where they have high status within the peer group and are popular. However, studies both in the USA (Roff and Wirt, 1984) and in the UK (West and Farrington, 1973) show that delinquents are usually unpopular with their peers. It seems paradoxical for offending to be a group phenomenon facilitated by peer influence, and yet for offenders to be largely rejected by other adolescents (Parker and Asher, 1987). However, it may be that offenders are popular in offending groups and unpopular in non-offending groups. More worrying is the suggestion that some people act as 'recruiters', constantly dragging more people into the net of offending (Reiss, 1988).

Just as association with delinquent peers may facilitate offending, social isolation may act as a protective factor. In the London survey, boys from typically criminogenic backgrounds (with three out of: low family income, large family size, convicted parents, poor parental child-rearing behaviour, and low intelligence) who, nevertheless, were not convicted up to age 32 were investigated (Farrington et al., 1988a, 1988b). The most characteristic feature of these boys was that they had few or no friends at age 8. While they were genuinely well-behaved at age 32, they were often leading relatively unsuccessful lives, for example living in dirty home conditions, not being home owners, living alone, having never married, having large debts, and having low status, lowly paid jobs. Therefore, while peer influence may facilitate offending for boys from vulnerable gackgrounds, social isolation may lead to other kinds of social problems.

Schools

It is clear that the prevalence of offending varies dramatically between different secondary schools, as Power et al. (1967) showed more than 20 years ago in London. However, what is far less clear is how much of the variation should be attributed to differences in school climates and practices, and how much to differences in the composition of the student body. As Wilson and Herrnstein (1985, pp. 279–80) pointed out:

> Perhaps the best way to find out whether schools contribute to crime independently of the personal attributes of their pupils is to see whether different kinds of schools lead to different rates of delinquency, controlling for the characteristics of the students. It is remarkable and a bit dismaying, given the great attention devoted to schools as influences in delinquency, that so little effort has been made to find out if different kinds of schools lead to different behavioural outcomes.

In the London longitudinal survey, the effects of secondary schools on offending were investigated by following boys from their primary schools to their secondary schools (Farrington, 1972). The best primary school predictor of offending was the rating of troublesomeness at age 8–10 by peers and teachers. The secondary schools differed dramatically in their official offending rates, from one school with 20.9 court appearances per 100 boys per year to another where the corresponding figure was only 0.3. However, it was very noticeable that the most troublesome boys tended to go to the high delinquency schools, and *vice versa*. Furthermore, it was clear that most of the variation between schools in their delinquency rates could be explained by differences in their intakes of troublesome boys. The secondary schools themselves had only a very small effect on the boys' offending.

The most famous study of school effects on offending was also carried out in London by Rutter et al. (1979). They studied 12 comprehensive schools, and again found big differences in official delinquency rates between them. High delinquency rate schools tended to have high truancy rates, low ability pupils, and low social class parents. However, the differences between the schools in delinquency rates could not be entirely explained by differences in the social class and verbal reasoning scores of the pupils at intake (age 11). Therefore, they must have been caused by some aspect of the schools themselves or by other, unmeasured factors.

In trying to discover which aspects of schools might be encouraging or inhibiting offending, Rutter et al. (1979) developed a measure of 'school process' based on school structure, organization and functioning. This was related to school misbehaviour, academic achievement and truancy independently of intake factors. However, it was not significantly related to delinquency independently of intake factors.

Many aspects of the schools were not related to their delinquency rates: the age of the buildings, the number of students, the amount of space per student, the staff/student ratio, the academic emphasis (e.g. amount of homework or library use), the rate of turnover of teachers, the number of school outings, the care of the school buildings, and so on. The main school factors that were related to delinquency were a high amount of punishment and a low amount of praise given by teachers in class. However, it is difficult to know whether much punishment and little praise are causes or consequences of antisocial school behaviour which, in turn, is probably linked to offending outside school.

The research of Rutter et al. (1979) does not show unambiguously that school factors influence offending. This is partly because of the small number of schools involved in the study (only 9 containing boys), and partly because far more is known about individual-level risk factors for offending than about school-level risk factors. Because this was a pioneering study, important school-level risk factors may not have been measured. In order to advance knowledge about possible school effects on offending, a study is needed in which many factors are measured for primary school children, who are then followed-up to a large number of secondary schools. This might make it possible to conclude confidently that school effects explained differences in offending rates independently of individual-level factors present at intake.

Several researchers have suggested that, if school failure is linked to offending, sending troublesome children to alternative schools where failure experiences are minimized might lead to a decrease in their offending. Gold and Mann (1984) studied three alternative schools in Detroit for disruptive and delinquent juveniles, which aimed to increase their success experiences through individualized curricula and grades based on a student's own progress (i.e. not in relation to other students). They found that students allocated to the alternative schools showed less disruptive behaviour than controls allocated to regular high schools. Similarly, Gottfredson (1987) evaluated several alternative school projects and found that some led to decreases in offending. Therefore, there is some evidence that school organization can affect offending. (For an extensive review of schooling and delinquency, *see* Hawkins and Lishner, 1987.)

Socio-economic Deprivation

In many projects, offenders and non-offenders are matched on social class before being compared on other factors. This indicates a widespread belief in the importance of social class but, of course, also prevents this belief from being tested.

Historically, social class, or socio-economic status, has been an important variable because of the belief of sociologists that human behaviour could be explained by reference to societal variables. Borrowing freely from geology, their model of society was somewhat analogous to the earth, characterized as it was by a series of strata. Each person's behaviour was thought to be determined to some extent by his position in strata of wealth, power or prestige. Generally, the social class of a family has been measured primarily according to rankings by sociologists of the occupational prestige of the family breadwinner. Persons with professional or managerial jobs were ranked in the highest class, while those with unskilled manual jobs were ranked in the lowest.

There are many problems with this measure of socio-economic status. Occupational prestige scales may not correlate very highly with real differences between families in socio-economic circumstances. In general, the scales date from many years ago, when it was more common for the father to be the family breadwinner and for the mother to be a housewife. Because of this, it may be difficult to derive a realistic measure of socio-economic status for a family with a single parent or with two working parents (Mueller and Parcel, 1981). Also, the social class of a child is sometimes defined not according to the circumstances of his parents, but according to the characteristics of his area of residence (e.g. Wolfgang et al., 1972) or even his school (Roff and Wirt, 1984). Clearly, characteristics of individuals cannot necessarily be inferred from characteristics of areas or schools.

Over the years, many other measures of social class have become popular, including family income, educational levels of parents, type of housing, overcrowding in the house, possessions, dependence on welfare benefits, and family size. These may all reflect more meaningful differences between families than occupational prestige. Family size is highly correlated with the other indices of socio-economic deprivation, although its relationship with offending may reflect child-rearing factors (e.g. less attention to each child) rather than socio-economic influence.

As Thornberry and Farnworth (1982) pointed out, the voluminous literature on the relationship between social class and crime is full of inconsistencies. However, most of the studies have been essentially correlational in nature and have not investigated social class as a precursor of offending. Perhaps rather surprisingly, the majority of American researchers who have carried out major community surveys have found very little relationship between social class (usually measured by parental occupation) and offending (whether measured by official records or self-reports). This was the result obtained by Thornberry and Farnworth (1982) in the Philadelphia cohort study. In the first major comparison of self-reported and official delinquency in a nationally representative sample of over 800 American adolescents, Williams and Gold (1972) came to the same conclusion.

Beginning with the pioneering self-report research of Short and Nye (1957), it was common to argue that low social class was related to official offending, but not to self-reported offending, and hence that the official processing of offenders was biased against lower class youth. However, in their careful review of the literature, Hindelang et al. (1981) found that the belief that low social class was related to official offending was entirely based on ecological (area) correlations. Studies based on individuals showed no discrepancy between official and self-report measures and no relation between offending and occupational prestige.

More consistently than correlational studies, longitudinal surveys tend to show that children from socio-economically deprived families are particularly likely to become offenders, especially when socio-economic deprivation is measured by poverty and poor housing. Robins (1979) reported in two surveys that children from poor families, in slum housing, and those whose parents or guardians had low status occupations, tended to become offenders. In the English national survey, Douglas et al. (1966) showed that the prevalence of recorded juvenile offending in males varied considerably according to the occupational prestige and educational background of their parents, from 3% in the highest category to 19% in the lowest. Also, Wadsworth (1979) reported that offending increased significantly with increasing family size in this survey. Similar results were reported by Kolvin et al. (1988) in their follow-up of Newcastle children from birth to age 33, and by Ouston (1984) in her longitudinal survey in London.

European surveys have also generally found a relation between socio-economic deprivation and offending. In major Swedish longitudinal surveys, Janson (1983) reported that official offending varied inversely with occupational prestige, and Magnusson et al. (1983) showed that it varied inversely with parental education. A similar inverse relationship between occupational prestige and official offending was obtained in Denmark by Hogh and Wolf (1983), while in West Germany Remschmidt et al. (1977) showed that low occupational prestige was correlated with high self-reported offending. Similar results were obtained in New Zealand by Moffitt and Silva (1988c). The research of Van Dusen et al. (1983) with adopted children in Denmark is especially interesting in showing a relation between official offending and the occupational prestige of both biological and adoptive parents.

In the London longitudinal survey, self-reported and official offending were predicted by low family income, unsatisfactory housing, neglected accommodation, support by social agencies, physical neglect by parents, and an erratic paternal work record—but not by occupational prestige (West and Farrington, 1973). Thus the measure of occupational prestige used did not adequately reflect differences between the families in socio-economic conditions, and the best measure of socio-economic deprivation was low family income. Somewhat similar results were obtained in the major American self-report survey by Hirschi (1969) of over 4000 children in California. While offending was not related to paternal occupation or education, it was related to paternal unemployment and to the welfare status of the family.

In the London survey, the ability of low family income to predict offending did not merely reflect its association with other factors such as criminal parents or poor parental child-rearing behaviour, since low income predicted offending independently of these other factors (West and Farrington, 1973). Also, low family income at age 8 was the best childhood predictor of general social failure at age 32 (Farrington, 1989a), and poor housing at age 8–10 predicted convictions up to age 32 independently of all other variables (Farrington, 1990a). It seems clear that, when socio-economic deprivation is measured meaningfully by income and housing, it predicts the onset or prevalence of offending.

Socio-economic deprivation of parents is usually related to offending by sons. However, when the sons grow up, their own socio-economic deprivation can be related to their own offending. In the London survey, just as an erratic work record by the father predicted later offending by the boy, an unstable job record of the boy at age 18 was one of the best independent predictors of his convictions between ages 21 and 25 (Farrington, 1986b). Also, between ages 15 and 18, the boys were convicted at a higher rate when they were unemployed than when they were employed (Farrington et al., 1986), suggesting that unemployment in some way causes crime and, conversely, that employment may lead to desistance from offending.

Community Influences

Offending rates vary systematically with area of residence. For example, Clark and Wenninger (1962) compared four areas in Illinois and concluded that self-reported offending rates were highest in the inner city, less in a lower-class urban area, less still in an upper middle-class urban area, and lowest of all in a rural farm area. In their national self-report survey of American juveniles, Gold and Reimer (1975) also found that self-reported offending was highest for males living in the city centres and lowest for those living in rural areas. More recently, Shannon (1988) documented how police contact rates over a long period were highest in the inner city (of Racine, Wisconsin) and lowest in the more peripheral areas.

The classic studies by Shaw and McKay (1969) in Chicago and other American cities also showed that juvenile delinquency rates (based on where offenders lived) were highest in inner city areas characterized by physical deterioration, neighbourhood disorganization, and high residential mobility. A large proportion of all offenders came from a small proportion of areas, which tended to be the most deprived. Furthermore, these relatively high delinquency rates persisted over time, despite the effect of successive waves of immigration and emigration in changing the demographics of the population in different areas. Shaw and McKay concluded that variations in offending rates reflected variations in the social values and norms to which children were exposed which, in turn, reflected the degree of social disorganization of an area.

Later work has tended to cast doubt on the consistency of offending rates over time. Bursik and Webb (1982) tested Shaw and McKay's cultural transmission hypothesis using more recent data in Chicago and more sophisticated quantitative methods. They concluded that the distribution of delinquency was not stable after 1950, but reflected demographic changes. Variations in delinquency rates in different areas were significantly correlated with variations in the percentage of non-whites, the percentage of foreign born whites, and the percentage of overcrowded households. The greatest increase in offending in an area occurred when blacks moved from the minority to the majority. These results suggested that Shaw and McKay's ideas, about commuity values which persisted despite successive waves of immigration and emigration, needed revising. It was necessary to take account both of the type of area and of the type of people living in the area (e.g. Simcha-Fagan and Schwartz, 1986).

Similar ecological studies have been carried out in the UK (for a review, see Baldwin, 1979). Wallis and Maliphant (1967) in London showed that official crime rates correlated with rates of local authority renting, percentage of land used industrially or commercially, population density, overcrowded households, the proportion of non-white immigrants, and the proportion of the population aged under 21. However, crime rates were negatively related to suicide and unemployment rates and not related to illegitimacy or mental illness rates. Power et al. (1972) carried out a similar study in one working-class London borough and found that official delinquency rates varied with rates of overcrowding and fertility and with the social class and type of housing of an area.

In Wallis and Maliphant's (1967) project, it was generally true that crime rates were higher in the inner city, and it is important to investigate why this is so. One of the most significant studies of inner city and rural areas is the comparison by Rutter et al. (1975a) of 10-year-old children in inner London and in the Isle of Wight. They found a much higher incidence of conduct disorder in their inner London sample. These results are relevant to crime, because of the link between conduct disorder in children and offending in juveniles and adults. Rutter, Yule et al. (1975c) investigated factors that might explain this area difference. They found that four sets of variables—family disorder, parental deviance, social disadvantage, and school character-istics—were correlated with conduct disorder in each area, and concluded that the higher rates of disorder in inner London were at least partly caused by the higher incidence of these four adverse factors.

It is not always true that crime rates are higher in inner city areas. In Sheffield, Baldwin and Bottoms (1976) found that the key factor influencing where offenders lived was the type of housing. Offender rates were lowest in owner-occupied areas and highest in areas of council housing and private renting, and the high crime areas were not all near the centre of the city. They concluded that council housing allocation policies played a role in creating high offender rate areas. This again raises the issue of how far crime rates reflect the influence of the area or the kinds of people living in the area.

Reiss (1986) pointed out that a key question was why crime rates of communities changed over time, and to what extent this was a function of changes in the communities or in the individuals living in them. Answering this question requires longitudinal research in which both communities and individuals are followed-up. The best way of establishing the impact of the environment is to follow people who move from one area to another, thus using each person as his own control. In the London longitudinal survey, Osborn (1980) found that moving out of London led to a significant decrease in convictions and self-reported offending. This decrease may have occurred because moving out led to a breaking up of offending groups. Also, Rutter (1981a) showed that the differences between inner London and the Isle of Wight held even when the analyses were restricted to children reared in the same area by parents reared in the same area. This result suggests that the movement of problem families into problem areas cannot be the whole explanation of area differences in offending.

Clearly, there is an interaction between individuals and the communities in which they live. Some aspect of an inner-city neighbourhood may be conducive to offending, perhaps because the inner city leads to a breakdown of community ties or neighbourhood patterns of mutual support, or perhaps because the high population density produces tension, frustration or anonymity. There may be many interrelated factors. As Reiss (1986) argued, high crime areas often have a high concentration of single-parent female-headed households with low incomes, living in low cost, poor housing. The weakened parental control in these families—partly caused by the fact that the mother had to work and left her children unsupervised—meant that the children tended to congregate on the streets. In consequence, they were influenced by a peer subculture that often encouraged and reinforced offending. This interaction of individual, family, peer and neighbourhood factors may be the rule rather than the exception.

Ethnic Origin

Most research on ethnic origin has compared 'blacks' (Afro-Caribbeans) and 'whites' (Caucasians). In London, black people are far more likely to be arrested than white people, especially for violent offences and particularly for robbery. For example, of those arrested for robbery in 1987, 41% were white, 54% were black, 2% were Asian, and 3% were other or not known (Home Office Statistical Bulletin, 1989). These figures can be compared with the estimated resident population of London, aged 10 or over, which was 85% white, 5% black, 5% Asian, and 5% other or not known. The comparison of these figures gives a black:white ratio for robbery of 22:1. This ratio is increasing over time, since it was only 11:1 in 1977. The comparable American ratio for index arrests for robbery was 10:1 in 1986, and the same in 1976 (Federal Bureau of Investigation, 1988). The comparable American figure in 1986 for all violent arrests was 5:1 and for all index arrests was 3:1.

The black:white ratio based on victim reports of the offender's appearance is even higher. For example, in 1985 (the last year for which this information was compiled), London robbery victims said that their offender(s) were white in 19% of cases, non-white in 56%, mixed in 7%, and not known in the remaining 18% (Home Office Statistical Bulletin, 1989). Making the assumption that a negligible proportion of non-white offenders were not black, the black:white ratio from victims is 50:1. The discrepancy between the 50:1 ratio from victims and the 22:1 ratio from arrests may mean that the average black robber commits twice as many robberies as the average white robber, or that white robbers are twice as likely to be arrested as black robbers. From reports in the USA by victims of personal crimes (rape, robbery, assault and theft from a person), Hindelang (1981) calculated that 85 of these crimes per year were committed by every 100 black males aged 18–20. The comparable figure for white males of this age was 15, yielding a black:white ratio of approximately 6:1.

Longitudinal surveys yield lower black:white ratios, at least for prevalence. This is because prevalence ratios are constrained by the maximum of 100%, whereas ratios like those above, based on numbers of offences, have no such constraint. In the first Philadelphia cohort study of Wolfgang et al. (1972), 50% of black males and 29% of white males had police records for non-traffic offences by the age of 18. The comparable figures for the second cohort (see Table 6.1) were 42% and 23% (Tracy et al., 1985). Up to age 30, 69% of black males and 38% of white males in the first cohort had police records for non-traffic offences (Wolfgang et al., 1987). Clearly, if 38% of whites are arrested, the maximum possible black:white ratio is 100:38 or 2.6:1. Extensive reviews of the prevalence of official offending by Gordon (1976), Hindelang et al. (1981) and Visher and Roth (1986) show consistent black:white differences averaging about 3:1 over different offences.

The most reliable English survey figures on ethnicity and crime are probably those obtained in Ouston's (1984) follow-up of over 2000 inner

London children. She found that 39% of black males were convicted or cautioned as juveniles, in comparison with 28% of white males. There are no comparable figures for Asians (originating in India, Pakistan or Bangladesh); however, studies elsewhere in England suggest that they have a lower crime rate than whites. For example, Mawby et al. (1979) calculated the annual rate of convictions and cautions in Bradford per 100 juveniles as 3.2 for Asians and 6.3 for others (mostly whites).

Differences between blacks and whites in self-reported offending are much less than differences in official offending, as Williams and Gold (1972) pointed out in their national American survey. Probably the most extensive self-reported offending figures have been obtained in the 'Monitoring the Future' project. In this, nationally representative samples of American high school students are interviewed each year, and usually about 400 of the 3000 respondents were black. Over the 10 years 1976–85, black:white prevalence ratios were close to 1:1 for most offences (Jamieson and Flanagan, 1987). Even for robbery using a weapon, the black:white ratio was only 1.7:1, since it was admitted by an average of 3.9% of blacks and 2.3% of whites. Similar results were obtained in the US National Youth Survey (Huizinga and Elliott, 1987). There seem to be no published large-scale comparisons of blacks, whites and Asians on self-reported offending, no comparable figure for older age groups, and no repeated English national self-report surveys.

To summarize, blacks are more likely than whites to commit offences (and especially violent offences) according to official records, but the differences in self-reports are much smaller. Williams and Gold (1972) suggested that blacks and whites were treated differently by the police and the courts, and there is some evidence of ethnic bias for juveniles in Philadelphia (Thornberry, 1973) and London (Landau, 1981). However, there is no evidence of ethnic bias in national English figures for Crown Court sentencing (Moxon, 1988). In any case, the fact that victim reports of offenders reveal substantial black:white ratios indicates that the differences between blacks and whites are not entirely attributable to bias in official processing.

A plausible explanation for the discrepancy between official and self-report figures is that self-report instruments are differentially invalid by ethnicity. In a validity check, Hindelang et al. (1981) found that the percentage of officially recorded offences which were not self-reported was 10% for white males, but 33% for black males. Similarly, Huizinga and Elliott (1986) discovered in the National Youth Survey that black males under-reported arrests more than white males (39% versus 19%). It is possible that black males are more likely to be falsely arrested. Also, black males, and especially those who are the most serious offenders, are likely to be under-represented in samples interviewed, because they are differentially institutionalized, uncooperative or difficult to locate.

The weight of evidence indicates that black males are more likely to commit offences than white males, both in the UK and in the USA. Most theories proposed to explain black-white differences suggest that ethnicity in itself is not an important causal factor, but that blacks and whites differ on known precursors of offending such as low family income, poor parental child-rearing behaviour or low intelligence. Rutter et al. (1975b) outlined the socio-economic deprivation suffered by their black families, especially in regard to poorer quality housing and lower status jobs. Wilson and Herrnstein (1985) commented on socio-economic deprivation and also proposed that, partly because of the high proportion of black single-parent female-headed households, parental control and supervision was less adequate in black families. Gordon (1976, 1987) suggested that black-white differences in the prevalence of offending reflected black-white differences in intelligence. In testing these and other theories, it is important to determine whether observed ethnic differences in offending hold independently of these known precursors. For example, Ouston (1984) showed that her black-white differences in official offending did not hold independently of differences in social class or school attainment.

In general, research on the link between ethnicity and offending has paid too little attention to ethnic groups other than whites and blacks. Results obtained with orientals in the USA and with Asians in England suggest that minorities (even those suffering socio-economic deprivation) can be less criminal than the majority white population, and it is important to establish why this is so. The low offending rate of Japanese-Americans has often been attributed to their closely-knit family system, characterized by strong parental controls (e.g. Voss, 1966), and a similar explanation was proposed by Batta et al. (1975) and Mawby et al. (1979) for the low offending rate of Asians in England. Hence, different child-rearing techniques might explain low offending rates by different ethnic groups as well as high ones.

Explaining Crime

So far in this chapter, the most important psychosocial predictors and correlates of offending have been reviewed. The fact that most possible predisposing factors tend to be inter-related makes theoretical interpretations difficult. Children who live in deprived inner-city areas tend to have parents with low paid jobs or an erratic work record, tend to have friends who commit offences, tend to be impulsive, and tend to fail in school. They also tend to be exposed to harsh and erratic child-rearing practices, and parental criminality, conflict, violence and alcohol abuse; and so on. It is not entirely clear from existing research how far these factors are independently related to offending, and so it is reasonable to include all of them in a theory. Also, most studies provide information only about the prevalence of offending, not about onset, continuation or frequency of offending, and desistance separately.

Several modern delinquency theories have aimed to achieve increased explanatory power by integrating propositions derived from other theories (e.g. Elliott et al., 1985; Hawkins and Weis, 1985; Pearson and Weiner, 1985). A previous attempt has been made to explain some of the findings of the London longitudinal survey in a speculative way by integrating elements of five other theories (Farrington, 1986b). These were Cohen's (1955) delinquent subculture theory, Cloward and Ohlin's (1960) opportunity theory, Trasler's (1962) social learning theory, Hirschi's (1969) control theory, and Sutherland and Cressey's (1974) differential association theory. It was proposed that offending was the result of a four-stage process. Motivations arose that could lead to offending, then an illegal method of satisfying the desire was chosen, then this could be magnified or opposed by internalized beliefs, and finally whether an offence occurred depended on immediate situational influences.

This chapter extends that theory in three major ways. First, acknowledging that crimes arise from the interaction between the individual (with a certain criminal tendency) and the environment (which includes both physical opportunities and social influences); these two aspects will be separated more explicitly. Second, more attention will be given to explaining the different stages of a criminal career: onset, continuation or intensification, and desistance (see Blumstein et al., 1988a,b; Farrington et al., 1990a). Third, partly to incorporate labelling ideas (e.g. Lemert, 1972), the learning process that follows offending and its consequences will be included more explicitly in the theory.

It is assumed that criminal tendency depends partly on motivation and partly on internalized beliefs. The main motivations that ultimately lead to offending are desires for material goods, status among intimates, and excitement. These desires could be culturally induced or could be a response to a specific situation (e.g. a desire for excitement arising from a state of boredom). The desire for excitement may be greater among children from poorer families, perhaps because excitement is more highly valued by lower class people than by middle-class ones, because poor children lead more boring lives, or because poor children are less able to postpone immediate gratification in favour of long-term goals (which could be linked to the emphasis in lower-class culture on the concrete and present as opposed to the abstract and future).

These motivations produce criminal tendency if illegal methods of satisfying them are habitually chosen. Some people (e.g. children from poor families) are less able to satisfy their desires for material goods, excitement and social status by legal or socially approved methods, and so tend to choose illegal or socially disapproved methods. The relative inability of poorer children to achieve goals by legitimate methods could be because they tend to fail in school and tend to have erratic, low status employment histories. School failure, in turn, may often be a consequence of the unstimulating intellectual environment that lower-class parents tend to provide for their children, and their lack of emphasis on abstract concepts.

Criminal tendency also depends on internalized beliefs and attitudes about law-breaking that have been built up in a learning process as a result of a history of rewards and punishments. The belief that offending is wrong, or a 'strong conscience', tends to built up if parents are in favour of legal norms, if they exercise close supervision over their children, and if they punish socially disapproved behaviour using love-oriented discipline. The belief that delinquency is legitimate, and antiestablishment attitudes generally, tend to build up if children have been exposed to attitudes and behaviour favouring offending (e.g. in a modelling process), especially by members of their family and by their friends.

The relative ordering of people on the criminal tendency spectrum tends to stay reasonably consistent over time. This may be partly because internalized beliefs are built up in childhood and thereafter do not change much, or partly because relative opportunities for achieving aims do not change much. However, absolute levels of criminal tendency are probably lower in adulthood than in the teenage years, partly because the strength of desires decline and partly because there is more opportunity to satisfy them legally.

Whether a person with a certain degree of criminal tendency commits a crime in a given situation depends on opportunities, costs and benefits, and on the subjective probability of the different outcomes. The costs and benefits include immediate situational factors such as the material goods that can be stolen and the likelihood and consequences of being caught by the police, as perceived by the individual. They also include social factors such as likely disapproval by parents or spouses, and encouragement or reinforcement from peers. In general, people are hedonistic, and make rational decisions. However, more impulsive people are less likely to consider the possible consequences of their actions, especially consequences that are likely to be long delayed.

The consequences of offending feed back to criminal tendency and to the cost-benefit calculation as a learning process. If the consequences include official labelling, stigmatization, and isolation with other offenders, this may make it more difficult for an offender to achieve his aims legally, and hence it may lead to an increase in his criminal tendency (Gold and Williams, 1969; Farrington, 1977). If the consequences of crime are reinforcing (e.g. gaining material goods or peer approval) or punishing (e.g. legal sanctions or parental disapproval), this may affect the person's future subjective estimations of costs, benefits and probabilities.

Applying the theory to explain some of the results reviewed here, children from poorer families are likely to offend, because they are less able to achieve their goals legally and because they value some goals (e.g. excitement) especially highly. Children with low intelligence are more likely to offend, because they tend to fail in school and hence cannot achieve their goals legally. Impulsive children are more likely to offend, because they do not give sufficient consideration to the possible consequences of offending. Children who are exposed to poor parental child-rearing behaviour, disharmony or separation are likely to offend, because they do not build up internal controls over socially disapproved behaviour, while children from criminal families and those with delinquent friends tend to build up antiestablishment attitudes and the belief that offending is justifiable. The whole process is self-perpetuating, in that poverty, low intelligence, and early school failure lead to truancy and a lack of educational qualifications which, in turn, lead to low status jobs and periods of unemployment, both of which make it harder to achieve goals legitimately.

Taking into account the ages at which different events occur, poverty, low intelligence and poor child rearing may be particularly related to the onset of offending. Antisocial parents and siblings, and delinquent peers, may influence why offenders continue after onset or the frequency of offending: while getting married, achieving a satisfactory job and moving out of criminal areas may be linked to desistance.

Offending may increase to a peak between ages 14 and 20, because boys (especially lower-class school failures) have high impulsivity, high desires for excitement, material goods and social status between these ages, little chance of achieving their desires legally, and little to lose (since legal penalties are lenient and their intimates—male peers—often approve of offending). In contrast, after age 20, desires become attenuated or more realistic, there is more possibility of achieving these more limited goals legally, and the costs of offending are greater (since legal penalties are harsher and their intimates—wives or girlfriends—disapprove of offending).

Implications for Prevention and Treatment

Interest in rehabilitative treatment for offenders declined in the mid-1970s, as the influential reviews by Martinson (1974) in the USA and Brody (1976) in England suggested that existing treatment techniques had no differential effects on the recidivism of detected offenders. This conclusion was substantially confirmed by the US National Academy of Sciences panel in an impressive, methodologically sophisticated review (Sechrest et al., 1979). Hence, the best hope for a long-term decrease in offending may lie in prevention rather than treatment.

Methods of preventing or treating offending should be based on theories about causes. The implications reviewed here are those for which there is some empirical justification, especially in randomized experiments. The effect of any intervention on offending can be demonstrated most convincingly in such experiments (Farrington, 1983, 1990b; Farrington et al., 1986).

It is difficult to know how and when it is best to intervene, because of the lack of knowledge about developmental sequences, ages at which causal factors are most salient, and influences on onset, continuation and desistance. For example, if truancy leads to delinquency in a development sequence, intervening successfully to decrease truancy should lead to a decrease in delinquency. On the other hand, if truancy and delinquency are merely different behavioural manifestations of the same underlying construct, tackling one symptom would not necessarily change the underlying construct. Experiments are useful in distinguishing between developmental sequences and different manifestations, and indeed Berg et al. (1979) found experimentally that decreases in truancy were followed by decreases in delinquency.

Causal factors may be more salient at some ages than others. For example, parental child-rearing factors are likely to be most influential before the teenage years, so that the same intervention technique targeted on parents may be more effective for children aged 8 than for those aged 15. Similarly, causal factors may have different effects on different stages of the criminal career. As an example, if delinquent peers affected continuation but not onset, an intervention technique targeted on peers should be applied after the criminal career has begun (as treatment) rather than before (as prevention).

If low intelligence and school problems are causes of offending, then any programme that leads to an increase in school success should lead to a decrease in offending. One of the most successful delinquency prevention programmes was the Perry preschool project carried out in Michigan by Schweinhart and Weikart (1980). This was essentially a 'Head Start' programme targeted on disadvantaged black children, who were allocated (approximately at random) to experimental and control groups. The experimental children attended a daily preschool programme, backed up by weekly home visits, usually lasting 2 years (covering ages 3–4). The aim of the programme was to provide intellectual stimulation, to increase cognitive abilities, and to increase later school achievement.

More than 120 children in the two groups were followed up to age 15, using teacher ratings, parent and youth interviews, and school records. As demonstrated in several other Head Start projects, the experimental group showed gains in intelligence that were rather short-lived. However, they were significantly better in elementary school motivation, school achievement at 14, teacher ratings of classroom behaviour at 6–9, self-reports of classroom behaviour at 15 and self-reports of offending at 15. Furthermore, a later follow-up of this sample by Berrueta-Clement et al. (1984) showed that, at age 19, the experimental group was more likely to be employed, more likely to have graduated from high school, more likely to have received college or vocational training, and less likely to have been arrested. Hence, this preschool intellectual enrichment programme led to decreases in school failure and to decreases in offending.

Impulsivity and other personality characteristics of offenders might be treated using the set of techniques variously termed 'cognitive-behavioural interpersonal social skills training' (*see* Michelson, 1987). For example, the methods used by Ross to treat juvenile delinquents (Ross et al., 1988; Ross and Ross, 1988) are solidly based on some of the known individual characteristic of delinquents. Ross pointed out that delinquents are impulsive, since they often fail to stop and think before they act, and fail to think even after they act. Hence, they do not learn to modify their behaviour as a result of punishment. They are concrete in their thinking, and their poor capacity for abstract reasoning makes it difficult for them to understand the reasons for rules and laws. They also find it difficult to appreciate what other people are thinking and feeling, and hence lack the skills necessary to form close personal relationships.

Ross also pointed out that many delinquents are 'external'. They believe that what happens to them depends on chance or luck, not on their own actions, and hence do not set goals or persist in trying to achieve them. They tend to have poor interpersonal problem-solving skills. They find it hard to think of ways of solving interpersonal problems, may not realize when they have such problems, and do not understand the cause and effect relationship between their behaviour and other people's negative reactions to them.

Some delinquents also tend to be egocentric. They see the world only from their perspective, and do not think how others are feeling. They may be selfish and callous, failing to appreciate the effects of their behaviour on others (such as their victims). They may see other people as objects, not as individuals with their own needs and motives. Overall, delinquents tend to have thinking errors. They put the blame for their acts on other people or on things beyond their control, and they expect people to believe far-fetched stories. These thinking errors are greater when delinquents are emotionally aroused.

Ross believes that delinquents can be taught the cognitive skills in which they are deficient, and that this can lead to a decrease in their offending. His reviews of delinquency rehabilitation programmes (Gendreau and Ross, 1979, 1987) show that those which have been successful in reducing offending have generally tried to change the offender's thinking. Ross carried out his own 'Reasoning and Rehabilitation' programme in Canada, and found (in a randomized experiment) that it led to a significant decrease in reoffending for a small sample in a 9-month follow-up period. His training is carried out by probation officers, but he believes that it could be carried out by parents or teachers.

Ross' programme aims to modify the impulsive, egocentric thinking of delinquents, to teach them to stop and think before acting, to consider the consequences of their behaviour, to conceptualize alternative ways of solving interpersonal problems, and to consider the impact of their behaviour on other people, especially their victims. It includes social skills training, lateral thinking (to teach creative problem solving), critical thinking (to teach logical reasoning), value education (to teach values and concern for others), assertiveness training (to teach non-aggressive, socially appropriate ways to obtain desired outcomes), negotiation skills training, interpersonal cognitive problem solving (to teach thinking skills for solving interpersonal problems), social perspective training (to teach how to recognize and understand other people's feelings), role-playing and modelling (demonstration and practice of effective and acceptable interpersonal behaviour).

If poor parental supervision and erratic child-rearing behaviour are causes of offending, it seems likely that parent training might succeed in reducing offending. The behavioural parent training developed by Patterson (1982) is one of the most hopeful approaches. His careful observations of parent-child interaction showed that parents of antisocial children were deficient in their methods of child rearing. These parents failed to tell their children how they were expected to behave, failed to monitor the behaviour to ensure that it was desirable, and failed to enforce rules promptly and unambiguously with appropriate rewards and penalties. The parents of antisocial children used more punishment (such as scolding, shouting or threatening), but failed to make it contingent on the child's behaviour.

Patterson attempted to train these parents in effective child-rearing methods, namely noticing what a child is doing, monitoring behaviour over long periods, clearly stating house rules, making rewards and punishments contingent on behaviour, and negotiating disagreements so that conflicts and crises did not escalate. His treatment was shown to be effective in reducing child stealing over short periods in small-scale studies.

If having delinquent friends causes offending, then any programme which reduces their influence or increases the influence of prosocial friends could have a reductive effect on offending. Feldman et al. (1983) carried out an experimental test of this prediction in St Louis. Over 400 boys who were referred because of antisocial behaviour were randomly assigned to two kinds of activity groups, each comprising about 10–12 adolescents. The groups consisted either totally of referred youths or of one or two referred youths and about 10 non-referred (prosocial) peers. On the basis of systematic observation, self-reports by the youths, and ratings by the group leaders, it was found that the antisocial behaviour of the referred youths with prosocial peers decreased relative to that of the referred youths in unmixed groups.

Several studies show that school students can be taught to resist peer influences encouraging smoking, drinking and marijuana use. For example, Telch et al. (1982) employed older high school students to teach younger ones to develop counter-arguing skills to resist peer pressure to smoke, using modelling and guided practice. This approach was successful in decreasing smoking by the younger students, and similar results were reported by Botvin and Eng (1982). Murray et al. (1984) used same-aged peer leaders to teach students how to resist peer pressures to begin smoking, and Evans et al. (1981) used films. These techniques, designed to counter antisocial peer pressures, could help to decrease offending.

If socio-economic deprivation causes offending, then providing increased economic resources for the more deprived families, perhaps by means of an income maintenance programme, should lead to a decrease in offending by their children. This prediction was not borne out in an evaluation of the

Seattle and Denver income maintenance experiments by Groeneveld et al. (1979), although, because of the complexity of the data, they had difficulty in drawing any conclusions. There were no significant differences between the experimental and control groups in the later official offending records of children who were aged 9–12 at the time of the treatment. However, extra welfare benefits given to ex-prisoners can in some instances lead to a decrease in their offending (Rossi et al., 1980), and employment programmes might foster desistance.

If some feature of inner city areas causes offending, and if that feature could be identified and changed by some kind of community action, then offending might decrease. Unfortunately, the specific causal feature is not known. Shaw and McKay (1969) argued that, since offending was caused by social disorganization, it could be prevented by community organization. This idea led to the Chicago Area Project, which aimed to coordinate community resources to increase the educational, recreational and occupational opportunities for young people. However, the success of this programme in reducing offending has never been rigorously demonstrated (Schlossman and Sedlak, 1983).

Conclusions

A great deal has been learned in the last 20 years, particularly from longitudinal surveys, about the psychosocial milieu of the offender. Offenders differ significantly from non-offenders in many respects, including intelligence, personality (especially impulsivity), family background, peer influence, socio-economic status, and area of residence. The differences are often present before, during and after criminal careers.

It is plausible to suggest that there is an 'antisocial personality' that arises in childhood and persists into adulthood, with numerous different behavioural manifestations, including offending. This idea has been popularized by Robins (1979), and is embodied in the DSM–III R diagnosis of antisocial personality disorder (American Psychiatric Association, 1987a). The antisocial male adult generally fails to maintain close personal relationships with anyone else, performs poorly in his job, is involved in crime, fails to support himself and his dependents without outside aid, and tends to change his plans impulsively and to lose his temper in response to minor frustrations. As a child, he tended to be restless, impulsive, and lacking in guilt, performed badly in school, truanted, ran away from home, was cruel to animals or people, and committed delinquent acts.

A similar pattern is seen in the London longitudinal survey (Farrington and West, 1990). The typical offender—a male property offender—tends to be born in a low income, large-sized family and to have criminal parents. When he is young, his parents supervise him rather poorly, use harsh or erratic child-rearing techniques, and are likely to be in conflict and to separate. At school, he tends to have low intelligence and attainment, is troublesome, hyperactive and impulsive, and often truants. He tends to associate with friends who are also delinquents.

After leaving school, the offender tends to have a low status job record punctuated by periods of unemployment. His deviant behaviour tends to be versatile rather than specialized. He not only commits property offences such as theft and burglary, but also engages in violence, vandalism, drug use, excessive drinking, reckless driving, and sexual promiscuity. His likelihood of offending reaches a peak during his teenage years and then declines in his twenties, when he is likely to get married or cohabit with a woman.

By the time he is in his thirties, the offender is likely to be separated or divorced from his wife and separated from his children. He tends to be unemployed or to have a low paid job, to move house frequently, and to live in rented rather than owner-occupied accommodation. His life is still characterized by more evenings out, more heavy drinking and drunk driving, more violence, and more drug taking than his contemporaries. Hence, the typical offender tends to provide the same kind of deprived and disrupted family background for his own children that he himself experienced, thus perpetuating from one generation to the next an antisocial personality syndrome of which offending is only one element.

Research is urgently needed on methods of preventing and treating this antisocial personality syndrome. Some hopeful techniques were reviewed in the previous section, but the most that can be said about them is that they warrant large-scale testing. In order to advance knowledge about the causes, prevention and treatment of offending, it has been argued elsewhere (Farrington, 1988a; Farrington, Ohlin and Wilson, 1986) that a new generation of longitudinal studies on offending and antisocial behaviour are needed, including testing of the effects of experimental interventions on the natural history of delinquency and crime.

Because of the link between crime and numerous other social problems, any measure that succeeds in reducing crime will have benefits that go far beyond this. Any measure that reduces crime will probably also reduce alcohol abuse, drunk driving, drug abuse, sexual promiscuity, family violence, school failure, unemployment, marital disharmony and divorce. It is clear that problem children tend to grow up into problem adults, and that problem adults tend to produce more problem children. Major efforts to tackle the problem of antisocial personality and its numerous manifestations, informed by reviews of the literature, are urgently needed.

7
Organic Disorders, Mental Handicap and Offending

Edited by
Pamela J. Taylor

Written by
Paul d'Orbán
John Gunn
Anthony Holland
Michael D. Kopelman
Graham Robertson
Pamela J. Taylor

Brain Disease and Crime

Crime embraces everything from murder and treason to riding a bicycle without lights. There are many interacting reasons why all of us break the law from time to time. Whilst the majority of these reasons will concern learning, habits, social pressures and neurotic mechanisms, organic or neuropathological factors may also play a role. This chapter examines some of the efforts that have been made to link brain disease and antisocial behaviour, and details some specific disorders which are important to clinical forensic psychiatric practice.

Localized Brain Damage and Offending

Relatively circumscribed brain damage, such as may result from a penetrating head wound or a tumour without raised intracranial pressure, has been cited as evidence for certain areas of the brain being of critical importance in the release of violence. It has been suggested that one of the more tragic mass murderers in the USA had a glioblastoma multiforme, probably in one medial temporal lobe (Sweet et al., 1969). Hadfield was a craftsman of high repute for his skills and personal attributes until his penetrating head injuries in battle. His post-injury attempt on the life of George III was among the more terrible aspects of the changed man. At postmortem, he was found to have had substantial frontal lobe lesions in the brain. Lishman (1968) found that, among head injury patients, post-traumatic antisocial behaviour was almost exclusively confined to those with injuries of the frontal lobe, but rare. Subsequent studies have reconfirmed the importance of frontal or fronto-temporal damage, but also emphasized that pre-morbid personality traits may be as important as the location and extent of the injury in determining subsequent behavioural disturbances (Bond, 1984; Brooks, 1984; Prigatano, 1987).

Genetic Links

Genetic mediation of violence has been explored. Some strains of mice and rats breed true for high or low levels of both affective and predatory aggression, and some breeds of dog, such as the pitbull terrier, are actually selected and bred for their aggressive proclivities. As both the brain and social structure of the animal becomes more complicated, however, it also becomes more apparent that, while such physical indicators may be a factor in aggression, the relationship is not simple and the progression to pathological violence far from inevitable. The study of genetic influence on crime generally is discussed more fully in Ch. 6, and models for understanding any linkages together with the specific case of one chromosomal variant—XYY status—on pp. 314–16.

Inferences from Animal Work

Animal studies have depended on the stimulation or ablation of parts of the brain and a demonstration of apparently consequent excessive aggressive or unusual tameness following such interventions. While it is unclear how far it is relevant to extrapolate from evidence of behavioural links in animals such as the cat, whose brain is not only simpler, but of very different organization from the human brain, even in non-human animals the complexity of the interaction between stimulation of specific areas of the brain and social status and activity of the animal has been demonstrated (e.g. Delgardo, 1969).

Neurophysiological and Neuropsychological Correlates of Organic Brain Disease

Perhaps the largest body of human work in this field has to do with establishing whether neurological deficits or dysfunctions and certain kinds of violent or other antisocial behaviours are more than merely chance associations. The neurological deficits are usually measured or inferred from neurophysiological or neuropsychological tests, and the offending activity by its extreme form, occasionally in terms of its seriousness, but usually in terms of its frequency.

The choice of frequent violence for study is the selection of a repetitive phenomenon, in some cases perhaps almost perseverative, and should certainly maximize the chances of finding at least a hint of organic disorder. Aside from the infrequent role of epilepsy, discussed below (pp. 299–307), the notion that cerebral dysrhythmia short of epilepsy may account for violent behaviour has been popular. Maudsley (1876), for example, proposed the concept of 'masked epilepsy' to account for any sudden, devastating, inexplicable act on the part of a patient. Subsequently, Hill and Watterson (1942), Stafford-Clark and Taylor (1949), and Williams (1969) all claimed that electroencephalographic (EEG) abnormalities were more common among habitually and dangerously violent men than those who were not violent, or only occasionally so. Williams' sample was substantial—206 men with habitual aggression and 127 who had engaged in an isolated act. Evidence of structural brain damage was equivalent between the groups (26% and 23% respectively). If those with gross structural brain damage or frank epilepsy were excluded, the habitually violent were still very significantly more likely to show non-specific EEG abnormalities (57% of the habitually aggressive; 12% of the others). There was no suggestion, however, that the dysrhythmias, although most often temporal in origin, were specific or pathognomonic. A substantial minority of the habitually violent men had no EEG abnormalities, and there was little attempt to evaluate other interactional factors or to calculate the level of variance that could be accounted for by the EEG abnormalities. Above all, the examinations of the EEGs in these studies were not conducted blind to the level of violence, and Kligman and Goldberg's (1975) criticisms of work linking temporal lobe epilepsy and aggression become even more pertinent the 'softer' the EEG findings. Smith et al. (1973) examined, blind, the EEGs in a series of child batterers, and did sustain the finding of a higher rate of EEG abnormalities among the repeatedly violent. Fenton et al. (1974), in a much larger series of special hospital patients, did not. Krynicki's (1978) comparative study of repetitively assaultive adolescents with minimally assaultive behaviourally disordered patients, and with patients with frank organic brain disease, involved small numbers, but blind examination of the EEGs established significant differences between the groups. Paroxymal frontal activity was the most important characteristic of the repetitively assaultive group. A number of American workers (Mark and Ervin, 1970; Bach-y-Rita et al., 1971; Maletzky, 1973; Monroe et al., 1978) have postulated an 'episodic dyscontrol syndrome', as an epileptic equivalent, to account for a supposed association between cerebral dysrhythmia and habitual episodic violence. They recommended treatment of the violence with anticonvulsants. It remains unclear whether such an interpretation of abnormal EEG findings is appropriate, not least because alcohol use is very often implicated in such patients. Milstein (1988) reported, from preliminary brain mapping studies, that although his series of aggressive patients had a high rate of EEG abnormalities, and many showed some change on clinical improvement, there was no characteristic map occurring in the context of the aggressive phase of behaviour nor consistent pattern of change on improvement.

Comprehensive evaluation of offender or violent patients using other physical indices of brain damage is unusual. This is in marked contrast to the situation for other psychiatric patients defined primarily by diagnosis, such as schizophrenia, for whom computerized tomography (CT) scans, cerebral bloodflow studies and even postmortem examinations are among the range of techniques of assessment reported. Volkow and Tancredi (1987) reported on four repetitively violent patients in whom EEG, CT and positron emission tomography measures had been undertaken. Each patient had a different diagnosis. One had a manic-depressive illness, another schizophrenia, another borderline personality disorder and the fourth had post-traumatic stress disorder with alcohol abuse. The EEG was reported as within normal limits for the man with schizophrenia, as was the CT scan for both psychotic men. All patients, however, showed a reduction in blood flow and metabolism in the left temporal cortex. The insensitivity of the CT scan among psychiatric patients, and the difficulties in interpreting it are well documented (Luchins, 1983). Bloodflow studies offer promise as a dynamic measure of cerebral activity, but their use among offender and violent patients remains largely untried.

Neuropsychological testing as a means of highlighting brain dysfunction is even more difficult to interpret than the physical measures just outlined. A number of studies have identified abnormal patterns of responses to standardized neuropsychological test batteries (e.g. Krynicki, 1978; Berman and Seigal, 1976; Yeudall et al., 1982). Although some of the criticisms applied to the results have now been met, such as the concerns about results being more reflective of the effects of long-term residential settings than intrinsic abnormalities since Robbins et al. (1983) replicated findings of neuropsychological deficits in community-placed delinquents, many problems of interpretation have not been fully addressed. How far do social background, educational levels and cultural experiences influence results— rendering the test more reflective of social learning problems than of deficits in the organic substrate? As with the EEG findings, with which they are sometimes coupled, the results tend to be very variable, and studies which resort to group means may diminish rather than overstate relevant deficiencies. Almost all studies have worked from a sample identified by their delinquency or criminality, so perhaps one of the most important studies in this field is that of Spreen (1981), since it focused prospectively on a group of 208 children, aged 8–12, with learning disabilities. At follow-up at an average of 10 years later, no evidence was found for an association between brain damage, learning disabilities and crime. Spellacy's (1978) study is slightly unusual in this field in reporting on the evaluation of adult offenders. Using a neuropsychological test battery he identified 'impaired brain function' as a distinguishing feature of the violent group, which he sought to distinguish from brain damage. Discriminant function analysis of the results of a neuropsychological test battery has been an increasingly common approach to such study, and seems rarely to fail to distinguish between violent and non-violent offenders of any age with a 75% or more degree of accuracy. Three of us (Robertson et al., 1987) were also able to report such success, but questioned whether the statistical significance of our findings had any clinical importance. Miller (1987) and Jackson and Hopewell (in press) provide useful and fuller reviews of the literature.

In examining the relationship between brain damage and the most serious violence, homicide, Hafner and Boker (1973) could only observe that the two occurred together rarely. Only 6% of the sample of 533 mentally abnormal offenders had dementia, 5% had epilepsy and 6% other brain damage. Mental retardation, with its presumed organic underpinning, accounted for a further 13% of the mentally abnormal homicides, but functional psychoses, and schizophrenia in particular, were much more prominent. A survey of sentenced prisoners in England and Wales (Gunn et al., 1991b), evaluating a much wider criminal constituency, including non-violent offenders, found that only about 1% of them suffered from organic brain disorder. Such disorders were more common among female than male prisoners. These are not exceptional findings in emphasizing the small contribution of recognized organic disorder to recognized crime and violence. Given that cerebral damage and dysfunction have been a focus of considerable interest, and are now widely accepted as major factors in explaining the schizophrenic state (e.g. Helmchen and Henn, 1987), it is perhaps surprising, however, that so little attention has been paid to the possibility of cerebral dysfunction as a common basis for psychosis and abnormally offensive or violent behaviour. It is a difficult area to study, because samples of seriously violent *and* psychotic patients who are willing and able to cooperate with extensive testing are likely to be small, and are possibly biased by the fact that the greater the disability the less likely it is that they can cooperate with testing. Two of us (Robertson and Taylor 1985), completed one study in which 61 men with schizophrenia and 30 with affective illnesses completed evaluation on a battery of cognitive tests. The symptoms most consistently associated with violent acting in both the affective and schizophrenic groups were delusions, and these were associated with deficits on visual recognition tasks. In the case of the men with schizophrenia, it was the verbally biased tasks, and for the men with affective illnesses the visuo-spatial tasks that were abnormal (Robertson et al., in preparation).

Among the features that interested Lombroso (1874) was the imbalance that he believed existed between the cerebral hemispheres in criminals. Although no longer wholly ignored (Robertson and Taylor, 1985; Nachshon, 1988), perhaps one of the great difficulties in studying possible organic damage and dysfunction in a violent offending group rests in contemporary discomfort with Lombroso's ideas and concepts such as 'the stigmata of degeneracy' (Talbot, 1898). General psychiatrists have long since overcome any distaste for such archaic language with respect to people who have psychosis, and have advanced the understanding of the disorders considerably by searching for ever more objective and hard evidence for organic damage and physical markers of the disease. Offender patients are perhaps more difficult to study in these terms, because the most seriously disordered, of central importance to such evaluations, tend to be held in security where some of the test facilities may not be immediately available or, in any event, questions of competence to consent to procedures which may not immediately benefit the individual patient can sometimes prevent research. Nothing in the softer organic findings yet points to the potential for definitive guidance in risk assessment, nor to undisputed lines of treatment, although some psychological work has found that special skills training where specific neuropsychological deficits have been identified may be helpful in reducing recidivism for violence or offending as well as improving the specific deficits (e.g. Gendreau and Ross, 1984; Feldman, 1989, and pp. 282–3).

Amnesia and Offending

When defendants claim amnesia for their alleged crimes, psychiatrists or psychologists may be asked to assess the relevance of this amnesia. It is, therefore, regrettable that there is a relative dearth of studies investigating this intriguing form of forgetfulness. More fully reviewed elsewhere (Kopelman, 1987a), this situation contrasts with the study of eyewitness testimony, which has re-emerged in the past decade as a popular topic for scientific enquiry (e.g. Loftus, 1979; Wells and Loftus, 1984; Gruneberg et al., 1988). Details of the legal issues are covered in Ch. 2 (pp. 46–7, 63, 66).

Prevalence and Characteristic Features of Amnesia for Offences

Amnesia has been reported most commonly in cases of homicide. Table 7.1 summarizes the rates of amnesia obtained in the principal studies of subjects convicted of homicide. It can be seen that between 25% and 45% of these offenders claim amnesia for the killing. Somewhat higher figures are obtained if vaguer descriptions of memory loss are accepted—the figure in the Bradford and Smith (1979) study is 60% if cases of 'hazy' memory are included, and Tanay (1969) reported that 70% of his cases were in a 'dissociative state . . . (involving) . . . spotty memory'.

Claims of amnesia also occur after other types of crime. Table 7.2, adapted from Kopelman (1987a), summarized the results of three studies which looked at the types of crime associated with amnesia. It appears that violent crime is particularly associated with amnesia, although the definitive prevalence study, examining rates of amnesia following a range of offensive behaviour that does not necessarily come to court, has never been conducted.

Table 7.1
Amnesia for the Offence among those Convicted of Homicide

Authors	Date	N	Amnesic
Leitch	1948	51	31%
Guttmacher	1955	36	33%
O'Connell	1960	50	40%
Bradford and Smith	1979	30	47%
Taylor and Kopelman	1984	34	26%
Parwatikar et al.*	1985	105	23%

* Pretrial evaluations only; rate for convicted homicides not given.
Reproduced with permission from Kopelman (1987b).

The three studies included in Table 7.2 were carried out in very different settings (a secure hospital in Britain, a Canadian forensic psychiatry service, and a British remand prison), yet the association with violent crime was evident in all three studies. It has to be emphasized, however, that the total non-violent groups in the maximum security hospital and in the remand prison were very small indeed.

Despite the substantial agreement about the prevalence of amnesia in homicide and its particular association with violent crime, there is considerable disagreement over the characteristic features of such amnesic episodes Kopelman (1987a). O'Connell (1960), for example, reported that this form of amnesia is often transitory, whereas Leitch (1948) described a man in whom it had lasted 'several years', and Bradford and Smith (1979) stated that the amnesia was 'permanent' in all their cases. Similarly, Leitch (1948) maintained that the amnesia might 'cover the whole life of the individual', whereas Bradford and Smith (1979) found that the duration of the amnesic gap was less than 24 hours in all their cases, and was less than half an hour in the majority (60%) of their cases.

Table 7.2
Relationship between Amnesia for Offending and Type of Offence

	Study		
	Hopwood & Snell (1933)	Lynch & Bradford (1980)	Taylor & Kopelman (1984)
	Maximum security hospital (UK)	*Forensic psychiatry service (Canada)*	*Remand prison (UK)*
Crime	*Percentage of amnesic patients*		
Homicide/attempted homicide	90%	23%	47%
Other violence	8%	63%	53%
Non-violent crime	2%	14%	0%
Total	100%	100%	100%

Principal Factors Associated with Amnesia for Crime

The factors most commonly associated with claims of amnesia are:

1. violent crime, particularly homicide;
2. extreme emotional arousal;
3. alcohol abuse and intoxication;
4. depressed mood;

(*see also* Taylor and Kopelman, 1984; Kopelman, 1987a).

1. Violent crime.   As well as after homicide, amnesia has been reported in cases of rape, assault, arson, armed robbery and criminal damage (Hopwood and Snell, 1933; Lynch and Bradford, 1980; Taylor and Kopelman, 1984). The association with violent crime may be secondary to the extreme emotional arousal and/or alcohol abuse commonly involved in such offences, and it is intriguing that studies of the victims and eyewitnesses of offences have also revealed that impaired recall is related to the violence of the crime (e.g. Kuehn, 1974; Clifford and Scott, 1978; Yuille and Cutshall, 1986).

2. Extreme emotional arousal   appears to be particularly important in homicide cases in which the offence is unpremeditated (Hopwood and Snell, 1933; O'Connell, 1960; Bradford and Smith, 1979; Taylor and Kopelman, 1984). In these cases, the victim is usually closely related to the offender— in one series the victim was a lover, wife, close friend or family member in 88% of the cases (Taylor and Kopelman, 1984). There is often an accompanying diagnosis of depression, and sometimes a diagnosis of schizophrenia.

3. Alcohol abuse and intoxication.   Various studies have shown that there is commonly a history of chronic alcohol abuse and/or acute intoxication at the time of the offence in amnesic subjects (see Table 7.3). Three studies have implicated abuse of other drugs, although the types of drugs involved were not specified (Bradford and Smith, 1979; Lynch and Bradford, 1980; Parwatikar et al., 1985). In cases of homicide committed during intoxication, the victim seems less likely to be related to the offender than in cases where extreme emotional arousal occurs in the absence of alcohol abuse (Taylor and Kopelman, 1984).

Goodwin et al. (1969) described three types of memory loss for significant episodes seen in hospitalized alcoholics (*see also* Kopelman, 1987a,b).

1. *State dependent* effects, in which subjects cannot remember events or facts when sober, which are easily recalled as soon as the subjects are intoxicated again (e.g. where money is hidden);
2. *Fragmentary* blackouts in which subjects become aware of their memory loss on being told of an event later. There are 'islets' of preserved memory, and the amnesia tends to recover partially through time by a

Table 7.3
Relationship between Alcohol and Amnesia for Crime

Study	Date	Amnesic cases	Non-amnesic cases
(a) Chronic abuse			
Hopwood and Snell	1933	38%	No comparison group
Lynch and Bradford	1980	72%	No comparison group
Taylor and Kopelman	1984	42%	10%
Parwatikar et al.	1985	71%	58%
(b) Intoxicated at time of offence			
O'Connell	1960	30%	13%
Bradford and Smith	1979	30%	10%
Taylor and Kopelman	1984	42%	20%
Parwatikar et al.*	1985	87%	42%

* The figure given is for alcohol and/or drug abuse in this study.
Reproduced with permission from Kopelman (1987a).

shrinking of the amnesic gap, similar to that which occurs in head injury;

3. *En bloc* blackouts, in which subjects become abruptly aware of a memory gap (e.g. on waking up), and they describe a sense of 'lost time'. The amnesic gap has a definite starting point, islets of preserved memory are rare, and the memories are very seldom recovered.

Mild degrees of persistent memory impairment are sometimes found on standard (anterograde) tests in subjects claiming amnesia for an offence when alcohol abuse is implicated (Kopelman, 1987a). The degree of impairment is consistent with that found in other (non-criminal) alcoholics, and it may be accompanied by a mild degree of cortical atrophy demonstrable on CT scan (Ron, 1983).

4. Depressed mood. Hopwood and Snell (1933) reported that amnesia occurred 'with some frequency' in states of depression; the precise figure was not given. Using the Minnesota Multiphasic Personality Inventory (MMPI), Parwatikar et al. (1985) reported that 'amnesic' killers showed significantly raised scores on the depression scale in comparison with 'confessed' killers. Two of us (Taylor and Kopelman, 1984) found no overall difference between amnesic and non-amnesic offenders in the rate or type of ICD-9 psychiatric diagnosis, apart from a raised prevalence of alcohol abuse, but evidence of depressed mood was much more commonly present in the amnesic cases as rated at semistructured interview (The Comprehensive Psychiatric Rating Scale; Åsberg et al., 1978) or on a self-rating scale (The Beck Inventory for Depression; Beck et al., 1961). There was usually evidence that the depressed mood had been present for weeks or months preceding the offence. This association of amnesia with depressed mood in the absence of a clinical diagnosis of depression is consistent with similar findings obtained in studies of fugue states (Kanzer, 1939; Stengel, 1941; Berrington et al., 1956). In the middle-aged and elderly, an association between depression and shoplifting has been described (Gibbens et al., 1971), and these subjects occasionally claim amnesia for their offences.

Other Psychiatric Disorders and Amnesia for Offending

Psychosis

In the pretrial prisoner study already referred to (Taylor and Kopelman, 1984), a small group of men with schizophrenia was identified who had damaged property during floridly psychotic episodes and who, while not denying the acts, presented accounts of what had happened which were at complete variance with what others had observed. Their trivial acts of aggression and paramnesic accounts could be given little meaning except in terms of their psychoses. Perhaps the phenomena were best described as delusional memories.

Hysterical States

O'Connell (1960) noted that claims of amnesia were associated with a hysterical personality, while Parwatikar et al. (1985) reported that amnesic killers showed significantly raised scores on the hysteria and hypochondriasis scales of the MMPI, relative to confessed killers. In this connection, mention should perhaps be made of the Ganser syndrome (*see* pp. 424–6).

A fugue state is a syndrome involving a transient loss of memory and of sense of personal identity accompanied by a period of wandering. A fugue only very exceptionally accounts for amnesia for crime (Schacter, 1986; Kopelman, 1987a), but an offence may very occasionally precipitate a fugue (Wilson et al., 1950; Berrington et al., 1956). Instances have been reported in which the assessment of a fugue is made particularly difficult by the subject's having a possible motivation for using such a state as a defence in law (e.g. Kopelman, 1987b).

Organic Brain Disorder and Amnesia

Although relatively rare, organic brain disorder is an important concomitant of amnesia for crime (Kopelman, 1987a). Hopwood and Snell (1933) reported that 20% of their cases had a history of head injury, 12% of previous amnesia, and 9% of epilepsy. In contrast, other studies have failed to find an increased frequency of organic disorder or EEG abnormalities in amnesic offenders, relative to non-amnesic offenders. O'Connell (1960) attributed 2 of his 20 amnesic cases to organic disorder (epilepsy, hypoglycaemia), but failed to find organic disorder in the remainder. Bradford and Smith (1979) failed to obtain any association of amnesia with head injury or EEG abnormalities. In the pretrial prisoner study (Taylor and Kopelman, 1984), no differences between amnesic and non-amnesic groups were found in terms of a past history of head injury or other neurological disorder. In all these series, the amnesic samples were relatively small and the base rates for organic disorder would have been low. Taken together, they do perhaps indicate that organic brain disorder is a relatively uncommon determinant of amnesia for an offence, although this should perhaps be qualified by a reminder that alcohol abuse is such a common accompaniment of amnesia for offending that it may only be the more gross, 'measurable' organic brain states, or irreversible disorders that are rare in these circumstances. An assessment for organic disorder in such cases remains very important because, although amnesia *per se* does not affect the subject's fitness to plead or the issues of responsibility in England and Wales, these issues may become pertinent in cases in which an organic factor is implicated, such as epilepsy or hypoglycaemia.

Epilepsy.   Only very infrequently can crime be attributed to epileptic automatisms or postictal confusion (pp. 302–5). When this does occur there is always bilateral involvement of the limbic structures involved in memory formation, including the amygdaloid-hippocampal complex and the mesial diencephalon (Fenton, 1972). Hence, amnesia for the period of automatic behaviour is always present and is usually complete (Knox, 1968).

Hypoglycaemia.   Any patients with diabetes, alcohol intoxication, the 'dumping' syndrome or insulinoma or subjects abusing insulin may suffer hypoglycaemia. Insulin abuse has been implicated in a number of serious offences, including violent crime against children (Scarlett et al., 1977; Lancet, 1978). Where hypoglycaemia results from the administration of an external agent such as insulin, the case for a 'non-insane' automatism can be argued (indicating acquittal).

Head Injury.   Where head injury is associated with amnesia for an offence, there is a brief period of retrograde amnesia, which may shrink through time, a longer period of post-traumatic amnesia (PTA), and there may be islets of preserved memory within the amnesic gap (Kopelman, 1987a). Occasionally, there is a particularly vivid memory for images or sounds occurring immediately before the injury, on regaining consciousness, or during a lucid interval before the onset of PTA (Russell and Nathan, 1946). The length of PTA is assumed to reflect the extent of diffuse brain pathology, resulting from rotational forces, and it is predictive of eventual psychiatric, social and cognitive outcome (Lishman, 1968; Brooks, 1984; Kopelman, 1987b).

Other Organic Brain Disorders.   Other disorders which produce a discrete or transient episode of memory loss, such as toxic or post-ECT confusional states, transient ischaemic episodes, or the transient global amnesia syndrome are very unlikely to be associated with crime (Kopelman, 1987b). Similarly, severe states of chronic or persistent amnesia are very seldom associated with crime, although occasional instances do occur in cases of mental retardation or dementia (e.g. Brooks et al., 1987).

Authentic Amnesia or Deliberate Malingering?

Many lay observers consider that the amnesia claimed by offenders is a deliberate strategy to try to avoid the legal consequences of their offence. This view has been reiterated by Schacter (1986), a psychologist, who declared that 'many claims of amnesia after crimes are simulated'. On the other hand, Hopwood and Snell (1933) conducted a retrospective review of follow-up information in the case notes of 100 Broadmoor patients who, at the time of their trials, had claimed amnesia for their offences and concluded that 78% of the amnesias had been 'genuine', 14% had been 'feigned', and 8% were 'doubtful'. Unfortunately, there appears to be no more recent evidence which would help evaluate Schacter's statement, but there are a number of reasons for supposing that many cases of amnesia are indeed authentic, although the issue may be less clear-cut, and perhaps less critical, than it sometimes appears (Kopelman, 1987a *see also* p. 424).

Firstly, there may not be any distinct demarcation between 'conscious' malingering and 'unconscious' hysteria. O'Connell (1960) favoured the view that the difference between them was a matter of degree rather than kind, and he provided examples of what he called the 'passive disregard' towards their crime, which was evident in the remarks of both amnesic and non-amnesic subjects. One non-amnesic offender, for example, described letting the memory 'drift into the background . . . like putting something into . . . a safe and locking it away'. By comparison, amnesic subjects described having 'buried everything about (the) case' and feeling that recall was prevented because the memory gets 'all jumbled up again'.

Secondly, many amnesic cases have been described in the literature, who either have reported their own crime or have failed to take measures to avoid their capture (Hopwood and Snell, 1933; Leitch, 1948; Gudjonsson and MacKeith, 1983a; Taylor and Kopelman, 1984; Gudjonsson and Taylor, 1985). This makes an account of amnesia as simulation to avoid punishment seem less plausible.

Thirdly, it should be noted that the factors which have been associated with amnesia in offenders are similar to those which have been implicated in cases of impaired recall by the victims or eyewitnesses of crime—notably, violent crime, extreme emotional arousal and alcohol intoxication (*see* e.g. Kuehn, 1974; Clifford and Scott, 1978; Yuille and Cutshall, 1986; Deffenbacher, 1988, Yuille, 1987).

Fourthly, it should be reiterated that in England and Wales amnesia *per se* does not constitute a defence or a barrier to trial (*see* pp. 46–7, 63, 66), and for these matters to be considered other issues, such as epilepsy, have to be raised. Consistent with this, two of us (Taylor and Kopelman, 1984) found that there were no significant differences between the groups of amnesic and non-amnesic prisoners in terms of fitness to plead, the types of plea made, or the reasons offered for those pleas.

Assessment of Amnesia and its Causes

Amnesic patients require detailed interviewing, with particular attention to the pattern and extent of the amnesic gap, and, if possible, noting how this changes through time. It is particularly important to obtain corroborative evidence about the subject's behaviour at the time of and after the offence from all available sources, including the legal documentation, the results of social and probation enquiries, and any available family member or other informant. Any previous episode of amnesia or of an associated condition such as head injury, epilepsy, or other neurological disorder must be noted. Evidence of alcohol or drug abuse should be sought and, if there is any suspicion of current memory impairment, this will require detailed neuro-psychological and neuropsychiatric investigation. To supplement the result-ant clinical formulation, various specific techniques have been proposed for assessing the authenticity of amnesia following an alleged crime (*see* Kopelman, 1987a).

Aside from deliberate simulation, various mechanisms have been proposed to account for amnesia for crime, including repression, dissociation, a failure of initial encoding, an encoding-retrieval interaction, and state-dependent retrieval problems (Kopelman 1987a,b). The various theories can be grouped into those which place emphasis on the failure of memory at the time of initial encoding, which may be particularly true of those cases in which alcohol is implicated, and those which place emphasis on a failure of memory retrieval, which is possibly more true of unpremeditated homicide cases taking place in a state of extreme emotional arousal. In the present state of knowledge, any theory about the nature of amnesia for crime is bound to be somewhat speculative, but it seems unlikely that any one explanation will cover all cases. The intriguing similarity between the factors which produce impaired recall by the victims, eyewitnesses and perpetrators of crime alike should perhaps direct further investigation in the field.

Summary of Issues in Amnesia for Offending

Amnesia is most commonly seen in homicide cases in which it is claimed by 25–45% of offenders, but it may also follow other types of violent crime and, occasionally, non-violent crimes. It is particularly associated with states of extreme emotional arousal, alcohol intoxication and depressed mood, and it is occasionally associated with episodes of florid psychosis. Overt organic brain disorder is infrequently the precipitant of amnesia for crime, but it is essential to identify any organic factor, such as epilepsy, head injury or hypoglycaemia, because of their potential medico-legal importance. In the absence of organic disease, the presence of amnesia carries no legal implications in England and Wales, and, for these purposes, the differentiation between 'authentic' and 'feigned' amnesia is probably not critical. Many amnesic subjects have either reported the crime themselves or made no attempt to conceal it, which argues against the view that these amnesias are deliberately simulated to avoid punishment. Detailed, longitudinal studies are required to elucidate further the precipitants, characteristics and outcome of this intriguing form of amnesia.

Epilepsy in Relation to Offending

The Nature and Classification of Epilepsy

The diagnosis of an epileptic fit depends upon clinical judgement. Very rarely it may be possible to have a patient's EEG monitored during the course of a fit, and the diagnosis made on electrical grounds, but this is generally only possible when fits are frequent. The EEG between seizures may be normal, and even an abnormal EEG between seizures, showing spike phenomena, does not prove that the seizures are, in fact, epileptic.

A pragmatic definition which has proved useful is:

> An epileptic seizure is an intermittent, stereotyped disturbance of behaviour, emotion, motor function or sensation which, on clinical grounds, is judged to be the result of pathological cortical neuronal discharge (Gunn, 1977)

Epilepsy is the condition in which such seizures are repeated or have to be repressed by medication. The many types of epilepsy can be classified in a variety of ways. That described below is a consensus system developed in 1970 by the International League Against Epilepsy (Lishman, 1987).

Varieties of Epilepsy
1. Generalized epilepsies
   (a) Primary generalised epilepsy (petit mal, grand mal)
   (b) Secondary generalized epilepsy
2. Focal epilepsies ('partial' or 'local' epilepsies)
   (a) With elementary (simple) symptomatology (e.g. motor Jacksonian epilepsy)
   (b) With complex symtomatology (mostly temporal lobe in origin, e.g. with cognitive or affective symptomatology, psychomotor attacks, psychosensory attacks)
3. Unclassifiable and mixed forms

The complete phenomena of epilepsy can be divided into three phases: pre-ictal, ictal and post-ictal. Pre-ictal prodromes may include affective changes and irritability and are experienced by the patient as a warning that a fit is coming on; they may last several hours or even a day. An aura is the initial focal onset of the attack and may be a sensation, a feeling or a movement lasting from a few seconds to a minute or two, thus giving some patients the opportunity to protect themselves slightly from the forthcoming loss of consciousness.

Almost any form of motor or sensory activity can be involved during the fit, or ictus, itself. The classic tonic-clonic movements in an unconscious patient, with or without tongue biting and loss of bladder control, are quite common, but not invariable. A description of the full range of phenomena to be seen is contained in Lishman (1987). Psycho-motor seizures are perhaps the most important form of epilepsy in relation to offending. These may entirely replace tonic-clonic fits, or accompany them. Consciousness may be completely or only partially lost, there may be automatic behaviour, confusion, wandering, strange or repetitive speech, affective changes such as panic, terror, anger or ecstasy, visual and/or auditory hallucinations, and delusions, especially of the paranoid kind.

After a fit, further confusional states, which resemble psychomotor phenomena, may also be experienced. It is sometimes difficult to determine when the fit stopped and the post-fit phase began.

Psychological Factors and Epilepsy

In the past, special laws have been enacted to restrain people with epilepsy. As recently as 1939, a law was enacted in North Carolina, USA, to control the marriage of people with epilepsy. Such antimarriage laws were drawn up in Sweden as early as 1757, and many states in the USA still have such laws on their statute books, even though they no longer operate them. Gallup poll data from the UK indicates that attitudes towards epilepsy are improving, but even in 1979, 12% of the sample interviewed in the Gallup survey thought that people with epilepsy should not be employed like others, and 5% said they would object to having their children associate with children who had fits (Gunn, 1981, 1991b). In a time of full employment, Pond and Bidwell (1960) found that 40% of patients with epilepsy in their survey had had serious difficulties finding employment at some time.

Economic and occupational frustration is not the only burden to be carried by the individual with epilepsy. As Taylor (1969a) pointed out:

> Every fit reinforces the view of witnesses that the epileptic cannot be relied upon to participate fully in society, since he is liable, at any time, to go out of control.

The damage to self-esteem of someone who has to suffer such feelings must be considerable.

Affective illnesses and schizophrenia have both been reported to occur with an increased prevalence in people with epilepsy. Irritability is classically associated with brain damage and brain damage is an aetiological factor in a high proportion of epilepsies; irritability can also accompany mood change. Some authors regard explosive, immature aggressiveness as especially characteristic of patients with temporal lobe epilepsy, occurring as a prominent feature in about one-third of patients who present for temporal lobectomy (Falconer and Taylor, 1970). Falconer (1973) reported a marked reduction in aggressiveness in such patients following the operation. Improvement is said to be related to improved fit control, and is shown by an increase in frustration tolerance and a diminution in irritability.

Unfortunately, there are no properly controlled epidemiological studies to determine whether these apparent associations between irritability and epilepsy are valid or in excess of what would be expected in any population suffering from a chronic debilitating disorder.

There does seem to be clear evidence that people with epilepsy are prone to suicide more often than others. Prudhomme (1941) estimated that the incidence was twice that of the general population, and five times greater when the figures were corrected for age. Henriksen et al. (1970) found the rate to be about three times the general population rate.

Prevalence of Epilepsy

In view of the subjectivity of diagnosis, it is clear that estimates of the prevalence of epilepsy will be contentious. Nevertheless, most European authors place the population figure at about 5/1000 (Gunn, 1977; Lishman, 1987). Surveys in the USA suggest a slightly higher prevalence (Hauser and Kurland, 1975; Whitman et al., 1980). These figures are very rough and ready and conceal important associations, for example that epilepsy is commoner in younger than in older people. There are many causes of epilepsy. Some people have 'idiopathic' epilepsy or epilepsy of unknown aetiology, although this type of epilepsy may run in families. Other cases are due to birth injury or congenital malformations, some to damage caused during febrile convulsions in infancy. Head injury, infections of the brain and meninges, cerebrovascular disease, cerebral tumours, degenerative disorders, drugs (such as alcohol) and toxins (e.g. uraemia) may all cause epilepsy. Some of these precipitating disorders are themselves associated with social conditions such as poverty, poor maternal care or drunkenness and these sociable variables may, in part, explain the varying prevalence rates found in different communities. In their review of the socio-economic correlates of epilepsy, Whitman et al. (1980) conclude that 'poor people have more epilepsy'.

An important study in the Illinois prison system (Whitman et al., 1984) found a prevalence rate of 24/1000, four times the rate among 20–29-year-old males in Rochester, Minnesota. Head trauma was the probable cause of epilepsy among 45% of the prisoners with epilepsy, a much higher percentage than that reported in studies of other populations.

An earlier, English, study of prisoners (Gunn, 1977) found the prevalence of epilepsy to be 7.2/1000. This excess prevalence over the general population could not be accounted for by the relatively youthful age structure of the prison population. Indeed, there was evidence in this survey (conducted in 1966), that the figure of 7.2/1000 was an underestimate of the number of people with epilepsy in prison, an undiagnosed group having been found among the supposedly non-epileptic control sample. Even with this in mind, it is unlikely that the prevalence figure would have been commensurate with the results obtained in the North American study. A more recent prison survey of England and Wales (Gunn et al., 1991b) has confirmed the lower English figure.

Relationships between Epilepsy and Crime

The excess prevalence of epilepsy among prisoners, the clinical impression of increased irritability in some epileptics, and the frightening idea that people with epilepsy may do dangerous things when they are unconscious, all lead to the expectation that there will be an excess incidence of criminal activity in an epileptic population. There is quite good evidence that there is no particular association between epilepsy and violent crime. For crime in general, the Gudmundsson survey (1966), found that 8.3% of the epileptic population of Iceland had a police record, three times the rate for the general population of that country. This is an important finding as a complete national sample of a relatively stable population. However, many of the offences were drunkenness or breaches of customs and price control regulations. Juul-Jensen (1964) studied a Danish population of people with epilepsy and found a criminal prevalance of 9.5% among the men and 1.9% among the women, figures similar to those found among the general population. An earlier Swedish report (Alström, 1950) found that patients attending a neurological clinic had much the same prevalence of criminality as the general population, if the epileptic population was standardized for geographical area, social class and age.

In spite of the different rates in the British and US prison studies, both came to the same conclusion in respect of offending. The epileptic and control prisoners had similar rates of violent and sexual offences. The British survey looked particularly carefully for any cases of ictal violence. Automatic behaviour of any kind in association with a fit is rare (10% cases), but acts of violence in this context exceptionally rare (Knox, 1968). No prisoner in the English survey (Gunn, 1977) met the criteria for having a violent outburst or incident during the fit itself. Only 10 men reported fits within a 12-hour period after the offence; 4 said they had had a fit just before the offence, 5 just after, and 1 man claimed both. Very little direct relationship between the crimes committed and the men's epilepsy could be detected (Gunn and Fenton, 1971). This is in line with other work. Macdonald (1969) in the USA found only two crimes committed as a result of an epileptic seizure in a series of 1000 cases, while according to Delgado-Escueta et al. (1981) only 15 cases in the whole of the USA had cited epilepsy as a defence in law against violent or disorderly conduct between 1889 and 1980. Treiman and Delgado-Escueta (1983) reviewed the world medical literature between 1872 and 1981 and found only 29 cases in which violent events were reported to be due to a seizure. This included the two cases from Broadmoor mentioned below (Gunn and Fenton, 1971). In his comprehensive review of the relationship between epilepsy and violence Treiman (1986) concluded that although violence may occur more frequently in people with epilepsy than in control populations, this is probably due to associated brain lesions or to adverse social factors rather than to the epilepsy directly.

In the English study (Gunn, 1977), a survey of patients with epilepsy in special hospitals was conducted to amplify the prison data. Only 3 patients were found to have had a definite epileptic seizure within the 24-hour period around the offence. Of these 3, 2 men probably did commit dangerous offences in a state of altered consciousness. The first was a 32-year-old man who had developed convulsions at the age of 18. Two-and-a-half years later, he had a generalized fit early in the morning while getting ready for work. On recovery 20 minutes later, his speech was slurred and his eyes seemed 'vacant'. He attacked an elderly man who lived in the house, striking him with a spade and kicking him. The victim died as a result of the severe head injuries he received. The man then attacked his girl friend and the victim's wife, smashed some panes of glass, and cycled away aimlessly with blood on his arms. Some way down the road he fell off his cycle and, on admission to hospital, was mentally confused and amnesic for all events following the seizure. In the second case, the man concerned developed a fit after an evening spent pigeon shooting. The following morning, still in a state of confusion, he rose early, took his shotgun into the street and brandished it about, firing it occasionally. Fortunately, nobody was killed.

It seems, then, that 'automatic' criminal behaviour in epilepsy is very rare indeed. Aggressive behaviour during a post-ictal confusional state is slightly less rare, though that too is extremely uncommon. Lishman (1987) neatly summarizes the criteria for suspecting that a criminal act may be the result of epilepsy or a post-ictal confusional state.

1. There must be unequivocal evidence of epilepsy, though not necessarily a previous history of automata;
2. The crime will have been sudden with an absence of obvious motive, and no evidence of planning or premeditation;
3. The crime will appear senseless and, typically, there will have been little or no attempt at concealment or escape;

4. The abnormal behaviour will usually have been of short duration, lasting minutes rather than hours, and will never have been entirely appropriate to the circumstances;
5. Witnesses may have noticed impairment of awareness, for example inappropriate actions or gestures, stereotypic movements, unresponsiveness or irrelevant replies to questions, aimless wanderings or a dazed and vacant expression on the person concerned;
6. Amnesia for the crime is the rule, but there should be no continuing anterograde amnesia for events following the resumption of conscious awareness.

This guidance is probably the best available, but it is only guidance and one of us (Gunn, 1978) has reported a case which flouted many of these guidelines. The man concerned had no known history of epilepsy and had killed his wife with a hammer before fleeing their home. He was convicted of manslaughter and sentenced to imprisonment. His EEG was strongly suggestive of epilepsy, and he subsequently showed evidence of this disorder in prison. As time went by, it became clear that he had killed his wife in a post-ictal confusional state during which he developed paranoid delusions.

There is no evidence that sex offending is commoner among people with epilepsy than among others. There are reports that sexual disturbance is associated with temporal lobe epilepsy, but the commonest disturbance is hyposexuality. Taylor (1969b) found poor sexual adjustment in two-thirds of 100 consecutive cases referred for temporal lobectomy, the commonest problem being lack of sexual drive. Hypersexuality appears to be rare. Transvestism has been reported, as have unusual forms of fetishism (*see* Lishman, 1987). The English prison sample (Gunn, 1977) consisted of 158 male prisoners with epilepsy and included 14 who had been convicted of sexual offences. These covered a wide spectrum of crimes from indecency, living off immoral earnings, bigamy and exhibitionism to incest and, in the case of three men, rape. These rates were not significantly different from the control group and in none of them was epilepsy thought to be of direct relevance.

The relationship between epilepsy and imprisonment is extremely complex. Indeed, epilepsy may be regarded as an example of the subtle yet important interactions between health, behaviour and society's response to that behaviour. There are at least seven possible explanations which might contribute to the increased rate of epilepsy among prisoners.

1. People with epilepsy have always been more likely than the general population to be placed in institutions of some kind;
2. The widespread belief that people with epilepsy are liable to behave in an antisocial way has largely been discredited, but attitudes linger;
3. The epilepsy may be caused by brain dysfunction which may itself result in behaviour disorder, for example where brain damage causes

both frontal lobe disinhibition and seizures. One man in the English prison study provides a good example of this. At the age of 29, he sustained a severe fracture of his skull and meningitis as the result of a motor-cycle accident. At that time, he was happily married and had a good work record having enjoyed an apparently normal childhood in a well-integrated home. Neurosurgery was required after the accident, and he was left with a right-sided weakness and some disorientation. Following discharge from hospital, he returned home but his marriage disintegrated and he failed to retain his job. He soon became an unemployed drifter, stealing frequently and living rough or in hostels. In the 10 years following his accident, he acquired 15 convictions for theft;

4. Low self-esteem in the person with epilepsy, related to social rejection, may be a precursor of antisocial behaviour. In a survey of children, Graham and Rutter (1968) concluded:

> The widespread community prejudice against epilepsy was probably an adverse factor in the epileptic child's development and it may have been one reason for the high rate of (psychiatric) disorder in the epilepsy group.

5. Epilepsy carries an increased risk of mental disorder, particularly schizophrenia-like psychoses, affective psychoses and suicidal behaviour. These psychiatric problems can, on occasion, lead to antisocial behaviour, especially petty theft and property damage offences;

6. Poor environments may cause both epilepsy and antisocial behaviour. A number of studies have shown an association between maternal care and quality of childhood environment, and the likelihood of developing fits (e.g. Miller et al., 1960). This association could be mediated through many channels, but child battering is an extreme example which illustrates the point. Kempe et al. (1962) reported on 302 children who had been attacked by their parents. Of these, 33 had died and 85 had suffered permanent brain injury. Modelling, learning by imitation, is a powerful force in determining behaviour and attitudes. It does not seem unreasonable to suppose that a brutal uncaring home environment during childhood will increase the likelihood both of developing brain damage and of coping with the adult world in a brutal uncaring fashion;

7. Behaviour disorders may lead to accidents which produce brain injuries. One prisoner in the English study came from a disturbed background, his parents continually rowing and separating until the final break when he was 9 years old. At the age of 12, he was convicted for stealing a lorry and was sent to an approved school. Thereafter, he was in trouble frequently and at the age of 17, shortly after joining the army, he smashed up one of their vehicles and sustained a head injury. Following this accident, he developed typical tonic-clonic seizures.

The Treatment of Offender Patients with Epilepsy

The treatment of epilepsy in any circumstances is much more than providing medication to obtain fit control, but the range of needs is likely to be especially high in an offender group. People with epilepsy frequently present with a wide range of problems, including mood disturbance, low self-esteem, suicidal ideas, irritability, a poor work record, difficulty in personal relationships, accommodation problems and a history of frequent injuries. All these matters require attention. The basis of treatment is the establishment of a trusting long-term relationship between doctor and patient. General support and the boosting of self-esteem are the first requirements. It is also important to explore the patient's fantasy life, discover what he really feels is happening to him during a fit and provide as much reality orientation as is feasible. Within this context, compliance in taking anticonvulsant drugs is likely to be much greater than it might otherwise be.

Drugs have to be given on an empirical and pragmatic basis, but every effort should be made to keep the regimen simple and to control the fits with one type of drug only. This is a counsel of perfection and, on occasion, more than one will have to be used, but this should be a last resort. All anticonvulsant drugs have their pros and cons. The more disturbed and non-compliant the patient population, the more important it is to avoid toxic drugs if possible. Carbamazepine and sodium valproate have toxic side-effects, but are probably less dangerous than some of the other drugs. Phenytoin is an effective anticonvulsant, but highly toxic to the cerebellum and is best reserved for otherwise intractable cases. Barbiturates in various forms, including phenobarbitone and primidone, may be useful on occasions, but induce drowsiness and depression and are dangerous in overdose. Benzodiazepines are very good anticonvulsants and are very safe drugs, but they are highly addictive and the dose required for seizure suppression can rise quite quickly. They are the drugs of choice in status epilepticus. Diazepam is probably better avoided as a regular anticonvulsant medication because tolerance to it develops very quickly; clonazepam and clobazam are more recent and are probably better in this regard.

Counselling should include advice about self-protection and life style. Public protection also has to be considered in counselling and, on rare occasions, it may even be necessary to break medical confidentiality and tell a potential employer of the patient's condition. This would be imperative, for example, if a patient were training to be a bus or train driver and refused to disclose his fits himself. Such a breach of confidentiality is often disasterous for the therapeutic alliance.

Suicidal ideas and behaviour are common and problematic. Self-destructive behaviour may be manifest in either direct or indirect ways (e.g. recklessness) and the patient will need careful counselling and support.

Alcohol may also be a special problem for the person with epilepsy. Some use it as an anticonvulsant (with a modicum of success), but more often it increases fit frequency and sometimes fits may be induced by alcohol withdrawal.

Anticonvulsant blood levels should always be regularly monitored. The correct dose for a particular patient is the minimum dose that will reduce fit frequency to an acceptable level without producing serious unwanted effects. This has to be discussed with the patient. It is wrong to prescribe exclusively according to the serum reports from the laboratory, but such reports do give some indication of compliance, upward or downward trends, and when toxic levels are being reached. Liver function tests, blood counts and serum folate should also be done at fairly frequent intervals to check on the more common unwanted effects.

One special problem for the person who has a criminal record as well as epilepsy is accommodation. There have been some improvements in this area (Channon, 1982) but the double stigma is sufficient to make placement in a hostel extremely difficult. There are still one or two specialized centres exclusively taking patients with epilepsy and, on occasion, these centres will admit patients with a history of antisocial behaviour. The pool of accommodation for such patients, however, remains small. A specialized hostel for ex-prisoners with epilepsy established in South London (Gunn, 1977; Channon, 1982; Gunn 1991c) and has proved to be of considerable value.

Management of Prisoners with Epilepsy

The general principles of treatment are identical within and without institutions. Prisoners may need extra psychological support because of the severe stigmatization they can receive at the hands of other prisoners. The prisoner should be asked for details of any previous treatment, every effort should be made by the prison doctor to contact the prisoner's immediate previous GP or specialist to check the nature and dose of any medication and, as far as possible, the medication should be maintained as outside prison. Epilepsy is a potentially fatal condition, and it has been known for prisoners to die through failure to follow these simple rules. Paradoxically, prisoners may require slightly less medication—regularity of dose and the absence of alcohol are important in this respect—but, for some, the stress of imprisonment results in an increased fit frequency. If in doubt, expert advice should always be sought. On discharge, epileptic prisoners should always be offered the opportunity of attending a psychiatric clinic, and, unless the prisoner explicitly objects, an appointment be made for him to attend a clinic appropriate for his health needs and his place of residence in the community. He should be given this appointment with clear directions as to how to get to the clinic, and an adequate supply of medication should be provided to cover him at least until the date of the appointment.

Violence in Sleep

The parasomnias are a group of sleep disorders in which behavioural phenomena that are inappropriate to the sleeping state occur during sleep (Fenton, 1975). They are commoner in childhood, but may continue into, or develop for the first time in adult life. Sleepwalking and night terrors are parasomnias which may sometimes be associated with serious violence or self-injury. These phenomena are of special interest in forensic psychiatry because, until very recently, they were regarded in law as 'non-insane' automatisms which occur in sleep and are not the result of disease. Since Lord Devlin's judgment in *Kemp*, the courts have made a distinction between insane and non-insane automatism. The insane variety is the product of 'disease of the mind', so that the McNaughton Rules apply and the accused is detained in hospital. By contrast, a successful defence of non-insane automatism leads to complete acquittal. Examples of non-insane automatism that have been recognized by the courts include acts committed in a state of concussion, involuntary intoxication, insulin-induced hypoglycaemia and, until recently, sleepwalking. In *Quick and Paddison*, Lord Justice Lawton introduced a distinction between external and internal factors causing the abnormality of mind, and since then abnormalities due to external factors are regarded as non-insane automatisms, whereas those due to internal factors are regarded in law as insane automatisms due to 'disease of the mind'. Patients with epileptic automatisms became the best known victims of this rule of thumb, as epileptic automatisms then came to be regarded in law as insane automatisms due to internal factors, and hence as a disease of the mind leading to the special verdict of not guilty by reason of insanity (*Sullivan*).

A further extension of the rule in *Quick and Paddison* occurred in March 1991, when the Court of Appeal ruled that sleepwalking was 'an abnormality or disorder, albeit transitory, due to an internal factor' and that it should, therefore, be regarded as an insane automatism (*Burgess*). Burgess was tried in July 1989 at Bristol Crown Court on charges arising from an attack on his girlfriend. His defence was that he had committed the attacks during a sleepwalking episode. At trial, he was found not guilty by reason of insanity and he was committed to hospital under the Criminal Procedure (Insanity) Act 1964 (Fenwick, 1989). His appeal in March 1991 failed (*Burgess*; Brahams, 1991). It appears that acts of violence committed in sleep, like those in epilepsy, are labelled as insanity. The effect of the special verdict of not guilty by reason of insanity has been changed, and the verdict no longer leads to indefinite detention in hospital. Under the Criminal Procedure (Insanity and Unfitness to Plead) Act 1991, the courts may make a hospital order, guardianship order or a supervision order, or grant an absolute discharge (Dyer, 1991). Nevertheless, acts of violence committed in sleep now no longer result in complete acquittal.

Many reports of violence in sleep predate the modern understanding of the physiology of sleep disorders, but they often give convincing descriptions of what is now known about these phenomena. Walker (1968) gives an interesting historical account of cases. Howard and d'Orbán (1987) reviewed the medical and legal literature and distinguished four groups.

1. **Violence associated with confusion on sudden awakening** (sleep drunkenness) was described in the continental literature as *l'ivresse du sommeil* or *Schlaftrunkenheit* (Gudden, 1905; Broughton, 1968). It is characterized by confusion, disorientation and misinterpretation of reality on sudden arousal from deep (stage 3 or 4) sleep. The subject may act as though defending himself against an imagined attack, but has no subsequent recall. A major German review of the forensic aspects by Schmidt (1943) collected 15 cases of homicide and 20 cases of wounding committed in these circumstances. An English review of the forensic aspects was provided by Bonkalo (1974). The condition is well illustrated by a 19th-century law report from Kentucky (*Fain*). A guest shot a hotel porter three times with his pistol when the victim attempted to wake him; he was sentenced to 2 years for manslaughter, but was acquitted on appeal as he was 'unconscious when he killed the deceased'.

2. **Violence associated with sleep-walking.** Complex, co-ordinated actions resulting in destruction of surrounding objects, self-injury or injury to others can occur in sleep-walking. As would be expected in these circumstances, the victim is most often a spouse (Hopwood and Snell, 1933; Gibbens, 1983; Tarsh, 1986), but the best known case was that of Boshears, an American airman who was acquitted in 1961 of strangling a girl in his sleep (Watkins, 1976). Oswald and Evans (1985) reviewed the subject and reported three cases, including a boy aged 14 who stabbed his 5-year-old cousin and was charged with attempted murder. They emphasized that sleep-walking is not a hysterical condition and that 'injustice could result if such ideas influenced medical evidence presented to courts'.

3. **Violence associated with night terrors** is probably the commonest of such disorders in sleep. Afterwards, there is either some recall of frightening dream material, or behaviour suggestive of a night terror is witnessed by others. Howard and d'Orbán (1987) cited a number of cases from the psychiatric literature and from law reports, and described two new cases acquitted on charges of murder and attempted murder. In law reports, there are several South African appeal cases which fit into this group (*Nhete*; *Dhlamini*; *Ngang*). The only British case mentioned in law reports is a Scottish one, *Fraser*. Fraser had a history of sleepwalking and killed his baby son by throwing him against a wall, while dreaming that he was struggling with a wild beast. The jury found him not responsible, and he was released after giving an undertaking to sleep alone in future. The case was also described by Yellowlees (1878) who gave expert evidence at his trial.

4. **Rapid eye movement sleep behaviour disorder**   is a more recently recognized category of parasomnia, first described by Schenck et al., 1986, 1987. It occurs predominantly in elderly men and half the cases were associated with neurological disorder, but none showed psychiatric abnormality. Violent behaviour or self-injury as a result of dream enactment occurred in REM sleep, which is normally associated with flaccid paralysis. One patient, for example, attempted to strangle his wife while dreaming of fending off a mauling bear, and another grabbed his wife's neck while dreaming of killing a bear by breaking its neck.

There may be some overlap between these groups, as night terrors and sleep-walking both arise in slow wave sleep and the two conditions often coexist in the same individual (Kales et al., 1980a). Similarly, descriptions of sleep-drunkenness often resemble night terrors, which are accompanied by extreme autonomic arousal, vocalization and massive bodily movements. Night terrors usually occur in the first hour-and-a-half of sleep (Fisher et al., 1973; Kales et al., 1980a). The mental content, when it can be recalled, is one of extreme fear, with the subject fighting or struggling to escape from mortal danger (Howard and d'Orbán, 1987). Recall tends to be less detailed than after nightmares. The latter are quite distinct from night terrors; they arise in REM sleep, are not normally accompanied by physical activity, and autonomic arousal is much less.

Earlier writers regarded sleep-walking as a form of hysterical dissociation, with purposive behaviour motivated by unconscious conflicts (Sours et al., 1963). Kales et al. (1980a,b) considered that a high proportion of adults who sleep-walk or have night terrors suffer from personality disorders or neurotic illness. More recent authors, however, have noted the absence of any concomitant psychiatric disorder (Hartmann et al., 1982; Hartmann, 1983; Oswald and Evans, 1985; Tarsh, 1986; Howard and d'Orbán, 1987). Violence in sleep is, therefore, not obviously correlated with any particular mental disorder and often occurs in otherwise normal individuals. Indeed, there is no evidence that the mental content of night terrors is related to preceding psychological disturbance, as attacks can be experimentally induced in the sleep laboratory (Fisher et al., 1973). Known precipitating factors suggest a physiological causation: they include fatigue, sleep deprivation, a change in sleeping environment and a variety of psychoactive drugs (Flemenbaum, 1976; Huapaya, 1979).

Fenwick (1987) drew up a list of 14 criteria to establish diagnosis of sleep-walking or night terrors in a forensic context. Whilst such a list is useful, it is only a guideline, and some cases will not fulfil *all* these criteria. The most striking feature of violence in sleep is the absence of any psychologically coherent explanation for the act. On waking, the subject is bewildered and usually seeks immediate assistance. Clinical assessment should rule out a metabolic disturbance, epilepsy or other neurological disorder, and sleep laboratory evaluation should be carried out if practicable.

The risk of recurrence must also be considered. Few reported cases mention any follow-up (Hartmann, 1983; Tarsh, 1986), but there is no recorded instance of a person committing further acts of violence after acquittal, and the recurrence of dangerous behaviour usually appears very unlikely (Howard and d'Orbán, 1987). Specific treatment may involve benzodiazepine hypnotics (Hartmann, 1983) and REM sleep disorders respond well to desipramine or clonazepam (Schenck et al., 1987). Possible precipitating factors should be eliminated. Explanation and supportive psychotherapy are important, as both perpetrator and victim (who are often marital partners) may be profoundly distressed and puzzled by the violent behaviour.

Genetic Disorders and Offending

The link between inheritance of a specific genetic abnormality and being charged and found guilty of a criminal offence is, at best, tenuous. Two factors are of particular importance. First, whether having a specific genetic disorder increases the propensity to deviant behaviour and second, whether having such a disorder makes the chances of being apprehended, charged and found guilty more or less likely.

It would seem probable that disorders affecting the brain, either in its development or by causing cognitive or mental state abnormalities, are the most likely to predispose to abnormalities of behaviour and thus possibly to offending. Some genetic disorders, for example, give rise to renal or liver disorder and thus to confusional states. Others can directly affect the brain and give rise to intellectual impairment and the possibility of mental handicap. All these different factors could increase the likelihood of inappropriate behaviour.

Theoretically, other phenotypic characteristics, independent of any effect on brain function, could also increase the risk of being arrested and charged. Aggressive behaviour may be regarded more seriously in a male, for example, compared to a female, or in a large rather than a small person. Further, being unusual in size, shape or other obvious characteristics may lead to being teased or excluded and thus to reactive aggression. On this basis alone, it might be expected that people with Turner's Syndrome (XO) would be less likely to have criminal convictions than those with Kleinfelter's (XXY) or the XYY syndrome. Furthermore, people who are intellectually impaired may have an increased chance of being apprehended whilst committing an offence, and may more readily confess to a crime whether guilty or not.

Any link, therefore, must be a complicated one, but is worthy of exploration for two reasons. First, if such a link is found to exist between a specific syndrome and offending, then an understanding of this could lead to the development of specific management strategies or specific treatments in those particular cases. Second, the study of rare genetic syndromes and their physical and behavioural manifestations can sometimes give rise to important insights into the causation of, or predisposition to, particular physical abnormalities, illnesses or behaviours. There are at least five possible links between such syndromes and offending behaviour.

1. A genetic syndrome may be associated with cognitive and/or mental state changes which, in turn, result in behavioural changes. Huntington's Chorea provides a specific example of this. In these cases, either the mood disturbance or the cognitive decline are the factors which increase the risk of behavioural problems, which may be the presenting features. In some disorders, the association might be with social impairment as part of the autistic syndrome which may result in oddities of behaviour. Dewhurst et al. (1970) found that 18 of the 102 patients in their series had serious criminal convictions. Sexual disturbances, including violence, were common. Promiscuity with unwanted pregnancies and serious neglect or abuse of those children were also serious problems.
2. Certain genetic disorders are associated with a markedly increased risk of epilepsy, with its possible associations with behavioural problems (*see above*).
3. In rare cases, a genetic syndrome may be associated with a particular behaviour which, in turn, may increase the risk of a specific offence. People with the Prader Willi Syndrome, for example, have an excessive craving for food, which might result in shoplifting (*see also* below p. 313). The connection between the disorder and the crime in such cases is relatively direct.
4. There may be genetic disorders which are associated with a failure of normal personality development. The personality disorder may, in turn, increase the risk of offending behaviour.
5. Genetic disorders may be associated with intellectual impairment and, for this reason, regardless of the cause of the impairment, there may be an increased risk of being apprehended and found guilty of an offence. Furthermore, people who are intellectually impaired may be socially impaired.

Causes of Genetic Disorders

Genetic disorders fall into two broad groups. The first include disorders which are due to the absence or abnormality of a single gene and the second, those caused by abnormalities of the chromosome itself.

The single gene disorders or 'inborn errors of metabolism' can be inherited in an autosomal recessive, autosomal dominant or X-linked manner or, particularly in the case of certain dominant disorders, may be due to new mutations. In these cases, the genetic abnormality results in the total absence or the deficiency of a specific enzyme. The absence or decrease in the enzyme activity may directly affect a specific metabolic pathway or lead to abnormal storage of metabolites, thus affecting brain development.

Chromosome disorders can be due to the loss or addition of sex chromosomes, the loss or addition of autosomes or small deletions or rearrangements of chromosomes. The loss or addition of whole autosomes frequently gives rise to a non-viable foetus or severe handicaps and multiple abnormalities which are present from birth. Lesser chromosomal abnormalities have less serious phenotypic effects. The best known example of an autosomal chromosome disorder is Down's Syndrome (Trisomy 21) (Corbett 1985; Gibson, 1978). Among the sex chromosome disorders, Kleinfelter's Syndrome (XXY), the XYY Syndrome and Turner's Syndrome (XO) are best known (Cowie, 1977).

Genetic Syndromes and Intellectual Impairment

Chromosome and certain single gene disorders are frequently associated with varying degrees of intellectual impairment. People born with a genetic syndrome and who are severely mentally handicapped may well present with difficult behaviour, but in these cases such behaviour is unlikely to lead to arrest and prosecution. This group of people will probably need continuous care and, in the majority of cases, criminal proceedings would be inappropriate. While special care has to be taken at all stages of proceedings against people with lesser degrees of intellectual impairment (*see* pp. 316–25), there is a whole range of factors which will determine the extent to which they become involved with the courts.

People with intellectual impairment constitute a very heterogeneous group. As with the non-handicapped population, they vary in personality, appearance and intellectual ability, and the aetiology of their handicap differs greatly. Some may have a genetic disorder affecting brain development in subtle and varied ways, while others may have suffered one of a number of possible environmental insults. Within the less handicapped group, however, certain rare genetic disorders are associated with specific types of abnormal behaviour. The Lesch Nyham Syndrome, for example, an X-linked single gene disorder affecting males only, is associated with severe self-injurious behaviour (Lesch and Nyham, 1964). Another disorder, the Prader Willi Syndrome, is characterized by mild intellectual impairment, failure of normal secondary sexual development and severe overeating, likely to lead to gross obesity and increased morbidity and mortality (Laurance, 1967; Hall and Smith, 1972; Corbett, 1985). Over 50% of people with this disorder have been reported as having a deletion or translocation involving the proximal part of the long arm of chromosome 15 (Ledbetter et al., 1981). Some parents report that as their children become more independent, they start shoplifting for food and other goods.

Autosomal dominant disorders such as tuberose sclerosis and neurofibromatosis are associated with varying degrees of intellectual impairment, epilepsy and psychiatric problems. The occurrence of epilepsy in these and other disorders may be associated with aggressive behaviour (Fenwick, 1986). Tuberose sclerosis is also associated with autistic type handicaps, characterized by social impairment, poor language development, frequently with more generalized intellectual impairments and sometimes with ritualistic behaviour (Hunt and Dennis, 1987). Social impairment as part of the autistic syndrome has been reported to occur in as many as a third of adults who are intellectually impaired (Shah et al., 1982), as is the case with a possibly related disorder, Asperger's Syndrome (Wing, 1981).

The XYY Syndrome

Jacobs et al. (1965) reported finding an excess of individuals with the XYY genotype in special (maximum security) hospitals, suggesting that people with this genotype were either more prone to criminal behaviour, to have been referred more frequently, or kept for longer periods in special hospitals. The study by Jacobs and his colleagues had been carried out following the observation of Forssman and Hambert (1966) that an excess number of men with the XYY genotype was found in Swedish institutions for the criminal and 'hard to manage', the first description of an XYY man being attributed to Sandberg et al. (1961). Jacobs et al. (1965) suggested that an extra Y chromosome might predispose to violent behaviour. Hook (1973), in his review, reported that a further 20 studies found a similar excess of males with the XYY genotype in 'mental/penal' institutions compared to purely 'mental' or purely 'penal' institutions, or compared to the observed population base rate of 0.4% established by Dorus et al. (1976) and Noel et al. (1974). This is a higher rate than the figure given by Ratcliffe et al. (1970) of 0.14% in their study of a consecutive series of newborn infants in Scotland, although Noel and colleagues noted a rate of 1 per 1000 if height had not been taken as a selection factor, and this concurs with findings from the population cytogenetic studies of Zang and Leyking (1981). A myth had been born.

Price and Whatmore (1967) described the behavioural characteristics of 9 men with the XYY genotype in a special hospital. None had suffered from a psychotic illness and all were categorized as having a severe personality disorder, 7 also being mildly mentally handicapped. Their behavioural problems were reported to have started in childhood and their family backgrounds were unremarkable. The authors commented that these 9 people were a highly selected group and that the number of people with the XYY genotype who do not have behavioural problems was unknown. Griffiths (1971) reported that the IQ scores of 12 individuals with the XYY genotype were several points lower on average than those of a control group. Hook (1973) discussed three possible explanations for deviant behaviour.

Firstly, that males with the genotype may more often be born into potentially deviant environments, he thought unlikely. Secondly, he suggested that increased height, or some other factor results in different 'channelling' by social forces, and thirdly, that there might be an underlying neural abnormality which predisposes to impulsivity and to behavioural problems. He favoured the hypothesis of an interaction between a pre-exisiting propensity to deviant behaviour, which is independent of the XYY genotype, and the effects of the genotype on neural development. The more likely presence of minor neurological signs (Daly, 1969) and cortical evoked potential abnormalities (Paty and Benejech, 1978) in males with the XYY genotype compared to matched controls provides some support for the hypothesis.

More powerful data from double-blind evaluations of XYY men, and controls matched for such features as age, height, educational level and socio-economic status, challenge the old stereotype of the hyperaggressive, dangerous male. Noel and Revil (1974) and Noel et al. (1974) compared 7 XYY men drawn at random from the general population with such controls and concluded that for the men established by chromosomal analysis to have an XYY configuration, the most important quality was 'their apparent inability to integrate aggression normally into their perception of reality'. They considered that the XYY genotype had achieved syndrome status. None of these XYY men, however, had engaged in criminal activity. Witkin et al. (1976) emphasized that, on evidence extracted from social and criminal records, aggression against the person was not a feature of XYY or XXY males. Similar findings emerged when Benezech et al. (1974) extended Noel's sample to 14 XYY men, and matched controls from the general population. They interpreted them differently, however, and conceded no more than a possible predisposition or increased vulnerability to problems, a '*fragilité psychique*'. These samples may appear small, but it is perhaps worth tracing the route by which Theilgaard (1984) identified her sample. From all males (31,438) born in the municipality of Copenhagen between January 1944 and 31 December 1947, the tallest 15% (4591) were selected for examination. Buccal smears and blood samples were taken from 4139. This resulted in the identification of 12 XYY men and 16 XXY men. All of the former, 14 of the latter and 52 matched XY controls participated in detailed neuro-psychosocial evaluations.

Theilgaard addressed all the complexities of relationship between exceptional inborn characteristics and environmental experiences through childhood and adult life (the latter may or may not have been secondary to those characteristics); she explored cognitive and personality styles as well as aggression and sexuality. In brief, both XXY and XYY groups showed, overall, a slight general deficit in general intelligence, but in neither group was the chromosome constitution incompatible with superior intelligence. Measures of aggression revealed few differences between the groups, with the only significant difference on actual verbal aggression being that the XXYs were exceptionally submissive. In terms of general aggressive behaviour, there were again few differences, but the XYYs reported more impulsivity and more domestic aggression, mainly directed towards the wife, than either controls or XXYs. Both chromosomally abnormal groups had been more frequently arrested, but not convicted, than the controls, which, since these men had been selected for size might say more about the attitudes of society than real qualities in their behaviour. Theilgaard emphasized that the XYYs were significantly more likely to have reported that the quality of their childhood was poor (on the basis of a number of standardized observations) than either the XXYs or the controls. She modestly concluded:

> The outcome of the present study strongly supports the statement that the problems of the XYY and the XXY constitutions are not of a magnitude that need concern society in the sense of requiring special precautions. . . . Direct straight-line cause-and-effect connections should be avoided. . . . The problem of not permitting the genetic information to prejudice the upbringing of the child should be discussed.

The XYY story thus presents a cautionary tale. The super-male, threatening stereotype must be discarded. Instead, there is a model for appreciating the complexities of social development and interaction for anyone who appears unusual. The pitfalls of accepting 'new syndromes' too quickly, are also apparent.

Mental Handicap and Offending

There is no evidence of a general causal link between the many conditions subsumed under the clinical label of mental handicap and a propensity to offend. For most of this century, however, the law in the UK has made special provision for mentally handicapped people who offend, by allowing courts to send them to hospital or make them subject to guardianship orders in the community. People who are mentally handicapped should not be placed into one category. From the practical standpoint, profoundly handicapped people, those whose capacity to understand and control their environment is minimal, are extremely limited in their range of behaviour, so that the notion of their behaving 'criminally' need not be considered. Of the 73 patients in the English special hospitals classified under the Mental Health Act 1983 as severely mentally impaired, only 5 were thought to need the maximum secure provision (Taylor et al., in press).

A distinction must also be made between low intelligence, the clinical understanding of what constitutes mental retardation, and the UK legal definitions of mental impairment (formerly subnormality), which is essentially behavioural. Misunderstanding has occured in the past for lack of adequate distinction between these three terms. For the sake of consistency, the term 'mental handicap' has been employed in this text, regardless of the particular wording employed in the legislative instrument being discussed.

The Legal Category of Mental Impairment

The legal position of the handicapped and the legal definition of mental impairment is contained in Ch. 2. The history of the law in relation to the mentally handicapped has been descibed by Walker (1968) and Walker and McCabe (1973), and an international review of past and present legislation in the area has recently been published by Smith and Kunjukrishnan (1986).

It is only when the legal process has reached the sentencing stage that there is any indication of the number of mentally handicapped people within the judicial system; even here the measure is extremely crude and potentially misleading. If interest is restricted to this century and to England and Wales, the operation of four Acts of Parliament must be considered; the Mental Deficiency Acts of 1913 and 1927, and the Mental Health Acts of 1959 and 1983. The MHA 1959 brought mental illness and subnormality within the same legislative instrument, but emphasized the disease aspects of the disorder and the clinical needs of the patient. The MHA 1983 gives a much more restrictive definition, which is essentially that of psychopathic disorder with 'arrested or incomplete development of mind'. Although this change has meant that compulsory detention can only be employed providing the individual in question qualifies as 'treatable', many have deplored the implication of some inevitable association between mental retardation and irresponsible or aggressive behaviour that this definition implied.

The full extent of the Mental Deficiency Act 1913 was not felt until the end of the 1914–18 War. Board of Control figures from 1920 onwards reveal a steady rise in the number of mentally handicapped people detained under the criminal provisions of the 1913 Act. Between 1920 and 1938, the population so detained in both state and local institutions increased from 690 to 4558 (Board of Control, 1921; 1939). This rise reflected the growth which had taken place in the provision of institutional places for mentally handicapped people by local authorities, a development encouraged by the 1913 Act. As the century progressed, so too did the building of such institutions. At the end of the First World War, there were 8686 residents in mental deficiency colonies; by 1938, that number had risen to 50,895. The situation paralleled the growth in provision of asylum places for the mentally ill which had taken place in the latter half of the 19th century. All such developments were underpinned by a firm belief in the benefit of institutional care. The following, from the Annual Report of the Board of Control for 1927 (Board of Control, 1928), was written by the then Medical Superintendent of Rampton State Hospital:

Of the 153 patients admitted during the year . . . 36 . . . had not previously resided in any institution certified under the mental deficiency Acts. . . . In surveying the general characteristics of this group I found that the only common factor was their mental defect. But it is possible from a study of the 'case histories' to express the firm opinion that, had the mental defect been recognised and dealt with at an earlier stage of their careers, no such sorry spectacle as a number of mental defectives brought before the courts would have been possible. . . . For the benefit of society and for the happiness of the mental defective it is of great importance that care and training in an institution should commence at least several years before the period of adolescence.

It is not clear from the account how it was that the 117 handicapped people who had been exposed to mental deficiency institutions came to be convicted of serious offences. Although such attitudes seem eccentric by present standards, they must be understood in their historical context. The then new institutions offered care and protection in place of the neglect and exploitation too often evident in the treatment meted out to handicapped people in the community.

Official statistics were not produced during the Second World War but, by extrapolation from the resident population figures by the end of it (Board of Control, 1947), it seems likely that the number of handicapped people being sent to hospital from the courts had remained at its prewar level. A full account of the use made of the 1913 Act in the courts is given by Walker and McCabe (1973). In the four years prior to the implementation of the MHA 1959, an average of 322 disposals were made in magistrates and Assizes courts under section 8 of the 1913 Act. The figure is very similar to the average of 325 such disposals in the 4-year period before the outbreak of the Second World War. Seen in this context, the number of orders made in the early years of the MHA 1959 operation, represents a marked change in the practice of the courts. In 1961, 443 hospital orders were made for mentally handicapped people. The increase in use of such disposals continued throughout the early 1960s, averaging 446 orders, a proportional rise of 38% from the pre-MHA 1959 period. Assuming there was no sudden rise in the number of mentally handicapped people coming before the courts, the increase may be attributed to what Walker and McCabe call:

> The stimulating effect of what was presented as a 'new deal' for hospital psychiatry in general and for forensic psychiatry in particular.

Figure 7.1 presents a graph of the number of unrestricted court/hospital orders made in respect of all categories of mentally disordered offender defined in the MHA 1959 and MHA 1983. For orders under mental handicap, there has been a rapid decline in use, from 478 in 1966 to 124 in 1976, and 41 (under mental impairment) in 1984. As is clear from the graph, the number of orders made in respect of mentally ill people has shown relatively little change over the same period.

If it can be assumed that there has been no real fall in the number of mentally handicapped people appearing in court, the decline is likely to be due to changes in the admission policy of mental handicap hospitals over that period, and must be viewed in the context of developments which had been taking place in the care and treatment of mentally handicapped people (Primrose, 1984). There has been a shift of opinion toward regarding institutional care as inappropriate for most mentally handicapped people,

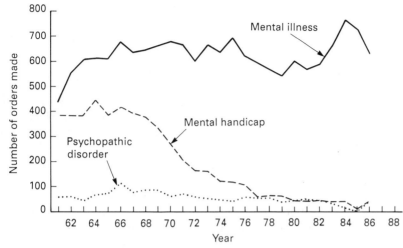

Fig. 7.1   The use of unrestricted hospital orders throughout the 1959 and 1983 Mental Health Acts.

care in the community now being the favoured model. The number of residents in mental handicap hospitals has fallen steadily since 1968, when it reached its peak of over 59,000. Five years later, in 1973, the resident population was under 52,000, in 1977 it was 48,000 and in 1985 the figure was 36,000 (Department of Health and Social Services, 1988a), a reduction of 23,000 beds from 1968 and a proportional fall of 39%.

Two questions arise. Has the mentally handicapped offender suffered in consequence of these changes and how have courts been disposing of such offenders if they are no longer being sent to hospital? No direct evidence exists to answer either question, but there is some indirect evidence to suggest that the change may have benefited the majority of mentally handicapped offenders and that, in the early years of the MHA 1959, mentally handicapped people had been rendered vulnerable to inappropriate hospitalization.

The study of hospital order patients conducted by Walker and McCabe (1973) was carried out during the early years of the operation of the MHA 1959, when the use of such orders (made by the courts) for mentally handicapped people was at its height. Referring to the 15-to-20-year-old group of mentally handicapped people in their sample, they found it surprising that 'so few are committed by compulsory procedures which do not involve the courts' (Walker and McCabe, 1973). Furthermore, within this group 'three-quarters of the males and four-fifths of the females had no previous institutional histories'. A 15-year follow-up of that population (Robertson, 1981) revealed that whereas only half of the mentally handicapped had been inpatients prior to receiving their hospital order, more than 80% of the mentally ill and the psychopathically disordered had received such care (p < 0.0001). If so few had required inpatient care before their court appearance, and very few were ever made subject to civil detention, it seems likely that their detention in hospital following conviction often represented an inappropriate hospital admission, albeit from the best of motives. It was also found that almost one in five of mentally handicapped offender/patients had been discharged from their hospital order around the period when the order expired (i.e. 12 months after admission). This picture contrasted markedly with the curvilinear pattern of discharges which had taken place among their mentally ill counterparts, suggesting that, in many cases, discharge was occurring for administrative reasons rather than for consideration of any therapeutic criteria.

Some may have been damaged by the experience. A paper by Tutt (1971) is revealing. In it, the characteristics of 44 men admitted between 1965 and 1970 to a 'psychopathic' unit situated in a mental handicap hospital were described. Their IQ scores ranged from 51 to 109, 50% of such scores falling within the normal range of intelligence. Only 40% had required special education. A majority (73%) had been admitted following conviction for property offences and all were young, their ages ranging from 16 to 33. Among the problems caused by housing young men of dull-normal or borderline intelligence in a mental handicap hospital, Tutt noted:

> The marked deleterious effect on the unit members by drastically disturbing their self image and subsequently producing lower aspirations and expectations. . . . Their admission to the unit often served to damage further an already damaged personality.

The declining use of hospital orders for mentally handicapped offenders probably need not, then, be regarded as detrimental to the well-being of most such people. As to other disposals being used by the courts, the follow-up of Walker and McCabe's population (Robertson, 1981), found that probation orders were frequently used for those who were reconvicted.

Probation represents a very similar type of disposal to guardianship under the mental health legislation, but perhaps does not stigmatize the mentally handicapped offender as being different from other offenders.

Offenders with Clinically Defined Mental Retardation

Court-based Epidemiological Studies

Walker and McCabe (1973) provided an example of the greatly exaggerated claims made for the association between crime and mental handicap in the early part of this century in the USA.

> The initial failure to distinguish between educational attainment and innate intelligence led to astounding over-estimates of the prevalence of feeble-mindedness amongst offenders: the Psychopathic Laboratory of the Chicago Municipal Court reported that 85 per cent of their female and young male offenders were 'distinctly feeble-minded'.

Later court-based surveys in the USA such as those of Messinger and Apfelberg (1961), reported that 2.5% of the 57 000 people examined in the New York County Court were mentally handicapped and needed to be considered for special disposal. No court surveys on this scale have been reported in the UK.

Prison Studies

The proportion of prison inmates deemed to be mentally handicapped has diminished steadily over the century, although exaggerated estimates of the number of such people in prison continue to be reported. The apparent decline in prevalence may have been due in part to increasing sophistication in psychometric testing, but this factor alone would not account for the decrease witnessed in the very early part of the century when, as described above, the opening of special institutions for the handicapped probably resulted in a shift of population from the prisons. Between 1976 and 1982, only 35 requests were made for the transfer to hospital of prisoners described as mentally handicapped, under the provisions of the MHA 1959, an average of 5 per year (Home Office 1977, 1978b, 1979, 1980a, 1981, 1982, 1983). In contrast, an average of 118 transfer requests were made in respect of mentally ill prisoners. These figures do not reflect the number of mentally handicapped people in the penal system, but may be taken as a guide to those who present special problems in their management. It may be noted that 63% of applications made in respect of mentally ill people were successful compared with only 29% of the small number of requests in respect of mentally handicapped prisoners.

The picture would seem to be similar in the USA. In his prison-based study, Guze (1976) concluded:

> Most investigators agree . . . that severe mental deficiency is present in only a small percentage of criminals, even though it may be present in a higher percentage of criminals than of the general population.

The problem which the mentally handicapped present to the prison authorities is one of management; the handicapped prisoner must be protected from exploitation, bullying and unnecessary stress.

Offenders of Low Average Intelligence

Juvenile Delinquent Groups

The apparent improvement in mean IQs reported within delinquent groups as the century progressed was due largely to increasing sophistication in testing procedures (Woodward, 1955; Caplan and Siebert, 1964). It is also clear, however, that populations of delinquents contain a higher than average proportion of youngsters of below average ability. Eilenberg (1961) in a study of boys in a London remand centre, reported that, although only 2% were 'defectives', 58% could be classified as being intellectually dull. A full account of relevant studies is presented in West and Farrington (1973). This longitudinal study of 411 boys provides the best available evidence of the role of low intelligence in the development of delinquency (West, 1969; West and Farrington, 1973, 1977). Defining delinquents as those with one or more convictions, Gibson and West (1970) found that, by the age of 14, 17% of those with IQs of 90 or less were delinquent compared to 5% of those with IQs of more than 90. The test used to measure intelligence was the non-verbal Raven's Progressive Matrices. The statistical relationship was sustained, though much less powerfully, when the 'social handicap' of the boys was taken into account. By the age of 18, when some 20% of the survey population had been convicted of at least one offence, non-verbal intelligence remained 'significantly predictive of delinquency'. The authors pointed to the large degree of overlap, however, between the delinquent and non-delinquent groups of boys, the mean difference in IQ being only 6 points. By the age of 21, 31% of those boys who could be traced had a criminal record, and those with low IQs, defined again as 90 or less, were twice as likely to be found in the group with juvenile and adult convictions than in the non-delinquent group (40% compared with 20%).

Adult Offenders

It is in reporting the intelligence of adult offenders in penal institutions that most confusion has arisen between low intelligence and mental handicap. In particular, two studies by Roper (1950, 1951), a medical officer at Wakefield Prison, have been misinterpreted as providing evidence that as many as 45% of prisoners are 'subnormal'. Roper himself states: 'The picture is that 50% of the prisoners fell into the subnormal intelligence groups', but he adds: 'The proportion of mental defectives was about ½ percent.' It is clear from the text and the accompanying tables that, by 'subnormal

Table 7.4
Distribution of Test Scores on Raven's Progressive Matrices among Adult and Juvenile Offenders

Population studied	Author	Distribution of scores on progressive matrices				
		A	B	C	D	E
		%	%	%	%	%
General population norms		10	20	40	20	10
Borstal boys N = 200	Gibbens, 1963	8	20	38	19	15
Wakefield prisoners N = 1079	Marcus, 1955	8	23	37	19	13
Five local prisons N = 674	Blackler, 1968	1	–	78	–	21

intelligence' Roper meant, of below average intelligence. Confirmation of this interpretation is contained in a paper by Marcus (1955), a psychologist in the same prison. Using the test referred to by Roper, Marcus reported the distribution of scores for 1079 prisoners. They resembled those of the general population (*see* Table 7.4). He found no correlation between IQ scores and age at first conviction or frequency of conviction. A study of 200 Borstal boys carried out by Gibbens (1963) produced an almost identical picture to that obtained by Marcus.

Gibbens' comments are revealing:

> Professional observers are usually struck by the apparent dullness of any normal population, because they are used to dealing with a more intelligent sample.

After examining the performance of the same young men on verbal and spelling tests, he concluded:

> The more the tests are influenced by what is learnt in school, the more the results deviate from the normal distribution.

A more recent report by Blackler (1968) produced a higher proportion of men in the lowest 10% of the population (*see* Table 7.4) which may be due to the fact that the study was carried out using men in local prisons rather than the more highly selected Wakefield prison population. In all these studies, the modal group, the middle 80% of the normal population, is represented by almost identical proportions of prisoners. As Gibbens points out, however, although dullness is no longer of much general significance, for the individual or the clinician dealing with him, intellectual level is an important factor. Three of us (Robertson et al., 1987) reported a variant on this theme. Among 76 remanded (pretrial) prisoners without classifiable psychiatric disease, the violent group was of significantly lower mean intelligence than the non-violent group. The *importance* of these findings was, however, difficult to interpret, since both groups showed mean scores that were well within the average range.

Types of Offence Associated with Mental Handicap

It clearly emerges from both court- and hospital-based reports that within the spectrum of criminal offending, there is an association between mental handicap and sexual offences (Shapiro, 1968; Tutt, 1971; Walker and McCabe, 1973; Fowles, 1978). In the Walker and McCabe study, the third of their sample who had been labelled mentally handicapped accounted for 59% of the 155 sexual offences committed. Sexual offences comprised 16% of total offences among this group. Many offences involved children and ranged in seriousness from child-like mutual exploration to fatal and near fatal encounters. As Prins (1980) stated

> The attitudes to legitimate expression of sexuality of some mentally subnormal patients may be naive, primitive or unrestrained.

It is also true that many mentally handicapped people are rejected and are thus denied 'legitimate expression' of their sexuality. This rejection plays a part in the frequency with which some of them engage in sexual activity without the consent of the other. The majority of sexual offenders described in these studies were men of an age when they were at their most sexually active. In their special assessment and rehabilitation unit, Spry and Craft (1984) found many of their patients to be—

> sexually ignorant as to how to channel their sexual tensions and needs or even how to approach a female in a way which might elicit a positive rather than a negative response.

To counter this, they set up a programme to teach about health and sexual matters by group and individual counselling.

To a lesser extent, mentally handicapped offenders have been found to be disproportionately represented among arson offenders. Walker and McCabe (1973) found that one-half of the offences of arson had been committed by the third of their sample who were handicapped. Such offences numbered only 16 among mentally handicapped people, however, and constituted only 5% of the offences for which the handicapped people in their study had been convicted.

The types of offence for which most mentally handicapped people are convicted are acquisitive. In this, they do not differ from the rest of the offender population. The pattern of offending among mentally handicapped men has been described by one of us (Robertson 1981). Unlike the mentally ill, who often presented atypical criminal careers which began in their mid to late twenties, the majority of mentally handicapped men studied (73%) were first convicted in their teens. As a group, they presented a pattern of criminality fairly similar to the normal, though perhaps slightly delayed in onset.

Overview of the Position of the Mentally Handicapped Offender

The implementation of the MHA 1959 occasioned an atypical surge in the number of people being sent to mental handicap hospitals by the courts, but since the mid 1960s, there has been a steep decline in the practice. It seems unlikely that the majority of mentally handicapped offenders have thereby been disadvantaged; many have received non-custodial sentences. For those of low or below average intelligence that are imprisoned, protection from exploitation in prison may be necessary. Prisons contain a higher than expected proportion of men in the bottom 10% of the normal range of intelligence, but the vast majority of prisoners produce non-verbal IQ scores which are within the normal range.

Low intelligence plays a role in early delinquency, possibly because of consequently increased vulnerability to the adverse influences of environment and home background and may also lead to being more easily apprehended. Most mentally handicapped offenders are convicted of acquisitive crimes. Within the population of mentally disordered offenders, sexual offending, and to a lesser extent arson are statistically linked with mental handicap, but it should be remembered that the vast majority of offenders in both categories are not mentally handicapped people. By virtue of their disability, the mentally handicapped may be more likely than most to become victims of all types of offending.

Old Age, Psychiatric Disorders and Offending

People of 60 and over constitute the most rapidly growing age group in the populations of many western countries. From 1980 to 1985 there was a 22% growth in the number of elderly people in residential care, mainly among those aged 75 and over (National Audit Office, 1987). Perhaps the most likely contact the old will have with the law is in civil matters, where competency of some kind is in question. A number of American publications have addressed this issue (e.g. Stanley, 1983; Nolan, 1984; Baker et al., 1986). Although much American law differs in detail from that in Britain, for example there is no 'living will' law in Britain, the principles of the necessary evaluation are essentially the same. In relation to criminal behaviour, it seems that under Chinese law of the Ch'ing dynasty, of 1644–1911, extremes of old age, just as extremes of youth, were in themselves allowed in whole or partial exemption from responsibility for offences, other than rebellion or treason (Bodde, 1973). In the western world, the criminal responsibility of the elderly offender, as his competency, is judged in the same way as for any other adult accused of crime.

Criminal Characteristics of Elderly Offenders

Within the criminal justice system, old age generally arrives in the fourth decade. Greenberg (1983), however, cautioned against false impressions of the extent of the decline in criminal behaviour with advancing age. He cited the greater tendency of the young to commit crime in groups, the discrepancy between arrest and real crime rates which might be exaggerated by experience, and annual cohort effects, as being among possible confounding variables. Nevertheless, across national boundaries, the contribution to crime of those aged 60 and over is consistently very small (Hough and Mayhew, 1983; Clarke et al., 1985). In England and Wales, less than 200 per 100 000 men of 60 and over, per year, are found guilty of or cautioned for an indictable crime. The rate is about half this for women. In 1986, in total, only 3000 men and 600 women of 60 or over were found guilty of an indictable crime. Comparable figures for men aged between 21 and 30 were nearly 112 000 and for women 19 000 (Home Office 1987a). Nevertheless, there is evidence to suggest that women aged over 60 form a relatively higher proportion of the offender population than men in that age group (*see also* p. 60).

Feinberg (1984) examined comparable US national statistics for 1966–1980 inclusive. He found that, although overall crime arrest rates had fallen over the period of his study, the rate of index crimes, roughly equivalent to indictable crimes, had risen, and at a greater rate, in the older than in the younger age groups. For all ages, the increases in arrests for index crimes was 115%, but among those of between 55 and 64 it was 136% and for those of 65 and over it was a steady 165%. He found that, for all arrests, driving while intoxicated and disorderly conduct were the most common apparent breaches of law among the elderly, but that larceny was the most common index crime.

The importance of alcohol in elderly offending has been consistently emphasized in US studies (e.g. Moberg, 1953; Keller and Vedder, 1968; Shichor, 1984). In California, where the arrest rates for drinking were as high as one in two for men under 60, no fewer than four in five of men who were arrested over that age were on drunkenness charges (Epstein et al., 1970). In an English series of remanded male prisoners, the proportion who showed withdrawal symptoms on admission to prison increased with increasing age (Taylor and Parrott, 1988). Less than 1% of those of 21 or under, and 6% of those between 25 and 34 showed withdrawal, compared with nearly 25% of those between 55 and 64 and one-third of those over 65.

For the rest, patterns of crime among elderly offenders seem remarkably similar to those of their younger peers. There are few offence categories in which the elderly do not figure at all. Indictable drug offences, however, are very rare, at least in England and Wales. In 1979 (Home Office, 1980b), only 7 of the 10 164 indictable drug offence convictions were committed by those of 60 or over. Proportionately, the elderly contributed more in the same year to the sex offending figures, but still those over 60 accounted for only 1% of indictable sex offending, rather less than the figure of 5% in the USA in the same year (Shichor, 1984). The British figures do not include exhibitionism, which may account for some of the difference. There has been considerable consistency, over the last fifty years, in the relative importance among the elderly of sex offending. Moberg (1953) showed that, in the 1930s, the quotient of decrease with age in sex offending other than rape and prostitution, was the lowest of any offence examined (2.2). By contrast, the quotient of decrease of car theft from the peak ages of 16–20 to the 50-plus age group was nearly 123.

Physical and Mental Health Problems of Elderly Offenders

All those who have written about elderly offenders remark on their extensive health problems. In the English samples of 1241 remanded male prisoners studied by case note review (Taylor and Parrott, 1988), active symptoms of psychiatric disorder on admission to the prison were identified in nearly half of those aged 55–64, and 55% of those of 65 and over, but were apparent in a minority of younger men. Only 15% of those aged 65 and over were without a history of psychiatric treatment. Apart from alcoholism, affective psychosis was the most important illness among older men, although the actual number was small. Schizophrenia played little part and dementia was not certainly identified at all. The former was particularly interesting because, compared to the general male population, men with schizophrenia made a disproportionately high contribution to the offender group up to the age of about 45, but beyond 50 a disproportionately low contribution.

The apparent absence of dementia was also intriguing, because it is a relatively common problem among the elderly. Kay and Bergmann (1980) calculated a prevalence of 6.5% for moderate or severe dementia in those over 65. The rate increases with age, being 2.1% among the 65–69-year-old group but 17.7 among those over 80. It is likely that dementing patients with all but the most serious antisocial behaviour can be contained within the health care system, and that those with social ties still are. Roth (1968) outlined the likely associations between senility and offending, in particular the link between disinhibition of behaviour and sexual offending. He suggested that inappropriate sexual behaviour may be due to the loss of control exercised by the higher centres of the brain, but it could equally be linked to increased loneliness among elderly people. While violence is probably more often directed towards the self than shows among the elderly, it sometimes happens that partners or other close relatives of a dementing person are killed, the homicide occurring after some trivial row (Roth, 1968). Deutsch et al. (1991) described physical aggression in nearly one-third of patients with Alzheimer's Disease attending a research clinic in the USA (Johns Hopkins). Frank psychotic symptons occurred commonly among those patients (over 40%), but accounted for only a tiny proportion of violence precipitation. Other factors like premorbid social relationships were clearly important too.

The Elderly in Custody

Upon conviction, about one-third of the men in the English remand prisoner series (Taylor and Parrott, 1988) were sentenced to imprisonment, a figure only sightly lower than the rates of imprisonment for the younger age groups in the study. There have been a number of reports of the elderly serving custodial sentences in the USA, but little interest in them in Britain. Golden (1984) reported that about 3% of jail (local prison) inmates in the USA were aged 55 or over. She described the typical elderly inmate as a white, unemployed, poorly educated male, charged or convicted of a petty offence. To this might be added a picture of social isolation. In the English remand study, no man over 65 was still living with a spouse at the time of his arrest, although two-thirds had at one time been married; furthermore, 75% were without fixed addresses of any kind, only slightly more than in the 55–64 age group. Rubenstein (1984) and Goetting (1983) reviewed a wider literature on the elderly in prison: their profile as offenders, their profile as prisoners (generally solitary and compliant with rules) and the problems they faced within the facilities. Prisons, they pointed out, are geared for younger offenders and, thus, not only make inadequate provisions for the many medical needs of the older prisoners, but fail them too in their special policies, programmes and rehabilitation facilities.

Imaginative approaches to sentencing (Feinberg et al., 1984) and changes in public policy (Newman and Newman, 1984) have been described in the USA, and in England at least one police force has a special group of officers to deal with the elderly offender, to facilitate contacts with medical or social services for them. Most elderly offenders presenting in the prison system have well established criminal histories (Goetting, 1983; Taylor and Parrott, 1988). Further imprisonment thus seems unlikely to be an effective deterrent for them. Given the poor health and isolation of many elderly offenders, community alternatives to imprisonment for them seems by far the most important way forward.

8
Psychosis, Violence and Crime

Edited by	*Written by*
Pamela J. Taylor	Paul Mullen
	Pamela J. Taylor
	Simon Wessely

This chapter is concerned with psychosis as a clinical condition in its association with violence and antisocial acts. Much of what is said will have implications for management—although this is most directly addressed in the chapters on service provision and on treatment.

The relationship between legal concepts of insanity and clinical concepts of psychosis is slight, as has already been emphasized in Ch. 2. Even when insanity *per se* is not an issue, the formulation of diagnostic material tends to become distorted in reports prepared for legal purposes. Simple opinions and certainties are preferred to scientific probabilities; the nature of illness or the patient's best interests are not often the dominant issues among the range of matters to be considered at law, and psychiatrists may even embrace these tendencies for their own ends, favouring legal classifications that will protect their services from the chronically psychotic, disruptive, but poorly compliant, patients that may be demanding and costly in the long term if taken on for treatment (Coid, 1988). The potential unreliability of court reports as a source of clinical data poses particular difficulties for the compilation of a valid review of associations between psychosis and antisocial acts since much of the existing literature depends on reports for the courts. In Canada, for example, Langevin et al. (1982) used a retrospective chart assessment, heavily reliant on such reports, to make diagnoses in a consecutive series of killers referred to the Forensic Psychiatric Services at the Clarke Institute in Toronto, and compare them with those of non-violent offenders. The interrater reliability of the research diagnosis was no better than chance. The correlation between a trial outcome of not guilty by reason of insanity, as made by the reporting psychiatrist, and a psychotic diagnosis was only 0.23. The distorting impact of the courts is not only on clinicians. Holley and Arboleda-Florez (1988), for example showed that on research forms police indicated that 27% of arrestees needed psychiatric assessment, but, on official arrest reports, only 2% of such recommendations were made to the magistrate.

Violence and crime are almost exclusively socially defined. Some forms of violence are not only accepted, but also required by society. Enquiry into the association between violence and psychosis has been wholly concerned with unacceptable violence, whatever that may mean. Crime is also more or less acceptable, attitudes ranging from those of the actively dissocial community, through those of the family or group tolerating a petty misdemeanour, because of affectionate bonding, to the frankly intolerant. Definitions, and interpretations of definitions, are fluid, and definitive statements about whether the mentally disordered are disproportionately likely to be identified as offenders, compared with the mentally normal, are never likely. Hypotheses have been advanced in favour of under, over and equivalent representation of the mentally disordered in violent and criminal groups. Scientifically gathered data has been offered in support of all the positions. It matters very little whether the mentally disordered are more or less violent or criminal than their normal peers. An estimate of the frequency of association between the various kinds of disorder, violence and crime is, however, of value in helping to determine the nature and extent of facilities required for appropriate treatment.

Estimating the Frequency of Association between Violence, Crime and Psychosis

Monahan and Steadman (1983) comprehensively reviewed the numerical relationship between violence, crime and mental disorder. They emphasized the distinction between 'true' rates of crime and mental disorder (that is the rates at which crime and mental disorder actually occur) and their 'treated' rates (that is the rates at which the criminal justice and the mental health systems respond to them). Most published research, they found, focused on true rates of disorder among 'treated' criminals or true rates of crime among 'treated' patients. Many studies referred to mental disorder or illness in broad terms and estimation of the contribution of psychosis was difficult. A few studies stand out as addressing at least some of these concerns.

Monahan et al (1979), in the USA, reported police officer perceptions of mental disorder present in a random group of people arrested for any criminal behaviour except public drunkenness. Of those arrested, 2% were described as 'seriously mentally ill', 10% as moderately mentally ill and 18% as 'somewhat mentally ill'. The authors interpreted severe mental illness as psychosis, and thus suggested from their figures that people with psychosis were represented in an offender group in roughly the same proportions as might be expected in the general population.

Teplin (1985) reported a similar study of 183 randomly selected police officers in encounters with the public in an urban area of the USA, although these encounters were with victims and people needing assistance as well as possible offenders. Psychology graduates shadowed the police and made the 'diagnosis', a small validity study showing that there was 93% agreement between the observational measure of 'severe mental disorder' and a research diagnosis of psychosis. Only 4% of the sample of 2000 showed signs of such mental disorder, a small proportion, but two or three times that of the expected rate of psychosis in the general population. Although less likely to be victims or complainants, the severely mentally ill were twice as likely to be 'subjects of concern or assistance' as the other people studied. They were also rather more likely to be suspects of crime. Ten per cent had been involved in violent personal crime, compared with only 3% of the non-mentally disordered, but the former represented only three people in the 'criminal' subgroup. No other significant differences emerged.

Lindqvist and Allebeck (1990a) were more specific in the disorder that they studied—schizophrenia. Their sample included all people with this diagnosis, born between 1920 and 1959 and discharged from a mental hospital or psychiatric clinic in Stockholm county in 1971. The sample was thus, strictly, of the 'treated' mentally ill, but it was otherwise complete for a substantial urban area of Sweden and, in extracting offending data from the central police register, contained information on all significant police contacts, so the authors came closer to studying true crime rates than those who focus on criminal statistics. Of the original cohort, 142 died during the 14-year follow-up, leaving just 644 for whom there was offending information. The crime rate varied with gender, being the same as for the general population among the men, but twice as high among the women. The rate of violent offences was four times as high among the people with schizophrenia—the violence, however, rarely being more than minimal.

Studies of all police encounters may offer a truer picture of the frequency of association between psychosis and crime than recording only charges or convictions, but they do not include those people with mental disorder who effectively offend but by-pass the police altogether, usually through presenting at mental hospital. Information bias remains a serious problem. Lagos et al. (1977) examined 321 consecutive admissions to hospitals in New Jersey in 1974, most of these suffering from psychosis; 18% had committed actual violence and a further 18% had threatened violence, but less than 1% had actually been arrested. This order of violence in admission samples has been confirmed on both sides of the Atlantic, albeit Tardiff and Sweillam (1980) finding it principally self-directed in about half of the cases. In a British series of patients at their first admission with schizophrenia, 19% had exhibited behaviour potentially threatening to the life of others, a third of these repeatedly so (Johnstone et al., 1986). Only 39 of the total (15%) had exhibited none of the behavioural disturbances (including also threat to own life 26%; inappropriate or bizarre sexual behaviour 15%; damage to property 29% or inappropriate behaviour not otherwise classified 60%). The police had been involved in 55 admissions (22%), but charges were brought in only 11 cases, well under 1% of the total. Conversely, various forms of systematic bias have been identified, for example that the mere presence of psychosis may increase the chances of arrest and criminal charges. Robertson (1988) showed that the mentally ill—almost all psychotic—were much more likely to have been arrested on the day of and at the scene of their offence, with witnesses present, than their non-psychotic peers. These, and other potential sources of bias in calculation of crime and disorder rates are discussed more fully in Wessely and Taylor (1991).

Two studies are worth emphasizing for the completeness of the samples studied. Small island communities provide a particularly valuable source of epidemiological data, not only because it is likely that their study can be comprehensive, but also because the population is not subject to major shifts over time, for example an influx of more deviant individuals as often happens in mainland urban communities. Petersson and Gudjonsson (1981) studied all 52 homicides in Iceland between 1900 and 1979. There were 45 incidents, involving 47 offenders. Although absolute numbers were thus small, the proportion with a psychotic illness—28%—is striking, and the group without psychiatric abnormality at all hardly bigger. The majority of the psychotic had schizophrenia. Swanson et al. (1990) reported on a broader spectrum of violence from the NIMH Epidemiologic Catchment Area Project, using the Diagnostic Interview Schedule (DIS). The level of violence was, thus, not tightly defined, but included hitting people, getting into physical fights or using a weapon in a fight, and was not confined to criminal violence. The importance of the work was that the findings were based on a true community survey (Regier et al., 1984)—in this particular study of about 10 000 residents of Baltimore, Raleigh-Durham and Los Angeles over 3 years. Although violence was associated with familiar risk factors such as youth, male gender and low socio-economic status, mental disorder did add to the risk. Multiple diagnoses and alcoholism carried the worst risks, but even so, over 8% of people with pure schizophrenia reported violence over a 12-month period and 13% where the illness was complicated with substance abuse or other disorders. These rates were several times higher than for the general population without any diagnosis (2%). It is interesting that the male : female ratio for violence became almost 1 : 1 within the psychotic and the alcohol abusing groups.

A further difficult, but important issue is the interaction between mental health care practices and psychosis-crime relationships. The work of Penrose (1939) is often and misleadingly quoted in this context. Penrose took the numbers of patients recorded in mental illness and handicap institutions in a country as an index of its provision of mental health services. He took the numbers of sentenced prisoners as an indicator of crime rates. He then subjected these two very crude variables to comparisons of their national rates, a practice subject to the ecological fallacy and providing the weakest form of epidemiological data. He described negative correlations between mental hospital and prison occupancy, and even between mental hospital occupancy and certain crimes. He presented, however, no data on the other attributes of the societies at the time and, without context, the comparison of two or three such isolated social variables is virtually meaningless.

Superficially, an aggregate of research from the USA would suggest a fairly recent rise in violence, arrest or conviction rates among those who have been inpatients in mental hospitals, the majority of them having a schizophrenic illness. Virtually all the work from the first half of this century showed that mental hospital patients were less likely to commit violent acts than the general population (e.g. Ashley, 1922; Pollock, 1938; Cohen and Freeman, 1945; Brill and Malzberg, 1962; Brennan 1964). Later studies showed that the rates for violent crimes among mental hospital patients appear higher (e.g. Rappeport and Lasson, 1965; Giovannoni and Gurel, 1967; Zitrin et al., 1976; Grunberg et al., 1977, 1978), although non-violent offending may still be lower (Giovannoni and Gurel, 1967). Only Durbin et al. (1977) showed substantial dissent in this trend. Based on a rural rather than an urban sample, not one man diagnosed as having schizophrenia had been arrested for a crime against the person in the 10 years of follow-up. Steadman et al. (1978), however, suggested that the real increase in arrest rates among mental patients lies within a recidivist group. Comparing their sample of 1975 with their own sample of 1968, and a sample of Brill and Malzberg (1962), collected in 1947, they showed that among ex-mental hospital patients, without prior arrests, the proportion subsequently arrested has remained remarkably constant over this 30-year period. By contrast, the arrest rate of those with at least one prior arrest has been escalating over the years. What seems to have been happening is that offender patients have become increasingly trapped in a cycle of reoffending and are disproportionately represented in the reduced inpatient population of mental hospitals. There appears to be a minimal compensatory rise in the proportion of prisoners with mental disorder (Steadman et al., 1984). They compared the numbers of men entering prison with a history of mental hospitalization in the year 1968 with those entering in the year 1978 in six representative states of the USA. This was a time when the numbers of patients in state mental hospitals fell from 64 400 to 24 731. The number of admissions, however, had fallen only slightly—from 66 077 male admissions to 60 161. The number of male prisoners with a history of prior hospitalization increased significantly in California, Texas and Iowa between 1968 and 1978, while the proportions in New York, Arizona and Massachusetts fell slightly. Steadman and his colleagues went on to show that the rapid growth in prison population was certainly not attributable to discharge from mental hospitals in any of the states; for example, in Texas, the state with the largest influx of former mental patients to the prisons, former patients still only accounted for 16.5% of the increase in the prison population. Their evidence does not discount the translocation of a few discharged mental hospital patients in at least half of the states studied, but it keeps it in perspective. According to the figures, the numbers of former mental hospital patients appearing in Texan gaols (1004) may well correspond fairly closely to the numbers that have fallen out of the revolving door system of mental hospital placements, but the proportion of previously hospitalized patients in Texan prisons is still under 1%. It is the increasing challenge to the hospitals of dealing with rising numbers of offender patients which seems more obvious. Unfortunately, there is no comparable study in Britain.

In spite of the evidence that the proportionate contribution of the mentally disordered to the rise in prison populations is small, it must nevertheless be of concern that there are substantial and rising numbers who are probably misplaced, and who may have unmet treatment needs. Glueck (1918) found 12% of over 600 men starting a prison sentence in the USA to be psychotic. In the 1970s, USA (Guze, 1976) and British (Gunn et al., 1978) surveys were remarkably consistent in finding that no more than 1% of sentenced prisoners had a schizophrenic illness. Over the entire prison system, these still represented substantial numbers of people. A more recent survey of a 5% representative sample of all sentenced prisoners in England and Wales found the rate for schizophrenia to be 1.5% and all psychosis 2.4% (Gunn et al., 1991b). Any suggestion that this may indicate a rise in the proportion and numbers of people with schizophrenia being imprisoned should be treated with caution, since the percentage extrapolation is from quite small numbers of people actually interviewed in each survey. Suffice it to say that numbers are certainly not declining. Higher rates of psychosis have been reported by Roth and Ervin (1971), 8%, Faulk (1976), 3%, and James et al. (1980), 5%, but are based on single prison studies rather than nationally representative samples. There is evidence that the contribution of people with a psychotic illness to the more behaviourally disturbed prisoner groups is much higher (e.g. Bach-y-Rita and Veno, 1974; Gunn et al., 1991b).

A case-note review from the largest remand prison in Europe (Taylor and Gunn, 1984) showed higher rates of psychosis (9%) than the average among sentenced prisoners. This was expected, since the overt reason for remand is preparation of pretrial medical reports, but another is the social containment and care of the mildly disruptive mentally ill not otherwise receiving services. Nevertheless, while twice the proportion of men without disorder were, on conviction, sentenced to imprisonment than those with schizophrenia, still over 20% of men with schizophrenia received prison sentences. At least half of these had a pure form of the disorder and were apparently symptomatic at the time of the offence.

There have been few attempts to quantify the ultimate risk posed by the person with a psychotic illness. Ekblom (1970) evaluated the most serious violence among all patients in Swedish mental hospitals, between 1955 and 1964 inclusive. Hafner and Boker (1973) jointly offered the other estimate, from an offender sample in West Germany, over the same time period. Ekblom found 25 cases of major personal assault, eight of them fatal. The majority of the patients involved had a psychotic illness and over half had schizophrenia. Adjusting for length of exposure, however, the risks appeared small. The risk of being killed by such a patient was 1 in 250 000 000 working hours for staff and 1 in 350 000 000 inpatient hours for patients. Hafner and Boker were similarly primarily interested in homicidal attacks. They set their findings against the background of relevant statistics for normal and abnormal populations and calculated that the risk of a homicidal attack was 0.05% among people with schizophrenia, and ten times less among those with affective psychosis. Swanson et al., 1990, confirmed schizophrenia as the illness giving rise to most violence across a broader spectrum, while McGlashan (1986), in a 15-year (average) follow-up of people with schizophrenia, found psychotic assaultiveness to be an important characteristic and one of only three consistent predictors of poor outcome. Within the latter group, almost all of the risk seemed accounted for by the depressive type. Hafner and Boker found just one person with mania among the 533 mentally abnormal and homicidal offenders amassed over the 10 years of their study. Craig (1982) did not record a single episode of violence among twenty consecutive manic admissions, despite finding high levels of agitation and anger among the patients. Swanson et al. (1990), in their community survey, found that no one with hypomania reported hitting anyone other than a spouse, partner or child and none reported using a weapon. Homicide is particularly rare. Schipkowensky (1968) found only 4 over a 40-year period up to 1965 in Sofia, compared with 21 depressive killings, this in the context of a calculated 3523 people with affective psychosis in Bulgaria in 1965.

The risk of homicidal attack by seriously mentally ill patients is thus small, and the risk of suicide about a hundred times greater. Lesser forms of violence are possibly similarly balanced but, as Swanson and colleagues (1990) point out, while public fear even of people with schizophrenia living in the community is largely unwarranted, it is not wholly groundless. The remainder of the chapter will explore ways in which psychosis may precipitate or contribute to violence, and amasses evidence that suggests that the risks that do exist could be reduced to negligible levels with adequate service provision.

The Nature of Relationships between Psychosis and Offending

Illness Activity and Offending

A major problem in attempting to determine whether there is a direct relationship between psychotic illness and offending is that the majority of studies are based on case record scrutiny. Researchers are thus heavily dependent on the unlikely chance that clinicians have recorded all aspects of the mental state in detail, and preferably noted any links between symptoms and behaviour. One of us (Taylor, unpublished data), in studying case records of previously hospitalized psychotic men in the interview study of psychotic offenders in Brixton Prison (hereafter known as the Brixton study) found that in more than 25% of such cases nothing had been previously recorded to indicate whether they had shown any of the first rank symptoms of schizophrenia (Taylor, 1985b). It was never clear whether mere absence of such recording could be taken as a significant negative, but it seemed unlikely (compare Taylor and Gunn, 1984, observations on recording suicidal behaviour). Some of the biases in court report studies have already been noted; further, few state how long after the offence data were collected for the reports. In Britain, a lapse of many months between the offence and any such report is common in all but the most trivial cases. It is not surprising, therefore, that some studies cast doubt on the presence of active symptoms of disorder at the time of offending, let alone an influential relationship. Virkkunen (1974), dependent on court reports, identified only 37% of acts of violence among people with schizophrenia, and an even smaller proportion of firesettings as occurring during a psychotic episode defined by the presence of hallucinations and delusions. At the other extreme, Planansky and Johnston (1977), with a hospital-based case record sample, found that all violent or aggressive behaviour had occurred in the presence of active symptoms, which is not necessarily the same as being directed by them. It is difficult to know whether this order of discrepancy in the presence of active symptoms is a true reflection of reasonably appropriate selection operating, with the very sick people going to hospital, or whether poor data from remand records cheated Virkkunen. In the more detailed examination of records by Hafner and Boker (1973), 17% of the violent patients were said to have had simple schizophrenia, implying a low rate of positive symptoms in this group. There is a later indication, however, that as many as 65% of the sample as a whole, and 80% of violent schizophrenics, were suffering delusions at the time of their offence, while affective disorders were also common, including cold, suspicious, sad, apathetic and labile affects. This second stage of the Brixton study (Taylor, 1985b) was the first to use interviews to supplement data from a variety of records, over half the interviews taking place within 3 weeks of the index offence and 85% within 6 weeks. It was found that only 9 of 121 psychotic offenders were without positive psychotic symptoms at the time of their offence.

Dangerous Symptoms?

Delusions

Delusions are the positive symptoms most widely experienced among people with schizophrenia (e.g. Lucas et al., 1962; Taylor et al., 1982). The latter found that only 26 (11%) of all 232 inpatients in one large mental hospital who had a research diagnosis of schizophrenia had apparently never experienced a delusion. This compared with Mellor's (1970) estimate that 21% of his sample had never experienced one of Schneider's first rank symptoms, for so long regarded as almost pathognomonic of schizophrenia. Delusions are firmly held beliefs, which are generally held to be false or fantastic in the context of the sufferer's social and cultural background. In fact, they are not invariably false or fantastic (Mullen and Maack, 1985), or even falsifiable, and some hold that absolute conviction is not essential (Sacks et al., 1974; Rudden et al., 1982). Further, not all beliefs held to be false are necessarily regarded as delusions. Taylor (1979) provided perhaps the most practical clinical direction through this maze in distinguishing between 'normal delusions', which he held to be false beliefs because they are held by a political opponent or someone of another culture, and 'psychotic delusions', which amounted to 'an absolute conviction of the truth of a proposition which is idiosyncratic, incorrigible, ego-involved and often preoccupying'. Socially acceptable belief systems powerfully motivate human beings, and it would hardly be surprising if pathological belief systems did not also, on occasion, drive the believer to action. There is evidence that delusions may sometimes become dangerous. This can be considered broadly under three headings:

1. A statistical link between the presence of delusions and violence. Remarkable though it may seem, there has been minimal enquiry into the occurrence or otherwise of a simple statistical association between delusions and violence or crime. Hafner and Boker (1973), examined in detail the case records of 533 men and women who had killed, the majority with schizophrenia (53%), but 7% with affective psychosis and the remainder with a range of disorders, almost all with an identifiable organic basis. These they compared with the records of a group of patients admitted to their local regional mental hospital over the same time period, matched for age, sex and diagnosis. Within the homicidal group, 65% were recorded as being deluded at the time of their offence compared with just 47% of the patient group at the time of enquiry. Within the psychotic subgroups, significantly more of the offenders with schizophrenia (89%) had been delusional compared with the non-violent patients (76%), and of the affectively ill killers (56%) compared with the non-violent (26%).

2. The relative frequency of the subtypes of schizophrenia associated with violence. The term 'paranoid schizophrenia' is a rather loose construct, but both ICD-9 and DSM-III R emphasize the distinctive features as 'relatively stable delusions' or 'preoccupation with one or more systematized delusions' respectively. DSM-III R specifically excludes most other symptoms of schizophrenia except hallucinations related to the delusions, while ICD-9 is more equivocal about associated features. The importance to this diagnosis of the presence of delusions is, and always has been, sufficiently clear as to allow some inference about the relationship between delusions and violence from studies which show that paranoid schizophrenia is the form most commonly associated with violent behaviour. Unfortunately, the task of weighing the data from such studies is made difficult by the fact that few comment on the relative frequency of paranoid schizophrenia in the base population of people with schizophrenia. Thus, Shader et al. (1977), examining a modestly violent group of hospital inpatients with schizophrenia, found that the people with paranoid schizophrenia made up by far the highest proportion of the violent sample. They also, however, calculated the prevalence of the subtypes of schizophrenia within the hospital and found that allowance for the over-all distribution of the subtypes demonstrated that the schizo-affective patients (regarded as having a subtype of schizophrenia in this study) were the most vulnerable to violent outbursts, repeated outbursts being especially characteristic. Tardiff and Sweillam (1980), in an admission sample, and Planansky and Johnston (1977) in their inpatient sample, were among those to draw attention to the strong association between paranoid schizophrenia and violence, without making this adjustment. Rofman et al. (1980) in their study of hospital inpatients did so. Evaluating, in this context, only those incidents which resulted in actual personal violence, over 16% of the patients with paranoid schizophrenia, but less than 5% of others, were involved. This, however, reflected only six and four assaultive patients respectively. The other diagnostic subtypes to be considered in this context are the paranoid states (ICD-9) or the delusional disorders (DSM-III-R), representing an almost pure form of delusional presentation. Hafner and Boker (1973) found that 15.5% of the violent, but only 6% of the non-violent controls had these diagnoses.

The most convincing indirect evidence of the association between delusions and violence through the evidence of the subtype of the illness comes from a second, wholly independent sample from Brixton Prison (Robertson and Taylor, 1985a, b). It was found that the group of men whose schizophrenia had followed an almost exclusively delusional presentation and course were very much more likely to have been seriously violent than those whose delusions had, over their course, been diluted by other symptoms. These, in turn, had behaved more dangerously than those who had shown no more than transient delusions (*see* Table 8.1).

3. Delusions as direct motivation for violence.   Psychiatrists are usually reluctant to discharge violent patients from hospital unless they 'understand' their behaviour. Kroll and McKenzie (1983) suggested that if admission symptoms are related to violence or threat of violence, then the patient cannot be discharged if his symptoms have not been adequately treated or if he is unlikely to stay in relevant treatment. There is, however, very little research indeed that addresses the issue of a causative link between symptoms and behaviour.

Lanzkron (1963), who studied the records of 153 consecutive patients of all diagnoses committed to a state mental hospital in the USA on murder charges, said that 37% of his sample had killed because of hallucinations or delusions. His criteria, however, for judging motives are not clear. Gibbens

Table 8.1
The Presence of Delusions and Violence Among Remanded Prisoners with Schizophrenia

	Violence rating scores* Lower range (0–3)		Higher range (4–8)	
Sub group of Schizophrenia	N	%	N	%
Delusional group	5	29	12	71
Mixed symptom group	17	55	14	45
Simple (negative symptom) group	6	86	1	14
Atypical group	3	50	3	50

N = 61
Excluding the atypical group, $X^2 = 6.72$; $p < 0.04$
* Calculated by adding scores for present and past violence scales (Gunn and Robertson, 1976)

(1958a) examined the records of 155 mentally abnormal and homicidal delinquents (not all psychotic) admitted to another USA state mental hospital and 120 individuals convicted of murder and manslaughter but judged sane for evidence of motivation. Delusions were found to be the main motivating force in 25% of the mentally abnormal, but in none of the normal group. Wolfgang (1958a) reported broadly similar findings, again exclusively from records and in relation to homicide. McKnight et al. (1966) studied the records of 100 of the mentally abnormal homicides admitted directly from the courts to the maximum security hospital of Ontario, Canada, over 30 years. Over 40% of these patients had a paranoid psychotic illness of some kind, but just 25% seemed to have been acting specifically on paranoid delusions. Petersson and Gudjonsson (1981) were able to study the records of all the unlawful homicides committed in Iceland this century, up to and inclusive of 1979. Thirteen of the 47 offenders (28%) had a psychotic illness. Five of these (38%) were regarded as having been driven by their delusions; again, none of the offenders with non-psychotic disturbances and none of those free of mental disorder attempted a delusional explanation.

Hafner and Boker (1973), in Germany, with a larger but otherwise similar data base to those already cited, offered a slightly more complex analysis of delusional role. The violence was judged to be directly attributable to delusions of threat or persecution in only about 16% of cases and to jealousy in about 15%, but motives of revenge, which had delusional causes or components, accounted for about 40%. Among people with schizophrenia, 70% had a delusional relationship with their victim, 76% of the men and 41% of the women, for example, delusionally perceiving their victim as an enemy.

For the Brixton study, 203 men, remanded in prison on a range of violent and non-violent criminal charges including murder charges, were interviewed, and hospital, criminal, prison, police and social work records were searched (Taylor, 1985b). Of the psychotic subsample of 121 men, 93% had been symptomatic at the time of their offence, but the illness had not always appeared directly relevant. The nature of some psychotic illnesses leads to incoherence in the patient's accounts of behaviour. It was thus necessary to make a distinction between offences that had definitely been driven by delusions, and those that had probably been so. In both cases, all the independent data suggested delusional drive, but only in the former group was a clear description of motivation available from the man himself. No matter what the offence, madness was never seen as an attractive excuse. No one in the non-psychotic group offered a delusional explanation for their behaviour. Just 18 of the men with psychosis (15%) gave a coherent account compatible with delusional drive, although most of these had no insight into the delusional nature of their claims. A further 29 men—increasing the proportion to 39%—were probably delusionally driven. Delusions were the main psychotic symptoms to have such a role in offending. Just 5 men apparently responded to hallucinations. No other psychotic features appeared to trigger violence.

It is important to note that this did not mean that in the remainder of the cases either specific symptoms or the illness as a whole were irrelevant. Particularly among the non-violent psychotic offenders, a 'rational mad' explanation was frequently offered. One man, for example, who was almost continuously hallucinated, stole a book on Jung from the library, to try to understand himself and his symptoms better. He insisted that his behaviour was a rational response to a mad experience. This sort of motivation was treated, for the research, as quite different from that where there was no such intervening thought process between symptom and behaviour. If these sorts of cases were added, about 82% of psychotic offending was attributable to the illness (Taylor, 1985). Thus, whether data are collected from case records, direct interview, or both, the frequency of influence by delusions, the only psychotic symptoms regularly implicated in a drive to offending, appears consistent at nearly 40%, the probability of a less direct influence being much higher. A further important point relates to the seriousness of the offending thus driven. Many studies have described people who have killed, giving rise to a suspicion that delusional drive may be a very dangerous phenomenon. This was confirmed in the Brixton study. Men within the group of psychotic offenders, who were delusionally driven, were significantly more likely to have engaged in serious violence than their psychotic, usually deluded, but more rationally motivated peers (Taylor, 1985).

Types of Delusional belief particularly associated with serious violence. The classification of delusions has taken several forms. Most of the seminal papers this century can be found in Cutting and Shepherd's (1986) collection. In evaluating delusions and their impact on behaviour it seems that at least four aspects of belief must be considered:

1. The structure of the belief, expressed in terms of form or organization. In these terms, a belief may be coherent and internally consistent or incoherent and chaotic;
2. The conviction with which the belief is held;
3. The content of the belief, reflecting both the degree to which the life experience of the deluded patient colours the belief or otherwise, but most particularly the quality of the experience, e.g. persecutory, religious;
4. The effect of the delusion on the patient in such terms as distress or intrusiveness and preoccupation.

To these characteristics might be added, for purposes of evaluating the capacity to act on delusions, the issue of interaction between delusions and other symptoms or factors in the environment. Thus, Ellinwood (1971) noted that an extraneously induced disturbance of behavioural habits, such as sleep deprivation, could precipitate a rapid intensification of delusional beliefs and mean the difference between internal containment and acting on them.

The organization-disorganization characteristic could transcend mental state and specific symptoms to include social existence generally and offending behaviour particularly (Taylor, 1981). The Brixton research confirmed that delusionally driven men were more like the non-psychotic in terms of social organization, being more likely to have retained a stable home and some close social ties, and unlikely to have a general history of offending. Those with a more mixed expression of mental state were more likely to be without a fixed home, relationships or employment and also to have offended in various petty ways against property, while rarely being organized enough to inflict serious harm or even threat of harm against another person. Hafner and Boker (1973) found that systematization of delusions was almost twice as frequent among violent schizophrenics (77%) as among the non-violent control group with this diagnosis (45%).

The Present State Examination (Wing et al., 1974) distinguishes between partial and full delusions. In the Brixton study, the delusionally motivated psychotic men were consistently rated as more ill on a global psychopathology item of the Comprehensive Psychiatric Rating Scale (Åsberg et al., 1978) than the others. This best reflected the greater likelihood of delusions, when held, to be held with total conviction (Taylor, 1993). Table 8.2, gives two examples within the delusionally motivated subgroup to demonstrate the further link between delusional conviction and a higher rate of serious violence. Subsequent research with 83 consecutively hospitalized patients with delusions (the Maudsley sample) has confirmed the importance of the link between acting on delusions—not necessarily violently in these cases— and full delusions (Wessely et al., in press).

The prediction that paranoid, and in particular persecutory delusions, would be most closely linked to the genesis of violence (Macdonald, 1963),

Table 8.2
Delusion Strength and Violence Among Delusionally Motivated Men*

	Passivity delusions				Delusions of paranormal influence			
	Violence				Violence			
	Low (0–2)		High (3–4)		Low (0–2)		High (3–4)	
	N	%	N	%	N	%	N	%
No delusions	13	(68)	6	(38)	14	(74)	8	(50)
Partial delusions	3	(16)	1	(6)	3	(16)	0	(0)
Full delusions	3	(16)	9	(56)	2	(11)	8	(50)

$X^2 = 6.37; p < 0.04$ $X^2 = 7.60; p < 0.02$

N = 47; delusion ratings uncertain in 12 cases.
* Calculated for index offence from Gunn and Robertson (1976a) scale
0 = No violence
1 = Verbal aggression; threats; minimal property damage (pd)
2 = Non-violent sex offence; limited pd; ABH
3 = GBH; extensive pd e.g. by fire
4 = Life endangered or ended

has good face validity. There is little evidence, however, to suggest that this is true, an exception being Shore et al. (1988, 1989). Neither Hafner and Boker (1973) nor Taylor (unpublished data) found that persecutory, grandiose or reference delusions *per se* carried any greater association with serious violence. Hafner and Boker demonstrated a link between 'delusions of physical influence' and 'bodily hallucinations' among people with schizophrenia and an increased risk of violence, in other words a perception of a serious threat to the life or physical integrity of the patient did seem disproportionately likely to provoke serious violence. Findings from Mawson's (1985) uncontrolled descriptive study of patients in a maximum security hospital may be taken as in line with this, demonstrating serious violence which seemed to have been associated with delusions of being poisoned. Mawson also emphasized Mowat's (1966) finding that, on the whole, in a sample of morbidly jealous people who had attempted or succeeded in killing others, delusions of poisoning did not persist after the killing. In Mowat's series, no less than 32% of the 57 men had experienced such delusions at the time of their offence and 4 of the 7 women. Subsequently, just 5 men and no women were so deluded. All these findings were based on highly selected samples of very dangerous people. Not dissimilar evidence for the importance of delusions of poisoning has emerged from a sample of people with schizophrenia, wholly unselected for violence. Fifty-two (20%) had behaved in a way threatening to the life of others (Humphreys et al., 1992). The most important illness characteristics associated with such threat were length of illness and the presence of delusions of being poisoned. Delusions of misidentification have also been cited as particularly dangerous (De Pauw and Szulecka, 1988). Evidence for this, however, is merely anecdotal.

In the Brixton study (Taylor, unpublished data) passivity, religious and paranormal delusions seemed to hold most potential danger for offending violently, in that they were significantly more likely to present concurrently with delusional drive. It was not necessarily, however, the passivity or religious delusions *per se* that had driven the man to offend. Perhaps these delusions were more important for their overall effect on the patient, lowering his ordinary socialized resistance to acting on even more fantastic or disturbing beliefs. More recent research with the Maudsley Hospital sample found that the content of the delusions most closely linked with acting on them—not necessarily violently—varied with the informant (Wessely et al., in press). The subjects themselves related delusions of catastrophe, and possibly passivity, to their actions, but it was the persecutory delusions that were remarked upon in this context by observers, most of whom were friends or relatives untrained in psychiatry and thus, perhaps, without a sophisticated enough knowledge to enquire about or observe more subtle delusions. Remarkably little attempt seems to have been made to examine systematically the effect of delusions on patients in terms of the distress or preoccupation they engender. In the Brixton study it was found that, although the rate of neurotic symptoms was fairly high among psychotic offenders, depression for example being present in 20%, high arousal, anxiety and unhappiness were all more or less evenly distributed between the delusionally driven and the more rationally motivated groups. The groups did not even differ in suicidal ideation, although attention has previously been drawn to a dichotomy between suicidal and homicidal behaviour (e.g. Albee, 1950), capacity to distinguish self from the environment being postulated as critical in the direction of the violence. The finding of similar suicide rates among people with schizophrenia to those with depression, but the very much higher homicide rates by the former may lend weight to this idea. Buchanan et al. (in press) have started to remedy the gaps in this area. Work with the Maudsley Hospital sample revealed that patients who had acted on their delusions were more likely to report having been made sad, frightened or anxious by them. Reported activity in seeking evidence for the beliefs also seemed crucial. All patients who had acted on their beliefs said they had evidence to corroborate them, but so did the majority of non-actors. Significantly fewer (20%) of the non-actors, however, had done anything to seek this information; nearly 60% of the 'actors' had been busy acting in this sense too. A brief semistructured interview schedule has been devised to assist clinicians in the evaluation of delusions and their likely impact (Taylor et al., in press).

Hallucinations

In a psychiatric hospital intensive care setting, Werner et al. (1984) noted that the best predictor of assaultive behaviour among 40 male patients, better even than their preadmission assault record, was hallucinatory behaviour as specified in the rather all-embracing category provided by the Brief Psychiatric Rating Scale (Overall and Gorham, 1962). The correlation coefficient, however, was only 0.37.

Hallucinations occur in all sensory modalities, but visual and tactile hallucinations have never been cited as strong candidates for provoking violence. Mawson (1985) noted that, in both his own series of violent, and psychotic patients and Mowat's (1966) sample of homicidally jealous people, patients commonly reported smells or tastes which they took as evidence for their beliefs. In the Brixton series of psychotic offenders, only two men reported disturbing, strong olfactory hallucinations. Although they did not appear to have triggered the extremely savage behaviour which followed in both cases, the men concerned thought their association important. The hallucinations were construed as being congruent with the delusional system, for which neither man had any insight at all.

Auditory hallucinations have created perhaps the most interest. Hafner and Boker (1973) expected to find that command hallucinations were of most importance in triggering offending. Comparison of the homicidal schizophrenics with the non-violent hospitalized group, however, revealed only a small excess in the frequency of auditory hallucinations overall in the violent group (67%), compared with the others (56%), with a slight but non-significant tendency for imperative voices to be more common in the violent group and abusive voices more common in the non-violent group. In the Brixton study, there was no difference in the occurrence of hallucinations between groups of offenders with psychosis, and only five men seemed to have offended because of their voices. All the offences in this tiny group were trivial; one man was arrested carrying a knife for protection, three broke windows and one who was first charged with threatening behaviour went on to hit the arresting police officer. Two said they were acting under instructions, three said they were attempting to escape from their voices. Rogers et al. (1988) reviewed the sparse literature on command hallucinations relevant to criminal or antisocial behaviour. In his series of 385 people under evaluation for the insanity defence in Toronto, Canada, nearly 6% were said to have acted antisocially at the direction of their voices.

Hellerstein et al. (1987) surveyed hospital inpatients. Reviewing the records of 789 consecutive admissions, they found 151 patients for whom hallucinations had been recorded. Just over one-third of them had been experiencing commands, the same as in an earlier sample of hallucinating patients (Goodwin et al., 1971). Hallucinations were most commonly recorded among patients with schizophrenia (40%), but those with affective disorder (13%) and personality disorder, usually of the borderline type

(11.5%) also experienced them. Command hallucinations were particularly rare in the last two groups. In the Hellerstein study, neither the self nor other directed violent behaviours of the hallucinating patients, whether overall or by subgroup, seemed significantly different from those of the non-hallucinating patients. The treatment of the hallucinating patients had, however, been rather different. Overall, they were significantly more likely to have been put in seclusion or to have been under one to one staff assignment than their non-hallucinating peers, so the absence of excessive violence could rather have demonstrated that clinical management strategies were successful rather than that the symptoms were innocuous.

It is perhaps important to note that disruptive acting out on the basis of auditory hallucinations may be more likely in an acute hospital admission sample than in an offender group. Depp (1983) found that 15% of a sample of 60 assaultive psychiatric inpatients had been acting on hallucinated commands. This would fit with the suggestion that violence secondary to hallucinations, while often of very high nuisance value, is generally trivial, and thus rarely comes to the attention of the law. Similarly, in a consecutively hospitalized sample of deluded patients, it was found that nearly half also had auditory hallucinations, three-quarters of which were command hallucinations (Reed et al., in preparation). Over half reported trying to escape the hallucinations in the month prior to interview, but as many as two-thirds said they had obeyed the hallucinations at least once. Nearly two-thirds said the commands were to commit some sort of violence to self or others. Junginger (1990) studied 40 hospital inpatients with command hallucinations. Nearly 40% reported compliance, half of those reporting harmless commands and 8 of the 20 dangerous ones. He also noted, however, that those reporting harmless commands were less likely to remember whether they had obeyed or not, suggesting a potential bias in favour of finding compliance with dangerous imperative voices.

Falloon and Talbot (1981) were more concerned with coping strategies, but they noted that during 6 months follow-through of community-based patients who had heard voices talking about them for at least 1 year, as many as a third reported listening attentively at least some of the time, and often accepting their guidance. In this series, violent acting against others did not seem to be an issue, but nearly one-third had attempted suicide.

Of all hallucinatory experiences, evidence is persuasive, but not conclusive, that descriptions of noxious tastes or smells are particularly ominous when they occur in conjunction with related paranoid delusions. There is growing evidence that patients are both more subject to command hallucinations and more prone to act on them than first thought. Dangerous acting is probably less likely than harmless acting, but nevertheless is a risk. Chronicity of command hallucinations, their consistency with the patient's wishes, their relevance to the patient (Rogers et al., 1988), association with a delusional belief given as evidence for the hallucinations (Junginger, 1990), association with avoidance behaviour consequent on delusional belief and frequency of experience (Reed et al., in preparation), all seem to be factors that increase the risk of obedience to the orders, and thus should perhaps be areas for enquiry in patients where command hallucinations have been identified.

Other psychotic symptoms

None of the positive symptoms of a psychotic illness other than hallucinations or delusions has been shown to be of any great relevance to actions (Hafner and Boker, 1973; Taylor, 1985b). The only other phenomenon worth considering is 'motivelessness', which is not strictly a symptom but was at one time taken as almost pathognomonic of a psychotic killing. Generally, a motiveless crime is taken to be one in which there has been very definite action on the part of the offender, but it has not been possible to formulate any reason at all for it, at least up to the time of trial. It is a commonly expressed lay view that a 'senseless' crime must imply mental abnormality, although psychiatrists should always try to demonstrate disorder from evidence independent of the crime. Wilmanns (1940) described 18 killers who showed no clear evidence of psychosis at the time of their crime, but went on to develop schizophreniform psychoses in prison. Gillies (1965) noted, in a different series, that, although some went on to develop florid symptoms of psychosis, others merely remained affectless and withdrawn, much as at the time of the offence. It must remain in some doubt as to whether those in either series who went on to develop a florid psychosis had really been free from illness at the time of the offence. Lanzkron (1963) presented the view that no less than 27% of his series of homicide offenders had become psychotic after their offence. It may not be unreasonable to suppose that psychiatric illness, including all of the psychoses, could be precipitated by such major life events as a killing, trial and imprisonment.

Hafner and Boker (1973) found that motive was unrecorded for less than 20% of the German mentally abnormal homicide group, and that this proportion was not peculiar to those with psychosis. It varied little between diagnostic groups. Among the men remanded in Brixton prison, there was a much lower proportion who could give no account of motives—8% among the psychotic group and 7% in the non-psychotic group (Taylor, 1985b). This lower proportion perhaps best reflects the methodological differences, the latter work including direct interviewing. This demonstrated that people with psychosis were occasionally motiveless in an entirely different sense. No positive motive could be recorded as their 'antisocial behaviour' almost amounted to a negative symptom of their illness, aimlessness possibly being a better word to describe the reason for what had happened. The latter men were not violent, but had been arrested for 'suspicious behaviour' or trespass.

Mood changes and neurotic symptoms

Disorders of affect may accompany a schizophrenic illness or be the leading features of a primary affective disorder. The risk of criminal behaviour among people with a primary affective disorder is extremely hard to estimate, not least because of the range of disorders subsumed under the general category of affective disorder, and the continuing doubts about the validity of many existing classifications. The potential for confusion between personality disorder and the affective disorders, perhaps particularly hypomania, is considerable (Akiskal et al., 1977; Thorneloe and Crews, 1981).

Kendell (1970) considered the hypothesis first propounded by Dollard et al. (1939), and modified by Berkowitz (1962) (*see also* p. 493), that depression, as a mood and as a syndrome, is caused by the inhibition of aggressive responses to frustration. He reviewed the relative distribution among communities, gender and age groups of manifest aggression and of depression and concluded:

> There is no flagrant discrepancy between existing evidence and the requirements of the hypothesis.

He was able to show, in general terms, something of an inverse relationship between aggression and depression, but the aetiological connections required for the hypothesis were far from evident. Much of the more criminological literature emphasizes violence in association with affective disorder, rather than other forms of criminal behaviour, and Harrer and Kofler-Westergren (1986), in particular, stressed the seriousness of a small number of acts rather than a numerically extensive delinquency. They cited 255 cases of extended suicide from the German literature between 1933 and 1985. Women predominated (68%), a common pattern being of a 30–40-year-old women killing her children before attempting to kill herself. Earlier, Batt (1948) had even noted the older age of the mother as an important point of distinction between depressive and non-depressive child killings, the 'non-psychotic' women commonly being between 16 and 20 in age. West (1965) found that in his series nearly all women who killed their children were depressed. From their study of homicidal people, Hafner and Boker (1973) confirmed that the depressive group was the only one in which the women out numbered the men, by 6 to 1, when the assault actually resulted in the death of the victim. Neither puerperal psychosis nor depressive illnesses are, however, the commonest causes of maternal filicide (*see* pp. 610–12).

Harrer and Kofler-Westergren (1986) emphasized that the mild, perhaps reactive and neurotic depressions appeared to account for more disorder than endogenous or psychotic depressions, and that, in cases other than homicide, the importance of depression in association with offending may thus be overlooked. Good (1978), reviewing data on prisoners, also argued that affective disorders are underdiagnosed. In the review of Brixton's remanded prisoners' records (Taylor and Gunn, 1984), neurotic disorders were underdiagnosed by prison medical officers compared with researchers working to research criteria. Batt (1948) suggested another problem, without quantifying it, that depressive symptomatology may have resolved by the time of psychiatric assessment after a killing. Dell (1984) presented evidence for this in her survey of people found guilty of manslaughter by reason of diminished responsibility. Herjanic et al. (1977) provided strong evidence for the differential prison identification of depression by gender for a full range of offenders and not just for those committing homicide. From a record search, 4% of a consecutive series of 1068 male offenders compared with 13% of 127 women were found to have a primary affective disorder. One explanation offered for under-reporting by British prison medical staff was that they were required to focus predominantly on disorder that was relevant to the court process or disorder that was immediately life threatening. Neurotic disorders, they suggested, were neither. Maybe this applies overseas too. Good (1978), however, suggested that the main reason for under identification lay with the disorders which, at least in the more common depressive form, tended to make such prisoners exceptionally compliant. They may be less resentful of punishment, as compatible with their feelings of guilt, and may have less drive to be troublemakers.

Bipolar disorders probably account for more offenders recognized as ill than do unipolar depressive disorders. In one series of patients admitted to a forensic psychiatry facility in Washington D.C., having been found not guilty by reason of insanity (London and Taylor, 1982), 34% had such diagnoses. By contrast, in a study of 5081 consecutive discharges over an 8-year period from a forensic psychiatric ward in New York, Wulach (1983) identified only 100 people with a diagnosis of mania. He pointed out that, although they had come from both prisons and courts, the majority of those transferred from prison had been noted as extremely difficult to manage, even within a prison hospital setting. Their crimes were predominantly assaultive, whether to people or property, but resulted in relatively little damage. Two, however, had killed through negligence in driving. The theme of the rarity of serious harm following from a manic episode is consistent throughout the literature (e.g. Schipkowensky, 1968; Craig, 1982; Hafner and Boker, 1973/1982), but it does occur (Podolsky, 1964). The truly dangerous potential seems to be chiefly in acts of omission rather than commission, such as distractability during driving.

There have been attempts to define better those manic patients likely to be most disruptive or dangerous. Beigel and Murphy (1971) postulated two types of manic patient, one elated and grandiose with little destructive behaviour, and the other paranoid and destructive with minimal euphoria and grandiosity. Carlson and Goodwin (1973) argued that the differences related to phases of the illness rather than distinct patient types. They found that 15 of 20 manic patients in their series passed through a harmless euphoric phase, but then entered into a phase characterized by hostility, anger and aggression, finally resolving towards a third harmless phase with predominantly anxiety symptoms. Wulach (1983), with by far the largest series to date, failed to find evidence for any such neat classification. Of interest is Blackburn's (1974) account of hostility traits in affectively ill patients. Hostility, as measured by such questionnaires as Blackburn employed, is by no means the same as violence. Nevertheless, it is interesting that for all of the affectively ill subject groups, except those with mania, hostility traits so measured were stable. The manics showed high scores during the active phase of illness, lowering with recovery.

In spite of the reassuring evidence about the violence of people with mania or hypomania, more than many other patients they retain the capacity to induce fear (Rossi et al., 1986). In relation to inpatient or other institutional settings, this cannot be dismissed simply in terms of the disconcerting nature of the direct, often belligerent stare which is often the principal form of eye contact. The manic patient tests limits and is uninhibited about exploiting the vulnerabilities of others (Janowsky et al., 1970; Foville, 1882). This can lead to violent confrontations with staff (Binder and McNeil, 1988) and renders interactions with violent prisoners or poorly controlled patients potentially very explosive indeed. The manic patient might still retain his innocence of a violent act but, through his illness, have nevertheless created considerable dangers.

Protective symptoms

Although a lot of attention has been given to symptoms of mental illness which may precipitate violence or offending, the possibility that some symptoms may be protective has barely been addressed. A logical extension from the material just described is that grandiose delusions, delusions of omnipotence in particular, may make for disruptive but, rarely, directly dangerous behaviour. Here it is likely that the 'conviction rule' works in the opposite direction, that is the more unshakeable the belief in personal omnipotence, the less likelihood there would be of acting violently. Other 'attractive' delusions may similarly safeguard the sufferer from inflicting any kind of serious harm. In the first Brixton interview study (Taylor et al., 1983), this was considered in relation to firmly held convictions about a delusional lover. Only when doubts about the fidelity or intentions of the lover emerged, did it appear that anyone became at risk of harm.

Planansky and Johnston (1977) argued, in relation to a single case, that obsessional symptoms in conjunction with a schizophrenic illness were possibly protective. It is doubtful whether too much weight should be put on such a suggestion, given that ruminative behaviour appears to precede at least some violent depressive acting, and that meticulous planning or preparation is sometimes seen to precede some of the more aggressive responses to pathologically perceived persecution. The possibility that a predominance of the negative symptoms of schizophrenia, the apathy, anhedonia, anergia or ambivalence would weigh against violent or criminal behaviour does seem partly borne out in clinical practice, but remains to be tested in any systematic way.

Pathologies of Passion

The pathologies of the passions of love, jealousy and entitlement may all form parts of a major psychiatric illness or manifest as the central, and occasionally, sole feature of a patient's disorder. De Clérambault (1942) argued that delusions of passion were to be distinguished from the persecutory delusions of paranoid disorders. Their special characteristics included having an aim or desire at their core which, from the outset, leads to striving for specific ends and clear-cut demands (Baruk, 1959). Patients with these disorders are actively engaged in a struggle for love or vindication, in contrast to those with persecutory delusions who seek explanations in a hostile and constantly changing world, a world which leaves them fearful and largely passive. This subtle distinction has had little impact outside France, though De Clérambault's attempt to illustrate his conceptualization, by a reworking of erotomania, has led to a largely inappropriate link between his name and this particular syndrome. This separation of persecutory and passionate delusions is rarely so clear-cut in clinical practice. This distinction does, however, offer an explanation of why disorders of passion so often lead to conflict and to offending.

Those with disorders of passion have an overwhelming sense of entitlement and are convinced that others are abrogating their rights. The jealous believe they are the victims of infidelity, and are deprived of the fealty which is their due; the litigant and the querulant have profound convictions of injustice and deprivation. They can identify who is offending against them or depriving them of their supposed rights, and usually assail those individuals with accusations of infidelity, misfeasance, or failing in the obligations of a lover. They know what they want, and who stands in their path to vindication. In their different ways, they may act to assert their supposed rights with a self-righteousness which puts at nought the obligation to conform to the law or the constraints on acceptable behaviour.

Morbid jealousy, erotomania and pathological querulance can emerge as symptom complexes forming part of more extensive mental disorders, such as schizophrenia, or as pathological reactions. The distinctions between symptomatic and reactive disorders are illustrated in Table 8.3. In clinical practice, there may be considerable overlap between these ideal types and the models should, therefore, be applied with flexibility.

Delusions of infidelity, love or entitlement may emerge in both the symptomatic and reactive forms of these disorders. In some cases, where clear-cut delusions are absent, the attribution of pathology rests on the judgment that the intensity and facility with which the responses are evoked is abnormal. The distinction between pathological reactions and the more extreme variants of the normal presents formidable problems when concerned with such issues as jealousy, love and injustice. When does a passionate concern for fairness and an intense commitment to obtaining justice become querulousness, and where is the line between the proper

Table 8.3
Reactive and Symptomatic Disorders of Passion

Reactive	*Symptomatic*
Arise in response to a real provocation understandably related to subsequent reaction	Arise in the context of a mental disorder without an understandable provocation
Subject rendered susceptible by:	The passion is accompanied by other clinical features of the underlying mental disorder

a. a personality vulnerability
  b. a previous sensitizing experience
  c. a mental disorder usually depressive
  d. any combination of the above	

An exaggerated response in terms of:
  a. state of mind
  b. behaviour	

The course is dependent in part on the actual situation and the behaviour of others	The course is closely related to the evolution and resolution of the underlying mental disorder

pursuit of civil redress and morbid litigousness? In theory, such distinctions may seem impossible; in everyday life they can often appear obvious to everyone except the one most directly concerned; in clinical practice, there is no substitute for building up a detailed historical account of the development, maintenance and correlates of the beliefs from as wide a range of informants as possible in addition to the patient.

Morbid jealousy

Jealousy is a passion which can involve dramatic changes in the actions and state of mind of otherwise normal individuals. White and Mullen (1989) have reviewed general as well as clinical concepts, and considered the influence of social and cultural factors. The recognition of morbid jealousy is crucial for the safe clinical management of affected patients, and it may be critical to legal issues of defence or mitigation.

Restricting morbid jealousy to cases where clear delusions of infidelity are present has the advantage of clarity and consistency (Krafft-Ebing, 1886; Todd and Dewhurst, 1955; Dominik, 1970), but excludes individuals whose jealous responses could be regarded as pathological by virtue of the intensity and abnormal facility with which they are evoked (Mairet, 1908; Jaspers, 1910; Shepherd, 1961).

When jealousy emerges as a symptom of an underlying mental disorder, the recognition of its pathological nature is usually straightforward. Jealousy may form part of the symptomatology of a wide variety of disorders. Shepherd (1961) reported that 14% of a large series of patients with delusional disorders had jealousy as a prominent feature. There is also a link between depressive disorders and jealousy. In one series of morbidly jealous people, over 50% had a primary or associated diagnosis of depression (Mullen and Maack, 1985). Alcohol abuse has traditionally been linked to morbid jealousy (Krafft-Ebing, 1886), although the closeness of the association has been questioned (Lagache, 1947). The only systematic study of an alcoholic population claimed an incidence of 27% in men and 15% in women (Shrestha et al., 1985). In most large series of morbid jealousy, alcoholism is reported to be present in between 10 and 20% of cases (Langfeldt, 1961; Shepherd, 1961; Vauhkonen, 1968; Mullen and Maack, 1985). A wide range of organic psychosyndromes may also give rise to morbid jealousy (Shepherd, 1961; Cummings, 1985).

The truth or falsity of the jealous individual's suspicions is no guide to whether the jealousy is pathological for, even with delusions of infidelity, the central accusation may be correct without these beliefs being any the less morbid (Jaspers, 1946, 1963; Mullen, 1985). Ødegaard (1968) commented on the frequency with which the spouses of jealous partners, who had separated on clinical advice, married or became sexually involved with the subjects of their former spouse's delusions. Mullen and Maack (1985) also found that the core concerns about infidelity often had substance, while the thought processes and behaviour that attended them were clearly abnormal.

Jealousy is dangerous for it not only evokes anger, but also arms the jealous with a sense of righteous indignation to justify their acts of aggression. Jealousy focuses primarily on the partner, as Spinoza (1677) argued

> The hatred towards an object loved, together with the envy of another, is called jealousy.

Mowat (1966), in his study of 110 subjects who had killed or committed serious assaults in the grip of jealousy, found that the loved ones were the victims in 94 instances, and the actual or supposed rivals were assaulted in only 7 cases. This pattern is confirmed by most studies of jealous violence (Lagache, 1947; Psarska, 1970; Mullen and Maack, 1985), although a study from Detroit of 58 jealous homicides reported almost as many rivals as lovers being slain (Daly et al., 1982). Jealousy motivates a significant proportion of serious violence. Gibbens (1958a) reported jealousy to have precipitated 43 (22%) of a series of 195 homicides. Daly and colleagues (1982) suggested that male sexual jealousy may be the source of conflict in the overwhelming majority of spousal homicide in North America. In the Brixton study (Taylor, 1985b), it was also found that jealousy not uncommonly motivated criminal violence. In a number of studies of battered and abused wives, jealousy has been identified as a major factor in the violence (Whitehurst, 1971; Gayford, 1975a,b; Hilberman and Manson, 1977). A study of a series of 138 morbidly jealous patients found that over half had physically assaulted their partners, some inflicting injury, though none had been charged with an offence as a result (Mullen and Maack, 1985). The criminal law recognizes that certain events may provoke such a passionate response that an ordinary man may suffer a temporary loss of control. If, in the grips of this passion, a person attacks his provoker, he may have a defence, should he kill the provoker, to a charge of murder, or grounds for mitigation if the victim survives. The infidelity of a spouse is the most frequently advanced example of such a provocation. Blackstone, the 18th century English jurist, commented that killing in a situation where the spouse was discovered in adultery—

> is of the lowest degree of [manslaughter] . . . for there could be no greater provocation (quoted in Smith and Hogan, 1988) (*see also Manning*).

In most jurisdictions in the USA, if a spouse or lover is killed in response to the provocation of blatant adultery, then the crime is voluntary manslaughter rather than murder (La Fave and Scott, 1972). Some jurisidictions, such as New Mexico and Utah, go even further, allowing such provocation to be advanced as a complete defence to the charge (Perkins, 1969). The provoking event has been extended beyond encountering the spouse *in flagrante delicto* to suddenly being told of infidelity or to the cumulative provocation of infidelity which evokes increasing jealousy over weeks, months or even years (Wasik, 1982). The leniency with which the jealous killer may be dealt has produced occasional protests from both jurists and the public. Williams (1978), after noting:

> Killing in jealousy is one of the best established instances of provocation

argued that adultery is common—but killing rare and that:

> to say that the ordinary man or woman kills for adultery is a grotesque untruth.

The continued indulgence shown towards the violence of jealousy is a judgement on both the prevailing social mores and our attitude to women, who are almost always the victims.

Erotomania

The idea that love may form the basis of a mental disorder is an ancient one (Enoch and Trethowan, 1979). The term, erotomania, dates back at least to Ferrand's 17th century text on erotomania (Hunter and MacAlpine, 1963). Esquirol (1838) placed erotomania among his monomanias, characterizing it as an exaggerated and irrational sentimental attachment, usually to someone who in reality has little or no relation to the sufferer. Krafft-Ebing (1886) considered the nucleus of the malady of erotomania to be the delusion of being loved by a distinguished or powerful person. Like Esquirol before him, he emphasized that the love was romantic and enthusiastic, rather than carnal although, in contradistinction to most other writers on the subject (Raskin and Sullivan, 1974; Hollender and Callahan, 1975), he considered it more common in males. Rudden et al. (1990) found that 75% of a sample of hospitalized patients with erotomanic delusions were women, compared with

48% of patients with other delusions, but it may be that it is an artefact of hospital sampling that produces this effect. Schacter (1977) advanced this argument, while Taylor et al. (1983) found that the disorder occured in around 3% of psychotic men in a prison. Kraepelin (1896) and Bleuler (1916) also focused on the individual's delusional conviction of being loved by someone of high rank. Kretschmer (1930) considered erotomania to be based on a simple and straightforward exaggeration of those dispositions to be found in normal lovers and, therefore, could involve both beliefs that one was loved and the experience of being in love. De Clérambault (1942) confined his cases to those who believe they are loved and deny that they love in return, or at least to the same extent. Like many previous authorities, he argued that erotic delusions may exist in isolation or form part of a variety of psychotic disorders. He also suggested that the disorder began with hope and pride, but deteriorated into resentment directed either to the object of the delusion for failure to declare their love, or to those supposed to stand in the path of this true love. The debate about whether the delusions are invariably associated with a more general psychotic process or whether they may form part of a discrete syndrome has continued (e.g. Hollender and Callahan, 1975; Seeman, 1978). Rudden et al. (1990) once again confirmed the heterogeneity of presentations, and indeed prognosis, and found that a 25% subgroup of the sample had a monodelusional presentation without other significant symptoms. Those whose symptoms seem to be part of a schizophrenic illness had the worst prognosis in terms of chronicity, and those with the more 'pure' state probably the best, tending to be relatively isolated, but to be able to stay in employment, often of a very responsible kind.

Erotomania may lead the sufferer into conflict with the law. The delusion may precipitate the patient into a fanatical pursuit of the supposed lover which often involves unwelcome approaches, letters and physical pursuit at any time of day or night. Victims of such attentions are not infrequently very frightened, and driven to use the law to protect their privacy and this may, eventually, bring the erotomanic before the courts. Taylor (1979) noted the embarrassment, and even danger, which such patients may create for psychiatrists should they fix their attentions upon them. Jealousy may also complicate erotomanic attachments and lead to assaults either on supposed rivals or the object of the delusions themselves. Savage (1892) described the case of a patient who, in pursuit of an erotomanic attachment to her doctor, attempted to poison his wife. Sexual attacks and violence directed at the object of the erotomanic beliefs are said, by some observers, to be rare. They certainly occur, but may be less common than attacks on rivals or others. Probably, unlike much other delusionally driven behaviour, the greatest risk arises when the conviction with which the belief is held is not complete.

Morbid querulousness

This group of patients share the conviction that they have been deprived by others and that they are entitled to redress. There appear to be three broad and, to some extent, overlapping varieties:

1. those people who get involved in lengthy legal battles for redress of their grievances and become known as 'vexatious litigants';
2. the querulants who lay repeated complaints against those supposed to have wronged them, but without recourse to the law;
3. the hypochondriacal claimants who usually direct their resentment against doctors they believe have failed to cure them, either by providing the wrong treatment or withholding the necessary treatment.

Those with these disorders become passionately engaged in restoring their supposed rights to the exclusion of all other interests or claims upon them. Their repeated failures to obtain satisfaction lead to increasing bitterness, and often to the belief that they are the victim of orchestrated persecution. Krafft-Ebing (1886) noted:

> Their constantly more voluminous recriminations, requests and denunciations are filled with invectives and insults to officials which attract the attention of the law . . . they use up their property, insult the courts and disturb public order.

The litigants tend only to come to psychiatric attention when they resort to extralegal mechanisms, or when their law suits are obviously grotesque from the outset. Rowlands (1988) reviewed the development of legal restraints in England. First applied under the Vexatious Actions Act 1896, the situation now is that the Attorney General may make application in the High Court, under section 42 of the Supreme Court Act 1981, prohibiting an individual from continuing or initiating legal actions. The names of such people are published in the London Gazette. On average, only five or six orders per year are made.

In many cases, there is an understandable grievance at the centre of the claims of the morbidly querulous, and it is only with time that those trying to assist them begin to suspect the presence of any pathology. The querulants issue complaints and accusations, usually against individuals, but occasionally against organizations. They come to notice by making a nuisance of themselves in writing abusive letters or accosting the supposed offender. One patient began by picketing her ex-employer's home with accusations of wrongful dismissal, escalated to poison pen letters and 'phone calls at all hours of the night, and finally throwing stones through his windows and vandalizing his car. Another pursued his complaint against a government department through his Member of Parliament and the newspapers, bombarding both with dozens of letters, often several a day; then he progressed to daubing accusations on the department's walls, and finally issuing death threats. Given the all too human tendency to believe the worst of others and take pleasure in the exposure of their failings, the querulant can recruit sympathy and support, at least initially. It is usually only when the gross disparity between the querulant's pursuit of the complaints and the actual or supposed offence becomes obvious that isolation follows.

Hypochondriacal claimants are convinced that they have been deprived of the correct treatment for what ails them. They may pursue their resentment against individual doctors through complaints, accusations and even by attacks on the property or person of the unfortunate practitioner. These patients are different from those with dysmorphophobia, although the clinical features can overlap on occasion.

One patient, who was convinced she had a rare endocrine disorder which she had seen described in a television documentary, pursued a number of doctors whom she believed were refusing to provide the treatment her life depended upon. She plagued these physicians with requests, complaints and intrusive visits to both their practices and private homes. Unlike many such patients, this particular lady had a pleasant manner and never became offensive or aggressive, though she created considerable disruption.

Another patient repeatedly visited dentists with a vague complaint about a problem in his teeth and jaw, which he claimed had rendered his life unsupportable. He managed to pursuade various dentists to remove every tooth in his head and to chip away at his mandible on several occasions. When this produced no relief, he became convinced that one particular dentist was responsible for his miseries. He made repeated visits demanding corrective treatment and, when this was not forthcoming, began making threats, both verbally and by letter, which created understandable alarm.

On occasion, such patients launch serious attacks upon those health professionals they believe to be responsible for their miseries. They may also resort to suicide and certainly wreak much destruction of other kinds in their own lives.

As with other disorders of passion, the primary disorder of the morbid querulent may be various (Stalstrom, 1980). Rowlands (1988) described a case illustrative of each of the main classes recognized with consistency. McKenna (1984) asserted firmly:

This syndrome (the querulous paranoid state) remains the standard clinical example of an overvalued idea

and argued strongly for the case that the condition only arises in people with well marked personality abnormalities. Others have emphasized the frankly psychotic nature of some querulants, but most agree that this is unusual, and that even when the grievance is delusional, recourse to litigation is even more rare (Astrup, 1984). It is interesting that the possibility of morbid querulousness being a varient of a primary affective disorder has apparently not been entertained, although all authors seem to agree that considerable affect is invested in the beliefs that the onset of the disorder tends to be between 40 and 60 and that, while the grievances may be relatively chronically held, the level of consequent activity tends to be fluctuant, with periods of quiescence followed by vigorous outbursts.

Patterns of Illness

Length of illness

Wilmann's (1940) work on murder in the prodromal stages of schizophrenia consolidated a view of the time, that early or very acute forms of psychosis would pose the greatest risk to others. This is not generally so. Hafner and Boker's (1973) study provided perhaps the best contrasting evidence. Just 8 of the 284 people with schizophrenia in the homicidal sample had committed their crime within the first month of their illness. Eighty-four percent had been ill for over a year and 55% for more than 5 years. Johnstone et al. (1986) found that nearly 20% of their sample of people presenting in their first episode of schizophrenia had behaved in a way threatening to the lives of others. This did not, however, necessarily imply recent pathology. Life-threatening behaviour was commoner the longer people had been ill, and half of these incidents took place when the patient had been ill for at least a year (Humphreys et al., 1992).

Walker and McCabe (1973) did not examine length of illness *per se* at the time of offending, but their data were suggestive of its importance. They compared 942 men and 218 women, who were the majority of those who had been made the subject of hospital orders in the courts in England and Wales between April 1963 and March 1964, with everyone found guilty of indictable offences in 1963, and with all admissions to a mental hospital in 1964 recorded at the Ministry of Health. People going into a maximum security hospital were excluded from the hospital order group. People admitted under a hospital order for schizophrenia were, on average, significantly older than those admitted to hospital informally or under civil orders, whether first admissions or subsequent admissions were examined. For the depressive groups, the position was more complicated. None of the very young had depressive illnesses, but a similar overall trend towards the offender group being older was negated by the substantial numbers of elderly people (over 65) among the ordinary admissions. Overall, the mentally abnormal offenders were very significantly older than the total population of offenders.

The older age of mentally abnormal offenders relative either to mentally abnormal non-offenders, or to mentally normal offenders is now well documented. East (1936) may have been among the first to draw attention to it among homicides. Mowat (1966) suggested that not only are the mentally abnormal homicides on average older, but that some subgroups of the mentally abnormal may be older than others. Mowat's particular interest was in morbid jealousy, and he argued that the older age of offence allowed for the development of the delusions. Hafner and Boker (1973) found that, on average, their 533 mentally abnormal offenders were 8.5 years older than the mentally 'normal' offenders, but that there was considerable differential between people by diagnostic subgroup. For the people with schizophrenia, the offending was on average 10–15 years later. It was also apparent in this series, however, that the non-violent people hospitalized with schizophrenia were, on average, older still. Unlike those in Walker and McCabe's (1973) sample, Hafner and Boker's offenders had all made homicidal attacks, and this may be relevant. The illnesses within the Hafner and Boker series differed in symptomatic presentation. Systematized delusions were signficantly more common in the offender group, adding weight to the developmental time-lag hypothesis. The people with affective psychoses, with a generally later onset than schizophrenia, showed an even larger age difference from the 'normal' offender sample. In the Brixton study, Taylor (1993) examined age at index offence for psychotic and non-psychotic offenders, but also considered age differences at other crucial times, namely the timing of the first recorded offence involving violence of any kind including threats, and the timing of the first incident involving actual personal injury. At each point, the men with a psychosis were significantly older than the men without, on average by 3–4 years. Stronger evidence for the impact of the illness on violent behaviour, but not necessarily on criminal behaviour more generally, was generated by comparing the age of onset of the illness with these other landmarks, in nearly all cases independently verified. A criminal record *per se* was as likely to have been accrued before the onset of illness as after it. By contrast, among the schizophrenic men who had ever been violent, 79% had first acted in a way that could have been construed as violent after the onset of their illness but, where actual injury had been inflicted on another, it followed the onset in 88% of cases. The patterns were almost exactly the same for the men with an affective psychosis.

Course of illness

Too little is known about the ordinary course of psychotic illnesses, and in particular schizophrenia, to allow much further comment on the association with offending, although some studies are beginning to show promise in their potential for demonstrating details of mental state over time (e.g. Harding et al., 1989) rather than simple statements of 'improvement' or discharge from hospital. Two issues are sometimes considered which seem likely to have some bearing on behaviour: firstly the influence of the recurring, acute forms of illness versus the chronic deteriorating forms, and secondly the disorganized/disintegrated symptom pattern versus the organized and integrated.

Shader et al. (1977) suggested that the periodicity as much as the affective loading of the schizo-affective psychoses, the subgroup of schizophrenia most commonly associated with violence in their series, could be responsible for the increased risk. Hafner and Boker (1973), however, in their much larger series, albeit of homicidal people, could find no distinction between violent and non-violent patients in periodicity of illness and, indeed, found that, where an exacerbation of symptoms had been noted by relatives prior to institutionalization, it was generally in the non-violent group. They made the important point that a decision about a violent act, and its anticipation, might have some calming or mood elevating effect, perhaps comparable to the improved mental state sometimes commented upon retrospectively as having existed in a presuicidal state. Another potentially important area for consideration is whether, where specific symptoms seem to have been associated with violence, they are useful in risk prediction by virtue of their likely repetition in each subsequent episode.

It has been noted (Taylor, 1981, 1987) that people with psychoses who have highly organized delusional systems, largely to the exclusion of other symptoms, tend also to be relatively organized in their social lives and even in their offending patterns. Their offending, and in particular their violence, may be less frequent, but more 'effective'. Conversely, those who have multiple, chaotic symptoms appear correspondingly chaotic in their social life and offending patterns, albeit indulging in offending of a less serious nature. These patterns of organization would bear further examination, but some parallels with the work on overcontrolled and undercontrolled personality types proposed by Megargee (1966) and expanded by Blackburn (e.g. 1970) are discussed further below.

The impact of treatment

There are no studies which follow prospectively a patient from the point of a violent or criminal incident through an institution and out, back to the community, although it is possible to generate some impression of the impact of contact with services from a combination of studies that look at a part of the process of psychiatric involvement, usually retrospectively. Few studies detail treatments received. It is of some importance to know whether admission to a psychiatric hospital or unit brings benefit or not, but it would be of much more value to know what elements of treatment—the milieu, the specific physical treatments, the specific psychological treatments or something else—brought change. Krakowski et al. (1988), studied a consecutive series of 44 patients (including 25 with schizophrenia and 6 with affective disorder) admitted to a special care unit after at least two violent incidents in the previous month. The patients stayed on average between 7 and 8 weeks and measures were reported for the first, the middle and last week of their stay. A decrease in psychiatric symptomatology was accompanied by a decrease in violence in the first, but not the second, half of the stay, while improvement in social functioning was consistently paralleled by a decrease in violence throughout. This led to an inference that ward milieu and some forms of psychological or social treatments were important, since the simple expedient of separating the patient from a provocative environment at the point of admission would be unlikely to show a cumulative effect. It also suggests that specific treatments for psychosis were relevant too. The different treatments were, however, neither defined nor analysed separately.

Previous studies similarly tended to deal with treatment in crude global terms. Hafner and Boker (1973) noted that a majority of their homicidal people with schizophrenia (59%) had previously been in hospital for treatment, as had nearly half of the people (49%) with affective psychoses. The proportion of the non-violent patients with schizophrenia who had previously been treated was significantly higher, although the proportion of those with affective illnesses who had had previous treatment were little different. Men in the Brixton study were asked about their previous experiences of treatment or prison. Only 10% of the men remanded in prison with a psychotic illness were new psychiatric cases, and as many as 87% had undergone previous inpatient psychiatric treatment. Although this had not necessarily been close in time to the offence, over 20% had been in hospital or prison, and in the latter case in contact with a doctor, within a month of the index offence. Nearly 70% had been back in the community from such an experience for less than a year (Taylor, 1993).

Hafner and Boker (1973) examined the way in which those patients who had been treated had left treatment. The vast majority of the violent offenders (88%) were discharged with the full agreement of the treating staff, and for only 7% was some doubt expressed about their fitness for discharge while just 5% had absconded. These proportions were significantly higher than for the non-violent group but, nevertheless, reflected a tiny minority of the patients. Throughout the relevant literature, there are references to offender patients, and patients brought to hospital by police, being less compliant with treatment than either patients admitted voluntarily or under civil compulsion (e.g. Bowden, 1978b; Szmukler et al., 1981; Moodley and Thornicroft, 1988), but all clinicians would do well to remember that formation of a therapeutic alliance is at least as dependent on clinical staff as on the patient. Non-compliance may be covertly encouraged in a demanding, hostile, disruptive individual, and full agreement that a patient is untreatable and thus appropriate in his/her demands to leave perhaps not hard to obtain.

Bowden (1978b) followed the progress of men remanded into custody for medical and psychiatric reports, following a criminal charge. The prospects of benefiting from treatment were very poor at any stage. Of 634 men entering custody on this basis, only 87 received recommendations for treatment, 82 of whom were actually referred to a hospital and just 59 traceable after 14 months. Only about one-third of these did well in treatment. Thus, only 5% of men entering prison for reports clearly benefited in terms of improved mental state. Again, it is more than possible that this reflects as much on the attitudes, skills and facilities of their prospective psychiatrists as the nature of their disorder.

Gibbens and Robertson (1983) followed, from records, the subsequent careers of Walker and McCabe's (1973) mentally disordered offenders compulsorily admitted to hospital after an offence. Of the mentally ill group in the hospital order series, 81% had schizophrenia and 13% affective illness, while in the notionally more dangerous group for whom Home Office restrictions on discharge had been imposed, 64% of the mental illness group had schizophrenia and 30% had an affective illness. The subsequent offending rate of the mentally ill was extremely low, just 4% of the hospital order group committing serious offences and repeated minor assaults. Within the restriction order group of 72, one patient subsequently killed and two engaged in serious assault; however, the period spent in hospital was long, and 14% of the mental illness sample was still detained after 15 years.

Continuing, or subsequent psychiatric treatment was much more likely than involvement with the criminal justice system in both groups, at least half of the hospital order group patients being readmitted to psychiatric hospital at some point. The greatest risk, and this cannot be too frequently stated, seemed to be to the patients themselves. In the hospital order group, 112 (16%) of the patients had died, only half of these from natural causes. More than half of the deaths occurred before the age of 50. In the restriction order group, the death rate was even higher, 21 of the original 100 patients having died and 7 being untraceable. Of the treatment, nothing is definitely known other than the fact that it meant that time was spent as a psychiatric inpatient. About one-third of the hospital order patients had left hospital within 3 months and a half within 6 months, many absconding, so treatment could only have been relatively cursory. The restriction order patients did stay longer, with a mean of 28 months for the time limited orders and 74 months for the indefinite orders. If their treatment had much in common with that received by mentally ill patients detained in maximum security under restriction orders, as from clinical impression seems likely, the main treatment would have been neuroleptic medication (Dell and Robertson, 1988).

Psychoses, Offending and Pathological Personality: Integral or Interactional?

Even when a psychotic symptom can be clearly associated in time with a violent or criminal act, and when the patient acknowledges a causative link, there is generally doubt about whether the symptom is a sufficient explanation for the act. A man may, for example, stab his mother because he believes she is poisoning him but, even if she were in reality poisoning him, a range of possible responses would be available to the man, and something else in his internal or external environment must be postulated as having contributed to his choice of the physically violent option. Disorder of personality is probably the principal among the alternatives or additional internal variables to be considered as a cause of violence, but its status and contribution is confused. The confusion arises in part from basic limitations in operational definition or core concept of personality disorder, but also because the framework for the consideration of the interaction between personality and psychosis is rarely explicit. Disorder of personality may arise independently of psychoses or be intrinsic to it. If the disorders are independent in aetiology, then further possibilities to be examined are that the psychosis is wholly coincidental to the personality structure or that it may be in some way interactional, the one disorder contributing to the expression of the other. If, as claimed in the International Classification of Diseases (WHO, 1978), personality disorder is fundamental to the diagnosis of schizophrenia, then is it evident as a core process, even as a constant marker of disorder between more florid attacks or does it constitute evidence of deteriorating function within the brain?

Psychoses as co-existent with but coincidental to personality disorder?

If clinical practice is an indication of clinical beliefs, then many practising clinicians do not view personality disorder, at least in its antisocial elements, as intrinsic to psychosis, being almost as unlikely to accept patients with both disorders as they are the patients with personality disorder alone. The Brixton record review study of pretrial prisoners (Taylor and Gunn, 1984) found that 44% of those with 'pure' schizophrenia and 53% of those with 'pure' affective disorder subsequently received hospital orders in court, the precondition to such a disposal being that there is a psychiatrist willing to commit himself to offering a bed and treatment. The proportions were just 13% and 12% respectively when the offender had a psychotic illness, but complicated with personality disorder and/or substance abuse. These findings echoed those of Bowden (1978b), who studied an earlier, independent sample from the same prison. The men who were recommended for treatment in hospital were mentally ill without heavy drinking, evidence of financial gain from crime or extensive criminal records.

The evidence for real independence between personality disorder and psychoses is slight. It has been argued, for example, that evidence of well-established antisocial behaviour prior to the onset of psychosis would favour the independent model. It has been shown that more trivial patterns of offending, which constitute one form of antisocial behaviour, as commonly precede the onset of psychosis as follow it (e.g. Taylor, 1993). This sort of data has, however, been used in making the diagnosis of schizophrenia. Premorbid social decline in achievements, in sensitivity to one's peers and possibly in moral standards too may be crucial elements in distinguishing schizophrenia from other functional psychoses. They may be evident even in childhood (e.g. Offord, 1974).

Evidence of consistent offending patterns in the context of fluctuating mental state could confirm the role of personality disorder, although without greatly clarifying the nature of its relationship with the psychosis. There is such evidence. Bowden (1978b), showed that there were differences in response to treatment in the 59 of his series of 82 remanded male prisoners ordered to hospital. Thirty-eight percent showed no benefit from their hospitalization; they were mainly men with schizophrenia who were poorly compliant with treatment, but included some alcoholics. Twenty-six percent, mainly men with schizophrenia, showed remission of the positive symptoms of their psychoses, but their behaviour remained unsocial in that they were wanderers, drinkers and were aggressive. For only one-third of the sample, a group of men with schizophrenia or manic depressive disorder, but without an additional diagnosis, was treatment really effective. Further evidence that there may indeed be differences between groups in the relative influence of illness and personality within a psychotic population comes from the Brixton study. Men who appeared to have been driven to offend by their delusions were rather less likely to have a criminal record than their more rationally motivated and less seriously violent peers, but significantly less so (59% : 78%) in relation to non-violent, usually recidivist offending (Taylor, unpublished data). Gibbens and Robertson (1983), who studied the criminal careers of male offenders receiving hospital orders, with or without restrictions, found that the criminal careers differed quite markedly between the offenders with affective disorder, those with other psychotic disorders and those with primary personality disorder, the likelihood of recidivism increasing in that order. Furthermore, within the restriction order group, those with paranoid illnesses were much less likely to have committed offences before or after the index offence than those with other schizophrenic illnesses.

Personality disorder, psychoses and offending : interactional effects

Much of the work that has been done on interactional effects between personality, psychosis and crime started with international observations that only about half of those convicted of unlawful killings are persistent criminals (e.g. West, 1965, 1968; Gillies, 1965; Pokorny, 1965; Cole et al., 1968). Weiss et al. (1960), on the basis of case records, compared 13 people for whom a murder was a first offence with groups of habitual criminals and sex offenders. All shared feelings of inadequacy and isolation, but the murder group alone showed motivation and behaviour towards conformity. Four of the murder group had schizophrenia, but none in the other groups. Megargee (1966), following a similar theme, acknowledged the force of environmental provocation towards aggression, or of internal provocation such as delusions, but argued that the expression of that aggression depended on the nature and strength of inhibitory personality traits. He proposed two broad personality types: the undercontrolled, with few inhibitions, who tended to be repeatedly assaultive, and the overcontrolled, with strong inhibitions, who only acted violently when provocation reached a very high level. He provided some support for this hypothesis among delinquents, but it was Blackburn who first systematically evaluated the contribution of personality traits among mentally ill offenders.

In an early study, Blackburn (1968), compared 24 men admitted to a maximum security hospital with paranoid schizophrenia and 24 with non-paranoid schizophrenia using the Minnesota Multiphasic Personality Inventory (MMPI). The groups were similar in age and intellectual level. Those with paranoid schizophrenia were significantly more extraverted than the others, and significantly more likely to have had a history of violence and aggressive behaviour. There was a significant inverse relationship between extreme assaultiveness and persistent aggression, and Blackburn argued that, among people with schizophrenia, personality factors might be more important than the disorder *per se* in accounting for aggressive behaviour.

He went on to study all 62 male homicides admitted to one English maximum security hospital in Britain during 28 months in the late 1960s (Blackburn, 1970), of whom 56 completed the MMPI. Four distinct groups were identified by cluster analysis, two broadly conforming with the under-controlled classification and two with the overcontrolled. The 'overcontrolled represser type' had a marked tendency to make use of denial and avoidance mechanisms. They were usually older, first offenders, not regarded as personality disordered by the legal or medical systems, and about one-third carried a diagnosis of schizophrenia. The related depressed inhibited type (Blackburn type 3) were less denying, but indicated strong impulse control, introversion, social anxiety and depression. Nearly all of them were regarded as ill, and the majority as having schizophrenia. The 'paranoid aggressive type' (Blackburn Type 2) were the most disturbed showing abnormal scores on depression, hypochondriac, psychopathic deviate, anxiety and hostility scales, but with some social anxiety and introversion. Their most frequent medical diagnosis was paranoid schizophrenia. Somewhat impulsive, they probably fitted least well into the simple Megargee model of classification. Type 4 was the smallest group, and the closest to the concept of an 'undercontrolled personality type', showing moderate anxiety and paranoid ideation, but poor socialization, high impulsivity and extraversion and outwardly directed hostility. No person with schizophrenia fell into this group.

Blackburn's personality typology was originally based on identification through clustering of traits. An alternative to this classification is the dimensional approach, in which variables are combined in a linear fashion, some would say giving a more exact description of the individual and individual differences. Blackburn (1974) expressed doubt about the supposed advantages of the dimensional approach, but tested it, again using the MMPI, with a larger series of maximum security patients (175), three-quarters of whom were mentally ill. He found that three dimensions—anxiety (or neuroticism 'n'), impulsivity and general extraversion supported the four clusters of his earlier work. Thus, by more than one approach to measurement, pathological personality traits were identifiable among the psychotic as well as the primarily personality disordered patients, typological and dimensional differences coming close to distinguishing them on personality classification alone.

In the tripartite association between personality, psychotic illness and offending, the assumption so far has been that the combination of most interest is that of some disorder of personality interacting with the illness, resulting in the release of antisocial behaviour. In any tripartite association, however, the other combinations must be considered. There is some evidence, principally anecdotal, that the offending behaviour may be cathartic, and the symptoms of illness relieved. Offending could also, if serious, constitute a life event sufficiently powerful to provoke symptoms in vulnerable individuals. No evidence of significant changes in mental state was found among psychotic offenders, the majority of whom were suffering from schizophrenia, at 4 to 6 weeks after their index offence (Taylor 1985b). Lanzkron (1963) noted the onset of psychoses in prison after a major offence in a substantial minority (27%) of cases. One factor in the development, or relief, of psychosis under these circumstances of stress may be the nature of the underlying personality. This may well, too, be the basis of the so-called prison psychosis or Ganser state (*see* pp. 424–6).

Personality disorder as integral to psychotic illness

An important way of clarifying the nature of any association between personality traits, psychotic symptoms and behaviour is to extend study beyond the individual to his family. For both of the major functional psychoses, relevant disorders of personality have been noted in first degree relatives. In relation to schizophrenia, Kraepelin was among the first to note:

> Not infrequently . . . among the brothers and sisters of the patient there are found striking personalities, criminals, queer individuals, prostitutes, suicides, vagrants, wrecked and ruined human beings . . . (Kraepelin, 1896).

Kendler (1985) reviewed the similar observations of successive phenomenologists. These have led to a general acknowledgement that certain kinds of personality disorder, especially the schizotypal, which may include manifestations of antisocial behaviour, may be among the many and heterogeneous presentations of disorder among the relatives of people with classical schizophrenia. The evidence for direct links between these abnormalities of personality and the illness is regarded as sufficiently strong that the deviant personalities are often referred to as schizophrenia spectrum disorders. One recent study (Sherrington et al., 1988), attempting to localize the genetic susceptibility to schizophrenia, found markers on chromosome 5 which were shared, among others, by those with recidivist antisocial traits and those with manifest schizophrenia. Earlier, Schinzel (1981) had drawn attention to some autosomal chromosome aberrations associated with behavioural problems without mental retardation. He cited, for example, an important minority of patients with a ring 18 chromosome and a presumed break point at the terminal bands who showed a severe degree of aggressivity, very poor frustration tolerance and signs of schizophrenia in early adolescence. Krag-Olsen et al. (1981) located ten cases of chromosome 18 abnormality and described an association between psychosis and behaviour disorder in all three cases surviving to 15 years or older.

Similar arguments and evidence have been supplied in support of integral links between personality disorder and affective illness, and indeed here frank clinical confusion between the disorders may occur. Akiskal et al. (1977) studied a series of cyclothymic patients and found that 66% had previously been diagnosed as hysterics or sociopaths. There was no doubt that some of their behavioural traits overlapped with those commonly taken as criteria for antisocial personality disorder, for example aggressive explosive outbursts and repeated changes of job, but in later studies (Akiskal et al., 1980; Akiskal, 1983) two subgroups of such patients were identified, one who showed physiological changes (rapid eye movement latency) on testing, characteristics of unipolar depressives, and who responded well to tricyclic antidepressants, and the other a more heterogeneous group with poorer prognoses. The inference of the presence of a particular disorder from the nature of its response to treatment must always be made with caution, particularly when the mechanism of drug action is poorly understood or the drug may have a range of effects. Response of non-psychotic symptoms to neuroleptics, for example, would not generally be considered as indirect evidence for schizophrenia, because of the general tranquillizing properties of the drugs. It is unclear whether the apparent control of some aggressive behaviour with lithium (Rifkin et al., 1972; Sheard et al., 1976) is similarly non-specific sedation or indicative of a link between some forms of personality disorder and affective illness. Response to antidepressants as indirect evidence of affective disorder is, however, somewhat more impressive.

The spectrum disorder concept has been applied to affective disorders, just as to the schizophrenias, but with a qualifying sex differentiating factor (e.g. Winokur et al., 1970; Winokur, 1972). The hypothesis is that the expression of a genetically transmitted vulnerability is likely to be as alcoholism or sociopathy among men and depression among women. There is some evidence to support this view, although the rate of association between personality disorders and affective illnesses in first-degree relatives appears to depend to some extent on the type of depression.

The Influence of Environment

Family Relations

Psychotic illnesses have been variously presented as the product of social environment and as disruptive of it. This is also true of criminal and violent behaviour, when the product of social environment, early childhood experiences, recent life events and current stresses have all been evoked. Early work emphasizing an association between certain childhood experiences, especially loss (e.g. Wahl, 1956; Brown and Harris, 1978), and mental disorder, including the psychoses, has been called into question on method-ological grounds (Tennant et al., 1980), and subsequently in the light of random community sampling (Tennant et al., 1982). Similarly, ideas about the relevance of an environment disrupted in other ways, for example through a powerful and pathological maternal relationship, (e.g. Fromm-Reichman, 1948; Bateson et al., 1956) have undergone considerable modifi-cation, giving more credance to elements in overall interpersonal family dynamics than to intense individual relations (e.g. Alanen, 1968; Hirsch and Leff, 1975). Increasingly, however, various forms of violence or sexual abuse are under study as important in contributing to later mental disorder, poor social adjustment and offending (e.g. Harter et al., 1988; Mullen et al., 1988; Burgess et al., 1987). Current thinking about other childhood experi-ences in relation to offending is reviewed elsewhere (Ch. 6). Almost no work specifically deals with the early experience of people who have both psychotic and antisocial or violent behaviour. In the Brixton study, a high prevalence of early childhood loss of a parent was common to all groups of offenders. The delusionally driven, more seriously violent psychotic offenders were the only group to show an important exception in this regard. The undiluted presence of a dominant and often disordered mother was more likely in this group than in any other (Taylor, unpublished data) and was in line with findings among people with schizophrenia in a French maximum security hospital (Addad et al., 1981).

The status of social relationships current to offending among psychotic offenders should be easier to tease out, but again such considerations have tended to focus on either the psychotic or the violent, but not people with both problems. The nature and quality of relationships within families with one member who has schizophrenia have been much studied. Expressed emotion (EE), which includes high levels of critical comment and over involvement, has been shown to correlate strongly with relapse in patients in close contact with their relatives (Brown et al., 1972) and even named as a causative factor (Vaughn and Leff, 1976). Demonstration that relapse rates could be reduced by social interventions that lowered EE in relatives seemed to confirm the association (Leff et al., 1982). The findings have, however, been challenged on the basis of small sample size and nature of sampling (MacMillan et al., 1986; McCreadie and Phillips, 1988), but received some independent and objective support from psychophysiological studies (e.g. Tarrier et al., 1988). Conversely, an absence of close, and particularly close-confiding relationships seems to be more implicated in relation to onset of depressive disorders (Brown and Harris, 1978; Birtchnell, 1988). Relation-ships within families with a violent member have also been studied (e.g. Martin, 1978; Dale et al., 1986a), although in this area knowledge of the demographics is perhaps more extensive than a recorded understanding of emotional interactions. Such research as there is into the family and social relationships of people who are psychotic and violent holds hints that at least among those with schizophrenia, the EE issues may be very important.

'Closeness' seems dangerous. In the German series of mentally abnormal homicides, 39% of the violent schizophrenics were married, compared with only 28% of the non-violent hospitalized group (Hafner and Boker, 1973). Planansky and Johnston (1977), working with an entirely hospitalized group, found that 41% of those who had made homicidal threats or attacks were married, compared with only 28% in the non-aggressive group. In the Brixton sample, a similar picture emerged. Two-thirds of the delusionally driven men, who were the most likely within the psychotic sample to be seriously violent, were living with someone, be it spouse, cohabitee, friend or some other family member, although a minority (36%) of the chaotic, generally minimally violent men were in such a position, half of them having no home at all. Social distancing, whether by accident or design, may have been protective, although it was striking that a sort of distancing had occurred even among those psychotic people who did assault others. There was little feeling for their victim, or interaction with them at the time of the offence, which was in marked contrast to the non-psychotic men (Taylor, 1993).

Wider Culture : Social Status and Ethnic Factors

It is always difficult to be confident about associations between social status and crime, because it is plausibly argued that those belonging to higher socio-economic groups are better able to conceal or defend their crimes than those of the lower groups, any apparent weighting towards an excess of crime in lower socio-economic groups thus being spurious. For some forms of mental illness the nature and direction of the relationship are well defined. Social standing is more-or-less irrelevant to the onset of a schizophrenic illness, but the illness itself brings decline in status (e.g. Goldberg and Morrison, 1963; Wiersma et al., 1983). Again, there has been little or no examination of these effects when illness and violence occur together. Given that violence tends to be a late associate of the illness, it might be inferred that criminal and violent behaviour of the mentally ill will be more likely to be associated with low socio-economic status, behaviour and status declining in parallel. Many of the more violent psychotic men in the Brixton study, however, had retained a home and family in some form, which raises the possibility that violent crime, and chaotic poverty, may be alternative forms of decline for those with psychoses who deteriorate over the years.

Rather more has been written about the specific issue of ethnic group and mentally abnormal offending, because in those areas of the British Isles with a relatively high representation of residents from ethnic minority groups, the numbers entering mental hospital compulsorily, either by direct referral from the police or by the courts, seem disproportionately high.

In relation to direct referrals from the police, the evidence is mixed. Sims and Symonds (1975), for example, studied psychiatric referrals from the police in Birmingham over an 11-year period (1962–73). In common with all such studies, the great majority of patients who were referred had a psychotic illness. Ten percent of this sample had been born in the West Indies, compared with 2.5% in the general population, and 10% in Eire (compared with 4.4%). By contrast, other ethnic minorities were not over-represented. Szmukler et al. (1981) compared two consecutive series of patients (1976/77 and 1977/78) compulsorily admitted to hospital with non-compulsory admissions, both from a North London borough. Neither among the compulsory admissions generally, nor formal admissions initiated by the police under section 136 of the Mental Health Act 1959, were there any differences by ethnic group. Only a little later (1984/85) in South London, however, another inner city area, Fahy et al., (1987), found marked differences. Thirty-four percent of admissions were of New Commonwealth or Pakistani origin, their representation in the general population being estimated at about 25% for that borough at that time. Compulsory emergency admissions under the civil provisions of the Act were also high, at 32%. The majority affected were of afro-caribbean origin. Moodley and Thornicroft (1988), also with a South London sample, suggested that men of West Indian origin were more likely to be brought to the hospital by police—4 of 13 men compared with none of the indigenous white men. Certainly, outwardly directed violence seemed a greater problem for the West Indian men, although not the women, 12 of the 13 men compared with 17 of 32 in the white group having been violent. Virtually all of the patients had a psychotic illness. In spite of police attention, none of these patients had been labelled as an offender at the time of admission, nor had they necessarily been engaged in anything approaching criminal activity, since the interests of the affected person are key considerations for this type of admission.

The debate about the relative likelihood of offending by those of different ethnic groups continues. An analysis of criminal convictions by birth place in the 1950s and 60s (McClintock, 1963) showed some excess of Irish and Commonwealth immigrants among the convicted, much of the excess being accounted for by domestic disputes. Stevens and Willis (1979) found no difference in rates for reported crime for areas with low and high immigrant populations, but did find a higher arrest rate in London Metropolitan Police districts in 1975 for Afro-Caribbean groups. The possibility of police attitudinal bias in arrests, however, seemed strong. The chances, for example, for a black person being arrested on 'suspicion' were 14–15 times higher than for a white person, calling into the question the validity of any arrest rate data, at least up to that time. In the Brixton record review of remanded prisoners (Taylor and Gunn 1984), there was no special association between violent offending and birth place of offender, nor of birth place of the offender's parent. The subgroup of men born in the West Indies, however, had a significantly higher rate of schizophrenia, a higher rate of recorded active symptoms of illness at the time of admission to prison and more chance of disposal by hospital order than had Caucasian groups (Taylor, 1988b). Given the difficulties in finding a hospital bed for offender patients, this latter finding is remarkable in itself. Although circumstances may be very different in the USA, it is interesting that Scheiffer et al. (1968) were impressed by the exceptional severity of illness among the black men transferred from jail to Maryland hospitals compared with their white peers, and argued that far from being too readily admitted to hospital, the black groups were disadvantaged in this respect. McGovern and Cope (1987) studied the records of all male patients between the ages of 16 and 65 compulsorily admitted to hospital together with a 50% sample of informal male patients over periods in the late 1970s and early 1980s in Birmingham. Rates for admission, compulsory or not, were similar for indigenous whites and Asians. Men of West Indian origin, whether first or second generation immigrants, were very significantly more likely to be admitted compulsorily, and especially as offender patients.

Use and Abuse of Patient-Selected Substances which Affect Mental State

Relationships between alcohol, other drugs, mental illness and offending are covered mainly in Ch. 11. Two principal concerns arise in relation to a person with an established psychotic illness. One is that substance abuse may trigger a rapid deterioration in psychotic state, which in turn leads to offending, and the other is that some substances may be as disinhibiting for people with psychosis, as for relatively healthy people. Since many psychoactive substances including alcohol, cannabis and amphetamines have been implicated in the development of toxic confusional states with psychotic symptoms, schizophreniform states or both, there is a common assumption that those same substances provoke deterioration or relapse in established illnesses, but there is little or no hard evidence for this. In some cases, it seems likely that patients turn to substance abuse in an attempt to make their symptoms more tolerable. Each case must be assessed on its own merits.

There is growing evidence that alcohol is less associated with offending among people with schizophrenia or affective psychosis than among the general population. Among 9365, mainly non-offender patients admitted to New York public hospitals in one year, Tardiff and Sweillam (1980) found an inverse relationship between alcohol abuse and assaultative or suicidal behaviour. This was mainly due to the relative absence of alcohol abuse among people with schizophrenia, psychotic depression or organic brain syndromes. Virkkunen (1974) found no relationship between alcohol use and offending among offenders with schizophrenia. In their homicide sample, Hafner and Boker (1973) found that, although two-thirds of the chronic alcoholics and one-third of each of the epileptic and the mental handicap groups had taken alcohol at the time of their offence, this was true of only 10% of the people with schizophrenia and 5% of those with an affective psychosis. Drugs of other kinds played little role in the backgrounds or in direct temporal relation to the offence of either the psychotics or the non-psychotics. Among men interviewed in the first Brixton study, alcohol use in the 12 hours prior to the offence was significantly less likely among the men with a psychosis than those without, and it was also significantly less likely to have been used by the victims of the psychotic men (Taylor, 1993). People recognized as dependent on other drugs were excluded from the sample, but users were not. Drug use in relation to the offence was unusual in either group. Abram and Teplin (1991) and Lindqvist and Allebeck (1990b), by contrast, both found substance abuse to have been a major problem within their psychotic offender samples, but only the latter addressed its association with the offence. The abuse appeared to be mainly by socially disintegrated, more trivial offenders, which is not wholly incompatible with our findings.

Effects of Institutionalization and Treatment

If factors in the environment do influence the facility with which crime is committed or the development of psychotic illnesses—probably both—then it follows that one of the most powerful interventions must be the removal of the affected individual from the provocative environment and the substitution of another, less provocative one. This is the basis on which much imprisonment and hospitalization should take place, but evidence for its impact on violence or offending is difficult to gather, partly because of the low base rate of serious violence and many other offences. Follow-through studies have rarely been attempted at all, but for the offender-patient none separate out the relative effects of admission *per se* to hospital or prison and more specific management approaches or treatments that may be offered there. Work with non-offender patients would suggest that a hospital milieu has powerful effects in itself, but can be enhanced by specific treatments (Ch. 17).

Conclusions

Evidence from symptom associations with offending and from illness development in relation to criminal career suggests that, for people with psychotic illness, the illness itself is an important factor in precipitating some non-violent antisocial behaviour and probably most violence. There is growing recognition of the symptoms that make people most vulnerable. It follows that where features of the illness can be identified as directly pertinent, these must not only be treated in the short term, but a continuing programme of care should be implemented to ensure that the symptoms are held at bay. Although specific symptoms are likely to be important, and people with schizophrenia or affective psychosis tend to have more autistic qualities than healthy offenders, no psychotic person acts wholly independently of his environment. Pathological relationships must be identified, understood and managed. Special difficulties arise when personality disorder coexists with the psychosis, as motivation for treatment on the part of both patients and clinicians seems to become impaired. Both the patients and their therapists may need special support to maintain treatment.

9
Personality Disorders

Edited by
John Gunn

Written by
Ron Blackburn
John Gunn
Jonathan Hill
David Mawson
Paul Mullen

Personality disorders are an ill defined yet substantial group of diseases which being the concern of all branches of psychiatry are dealt with in general textbooks. Yet a textbook of forensic psychiatry would not be complete without a chapter on personality disorders, or at least that group of personality disorders that gives rise to objectionable behaviour. They are the most contentious aspect of modern psychiatry. They may represent within a medical framework the process of extrusion of unwanted individuals which is universal in social animals. To some extent they provide the drive for the development of forensic psychiatry. This chapter deals with the nosological and descriptive aspects of personality disorder and gives some preliminary indications about management.

The *Oxford English Dictionary* defines personality as:

> The quality, character, or fact of being a person as opposed to a thing; that quality or principle which makes a being personal, and
> The quality or assemblage of qualities which makes a person what he is, as distinct from other persons.

This circularity suggests that lexicographers are as challenged as the rest of us by this fundamental concept which we all think we understand, yet find hard to enunciate. The dictionary definition implies that we usually ascribe to other people a single all embracing quality called 'personality'. Such a singular concept has its uses for it emphasizes the uniqueness of each human being. For practical purposes, however, it seems sensible to break this all embracing higher order concept of personality into its component parts which includes attitudes, skills, beliefs, affective responses, aggressiveness, intelligence, and behaviour.

In an extensive review of the terminology used both publically and professionally Rutter (1987) argued that there are three different types of concept. *Temperament* is a:

> relatively small number of simple, non-motivational, non-cognitive, stylistic features of which emotionality, activity, and sociability are the best validated.

Personality refers to:

> the coherence of functioning that derives from how people react to their given attributes, how they think about themselves, and how they put these together into some form of conceptual whole.

Personality disorders, include variants of conditions like affective disorder, autism and schizophrenia together with persistent pervasive abnormalities in social relationships and social functioning generally. As Rutter put it:

> These personality disorders are clinically important in terms of both their incidence and their chronicity. They deserve much greater attention than they have received in the past.

The International Classification of Diseases, 9th revision (ICD-9) defines personality disorder as:

> Deeply ingrained maladaptive patterns of behaviour generally recognizable by the time of adolescence or earlier and continuing throughout most of adult life, although often becoming less obvious in middle or old age. The personality is abnormal either in the balance of its components, their quality and expression or in its total aspect. Because of this deviation or psychopathy the patient suffers or others have to suffer and there is an adverse effect upon the individual or on society.

DSM-III R defines personality disorder thus:

> Behaviours or traits that are characteristic of the individual's recent (past year) and long-term functioning (generally since adolescence or early childhood). The constellation of behaviours or traits causes either significant impairment in social or occupational functioning, or subjective distress.

A major difficulty which is apparent from these definitions is that the concept of personality disorder is both vague and all-embracing. Furthermore, it can acquire pejorative overtones. Nevertheless, Tyrer (1988) concludes:

> Personality disorder is a necessary concept in clinical psychiatry because it describes a class of abnormality not included elsewhere in classification.

Even so 'personality disorder' to some extent remains a nosological dustbin of residual diagnoses.

Classification of Personality Disorders

DSM-III R describes eleven personality disorders, and ICD 9 eight. In DSM-III R, categories are grouped on the basis of common features into three clusters (ICD-9 equivalent terms are given in parentheses).

A. Disorders characterized by 'odd' or eccentric behaviours; paranoid 301.00 (paranoid), schizoid 301.20 (schizoid), and schizotypal 301.22;
B. Those disorders in which individuals display dramatic, emotional, or erratic behaviours; histrionic 301.50 (hysterical), narcissistic 301.81, antisocial 301.70 (personality disorder with predominantly asocial or sociopathic manifestations), and borderline 301.83;
C. Those disorders comprising individuals with anxious or fearful tendencies; avoidant 301.82, dependent 301.60 (asthenic), obsessive compulsive 301.40 (anankastic), and passive-aggressive 301.84.

This clustering has little theoretical rationale. These diagnoses are all listed on axis II of DSM-III R which lists developmental and personality disorders. Diagnoses such as major depression, panic disorder, and schizophrenia constitute axis I.

One problem with both the ICD-9 and DSM-III R classifications is that they mix and muddle different conceptual frameworks. Some types of personality disorder are derived, in large part, from what were once conceived of as descriptions of the fundamental or prodromal disturbances from which more serious mental disorders arose. These little mental disorders include the schizoid personality disorder which may be a forme fruste of schizophrenia, the cycloid personality disorder which is an attenuated form of bipolar (manic depressive) disorder and obsessive compulsive (anankastic) personality disorder which verges upon obsessive compulsive disorder. Other personality disorders have their origin in the totally distinct theoretical framework in which disorders are conceived as being at the extreme ends of the normal variation. This model associated with psychometrics and clearly articulated within psychiatry by Schneider (1950) assumes that personality traits have a normal distribution (in a statistical sense) within the population and objective measures, or at the very least value-free judgements, can be applied to the recognition of significant deviations within that normal range. To some extent this model pervades all the currently described personality disorders, but is seen clearest in our use of such terms as dependent, avoidant and passive–aggressive.

Current classifications have their origins in personality typologies proposed by European theorists at the turn of the century (*see* Lewis, 1974; Millon, 1981), and to a lesser extent in the character types of psychodynamic theory. However, DSM-III R drew on the classification developed by Millon (1981), and on recent psychodynamic formulations of abnormal personality (Kernberg, 1975). Millon's scheme combines four patterns of self-other orientation (dependent, independent, ambivalent, detached) with approach or avoidance (active versus passive) to yield eight basic coping patterns. For example, histrionic and dependent disorders are held to be active and passive variants, respectively, of a dependent orientation.

Traits, Symptoms and Socially Deviant Behaviour

Everyday use of the term 'personality' implies that it is something a person has or is. This somewhat misleading connotation of a force or entity is seen in ICD-9 which refers to 'the personality'. However, in personality theories, 'personality' denotes nothing more specific than individual distinctiveness and differentiation. While theories emphasize different causal processes, they typically describe human variation in terms of stable dispositions or traits. Traits are also central to the DSM-III R concept of personality disorders, and are defined as 'enduring patterns of perceiving, relating to, and thinking about the environment and one's self'. They are said to constitute personality disorder when they are 'inflexible and maladaptive' and result in impaired social functioning or subjective distress.

Current nosology in this area pays little attention to the extent to which expressions of so-called personality vary in different social and interpersonal contexts. Most people have a range of interpersonal styles which they employ as appropriate in differing contexts. Clearly most of us present different aspects at work, on the sports field, attempting to redress a personal wrong, and at home with our family. In part, those we call personality disordered exhibit greater rigidity and less flexibility in their ways of experiencing and responding to differing social contexts. Thus a belligerence which can be functional in situations of social and sporting conflict, when it is evinced in interpersonal spheres where it is counterproductive for the individual, or damaging to others, may lead to the individual being labelled as having an antisocial personality disorder. Personality disorders are, in part, inflexible dispositions which become maladaptive by their use in inappropriate social contexts.

Foulds (1971) pointed out the logical distinction between personality traits and symptoms of illness. Traits refer to enduring attributes which vary universally, whereas symptoms are neither enduring nor universal. In fact, symptoms are signposts pointing to some underlying morbid condition. The traits of personality disorder represent departures from the norms of interpersonal behaviour, while symptoms of illness signal a breakdown of function and a departure from a person's own norms. Foulds argued that mental illness and personality disorder, therefore, entail different universes of discourse, and that a person may belong in either, neither or both. This position is adopted in DSM-III R, which requires the clinician to make diagnoses on both axis I (clinical syndromes) and axis II (personality disorders). Previous classifications have tended to encourage either/or diagnoses, resulting in estimates of the prevalence of personality disorders in psychiatric populations of between 5 and 17%. Studies using DSM-III R, however, indicate that between a third and a half of psychiatric samples meet the criteria for one or more personality disorders, while within antisocial or asocial populations the proportion is substantially higher.

Utility of Current Classifications

Categories of psychopathology have the status of scientific constructs, and serve a number of communicative and predictive purposes. The diagnosis of a particular personality disorder should indicate the salient traits which impair the patient's functioning, permit the formulation of explanations and clinical predictions regarding intervention and outcome, and provide a basis for research. The utility of classification is dependent on the reliability with which a person's behaviour can be assigned to a category, and the theoretical and predictive validity of the category concept.

Reliability of DSM Classifications

The reliability of clinical judgements of personality disorder is low. For example, field trials for the earlier DSM-III classification (American Psychiatric Association, 1980) revealed a mean inter-rater reliability of 0.56 (kappa coefficient; range 0.26 to 0.75). Mellsop et al. (1982) reported even lower figures (mean 0.41; range 0.00–0.49). This low level of agreement between clinicians on assignment of patients to categories seriously restricts the general utility of the classification.

There are several reasons for this lack of consistency. The criteria range from the readily observable to the highly inferential. Also, the clinician must make dichotomous judgements about traits, which are summary abstractions of behaviours varying in frequency and intensity. Moreover, state factors, such as depression, may obscure a patient's more typical characteristics through their influence on self-description or current behaviour.

Attempts to improve reliability have been made with varying degress of success, by using personality questionnaires, trait rating scales, or structured interviews. Widiger and Frances (1985) suggested that the trait criteria require redefinition in terms of specific behavioural indicators. They drew on cognitive research which has shown that the class concepts of both scientific and natural language are not typically applied on the basis of necessary and sufficient criteria, but rather through the identification of central and prototypical features shared by most, but not all, members of a category. For example, the ability to swim is a less prototypical defining attribute of the class 'bird' than is the possession of wings and feathers. Livesley (1986) has shown that the trait concepts of personality disorders can be identified more reliably by reference to specific acts which are prototypical for a particular trait. This represents the most promising development in improving reliability.

Validity of Classification

DSM-III R does not assume absolute homogeneity of class members in the traits they exhibit, and specifies polythetic criteria for all categories, i.e.

not all criteria need be present for class membership. It also recognizes overlap between categories, and recommends multiple diagnosis when a person meets criteria for more than one disorder. Nevertheless, to establish validity it needs to be shown that the criteria contribute to the identification of categories which are distinguishable from each other.

Evidence for the validity of specific categories is limited and on the whole weak (Blackburn, 1988a). The most well validated is the concept of obsessive-compulsive personality (Pollack, 1979), although neither the current obsessive-compulsive nor anankastic categories are precisely equivalent to this construct. There is modest support for the validity of hysterical, dependent, borderline, and schizoid disorders. However, it has been suggested that hysterical and antisocial disorders are sex-linked stereotypes of the same disorder (Warner, 1978). Moreover, several studies have indicated sufficient overlap between histrionic, narcissistic, antisocial and borderline disorders to question the need for distinct categories, while the passive-aggressive category may be redundant (Pfohl et al., 1986). It therefore seems unlikely that the categories currently specified represent the optimal clustering of inflexible and maladaptive dispositions.

Alternative Classifications

Current classifications continue to lack a firm basis in a consistent theoretical or empirical scheme. Moreover, while clinical concepts of personality disorder often assume quantitative rather than qualitative variations from normality, the use of categorical classification spuriously implies a discontinuity between disorders, and between disorder and normality. Several attempts have, therefore, been made to describe personality disorder in terms of dimensional classification.

One approach is to derive dimensions empirically through factor analysis of maladaptive traits, but studies sampling a wide variety of such traits have so far been few. Tyrer and Alexander (1979) describe an analysis of a number of ICD-9 traits, and identified three dimensions labelled sociopathy, passive dependence and dysthymia. Patterns of scores indicated four main clusters of patients, suggesting that for some purposes the ICD-9 categories of personality disorder could be reduced in number. The problem with this approach is that only a limited number of traits have so far been considered. For example sadism, a key trait in forensic psychiatry, is omitted.

The current categories may also be translated into established dimensional systems of personality description (Frances, 1982). Particularly relevant is the interpersonal circle, which relates interpersonal traits to two dimensions of dominance versus submission and hostility versus affection (Leary, 1957; Widiger and Frances, 1985). Combinations of these two yield differing interpersonal styles, more extreme or rigid styles representing personality disorder. This approach has the advantage of emphasizing that a central characteristic of personality disorder is an inability to sustain satisfactory social interactions.

There is currently a lack of evidence about which dimensional system is most appropriate for describing personality disorders, and Kendell (1975) has argued against the use of dimensional systems in psychiatric diagnosis on the grounds that clinicians typically think in terms of categories. However, it should be noted that typologies can be derived from dimensional systems, and the potential of a dimensional approach for clarifying the classification of personality disorders should not be overlooked.

The term 'personal functioning' refers to the traits involved in thinking, feeling and behaving which make up an individual's personality (Gunn, 1988). Each of these functions (e.g. mood, irritability, callousness, stubbornness, aggressiveness, self-esteem, suggestibility) could be measured on a reliable scale and assessed by clinical interview just as other elements of psychological functioning are assessed and measured in the routine mental state evaluation made by psychiatrists. In this way, the clinician would have both a categorical diagnosis and a personal function analysis available for evaluation and treatment, in the same way as he currently has both a diagnosis and a mental state analysis available in a fully assessed case.

Example

A man might be labelled in ICD-9 terms as suffering from asocial personality disorder. An evaluation of his personal functions at the time of initial contact will be more revealing.

Thinking
  A low self-esteem
  Believes people are generally against him
  Determined not to be dominated
  Manliness necessarily involves aggressiveness
  Heavy drinking is prestigious and improves potency
Feeling
  Constant severe anxiety
  Upsurges of super-added tension
  A constant sense of suspiciousness
  Frequent feelings of anger which may turn into uncontrollable rage
  Despair, hopelessness
Behaviour
  Periods of effective work punctuated by dismissal following arguments
  Periodic heavy drinking following arguments
  Intensive aggressiveness on occasions including homicidal attacks
  Resorts to fire as a weapon on occasions

Setting out a functional analysis in this way (which is given here in abbreviated form) gives a clearer picture of the therapeutic task and provides separate aspects of the patient, which can be tackled each in their own right, perhaps in several treatment approaches simultaneously (e.g. pharmocotherapy, dynamic psychotherapy, cognitive therapy). The analysis also gives a clue to criteria which might be used to assess progress. Simply discussing the analysis with the patient can be helpful; he begins to see himself in a different way and can join in a crude assessment process.

Development Processes

Simple notions of normal personality development have to be discarded (*see* Rutter, 1980; Hill, 1984). It is clear that experiences are not written on a blank sheet, so the developing child cannot simply be moulded by particular experiences of forms of learning. Equally there is no 'wired in' personality that simply unfolds irrespective of environmental influences. The development of personality is interactional in that the parent influences the child and the child influences the parent; furthermore influences impinge from the wider family, social and educational networks. For instance it is clear that infants and young children differ in their style of behaving and relating, and these differences have been characterized in terms of 'temperamental traits' such as emotionality, activity and sociability. Such temperamental traits might appear to be good candidates for biologically or genetically determined qualities, and it is likely that to a certain extent this is the case (Buss and Plomin, 1986). However, the temperamental characteristics of the infant influence the responses of caregivers. Lee and Bates (1985) found that at 2 years temperamental traits that might lead to a child being seen as difficult were associated with an increased likelihood of confrontations with the mother, and of the mother using intrusive control strategies with the child. Furthermore, there was some evidence of an association between temperamental traits at 6 months and subsequent parent-child interactions at 2 years. Evidence from Patterson's work (1982) with older children shows that similar parental responses, which he termed 'coercive', can prolong sequences of aggressive behaviour from children. This raises the question of the extent to which parental behaviour had already contributed to the origins of difficult 'temperament' in the 2 year olds studied by Lee and Bates.

The mechanisms involved in the interplay between the child's characteristics and parental behaviour are complex. They are likely to include a wide range of factors such as the parents' perception of the child, the level of previous success or failure in exerting control over the child, the overall level of organization within the family, and the extent to which there is marital discord or support. The way in which such processes may influence later outcome are illustrated in Thomas and Chess's case vignettes from their New York longitudinal study (1984) of 141 children from infancy to early adult life. One girl was 'difficult' as an infant in that she showed predominantly negative emotions and was not adaptable to changing situations. Her father was critical and punitive towards her, and at the age of 6 she had quite marked behaviour problems. The mother appeared to be intimidated by her husband and her daughter, and was anxious and vacillating in her handling of the child. Then it emerged that the girl had musical and dramatic talents, and the father started to see his daughter's difficult behaviour as evidence of her 'artistic temperament', and changed his attitude and behaviour towards her. By the age of 17 she was a lively well-adapted young lady. Here temperament, and interactions both between each parent and the child, and between the parents, played a part in the origins of the disorder, and apparently a change of perception of the child contributed to a good outcome.

Whilst the interaction of temperamental characteristics and parental behaviour is crucial to personality development, so is the development of relationships. The definition and characteristics of relationships are complex (Hinde, 1979) in that they involve what is done between individuals, how that is perceived by the partipants and what is internalized by each individual as an enduring image of the other. It is striking that the developing infant forms selective attachment relationships during the latter half of the first year, and there then follows a life-long immersion in and preoccupation with, relationships. Individual characteristics and relationship characteristics become indivisible so that, for instance, the same infant can show signs of secure attachment with one care-giver, and anxious attachment in relation to another (Main and Weston, 1981); in other words the behaviour is both the property of the individual and the relationship. The presence of a secure attachment relationship in the first two years of life is associated up to three years later with a range of personal and interpersonal qualities such as self-confidence, curiosity, and a combination of independence and a capacity to form close relationships with other children (Sroufe, 1986). This suggests that these early relationships may be important to satisfactory personality development. Whether the corollary applies and absence of such relationships is inevitably damaging is not clear. In general, new learning can take place throughout childhood and, for instance, intellectual deficits can be made up throughout childhood. However, some evidence suggests that even in the face of subsequent good caretaking, the experience of multiple caretakers (and, therefore, a lack of enduring attachment relationships) in the first years of life may have an effect on an individual's social development extending at least into adolescence (Hodges and Tizard, 1989).

It is important to note that a range of processes may mediate continuities between early experience and later development (Rutter, 1987). Sroufe (1986) and others have argued that it is the internal model of the attachment relationship gained at an early age by the child that is crucial to the individual's subsequent capacity to be an attachment figure. In support of this, a number of studies have demonstrated an association between the parent's internal model of relationships with his or her own parents (adult attachment representation), and the security of attachment of the infant to that parent (Main et al., 1985; Grossman et al., 1989; Fonagy et al., 1991).

It remains to be established what factors influence the development of such an internalized model and what determines the extent to which it is available to influence subsequent relationships, but there are Freudian and social learning theories of how 'identification' occurs (*see* Bandura, 1986). It seems plausible that one route linking childhood experiences and adult functioning is via such internalized models of relationships, or internal objects (Main et al., 1985). Child-adult links may, however, be mediated in other ways, for instance through continuity of environmental influences. Thus many children who face adversity in early childhood also face it later, and therefore enter adult life still facing obstacles which can lead to problems independently of their own strengths and weaknesses. Frequently, there is an interaction throughout childhood so that, for instance, parenting influences the security of attachment and this, in turn, influences the extent to which the child is a rewarding son or daughter to parents, playmate for peers, and pupil for teachers; this, in turn, is likely to influence whether the parents continue to be available for social development, and whether teachers continue to promote the child's education.

The Development of Personality Dysfunction

Some forms of adult personality dysfunction also seem to arise from a similar complex interplay of factors. This can be illustrated with reference to the follow-up studies of men and women who were in institutional care as children (Quinton et al., 1984; Rutter et al., 1990). The in-care children had a poorer outcome in terms of personality functioning than a control group brought up in families, but, within the in-care group, outcome was significantly worse for those who experienced early disruptions in the form of short-term admissions to fostercare, multiple separations through parental discord or disorder, persistent family discord or early admission into longtime care. Whilst such early experiences appeared to exert an influence on adult outcome, so did numerous later influences. In the case of the women, the interaction of individual factors and environment in adolescence was clear. Those who returned from care to discordant homes (and were, therefore, exposed to a continuity of environment) were more likely to leave home precipitously, marry a man with personality problems, and have an early unwanted pregnancy, thereby increasing their risk of later problems. There were, in addition, protective factors which operated in a similarly interactive fashion. Good outcome was associated with having had positive experiences at school, and this arose because those with good school experiences were more likely to show planning in their choice of spouse, and this, in turn, influenced whether or not they formed a stable supportive relationship with a non-deviant spouse. The presence of the latter was associated with a good outcome irrespective of early childhood experiences. Therefore, a lack of enduring attachment relationships in early childhood had an effect on personality functioning in adult life because it increased the likelihood of a non-supportive relationship with a deviant spouse; however, the presence of a stable relationship in adult life almost completely ameliorated the effects of childhood adversities. There was also evidence that genetic factors played a significant if modest role and that, particularly for boys, conduct disorder in childhood increased the likelihood of later disturbance, either through a straightforward continuity of individual disturbance, or by an interactive process of the form described earlier.

Whilst some forms of personality dysfunction are the outcome of such a complex interplay of individual (possibly constitutional) and environmental factors, there are other possibilities. For instance, it is possible that some forms of personality disorder could arise in a way analogous to that of autism in which a constitutional deficit is the overwhelming influence on outcome, and environmental factors are relatively insignificant (Rutter, 1985). A further possibility could be that a constitutional vulnerability means that the individual will develop personality problems in the face of very specific environmental factors. Currently, there is no evidence regarding these latter two possible mechanisms. However, anecdotal evidence might be found to support one or other of them in Cleckley's (highly selected) case histories of psychopathic patients, which as described are remarkably lacking in the childhood adversities so characteristic of the histories of individuals with juvenile delinquency and adult criminality in general (Cleckley, 1976).

From a developmental perspective, a concept of personality functioning that includes development in adult life is required. It is not appropriate to consider personality disorder as static, a state in which outcome has been reached. It was clear in the in-care studies that the presence of a stable confiding relationship in adult life made a difference to the outcome in terms of personality functioning. The outcome measures in Robin's (1966, 1979) follow-up study of children with psychiatric disorder provide evidence of the importance of examining development within adult life in an offender population. For instance, in the group with 'sociopathic' personality disorder, the rates of marital difficulties, divorce, and marriage to a deviant partner were very high. These problems can be seen as an outcome in that they provide evidence of personality difficulties at the time of the study, but also may constitute a risk factor for further development. Conversely, a substantial number of 'sociopaths' are recorded as not being married to a deviant spouse which, along lines described earlier, might constitute a protective factor in a study of subsequent outcome. The point concerning adversity is particularly striking when considering the effect of convictions and sentencing. In Robin's series (1966, 1979) 38% of 'sociopathic' subjects served prison sentences of 5 years, a level of 'intervention' that might well make an impact on development in adult life. That is to say it might increase the likelihood of further problems such as poor work or marital history which are features of sociopathic personality disorder. The general point to be made is that outcome in developmental terms is only a description of the functioning of an individual at a particular time; functioning that is likely to open or close avenues of future development. The concept of personality disorder, therefore, needs to be considered in this light.

Development of Criminality

The origins of juvenile delinquency and adult criminality are so central to forensic psychiatry that they are dealt with separately as Ch. 6.

Personality Disorders in Forensic Psychiatry

In spite of the general usefulness of a trait approach to personality dysfunction, psychiatry is, as Kendell (1975) indicated, wedded for the time being to a categorical or disease approach to personality disorder. We have already seen that the important classifications of disease list just over a dozen different types of personality disorder and yet the nosology is unsatisfactory; the categories overlap, and severely disabled individuals fit into several categories at the same time.

The reader is referred to textbooks of general psychiatry for the full range of personality disorders. The ones briefly outlined here have special relevance for forensic psychiatry. They serve to illustrate an approach to the problem of personality disorder and, in particular, its treatment and management. The selected topics are psychopathic personality, dyssocial personality disorder, impulsive personality disorder, narcissistic personality disorder, borderline personality disorder, sadistic personality and Asperger's syndrome. Multiple personality disorder is dealt with in Ch. 10. There is also a subsection on power and control in the section on sadistic personality (p. 392).

Psychopathic Disorder

We begin with a central topic which has lost its place in the official classifications. 'Psychopathic' means literally 'psychically damaged', and was introduced in 19th century Germany to cover all forms of psychopathology. It was later narrowed to refer to psychic anomalies which were not mental illnesses, and Schneider (1950) followed Kraepelin (1896) in describing a typology of psychopathic personalities. He explicitly excluded antisocial behaviour from the criteria for abnormal personality, which he construed in statistical terms as a deviation from average. Psychopathic personalities were those abnormal personalities who cause suffering to themselves or others. This is now the notion of personality disorders adopted in DSM-III R, and the classifications of ICD-8, ICD-9 and DSM-III originate in Schneider's typology of psychopathic personalities.

This classification was never widely adopted in Britain, where the influence of Prichard's notion of moral insanity (*see* Leigh, 1961) resulted in the statutory category of moral imbecile in the Mental Deficiency Act 1913, and eventually in the category of psychopathic disorder of the, English, Mental Health Act 1983:

> A disorder or disability of mind . . . which results in abnormally aggressive or seriously irresponsible conduct on the part of the person concerned.

Although the term 'psychopathic' is adopted from the German, there is no resemblance between this category and Schneider's concept. The definition, in fact, contains no reference to any concept of personality, the only defining features being the antisocial conduct from which a 'mental disability' is inferred.

A similar transformation of the term 'psychopathic' and its equation with 'antisocial' has occurred within American psychiatry, where it has been used interchangeably with 'sociopathic', a term denoting any form of socially deviant behaviour. To further complicate matters, psychopathy was specifically associated in the American literature and legislation with sexual deviance and offending. Karpman (1948) explicitly rejected Schneider's concept of psychopathic personalities and, indeed, the notion of personality disorders. He proposed that some of Schneider's categories were 'primary psychopaths', whose antisocial behaviour is related to uninhibited instinctual expression unmodified by conscience or guilt. The remainder he suggested were 'secondary psychopaths' whose antisocial behaviour results from dynamic disturbance, and who were more properly classified with the neuroses or psychoses. Cleckley (1976) took a similar view, seeing most categories of personality disorder as neurotic or psychotic disorders, but he proposed a 'distinct clinical entity' of psychopathic personality. He suggested sixteen criteria, including superficial charm, unreliability, lack of remorse, egocentricity, and interpersonal unresponsiveness, with antisocial behaviour being just one among the many criteria. Cleckley's concept has been influential in guiding research (Hare, 1986), and there is evidence that his criteria define a broad dimension of personality deviation. Although Cleckley's concept refers only to 'primary psychopaths', the concepts of 'primary' and 'secondary psychopath' have been adopted by some researchers to distinguish non-anxious from anxious deviant personalities in antisocial populations.

The term 'psychopathic personality', then, has been used in three ways. The first corresponds to the current concept of a broad class of personality disorders defined by reference to personality traits alone. The second identifies a class of abnormal individuals on the basis of social deviance. It is represented by the, English, MHA 1983 category of psychopathic disorder. The third is a hybrid referring to a specific category of social deviance, but defined by certain personality traits such as egocentricity. This last category is often equated with the antisocial category of DSM-III R, but it probably includes all those within the 'dramatic' cluster B of DSM-III R who are also antisocial. By emphasizing socially deviant behaviour, more recent conceptions of psychopathic personality have retarded understanding of personality disorders, and the concept appears to have outlived its usefulness.

During the course of this century, reams have been written under the broad heading of psychopathic disorder, yet without much enlightenment. Lewis (1974) called it 'a most elusive category', 'a life-long propensity to behaviour which falls mid-way between normality and psychosis'. After a thorough review of the literature Lewis concluded:

> The whole matter is somewhat gloomy . . . psychopathic personality . . . will not be firm until much more is known about its genetics, psychopathology and neuropathology.

Succeeding years have revealed no such knowledge. This may be because we are only at a rudimentary stage of scientific endeavour in understanding human personality. It may be because the elusive category just cannot be captured because it does not, in fact, have any real meaning. In 1974 Shepherd and Sartorius opined that 'some working concept of psychopathic personality is essential for the practice of clinical psychiatry'. Yet some workers (e.g. Lewis and Balla, 1975) argue for the term not to be used as it 'hinders the search for other symptomatology'. The Butler Committee (Home Office, Department of Health and Social Security, 1975) recommended that the term be abandoned. A brief review (Gunn and Robertson, 1976b) suggested that there are five agreed facts about the term psychopathic disorder:

1. it is unreliable;
2. authors disagree about its definition;
3. it is used in the vernacular as a term of derogation;
4. it has a legal use in England and Wales;
5. many doctors use the term to indicate that a patient is incurable or untreatable.

In a study of prisoners all labelled psychopathic, sent to Grendon prison, it was found that inter-rater reliability of the traits which people use to describe psychopaths was difficult to obtain and no general factor emerged; indeed the differences between the Grendon men were more impressive than the similarities. They all had some anxiety and depression, and there was a correlation between anxiety and a history of disturbed interpersonal relationships.

A conceptual review (Blackburn, 1988b) has concluded:

> The current concept of psychopathic or antisocial personality remains a mythical entity. The taxonomic error of confounding different universes of discourse has resulted in a diagnostic category that embraces a wide variety of deviant personalities. Such a category is not a meaningful focus for theory and research, nor can it facilitate clinical communication and prediction. Indeed a disorder defined by past

history of socially deviant behaviour is permanently fixed, and cannot provide a point of reference for clinical intervention. Such a concept is little more than a moral judgment masquerading as a clinical diagnosis.

The best that can be said for 'the elusive category' is that it is a ragbag containing a wide range of behavioural problems which tend to produce negative emotions and reactions in other people. It is essentially a social concept (which may account for many people switching to the term 'sociopath'), yet frequently it indicates a group of people with pathology, sometimes serious pathology, patients needing medical attention. The task for psychiatry is to identify the pathology more clearly and perhaps concentrate on the management/treatment of particularly troublesome traits, like aggressiveness or self-centredness. Provided this is done, psychiatry can get along quite effectively without the terms 'sociopath' or 'psychopath'.

What follows is a selection of disorders/diseases which have largely replaced psychopathic disorder as a clinical concept.

Dyssocial Personality Disorder

ICD-10 (World Health Organisation, 1992) introduced a new term 'dyssocial personality'. This disease is probably the closest that modern terminology comes to the old concept of psychopathic disorder. It is defined in terms of a gross disparity between the individual's behaviour and the prevailing social norms. It is characterized by:

1. callous unconcern for the feelings of others and a lack of capacity for empathy;
2. gross and persistent attitudes of irresponsibility;
3. an incapacity to maintain enduring relationships;
4. a very low tolerance to frustration and a low threshold for discharge of aggression;
5. an incapacity to experience guilt and to profit from experience;
6. a marked proneness to blame others; and
7. persistent irritability.

This disorder like all personality disorders overlaps and intermingles with others on the list. It has similarities to antisocial personality disorder of DSM-III R.

Impulsive Personality Disorder

ICD-10 also included a closely related impulsive personality disorder. It is characterized by:

1. a tendency to act unexpectedly and without consideration of the consequences;
2. a conspicious inability to plan ahead;
3. an unpredictable capricious mood;
4. a liability to outbursts of anger or violence;
5. an incapacity to control behavioural explosions;
6. a tendency to quarrelsome behaviour; and
7. difficulty in maintaining any course of action that offers no immediate reward.

Narcissistic Personality Disorder

Narcissistic personality disorder is a recognized disease in the USA, but not apparently in the rest of the world, as it is omitted from the International Classification. To fulfil the DSM-III R criteria the patient should be described in at least five of the following ways:

1. reacts to criticism with feelings of rage, shame, or humiliation;
2. is interpersonally exploitative;
3. has a grandiose sense of self-importance;
4. believes that his problems are unique;
5. is preoccupied with fantasies of unlimited success, power, brilliance, beauty, or ideal love;
6. has a sense of entitlement;
7. requires constant attention and admiration;
8. has lack of empathy; and
9. is preoccupied with feelings of envy.

It should be noted how subjective and inherently difficult it is to measure these features, even though clinical experience suggests that they are central to the problems of many offender patients. Adler (1986) talks of 'a spectrum of narcissistic disorders', between a borderline personality organization in which the patient has a need for self-sufficiency and does not wish to acknowledge the existence of others, because he cannot tolerate his envy of others, and the narcissistic person who needs a 'self-object' to regulate his self-esteem, a bit like a child's need for a parent.

As with other types of personality disorder, not only do the phenomena need refining, but the aetiology, the epidemiology and the prognosis of the disorder needs to be delineated, tasks yet to be fulfilled.

Borderline Personality Disorder (BPD)

Psychiatry is subject to the vagaries of fashion; borderline personality disorder is gaining ground. In 1938, Stern described patients who become very angry and disturbed during the course of psychoanalysis. He said they had a 'negative therapeutic reaction' and formed a 'borderline group of neuroses'. Since that time the term has never looked back, finally reaching the accolade of a place in DSM. DSM-III R gives the diagnostic criteria for BPD as at least five of the following eight symptoms:

1. a pattern of unstable and intense interpersonal relationships, alternating between over idealization and devaluation;
2. impulsiveness;
3. affective instability;
4. inappropriate intense anger or lack of control of anger;
5. recurrent suicidal or self-mutilating behaviour;
6. uncertainty of identity such as self-image, gender, long-term goals, values and loyalties, e.g. 'whom am I?';
7. chronic feelings of emptiness or boredom; and
8. frantic efforts to avoid real or imagined abandonment.

The overlap between this disorder and narcissistic personality disorder is self-evident. There has been considerable debate about the usefulness of the concept, although a recent review claimed it to have established itself as a psychiatric diagnosis (Tarnopolsky and Berelowitz, 1987). What then is it borderline between? Why will other labels not suffice? Is there any reliability between users of the term? Kernberg (1975) for example defines it as:

> An absence of a stable sense of identity with a use of the primitive defence mechanisms of splitting and projective identification, but with partial retention of reality testing.

This suggests that the condition is borderline between psychosis and neurosis, a view not taken by other workers.

Andrulonis et al. (1982), using DSM-III R criteria, examined the aetiology of the condition. They suggested that there are three distinct subcategories of BPD: those with no organic history, those with a history of cerebral trauma, and those with learning disabilities. They showed the first group to have transitory and periodic minipsychotic episodes with a tendency towards both recurrence and recovery. The other two groups showed aggressive and hyperactive behaviour and were recommended for cognitive therapy, special education and vocational training. They concluded:

> Clinicians and researchers need to cross-fertilize their eclectic view and treatment of borderline patients with knowledge from the psychoanalytic, developmental, and neuropsychiatric literature.

Gallwey (1985) disagreed with attempts to make borderline personality disorder a separate diagnosis. He said:

> It is puzzling why so many authors appear to feel there must be single condition to which this term properly refers . . . historically the term has often been linked to . . . latent schizophrenia or pseudo-neurotic schizophrenia. . . . It is odd that a professional group who would not dream of using, say, 'bisexuality' as a diagnostic

category, should have engaged in a determined endeavour to make an entity out of a perfectly respectable and useful general descriptive label.

Gallwey explained that the term 'borderline' in psychoanalysis has become bound up with the concept of narcissism, both terms meaning that some aspect of a patient is felt to have a link with the psychopathology of psychosis. He believed there are two kinds of patient worthy of the label 'borderline personality disorder'. Both of them are liable to episodes of psychosis and/or pathological aggression. Type A is a schizoid type who has the better immediate prognosis, but tends to relapse unexpectedly. Such patterns are difficult to treat supportively, although they seem easier because of a capacity to revive well-functioning areas of their personality. Because of early mother deprivation, they have a deformed sense of indentity with disturbance in body image and feelings of depersonalization, plus escalating anxiety and loss of impulse control with clinging, ambivalent jealousy and a profound sense of loss and unworthiness accompanied by a deep sense of having been cheated. Type B patients are ego deficient and seem more difficult because of their dependency needs, but their disturbance is more available for psychotherapy. Some of these patients become offenders, but others do not; the offenders deal with their ego-dystonic impulses by carrying out some catastrophic antisocial behaviour, the non-offenders develop para- noid psychoses. In each type, the resultant crimes tend to be the presenting features, although they may present with no overt abnormalities at the time of interview and very little explanation for what happened. Gallwey dis- tinguished the psychotic ones from schizophrenia because they have no personality deterioration between episodes.

Sadistic Personality

Working in the Scottish State Hospital (Carstairs), Brittain (1970) described what he called the 'syndrome' of the 'sadistic murderer'. This was a useful and novel description at that time. For Brittain the sadistic murderer was male, introspective, withdrawn, solitary, obsessional, tidy, well-dressed, and very clean. Such a person, said Brittain, may compensate for feelings of inferiority and even obtain feelings of superiority from the planning and contemplation of his killings, so that others instead of being superior become inferior creatures, without rights, to be used for personal gratification. He may be prim and proper, even prudish, condemning sexual conversation. He is also vain, narcissistic (in the non-technical sense), egocentric and hypochondriacal. His fantasy life is rich in violence, atrocities, and cruelty. He is unmoved to compassion or pity by the suffering of others. Sexually he may be unsuccessful or even impotent, usually unmarried and without girlfriends. He may also be religiose, even sanctimonious. There may be brief psychotic episodes.

The work records of such men may be poor. . . . A surprising number have worked as butchers. . . . Not infrequently there is an inordinate interest in weapons, guns, knives, etc. . . . he may 'love' them. . . . He has strong feelings about them and he can even have 'pet' names for these.

Other characteristics described by Brittain included a strong ambivalent relationship to the mother, an authoritarian, punitive father, and a close attachment to a grandparent. They may be cruel to animals except to one owned by the sadist himself, which may be the object of tenderness. A common fantasy involves Nazism, including antisemitism, Nazi uniforms and medallions; another is black magic. The murder itself, believed, Brittain, is usually planned in advance. At the time of the crime, the sadist gets excited and is transformed from his usual shy, timid self. The sight of suffering excites him especially, and the death itself may be an anticlimax; this may partly explain the common use of ligatures in such killings. The desire to have power over others is an essential part of the abnormality. Sexual intercourse and/or orgasm does not always occur, but sometimes the murderer masturbates beside his victims, sometimes he uses a phallus-substitute, such as a piece of wood which is rammed into the vagina or rectum with great force.

This classical description has been quoted at some length because it has largely stood the test of time, yet ICD-9 makes no mention of it. DSM-III R includes it, but only as a possible category for future editions in the appendix which lists categories 'needing further study'. It certainly requires that. Perhaps the limited study and limited professional interest is related to rarity. However, there is a considerable public interest in such individuals as evidenced by the biographies of such people that are published, e.g. *The Shoemaker* (Schreiber, 1984), *The St Albans Poisoner* (Holden, 1974), *Killing for Company* (Masters, 1985), *Brady and Hindley* (Harrison, 1987).

The DSM-III R provisional definition is of a pervasive pattern of cruel, demeaning and aggressive behaviour directed toward other people, beginning by early adulthood. The definition allows for the inclusion of some indviduals who are never actually physically violent. Further, it is noted that the behaviour is usually egosyntonic and the person rarely comes to attention except via other complaints or by legal process. The manual notes that the disorder should be distinguished from sexual sadism in which an individual engages in sadistic behaviour for the purpose of sexual arousal. Sometimes both diagnoses are appropriate.

These descriptions all acknowledge the problem of drawing boundaries between one category and another. The sadistic personality may well experience episodes of psychosis, indeed some are reported to go on to chronic psychoses, which implies that, although sadistic personality disorder may be egosyntonic, it may also reflect serious ego weaknesses which collapse under the pressures of stress and time. Sadistic personality traits also include obsessional and narcissistic traits. This observation can lead to a way of understanding some of the troublesome personality disorders which confront forensic psychiatry.

Power and control

Man is a social animal. Any social system depends upon order and structure; the currency of order is power in various forms with its corollary of submission. Individuals further up the hierarchy have more power. Those with more power have more control. Competition for power and status is an essential element in social systems (Leary, 1957). Powerlessness, and feelings of powerlessness are conditions to be avoided, yet they are common. Individuals and groups in such a situation will cope with this problem in a variety of ways. Some will compete more or less successfully and adjust to the niche they find, others will react in less successful ways. For example, violence is often a response to feelings of powerlessness and yet it is frequently unsuccessful (for an elaboration of this point *see* Gunn, 1991d).

In such a system, it is hardly surprising that traits concerned with control develop in human beings and colour their lifestyles. Fromm (1974) developed a theory of aggression in terms of mechanisms concerned with control. The theory provides a model of some personality disorders which are placed on a spectrum of control, or perhaps more graphically a spectrum of despair relating to control.

At one end of this theoretical spectrum lies *obsessive-compulsive personality disorder*. Individuals suffering from this disease are described as people constantly striving for perfection with an adherence to their own overly strict and often unattainable standards. Preoccupation with rules, efficiency, trivia, and procedures interfere with the ability to take a broad view of things. People with the disease are always mindful of their relative status in dominance-submission terms. Although they resist the authority of others, they stubbornly and unreasonably insist that people conform to their way of doing things. Decision making is avoided, postponed or protracted, perhaps because of an inordinate fear of making a mistake. Such people are excessively conscientious, moralistic, scrupulous and judgmental; they are also stingy with their emotions and possessions. They have an unusually strong need to be in control and when they are unable to control others, they often become angry (DSM-III R). Freud (1908) described this type of personality as 'anal'; such a person feels safe if he hoards, if he controls his dirt, if he is orderly, punctual, clean.

What we call here Fromm's control hypothesis suggests that the obsessional personality (anal character), the sadistic personality and the 'necrophilous' personality lie on a continuum of increasing severity, the severity being determined by (1) an increasing desperation to control the environment, and (2) an increasing degree of narcissism or self-concern. The weakness of this hypothesis is, of course, that two variables must be able to vary independently, thus producing a cruciate distribution instead of a linear one, but if the variables, although independent to some extent, are in fact significantly correlated, then the linear model can be approached.

The hypothesis introduces a new concept by Fromm the *necrophilous personality*. Fromm described the basic element of *non-sexual necrophilia* as, the desire to handle, to be near to, and to gaze at corpses, and particularly the desire to dismember them. But he meant much more than that and elaborated it to mean:

> A passionate attraction to all that is dead, decayed, putrid, sickly; it is the passion to transform that which is alive into something unalive; to destroy for the sake of destruction; the exclusive interest in all that is purely mechanical. It is the passion to tear apart living structures.

According to Fromm, the necrophilous character dreams of death and putrefaction, of faeces, of dismembered limbs, of skeletons, of tombs, of dirt. He described the myth of Midas as necrophilous, as it transforms everything alive into things dead (symbolically dirt or faeces). At a milder level, the necrophilous person may have a marked interest in disease, in obituaries, and in attending funerals; such a person may also be a kill-joy with a predilection for dark colours. Another aspect may be the substitution of mechanical devices for living things, a delight in machinery that knocks things down, blows things up, and generally replaces living things with inanimate things.

The Fromm hypothesis is that this necrophilous character is a malignant form of the anal character. The continuum of severity is anal character → sadistic character → necrophilous character. In simple terms, the obsessional personality disorder is one in which attempts are made to control the threatening external world by imposing one's own order and routine. If this fails, then stronger measures are required which incorporate aggression and violence. The obsessional state is narcissistic and, as anxiety about the external world and narcissism increases, so less and less regard is paid to the needs of others and the controlling processes get more aggressive; indeed, the narcissism can induce personal satisfaction and pleasure in the aggressive means of control. At this point, we have reached sadistic personality disorder. If this fails also, then the penultimate form of self-centred control is aggression which destroys, converts life to death, other people's order to chaos, the necrophilous personality response. The ultimate form of control is total destruction, including destruction of the self and its works.

The point of Fromm's hypothesis is that it gave him a way of understanding and describing the personalities of the Nazi leaders, especially Hitler. Whether he achieved this is open to debate for there are gaps in the historical record about Hitler himself, but in one version of events, he was preoccupied with death and destruction, and the manufacture of systems of genocide. He took delight in watching a film of his enemies squirm as they hung on piano wire, and allowed the ultimate carnage of Germany. Perhaps a better example is Denis Nilsen, convicted in England on 4 November 1983 of six murders. He lured a number of men to his house for the pleasure of killing, of sexual encounter, and of possession of a body. He had the privilege of a first-rate biography, written by Masters (1985), called *Killing for Company*. He fitted the DSM-III R criteria for sadistic personality, but that diagnosis does not go far enough to evoke the special qualities of this man, who seemed preoccupied with death itself and liked to have corpses around him (hence the title of the biography).

For forensic psychiatry the hypothesis, although speculative, is useful at the level of describing and understanding a small, but significant, group of people more completely. It also emphasizes the importance of two character traits: narcissism and obsessionality. It further emphasizes the centrality of power and control in any understanding of human nature and human social systems. What it fails to explore is the relationship between these phenomena and the breakdown of ego boundaries, which seems to occur in a significant proportion of cases. For further speculation it may be worth noting that obsessional (anal) characteristics are also central characteristics in schizophrenia, which also may produce sadistic and/or destructive violence in a few afflicted individuals.

The theory could be elaborated further by considering other factors. For example, it has been suggested that control is orthogonal to hostility as a character trait (Leary, 1957). If so, those individuals who control with hostility (the Fromm sadists) may differ from those who control with affection.

Asperger's Syndrome

The work of Hans Asperger, an Austrian paediatrician, was introduced to English readers by Van Krevelen (1971), nearly 30 years after the original work (Asperger, 1944). His syndrome of 'austistic psychopathy of childhood' was a persistent impairment of social adaptation usually associated with a lack of interpersonal empathy, solitariness and the pursuit of idiosyncratic goals. The patients showed abnormalities of gaze, poverty of expression and gesture, and had unusual voice production. Asperger noted the original and often inventive creativity of the more intelligent, in contrast to the unproductive activity of the less able. The patients evinced marked personal sensitivity, egocentrism, callousness and even sadism. In adult life, they often failed to develop an interest in sex. All of his patients were male, but he suggested that in girls the condition may not become apparent until after puberty.

The profound inability of such patients to perceive the feelings of others, or to accurately interpret non-verbal behaviour is striking. Their speech and cognition may be centred on one particular topic, such as astronomy or chemistry, and they will frequently speak at length on the favourite subject, quite unaware of the reaction of the listener. Gait and posture are frequently clumsy, manneristic and ill coordinated.

The syndrome is not referred to eponymously in the major classifications. ICD-9 has childhood autism and schizoid personality disorder, but the latter does not really do justice to Asperger's description. DSM-III R includes both schizoid personality disorder and, on Axis I, autistic disorder as a pervasive development disorder, the diagnosis depending on a complex combination of symptoms from three groups, the first dealing with impairment in social interactions, the second with communication (verbal and non-verbal) and the third with activities and interests. A good introduction to the strange combinations of skills and deficits which may be found in the sufferer is given by the film *The Rainman*.

In her review of the syndrome, Wing (1981) noted certain additional features including a lack of the normal interest and pleasure in human company from an early stage with a decrease in the babble, gesture, movement and smiles that the normal baby shows. Also, imaginative pretend play does not occur at all in some of those with the syndrome, and in the few that do have pretend play, it is rigidly confined to one or two particular topics. Wing disagreed with two of Asperger's observations. Asperger said that speech develops before walking, and described 'an especially intimate relationship with language', whereas in Wing's series nearly half walked at the usual age, but were slow to talk. Speech delay, and impoverished speech content, and idiosyncratic or highly selective use of terms was noted. Obscure, long words might be known, but not those of everyday use. Wing also disputed the finding of originality and creativity in a chosen field. She suggests instead that the thought processes are confined to a 'narrow, pedantic, literal, but logical chain of reasoning'. The special abilities involved mainly memory, while comprehension of real meaning is often poor. She noted a conspicuous lack of common sense of patients in her series.

It may be that infantile autism and Asperger's Syndrome are on the same continuum of pathology. One study (Burgoine and Wing, 1983) of identical triplets with Asperger's Syndrome found overall similarity between the three 17-year-old boys, but the authors noted a relationship between the amount of peri- and postnatal trauma, the degree of intellectual impairment and the number of autistic features. Greater birth trauma yielded low intellect and more of the autistic features.

Asperger's cases in a number of instances displayed considerable violence and aggression. Fritz for example always played alone and, if other children irritated him, he would hit out at them with anything to hand including (on one occasion) a hammer. Fritz was noted for 'utterly calculated' maliciousness towards other children. Asperger noted another case to be obsessed with poisons. He had a most extensive knowledge in this subject, possessed a large collection of poisons and had stolen cyanide from his school. Asperger also commented on the calculated acts of malice, especially within the family. Some children had sadistic traits. One 7-year-old boy remarked: 'Mummy, I shall take a knife one day and push it into your heart, then blood will spurt out and this will cause a great stir.' Once, when the mother cut herself he said: 'Why isn't there more blood? Blood should run.'

Wolff (1984a), who has urged more study of perpetrators of apparently motiveless or oddly motivated, callous crimes, noted frequent irrational violence in a number of 'schizoid children' (Wolff 1984b). One child stabbed other boys in a school bus with a compass; another became violent in a crowded outpatients clinic, another boy eventually went to the State Hospital, Carstairs, because of violence. A case has also been described from the English special hospitals in which the patient's dangerousness was thought to be related to Asperger's Syndrome (Mawson et al., 1985). Before his admission to a special hospital at the age of 30, he had had much contact with psychiatric services, usually following impulsive acts of violence on children whose high pitch crying irritated him, or following acts of violence towards women, whom he had either envied or had been aroused by. Psychological assessment at the time of his 17th birthday found him to have a verbal IQ of 133. It was reported that:

> His strength lies in tracing new relationships in given data, especially in organic chemistry. . . . His thinking tends to be schizoid, but he appears to have the outlook of a research worker in pure science.

Treatment and Management

Schizophrenia is a good model for the therapist to keep in mind when he is treating the conditions more commonly referred to as personality disorders. It may seem paradoxical to consider schizophrenia when considering the treatment of personality disorder; yet few afflictions of mankind are as destructive of the personality as schizophrenia, indeed the International Classification of Diseases (ICD-9) starts off by defining schizophrenia as a disorder of personality. Despite this, schizophrenia is not termed a personality disorder, the effects of personality are often either ignored, seen as independent of the schizophrenia or, worse still, in some ways seen as casting doubt on the diagnosis of schizophrenia itself.

The principles of good general psychiatry which apply to the management of schizophrenia also apply to the management of personality disorder. Such management involves not only the control of symptoms and high arousal with medication, but also helping the patient relate to his environment, helping the family relate to the patient in an accommodating and non-provocative manner, occupational training and therapy, supportive and, on occasions, more dynamic psychotherapy, behavioural treatments, especially cognitive and interpersonal treatments, and so on. This is also the model appropriate in the field of personality disorder.

The analogy with schizophrenia points to a special complication. In current jargon, schizophrenia is an 'illness', personality disorder is not. The mental health acts of Britain reinforce these clinical ideas with a legal structure, arrangements being different for the mentally ill as opposed to the psychopathically disordered. As noted in Ch. 2, these distinctions are difficult to make and most people tend to fall back on lists; if the disorder is on one list, it is an illness, if it is on the other, it is a personality disorder. In spite of its ICD-9 definition schizophrenia is an illness. What is Asperger's Syndrome? It is classified on axis I as an illness in DSM-III R, but it is clearly, like schizophrenia, a severe disorder of personality. Is it also an illness for the purposes of the British mental health acts? Such interesting judgements are left to individual clinicians.

Treatability is in England a crucial issue as far as the personality disordered patient is concerned. The MHA 1983 says that compulsory treatment can only be given to the psychopathically disordered if 'such treatment is likely to alleviate or prevent a deterioration of his condition'. At first sight a not unreasonable criterion, but then it will be noticed that such a barrier is not placed in the way of the 'mentally ill' or those suffering from severe mental impairment. Such blatant legal discrimination between categories of patients is unusual, but it is heuristic. It illustrates what the stigmatized patient is up against and, in practice, very few such patients get into hospital under compulsory arrangements unless they are sent there by courts or unless they are temporarily redesignated at 'ill', e.g. after a suicide attempt.

A recent 23-year follow-up of mentally disordered offenders (Robertson, 1987) has shown that for the group as a whole, they have a very high risk of 'unnatural death', i.e. death from accidents, suicide, or homicide. At the age of 40 years, when violent death accounts for about 12% of deaths in the general population, it accounts for 50% of deaths among the mentally disordered, suicide for example is five times more common than in the general population for the third decade of life. The point of considerable interest here is that these trends occur across all diagnostic groups, the personality disordered were just as vulnerable to premature death as those with schizophrenia, affective disorder, and mental handicap. This information is unlikely to impress those who wish to define and reject the personality disordered patient as 'not ill' or not suffering from 'formal mental illness' (*see* p. 7) but it should impress the thoughtful psychiatrist.

How then should we deal with the treatability criterion? Quite simply on clinical grounds after as thorough an assessment as possible. Treatability is not synonymous with curability. If a patient has renal failure, the only effective treatment available may be renal dialysis—this has to be done frequently and will not cure him. Such treatment keeps the patient alive and ameliorates his distress. For the personality disordered patient, his life line may be weekly support, a group, or even inpatient care. The fact that he may relapse when the treatment is stopped is not a reason for not providing it. For a patient to be deemed 'untreatable', he would need to be so resistant to treatment as to be unaffected by nursing, or support, or counselling, so unaffected as to make these techniques completely irrelevant to his management; a rare case (*see also Dillon* and pp. 401–4).

The assessment should be more concerned with symptoms and traits than with diagnostic categories. The features of interest can be listed under five headings:

1. Feelings and emotions
2. Thinking
3. Behaviour
4. Social Functions
5. Insight

These each have to be considered in the context of the patient's life history. This approach is, therefore, the traditional psychiatric approach, but here special attention should be paid to duration of symptoms and witnesses' accounts (particularly of behavioural problems). An effort should be made to list the abnormalities or dysfunctions in order of significance. In addition, and this is rather important, an effort should be made to list strengths as well as weaknesses.

Assessment may take 3 to 4 hours in separated interviews. At the end, it is worth summarizing the problem for the patient. This is a precursor to establishing an understanding about aims and goals. It also helps to test insight and motivation. The patient with no motivation or wildly unrealistic aims presents different problems to the one who has modest expectations and is eager to try things out. In the latter case, the initial phase of treatment will be concerned with bridging the gap of understanding.

Insight is included on the list for all patients, whether the observer decides to call them psychotic or not. David (1990) suggested that there are three components to insight: the recognition that one has a mental illness, compliance with treatment, and the ability to relabel unusual mental events as pathological. All these elements should be considered in any patient. There is a further more subtle test which is equally useful and that is the ability to integrate thoughts, feelings and actions. It relates to 'compliance', but is slightly different. A patient may say that he is, for example, quite calm, but show in behaviour that he is not. He may say that he has stopped excessive drinking, when he is consuming many pints each day. If these tests of insight are applied to all patients, it will quickly be seen that some 'non-psychotic' patients have, in fact, very poor insight. The level of insight in any patient, whatever label is given, should help to determine the type of treatment to be offered and the degree of paternalism with which it is offered (*see also* pp. 11–13). It is in these terms that a personality disordered patient may become eligible for compulsory care.

A variety of techniques of treatment is available including both psycho-therapy and pharmacotherapy. Psychotherapy here is taken to include behavioural treatments. Specialist advice from psychologists, and dynamic psychotherapists may be appropriate once specific problems have been identified and the global 'personality disorder' with its pejorative overtones is less prominent. Pharmacotherapy using major and minor tranquillizers, antidepressants, night sedation, mood stablizers, libido suppressants and the like should be considered on a symptomatic basis. Indeed, it is important to note that atypical mood disorder may present as so-called personality disorder.

The strengths mentioned above are of particular importance. Stigma is reinforcing; once a patient is labelled a 'psychopath', he and everyone else knows this means he is a hopeless case and universally disliked. Focusing on strengths is a first step towards an improvement of self-esteem; it also allows other practical adjunctive decisions. The patient may show artistic aptitude or evidence of manual skills. With help from an occupational therapist, a skills-building programme can be developed. The patient may have one warm, close personal attachment, perhaps to his mother. This can form the focus of discussion for simple goal setting. Strengths such as charm and intelligence should not be redefined as problems simply because they are not associated with a full house of other desirable traits. Strengths in the patient are also important for the therapist. One reason for the constant rejection of such patients is the feeling of impotence they engender in medical and paramedical staff. Reinforcement of strengths dilutes this negative aspect. A further way of coping with this negativity is to ensure that the goals set are limited in extent and time, and are reviewed regularly. Most important of all, for very difficult cases, is the avoidance of professional isolation: ensure that several disciplines work with such a patient and meet regularly.

One technique that should be readily available, but is now in very short supply is inpatient admission. The criteria for admission of the personality disordered are the same as for all other patients, in spite of the legal treatability criterion. They include emergency admission to avert a crisis (such as suicidal or homicidal episodes), planned admission to prevent social deterioration, to relieve domestic pressures, to stabilize medication, for fuller observation and assessment, and to begin difficult psychotherapy. Centres, like the Henderson Hospital, have a special therapeutic milieu which may be suitable for a particular patient (Norton, 1992).

Long-term treatment as an inpatient is rapidly becoming unavailable for any patient whatever the diagnosis. This is a pity, because some of these patients do require lengthy periods of support, training, nursing, mood normalization and psychotherapy in a protected environment. Changes in such people are slow unless they are pushed out of hospital, when they may deteriorate rapidly and become a nuisance or even dangerous.

Compulsory treatment for the personality disordered is a vexed question, vexed because of the attitudes previously referred to, and vexed because of the interpretation of the treatability clause in the MHA 1983, but vexed, above all, because of the declining provision of inpatient resources. Very few such patients are treated compulsorily in ordinary hospitals. District general hospitals have heavy pressures on beds and do not have the relaxed environments which are required. Older mental hospitals have low staff-patient ratios and no security, so unless the patient is very damaged, or dull, he can walk away when he wishes. Medium secure beds in the NHS are in very short supply and only take a few such patients, usually for relatively short periods. Special hospitals have a few compulsory and long-term patients admitted by courts under the category of 'psychopathic disorder', but in national terms this does not make much impact on the problem. The truth is that unpopular people, some of whom have done terrible things (e.g. rape, torture, murder) are not likely to get many health resources when such resources are in short supply. The few patients who are admitted to special hospitals are, therefore, of particular importance for they serve to emphasize that there is an alternative to abandoning such people, and that the skills for their treatment still exist.

It might be helpful to list some of the techniques which are particularly useful in the treatment of the personality disordered patient who breaks the law.

Support

Support is a difficult, time-consuming, irksome art. It is not necessarily best given by a doctor, but all forensic psychiatrists need to be skilled in it. It involves being able to accept unpleasant demanding individuals (without accepting their unpleasant behaviour), having patience in the face of provocative behaviour, availability, and commitment to a long period of treatment, often lasting years. Such support is best given by a long-term member of a clinical team, so that relationships are not being continually broken. The consultant is often in the best position to provide such support, and it may well be an economic use of his time to do so because relapses are less likely.

Directive Psychotherapy

The usual emphasis in psychotherapy is on non-directive techniques, allowing the patient to air his thoughts, and receive interpretations, but eschewing direct advice. Some personality disordered patients show characteristics which are labelled as 'immature', at least they would gain a low score in Interpersonal Maturity assessment systems used in the California Treatment Project for delinquents (Warren 1969). In that study, it was suggested that people with such scores respond best to therapists who are directive (Palmer 1973).

Group Psychotherapy

Group psychotherapy has a traditional place in the management of the personality disordered with antisocial features. Certainly it has been used effectively at Grendon prison and at the Henderson Hospital. A prison study produced some evidence that it is more effective than individual treatment amongst recidivist prisoners (Gunn et al., 1978).

Crisis Intervention

Crisis intervention is a corollary of support. For it to be fully effective, there has to be close attention to the details of each patient's life so that crises can be averted rather than dealt with after the event. Ideally, a clinical team should be prepared to carry out domiciliary visits at short notice, and to spend time dealing with employers, social security officers, and other key figures in the patient's life. It may be particularly important to admit a patient to hospital as an emergency. For an elaboration of these points *see* Gunn (1983).

Hospital or Prison

A subsidiary, but important, issue in British forensic psychiatry is the court decision to send a convicted 'psychopath' to prison or to a hospital. In practice, most personality disordered people who commit serious offences end up in prison and receive no treatment. In Britain, a few get to Grendon prison, and a few are transferred to the hospital system (usually a special hospital) during the course of their sentence. Yet in Britain, it is perfectly possible for a court to send any offender with psychopathic disorder to hospital provided the hospital is willing to have him and provided two medical recommendations are made to that effect. Why then are only a few actually sent? There are several reasons: first there is a shortage of hospital places; next there is a fairly widespread belief among psychiatrists, especially those who are not forensic psychiatrists, that so-called 'psychopaths' are 'untreatable'; finally, there is the view that it is unfair to 'psychopaths' to 'sentence them to hospital' because they are, thereby, likely to be detained in custody longer as 'dangerous' than they would have been in prison, even though there are no data on this point.

In 1983, one of us, a special hospital consultant, recommended that individuals identified as suffering psychopathic disorder might be most appropriately referred to a special hospital while serving a sentence rather than at the time of trial. It was argued that there were many difficulties in assessing probable motivation, compliance and treatability when someone is seen on remand, and that removal to a special hospital following the trial would make it more difficult for the patient to perceive the difference between the therapeutic and penal aspects of compulsory detention. It was argued:

> Instead of going to, say, Broadmoor Hospital on what is effectively an indeterminate sentence, he can go to prison and later seek or be offered treatment during the course of what will more usually be a determinate sentence.

Also:

> If the patient goes from prison to special hospital on a section 72 (now section 47), and is found unwilling or unable to use the facilities of the hospital, he can

return to prison and somebody else can take his valuable hospital place (Mawson, 1983).

In numerical terms, this might also make sound sense, for instead of having one patient in the hospital for 20 years, it may be that a much larger number of patients could receive beneficial periods of treatment during the same period but it happens very rarely.

It has to be remembered, though, in considering this argument that the Court of Appeal has recommended that serious offenders who have a psychiatric disorder, who are not offered hospital beds, should be given indefinite, or life, sentences anyway (Thomas, 1979).

It was further argued (Mawson, 1983) that there are a number of people in special hospitals who fail to respond to treatment, remain dangerous, therefore cannot be released, and thus convert the hospital into a place of custody. This it was said has an impact on staff and other patients which is 'appalling'. Those who did not wish for hospital treatment or who have changed their mind can also become a nuisance and highly disruptive.

This somewhat pragmatic suggestion has had a considerable impact on British discussion about the treatment of psychopaths (NB. on the discussions, not on the treatment itself!). Indeed, the idea was taken up vigorously by Grounds (1987) and later by Dell and Robertson (1988).

Grounds assumed that no treatment works and argued that it is unjust to send patients who cannot be cured of their psychopathy to hospital. He began by stating that in his view the diagnosis of psychopathic disorder has no explanatory, descriptive, prognostic, or therapeutic function, it is therefore a 'pseudo-diagnosis', used just to get patients 'through the customs-barrier of the courts if he wants to'. Thus, it is no basis on which to prescribe treatment. He further argued that under the present arrangements an accused 'psychopathic' offender is offered treatment instead of justice, and that indefinite detention in conditions of maximum security is damaging. He moderated these views by pointing out that personality disordered patients should be offered treatment and so he supported the view that a determinate sentence with later transfer to hospital is the just approach. He wanted in addition change in the law such that most transferred prisoners could not be contained in hospital beyond their release date, but be released; the exceptions would need a civil treatment order made separately at that point. He concluded by quoting C. S. Lewis to the effect that it is inhumane to substitute mercy for justice.

One problem with this moral argument is that it is one sided. If it is 'unjust' to send mentally disordered people to hospital because treatment might take a long time or end up as permanent hospitalization, is it any more just to send them to prison for long, frequently indefinite periods of time? It is anybody's guess as to whether patients in one system stay longer or shorter periods than they would if they had been in the other. To test this would require a random controlled trial and that is, to say the least, highly unlikely in a legal system. Furthermore, it is difficult to see why these morals should apply to one set of mentally disordered offenders, but not another. Why should it be wrong to be merciful (or unmerciful depending on the observer) to the psychopathic patient, and lock him up in a hospital rather than a prison, but not wrong to take similar action with a schizophrenic patient? Another problem with the argument is that it is based on an outmoded view of psychopathic disorder as a clinical entity. If the argument is shifted to all those patients who are carefully assessed and diagnosed as suffering from one of the recognized variants of personality disorder, then it is harder to sustain.

It could be argued that the injustices of indefinite hospitalization could be ameliorated for *all* diagnostic groups by an increased use of timed restriction orders. When a restriction order is added, by a judge, to a hospital order, the restrictions do not have to be 'without limit of time', they could be for a specified period—say 5 years, such that the tariff element is catered for by handing control to the Home Office for the same period that the Home Office would have controlled matters if a prison sentence had been given. The problems with this suggestion are that psychiatrists, on the whole, do not like the idea. They welcome the indefinite period of Home Office control for their patients, especially the outpatient licence. It also has to be acknowledged that these patients, if sent to prison, would usually get a life sentence anyway, because of the Court of Appeal direction mentioned above, and an earlier Lord Chief Justice decided that fixed-time restriction orders were a bad idea (Thomas, 1979), and that powerful opinion still holds sway.

These discussions reached the ears of a Minister who wondered whether it would be a good idea to remove the power to give hospital orders to psychopaths, thus forcing all such patients to receive prison sentences. It soon became clear that the reason for this piece of support for the moral position taken above was because the Minister had discerned that it would give the Home Office more control over such patients and weaken the medical component in arguments about their rehabilitation and release. It is no surprise that he ran into medical and civil rights opposition. One matter he had not realized was the inexactness of the legal diagnostic classifications in the MHA 1983. Psychiatrists pointed out that if patients requiring treatment in hospital needed to be called 'mentally ill' to get it, then that is what they would be called. This interesting episode has been well documented by Peay (1988).

Considering that this chapter, is authored by advocates of both positions in the argument, it is useful to see what issues unite both sides. All are agreed that the term 'psychopathic disorder' is clinically unsatisfactory and is increasingly being reserved for legal and social purposes. All are agreed that those who fall into this nosological dustbin need a better deal from the criminal justice system. Some would argue for better treatment facilities in prison (e.g. an expansion of the Grendon prison type of service), others prefer to see more resources given to the special hospitals to create better services there. Some would like to see both. All are agreed that transfers from the prison to the hospital system should be made easier and more numerous. The whole of *Criminal Behaviour and Mental Health* (1992) vol 2, no. 3 was devoted to these issues.

Clinical Examples

Case 1

A man born to parents, each in bad health, who largely neglected his care and left it to his older sister. The family structure was such that he stayed away from school a great deal and, in his turn, had to look after his younger sister and manage the house. He harboured feelings of resentment against his parents. At the age of 17 he began a series of convictions, mainly for shopbreaking and housebreaking. He had no educational achievements and did not find a job lasting more than a few days until he worked as a warehouseman. After a month or two, he set fire to the warehouse, completely destroying it. He was not detected, but went on to set a series of other fires. He also took to heavy drinking. One night, when drunk, he took a girlfriend back home to her house, set fire to some papers, went upstairs and went to bed with her. Later they were disturbed by smoke. He helped rescue some residents, but three people died in the fire. He was still not detected. The drinking and fire-raising continued and on two occasions he tried to kill himself.

Whilst in prison for a theft offence, he revealed his previous activities and was convicted of manslaughter. A psychiatric report described him as suffering from 'longstanding emotional instability' with a diagnosis of 'psychopathic personality disorder'. The reporting psychiatrist said 'he must be regarded as a very dangerous individual whose prognosis, even with treatment, is poor'. He was sent to a special hospital. He remained in hospital as an inpatient for 7 years. He was noted to have very considerable difficulty with authority figures and in sustaining any kind of occupational activity. Further assessment revealed that his fire-setting behaviour stretched back to the age of 8 years. An EEG was normal, his IQ was average. A programme of counselling by nursing staff together with occupational training was instituted. He responded well to this and gradually made progress through the hospital hierarchy of increasing responsibility. During the course of his treatment, special attention was given to his drinking problems and he became a member of Alcoholics Anonymous. A predischarge assessment viewed his fire-raising as an instrument of power which he, a weak individual, could use to score over adversaries. Most of the fires were related to feelings of grievance against employers or owners of property. All were committed when he was drunk. He was considerably distressed by the deaths he had caused, these ideas disturbed him to the point of despair and depression, hence the suicidal attempts. He formed an attachment to a female visitor and they decided to marry. He was discharged directly from special hospital to the community, under the supervision of a forensic psychiatry team which included a psychiatrist, a nurse and a social worker. At first, he was on trial leave, but further successful management converted it to full leave and, after 3 years successful care, he was given an absolute discharge from his restriction order and continues to make progress under voluntary supervision.

COMMENT

A man 'whose prognosis even with treatment is poor' does rather well with the structure, support, nursing and psychotherapy of a maximum security hospital, albeit over a long period, some twelve years.

Case 2

A further case is extracted from *Portrait of a Psychopath* written by Lloyd and Williamson (1968), to which the reader is referred for the full flavour of the destructiveness of 'psychopathic disorder'. Harry was born to a 16-year-old, unmarried mother, in Lancashire. They never had a settled existence. The first four or five years of his life were harsh and chaotic. He did not have a father, but the shadow of 'a sort of ogre figure he could not recall, but knew had been cruel to his mother'. He had no proper home just a succession of holes and corners where he was mostly left to the mercies of elderly domineering women. At the age of six, he started to steal from shops, he was always in trouble at school, and frequently in fights. At the age of 9 years, he was sexually assaulted by an older man. At the age of 11, he was sent to an approved school (for delinquent boys). On the way to the approved school, he was in a remand home for a period where he tried to hang himself. He developed a brief but intense liking for a girl who became pregnant by him, only to jilt him soon afterwards. Offending continued after leaving school, mainly theft. He went to sea, and joined the army. He also served time in borstal. At the age of 19, he began to take an interest in what he called 'blood letting'. He became a blood donor, but he also used to slash his arms with a razor blade to release a lot of blood which made him feel 'better'. Army life was followed by married life, or at least a brief marriage after a one night stand. At this stage, he began to complain of 'blackouts' by which he meant periods of lost memory in which he would commit violence. Imprisonment was inevitable and his period there included a further suicide attempt. An unsuccessful period as a trawlerman was followed by more imprisonment for grievous bodily harm. After this more charges, this time for flourishing a revolver at his mother. Instead of imprisonment for this offence, he received a hospital order and a leucotomy.

He was disappointed with the operation as he expected it to obliterate all his bad memories which it failed to do. He discharged himself and returned to thieving, which resulted in a further period of imprisonment. In prison, he rebelled further and was regarded by other prisoners as 'a nut case'. During this period he began a new activity, swallowing foreign bodies. He began with spoon handles, bed springs, an electric bell, and an electric light bulb. These were followed by bathroom and lavatory chains, and he acquired the nickname 'Flush'. The swallowing was sometimes followed by an operation. Sometimes he would swallow needles and open safety pins. He was told that he would die if he continued. 'Well, I got into trouble and thought, if I were to die, so what? I wouldn't have to go to court, what I had done would be forgotten.'

After release from prison he met and married another girl. She suffered his violence for a while and nearly died from strangulation. Harry was readmitted to a mental hospital, but he did not like it any more than the first time and discharged himself, only to be picked up on an outstanding charge. In the police station, he swallowed some spoons which had to be removed by an operation. Further imprisonment was followed by more swallowing and operations. Eventually, he found a new job as a laundry man on a tanker. He remained a seaman for 3½ years. This pattern of events continued and on one occasion he was recommended for Grendon prison, but he was not selected. One day in an agitated state, he swallowed a series of open safety pins, possibly to avoid a forthcoming charge for misdemeanour. One of the pins pierced his oesophagus and his heart. He refused a blood transfusion: 'I give blood, I don't take it.' He died. He was 39 years old.

COMMENT

This case illustrates the combination of self-destructive and aggressive features seen in so many severely personality disordered patients. It also emphasizes the life-threatening nature of the disease. Treatment seems to have been inappropriate. Presumably the leucotomy was to deal with chronic feelings of tension, but it is doubtful if it would be advised these days given the underlying problem of impulsiveness. Psychotherapy seems not to have been tried, nor does nursing in a controlled environment.

Case 3

The final case further illustrates the serious medical problems suffered by 'psychopathic' patients. It also portrays difficulties such patients encounter on the way to hospital.

A woman whose early years are uncertain and who was fostered a good deal. Her schooling was poor and she was eventually sent to a residential school because of disturbed behaviour which included truanting, mis-using telephones and threatening behaviour. At one point, she was admitted to a mental hospital, but discharged by a mental health review tribunal (MHRT). Following that, she was readmitted to another mental hospital where she attempted to strangle other patients and set fire to curtains. She was transferred to a special hospital. At the special hospital she continued to express homicidal urges and attacked staff. She began to have epileptic attacks. A further discharge by an MHRT left her in the community until she was convicted of theft and made subject to a hospital order back in a special hospital, but not before she gave birth to a boy. Yet another discharge by an MHRT was followed by a plea from her to a psychiatrist because she was hearing voices. An informal admission was ended by a self-discharge, and more theft. After a prison sentence she went to a hostel which she smashed up. She soon returned to a special hospital, but for a fourth time was discharged by an MHRT.

After an assault on a nurse at a health centre she was seen by a psychiatrist who described her as 'overbearing and paranoid' and also a very damaged person, but intelligent. She was convicted of criminal damage and sentenced to 6 months' imprisonment. Further convictions led to a probation order and a condition of residence in hospital. Later she developed a sexual relationship and went to live with her man in a guest house. They were turned out after a series of arguments with the landlord. Amidst much mutual abuse, the patient set fire to the basement of the guest house and was remanded in custody as a consequence. A medical report said 'she displays no real contrition and inclines to justify her actions. At the same time, she is not a cold unfeeling person who would not care whether she burnt people to death or not. I think, like a typical psychopath, she has no thoughts at all. It seems she was homeless and in difficulties and once more responded to the situation by acting aggressively. . . . I do not feel justified in making an application for her return to special hospital. . . . I think she will continue to mature and perhaps a further period of institutional care will be of value in this situation. I think it must be brought home to her that she must think before she acts.' She was sentenced to life imprisonment. On appeal, this was quashed and a hospital order with restrictions substituted.

In special hospital she was noted to have a low IQ and soon developed a number of ideas about being homosexual and discharging male sperm. Other paranoid ideas were expressed. She was rediagosed as suffering from schizophrenia, placed on intramuscular antipsychotic medication and anticonvulsants. She was given considerable nursing support and education and occupational training. After 15 years she was transferred to a medium secure unit. A few months later, she was moved to a hostel under supervision and continues to make good progress with psychiatric treatment and support.

COMMENT

This case picks up a common theme for work with the severely personality disordered, the difficulty in knowing when a patient has actually become psychotic and in recognizing schizophrenia in its early stages. If the philosophy espoused in this book is adopted, that matters only up to a point, because with or without the label of 'schizophrenia', this patient needed hospitalization, support, psychotherapy and tranquillizers. Clinically, it would be better if treatment was more directed to symptoms and less to global assessments.

10
Deception, Self-deception, and Dissociation

Edited by	*Written by*
Paul Mullen	John Gunn
	David Mawson
	Paul Mullen
	Peter Noble

I have done that—says my memory. I could not have done that—says my pride and remains inexorable. Eventually memory gives in.

Nietzche, 1886

Deception occupies a central and privileged place in forensic psychiatry. The founding fathers of the speciality, such as Haslam (1817), Ray (1838) and East (1927), were all much concerned with the need to recognize fraudulent claims in the accused, the claimant and the conscripted serviceman, to potentially mitigating, compensable or exempting disorders. The touchstone of the experts skill used to be in distinguishing between the genuine and the simulated. Although this particular question has lost much of its urgency, what remains central are issues surrounding those human, all too human, tendencies to deny, to lie to others, and to lose oneself in self-deception.

The tendency to modify our experiences of current reality by how we think rather than by what we do, and to interpret and edit memories of the past in pursuit of present needs is universal. We try to escape the contingencies of reality by a variety of mechanisms.

Substituting available alternatives for those objects of our desire which appear beyond reach. Jaspers (1946) quotes Plutarch as saying of people who waste their feelings on guinea pigs and pet dogs:

> The element of love in all of us when deprived of any adequate object seeks out something trivial and false rather than let itself remain unengaged.

So the psyche in its passions prefers to deceive itself, or even in spite of itself, invent some nonsensical object, rather than give up all drive or aim. The displacement of desire, or aggression, on to a more available, or vulnerable object, is common. In some claimants and litigants this mechanism can be at work. The bereaved, deprived of their loved one, may displace their energy from the pursuit of the lost love on to the pursuit of compensation. At first glance, their actions may appear venal and self-serving, but behind this appearance can lie a tragic attempt to restore an unbearable loss through pursuit of the substituted goal.

Daydreaming   in which we turn away from the daunting task of wresting the desired from reality, or from the conflicts inherent in current obligations, into a world of fantasy and make-believe. In children, the world of private make-believe and public reality can merge and mix. In some adults, the dividing line between the internal world of fantasy and the shared external world of consensual reality remains wavering and uncertain. The French concept of mythomania, often treated as synonymous with pathological lying, captures this quality of being caught up in one's own fantasies and imaginery adventures.

Lying,   or to use the minimally less pejorative and far broader term 'deception', is near universal. Advertisers 'put a gloss' on their products, companies fail to disclose the whole story, politicians distort, sportsmen break rules when they think they will not be detected, and we all deceive on occasions to obtain advantage or avoid embarrassment. Lying may even be part of normal development and individuation (Ford et al., 1988). Hartshorne and May (1928) conducted a series of elegant experiments demonstrating the frequency of deceptive behaviour amongst youngsters. Most authors agree that lying involves the consciousness of falsity, the intent to deceive, and a preconceived goal or purpose. Normal prevarication is instrumental and, at least initially, the liar is aware of the deception. In practice, the intentional lie emerges into self-deception and we move, all too easily, from knowingly fabricating into believing our own stories.

In pathological lying (pseudologia fantastica; *see* below), there is created a tissue of fantastic lies in which the deception is not merely about matters of fact, but aims to create a whole new identity. The lies, though they may begin as instrumental, in the sense of bringing pecuniary advantage or prestige, rapidly develop to a stage where they are disproportionate to any discernible end or personal gain. The lies of the commonalty deceive about matters of fact, the fabrications of the pathological liar deceive about who and what he is; they are about creating a new identity and recreating the world. Pseudologia fantastica is about lying, but it is also about fantasy run riot which involves self-deception as much as deceiving others.

Denial   of current reality is one way of coping with the disturbing and the threatening. Denial differs from lying in that it is not an attempt to convince others, or oneself, of a different reality, but involves turning away from the unacceptable. Clearly, denial involves deception and self-deception, but lacks the intention to affirm a new and false reality. In practice, denial often slips into fabrication. Denial involves the claim that something did not occur or, if it did, the subject has no memory for the events.

Amnesia is an inability to remember or a denial of memory. Selective memory which leaves convenient blanks is a common enough indulgence, and is to be expected in those where forgetting may bring considerable advantage. The distinctions and overlaps between so-called psychogenic amnesia and organic memory disturbances are considered later in this chapter and on pp. 297–8.

Self-deception is a concept presenting profound theoretical ambiguities, but is none the less potentially of wide applicability in psychiatry. Many aspects of what we term unconscious, dissociative, hysterical, or even abnormal illness behaviour can, from a different perspective, be spoken of as types of self-deception.

The central paradox of self-deception was described by Fingarette (1969) in his excellent book on the subject:

> For as deceiver one is insincere, guilty: whereas if genuinely deceived, one is the innocent victim.

Is then the self-deceiver both perpetrator and sufferer? The psychiatrist's view of self-deception is often influenced by the Freudian vocabulary which articulates the phenomenon as one of helplessness in the grip of unconscious conflict, for the self-deceiver is spoken of as the victim of the compulsive force of the unconscious. Similarly, the Marxist notion of false consciousness places the self-deceived in the role of victim of forces outside of his control and thus choice. Existentialists, such as Kierkegaard (1845) and Sartre (1953), by using a different vocabulary, that of wilful ignorance, bad faith and inauthenticity, focus on the self-deceiver as perpetrator, as agent of his own spiritual cowardice. There is an implied assumption that the self-deceiver could tell the truth if he would, and with this assumption comes moral judgment.

Self-deception is in part about how information is interpreted and what aspects are acknowledged but, more important, it is about self-presentation; it is about what we avow as our motivations and what we accept has been our behaviour. The simplest model of self-deception is of holding two incompatible beliefs, one of which is not noticed or acknowledged. Self-deception is not just persisting in beliefs in the face of contrary evidence, nor merely holding incompatible beliefs, for it implies and active engagement which strives to maintain ignorance. The characteristics of self-deception as viewed from the vantage point of an observer include:

1. activities which appear incompatible with the individual's previous claims or behaviour;
2. the refusal of the self-deceiver to give adequate (or at least acceptable) justifications for his activities;

3. a refusal to accept responsibility for activities and their consequences which appears to stem not from disregard of those responsibilities, but from an inability to recognize the transgressions;
4. an adherence to the deception which persists even when it becomes personally disadvantageous.

The latter two characteristics which speak of loss of self-control tend to soften, or even remove, the moral condemnation of the self-deceiver. What of the experience of self-deception for the self-deceiver? This is difficult to pin down. Totally successful self-deception would presumably be experienced as having a conviction or desire no different from any other. We assume that some discomfort and disequilibrium accompanies most self-deceptive engagements, which may be experienced as unease or a puzzlement at one's own apparently disproportionate vehemence.

Self-deception covers a wide range of human activity. It covers the exuberant, if shallow individuals, who commit themselves to a course of action in the enthusiasm of the moment, only to later disavow that commitment. It includes the envious, who undermine and damage those around them under the guise of friendship, apparently in ignorance of their own motives. It includes those who convince themselves of their own illness and disability, then dedicate themselves to having this belief confirmed. It includes most of us as we try and impose coherence and create a flattering tale out of our past and present activities.

Occasionally, it is possible to see self-deception emerging. A young man who had strangled his girlfriend was examined a matter of a few hours after the event. He gave, at that time, an account of the killing marked by great distress and genuine perplexity about how he came to commit such an act. A few days later he claimed to have only the vaguest memories of the event leading up to the killing and none for the act itself. A week or so later, a story began gradually to emerge as he 'remembered' what had really happened and the provocations which had occasioned the act. The following month, he gave a clear account of intolerable provocation which culminated in his loss of control and which 'must have led to the killing', although he said he could not recall committing the deed. Somewhere in that progression, self deception must have played a part but, by the time this man went to trial, he seemed to honestly believe his own account of the events, and certainly he was filled with a genuine sense of grievance and injustice when his defence foundered.

Self-deception involves the editing and reorganization of memory to serve the needs of current imperatives. In fact, such restructuring of memory is to some degree a normal process which is going on constantly. The view of human memory as analogous to a massive filing system or the hard disk of a computer, which assuming you employ the correct access codes calls up exactly what was filed away, is increasingly coming under critical scrutiny. Memory is, at least in part, a functional and selective system which is constantly evolving and adapting to current needs (Rosenfield, 1988). In a mundane way, we all re-write our own histories so as to ease the disjunctions between our present attitudes and positions and our past actions and views. Self-deception is essential to righteousness, or any other form of pomposity. Equally, it plays a prominent role in creating and maintaining some of our patient's difficulties.

Confabulation   has been defined as:

> The falsification of memory occurring in clear consciousness in association with an organically derived amnesia (Berlyne, 1972).

Confabulation is, on occasion, considered as the fabricating of false statements by someone with impaired memory in order to cover their embarrassment at forgetting. The implication of intentional falsification has been, quite rightly, challenged (Whitlock, 1981). Confabulation is typically encountered in amnesic disorders where the patients lack insight into their impairment and, therefore, would be incapable of constructing falsifications to cover a deficit which they were unaware existed. Bonhoeffer (1904) distinguished between 'momentary' confabulation, where the patient, when asked specifically about recent events, responds by recounting more distant unrelated memories and 'fantastic' confabulations which involved spontaneous creations, often grandiose or absurd. The fantastic, or spontaneous, confabulations tend to be associated with amnesias in which there is associated frontal lobe dysfunction, whereas the provoked, or momentary confabulations, are the result of an attempt to respond to specific enquiries in those with a defective memory and is found in amnesic patients and, to a lesser extent, in normal subjects whose memory fails them for some reason (Kopelman, 1987c). It is not a form of intentional deception.

This chapter is concerned with a variety of conditions, disparate in many ways, but in which deception, both of others and the self, plays a part. The introduction was intended to emphasize the extent to which there is a continuum between the experiences and activities of us all and the disorders to be described. Deception is, however, a term redolent of judgement and rejection. Here the emphasis is on the recognition of distress and disorder, so that it can be treated rather than identifying deceptions in order to confound or condemn them.

Pseudologia Fantastica (Pathological Lying)

Lying, as has been noted, is a frequent, possibly universal, human activity. A group of disorders have been reported which involve fantastic lies that are developed into complex systems of deception. The terms employed for this condition include pseudologia fantastica, mythomania and pathological liars

(Delbrueck, 1891, Healy and Healy 1915; King and Ford, 1988). The following are the clinical characteristics:

1. extensive and gross fabrications;
2. the content and extent of the lies are disproportionate to any discernible end or personal advantage;
3. the lies deceive not just about matters of fact, but attempt to create a new and false identity for the liar;
4. the subject appears to become caught up in his own fabrications which take on a life of their own in which the subject seems eventually to believe;
5. the lying is a central and persistent feature of the patient's life and the mythologism of a lifetime comes to supplant valid memories.

When pathological liars are enmeshed in their fabric of lies, the degree of self-deception may make it difficult to distinguish them from patients in the grip of a delusional system. Kraepelin (1896) included some patients with systematized delusions under pseudologia fantastica and Krafft Ebing (1886) used the term 'inventive paranoia' for both pathological liars and deluded subjects. Most authorities, however, exclude deluded or otherwise psychotic subjects (e.g. Healy and Healy, 1915). Closely related conditions are Munchausen's Syndrome (Asher, 1951) and feigned bereavement (Snowdon et al., 1978).

Two clinical examples may help illustrate this disorder:

A patient was brought to the outpatient department by his landlady who was concerned with his increasing depression which she feared might lead him to harm himself. She explained that he was now living in much reduced circumstances, having suffered major financial losses and the desertion of his erstwhile friends. It became clear that he had been living rent free for some considerable time, and the landlady was providing all his meals and a regular supply of pipe tobacco, to say nothing of comfort and support. The patient was a well-dressed man in his early 60s, who wore tinted spectacles and assumed an air of profound sadness. He was induced to give his history despite several claims that he did not want to go over the past. The personal history provided was of humble origins from which he escaped via a university scholarship. He claimed to have left university prematurely to join the government forces fighting in Spain. At the end of the Civil War, he reported a brief period in Rhodesia before joining the British army during the Second World War. A distinguished army career was followed by a period working in the United Nations. The tale continued with a series of great successes followed by undeserved disasters until he reached his present homeless, lonely plight. The stories had plausibility and a wealth of detail. Suspicions as to their authenticity were raised by the remarkable similarity of some aspects of his account to the memoirs of such figures as Orwell and Wingate. Over subsequent months, it emerged that the patient had lived most of his life in London, he had never been in the army, far from being unmarried he had been married on a number of occasions and his reported childlessness ignored a number of offspring. Following the exposure of his identity, the patient disappeared, but was encountered some years later having created for himself a new persona and an equally dedicated supporter in the form of another middle-aged lady sponsoring the ageing and misunderstood artist. At a second encounter, he greeted his doctor with apparent pleasure and without a blush, or any visible unease, told of his new circumstances. He did not seem to be concerned about, or even aware of, the possibility that his new identity might be threatened. He believed in himself, or at least he evinced no insecurity.

The second case was admitted from prison where he was said to have become depressed and suicidal. He was a small young man who, though in his early 20s, could have passed for

12 or 13 years of age. He gave an account of having been raped in prison with the connivance of a number of prison officers. He had made these allegations previously, and they had been extensively investigated without any basis having been found. He gave a history of having been seduced in his early teens by the mother of a school friend, and described a number of romantic adventures prior to his arrest on arson charges. Other aspects of his history included a graphic account of child abuse, remarkable academic and artistic success, cut short by circumstance, and a period of army service. This young man attempted to create by his stories an identity characterized by remarkable talents and charm, but a personal history replete with disadvantage and tragedy. Misunderstood, abused, cheated and victimized, nevertheless, he struggled to realize his potential. Different stories were given to different members of staff and even more dramatic discrepancies emerged between his self-presentation to other patients and that to the staff. During his time on the unit, his use of mimesis became obvious. He latched on to a patient and later a staff member whom he found admirable and began not only to talk like his new found models, but tried to present himself in an identical manner. He even borrowed aspects of the personal histories of these two admired individuals, and presented them as his own.

Schneider (1959) classifies this group of patients under the general heading of attention-seeking psychopaths who love to boast about themselves, and invent or act out fairy tales of self-aggrandizement. He noted that the true pathological liar begins as a story teller, but becomes so caught up in his fabrications that 'they forsake actuality and finish up on the stage of their own mind'. Taylor (1979) took a similar view describing the stories as hysterical confabulations. He believed that recent reminiscences are temporarily replaced by hallucinated reminiscences, which are true memories to the patient, at least for a time. Kräupl Taylor emphasized the negative or disadvantageous aspects of this behaviour. Whilst the pathological liar has the gratification of an occasional audience that is impressed, this pleasure is short-lived, only to be followed by the humiliation of being treated as a liar. Such patients are soon generally disbelieved, and they may be teased mercilessly. Such behaviour does merge into more externally goal-oriented deception.

Pathological lying is usually encountered in forensic practice in those accused of fraud, swindling, making false accusations or false confessions (Powell et al., 1983; Sharrock and Cresswell, 1989). Once the counterfeit is exposed, the pathological liar will often give up his deceptions and readily confess, sometimes to offences in which he was not involved, thus beginning a new cycle of attention-seeking mythologies in the very act of acknowledging the previous deceptions. The frauds and swindles perpetrated by the pathological liar usually form part of an attempt to create a false identify. Such frauds are often flamboyant and have little in common with the furtive and carefully planned dishonesty of the more typical fraud. Pathological liars are closer to confidence tricksters, though unlike them, they do not take the money and run, but persist in the pretence long after exposure is inevitable. Their lies are rarely aimed at excusing or exculpating their offences, but more frequently, at attracting notice and inflating their importance.

Abnormal Illness Behaviour

Parsons (1951) regarded illness and health as socially institutionalized role types. A sick person's role was legitimated and allowed if its undesirability and the need to cooperate with others to get well was accepted. While in the sick role, normal obligations are suspended and responsibilities are reduced, but the role might not be granted unless adequate evidence of disease were available. Mechanic (1962) described 'illness behaviour' which referred to—

> the ways in which symptoms may be differentially perceived, evaluated and acted (or not acted) upon by different kinds of persons.

In a more recent review of the topic, Mechanic (1986) emphasized that in his view illness and illness experience are shaped by socio-cultural and socio-psychological factors, irrespective of their genetic, physiological and other biological bases.

> Away from the research laboratory illness is often used to achieve a variety of social and personal objectives, having little to do with biological systems or the pathogenesis of disease.

He went on to ask himself why 50% of patients entering medical care have symptoms and complaints that do not fit the International Classification of Diseases? Why are rates of depression and the use of medication relatively high among women, whereas alcoholism, hard drug use and violence are particularly common among men? Why among the Chinese are affective expressions of depression uncommon, but somatic symptoms relatively frequent? Why are rates of suicide among young black people in the USA relatively low, but rates of homicide high? Rather than attempting answers to such questions, he urged us to look beyond individuals to their social environment. He pointed out that the 19th century phenomenon of female hysteria has all but disappeared in the west, perhaps due to a change in social response to the characteristic symptoms. Illness behaviour is more than a psychological response among persons faced with a situation calling for assessment. It arises in response to troubling social situations, and may serve as an effective means of achieving release from social expectations, as an excuse for failure, or as a way of obtaining a variety of privileges, including monetary compensation. A complaint of illness is one way in our society of obtaining reassurance and support.

Pilowski (1969) has proposed 'abnormal illness behaviour' as a subcategory of illness behaviour for those patients who have physical symptoms for which no organic explanation can be found. This is a useful extension of the concept of illness behaviour, even though it is not clear why it should be confined to physical symptoms and organic disease. The forensic psychiatrist may be called to see a number of conditions which in some ways can be regarded as variants of malingering, but which can also be regarded as gross abnormalities of illness behaviour, abnormalities of such a degree that instead of eliciting support and sympathy, they produce rejection and anger on the part of doctors, which are sometimes coupled with frankly punitive responses.

Compensation Neurosis

Compensation neurosis is a pejorative term which has many pseudonyms, e.g. 'accident neurosis', 'greenback neurosis', 'profit neurosis', 'railway spine', and 'unconscious malingering'. Kennedy (1946), gave expression to such prejudice in the following aphorism:

> A compensation neurosis is a state of mind, borne out of fear, kept alive by avarice, stimulated by lawyers, and cured by a verdict.

The difficulty is that the emotional effects of an injury manifest themselves within a personal and social context. Least psychological damage occurs when injury can be accepted as part of a natural order. Feelings of anger and resentment exacerbate physical and psychiatric symptoms. Litigation is almost always protracted and involves repeated medical examination. The patient's attention is focused on his grievance and symptoms. Finally, in court, disability is financially rewarded and any recovery may reduce the level of compensation. This process exacerbates psychological symptoms and hampers recovery. The experience in New Zealand of a government-run accident compensation scheme has, however, amply demonstrated that merely removing the courts and the litigation process in no way reduces either the psychological problems or the temptation to exaggerate or fabricate compensatable injuries. In fact, it may increase these problems, as all injuries become potentially compensatable irrespective of whose responsibility they may have been.

The problem is neatly illustrated by considering the effects of minor concussional head injury. Virtually every individual who leads an active life has sustained an injury causing a brief interruption of consciousness. Recovery is almost always prompt and complete, except where litigation is involved. Thus, if a man falls off his own ladder and bangs his head he recovers quickly, but if he falls off his employer's ladder and becomes involved in compensation, persistent disability may be more likely. An extensive literature has developed in response to this paradox.

In 1942 Lewis referred to the postconcussional syndrome as:

> That common, dubious, psychopathic condition—the bugbear of the clear-minded doctor and lawyer.

Lishman (1968) commented:

> Central to most descriptions are headaches and dizziness, but to these may be added abnormal fatiguability, insomnia, sensitivity to noise, irritability, and emotional instability. Anxiety and depression are often prominent. Difficulties with concentration and memory may feature strongly among the complaints, and some degree of overt intellectual impairment may on occasion be detected. With

this mixture of quasi-organic and subjective symptoms, variously reported, it is scarcely surprising that the concept lacks clarity and that its aetiology has remained in doubt. Nevertheless, its ubiquity following even minor blows to the head, and the regularity with which it features among claims for compensation, have ensured that it persists as an important subject for medical interest and debate.

In the early days or weeks after injury the postconcussional syndrome is probably directly related to the cerebral trauma but, subsequently, it becomes overlain by psychological factors and in some cases deliberate exaggeration.

The literature on the recovery of psychological symptoms after settlement is confused. The most optimistic work is that of Miller (1961; 1966) who followed-up an unrepresentative sample of 50 neurotic patients from a total of 200 head injury cases and found that 90% returned to the same or similar employment after their cases were settled. Kelly (1981) documented 100 'post-traumatic syndrome' patients, but traced only 43 after a follow-up period averaging 2.8 years. No patients were personally interviewed. Many patients had improved and returned to work by the time the case was settled, but of the 26 not working by settlement, 22 were still not working at follow-up, which led him to conclude that the 'cured by a verdict' jibe is not correct.

A high proportion of the surveys showing long-term disability after work injury are from Australia (Cole et al., 1968; Balla and Moraitis, 1970; Ellard, 1970). Balla and Moraitis (1970) attributed chronic disability in trivially injured Melbourne Greek immigrants to 'psychological factors'. It was suspected that many of these so-called 'disabilities' stem from the laxity of a social security system which allowed widespread fraud.

Perhaps the most comprehensive review is by Mendelson (1984). He looked at 18 follow-up studies of personal injury litigants. Of these only three studies, including the one by Miller, favoured the view that claimants improved within a fairly short time of the finalization of their claims. Six studies were discounted because of the small number of patients examined. Nine studies indicated that of patients who stopped work following a head injury, between 50 and 85% failed to return to work after a settlement. For patients with a low back injury, 35% were unemployed after a minimum of 3 years following settlement. Patients with neck injuries had persistent disability of a severe degree, in from 12–60% of cases 5 years after the injury. Tarsh and Royston (1985) carried out a follow-up of 35 claimants who had an 'accident neurosis'. Patients were followed-up from 1 to 7 years after compensation was received. Few recovered and such recovery as did take place was unrelated to the time of compensation. Most cases still had continuing and often severe symptoms at follow-up, and about one-third of the group seemed certain to be always going to lead lives of invalidism, totally dependent on other family members.

It is not easy to apply these findings to individual cases, but some general considerations are helpful. 'Recovery' and 'return to employment' are very different. Many complainants are manual workers in mid-life who have little motivation to return to the sort of poorly paid employment which would leave them little better off than when in receipt of state benefit. The boundary is blurred between what is genuine, what has a genuine basis, but is exaggerated, and what is gross malingering. Often one develops chronologically from the other. It may be that the immediate response to injury, be it physical or psychological, is almost always genuine and would have occurred in the absence of any compensation claimed. The lengthy process of pursuing compensation hampers recovery and encourages exaggeration and sometimes naturally occurring recovery is not frankly admitted. As the litigation progresses over years, some suggestible individuals elaborate gross syndromes and these tend to carry a poor prognosis. The plaintiffs account of the past is often distorted and preaccident physical and psychological disabilities may be concealed. Careful examination of the full family practitioner case notes and correspondence is often revealing. Malingering can occur, but is difficult to detect on the basis of a single psychiatric examination (*see* below). Sometimes enquiry agents' reports and videos indicate that allegedly disabled subjects are, in fact, working clandestinely and leading comparatively normal lives.

Feigned Mental Illness

In the 19th century, there was considerable interest in identifying malingerers who simulate mental disorder. It was considered that diseases were feigned from fear, shame, or in the hope of gain, and that avoiding military service and escaping the punishment of crimes were frequent motivations. Beck (1829) devoted considerable space in his text on medical jurisprudence to the recognition of feigned diseases and, in particular, offered no less than twelve strategies for unmasking those pretending madness. Tuke (1892) noted that simulators of insanity make errors in such matters as adding 3 and 4, or the number of shillings in a sovereign, or in identifying commonplace objects. He stated that the unskilled malingerer answers nothing right, constantly falling into absurdities quite foreign to true insanity. Maudsley (1867) also noted:

> Imposters generally overact thinking the lunatic widely different from a sane person . . . pretends he cannot remember things such as what day follows another, or how many days there are in a week, that he cannot add the simplest figures . . . answers stupidly where a real lunatic who was not an idiot would act cunningly and answer intelligently.

The commonality between such descriptions and Ganser's syndrome have been noted (Enoch and Trethowan, 1979).

Malingering and Simulated Psychosis

The question of what is malingering is claimed by some to be straight-forward. An early authority, whose text on the subject was dedicated 'to my friend the British workman, to whom I owe so much' (Collie, 1917) cited Lord Justice Buckley. The judge defined a malingerer as 'one who is not ill and pretends that he is'. Collie also cited Bramwell who distinguished between 'malingering' (conscious, deliberate simulation of disease, or exaggeration of symptoms) and 'valetudinarianism', where the process is unconscious or subconscious. In a more recent study of feigning after brain or spinal injury, Miller and Cartlidge (1972) defined malingering as:

> All forms of fraud relating to matters of health. This includes the stimulation of diseases or disability which is not present; the much commoner gross exaggeration of minor disability; and the conscious and deliberate attribution of a disability to an injury, or accident that did not in fact cause it, for personal advantage.

Other than in occasional cases of psychosis, the authors held that medical simulation occurs only where it is hoped that it will yield personal, economic or social gain.

In a lecture, a psychiatrist with a medicolegal compensation practice in Australia (Parker, 1988), claimed:

> A week will not go by without seeing at least two malingerers, and about the same number with gross conversion hysteria.

Nevertheless, he went on to warn, using the words of Asher (1958):

> The pride of a doctor who has caught a malingerer is akin to that of a fisherman who has landed an enormous fish; and his stories (like those of fishermen) may become somewhat exaggerated in the telling.

It could be that there is a special form of malingering, the feigning of psychotic illness. The following kind of argument may not be uncommon.

> The trouble is that as soon as the language of 'patient-treatment-disease' is used, it is hard to diagnose insanity in anyone who commits a really horrible act; for to be cured of mental disease is to be sane, and a sane man does not do such things; there is a merging of the language of medicine and the language of morality; if bad is sick, then sick is bad, and sane must be good. The more we treat someone as a patient, the more likely we are to give his sincerity the benefit of the doubt. We tend to ask 'What makes him behave like that' instead of 'is he telling the truth?' and 'could he behave differently if it was to his advantage?' (Mount, 1984).

It is certainly a robust statement of the antipsychiatry position. Yet medical practitioners can also have considerable scepticism about mental disorder in those charged with serious crimes. An anecdote from Ray (1838) is, of course, out of date and could never be matched today, but it illustrates just how far preconceptions about deception, malingering and moral responsibility will take even the experienced observer.

> Jean Gerard, a bold villain, murdered a woman at Lyons in 1829. Immediately after being arrested, he ceased to speak altogether and appeared to be in a state of

fatuity. He laid nearly motionless in his bed, and when food was brought his attendants raised him up and it was given to him in that position. His hearing also seemed to be affected. The physicians who were directed to examine him concluded that if this was actually what it appeared to be, paralysis of the nerves of the tongue and ear, actual cautery applied to the soles of the feet would be a proper remedy. It being used, however, for several days without any success, it was agreed to apply it to the neck. For two days no effect was produced, but on the third, while preparations were making for its applications, Gerard evinced some signs of repugnance to it, and after some urging, he spoke, declaring his innocence of the crime of which he was charged. His simulation was thus exposed.

To try to understand just how easy or difficult it is to simulate mental disorder, Anderson et al. (1959) carried out a study in Australia. Eighteen psychology students were asked to simulate mental disorder. Six were asked to imagine that they had committed murder and they were to feign insanity to escape the consequences. Twelve were asked to feign insanity for their own reasons. The subjects were then subjected to a standard psychiatric examination. None of the pictures presented resembled well-defined psychiatric disorders. Even the better performances lacked consistency and persistence. The commonest simulation was of depression, in two people accompanied by amnesia, three also simulated paranoid features. On cognitive testing, errors were produced, especially approximate answers. One tried to make out he was an epileptic, another tried to simulate feeble-mindedness. Unfortunately, the psychiatric examinations were not carried out blindly, so although the experimenters were not very impressed by their students' acting, it is difficult to know whether they could have actually been fooled.

Perhaps the most famous test of simulated psychosis is 'on being sane in insane places' (Rosenhan, 1973). Eight volunteers, a psychology student, three psychologists, a paediatrician, a psychiatrist, a painter, and a housewife, (three were women) became pseudopatients and gained 'secret admission' to 12 different hospitals. The pseudopatients complained that they were hearing voices, they changed their names and occupations, but otherwise told the truth. The 'voices' were stopped immediately on admission. Each was diagnosied as schizophrenic, but soon discharged as in remission (length of stay varied from 7–52 days). Other patients sometimes recognized the pseudopatients as frauds. Rosenhan concluded, 'it is clear we cannot distinguish the sane from the insane in psychiatric hospitals'. A torrent of replies disagreed. The strongest criticism was perhaps by Spitzer (1975), who pointed out that it is not very surprising that psychiatrists do not diagnose pseudopatients when they are not looking for them. He concluded himself, however, that the data actually supported the view that psychiatrists are good at distinguishing the sane from the insane.

None of this is much help if a psychiatrist is faced with a patient in a situation in which having a psychosis would be a distinct advantage. There is no simple answer and the principles of assessment and management will be the same as if simulation of physical disorder is suspected. As much information as possible should be collected from as many sources as possible, and a professional relationship should be built with the patient. In this way, the nature of the patient's problem (for the one thing that will be true, unless he is one of Rosenhan's research workers, is that he will have a problem) will emerge. Whether it is primarily financial, social, psychological or organic will determine the type of appropriate response.

Malingered psychiatric disorders are encountered both in situations where compensation is at issue and in those facing criminal charges. Malingered psychiatric disorders may occasionally be encountered in those seeking admission or transfer to a psychiatric hospital from prison. The malingerer sometimes believes he has to appear mad or idiotic in every sphere of function and thus presents such an exaggerated picture that suspicions are raised, even in the most trusting. This type of malingerer, who counterfeits a disorder too mad to be mad, often claims gross disorientation under the misapprehension that the mentally disordered suffer a global confusion. More subtle malingerers draw on their experience with mentally disordered individuals. They may claim to be hallucinated, in which case the hallucinations tend to be described as omnipresent, distressing and without the usual association with mood changes or delusional developments. The flamboyant claims about the content and extensive nature of the hallucinations often contrast with the meagre and vague account provided of the form of the experience in terms of being experienced in objective space, having directional qualities, the effects of extraneous events such as other noises, or whether it is worse when alone. Malingered hallucinations may also take atypical forms as when a vision of a person is described which talks to the patient and may even enter into conversation. Occasionally, command hallucinations are offered as an explanation of offending. These should be treated with some scepticism when presented in the absence of other features of psychotic illness.

Command hallucinations have a particular appeal to the malingerer as they offer both evidence of mental disorder and at the same time incorporate a direct exculpatory element. Claims are made by offenders that they committed criminal acts because the voices told them to do so, and they were unable to resist the instruction. These claims should be judged in the context of our knowledge that command hallucinations occur not infrequently in the schizophrenias and, when they do occur, they are often ignored or resisted (Hellerstein et al., 1987). Occasionally, distressed and disturbed individuals will report command hallucinations to dramatize their suicidal or homicidal impulses; such individuals should be taken seriously, less they feel impelled to prove the gravity of their threats.

Fabricated delusions are less common. Malingerers usually present a straightforward account of persecution or control which accounts conveniently for their acts or makes necessary their transfer. The accounts differ from actual delusional experiences both in providing an unusually clear story line and paradoxically containing elements of the totally fantastic. One young man gave an account of being followed and persecuted by shadowy figures whom he claimed had arranged for him to be locked in a cell on board a ship which was about to be sunk. When questioned, he went to the prison window and pointed out at the surrounding sea, then abruptly fled under the table claiming the boat (prison) was sinking. Fabricated accounts, unlike true systematized delusions, rarely contain the typical mixture of self-referential material and laboured constructions placed on minor points proving, to the patient's complete satisfaction, the delusional claims. Malingered delusions are often said to have emerged at a particular point, usually relatively recently, and to have, from the outset, their fully fledged content. In genuine delusions, it is usually possible to discern their gradual development from the initial intuition through an extended process as the patient uncovers the full extent of 'the truth.'

Language disorders are rarely, if ever, malingered. Manic states are difficult to imitate, but depressive syndromes relatively easy. Most of us have sufficient experience of despair and despondency to mimic depression. Where suicidal intent is claimed in the context of an account of depression which appears so atypical as to raise suspicions about malingering, it is probably wiser to give the benefit of the doubt to the individual until he can be observed carefully. In disorganized and disturbed personalities, so common in forensic psychiatry, instability of mood and markedly atypical depressive syndromes occur not infrequently and they are all too often coupled with self-destructive behaviour.

Malingered mental disorders are often presented flamboyantly and insistently. Any questioning of the reported experiences is likely to be greeted by assurances that it is 'the truth', or with the accusation that you don't believe the patient. In schizophrenia, the patient is often reluctant to share disturbing experiences and may go to considerable lengths to minimize or deny abnormal phenomena. In contrast, malingerers usually flaunt the claimed disturbances and insist on their presence. In a malingerer, the symptoms are presented early in the interview and few additional details are added later. In genuine disorders, the abnormalities of mental state usually emerge gradually as the interview progresses. Some malingerers are suggestible and can be induced to add contradictory and absurd symptoms to their account, but more calculating malingerers will stick doggedly to their basic story.

To summarize, the detection of malingering is a difficult, but not entirely mysterious art. The longer the patient is studied, the more carefully the information is gathered and checked, the easier it becomes to detect malingering. Malingering patients tend to have an air of exaggeration, a disproportionate bias in their symptoms, and their complaints do not fit with objective observations from others. They tend to tell lies and so their accounts differ from time to time. However, it also has to be remembered that differences between objective and subjective accounts may be due to many factors other than malingering. Inconsistencies between interviews may be entirely compatible with the memory failures of normal recall, and with clinical change as the disorder progresses. Exaggerated, overoptimistic, or even pessimistic accounts may be due to mood changes. Self-deception may replace conscious lying and dissimulation. There are no absolutes in the detection of malingering, but standard techniques of cross-checking, observation, repeated interviewing, together with the skill of an experienced interviewer who is alive to the possibility of malingering are the best that can be done. It is worth remembering that hostile questioning of distressed patients will probably increase rather than reduce error.

Munchausen's Syndrome

Munchausen's syndrome was described and named by Asher in 1951. Like the famous Baron whose tales were bowdlerized and published by Raspe (1786), the affected persons had travelled widely, and they related tales which were both dramatic and untruthful. Typically, such patients will be admitted to hospital with an acute, harrowing, but not entirely convincing history; their manner is evasive and truculent; and, on enquiry, it may be revealed that they have attended and deceived other hospitals, often discharging themselves against advice.

Most cases resemble organic emergencies and favour three main variants:

1. the acute abdomen type which is usually accompanied by a multiplicity of abdominal scars;
2. the haemorrhagic type, usually reporting haemoptosis, haematemesis, or haematuria;
3. the neurological type, with headache, odd fits, or loss of consciousness.

Asher's title for this group of patients seems well established, although 'hospital addiction' (Enoch and Trethowan, 1979), and even Kraepelin's original appellation of 'hospital swindler' are also used. The patients tend to be emotionally labile, lonely, attention-seeking and establish little rapport. Multiple aliases and repeated admissions are central features and some cases also fulfil the criteria for pseudologica fantastica.

A sinister variant of hospital addiction has been described as Munchausen syndrome by proxy (Meadow, 1977, 1982, 1989; Black, 1981). This involves children whose mothers or care givers invent stories of illness about their child and in some cases fabricate false physical signs. Older children may even be coached by the parent on how to deceive the doctor. Meadow (1989) describes the consequences for children who are falsely labelled as ill:

1. they receive needless investigations and treatment;
2. real injury may be caused by the mother's action, for example by giving drugs to induce unconsciousness;
3. they are at risk from becoming chronic invalids or hospital addicts in their own right.

The parents' motivations have been considered to include a desire for the status and attention provided by being the mother of a sick child, the enjoyment of help from the various medical professionals, and as a way of resolving or avoiding marital conflicts.

Self-mutilators

A related, and to some extent overlapping group of patients are those who obtain medical attention, if not care, by repeated self-injury. There is usually no attempt at mimicking of genuine medical disorders, although occasionally bizarre skin lesions are induced which raise questions as to their origin. In one case, the patient injected air under the skin and persuaded one hospital to treat her for gas gangrene (*see also* pp. 617–18, 816–18).

Pseudoepileptic Seizures

Fenton (1986) favoured the term 'pseudoepileptic seizures', as this acknowledged the resemblance of the fits to genuine fits but avoided any implications of common underlying mechanisms to 'simulated epilepsy', with its implication of deliberate malingering. Important antecedent factors in those with such fits are an emotional precipitant, and they may have a personal or family history of epilepsy or have worked in some capacity in a medical environment. A family and personal history of psychiatric illness, a personal history of self-harm, sexual maladjustment, disturbed relationships and evidence of mood disorder (past self-harm; concurrent affective symptoms) have also been reported (Roy, 1977).

Suspicion of pseudoepileptic seizures should be raised by the following features:

1. restraint of the convulsive movements leads to struggling, even combativeness;
2. an absence of cyanosis;
3. normal pupil responses and corneal reflexes present;
4. pressure on the supraorbital arch causes head withdrawal;
5. the level of consciousness fluctuates during the seizure;
6. there tends to be marked emotionality after the episode.

Pseudoseizures are often preceded by auras involving somatic or visual symptoms and headache. Unlike true epilepsy, in which the onset is usually abrupt, the pseudoseizure may be gradual in onset. Pseudepileptic seizures rarely result in injuries either from falls or biting of the tongue. It should be remembered that epilepsy is more often misconstrued as hysterical than the other way round. Fully deliberately simulated seizures are rare.

Amnesia

The most frequently feigned mental disorder is amnesia (Anderson, 1960). Distinguishing between genuine and feigned amnesia presents considerable difficulty (Schacter, 1986) and may not be meaningful (*see* pp. 297–8). Early accounts suggest that amnesia was the most commonly alleged symptom in those maintaining the old insanity defence (Hopwood and Snell, 1933) and among prisoners (East, 1927). In more modern practice, it is still the case that those claiming amnesia among remand prisoners are very frequently charged with murder. Taylor and Kopelman (1984) found nearly 10% of a sample of men on remand in custody claimed amnesia for the alleged offence, a finding only elicited in those charged with offences of violence. Within the amnesic group, nearly half were charged with murder.

Lishman (1987) has suggested that the traditionally rigid distinction between psychogenic and organic memory disturbance may be an artificial one. Pathophysiology of some kind accompanies psychogenic amnesia, just as a psychological basis underlies the influence of emotion and motive on normal forgetting. Possible underlying mechanisms in psychogenic amnesia are considered at length by Lishman.

Clinically, psychogenic amnesia is either global and dense or more circumscribed. Amnesia for long periods of life may occur, which is only seen in organic states when accompanied by severe disruption of orientation or cognition. Psychogenic amnesia may cover emotionally important events or issues, and the subject may show inconsistency in the history. Normal ability to learn new facts, but severe problems or recall of past events hints at psychogenic amnesia. A total inability to retain new information, even briefly, also favours the psychogenic form.

Kennedy and Neville (1957) described abrupt onset of failure of memory in 74 patients, some of whom had a loss of personal identity. About 40% seemed to show psychogenic mechanisms alone, and a similar proportion showed both organic and psychogenic features. Sixteen per cent showed organic features alone. The authors regarded neither aetiology as excluding the other. Brain damage was felt to predispose to the development of primitive escape mechanisms, and antecedent difficulties in money, mood disorder or marriage were evident. The case of *Podola*, who claimed amnesia after being charged with the murder of a policeman is dealt with in Ch. 2.

Ganser States

Prisoners are placed under considerable stress by incarceration and, in addition, those on remand face the apprehension associated with their forthcoming trial. The dependent, socially incompetent and psychologically impaired are over-represented in the prison population. Given such a concatenation of vulnerabilities and environmental pressures, increased rates of psychiatric disorders might be expected. At one time, it was considered that prisons generated a number of specific mental disorders. Kraepelin (1896) for example, described a prisoner's insanity (*Gefansenenwahsinn*) characterized by grandiose ideas and depressive symptoms, and Bleuler (1924) reported an imprisonment complex associated with delusions of having been pardoned or liberated. The concept of a specific prison psychosis has not stood the test of time, although some still use it to describe reactive psychoses that occur under the pressure of imprisonment. The 'peculiar hysterical state' described by Ganser (1898) was often regarded as a 'prison psychosis' and, despite its rarity, it continues to claim attention. The clinical features are:

1. approximate answers;
2. clouding of consciousness with disorientation in time, place, and occasionally person;
3. vivid hallucinosis, both visual and auditory;
4. areas of analgesia and hyperalgesia with, on occasion, motor disturbances which were considered 'hysterical stigma';
5. complete and often sudden clearing of the disorder, leaving the patient with a total amnesia for the period of the disorder (*see also* Lishman, 1987).

The description of the peculiar way of answering questions was the feature which intrigued subsequent investigators and guaranteed the survival of the putative syndrome (Auerbach, 1982). The phenomenon of approximate answers (*Vorbeireden* or *Vorbeigehen*) was described by Anderson and Mallinson (1941) as:

A false response of a patient to the examiner's question, where the answer, although wrong, is never far wrong and bears a definite and obvious relation to the question, indicating clearly that the question has been grasped.

They go on to make clear that this is not merely giving random responses. Among Ganser's examples was a prisoner who, when asked how many fingers he had, replied 11 and said a horse had three legs, but an elephant five. Counting, simple arithmetic, identifying letters of the alphabet and reading, are all reported to produce obvious errors and omissions. One of our cases, when shown a chessman and asked what it was, replied after several minutes of puzzled examination that it was a little statue whose function quite escaped him. This same man correctly identified a watch and could tell the time, but called a key a knife, and added a little pantomime of horrified withdrawal. One of Ganser's own cases identified a key as a revolver.

There are some similarities between approximate answers and responses which can occasionally occur in organic dysphasias, in a variety of psychotic states (Weiner and Braiman, 1955; Arieti and Bemporad, 1974) and in normal individuals asked to try and simulate insanity (Anderson et al., 1959).

Clouding of consciousness is evidenced by disorientation and difficulty in sustaining attention. There may be either an air of perplexity or apathetic indifference. A number of cases are reported as having lost personal identity with, in some, apparent total amnesia for their past life, including even their name. In others, a state resembling depersonalization is described. Hallucinations, when present, may be vivid and produce flamboyant responses in the patient. The hallucinations may involve the re-enactment of emotionally charged episodes (Enoch and Trethowan, 1979). One of our cases claimed to see his mother standing in the room admonishing him, and in response to this vision, he crouched in the corner, loudly begging forgiveness. Case reports include a range of neurological symptoms, particularly analgesias, parathesias, paralysis and dramatic disturbances of posture and gait which are usually described as hysterical in type. In the classic Ganser state, the condition lasts from a few days to a few weeks, then recovers suddenly and spontaneously, often leaving the patient reporting total amnesia for the episode.

Ganser's original descriptions were in a series of prison inmates. Subsequently, the condition has been described in a variety of settings outside of prisons (Whitlock, 1967; Enoch and Trethowan, 1979). Many of the cases did, however, occur in the context of overt stress of a severe kind from which the patient might understandably wish to escape. The disorder is usually considered rare, but was reported in 50 cases amongst 8000 US army prisoners and in six of just over 1000 psychiatric hospital admissions (Weiner and Braiman, 1955).

Ganser syndrome is advanced as an independent clinical entity by recent authoritative reviews, although one which may manifest as part of other disorders such as schizophrenia and organic brain syndromes, usually in the context of overwhelming stress (Enoch and Trethowan, 1979; Auerbach, 1982). The possibility that the Ganser state is a manifestation of the conscious simulation of mental disorder is considered frequently in the literature, usually to be dismissed in favour of unconscious mechanisms, or the impact of major stress on somebody who already has a mental disorder. What Ganser added to previous descriptions of feigned mental disorder in prisoners was his personal assurance that 'it could not be doubted' that the prisoners being examined were not malingering, but 'truly sick'. Perhaps more scepticism and less acceptance of the explanatory power of the unconscious is indicated in approaching such states, but then, again, perhaps it is better to follow Scott's (1965) pragmatic advice to avoid guesses or inferences about their motivation and to concentrate on observing with greater precision, the clinical picture of these odd states.

Dissociative Disorders

This section covers a group of syndromes which all involve a constitutional or acquired tendency to react, when confronted by stress, with an alteration in consciousness. These periods of reduced, or otherwise disturbed, consciousness are often followed by a partial or total amnesia. Disorders such as multiple personality disorder and fugues tend to have a flamboyant, not to say histrionic, quality and all are reported to be associated, on occasion, with anaesthesias and motor weaknesses of the type found in hysterical conversion. These syndromes may manifest as symptoms of other psychiatric disorders, usually in the context of overwhelming stress. Depressed mood is a frequent prodrome or association, and such states as fugues and multiple personality disorders have been conceptualized as equivalents, or alternatives, to suicide.

The overlap in the clinical descriptions of these states can be considerable. The DSM-III R criteria for a 'psychogenic' fugue includes the assumption of a new identity. Stengel (1941) included a case which could be considered a classic multiple personality disorder among his cases of fugue states. Multiple personality disorder and pseudologia fantastica may also overlap: one of Burt's (1923) cases of pathological lying, for example, has subsequently appeared in the literature as illustrative of typical multiple personality (McKellar, 1979). Possession and trance states often occur in those prone to elaborate fabrications and conversion symptoms. To complete the circle, a considerable proportion of fugue states are said to occur in those with a tendency to habitual lying which amounts in some to pseudologia fantastica (Stengel, 1941). They also all share the potential for creating problems for forensic psychiatrists.

Multiple Personality Disorder

Multiple personality has been described as:

> The presence in one patient of two or more personalities each of which is so well defined as to have a relatively coordinated, rich, unified, and stable mental life of its own
>
> (Taylor and Martin, 1944).

These differing personality systems tend to lose communication with each other and amnesic barriers commonly divide and prevent integration between them (Hilgard, 1977).

Cases of dual or multiple personality were reported in the scientific literature from the late 18th century onward and, by the end of the 19th, they had become a popular theme for philosophers, psychiatrists and novelists (Ellenberger, 1970; McKellar, 1979). Robert Louis Stevenson's *Strange Case of Dr Jekyll and Mr Hyde* is the most celebrated literary example. Prince's (1906) account of the case of Christine Beauchamp and her three personalities and James's (1890) account of Ansel Bourne, led to considerable interest in the topic, particularly in America. There was a later wave of reaction against the concept of multiple personality. It was argued that the cases were often the creation of therapists who, by selective reinforcement and suggestion, produced iatrogenic syndromes or, that the clinicians were themselves the gullible dupes of liars and histrionic attention-seeking patients. In 1941, Stengel commented:

> The condition seems nowadays to occur in textbooks only . . . in reading (such accounts) one cannot help feeling that some of them were artefacts of a bygone age of psychiatry, while in others a careful personality study would have revealed that the actions of the double were by no means foreign to the primary personality.

In the 1950s, multiple personalities re-emerged from the pages of old textbooks. A surge of reports, both in the popular and scientific literature, followed publication of Thigpen and Cleckley's (1957) case of Eve and her three faces. In the USA this has grown into a virtual epidemic (Boor, 1982).

The central clinical feature described in DSM-III R is the existence within the individual of two or more distinct personalities. The recognition of this extraordinary state of affairs may be complicated by the primary personality being unable to provide any account of the *alter egos* which are hidden behind a barrier of amnesia. A number of diagnostic signs have been described to assist the clinician (Greaves, 1980). The patient may report time distortions or unexplained memory lapses for the period when the other personality is in residence. Accounts may be provided by independent observers of discrepant behaviour patterns and patients calling themselves by different names. Writings, drawing, or other artefacts by patients may be discovered which they have no memory of producing. Other features include headaches, deep sleeps, employing 'we' rather than 'I', and pseudohallucinations. The condition is said to begin in childhood or adolescence, often in the context of abuse, neglect, or trauma (Congdon and Abels, 1983). Histrionic personalities, other dissociative states, superior intellect and high hypnotizability, are all claimed to be associated with multiple personality disorder.

The origins of multiple personality have been hypothesized to lie in repeated dissociations. These patients are peculiarly prone to dissociative states in response to stress. They defend against fear, anxiety and depression by either denying that it is happening to them or escaping into the new personality (Ludwig et al., 1972; Spiegel, 1984). These repeated dissociations are said to produce a separate store of memories which ultimately leads to different chains of integrated memories with groups of specific behaviours that can be separated by impermeable barriers (Braun, 1984). William James put this more elegantly:

> Alternating personality in its simplest phases seems based on lapse of memory . . . any man becomes, as we say, inconsistent with himself if he forgets his engagements, pledges, knowledge and habits, and it is merely a question of degree at which point we shall say that his personality is changed
>
> (James, 1890).

The authenticity of multiple personality as a clinical entity has been repeatedly questioned, although its advocates, such as Greaves (1980), consider its existence to be demonstrated beyond reasonable doubt. He claims, moreover, that its infrequency reflects not rarity, but clinical oversight on the part of those who cannot, or will not recognize the condition. Cases of multiple personality are frequently described—what remains in doubt is what the syndrome represents. Is it an entity with its own unique psychopathology, or is it a culture bound syndrome wrought out of the dissociative potential and suggestibility of distressed and confused people looking for a way out of their predicament? It is widely acknowledged that, in practice, the new personalities allow the patient to avoid the constraints, limitations and stresses of their normal life (Prince, 1906; Taylor and Martin, 1944; Ludwig et al., 1972; Mckellar, 1979). In two of our cases, the gains from the abnormal state were obvious both in terms of becoming the centre of considerable attention and in avoiding responsibility for antisocial acts in one case, and insufficiently morally restrained ones in the other. Both of these patients were imaginative individuals who had habitually hidden from the very real difficulties and abuse of their childhood in a world of fantasy. Both were well aware of the culturally accepted notions of multiple personality. One had had the benefits of hypnotherapy, the other of interpretive psychotherapy, which had brought their *alter* personalities to light.

The potential significance of multiple personality for questions of responsibility and culpability were quickly recognized. These are dealt with in Ch. 2, p. 65. Some theories of reduced or absent responsibility presuppose that the sufferer is in the grips of an *alter* personality which dominates his normal and presumably 'real', non-offending, non-raping self. An argument of 'unconsciousness' has been advanced by French and Schechmeister (1983), resting on the analogy between the somnambulist and the multiple personality when in a state dominated by a subsidiary personality. These contentions appear to be based on the following assumptions:

1. there is only one real or primary personality and that the other personalities are excrescences created by disease or disorder, for which the sufferer cannot be held responsible;
2. the primary personality is incapable of controlling the actions of the secondary personality; and
3. when an amnesic barrier exists between the innocent primary personality and the guilty secondary one, this is tantamount to the primary personality being unconscious at the time of the offending.

The first point is put in question by those who argue that multiple personalities emerge out of splitting, or dissociation, in response to unpleasant realities, and are a way of coping with stress. This latter argument places the condition in the category of an exaggeration or distortion of normal mental mechanisms. It is seen as a development or reaction rather than a disease process. It is believed to involve a separation of different elements in the subject's character and behaviour, but these elements, nevertheless, arise from the individual's responses to the real world. Such personalities may, perhaps, be better regarded as different aspects of self, albeit compartmentalized, rather than different selves. The appeal of the Dr Jekyll and Mr Hyde story is surely, in part, that we all recognize the splits and incompatibilities in our desires, fantasies and even actions, and that most of us have done things which retrospectively, or even at the time, seemed foreign to our personalities and 'really wasn't us'. If the multiple personality is to be given the benefit of repudiating legal responsibility for forbidden actions, why not all criminals who can argue they acted out of character and were thus not themselves at the time? In criminal cases it always appears that offending is confined to the multiple personality's *alter ego*, although in the literature on non-forensic cases the 'normal' personality is recognized on occasion to be 'more pathological' (James, 1890; Ellenberger, 1970).

A more subtle argument has been advanced that in multiple personalities each personality manifests traits which are unbalanced by the factors which would constrain the expression in a normal and complete individual. This implies an immaturity in the various *alter* personalities and a lack of self-control, the recognition of which, it is contended, should modify our moral and forensic response (Gillett, 1986). This speaks not to intent or fitness to plead, but to mitigation and to future management and as such has greater appeal.

Fugues

Fugue literally means to take flight or escape, but its use in psychiatry is best confined to transitory abnormal behaviour characterized by aimless wandering with alteration of consciousness, often associated with subsequent amnesia (Stengel, 1941). Fugues are encountered as part of the symptomatology of a wide variety of psychiatric disorder, though their manifestation probably depends on a predisposition to disturbances of consciousness and dissociation. A traumatic event may act as the precipitant of the actual fugue state.

Fugues may be encountered in forensic practice in subjects who, following committing a criminal act, or in the context of imminent detection, suddenly wander off apparently in a state of disturbed consciousness. One of our cases, a young accountant, disappeared suddenly from work, only to turn up 5 days later in a state of total exhaustion and inanition wandering in the outskirts of Paris. When questioned by the French police, he claimed no knowledge of the events of the previous days, or how he had managed to cross the Channel and enter France, apparently without any passport. Subsequently, it emerged than an audit was in progress at his place of work which revealed that he had been misappropriating funds. The man had a history of depressive illness and had been recommenced on treatment only days before. In another case, a man of previous good character, who had stabbed an acquaintance in an argument, wandered off into the freezing cold of a winter's night without a jacket or overcoat. When apprehended some hours later, he was walking apparently aimlessly and in a perplexed and disoriented state. He claimed total amnesia for the night's events. Occasionally, acts committed during a fugue state may lead to criminal charges. A young hospital worker of histrionic disposition and with a past history of depression and suicidal behaviour was charged with arson. Immediately prior to the fire setting, the man had been rejected by a nurse with whom he had had a relationship. He turned up 12 hours later standing perplexed outside a house in which he had lived in as a child. There was a history, in this case, of a previous fugue state. On the previous occasion, he had wandered for several days before being discovered by the police on a motorway, apparently oblivious to his situation. This man was not totally amnesic, but described walking as if in a dream, with tunnel vision and islands of memory.

Possession States

Possession states, which are a rare form of dissociative disorder in western societies, are characterized by claims to be taken over by a spirit or some external power. They have to be distinguished from the passivity experiences and delusions of control found in the schizophrenias. In one case, a young man charged with killing his wife claimed to have committed the act whilst possessed by a spirit. He gave a 5-year history, which was confirmed from several independent sources, of brief periods of possession during which he would enter a trance-like state. He reported that a warrior periodically manifested to him, sometimes in the form of an auditory pseudohallucination, sometimes as a vivid visual mental image. Less frequently, this spirit would, he claimed, enter into his body and take possession of his mind. The warrior was a comfort and support to him at times of distress, but could also advocate acts of violence usually in the context of avenging slights and reverses. The warrior had undoubtedly in the past provided both a source of reassurance and an excuse for his angry and destructive impulses and actions. In the context of escalating domestic disputes, the warrior had, he claimed, been increasingly active in advocating violence. A short time before the offence, he had undergone an excorcism at the hands of a local clergyman. Immediately prior to the fatal attack, in the context of another angry domestic dispute, he claimed to experience the presence of the warrior, he then described a state of derealization followed by a sense of being engulfed by the spirit. He said he had no further memory for events until the police arrived some time after the attack on his wife. This man had a history of extensive abuse and physical and emotional deprivation during childhood. He was an intelligent man, who despite lacking formal education, had acquired a remarkable facility with the spoken and written language. His previous personality had marked histrionic and attention-seeking aspects which, coupled with a vivid imagination, had given him a reputation as boastful and unreliable. Fantasy and denial were his habitual ways of dealing with stress. The possession by the warrior could be interpreted as a dramatic extension of these mental mechanisms.

In cases where fugue or possession states are claimed to have been present at the time of a serious act of violence, the defence may raise the issue of non-insane automatism [*see* Ch. 2, p. 56].

Dissociative disorders have been claimed to lay a basis for a defence of non-insane automatism. A test case was that of *Mawonani* in preindependence Rhodesia (*see* Mackay, 1983). The accused stabbed and killed his brother whilst in a trance at a tribal ceremony during which he claimed he was possessed by his grandfather's spirit. He said he had no memory for the attack on his brother. Psychiatric evidence was given that at the time of the offence the accused was in a state of 'hysterical dissociation'. Beadle C. J. dismissed the defence of non-insane automatism stating:

> A person who is suffering from a state of hysterical dissociation and because of this is unable to appreciate the nature and quality of his acts, must be suffering at the time from some disability of mind.

Thus in dissociative states, if they do indeed render the sufferer incapable of voluntary control, then the defence is one of insanity not of non-insane automatism. This position has much to recommend it both from the legal and the psychiatric point of view, and its consistent application would prevent some of the more troubling attempts to employ the defence of non-insane automatism in cases of claimed dissociation.

Amok and Windigo

Amok (or amuck) is a term that has been applied to any sudden outbursts of violence, but in psychiatry it has tended to be confined to a so-called culture bound reactive syndrome involving the peoples of the Malay archipelago (Linton, 1956; Yap, 1969, Carr and Tan, 1976). Amok in Malay has the meaning of rushing in a state of frenzy to the commission of indiscriminate murder (*Oxford English Dictionary*). There were reports from Java by early Dutch and British colonists of Malays running amok (Spores, 1988).

Amok was claimed originally to have three phases (Gimlette, 1901; Burton-Bradley, 1968; Westermeyer, 1982):

1. a prodrome characterized by social withdrawal and anxious brooding;
2. a sudden furious outburst in which a number of people are attacked at random; and
3. sudden termination of the attacks, sometimes in extended stuporous sleep, but always with subsequent amnesia for the events.

This description is probably, at least in part, overlain by mythology (*see below*).

A number of precipitants have been described, the most common involving some overwhelming blow to the individual's self-esteem and social prestige. Others include acute intoxication (Westermeyer, 1973), organic brain syndromes (Van Loon, 1927), social stress as in migration, and relationship difficulties such as jealousy (Carr and Tan, 1976). The Malay culture is said to place a strong emphasis for males on retaining social prestige and avoiding loss of face. A powerful interdiction exists towards suicide. The act of running amok (becoming a pengamok) in traditional Malay culture, allowed a discredited or shamed male to bring about his own destruction, as the amok was often terminated by the killing of the pengamok or, if he survived, restoring his prestige. Amok was a recognized, if not sanctioned, social performance. The British colonial administration is said to have dramatically decreased the incidence of amok by legislation introduced in Pengang in 1893. This led to pengamoks being captured alive, often employing a specifically designed instrument consisting of a noose or trident on a long handle to subdue the victim at a safe distance. Following capture, they were transferred to the local lunatic asylum. This substitution of an extended and shameful incarceration for death or vindication appeared to reduce successfully the behaviour for some time.

A study of 21 subjects, who were in a secure psychiatric unit following running amok, cast doubt on some of the classical features of the condition (Carr and Tan, 1976). The attacks were often not as motiveless as they appeared at first sight. There was clear evidence for purposiveness. Two Malay subjects, who both harboured great resentment against the local Chinese community, carefully selected out Chinese victims during their amok and one revenged himself on his wife and her supposed lover (Carr and Tan, 1976). Burton-Bradley (1968) also noted in his cases, that the amnesia for the amok might be absent or only partially present (*see also* Spores, 1988).

Windigo is a related syndrome described in the Ojibwa Indians of sub-Arctic North America. The males of this tribe spend the long winter months hunting alone in the frozen wastes. Their prestige depends on success, and failure brings shame (Friedmann, 1982). The windigo is believed to be a giant phantom compounded of all those who have starved to death in the past (Meth, 1974). This phantom is believed to be capable of possessing a man and metamorphosing him into a murderous cannibalistic monster. The development of windigo is associated with failure in the hunt and especially famine. A prodrome of sleeplessness, depression and brooding is described, followed by an outburst of murderous activity in which the family as well as fellow members of the tribe are attacked and attempts made to consume their flesh (Landes, 1938). The state is terminated by the killing of the windigo or by his suicide. As with amok, this picture is at least in part mythological. There are no non-Indian eyewitnesses to murder or cannibalism ascribed to windigo, but this may testify to infrequency rather than to complete mythology. Famine cannabalism has been observed by outsiders.

Analogies have been drawn between amok and the sudden outbursts of murderous violence directed at a number of victims which occur periodically in western societies (Teoh, 1972; Westermeyer, 1982). Superificial similarities certainly exist in that they both involve a public display of apparently motiveless violence, often terminated by the killing or suicide of the perpetrator. Both seem to have elements of contagion in that amok violence has been described as spreading epidemics through some Asian communities (Westermeyer, 1973) and spectacular mass killings can spawn copy-cat killings. The analogy, however, obscures more than it illuminates. Mass killers in western societies are a heterogeneous mixture including disgruntled teenagers, gun-obsessed inadequates, deluded psychotics and misguided fanatics. There is fortunately no culturally accepted model of personal vindication through killing, although with Rambo movies and the like, one could presumably develop. Those who live to tell of their outbursts are not reported to claim amnesia for the events. One of our subjects was a depressed teenager with an excessive interest in guns and things military, which had unfortunately been indulged by his father. This young man's murderous outburst began with the unplanned, and probably inadvertent, slaying of his mother. What followed owed much to panic and despair. In another case, which fortunately led to no fatalities, a severely depressed and deluded young man attempted to end his own life by provoking the police into killing him by running through the streets discharging a pump-action shotgun. To describe a sudden outburst of violence as amok, in the technical rather than lay sense, evokes a spurious confidence that we have somehow understood the events. This could inhibit the proper exploration of the actual context and state of mind of the perpetrator.

Human behaviour, however apparently extraordinary, is the endpoint of a wide variety of interacting processes and influences. Amok is probably best viewed as a piece of behaviour which may occur in certain specific cultures as the result of provocations as varied as intoxication and marital discord. The culture acts to shape the behaviour and, perhaps even more importantly, moulds the attacker's subsequent understanding and justification of his behaviour.

11
Addictions and Dependencies; their Association with Offending

Edited by
Pamela J. Taylor

Written by
Alcohol:
John Hamilton
Michael D. Kopelman
Anthony Maden
Pamela J. Taylor

Other drug abuse:
John Strang
Andrew Johns

Gambling:
John Gunn
Pamela J. Taylor

ALCOHOL AND ITS ABUSE WITH SPECIAL REFERENCE TO ENGLAND AND WALES

Background to Legislation

Alcohol is an important economic commodity; it is also a dangerous drug and all modern societies make use of the criminal law to control its supply and consumption. The law relating to alcohol is of interest for several reasons:

1. it defines a number of offences; many of these are common, particularly in young people, and have considerable cost implications for the criminal justice system;
2. the law can be used as an instrument of social policy. The British Medical Association (BMA) regards legislative and fiscal changes as essential elements in a coordinated campaign to tackle alcohol abuse (Paton, 1985); the World Health Organisation recommends that member governments 'should begin to reduce *per capita* consumption by reducing the availability of alcoholic beverages' (Moser, 1985);
3. the structure of the law and the way in which it is applied can often be seen to reflect society's ambivalent attitudes towards alcohol and the conflict between economic and public health considerations; £16 billion

were spent on alcohol in the UK in 1985, earning the government £6 billion in taxes, whilst it spent less than £1 million on campaigns to combat abuse (Royal College of Psychiatrists, 1986).

Under UK law, alcohol is subject to legal controls in three main areas:

1. the licensing laws regulate retail supply;
2. legislation on drunkenness defines intoxication as an offence under certain circumstances;
3. road traffic legislation makes driving an offence when the blood alcohol level exceeds a certain value.

The Laws

The Licensing Laws

The UK licensing laws were introduced during the First World War in response to concern that munitions workers were spending too much time in public houses rather than in the factories. Modified since that time, these laws not only regulate the time and place at which alcohol may be sold, but are also intended to control under-age drinking. They state that those under 14 years may not be in the bar of licensed premises during permitted hours; those under 18 may not purchase or be supplied with alcohol in a bar or off-licence, nor may they consume alcohol in a bar (Licensing Act 1964). In addition, the Children and Young Persons Act 1933 makes it an offence to give intoxicating liquor to a child under the age of 5 years, except on medical orders. The law does allow, however, that persons of any age may be present in registered clubs and that those over 5 years may consume alcohol there. Over-5s may also consume alcohol in an eating area on licensed premises if bought by an accompanying adult. Those aged over 14 years may be in the bar of licensed premises during permitted hours and those over 16 years may purchase beer, porter, cider or perry with a meal in an eating area on licensed premises.

Apart from these restrictions, it is worth noting that people under 18 may lawfully consume alcohol at home, or anywhere other than a bar in licensed premises.

The allowing of under-age drinking in some situations but not others is seen as anomalous by many people. There is good evidence that most under-age drinking does not take place within the law. Surveys of drinking behaviour in the young show that a sizeable minority of school children are regular alcohol drinkers; the proportion rises towards the school leaving age and around a half of all 17-year-olds drink regularly, with the pub reported as the commonest source of alcohol for most (Home Office, 1987a). The

Home Office Working Group concluded that the major problem was not the law itself, but the fact that it was widely flouted. Prosecution for under-age drinking is rare in relation to the frequency of offending, and evidence of under-age drinking is rarely used by the courts as a reason for failing to renew a liquor licence.

Popular concern over the link between alcohol and violence has led to curbs on the sale of alcohol at football grounds, restrictions on drinking in public places and stricter penalties for publicans who serve under-age drinkers.

Conversely, the law on hours of opening has been relaxed. From 1976, opening hours for public bars in Scotland were extended for one hour in the evenings. A study designed to assess the impact of the Scottish changes concluded that they had no significant effect on the incidence of alcohol-related problems; a decline in drunkenness convictions is attributed to changes in police policy rather then the change in the law (Duffy and Plant, 1986). Others have criticized this study, arguing that difficulties in interpreting the data are so great that no firm conclusions can be drawn (Eagles and Besson, 1986). If the effect of the extensions remains in doubt, their popularity does not (Office of Population Censuses and Surveys, 1985). In England and Wales it is legal for bars to remain open all day.

The contradictory nature of attitudes towards alcohol is reflected in these changes and is likely to hinder the development of a consistent policy for dealing with abuse.

Drunkenness

Drunkenness is covered by the Licensing Act 1872, making it an offence to be drunk in any public place (simple drunkenness, encompassing drunk and incapable), or to be drunk and disorderly or drunk and indecent (aggravated drunkenness). The maximum penalty is 1 month's imprisonment, although fines and other sentences are open to the court. In 1985, there were 83 000 cautions or convictions for drunkenness offences in England and Wales; 22 000 of these were committed by people under 21. Of these, over 80% were for aggravated drunkenness (Home Office, 1987a).

The peak age for drunkenness prosecutions is 18 years; a caution or conviction in this age group is almost twice as likely as in those aged 21–29 years. Even in 17-year-olds, the rate is higher than for those over 21. For all age groups, the ratio of male to female offenders is 10:1. To some extent, these figures may reflect differences in the response of police and prosecutors, but it seems certain that they also reflect a real problem of drunkenness concentrated in young males. Statistics such as these have been used to argue in favour of a tightening of the licensing laws as they relate to young drinkers.

Drinking and Driving (*see also* pp. 112–15)

The problem of the drunken driver is not new; the Licensing Act 1872 makes it an offence 'to be drunk while in charge of any carriage on a highway' and the legislation was updated in the Criminal Justice Act 1925 to refer to 'mechanically propelled vehicles'.

The history of subsequent legislation reflects a concern that driving is impaired at levels of intoxication which do not amount to being 'drunk' and that this state is difficult to define. The wording was altered several times before the Road Traffic Act 1962 directed courts to take full account of the blood alcohol level and the Road Safety Act 1967 further reduced ambiguity by making it an offence to drive in the UK with a blood alcohol level exceeding 80 mg/dl. This limit remains in force. The only significant changes came in 1983, when breath replaced blood as the usual evidential sample and an attempt was made to define a class of 'high risk' offenders who should be further investigated for problem drinking.

Looking at the application of the law, it is apparent that the impact of the 1967 legislation was short-lived; after an initial fall in drunken driving, its frequency has risen again, probably as it is perceived, correctly, that the chance of detection is low (less than 1 in 250 according to Home Office estimates cited in Clare and Bristow, 1987; for further discussion see also Institute of Alcohol Studies, 1985). In those who are convicted, the peak age is 21 years and 32% of all convictions are in those aged under 25. As the majority of offenders are never detected, caution is needed in generalizing from these figures; the risk of accidents is greater in the young and the older drink-driver may simply pass unnoticed.

The true prevalence of drinking when driving is not known. In the 1960s, figures from the USA and Sweden suggested that the number of problem drinkers among those convicted may range from 10 to 57%, depending on the sample and methods used (Glatt, 1964; Selzer, 1963). Since an extensive international review of the field (Cohen, 1963), the only information on the drinking habits of drunken drivers in the UK comes from the Tayside Safe Driving Project (Dunbar et al., 1985). Alcohol metabolism in the body is speeded up by enzymes which are made in the liver. Large doses of alcohol stimulate these enzymes, their levels rise and this can be measured in the blood. One of these enzymes, gamma glutamyl transpeptidase (gamma-GT), was measured in blood samples taken from 440 offenders at the time of arrest; significantly raised levels were found in one-third of drivers aged over 30 years. This study also showed that present Department of Transport criteria for high risk offenders (two convictions within 10 years, alcohol concentration over two-and-a-half times the legal limit or refusal to provide a specimen) failed to detect the majority of these subjects. The overall conclusion is that a substantial minority of drunken drivers have a drink problem that is unknown to their general practitioner and to the court. Raised gamma-GT is only a moderately sensitive indicator of problem drinking. The true prevalence of problem drinking among drunken drivers is likely to be much higher than even this measure suggests. Given that drunken driving is known to cause over 1000 deaths annually, the failure to give priority to basic research in this area is a cause for concern (Clare and Bristow, 1987).

Similar criticisms can be made of the failure to provide facilities for the treatment of those problem drinkers who are detected. In the UK, there is no official policy on rehabilitation; local initiatives have produced a number of small projects. Other countries have more adventurous approaches. In the USA, many states operate rehabilitation programmes which, with the offender's consent, are available to the court as an alternative to other types of sentence. The programmes vary greatly; some are based on an educational model, aimed at all offenders, whilst others adopt a medical model, designed to identify and treat problem drinkers within the larger group of offenders. The latter approach is described in Siegal (1985), along with claims for its success in terms of clinical outcome and reconviction rates.

Such programmes are difficult to evaluate adequately and many have not been in existence long enough to allow firm conclusions to be reached. In addition, the element of compulsion involved raises important ethical questions. Even so, neither of these reservations can explain the virtual absence in the UK of any debate on these more imaginative responses to the problem of drunken driving.

Future Trends in Basic Alcohol Legislation

In 1975, concern over the fading impact of the breathalyser in the UK led to the setting-up of the Blennerhassett Committee of Enquiry (Department of the Environment, 1976); this concluded that the current legal limit is satisfactory, but enforcement should be improved by the introduction of discretionary or random breath-testing. At present, a motorist may be tested only if police have reasonable cause and the government rejected the proposed changes as an infringement of civil liberties, a burden on resources and damaging to police relations with the public. The question of random testing has remained a central topic of debate. Dunbar et al. (1987a) described its success in Finland. They concluded that it deters the social drinker, aids detection of the problem drinker and is a generally popular measure. Noting that similar legislation has now been adopted by two Australian states, they argued that it is only a matter of time before it reaches the UK. Dunbar et al. (1987b) made a case for lowering the legal limit from 80 mg/100 ml to 50 mg/100 ml, based on studies which show many aspects of psychomotor performance to be significantly impaired at blood alcohol levels which fall between these figures. It is also argued that Britain should follow the example of several Australian states by setting a zero limit for inexperienced drivers.

Whilst opinion is divided on appropriate limits, there is general agreement that all limits are irrelevant unless enforced, and there is pressure from many quarters to introduce random testing. Reluctance to do this can be seen as a further reflection of society's ambivalence towards alcohol, which places such a high value on the civil liberties of the drinker.

Alcohol and the Mental Health Acts

Under the MHA 1959, the wide definition of mental disorder allowed for the possibility of compulsory detention of alcoholics or drug addicts as suffering from 'any other disorder or disability of mind'. This provision was rarely used and the Butler Committee (Home Office/DHSS, 1975) concluded that the use of compulsory powers for the admission of alcoholics was inappropriate. It was argued that alcoholism, along with drug addiction and sexual deviation, was better regarded as a social or behaviour problem rather than a mental disorder. The MHA 1983 includes the stipulation that alcohol dependence alone is not a sufficient reason for compulsory admission, there must be a coexisting mental disorder. A mental disorder which has arisen as a consequence of alcohol abuse is not precluded.

Alcohol and the Possibility of Defence against Criminal Charges

Self-induced intoxication is generally *no* defence to a criminal charge. There are, however, some crimes which incorporate within their definition the concept of 'specific intent'. They require demonstration of a capability to form intent beyond the prohibited act (e.g. murder as opposed to manslaughter). Intoxication may be a defence to such charges, although conviction on a lesser charge, requiring only 'basic intent', would be usual if the facts sustained it. These issues, together with an account of circumstances in which alcohol may have been a contributory cause of relevant mental disorder are dealt with more fully on pp. 59–64.

Alcohol and Offending Behaviour: Relevant Alcohol-related Pharmacological and Psychological Factors

The Alcohol-dependence Syndrome

Some psychiatrists have deplored the notion of alcoholism as a disease (e.g. Scott, 1968); and classifications of alcoholism, such as that of Jellinek (1960), have been found to be insensitive to the gradations and complexity of the disorder. In order to circumvent these difficulties, Edwards and Gross (1976) provided a behavioural description of what they called the 'alcohol dependence syndrome'. This has the following characteristic features:

1. a narrowing of the drinking repertoire (so that it becomes increasingly stereotyped);
2. a progressive increase in the salience given to drink-seeking behaviour over other activities;
3. increased tolerance to alcohol;
4. repeated withdrawal symptoms;
5. relief or avoidance of withdrawal symptoms by further drinking;
6. subjective awareness of the compulsion to drink;
7. rapid reinstatement of the features of the syndrome, when a severely dependent subject resumes drinking again after a period of abstinence.

This behavioural description of the dependence syndrome provides a potential means of developing quantitative and relatively objective methods of assessing alcohol abuse in offender populations (*see* e.g. Edwards et al., 1971), but it is not without difficulties and, in practice, has seldom been used in such studies.

The search for the causes of alcohol abuse has encompassed genetic, metabolic, neurotransmitter, psychoanalytic, personality, behavioural and socio-cultural theories. Many commentators accept a multifactorial approach, in which the contributions of predisposing personality traits, learned maladaptive behaviour, and the socio-cultural environment are all acknowledged (Clare, 1979). Vaillant and Milofsky (1982) followed-up 456 delinquent adolescents at risk for alcoholism until they reached the age of 47, and found that 110 became alcohol abusers at some stage (modal age-31). By the age of 47, approximately one-third of these alcohol abusers had been abstinent for a year or more, another third were described as 'progressively alcoholic' and the remaining third were either 'social drinkers' or 'suspected abusers'. The factors which tended to promote abstinence were:

1. a substitute form of dependency, e.g. gambling, illicit drugs, smoking, compulsive work, religion;
2. 'naturalistic' behaviour modification, e.g. medical illness, compulsory supervision;
3. a stable source of increased hope and self-esteem, e.g. Alcoholics Anonymous; and
4. 'social rehabilitation'—a new close relationship with a mentor or lover.

Attendance at a clinic seemed to have relatively little effect (*see also* Orford, 1978).

The complications of alcohol abuse encompass social, employment, marital, neurological, and general medical and surgical problems as well as the psychiatric and psychological (for review of these wider aspects of alcohol abuse, *see* Lancet, 1981; Murray, 1986; Lishman, 1987).

Psychiatric Complications of Alcohol Abuse

The specifically psychiatric complications of alcohol abuse have been well reviewed by Cutting (1979). Cutting classified alcohol-related psychiatric disabilities in four main groups: intoxication phenomena, withdrawal phenomena, chronic nutritional conditions and associated psychiatric disorders. These will be considered in turn.

Intoxication phenomena

Simple intoxication.   Alcohol is a central nervous system depressant, even the apparently excited behaviour seen at lower doses following from depression of neural activity, in this case of inhibitory control systems. Levels at which symptoms may appear to the casual observer are enormously variable, depending on such factors as the subject's habituation to alcohol, whether it was taken with food (particularly other carbohydrates which tend to slow absorption), or the rate at which it was consumed—a rapid rise in blood alcohol tending to produce effects at a lower level than a gradual rise. In addition, social conditions or mood state at the time of drinking may influence behaviour, but there is little doubt that testing of various kinds reveals deficits in performance at comparatively low doses, and at a time when the subject may be denying of problems.

Smith et al. (1975) showed that use of language, both in terms of cognitive ability to identify or recall words and in skills associated with social speech, declined from the commencement of drinking. In a neat and practical study, Cohen et al. (1958) examined the performance of experienced, professional bus drivers in Manchester, all of whom had received awards for safe driving. After consumption of alcohol, they were asked to estimate the size of gap through which they thought they could drive their bus, and then given a driving test, first to determine the smallest gap they would attempt from choice, and second their behaviour when required to drive through gaps regardless of their opinion. At any blood alcohol level, there was a probability of impairment of judgement, nevertheless, no driver lacked confidence in his judgements. Other studies have further demonstrated poverty of judgements after alcohol consumption. Drew et al. (1958), for example, in a simulated driving experiment, found that even on small doses of alcohol, subjects' steering wheel movement and timing as well as speed of driving became increasingly faulty. The quality of the mistakes varied to an extent with personality type. The legal limit for blood alcohol in the UK is perhaps overgenerous, given that the risk of road accidents is more than doubled at this level and, at 160 mg per 100 ml, it has increased tenfold. Thus, the risk of one sort of dangerous behaviour is certainly increased, even at quite low levels of intoxication.

The increased risk of other kinds of dangerous offending behaviour is less clear, many studies of any association between offending and alcohol consumption tending to focus on the alcoholic or recognized problem drinker rather than the inebriate. In practice, blood alcohol levels, at least in the UK, are infrequently measured even after a serious crime, presumably because the legal importance in relation to the individual is generally regarded as minimal. Shupe (1954), however, inferred from urine alcohol levels in a substantial series (882) of people arrested for a serious offence that 64% were under the influence of alcohol 'to an extent to reduce their inhibitions' at the time of their offence. This is very similar to the proportion (54%) in Washbrook's (1977) much larger series of consecutively sentenced men (5000) entering Birmingham prisons who admitted at interview to having consumed alcohol during the 24-hour period leading up to the offence.

Pathological intoxication, also known as pathological reaction to alcohol, acute alcoholic paranoid state and *mania à potu*, has been reviewed at regular intervals (Banay, 1944; May and Ebaugh, 1953; Coid, 1979). It has been described in ICD-9 as 'acute psychotic episodes induced by relatively small amounts of alcohol . . .', or, in an operational definition in DSM-III R as having three requirements:

1. maladaptive behavioural changes occurring *within minutes* of ingesting an amount of alcohol insufficient to induce intoxication in most people;
2. the behaviour is atypical of the person when not drinking; and
3. it is not due to any other disorder.

It is extremely doubtful whether such a condition exists. Cutting (1978) found no cases among patients with alcoholic psychoses admitted to one hospital over 27 years. Bach-y-Rita et al. (1970), infused alcohol into 10 patients with this alleged diagnosis and obtained no evidence of either 'behavioural arousal' or abnormal EEG activity. Others have had more success in inducing symptoms and signs, but not consistently so, including Maletsky (1976) and Wolf (1980). None of the simulation studies involved a comparison group, and Coid (1979) found that the clinical descriptions of the disorder used in the studies tended to be vague and contradictory. Some supposed cases may result from alcohol-induced hypoglycaemia (Marks and Rose, 1965), others from alcohol-induced seizures, head injury, or other organic disorder, and a third group from psychiatric disorder or underlying personality predispositions.

Alcoholic blackouts. Alcoholic blackouts are described by alcohol abusers (Goodwin et al., 1969), and are commonly implicated in the amnesia claimed by offenders for their crime (Kopelman, 1987a). They may be of the fragmentary or *en bloc* variety (*see also* p. 63). They appear to be related to the level of blood alcohol (Goodwin et al., 1969; Tamerin et al., 1971); but they do not appear to be predictive of either chronic cognitive impairment (Tarter and Schneider, 1976) or neuroradiological evidence of cortical atrophy (Ron, 1983).

Abstinence and withdrawal states

Withdrawal phenomena may be precipitated by custodial confinement after an arrest, but otherwise carry no implications for offenders. Since, however, at least 4% of remanded prisoners show withdrawal symptoms or signs on arrival in prison (Taylor and Gunn, 1984) it is important that prison medical staff and visiting psychiatrists are aware of this potential. In the most serious form of withdrawal state—delirium tremens—there is a mortality of up to 5% (Victor, 1966).

Treatment of minor, even moderate withdrawal symptoms may be dealt with on an inpatient or outpatient basis, and thus it may be safe to manage them within a prison, providing observation is good. Drug treatment is adviseable, to reduce symptoms and discomfort, but also to minimize the risk of withdrawal fits. Drugs with cross-tolerance with alcohol should be used, usually in a reducing dose over 1 week. Benzodiazepines are one option, especially chlordiazepoxide or diazepam, but many prefer chlormethiazole. A typical regime for the latter would be to start on 4 g a day in divided doses and then reduce by 1 g every other day until the patient is off medication.

Patients with a history of seizures, whether alcohol-induced or not, or with any indication of impending or established delirium tremens *must* be admitted to hospital immediately. It is important to exclude or identify likely coexisting pathologies. Head injury, simultaneous intoxication with other substances, especially barbiturates or benzodiazepines, or infections are probably most likely, but liver or heart failure and gastric or oesophageal bleeding are possibilities. Once a diagnosis of delirium tremens is established, then the mainstays of treatment are fluid replacement, which may need to be given intravenously, sedation and a quiet, minimally stimulating environment where observation by medical and nursing staff experienced in treating the condition can be close (Edwards, 1982).

Other associated psychiatric conditions

Schacter (1986) was unable to find any reported case in the literature of a patient with severe, chronic amnesia, such as that found in the Wernicke/Korsakoff syndrome, being involved in an offence. A likely case has now come to our attention on a charge of murder, but was found unfit to plead and so is detained in a maximum security hospital without a trial of the facts. Milder degrees of cognitive impairment, which Cutting (1979) called 'psychological deterioration', sometimes with an associated mild degree of cortical atrophy on CT (computerized tomography) scan, are commonly found in alcoholics charged with an offence (Kopelman, 1987b); such changes, however, are no different from those found in non-criminal alcoholics (Ron, 1983; Brandt and Butters, 1986). A case in whom a mild degree of organic memory impairment may have provided the substrate upon which a psychogenic amnesia was based has been reported (Gudjonsson and Taylor 1985).

Cutting (1978) found that many people with 'alcoholic hallucinosis' manifested features suggestive of an underlying schizophrenic or affective disorder, and that only small numbers of patients exhibited the classical persecutory hallucinations and secondary delusions in the absence of other abnormal phenomena. The nature of any relationship between alcohol abuse, schizophrenia and offending remains to be elucidated (*see also* pp. 370–1). Winokur et al. (1971) have suggested a genetic link between alcoholism in males and depression in females—others have noted that depression may first appear in the context of alcohol dependence, and that there is a high suicide rate amongst alcoholics (Beck et al., 1976). Paranoid disorders, including morbid jealousy are sometimes associated with alcohol abuse (Shepherd, 1961; Cobb, 1979), and 2–4% of cases of morbid jealousy end in homicide (Cobb, 1979) (*see also* pp. 351–3).

The Association between Alcohol Use and Abuse and Criminal Behaviour (other than that defined by Drunkenness Laws)

An apparent statistical association between alcohol and crime in western society should, perhaps, be unsurprising given the widespread and probably increasing use of alcohol. The fact that even the presence of alcohol in likely excess of the legal limit for driving is regarded by criminal courts as wholly irrelevant to any but specifically drink-related crimes may have contributed to the general paucity of the literature on the role of alcohol in crime. Greenberg (in Collins, 1982) provide an excellent methodological critique of the role of alcohol in the criminal situation, and the different, but related, issue of the prevalence of alcoholism among criminals and the criminal history of alcoholics. Blum, and Roman (both in Collins, 1982) enlarged on the complex matter of context in which drinking and crime occur. The book provides a useful framework for tackling the field.

The Frequency of Overall Association between Alcohol Use and Offending

Amark's (1951) study remains extremely important and interesting, for its size, its thoroughness and its comparative approach. Three groups of alcoholics were included, 103 attending a clinic in Stockholm, 100 in a range of institutions provided for alcoholics and over 400 'temperance board cases'. Subjects and their relatives were interviewed and a remarkable range of independent data, from community sources, such as the clergy, to national criminal statistics, were obtained. A high rate of convictions for drunkenness in the temperance board group was inevitable, one of the reasons for intervention by the board being repeated drunkenness convictions. The institutional group showed a similar rate, but the clinic group a much lower. Crime rates were between four and eight times higher across the alcoholic group than in the general population, with an interesting pattern. The alcohol abuse appeared relevant since the first criminal sentence was on average at 28 years old, a rather late entry to the criminal system, and it occurred usually between the onset of abuse and the first appearance or recognition of psychiatric symptoms. The criminal alcoholics were found to differ from the others in that they appeared to have started drinking at an earlier age. The extension into family studies raised particularly interesting questions. The male siblings of the alcoholic were also significantly more likely to have convictions for both drunkenness and other crimes than the general population.

Lindelius and Salum (1975), also in Sweden, compared three groups of men identified primarily by their alcoholism—a voluntary, psychiatric hospital group (I), those hospitalized for the acute sequelae of excessive drinking (group II), and homeless men. The rate of criminality was similar to that in the general population in group I, and highest among the homeless men. Types of offending were varied.

Banay (1942) conducted an extensive survey of over 3000 men in Sing Sing Prison between 1938 and 1940. They were subjected to complete physical, laboratory, psychometric and psychiatric examinations and statements about drinking were checked with informants. Three groups emerged: alcoholic criminals, criminals who were alcoholic (i.e. their drinking was judged to be coincidental to their offending) and non-drinkers. Banay emphasized the likelihood of at least one other group not appearing in the sample—the chronic drinker who, in spite of frequent intoxication, manages to complete life without violating more than the conventions of civilized conduct. The alcoholic criminals were a heterogeneous group, but differed from the others primarily in terms of their higher incidence of assault.

Gibbens and Silberman (1970) studied a stratified sample of over 400 prisoners and ex-prisoners from different London prisons. Within this sample, 22% had previous convictions for drunkenness and a further 18% admitted to excessive drinking to the extent that it had interfered seriously with their social adjustment. The overall rate of drunkenness and excessive drinking varied from 17% in an open prison for convicted men, through 27% of first offenders in a male remand (pre-sentence and generally pre-conviction) prison to 47% of male recidivists serving long sentences in a third prison.

Edwards et al. (1971) applied different criteria for problem drinking. They compared groups of offenders with samples of London flat dwellers and the occupants of a reception centre in terms of the proportion of subjects who reported drinking 10 pints or more a day, subjective awareness of a drink problem, and a history of alcoholic blackouts or of an arrest for drunkenness. They found that subjects serving a short sentence (less than 3 months) had particularly high rates of such alcohol-related problems. With a different sample, Edwards et al. (1977) subsequently reported that 30% of male and 17% of female inpatient alcoholics had a criminal record.

Guze (1976) in North America reported that 43% of a consecutive series of male sentenced prisoners were alcoholic, and, with others, (Guze et al., 1974) found that 13% of a sample of 70 alcoholic outpatients had committed a criminal offence.

More recently (Taylor and Gunn 1984), it was found that 4.1% of a sample of 2743 men newly admitted to a British remand prison fulfilled criteria for alcoholism in terms of showing symptoms of withdrawal after admission. A further 8.4% of the total sample were also noted to be abusing either alcohol or drugs without obvious signs of dependency, although, on the basis of the reliability study, this probably underrepresented the problem considerably.

There are, thus, substantial rates of problem drinking among offenders, and criminal behaviour among alcoholics, but the case for a statistically significant association between alcohol and crime generally remains unproven. Washbrook (1977) comparing self-reports of the drinking habits of convicted male prisoners with those of men working in a nearby factory found little difference between the samples. Just over 4% of the factory sample admitted to a serious drink problem, probably amounting to alcoholism, compared with 7.5% in the prison sample, but about one-third of both groups admitted heavy drinking. By contrast Bell and Champion (1979) suggested a significant association from a study of over 500 prisoners, probation clients and delinquents and more than 7000 school and college students, matched for age. Over 70% of the delinquents and prisoners used alcohol at least once a week compared with 30–40% of the school attenders and up to 54% of college students. There was a tendency for heavy alcohol use (eleven or more drinks on each drinking day) to be associated with recidivism.

Alcohol and Specific Offence Categories

Homicide

> *'That which hath made them drunk hath made men bold'*
> (Lady MacBeth—*MacBeth*, Act 2, Scene 1, Shakespeare)

Wolfgang and Strohm (1956) extensively reviewed literature examining links between alcohol and crime and then described all 621 homicides in Philadelphia between January 1948 and December 1952. Nearly two-thirds of the killings had taken place in the context of alcohol usually with both parties indulging. In New Jersey, Gibbens (1958a) found that drunkenness played a large part in crimes of homicide; further, there were eight murders by drunken men in which ordinary motives were lacking. Thirty of the 235 cases were chronic alcoholics, a remarkably similar proportion to that found by Gudjonsson and Petursson (1982) in their complete sample of homicides in Iceland this century (to 1979). Only London's (Taylor, 1986) figures were higher, but for a more selected group—men and women serving life sentences, mainly for murder. Scott (1968) and Adair (1973) found slightly lower rates of alcoholism while, in Scotland, Gillies (1976) focused on intoxication. A bare majority of male victims and killers alike had been drunk at the time of the crime, as had a substantial minority of the women. These drunken killers were usually otherwise psychiatrically 'normal'. The possibility of an exceptionally low rate of alcohol use among mentally abnormal killers and serious offenders is discussed elsewhere (pp. 370–1). In England and Wales, Zacune and Hensman (1971) reported that up to 42% of murderers had been drinking before their offence.

In summary, it seems that alcohol use at the time of a killing by both victim and offender is common, especially among those regarded as mentally normal, but the rates of serious problem drinking seem low. Within these broad generalizations, it is likely that, in addition, there are cultural variations. Further, the studies cited are concerned only with murder or manslaughter. The other group of alcohol-related homicides—those killers who were driving a car when over the legal limit of blood alcohol—are rarely, if ever, included in these figures.

Rape and sexual assault

Coid (1986) summarized the major studies of rape during the last 30 years, and found that alcohol had been consumed shortly before the offence by the offender, the victim or both in between 34 and 72% of cases. Coid, however, emphasized the lack of comparison groups in these studies, the very wide variation in range of figures given, and the consequent difficulty in interpreting their importance. He commented that a lack of major differences between the nature of sexual assaults when alcohol is present and those when it is absent is generally striking, although there is some evidence that alcohol may be more associated with the sexual humiliation of the victim or with violence (e.g. Amir, 1967). Amir also found that alcohol was most commonly present in cases of group rape, being involved in 63% of these incidents. Indecent exposure and exhibitionism have also been associated with alcohol abuse, especially in older subjects (Rooth, 1971).

Other violent crime

Banay's (1942) finding of higher rates of assault among alcoholic criminals has already been noted. Gibbens and Silberman (1970) in their series of English prisoners found that a history of two or more aggressive offences was much commoner among alcoholics. Shupe (1954) reported an American series of 882 offenders in whom a high level of intoxication was more commonly involved in serious assaults, particularly when a weapon was used. Coid (1982) provided a more extended review of the field and (1986b) explored some of the complexities of the interaction between alcohol, other socio-cultural factors and aggression.

It is a common clinical impression that alcohol is implicated in domestic violence, but the evidence is mixed. Two examples illustrate the conflict. Gayford (1975a, b), for example, found that alcohol was commonly a problem. In studying 100 battered wives, he found that more than half the husbands engaged in frequent heavy drinking, with drunkenness on approximately a weekly basis, usually violence only occurring after the husband had been drinking. McClintock (1978), however, reporting only on cases in which the police had been involved, found that in 82% of cases there was no indication of alcohol having been taken 'immediately prior' to the offence by either offender or victim. This figure may indicate best a lack of police curiosity about drinking behaviour, since information was collected from police records in this study, but from the victims in Gayford's study. The police were said to have distinguished between 'some' and 'heavy' drinking, but it is unusual in Britain for alcohol consumption in relation to crime to be recorded.

Non-violent crime

Edwards et al. (1971), within their prison sample, found that it was particularly the offenders serving short sentences (less than 3 months) who showed evidence of problems with alcohol. Some of these subjects had been arrested for public drunkenness, or for non-payment of a fine in connection with such an offence, and there was a tendency for alcohol abuse to be inversely associated with violence. Drunkenness apart, few admitted a direct relationship between alcohol abuse and offending; 6% admitted to fraud and 6% to an acquisitive offence in order to pay for drink, and 2% to drinking in order to pluck up courage to commit the offence for which they were convicted.

Alcohol and Crime: a Summary

Five possible ways thus emerge in which alcohol might be related either to violence or to crime in general:

1. alcohol may be a direct precipitant of crime through a toxic or pharmacological 'disinhibiting' effect;
2. alcohol may be a facilitator for offending arising from associated social relations or desires, also mediated through its pharmacological properties;
3. alcohol may precipitate psychiatric disorder, often through measurable brain damage, which may itself predispose to offending;

4. alcohol abuse may result in an increase in crime to support the habit;
5. alcohol abuse and offending may be related by a common aetiology.

Easy assumptions about the relationship of alcohol abuse to violent crime have been undermined by the anthropological study of MacAndrew and Edgerton (1969), who found a differential interaction between social mores and alcohol consumption. These authors observed that in certain Indian tribes in North and South America alcohol intoxication produced 'changes for the worse', whereas in other tribes it did not. The effect of alcohol abuse was mitigated by the time and circumstances of the drinking behaviour, by social controls, and by the presence or absence of particular 'target groups' or victims. They are not the only researchers to have emphasized the importance of the social context of drinking in terms of its consequences (e.g. Collins, 1982).

Alcohol and Reoffending

The sociological viewpoint of criminality as a career suggests that it is a career which, like that of entertainer or doctor, carries an increased risk of alcoholism. The London Longitudinal Survey (West, 1982) followed the careers of a random, non-institutional sample of 400 8-year-olds and traced their development into adulthood. At the age of 18, the most popular leisure pursuit for the entire sample was 'going to pubs' (reported by 89%), illustrating the central social role of drinking in this section of the population. Nevertheless, heavy alcohol consumption was more than twice as common in the 101 delinquents (45%) as in the non-delinquent controls (18%). By the age of 24 years, the frequency of delinquency and of heavy drinking within the group had decreased, but the association remained; furthermore, the persistent recidivist offenders showed an increased prevalence of excessive drinking relative to both the non-delinquents and the temporary recidivists, whose offending careers ended before the age of 21 years.

Studies of young offenders in custody lend further support to an association between alcohol abuse and recidivism. Heather (1981a, b) studied 200 consecutive admissions to a Scottish young offenders institution and found that 63% reported being drunk at the time of their offence. Almost 80% of these drunken offenders showed evidence of physical or psychological dependence on alcohol and 40% of them had 10 or more previous convictions, compared to 19% of the other receptions. Within this group, severity of problem drinking was found to be associated with degree of recidivism. Moreover, whilst the majority of their previous offending was in some way drink-related, the association of alcohol abuse with recidivism remained even when such offences were excluded. With regard to the nature of the present offence, it is of interest that there was no significant difference between drunken offenders and others; crimes of violence and hooliganism were slightly over-represented, but so was theft, by far the commonest offence in both groups. In a similar study of receptions to an English youth custody centre, Hollin (1983) found that a smaller proportion reported offending under the influence of alcohol (38%), but the association between alcohol abuse and recidivism remained.

For adult offenders, most data comes from cross-sectional surveys of prison populations. An exception is the longitudinal study by Sapsford and Fairhead (1980) who used data collected in the South East region prison survey to identify predictors of reconviction in the 2 years following release. Excluding those men whose original sentence was for drunkenness, they found reconviction rates of 65% for those with a drink problem compared to 47% for those without. Detection of problem drinking was from information in prison records, so a high number of false negatives may be expected; the findings probably underestimate the significance of problem drinking in predicting reconviction.

Surveys of the adult prison population provide further information about the criminological, social and psychological characteristics of those prisoners with alcohol problems. The Gibbens and Silberman (1970) study has already been mentioned p. 448. Although excluding prisoners serving sentences of under 28 days, and thereby eliminating all but 5% of men sentenced for drunkenness itself, problem drinking was found in 47% of recidivists, compared to 27% of those serving their first custodial sentence. Of those men with more than six previous sentences, two-thirds were excessive drinkers. Despite this, only a small minority had a previous record consisting mainly of drunkenness offences; most were indistinguishable from other recidivists, except for a slight increase in the rate of conviction for aggressive offences. Heavy drinkers did differ from other prisoners in being more likely to have a background of poverty, social isolation and a poor work record.

Other surveys of prison populations have produced similar findings. Unfortunately, demonstrating a relationship between alcohol abuse and recidivism falls far short of explaining it; in this sense, the problem is similar to that of the relationship between alcohol and crime in general. Recidivists as a group, however, are distinguished by a number of characteristics, other than their drinking behaviour. West (1982) describes his group of 24-year-old persistant recidivists as a 'disfavoured and deviant group' characterized by unemployment, substandard housing, disrupted family and peer relationships and a high incidence of antisocial behaviour in the form of frequent fighting and drug abuse. Rutter and Giller (1983) characterized the young recidivist as more likely to suffer from various neurotic symptoms and discordant relationships, in addition to material, educational and social disadvantages.

The fact that recidivists as a group differ in many ways from other offenders and from the general population in itself, militates against any simple explanation of the role of alcohol. It also suggests that future research should take account of these variables, particularly in selecting control populations (Vingilis, 1981). Disentangling these influences presents a formidable task. For the moment it can be concluded that, however the alcohol-abusing recidivist came to be that way, his drink problem is unlikely to be a positive influence in a life that already has many negative ones.

Habitual Drunken Offenders

Two hundred years ago, Thomas Trotter (1788) described habitual drunkenness as a disease necessitating the attention of doctors and said that 'the habit of drunkenness is a disease of the mind'. Controversy has continued from then until now as to the respective roles of penal, medical and social services in the management of habitual drunken offenders.

The 'gin lane' days, depicted by Hogarth in the 18th century were followed by epidemics of drunkenness in the 19th century, with a rate of public drunkenness six times the present-day figures. Consequently, two pieces of legislation were enacted towards the end of that century which are now in disuse. The Habitual Drunkards Act 1879 provided for the establishment of 'retreats' to which habitual drunkards could be admitted voluntarily for treatment, for a maximum of 2 years unless released earlier by licence. Compulsory detention was introduced with the Inebriates Act 1898, by which 'any habitual drunkard convicted on indictment of an offence punishable by imprisonment, if the offence was committed when the defendant was under the influence of drink; or if drunkenness was a contributory cause' could be sent to a state or certified inebriate reformatory for up to 3 years. Any person guilty of four drunkenness offences in the course of 12 months could be sent, with his consent, by magistrates to an inebriate reformatory or by a higher court without his consent. Fifteen state and inebriate reformatories were established, but all had closed by 1921.

The ineffectiveness of imprisonment in preventing recidivism has long been recognized and led in the 1960s to the Home Office setting up a working party on habitual drunken offenders which reported in 1971 (Home Office, 1971b). Amongst their 105 conclusions and recommendations, the working party stated:

> Persons who under present arrangements would be arrested for being drunk in public should be taken by the police to special detoxification centres and there detained while they are dried out and any necessary medical and social investigation is carried out.

They recommended the provision of places for 2000 males and 200 females, but thought the number of potential users of such facilities might be nearer 5000.

The Criminal Justice Act 1967 removed the penalty of imprisonment for drunken offenders, but also stated that a statutory order implementing this change would not be made—

> unless the Secretary of State is satisfied that sufficient suitable accommodation is available for the care and treatment of persons convicted of being drunk and disorderly.

The Criminal Justice Act 1972 provided police with the power to arrest the drunk and incapable or drunk and disorderly and to take them to any place approved by the Secretary of State as a medical treatment centre for alcoholics.

This change in the direction of diversion from the criminal justice system was accompanied by the issue, in 1973, of a circular from the Department of Health and Social Security *Community Services for Alcoholics* (DHSS Circular 21/73), which enabled capital and revenue grants to be made for a period of 5 years to voluntary organizations who were seeking to establish detoxification and hospital services for alcoholics. Some 70 projects were developed as a result of these arrangements, but subsequent problems about funding led to increasing competition for scarce resources, and the impetus to provide comprehensive community services was lost.

Under the Criminal Justice Act 1972 detoxification centres were set up in Manchester and Leeds. Other detoxification services developed separately in Edinburgh, Oxford and London. Orford and Wawman (1986) have evaluated the effectiveness of these and other centres in the UK and North America and commented on the difficulties intrinsic in such an evaluation, as different projects had differing aims. These include firstly the management and treatment of intoxication and withdrawal in humane and safe conditions with the provision of medical attention for associated physical problems, secondly the diversion of the management of drunken offenders from penal to medical and social welfare agencies and thirdly rehabilitation. Projects also developed services for varying client groups and used a variety of hospital and non-hospital settings for detoxification. The authors found that only a minority of patients admitted for detoxification were referred for further treatment or rehabilitation. A similar minority had a very high rate of readmission.

Orford and Wawman found only the Edinburgh study (Hamilton et al. 1978), examining the medium to long-term outcome for individual users of alcohol detoxification services, to have employed an adequate research design. They used random assignment of habitual drunken offenders to detoxification and control groups and compared the progress of each group, both in an experimental year and in the previous year. The results of this project suggested that the handling of most of this difficult group of clients could successfully be transferred from the criminal justice to the health care system. Doing so led to early signs of producing beneficial changes in lifestyle.

Finn (1985) expressed the belief that such detoxification centres should provide—

some relief to the criminal justice system, rehabilitating a few public inebriates permanently, and facilitating temporary but beneficial periods of abstinence for many.

This setting of modest goals is supported by Orford and Wawman's conclusions that, where detoxification services appear not to have met their objectives, this may have as much to do with unrealistic objectives and poor planning than with a failure of the basic idea. They pointed to the need for considerable thought and effort being put into joint planning and liaison between the differing agencies involved in taking clients into the service, working with them whilst they remain in the service or at the stage of discharge or onward referral. Where decriminalization is chosen as a high priority aim, joint planning and liaison with the police is of paramount importance. The authors also said that there is a need to devote careful attention to staff training and support, and to staff attitudes and morale, both within the detoxification service itself and the larger organization or institution of which the service may be a part.

With the failure of a comprehensive development of detoxification services for habitual drunken offenders on a national basis, police forces in different parts of the country have instituted schemes for 'cautioning' regular offenders. In 1984, new guidelines on the criteria to be applied when deciding on a prosecution or other action were set by the Attorney General and are based on a presumption that police will caution rather than prosecute drunken offenders. The guidelines stipulate that drunken offenders will only be prosecuted if arrested more than three times in any period of 4 weeks. Whilst such cautioning schemes have led to a reduction in the numbers of drunken offenders being sent to prison in default of payment of a fine (from 2400 in 1983 to 923 in 1986) (Home Office, 1987b), they almost certainly do not help in any real reductions in offensive drunken behaviour and they do not solve the problem of how to provide the treatment and rehabilitation the individuals need and deserve.

Light (1988) suggested that the issues surrounding the management of habitual drunken offenders must be seen on a wider setting. Police are not trained or equipped to deal with these problems: more than 100 people die in police custody each year and over half of these deaths are drink-related. Light recommends the improvement of police custody facilities, which are often inadequate and degrading, and recommends a thorough examination of the full range of service requirements for the skid row population, including housing and health care. This, however, is to imply that police custody, if only a little more congenial, would be a satisfactory place for the intoxicated. No doctor would recommend such a placement for any other form of poisoning. This Edinburgh experience offers real guidance for a way forward. What is needed is a commitment to providing the necessary resources.

Treatment of Alcoholic Offenders in Prison and other Penal Establishments

The treatment of withdrawal symptoms is described on p. 444. While this is important, and maybe life saving, it is likely to have little impact on the underlying drinking habits. Edwards et al. (1971) ended their survey of drinking problems in prison with an urgent call for 'an experimental treatment programme within the prisons', and in the face of the failure of community provision the pressure is always there to do so. Treatment facilities within prisons, however, also remain inadequate, and may even be deteriorating (House of Commons, 1986b). Provision is very variable; there is no overall policy for treatment and no comprehensive account of the service provided at different establishments, although the latter is in preparation (McMurran and Baldwin, 1989). The best existing description is that contained in the Report of the Home Office Working Party on the Habitual Drunken Offender (Home Office, 1971b), now almost twenty years old.

The commonest source of help is Alcoholics Anonymous (AA), which visits most prisons and youth custody centres on a weekly or monthly basis. This is the only service provided at some institutions, but others have groups for alcohol abusers run by a psychologist or probation officer; these have an educational or self-help orientation (McMurran, 1989). In addition, some doctors within the prison system provide group or individual treatments, often with a psychotherapeutic orientation; Wormwood Scrubs Annexe is an example (Gunn et al., 1978).

Some general points can be made concerning these services. Variation between establishments has already been mentioned; services are likely to be minimal in the overcrowded and understaffed local prisons where the majority of alcoholics are to be found. The 1971 Working Party accepts that no treatment, beyond drying out, is provided to those serving short sentences and only a tiny minority of those serving a longer sentence will receive help.

When treatment is provided it is, generally, for a maximum of one hour a week. Most treatments stress the need for the drinker to accept responsibility for his own actions, yet the remainder of his time is spent in an institutional setting which regulates most aspects of life.

Institutional restrictions may even prevent attendance at AA groups; again, a particular problem in local prisons where low staffing levels mean longer periods confined to a cell.

Treatment in prison may be rudimentary, but the House of Commons (1986c) Social Services Committee expressed even greater concern at the absence of any form of after-care or liaison for most alcoholics leaving prison. This is partly due to a general shortage of treatment facilities in the community, but it also appears that little attempt is made to use the resources which do exist. It is worth looking in more detail at some of the reasons for this lack of services in the face of obvious need.

In general, it appears that disillusionment with the 'therapeutic' model of imprisonment has resulted in a nihilistic tendency to see all treatments for prisoners as pointless. In fact, the philosophy of humane containment should imply an obligation to make available treatments for all psychiatric conditions in prisoners.

The treatment of alcoholism is further complicated by the ambivalent attitude of many doctors towards alcoholics. Generally, they are unpopular patients and the alcoholic recidivist is likely to be even less favoured (Ross, 1971). Edwards et al. (1971) found that many alcohol problems were not even identified within prison, a finding confirmed in the much later Brixton remand study (Taylor and Gunn, 1984). This may be because the authorities do not regard anything other than acute withdrawal as a priority, or because prisoners conceal their problems from prison doctors, where they can, fearing an adverse effect on parole or their treatment within the institution.

Finally, it has been argued that the artificial environment of prison, where alcohol is not available, occasional illicit prisoner-brewed substances aside, prevents meaningful treatment. Both short and long sentences have been put forward as obstacles to effective action, on the grounds that there is not enough time for useful treatment in the former case and, in the latter, it seems irrelevant. Whilst prison undoubtedly limits the scope for treatment, it also provides a sober and, literally, captive audience of people who may have little contact with treatment agencies outside. It can be seen as an opportunity to begin the work of treatment which could be extended later when a prisoner is released on parole. Ideally, prison and community facilities could be developed simultaneously, with liaison systems between the two established from the outset.

DRUG ABUSE AND DRUG DEPENDENCE

An analysis of the relationship between use of drugs and offending must extend beyond consideration of the particular drug itself. In different doses, by different routes and in different circumstances, the effect of the drug use will vary considerably; and the effects on a naive user will differ considerably from those that occur in the experienced drug taker and will differ yet again from those that occur in an individual who has developed tolerance to the drug.

It is convenient to consider drug taking as either experimental, recreational or compulsive/dependent (Yates, 1985). Initial use of a drug is probably always experimental, being prompted by curiosity on the part of the prospective drug taker rather than pursuit of a particular effect. Having satisfied this curiosity, the individual may then choose to continue to use this drug 'recreationally', in pursuit of an effect perceived as positive and pleasurable. For some individuals, pursuit of the drug and its subsequent consumption become all-important, with a consequent narrowing of the repertoire of interests and activities. There may also be a change in the effect sought—away from pursuit of positive effects to a state where the drug is being used in order to abolish negative feelings which may be drug-related (e.g. withdrawal symptoms), or may be independent (e.g. anomie, recent bereavement or unemployment). At each of these stages, the drug taker may experience unwanted and unanticipated effects. It is probable that these are more likely to occur with an episode of drug use by a drug-naive experimental user rather than with the regular user, who is more likely to be aware of possible adverse reactions and of emergency management in such an event.

The Physical and Mental Effects of Drug-taking

The effect of a drug will be influenced by many factors including the dose, the route, the context and the physiological state of the individual. The ways in which use of drugs might alter mental state and behaviour may be due to one of the following:

direct drug effect;
intoxication;
drug-induced special mental states (e.g. psychosis);
drug dependence;
drug withdrawal.

Direct Drug Effects

Effects which follow directly from the pharmacological properties of the drug will occur after its intake and will include the effects for which it was taken. Thus, the wakefulness and overactivity following cocaine use and the perceptual distortions and hallucinations after use of LSD are effects which will generally have been anticipated by the drug taker and for which purpose the drug has been taken. Other direct effects on mental state and behaviour may be seen as either neutral or unwanted but are, nevertheless, directly associated with use of the drug and are predictable. These include the slowing of reaction times and impaired coordination following barbiturate use and the sense of agitation following use of amphetamine. The most obvious example of a direct drug effect with a major influence on mental state and behaviour is the state of distortion of sensory input and, in particular, altered perception of stimuli which occurs after ingestion of LSD. These, again, are predicted effects, even though the overall effects associated with the experience will vary considerably from one drug-taking episode to the next, and will be referred to as either a 'good trip' or a 'bad trip'.

States of Intoxication

States of intoxication of varying degree, with associated impaired motor coordination, are classically associated with drugs with a central nervous system depressant effect (e.g. barbiturates, benzodiazepines, alcohol). Apart from the novice, most drug takers will be aware of the likely effect that will be produced by a given dose of a particular drug, especially when the specific drug taken has already been identified by the drug user and is in the form of a pharmaceutical preparation. Unanticipated intoxication would otherwise only occur in the drug user in whom a period of voluntary or enforced abstinence had brought about a marked alteration in the degree of tolerance to the drug, so that a much greater effect occurred from a dose which may previously have merely maintained the drug-taking status quo. Indeed, the considerable number of deaths of former drug addicts in the days immediately following their release from remand or custody is thought to be associated with a lack of recognition of loss of tolerance to the drug.

Drug-induced Special Mental States

Abnormal mental states, such as drug-induced psychoses are classically associated with the amphetamines (Connell, 1958) but also occur with other stimulant drugs such as cocaine (Jaffe, 1980) and pharmaceutically available amphetamine-like drugs, such as methylphenidate (Ritalin). Experimental psychoses can be precipitated in volunteers once a sufficiently high dose of such drugs has been given, although the threshold at which these drug-induced psychoses occur will vary from one subject to the next (Griffith et al., 1972; Ellinwood and Petrie, 1976). Typically, the drug taker will become increasingly irritable and suspicious as dose increases, prior to developing a time-limited psychosis which, apart from the evidence of the stigmata of drug use, resembles closely acute paranoid schizophrenia. The tell-tale indications of aetiology may include dilated pupils, venepuncture marks and positive identification on urine analysis. Such dose-dependent psychoses have been described with cannabis (Ghodse, 1987) and phencyclidine (Luisada and Brown, 1976; Lerner and Burns, 1978). Phencyclidine (PCP, angel dust) is widely used in most parts of the USA, where it is thought to be second only to cannabis in terms of extent of use of illicit drugs, but has never made more than a fleeting appearance on the UK drug scene. Mania has been reported following use of the anticholinergic drug, procyclidine (Coid and Strang, 1982).

Drug Dependence

Once dependence on a drug has developed, and tolerance to many of the effects of the drug has become established, then the continued intake of the regular daily dose is unlikely to produce marked alterations in mental state and behaviour other than might be accurately predicted by the drug user. Only when the dependent drug addict departs from his usual drug of abuse, or uses a product of unknown purity, as he may in police custody or prison, is there any likelihood of unanticipated adverse reaction. Considerable tolerance develops at metabolic and target-cell levels to most drugs of dependence, so that in individuals who have unrestricted supply to drugs such as heroin, daily intake can gradually increase to many times the original psychoactive dose.

Drug Withdrawal (Abstinence) Syndromes

A withdrawal syndrome can only occur once physical dependence on the drug has developed, with associated neuroadaptive tolerance. Although early adaptive changes can be identified after only a few doses of some drugs, it would usually require daily intake of the drug (or of another drug from the same pharmacological group), for a continuous period of at least several weeks or months for physical dependence to be established to such an extent that a withdrawal syndrome would be observed clinically. Thus it is essential to look for evidence to substantiate a claim of daily use of a drug in any patient who claims, for straightforward clinical or legal reasons, to be suffering from (or have suffered) a drug withdrawal syndrome. The exact characteristics of the withdrawal syndrome are determined by the group of drugs to which the individual has become dependent (e.g. opiates, barbiturates, amphetamines), although the speed of onset and duration of the withdrawal syndrome will be determined by the pharmacokinetics of the drug which was taken on the last occasion. The opiate withdrawal syndrome seen in a heroin addict after abrupt cessation of intake of heroin, for example, will comprise the same features as those seen in the same individual after abrupt cessation of methadone, except that the time-scale and possibly the intensity will be different. Thus, after the last dose of heroin, the opiate withdrawal syndrome is likely to commence within 6–12 hours, reaching peak intensity at about 36–48 hours and subsiding thereafter over the next few days, so that by a week later the most intense features have largely passed. On the other hand, the opiate withdrawal syndrome after the last dose of methadone may take a day or more before it becomes evident, and may not reach peak intensity for several days, after which it may persist at moderate levels of intensity for several weeks (*see* Gossop et al., 1987).

Different Routes—Different Effects and Different Complications

Not only will the effect of a particular drug be influenced by the setting in which it is taken, but the route by which the drug is taken may make a considerable difference. With intravenous use of drugs, there is an immediate flash or buzz which is intense in nature and has sometimes been likened to sexual orgasm. A similar effect occurs after use of cocaine by 'free basing' as 'crack'. During the early 1980s, cocaine began to be used more widely by freebasing which involved further processing of the blackmarket cocaine to separate the hydrochloride and hence left the freebase (a process frequently involving ether or ammonia), whilst at the same time smoking the volatile-free cocaine through a custom-made pipe. Subsequently, blackmarket technology has moved on (*see* Strang, 1990) and the cocaine is now refined into a more suitable freebase form (often known as crack or rock cocaine) which is likewise taken as a volatilate through a crack pipe. Intravenous use of a drug is more likely to be associated with unpredictable effects and behaviour or inadvertent intoxication in that the very act of sudden injection removes any opportunity to titrate dose against effect or to take precautionary action, as may occur with smoking or snorting of a drug. The cocaine snorter will typically chop the black market cocaine into a fine powder on a mirror with a razor blade and will then sort the cocaine into lines on the mirror ready for individual or collective snorting—inhaling the line of cocaine up a tube (typically a rolled up banknote) into the nostril in one inhalation (Strang, 1990). This is particularly likely to occur when the drug being used has been manufactured illicitly so that purity and dose are not known. The knowledgeable drug user is less likely to take an accidental overdose with pharmaceutical products as the dose can be gauged more reliably.

Legal Aspects of Drug Use in the UK

Before the middle of the 19th century, there were no legal restrictions in Britain on the sale of poisons or drugs. Opium was freely available and bought largely for self-medication. The first measure of control was the Pharmacy Act 1868 which, among other measures, allowed only pharmacists to sell opium. This had little effect on overall consumption, and use of such drugs remained largely unchecked until the First World War, when the Government became concerned about the recreational use of cocaine by troops, sometimes in association with visits to prostitutes. In 1917, Regulation 40B of the Defence of the Realm Act 1914 made it an offence for anyone other than doctors, dentists and pharmacists to possess cocaine or opium (other than on prescription).

The Dangerous Drugs Act 1920 added morphine and heroin to the list of controlled drugs and further restricted the importation and possession of opiates. In 1926, the Departmental Committee on Morphine and Heroin Addiction, chaired by Sir Humphrey Rolleston (Ministry of Health, 1926), concluded that it was legitimate to prescribe opiates for analgesia, for detoxification and also to those addicts for whom other treatments had failed. Thus, Britain went in a different direction from the USA, where almost total emphasis was placed on control. With the passing of the Harison Act 1920, America entered the prohibition era (Musto, 1973). The 'British approach' was further endorsed in 1961 (Ministry of Health and Department of Health for Scotland, 1961) by an Interdepartmental Committee of the Ministry of Health chaired by Lord Brain. Yet heroin use in Britain was evidently increasing and the Brain Committee was hastily reconvened, issuing a second report in 1965 (Ministry of Health and Department of Health for Scotland, 1965). It was then recommended that the prescription of heroin or cocaine to addicts should be limited and that doctors should be obliged to report their addict patients to the Home Office. These recommendations were incorporated in the Dangerous Drugs Act 1967, now superseded by the Misuse of Drugs Act 1971. Much has been made of the 'British system' up to 1968, even though no system ever existed. Enthusiastic commentators have concluded that there was virtually no drug problem in Britain because the 'British system' worked; in reality, the 'British system' probably worked precisely because there was no drug problem. (For a fuller review *see* Strang, 1989.)

Current Legislative Control

The two main statutes regulating the availability of drugs in the UK are the Medicines Act 1968 and the Misuse of Drugs Act 1971.

The Medicines Act 1968

The Medicines Act 1968 governs the manufacture and supply of all medicinal products and divides drugs into three categories. The most restricted (prescription only) can only be sold or supplied by a pharmacist if prescribed by a doctor, and this category includes all controlled drugs. The least restricted (general sales list) can be sold by any shop. All the remaining products (pharmacy medicines) can be sold without prescription, but only by a pharmacist.

The Misuse of Drugs Act 1971 and Misuse of Drugs Regulations 1985

Although the Misuse of Drugs Act 1971 is the main statutory instrument controlling the non-medical use of drugs, the scope of the Act has since been extended by the Misuse of Drugs Regulations 1985 and other orders. The effect of this legislation is to define categories of controlled drugs and to establish restrictions on their licit use, together with sanctions on illicit use.

Categories of controlled drugs.   Controlled drugs are defined in the Misuse of Drugs Act by reference to Schedule 2. This lists all drugs subject to control in three classes—A, B and C, in decreasing order of their perceived dangerousness. Preparations of Class B drugs designed for injection are designated as Class A. These classes are retained (and given below in brackets) even though Schedule 2 is now amended by the Misuse of Drugs Regulations 1985, which gives the following schedules.

Schedule 1. This contains naturally occurring substances or non-pharmaceutical preparations, i.e:

cannabinol (A)
cannabis and cannabis resin (B)
coca leaf (A)
lysergamide and derivatives (A)

mescaline (A)
poppy straw (A)
psilocin (A)
raw opium (A)

Schedule 2. This contains largely pharmaceutical preparations, i.e:

cocaine (A)
codeine (B)
dextromoramide (Palfium) (A)
dextropropoxyphene (C)
diamorphine (A)
diphenoxylate (in Lomotil) (A)
dipipanone (in Diconal) (A)
dihydrocodeine (DF118) (B)
fentanyl (Sublimaze) (A)
glutethamide (Doriden) (B)

levorphanol (Dromoran) (A)
methadone (Physeptone) (A)
methaqualone (B)
methylphenidate (Ritalin) (B)
morphine (MST) (A)
oxycodone (A)
pethidine (A)
phencylidine (A)
thebaine (A)

Amphetamine, amphetamine/dexamphetamine (Durophet), methylamphetamine (Methedrine), stereoisomers and salts of these (all B).

Schedule 3

buprenorphine (Temgesic) (C)
diethylpropion (Tenuate dospan) (C)
meprobromate (Equanil) (C)
methylphenobarbitone (B)

pentazocine (Fortral) (B)
phentermine (Duromine) (C)
any 5.5 disubstituted barbituric acid
    (i.e. all barbiturates) (B)

Schedule 4 (all category C). These products are excepted from prohibition on import, export and, when in the form of a medicinal product, possession.

chlordiazepoxide (Librium)
clobazam (Frisium)
clonazepam (Rivotril)
clorazepic acid (Tranxene)
diazepam (Valium)
flurazepam (Dalmane)

ketazolam (Anxon)
lorazepam (Ativan)
nitrazepam (Mogadon)
temazepam (Euhypnos)
triazolam (Halcion)
and 22 other benzodiazepines.

It will be seen that some substances of misuse are not scheduled above; these include dichloralphenazone (Welldorm), khat and volatile solvents.

Offences under the Misuse of Drugs Act and Regulations.   Other sections of the Misuse of Drugs Act 1971 define a series of offences, including unlawful supply, possession with intent to supply, unlicensed import or export of a controlled drug (all of these are known as 'trafficking offences') and unlawful production. The Act also prohibits unlawful possession, and to enforce this the police have the power to stop, detain and search people on 'reasonable suspicion' that they are in possession of a controlled drug. If a doctor contravenes the regulations relating to the prescription of controlled drugs to addicts, then he does not commit any offence under the Act, but may be referred to a tribunal which has the power to restrict his ability to prescribe those drugs. The Act also established an Advisory Council on the Misuse of Drugs to advise ministers on drug misuse and preventive measures. Clear distinctions are made between the seriousness of the offence of straight possession compared with possession with intent to supply, and this is reflected in the different sentencing policies. Straight possession is much less likely to be associated with a custodial sentence than other offences which reflect involvement in drug dealing.

The Misuse of Drugs (Notification of and Supply to Addicts) Regulations 1973

The Misuse of Drugs regulations deal with:

Notification. Regulation 3 requires any doctor to notify, in writing, the Chief Medical Officer at the Home Office, within 7 days of attendance, the particular details of any patient he considers, or has reasonable grounds to suspect, is addicted to any of the following drugs: cocaine, dextromoramide, diamorphine (heroin), dipipanone, hydrocodone, hydromorphone, levorphanol, methadone, morphine, opium, oxycodone, pethidine, phenazocine and piritramide.

Prescription of heroin, cocaine and dipipanone. Regulation 4 prevents any doctor from prescribing heroin, cocaine or dipipanone except for the treatment of organic disease or injury, unless licensed to do so by the Home Secretary.

The effect of these regulations is to allow any doctor to prescribe controlled drugs to a patient to treat organic disease or injury and for any doctor to prescribe controlled drugs (except heroin, cocaine or dipipanone) to addicts for the purposes of treating their addiction. A person may be in lawful possession of controlled drugs if they are lawfully prescribed for him by a doctor.

The Intoxicating Substances (Supply) Act 1985

The Intoxicating Substances (Supply) Act 1985 makes it an offence to supply a substance to a person under the age of 18, if the supplier believes that the recipient is likely to inhale it for the purposes of causing intoxication.

The Drug Trafficking (Offences) Act 1986

The objective of the Drug Trafficking (Offences) Act is to make provision for confiscating the assets of drug traffickers to reduce the extent of profit from trade in controlled drugs. The Act leaves intact the existing forfeiture powers, under the Customs and Excise Management Act 1979 and the Misuse of Drugs Act 1971, and establishes new powers of confiscation orders, which are made in the Crown Court, and which are enforced as if they were a fine, but subject to periods of imprisonment of up to 10 years in default. (For discussion of the possible approaches and benefits of forfeiture proceedings *see* Nagler, 1984.) Section 34 of the 1979 Act adds a new section 9A to the Misuse of Drugs Act 1971 prohibiting the supply of articles for administering or preparing controlled drugs. Clarification has been given that this does not relate to needles and syringes. It is intended to prevent the sale of cocaine sniffing kits or other apparatus which may be used to prepare or take drugs.

Penalties and Sentencing

Maximum sentences differ according to the nature of the offence—less for possession, more for trafficking or production. They are also related to how harmful the drug is thought to be. Class A carries the highest penalties (up to 7 years' imprisonment plus an unlimited fine for possession; up to life imprisonment plus fine for production or trafficking). Class B has lower maximum penalties (up to 5 years' imprisonment plus fine for possession; up to 14 years' imprisonment plus fine for trafficking) and Class C has the lowest penalties (up to 2 years' imprisonment plus fine for possession; up to 5 years' plus fine for trafficking) (Bucknall and Ghodse, 1986). Sentences for possession of small quantities of drugs (for the sole use of the accused) attract lower sentences than those which are attached to a charge of possession with intent to supply (commonly known as dealing). Accurate recording of the presence or absence of any symptoms or signs of present/ past drug use may be of considerable importance in later discussions as to whether or not the patient was indeed a drug user and might or might not have been holding the drugs for personal consumption.

The Court of Appeal has laid down sentencing guidelines (*Aramah*) which indicate that in importing Class A drugs (principally cocaine and heroin), where the street value of the consignment exceeds one million pounds sterling, the offence should merit a sentence of 12–14 years' imprisonment and that seldom will an importer of any appreciable amount receive less than 4 years. Suppliers of heroin or cocaine should seldom receive less than 3 years' imprisonment. Wholesale importation of Class B drugs, particularly cannabis, will justify sentences of approximately 10 years' imprisonment.

In subsequent correspondence about the *Aramah* guidelines, criticisms have been made of inconsistent practice in estimating street value, and it has been suggested that weight of drug would be a more appropriate guideline for stratifying sentencing bands, unless a more sophisticated formula is used for estimating true street value as proposed by Kay (1987). Sentences for trafficking in large amounts of Class A or B drugs have increased over recent years, reflecting concern at the increasing extent and dangers of drug dependence. The importation of small amounts of cannabis for personal use, however, is considered as simple possession, which can be dealt with by a fine. Indeed, Customs and Excise in parts of the UK now operate a discretionary on-the-spot fine and confiscation for first-time possession of small quantities of cannabis (Institute for the Study of Drug Dependence, 1982). Over 80% of all drug offenders are convicted of unlawful possession and, although maximum penalties are severe, only 1 in 6 offenders receive a custodial sentence. In 1984 three-quarters of fines were £50 or less (Institute for the Study of Drug Dependence, 1984).

Compulsory Screening for Substance Misuse

Compulsory screening for illegal substances may be offered as a condition of employment in some sports or in industry. In the USA, it has been recommended that drug testing should be mandatory for all Federal employees (Edwards, 1986). This has led to a legal and ethical controversy which has yet to be resolved.

In Britain, no mandatory screening is in use, except as part of some condition of continued employment as when a doctor with a drug problem is required by the General Medical Council to furnish evidence of abstinence.

The Examination of the Drug Taker

The psychiatrist may be asked to conduct such an examination either to advise on suspicions or claims of drug dependence or to advise on treatment that should be instigated. It is not possible, in the space available, to describe the many and various observations that must be undertaken in the examination of the acutely intoxicated patient. A detailed account is available in Ghodse (1989) and Morgan (1990).

Satisfactory evaluation of the suspected drug addict will usually involve serial examinations so as to gather evidence on changes in the clinical condition over time. Valuable information may be available from external agencies if the individual has previously received treatment for drug dependence itself or for complications of the drug use. Additionally, confidential information on a named patient basis can be obtained from the Home Office Addicts Index as to whether or not the patient has previously been attended by a medical practitioner who diagnosed dependence on a notifiable drug (mainly the opiates and cocaine: see 'notification' above). The Index is held for information purposes only. It is emphatically not a register which implies 'entitlement' to listed drugs. Information about substances or drug paraphernalia found on the individual or in his possession may give an indication as to the substance and route of use.

Signs of intoxication or of withdrawal should be sought, although neither may be evident in a physically dependent addict who has recently taken his normal dose or a dose sufficient to maintain the *status quo*. However, even in individuals in whom neither intoxication nor withdrawal is evident, there are some responses to which tolerance develops either extremely slowly or not at all; even in long-term opiate addicts who have become highly tolerant to most of the effects of the drug, the pupils will be constricted after use of the drug and will become widely dilated during withdrawal. Serial examination of an asymptomatic patient may find that a withdrawal syndrome develops over time, indicating that the original examination was at a time too soon after the last intake of the drug. It is doubtful whether it is ever justified to give an injection of the opiate antagonist naloxone (Narcan) merely to confirm or refute a possible diagnosis of opiate dependence. Such a procedure is potentially hazardous and provides no more information than will become evident in due course with serial examination.

A search for venepuncture sites is essential; the most frequent sites are in the antecubetal fossae, on the front and back of the forearms, on the back of the hands, on the dorsum of the feet and malleolae of the ankles and in the groins above the femoral vein. Rarely, other veins will be used, or the addict may have moved on to intramuscular injection, having sclerosed all available superficial veins, but in such cases there will be clear evidence of considerable previous intravenous drug use. To some extent, it is possible to give an opinion on whether or not such intravenous injection of drugs has occurred in the near or distant past. Evidence of fresh or clotted blood at the venepuncture site indicates recent use of the vein, and a visible puncture mark is also indicative of recent use. Fresh bruising would indicate that the injection had occurred within the last couple of days, after which the bruise will become characteristically yellow/brown before eventually disappearing within 2 weeks. Longstanding, frequent injection into the same site results in scarring over the vein causing lines of scar tissue, which follow the course of the superficial vein—known as track marks.

Examination of the eyes may reveal the constricted pupils of opiate use or the dilated pupils of use of stimulants such as amphetamines and cocaine; the opposite effect is found in the withdrawal syndromes from each of these types of drug in subjects who have become dependent. It is more difficult to identify the sluggish reaction of the pupils in the barbiturate addict, although this may become obvious by an associated coarse nystagmus. Additionally, examination of the eyes may find the typical red injected conjunctivae which occur after cannabis use.

There are also some signs which are associated with particular substances of abuse, such as the distinctive smell of solvents on the breath of glue sniffers in whom there is also likely to be a rash of acneiform spots around the mouth and nose, known colloquially as glue-sniffers rash (Watson, 1977; Watson, 1986). Intravenous abuse of barbiturates is now much rarer than it was in the 1970s in the UK, but in such individuals there may be current or healed cold abscesses and areas of open ulceration which are caused by the direct effect of barbiturates on the tissue surrounding the vein when there is leakage.

Interview is often difficult with a patient who does not wish to discuss his use of and/or dependence on drugs, and this is most likely to occur when the drugs of use have been obtained illegally. Apart from eliciting a history of use of the drugs and of the occurrence of possible withdrawal signs and symptoms when the drug has been unavailable, mental state examination will be mainly concerned with eliciting signs and symptoms. As volunteered information may not be reliable, clinical signs take on special importance. The amphetamine or cocaine user will be overactive, wakeful, garrulous and may become agitated, irritable and suspicious. At still higher doses, the stimulant user may develop an acute paranoid psychosis which only passes with the passage of the drug. On withdrawal from amphetamines, there is rebound depression and hypersomnia, although the quality of the sleep is often poor and there may be demands for sedatives to ease the 'crash'. The opiate user will not show any obvious signs which would be detected on mental state examination after taking a dose of the drug similar to recent use. If an opiate withdrawal syndrome subsequently develops, however, the addict will become restless, distressed, in pain from abdominal cramps and general body aching (especially in the back and legs) and will fall into a restless, interrupted sleep interspersed with hot and cold flushes, rhinorrhoea, nausea and possibly vomiting, diarrhoea as well as piloerection (hence the phrase 'cold turkey'). It cannot be overemphasized that accurate diagnosis usually requires results from observations over a period of time and will probably involve serial examination.

The clinician should make maximum use of laboratory facilities for urine analysis. Urine provides a convenient body fluid which is not only easy to collect, but also provides results from a wider window of time than would be achieved by blood specimens. It is often difficult to obtain venous blood specimens from drug addicts, who may have damaged their superficial veins, and concerns about HIV and hepatitis B militate against unnecessary venepuncture. Many laboratories will be able to examine urine specimens using thin layer chromatography (TLC) to detect the presence of metabolites from a range of drugs including the opiates, amphetamines and barbiturates. In cases where accurate diagnosis is particularly important, however, it is probably wiser to arrange for the analysis to be undertaken by a laboratory specialized in providing such a service, who will also be able to confirm the actual drug within the group, using gas chromatography (GC) and/or high pressure liquid chromatography (HPLC) and/or immunoassay techniques such as the EMIT (Enzyme Multiplied Immunoassay Technique) system for confirmation of the identification. (For a more detailed summary of urine testing for drugs of abuse see *Lancet*, 1987.) Preliminary work has been undertaken looking at the feasibility of analysis of hair samples which could provide a valuable longer-term result with approximate dating of positive findings according to the distance from hair root (Baumgartner et al., 1979;

Valente et al., 1981), but as yet this technique has not found a place in standard clinical practice. Exploratory work is also in progress looking at whether it might be possible to gauge the extent of dependence by use of naloxone eye drops, but this approach has not yet been employed outside the experimental setting (Ghodse et al. 1986).

Drug-induced and Drug-precipitated Mental Illness

Hallucinogenic drugs such as LSD and stimulant drugs such as cocaine and the amphetamines can cause a psychotic illness which is a direct effect of the drug and can be regarded as an experimental psychosis. As the effect of the drug wears off, so the psychotic features moderate and then disappear, and full recovery is to be expected from such a drug-induced psychosis. Connell's monograph on amphetamine psychosis is a classic description of a drug-induced psychosis (Connell, 1958). In the absence of further use of the drug, the likelihood that the patient will experience further psychotic episodes is no greater than normal. Indeed, clinical procedures which hasten the elimination of the drug (such as the acidification of the urine in cases of amphetamine psychosis) result in direct clinical benefit with shortening of the duration of the psychosis; in the case of phencyclidine (PCP) psychosis, the severity of the psychosis may go through stages of greater and lesser intensity which reflect the variable release from fat stores of phencyclidine and its active metabolites (Aniline, 1980). Cannabis has been described as directly inducing psychosis (Ghodse, 1987), but this area remains controversial (Johnson, 1990).

In addition to these direct drug-induced psychoses, there will be cases in which use of a drug has precipitated an otherwise independent mental illness. Use of LSD, amphetamines or many other drugs, for example, may act as a stressor which makes clinically manifest a previously subclinical condition; and it is particularly likely that unpleasant drug experiences (such as a 'bad trip' on LSD or a sense of loss of control with amphetamines or cannabis) may act as a significant life event which may trigger an initial episode of mental illness or may cause a recurrence of a previous clinical condition. Treffert (1978) described how use of cannabis may precipitate a clinical recurrence in patients who have already received a diagnosis of schizophrenia, and Negrete et al. (1986) described how cannabis causes a worsening of the clinical condition. Ablon and Goodwin (1974) reported that further episodes of depression have occurred after dysphoric reactions to use of cannabis in patients who have previously received treatment for depression. Occasionally, the psychiatric disturbance will occur in subjects in whom there is no evidence of prior psychopathology such as panic attacks after use of cannabis (Pillard, 1970). It is probable that some of the reports of chronic psychiatric illness including schizophrenia which have been reported in association with use of stimulants, LSD and cannabis may relate to cases in which the event of adverse reaction to the drug use was a critical factor in the development of a psychiatric illness which was otherwise (and subsequently) independent. It is also possible that some people developing symptoms attempt to make use of the sedative properties of a drug like cannabis and the drug taking is, in fact, secondary to the onset of the psychosis. Occasionally, patients have also described using drugs because they produce symptoms similar in quality to those occurring as part of the illness, and thus they felt able to attribute all their symptomatology to drugs and regain some sense of control over their destiny. In individual cases, the direction of the relationship between drug taking and psychosis is often extremely difficult to disentangle, but it is important that treatment is not denied to people in these circumstances in the naive belief that symptoms will necessarily be self-limiting, or are the sole responsibility of the patient because he chooses to take the drug. Both attitudes have been encountered in practice to the detriment of the patients. Equally, any treatment specifically for the psychosis must be kept under close review.

Personality and Drug Abuse

The psychological characteristics of drug users have long been studied in an attempt to establish whether some aspects of personality are associated with the use of drugs. In classical psychoanalytical theory, addiction is regarded as resulting from oral fixation and as a substitute for normal heterosexual expression. Until the 1970s psychological research focused on factors in the abuse of specific drugs, but as polydrug use became more prevalent, later studies correlated the frequency and extent of drug use with scores on personality inventories. A common methodological approach involved applying some measure of personality such as the Minnesota Multiphasic Personality Inventory (MMPI) to a drug-using sample and comparing the results obtained from various non-addict groups. Most MMPI studies report abnormal profiles, mostly those of psychopathic or sociopathic characteristics; that is a need for immediate gratification, lack of impulse control, low frustration tolerance, poor socialization and hostility (Craig, 1982). The MMPI includes an He (heroin) scale which predicts addict group status, but is less successful in discriminating heroin users from alcoholics or polydrug abusers. Opiate users do not appear to differ from normals on the Eysenck Personality Inventory (EPI) extraversion scale, but score higher on neuroticism than normal, though less than neurotic or alcoholic patients (Mott, 1972). A separate approach was adopted by Gossop and Eiser (1979) in which they identified two factors ('hooked' and 'sick') which enabled identification of two groups of opiate addicts, one of which referred to those addicts who saw their drug use as related to illness.

These findings are supported by Woody et al. (1983) who identified 15% of a male veteran group of opiate users as antisocial according to the Research

Diagnostic Criteria (RDC), and by Rounsaville et al. (1980) who found 20% antisocial, using the RDC in a male community inpatient drug programme. As RDC are more restrictive than DSM-III criteria, use of the latter generates a still higher prevalence of antisocial personality in drug users. Other personality findings include schizotypal features (RDC) in 8% of opiate addicts; borderline personality disorder (DSM-III) in 3% and dependent personality in 2% (Rounsaville et al., 1980).

While no one personality type appears directly related to drug use, Penk et al. (1981) accept the possibility of vulnerability in several personality types and suggest that personality factors do, in some unspecified way, contribute to drug abuse. They may, for example, influence how an individual responds to an established dependence, or to withdrawal. Phillips et al. (1986) confirmed previous observations that psychological factors play a major part in the opiate withdrawal syndrome and, in particular, that the personality factor of neuroticism, as measured by the EPI, is strongly related to the maximum level of withdrawal distress.

Following the identification of the alcohol dependence syndrome (Edwards and Gross, 1976), work was undertaken to develop a questionnaire which measured the extent of alcohol dependence, resulting in the Severity of Alcohol Dependence Questionnaire (Stockwell et al., 1979). More recently, a similar scale has been developed for assessment of opiate dependence—the Severity of Opiate Dependence Questionnaire (Sutherland et al., 1986; Phillips et al., 1987), although the clinical and research applications of this questionnaire have not yet been adequately explored.

Other Disorders and Drug Abuse

Central nervous sytem sequelae of drug use may either follow a particular method of use, i.e., the route-specific complications of injecting drugs, or they may be due to the specific effects of a drug.

Technique (route)-specific Complications

Many hazards are related to the manner in which the drugs are taken. Injecting drugs is a hazardous pursuit. The dose taken is rarely known, adulterants may be present and, unless sterile equipment is available, the risk of injection is high—especially when sharing occurs between users. A major new risk is presented by the HIV/AIDS virus; human immunodeficiency virus (HIV) prevalence among injecting drug users exceeds 50% in areas such as Edinburgh (Brettle et al., 1987), Dundee, Milan and New York, but is as yet much lower elsewhere. HIV infection may cause cognitive impairment, either due to the direct neuropathic effects of the virus, or as a consequence of CNS infections secondary to immunodeficiency (Riccio, 1987).

The onset of cognitive impairment may be insidious with initial changes in personality, motor slowing, loss of concentration and memory loss, affecting delayed recall more than immediate or long-term memory. These changes can precede the development of AIDS, which once established is associated with a high prevalence of dementia.

Drug-specific Complications

Amphetamines can cause an occlusive vascular disease of the cerebral vessels with focal neurological signs (Sapira and Cherubin, 1975) and, like cocaine (Estroff, 1987), usage can lead to a hypertensive intracerebral haemorrhage. Intravenous use of Diconal (dipipanone and cyclizine) can also lead to cerebral haemorrhage following arterial spasm (Thorley, 1983).

Synthetic analogues of the opiate fentanyl are known in the USA as 'designer drugs' and, during their illicit manufacture, by-products may be formed which induce severe Parkinson's Disease in users (Banks and Waller, 1988). Their use has not been reported in the UK. The use of ecstasy, an amphetamine analogue is becoming more common in Britain, and large doses may lead to tremors, convulsions or death.

Sterile abscesses are associated with the intravenous use of barbiturates and are due to the local necrosis which occurs following clumsy intravenous technique when the drug user may miss a brittle vein, or even as a result of extravasation of barbiturates around the venepuncture site.

Volatile solvent abuse (frequently involving toluene which is present in many adhesives) can cause transient cerebellar signs which may, however, be prolonged with long-term use. It is difficult to judge if volatile solvent abuse leads to neuropsychiatric deficits, and whether, if present, these are transitory or permanent (Ron, 1986).

Drug Use, Crime and Violence

Overall Patterns

Although obtaining and possessing drugs of abuse may be illegal acts in themselves, the nature of the association between drug use and crime is complex. There are many pathways to opiate addiction and the users are a very heterogeneous group. Rounsaville et al. (1982) took detailed histories from 360 opiate addicts and identified three subgroups on the basis of antecedents to illegal drug use. In about a third, childhood trauma such as abuse or separation was associated with later personality difficulties which were associated with later drug use. For some 24%, opiate addiction was an extension of early patterns of antisocial behaviour in that delinquency preceded drug use while, in the remaining 45%, drug use preceded major developmental disturbance or criminal activity.

The chronological relationship between crime and use of heroin was further examined by Fazey (1988), who reported that among 436 patients attending a Liverpool drug dependency clinic, 82% had criminal convictions of whom three-quarters were convicted before they became dependent on drugs. For the remaining quarter of those with convictions their identified criminality had coincided with or followed their drug dependence. These studies serve as a reminder that a full assessment of the individual drug user is crucially dependent on an understanding of the contribution of antecedent behaviours and events.

Given that opiate use and crime are associated, amongst opiate-using criminals the need for opiates may cause crime on a day-to-day basis, or both may be determined by some other factors. From interviews with 151 Scottish prisoners and non-prisoners, it was found that heavy opiate users committed crimes significantly more often than did moderate opiate users, cannabis users or alcohol users (Hammersley et al., 1990). Moderate opiate users did not commit crimes more frequently than other groups. Polydrug use (including cannabis) was more related to theft and delinquency than was opiate use. It was concluded that crime was not simply caused by need for opiates, but that crime and drug use influenced each other. For example, a drug user may burgle to sustain the cost of his habit, but if he makes a lot of money, then his drug use may increase.

Crime related to the use of drugs may be categorized as follows. Commonest are offences such as possession and trafficking, which result directly from the legal sanctions against the illicit use of drugs; then follows the predominantly acquisitive 'drug-related crime' or 'street crime' which arises from the high cost of illegal drugs; less commonly, an offence may be committed during an abnormal mental state related to drug use, such as that induced by drug intoxication or withdrawal. With certain specific drugs (such as amphetamines and cocaine) criminal behaviour may occur in the context of a drug-induced psychosis, but there is no evidence that crime occurs as a direct result of the pharmacological action of a drug.

Illicit Possession and Trade in Drugs

These activities lead to the majority of drug criminal convictions in the UK. In 1987, 29 665 people were found guilty or cautioned for drug offences, of whom 87% were male and 54% aged less than 25 years (Home Office, 1988a). Most of these offences involved the unlawful possession or production of cannabis, and then in decreasing order of frequency, heroin, amphetamines, cocaine, LSD and methadone. Regarding disposal, only 15% received an immediate custodial sentence and the majority were fined.

Drug Use and Acquisitive Crime

Home Office statistics for opiate addicts, first notified in 1979–81, show that 42% were first convicted for theft, 19% for drugs and 18% for burglary. Among the convicted population in general, the figures are 60, 2 and 11% respectively (Home Office, 1985b).

The relationship between drug use and acquisitive crime has been examined in the Wirral, an area of Merseyside known to have a serious drug problem. Parker et al. (1987) showed that the annual prevalence of opioid use during 1984–85 was 4.4 per thousand of the adult population; this rate was higher for males (6.2 per thousand) and for 16–24-year-olds (over 18 per thousand). The typical quantity of heroin used was 0.25–0.5 g a day, costing up to £300 sterling a week. Well over 80% of these drug users were unemployed. The hypothesis was then tested (Parker and Newcombe, 1987) that the prevalence of young, unemployed heroin users in the community was directly related to a parallel rise in acquisitive crime. There had, for example, been a 200% rise in recorded domestic burglaries in the Wirral, since 1979, compared with an 89% increase nationally. On examining the records of those convicted of serious crimes, it was found that the highest rate of known drug use was among those convicted of burglary (55%) followed by theft (33%), compared with those convicted of car taking (13%) and criminal damage (5%). The results showed that there was a strong tendency for heroin users to commit acquisitive, rather than non-acquisitive crime. Subsequent study of addicts attending three drug dependence units supported these findings (Jarvis and Parker, 1989; Jarvis and Parker, 1990).

Drug Use and Crimes of Violence

Most drugs of abuse do not cause violent criminal behaviour, and personality, situation and cultural background remain critical determinants. Among notified addicts, crimes of violence comprise only 6% of convictions, compared with 12% for the general convicted population (Home Office, 1985b).

Opiates and barbiturates

Central nervous system depressants, such as heroin, are taken for their euphoriant and tranquillizing effects; use of heroin and other opiates does not usually lead to aggression, although this could result from a disinhibited state, especially if alcohol is consumed as well. Withdrawal from opiates, though uncomfortable, is not directly associated with violence. Although barbiturates are also central depressants, their long-term use often leads to chronic intoxication, marked by irritability and aggression.

Benzodiazepines

Occasionally, benzodiazepines produce apparently paradoxical stimulation, leading to hyperactivity, aggression and outbursts of violence (Hall and Zisook, 1981). These effects are also exacerbated by alcohol and have been attributed to disinhibition of behaviour normally suppressed by anxiety, fear or social restraints. They are most likely to occur in anxious or aggressive individuals. Disinhibition, combined with memory loss and confusion, may lead patients on low doses of benzodiazepines to commit a range of acts from shoplifting to sexual offences (Ashton, 1987). The benzodiazepine withdrawal syndrome (Ashton, 1984) can include acute psychotic reactions with hallucinations, delusions, paranoia and acute confusion; violence may occur in such an abnormal mental state.

Stimulant drugs

The use of amphetamines or cocaine can induce a drug-induced psychosis without toxicity (Connell, 1958) or an acute toxic psychosis. Agitation, irritability and paranoid delusions are characteristic, as a result of which aggression may occur. Some patients may abuse anticholinergic drugs such as procyclidine, and these can cause a hypomanic disinhibited state (Coid and Strang, 1982). In the USA, it has been suggested that chronic use of cocaine and its derivative 'crack' is associated with a state of marked irritability in which the threshold for violent behaviour may be lowered. A high proportion of American 'crack' users are reported to commit acts of violence (House of Commons, 1989).

Cannabis and hallucinogens

Although there is no direct association between use of hallucinogenic substances and violence, hallucinogens such as cannabis, phencyclidine and lysergic acid diethylamide (LSD) may induce an agitated and psychotic state. In the USA, it is well recognized that consumption of even low doses of phencyclidine (PCP or angel dust) may produce an agitated and combative state (Young et al., 1987).

Volatile solvent abuse and crime

Inhalation of volatile solvents generally leads to an elated and disinhibited state in which aggression is rarely a feature, although violence may arise from persecutory thoughts (Evans and Raistrick, 1987a).

In a study of young people who abused volatile solvents such as toluene and butane, Evans and Raistrick (1987b) reported, however, that most had a criminal record, usually of theft, to support the habit. Regular use of solvents was associated with antisocial and destructive acts and nearly half showed an associated misuse of alcohol and illicit drugs.

Female Drug Users and Crime

Women comprise about 30% of notified addicts and 20% of drug users reported in community surveys (Parker et al., 1987). Earlier British studies of this group (d'Orbán, 1974) showed that a record of conviction prior to drug use carries a more adverse prognostic influence than in men. Women drug users also commit acquisitive crime to sustain their habit, but clinical experience suggests that this is more likely to involve shoplifting than burglary. Prostitution is reported by about 5% of clients attending syringe-exchange schemes and may be as common among men as women.

The Effect of Clinical Practice on Criminal Activity

Given that many addicts have criminal convictions which predate their addiction, it may be unrealistic to expect that clinical practice will 'decriminalize' these drug users. It has, however, been suggested that a policy of liberally prescribing heroin to opiate users would have this effect (Ditton and Speirits, 1981). To examine this matter, Bennett and Wright (1986) selected groups of addicts who obtained their drugs from a variety of different sources and ascertained the amount of drug-related offences they had committed. Their findings showed that addicts reported fewer non-drug crimes when receiving a prescription than in the period before receiving one, but the degree of reduction was not statistically significant.

Hartnoll and colleagues (1980) reported on their study of 96 heroin addicts who were randomly allocated to a group which was offered injectable heroin maintenance and a group offered oral methadone maintenance. The two groups were followed-up for the next 12 months by independent research staff. The prescribing of injectable heroin appeared to maintain the drug taking *status quo*, with the majority continuing to inject on a regular basis and to take additional black market drugs while maintaining an involvement in the drug subculture and being involved in continued criminal activity. The refusal to prescribe injectable heroin while offering oral methadone appeared to force a polarization of the responses, so that a higher abstinence rate was achieved whilst also resulting in a greater proportion who were dependent on black market drugs. At the end of the 1-year study period, crime was a major source of income for 61% of the oral methadone group compared with 43% of the injectable heroin group, whereas the same number reported no criminal activity in the last month (35 and 36% respectively). Similar figures were found with regard to arrests during the 1-year period with 71% of the oral methadone group having been arrested at least once compared with 52% of the injectable heroin group.

On the basis of these findings, it seems likely that a policy of more liberal prescribing for opiate addicts would not eliminate the occasional use of illicit drugs, though it may be that there would be a reduction in the overall number of crimes committed by addicts.

Treatment of Drug Abusers

Treatment in Prison—Special Aspects

Given the high rate of reported pre-arrest drug use among men serving prison sentences (Maden et al., 1991) and the even higher rate among women (Maden et al., 1990), it is disappointing how little opportunity is taken for treatment and rehabilitative work with drug users in prison. A 1988 Home Office policy statement (Home Office, 1988c) reflects only small initiative since the report of the Advisory Council on the Misuse of Drugs (1979). This has become even more disturbing since the awareness of the spread of HIV amongst injecting drug users, and the recognition that such drug taking (Carvell and Hart, 1990), as well as uncharacteristic sexual practices, may be adopted by prison inmates, which may expose them to risks from homosexual acts or needle sharing to which they would not normally be exposed. The report on *AIDS and Drug Misuse* (Advisory Council on the Misuse of Drugs, 1988) drew attention to a lost opportunity for intervention, noting that a substantial proportion of injecting drug users will have a period on remand or in custody during any 12-month period, at which time they would presumably be available for educational efforts.

The report of the Medical Working Group on Drug Dependence was published by the DHSS in 1984, and included a brief chapter on guidance for police surgeons and prison medical officers which supported the Advisory Council's view . . . 'that supervised withdrawal should take full advantage of the techniques developed by specialised units in the National Health Service'. The recommendation was made that parole release schemes for former drug addicts should be established and one such scheme exists on an experimental basis run as the parole release scheme managed by the Cranstoun Project (Tippell, 1989). Published data on its effectiveness are not yet available. Attempts have been made in the UK to set up therapeutic communities for former addicts within the prison system. The only well-developed example of such an approach has been described by Glatt (1977, 1985), although this was not exclusively for addicts.

Treatment in the Community

Arrest for possession of drugs or for burglary or shoplifting to raise money for drugs is often the first indication to the family that drugs are being used. For the drug taker himself, the arrest may herald a new awareness of the problems associated with his behaviour and the period in police custody or on remand may be the first separation from use of the drugs and may be accompanied by the first experiencing of a drug withdrawal syndrome. It is possible that the sudden realization of the adverse consequences of drug taking may provoke help-seeking behaviour for the first time, and promote flow through the process of change which has been described by Prochaska and DiClemente (1983; 1986).

NHS drug dependence units in the UK are often reluctant to accept referrals of drug addicts who have pending court cases on the basis that this constitutes a contamination of the pure motivation which they wish to see evident in the drug addicts. In fact, better results are often achieved in a range of treatment programmes with drug addicts who have a pending court case or receive treatment as a condition of the courts (Lissner et al., 1976; Gossop, 1978; DeLeon and Schwartz, 1984; Strang and Yates, 1984; Pompi and Resnick, 1987). There are, too, studies which have failed to show such an association (Harford et al., 1976; Rinella, 1976; Wexler and DeLeon, 1977; Sansone, 1980). An experimental arrest referral scheme has been set up in south London in an attempt to turn the events of arrest or caution into a therapeutic event by interviewing the drug taker at this time and offering an opportunity to seek treatment. In contrast to the NHS drug clinics, many drug-free therapeutic communities regularly offer accommodation to people for whom residence is a condition imposed by the courts. Agencies in the voluntary sector have become adept at securing places in appropriate drug-free therapeutic communities and then liaising with the courts and/or the funding authorities so that realistic alternatives to custody can be presented to the courts. The Lifeline project in Manchester runs a special 2-week induction programme during which the drug user is placed in a drug-free hostel at night and attends the induction programme daily during which he explores the options available to him prior to reappearing before the courts 2 weeks later (for description see Yates, 1981). The factors which influence help-seeking behaviour are currently the subject of study (Drug Indicators Project, 1989).

The Transition from Custody to Community

Little else has been developed despite the recommendations of the Advisory Council on the Misuse of Drugs (1979) that special therapeutic programmes should be available for former drug addicts, which would include liaison work to facilitate the return of former drug-taking prisoners to the community. They recommended that drug specialist agencies should be invited in to see former drug-using inmates in the months leading up to their release, so as to prepare them for release and to reduce the likelihood of their relapse back into drug taking and to reduce the risk of inadvertent overdose due to the loss of tolerance.

Agencies such as the Langley House Trust have set up hostels which provide after-care for former prisoners who may have previously been addicted to drugs. Some of these hostels will be specific to the ex-addict population, while others will absorb them into general after-care services. In the mid-1980s, the parole release scheme was established, with its aim of increasing the opportunities for former drug users after they leave prison. It also operates a hostel for such former drug users in London (Parole Release Scheme, 1988; Trace, 1988).

A few drug projects in the UK provide residential accommodation specifically for drug addicts while they continue to use drugs. The Rehabilitation of Metropolitan Addicts hostel in London aims to provide an opportunity for drug users to stabilize their life style with much less emphasis on dose reduction and withdrawal. The hostel's main contribution is to provide an opportunity for interim stability for longstanding drug addicts who have often been extremely chaotic prior to entry. Management of this group within the hostel often remains difficult and the preceding chaotic nature of the group is likely to account for the unusually high mortality rate in ex-residents from this hostel (Glanz and Taylor, 1987).

A number of prisons in England and Wales have agreed to host meetings of the self-help group Narcotics Anonymous, but English prison authorities have had difficulty accepting that some or all of the therapists of these agencies may themselves be ex-addicts.

In the alcohol field, there has been discussion and some implementation of 'third person Antabuse' in which a third party assumes responsibility for ensuring that the patient takes the medication. Occasionally, this third person may be a probation officer and there have been instances when the probation officer or husband/wife have been instructed by the courts to ensure that the former alcoholic takes the Antabuse (disulfiram). This is a highly contentious practice. An orally-available opiate antagonist, naltrexone, has received a product licence in the UK for use in conjunction with, and under the supervision of, specialists in the drug field. This constitutes a new type of medication for the treatment of drug addiction, but in our view it should not be used in a similar way to 'third person Antabuse'. It may, eventually, find a place in orthodox treatment of recovering drug addicts.

Drug Users and HIV Infection in England and Wales

The advent of HIV has brought about a reappraisal of treatment policies for drug users. In particular, there is now a greater recognition of the importance of technique-specific hazards and harm-reduction interventions in which behaviour change in the individual who continues to inject drugs may result in a lowering of the likelihood of infection or of transmission of the virus. There is an increasing body of evidence to support the view that it is within the repertoire of many drug addicts to change the nature of their drug taking, and it has been suggested that it may be more effective for drug treatment services to place greater emphasis on the negotiation and achievement of intermediate goals, than on total abstinence. Such a view may be more realistic and appear more relevant to the drug taker (Strang et al., 1987; Strang, 1988; Advisory Council on the Misuse of Drugs, 1988).

The World Health Organization (1987a and b) has established a Special Programme on AIDS and has published a document in which it draws attention to the importance of applying similar general principles of AIDS programmes to the prison population as to the general community. In their 1988 report on *AIDS and Drug Misuse*, the Advisory Council on the Misuse of Drugs devoted one chapter of the report to prisons and made various recommendations, including the development of policy and practice which would encourage drug users to identify themselves; the greater involvement of the probation service under the English Prison Department's new policy on through-care; the improvement of education of prisoners about HIV and risk reduction (including involvement of outside agencies); and the increased use of existing filters so as to minimize the number of drug misusers in prison or remanded in custody. The report noted the dilemma that existed on the subjects of provision of injecting equipment and availability of condoms in prisons, but was particularly concerned that prisoners are likely to engage to a greater extent in atypical high-risk activities, such as anal intercourse and shared injectable drug use which would thus create an extension of the population at risk of HIV infection (*see also* p. 818).

An additional problem for prisons is whether or not they should have a policy of segregation of HIV positive prisoners. The UK consensus is that the assurance of confidentiality is of paramount importance, so as to increase the likelihood that individuals who have engaged in at-risk behaviour will present themselves to services. Most drug treatment services in the NHS and voluntary sector have found that it is most straightforward to operate a policy of presumption of positivity in which precautions for the whole service are raised to an appropriate level for all patients/residents rather than trying to identify specific cases for whom this higher level of precaution may be necessary. In view of the substantial number of individuals who may choose not to be tested, and the possibility that prisoners may be infectious at times when they have not yet HIV antibody sero-converted, it is clearly important to avoid a policy which presumes that precautions are not necessary for those who are untested or have not yet developed antibodies. At present, individual prison medical officers decide on the degree of infectivity of each individual prisoner, applying an operational 'need to know' system for informing any other staff about the prisoner's HIV or hepatitis B status, and they must also decide whether or not to place the prisoner under viral infectivity restrictions.

The policy statement from the Prison Department on the through-care of drug misusers in the prison system in England and Wales provides a constructive framework for the necessary improvements in the services for the drug addict prisoner and opens up possibilities for preventative education and intervention to tackle the compound problem of HIV and drug misuse.

Drug Use and Parenting

Although drug use is hazardous in pregnancy and the demands and consequences of further use may impair child care, it should not be assumed that drug-using parents are invariably poor at parenting. Any assessment of their ability to care for their children depends on a detailed understanding of the effects of drug use in that family, while mindful that the welfare of the child is paramount.

Assessing parental competence requires an understanding of the following key areas:

1. the pattern of parental drug use: what drugs are taken and by what route, the frequency and complications of use, intoxication and withdrawal, and the coping skills exercised;
2. how the drugs are procured: is there prostitution, theft or dealing in drugs, and do these occur on premises where there are children?
3. basic provision for children: is there adequate food, clothing and warmth, are their emotional needs met and are there health risks to them?
4. family supports and contacts; are relatives involved, do the parents associate with other drug users or with non-users, or with both?
5. parental perception: do the parents understand the degree of risk to each child?

Such an assessment should involve the multidisciplinary team, as the views of the general practitioner, social worker, health visitor and drug workers are all relevant. Legal interventions in England and Wales may include care proceedings under the Children and Young Persons Act 1969, and it has recently been held (*Re.D.*) that consideration may now be given to the time before the child is born. In the Children Act 1989 an emergency protection order was introduced to replace the place of safety order, and criteria were widened for care orders, to cover cases of predicted as well as actual harm. A restriction on the local authorities' use of wardship proceedings was also included. The Advisory Council on the Misuse of Drugs (1988) has stated:

> If drug misusing parents are not to be deterred from seeking help, social services departments should work hard to ensure that drug misuse *per se* is never, and is never seen as, a reason for separating parent and child.

International Aspects of Drug Misuse

The cultivation, refinement and international traffic in blackmarket drugs has become increasingly big business over the last two decades, with the emergence of many more laboratories and refineries near to the growing fields. This has brought with it problems for the producer countries themselves in which there are burgeoning indigenous drug problems associated with the more refined products and the new technologies for self-administration. Increased international cooperation by control forces has resulted in some spectacular seizures, but it is likely that these seizures are but the tip of the iceberg, and it is rare for any individual seizure to cause more than a temporary increase in blackmarket price on the street. In considering control options, it must also be borne in mind that many of the producer countries in the third world now have economies which are to a large extent dependent on the income which derives from the drug trade. Despite the increase in international travel, there is still great variation evident between and even within nations in styles of drug abuse and availability of substances. Phencyclidine, for example, is absent from the UK drug scene despite its widespread use in the USA, and the cocaine epidemic has been slow to spread to Europe from the USA. It is evident that the spread of a drug epidemic is under the influence of a wider range of factors than legal controls, and future analyses of such epidemics will need to pay greater attention to the contexts within which drugs are used and the methods by which they are acquired and taken.

PATHOLOGICAL GAMBLING

Gambling as a Social Phenomenon

Gambling is a ubiquitous phenomenon in western society, reaching the point in Britain where it merited a major investigation by a Royal Commission (1978), and, in the USA, a congressionally mandated commission (Commission on the Review of the National Policy toward Gambling, 1976). The Royal Commission quoted a Social and Community Planning Research Survey carried out in 1977 showing that 35% of the British adult population gambled on the football pools every week, 9% bet on horses or dogs once a month and 4% played bingo regularly. £873m were spent on gambling compared with £5980m on alcohol, £3106m on tobacco, and £1317m on other entertainments during 1976. According to the US commission, reporting on figures for 1974, 60% of the adult population of the USA engaged in some form of gambling, with at least $22.4 billion spent in the year. In many western countries gambling is not only permitted by the state, but used as a direct form of revenue. A number of countries in Europe run national lotteries, and states of the USA state lotteries. In Britain, Premium Bonds constitute a form of government-run gambling.

Cornish (1978), reviewing the field, concluded that the evidence—

> patchy and tentative though it is at present seems to show that most punters, regardless of which form of gambling they engage in, are able to exercise considerable self control over their involvement . . . there is little evidence, so far as the average punter is concerned of any adverse effects.

Besides providing pleasure, jobs and revenue for the exchequer, however, gambling also produces considerable misery for an unknown number of people. The USA Commission estimated that not far short of 1% of the adult population of the US were 'probable compulsive gamblers', a figure criticized as too low by Nadler (1985). Volberg and Steadman (1988), in a telephone survey of a representative sample of 1000 residents of New York State found that 2.8% were 'problem gamblers' and 1.4% 'probable pathological gamblers' on the basis of their scores on the South Oaks Gambling Screen (Lesieur and Blume, 1987). The misery of gambling may include slavish adherence to it, social deterioration, despair, even suicide. It also may generate a good deal of crime such as large scale rackets in casinos, the doping of horses and dogs, and the fixing of odds. For the excessive gambler, there may be need to steal money and to gamble further to pay debts.

> Each day for the pathological gambler . . . becomes a matter of stratagems by which to obtain more money for gambling. The man awaits the early racing results as eagerly as the alcoholic awaits opening time. He may hasten from betting shop to gaming room hoping to recoup his losses. But if the big win which should settle all his debts is made the money only goes on more gambling. Betting becomes secretive; an employer may be swindled. The man's whole personality may deteriorate—his wife reports that he is a totally changed person, that he is selfish, irritable, moody and utterly untrustworthy. (*British Medical Journal*, 1965)

Causes of Excessive Gambling

In considering the possible causes of excessive gambling, Cornish (1978) concluded that simple social or personality theories will not, in themselves, fully account for why a particular individual takes up gambling. He then suggested that persistent gambling and excessive gambling can best be understood by seeing how the recruit to gambling has his gambling behaviour reinforced. Dickerson (1984) found that variable ratio schedules of reinforcement (i.e. occasional winnings at variable time intervals) have the most powerful effect. Such a behavioural model of gambling suggests that the number of pathological gamblers will be related to the number of gamblers in the community generally and this number, in turn, will be related to the number of gambling opportunities available. This could lead to preventive policies. Fruit and video game machines are, however, very common and Graham (1988) showed that although nearly one in two boys between the ages of 10 and 16 played at least once a month, a tiny number developed playing habits which were intrusive on their time and money.

Psychodynamic theories of gambling antedate behavioural ones. Freud (1928) analysed the personality of Dostoevsky and described his gambling period as:

> an unmistakable fit of pathological passion. . . . Dostoevsky's sense of guilt had taken a tangible shape as a burden of debt, and he was able to take refuge behind

the pretext that he was trying by his winnings at the tables to make it possible for him to return to Russia. . . . But this was no more than a pretext. . . . He never rested until he had lost everything. For him gambling was a method of self-punishment as well. Time after time he gave his young wife his promise or his word of honour not to play any more . . . and . . . he almost always broke it. When his losses had reduced himself and her to direct need, he derived a second pathological satisfaction from that. He could then scold and humiliate himself before her, invite her to despise him . . . and when he had thus unburdened his conscience, the whole business would begin again the next day . . .

Bergler (1958) believed that pathological gambling is a truly masochistic neurosis. He postulated that what he called the 'classical gambler' has never relinquished the omnipotent phase of childhood. In this theory the gambler expects that he will win because he wants to win. In another sense, however, the gambling is aggressive, the bets are placed in defiance of those adults who tell him that he is not omnipotent. In turn, this aggression makes him feel guilty, and the guilt is expiated by losing, therefore the unconscious wish to lose also becomes an integral part of the neurosis. Bergler went on to provide a detailed subsclassification in psychodynamic terms.

Taber et al. (1987a) have elaborated an aetiological model of gambling which overlaps with some of these earlier hypotheses in its affective roots. They found that 23% of 44 consecutive admissions to a gambling project had experienced major traumatic events and constituted a group different from the other gamblers in being more depressed, anxious and avoidant in personality style, and also more likely to be abusing alcohol or other drugs. From these data the authors inferred a concept of 'learned dysthymia', a state of chronic negative affect related to cumulative life events. They identified a characteristic pattern of scores on subscales of the MMPI for this group who seemed to use the high arousal created for them by the gambling to alleviate their depression.

Clinical Features

According to Moran (1970) recognition of pathological gambling depends on four features:

1. concern on the part of the gambler and/or the family about the amount of gambling;
2. the presence of an overpowering urge to gamble so that the individual may be intermittently or continuously preoccupied with thoughts of gambling. This is usually associated with the subjective experience of tension which is found to be relieved only by further gambling;
3. the subjective experience of an inability to control the amount of gambling;
4. economic and/or social and/or psychological and/or family disturbances which result from the gambling.

The International Classification of Diseases (ICD-9) (WHO, 1978) recognizes no specific category of pathological gambling, but pathological gambling was introduced into the American Psychiatric Association Diagnostic and Statistical manual of 1980 and is in ICD-10. DSM-III R provides an improved operational definition. It requires that at least four of nine features are present. They have considerable overlap with Moran's features, but include also the concept of developing 'behavioural tolerance', i.e. 'a need to increase the size and frequency of bets to achieve the desired excitement'. More recently a useful screening tool, a short self-rating questionnaire, has been devised by Lesieur and Blume (1987). Its reliability has been established and it has been shown to correlate closely with DSM-III R criteria.

After reviewing 50 patients, Moran (1970) suggested five subtypes of pathological gambling:

1. *Symptomatic gambling* associated with mental illness, for example a depressive illness, giving rise to guilt feelings which are then expiated by gambling. It is sometimes difficult to distinguish a depression causing the gambling from a depression which is reactive to the gambling;

2. *Psychopathic gambling* as part of a generalized antisocial response to life, mixed with stealing and other criminal activities (not only related to gambling) and poor social adjustment in terms of work and personal relationships;

3. *Neurotic gambling* as a response to stress such as a disturbed marriage. One partner in such a marriage may use the gambling as a means of punishing the other. Adolescent stress is another possible cause of gambling;

4. *Impulsive gambling*, characterized by loss of control which cannot be readily accounted for by illness, or the environment and is not part of an antisocial response to life. Sometimes it is controlled when the money runs out. It is usually feared by the gambler who is aware that he loses control to his own detriment, but it also brings relief from craving;

5. *Subcultural gambling* or socially acceptable heavy gambling.

A possible association between gambling and affective disorders has been postulated (e.g. Moran, 1970; Taber et al., 1987a). It is tempting to compare this with the association described between affective disorders and alcoholism (e.g. Winokur et al., 1970). McCormick et al. (1984) reported that, in a group of 50 men, highly selected by virtue of their admission to an inpatient treatment unit for gamblers, 76% had a major depressive disorder, 38% hypomanic disorder and 8% manic disorder, while 36% had at least one important cross-addiction to alcohol or drugs. Subjects also showed a very high rate of suicidal behaviours, only 10 not having shown any apparent tendency in the year prior to admission, and nearly half the group having shown at least moderately severe behaviour, e.g. having thought of a specific plan. Six had made a lethal attempt. Linden et al. (1986), studying people attending Gamblers Anonymous (*see* p. 488) meetings, also found that over 70% of their sample had had a major depressive illness at some time in their lives. Findings of abnormalities on the dexamethazone suppression test (Ramirez, 1988) and in monoamine levels and peptides in the cerebrospinal fluid, plasma and urine of gamblers (Roy et al., 1988) have lent some weight to these associations.

Moran also studied a group from Gamblers Anonymous and found that the incidence of attempted suicide among his pathological gamblers was 20%. This compared with their spouses who had an incidence of attempted suicide of 12%. An interesting clinical observation was made by Seager (1970) who took on 16 patients for aversion treatment. He found that none of them was aggressive, even verbally; when provoked, they could not even chastise their own children.

Management

The prognosis in many cases of excessive gambling is poor. There is ambivalence on the part of the patient, social pressure to continue gambling, psychological dependence intermittently reinforced, and perhaps powerful unconscious destructive drives. Psychiatric and psychological treatments have limited success. Traditional punishments, however, such as fines and imprisonment are unlikely to improve an accused and may even make him worse. The pathological gambler is quite likely to try and win his fine on a racehorse!

Prisons are ideal places in which to gamble, since boredom is excessive, everybody is short of money, tobacco, and other desirables, and important support systems such as employment, wife, family are removed, maybe permanently.

The efficacy of treatment for gamblers may be as much affected by the quality and extent of the service delivery as the treatment itself. Volberg and Steadman's (1988) telephone survey of the prevalence of pathological gambling in New York illustrated how one service delivery seemed to be failing. Thirty-six percent of problem gamblers were women, but only 7% of clients coming into one of the three treatment programmes in New York State; 43% of the survey gamblers were non-white, but 91% of treatment places were taken up by a white clientele; only half the expected group of young people presented for treatment. All the differences were significant. A disproportionate number of women, non-white people and young folk were thus failing to connect with services.

The Importance of Extended Assessment

Cases of excessive gambling are difficult to assess briefly, and require a detailed knowledge of the patient's background, current social environment and psychopathology before a management programme can be advised. Particular care should be taken not to miss depressive disorder or suicidal ideation. It is almost never possible to treat gamblers successfully without involving spouses or close contacts, as the behaviour and the treatment will profoundly affect their life also. This is especially true in Moran's type (c) cases, where family stress may be the main pressure to gamble.

Building a Supportive Network

The two elements of management which are universally important are support and counselling. The necessary qualities of support include accepting the individual without accepting his behaviour, making and keeping to a long-term commitment, refusing to reject the patient/client when others reject because the problem seems hopeless. In addition, where the gambler has retained family and friends, support should be extended, as far as possible, to them too, whether directly or through other professional or voluntary bodies. Counselling will include a discussion about the patient's behaviour and its consequences, and advice about restructuring his life.

The Role of Hospital Admission

Inpatient treatment for gambling *per se* is unusual, but a number of programmes have grown up in the USA, modelled on acute treatment packages for alcoholics or other substance abusers. Taber et al. (1987b) described the outcome of one such highly structured 28-day programme, housed within an alcohol treatment unit. Of 66 consecutive male admissions, all met DSM-III criteria for pathological gambling and averaged 18 years of such gambling, with the longest period of abstinence being an average of 11 months. Most had tried and failed some sort of outpatient treatment for gambling. Fifty-seven patients completed the 6 months follow-up, 32 (56%) reported abstinence for the full 6 months after treatment. There was also an improvement in other features such as depression and suicidal ideation in many, but not all of the abstainers. Although these results are encouraging, given the average length of abstinence (11 months) achieved by this group at some time during their years of pathological gambling, it will be the 12 and 18 month follow-up figures that will be most useful.

Psychoanalysis and Dynamically Oriented Psychotherapies

A good deal has been written about the psychodynamics of gambling, but there are few reports of the use of psychotherapy. Bergler (1958) wrote of 60 gamblers he treated by psychoanalysis. Twenty-five percent gave up treatment after a 4–6-week trial period, but he implied that the other 44 patients all gave up gambling, although only three-quarters of them would be regarded as cured, because a quarter of the cases stopped treatment after they had given up gambling in the mistaken belief that they had no other problems. These apparently remarkable results, need replication before any generalization can be made.

Behavioural Treatments

Treatments based on general behavioural principles

Greenberg and Rankin (1982) described a series of 26 compulsive gamblers seen in a London hospital over an 8-year period, all of them male and 15 with criminal records. They had been gambling for an average of nearly 14 years. This was not a planned study, but a report of treatment outcome. Each man underwent a detailed assessment to elucidate stimuli associated with gambling (e.g. walking past a betting shop) or other factors (e.g. pay day) and was required to keep a record of behaviour. Five men attended on only one occasion. The rest were treated according to one of two main patterns, with advice about avoiding precipitants of gambling, or by the therapist accompanying the patient to provocative situations. Each man's treatment group was fortuitous. Five men gained good control over their gambling over 9 months to 4½ years. A further seven gained intermittent control, but whether either of the treatment approaches had a more beneficial effect is not clear. For various reasons, including poor compliance, over half of the referrals had not been helped at all by a behavioural approach in an ordinary clinical setting.

Paradoxical intention

In 1967 Victor and Krug reported a case in which they instructed a 36-year-old gambler, who had been in group therapy for 7 months without much success, to go on gambling. He became angry with his doctor whom he accused of trying to control and ruin him. When the doctor advised him to sell his watch, he gave up gambling! Unfortunately, single case reports account for much of the literature on behavioural treatments, and are little more than pointers for future research.

Aversion therapies and imaginal desensitization

Several reports exist in the literature of the use of aversion treatment (Barker and Miller, 1968; Goorney, 1968; Seager, 1970). If the Freudian and Berglerian models of the masochistic origins of pathological gambling (described above) are correct, then this is surprising. The most thorough of these earlier reports (Seager) was on 1 female and 15 male patients who were referred for treatment. Two rejected the offer of treatment and two more left prematurely after only a few sessions. The others received between 11 and 164 shocks each in relation to their gambling stimuli (e.g. sporting newspapers, slides of betting shops). Treatment was stopped when they no longer felt the urge to gamble. Of the original 16 patients, only 5 remained free from gambling for 1–3 years. As the author concludes, this is not a very satisfactory result.

McConaghy et al. (1983) randomly assigned 20 compulsive gamblers to receive either aversive therapy or imaginal desensitization, the assessor remaining blind to the treatment condition. In the aversive therapy group, four stopped gambling in the first month after treatment, and two more were considerably helped, a pattern only marginally less good than for the imaginal desensitization. At 1 year after treatment, however, none in the aversive group were abstaining and only two were improved compared with two confirmed abstainers and five controlled gamblers in the desensitization group. Furthermore, those in the desensitization group reported significant reduction in state anxiety at 1 month and state and trait anxiety at 1 year after treatment.

Group Treatments

A variety of approaches to group work have been tried, but again very few evaluative reports exist. An interesting idea, in view of the prominent marital problems in some cases, was reported by Boyd and Bolen (1970) who treated husband and wife pairs. Of nine pathological gamblers and their wives, one pair dropped out leaving four pairs in each of two groups. All improved, five nearly stopped gambling, three actually stopped, all the marriages were reported as improved. These are promising results, but need replication.

Perhaps the most interesting form of group treatment for gamblers is that run by the gamblers themselves. As in alcoholism, a self-help group Gamblers Anonymous has gained a prominent place in treatment and should always be considered as one option a patient may take. A description of the California branch where it all began is given by Scodel (1964). Again following the lead of the sufferers from alcoholism, another self-help group has sprung up for spouses of gamblers—Gam-Anon.

Gambling and Crime

Of the three major dependencies discussed in this chapter, gambling is the least criminalized—neither gambling itself nor the organization of systems to enable gambling being illegal. The evidence for an association between gambling and crime is mixed. Dickerson (1984) found that, among problem gamblers attending Gamblers Anonymous or for treatment, almost half reported offending, often to support the habit. West and Farrington (1977) found that heavy gambling was more common among delinquents than non-delinquents, while Huff and Collinson (1987), studying inmates in youth custody, identified a possibly distinct subsample of people who had stolen to play video machines. They tended to have started playing earlier, spent all their money more frequently and reported more associated problems than non-criminal video players. Sample sizes were, however, very small. Graham (1988) was not impressed with any criminal tendencies in his sample of 10–16-year-olds. Two of us took part in a survey of 404 incarcerated young offenders and found that 12% were excessive gamblers (Maden et al., 1992). The impression was that gambling and other behaviour disorders, including offending, were associated by a common aetiology in oppressive, deprived or uncertain backgrounds, rather than the one being characteristic of the other.

12
Non-psychotic Violence

Edited by	*Written by*
John Gunn	Ron Blackburn
	John Gunn
	Pamela J. Taylor

Violence is a universal phenomenon, an integral part of any social system. Social activity does not exist without it. For human beings it is a very wide term which embraces everything from boxing matches to baby battering, armed robbery and war. Nevertheless, it is a very unusual activity, whilst lesser forms of aggression are occurring continually. In most societies rigorous attempts are made to control levels of violence, and legal distinctions are made between sanctioned and unsanctioned violence.

The reasons that violence exists and persists in social systems are complicated. Even so, those who work with offenders are advised to have some understanding of the universality of violence in social mammals, the functions it performs, and the ideas which have been generated to explain these phenomena. For more detailed understanding therefore the reader is referred to other sources (Daniels et al., 1970; Gunn, 1973; Kutash, et al., 1978; Hays et al., 1981; Klama, 1988; Gunn, 1991d).

Injurious or harmful behaviour takes a variety of forms, such as physical violence, verbal derogation, or passive obstruction, and its effects range from loss of life to wounded pride. Distinction is commonly made between angry aggression, in which injury to the victim is a goal in itself, and instrumental aggression, in which injury facilitates the attainment of non-aggressive aims. As this distinction implies, anger, an emotional state with physiological, cognitive, and expressive components, is relatively independent of aggression.

Although the arousal of anger makes aggressive behaviour more likely, aggression is not a necessary consequence of anger, nor is all aggression accompanied by a state of anger.

Theories of aggression vary in the extent to which they emphasize unlearned or learned components, affective or cognitive processes, and internal or external determinants. They therefore differ in how they address three critical questions:

1. How does aggression originate?
2. How is it provoked or instigated?
3. How is it maintained and regulated?

Biological Perspectives

Ethological studies of lower vertebrates led Lorenz (1966) to propose that there is a universal instinct of aggression which functions to ensure population control, selection of the strongest animals for reproduction, brood defence, and social organization. Instinct relates to a spontaneously generated energy source in the nervous system which discharges through fixed action patterns in response to specific releasing stimuli. Lorenz saw parallels between human militaristic displays or competitive sports and aggressive activities in geese and other animals. The theory postulated that human behaviour is governed by a constant need to discharge aggressive energy. There is, however, no evidence to support this hydraulic model of a reservoir of energy, even in lower animals, and Lorenz has been criticized for anthropormorphic extrapolation and his neglect of the role of learning.

Phylogenetic continuity of anatomical structure and behaviour was also assumed by Moyer (1981), who drew on studies of the effects of electrical brain stimulation and surgical lesions in animals and in patients with organic pathology. He suggested that there are organized neural circuits in the brain which are sensitized by hormones and blood constituents, and which when fired in the presence of a relevant target, produce integrated attacking behaviour. Human learning can influence the selection of targets and the inhibition of behaviour, but feelings of hostility will be experienced, whether or not aggressive behaviour occurs. Mark and Ervin (1970) similarly proposed that there are limbic centres which control aggressive behaviour, and that these are damaged in a substantial proportion of violent people. However, brain stimulation and ablation research has not produced reliable findings, and there is no evidence for brain systems exclusively concerned with aggression (Valenstein, 1976). In studies where aggressive effects have been demonstrated, these may be the result of changes in general excitability.

All these theories of human aggression attribute both instigation and regulation to internal physiological mechanisms which can override voluntary control. Their limitations lie in their lack of attention to human symbolic capacities and individual learning.

Psychodynamic Perspectives

There is no single psychodynamic theory of aggression, but again an aggressive instinct or drive is commonly assumed. The main interest has been in how aggressive drive is accommodated within the hypothesized psychic structures, and how it comes to be channelled and controlled in the course of individual development.

In his earlier writings, Freud saw aggression as a reaction to frustration and pain. He later introduced the notion of a death instinct (Thanatos), a tendency to self-destruction which is diverted by the self-preserving libidinal instinct (Eros) to the external world (Freud, 1920). Some psychoanalysts accept an instinct of aggression, but reject the notion of a death instinct. Others see aggression as reactive, but attribute extreme violence to the eruption of destructively motivated energy. Manifestations of aggressive instinct are said to include the rage reaction to frustration, which mobilizes the organism for combat, but aggressive drive is also subject to the same developmental vicissitudes as the libido. It is, therefore, thought to be manifest in biting (oral sadism) or faeces retention (anal sadism). The theory also suggests that through fixation these reactions may be transformed into hostile character traits. Instinctual discharge is thought then to occur through fantasy or overt aggression and is also occasioned by rivalry with siblings or parents, which may have counterparts in later life.

Ego psychologists have elaborated on the transformation of aggressive energy. Hartmann et al. (1949) proposed that the destructive aims of aggression become modified by displacement or sublimation, and through neutralization, constructive energy is supplied to the ego, enabling it to fulfil self-assertive and adaptive functions. Superego development is thought to permit the internalization of aggressive energy in the form of guilt, but the theory suggests that instinctual energy is nevertheless still generated and may conflict with the demands of the libido, the superego, or reality, so that continuous sublimation or neutralization is necessary for healthy functioning.

Neo-Freudian psychoanalysts criticize the instinct concept, and argue for socio-cultural origins of aggression. Fromm (1973) distinguished defensive or benign aggression, a biologically programmed reaction to threat, from destructive or malignant aggression, which is a specifically human phenomenon arising when socio-economic conditions prevent the fulfilment of existential needs for interpersonal ties or personal effectiveness. Fromm saw malignant aggression in cruelty, torture, or disproportionate revenge, and believed it typifies sadistic characters who need to control others. He suggested that it is not derived from benign aggression, and is distinct from instrumental aggression (*see also* pp. 392–4).

The shortcomings of an hydraulic concept of instinct have already been noted, and the proposal that non-aggressive behaviours, such as constructive self-assertion, are manifestations of transformed destructive energy allows virtually any activity to be construed as aggressive. For this and other reasons the intuitive view of aggression has largely withered outside of psychodynamic theory. However, psychodynamic perspectives do emphasize early learning of aggressive solutions to conflict and processes of regulation which have parallels in other theories.

Learning Perspectives

While accepting the possibility of some archaic connections between threatening events and motor responses, learning theorists see aggression as acquired and maintained by rewarding or reinforcing contingencies. Theoretical attention focuses on how particular classes of antecedent and consequent events promote aggression.

Dollard et al. (1939) drew on early Freudian theory in formulating the frustration-aggression hypothesis, and asserted that aggression is a consequence of frustration in the form of thwarting of goal-directed activity. Frustration thus instigates a motive to injure the source of frustration, its intensity depending on the value of the blocked goal and the degree of frustration. The theory suggests that aggression is a function of prior reinforcement or punishment. If punishment is anticipated, the response is inhibited unless displaced to an alternative target.

Although influential, the original theory has not been widely accepted since frustration instigates responses other than aggression, and aggression is equally provoked by insult or attack, threats to self-esteem or pain (Berkowitz, 1989). Anger can increase attempts to injure, and that injury is sometimes a positive reinforcer for further aggression. Frustration, however, only leads to anger when it is perceived as unjustified. Other workers have shown that aggression is negatively reinforced by the termination of an aversive state, and question the notion of a specific aggressive drive (Patterson, 1979). Tension produced by frustration or other aversive events can be reduced by direct aggression, but also by non-aggressive behaviour which removes aversion. This casts doubts on the psychodynamic notion that aggression can be reduced by catharsis, e.g. the 'purging' of aggressive tension by means of substitute aggressive expression. Instrumental aggression, on the other hand, is positively reinforced by the attainment of rewards such as material goods, status, or approval. In these terms, persistent aggression may be not only the result of positive or negative reinforcement for aggressive behaviour, but also the failure to learn non-aggressive ways of coping with aversive events or obtaining desired rewards.

Although the anticipation of punishment is considered to be the major inhibitor of aggression in both psychodynamic and learning theories, its effects are variable (Baron, 1983). Actual punishment is frustrating, and unless incapacitating, may increase angry aggression. It also constitutes counteraggression and provides a model for aggression. Threatened punishment has been found to deter angry aggression of low intensity and instrumental aggression motivated by modest gains. It is less likely to reduce aggression motivated by strong positive reinforcers, or by intense anger, which impairs consideration of future consequences.

Social Cognitive Perspectives

Learning theories evolved from studies of conditioning processes in animals. Some theorists question whether these processes apply in any simple way to human aggression, and stress complex cognitive mediation as the source of aggression. The effects of frustration and punishment, for example, depend on whether the recipient perceives them as justified. This clearly entails normative judgments and cognitive appraisals about the intent of a frustrator. Similarly, physiological arousal energizes aggressive behaviour, but only when it is attributed to frustration or provocation. When people are provoked to anger, further arousal from extraneous sources, such as noise or heat, may be 'misinterpreted' and intensify aggression (Zillmann, 1979).

A comprehensive cognitive theory of aggression is the social learning theory of Bandura (1983). He saw reinforcing contingencies as providing information about the effects of behaviour, but held that such information is most readily acquired through observational learning or modelling. Aggression originates in modelling and reinforcement, through which people develop expectations about the likely outcomes of different behaviours in meeting their goals. These, however, include consequences for the self, and behaviour is adjusted to meet personal and social standards through the self-regulatory process of self-reward and punishment. Standards may, nevertheless, be overriden or neutralized by cognitive distortions such as blaming or dehumanizing the victim.

Bandura, like most workers, rejected the notion of a specific aggressive drive, and proposed that both aversive experiences and positive incentives produce a general increase in emotional arousal. This motivates whatever relevant responses are strongest in the behavioural repertoire. In coping with aversive experiences, aggression is only one of several possible strategies, which might include avoidance or constructive problem-solving, depending on the individual's skills.

Zillman (1979) suggested a similar model which emphasized the interaction of arousal and cognitive guidance of aggression. Social events influence behaviour through the causal attributions people assign to them, but also through moral evaluations of behaviour, including one's own, relative to social norms. Thus the attribution to another of an intentional infliction of aversion will result in compensatory retaliation to a level dictated by social norms of equity, due account being taken of personal rewards and costs. Aggression then, in this theory, is to a degree rational. However, the cognitive control of aggression is determined by the level of physiological arousal. At high or low levels, cognitive guidance is minimized, and aggression is likely to be impulsive and under immediate situational control.

Social cognitive approaches are consistent with recent proposals that human emotional behaviour has significant cultural components and serves social functions of communication (Averill, 1983). While not wholly incompatible with biological or psychodynamic perspectives, such a view dictates an analysis of human aggression in terms of its meaning for the individual and the social context in which it occurs.

An important book, written by a group of scientists interested in animal behaviour, anthropology, and human development (Klama, 1988) argued that aggression is not a thing or a class of things that can be located somewhere in the brain, neither is it a core of impulses overlaid by cultural modifiers and restraints. They drew heavily on the ideas in game theory and particularly Axelrod's theory of the evolution of cooperation (Axelrod, 1984) which incorporated an analysis of the prisoner's dilemma. The essence of the argument is that individuals (not species) evolve in an environment of dilemmas, conflicts, and pay-offs, such that the costs and benefits of any particular strategy or tactic by an individual are complex. Some circumstances give advantages if an individual is very nasty to his fellows and other circumstances give advantages to being very nice.

Axelrod's analysis of the prisoner's dilemma is about the problem faced by two prisoners, arrested and separated, who have committed a series of crimes together. There may be advantage for each in saying nothing, and going to prison for a short period or, alternatively, there may be advantage in grassing (defecting) on their colleague in return for a let-off. Everything depends on what the other one does. The usual analysis is that it is better to defect, because that produces the best overall risk-benefit profile whatever the other prisoner does. However, Axelrod said that if the game is played more than once by the same two people, then the best profile is produced by saying nothing and thus cooperating with the other prisoner. This is because each knows that the other can either follow suit and cooperate next time round, or retaliate next time, and it is better to avoid retaliation. Axelrod suggested, therefore, that an individual playing the game this way can help himself (and his opponent) best by not being envious, not being the first to defect, reciprocating both cooperation and defection, and not being too clever.

Aggression seen this way is a spectrum of activity, which varies widely and is highly flexible. Perhaps a useful concept to add to this view of aggression is the concept of power. Powerlessness, the search for control, subjective feelings of weakness and helplessness, distorted perceptions of power, are all factors found in human aggression. A theoretical understanding of the distribution of power in any social system enables ideas of intervention for treatment to be generated and tested.

On the face of it, the discussion of the iterated prisoner's dilemma, and the distribution of power is all concerned with rational activity, thus apparently leaving out irrational, motiveless violence. However, it is even possible to attribute these rational ideas to psychotic individuals to some extent. Equally, irrationality is a judgment passed by one observer on another. Once a patient's sense of helplessness, his terror of being attacked by neighbours, rays, gas, or whatever, and other aspects of his inner world have been understood, then aggressive behaviour from him also becomes understandable.

An important additional dimension, as far as human beings are concerned, which must be added to these perspectives of violence and aggression, is the dimension of self-destructiveness. Human beings are not the only animals that destroy themselves but, presumably because of the great cognitive

component of all human behaviour, they are more likely to destroy themselves in a planned way. Self-destruction and destruction of others seems to
be closely linked in human thinking and behaviour, therefore self-destruction
has to be kept in mind as an important and specially human factor when
matters of violence are considered.

Television and Violence

A separate subsection on television and violence seems necessary because of
the persistent public interest in it. This is in spite of the fact that television
can only ever be one of many influences which shape our behaviour. The
reasons for this interest seem to be related to its ubiquitousness with most
people in richer countries having access to a TV set, and the large number
of programmes shown which portray violence, whether real or fictional.
People are also aware that manufacturers and politicians will pay money to
have their products and ideas advertised—presumably, therefore, those
manufacturers and politicians have evidence that they can alter the viewer's
behaviour.

To maintain perspective, it has to be remembered that violence is not a
new phenomenon that has appeared since the advent of TV. Recorded rates
of violent crime in Britain have gone up in recent years, but we are not clear
how far this is a real increase, how far it relates to a shift in the type of
violence (e.g. from domestic to public) and how far it relates to decreased
public tolerance with an increase in reporting (e.g. of street fights). Learning
from TV is largely cognitive and is diluted by many other daily influences.
It is, for example, unlikely that an angry hostile attitude to women in a
violent rapist will have been gleaned from TV cop movies; it is more likely
it was learned from adverse early experiences, from modelling on powerful
adult figures actually in the household, and a range of internal psychological
problems. One of the assumptions sometimes made about the adverse effects
of TV violence is that the viewer (especially the child viewer) does not
understand the difference between fiction and fact, and is unable to
distinguish make-believe from reality. It is equally plausible that children
are good at such distinctions and will model on reality and entertain
themselves with fantasy.

What of the research? There are mountains of reports. The reader is
particularly referred to the US Surgeon General's report (US Public Health
Service, 1972), a Home Office report (Brody, 1977), an overview from New
York (Liebert and Sprafkin, 1988), and a review taking a much broader
perspective of the influence of television on children (Gunter and McAleer,
1990).

Most studies focus on children and young people. Rothenberg (1975)
pointed out that, on leaving school, the average American child will have
watched 15 000 hours of television, but received only 11 000 hours of formal

classroom instruction. He will have witnessed some 18 000 murders and countless examples of lesser violence. Rothenberg reviewed 50 studies involving 10 000 children and adolescents from 'every conceivable background', and argued that the evidence was consistently supportive of the view that viewing violence produces increased aggressive behaviour in young people. The Eisenhower Commission (National Commission on the Causes and Prevention of Violence, 1969) was only slightly more modest in its conclusions:

> We do not suggest that television is a principal cause of violence in society. We do suggest that it is a contributing factor.

By contrast, the conclusion of the Surgeon General's report (US Public Health Service, 1972) was much more equivocal, but widespread criticism followed because of the alleged influence of the television industry on the membership of the committee (see Rothenberg, 1975; Somers, 1976) and individual members of the Committee dissented from its final conclusion (e.g. Rubenstein, 1974).

Brody (1977) examined the four basic hypotheses about the generation of social violence from screen violence, by imitation, by arousal of aggressive feelings, by emotional reactions, by the debasement of social and moral values. He concluded that young children do imitate novel actions, including aggressive ones, boys imitate aggression more than girls, but all this has to be seen in an emotional context which may outweigh all other factors, and the research has been subjected to much technical criticism. As for arousal of aggressive feelings, laboratory experiments have repeatedly shown that college students are more ready to administer powerful electric shocks to strangers after they have seen violent films, but there is little evidence that these data can be generalized to ordinary social circumstances. The idea that emotional responsiveness can be blunted by repeated exposure to violence seems to be supported by the fact that people are less upset the second time they see a violent film than they were the first time, but there is also evidence that this is highly situationally specific with little or no generalization. The debasement of moral values is the most serious charge against violent films. Whilst there is evidence that a specific film may change specific ideas, just as educational films are intended to, there is very little data on whether this generalizes very far. It is hardly surprising that Brody concluded:

> It can be stated quite simply that social research has not been able unambiguously to offer any firm reassurance that the mass media in general, and films and television in particular, either exercise a socially harmful effect, or that they do not.

This debate could run for ever as no-one can do the definitive experiment. What is needed is a prosperous, westernized town that has all aspects of modern life except television. Its violence levels would have to be measured accurately and then the town be provided with TV for a few years. Violence levels would again have to be measured. Finally, the TV sets would need to be taken away (just imagine!) and the violence levels measured again. The nearest we can come to this experiment is the study by Hennigam et al. (1982) which compared crime rates in American cities with and without TV between 1949 and 1952. The introduction of TV did not increase violent crime, but it was associated with an increase in larceny! Could this have been due to an increased awareness of relative poverty on the part of some people?

An early British study has not yet had its conclusion overturned:

> The whole weight of research and theory in the juvenile delinquency field would suggest that the mass media, except just possibly in the case of a very small number of pathological individuals, are never the sole cause of delinquent behaviour. At most, they may play a contributory role, and that a minor one
>
> (Halloran et al., 1970).

Liebert and Sprafkin (1988) were a little more definite.

> TV violence can provide instruction in antisocial and aggressive behaviour, which will sometimes lead to direct copying or disinhibition of such behaviours. These effects do not invariably occur, however, and depend upon the character-istics of the viewers and the situation. In contrast, the value shaping and cultivation effects of TV violence appear to be very widespread, suggesting that TV violence can work in subtle and insidious ways to adversely influence youth and society.

A broadly based review of the impact of television on children (Gunter and McAleer, 1990) has challenged the whole concept of television as a monster. These authors pointed out that it is the possible *negative* effects of television which receive all the publicity. There may be many beneficial effects which are less often discussed. They reviewed the known facts about British children's television viewing, and asked 'why do children watch TV?', finding a range of reasons from boredom to a desire to learn, from escapism to companionship. They found that children do not attend to the TV screen constantly or passively, the amount of attention they are prepared to give a programme is related to whether it means much to them. Hardly a surprising conclusion, but an important one. There is evidence that television influences the formation of social perceptions, as well as factual knowledge. They, like all other writers in this field, then reviewed the evidence for and against television directly influencing social behaviour, particularly violent behaviour, and came to no very definite conclusions, although they pointed to evidence that television may be a way of harmlessly dispersing hostile impulses, and also encouraging children to be more thoughtful towards others. They went on to look at the ways in which parents and schools influence viewing patterns. Their final message was:

> We believe there is a tendency to make television a scapegoat for some of society's ills. Television is often unjustifiably accused of misleading children on very flimsy evidence and a very poor understanding of how young viewers respond to programmes.

This digression into a topic of great public interest is necessary in a modern book dealing with aspects of human behaviour, yet, as we have seen, it is of only marginal relevance. There is no evidence that personality structure is fundamentally moulded by television; there are other more powerful social influences such as the family, friendships, neighbourhood beliefs and schools. Further, given the universality of violence through cultures and time, it seems inherently unlikely that television, a new invention, plays a major role in its genesis. Its marginal/pathoplastic role is still open to debate and study.

Crimes of Violence

Crimes are socially determined phenomena, defined as such by man-made laws and are therefore, by definition, closely linked to culture. Criminal patterns will differ from time to time and place to place. It is sometimes thought that we live in a violent age, and perhaps that is true compared with the 1920s and 1930s, but is it true compared with previous centuries? When Anthony Trollope was writing *Phineas Phinn*, he described after-dark street violence in horrifying terms. At the time, it was usual for personal protectors (e.g. truncheons) to be carried by men walking out at night anywhere in a large city and for women to stay indoors. In the 18th century, travel between towns was highly risky because of highway robbers. Table 12.1 illustrates variations in violent activity (including criminal violence) between different countries. It shows the death rates due to firearms in different countries in the mid-sixties, with a comment about each country's gun laws at that time.

As Mays said in 1970:

> Crimes of violence always arouse considerable emotional reactions and anxiety, yet they never seem to get above 5% of the grand total.

Walmsley (1986) gave the rounded figures for personal violence as recorded by the police in 1984 (see Table 12.2) and said:

> These 154 000 offences represent just under 5% of all notifiable offences recorded by the police.

Table 12.1
Deaths due to Firearms in Rates per 100,000 Population

Country	Homicide	Suicide	Accident	Laws
USA (1966)	3.5	5.3	1.3	Lax
Canada (1966)	0.5	3.1	1.0	Gun registration
Sweden (1966)	0.2	2.5	0.3	Gun registration
France (1965)	0.3	1.8	0.5	Police permits
GFRep (1965)	0.1	0.9	0.2	Hunters only
Scotland (1963)	0.1	0.4	0.3	Police permits
Eng & Wales (1966)	0.1	0.4	0.1	Police permits
Japan (1965)	0.1	0.1	0.1	Prohibition

These figures are quoted from Gillin and Ochberg, 1970 with permission from Little, Brown & Co.

Table 12.2
Offences of Personal Violence 1984

Wounding or assaults	circa	112 000 (73%)
Robbery	circa	25 000 (16%)
Sexual assaults	circa	15 000 (10%)
Causing death by dangerous driving	circa	200 ⎫
Other homicides	circa	800 ⎬ (1%)
Threats to murder	circa	800 ⎭
	actual	154 268

Based on figures given in Walmsley, 1986

There is, however, an anomaly in the figures. Crimes of personal violence recorded by the police rose by 72% between 1974 and 1984 (from 89 599 to 154 268), an increase similar to that for all recorded crime (69%), yet the most serious offenders of violence rose less rapidly (rape 37%, wounding endangering life 24%, and homicide only 3%). If homicide is simply one end of the spectrum of violence, then why is it so out of step? There are probably two factors. First, the amount of violent crime that is reported is a small proportion of that committed (the British Crime Survey, Hough and Mayhew, 1983, would suggest about a quarter), but serious violence may be reported much more commonly, so that if the apparent rise in crimes of violence is partly due to increased reporting or increased police efficiency, these factors will influence the homicide rate much less. Second, homicide rates are partly dependent on the efficiency of medical services which probably improved over that period. A good ambulance service, a blood transfusion service, and skilled surgery can convert a potential homicide statistic into a wounding statistic.

In his study of violence in Britain in the late 1950s, McClintock (1963) discovered that one-half of recorded violent crimes occurred in and around pubs, whilst family and domestic disputes accounted for another third; half the offenders and victims knew one another. The majority of fights were between males, and of the female victims, three-quarters were attacked by relatives or close neighbours. Half the victims required some form of hospital treatment, but only 20% were detained in hospital.

Even in the United States, where violence is much commoner, some of the same features are found. As Morris and Hawkins (1970) put it:

> Taken together, murders involving spouse killing, parent killing child, other family killings, romantic triangles and lovers' quarrels, and arguments between those previously acquainted with one another, account for 80% of all homicides in America. You are safer on the streets than at home; safer with a stranger than with a friend or relative.

In the USA, aggravated assault, rape and robbery only account for 13% of crime.

In his analysis of the 1984 English figures, Walmsley (1986) said that most of the people convicted of woundings are 'of course' male (93%). Half of them are aged 17–24 (three-quarters aged 14–29). He also noted that the recorded levels of violence in Britain are slightly lower than in most of our European neighbours and much lower than those in North America. Walmsley (1986) went on to give what he called snapshots of personal violence.

Homicide. In 1984 there were 11 victims of homicide per million population, children under the age of one being at greatest risk (32 per million). In 9 out of every 12 cases the victim was acquainted with the suspect. The commonest method of killing was a sharp instrument, followed by strangulation or asphyxiation. About half the offences were committed during quarrels or bouts of temper.

Wounding. Males were five times as likely as females to be victims of more serious wounding and three times as likely to be victims of less serious wounding. In about 1 in 8 recorded woundings, the offender was a member of the victim's family, the offender was a complete stranger in only about half the recorded cases. The more serious woundings occurred indoors and outdoors equally, but less serious woundings were more likely to occur outdoors.

Rape. Offenders tended to be of a similar age to their victims or slightly older. About half the offenders in 1984 were 16–24 and a further 40% were 25–39.

Sentencing. People convicted of murder receive, in Britain, a mandatory life sentence. Ninety per cent of those convicted of manslaughter in 1984 also received a custodial sentence (77% prison, 13% a hospital order with restrictions). The general pattern for violent offenders was that only 1% of them received a hospital order, this was true for both serious wounding and rape.

Domestic Violence

All the statistics point to the fact that the home is the scene of much serious violence. This has probably always been the case. The horrors of 19th century child abuse have been highlighted by novelists such as Charles Dickens (e.g. *David Copperfield*, *Nicholas Nickelby*) and Charles Kingsley (*Water Babies*). For a historical perspective the reader is referred to Radbill (1968) and May (1978); (*see also* Ch. 23).

Smith (1989) gave a useful overview of the topic from a feminist perspective. She acknowledged that domestic violence must have a multi-dimensional explanation, but was largely unhappy with the notion that the perpetrators of such violence should be regarded as psychiatric patients; the problem is too universal for that to be the case in her view. On the other hand, she chided general practitioners for remaining non-committal and for offering little advice other than for the women to leave home. An alternative explanation offered was that domestic violence reflected the unequal power of men and women in society. The curious thing is that the arguments advanced are all about male/female power systems (none relating to adult/child systems) and are perceived as a manifestation of males having more power than females. No attention is given to the fact that, however common domestic violence is, it is less common than domestic harmony. As yet, the parent who attacks a child, for example, is still the exception rather than the rule. A better explanation would be that in those cases where violence breaks out, the power system is unbalanced and the violent individual has or feels they have less power than other individuals in the system, and is using the violence vainly to try and redress the balance (*see* Gunn, 1991d). On the medical point, whilst Smith is right, there is more that doctors can do—it is surely not just with the victims. Individuals who, for whatever reasons, feel so threatened by their circumstances that they frequently lash out, deserve, at the very least, a full psychiatric assessment.

Violence to Children

A questionnaire survey in the USA (Gil, 1968) suggested that perhaps 3% of families cause deliberate injury to children in that country. In a British study of 134 children under the age of 5, located from hospitals and various social agencies in a two-year period in Birmingham and suffering from non-accidental injury, it was found that nearly half had serious injuries and 21 (16%) died (Smith and Hanson, 1974). The children were equally divided between the sexes. The injuries reported in all surveys embrace every conceivable type of injury and torture, from internal damage, to head injuries, broken bones, burns, starvation and wasting, and poisoning. Beatings with hands, fists, belts, sticks, bars, burnings and scaldings, are all quite common. Parental explanations for the injuries vary but are often vague; 'fell on his head', 'bruises easily', 'fell down the stairs', 'sat on the radiator' are the general pattern. In the Birmingham study the 'battered' children were younger than other children brought to hospital because of injuries. Over one-third of the children had an intracranial haemorrhage (usually subdural), one-fifth had serious burns or scalds. One-third of the dead children had been battered before. Neurological sequelae that required long-term rehabilitation developed in 15% of cases. Other findings were that, regardless of head injury, language retardation occurred in the 'battered' sample.

The Royal College of Psychiatrists in evidence to the House of Commons Select Committee on battered children relied on Dr J. Oliver's survey of North Wiltshire to estimate the prevalence of the problem (Royal College of Psychiatrists, 1977). His team estimated that:

1. 1 in 1000 children under the age of 4 years will be severely injured each year;
2. 1 in 10 of these children will die;
3. in England and Wales, some 3000 children aged 0–3 will be injured each year and 6 of them will die each week.

Mild to moderate injuries will be much commoner, perhaps four to six times as common. These issues are dealt with in more detail in Ch. 23.

The parents of these children are of special concern to the forensic psychiatrist. Various attempts have been made to classify the types of battering (e.g. *see* Ch. 15).

Kempe and Kempe (1978) suggested a ten-point checklist of factors in parental history, which they claimed can accurately predict risk to a child. They suggested that, to be of maximum value, these questions should be posed at the time of the child's birth.

1. As a child, was the parent repeatedly beaten or deprived?
2. Does the parent have a record of mental illness or criminal activities?
3. Is the parent suspected of criminal abuse in the past?
4. Is the parent suffering loss of self-esteem, social isolation or depression?
5. Has the parent experienced multiple stresses such as marital discord, divorce, debt, frequent moves, significant losses?
6. Does the parent have violent outbursts of temper?
7. Does the parent have rigid unrealistic expectations of the child's behaviour?
8. Does the parent punish harshly?
9. Does the parent see the child as difficult and provocative, whether or not the child is?
10. Does the parent reject the child or have difficulty in forming a bond with it?

Steele and Pollock (1968) studied and treated 60 child batterers. They came from all socio-economic strata, IQs varied from 73 to 130, ages ranged from 11–40 years (the 11-year-old was a babysitter, the majority were in their twenties), most had stable marriages even if sometimes it was a desperate dependent clinging together, and alcohol intake bore no significant relationship to the child injury. In terms of diagnoses, there was a wide spectrum from anxiety states and personality disorders to depression and schizophrenia, many patients having a mixture of diagnoses. Sociopathic traits were, however, rare in this sample.

In contrast Smith et al. (1973) in Birmingham likewise found that the parents were young, but in this sample they came predominantly from the lower social classes and 29% of the fathers had a criminal record. No special alcohol or drug problems were found, but the parents had had their first child at a particularly young age (mean = 19.7 years). Diagnostically, there was a wide spread, 4 mothers and 1 father (out of 214 parents) were psychotic, 17 mothers and 33 fathers had severe personality disorders. A national questionnaire survey carried out through the probation service by the Home Office (Sturgess and Heal, 1977) found that the probability of non-accidental injury is related inversely to the age of the potential victim, with 40% of all victims being under the age of 1 year. Boys are slightly more vulnerable than girls. Half of all offences were committed against the parents' first child.

Steele and Pollock went beyond the simple diagnostic label which psychiatrists frequently use, to try and understand the interaction between parent and child. They found that the parents expected and demanded a great deal from their children, much more than an infant could provide, a phenomenon sometimes called role reversal. They quoted Kaufman as stating that—

> the child is not perceived as a child but some symbolic or delusional figure; and the child
> may be perceived as the psychotic portion of the parent which the parent wishes to control or destroy. . . .
> other parents who are extremely infantile and wish to be babied themselves resent the dependency and needs of their child and express this resentment in hostile ways.

One of Steele and Pollock's patients said:

> I have never felt really loved all my life. When the baby was born, I thought he would love me, but when he cried all the time, it meant he didn't love me, so I hit him.

The authors note too how much common parlance about children underlay some of the pathological emotions, e.g. 'If you give in to kids, they'll be spoiled rotten'; 'You have to teach children to obey authority'. Carter (1974) has suggested that harsh punishment is part of a power game in which an insecure parent reacts to the uncontrollable demands of an apparently powerful baby like an unstable totalitarian ruler faced with a rebellion.

Perhaps the most important finding in the Steele and Pollock study was that:

> Without exception . . . there is a history of having been raised in the same style which they have recreated in the pattern of rearing their own children.

Several had been physically abused, all had experienced a sense of intense, pervasive, continuous demand from their parents. There are analogies from animal experiments suggesting that lack of mothering produces an adult with poor mothering skills and infant-battering potential (Harlow and Harlow, 1962).

Management

Initial steps. Forensic psychiatrists are rarely front line workers in dealing with child abuse of any kind whether by neglect, violence, or sex. However, they should be familiar with current social policy. For England and Wales, this has been set out in a pamphlet *Working Together* (DHSS and Welsh Office, 1988). The title emphasized the multi-professional approach which is required, yet, strangely, the booklet hardly mentioned the use of psychiatry at all, even though the guidance goes beyond the management of the initial crisis.

If child abuse is suspected, more than one opinion on the case should be sought urgently. Paediatric, general practice, orthopaedic, child psychiatry and social work opinions may all be relevant. If, on consultation, there seems to be a serious likelihood of child abuse, then the local authority social services department must be informed immediately. Social workers from that department should then consult with those who know the case and consider some preventive action. This may be advice to the parents, the provision of day care, a play group, a child minder, attendance at a family centre, advice about voluntary fostering and the like. In very urgent and serious cases, compulsory action may be considered, such as an emergency protection order.

Longer term. In the longer term, a care order or a supervision order may be provided by the courts for the child, and this may mean placement away from the parental home (*see also* pp. 245–51).

Every area of the country has to have a child protection register (often known as an 'at risk' register) which lists all the children in the area who have been abused or who are at risk of abuse. Five categories of abuse are considered for the register: neglect, physical abuse (e.g. violence, poisoning), sexual abuse, emotional abuse, grave concern (e.g. other children in the family have been abused). As the DHSS guidance states:

> The purpose of the register is to provide a record of all children in the area who are currently the subject of inter-agency protection plans and to ensure that the plans are formally reviewed at least every 6 months.

The register is maintained by either the local social services department or the NSPCC on its behalf. Twice-yearly case conferences are at the heart of the protection register scheme; they should allow for a frank multi-professional discussion about the child's progress, and will include a social worker, teacher, the family doctor, a liaison police officer, and other significant professionals. This should include psychiatric advisers, both to the child and the parents. If a psychiatrist treating a parent is not invited to the conference, he should make every effort to remain as informed about the conferences as possible and he should be prepared to swap sensitive information with the team (with the patient's knowledge of course). Parents are rarely invited to these conferences, but they could be and perhaps should be more often.

It would be helpful in all child abuse cases, if the parents or abusers were referred for psychiatric examination. The needs of distressed adults are frequently overlooked when children have been hurt. It is right that the needs of children should be put first, but abusing parents are usually in severe psychological distress themselves. A psychiatric referral is not only humanitarian, it may also be a source of extra useful information which will help make better predictions and management plans for the child. In an ideal world, *each* member of a family in which abuse is occurring should have a personal counsellor. This may be a social worker, a nurse, or a psychiatrist, but should be someone who puts the interests of that individual high on the agenda of concern. Resources will limit the implementation of this ideal, but it should be approached as far as possible. This is not to neglect the needs of the child who will have suffered considerably, who will be a candidate to become a violent adult, and who should be referred for psychiatric and/or psychological treatment in his own right.

In England and Wales, the prosecution of abusing parents is a matter for the Crown Prosecution Service (CPS). This service is provided with evidence by the police. All cases of serious abuse should be reported to the police. The police and the CPS will decide whether the evidence is strong enough for prosecution and whether prosecution would be in the public interest.

Following a successful prosecution, the courts will decide on the disposal of an abusing adult. As Scott (1973) argued, the majority of seriously abusing parents, especially those who have killed a child, will be given prison sentences. He further argued that, as a result, therapeutic effort for these people should be focused on the prisons. There is some truth in this, but it is still very difficult in Britain for trained psychiatrists to conduct treatment in prison, and almost impossible to link any prison treatment with the family or with long-term community care. Scott believed that imprisonment, however, has a number of positive aspects in cases like these, such as appeasing public opinion, and allaying guilt feelings. On the other hand, a lengthy prison sentence is almost bound to break up the family if it has not been broken by the prosecution itself, child abusers in prison are vulnerable to savage attacks from other prisoners and, whilst motivation for treatment is certainly altered by imprisonment, it is rarely improved, it may alienate the violent patient completely. Further, it is not part of the psychiatrist's job to advise or recommend punishment such as imprisonment. If it is thought advisable for a family to separate, there are other ways of achieving this. If treatment in security is required, or it is clear that the court will not accept treatment unless it begins in security, then a hospital order is the correct recommendation. It may be that the hospital system would be overwhelmed if this advice were followed in every case, but that is a political matter concerning resources, and should be kept separate from the consideration of an individual case.

The details of the management of each individual child abuser will depend on a full psychiatric (including social and psychological) assessment. Diagnosis, family dynamics, personality characteristics should all be investigated in some detail so that a clear understanding of the processes of aggression can be obtained. Removal of one or more individuals from the family may be necessary (this should only be the child as a last resort), family discussions may be fruitful, practical assistance with access to a nursery or play group, and medication to effect symptom relief in depressed, anxious, or psychotic parents may be needed. Counselling to reduce drinking is occasionally helpful, above all support for the frightened, abusing parents must be forthcoming, especially if they are to be prosecuted.

When the parental problem can be identified as one of the severer forms of psychosis or personality disorder, then admission to hospital may be necessary for that person and maybe for months, even several years. Whenever possible, contacts between members of the family should be maintained during such hospitalization. Feelings of guilt and rejection in the various parties, particularly the children, can thus be reduced.

A running theme throughout this book is the need for forensic psychiatrists, all psychiatrists, to provide more and better psychotherapy. The battering family is certainly a good candidate for such services. We also believe that other professional groups could provide more in the way of advice, support, and psychotherapy. Ideally, every violent individual who seeks help should be provided with some kind of supportive long-term service. An adjunct to professional services of this kind might be some kind of self-help service, but these do not seem to exist in the UK. In the USA, there is Mothers' Anonymous, and a system of foster grandparents (*see* Kempe and Helfer, 1972).

Violence to Wives

Intramarital strife is common and may spill over into violence, sometimes severe violence up to and including homicide; it may also involve sadism and torture in some cases. Men are stronger than women, men are more likely to be extrapunitive, women intropunitive. Historically, women have had few legal protections in marriage. In Britain until 1878, wives were regarded as part of a man's property and could be forcibly detained in the man's home. The majority of serious physical injuries in marital conflict are, therefore, suffered by women.

Perhaps the most comprehensive British review of violence in marriage in recent years is the report of the Parliamentary Select Committee on Violence in Marriage (House of Commons, 1975b). The English Department of Health and Social Security (DHSS) gave evidence to that Committee that there are 'very few facts, and no reliable statistics' on the subject of wife beating, partly because of the paucity of research, partly because of the inherent difficulties of knowing what goes on behind the closed doors of the domestic environment. The DHSS quoted a citizens' advice bureau as receiving 25 000 enquiries about or on behalf of battered women in 1973. The Metropolitan Police suggested that in London there are between 6000 and 6500 reported wife assaults and 15–23 husband/wife murders each year. DHSS and the Welsh Office quoted a Colchester survey as suggesting that as many as one wife in 200 might be subject to violence.

The Committee was impressed by the large number of factors which lead to violence and concluded:

> We had no evidence that the husband alone is responsible for his violence. The behaviour of the wife is relevant. So, too, is the family's environment, their housing, their sexual relationship, and many other factors.

They highlighted three factors for preventive action.

1. Education, including school instruction on family dynamics.
2. Special investment in the children of a violent family to try and break the cycle of domestic abuse whereby victims become victimizers.
3. A publicity campaign against alcohol.

In respect of alcohol they concluded:

> No one can be sure whether excess drinking is the cause of violence or a result of the frustration which produced it. However, we have had considerable evidence indicating that excessive drinking is frequently a factor in domestic violence. This is not surprising in view of the known pharmacological actions of the drug alcohol.

Other psychiatric factors were given less prominence, but they did urge that battering husbands be offered considerate advice and discussion, help in court, and 'psychiatric advice'.

In its evidence to the Select Committee, DHSS had argued that not all battering husbands 'have a psychiatric problem'. They believed that of those who are in some sense abnormal, some are alcoholics, some—perhaps the majority—are 'psychopaths', some are borderline subnormals, others are neurotic men with anxiety states and a few may be frankly paranoid. They said:

> Some of these conditions can and should be treated but it would be a mistake to believe that all mental abnormality is susceptible to treatment—some is not, and even where treatment might help, the man might be unwilling to cooperate.

The evidence went on:

> Treatment with tranquillizers and anti-depressants is no solution for immaturity, irresponsibility, financial hardships, intolerable housing conditions or any of the other variety of factors in or affecting either partner, which may have contributed to the violence in the family.

The DHSS evidence contained some truth, but it also carried the remarkable implication that psychiatric treatment is the same thing as prescribing pills. No doubt some psychiatrists see it that way; if many do, it is no wonder that only a few wife beaters are helped effectively. Psychotherapy, support, admission to hospital, environmental manipulation all should play a role with these patients. It is true that doctors are not primarily responsible for curing housing problems, poverty, and other social difficulties, but they do have a role in making appropriate referrals. The hospital can sometimes be the place where these matters are first carefully evaluated; medical facts and recommendations can sway housing decisions. Good psychiatry goes hand in hand with good social work. If the little homily telling us that tranquillizers and anti-depressants are not solutions for 'irresponsibility' is meant to tell us that the thoughtless prescription of tablets without attention to other factors is bad practice then quite so; however, aggressive behaviour (to self and others) may be symptomatic of depression, of schizophrenia, of personality disorder, of alcoholism, all of which are treatable diseases. Hamberger and Hastings (1988) provide a useful review of their own work as well as that of others in exploring the personality characteristics of male spouse abusers. Many suffer from personality disorder.

A psychiatric profession that follows the DHSS approach leaves itself open to the kind of criticism that was levelled against it by Erin Pizzey (1974) in the 1970s:

> When a husband comes to court and is put in prison, the prison doctor or psychiatrist will often, if he sees the man is sick, try to have him put into a mental hospital for treatment, as prison is of no therapeutic value. However the prison doctor will run up against a major snag. Mental hospitals are geared to treating the mentally ill, but the majority of husbands have a 'personality problem'. In other words there is nothing organically wrong with their minds, but their personality needs re-educating. . . . So far our society has made almost no provision for the people we term 'psychopaths'. . . . The hospital usually reports that there is nothing mentally wrong with him and sends him home.

Pizzey exaggerated—but only a little. She brought the severity and extent of wife battering to the attention of a somewhat incredulous London public in 1971 by founding a refuge for battered women, Chiswick Women's Aid. One hundred of the women were studied by Gayford (1975b, 1978). He described some very severe injuries, including extensive bruising, burns and scalds, attempted strangulation (19 cases), biting, broken bones, unconsciousness (9 cases). Weapons included fists, cooking utensils, feet, cigarettes, and a specially heated red-hot poker! Some of the violence was clearly sadistic and premeditated. In 44 cases the violence only occurred after the man had been drinking. Jealousy was a common issue, 66 of the women claiming that their husband was constantly accusing them of infidelity.

Gayford also collected some tentative views about the men who caused this mayhem from the women in the survey. Gambling seemed to be a problem for a quarter. Over a half were said to have a prison record. Three-quarters of the men were said to be drunk at least once a month. One-quarter were said to have had psychiatric treatment. Seventeen were thought to be illiterate or semiliterate.

A closer examination of battering husbands was made by Faulk (1974). He looked at 23 men remanded in custody for seriously assaulting their wives. Like most samples, this is a skewed sample, but it may give some idea of the picture at the severe end of the spectrum. The mean age of the men was 39 (20–70). Fourteen of the men had a marked psychiatric disturbance, 5 were depressed, 3 had delusional jealousy, 2 suffered from personality disorder and 1 was dementing. Faulk described five types of relationship between battering husband and wife:

1. dependent passive husband with querulous demanding wife;
2. dependent suspicious husband, escalating to jealousy of the wife;
3. violent bullying men, often accompanied by heavy drinking;
4. dominating men, often successful at work, unable to cope with any challenge;
5. stable and affectionate relationship disrupted by illness, e.g. depression.

The first category raises the unpopular topic of the role of the victim. It is quite clear that to blame the victim of any type of violence, 'she asked for it', 'she must enjoy it, why doesn't she leave', is absurd and harmful to the process of prevention and management. Yet violence is interactive, even babies play a role in the provoking of violence. To understand domestic violence, the interaction between the participants has to be understood as fully as possible. Understanding interactions and analysing them is, or should be, very different from apportioning blame. In forensic psychiatry, the attribution of blame is rarely helpful.

Voluntary self-help is, as is so often the case with behavioural problems, quite helpful to some men who are violent at home. In conjunction with Chiswick Women's Aid a project called Men's Aid was established in North London. It provided accommodation for up to 6 men, a 24-hour telephone service, weekly counselling for both men and couples, home visits, and a daily drop-in centre (Melville, 1978).

The problems experienced by the victims are dealt with more fully in Ch. 23. Here it is worth emphasizing that battered women need a lot of help, not just social and legal, but also psychiatric.

Violence to Husbands

Domestic violence in this book has been largely interpreted as child and wife abuse, because those seem to be the commonest problems. Yet the old music hall gag of the wife-beating husband has some truth in it too. A battered husband wrote to the Select Committee on Violence in Marriage (House of Commons, 1975b) telling how his 63-year-old wife, described by a psychiatrist as emotionally immature, hit him with planks of wood and broomsticks, and on one occasion attacked him with a knife. Geller and Straus are reported in Freeman (1979) as finding that wives assault husbands just as frequently as the other way round. Presumably, if this is the case, the consequences are usually less serious because of superior male strength, and are even less likely to be noticed or reported.

Violence to the Elderly

As with babies, older individuals who make constant demands for attention and succour will stretch the patience of others, particularly those who have a vulnerable, brittle personality. If the dynamics between the younger individual and the elderly person include complex power struggles, then violence may ensue. As with children and women, the physically weak individual will fare badly.

A particularly vulnerable group of old people are those who suffer from dementia. They are both demanding and intensely frustrating; they can be aggressive and they provide few rewards, as they no longer respond with smiles or gratitude. Perhaps the most notable thing about so-called 'granny bashing' is the way in which it is tolerated. Whilst the public conscience about other forms of domestic violence has to some extent been awakened by increased knowledge, minimal action has followed the identification of violence to the elderly (Marsden, 1978).

Homicide

It is slightly artificial to divide violence up into categories such as we have in this text. The categories merge and overlap. Other ways of discussing the problem would be equally valid. The subheadings used are merely for convenience and partly because they are currently in common usage. A separate category for homicide is used because, when a victim actually dies, then different attitudes, different criteria, even different laws come into effect. Murder is said to be 'a crime apart'. Manslaughter runs it close.

In the subsequent discussion, it should be borne in mind that in biological terms homicide is simply at one end of a spectrum of violence, and the distinction between homicide and a lesser form of violence may simply be chance, the thickness of a victim's skull, the angle of a blow, the health of the victim, the efficiency and proximity of the medical services and so on. The discussion on homicide therefore, should be taken to include other types of dangerous violence which could have ended fatally.

An important minority of violent people are mentally disordered. This is especially true of homicide. In an analysis of the homicide offences in England and Wales between 1967 and 1972 Gibson (1975) showed that the proportion of males suspected of murder who were 'normal' in the legal sense varied between 42 and 51%, and the 'abnormal' male 'murderers' split into those who killed themselves (9–21%) and those found insane or of diminished responsibility (29–35%). In an analysis of international statistics Coid (1983) has suggested that throughout the world the proportion of abnormal homicides is similar between countries at around 0.16/100 000 population/year, whereas the wide variation in overall homicide rates are variation in 'normal' murders and probably related to social and cultural differences between countries.

An interesting study of a small country, Iceland (Petursson and Gudjonsson, 1981; Gudjonsson and Petursson, 1986) has shown how rates of homicide change with changing cultural patterns. Iceland, which has a population of 224 000, had only 45 homicide incidents in 80 years (52 victims and 47 offenders). The distribution of these cases was not even however, there were only 2 killings in the first 40 years of this century. The second 40 years (1940–79) produced 43 more (a rate of 0.72/100 000) and in that period the 10 years 1970–79 produced a rate of 0.97/10 000 or three times the rate for the previous 30 years. Of the 47 killers, 70% were regarded by the authors as psychiatrically abnormal.

'Normal' Murder

An earlier study by Gibson and Klein (1969) concluded that even for so-called normal murder the motives were usually emotional, i.e. rage, quarrel, jealousy, revenge; theft and gain were important motives, but numerically less so. Of victims, children were about one-fifth of the total, whilst the numbers of male and female victims were about equal for both children and adults. Women were usually murdered by members of their family, especially husbands, whereas men were usually murdered by acquaintances. Similar patterns were found for later years (Gibson, 1975), although there was an increase in 'normal' murder from the 1960s to 1970s. In the USA, where murder rates are very much higher than in the UK, Wolfgang (1958a) studied all the 588 homicides involving 621 offenders in Philadelphia in the years 1948–52. He concluded that important factors leading to homicide are accessibility to a weapon, and cultural traditions of carrying and using weapons. Saturday seemed to be the most dangerous day of the week, especially the hours 8.00 pm–2.00 am, the traditional drinking time. Alcohol was a factor in two-thirds of all killings and there was a further association between alcohol and the more violent types of homicide. As in Britain, the motives for killing were largely emotional—altercations, domestic quarrels, jealousy, revenge, with only 7% of killings being associated with robbery.

As two highly important factors in the precipitation of 'normal' murder are intensely aroused emotions and alcohol intoxication, 'normal' murder will merge into abnormal murder without a discernible dividing line between the two. A good overview of British homicide is provided by Morris and Blom-Cooper (1964) which gives a series of thumbnail sketches of all the 764 men and women who were tried for murder in England and Wales in the years 1957–62. As they pointed out:

> In this country murder is overwhelmingly a domestic crime in which men kill their wives, mistresses and children.

Sexual rivals (real and imagined) should be added to this list, but the comment is still true nearly thirty years later. It is also probably true everywhere in the world. Interpersonal relationships, especially those with a sexual component are associated with the most intense of human passions, including violent passions.

Criminological studies tell us that women usually die in the bedroom and men in the kitchen, and that weapons which are readily available are the ones most often used, e.g. stockings for strangulation, kitchen knives for stabbing. About a third of all homicides in Britain involve a sharp instrument, but less than 10% a firearm. The lack of general interest in firearms in Britain together with firearms controls result in only a small number of such weapons being available in homes and this may partly explain the wide gap between British and North American homicide rates (*see* Table 12.1 above, p. 499).

Organic Brain Syndromes and Homicide

In spite of the immense amount of interest in 'epileptic' murderers and a frequent legal search for 'organic factors' after a killing (presumably because it is more comfortable to excuse individuals with gross organic pathology than those with, say, neurotic disorders), little is known about the epidemiology of organic brain syndrome homicide. Hafner and Boker (1973) studied all the 533 men and women detained as legally irresponsible in the Federal Republic of Germany between 1955 and 1964 charged with homicide or attempted homicide and compared them with various control groups. They found the following distribution of organic cases in their study (Table 12.3).

Table 12.3 shows that patients with organic degenerative disorders are significantly *less* likely to commit homicidal violence than other patients, although the chances seem evenly distributed for people with epilepsy.

These results agree with clinical experience in that gross brain pathology is likely to impair motor efficiency in any activity, violent or non-violent. Furthermore, clinical experience would suggest that where an organic disorder is related to violence, it is via a functional complication. Thus

Table 12.3
Homicide and Brain Damage

	Mentally disordered homicidal offenders (N=533)	Mentally disordered non-offenders (N=3392)	
Organic cerebral degenerative disorders	40 (7.5%)	452 (13.3%)	$X^2 = 14.2$ p 0.001
Late acquired brain damage	43 (8.0%)	350 (10.3%)	
Epilepsies	29 (5.4%)	177 (5.2%)	
Other disorders	50 (9.4%)	614 (18.1%)	

These figures quoted from Häfner and Böker, 1973

several patients with brain disease, who have committed serious violence, may do this in the context of a paranoid mental state probably emanating from the brain disease. Violence may also result from damage to the frontal lobes; here, however, the violence is usually short-lived and ill directed, so it more often ends up as damage to property or a less serious wounding than as a sustained homicidal attack.

Many of these points were supported by a study on epilepsy (Gunn, 1977). It was found that even although epileptics were more liable to imprisonment than other members of the general population, this was not related to a special propensity to commit violence, it was much more likely to be due to a mixture of social factors and the special vulnerability offenders may have to brain damage. The social aspects of imprisoning epileptics have been confirmed in a recent American study (Whitman et al., 1980; Whitman et al., 1984). In the British study, among those epileptic prisoners who were violent, there was no special association with temporal lobe disorder; further, it seemed that violence committed by an epileptic patient during a period of unconsciousness (or automatism) was extremely rare (Gunn and Fenton, 1971).

Alcohol and Homicide

It is a common, everyday experience that alcohol can increase aggressiveness in some people in certain contexts. Many studies have shown a clear association with a killing and high level of alcohol in the bloodstream of either the assailant or the victim or both, e.g. Wolfgang and Strohm (1956) found that only in 214 out of 588 homicides (36%) was alcohol absent from the bloodstream of either victim or assailant and it was present in both in 256 cases (44%). Macdonald (1961) reviewed 10 studies and found that the proportion of killers who had been drinking prior to their crimes ranged from 19–83% with a median of 54%.

Alcoholism and Homicide

Although alcohol may lead to increased aggressiveness, there seems little evidence of an association between homicide and alcoholism. In the Hafner and Boker (1973) study there was no real evidence of an increased prevalence of alcoholism among the violent offenders as compared to controls. In his review of alcohol and violent mortality, Goodwin (1973) noted:

> It is interesting that although drinking is commonly associated with homicide, murderers are rarely diagnosed as alcoholics.

A Swedish study (Lindelius and Salum, 1975) showed that alcoholic patients of all sorts are largely non-violent. Violence was related to social deterioration such as homelessness. The association between alcoholism and homicide is also discussed in Ch. 11, pp. 447–8.

Parricide

A murder of parents by their children is rare (about 3% of British homicides—Bluglass, 1979). A son who kills his mother is usually an unmarried, unambitious young man with an intense relationship with the mother, feelings of social inferiority, and an absent or passive father (O'Connell, 1963). In other words, there is a good chance that the relationship has been eroticized and thus acquired much of the passion that goes with eroticism. The reasons for sons killing their fathers are more diverse with oedipal factors being prominent together with other kinds of rivalry and hatred in some cases. Both matricide and patricide may be associated with gross mental illness especially schizophrenia. Bluglass (1979) suggested that the killing of a mother by her daughter is 'invariably' schizophrenic.

Children Killed Outside the Home

Not all child killings can be regarded as 'domestic' or laid at the door of parents. Adelson (1961) studied 46 homicides in which the victims were children in Ohio; the killings took place over 17 years and constituted 3% of the homicides in the county studied. The 46 children were killed by 41 adults, 36 of them dying at the hands of parents or parent substitutes, one being killed by a psychotic grandparent, 8 were killed by a neighbour or stranger and one was a mystery, 5 (4 girls, one boy) of these 9 non-family killings were associated with sexual assault. A later study by Kaplun and Reich (1976) of 112 child killings in New York City has confirmed that the younger the child victim the more likely he or she is to have been killed by a parent (or paramour of the parent), 83% of baby victims were killed by their parents, 53% of preschool toddlers, 30% at school but under 10 years and 17% of children over 10 years.

Homicide Followed by Suicide

Killers who kill themselves are more likely to be responsible for several killings at the one time (e.g. the whole family, Gibson, 1975). In Wolfgang's (1958b) study in Philadelphia, of 621 killers identified between 1948 and 1952, 24 (4%) committed suicide, 22 of these were men, 10 of whom had killed their wives; in all, 18 of the killers murdered someone in their own family and in only 3 cases were the killer and the victim of the same sex. West (1965) studied 148 murder/suicide incidents in London and the Home Counties. There were considerable differences between these killers and those who survived:

> The most striking distinguishing features of murder-suicides were the large numbers of women offenders and child victims, the very small numbers of offenders with previous convictions, and the total absence of the young thug who kills in the furtherance of theft or robbery.

From an analysis of the files of the dead individuals, it was estimated that insane killers were outnumbered by sane ones, the majority killing their relatives and then themselves under the pressure of collapsing physical health or impending disaster. Many of the incidents could thus have been extended suicides in individuals who have a strong feeling for and close identification with their families. Further, the cases gave some support for the Freudian theory of the interchangeability of self-directed and other-directed aggression (Freud, 1917). Some individuals with a high level of aggression may turn the aggression against others or against themselves according to circumstances (e.g. the deserted husband who went looking for his wife and her lover in order to kill them both but who, when he could not find them, returned home and gassed himself and his children). West's conclusions are important:

> Commonly accepted generalizations such as the assumption that nearly all murders are committed by men, that most insane murderers are schizophrenics, or that the lower classes predominate among offenders, hold true only so long as the crimes followed by suicide are resolutely disregarded.
> If the present enquiry has done nothing else it has at least shown that the indiscriminating violence of the psychopath, the despairing mother who kills her children, and the unhappy couple who decide to die together, are not to be squeezed into any single motivational theory.

Mercy Killings

A small but important group of domestic homicides are the so-called mercy killings. These have been defined by Lord Justice Lawton as the killing of a person believed to be permanently subject to great bodily pain or suffering, or permanently helpless, or subject to rapid and incurable bodily or mental deterioration (Lawton, 1979). Dell (1984) found 10 such cases in her consecutive series of 253 diminished responsibility verdicts. All the victims were seriously ill, but in none was there evidence of planning—they seemed to be impulsive acts at a moment of great strain, e.g. the 71-year-old man who killed his wife who was dying of cancer; when hospital admission was refused on the grounds that she was untreatable, he decided that he could not let her go on suffering and killed her.

Children who Kill

Murder by a child is an infrequent crime, only two or three cases each year in Britain. The variety of child killings is as wide as the variety of adult killings, except that the places and events of childhood colour the incidents. Wilson (1973), a journalist, identified and described 57 incidents of homicide involving children under the age of 16 years, between 1743 and 1972. Forty-eight of the incidents, involving 75 children (12 girls and 63 boys) were British, but they are by no means a complete set of cases as Wilson relied upon newspaper reports, and apparently such things were not reported between 1865 and 1920!

Wilson made an attempt to categorize the 57 incidents into overlapping categories; this gives some idea of the motives and circumstances. Five girls and 1 boy each killed a baby in their charge, 10 incidents were drownings, 5 children killed more than one victim, 2 were cases of patricide, one of matricide, 2 killed their grandfathers and 3 their brothers. There were 16 incidents related to sex, 17 to theft, and 8 occurred in fights or brawls, 6 took place in schools or children's homes, and at least 15 of the children were likely to have been mentally disturbed. One boy (Wm Allnutt), aged 12, poisoned his grandfather with arsenic. Graham Young escaped inclusion because his first childhood conviction was only administering poisons, but by the time he was 9 years old, he was collecting dangerous chemicals, studying black magic and Naziism, Hitler was already an obsession, and he wore a swastika (Holden, 1974) (see also p. 185).

It is not possible from the material which Wilson was able to collect to glean much about the mental states of these children. Of the 15 described as mentally abnormal, several were subnormal in intelligence and in no case was there convincing evidence of delusions or hallucinations. In a number of cases, not only those where issues of psychiatric abnormality were raised at the trial, there is a suggestion of the early stages of either a schizophrenic illness, or a sadistic personality (*see* pp. 390–4), or sexual sadism (*see* p. 551). There were, for example, several strangulations of girls during or after intercourse, and one case in which a 15-year-old boy killed twice. There was the 16-year-old girl who gleefully planned, with her companion, to murder her mother and make it look like an accident, in her diary she wrote:

> Next time I write in the diary Mother will be dead. How odd, yet how pleasing! . . . I felt very excited and the night-before-Christmassy last night.

She told the psychiatrist she had set out to break all of the Ten Commandments and had succeeded.

Assassinations

Assassination has come to mean the killing of a prominent individual, often a political leader or head of state by a stranger or by a political opponent. It is usually carried out in public and in some ways can be regarded as at the opposite end of the homicide spectrum to domestic violence. Not surprisingly, it is of special interest in the United States of America, a country which has seen 10 presidential assassination attempts, 4 of them successful, 2 others wounding the President, and the shootings of such prominent politicians as Martin Luther King, Robert Kennedy and George Wallace. Nevertheless, assassinations occur throughout the world, e.g. President Allende of Chile, President Sadat of Egypt, and are often the basis of a *coup d'état*. Even in Britain, assassinations and attempts occur. Perhaps the most famous of all is Daniel McNaughton's attempt on Robert Peel. Queen Victoria was shot at three times and, in recent years, Queen Elizabeth II had blanks fired at her, Lord Mountbatten was killed by the IRA, the British Prime Minister, Margaret Thatcher, was also bombed by the IRA when she was staying in a hotel and escaped death by inches.

Assassinations can be broadly divided into the political and the mentally disordered, usually paranoid. The best description of a series of assassins is given by Taylor and Weis (1970) who briefly review nine presidential assassins from Lawrence to Oswald. They pointed out that they were all smaller than average in stature, all except Booth were unknowns, five were born outside the USA, eight of them were unmarried at the time of the attack, for seven of them there had been a striking socio-economic deterioration during the year leading up to the attack. Harris (1978) pointed out that most American assassins are later sons. Taylor and Weis regarded seven of the nine presidential assassins as mentally disordered. Ideas of persecution and/or grandeur were discovered in most of the individuals. McNaughten believed that the Tory party was plotting against him and, more recently, Hinckley had erotic delusions about a film star. Frank paranoid psychoses, especially schizophrenia seem not uncommon.

Rothstein (1964) speculated on what he called 'The Presidential Assassination Syndrome'. He studied ten schizophrenic patients in the Springfield Medical Center for federal prisoners, nine of whom were charged with threats to kill the President and one who expressed similar fantasies. This is, of course, somewhat different from a study of individuals who have done more than just threaten, but he does give the best available speculations on how the paranoid ideas against a head of state develop in the schizophrenic mind. Most of his cases suffered considerable maternal deprivation which he suggests has resulted in severe rage against women. None of his patients was able to form stable mature heterosexual relationships and homosexual ideas were prominent. The individuals also had weak or absent fathers which produced anger at men. This anger, Rothstein said, is reinforced by rage against a depriving mother. At adolescence, these individuals turn from an unsatisfactory family to institutions, usually the army, which it is hoped will provide controls, masculine identity, basic caring, and an absence of women. If and when the institution fails to fulfil these high expectations, it then becomes viewed as the frustrating object, especially in circumstances where (as in three cases) an older brother has been successful in the services. The rage is then further displaced on to the government, the state, and its head. The President is threatened as a negligent mother figure (*see also* Ch. 8).

Clearly these ideas cannot be generalized very far, but it is worth remembering that paranoid individuals with highly deprived backgrounds, constant failure, very low self-esteem, who are low down in a sibship, have sexual identity problems, no friendships, and who may have contemplated suicide can turn their anger outwards and on occasions direct it towards a prominent figure on whom they project their failings. Heads of state, royal families, and the like play a prominent part in many people's fantasy life so it is not surprising that these people become the focus of pathological fantasies too.

Multiple Homicide

The individual (usually a man) who kills repeatedly is clearly of special concern and a great deal of emotionalism, both professional and lay, develops around such a person. Doctors and public alike find discussions of these cases compulsive, fascinating and perhaps even pleasurable on occasions. A session on 'mass murder' at a psychiatric conference will fill the lecture room even though the speakers may produce unimaginative anecdotal accounts of cases they have known.

The term 'mass murderer' is best reserved for those rare cases who kill a number of people at once. One of the best known is Charles Whitman, a student at the University of Texas, who consulted a psychiatrist about his loss of temper control and his thoughts of shooting people. Later, he stabbed his wife and his mother to death, then climbed a 300 foot university tower carrying a variety of firearms and shot 44 people, killing 16, before being shot himself (Macdonald, 1968). A more recent British example was Michael Ryan who shot 16 people in Hungerford one day. Ryan committed suicide before he could be arrested, a not uncommon outcome.

Another type of mass killing can occur in a domestic setting, often as a result of a psychosis, when the killer sees his or her family as a single entity and aims to put everybody out of perceived misery or remove them from a perceived threat simultaneously. This type of multiple killing is often a form of extended suicide.

A third type of multiple murder in which repeated killings take place over a longish period (weeks, months or years) can be called serial murder. It is probably better viewed as the extreme end of the violence spectrum. In other words, the factors which lead individuals to kill may on occasion lead a particular individual to kill repeatedly. In a study of 31 murderers from Texas, Minnesota, New Jersey, New York, and Saskatchewan, Frazier (1974) found 8 multiple murderers who killed, 3, 5, 5, 6, 7, 12, 13, and 17 people respectively. His impression was that the selection of one victim or several victims was not related to personality, mental state or other factors that might be diagnostically predictive. Serial murderers will, therefore, sometimes be normal (e.g. terrorists), sometimes psychotic, sometimes sadistic, and sometimes necrophilic. It is difficult to specify why in some cases one killing leads to another. Clearly, the motive for killing has to be something other than a sudden impulse or a rage attack. It would seem reasonable to speculate that in some cases there is pleasurable reinforcement of a murderous drive by an actual killing, in other cases the problem to be solved by a killing (e.g. the elimination of persecution) is not solved so the search for peace goes on. A 1980s/1990s fascination for such killers has produced a crop of books and even films (e.g. Ellis, 1991, and *Henry, Portrait of a Serial Killer*). An excellent account of one such killer is a biography by Masters (1985).

The Medical Role

The beginning of this chapter stressed the ordinariness, even the healthiness of violent behaviour. The remainder of the chapter has shown, however, how difficult it is to draw lines between 'normal' and 'abnormal' violence. Further, it should now be clear that there is a legitimate limited medical interest even in 'normal' violent behaviour. The psychiatrist will often be asked to elucidate the cause or causes behind an act of violence and to prevent it happening again. He may be asked to do this partly because he is seen as a special kind of priest, a medicine man who brings understanding and reduces anxiety, but more importantly because there is an increasing realization that medical factors do play a part in many violent interactions.

A violent individual may manifest distress or abnormality in his mental state. This can vary from understandable feelings of hate and rage right through to pathological paranoia and other delusional ideas. Some violence is based on chronic feelings of inferiority, inadequacy, and insecurity, marked abnormalities of mental state which are frequently missed, or dismissed as 'normal', because they are common. Rage and anger are increasingly understood as separate affects with their own treatments. Sometimes violent individuals will be acting in a style to which they have been trained. Individuals who are unacceptably violent have often learnt to respond to stress and difficulty in a violent fashion through modelling of parental or other influential examples.

A great deal of ordinary social life, the hierarchy in which we work or live, the success and satisfaction we obtain from life depends upon subtle aggression. Yet sophisticated, successful non-violent aggression is difficult to learn and depends upon optimal biological function. Individuals, with poor skills and/or psychological dysfunctions may resort more readily to extreme forms of aggression in a desperate attempt to win some status or satisfaction. Optimal biological function implies an intact brain, and individuals with minor brain damage who are deficient in specific skills may resort to violence more frequently than other people because they are deficient in skills and because, for organic reasons, they are more prone to experience unpleasant ideas and affect, e.g. rage and paranoia. A similar pattern can be produced in some individuals with intact brains by intoxicating substances, such as alcohol. Thus the exact form which violence may take, and its seriousness will depend upon a complex interaction of a range of factors, such as the health, especially the mental health, of the violent individual, his repertoire of learned behaviours, the social context, levels and type of intoxication and such environmental matters as the availability of a weapon.

It is clear, therefore, that when a psychiatrist is asked to examine the background to a violent event, he has to try and construct the interaction which led up to it looking at developmental, social, organic, intoxicating and psychological circumstances. If he can construct a coherent explanation for the event, he then should try to evaluate which factors, if any, can be modified or treated. It may be an explosive incident that is unlikely to recur, but it may be that drunkenness, inferiority, brain damage, anger or depression, will require medical attention; it may be that a psychosis will be uncovered; it may be that the family dynamics are inducing the pathological aggression. In each case, it is reasonable to offer medical and/or social assistance. Anybody who asks for help with violence should always receive some help—that help will usually need to be multidisciplinary in nature, and it will usually need to be long term as well. Those who are sent for help with violence problems, against their own inclinations, pose more complex questions which are dealt with in other parts of this book.

13
Disordered and Offensive Sexual Behaviour

Edited by	*Written by*
Donald J. West	Don Grubin
	Gisli Gudjonsson
	John Gunn
	Donald J. West

The title of this chapter proved to be a problem, for almost any title that would give the reader a clue to its content also contains within it assumptions to which the authors do not necessarily subscribe. One problem is that sexual behaviour arouses powerful emotions; this is obvious within the act itself, but a discussion on sexual matters rapidly runs into emotionally charged material. Sexual ideas readily arouse moral beliefs, taboos, aggression and fierce antisexual attitudes. These passions vary between groups and between individuals. Another problem is that many people ('normalists') regard the main, perhaps the sole function of sexual activity as procreation. On this basis, sexual activity between fertile males and females is normal, other sexual activity is 'deviant'. Yet zoological, including human ethological, studies suggest that sexual activity has wider functions than fertilization. These include the development of affectional bonds. Such bonds are for the rearing of the young, say the normalists. Certainly there is evidence for this, but it seems highly likely that other functions are also served by the development of sexual bonds between individuals. In man, individuals who have no mate or other individual to confide in may be at a considerable social disadvantage and may even have greater health problems and/or mortality.

It is sometimes argued by those who have rejected the normalist position that since sexual activity has several functions, most sexual activity can be regarded as broadly 'normal' and, therefore, medicine and psychiatry should eschew the task of helping those labelled 'deviant' to conform to the fertile heterosexual model. Clearly, there is something to this argument. The old-fashioned view that if two men set up home together and have an active sexual life, then they are cases for 'treatment' has largely vanished. Furthermore, the English law is quite explicit that 'promiscuity' and 'sexual deviancy' are not in themselves grounds for detaining someone under the Mental Health Act 1983 (*see* p. 26). On the other hand, is the individual who has a sexual drive that can only be satisfied by torturing women or children to death also to be regarded as 'normal'? Such activity is unhealthy both for society and for that individual. Sexual distress of all kinds takes people to see doctors and psychologists. Sexual behaviour so clearly has its roots in anatomy, physiology and psychology that medicine is the obvious repository of appropriate knowledge to help those with sexual distress. The debate is about where to draw the line, where sexual difficulties merge with broader personality difficulties.

Theories of sex offending have been well reviewed by Lanyon (1991). He pointed out that theorists have concerned themselves with global explanations for sexual deviation. Freud (1905a), for example, regarded them as representing a single type of psychopathology and highly resistant to change. His explanations involved Oedipal conflicts and castration anxiety. At the other extreme, the behaviourists seemed to believe that there is no particular character disorder present in the sexual deviant, the behaviour itself is the disorder. In contrast to all this Flor-Henry (1987) suggested that 'sexual deviations are, overwhelmingly, a consequence of the male pattern of cerebral organization'.

In an extensive review of the neurochemistry of sexual aggression Prentky (1985) concluded:

> It is obvious that exogenous factors are important . . . it is apparent that the role of androgens in human aggression is neither direct nor obvious. The most compelling evidence to date underscores the powerful effect of social learning on the manner in which individuals cope with and react to the emotional experiences associated with hormonal changes. Thus . . . social learning may serve to facilitate or inhibit the expression of the behaviour. Nevertheless there remains convincing evidence to suggest that biological factors may have important influences on types of human sexual aggression.

'Biological' here seems to mean physiological. Indeed, the idea persists that abnormal neurological programming underlies some forms of deviance. Twin studies point to a genetic factor in the determination of sexual orientation (Heston and Shields, 1968). Paradoxical sex differentiation of the brain under the influence of fetal hormone imbalance is conceivable as a factor in the development of homosexuality (Gladue et al., 1984), although this is unconfirmed by recent research (Gooren et al., 1990), and temporal lobe pathology has been found unduly prevalent among trans-sexuals (Hoenig and Kenna, 1979).

An ethological explanation for sexual deviation has been offered by Wilson (1987) suggesting that it results from the male's struggle for access to young healthy females and that the difficulties stem from the problems which unsuccessful males have in managing their sex drive. This suggests that some sexual deviations are inevitable and should be tolerated rather than treated. Lanyon (1991) concluded his review with a bifactorial 'framework' to assist understanding of sexual deviation. He suggested that both predispositions and trigger factors play roles. Predispositions develop in childhood and are related to cognition. Triggers may be personal (alcohol, stress, psychosis), or environmental (stress, availability, stimuli). This theory, he argued, is consistent with the more usual preference/situational view of sex offending. He also argued that the importance of cognitive factors in the development and maintenance of sexual deviation has been underestimated; these are attitudes and fantasy. Attitudes to others, especially children and women is open, theoretically at least, to educational change. Lanyon also made the important point that the distress of unwanted fantasies has been virtually ignored.

The centrality of social attitudes in sexual behaviour and particularly sexual offending is lucidly developed in a paper by Bancroft (1991) who heads a research group in reproductive biology in Edinburgh. He has kindly allowed us to quote extensively from this paper.

Bancroft argued that whenever we try to understand sexual offending, we should ask: 'what are the sexual and non-sexual determinants of the behaviour and what is their relative importance'. Further:

> To what extent are these determinants individual in origin, reflecting perhaps psychopathology, or social in origin reflecting the social scripts provided by the offender's subculture or by society at large?

He pointed out that Holmstrom and Burgess (1980) suggested four meanings for sexually aggressive behaviour:

1. the assertion of power and control;
2. the expression of anger or hatred;
3. camaraderie in group rape;
4. sexual experience *per se*.

Bancroft suggested that (1) and (2) reflect social values about male-female relationships and the part that sex is seen to play in such relationships. If a man wants to exert power and control over or express anger to a woman, he does not need to rape her. The use of sex in the assault reflects a model of the dominant male in which sexuality becomes the vehicle for the dominance and aggression and a justification for it.

'To what extent are sexuality and aggression compatible?' asked Bancroft.

> It would appear that we humans are very variable in this respect. For many of us it is difficult to be sexual and angry at the same time. For others it would appear that the arousal associated with anger can facilitate a sexual response (Bancroft, 1989). This takes us to a crucial aspect of human sexuality, in particular male sexuality, the potential for secondary sexualization of our behaviour. It appears to be relatively easy, for some of us at least, for sexual response to be conditioned to a variety of behaviour patterns. The mechanism involved in this type of conditioning is not well understood, although I suspect that it is a peculiarly male type of learning because it depends upon the signalling effect of penile erection. Pre-pubertal boys often pass through a phase of enhanced erectile responsiveness, when erections occur to a variety of situations. not necessarily sexual, but sharing a degree of non-specific arousal or excitement (e.g. during contact sports, being chased by a policeman, flying in an aeroplane). Then follows a period of discriminative learning when such responses become linked to stimuli

which are more clearly sexual. The important question is what directs this learning process and decides for the adolescent boy what is, in fact, appropriately sexual. The peer group is probably the most important source of such guidance. For the individual isolated from his peer group, other sources, often translated through his own imagination, provide the meanings.

Bancroft suggested that there are three strands in sexual development: (1) gender identity; (2) sexual responsiveness; (3) the capacity for close, intimate dyadic relationships.

> During childhood these three strands develop relatively independently of each other, and each can be adversely affected by experience in a variety of ways. As the child approaches puberty and enters adolescence, these strands begin to integrate to form the sexual adult. . . . This process can go wrong. What I am proposing is that in a society in which the child is given values about sex which are predominantly negative, that sex must be contained, that it is dangerous, that it is wrong, where sexual relationships are often seen as exploitative, where sexual imagery is divorced from personal identity, then we should not be surprised to find the strand of sexual responsiveness diversified in its associations and functions. Sexual interest in children is one possible consequence of such a developmental process. In contrast, in a society which sees sex predominantly as a binding force in close, loving relationships, a truly positive feature of a good relationship, and in which men and women have equal status, then we should expect to find our sexual responsiveness more readily integrated into our close relationships.

Arguments about cultural relativity, moral absolutes or philosophical distinctions between pathology and natural diversity and even disputes about the aetiology of particular behaviour patterns have only indirect relevance to the clinical needs of those in trouble over their sexuality. Individuals have to adjust to the mores of the society in which they live. They may be distressed because they experience inconvenient or disapproved urges, or because they cannot achieve sexual satisfaction in ways others find acceptable, or because they are threatened with or subjected to legal punishments. These are all good reasons for wanting help. Even if the behaviour is deviant only with reference to certain arbitrary standards and its origins are obscure, the therapist has a role to play in identifying and clarifying the individual's problems and attempting beneficial intervention.

Bancroft argued that the sexuality of sexual offences reflects the sexual values of our society. He accepted that psychiatrists must find ways to work with sexual offenders to help them to avoid further offences, but urged that this should be tempered by realism about the limitations of psychiatric intervention, and a determination not to simply collude in dealing with a social problem by relabelling it as 'psychiatric illness'. Bancroft believed that there is little understanding by the judiciary of the relevance of psychiatry to these issues. The psychiatrist must strive to develop medical skills, to collaborate with other caring professions, and to understand the social influences which define the sexuality of an offence.

Pornography

One indicator of socio-sexual attitudes is the way in which sexual themes are dealt with in literature and the visual arts, and the social responses which sexual material, especially erotic material, evokes. Attempts to distinguish eroticism from pornography have a long history. Although the border between the two is constantly shifting, the hinterlands are probably best recognized by an appeal to the Greek derivation of the words: 'pornography' from *porne* (prostitute) and *grapho* (write), and 'erotic' from *erotos* (sexual love). Pornography, therefore, which originally referred to depictions of prostitutes, can be thought of as relating to a concept of sexual gratification as something to be bought without the need of a human relationship. Erotic art, however, employs sex for other, less exploitative goals.

Modern concern about pornography in Western societies consists of two strands. The first relates to the tension between moral and libertarian values which prevail within a community, while the second is concerned with the effects pornography may have on behaviour in general and sexual deviance and offending in particular. Although these strands cannot be completely separated, it is issues related to the latter which are of particular relevance for the forensic psychiatrist.

Government commissions from a number of countries have reported on the influence of pornography on behaviour and offending. The general consensus has been that what research evidence there is is conflicting, and that definitive statements about the effects of pornography cannot be made with confidence. Not surprisingly, these conclusions have been heavily criticized by experts supporting opposite sides of the pornography question.

Those who argue that pornography is an important contributor to sexual offending point to studies which demonstrate that the viewing of violent pornography by male university students increases their acceptance of sexual violence (Malamuth and Check, 1981) and that it decreases their inhibition for aggression against women (Donnerstein and Berkowitz, 1981). They also argue that the increased availability of hard core pornography in states and countries where pornography laws have been liberalized has been associated with an increase in violent sexual crime (Court, 1976), and that sex offenders have been shown to have a pattern of pornography use different from non-offenders (Goldstein et al., 1973).

Those who are sceptical about the effects of pornography, however, argue that short-term attitudinal changes amongst volunteer American university students in laboratory settings are not a good representation of conditions in the real world and that, in any case, these studies have not adequately taken into account subjects' pre-existing attitudes and personality characteristics. They also note studies which have reported a decrease in the incidence of voyeurism and child molestation when pornography laws have been liberalized (Kutchinsky, 1973). Furthermore, they point out that pornography use amongst sex offenders may be an effect of underlying deviance or preoccupation rather than a cause of offending. For instance, one study which compared pornography use in child molesters and rapists found that it was only in the former group that its use was more common, where it seemed to be an adjunct to their offending rather than a cause of it (Carter et al., 1986).

One of the best reviews of the research relating to pornography in Britain is by Howitt and Cumberbatch (1990). They concluded that there is little evidence that the use of pornography in Britain is rising, it may even be declining. They believed that USA evidence that the use of pornography is associated with crimes of rape is artifactual, both phenomena being related to an underlying third variable. On the other hand, they saw evidence that sex offenders may use pornographic material for sexual arousal before committing a sexual offence, but found no evidence to suggest that the use of pornography diminishes the risk of sexual crime. They also drew attention to the lack of consensus in the research literature and, indeed, the acrimony that can develop between researchers using similar experimental methods.

Howitt and Cumberbatch summarized their findings in twelve paragraphs.

1. Evidence of the adverse effects of pornography is far less clear cut than some reviews imply.
2. Sexual crimes may be carried out by people who seem to have a special interest in pornography, but the evidence does not point to a cause and effect relationship.
3. Variations in rates of sexual crime do not indicate any simple causal relationship with the circulation rates of sex magazines.
4. Very little is known about the possible inhibiting effects of pornography on the sex-crime prone individual.
5. We lack any understanding of the ways in which symbolic messages of pornography are communicated and interpreted.
6. It is not clear whether attitudes are becoming more or less conducive to sexual violence.
7. Laboratory findings and effects are not reflected in field studies.
8. There is a dearth of British research.
9. Self-reports from women suggest that pornography is associated with some forms of sexual violence.
10. The use of erotic material is common in normal people and in couples. Few people have never been exposed to pornography.
11. We know little about the role of pornography in the psychosocial development of children.
12. There are few educational initiatives to promote values which undermine sexual violence.

Research into the effects of pornography must clearly surmount a vast array of confounding variables (for other reviews of relevant research *see* Mulvey and Haugaard, 1986, or Murrin and Laws, 1990). But pornography does not exist in isolation, and its nature is likely to reflect values within a society as a whole. Liberalization of pornography laws, for instance, may be associated with other changes in society. More important than pornography use on its own may be a society's attitude to violence in general; in particular, as societies become more accepting of interpersonal violence, the incidence of both non-sexual and sexual violent crime tends to rise. Indeed, anthropological work has shown that societies which are more accepting of interpersonal violence in general are also more likely to be rape prone (Sanday, 1981). If changes in pornography content and usage actually reflect more fundamental movements which are occurring in a society as a whole, then a narrow concentration on pornography is unlikely to have much impact either on individuals or on the societies in which they live.

It should be added that whether or not pornography has a harmful effect on those who use it, and regardless of whether the production of pornography exploits those portrayed in it, the use of children in the making of pornographic material almost certainly will have a detrimental effect on the children involved (Burgess et al., 1984; Finkelhor and Browne, 1986).

The Range of Problematic Behaviours

Diversity and Abnormality

The conventions of courtship and the types of bodily interchange involved in sexual arousal and satiation are all regulated by traditions which vary bewilderingly between cultures, historical epochs and even to some extent contemporary social classes. Ever since publication of the famous report on *Sex and Temperament in Three Primitive Societies* (Mead, 1935), it has been acknowledged that the stereotype of the aggressive, macho male and the decorous, submissive female, appropriate as it may be in the study of some animal behaviour, is not a biological imperative in the human species. Gender roles can be modified, even reversed, in some social settings (Money and Ehrhardt, 1972).

Behaviour acceptable to one society can be seriously offensive to others. Sexual contacts between adults and children, strictly taboo in our own culture, were less so in traditional Moslem societies where child marriages were prevalent. Currier (1981) noted how some cultures are permissive and encouraging towards overt manifestations of sexuality among their children and allow parents to stimulate sexually both boy and girl infants as a means of pacification. In many parts of the world homosexual contacts are under all circumstances forbidden, yet other societies have institutionalized systems of initiation of adolescent boys into anal intercourse with older males (Herdt, 1984). The types of coital foreplay expected or permitted are also remarkably varied. Oral-genital stimulation and even kissing are taboo in some places and, in our own history, coital positions were once matters of concern to Christian moralists. The history of medical attitudes to masturbation, and the instruments that used to be employed to restrain children from the practice, illustrate the remarkable changes that have occurred in quite recent times in our own sexual mores (Hare, 1962).

So much variation makes for confusion about what is 'right' or 'normal'. At one time, unconventional behaviour, such as buggery, was considered simply as wrongdoing, no different in principle from thieving or any other punishable offence. More recently, assumptions have been made that non-conformity with current standards indicates abnormality, particularly if the behaviour in question seems to the majority alien and erotically unsatisfying. Homosexual behaviour, once thought to be a medical condition, has lost its 'disease' status, but it is thought to be 'wrong' outside narrowly defined circumstances, much more narrowly defined than for heterosexual behaviour.

The Paraphilias: Their Variety and Severity

Problematic sexuality tends to fall into two contrasting groups, the dysfunctional and the deviant. The primary feature of the dysfunctional group is loss of libido or impaired sexual arousal and functioning, manifest in varying degrees of impotence, frigidity or phobia and produced by physiological malfunction or psychological aversion. The deviant group, otherwise known as the paraphilias, consists of individuals who are sexually aroused by inappropriate stimuli. They may also experience reduced or absent arousal in conventional heterosexual situations, but that is not the primary complaint.

Sexually dysfunctional individuals, who are not otherwise deviant, rarely present to the forensic psychiatrist. Exceptions to this are the shy, inhibited, sexually inexperienced young men with bottled-up sexual feelings and fantasies who unexpectedly break out in some offensive outburst, which may be anything from indecent exposure to sexual assault or even homicide. They closely resemble the offenders Megargee (1966) described as 'overcontrolled', who allow their aggressive feelings no overt expression until suddenly, following a long period of provocation and frustration, they erupt in unexpected and often extreme violence. A high rate of overcontrolled hostility has been described in some sex offenders (Gudjonsson et al., 1989).

Some workers find it helpful to consider sexual deviance as a dimensional rather than a categorical phenomenon (Christie-Brown, 1983), arguing that sexual deviance shades into normal behaviour in a continuous fashion. Christie-Brown suggested that sexual behaviour varies along five dimensions: the gender identity of the individual, the object choice or direction of preference, the rate of arousability, the level of arousal, and the frequency of sexual activity. Thus, it is not the case that one is either homosexual or heterosexual, for instance, or attracted to children or to adults; depending on circumstances, an individual's position on each of the five dimensions may vary.

Table 13.1
Paraphilias

Arousal from	
Interaction with persons of the same sex	— homosexuality
Interaction with children	— paedophilia
Genital exposure to strangers in public places	— exhibitionism
Handling, possessing or wearing certain articles, e.g. underwear, rubber	— fetishism
Inflicting pain or humiliation	— sadism
Receiving pain or humiliation	— masochism
Spying on naked persons or sex acts	— voyeurism
Spraying urine ('water sports')	— uralagnia
Rubbing against strangers in crowded places	— frottage
Cross dressing	— transvestism
Contact with corpses	— necrophilia
Making obscene telephone calls	— scatologia
Sexual activity from non-human mammals	— bestiality

The paraphilias have been dignified by a multiplicity of invented terms indicative of the nature of the stimulus or activity that produces arousal. Table 13.1 shows some of the best known.

These are, of course, mere descriptive labels for a great variety of personalized sexual rituals and preferences. Masochism, for example, might include submission to bondage, caning, nipple biting, piercing or genital trauma, or the acting out of elaborate charades of humiliation such as boot licking or crawling on all fours in a dog collar. Even paraphilias which appear relatively harmless, such as an interest in amassing articles of underwear, can lead to a conviction for stealing from clothes lines or to a broken marriage when an outraged spouse discovers the hoard.

The rituals involved in paraphilias are for the most part exaggerations of commonplace sexual fantasies or practices. Most people can recall at least fleeting homosexual feelings at some stage of their sexual development. If incipient fetishistic inclinations were not so widespread, the purveyors of fancy lingerie would go out of business. Fantasies of forced sexual submission are said to be frequent among women (Kanin, 1982) although, as with other sexual images enjoyed in reverie, translation into reality might not be so pleasant.

Idiosyncratic sexual interests come to deserve the label paraphilia when they are so compulsive and intense as to detract from or replace heterosexual intercourse or when they take the form of behaviour that is illegal or unacceptable to prospective sexual partners. Some forms of paraphilia are supported by groups sharing similar interests and communicating through specialized pornographic publications or contact magazines (Gosselin and Wilson, 1984). The defunct *Paedophile Information Exchange* was one example and gay and lesbian organizations exist on a much larger scale, corresponding to the much greater prevalence of homosexuality. With the doubtful exception of milder degrees of sado-masochism, most other paraphilias are acted out with considerable secrecy. Even adult homosexuals do not enjoy complete liberty, for legal sanctions against males propositioning males, or sex between males in public places or involving anyone under 21, are heavier and more strictly applied than in the case of analagous heterosexual behaviour (Howard League, 1985).

The paraphilias are of interest to forensic psychiatrists because some of the practices are defined as criminal, some are both criminal and potentially harmful (e.g. indecent acts with young children) and some involve serious victimization (e.g. sexual exploitation of children by parents and assaults motivated by sadism). Most cases present to psychiatrists only after a confrontation with the law has occurred, although it is by no means unknown for men to come forward because they are scared of their own sexual behaviour or fantasies and fear they may commit some serious crime.

Paraphilias vary enormously in severity. Given a tolerant partner, a mild 'kinkiness' may be no more than a slight inconvenience. On the other hand, paraphilias, like drug addictions, can enslave the individual costing him employment, friends and liberty.

Paedophilia

Bancroft (1991) argued that attitudes about the sexual abuse of children are special in that psychiatric treatment is often considered. He did not believe, however, that this reflects greater compassion towards the paedophile, but an indication that we find adult/child sexual interactions more threatening. We are more likely to see it as alien and rare. So threatening is it that it is probably impossible to determine its true prevalence. Bancroft regarded the history of the psychoanalytic movement as encapsulating the ambivalence of public opinion.

> Freud started off attributing much of neurosis to sexual trauma in childhood. Then came the metamorphosis: the trauma becomes fulfillment. And for the next 80 years anyone inclined to reveal their sexual abuse during childhood, at least to a psychoanalyst, has been gently, but devastatingly, told that they reveal nothing but a wish-fulfilling fantasy. . . . Next we see a violent swing of the pendulum in the opposite direction; it becomes morally questionable to doubt a child's story of sexual abuse. Children never lie about such things, we are told. Is the pendulum beginning to swing back again?
>
> How can we account for such a situation . . .? I would suggest that one important factor is the considerable difficulty that many of us have in accepting

anything to do with the sexuality of childhood. The notion that anything sexual could occur between an adult and a child, particularly in the family, is deeply threatening, and yet, I would maintain that, providing it is securely contained by the parent within appropriate bounds . . . the sexuality of the parent–child relationship is an important part of normal sexual development. The difficulty is accepting that it exists in any form is, in my view, symptomatic of a social system which holds predominantly negative views about sexuality and hence has a vested interest in keeping sexuality out of the family. (Bancroft, 1991)

Grubin and Kennedy (1991) have shown that there are many similarities between incestuous and non-incestuous paedophiles. We are now aware that a proportion of offenders against children were themselves abused in childhood, although the explanation for the progression from abused to abuser is not yet clear.

From the cases brought before the courts, it would appear that the involvement of children in sexual activity with adults is the most frequent form of sexual misconduct. Some three-quarters of prosecutions for notifiable sex offences concern behaviour in which children under 16 are victims or participants (Walmsley and White, 1979). These offences are not all committed by persons who would be classed as paedophiles. For example, the crime of unlawful sexual intercourse with a girl under 16 might be the result of seduction by a confirmed paedophile, but it might also arise from a relationship between a sexually mature fifteen-year-old and her boyfriend of similar age or only a little older. The legal age of consent, which defines when a female can legitimately agree to any sexual act, varies erratically between different countries and from one historical period to another. In any event, no arbitrarily set chronological age will match individual differences in rates of physiological maturation or in socio-cultural expectations. There is no agreement or clear criterion to decide how young a child has to be, or how large the age gap between the child and the offender must be, before the behaviour is to be regarded as paedophilic. As the popularity of teenage prostitutes and pin ups confirms, girls on the borderline of the legal age of consent are sexually attractive to large numbers of men who would not be considered paedophiles. One rough and ready distinction is between attraction to prepubertal children with undeveloped secondary sexual characteristics (true paedophilia) and attraction to adolescents (hebephilia). An excellent review of paedophilia (Quinsey, 1986) concluded that child molestation has been observed in a wide variety of settings, from cultures which condone it (e.g. New Guinea) to those which punish it severely. It is common, however, in all societies.

Identified paedophile offenders are almost always male. Official complaints of sexual molestation of children or adults by females are extremely rare. When females are prosecuted for sexual assaults, it is usually as an accessory to a man friend's or husband's misconduct. Although it is true that in comparison with other types of offender—burglars for instance—detected sex offenders against children include a higher proportion of middle-aged or even elderly men, nevertheless, most are youngish adults and some are adolescents.

Whilst offenders are nearly always male, victims may be male or female with a preponderance of female victims (*see* Quinsey, 1986; Howells, 1981). Homosexual child molesters tend to prefer older victims, are less likely to be incestuous and have higher recidivism rates (Quinsey, 1986). Retrospective victim surveys in which unselected samples of adults are asked about their recollections of early sexual experiences have revealed that children have sexual confrontations with adults much more often than generally realized. Because of the difficulty in communicating with parents on sexual matters, most of these incidents go unreported at the time. Finkhelhor (1986), in a review of American research, noted that the reported prevalence of histories of child sexual abuse derived from different surveys varied from over 50% to less than 5%. Similar variations occur in British surveys (West, 1985; Baker and Duncan, 1985). Conflicting definitions of what constitutes child sexual abuse are largely responsible. The age range covered by the term 'child' is crucial, different investigators use cut off points at the 14th, 16th or 18th birthdays. If the term abuse is used in questioning, it directs attention away from seduction experiences not viewed as abusive by the young person at the time. It makes a big difference whether investigations include incidents that do not proceed to actual physical contact, such as encounters with a 'flasher' or exposure to verbal indecencies. In a Cambridge survey (West, 1985) the proportion of women claiming to have had some childhood sexual experience with an adult was halved—from an original 42%—when non-contact incidents were discounted.

A figure of 10% would be a very conservative estimate of the prevalence of childhood histories of sexual contact with an adult. Whatever the actual frequency of such incidents, the number of occurrences greatly exceeds the number coming to official notice. It would be a mistake, however, to equate the serious cases of molestation seen in clinical practice with the generality of childhood sexual encounters, many of which are comparatively trivial and without adverse sequelae. Clinical work with sexually abused children is largely taken up with intrafamilial situations in which a father, father substitute or trusted relative, has exploited a child's dependency to obtain sexual gratification repeatedly over a period of time. Most of these children experience confusion and guilt and may have longstanding problems of sexual adjustment as a consequence. Usually it is young girls who suffer in this way, but casual encounters outside the home with strangers or near strangers are just as common in female sexual histories and overwhelmingly more common in the case of boys' sexual encounters. These more casual situations from which children can normally extricate themselves without much difficulty if they want to do so are less likely to cause upset or to lead to referral of the child to a clinic. Boys who have been approached by men with sexual intent may find it anxiety-provoking at the time, but they rarely admit to sexual problems as a result. Indeed, homosexual men often report having welcomed or encouraged sexual approaches from older males when they were boys. Of course, coercive sexual acts are distressing to victims of any age, but most confrontations with paedophiles are more like attempted seduction than actual assault.

Unfortunately, where young children ignorant of sex are targeted, frightened and bewildered compliance with adult demands can lead an offender into the wishful, but mistaken, belief that his advances are being welcomed. On the other hand, many paedophiles develop a sensitivity to children's thoughts and feelings. This enables them to avoid causing shock and to establish friendships which gradually become sexualized. They provide the children with treats and rewards and they know how to exploit a natural fascination for sexual matters. On occasion, lasting relationships develop which act as a substitute for parental neglect and persist after sexual attraction has faded. Some of the more fickle or promiscuous paedophiles establish 'rings' of available children, especially boys, captivating them with the aid of pornography, sex 'games' and introductions to other adult patrons. It is important to be aware of these varied patterns of adult-child sexual interaction in order to deal with the attitudes and habits of paedophiles seen in therapeutic settings.

Whilst physical coercion is frequently involved in the more serious forms of child sexual molestation, physical injury occurs in only a small proportion of cases.

By no means all adults who seek sexual gratification from children are paedophiles in the sense of being erotically aroused only by children. The so-called 'regressed' paedophiles are individuals who have been married or have had adult sexual relationships but, in the face of difficulties in or loss of their relationships, they turn to children as the best and most readily available substitute. A regressive pattern appears more commonly in heterosexual than homosexual males. Some men indulge with children because their sexual or social inadequacies have temporarily blocked adult relationships. They may approach children of either sex, sometimes choosing boys simply because boys are less chaperoned and more amenable. For treatment purposes, it is necessary to distinguish these patterns from that of the lifelong fixated paedophiles with no interest in and perhaps a positive aversion to partners of mature age.

Quinsey (1986) explored the possibility of developing a theory of paedophilia. He noted that child molestation is found in a wide variety of contexts and that, where it is common, it is accompanied by cultural beliefs that support and structure its practice. Nevertheless, child molestation also persists in societies which condemn and punish it severely. Quinsey argued that:

> From an evolutionary viewpoint, it would appear that an exclusive preference for young children is a very costly error in male reproductive strategy. Because of this it seems plausible that such preferences are learned.

He further argued that some preferences are likely to be much more easily learned than others:

> Stimuli that are associated with reproductively viable females are plausible candidates for 'prepared' or easily conditionable status. These would include youthfulness, primary sexual characteristics, signs of good health, and secondary sexual characteristics. It is not difficult to imagine circumstances in which youthfulness might become the dominant cue particularly because a viable male reproductive strategy might involve forming a long-term relationship with an immature female.

Bell et al. (1981) suggested that men who prefer adult males as sexual partners develop those preferences at an early age. Others have suggested that paedophiles also develop their preferences at an early age. Child molesters report a high frequency of being sexually molested themselves as children. Paradoxically, however, they also report having been exposed to less pornography at young ages than normal subjects (Goldstein et al., 1973). Yet, as Quinsey emphasized, our understanding of the development of inappropriate sexual age preference is handicapped by our lack of knowledge about the development of normal sexual age preference.

Psychiatrists are likely to be as much involved with the child participant in sexual incidents with adults as with the offender. The probability of psychological damage being sustained by the child is greatest where there has been coercion or force, where the perpetrator is a father or father figure, where police interrogations and legal proceedings have ensued, where the victim experiences ridicule or rejection from other children or from neighbourhood parents, where the family is broken up or impoverished by the imprisonment of the offender or where the child is removed from home. On the other hand, many children, especially boys, among those who have had contacts outside the home of a casual sort or among those whose experiences have been truly consensual, appear to suffer no adverse consequences (Constantine, 1981). In fact, in some cases paedophile relationships are claimed subsequently by the supposed victims to have been rewarding and developmentally beneficial (Brongersma, 1986; Sandfort, 1987). In the absence of any spontaneous complaint or admission by the victim, where suspicion derives from the observations of a third party, caution is needed before action is taken that can be very detrimental. Sexual interference with young children often leaves no detectable physical sign, and even when suggestive signs are present, their significance may be uncertain (Paul, 1986; Enos et al., 1986). The danger of false accusations, especially in disputed child custody cases following divorce, where a malicious parent can influence a child's testimony, is now beginning to be appreciated (Schuman, 1986). In Britain, there have been a few cases of overzealous authorities conducting what amounts to a witch hunt against parents who are wrongly accused of paedophilic and incestuous behaviour. One of the best described of these incidents is the Cleveland one (Bell, 1988; Butler-Sloss, 1988).

The report of the inquiry into the Cleveland affair (Butler-Sloss, 1988), is almost like a textbook of child abuse. It gave, for example, the story of 'Samantha' who grew up without a mother, in the care of a father who was not only jealous and possessive of her, but who regularly sexually abused her. The essence of the Cleveland story (or *When Salem came to the Boro* (Bell 1988)) is that between February and July 1987, 125 children were diagnosed, in one area, as sexually abused, 121 of these by two doctors. Sixty-seven of the children became wards of the court. By the time of the inquiry, however, 98 of those children were living back at home. Mrs Justice Butler-Sloss concluded that an honest attempt had been made to address an increasing problem of child abuse, but it went wrong. Two paediatricians reached firm conclusions about child abuse on the basis of physical signs in the children, the children were then separated from their parents and admitted to hospital, thus compromising the work of social workers and the police. The report criticized the doctors for being over-confident. No comment was made about the failure to refer these children to child psychiatrists for detailed interviews. The conclusion, however, did recommend that adults should explain to children what is happening to them, that false promises of confidentiality should never be given, and that the views and wishes of the children should be listened to.

Incest

Incest did not become a criminal offence in England and Wales until 1908; prior to this, it was dealt with by the ecclesiastical courts. In law, the offence relates only to sexual intercourse, and only when this occurs between individuals of specified relationships: father-daughter, grandfather-granddaughter, brother-sister or mother-son. Sibling incest is probably the most common form, but incest between father and daughter is most often brought to the attention of the police. For the psychiatrist, however, this legal framework is clearly overrestrictive, and sexual activity of any sort between family members (including step relations) is of concern.

Although the relevant degree of relationship varies, incest has been outlawed in most societies throughout history. Occasionally, however, the activity has been encouraged, particularly amongst royal lines (Maisch, 1973). The strength, longevity, and near universality of the incest taboo suggests that it arises from strong human drives and that it serves important cultural functions, but what these functions are is unclear. To say that the taboo has arisen from magical or superstitious beliefs, related for instance to the mixing of blood, begs the question. We now know that there are good genetic reasons to avoid incest, but it is unlikely that ancient civilizations would have been aware of these (nor have modern lawmakers found it necessary to forbid those with hereditary diseases from having sexual intercourse). Freud saw the taboo as a cultural one aimed at curbing the desires of the child rather than those of the adult (Freud, 1913), a view which is no longer popular. The answer may lie in a combination of bio-logical and cultural evolution: individuals and societies in which inbreeding is discouraged are more likely to thrive.

With all sexual offences, cases known to the police are an underestimate of their true incidence. This is particularly true for incest where official statistics provide little guidance. During the 1980s, the number of cases recorded by the police in England and Wales ranged from 241 to 516 per year, accounting for just 1–2% of all recorded sex offences. Even accepting the narrow legal definition, other cases will have been recorded as unlawful sexual intercourse or rape, and instances of intrafamilial sexual activity not meeting the strict criterion for incest will be hidden within other offence categories such as buggery or indecent assault. Although reported cases of incest are more common in lower social classes, this is probably biased by the fact that many cases are discovered when the police are investigating other crimes.

Community surveys inevitably uncover a large number of individuals who report that they were sexually victimized when children (Kinsey et al., 1953; Baker and Duncan, 1985; La Fontaine, 1987; Mullen et al., 1988). As discussed above, definitions of sexual abuse vary between studies, and it can be difficult to match the length of time the abuse lasted, the relationship of victim with abuser, and the nature of the sexual activity. Moreover, most studies have concentrated on female victims, and there is now an increasing awareness of sexual victimization of male children by mothers and older siblings (Finkelhor, 1984; O'Connor, 1987; Grubin and Gunn, 1990). Keeping in mind these limitations, the prevalence of child sexual abuse involving physical contact may be as high as 10%; estimates of the proportion of this that occurs within the home range from less than a fifth to about two-thirds (Baker and Duncan, 1985; La Fontaine, 1987).

Theories about the aetiology of incest tend to focus on either family oriented or offender oriented issues, but these perspectives are not in fact mutually exclusive. Theories in which family pathology is considered primary consider incest to be a sexual expression of non-sexual difficulties, and describe the blurring of generational boundaries in the family with each member contrib-uting to the development and maintenance of the incestuous relationship and behaviour (Conte, 1986). Offender oriented theories, on the other hand, see incest as a form of paedophilia, and hence a sexually deviant behaviour.

Questions about the aetiology of incest are not simply of academic interest. Those who argue that incest is primarily a symptom of family pathology, and thus a distinct entity from paedophilia, see the incest offender as representing little danger to the community at large: the offender is considered appropriate for community treatment programmes so long as he can be kept separate from his family (so few female offenders are brought to the attention of the law, that discussion here is limited to the male gender). On the whole, evidence tends to support this view. Most phallometric studies of sexual arousal in incest offenders report a pattern closer to that of 'normal' men than to paedophiles (Quinsey et al., 1979; Marshall et al., 1986), although one small and unreplicated study did find significant arousal to children (Abel et al., 1981). Similarly, a 13-year follow-up of all men accused of incest brought before the English courts in 1961 found that although many (particularly those accused of sibling incest) had past or subsequent convictions for non-sexual offences, persistent sexual offenders were few (Gibbens et al., 1978).

It is certainly the case, however, that some incest offenders are driven more by sexual deviance than by family pathology. One American study, for instance, although marred by problems of methodology, reported that nearly half of self-reported father or step-father incest offenders had also abused children outside the family, and 18% had raped adult women (Abel et al., 1988). It is also known that some men target and subsequently marry or cohabit with single mothers in order to gain access to their children. Thus, as with any other sexual offenders, the psychiatrist must avoid blind adherence to aetiological theory, and needs to carry out a proper assessment to define and understand the paedophilic or otherwise deviant man before making recommendations for disposal or treatment.

Victims of incest are known to suffer from chronic as well as immediate psychological trauma, but the large number of hidden cases means that the true incidence, and the risk of psychopathology, are unknown. Promiscuity, prostitution, substance abuse, sexual dysfunction, homosexuality, and sexual offending have been reported in victims, but early studies were often based on populations from psychiatric or penal settings and so tended to overestimate the severity and incidence of negative sequelae.

Certainly at the time of the offending, a variety of problems may become evident in children, from sexualized play to poor performance at school to overt depression. A number of studies have now addressed the type and incidence of longer-term effects of childhood sexual abuse in random community samples. These have shown that about 20% of victims of childhood sexual abuse have adult psychiatric disorders (compared with 6% of controls), characterized primarily by depressive, anxiety or phobic symptoms (Burnam et al., 1988; Mullen et al., 1988). Other studies have found a high incidence of sexual abuse in the histories of parents who abuse their own children (Cormier and Cooper, 1982a), although the majority of victims of abuse do not go on to become abusers themselves.

Whether childhood sexual abuse will have detrimental effects on a victim will depend on the context in which the abuse takes place. As described above, protracted abuse of an invasive kind, particularly when carried out by an individual in a position of trust, is usually found to result in increased psychopathology. Furthermore, a lack of protective factors, such as the absence of a supportive caregiver, may also be important; one study found that sexual abuse in combination with caregiver instability was a strong predictor of sexual offending (Prentky et al., 1989). The victim of parental incest, therefore, would appear to be particularly at risk.

Homosexuality

Homosexuality is no longer viewed in Britain as necessarily antisocial, pathological or criminal (although it is still illegal in the armed services), and DSM-III R no longer defines homosexual orientation as in itself a psychiatric diagnosis, so it is open to question whether the topic should appear at all in a text on forensic psychiatry. The fact remains, however, that many people, especially the young, still feel anxious, guilty or otherwise deeply unhappy about homosexual inclinations, medical advice continues to be sought, and the legal restraints on homosexual behaviour are much stricter than on heterosexual behaviour. The 'diagnosis' of ego-dystonic homosexuality acknowledges the existence of worries about inability to conform to cultural expectation, whether in regard to gender roles or choice of sexual partner. Demands for the recriminalization of male homosexual behaviour in the wake of the AIDS epidemic and more stringent denunciations from the morally orthodox are reviving stigma. The shame and alienation experienced, particularly by those who feel obliged to conceal their sexuality from employers, relatives or others from whom they fear rejection, can still lead to secondary psychological problems. Nevertheless, sheer weight of numbers and the political influence that has developed through a sizeable minority being willing to declare themselves makes it unlikely that medical opinion will revert to equating homosexuality with personality disorder or severe neurosis. All the same, in spite of the numbers of persons involved and in spite of reluctance to apply pejorative labels, the limitation of sexual arousal exclusively or predominantly to the same sex must be regarded as a sexual 'deviation' from cultural, biological and statistical norms.

Sexual orientation remains of forensic significance because of the ways in which the law seeks to control male homosexual activities more strictly than heterosexual or lesbian behaviour. For example, the age of consent, which defines when sexual contact with a willing partner ceases to be a technical assault, is 21 for male homosexual acts, but 16 for heterosexual or lesbian acts. Conditions of privacy are more stringent; the presence of a third party makes any male homosexual act a crime. A man who importunes males commits a more serious, imprisonable offence than a woman who solicits men, and she only offends if her purpose is prostitution. In practice, males under 21 are not often prosecuted for sexual acts with each other, but older men who may have sexual relations with them are frequently prosecuted in circumstances that would not apply to relations with young women of similar age. Youths embroiled in these prosecutions, even if officially defined as victims or witnesses, suffer much embarrassment from the exposure. A substantial proportion of all convictions for importuning or for indecency between men occur as a result of the search for homosexual contacts in public places, notably public lavatories, and often by married men who are not free to seek contacts in the gay subculture.

Much the most frequent and serious circumstance in which homosexuals come to the attention of forensic psychiatrists is in connection with sexual incidents with male children. Although there is no evidence that persons of homosexual orientation are more likely than heterosexuals to seek contact with prepubertal children, those who do molest boys are often very persistent in their habit and some appear to organize their lives, including their employments, around this pursuit. Such offenders include higher proportions of older and middle-class males than is typical of, for example, rapists. The male boarding school teacher and the vicar with his choir boys are popular stereotypes but, in practice, younger offenders are also common. In a Home Office survey (Walmsley and White, 1979), it was found that 20% of offenders convicted of indecent assault on a male were under 21, 41% under 30. Many are isolated from ordinary adult society. Their interest in young boys does not make them particularly welcome in homosexual circles, and the enormous hostility their behaviour evokes renders them secretive and even paranoid. Once detected, they may become still further isolated as a result of rejection and loss of employment and their deviant behaviour may escalate as they have no other satisfactions to distract them and nothing much more to lose. As with heterosexual paedophiles, however, the individuals involved range from the mental dullard to the highly intelligent and from the pathetic social inadequate to the socially successful sophisticate capable of managing his indulgence with discretion. Needless to say, the former categories are more prominent among those detected and imprisoned.

The aetiologies of homosexual orientation remain matters of dispute, and arguments about them are of little help to individuals. Evidence of an hereditary factor (Heston and Shields, 1968), a hormone anomaly affecting sex differentiation of the brain (Dorner, 1988), a personality defect (Socarides, 1978) or an anomalous upbringing (Saghir and Robins, 1973) continue to be cited. As with most behavioural syndromes, a multiplicity of factors are likely to be involved. Some authorities distinguish primary homosexuality, in which responsiveness to heterosexual stimulation never develops or remains weak, from secondary homosexuality, in which the balance between heterosexual and homosexual arousal is potentially fluid, varying with circumstance or the passage of time (MacCulloch and Waddington, 1981). Survey evidence (Bell et al., 1981; Whitam and Mathy, 1986) favours the notion of the presence of a hard core of primary cases in which the direction of erotic desire becomes clear at an early age and is notoriously difficult to alter.

A homosexual orientation is not necessarily linked with any difficulty in the performance of culturally expected gender roles in other respects than choice of sex partner. Nevertheless, 'sissy' attributes in boyhood or tomboyish traits in girls are probably more common in the histories of homosexuals than among heterosexuals. Certainly boys who display effeminate behaviour to a marked degree are very likely to become adult homosexuals (Green, 1987). On the other hand, quite pronounced deviations from culturally defined gender roles or personality stereotypes—in the guise of masterful women or passive men—are not necessarily indicative of homosexual orientation.

Rape and other Sexual Violence towards Women

Until the Sexual Offences (Amendment) Act 1976 came into force, the legal definition of rape in England and Wales was based on the 17th century common law concept of 'intercourse without consent by force, fear or fraud'. The 1976 Act established that the issue was one of consent only. A man commits rape if—

1. he has sexual intercourse with a woman who at the time does not consent; and
2. he knows that she does not consent to the intercourse or he is reckless as to whether she consents or not.

Assaults on girls under 16 or on women whom the offender knows to be mentally impaired (as defined in the MHA 1983) are sometimes prosecuted as unlawful sexual intercourse simply because this avoids the need to prove the absence of consent.

The 1976 Act, though clarifying some important issues, left a number of oddities in the law. For instance, rape can only be committed by a man, and only a woman can be his victim: in English law, a man cannot rape another man. Nor did it recognize as an offence a husband living with his wife and having non-consensual sexual intercourse with her (although, if she is injured in the process, he may be guilty of another offence such as assault). Only in 1991 did the Court of Appeal rule that rape could occur in marriage (*R v R*). Even more curious, a boy under 14 is considered incapable by the law of having sexual intercourse and, therefore, of committing rape: legally, it is not simply that the act is not an offence, but that it cannot possibly happen (for a more complete discussion of the law as it relates to rape, *see* Smith and Hogan, 1988).

The need to differentiate rape from other forms of sexual assault can also be questioned. Indeed, since 1983 Canada has replaced the offences of rape and indecent assault with a new offence called sexual assault in which penetration is irrelevant and which applies to both men and women, and in 1991 Ireland extended rape to include penetration of the mouth or anus.

During the 1980s, the number of rapes recorded by the police in England and Wales more than doubled, from about 1200 cases in 1980 to nearly 2900 by 1988; similar dramatic rises have been reported in North America. The proportion of men charged with rape who are eventually convicted and sentenced, however, has fallen steadily over the decade from about 60–40% (Fig. 13.1).

It is unclear whether the increase in recorded rape represents an actual rise in the amount of sexual violence that is occurring in the community, or

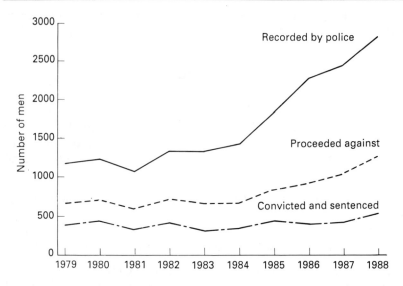

Fig. 13.1　Number of rapes recorded by the police, number of men charged with rape and proceeded against at magistrates' court, and number of men found guilty and sentenced for rape for the years 1979–88 (England and Wales).

whether it instead reflects a greater willingness of women to report rape offences to the police. That the latter may be the case is suggested by a Home Office study of rape convictions which found that the proportion of attackers known well by their victims increased from 14% in 1973 to 30% in 1985 (Lloyd and Walmsley, 1989). The decrease in the proportion of charges leading to conviction referred to above may thus be a reflection of more difficult to prove acquaintance rapes now being brought to the attention of the police. Thus although the number of recorded rapes has increased therefore, stranger rapes of the kind associated with fears of increased sex crime do not seem to have risen substantially.

Rape is an offence which involves both sex and violence. There is a tendency amongst people writing about rape, however, to emphasize the primacy of one or the other of these elements. Some argue that rape is a fundamentally sexual act in which aggression is used to achieve a sexual aim, while others claim that rape is in essence an act of violence expressed in a sexualized way. Indeed, Groth has downplayed the importance of sex altogether, calling rape a pseudosexual act in which power or anger, not sex, are the driving forces (Groth and Birnbaum, 1979). This view has found widespread support with feminist authors, many of whom argue, in addition, that more important in the aetiology of rape than either sexual or psychological factors *per se* are the cultural norms which determine the relative roles of men and women in society.

General statements about the nature of rape, however, should at present be viewed with caution. Rape is a crime which can result from a range of complex behaviours, and rapists form a heterogeneous group of individuals in whom social, cultural and psychological factors combine in a variety of ways. The search for unique attributes by which rapists can be categorized has included attitudes, hormones, pornography use, and sexual arousal patterns to name but a few (*see* Quinsey, 1984, for a review), but the most that can be said is that some factors are important for some rapists; none tends to separate rapists as a group from the general male population once variables such as age or social class are taken into account. In order properly to understand the phenomenon of rape, therefore, and before the question of psychiatric treatment for rapists can be sensibly addressed, more homogeneous subgroups within the rapist population need to be identified.

Most studies of rapist populations have described young men of lower social class background and limited educational attainment; ethnic minorities, particularly blacks, are heavily overrepresented. The majority already have past criminal records: up to a quarter have past convictions for offences of violence, and up to a third have convictions for past sex offences. However, rapists do not seem to differ significantly from other prisoners either in terms of background or general attitudes (Gebhard et al., 1965; Amir, 1971; Dietz, 1978; Lloyd and Walmsley, 1989; Grubin and Gunn, 1990). These studies, of course, are necessarily biased by the selection processes of the criminal justice system, and it is difficult to know to what extent they are an accurate reflection of men who rape. They are, however, probably representative of the more serious end of the offence spectrum. It is also of interest that a British study which compared men convicted of rape in 1961 with those acquitted found few differences between them in terms of their past or future offending behaviour (Soothill et al., 1980).

Among young men actually charged with rape, those who are generally delinquent are prominent. Analysis of criminal records alone suffices to identify a substantial proportion with convictions for non-sexual crime and many with at least one previous or subsequent conviction for personal violence (Gibbens et al., 1977b). These offenders are not unusual in their sexual aims and interests. They may choose victims under 16 but, as many are themselves still teenagers, this does not indicate true paedophilia. Like other delinquent youths, they are generally undersocialized, tending to resort to physical aggression or antisocial acts at slight provocation, especially after drinking. They are likely to be poorly educated, ill-informed about sexual relationships and identified with crudely macho ideas. Many convince themselves that the girl was 'asking for it' or that she 'led me on'. Sometimes they seek assurance from the victim, who may be willing to agree to anything to get away, that she enjoyed the experience. Indeed, some offenders are caught through making an appointment to meet the victim again. These young men are unlikely to view themselves as being in need of psychiatry, but educative programmes, social skills training, group discussion and even confrontational sessions with women who have been victimized are less resisted and more relevant.

Existing classification schemes for rapists, as for sex offenders generally, tend to be anecdotal and based on intuition and interpretation of motive rather than empirically derived and tested. Terms such as amoral delinquent, explosive assaulter, sadistic, impulsive and antisocial have a long history of use in describing types of rapist, but there has been little attempt to test their reliability or validity (*see* Knight and Prentky, 1989, for a review). Recent work, however, has shown that it is possible to form coherent classification schemes of clinical relevance based on motivational concepts such as anger or impulsivity, but only when these and similar terms are rigorously operationalized (Knight and Prentky, 1989).

Another approach to classification has been taken in a large English study of imprisoned rapists. In this study, simple, single variables relating to either the offence or the offender were found to offer some help in distinguishing types of rapist (Grubin and Gunn, 1990). Serial rapists, for instance, were characterized by the large amount of sexually disturbed behaviour found in their histories when compared with men who had raped only once, while sexual murderers were notable for their social isolation and reserved, overcontrolled personalities. Group rapists, on the other hand, seemed to be driven more by peer interaction than by issues relating to either sexuality or aggression.

Rapes and burglaries are looked upon as 'understandable' crimes, so the offenders are not perceived as abnormal or suitable for referral to a psychiatrist. Yet rapists include many disordered people and even a few with psychosis. Like any other act of violence, rape can be instrumental, expressive or a combination of both. It can be instrumental simply in the satisfaction of sexual urges, but it can also be an extreme example of the assertion of the macho stance of male power over women. It can be expressive of uncontrolled emotions other than sexual passion, notably anger, hostility or contempt towards a particular victim or towards women at large. For the sadist, the use of violence is a means of obtaining sexual arousal. Like other violent offenders, some rapists are undercontrolled characters who give way to impulses, whether erotic or aggressive, at slight provocation. A minority are overcontrolled, ordinarily shy and inhibited with the opposite sex, whose offences appear completely unexpected and out of character. A common variety of rapist, the overenthusiastic boyfriend, is a type rarely denounced, and still less rarely psychiatrically examined. In any event, he is unlikely to differ much from other young men of his age and social group or to require treatment beyond the stern lessons applied by the penal system when sexual misconduct happens to come to official notice.

As with other forms of criminal behaviour, the incidence of rape is much influenced by social circumstance and cultural factors. For example, incidents frequently follow on from social drinking and are commoner at weekends when socializing peaks. For whatever reason, fantasies of rape are very prevalent among normal men who have never been found guilty of any offence (Malamuth, 1981). In American cities, where crimes of violence and the criminal use of weapons are more frequent than in the UK, rapes are much more frequent and more often involve injury to the victim. Gratuitous brutality is especially likely to occur during gang rapes when young men seek to impress each other with their toughness (Katz and Mazur, 1979). Societies with restrictive attitudes to premarital sex, where males are dominant and women economically and psychologically subservient, are said to have more rapes than more 'liberal' societies (Sanday, 1981), (*see below*).

Malamuth and Donnerstein (1982) suggested that some men, but not all, are aroused by images of rape. What differentiates these groups is not clear. Bancroft (1991) suggested that the socially derived meanings of sexuality probably play an important part, and pointed out that Quinsey et al. (1981) found that responses of normal controls to rape stimuli were increased if subjects were told beforehand that it was 'normal' for men to be aroused in this way. Kanin (1985) identified 71 college students who admitted to having raped girls they had dated. In comparison with a control group of students of similar age, the rapists reported substantially more sexual experience. Kanin concluded that the high level of sexual success combined with an exploitative attitude to sexual relationships, resulted in greater frustration when confronted with a non-compliant partner. Bancroft stated:

> I think it unlikely that a man who throughout his life has viewed sex as an expression of a loving relationship would show this rape proclivity. On the other hand, a man who grows up in a culture which views the sexual dominance of women as a sign of masculine success and potency may react this way.

Sanday (1981) analysed 156 societies and concluded that 47% were rape free and 18% rape prone. A rape prone culture characteristically promoted male-female antagonism, whereas rape-free societies showed sexual equality and there were generally low levels of interpersonal violence. Bancroft (1991) argued that the UK is a rape supportive culture, because it promulgates the view that, where sex is concerned, the woman is seen as the responsible person and the property to be taken. It is a woman's responsibility to see that a man is not aroused or else she must accept the consequences. He suggested that the media portray the woman as temptress, the police are biased in their investigations of rape cases (as shown in Chambers and Millar, 1983) and, in a further Chambers and Millar study (1986), most women found the experience of going to court even worse than they expected, because they felt put on trial themselves. Bancroft quoted an illustrative case in which a man convicted of rape (after a series of unsuccessful prosecutions in previous trials) was released on bail, pending appeal, without the woman who had been raped being told. At the appeal the self-exonerating statement of the accused was re-examined.

> The appeal court heard the view that the fact that she, together with her daughters, had allowed this man into her house late at night and had given him

coffee and talked to him, was an indication of her consent to intercourse. The appeal court judges did not demur from this astounding statement. The court was further told that because the daughter, who having gone to bed to sleep, said she did not hear her mother call to her this was further evidence that she had in fact consented. . . . The sentence was quashed.

The treatment of rapists should follow the same principles as that used in the treatment of other sex offenders: contributory factors to offending should be identified, and then addressed in a therapeutic context. It is important, however, that goals other than a simple reduction in recidivism are chosen. Two long-term follow-up studies of convicted rapists, one of 12 years, the other of 22 years, found that about 15% were convicted of further sexual offences, and about a quarter of further offences of violence (Soothill et al., 1976; Gibbens et al., 1977b). Of particular interest was the finding that sexual reoffending continued throughout the follow-up period. Thus, even accepting the difficulties involved in monitoring reoffending, one would have to wait a very long time indeed for evidence that treatment was having a significant impact on recidivism.

Some rapists are potential candidates for psychotherapy and/or behaviour therapy, although they may not initially acknowledge their need. The seriousness of their offence demands attention, but how much persuasion is ethically justified to bring them into a treatment situation, and how such endeavours can be made to work within the constraints of conventional imprisonment are matters of continuing debate. Socio-sexual conflicts which everyone experiences to some extent cannot fully account for sexual attacks on strangers. Many rapists also have some of the personality traits and histories of neglectful, disorderly or violent upbringings commonly associated with a diagnosis of dyssocial personality disorder. Their conflicts become dangerous to others because of their propensity for expressing frustration in physical violence. These characteristics render treatment endeavours that much more difficult. In some individuals the link between coercive behaviour and sexual arousal—a link made use of by many people during harmless sexual foreplay—is allowed dangerous expression in overt and even homicidal sadistic acts. Abel and his collaborators (1977) developed assessment methods to identify the minority of rapists who need a violent situation in order to attain full sexual arousal. For them, they advocate reconditioning techniques to alter the arousal pattern, but this demands the subject's full and active cooperation. A few rapists are manifestly psychotic. Delusions of bewitchment, grandiose notions of ridding the world of immoral women or psychotic ideas of vengeance against the whole female sex have been found to underlie the otherwise inexplicable behaviour of some multiple sex murderers.

Rape of males

Some American research has suggested that male victims of sexual assault are more likely to be physically injured than female rape victims, and are more likely to be victims of multiple assailants (Groth and Burgess, 1980; Kaufman et al., 1980). Contrary to popular prejudice, the perpetrators of male rape are not all homosexual (Groth and Birnbaum, 1979). They include a number of heterosexuals, particularly in institutions, who sexually assault men they perceive to be homosexual or sexually deviant. These attacks appear to be an extension of 'gay bashing' and, as in female rape, can be an expression of anger and an attempt to humiliate the victim (Groth *et al.*, 1977). The rapist uses these assaults to defend against his own inadequate sexuality, and to assert his dominance over the victim. The most disordered rapists appear to be gender blind and attack both men and women (Sagarin, 1976).

Miscellaneous Anomalous Behaviours

Indecent Exposure

Indecent exposure 'of the male person with intent to insult a female' is the statutory definition of the offence colloquially known as 'flashing'. In clinical terms, it is the urge to expose the genitals, usually before strangers, in a public place. It is one of the most common of heterosexual offences but, judging from the large number of 'one time only' offenders, it is a form of behaviour that is not necessarily indicative of a persistent tendency. Sometimes, however, literally hundreds of such incidents occur before an offender is finally reported and apprehended, and some men are reconvicted repeatedly over the best part of a lifetime, seemingly incapable of resisting the temptation in spite of the most damaging social consequences to themselves. Exhibitionism is a form of sexual disturbance that, despite its superficially innocuous nature, can be extremely persistent and disruptive.

In Britain indecent exposure is a specific offence, but this is not the case in other European countries (Bancroft, 1989). Not all who are convicted of this offence are clinical exhibitionists. The act is sometimes a crude form of sexual invitation employed by the mentally impaired. Occasionally, the charge is brought against a man apprehended in the early stages of an intended assault. Usually, however, the offender is performing an habitual ritual that does not include any contact with the victim. A small minority of exhibitionists escalate their offending and in the course of time commit sexual assaults, but this seems to be the exception, in spite of the fact that some individuals are extremely persistent and resistant to treatment. Mohr et al. (1964) reported that, in a Toronto study, the reconviction rate for first offenders was 19%, 57% for those with a previous sexual offence, and 71% for those with previous sexual and non-sexual offences. In a follow-up study, those who received treatment did not differ in terms of reconviction rates from those who did not receive treatment.

Exhibitionism is mainly a disorder of males, but women sometimes indecently expose their genitals too. This may be to please intimates (e.g. during a prison visit). Morris and Morris (1963) described the 'flash' or 'flash up' during prison visiting when a wife, girlfriend, or even paid prostitute will briefly expose her breasts or lift her skirt having come to the prison without the relevant items of underclothing. Hollender et al. (1977) described a case of female 'flashing' which is akin to male exhibitionism, but where the drive was for attention rather than sexual excitement. When it is pathological, it usually indicates mental retardation, psychosis or a severe personality problem.

As with other types of deviant sex offender, clinical examination reveals contrasting personality types. The most common finding is a tendency to shyness, timidity and inhibition, with little confidence in courtship or sexual performance. Many contract marriages in which they feel unhappily domi- nated and frustrated by their wives. Incidents of exposing sometimes follow sexual failures or marital disputes. These men often struggle against what is tantamount to an addiction, experience considerable shame and may even feel relieved when caught. Other offenders are less inhibited, being aggress- ive, impulsive and antisocial in their ordinary life and often prone to alcohol abuse and non-sexual crime. Some are homosexual in orientation, some are misogynists.

The fantasies that accompany acts of exhibitionism, or during mastur- bation to memory of the scene, give some clue to the complex inner meaning of this superficially irrational behaviour. If the victims appear shocked, or at any rate impressed, this provides a feeling of sexual power and control, albeit at a safe distance, and compensates for feelings of inadequacy in real life (Rooth, 1971). The conditioning effect from constant repetition of their ritual may permit these men to attain maximal sexual arousal more easily in these situations than in what are for them more threatening personal relationships. One reason why these offences need to be taken seriously is that the victims chosen are often pubescent or prepubescent girls. Some of the offenders have clear paedophile tendencies (Rooth, 1973). Lastly whilst Gebhard et al. (1965) found that the majority of exhibitionists do not resort to violence, 10% attempt or contemplate rape.

Obscene telephone calls (scatologia)

During an exhibitionist encounter, a man may make obscene remarks to his victim. An extension of this behaviour seems to be the increasingly common offence of telephoning women and engaging them in erotic, obscene, and sometimes frightening conversations. Orgasm with or without concurrent masturbation may occur during the phone call. Such calls are mainly of nuisance value, but they can cause considerable distress and alarm;

indeed threats are often part of the communication, partly because they are erotic in themselves, partly because they hold the attention of the female victim which is essential for the caller's orgasm.

Such offenders are rarely caught. When they are, they usually have a number of other deviant sexual behaviours as well, such as exhibitionism, writing obscene letters, voyeurism, and sometimes assaultative urges. As the comprehensive Kinsey source book on sex offenders (Gebhard et al., 1965) put it:

> Obscene telephone communication is not a discrete behaviour and psychological entity . . . but . . . a pathological development of an interest common to most males—a symptom of some sexual and emotional difficulty.

Almost all lewd callers (as they are sometimes called) are men, they may find normal sexual relationships difficult, and they may have been sexually abused as children. One approach to treatment is behavioural: the patient is asked to imagine being caught, disgraced and thrown into gaol.

Voyeurism

Peepers or peeping Toms are adult males who obtain some sexual satisfaction by secretly watching women undress, perform their toilet, or make love. It is an extension of normal behaviour in that most males use visual material as part of their erotic stimulus, and it is quite close to watching strip-tease. Sometimes the disorder relates to others, e.g. a peeping Tom may suddenly draw attention to himself by, say, tapping on a window or by making a telephone call, to frighten the woman and enhance his own excitement. The peeping is frequently accompanied by masturbation to orgasm. Gebhard et al. (1965) found peepers to be a mixed group including the 'sociosexually underdeveloped, mental deficients, situational cases, drunks'. They noted that peepers rarely spied on relatives, but sought strangers for preference. Only a very few of them were married. One or two cases were men who had also raped or exhibited themselves. So whilst the disorder is largely of nuisance value, the peeping Tom who gets so excited that he goes on to rape or even kill (e.g. *Byrne*) must be remembered.

Freund has suggested (and produced some data in support) that voyeurism, exhibitionism, frotteurism and obscene telephone calling are all part of a basic disorder of courtship in which the sufferer is unable to accomplish precopulatory behaviour successfully (Freund et al., 1983, 1984).

Fetishism

Fetishism is arousal to symbols of sexuality (e.g. panties, silk underwear, rubber clothing, shoes). It is a commonplace phenomenon, but it can develop into a predominant or exclusive form of sexual outlet. It is interesting aetiologically because it is obviously a learned response rather than a physiologically determined reflex. This particular compulsion has little forensic significance save in cases in which the man (and it is virtually always a man) is impelled to steal the objects of interest, commonly knickers off clothes lines. Used garments that retain odours or other traces of wear may have a special attraction. The articles may be handled and admired and used to promote fantasies during solitary masturbation or to produce arousal during sexual intercourse. Some cross-dressing transvestites are not suffering from gender confusion, but merely satisfying fetishistic impulses.

Transvestism

A prediliction for putting on the clothes of the opposite sex, either during sexual activity or for parading in public, known as transvestism is compatible with active heterosexuality (Randell, 1970). The causes of this condition are not known, although analytic theories include the notion that the cross-dressing male may be attempting to emulate the feared women with a phallus. Krueger (1978) suggested that the onset of the condition is either aged 2 or 3, usually initiated by a female adult (e.g. mother) or during adolescence. He described the family of an adolescent male transvestite in which the father, also a transvestite, played a crucial role, although even in this family the mother was described as the classic 'dominant, overbearing "phallic" woman'.

Buhrich (1978) analysed the motives for cross-dressing in heterosexual transvestism in 33 members of a transvestite club. The men reported feelings of relaxation and comfort, together with a relief from masculine demands when they were cross-dressed. Only a minority were sexually stimulated by cross-dressing and to some this was an unwelcome side effect. Narcissistic desires to be beautiful seemed to be important for some and others reported the desire as an overwhelming urge. Some spent a lot of money on clothes and some took lots of photographs of themselves cross-dressed.

The condition is not recognized as such in women, but as Buhrich (1977) pointed out, in historical terms it is reported more commonly in women than in men, e.g. Joan of Arc, and not just in lesbians. He quoted the well-known example of George Sand who always dressed as a man, but who had numerous heterosexual affairs. Part of the explanation for the emphasis on male pathology is that it is much more socially acceptable for women to live as men than vice versa.

Treatment is not usually sought and all that is required is support.

Trans-sexualism

Trans-sexualism is a persistent drive, not just to dress as a member of the opposite sex, but actually to be reassigned to that opposite sex. Fully developed male trans-sexuality, typically expressed as a feminine being trapped in a male body, necessarily involves rejection of women as sex

partners and hence a homosexual orientation, although in many such cases
the prime preoccupation is with the assumption of a feminine social role
rather than with finding male sex contacts. Moreover, sexual relations are
viewed by the male trans-sexual as satisfactory only if he is in a passive or
'feminine' position, the ambition being in most cases to be enabled to have
sex as a woman following surgical castration and the construction of an
artificial vagina. The potential independence of sexual performance and
gender performance is amply illustrated by those male trans-sexuals who
manage to fulfil the role of husband for a period of years before finally
demanding a sex change (Morris, 1974). Reconstructive surgery as a
treatment for such people is highly controversial and a debate on this topic
is not appropriate here. The reader is referred to more specialized texts, e.g.
Bancroft (1989). Such patients are not particularly delinquent or likely to be
in court (although a few, inevitably, do offend). 'Criminal tendencies' are
according to Randell (1970) one of the absolute contraindications to surgical
gender reassignment.

Bestiality (zoophilia)

In law a form of buggery, bestiality is a person of either sex having sexual
intercourse with an individual of another species either *per annum* or *per
vaginum*. Sexual activity with non-human mammals is probably quite
common. It is largely undetected—the victims not being able to complain
(Kinsey et al., 1948; 1953). The Kinsey reports suggested that it occurs in
8% of adult males and 4% of adult females at some time in their lives, and
that it is commoner in rural than urban communities. It is also probably
commoner in those of low intelligence and the very lonely. Unless it is
attended by other features such as sadism, it is probably not useful to regard
it as a medical problem. Its legal significance comes from the fact that, in
Britain at least, it can still be regarded as a serious crime punishable by up
to life imprisonment! Most authorities, including the Howard League
Working Party on *Unlawful Sex* (1985), believe that in Britain the offence
should be abolished. Even the Criminal Law Revision Committee thought
that the maximum penalty should be reduced to 6 months' imprisonment.

Sado-masochism

A term that can cover anything from love bites to murder and sexual
mutilation, sado-masochism is a phenomenon that comes to forensic attention only in its more extreme and rare forms. The few researchers who have
inquired into sado-masochistic practices in the community at large (Spengler,
1977; Gosselin and Wilson, 1980) were clear that the majority of people who
enjoy giving or receiving pain or humiliation as an aid to sexual arousal
regard this as a form of 'fun sex'. The rules of the game are tacitly agreed so
that matters do not get out of hand. The level of stimulation is delicately

poised between the exciting and the unbearable, and the outward appearance of coercion and torture is something of a sham. As with some other forms of variant sex, there are sufficient numbers of persons interested to support contact advertisements, specialized clubs and specialized pornographic magazines. Sado-masochistic interests are common in both heterosexual and homosexual contexts and women as well as men are attracted.

The infliction of injury for purposes of sexual pleasure, even if the partner consents, is a criminal offence (*Donovan*) but in the ordinary course of events no one complains, significant injuries being unusual. Accidents may occur, of course, sometimes self-inflicted as a result of the insertion of unsuitable objects into body orifices, but these are normally dealt with medically without reference to the police. Rare instances of death from accidental strangulation in the course of solitary, self-administered bondage procedures are in the domain of the forensic pathologist rather than the psychiatrist.

Sadistic sexual assaults on non-consenting women or children, whether in sudden unpredictable attacks in the street, or upon victims lured into situations of vulnerability, are what mostly concerns forensic authorities. Sadistic crimes are distinguished from the generality of sexual assaults by the offender's enjoyment of brutality for its own sake. In investigations of men convicted of rape, those motivated by sadism are said to be distinguishable from ordinary rapists by being maximally aroused only when presented with visual stimuli that depict violence as well as sex (Abel et al., 1977). Sadism, however, may also arise from a desire to dominate rather than from a desire to harm *per se*.

Gratuitous brutality in the course of sexual assaults, the deliberate infliction of genital injuries, the slashing of breasts and the horrifying mutilations of 'Ripper'-type murders are not necessarily due entirely to pure sexual sadism. Peter Sutcliffe, the 'Yorkshire Ripper', suffered from schizophrenia and murdered most of his women victims without sexual interference, being under the psychotic delusion that he had a mission to eradicate prostitutes. Other sexual homicides are committed by men harbouring uncontrolled rage against women, a kind of misogyny run amok (West et al., 1978). Whether the motive is sexual or emotional satisfaction, or both, the commission of appalling sexual atrocities is hardly possible unless the offender has a highly abnormal personality disorder (*see* Ch. 9), or is an individual in the grip of psychotic or near psychotic emotions and thought processes. Fortunately, notwithstanding the attention given to such offenders in the media, they are rarities, although they tend to accumulate in special hospitals and among life prisoners.

Sexual asphyxia

An aspect of masochism that has interested a number of forensic psychiatrists in the USA and Canada is sexual asphyxia (Blanchard and Hucker,

1991). This is the induction of sexual pleasure by anoxia. It is usually a form of autoeroticism carried out in complex ways with ropes and slip knots, or plastic bags, or even anaesthetic agents. It is confined to males. Every medical student has some acquaintance with the practice, because of the prominence the topic is given in courses on forensic medicine (pathology) where the main interest is the determination of the cause of death in a sexual asphyxia episode that has gone wrong. Hazelwood et al. (1983) estimated that there may be 500–1000 such deaths per annum in the USA.

The legal problems created by this particular deviation are largely confined to issues about cause of death and possible wrangles about life insurance, i.e. can the death be classed as a true accident or should it be regarded as a form of suicide. If, of course, a man induces a partner to help him get sexual arousal this way and death results, then the partner would have serious legal problems.

The practice is highly dangerous and might be regarded as requiring treatment. Very few 'sufferers', however, come for treatment. Hazelwood et al. (1983) suggested that the typical man who indulges himself this way is middle class with very few other medical or psychiatric problems. Behavioural treatments (Haydn-Smith et al., 1987), libido reduction, and psychotherapy may also be useful methods of management.

Necrophilia

The Fromm concept of a necrophilous personality preoccupied with death, dirt and destruction is dealt with on pp. 392–4. The term necrophilia is more usually reserved for what might be called a corpse fetish, i.e. sexual arousal obtained from seeing, touching, and copulating with dead bodies, usually very recently dead bodies. It is a disorder confined to males and is usually an attraction to female bodies, although homosexual necrophilia does occur (Bartholomew et al., 1978, and the Nilsen case—Masters, 1985).

Unlike some paraphilias, this deviation, if acted on at all, is difficult to keep secret. It is possible for such a person to work in a mortuary and obtain private access to bodies, others would have to intrude in some way such as tomb robbing. Some documented cases such as Nilsen and Christie provided themselves with dead bodies by murder. It is likely that a number of sadistic killers are also partly necrophiliac and that the culmination of the sadistic thrill is intercourse with the now lifeless, motionless, totally submissive body. Also, unlike other paraphilias, but like sado-masochism, it is difficult to conceptualize the deviation of necrophilia in an otherwise normally functioning individual. Some argue that sexual deviation is always symptomatic of some other disturbance. This must surely be the case with necrophilia, and individuals usually show a range of personality difficulties that include obsessional traits, narcissism, sadism and a preoccupation with destruction. Most have poor reality testing and a few are frankly psychotic. The disorder is rare, of no known specific aetiology and can be treated in the context of a broad approach to the patient's personality. No recommendations for specific treatments are in the literature apart from a case study using behavioural treatment for a man with necrophiliac fantasies (Lazarus, 1968). In Britain, the majority of such patients are either sent to prison and given no treatment or sent to a special hospital where they will receive the package of treatments available to all types of sexual deviants, including individual counselling, group therapy, and social skills training.

Assessment and Treatment

It will be apparent from the introduction to this chapter and the foregoing description of problem sexual behaviour that there is no simple treatment model for particular problems or offences. One naive approach is for a man with a conviction for unlawful sexual intercourse against a child to be referred, a diagnosis of paedophilia to be made, and a ready made treatment package to be prescribed. People, including those with paedophilia, are more complicated than that. Another naive approach would be to assess another man charged with a similar offence, but this time note that he does not have paedophilia, the offence occurring as incest within his family, go on to diagnose his problems as social or marital and 'non-medical', and then reject him as unsuitable for psychiatric care.

The difficulty is to maintain a balanced, but therapeutic approach. At the start of this chapter Bancroft (1991) warned against overstating the role of psychiatry. He suggested that many of the sexual behaviours which turn up as 'problems' or even 'offences' are determined socially and, as Quinsey (1986) has hypothesized, are acquired early in life. Yet Bancroft also stressed that psychiatrists and psychologists do have useful skills and resources which can play their part in helping the sexually deviant individual, including the sex offender, to come to terms with his problems and circumstances. Whatever type of treatment is used, it is likely to be needed long-term if it is to be successful.

Assessment of Deviant Sexuality

Patients come to forensic psychiatrists and psychologists by many routes, but a common reason for referral is that charges have been laid against the potential patient. Some offenders are referred in connection with decisions concerning release on parole or discharge from hospital. Clearly the patient's social circumstances are highly relevant, as is his own view of his problems and their development, his expectations or wishes for change and the likelihood that he would be able or willing to cooperate in what might be a taxing therapeutic endeavour. On all these points, there is no substitute for the classic clinical history-taking interview. Comparison of the patient's version of his history and his offences with particulars in police records and from independent informants is also highly desirable.

Almost any psychiatric disease can present as a sexual problem so the primary assessment must be to look for evidence of any type of psychopathology. Diseases such as depression, schizophrenia, personality disorder and the like will need management in their own right and in conventional ways. Indeed, it is absolutely essential to attend to the patient's neurotic, social, and marital difficulties in every case. Sexual deviation can never be taken out of its complex context. In some cases, attending to the contextual factors will be sufficient to prevent the patient reoffending. For example, a patient who has persistent exhibitionist fantasies may break the law by exposing himself only when depressed, or anxious, or drinking. Such a patient can be greatly helped by attending to the affective state or the drinking, without much change in his sexual deviation taking place.

Some sexual deviations and/or offences may be opportunistic or situational rather than indicative of significant sexual disease. Family dynamics, and social adjustments will, in such cases, be of much greater significance than simple preoccupation with sexual fantasies.

Nevertheless, the deviant components present in any particular problem do always need assessment. Barlow (1977) provided a convenient framework for this aspect of the assessment of sexual dysfunction based on three basic components of sexual behaviour: arousal behaviour, heterosexual social skills, and gender role behaviour.

Arousal behaviour

Arousal behaviour is behaviour which accompanies or promotes genital excitement. It is the chain of events beginning with the onset of sexual arousal, through sexual contact or stimulation of some kind, to termination in orgasm. An important aspect of arousal behaviour is, of course, *erotic preferences*. People may have a variety of sexual interests or develop new ones in special circumstances (such as when in prison), but most have primary preferences (Langevin, 1983). A proper assessment of these preferences is very important. It includes sexual activity and thoughts and daydreams about sexual matters (Wilson, 1978).

Heterosexual social skills

Heterosexual social skills allude to levels of competence in meeting, dating and successfully interacting with persons of the opposite sex. According to Barlow (1977), there are three facets:

1. the social behaviours required to initiate contacts;
2. the chain of social and interpersonal behaviours that proceed to sexual behaviour; and
3. the ability to maintain heterosocial relationships.

Gender role behaviour

Gender role behaviour represents the public expression of the individual's private experience of gender identity. Gender identity disturbance refers to a degree of incongruence between an individual's actual behaviour and the behaviour defined as appropriate in a given culture for a person of his or her physiological sex.

An understanding of the relationship between sexual arousal and sexual behaviour in any given case is particularly important, since deviant sexual arousal or preference does not automatically lead to deviant sexual behaviour. There are complex mediating variables that determine behavioural outcome in a sexually aroused individual. These may be cognitive (such as a perception of the likely consequences of the desired behaviour), emotional (such as guilt, affection, anger or frustration) or environmental. Related to these mediating variables is the person's awareness of the factors which influence his behaviour, and an understanding of his ability to modify these.

These components of sexual behaviour, arousal, social skills and gender role, can each be assessed in three different ways: self-report, behavioural observations and physiological tests. Self-report data are generally obtained from interviews, questionnaires, card sorting procedures, and rating scales. Behavioural assessments require careful observations, e.g. in ward settings, in social settings, in role play (perhaps with video feedback), and by reports from informants, especially sexual partners. Several physiological measures have been used in the assessment of sexual arousal and preferences, such as electro-dermal responses, heart rate, respiration, pupil size and penile erection. All these different measures may accurately indicate arousal levels, but penile erection is the only direct measure of male sexual arousal. The pros and cons of penile plethysmography are well reviewed by Marshall and Eccles (1991). In clinical practice, self-report measures are the most widely used.

Generally speaking, the more direct the assessment the more intrusive it tends to be. It is important to remember that self-report may give the most useful and valid information about behaviours, attitudes, preferences and fantasies, especially among motivated subjects. However, many clinicians and researchers are reluctant to rely on self-report data alone when dealing with sex offenders, because they are known to deny, minimize or rationalize their acts (Laws, 1984). Physiological measures should not be overemphasized as a result. They can never replace self-report completely. Some characteristics, such as fantasies, can by their nature be studied only indirectly (*see also* Murphy et al., 1991).

Cognitive distortions

In recent years there has been increased recognition of the importance of 'cognitive distortions' among sex offenders such as child molesters and rapists (Salter, 1988). Cognitive distortions are learned beliefs that many sex offenders hold about their deviant sexual behaviour which help them justify their criminal acts.

Abel et al. (1984a) identified a number of common cognitive distortions found among those with paedophilia. These included the following beliefs:

1. a child who does not physically resist the adult's sexual advances really wants sex;
2. having sex with an adult is a good way of teaching the child about sex;
3. children who do not disclose to others that they are having sex with a parent really enjoy the sexual activity and want it to continue; and
4. children who ask adults questions about sex really want to have sex with the adult.

A number of scales have been constructed that measure a range of cognitive distortions about offending sexual behaviours (Abel et al., 1984b; Burt, 1980; Kennedy and Grubin, 1992). All, however, are open to manipulation by subjects seeking to give socially appropriate responses.

Cognitive distortions are thought to play an important role in the development and maintenance of sexual deviation. Therefore, an important part of any treatment programme is to modify these cognitive distortions in order to reduce the risk of reoffending (Salter, 1988). Finkelhor (1984) proposes a model of offending against children in which four preconditions need to be met: the offender wants to abuse; he gives himself permission; he creates the opportunity; and he overcomes victim resistance. By learning the cognitions associated with each stage an attempt can be made to intervene in the cycle.

Treatment Goals and Methods

Following assessment, the next step is to decide what can realistically be done about the offender's sexual problems. A radical solution is often impossible. A more modest goal, such as achieving better control over impulses to offend or reducing occasions of temptation, may be all that can be achieved. The development of an interest in partners of mature age is more feasible than the conversion of a man who loves young boys to heterosexuality (Serber and Keith, 1974). For example, if lack of social skills is the main problem this is, in principle, remediable by means of social skills training. Some offenders are very ignorant of female sexuality, so sex instruction and practice in role playing may be helpful for them. If, however, the offender is further handicapped by a degree of mental impairment, by unattractive personality traits, by paranoid attitudes towards the opposite sex, by lack of family support, then these problems need tackling as well with say, general education, medication, and social rehabilitation.

Context or setting

A useful account of the treatment of sex offenders has been given by Perkins (1991). He dealt with an issue which is easily overlooked, that of context. He pointed out that prisons in general are unlikely to be places where treatment can be carried out successfully, because prisoners are encouraged to deny, minimalize, and rationalize their deviant behaviour in order to survive in the brutal culture in which they are placed. Release from prison rarely depends on progress in treatment. Incentives in hospitals are strengthened if hospitalization is coupled with restrictions. In England, for example, a hospital patient may be detained under a restriction order which means that not only the doctor but also the Home Secretary will want evidence that either the deviant sexual drives have lessened, or that they have altered in direction, or that the patient has better control over them. In such circumstances, patients are more likely to talk about their problems, to try and come to terms with them, and eventually to take more responsibility for them.

Psychotherapy

If the main problem is one of neurotic attitudes, of emotional complexes preventing smooth relationships with the opposite sex, then psychotherapy, either group or individual, may be the treatment of choice. Techniques vary from supervisory chats through to classical psychoanalysis. For those offenders who have difficulty with solitary introspection, psychotherapy may be best conducted in group sessions where listening to others' experiences and noticing their rationalizations stimulates self-revelation. Further impetus can be provided by introducing two group leaders, male and female, so that members' reactions to either sex are more readily manifest. For group therapy to work, however, a minimum facility for verbalizing feelings is necessary. As already indicated, when offenders are inmates of penal institutions with an antitherapeutic ethos (for example, where known sex offenders are persecuted by fellow inmates or discriminated against by a hostile staff, or where personal revelations would involve risk of blackmail or deferment of parole), then the scope for the effective application of group psychotherapy is severely limited. In practice, in England and Wales, it is confined to one or two specialist prisons such as Grendon. Hospitals, particularly those with a degree of security have an important role to play in the provision of psychotherapy for offenders (*see* Grounds et al., 1987; Perkins, 1991). The most successful form of psychotherapy has followed a relapse prevention model similar to that used to treat substance abusers. It aims to increase self-control by enhancing the identification of risk situations, analysing the decisions that tend to the problem behaviour and developing strategies to either avoid or cope with the risk situations (*see* Pithers, 1990 for a review).

Some form of psychotherapy is an essential adjunct to all of the other forms of treatment discussed in this section. Furthermore, psychotherapy may need to be long term. Coming to terms with socially undesirable drives, or changing those drives, or relinquishing an important and pleasurable activity, are painful undertakings which involve loss of esteem, loss of pleasure, and loss of purpose. Quayle (1989) suggested that it is through identification with the victims of other offenders' offences that offenders gain most insight into their own offences and the effects these are likely to have had on their victims.

Life skills instruction

Life skills instruction has the advantage that it is acceptable to persons who do not have, or do not recognize they have, serious personality problems (Crawford and Allen, 1979; Brodsky and West, 1981). It includes role-playing exercises, instruction in the management of day-to-day problems such as financial management, cooking, shopping and situational awareness training. For instance, a patient whose offending is associated with drinking bouts may be helped to control his alcohol consumption, another whose inclinations are towards children can be steered away from occupations which present temptation and an exposer who spends a lot of time prowling may be persuaded to undertake some diversionary activity. Employment and housing are basic requirements before more subtle social problems can be tackled. For the offender who is not living in isolation, the involvement of significant others, notably wives or cohabitees, in helping him to reorganize his life style and avoid the stresses that provoke misconduct is highly desirable. Where marital conflict has contributed to a patient's problem behaviour, joint counselling is essential.

Social management and family counselling are frequently advocated in cases of intrafamilial child sexual abuse, where the offender is of generally sound personality and potentially responsive, and where other members of the family are keen to cooperate with a view to preventing a permanent break up of the home (Furniss et al., 1984). In such family situations, however, a therapeutic approach calls for smooth, difficult to achieve, cooperation between a variety of agencies—police, social services, probation officers, courts and psychiatrists—whose procedures and philosophies often clash. All too often, when indecencies within families come to light, the outcome, which may be reached only after protracted legal conflict, is felt by all concerned, including the victim, to be distinctly punitive and unhelpful. In places where such family situations can be handled without necessarily involving the criminal justice system, cases come to light more readily because victims or concerned family members have less to fear from disclosure (Christopherson, 1981). This is not to advocate collusion with illegal (and often damaging) behaviour, but it does suggest sensitive and open limitation of legal activity to the minimum required to achieve maximal benefit.

Table 13.2
Behaviour Treatments for Sexual Deviants

Aversion Techiques

Covert aversive conditioning
Overt aversion conditioning
Electric stimulation
Odour aversion
Taste aversion
Shame therapy
Negative practice

Reconditioning

Fading
Plethysmographic biofeedback
Masturbatory satiation
Masturbatory fantasy change
Masturbatory conditioning

Positive conditioning

Desensitization
Success imagery
Orgasmic conditioning
Olfactory conditioning
Amyl nitrate enhancement

From Maletsky, 1991

Behaviour modification

Behaviour modification techniques can be used to modify sexual arousal patterns and also to improve self-awareness and self-control through self-monitoring, self-evaluation and self-reinforcement. A detailed account of the techniques which can be used is given in Maletzky (1991). He listed a series of techniques in three groups, aversion techniques, reconditioning and positive conditioning (*see* Table 13.2). Some of these are mentioned here by way of illustration.

Covert sensitization (or aversive conditioning) is the self-administration of aversion exercises in which the patient has to imagine his deviant activity in progress and then picture all the punishing consequences that may follow through detection, shame, or loss of liberty (Cautela and Wisocki, 1971).

Conditioned aversion, achieved by presenting the patient with slides that stimulate deviant sexual arousal and then administering electric shocks, is a technique that has become less popular following criticism of it on ethical grounds. Its greatest practical disadvantage is that the aversive effects are unlikely to be lasting if the patient has no other, more acceptable, sexual outlet.

Satiation. A possibly better method of aversion, satiation, consists of requiring the subject to continue masturbation for a prolonged period after orgasm while simultaneously verbalizing his deviant fantasy (Marshall and Barbaree, 1978).

Shaming. Yet another aversive technique, shaming involves the subject describing or performing his deviant activity (such as penile exposure or cross-dressing) before a critical audience (Jones and Frei, 1977).

Orgasmic reconditioning techniques attempt to induce arousal to more acceptable targets (Marquis, 1990). In the simplest system, the patient is instructed to masturbate to his usual deviant fantasy and then, as orgasm approaches, aided perhaps by suitable erotic materials, to switch his thoughts to a non-deviant fantasy.

Fading. In the technique called fading (Barlow and Agras, 1973) the subject is shown a slide depicting his deviant interest (perhaps an under age girl) and as he comes close to maximum arousal, another slide of a less deviant image (in this example an older girl) is superimposed upon and finally obliterates the original image. This ensures that orgasm occurs while watching an acceptable sexual target.

Shaping (or plethysmographic biofeedback) refers to the reinforcement of incipient sexual arousal to a socially acceptable target. In one version, the subject is first dehydrated, then shown socially approved targets while linked to a penile plethysmograph, with any significant increase in penile circumference rewarded with a cool drink (Quinn et al., 1970). The monitoring of sexual arousal with the plethysmograph is an essential part of all these techniques. This provides some verification of beneficial changes in arousal patterns, although false impressions can be obtained if subjects attempt deception (Laws, 1984). Unfortunately, the extent that changes in arousal in the laboratory generalize to the more complex situations encountered in real life is unknown.

Libido reduction by physical means

Whilst there is a shortage of evidence that the direction of libido in a given individual can be changed, there is more evidence that the strength of libido is driven, at least in part, endocrinologically and can be reduced by intervention. Three types of intervention are theoretically available; drug treatments, orchidectomy (castration), and stereotaxic neurosurgery, which means either applying hormones to specific areas of the brain or destroying a small area of the brain such as the ventromedial hypothalamic nucleus.

Freund (1980) reviewed all three methods. Neurosurgery has, so far, little to offer. Castration, on the other hand, seems to offer the recidivist a reasonable chance of keeping out of trouble, but it is not legally accepted, even on a voluntary basis, for sexual dysfunction in Britain.

Drug treatments are available in all countries, but different places use different drugs. Some doctors prescribe small doses of butyrophenones such as benperidol or haloperidol, or phenothiazines such as chlorpromazine, as libido suppressants. Impotence and loss of libido are recognized side effects of these drugs and, in some patients, they are sufficient to take the edge off a troublesome sex drive (e.g. for exhibitionism) such that some self-control can be regained, but their effect is weak.

Drugs which compete with androgens or suppress their production are more powerful antilibidinals (Freund, 1980). At one time, oestrogens were used with some success in sexually deviant males, but the near certainty of feminization which included irreversible breast enlargement requiring surgery, has made the use of oestrogens unpopular.

Female hormones are still used in North America, but only progesterones. The drug usually given is medroxyprogesterone acetate. It is administered intramuscularly once or twice a week, and it causes a reduction in the circulating levels of testosterone. It may cause weight gain, lethargy, nightmares, hyperglycaemia and hypogonadism, but it is said not to cause feminization (Berlin and Meinecke, 1981). Cyproterone acetate is a steroid compound which acts as an antiandrogen. It is readily available in Europe, but not at all in the USA. It is given either orally, usually in doses of between 100 and 200 mg per day, or by weekly injection (which is not available in Britain).

Before starting antiandrogen treatment, it is essential to obtain written consent (after a full explanation of what the treatment does), to carry out a full physical examination recording the details, to undertake liver function tests, to obtain a base-line serum testosterone level, and a base-line sperm count. Patients with liver disease, alcoholism, diabetes, tuberculosis, osteoporosis, and who are below 20 years of age should not be given the treatment. Baseline sperm counts are essential as the drug reduces the sperm count; although this is reversible, pre-existing infertility could be ascribed to the drug. Liver function may be damaged in rare cases and should be constantly monitored. Serum testosterone and prolactin levels will give guidance on the dosage required and on compliance. Libido will not decline until the serum testosterone declines.

Antiandrogen treatment is somewhat crude and drastic, and it is only effective when libido is an important contributor to the offending. Careful assessment of the causes of the offending behaviour is therefore critical. Furthermore, most trials show that patients will not continue to take it for many years, and only in very exceptional cases should permanent treatment be the aim. Those who cooperate will get a sexual holiday. During that holiday, psychotherapy, social skills training, and behaviour therapy should all be pursued actively. The aim is that when the drug is stopped and libido returns, the man's underlying problems will be sufficiently modified so that he has more self-control, and the sexual drive itself will be less fixated in one harmful direction.

Unwanted effects of antiandrogen treatment are not particularly common, but liver and bone changes have been recorded. The commonest problem is feminization, the worst feature being breast enlargement. To avoid this, there must be regular enquiries about and checks on the breasts. If the breasts begin to enlarge, the dose should be reduced or the drug stopped altogether. It is little short of a psychological disaster for a man with severe sexual difficulties to notice that he is (as he would perceive it) changing into a woman! Cautious restarting of the drug may be tried, but if the problem returns no further attempts should be made.

In spite of all the difficulties, this treatment can help some serious sex offenders return to life in the community without endangering others and it therefore has an important place in forensic psychiatry. It is probably underused at the present time.

Treatment with androxyprogesterone or with cyproterone should not be confused with goserelin acetate (Zoladex) which is a gonadotrophin releasing hormone developed for the treatment of metastic cancer of the prostate and which is given by monthly injection. This drug does reduce libido, but is largely untested in that capacity, and it has the major disadvantage that the dose cannot be adjusted easily because of its depot administration. If unwanted effects arise one week after the injection, nothing can be done for another 3 weeks. Furthermore, the patient virtually relinquishes control of the medication. It is not sold in Britain for antilibidinal uses.

The use of antiandrogens in patients with mental handicap raises special problems. Such patients may not comprehend the nature and consequences of the treatment nor be able to give real consent. Much more discussion is needed to resolve this dilemma, but for the moment it is probably best dealt with by having the patient under guardianship and allowing the guardian to take the decisions about treatment.

Because sexual deviations and thus some sexual offences can be effectively controlled by the use of antiandrogen medication, there is a natural tendency for society to demand that serious offenders be compelled to have such treatment. Indeed, in the USA a judge has actually sentenced a sex offender to antiandrogen treatment by regular injection (*Gauntlett*; *see* Melella et al., 1989). This is inappropriate; medical treatments must be prescribed by doctors on a voluntary basis unless the patient is unable to judge the situation for himself, when special legal formulae and safeguards need to be developed. This is generally agreed, but to preserve this position there is sometimes an overreaction against valid prescriptions to consenting sexual deviants. Melella et al. (1989) described how some states in the USA have tried to ban antiandrogen medication entirely in prisoner populations, or insist that patients confess to child molestation before allowing them to receive the treatment. In England, the MHA 1983 has a special clause in it preventing the surgical implantation of hormones unless the patient has consented *and* had his treatment agreed by a Mental Health Act Commission appointed doctor (*see* pp. 37–8). This curious piece of legislation is largely redundant, as it refers to a mode of administration of female hormones which has not been used for some time in Britain.

A more subtle dilemma is posed by the notion that patients should not receive medical treatment under duress. It could be argued that a man convicted of a sex offence does not have an entirely free choice for, in reality, he may be facing either a prison sentence or medical treatment. Within his medical treatment he may be advised that to have antiandrogen treatment will take away his deviant urges and keep him out of prison, whereas to refuse it may lead to almost certain reoffending and imprisonment. We believe that this series of choices is reasonably free. It is at least as free as that facing a patient with progressive cancer, who may be told he can have either an unpleasant operation with a modest chance of cure or he can forego the operation and face a very short life expectancy. The important point is that the patient understands the choices and is not compelled to take any particular medical decision. These matters are also discussed in a special edition of *Criminal Behaviour and Mental Health* (1991, Vol. 1, No. 2) and in the *Bulletin of the American Academy of Psychiatry and the Law* (1989, Vol. 17, No. 3)

Treatment Evaluation

Almost insuperable problems confront attempts to evaluate effectiveness of treatment in the sex offender. The criterion of reconviction is notoriously unreliable. Sex offenders in general have a low, but persisting, probability of reconviction, so for research studies large samples and a long follow-up are needed to demonstrate a statistically significant reduction. Random allocation to treatment and non-treatment regimes is administratively and ethically difficult to accomplish in a rigorous fashion. Matched samples of treated and untreated offenders are always suspect, because matching never fully controls for variables that may be relevant. An individual's rate of offending before and after treatment provides a feasible guide in the case of minor, but highly persistent, offenders, such as certain exhibitionists. The relatively low rates of reoffending reported by some treatment centres in the USA is suggestive of benefit, but it has to be remembered that offenders admitted for therapy are always selected. Furthermore, most studies do not randomly allocate patients to treatment and non-treatment groups and those who drop out of treatment are frequently excluded from the analysis, thus skewing the results. More convincing are the objective observations of changes in sexual arousal produced by behaviour modification techniques

(Langevin, 1983) and by drug suppressant treatment (Bancroft et al., 1974). The attainment of limited goals, such as the avoidance of social encounters with children, is also open to validation. The problem remains that inhibition demonstrated in the laboratory or changes in social habits are not direct measures of offending behaviour in real life settings.

The technical difficulties in the way of obtaining greater scientific certainty should act as a spur to better treatment applications and better evaluations rather than as an excuse for abandoning sexual delinquents, many of whom are struggling with impulses the rest of us are fortunate to be spared. At present, only a minority of known sex offenders get the chance of a determined treatment endeavour.

Prison or Hospital?

A final thought should go to the setting in which any treatment for sex offenders is administered. In Britain at present the question is largely academic for very little treatment is offered in any setting. The principles should nevertheless be considered. There is probably a majority view among health professionals that hospitals have nothing to offer sex offenders and, therefore, any treatment is best left to prisons. Indeed, one or two prisons in Britain, such as Grendon prison or Wormwood Scrubs annexe do have groups available for sex offenders. General psychiatric hospitals find it difficult to offer sufficient inpatient care even for diseases most traditionally regarded as psychiatric, such as schizophrenia, and what inpatient services there are are biased towards the management of acutely or chronically psychotic patients. Such wards are not really suitable for the inpatient management of patients with sexual deviations. Special hospitals in Britain are more likely to provide treatment programmes for sex offenders. Such programmes will usually be a mixture of psychotherapy, behaviour therapy, sex education, general education and nursing support. Such patients usually live on a 'general' ward where once again the bias will be towards the management of patients with psychoses.

Antiandrogen treatment can be started in either prison or hospital, but it is pointless to start it there unless it can be quickly followed by outpatient care where its effects can be monitored. Outpatient care is not provided by the prison service, or by special hospitals. In either of these cases, therefore, it will be important to transfer a patient into the more community-based hospital services soon after the drug is started.

What is required is the development of a few specialized centres which provide assessment and treatment of patients with sexual deviations as a primary activity. Such centres will need to be linked in some way to community services if full rehabilitation is to take place. Whilst there is no objection in principle to some such centres being developed in prisons (provided the appropriate community linkage can be forged), it would make more sense to have the main thrust of such developments within hospital services. Prisons are primarily staffed with prison officers. Their task is the humane care of law breakers. Services such as the provision of psychiatric/ psychological treatment must necessarily be added on to that basic role. Hospitals, on the other hand, have no role other than treatment and are staffed with nurses, doctors, psychologists, social workers and occupational therapists. For them, it is security which may be the additional role. One way or another all hospitals should be linked to the community, so that outpatient care, day support and community nursing are available as patients move forwards.

As indicated in the Howard League report (1985), the value of treatment programmes for sex offenders is more readily accepted in America than in Britain (*see also* Brecher, 1978 and Knopp, 1984). The Howard League report identified a programme in South Florida State Hospital as a good example of what might be done. The programme is a rehabilitation one which focuses on group discussion, but it includes wives and girlfriends. When patients leave the hospital, they are given pocket telephones so that they can telephone another ex-offender volunteer for support at times of crisis. Another scheme in Washington State allowed courts to send sex offenders to hospital for assessment, for up to 90 days initially, but maybe indefinitely for treatment. Treatment was started in closed wards and moved through a phased programme of increasing responsibility, but this was monitored at every stage by the court. The focus of treatment is a group discussion programme. Trials of orgasmic reconditioning were undertaken in selected cases.

In case any reader is still attracted to the market forces philosophy of the 1980s, let the last word on the hospital/prison debate be a financial one. In 1989/90 the average cost of keeping someone in prison was £321 per *week* in England and Wales. The costs ranged from £218 to £554 per week according to the level of security provided (National Association for the Care and Resettlement of Offenders, 1991). The cost of keeping someone in hospital is much greater than this, but the costs of outpatient care are much less, e.g. the cost of having an offender on probation was £1100 per *year* in 1988/89. Even if these costs are trebled by the addition of outpatient psychiatric care (and that may be too high), there would be a saving of about £13 000 per offender per year as between prison and outpatient costs. Just 100 such cases would mean savings of over £1 million each year at 1989 values. If treatment effectively prevented, say, 10% of those cases returning to prison (and that could be a rather low estimate), and assuming a reoffender gets on average 3 years in prison (serving, say, 24 months), then besides all the victim pain which would be saved, a further £250,000 would be saved by offence prevention, at 1989 values.

14
Ninety-five Percent of Crime

Theft, motoring and criminal damage (including arson)

Edited by	*Written by*
John Gunn	Ann Barker
	David Forshaw
	Gisli Gudjonsson
	John Gunn
	Robert Sharrock

In criminal terms forensic psychiatry tends to focus on violent offences against the person, sex offences and substance abuse. This is entirely reasonable as those are the behavioural problems which are more likely to be related to psychiatric disorder. However, to get the matter in perspective it is important to note that such offences account for only a small proportion of crime. The 1988 recorded figures for serious (notifiable) crimes in England and Wales are shown in Table 14.1 (Home Office, 1989b).

The numbers of crimes actually being committed are very much higher than those recorded in this table. From the British Crime Survey (Mayhew et al., 1989), it looks as though the total figure should be multiplied by about four, with a wide variation for individual categories. Perhaps criminal

Table 14.1
Crimes Recorded, England and Wales 1988

		%
Violence to the person	158 200	4.3
Sex offences	26 500	0.7
Robbery	31 400	0.9
Burglary	817 800	22.0
Theft	1 931 300	52.0
Fraud	133 900	3.6
Arson	21 000	0.6
Other criminal damage	572 900	15.4
Other (including drugs)	22 700	0.6
	3 715 700	100

Table 14.2
Findings of guilt, England and Wales 1988

		%
Violence to the person	53 500	3.4
Sexual offences	7 200	0.5
Robbery	4 300	0.3
Burglary	48 400	3.1
Theft and handling	163 400	10.5
Fraud	22 700	1.5
Criminal damage	11 800	0.8
Drug offences	18 800	1.2
Other	24 900	1.6
Motoring	31 300	2.0
Summary non-motoring	455 200	29.3
Summary motoring	713 900	45.9
	1 555 400	100

damage should be multiplied by 10, but stealing motor vehicles (a category of theft) by 1.2.

If we simply attend to findings of guilt, then the figures recorded are very much lower indeed. Table 14.2 is also taken from the 1988 Criminal Statistics (Home Office, 1989b).

Psychiatrists are more likely to deal with violent, sexual and drug offences which account for approximately 5% of recognized criminal behaviour. Thus it is reasonable to conclude that the vast majority of crime has little to do with psychiatric disorder. However the other 95% of criminal activity will, on occasions, also be related to psychiatric disorder. Even though there may be few special reasons to link, say, property offending such as theft with psychiatric disorder, there will be some individuals who are stealing in association with, or as a result of, a range of psychiatric disorders, from personality disorders to confusional states. Even if the number of such cases is as low as 1–2% (and it could be a lot higher), this means that in England and Wales maybe 20 000 cases of theft each year have a psychiatric aspect to them, a figure comparable to all the cases of sex offending which are reported to the police (*see* Table 14.1).

Crime is heterogeneous and ubiquitous, embracing everything from parking on a double yellow line and exceeding the duty free allowance to rape and murder. This chapter simply aims to illustrate a few general principles by reference to some common and/or interesting problems.

Theft

Theft, or larceny, in Britain was once limited in common law to the taking of a tangible object from the possession of another without their consent.

Numerous reform and consolidation acts in the 19th century improved and clarified the law, but the Theft Act 1968 completely recast the criminal law of property into its present form giving new definitions of different types of theft. The two main provisions of this Act are theft and obtaining by deception.

> A person is guilty of theft if he dishonestly appropriates property belonging to another with the intention of permanently depriving the other of it and 'thief' and 'steal' shall be construed accordingly.

Obtaining by deception is defined as:

> A person who by any deception dishonestly obtains property belonging to another, with the intention of permanently depriving the other of it, shall on conviction on indictment be liable to imprisonment for a term not exceeding 10 years.

Dishonesty and deception are almost universal human phenomena. Hartshorne and May (1928) produced a remarkable series of studies showing that it is difficult to find a child who does not cheat, lie, or steal in some circumstances (although there were a few such children).

The type of deception employed varies greatly between individuals and between circumstances and, in the Hartshorne and May study (1928) about 15% of children took the opportunity to steal when presented with it. The authors concluded:

> No one is honest or dishonest by 'nature'. Where conflict arises between a child and his environment, deception is a natural mode of adjustment, having in itself no 'moral' significance.

Indeed, in zoological terms we can regard moderate degrees of dishonesty as adaptive. Durkheim (1901) used different, starker language to make a related point:

> Crime is present not only in the majority of societies of one particular species, but in all societies of all types . . . crime is normal because a society exempt from it is utterly impossible.

He goes on to argue that the simple fact of human diversity means that some people will always disagree with and flout the prevailing sentiments of a social system.

McClintock and Avison (1968) estimated that before we die, one-third of us will be convicted of an indictable (serious) crime, one-quarter of us of a property offence. As most crime goes undetected, this must mean a remarkably large proportion of the population carry out a serious property crime at some time in their lives, and an even larger proportion have carried out a minor property offence.

Yet, as Hartshorne and May (1928) showed, whilst stealing is common in childhood not all children do it; those who do are of special interest to child psychiatrists. Stealing is used, in DSM-III R, as a defining symptom of 'conduct disorder' with 'repeated serious thievery' contributing towards subclassifying the conduct disorder as 'severe'. Wolff (1985) suggests that stealing is the commonest antisocial disorder in childhood and occurs in about 5% of primary school children. Rich (1956) proposed a classification of childhood stealing. He identified marauding offences carried out by three or more boys which are unplanned or only semiplanned; proving offences which are attempts to prove toughness and/or manhood and include breaking and entering, as well as stealing to show off, and taking and driving away; comforting offences, either stealing from parents or impulsive pilfering; secondary offences, planned with a clear objective in view, and other offences for everything else.

It may be appropriate to develop the Rich classification into one for adults as follows:

1. *Needy stealing* is theft which takes place in the context of poverty and/ or deprivation and is largely instrumental (i.e. rationally purposeful);
2. *Status stealing* is theft akin to childhood proving offences, but related to adult fantasies of power and wealth. It embraces professional crime such as white collar crime and robbery;
3. *Delinquent stealing* is theft occurring in the context of a more generalized delinquent way of life;
4. *Attention-seeking stealing* is theft whose primary purpose seems to be to identify the thief as a person with problems; by definition the stealing is carried out in a manner which will ensure capture. A malign subcategory of this type is self-destructive stealing in which the attention drawn is harmful; for example, a policeman suffering from post-traumatic stress disorder carried out a series of shop break-ins taking nothing of value or use until he was caught, dismissed, disgraced and imprisoned;
5. *Compulsive stealing* is repeated theft, often of unwanted articles which is experienced by the thief as a symptom, an urge which it is difficult to control. It is sometimes called kleptomania. A subcategory of this type may be the morbid greed of Medlicott (1968) which included women with eating disorders. Some steal large quantities of food to eat and then later vomit. A paper from St George's Hospital, London (Crisp et al., 1980) suggested that stealing of food, usually from shops, occurs in at least 14% of patients with anorexia nervosa. They said that it usually occurs in those who are chronically ill and who couple overeating with vomiting and purging. Another subcategory may be fetish stealing in which men with masturbatory fantasies involving female clothing (usually underwear) also seem to need to obtain the fetish object by theft, although on occasions the reasons may be more mundane, e.g. a ballgown fetishist who could not afford the dresses!
6. *Symbolic stealing* is akin to comfort stealing. The object stolen is usually standing in for, symbolically, something important that has been, or is about to be, lost. It may occur when an individual is grieving from the

departure of a loved one, or the impending departure of a loved one. It may also occur when the individual's own life seems to be in jeopardy; illness related to cancer is a common theme in the patient's mind. Other forms of depressive stealing may also occur, but most are explicable in terms of loss, confusion or attention-seeking;

7. *Psychotic stealing* is theft which can only be accounted for in terms of delusional ideas or hallucinatory instructions;
8. *Absentminded or confused stealing* is not really theft at all, because the unsanctioned appropriation is erroneous in some way and related to cognitive deficits, which maybe as a result of stress, or mental illness, or other (organic) brain dysfunction.

It is clear that these categories are rough and ready and are not mutually exclusive. For example, a chronic schizophrenic patient may steal because his voices tell him to, he may also steal because he is hungry, and he may even steal in order to draw attention to his plight and get into a prison or a hospital. A particular act of stealing may embrace more than one of these motives. The first three types are less likely to lead to a psychiatric referral, and account for most of the acquisitive offences dealt with by the criminal justice system. For some reason shoplifting, which is not a term recognized in the law, has come to be more associated with psychiatric referral than other types of theft. It is, therefore, dealt with here in more detail, but it should be remembered that the principles which emerge from a consideration of shoplifting apply also to other forms of theft, indeed to many kinds of antisocial behaviour. Special consideration will also be given to car theft which is an antisocial behaviour of increasing importance, and one which is predominantly juvenile.

Shoplifting

Shoplifting is no longer a term of legal significance, stealing from a shop is simply theft. The term has, however, a long legal history, the Shoplifting Act 1699 made the theft of 5 shillings or more from a shop a *capital* felony!

Even today, shoplifting has a special status, a status which is largely unjustified. Most people undertake some stealing during their lifetime, but many only steal when the opportunity presents itself fairly blatantly (e.g. taking items from work), and when detection is highly unlikely. Shops present a very good opportunity for stealing, indeed the shopkeeper's philosophy is to thrust temptation at the shopper, hoping he will take attractive items and then pay for them. Payment is avoided for a number of different reasons, some of them are psychiatric, the majority are not.

The distinction between psychiatric and other reasons can be difficult to make (it can be in any criminal behaviour). At one time 'respectable' ladies were thought to be psychologically unbalanced simply because they stole, presumably on the basis that 'nice' ladies couldn't be 'bad' and, therefore, if they transgressed, they must be excusable, and psychological disturbance was the alternative construction. Abelson (1989) has a lot of fun scoffing at what she calls the 'medicalization of shoplifting'. Whilst she may be right in many cases, it is obviously an extreme and erroneous view to imply that there is no connection between disease and theft. Further, it is reasonable to suppose that disease factors leading to theft will be commoner in populations like middle class, well-heeled ladies, where social factors (such as poverty and peer group pressure) are uncommon.

Clearly, we do not know what proportion of people who steal from shops have psychiatric problems. We do not even know how many people steal from shops. The number of convictions for shoplifting gives a very low estimate of the actual number of shoplifters. Surveys which have followed shoppers at random have suggested that 1 in 12 shoppers in New York City, 1 in 23 in Boston, 1 in 13 in Philadelphia, and 1 in 18 in Dublin (Buckle and Farrington, 1984) are shoplifters. Buckle and Farrington recently conducted an observation study on a small department store in England, and they suggested that between 1 and 2% of customers entering a store take goods without paying for them.

It is sometimes asserted that women are more likely to shoplift than men (e.g. Abelson, 1989). We suspect this is partly because some important studies have been done exclusively on female shoplifters (e.g. Gibbens and Prince, 1962), partly because among women offenders shoplifting is proportionately a more prominent offence than it is among male offenders, and partly because female shoplifters are more likely to be referred to psychiatrists than male shoplifters. It is however untrue: there may be twice as many men as women who steal from shops (Buckle and Farrington, 1984). In 1988, in England and Wales 97 893 people were cautioned for or convicted of shoplifting, 18% less than in 1987 and 20% less than a decade before, 61% were males, 29% were young males (National Association for the care and Resettlement of Offenders [NACRO], 1990b).

In 1988, 216 200 shoplifting offences were recorded by the police in England and Wales, 6% of all crime recorded by the police that year. Between 1950 and 1960, recorded shoplifting rose by 250% and between 1960 and 1970 by a further 100% (NACRO, 1990b). In 1987, the average value of goods stolen by shoplifting was £53. In 33% of offences, goods less than £5 were taken. That same year 61 241 people were cautioned, i.e. 51% of the total of convicted or admitted shoplifters. They represented 47% of the males and 53% of the females. A further 58 529 people were convicted of shoplifting; of these two-thirds were males and one-third aged under 21. The way courts in England and Wales deal with shoplifters is set out in Tables 14.3 and 14.4 (NACRO, 1990b).

Shoplifters referred to psychiatrists after a court appearance are included as small percentages of discharges, probationers, fines, 'other' and suspended sentences. Overall only 7% of shoplifters receive a custodial sentence.

Table 14.3
Sentences of Male Shoplifters 1988

	10–16	(%)	17–20	(%)	21+	(%)	Total	(%)
					Age in years			
Non-custody								
Discharge	1088	(3)	1185	(3)	4078	(12)	6351	(18)
Probation/supervision	447	(1)	906	(3)	2513	(7)	3866	(11)
Fine	1035	(3)	3962	(11)	12 513	(36)	17 510	(50)
Community service	41		527	(2)	998	(3)	1566	(5)
Attendance centre	414	(1)	115		0		529	(2)
Care order	15		0		0		15	
Other	7		23		254	(1)	284	(1)
Total	3047	(9)	6718	(19)	20 356	(59)	30 121	(87)
Custody								
Young offender	71		534	(2)	2		607	(2)
Prison	0		0		2261	(7)	2261	(7)
Total	71		534	(2)	2263	(7)	2868	(8)
Suspended sentence	0		0		1746	(5)	1746	(5)
Total	3118	(9)	7252	(21)	24 365	(70)	34 735	(100)

Table 14.4
Sentences of Female Shoplifters 1988

	10–16	(%)	17–20	(%)	21+	(%)	Total	(%)
					Age in years			
Non-custody								
Discharge	559	(3)	1145	(7)	3485	(20)	5189	(30)
Probation/supervision	160	(1)	766	(4)	2236	(13)	3162	(18)
Fine	290	(2)	1680	(10)	5347	(31)	7317	(42)
Community service	10		156	(1)	301	(2)	467	(3)
Attendance centre	39		1		0		40	
Care order	9		0		0		9	
Other	2		6		40		48	
Total	1069	(6)	3754	(22)	11 409	(66)	16 232	(93)
Custody								
Youth custody	5		88	(1)	0		93	(1)
Prison	0		0		442	(3)	442	(3)
Total	5		88	(1)	442	(3)	535	(3)
Suspended sentence	0		0		614	(4)	614	(4)
Total	1074	(6)	3842	(22)	12 465	(72)	17 381	(100)

Women are more likely to be given a discharge or probation than men.

The women identified by Gibbens and Prince were studed in a 10-year follow-up (Gibbens et al., 1971b). Of the 525 women traced 20% were found to be reconvicted in the 10 years, and 44 of these were admitted to a mental hospital (three times the expected rate for women). The commonest reason for hospitalization was an attempt at suicide, other reasons were schizophrenia, manic depressive illness, dementia, alcoholism, and a few other non-specific diagnoses. The 24 who attempted suicide are a reminder of the potential for tragedy which this seemingly trivial and common activity has. In recent history, Lady Barnett, a TV personality, a medical practitioner, and a magistrate, killed herself when prosecuted for shoplifting. In more distant history, Mrs Leigh-Perrot, aunt of Jane Austin, was charged with stealing a card of white lace from a haberdashers shop in Bath in 1799. She was remanded in custody for 8 months and brought before the Assizes in Taunton. If found guilty, she could have been hanged, or transported, or branded. The evidence against her was overwhelming, but she was acquitted, although some £2000 poorer (James, 1976). Not quite financial ruin, but an appalling experience altogether (*see* MacKinnon, 1937 for full story).

Very few attempts to classify the psychological mechanisms of shoplifting have been made, but Cupchick and Acherson (1983) produced theirs after looking at 24 cases. They singled out reactions to stress, regressive symbolism, unconscious retribution, unconscious manipulation, conscious manipulation, and object loss. They were impressed with the fact that a number of their patients had experienced a very significant loss or were about to do so. The losses included loss of home, loss of spouse, and loss of life, especially from cancer (10 cases). Sometimes, the impending loss of life was to the individual themselves, and sometimes it was to a close relative. The conscious manipulation was in patients who seemed to be deliberately drawing attention to themselves, hoping to get caught. The unconscious manipulation was similar, but was in people who did not seem to be aware of the mechanism involved. One woman for example, an immigrant, longed to return to her own country, but was married to a Canadian (the country of the study). Her continuance in Canada as far as the immigration authorities were concerned depended on her not breaking the law; consciously, she could not understand why she was constantly doing just that. Unconscious retribution referred to the unconscious need to punish a relative, especially a spouse. Cupchick and Acherson (1983) admitted the difficulty of deciding which mechanism is operating, and they described a middle-aged woman who had been married for 28 years to a very senior businessman. She was confronted suddenly with her husband talking of possible separation. The day after this distressing conversation, he went out of town to a business meeting. She developed jealous ideas about him going to meet a lover. She went into the local town and stole goods amounting to $4.00 from a supermarket. The stealing could be interpreted in a number of ways; as a tiny comfort against the impending loss, a punishment to either herself or her husband, or it could have been an absent-minded response to the stress in that she was preoccupied with her personal problem to a degree that took her mind off the proper order of events in the shop.

Another Canadian paper (Bradford and Balmaceda, 1983) studied 50 shoplifters who were referred to a forensic psychiatry clinic and compared them with 50 other patients referred to the same clinic for pretrial reports, and 50 patients who were attending other non-forensic clinics in the hospital for non-criminal reasons. These authors found that although the groups were closely matched in terms of age, the shoplifters were much more like the general psychiatric population than they were like the other offenders. The typical profile of the shoplifter was a 37-year-old woman who came from the upper end of the occupational spectrum, who had been subject to a significant psychological stress, who was anxious and depressed with symptoms of dissociation, and who had stolen trivial items which she could easily have paid for. The study tends to support the view that pathological shoplifters are more like other neurotic patients and less like delinquents, but it should be noted that the sample was selected by the courts, and we are very ignorant of the processes which determine which offenders are sent to psychiatrists and which are not.

One explanation for shoplifting which may deserve more consideration than it gets is absent-mindedness. Reason and Lucas (1984) postulated that little lapses of memory or episodes of absent-mindedness are common events, especially in shops. In a questionnaire survey of 150 people not involved in shoplifting, 85% admitted they had on occasions forgotten why they had gone into a shop, 72% had left goods behind they had paid for, 67% had on occasion failed to wait for their change, 40% had bought something they did not want, 31% had started to push the wrong trolley round a supermarket, and 18% had left the shop without paying for something and had to go back. The authors postulated that as stress increases, so we become more preoccupied with thinking and pay less and less attention to the external environment. The authors also analysed 166 letters received by the Portia Trust, protesting their innocence of shoplifting charges: 53% of the protestors blamed the theft on absent-mindedness or confusion, 69% mentioned being distracted or preoccupied. Distractors were of two kinds, the first being novel features of the surroundings that demanded attention, for example losing a child, getting into a conversation, knocking over a display, and the second the triggering of distressing ruminations (e.g. a woman seeing her husband and his mistress together). Twenty-three per cent of the protestors were receiving medical help, and 50% were engaged in negative life events such as separation, divorce, illness or bereavement. All correspondents wrote of the great distress they experienced, several mentioned suicidal ideas, drink problems, loss of weight, and subsequent accidents.

It should also be noted that psychotic illnesses may lead to stealing in many guises. These are rarely referred as 'shoplifters', because the psychosis is more clearly the prominent feature. For example, a manic patient went into a small shop, distracted the attention of the shopkeeper by asking for something from a high shelf, leaned over the counter to grab the till, and was caught just outside the shop staggering under the weight of the till. He was referred to the hospital because of his madness, not because of his shoplifting. However, schizophrenia, serious depression, mania, alcoholism, drug addiction, may all present via a shoplifting charge. Shoplifting may also follow brain damage. There are the simple classic cases of patients with dementia being confused and forgetful, but other forms of brain damage must be kept in mind.

The term *compulsive shoplifting* overlaps with the term *kleptomania*, which is defined in DSM-III R as 'a recurrent failure to resist impulses to steal objects not needed for personal use or their monetary value'. The condition is associated with a build-up of tension immediately before the commission of the act and then a feeling of relief afterwards. It is not known what proportion of all arrested shoplifters fulfil the criteria of the condition, but probably fewer than 5% do so. A study of shoplifters (Gudjonsson, 1987b) pointed to the importance of low self-esteem and general dissatisfaction with life in the development of compulsive shoplifting. It was considered that these factors provide a starting point for a chain of developments where feelings of anger, frustration and lack of self-fulfilment become temporarily relieved through shoplifting activity.

A behavioural model of compulsive shoplifting (Gudjonsson, 1987a) included the basic premise that a distinction must be drawn between the motivation behind the initial shoplifting and the development of its compulsive features. Shoplifting becomes 'compulsive' because it provides some vulnerable individuals with psychological fulfilment and relief which are highly reinforcing. Compulsive shoplifting and obsessive-compulsive problems (e.g. checking and washing compulsions) may to some extent overlap (Gudjonsson, 1987a), but there is no evidence that compulsive shoplifting is an obsessive-compulsive disorder *per se*. It is better construed as a specific type of behaviour which is perceived by the shoplifter at the time as comprising 'an irresistible impulse'. It involves initial arousal enhancement, which momentarily relieves frustration and depressive mood, and sudden reduction in anxiety afterwards, which provides a temporary sense of well-being. It is probably the combination of the two stages, rather than each acting in isolation, which is reinforcing for the compulsive shoplifter. Mood elevation and anxiety relief may be particularly reinforcing for individuals with a depressive disposition. However, it is evident that only a small proportion of all depressives who shoplift become compulsive shoplifters. It has been argued elsewhere (Gudjonsson, 1988a) that much depends on such factors as the nature of the shoplifter's depressive problems, their current emotional and sexual relationships, and their ability to express dissatisfaction and anger to others satisfactorily.

It should always be borne in mind that the whole matter of assessing shoplifting is a complex business involving motivations at many levels, e.g.

one lady was referred for stealing two bottles of aftershave. She was in evident distress at the time of her shoplifting, which she did in an obvious and incriminating manner. She said that she did not want the aftershave. Her neurotic problem was a depressive illness following the double blow of a painful bereavement and the break-up of her marriage. However, this was not her first conviction for shoplifting. It turned out she was a successful professional cashmere thief who usually did not get caught. Stealing two bottles of aftershave served a different and a neurotic purpose.

Prevention and treatment of shoplifting

Most public prevention programmes for shoplifting focus on increasing awareness of the severity of the consequences associated with being caught or increasing the threat of detection. One successful technique was to place anti-shoplifting signs and posters throughout a shop (McNee et al., 1976). They reduced shoplifting significantly without reducing sales turnover. When commodities were publicly identified as being frequently stolen, the shoplifting of these items was almost eliminated.

It is not known to what extent arrest, prosecution, conviction and sentence reduce recidivism in the case of the shoplifter. Sometimes the act of arrest, even without the likelihood of conviction and sentence, may deter some people from further shoplifting. For example, in Iceland shoplifters are rarely prosecuted, but arrest does seem to deter them from further shoplifting (Gudjonsson, 1982). Motivation is important when considering behavioural treatment, for example Solomon and Ray (1984) found that 'rational-emotive therapy' was effective for treating shoplifters who stole out of rational choice, but ineffective with habitual and compulsive shoplifters. Prince (1980) argued that different motivation factors operate at different ages, young shoplifters may show signs of 'general social maladjustment' whereas, in older women, shoplifting may be associated with sexual problems and depression. Shoplifting often provides immediate gratification and reinforcement and thus, as the likelihood of apprehension and punishment is low, tends to lead to lack of motivation which may mean a failure to keep appointments, or complete prescribed homework. Compulsive shoplifters who steal to fulfil a psychological need may not be motivated to stop shoplifting unless the therapist can provide an alternative outlet for their need.

Both psychiatric and psychological techniques may be useful in the treatment of patients who steal. The first essential is a full assessment leading to a diagnostic formulation which embraces an understanding of how and why the stealing occurred. Treatment strategies should follow naturally from this formulation. Underlying illnesses and disorders should be treated in their own right. Support and psychotherapy aimed at the provision of insight, the raising of self-esteem and the acceptance of loss are also necessary. For some patients, psychotherapy can be provided in a group. In successful cases, support may need to be long term in order to prevent relapse; behavioural techniques are also being tried for selected cases.

Reports of behavioural treatment are often of single case studies. Keutzer (1972) successfully used aversive-conditioning with a female kleptomaniac. Gauthier and Pellerin (1982) showed that covert sensitization was effective in eliminating compulsive shoplifting in a patient. One of us (Gudjonsson, 1987a) has described a case of a middle-aged female compulsive shoplifter who was successfully treated by a programme which consisted of increasing time spent on self-rewarding activities, where the patient was able to fulfil her need for excitement, challenge and purpose, while simultaneously reducing the undesirable activity of shoplifting.

Other shoplifters have been treated by more cognitive means. R. H. Moore (1984) recommended short-term crisis counselling followed by education which encouraged the offender to see shoplifting as wrong and to appreciate the consequences of further offending. Solomon and Ray (1984) reported a high success rate for 94 adult shoplifters who participated in an intensive eight-hour group counselling based on rational-emotive therapy principles. Attention was aimed at modifying the irrational beliefs of shoplifters.

A case of shoplifting

Kathy, was a middle-aged housewife referred after several years of persistent shoplifting and five convictions, including a period of imprisonment. She was extremely anxious, suffered from phobias, panic attacks, recurrent depression and a good deal of marital disharmony. One aspect of this disharmony was the loss, as she saw it, of her home and friends. Her husband had moved to London from a small market town for a better paid job. She resented this bitterly and felt isolated. The frequent trips to court and the period of imprisonment hurt him considerably. Treatment took 4 years. Her anxiety was managed with behavioural treatment and beta blockers, her depression responded to antidepressants. Marriage counselling improved the quality of their relationship and, in this setting, her husband decided to go back to his old town. With much relief Kathy said goodbye to London. Two years later she wrote:

My probation officer used to think I shoplifted to get back at my husband. I wish sometimes that the reason was as simple as that. For some reason, I just wanted to shoplift, I just could not control this feeling I had at those times, I just had to do it irrespective of the consequences. Now I have got back my safety valve and I would not dream, I hope, of doing the things I did. I was so ashamed I could never tell anybody how bad the shoplifting was. At one time I had cases of things I did not know what to do with . . . at those times I often felt like killing myself, but that safety valve was *just* there, just. I feel nearly my old self. I know I will never really get over that awful 7 years, it was terrible.

Car Theft

Car theft is predominantly a juvenile crime, although in Britain it accounts for nearly one-fifth of the total of recorded notifiable theft, and amounts to a tenth of all recorded notifiable crime (e.g. Home Office, 1988a). It is also on the increase; between 1983 and 1987 the number of recorded thefts and unauthorized taking of motor vehicles rose by 19%, although the number of licensed vehicles increased by a little under 10%. Also, significant numbers of young offenders are imprisoned each year for auto-crime: of the 23 283 receptions of young offenders (under 21) into custody in 1987, 1208 related to auto-theft (Home Office, 1988a). Further, the financial loss as a result of auto-crime is large and increasing, with victim studies showing that lower income car-owners suffer most (Brill, 1982). It has also been estimated in the USA that the driver of a stolen vehicle is 200 times more likely to be involved in an accident, although there is no relevant data in this country (Home Office, 1988d). The poignant newspaper stories that appear of innocent people who lose their lives as a result of car chases with the police, highlight the personal tragedy that car theft can create.

Psychological factors

In spite of the severity of the problem, there has been surprisingly little research dealing specifically with car theft. A notable exception was the work of Gibbens (1958b) who contrasted the background characteristics of car-thieves with other offenders. He noted that most came from 'intact and affectionate homes', with a trend towards more neurotic symptoms in the car-thieves. His suggestion that unconscious sexual motives were responsible for some car theft is less likely to be agreed than his emphasis on the role of subculture and the influence of the delinquent group. In a study of case records on several hundred young offenders on probation, and considering many background factors that may have distinguished offender types, Davies (1969) found only one significant difference between car thieves and other offenders: they were more likely to be members of delinquent gangs. However, such research says little about those aspects of delinquent groups which promote car theft. It is possible that, in addition to peer 'pressure' or 'support', there are other, more subtle cognitive influences, such as the tendency of groups to alter individuals' perceptions of risk—the so-called 'shift to risk effect' (Wallach et al., 1964)—and thereby criminal decision-making.

Intervention

One school of criminology eschews social and personality-based explanations and emphasizes more the role of the immediate environment (e.g. Clarke, 1985). Rather than individual treatment, the aim of crime reduction is seen as best served by preventive measures, with a focus on what environmental factors can be manipulated to reduce crime. Security devices and better street lighting are obvious examples.

Yet such measures are unlikely to eliminate auto-theft completely; attention may simply be redirected to other, easier criminal targets (the so-called displacement effect). How, then, can the persistent car thief be dealt with? Imprisonment is a frequent disposal for recidivist young car thieves and it may not be totally ineffective: it will certainly prevent offending during detention. To examine longer-term effects of imprisonment, Kraus (1974) studied prospectively 223 young Australian offenders who were given either custodial sentences or probation orders, whilst being matched on other relevant factors including number of offences. The auto-theft offenders showed less subsequent crime (car theft and other offences) following imprisonment than the other offender groups in which there were no differences in outcome. However, on the basis of an isolated study and in the light of more general findings which indicate the long-term ineffectiveness of imprisonment, it should not be assumed that imprisonment is the preferred treatment of car thieves.

Far better, perhaps, to attend specifically to the interests and aspirations of young car thieves. Such is the approach of a number of 'motor projects' recently established by the English probation services, in which young motor offenders use their spare time to renovate and race cars before racing them in banger meetings. Although the ethos of individual projects varies, there is heavy emphasis on encouraging individual responsibility and awareness of safety issues. Pilot research suggests that participation in such schemes does have a significant effect in reducing the likelihood of offending, at least in the short term, although the psychological mechanisms responsible are unclear; it may be that the disincentive of losing a place which follows inevitably from reoffending is a preventive factor, or it could be that there is a change in the appraisal of risks involved in 'joy-riding' as individuals learn about the dangers of cars. Such schemes clearly warrant further research in evaluating their effectiveness.

For the forensic psychiatrist or psychologist, analysis of the individual case will normally reveal what motivates the offending behaviour: prime candidates are excitement and, occasionally, increased status in the peer group, often associated with a pre-existing interest in cars. The disinhibiting influence of drugs and alcohol should also be considered. The role of auto-theft as a means of combating boredom or depression should be investigated. The effect of depression on delinquency has been commented upon (e.g. Weiner, 1980), although usually in the context of aggressive behaviour. In a personal sample of over 20 car thieves (Sharrock, in preparation), one of us (R. S.) found a lad who had a pattern of offending which was solitary and which always resulted in detection, features which are both highly unusual for delinquents in general and car thieves in particular. Gentle inquiry revealed the behaviour to be a clear signal for help, and that the offender had been depressed following domestic problems. The treatment implications for such findings are clear, and remind us that the general principles of forensic psychiatry apply here just as in other types of stealing.

Road Traffic Offenders and Accidents

The Legal Background

Since motor vehicles are largely an innovation of the 20th century, little exists in common law to regulate their use. There is, however, in most countries a good deal of legislation that governs road traffic and related offences such as speeding, driving without a licence or without being insured, and careless driving, although even standard legal texts eschew a consideration of the plethora of such offences (e.g. Smith and Hogan, 1988). Motoring offences in England and Wales are dealt with by magistrates' courts and a newly introduced fixed penalty scheme. Penalties are usually of a relatively minor nature. The most serious offences are those of reckless driving (S.2 Road Traffic Act 1972); and death by reckless driving (S.1 Road Traffic Act 1972) which can carry a prison sentence of 5 years. Death by reckless driving was introduced in response to the difficulty which juries had in convicting homicidal drivers of manslaughter.

Accidents: the Problem of Prediction

In relation to the total amount of driving, road traffic accidents are relatively rare. Thus predicting a group at risk of an accident will identify erroneously many 'false positive' cases. The problems of prediction of this type of violence are much the same as those in other types (*see* Ch. 16).

Even so, it may be of some interest that when Tillmann and Hobbs (1949), compared 96 taxi-drivers with histories of motor accidents with 100 age-matched controls without a history of accidents, the accident-prone group were more likely to have had a history of legal proceedings not related to driving. The authors concluded that a man—

> drives as he lives. If his personal life is marked by caution, tolerance . . . and consideration of others, then he would drive in the same manner.

Other research has tended to confirm the role of temperamental factors (e.g. Mayer and Treat, 1977), even allowing for the complicating effects of alcohol.

Accidents probably arise from an interaction between a number of factors, including alcohol consumption (*see below*). These possibilities have unfortunately not always been carefully distinguished in the literature.

Stress and Life Events

There are a number of ways in which life stresses could lead to an increased likelihood of accidents (and traffic offences). First, the kind of intrusive thoughts that commonly accompany states of anxiety or depression (e.g. Watts and Sharrock, 1985) may well impair concentration and thus driving ability. This may be analogous to the absent-mindedness in shoplifting mentioned earlier. Second, states of anxiety may produce the tendency to drive quickly or aggressively (Shinar, 1978). Third, some highway collisions might reflect self-destructive behaviour including frank suicide or parasuicide attempts, as well as the abandonment of caution because of mood changes.

That a serious life event may be associated with increased risk of accident and road traffic offences was shown by McMurry (1970) who studied 410 people filing for divorce in Washington State, USA. There was a steady rise in risk from 6 months before filing for divorce to a peak risk at 3 months afterwards, by which time the outcome of the divorce would have been determined.

Psychiatric patients who have been hospitalized for suicidal behaviour have a considerably raised risk of both accident involvement and road traffic offences (Crancer and Quiring, 1969), with a disproportionate number of drinking and driving and reckless driving offences. Psychiatric inpatients in general have higher accident rates compared to the general population (Waller, 1965). Phillips (1977) found a substantially raised fatality rate on Californian highways after well-publicized suicide stories, possibly reflecting, he suggested, the imitative nature of sucidal behaviour.

Alcohol and Medication (*see also* pp. 114, 438–40)

As early as 1914 (*see* Buttigliere et al., 1972), it was suggested that, in the future, only total abstainers would be permitted to drive. Although this prediction has not yet been realized, research continues to point to alcohol as the single most common factor in accident involvement, contributing to up to 50% of accident fatalities. Indeed, Waller (1973) estimated that a third of all fatal accidents involved alcoholics. People with alcoholism have accidents and commit road traffic offences at approximately twice the normal rates (Waller, 1965). In Britain, an investigation of 2000 road accidents showed that 25% involved a drinking driver. By 1974, one in three of drivers who died in a road accident had blood alcohol levels over 80 mg/100 ml when they were killed (Dept. of the Environment, 1976). Mozdziera et al. (1975) compared two groups of alcoholics with either high or low rates of accidents or motor offences: those most at risk were found to be more aggressive and impulsive on personality tests. Therefore, alcohol may disinhibit or 'release' undesirable behaviours that are responsible for accidents (Smart and Schmidt, 1969).

In addition to behavioural effects, with increasing levels of alcohol ingested, driving skills are increasingly impaired, beginning with fine visual perceptual judgements, through cognitive decision-making to gross motor incoordination at about 0.15% blood alcohol level: these abilities interact to impair drivers' performance (Levine et al., 1975). Unfortunately, alcohol also seems to impair individuals' appraisal of their own abilities so that the cognitive effects of alcohol often go unrecognized.

In view of the extent of the problem of drunk-driving, there has been some interest of late in general educational and specific treatment programmes in recidivist offenders. The relative lack of success of general educational programmes (Scoles and Fine, 1977) may be because drunk drivers have a more generalized excessive alcohol problem. Connors et al. (1986) devised a behavioural treatment which emphasized self-control via self-monitoring, the use of portable breath-tests and a focus on the antecedents and consequences for the individual of drinking. They found modest effects of their treatment over a 3-year period, with one in three being rearrested for drinking and driving, which was better than might be expected on the basis of actuarial predictions. So it would be argued that a focus on environmental precipitants to drinking and driving may prevent a significant amount of drunk driving. Random breath-tests, subsidized soft-drinks and increasingly expensive alcoholic drinks are proposals that follow from such an approach. Nevertheless, individual treatment is important in those cases in which alcohol consumption is a means of dealing with stress.

A related important point is that psychotropic drugs also have effects on arousal, cognition and psychomotor functioning, and so must be used with extreme caution together with clear advice in patients who drive. It is especially important to point out how sedative drugs interact with one another and that psychotropic drugs plus alcohol are a dangerous combination. Noyes (1985) suggested, however, that an increased likelihood of accidents may also be associated with the illness being treated, and in some cases the drug treatment may improve the underlying disabilities.

Epilepsy (*see also* pp. 112–13)

The prevalence of epilepsy in adult life is at least four per 1000 adults which means that in Great Britain there are 130 000 adult epileptic people who are potential drivers (Pond and Espir, 1971). In a general practice survey, Pond and Bidwell (1960) found that about 15% of adult epileptic patients drove and Phemister (1961) estimated that it was even higher— 20%, and these studies were at a time when epileptic people had no permission to drive at all. This means that over 20 000 drivers in Britain may suffer from epilepsy. Over 17 years Raffle (1970) found that of 53 accidents resulting from loss of consciousness in bus drivers, 14 were due to epilepsy. Herner et al. (1966) found that in Sweden 10 out of 14 255 traffic accidents reported by the police were caused by epilepsy, but these seemed to be serious accidents.

Neurotic Factors

Parry (1968) tested the hypothesis that aggressive drivers and anxious or frightened drivers are more likely to have an accident than other drivers. He gave questionnaires to a randomly selected group of car drivers and found that quite a high proportion admitted to aggressive behaviour such as chasing another vehicle when annoyed, driving straight at another vehicle in anger, deliberately trying to edge another car off the road, and fighting with other drivers. These aggressive tendencies tended to diminish with age, and the aggressive feelings were correlated with the number of accidents. Combinations of high aggression and high anxiety made for an even greater degree of accident liability.

In contrast to the Tillman and Hobbs (1949) study quoted earlier, Parry was impressed by the non-aggressiveness in other areas of life which some of the aggressive drivers showed. He tended to think that people drive as they would like to live, and quoted a young bank clerk who confessed to getting a thrill out of pretending that the North Circular Road in London was a motor-racing circuit—he had always wanted to be a motor-racing driver.

Ageing and Driving

When corrections are made for the amount of driving, elderly people have accident rates that are higher than middle-aged people, and similar to very young people. McFarland et al. (1964) observed errors in old people's driving that pointed to lapses in cognition. However, these rates are almost certainly affected by the presence of a subgroup of people with either dementing or cerebrovascular illness, who are four times as likely to be involved in accidents as healthy individuals over 60 and who were only slightly more accident prone than other adults over 30 (Waller, 1967).

Homicide

Table 14.5 shows that causing death by reckless driving is the commonest type of criminal homicide (about one-third of all cases) in England and Wales. As Macdonald (1964) has pointed out, not only is death by car a relatively effective way of killing or being killed, it also offers opportunities for concealment. He found that patients at a mental hospital had a fatal accident rate some 30 times greater than that of the general population and many of them died in circumstances suggestive of suicide, while other patients in the hospital confessed to both suicidal and homicidal attempts by automobile.

In England and Wales these killings are excluded from the criminal statistics annual homicide analysis. A study of these drivers waits to be

Table 14.5
Criminal Homicide 1987 & 1988

	1987	1988
Murder	202	103
Diminished responsibility	80	50
Other manslaughter	188	118
Infanticide	1	6
Insane	7	0
Suspect died	1	2
Suspect committed suicide	58	42
Proceedings discontinued	10	4
Suspects acquitted	10	8
No one charge	37	38
Case pending	10	221
Causing death by reckless driving[1]	292	339
Total	896	931

[1] Police figures

From Home Office, 1988a, 1989b

carried out. In the absence of such a survey, it can be presumed that this reckless driving population is likely to contain a high proportion of alcohol abusers, a high proportion of abnormally aggressive people and one or two psychotic individuals. Almost none of them will be dealt with by the courts as seriously as other types of killer, yet it is not known whether they are any more healthy, or less likely to reoffend than any other case of homicide. At the very least, anybody who kills with a vehicle should be medically examined as thoroughly as anybody who kills with any other type of weapon.

Guidelines for the Practitioner

The complexity of interactions between causal factors and the potential problem of overidentifying at-risk cases makes the task of advising patients about their driving very difficult. Noyes (1985) suggested that high risk groups should be identified, for careful monitoring, and such patients and their families should be told about the risks they run, the possible effects of medication and how this may interact with alcohol; psychiatric help should also be provided where possible. If convictions result from impulsive driving, Noyes proposed 'counselling targeted to specific behaviours'.

The points for the psychiatrist to bear in mind are that anybody with a drink or drugs problem should be advised not to drive, those on sedative medication should either refrain from driving or, if on small doses that do not interfere with performance, they should totally abstain from drinking when driving. Professional drivers should be taken off driving duties while taking any psychoactive drug such as an antidepressant or a tranquillizer. Aggressive drivers should refrain from driving and receive treatment for the aggression; anger management may be helpful. Patients with anxiety states, particularly those which induce a lack of self-concern (e.g. post-traumatic stress disorder) should avoid driving. Psychotic patients with any degree of anger, suicidal feelings, paranoid ideas, hyperactivity, or other potentially dangerous affect should be forbidden to drive until their mental state improves.

Epilepsy is, in most countries, subject to special laws. According to Schmidt and Wilder (1988), in general, in the USA, most states only required a period of 1 year fit free before granting a driving licence. In the UK persons who suffer from epilepsy may apply for a driving licence if they have been fit free from any epileptic attack for 2 years. Persons who cannot fulfil that condition may still qualify for a licence provided they have had attacks only while asleep over a period of at least 3 years. Drivers of heavy goods vehicles and public service vehicles must have been seizure free from the age of 5.

In nine of the US states the law requires an attending physician to report epileptic patients to licensing authorities; in the UK this is left to the judgement of the doctor. As Fenwick (1988) pointed out, advising an epileptic patient about driving is a complex business for, in addition to the risk of seizures, there is also the possibility of drowsiness due to medication. Further, there are other coexisting medical and social problems, for example, some epileptic patients are mentally handicapped, others drink heavily.

The Medical Commission on Accident Prevention booklet *Medical Aspects of Fitness to Drive* (Raffle, 1985) has useful clinical advice on a number of conditions both physical and mental.

Criminal Damage

Criminal damage is dealt with by the Criminal Damage Act 1971. Section 1 of this Act deals with three types of damage, types which for convenience may be labelled simple damage, dangerous damage, and arson. They are triable either way, that is either by indictment or summary trial. *Simple damage* S1(1) is when—

> a person who without lawful excuse destroys or damages any property belonging to another intending to destroy or damage any such property or being reckless as to whether any such property would be destroyed or damaged shall be guilty of an offence.

This offence carries a maximum sentence of 10 years' imprisonment.

In *dangerous damage* S1(2), there is either intent to endanger life or recklessness as to whether life is endangered. In *arson* S1(3), the damage or destruction of property is by fire. Both dangerous damage and arson carry a possible maximum penalty of life imprisonment on trial by indictment.

It is clear from Table 14.1 that criminal damage in its various forms is a very common offence, indeed it is 16% of all reported notifiable crime. As Gibbens (1970) put it:

> There is no doubt that vandalism is common behaviour. It is the type of crime which everyone commits at some time.

Yet in spite of its ubiquity vandalism is of interest to the psychiatrist. It is not just that over half a million cases of criminal damage each year will inevitably throw up a few psychiatric cases, there is also the common clinical observation that altered, abnormal mental states can lead to the damage and the smashing of property. It may be the drunk who is annoyed, the spouse who has been emotionally hurt (e.g. by a threat of abandonment), the person with schizophrenia who is responding to voices, or the paranoid person who is seeking secret revenge. Prewer (1959) studied 98 window smashers who passed through a prison reception. They were aged between 20 and 75 years, 73 had previous criminal records, 65 were drunk at the time of the offence. The window smashers proved to be a rich source of psychiatric cases—some 34% having an identifiable mental disorder or severe mental impairment, with diagnoses ranging from schizophrenia, dementia, and personality disorder. Prewer suggested a classification of motives for the window smashing, which included accident, attention or care seeking, theft, revenge, despair, frustration and excitement. Certainly, any doctor attached to a police station, court or prison, should take a particular interest in the criminal damage clients.

To put the matter in perspective, however, a few facts from the *NACRO Briefing* of July 1989 on *Vandalism* (NACRO, 1989b) are worth noting. In 1987 the police recorded 587 878 offences of criminal damage, but only 62 116 offenders were caught (i.e. the number of cautions plus the number of convictions). These were 90% males, and 55% were under 21 years old, 26% were between 10 and 16 years. Many offenders are believed to be below the age of criminal responsibility (i.e. under 10 years). 16 444 people were cautioned for criminal damage in 1987. Of those convicted, 5% of males and 4% of females were given custodial sentences. The bulk (52% overall) were fined or discharged (20%).

Arson

Arson has always been of special interest to psychiatrists. It is defined in Britain under the Criminal Damage Act 1971 as a reckless or intentional act to damage or destroy property by fire, or (the more serious charge) as reckless or intentional damage to property in which the life of another is recklessly or intentionally endangered. It is a triable either-way offence, and arson endangering life carries life imprisonment. Damage to one's own property is criminal only when there is a further intent, such as endangering life, or fraud.

Medical interest in the subject of fire-raising or pyromania goes back to the 19th century and continental writers in particular, e.g. Marc, Planer, Meckel (Lewis and Yarnell, 1951). Several of the 19th century authors apparently thought that fire-raising was especially a problem among retarded servant girls, but there is no evidence to support this idea.

Probably the most comprehensive survey of arson ever undertaken is that by Lewis and Yarnell (1951). They studied 2000 files from the National Board of Fire Underwriters in the USA, eliminated those cases with very sketchy data and thus examined 1145 cases of males 16 years or older, 220 younger males, 201 adult female fire-setters and 18 young girls. Of the total (1584), 100 were interviewed. From this material Lewis and Yarnell developed a classification of fire-setters which has been the basis of many subsequent classifications (e.g. Scott, 1978; Prins et al., 1985). They had four basic groups:

1. Profiteers;
2. Accidental fire-setters;
3. Occasional fire-setters;
4. Habitual fire-setters.

They divided the motives for fire-setting into six categories:

1. Reactions to society;
2. Vengeance against an employer;
3. Simple revenge;
4. Jealous rage;
5. An opportunity for heroism;
6. Perverted sexual pleasure.

A revised classification is proposed later (p. 591), after the general features of fire raising have been considered.

Fire statistics

Of the many fires attended by the fire brigade (383 000 in 1989) in Britain, few are actually recorded as arson (23 715). Arson is renowned for the difficulty of detection as it may consume the evidence. Subsequent prosecution and conviction are also difficult with only 24% of the offences notified as arson in 1989 being cleared up.

Fire brigades are required by law to report on each fire which they attend, and, like criminal statistics, the fire statistics are published annually. Details include the number of dead and injured (nearly a thousand people die annually by fire in England and Wales), the time of the call (the majority occur in the afternoon and evening), and the site of the fire (25% of fires occur in occupied dwellings, and some 60% outdoors and in derelict buildings). Arson is today an urban offence occurring most prominently in otherwise highly vandalized vicinities.

Regular investigations of fires only started during the Second World War, and earlier figures for the prevalence of arson are, therefore, highly doubtful. Figures in the UK are hampered by the separate investigative approaches of the interested parties: the police, the fire brigades and the fire insurance agencies. The American concept of the 'arson squad', in which investigation is unified, is an advance, but still leaves estimates of prevalence at 'anywhere between 10 and 75% of fires' (Perr, 1979). One source of confusion is due to a lack of consensus on what is 'normal', and what is 'vandalism by fire', or 'arson'.

Interest in fire is almost universal in childhood, starting at about 2–3 years of age, with a high level of understanding of its dangerousness by the age of 8 (Kafry, 1980). Among children in particular, there is a need for a clearer definition of what constitutes abnormal behaviour, since with fire, experiment may rapidly turn into disaster and firelighting by children may range from simply playing with matches or fires to malicious fire-setting (Kosky and Silburn, 1984).

In view of the uncertainty of the extent of arson amid the general fire statistics, it is probable that the characteristics of identified arsonists represent a biased sample and psychiatric patients who set fires constitute a separate group.

Personal characteristics and background

Those detected committing arson tend to be young. Thirty-three per cent of all those arrested or cautioned for arson are under 13; 77% of those cautioned or arrested are under 21; and 65% of those imprisoned are under 25. The mean age of arsonists in the psychiatric literature is older than these norms, but this older age of cases may simply reflect a low referral rate for children.

Most criminal acts are commoner in youth than in adult life, but there does seem some evidence that this is especially true of fire-setting. For example in England and Wales in 1979 (Home Office, 1980b), there were 52 people under the age of 17 brought to trial for arson out of a total of 732 children and young persons tried for serious offences. In statistical terms, this means that 7% of young persons brought to trial for serious offences were charged with arson compared with an arson charge rate for all ages brought to trial in Crown courts of only 1.7%. These figures will, of course, only give a very minimal estimate of the amount of childhood fire-setting in a community, not only because of the low detection rate, but also because, as surveys by child psychiatrists have shown (e.g. Yarnell, 1940; Vandersall and Wiener, 1970), young children tend to set fires which do not get out of hand, and are rarely brought to court; indeed, in these surveys the fire-setting is often not even a presenting symptom. In 1979 only one boy in the

10–14 age group was tried for arson and he was acquitted; however, this was out of only 11 youngsters brought before the Crown courts.

Female arsonists are infrequent in psychiatric cohorts, but the statistics may be biased through underprosecution of women. Tennent et al. (1971), for example, found that only 46% of female arsonists in special hospitals had been prosecuted for the offence. The only adult psychiatric inpatient study of fire-setting behaviour (Geller and Bertsch, 1985) showed an equal sex incidence.

For children, there seems to be a low prevalence of female fire-setters. Yarnell (1940) found only 2 out of 60 (3%) when their general prevalence in the clinic was 35%, whilst Vandersall and Wiener (1970) had only 1 out of their 20 (5%), and she was mentally retarded. This low female prevalence amongst juvenile fire-setters is supported to some extent by the criminal statistics for England and Wales. In 1979, only one girl in the 10–17 age group was tried for arson (2%), whereas girls form 10% overall of the juveniles going through Crown courts (Home Office, 1980b), but this difference does not quite reach significance.

One aspect of the symbolism of fire commonly used in interpreting fire-setting has been its god-like power, either as an unconscious quest for a missing authority figure such as a parent, or a rebellion against one. In this respect, the childhood background of fire-setters seen by psychiatrists is noted for deprivation, but there is as yet no evidence that fire-setters are more deprived than any other types of juvenile delinquents.

Mental retardation, alcohol and mental illness

It is sometimes held that there is an association between arson and mental retardation. There is no doubt that fire-setting by a mentally retarded person may make institutional care a necessity, and within institutions a very great danger; it is, in addition, a poor prognostic factor (O'Gorman, 1979). There are, however, doubts as to whether the mentally retarded commit arson at a rate greater than their overall prevalence in the general population. Among recent studies of child cohorts, it is poor school performance rather than a lack of intelligence that appears significant.

There has been a long-known association of arson with alcohol, especially in the context of personality disorder (Koson and Dvoskin, 1982); the tendency is as great among females as among males (Harmon et al., 1985). Kammerer et al. (1967) noted that arson can be associated with any of the states seen in alcohol abuse: acute intoxication, chronic alcoholism, hallucinosis and dementia.

Drinking is common among those who die by fire in their own homes; a survey of victims in Glasgow found that 25% had blood levels over 150 mg/100 ml at the time of death, a level which at the least would severely inhibit their chances of escaping (Anderson et al., 1981).

Arsonists on the whole are probably not mentally ill; only about 2 per 100 convicted arsonists receive a hospital order each year in England and Wales and, of those arrested for arson, about 10% are mentally ill (Molnar et al., 1984). However, there is a disproportionate percentage receiving hospital orders (7%) in relation to the rarity of the offence, and arsonists constitute an eighth of all restriction order patients in England and Wales. The major categories of mental disorder found in most studies are schizophrenia, mental retardation, and personality disorder (*see below*).

A factor of concern emerging in recent studies (Koson and Dvoskin, 1982; Molnar et al., 1984) is the failure of psychiatric services to deliver health care to mentally disordered arsonists who 'had been involved with the agencies just prior to their act of fire-setting and either were rejected or lost to follow-up' (Koson and Dvoskin 1982).

Prognosis

Soothill and Pope (1973) conducted a 20-year follow-up of the 67 people convicted of arson in 1951 on whom they could get complete information (15 could not be traced). Only three men were reconvicted of arson by the end of 1971, 32 (48%) were not reconvicted of a serious offence at all. All three of the reoffenders seemed to be solitary offenders with problems of social adjustment. The first was a recidivist thief who set fire to a hay stack. Some years later he set a few fires in huts on a building site and was sent to hospital on a hospital order as suffering from schizophrenia. The second set fire to stacks of straw as a farm worker. The prison doctor described him as a 'pyromaniac' and one who got a 'deep feeling of satisfaction' when he lit fires. He was reconvicted some years later for three further cases of arson. The third man was also convicted of setting fires to a haystack, later fires included firing a Dutch barn and setting fire to a house. He had lots of shoplifting convictions as well and was a homeless vagrant who had spent time in a mental hospital.

Group fire-setters are thought to show less severe psychopathology, and to have a better prognosis for recidivism (Molnar et al., 1984).

Proposed classification

Profitable arson. The destruction of one's own property in order to claim, for example, the insurance money, or to be rehoused, is a well-established type of fraudulent activity and one which fire departments and insurers look out for. Under the heading of profitable arson, we can also place the arson which is designed to destroy evidence of other crimes, perhaps a murdered body, perhaps evidence of theft, or accounts books which reveal a fraud. We might also place in this category the protection gang fire, i.e. the fire set by a gang of extortionists when the owner of a property does not pay the dues demanded from him.

Political arson.   Perhaps the best-known political arsonist is Guy Fawkes and the tradition of catholic v. protestant political arson still exists in Northern Ireland. Political bombing can also be included here; bombing is a closely related activity to firesetting and, indeed, it does often cause serious fire. Urban rioting may lead to fires, some accidental, some set by petrol bombs, others set by other means. Very little of this activity has direct relevance for psychiatry.

Accidental fire-setting.   By definition, a truly accidental fire cannot be arson, or any crime at all, but the line between 'accident' and 'recklessness' is very difficult to draw. A skid row alcoholic with some evidence of brain damage found himself a 'skip' or squat for the night in a derelict warehouse. He felt cold, so he put a match to some cardboard refuse lying about. This set light to the whole building nearly killing one or two other down-and-outs taking refuge in the same building. He was convicted of arson and sentenced to life imprisonment. Nevertheless, in clinical terms this would probably best be regarded as an accidental fire. Perhaps childish pranks which get out of hand can also be included here, e.g. November bonfires that spread to woods or buildings.

Revenge fire-setting.   Lewis and Yarnell (1951) divided their revenge category into the subcategories of revenge against society in general (the boy who doesn't like school, so burns it down, the rioter who hates the police, so he fires the police station), revenge against employers (the disgruntled, sacked man who burns down his old bosses' premises), and jealous revenge usually in a sexual context.

A good deal of revenge fire-setting can be 'understood' if the individual's feelings and perceptions of his world are understood. Perhaps some of the easiest cases for courts to comprehend are the cases of straightforward sexual jealousy; so a man who set fire to his girlfriend's wardrobe with her treasured collection of clothes because she had jilted him, received the relatively light sentence of 2 years' imprisonment, even though the house was occupied at the time of the fire and was badly damaged. However, to regard fire-setting as a 'normal' consequence of jealousy would be mistaken indeed, and whenever possible much greater elaboration of the fire-setter's psychopathology is desirable. For example, a woman was referred for assessment after setting fire to the curtains in her own home, thus causing a lot of damage. This was in response to her husband having an affair with another woman and threatening to leave her. The reason for the fire became a little clearer when their mutual feelings about the house were revealed; he cherished it, she didn't. It was further revealed that their only child was asleep in bed upstairs at the time of the fire, was seriously endangered and had to be rescued by the husband. Tentative exploration of the woman's feelings suggested that either she was identifying the child with the husband, and was thus murdering him vicariously or, more likely, was putting him through a primitive ordeal, in that he had to rescue his beloved child to prove himself worthy of her and perhaps life itself.

The revenge fire-setter is probably best regarded as a special type of violent individual. Sometimes the vengeful fire-setter chooses fire as his weapon for its instrumental or convenience value and has no other attachment to fire itself. A patient who exhibited rage attacks when insulted or emotionally hurt illustrates the point. He was a married man with a good work record and an ability to make and keep friends. He suffered from some inferiority feelings which he covered with a macho style of life and heavy drinking. On several occasions when he had been drunk, he reacted to insults by highly excessive violence, e.g. when drunk in the street one night he responded to abuse from an upstairs window by climbing a drainpipe, forcing his way into the startled abuser's window and beating him up quite savagely. One day in his favourite pub, in front of his friends, he was called a 'queer' by a brazen newcomer. He immediately challenged the man, fought him, but lost. He then went back to his car, pulled out a spare can of petrol, spread some on the pub floor, threw a match into it, ran out and locked the door.

Fire-setting for pleasure and excitement.   Fire-setting for pleasure can be conveniently further divided into three subcategories (a) hero fire-setters; (2) fire-bugs and (3) erotic fire-setters.

1. *Hero fire-setters.*   Fire has a fundamental fascination for most people— there is drama and excitement in a building on fire, the fire engines themselves create a thrill, and quite a lot of people have fantasies about rescuing or being rescued from a fire. Some people, usually men, take a special interest in fires, collect pieces of fire fighting equipment, log the activities of the fire brigade, join the fire brigade, or volunteer as fire officer at work. Much of this is healthy sublimation but, for some people, such things do not sufficiently satisfy the need for fiery excitement and they, therefore, set extra fires to increase their own involvement in their favourite activity. A prisoner had been commended for bravery in fires no less than five times. He was a fire officer at his factory, and it took the firm a long time to work out that, since his appointment, the prevalence of fires had increased sharply and that he was always the first on the scene, saving lives and putting out the fire. He was eventually convicted of over 20 episodes of arson, and that was probably an underestimate. Fire chiefs and factory safety officers need to be constantly on the lookout for excessive zeal in members of their staff. Fire investigators should always take note of individuals who turn up to help the brigade especially if this happens more than once. Lewis and Yarnell (1951) found 51 cases of volunteer firemen who set fires.

2. *Fire-bugs.*   Fire-bugs are individuals (usually male) who derive intense satisfaction or relief from setting fires. A good description is given by Scott (1978):

He suffers from periods of mounting tension, becoming increasingly restless and edgy, and then suddenly his actions are out of control having been triggered off, for example by a quarrel at home or dismissal from work. The fire-bug has learnt that starting a blaze releases tension and so may begin a fire-setting spree. Some fire-bugs may find only one blaze sufficient to discharge tension while others start many fires within a short period. The fires are usually unplanned and lit in hallways, staircases, and passages where the general public have access . . . the fire-bug is . . . likely to thrust a match into a brimming dustbin and rush away to start others elsewhere in the neighbourhood, creating chaos and confusion. After such acts he may return home feeling calm.

The fire-bug can be particularly dangerous for he may resort to arson under stresses of all sorts.

It is tempting to link the fire-setting in these patients to their only too evident sexual problems, but they almost invariably have personality disorders with a galaxy of difficulties, especially interpersonal problems.

3. *Erotic fire-setters.*   There are constant allusions in the psychiatric litera-ture to the sexuality of fire, fire-setting, and fire fighting. Attention is drawn to the use of thermal words for descriptions of eroticism, e.g. hot pants, fiery passion, burning with desire. Attention is also drawn to the male penis being like a hosepipe. No doubt some of these views derive from direct clinical experience, but much must also be attributed to Freud. In *Civilisa-tion and its Discontents* he suggested that in man's struggle to gain power over the tyranny of nature, his acquisition of power over fire was quite exceptional:

> It is as if primitive man had had the impulse when he came into contact with fire, to gratify an infantile pleasure in respect of it and put it out with a stream of urine. The legends that we possess leave no doubt that flames shooting upwards like tongues were originally felt to have a phallic sense. Putting out fire by urinating . . . therefore represents a sexual act with a man, an enjoyment of masculine potency in homosexual rivalry. . . . It is remarkable how regularly analytic findings testify to the close connection between the ideas of ambition, fire and urethral eroticism (Freud, 1929).

Credence for these theories comes from a small, but interesting, group of men who do indeed describe erotic feelings in association with fire—some have erotic fiery dreams, others have what amounts to a fire fetish in that they need to fantasize fire to be potent, and they will masturbate over a conflagration. However, such men are, rare and are given a disproportionate degree of attention in the literature.

It is just possible that fire-setters as a group have more than their fair share of sexual difficulties. In their sample of Grendon (non-psychotic) prisoners who had set fires, Hurley and Monahan (1969) found that 54% showed some evidence of sexual maladjustment (homosexuality, transves-tism, exhibitionism, masturbating at fires (60%) etc); but they point out this may be no higher than in other groups of offenders with personality disorders. It is still an open question whether fire-setting is especially related to sexual problems or whether any relationship is via the underlying personality disorder which is usually present.

Sexual difficulties may also play a part in the genesis of fire-setting by women. Macdonald (1977) provided the only examples currently available in the literature of clearly sexually related female arson. One girl was raped in the rear seat of a car and she burned a number of cars by setting fires in the rear seats. Another had a boyfriend who served as a volunteer fireman, and she had a recurrent erotic dream of his masturbating over her. She saw his hose as an ejaculating penis and set fires in deserted buildings so she could watch him at work.

Psychotic and organic fire-setters. In the selected Lewis and Yarnell (1951) sample of fire-setters, by far the largest diagnostic category of mental disorder was schizophrenia. The only other prominent group was senile psychosis among the women. Other diagnoses also represented were alcoholic psychosis, epilepsy, encephalitis, depression and GPI. Another series of arsonists came from Poland (Fleszar-Szumigajowa, 1969); in this study, 311 referred cases of arson were examined at the Institute of Psychoneurology in Pruszkow over the 10-year period 1953–62. The Polish clinic had similar causes to the American study, the top five categories being: schizophrenia, mental deficiency, personality disorder, alcoholism and organic psychoses.

The Polish paper also analysed motives. Revenge and hatred were the commonest motivation, and were particularly associated with personality disorders. The need for heroism was uncommon as were fire bugs and erotic firesetters. Some of the fires were accidental (especially among the schizophrenic patients). A few were suicide attempts and others in response to persecutory ideas.

Suicide by fire. Self-immolation by fire as a sign of total detachment from the world before the attainment of Nirvana has long been a part of the tradition of Buddhist monks. Suicide by fire has also been a part of the cultural tradition in the East (in the form of suttee) for centuries and has been noted in Israel (Modan et al., 1970) and in Cuba (Davis, 1962) in modern times.

Suicide by fire became prominent in France following the widely publicized self-immolations of Buddhist monks in Saigon in 1963 as political protests against the Diem government, and later the self-immolation of Jan Palach as a political protest against the Russian invasion of Czechoslovakia in 1969 (Bourgeois, 1969). A similar 'epidemic' in Britain was carefully recorded by Ashton and Donnan (1981), following a political or quasi-religious suicide which was highly publicized. In the USA, Andreasen and Noyes's (1975) study in a burns unit had indicated suicidal intentions in 2% of patients with a very wide range of psychopathology, none of whom had any political motivation. It is probable that this method of suicide is too little suspected.

A paper on hospital inpatient suicides by fire (Jacobson et al., 1985) also indicated that although unusual, it is not by any means rare among suicidal patients. Death by fire is a known hazard in an institution. It may be difficult to know whether, say, a schizophrenic patient who dies in a self-induced fire was responding to suicidal ideas or has accidentally suffered from outwardly directed aggression such as the burning of a hated object. Some patients may also try to scare the staff by setting a fire which then overwhelms them. Topp (1973) described such an incident in an English borstal when three lads barricaded themselves in their cell as part of a more general protest against conditions. When their protest produced no immediate results, they threatened to set a fire and later did so. As the door was barricaded, it took staff some minutes to smash it down during which time all three were so badly burnt that they all subsequently died.

Child fire-setters.   In her important study of 60 children attending the Bellevue Hospital in New York, Yarnell (1940) divided her cases into children aged 6–8 years and older adolescents. The little children were usually referred for other antisocial behaviour such as stealing and truancy, most of the fires they set were at home and the fire-setting was coupled with intense anxiety, including anxiety about the fire. Their fantasies included aggression, anxiety and self-punishment and often a desire to burn a member of the family who either withheld love or became a serious rival for parental love. Most of the fires were easily controlled. All the children showed some evidence of sexual conflicts, but enuresis was infrequent and, unlike some of the mythology about arson would suggest, was not specifically associated with the fire-setting. Adolescents showed a number of similarities, but enjoyed their fire-setting much more, often doing it away from home, sometimes in pairs, deriving excitement from the flames and the fire engines.

Most of these features were confirmed by Vandersall and Wiener (1970). They drew attention to the ineffective role played by the father of the 20 children in their sample. In 10 cases the father was totally absent. The mothers were found wanting in being distant, rejecting or overprotective. These authors also confirmed the relative unimportance and non-specificity of enuresis as a symptom in fire-setting children. Unlike Yarnell they could not find any material which was directly suggestive of sexual conflicts.

> Their most demonstrable difficulty seemed more centred about issues of aggression and impulse control. A sense of exclusion, inadequacy and loneliness was conveyed by many of the boys, originating from a real or perceived lack of dependency gratification and low self-esteem.

Management and treatment

As with all psychiatric patients, good management of fire-setters is dependent upon an accurate diagnosis and formulation. It is not enough just to know which category a particular fire-setter comes into, although that is a good start. It is also important to understand as far as possible why a particular individual chose fire as a weapon and to know something of his fantasy life. Following that, treatment is along straightforward lines.

Political protests would seem to have nothing to do with psychiatry, but any so-called political protester who sets fire is worthy of a psychiatric examination. Fire-raising may be a primary problem with the political protest being used as the social guise to perpetrate it. Similarly, arson for profit, if that is what it really is, has nothing to do with psychiatry. However, an alcoholic, a patient with dementia, or confused individual who sets fires by accident should be regarded as a serious nursing problem and cared for within as structured a framework as possible. Sometimes such individuals are sent to prison for long periods of time, and that is not appropriate. However, a court may have no option unless a medical disposal, e.g. a hospital bed in a relatively secure setting, is forthcoming.

The problem is that hospitals, just like all other institutions, are very afraid of arsonists. It is hardly surprising that an old people's home will wish to rid itself of, say, a confused old lady who keeps lighting fires in her waste paper bin. Even though the diagnosis of her brain syndrome may be clear, a hospital will not relish her admission either, because she will require constant supervision and will create continuous anxiety about the safety of other patients. Such a patient should definitely not be admitted unless adequate supervision can be provided. On the other hand, it is the responsibility of public hospitals to make provision for the problems that actually present rather than the ones staff hope will present and any district psychiatric service *should* be able to care for such a patient.

Many more problems will be presented by the intelligent fire-bug who schemes to get opportunities to set fires and who is highly secretive in his activities. Most ordinary psychiatric hospitals decline to admit such patients and most of them go instead to prison. It should be possible for a regional security unit to nurse such an individual, at least on a short to medium-term basis, although a few of these patients are often best managed, particularly on a long-term basis, in special hospitals. In a security setting, the nurses will ensure that they know the whereabouts of the patient at all times, and they will ensure he has no access to fire-setting materials such as matches unless they are used under supervision. Within such a restrictive context, it will be important to try and give the patient as much pleasure as possible and to offer appropriate treatments, such as behavioural treatment, psychotherapy and anxiolytic drugs.

Outside hospital, the treatments available to the fire-bug are extremely limited. Sometimes adjustment of mood or level of anxiety by antidepressant or tranquillizing drugs is helpful. This may be especially true for the patient who is setting fires to relieve tension. Behavioural treatments may also be worth a try, although it must be noted that, as yet, there are no studies reporting successful outcome. We have tried such techniques as flooding in imagination, flooding in reality (48 hours stoking a bonfire), relaxation, stimulus avoidance in occasional patients, all without much success. Psychotherapy is traditionally the treatment of choice for the fire-bug; the sessions are likely to be rich in fantasy material, including sexual feelings if the patient is of average intelligence or above. However, some patients are of limited intelligence and find it difficult to be other than concrete. There are no data suggesting that psychotherapy is effective in controlling the urges to set fires, even though it seems likely that other elements of personality disturbance may improve.

It may be that, occasionally, where there is clear evidence that the fire-raising is erotic, a male patient may benefit from an anti-androgen such as cyproterone acetate. Experience gives no cause for great optimism. One of us treated a fire-bug who had a considerable number of personality problems, including marked interpersonal difficulties, severe mood swings, both high and low, and sexual difficulties. His fire-setting seemed to be erotic in nature as he always used fire in his sexual fantasies. A long period of psychotherapy brought little or no benefit, mood stabilizing drugs, including lithium, did not help either and so eventually he was offered antilibidinol injections. These he accepted with some benefit, his libido fell to zero, thus simplifying his life and producing a marked reduction in tension. His urges to set fires were unaffected and he had to be sent to a special hospital for long-term treatment.

The most satisfying group of arsonists to treat are probably those in which the fire-setting is secondary to a fluctuating disorder, e.g. depression or schizophrenia. The treatment in these cases is the treatment of the underlying condition plus the special management during the acute stage and the careful observation during follow-up which the fire-setting propensity deserves. Special attention should also be given in psychotherapy to the dynamics and other factors leading to fire as a choice of weapon or means of expression.

15
Female Offenders

Edited and written by
P. T. d'Orbán

with contributions from

Anthony Maden, Pamela J. Taylor

Women form only a small proportion of offenders and female crime remained a relatively neglected topic until recently. The rapid expansion of women's studies in the 1970s led to a growth of interest in female offenders and an enormous increase in the literature on female crime. The result has been a recognition that female offenders are of exceptional criminological and psychiatric interest. The reasons for their relative rarity are in themselves a fertile field for research. This chapter will review some of the gender differences in crime and examine some specific issues concerning psychiatric aspects of female crime.

Sex Differences in Crime

One of the most striking features of crime is that it is overwhelmingly a male activity. In all societies and throughout history women have been responsible for only a small proportion of recorded crime. The comparative figures for England and Wales can be calculated from the annual criminal statistics published by the Home Office. In 1986, of offenders found guilty or cautioned for indictable offences, 17% were women, and for summary offences (excluding motoring offences) women's share was 24% (Home Office, 1987b). Thus the male:female ratio was approximately 5:1 for indictable offences and approximately 3:1 for summary offences. A better estimate of the numerical differences is the number of convictions and cautions for indictable offences per 100 000 population; here the male:female ratio in 1986 was just over 5:1.

Although this male preponderance is a constant feature of recorded crime, the proportion of female offenders is subject to considerable variation over time. In the early 19th century in England, women comprised one-third of those convicted of crime, and in France, Germany and the Scandinavian countries between one-quarter and one-fifth of offenders were women (Hurwitz and Christiansen, 1983). The proportion of female offenders gradually declined during this century, partly due to the decriminalization of some offences, such as prostitution. The decline was particularly marked after the Second World War. In England between 1950 and 1969, women's participation in indictable offences remained fairly constant at around 13% of the total (d'Orbán, 1971). The increase to present levels occurred during the early 1970s, but in the past decade (1977–86) the proportion of female indictable offences has again stabilized at 17–18% of the total. By contrast, in the case of summary (other than motoring) offences there has been a doubling in the proportion of women, from 12% in 1977 to 24% in 1986.

The Offences of Women

There is a large variation in the male:female ratio for different types of offences (Home Office, 1987d). At one end of the scale are offences which by definition can only be committed by women (infanticide and soliciting). There are others in which women form a majority of offenders; these are mostly offences related to children (concealment of birth, cruelty to or neglect of children, or offences against the Education Act by failure to send children to school). Thirdly, there are a group of offences to which women make a substantial contribution; examples are child abduction and theft from shops. At the other end of the scale are offences which are rarely committed by women, for example sexual offences (O'Connor, 1987).

The broad categories into which indictable offences are classified in criminal statistics are differently distributed among male and female offenders (Home Office, 1987b). In 1986, 77% of female convictions for indictable offences were for theft and handling stolen goods, 7% for fraud and forgery and 6% for violence against the person. Sex offences and robbery each accounted for less than 0.5%. By contrast, the predominant indictable offences committed by men were theft (50%), burglary (16%) and violence against the person (11%). The male:female ratio for the various groups of indictable offences was, in decreasing order, 82:1 for sex offences, 25.5:1 for burglary, 21:1 for robbery, 12:1 for criminal damage, approximately 9:1 for violence against the person, just over 7:1 for drug offences, 3.5:1 for fraud and forgery and just over 3:1 for theft and handling stolen goods. Since the early 1970s these ratios have shown little change. What emerges from these comparisons is that sex offences, property crimes involving an element of planning or aggression, and crimes of violence are predominantly a male province, whereas women tend to commit relatively more theft or fraud although even in these fields men outnumber them by more than 3 to 1. The few offences in which women form an absolute majority are offences related to child-rearing or to sexual mores.

Age Differences between Male and Female Offending

The peak incidence of recorded crime in both sexes occurs at the age of 15. In males, there is a swift decline after the age of 30, but in women the decline is slower; thus the male:female ratio for offending varies with age. Based on the number per 100 000 population convicted or cautioned in 1986, the ratio is highest at the age of 18 (6.7) and then gradually declines to 2.7 in those aged 60 or over (Home Office, 1987b). Thus a relatively larger proportion of women participate in crime in the older age groups. In 1986, 11.5% of all women convicted or cautioned for indictable offences were aged 50 years or over compared with 5.5% of men. A similar trend was noted earlier by Mannheim (1965) in England and by Pollak (1950) in the USA. Gibbens and Ahrenfeldt (1966) found that in the Netherlands there was a similar 'second peak' of arrests of women aged 45–55, and they suggested that these women were mostly shoplifters or women who took to crime in order to support their children. The 'second peak' in female crime—especially shoplifting—was popularly linked with the menopause, but a study of shoplifters in Holloway Prison found no evidence to substantiate this (Gibbens and Prince, 1962). Clinical experience suggests that many of these latecomers to crime are socially isolated individuals with broken marriages who often suffer from depression and have drinking problems (d'Orbán, 1971). Middle-aged women who commit crime are of special psychiatric interest as the prevalence of psychiatric disorder in women prisoners increases with age (Gibbens, Goodman et al., 1971a). In the USA, Daniel et al. (1981) found that female offenders in mid-life (aged 40 to 54) were a specially vulnerable group with an increased prevalence of medical and psychiatric disorder. Compared with young adult offenders, they were found to have significantly more affective illness and alcoholism but fewer previous convictions. None of the women in the mid-life group was diagnosed as having antisocial personality disorder, whereas this was the most frequent diagnosis in the younger age group. Thus the older women are a relatively distinct group of first-time offenders who often require medical or psychiatric help, particularly for depression and alcoholism. Elderly male offenders also have increased rates of alcoholism and affective illness, but they are usually recidivists (Taylor and Parrott, 1988).

In Britain, two unusual groups of mid-life female offenders have been described. Chronic drunkenness offenders (with a mean age of 54) were found to have high rates of physical illness related to their life-style (accident injuries and cervical carcinoma) as well as suffering from alcohol dependence (d'Orbán, 1969). Another group are women in prison for contempt of court (mean age 41 years); a high proportion of them suffer from paranoid disorders (d'Orbán, 1985a).

Accounting for Sex Differences in Crime

The quantitative differences that are such a marked feature of criminal statistics apply to crime that is detected and recorded. One possible explanation that has been advanced for the male preponderance is that female crimes remain relatively hidden and undetected. Thus Pollak (1950) argued that the discrepancy between the sexes is more apparent than real, and that the lower female crime rate is largely due to the masked character of female crime. He suggested that women commit crimes that have a low rate of detection (e.g., shoplifting or domestic theft) and that even when detected, crimes tend to remain unreported (e.g., theft by prostitutes or domestic violence). The relatively recent recognition of non-accidental injury to children tends to support this argument. However, there must also be a similar area of male behaviour, particularly in the field of family violence, which remains undetected or unreported.

An attempt to elucidate this iceberg phenomenon and explore the unreported aspects of criminality has been made through self-report delinquency studies and through experimental observation of behaviour. The results of both these approaches suggest that, although the male:female ratio for criminal behaviour is much closer than in recorded crime, there is still a male preponderance. These studies also suggest that the pattern of delinquency in boys and girls is broadly similar, although boys are more involved in serious offences (Campbell, 1981; Morris, 1987).

Given that the differences in criminality between the sexes constitute a valid finding, two broad categories of explanatory theories have been proposed to account for the differences; one group seeks to attribute them to innate psychobiological differences, while the other points to a variety of social influences that affect men and women differently. These varying approaches to the problem need not be mutually exclusive; in view of the complex aetiology of criminal behaviour, it would be surprising if any single explanatory theory would be found adequate. As Walker (1977) noted, the quest for a general theory which will account for all instances of crime 'makes no more sense than would a search for a general theory of disease'.

The various theories of female criminality have been reviewed by d'Orbán (1971), Smart (1976) and Morris (1987). Modern psychobiological theories are concerned with the biological substrate of aggression, which is relevant to both the quantitative and the qualitative aspects of gender differences in criminal behaviour. Maccoby and Jacklin (1980) in their review of psychological sex differences argued that the greater aggressivity of men has a biological foundation. The sex differences are present from early childhood, are applicable across cultures and also to subhuman primates, and prenatal androgens (and in adult life circulating testosterone levels) affect aggressivity. However, while there is evidence to link aggression with hormonal influences, the actual mechanisms are extraordinarily complex. Reviewing the neurochemistry and neuroendocrinology of sexual aggression, Prentky (1985) concluded that the role of androgens in human aggression is neither direct nor obvious. Cognitive and environmental factors modify the endogenous ones, and social learning has a powerful effect on the manner in which individuals cope with and react to the emotional experiences associated with hormonal changes.

Sociological explanations of female criminality are equally complex and varied, but tend to focus on women's role and position in society. The fact that female participation in crime shows considerable variation across different cultures and at different points in time suggests that the female crime rate (like that of males) is sensitive to social change. Thus, even if biological factors do play a role, the somewhat simplistic biological determinism, which (according to Morris, 1987) still characterizes interpretations of female crime, is not an adequate or appropriate stance.

Recent Trends and the Women's Movement

During the 1960s in the USA, and in England during the 1970s, there was some increase in women's participation in crime. As a result much alarm was expressed about a 'new breed' of female criminal; in particular, it was thought that there had been an increase in offences of violence among young women and the changes were attributed to the influence of the feminist movement. In the USA, however, on the basis of FBI Uniform Crime Reports for 1966–76, Bowker (1978) found that, although the female contribution to arrests had increased from 12 to 16%, this was due to women committing more property offences, whereas the proportion of violent offenders remained stable. In England too, Morris (1987) found that there has been a proportionately greater increase in female than in male crime during the past 20 years, and that the greatest increase has occurred among girls aged 17–21. However, percentage increases can be misleading as the actual numerical increase has been small. Box and Hale (1983) devised various measures of female emancipation, but were unable to find any statistical relationship between these measures and the female crime rate during the period 1951–79. Instead, they found that female conviction rates were related to female unemployment and to changes in law enforcement practice. Reviewing the influence of feminism on the growth of female crime, Heidensohn (1985) concluded:

> The central hypothesis has been extensively explored and tested, to no final conclusive results—although it has been refuted to some degree.

Both Heidensohn and Morris emphasized that women's role in the economic sphere and in employment has changed relatively little. The majority of women continue to be employed in unskilled work, and there has been relatively little change in traditional social expectations. The Women's Movement has to a large extent been a middle-class phenomenon and has had little impact on working-class women, who constitute the great majority of women who come into conflict with the law.

A related argument has attempted to link the degree of female emancipation in different countries with the level of female crime, suggesting that changes in the social role and status of women leads to their increased participation in crime (Pollak, 1950; Gibbens and Ahrenfeldt, 1966; Adler, 1977). Differences in the sex ratio of crime are also found within a single country among people of different cultural backgrounds; for example, conduct disorders show a lower sex ratio in children of West Indian background in London than in children from Asian or Cypriot families, where female crime is very uncommon (Ouston, 1984). The argument, however, remains unresolved. While at the extreme end of the spectrum, in societies where there are rigid cultural and religious restraints on women, it may be argued that their opportunity to participate in crime is consequently also restricted, the interpretation and comparison of criminal statistics from different countries requires great caution (Morris, 1987). Simon (1975) found that there was little relationship between female crime and the level of economic development in different countries. Paradoxically, taking a long-term view Hurwitz and Christiansen (1983) pointed out that the emancipation of women in various countries over the past 100 years has been accompanied by a *fall* in the female crime rate.

Sex Differences in Juvenile Delinquency

The large discrepancy in recorded crime rates between the sexes is evident also among juveniles. Farrington (1981) calculated that 11.7% of boys can expect to be convicted before their 17th birthday, compared with 2.1% of girls. In their review of gender differences in juvenile delinquency Cowie et al. (1968) found that comparative studies consistently demonstrate that girl delinquents deviate more from social and psychological norms than their male counterparts. Delinquent girls were found to have a higher incidence of broken homes, illegitimacy, parental neglect, disturbed family relationships and psychiatric illness. More recent studies of non-institutionalized samples of delinquents show many similarities in the behaviour patterns and family background of delinquent boys and girls. Nevertheless, there is a consistent trend for boys to be more vulnerable than girls to developing conduct disorder in response to family stress and discord (Rutter and Giller, 1983). As with adult crime, both biological and sociological theories have been advanced as explanations for these differences. Biological theories suggest that girls are constitutionally less prone to delinquency than boys, and that they therefore only become delinquent when their relatively greater resilience is overwhelmed by adverse life events, environmental influences or increased personal vulnerability due to psychiatric disorder. However, adoption studies have failed to find any significant sex difference in genetic predictors of delinquency (Cadoret and Cain, 1980). Instead, a variety of sociological theories of delinquency (for example social control, social learning and subcultural approaches) seek to find aetiological factors which affect boys and girls differently.

The Premenstrual Syndrome and Crime

The view that female crime (particularly shoplifting and violence) is associated with menstruation was widely held in the 19th century (Pollak, 1950). Menstrual problems were at times successfully used as a defence to crimes of murder or theft (Smith, 1981). Since the description of the premenstrual syndrome by Frank (1931), a number of studies have investigated the relationship between phases of the menstrual cycle and the behaviour of female offenders. Some studies focused on aggressive behaviour in penal institutions (Dalton, 1961; Ellis and Austin, 1971) or in a special hospital (Hands et al., 1974) and found a significant correlation with the premenstrual or early menstrual phases of the cycle. Other studies have been concerned with the relationship between criminal offences and the menstrual cycle. Morton et al. (1953) found that 62% of women imprisoned for crimes of violence committed their crime during the premenstrual week. Dalton (1961) studied 156 women in Holloway prison convicted of theft, soliciting and drunkenness offences and found that nearly half had offended during the premenstrual or menstrual phases. She suggested that women with premenstrual symptoms are especially liable to commit crime during the paramenstruum (the first 4 and the last 4 days of the menstrual cycle) and that premenstrual tension is an important factor in female crime, especially theft. Later, she suggested a link with baby battering (Dalton, 1975) and described three cases in which women successfully pleaded diminished responsibility or mitigation to various offences on the grounds of the premenstrual syndrome (Dalton, 1980).

Dalton's findings were not confirmed by Epps (1962) who found no relationship between the offence and any phase of the menstrual cycle in shoplifters in Holloway prison; this applied also to the small proportion (13.5%) of women who had premenstrual symptoms. Other studies, although confirming an association between behavioural disturbance and the menstrual cycle, failed to find any relationship to premenstrual symptoms. Thus Ellis and Austin (1971) in their carefully designed prospective study of verbal and physical aggression in a North Carolina penal institution found that aggression correlated with the premenstrual and early menstrual phases. However, they found no relationship between aggression and feelings of premenstrual irritability. Similarly, d'Orbán and Dalton (1980) in a study of 50 women charged with impulsive offences of violence against persons or property found that, although a significant excess of offences occurred on the 28th and the first days of the cycle, a subgroup of women who complained of premenstrual symptoms did *not* show any significant tendency to commit offences during the paramenstruum. Only 2 of the 50 women were subjectively aware of a possible connection between their menstrual cycle and their aggressive behaviour. Thus, mood disturbance or other premenstrual symptoms are not diagnostically helpful in identifying women who are prone to commit offences in the paramenstruum; instead, cyclically recurrent behavioural disturbances should be looked for.

Although many studies in this field have serious methodological flaws (Parlee, 1973; Clare, 1983), there is considerable evidence of an association between behavioural disturbance, including impulsive criminal behaviour, and the paramenstruum. This does not imply that women in general are more likely to commit crime during their paramenstruum; the association may apply only to a vulnerable group of women who are prone to impulsive behaviour and in whom premenstrual disorder acts as a triggering factor rather than as a cause of their disturbance. The evidence also suggests that offences are associated with behavioural rather than affective symptoms of the premenstrual syndrome, and the role of premenstrual tension, depression or irritability as precipitants of female crime has been overemphasized in the past.

A variety of factors have been proposed as explanations for the correlation between crime and the menstrual cycle. They include social and psychological factors such as social learning, the influence of expectations and beliefs about menstruation, and the effects of psychological stress which may delay menstruation or precipitate its onset. Alternatively, a variety of hormonal factors have been proposed, but the aetiology of the syndrome remains uncertain and there are no consistent hormonal or biochemical abnormalities; the diagnosis has to be made on clinical grounds. This may be particularly difficult in patients charged with a criminal offence, as their history is open to falsification, whether deliberately or by suggestion. Even if a diagnosis of premenstrual syndrome is made, there can be great difficulty in attributing offence behaviour to it; such single-cause explanations are naive and it would seem more appropriate to regard the syndrome as triggering or exacerbating pre-existing psychological problems. In the forensic context, confusion often arises between premenstrual syndrome and psychiatric disorder. Clare (1983) has shown that there is a significant and positive association between them. Physicians and lawyers sometimes seize on premenstrual complaints as a sole 'explanation' of behaviour and ignore the associated social and psychiatric problems.

The Premenstrual Syndrome as a Defence

In England, the courts have accepted the premenstrual syndrome in mitigation in the same way as they accept other factors related to social or psychological stress, or physical or mental illness. The syndrome has also been successfully used in three murder cases as a basis for a diminished responsibility defence under Section 2 of the Homicide Act 1957. Dalton, a strong proponent of the progesterone deficiency theory of the syndrome, gave evidence in all three cases, which created considerable controversy. The most recent case was that of an 18-year-old girl who was convicted of the murder of her mother and sentenced to life imprisonment, despite undisputed medical evidence of diminished responsibility on the grounds of depression. On appeal, further medical evidence was given to support the original plea of diminished responsibility, including an additional opinion that she suffered from premenstrual syndrome. The appeal succeeded and she was put on probation with a condition of medical treatment (d'Orbán and O'Connor, 1989; Reynolds, 1991). Although legally the premenstrual syndrome has been accepted by the courts as a 'disease of the mind' (Brahams, 1981; d'Orbán, 1983), from the medical point of view there are a number of problems surrounding the disease concept of premenstrual syndrome, including its high prevalence rate, its uncertain aetiology, and the high rate of placebo response to a variety of treatments. d'Orbán (1981) suggested that the legal concepts embodied in the Homicide Act could best be reconciled with current medical views and with common sense by regarding the syndrome not as a disease, but as an 'inherent cause'. However, the clinical details available suggest that all three women would have qualified for a defence of diminished responsibility on grounds other than premenstrual syndrome.

The question of premenstrual syndrome as a special defence negating criminal responsibility was tested in the Court of Appeal in 1982. Sandra Craddock, one of the women who had been acquitted of murder in 1980 on the grounds of premenstrual syndrome, appealed against her subsequent conviction (under the name of Smith) for threatening to kill a police sergeant (*Smith*; Brahams, 1982). Her appeal was based on arguments that included 'transient derangement of her understanding', automatism, irresistible impulse and lawful excuse. The appeal was dismissed, and it would seem very unlikely that any of these propositions could be supported on medical grounds.

In the USA, there have also been pleas for the recognition of the premenstrual syndrome as a special defence on the grounds of temporary insanity (Oleck, 1953; Wallach and Rubin, 1972), but the issue has not been tested in the criminal courts and, if it were, it would be unlikely to succeed (Benedek, 1985). However, the disorder has been used in plea-bargaining in *Santos*, a case of child abuse. In a civil case of bankruptcy (*Lovato*), involving a lesbian couple in a stormy relationship, the plea of premenstrual disorder failed as the judge found that there were numerous acts of violence dissociated from any cycle, some of which were planned and deliberate (Benedek, 1985; Sampson, 1987). In Canada, the premenstrual syndrome has also been rejected as a special defence, but it has been used in mitigation. In a case in Alberta in 1984, a woman was acquitted of shoplifting on the grounds that the disorder (in conjunction with other factors) indicated lack of the specific intent required for the offence (Meehan and MacRae, 1986).

Prostitution

Prostitution is not in itself an offence, but the Street Offences Act 1959 provides that—

> it shall be an offence for a common prostitute to loiter or solicit in a street or public place for the purpose of prostitution.

Being a 'common prostitute' in this context means that a woman has persisted in conduct for which she has previously been cautioned by a constable. The cautioning system is not statutory, but two formal cautions are allowed before a woman is charged with soliciting (Home Office, 1974).

In 1986, there were 9098 convictions for soliciting (Home Office, 1987b); this represents an almost three-fold increase since 1979. Section 71 of the Criminal Justice Act 1982 made soliciting a non-imprisonable offence, partly as an expedient to reduce overcrowding in prisons. In the preceding 4 years about 180–200 women were sentenced to imprisonment each year for soliciting. The result of the 1982 Act has been an increased use of fines and a steep rise in the number of women sent to prison for fine-defaulting (Edwards, 1987).

Prostitution has been defined by Goldstein (1979) as non-marital sexual service for material gain. It can clearly encompass a variety of situations and its characteristics will vary over time and in different societies. James (1976) emphasized the economic motives that lead women to prostitution; it is perceived as a good occupational option and at the same time it provides adventure and excitement. James also found, however, that a high proportion of prostitutes had experienced parental abuse and neglect, sexual abuse and rape, and 35% had had lesbian relationships. There are very few data on the psychiatric aspects of prostitution, but Gibbens (1971) thought that 'prostitution occupies a central position in the psychopathology of crime by women'. He found that, of women aged over 21 admitted to prison, between a quarter and a third were or had been prostitutes, whatever their current offence. Prostitutes in prison are not likely to be representative: the efficient and well-organized call girl is rarely seen there, and it is the failures who drift into prison. Among prostitutes in prison, Gibbens found a concentration of women with personality disorders and multiple social deviance. A history of suicidal attempts, alcoholism and drug dependence were each found in a quarter of prostitutes, and a quarter suffered from physical illnesses, mostly gynaecological problems. Sixteen percent were lesbian or bisexual. The relatively few prostitutes who come to psychiatric attention outside the prison setting are likely to be young women with drug or alcohol dependence problems and to have a history of family disruption and sexual abuse; their own sexual orientation is often markedly uncertain.

The relationship between prostitution and drug dependence has been studied in the USA by Goldstein (1979). He found that the relationship varied depending on the level of prostitution. Among high-class prostitutes, prostitution mostly preceded addiction. The most common addiction was to stimulants which served a functional purpose for their work. By contrast, among low-class prostitutes addiction tended to predate prostitution. In this group, the most common addiction was to heroin, and prostitution was mostly motivated by the need to buy drugs. In Britain during the 1970s, prostitution was not a common practice among female opiate addicts, and there was no evidence to suggest any causal link between opiate dependence and prostitution (d'Orbán, 1970, 1973; Wiepert et al., 1979). The reason for this relatively benign situation may have been the availability of opiates through legitimate medical prescribing. The pattern of drug related crime may have changed in recent years as a result of the growth of illicit drug use since 1980. Nevertheless, a recent survey of women serving a prison sentence in England found that 8% had a record of prostitution-related convictions and 23% had been drug dependent prior to their sentence, but there was no significant association between these features (Maden et al., 1990; Gunn et al., 1991b).

Homicide by Women

Gender differences in crime are well illustrated by crimes of homicide. In his classic study of homicide in Philadelphia, Wolfgang (1958a) found that, for both white and non-white ethnic groups, the female murder rate was a little over one-tenth of that of males. In female homicides, the relationship to the victim was more often an intimate one, and victim precipitation was twice as common. Alcohol intoxication is less often a factor in women (Gillies, 1976). On the other hand, psychiatric factors are significantly more often a feature of female homicide. Gibson (1975) distinguished between 'normal' homicides (convicted of murder) and 'abnormal homicides' (where the offender was found insane, convicted of manslaughter on the grounds of diminished responsibility or of infanticide, or where the suspect committed suicide). Her study showed that during 1967–71, 68% of female homicides were in the 'abnormal' group compared with 28% of male homicides. Women were responsible for 35% of all 'abnormal' homicides, but for only 2.5% of 'normal' homicides. 'Normal' killing is an almost exclusively male offence. During an 8-year period 1980–87, the average number of murder convictions for women was only 6.5 compared with 154 for men. During this period only 4% of persons convicted of murder were women, but the proportion of female offenders increased to 12% of manslaughter and 20% of diminished responsibility manslaughter convictions (d'Orbán, 1990a).

The victims of female homicide are predominantly family members; for example in Gillies' (1976) Scottish study nearly 80% of the victims of females charged with murder had a family relationship with the offender, compared with 30% for the males. The two largest groups of victims were children and spouses. In England, the findings are similar. In Holloway prison (a remand prison for London and South Eastern England), 233 women were remanded on initial charges of murder or attempted murder during a 6-year period (1970–75). In 191 cases (82%) the victim was a family member; children accounted for 104 cases (45%) and spouses for 70 (30%) (d'Orbán, 1990a).

Maternal Filicide

During the decade 1977–86, 15% of all victims of homicide were children aged under 16 years. Children aged under one year are the age group at highest risk, with 34 homicides per million population compared with the average risk of 12 per million (Home Office, 1987a). The majority of victims in this age group are killed by their mothers (Gibson, 1975).

Resnick (1969, 1970) classified maternal filicide by motive, and Scott (1973) by the source of the impulse to kill. Scott's classification has been modified, and Resnick's category of neonaticide added because of its distinctive characteristics and medicolegal interest (d'Orbán, 1979). In a series of 89 women charged with the killing or attempted murder of their children who were examined in a remand prison over a 6-year period there were six groups given in order of frequency.

1. *Battering mothers* (36 cases, 40%). These are cases of fatal non-accidental injury. Here the killing occurs as a sudden, impulsive act in a violent outburst of temper. The immediate stimulus to aggression allegedly arises from the child. The psychiatric problems associated with this group are personality disorder, reactive depression and low intelligence. The relative importance of these psychiatric factors is, however, overwhelmed by a concentration of social problems and stresses in this group. These women have chaotic and often violent home backgrounds. Compared with the other filicidal women, they experienced significantly more parental separation in childhood, marital violence, financial and housing problems. At the time of their offence, they are significantly more often pregnant, have other children to care for, or have children who are ill. Other indices of social and family disturbance, although not reaching significance, are also commoner in battering mothers than in other filicides: the battering mothers tend to come from large families, have a history of maltreatment in childhood, parental discord, a family history of crime and a criminal record. Ethnic minorities are over-represented in this group.
2. *The mentally ill* (24 cases, 27%). This group includes acute reactive

depression associated with a suicidal attempt, personality disorders with depressive symptomatology of sufficient severity to merit hospital admission, and psychotic illness. This group usually attempts or contemplates simultaneous suicide. The women usually have multiple victims as they kill or attempt to kill all their children. Psychosis was diagnosed in 14 cases (16% of all filicides); 7 had puerperal psychoses with mixed schizoaffective symptomatology, 4 had schizophrenia, 2 had paranoid psychoses and 1 had psychotic depression.

3. *Neonaticides* (11 cases, 12%). These women kill their children within 24 hours of birth (Resnick, 1970). They rarely suffer from psychiatric disorder (2 cases of personality disorder and 1 case of subnormality in this series). They are significantly younger than other filicides, and are single or separated women who conceal their illegitimate pregnancy and kill their child almost immediately after birth. There is usually no premeditation as these women dissociate from their pregnancy. The degree of dissociation and denial may at times amount to a gross hysterical defence mechanism (Green and Manohar, 1990). These women usually do not seek antenatal care or medical help at the time of birth.

4. *Retaliating mothers* (9 cases, 10%). Here the aggression directed against the spouse is displaced on to the child: the Medea Complex described by Stern (1948). These women have severe personality disorders with aggressive or impulsive behaviour, suicidal attempts and frequent psychiatric hospital admission. Their marital relationships are hostile and chaotic, and they use their children to manipulate their spouses.

5. *Women who kill unwanted children* (8 cases, 9%). They are either impulsive, antisocial personalities with a history of delinquency and often drug abuse, who kill their children by active and deliberate aggression rather than through loss of temper, or passive, immature personalities who are separated from their spouses and beset by social problems, and who kill their child by neglect. This latter group often shows dissociative mechanisms reminiscent of the neonaticide group.

6. *Mercy killing* (1 case). Here there is a real degree suffering for the victim, and an absence of secondary gain for the mother.

From the relative frequency of the six types of filicide, it is apparent that, in Britain, cases of fatal non-accidental injury are in the majority. Contrary to medicolegal tradition, maternal filicide is not significantly associated with puerperal psychotic illness, which is a relatively rare cause (8% in d'Orbán, 1979). It is also apparent that neonaticides (the other group for whom the special legislation on infanticide was intended) do not usually suffer from mental disorder; they are young women of immature personality who kill their newborn children for social reasons, usually to avoid the stigma of illegitimate childbirth (Resnick, 1970). The Infanticide Act 1938 and its operation is described on pp. 49–50. It remains useful because it enables women with relatively little or no psychiatric abnormality (who would not qualify for the diminished responsibility defence) to avoid a murder conviction, and to be dealt with in a humane and flexible way.

In some countries the relative frequency of various types of maternal filicide is difficult to disentangle from child killing in general. Australian studies include male offenders (Wallace, 1986), or specify the sex of the victim rather than the offender (Wilkey et al., 1982), but in both studies the largest number of deaths (more than a third) were due to non-accidental injury. In Hong Kong, Cheung (1986) found mentally ill women slightly outnumbered the non-accidental injury cases. A rare form of filicide by suffocation, which is sometimes serially repeated with consecutive children, is associated with Munchhausen's Syndrome by proxy (d'Orbán, 1990b). Other types of serial filicides are usually neonaticides; although rarely reported from European countries, they are not uncommon in Japan (Funayama and Sagisaka, 1988), where it may be practised as a traditional form of population control (Sakuta and Saito, 1981).

Child Abduction

Most cases of child abduction involve parents who are separated or divorced, but remain in dispute over the custody of their children. The increase in such cases is attributed to the rising divorce rate and more frequent intermarriage between people of different nationalities. Children who are abducted by strangers form a smaller group. Until recently, the latter offenders were charged with child stealing (Section 56, Offences Against the Person Act 1861), whereas abduction by a parent was not a criminal offence (although, if a court order was flouted, proceedings could be taken for contempt of court). The Child Abduction Act 1984 reformed the law by encompassing both types of abduction, thus bringing abduction by a parent within the ambit of the criminal law. Section 1 deals with abduction of a child under the age of 16 by a parent if the child is taken out of the UK without appropriate consent. Section 2 repealed the offence of child stealing under the Offences Against the Person Act 1861 and made it an offence to 'take or detain' a child under the age of 16 within the UK. Whereas child stealing required proof of force or fraud, the Child Abduction Act 1984 focused on lack of consent by the parent or lawful guardian to the taking away of the child.

There are no studies of parents who abduct their children, but psychiatric factors are unlikely to play an important part. The children are used as a means of retaliation against the spouse, or to manipulate a financial settlement. Terr (1983a) has emphasized the psychological harm that abducting parents can cause to their children. By contrast, abduction by strangers is relatively rare, but psychiatric abnormality in the offender is a prominent feature. Criminal statistics since 1985 deal with child abduction which includes both categories of offender (parents and strangers): in 1986, 20 men and 8 women were convicted (Home Office, 1987b). The previous offence of child stealing which dealt only with abduction by strangers was also more often committed by men, but since the late 1970s men and women were equally involved.

Three patterns of child stealing have been distinguished (d'Orbán, 1972, 1976).

1. *Comforting offences* are committed by young girls with immature or hysterical personalities; some also have mild or borderline mental handicap. They usually have a previous history of petty delinquency and of psychiatric treatment for depression, parasuicide or adolescent conduct disorder. Characteristically, they have deprived backgrounds; their offences are motivated by their need to comfort feelings of deprivation and to mother a baby whom they can fantasize as their own. They snatch babies from unattended prams or sometimes abduct children for whom they have been baby-sitting. They rationalize their offence by claiming that the parents were neglecting the child; they project their own feelings of rejection and identify with the supposedly unwanted child. They are often preoccupied with thoughts of pregnancy and having children. Many have a history of their own children having been taken into care or adopted, because of their inability to care for them.
2. *The psychotic group* are usually women in mid-life with chronic schizophrenia whose children have been taken into care; often they have been sterilized. The offence is committed during an acute relapse and they usually have a delusional belief that the child is their own.
3. *The manipulative group* commit their offence in the setting of an insecure relationship; feeling themselves under threat of rejection or desertion they simulate a pregnancy or develop pseudocyesis (d'Orbán, 1982). They then steal a newborn baby (often from a maternity hospital) pretending to their partner that the child is his.

The stolen children are usually well cared for and rarely come to any harm. Most are quickly recovered except from those in the manipulative group who plan the offence and carefully conceal it. Because of premeditation and the absence of mental illness in this group, the women tend to be dealt with more severely by the courts. However, it is in the manipulative group that repetition of the offence is least likely; the offence is a response to a crisis in interpersonal relationships which is likely to remain unique and is resolved one way or another after discovery.

Men who abduct children are usually paedophiles. A small series was described by d'Orbán and Haydn-Smith (1985). None was mentally ill; they had a previous history of sexual offences against children and had a preference for a specific sex and age group.

Women in Prison

The Demographic and Offending Characteristics of Imprisoned Women

Women form between 3 and 4% of the prison population in England and Wales. From the 1930s to the early 1970s, their numbers remained stable at between 800 and 1000, but there was then a rapid growth from the mid 1970s onwards. The average population in women's prisons in 1986 was 1607 (Home Office, 1987d). Approximately a quarter of the female prison population are remand prisoners. Of those remanded in custody, over two-thirds do not subsequently receive a custodial sentence (NACRO, 1985; O'Dwyer et al., 1987). Of sentenced prisoners, approximately 30% of receptions are fine defaulters, and in Scotland the proportion is between 50 and 60% (Carlen, 1983). However, because of their brief stay in prison, fine defaulters only form 3% of the daily average population. When considering the average sentenced population in custody, the largest group (38%) are imprisoned for offences against property (theft, fraud and handling stolen goods). Offences of violence account for only 17%. A recent change has been the marked increase in the number of drug offenders in the 1980s, from 50 to 60 annually during the 1970s to 316 in 1985. Most of these women are not themselves addicts, but are convicted of illegal importation of drugs. Forty percent of women serving a sentence for drug offences are from overseas, mainly from Nigeria, and this group now makes up about 13% of the sentenced female population (Maden et al., in preparation).

Relatively little is known about the demographic characteristics of female prisoners. By 1988, 70% of the female prison population were white, and 20% were of Caribbean or African origin (Home Office, 1989c). As expected, female prisoners are young, with over 60% of sentenced prisoners aged less than 30 years. Fifteen percent have no previous convictions (compared with 6% of male prisoners), but in nearly one-third of women no information is available on their previous criminal record (Home Office, 1987c).

Psychiatric Disorder in Female Prisoners

Both in Britain and in the USA, early psychiatric surveys of the female prison population highlighted factors such as economic and social disadvantage, educational backwardness, low intelligence and neurotic illness or personality maladjustment rather than major psychiatric disorder (Fernald et al., 1920; Glueck and Glueck, 1934). Pailthorpe (1932) writing from a psychoanalytic perspective suggested that 93% of women prisoners in Birmingham and Holloway were suffering from psychiatric abnormality.

Until 1989, subsequent British surveys were all carried out in Holloway Prison. Woodside (1962) found evidence of psychiatric abnormality in 49% of women serving sentences of 6 months or longer. Gibbens et al. (1971a) in a 1 in 4 sample survey of all receptions in 1967 (638 women and girls) found that mental ill-health was a major problem in 22% of the women. Major psychiatric disability increased with age, reaching 40% in those aged over 50. One-quarter of the women had a history of admission to psychiatric hospitals and 22% had a history of attempted suicide. In an unpublished report from the same study, it was reported that, at reception or during the preceding year, a diagnosis of psychosis was made in 5%, neurotic illness in 5%, psychopathy or personality disorder in 21%, alcoholism in 8% and drug dependence in 5%. The remarkably similar proportions of women with psychosis and with neurosis are perhaps surprising. A total of 44% had some form of psychiatric disorder, a proportion very similar to Woodside's findings. The study by Turner and Tofler (1986) was of 708 women screened on admission to prison. They did not do a full psychiatric assessment, but found that over one-quarter had a history of self-harm and nearly one-third were taking some form of psychotropic drug (14% were heroin or other opiate addicts). Eighteen percent had a previous history of psychiatric treatment. These figures were probably an underestimate, as 63 women bypassed the routine admission procedure due to their disturbed mental state or urgent need for treatment for drug withdrawal. Overall, just over one-half of the women had one of the triad of self-harm, drug abuse and past psychiatric illness which were used as indicators of psychiatric disorder. Maden et al. (1990), surveying sentenced women prisoners, found that 23% were dependent on drugs, mainly opiates, at the time of arrest.

Taken together, the results of three psychiatric surveys at Holloway over the past 25 years show fairly close agreement and suggest that about half the population suffers from some degree of psychiatric disorder; it appears that the nature of this disturbance is largely in the field of personality disorder, drug and alcohol abuse and self-harm. This is in keeping with the work of Guze (1976) in Missouri, USA, although not strictly comparable, since Guze's work was exclusively with sentenced prisoners and the Holloway studies included remanded women. He found a high prevalence of psychiatric disorder among both male and female criminals, and concluded that the psychiatric disorders associated with criminality are sociopathy, alcoholism and drug dependence in both sexes, and hysteria in women. Schizophrenia, primary affective disorders, the neuroses and organic brain syndromes were not associated with sentence to imprisonment. Guze's findings are of special interest because he found a similar prevalence of psychiatric disorder in a comparable group of male prisoners. However, the prevalence of psychiatric illness was twice as high in the relatives of female criminals as among the relatives of male criminals.

In Canada too, a study of female offenders admitted to a remand centre in Winnipeg found a high incidence of psychiatric disorder, but this was predominantly accounted for by antisocial personality disorder (60%) and alcohol abuse (34%); only 4% suffered from psychotic illness (Robertson, Bankier and Schwartz, 1987).

Although many studies show that a high proportion of female prisoners suffer from psychiatric abnormality, variations in sampling and diagnostic criteria preclude direct comparison between male and female prisoners. Eysenck and Eysenck (1973) compared the responses of male and female prisoners to a personality inventory and found higher scores for 'psychoticism' among the women in Holloway, suggesting that they have a higher prevalence of psychiatric disorder. The source and characteristics of the sample of male prisoners, however, is not described. The Holloway population is a mixed group of remanded and sentenced women, whereas psychiatric surveys of sentenced male prisoners also found that a high proportion have personality disorders (Faulk, 1976) or are psychiatric 'cases' (Gunn et al., 1978). It may be that the traditional view that female offenders are more 'disturbed' than male offenders is in part due to an underestimate of the extent of psychiatric problems among male prisoners (Allen, 1987). One comparison that has been made between male and female offenders is in the relative proportion who receive some form of psychiatric disposal in court. Walker (1965) noted that significantly more female offenders are dealt with as mentally disordered by various procedures under the Mental Health Act 1983 or under probation orders, or are found insane or unfit to plead. Allen (1987) found that this has been a consistent trend and that over the years 1950–85, the rate of 'psychiatric disposals' for women are about twice the rate for men. She suggests that the discrepancy cannot be accounted for by differences in the prevalence of mental disorder, and that at each stage of the process of criminal justice factors operate which favour a psychiatric disposal for women as against men.

The only study which has applied identical methods to comparable random samples of sentenced male and female prisoners is the Institute of Psychiatry national survey of prisoners, which found that 57% of women and 38% of men received at least one psychiatric diagnosis (Gunn et al., 1991a). Most of this difference was accounted for by drug dependence (found in 11% of men and 23% of women), personality disorder (10% of men, 18% of women) and neurosis (6% of men, 16% of women). There was no significant difference in rates of psychosis (1.6% of men and 1.9% of women). An increased rate of neurotic disorders in women would have been predicted from prevalence rates in the community (Regier et al., 1988), but the differences in the rates for personality disorder and drug abuse are in the opposite direction.

Behavioural Problems of Women in Prison

Women prisoners have traditionally been regarded as more difficult, disturbed and unstable than their male counterparts. However, organized, collective demonstrations or rioting are unusual among women prisoners and most behavioural disturbance or rule infraction is on an individual basis. A whole range of behaviour may be manifested—self-mutilation, fire-setting, barricading, assaults, or destruction of clothes, bedding and furniture—much of which is aimed at relieving tension and is correlated with boredom, inactivity and confinement. Such behaviour is routinely dealt with through the disciplinary system, and women are put on report for a wide variety of offences against prison rules and regulations. Dobash et al. (1986) suggest that:

> Women in prison are more closely observed and controlled, more often punished, and punished for more trivial offences than are men in prison.

The rate per 100 population for all offences in women's establishments is more than twice the rate for males (Home Office 1987b). About 50% of these offences are for 'disobedience or disrespect' and only 4% are for violence. Interpretation of these figures, though, is complicated by differences in the general prison regime for men and women. Even 'closed' female prisons such as Holloway and Styal provide considerable freedom of movement within a secure perimeter without the prolonged lock-up periods that characterize many male prisons. With decreased physical constraints comes an increased likelihood of breaking prison rules which rarely impinge on those prisoners confined behind a cell door for most of the day. The number of incidents of self-injury 'without apparent suicidal intent' in 1985/86 was 619 in women and 692 in men—almost equal numbers, despite the disparity in the size of the respective prison populations (Home Office, 1986b).

In Holloway, Cookson (1977) found that self-mutilators tended to be young, to have a high degree of previous institutional experience, and to have committed more violent offences. Incidents of self-injury tended to occur in epidemics and were learnt and imitated by others. Cookson suggested that self-mutilation is a response to feelings of frustration and helplessness in a closed institutional setting, and that it helps the inmate to gain momentary relief from depression, tension or depersonalization. At the same time, by producing a response from the environment, it also reduces helplessness and provides a way in which the inmate can gain some control over her environment. Wilkins and Coid (1991) found that 7.5% of admissions to Holloway Prison had a previous history of self-mutilation. Compared with controls, self-mutilators had histories of severe deprivation in early life with more extensive experience of physical and sexual abuse. In adulthood, many showed abnormal psychosexual development. Their criminal histories were characterized by early onset of persistent offending with significantly more criminal damage and arson offences. Wilkins and Coid concluded that self-mutilation is an indicator of severe psychopathology (mostly antisocial and/or borderline personality disorder). Whatever the role of the prison environment, these women were already highly prone to impulsive antisocial behaviour, including repeated self-mutilation. In a large survey of sentenced prisoners (Gunn et al., 1991b), the lifetime prevalence of deliberate self-harm was 32% in women and 17% in men, but 5% of inmates of each sex reported deliberate self-harm during the current period in custody (Maden et al., in preparation).

The relatively more disturbed behaviour of women as compared with men in institutional settings is not confined to prisons, but is seen also in hospitals. For example, McKerracher et al. (1966) in Rampton Hospital found that mentally subnormal female offenders showed significantly more aggression to persons and property, self-mutilation and noisy disturbance. In general psychiatric hospitals, too, violence to self or others has been shown to be more common in women (Fottrell, 1980). These observations suggest that behaviour disturbance in institutional settings is not solely due to the severity of psychiatric disorder, but that it is also gender-related, and that women tend to react differently to an institutional environment.

Mandaraka-Sheppard (1986) explored the causes of misbehaviour in prison, emphasizing the importance of environmental factors rather than pre-existing personality disorders. She studied a representative sample of sentenced women in six women's prisons. Rule violators tended to be young, single and without children. Type of offence, previous criminal record and length of sentence were not correlated with either minor or serious misbehaviour; thus a violent offence or a violent criminal record was *not* a predictor of violent behaviour in prison. Mandaraka-Sheppard concluded:

> To a very large extent serious misbehaviour of women in prison is directly a function of their responses to the particular negative aspects of the institution.

Mandaraka-Sheppard (1986) also studied the ways in which women adapted to the prison regime. She found that women did not organize into cohesive anti-institutional groups; anomie prevailed and the most common response to imprisonment was 'ritualistic compliance'—remaining on good terms with staff and other inmates, but having no commitment to the norms of the institution. Social relationships were most commonly with one or two other inmates, but withdrawal and indifference were also common. In contrast to findings in American studies of women's prisons (Giallombardo, 1966; Ward and Kassebaum, 1966), there was no evidence of the formation of extended family structures and far less involvement in homosexual relationships (25% compared with 80% in the American studies). Mandaraka-Sheppard suggested that the difference between English and American patterns of adaptation to prison may be attributable to the extended family structure among black Americans, who predominate in the American prison population, and that longer prison sentences and the mixing of age groups in American prisons may be contributing factors. However, age-mixing does not seem a likely explanation for the differences. Since the introduction of Youth Custody in Britain in 1983, and with it a deliberate policy of age-mixing in women's establishments, Genders and Player (1986) noted that the majority of women made friends only within their own age groups. Homosexual relationships, like other forms of friendship in prison, tended to occur between prisoners of a similar age, and there was no evidence to justify the prison staff's fears that young offenders would be 'led astray' by older women. The young offenders did, however, learn new criminal skills about various types of fraud and about drug abuse from the older women.

Medical Aspects of Women's Prison Regimes

In the 1960s penal philosophy in the women's prison system was strongly influenced by overoptimistic views on the efficacy of psychotherapy in 'curing' crime. There was also a prevalent belief that most female criminals were psychologically abnormal, and that they required treatment rather than punishment. This 'medical model' of female crime received some support from the psychiatric survey of Holloway Prison by Gibbens et al. (1971a), which was commissioned by the Home Office in preparation for the redevelopment of Holloway. The survey was carried out in 1967 and the following year the Home Secretary announced the rebuilding of Holloway as a 'secure hospital' to act as the hub of the female prison system, with medical and psychiatric facilities as its central feature (Home Office, 1985c). The planning of Cornton Vale, the only women's prison in Scotland was influenced by similar ideas and the role of the psychiatrist was explicitly stated to include involvement in the general policy and management of the institution, which was envisaged as a therapeutic community (Dobash et al., 1986). By the late 1970s, there was a dramatic shift in the Home Office's views on women prisoners. In their evidence to the Expenditure Committee of the House of Commons in 1978/79 on Women and the Penal System, they suggested that the female prison population is 'depressingly normal' and the Director of Medical Services claimed that there had been a change in the characteristics of women who are sent to prison, with proportionately fewer who are 'psychiatrically disturbed' (Dobash et al., 1986). It was considered that female prisoners 'possessed many characteristics which are similar to those of the male inmate population' (Home Office, 1985c). However, apart from an increase in their numbers and a lengthening of their sentences, no evidence was produced to support the claim that there had been a change in the prevalence of psychiatric disorder among women prisoners. Much of the misunderstanding and disagreement about the prevalence of psychiatric disorder in the female prison population is based on the fact that Holloway, the largest of the women's prisons, is also a remand centre for South Eastern England. With the general increase in the prison population and the redevelopment of Holloway, a larger proportion of Holloway inmates are on remand, and psychiatric disorder is particularly associated with remand prisoners rather than those who are sentenced.

Having abandoned any pretensions of being a hospital, Holloway, like other women's prisons, now functions according to a penal model. Nevertheless, it recognizes that a significant minority of its clients are likely to have medical and psychiatric needs and provides some hospital facilities in the prison. Smith (1984) discussed the medical needs of women in prison. Specialist medical and gynaecological services are provided by visiting consultants. The pattern of psychiatric services is very similar to that found in men's prisons, with remand prisoners accounting for most assessments and transfers to hospitals in the NHS. In the hospital section of Holloway in 1985, about 90% of women were on remand, and over 70% were awaiting medical reports. Hospital officers in women's prisons are all trained nurses; only a minority of hospital officers in men's prisons have a nursing qualification. In response to the high rate of drug addiction among women in prison, Holloway is the site of a pilot scheme for the treatment of drug dependent prisoners, in liaison with treatment agencies outside prison.

The Holloway unit was comparable to the observation wards that existed prior to the MHA 1959; it functioned as a diagnostic and assessment centre and had a constantly changing population with a high turnover. Half of the hospital population was suffering from major mental illness (32% with schizophrenia and 18% with affective disorder). In addition, about one-third of the women had serious personality disorders and about 10% were awaiting assessment for admission to a special hospital (d'Orbán, 1985b). The most difficult problem was presented by women with a combination of mild mental handicap and personality disorder; they respond poorly or slowly to treatment and are least likely to be accepted by NHS hospitals for admission. Despite the nature of the population, the regime was a prison regime governed primarily by security and disciplinary considerations, and was quite inappropriate for the creation of a therapeutic milieu and the treatment of the mentally disordered. The unit was also grossly understaffed, occupational and recreational facilities were inadequate, and long periods of confinement led to disturbed behaviour and self-mutilation. The attempt to create a multidisciplinary team approach with joint staffing by nurses and prison officers was a failure and the Holloway Project Committee, on unanimous medical advice, recommended that the unit should be staffed by psychiatrically trained nursing staff. They fudged, however, the crucial issue of medical versus prison governor management by stating that, although the unit should 'eventually' be a hospital unit managed by a doctor, for the immediate future there should be joint management by medical and governor staff (Home Office, 1985c).

The possibilities of treatment in such a setting are limited. The remand period, with its uncertainties, is a particularly stressful one for women. Many who are subsequently sentenced, who are not psychiatrically ill and appear to adjust reasonably well to their sentence, nevertheless pass through a period of severe anxiety while on remand, and during this period they need psychotherapeutic support and at times also medication. The use of psychotropic drugs in women's prisons has at times attracted adverse and ill-informed comment. The Prison Department's statistics on the 'number of doses of medicine administered' in various establishments is of very limited value, but it is, nevertheless, apparent that more psychotropic medication is used in women's establishments (Home Office, 1986b). However, this is in part a reflection of gender differences in psychotropic drug use in the community. Thus the proportion of women who are prescribed psychoactive drugs in general practice is more than double that of men (Skegg et al., 1977). Gibbens et al. (1971a) in their survey of Holloway in 1967 found that, on admission, 45% of the women were on a prescription for psychotropic drugs, or had a history of illicit drug use. With the increased use of benzodiazepines, this proportion is likely to have increased in recent years. In a remand prison such as Holloway, the use of psychotropic drugs also reflects the high proportion of women who are acutely distressed or psychiatrically ill. Indeed, the problem is the opposite of that depicted in the media in that prison doctors try to resist demands for psychoactive drugs rather than foisting them on their patients without proper indication or consent. The fact that patients in a prison hospital are not subject to the provisions of the MHA 1983 means that they cannot be given medication without their consent, except under common law powers in case of emergency. This can cause considerable difficulty in remand prisons where psychotic patients may spend long periods prior to hospital admission, and it may contribute to behavioural disturbance in prison hospitals.

Various aspects of the ordinary prison regime for sentenced women have been described by Carlen (1983), Edwards (1984), Mandaraka-Sheppard (1986), Genders and Player (1987) and Morris (1987). There is much criticism of the limited training and occupational facilities in women's prisons; existing facilities are seen by some critics as attempting to fit women into stereotyped gender roles. The problems are exaggerated in relation to life sentence or high security risk (category A) women for whom there is only one small unit for the whole of England and Wales, in Durham jail, regarded as suitable for the early years of their sentence (Lester and Taylor, 1989). This unit is geographically isolated from the home communities of most English women, but it poses even more problems for those from ethnic minorities or from abroad who become isolated from their culture as well as their family and, in the overseas cases, embassy support. The problems inherent in providing work for such a small group in a prison has meant that workshop activities intruded on educational and therapeutic activities simply in order to maintain the possibility of work.

Mothers and Babies in Prison

The provision for pregnant women and young children is a controversial issue. From the child's point of view, the potential harm resulting from separation has to be balanced against the unsuitability of the prison environment. The Prison Department's policy is to allow babies to stay until they are 9 months old in closed prisons (Styal and Holloway) and up to 18 months old in an open prison (Askham Grange). The three existing mother and baby units provide a total of 34 places, but a census in February 1985 found that only 21 places were in use (TUC, 1987). The extent of the demand for places is not known. A census of 11 establishments in August 1986 showed that there were 340 women prisoners with 566 children aged under 5; of these, 111 were aged under 18 months (Elton, 1987). However, many of the mothers may not be looking after their children. A survey in Holloway Prison found that at the time of the mother's imprisonment, 45% of dependent children were not living with the mother; 20% were being cared for by relatives and 25% were in care or fostered (Posen, 1979). These findings are very similar to the result of the Holloway survey in 1967 (Gibbs, 1971). Gibbs also noted that single parents were particularly vulnerable to having their children taken into care, and that cohabitees and stepfathers rarely maintained parental responsibility once the mother was sent to prison. Although the courts generally try to avoid prison sentences for women with young children or women in advanced pregnancy, there are cases in which a prison sentence will still be imposed, and it seems more humane to make some provision for mother and baby units rather than adding to the burden of these women by separating them from their children. The existence of mother and baby units, however, will prevent separation only if the length of sentence is such that the child would not have to remain in a unit beyond the age of 18 months. In the USA separation appears to be the general policy, and there is only one prison where children may stay with their mothers until the age of one (Morris, 1987).

How is the physical and psychological development of babies affected by a period spent in a prison mother and baby unit? This question was addressed by a research project commissioned by the Home Office from the University of Sussex (House of Commons, 1986c). Using the Griffiths Mental Development Scale, the study compared babies' development during their stay in prison nurseries, and for a short period after their release, with babies of a similar age and background who remained with relatives, friends or in care during their mothers' imprisonment. There were no statistically significant differences between the overall developmental scores of the unit babies and the controls, and scores of both groups fell within recent British norms. However, a subsample of babies who spent 4 months or longer in the unit showed a gradual and statistically significant decline in their locomotive and cognitive areas of development (Catan, 1988). Catan concluded that, although there was no evidence that either short stay in a prison nursery or brief separation from the imprisoned mother in itself severely damages the development of children, thinking about child care in prisons must move beyond the goal of preventing obvious harm and gross deprivation.

> There is thus a need to re-emphasize the developmental needs of young children, especially in the areas of freedom of movement and exploratory play, when planning physical facilities, staff specialties and daily regimes in the Unit (Catan, 1989).

Alternatives to Imprisonment for Women who Offend

Although women account for a tiny minority of the prison population, all the evidence suggests that even fewer should spend time there—on three counts. First, in many cases, the nature of the behaviour which results in imprisonment probably should not do so. Two-thirds of custodially-remanded women, for example, do not subsequently receive a custodial sentence; the case for imprisoning fine defaulters is weak. Second, there is some evidence that prison may have a maximally disturbing effect on women—illustrated by their excessive rates of self-harm, mutilation, and possibly of disciplinary reports too. Third, many women have small children and the consequent enforced separation for most of them may damage the children as well as the mother.

Alternatives to prison are dealt with mainly in Ch.19, and for the most part apply as well to women as to men. There are some aspects of negotiating such alternatives which may be exceptionally hard in relation to women, such as finding appropriate accommodation. Many female offenders are from traditionally disadvantaged groups in this regard. They include disproportionate numbers of young single people, alcohol and other drug takers, people with behavioural disturbance, including fire setting, or single parents with young children. Where a hostel is the most likely option, few cater specially for women. Many female offenders, however, have been previously abused by men and prefer, at least initially, to avoid mixed accommodation. Carlen (1990), in a practical guide, lists some of the residential places available specifically or principally for women. She also reviews educational, training and recreational facilities for daytime use.

16
Dangerousness

Written and edited by
John Gunn

With an American perspective by
John Monahan

Dangerousness is an important topic for psychiatry. Whether they like it or not, psychiatrists are expected by the population at large to select mentally disordered people who are dangerous to themselves or others, and to treat them. Psychiatrists are even given special powers to treat such people compulsorily, usually in a hospital, if patients object to the treatment which is offered. This seems to be true in every country in the world. It is, of course, especially true for those patients who have already offended in some way. The English Mental Health Act (1983) gives powers under its sections 2 and 3 for the detention of a mentally disordered patient for 'his own health or safety or with a view to the protection of other persons'. British courts have special powers to apply restriction orders to prevent the discharge of patients by doctors if they think 'it is necessary for the protection of the public from serious harm so to do' (*see* Ch. 2 for details).

So, although the word 'dangerous' is hardly used in British legislation, and British psychiatrists tend to play down their role in the assessment of dangerousness, it is an inescapable part of everyday psychiatry to make judgements about dangers and risks which the patient poses to himself or to other people. Much of the mystique of psychiatry comes from the public awareness of this role. Indeed, some of the public hostility to psychiatry is also related to this role, which is sometimes construed as the psychiatrist relinquishing his medical function for a police one! This chapter will include theoretical issues, clinical matters, a word about justice and a view from the USA. The American view is particularly important here not only because most of the empirical research on this topic has been conducted in the USA, but also because American mental health professionals give the topic a much greater prominence and is are more candid about the immense difficulties surrounding it.

Theoretical Issues

The word, dangerous, is a common one, and is attributed to all kinds of objects, concepts, and people, e.g. snakes, aeroplanes, the dark, guns, communists, fascists, the insane and so on. The *Concise Oxford Dictionary* defines danger as 'liability or exposure to harm, risk or peril'. This definition is not entirely adequate. A journey involving land, sea and air travel may be perceived as 'dangerous' at different points. Many individuals might feel that the air travel is the most dangerous part. The word 'feel' in this context is important because, if the traveller were able to determine accurately the actual risk, he might be surprised to find that the risk is at its height on the road leading to the airport. In other words, dangerousness is something attributed to people or things, partly taking account of actuarial risk which can be calculated, and partly subjective fear. A good illustration of the complications caused by this semantic confusion is the unceasing political debate about the dangerousness of nuclear power stations. Actuarially, the risk to the community from a nuclear power station is very low, maybe even lower than from conventional power stations, certainly lower than from cigarettes, motor cars and other common hazards, but this is not how the risk is perceived (*see* Slovic, 1987 and 1989 for an analysis of the perception of risk).

The same subjective element is a complicating factor in determining risk from individuals. To illustrate, let us take some well-known examples. Almost every English person knows the names, or at least the folk names, of some violent criminals—Ian Brady, Myra Hindley (the Moors Murderers), Peter Sutcliffe (the Yorkshire Ripper), Peter Cook (the Cambridge Rapist) are all regarded as 'dangerous' people. Collectively, they have killed or harmed a few dozen people. Even if unrestrained, they would be unlikely to further kill or harm more than a few more. Set alongside a pilot who crashes his plane into a mountain, a factory owner who causes an explosion or releases toxic waste into the atmosphere, or a ship owner who is negligent about safety regulations, they may present a relatively small threat to society. Yet all four of the named criminals will be on almost everybody's priority list for antidangerousness measures. This may be partly because the word 'dangerous' can be a pejorative word in some circumstances, but it must also be related to the fact that people are simply afraid of such individuals, more afraid than they are of, say, the negligent factory owner. The concept of a deranged man stalking the streets at night over a long period of time, picking off an occasional victim is terrifying. It is, therefore, important to understand that dangerousness is a subjective concept which is attributed to individuals, and its attribution is not necessarily a good guide to the statistical risk that those individuals actually pose. Above all, it is not a medical diagnosis.

Prediction

At one time, it was the vogue in psychological literature to say that prediction of violent behaviour for any given individual was an impossibility, or at least so inaccurate as to be useless. This nihilistic approach now appears to be receding. Monahan (1978) has urged a reconsideration pointing out that most of the research on the prediction of violence is concerned with the release of institutionalized individuals into the community. The classic study of this type is perhaps that concerning the so-called 'Baxstrom' patients (Steadman and Keveles, 1972; Steadman and Cocozza, 1974). In 1966, Johnnie Baxstrom was held in New York's Dannemora State Hospital for the criminally insane before his release. He had been convicted in 1959 of assault and sentenced to imprisonment. Whilst he was serving his sentence, he was diagnosed as mentally ill and was transferred to Dannemora but, when his sentence expired in 1961, he was retained within the hospital as continuing to be mentally ill. In February 1966, the US Supreme Court upheld Baxstrom's petition by stating that he had been denied equal protection under the Fourteenth Amendment. He was released. The New York State Department of Mental Hygiene decided there were 966 other patients who could also petition against detention, so all 967 patients within Dannemora and Mattewan (the state's other hospital for the criminally insane) were transferred to civil mental hospitals between March and August 1966. This caused a great deal of anxiety because these patients had all been labelled as 'dangerous'. Steadman and his colleagues followed up these cases. Four years later about half remained in civil mental hospitals, 27% were discharged to the community, and 14% were dead. Only 3% were in a correctional facility or hospital for the criminally insane. In all, there were 16 convictions sustained by 246 patients during the follow-up period, the 16 convictions involved only 9 patients, and only 2 of the 16 convictions were for felonies.

Low frequencies of violent behaviour have been recorded in all studies of patients leaving institutions, but it is wrong to generalize from this statistical finding to all circumstances in which patients are hospitalized on account of so-called 'dangerousness' (Monahan, 1978). Nevertheless, an international study (Harding and Montandon, 1982) has shown how weak the psychiatrist is at static predictions of this kind; 193 raters, including 62 psychiatrists, rated 16 case histories for dangerousness. The levels of agreement between the rates ranged from less than 35% to (in one case) 86%. However, the psychiatrists did not agree among themselves any more than the other professionals did.

Human beings have always tried to foretell the future and, of course, they have never been able to do it exactly. Even when we are concerned with frequent, fundamental, biological phenomena, such as predicting the number of births and deaths in a stable population, a problem which can be forecast with a high degree of accuracy, we cannot say much about any particular individual. We may know the probability of a woman, aged 30, giving birth to a male child within the next 12 months, but we cannot know who will fall in love with whom, have intercourse with whom, and give birth to which sex. Indeed, some of these elements are subject to that chancy process we call individual choice. However, it is worth noting that the extra randomness introduced by individual choice, also gives us a bit more predictive power if we can talk to some of the individuals concerned. We can ask people about the choices they are likely to make.

Yet, paradoxically, we daily do make predictions about human behaviour which we rely upon and act upon. We know which friends to trust and for what purpose. We know to whom it is safe to lend money and to whom it is not. We know who will succeed in carrying out a difficult task, and who will fail. The method we use is quite simple, we forecast the future by referring back to previous behaviour. Banks and other businesses formalize this by careful research into an individual's financial and business history. In this way, society goes about its affairs in an orderly fashion and, although some disasters occur, by and large, the predictive system bears fruit. Why should this be easier than the prediction of dangerousness?

If we turn to the criminological literature we find that there are several problems. Simon (1971) showed that criminological prediction studies, whether they relate to recidivism among juvenile offenders, probationers, or persons released from correctional institutions, rarely achieve a correlation of more than 0.4 between predicted and observed probability of recidivism. This means that, although small groups of good or bad risks can be distinguished, for many of the cases little discrimination is achieved. Simon suggested that this very low power is probably related to the considerable environmental influences under which any individual comes, but which are not as easily or as systematically measured as demographic details such as age, sex, numbers of previous convictions and so on. Nevertheless, like most workers in this field, Simon showed that the best predictor of future criminal behaviour is early delinquent tendencies.

If the field of interest is narrowed to violence, then the same general proposition holds true; the best predictor of future violence is previous violence, for example Black (1982) has reported a 5-year follow-up study of patients released from Broadmoor, and confirms that the best predictor of future criminal behaviour is previous criminal behaviour (*see also* p. 706).

Kozol studied 592 male offenders most of whom had been convicted of violent sex crimes. Each offender was examined independently by at least two psychiatrists, two psychologists and a social worker. Of the 592 patients, 435 were released; of these 435, Kozol and his colleagues recommended that 49 should *not* be released because of their dangerousness. During the 5-year follow-up period, 8% of those predicted not to be dangerous committed an assault, as did 34.7% of those who were predicted to be dangerous. In other words, Kozol and his colleagues were right in a third of their predictions of dangerousness, but they were wrong 65% of the time. As Monahan (1981) indicates this kind of result has been found more than once. Its interpretation is, however, complex; in the Kozol study, 163 patients were detained because of the psychiatric recommendation, which meant that the judges agreed with the psychiatrists. There is no way of knowing what their violent recidivism rate would have been if they had been released. It probably would be higher than the 35% in the released cases, which must have been borderline because of the disagreement between psychiatrist and judge.

Only 20% of the Baxstrom (Steadman and Cocozza, 1974) patients were assaultative during the 4-year follow-up period, and 3% were readmitted to hospitals for the criminally insane. The best predictors of any violence were presence of a juvenile record, the number of previous arrests, presence of convictions, presence of convictions for violent crimes, the severity of the original offence, and age. Cocozza and Steadman (1976) applied a 15-point Legal Dangerousness Scale to the patients released into the community. Of the 20 patients who were arrested later for violent crime, 17 had a legal dangerousness score of 5 or more and were under 50 years of age. Yet despite this, the authors point out that for every patient with these criteria who did commit a violent offence, 2 did not and that the best statistical strategy for predicting violence would be to assume that none of them would be dangerous. By this the authors meant that the best way to reduce the total error rate (i.e. false positives plus false negatives), would be to guess that none would be violent again. However, as Monahan (1981) indicates, this assumes that all errors are of equal importance, and it makes no attempt to weight or cost different kinds of mistakes.

The data from these and other studies are quite clear and consistent. Whatever the theoretical position, in practice, psychiatrists and others are bad at predicting the future violence of inmates released from institutions, and they are also conservative in their release policies. This has led many people to urge that predictions be not made, a position which has superficial appeal, but leaves out of account the subjective element of fear mentioned earlier, the consequent political reality of public demand for dangerousness predictions of one sort or another to be made, and the fact that we know that ordinary judgements about our friends are more often right than wrong. One aspect of prediction which is of great importance, but so far not considered, is the specification of limits to the predictive judgement. Sometimes it is said that the only prediction worth making about an offender is whether or not he or she will *ever* be violent again. In other words, prediction is being demanded for a period which may span 40 or 50 years. One only has to think of the declining accuracy of weather forecasting over increasing periods of time, or the way in which human personality changes as we grow older, or the major environmental changes to which we are subject as our life develops, to realize that such a task is a tall order indeed, and for all practical purposes should be regarded as impossible. Short-term prediction in almost any field of human or biological activity is much more likely to be accurate.

Another crucial variable in predicting behaviour is the context or environment influencing that behaviour. If we wanted to predict weeping instead of violence, we would be surprised if we were expected to do this by reference to individual variables only. Individual variables would no doubt tell us who is a weepy sort of person and who is not, we may find that children weep more than adults, women more than men and so on *but*, for accuracy, we would want to know about the individual's recent experiences and inner feelings as well. So it is with violence also.

Steadman (1982) found that if people are asked about recent violent events, some unsurprising systematic associations between context and the seriousness of violence emerge, e.g. violence is greatest when the dispute is outside the home, late at night, when alcohol or drugs have been used by either party involved, in the presence of third parties, where strangers are involved and where the antagonist is larger and stronger than the respondent. The major exception is that psychiatric patients are more likely than other offenders or the general population to involve family members in their more violent disputes. Another qualification is that alcohol and drugs are especially involved in offender violence. Steadman goes on to urge that if a prediction is made, it should focus on the environment to which the person with violent propensities is to be returned and that, if intervention strategies are sought, controllable factors in the environment should be attended to.

A further aspect of prediction which is of critical importance is an individual's mental state. We can never be sure exactly what another human being is feeling or thinking. He may not be able to tell us, or he may mislead us, but we do have better communications with one another's brains than does any other creature. We should always make use of this remarkable facility. For example, the terrorist who says that whenever he is released from prison, he will take up arms again has to be regarded in a different light to a similar offender who can give good reasons, coupled with plans, for starting a new life. Equally, the man who feels that life is not worth living and that he and his family would be better off dead should be listened to.

It may be that these aspects of time limits, environmental factors, thoughts and intentions are the factors that differentiate the relatively poor predictive power of decisions made on statistical paperwork in the studies quoted from the better experience we all have of making predictions about our friends and acquaintances in everyday life. Future research on prediction should take all three factors into account before determining whether predictions are accurate or not.

Finally, when dangerousness predictions are made, they are almost exclusively confined to predictions made on treated patients about to return to the community from hospital or prison. It may be that acute assessments where admission is contemplated are easier and more accurate.

Clinical Issues

The Role of Psychiatry

Psychiatrists, like any other professional group, are the product of societal attitudes and beliefs. To some extent the psychiatrist is the medicine man who heals anxiety. The doctor we call upon to take away our fears. This is partly why we give him legal powers to protect us from insane violent people. The psychiatrist will protect us from insane people, he will lock them up in his hospital. He will understand their insanity, and by his understanding learn how to control it and render it harmless.

Should the psychiatrist accept these attitudes or try to resist them? In practice, psychiatrists *do* know more about madness than other people, they *do* help some mentally disordered people to recover, they *do* reassure frightened patients, frightened families and frightened communities. It is, therefore, not suprising that psychiatrists are summoned to act as agents of reassurance when life becomes disorganized and threatening. Psychiatrists do have special knowledge of human psychology, both normal and abnormal. Nevertheless, it is important that the psychiatrist sticks strictly to the limits of his skills and also teaches the fearful public just how much he does *not* know.

The traditional medical skill which seems very relevant to the prediction of dangerousness is the art of making prognoses. Prognosis is simply a medical prediction. Patients with nasty diseases, such as cancer, wish to know what course their illness will take, and how long they have to live. The patient with depression may also ask how long his miseries will last, and whether he can expect them to return if they clear up. Doctors are paid, in part, to know about these things and give sensible answers. However, it should be noted that it is the *patient* who wishes to know, and the doctor gives him information on which to act. The predictive information here is a private communication between the doctor and his patient, it is clearly understood that it is hedged with uncertainty, and it is for the patient to decide what to do with the information.

When it comes to dangerousness, the psychiatrist is asked to do something different. He is asked to say whether or not a particular person is likely to act violently in the future. The client in this interaction is not necessarily the patient. The client is usually some legal authority or social system. This poses ethical questions, which are not inherent in ordinary medical prognostication. A psychiatric prognosis for a patient who is deemed either dangerous or lacking in responsibility may result in taking away the patient's liberty. Can this ever be justified? Can we accept the controlling paternalistic role which society has given the psychiatrist?

Paternalism for the mentally abnormal exists in every society. It is related to the concept of responsibility or competence. We do not attribute very much responsibility to children, those with poor brain function, those who are under great stress, and the insane. In terms of our own social mores, it could be argued that a society which makes no allowance for mentally abnormal people is not humane. Every society makes provision to override the wishes of mentally abnormal people under certain circumstances. It is easier to allow that this may be a reasonable and humane course of action if it is entirely for the benefit of the patient. It is perhaps more difficult to allow that some kind of psychiatric procedure should, on occasion, take away the liberty of a patient largely for the benefit of other people instead of purely for the benefit of the patient; however, preventing a psychiatric patient harming other people is almost always for the benefit of the patient as well. Nevertheless, there may be exceptions to this rule. So the question remains: is it reasonable for a doctor to restrain a patient for the benefit of other people? Psychiatry is a branch of medicine which has been generated by patient's wishes and broader social desires, and those desires include a desire to be safe from aberrant behaviour. The code of ethics drafted in Geneva for the governance of the medical profession in 1948 (*see* p. 1015) puts 'service to humanity' above all else including consideration of individual patients. Few doctors have qualms about preventing an epileptic patient, liable to have sudden loss of consciousness, from driving a train, a bus, or an aeroplane. It seems entirely reasonable for the doctor likewise to accept the role of protecting the public from damage caused by psychological disorders. However, there is a substantial qualification which we should perhaps add to this perspective. Psychiatry should only restrain patients purely for the benefit of others in collaboration with other non-medical people. Such non-medical people might include relatives, social workers, hospital managers, lawyers or judges.

In the light of this, let us see how the prognostic process can be applied to dangerousness. A first step would be to decide whether the patient concerned has a demonstrable mental disease. The next step is to try and determine the connection, if any, between the aggressive or feared behaviour and the mental disease. If it is clear there is no connection, that should be stated and that should be the end of the prognostic statement. If, as happens with the majority of the mentally abnormal and violent, one is suspicious or convinced of a connection between the disease and the violence, then it is reasonable to spell out how that connection comes about and what aspects of the disease are behind the violent behaviour. In such cases, the prognosis of the violence and the prognosis of the disorder are linked. Action to alleviate the disease will be action to reduce dangerousness.

A simple example will illustrate. A man is subject to recurrent depressive episodes during which he becomes deluded to the point where he believes that life is useless, he is worthless, and the only practical remedy is to kill himself and destroy his world. During one such episode, he kills his wife and tries to kill himself. He has no other history of violence, so it is reasonable to regard him as not dangerous during his well phases, but as potentially suicidal and perhaps homicidal if the psychotic depression returns and, also, to regard a future close relationship with a woman, or a future marriage, with especial concern.

At first sight it may seem odd, but such a clinical opinion can help in the *discharge* and *rehabilitation* of the man concerned, because in a strictly supervised aftercare programme, problems in relationships with women or the return of depression could be identified and acted upon. This, in turn, gives confidence that the risk of a planned supervised discharge is worth taking. So compulsory care, in hospital at first, on licence later on, can be for the mutual benefit of patient and public alike.

It is more difficult to illustrate the theoretically possible circumstances in which a patient is restrained by the medical profession purely for the benefit of the public and not at all for the patient. Perhaps the nearest example would be the patient who has recovered from a brief psychosis during which he was severely violent and killed someone, but who is not released from hospital because the psychopathology has never been understood, and because there is no medical confidence that the psychosis will not return.

Assessment

Assessments of suicidal behaviour (i.e. risk to self) are well understood within psychiatry. Assessments of risk to others are much the same, and use the same principles, with a slightly different emphasis.

Step 1 is a detailed history from birth using every available informant and agency for validation;

Step 2 is special attention to substance abuse especially alcohol, with information about dosage taken, reasons for taking it, and its effects;

Step 3 is special attention to sexual interests, attitudes and ideas;

Step 4 is a detailed account of any criminal and/or antisocial behaviour; police records should be sought whenever possible, remembering that an uncorroborated account from the patient is insufficient. The account should be discussed with the patient in terms of his thoughts, fears, feelings at the time. The account should, if possible, give a description of the build-up to the antisocial behaviour and the situation in which it occurred;

Step 5 is a psychological assessment, including an assessment of intelligence, an assessment of personality and, if relevant from step 3, a detailed assessment of sexual feelings and sexual response;

Step 6 is a mental state assessment, not just a mental state assessment at the time of one interview, but a description, if possible, of thoughts, moods, fears over the period of time covering any antisocial behaviour; an attempt should be made to relate any abnormalities to the antisocial behaviour. Particular emphasis should be given to feelings of anger and temper control;

Step 7 is a description of behaviour, attitudes and responses to any treatment.

A detailed assessment of this kind will usually take quite a long time, and the time is best divided between several interviews, because conditions change over time, a more trusting relationship can be established by repeated interviews and facts can be tested between interviews. If time is limited, then any assessment or opinion should be qualified by a comment to that effect. Of course, a limited interview may still be supplemented by detailed information collected by others.

In an emergency, only a small amount of information will become available. Attempts should be made to maximize this by deferring any decision as long as possible, even if only for an hour, interviewing as many informants as possible, and checking on the availability of old records. A judgement is then required, and, as with suicidal behaviour, cautious decisions are frequently the best. For example, admission to hospital, sedation, removal from provocative surroundings, all give time for more information gathering and are usually not damaging to the patient. It is usually much simpler to reverse and correct an over-cautious decision than pick up the pieces of an incautious one. Table 16.1 shows the important variables in the prediction of risk as suggested by examination of the literature on violence and clinical experience.

Details about each of the points on Table 16.1 should be obtainable from the 7-step assessment mentioned above. The asterisks indicate variables which are subject to change and it will be noted that they are in the majority. These are the items upon which any treatment plan should be concentrated.

Here, perhaps, is the key to the psychiatric approach to dangerousness. The aim is to assess the factors which have led the patient to be aggressive, to ascertain how many of those factors are amenable to change, and then to intervene to alter the factors, so that risks of aggression are reduced. Assessment of dangerousness is, therefore, important in psychiatry, but only as a first step, the really important issue (which depends on good assessment) is *management*.

Management of Dangerousness

The management of 'dangerousness' is, for the most part, the management of 'risk'. However, the feelings and fears of relatives, neighbours, former victims and others should have great consideration in the management of a patient of whom they are afraid. Rehabilitation plans should be discussed with such people; local police forces should be informed of what is happening; admission to hospital decisions may be tipped one way or the other by such considerations; and; in some cases it might be appropriate to rehabilitate someone in a new area of the country. At the very least, local fears should be attended to, discussed and support given. Even when relatives are acquiescing or encouraging about a particular course of action, the practical and emotional effects of that action should be carefully considered. For example, a patient killed his mother in a deluded, hallucinated state. It emerged that he had previously terrorized his father and his sister in the family home for some years. The patient responded well to hospitalization plus medication. After 2 years' treatment, it was proposed that he should return home for outpatient treatment. The family apparently agreed to this. After some case work and counselling with the family, it

Table 16.1
Important Variables in Risk Prediction

Demographic Facts

Previous violence
Previous sexual assaults
Age*
Sex
Race
Socio-economic status*
Drug and/or alcohol abuse*
Intelligence*
Marital status*

Environmental factors (Stressors)*

Family supports
Personal relationships
Employment
Accommodation

*Interests**

Sexual (including paedophilia, sadism)
Violence
Cruelty
Social domination (e.g. Nazi party)
Racism

*Contextual factors**

Availability of potential victims
Availability of weapons
Availability of drugs and/or alcohol

*Declared intentions and attitudes**

To previous victims
To future potential victims
To caring staff

Physical features

Size
Strength*
Brain dysfunction*

*Mental state**

Feelings of tension
    depression
    paranoid ideas, especially delusions
    hallucinations, especially instructions to harm
    intense reliosity
    jealousy
Anger, especially rage attacks

---

* Variables which are subject to change.

became apparent that they agreed out of loyalty and because of guilt feelings. Eventually, the patient was rehabilitated via sheltered accommodation (a hostel), after 2 further years in hospital.

The management of violent patients is considered in Chapter 17 (*see also* Roth, 1985). Here emphasis is given to three features which are at the centre of risk management: *security, supervision, support.*

Security. The level of security applied to a patient should always be the *minimum* level which is compatible with safety and good management. Excessive caution, i.e. putting patients in greater degrees of security, or retaining them there longer than absolutely necessary, is bad clinical practice. In the British system, there will be disputes between doctors and politicians about the appropriate level of security. That is inevitable and healthy. The British security hospital network is basically a simple heirarchy as shown in (Fig. 16.1). There is a major gap in this system which is not apparent from the diagram. Special hospitals provide maximum security and regional security units provide medium security (*see* ch. 20). Special hospitals provide long-term care, regional security units provide medium-term care (up to 2 years). This means there is nowhere for the patient who requires long-term medium security and, very often, short-term security is also difficult to provide.

Fig. 16.1 A hierarchy of supervision and security in the English hospital system.

The decision about which level of security is first made by the doctors and nurses who are closely involved in the patient's care. A nursing assessment, for example, is essential to determine whether or not a particular patient will fit into a particular setting, but often there is also a political dimension to special hospital care, and ministers will have the last word for both admission and discharge decisions relating to some patients, and to the special hospitals.

The practicalities of the security heirarchy mean that special hospitals take four types of patient: those who present an immediate risk if they escape;

those who are proving unmanageable and dangerous to staff in hospitals lower down the hierarchy: those who would create political embarrassment for the Minister if they escaped; and those who need some significant degree of security on a long-term basis. Regional security units take patients who present less problems, but are unsuitable for safe management in a general psychiatry ward (closed or open), plus patients who need a forensic psychiatry team (as opposed to a general psychiatry team) for the long-term management. Locked wards are usually intensive care areas which do not have any special emphasis on or training in the arts of managing mentally abnormal offenders. These facilities are useful for the patient who is normally quite safely managed on an open ward, but who develops an acute reaction, perhaps an affective or a psychotic state, which creates behavioural problems and/or danger to the patients or others on a short- to medium-term basis.

Patients who have to spend a long time, maybe many months, or even years, behind locked doors should not be kept in small intensive care units if possible. The patient's quality of life is a special responsibility for medical and nursing staff if liberty is curtailed. Small units can only provide a limited environment. Security units and special hospitals usually have a full range of occupational and recreational arrangements available. Furthermore, larger hospitals are more likely to be able to provide specialized services such as remedial education, counselling, individual and group psychotherapy.

The decision about level of security is a judgement which should be taken with the maxiumum of information and the factors leading to the decision include:

seriousness of previous aggressive behaviour;
severity of mental disorder;
type of mental disorder and its prognosis;
expected length of risk from aggressive behaviour;
likelihood of return of aggressive behaviour;
the range of therapeutic and educational services available.

Supervision.   Supervision should be present at all levels of security. It is an inherent part of good medical management. The degree and type of supervisions offered depend upon the number of staff available and their skills. Supervision also depends upon consent, the non-consenting patient is supervised differently from the consenting patient.

Supervision is an inherent part of nursing and is, for the inpatient, difficult to distinguish from nursing care. The term supervision is used here to imply continuous assessment of risk to self and others, with a readiness to intervene if the risk increases unacceptably. It includes the skills of counselling and of psychotherapy, it includes paternalism such as the provision of medication even when undesired (*see* the view from the USA below), it includes basic visual monitoring of movements. Supervision in a security setting has the extra dimension of knowing where all dangerous objects (knives, tools, matches, etc.) are, and knowing which patients present which risks in which situations. Supervision in security also includes a knowledge of all patient movements. Patient movements should always be understandable and agreed in advance. Equally important, supervision should not be very intrusive nor should it be oppressive. It should be friendly and the patient should understand it and be allowed some opportunity to challenge it. As with security, it should always be the minimum which is compatible with safety and good management.

Outpatient supervision is necessarily more distant. It is, though, the key to keeping patients who present risks in the community. It may include visits to the patient's home, or visits by the patient to a clinic, day centre, or other service. It will include counselling, advice and paternalism (i.e. persuasion about taking medication, sticking to court requirements, keeping within the law). It should include a strong relationship between supervisor and patient, such that the patient will express problems, fears and plans to the supervisor before taking action. It will include a clear understanding by both parties about the absolutes, the firm dos and don'ts, and the consequences of breaching any prearranged limits.

Supervision also includes direct environmental manipulation, i.e. advising about and sometimes determining where the patient is to live, where to work, with whom to cohabit and so on. Again, such intrusions must be kept to a minimum and only applied for very good reasons. An example might be the patient who killed her lesbian lover by poisoning. During rehabilitation, she applied for a job at a chemical factory. Advice and eventually intervention were necessary to ensure that she told her employer of previous problems so that a proper account could be taken of them. Later, she developed a crush on a woman at work, and the woman proposed to move in with the patient. At this point, joint sessions, including disclosure to the other woman, were essential. In extreme circumstances of this kind, it may be necessary to forbid the cohabitation.

This abbreviated account may give an impression of unnecessary authoritarianism, so it should be emphasized that each patient should have more than one supervisor—for outpatients this is usually a doctor and a social worker. As far as possible, each step should be agreed between the supervisors and the patient, each supervisor should have a peer group available for advice, and others knowledgeable about the case (e.g. civil servants) should also be consulted.

Support. Support is often thought of as something provided universally in a psychiatric clinic. In reality, it is frequently not provided. The provision of support requires skill, commitment and hard work. It involves being available at inconvenient times, it involves special arrangements (maybe admission, maybe giving evidence in court, maybe a home visit) at moments of crisis. It involves a degree of mutual trust between therapist and patient which is akin to domestic trust, i.e. it is important for each to know how to get hold of the other, and for the therapist to make some deputy arrangements when completely out of touch. However, it should never go beyond a professional relationship, so that contact is always focused on neutral professional territory (e.g. the hospital); the therapist's private address and telephone number should never be disclosed.

Support can include psychotherapy, but does not necessarily do so. It can be provided without much interpretation. However, support always involves the development of a special relationship between the patient and his supporter. This relationship will, in turn, develop strong feelings between the two people. These feelings are often called 'transference' feelings, because they may relate to strong feelings developed in previous relationships which are transferred into the contemporary supportive relationship (*see also* p. 678). The feelings may well become eroticized. The verbal interactions between the parties may be supplemented by powerful non-verbal communications which are never discussed and in some cases not given or received consciously. It does not take much imagination to realize that strong feelings developed in this way can lead to difficult, violent, and/or sexualized behaviour. For these reasons, some understanding of 'transference' feelings and the special relationships that develop in psychological treatments is essential. Further, supporters need their own supporters and should be able to turn to their colleagues for advice from time to time.

The reduction of risk

This chapter began by considering the prediction of dangerousness. We now change the terminology and consider the reduction of risk. Lawyers, and maybe criminologists, will want to retain the dangerousness concept; it has its place. The therapist/supervisor, the doctor, the psychiatrist dealing with an individual patient will, however, want to eschew 'dangerousness' and concentrate on risk. The question: 'Is this man dangerous?' can be recast. First, it can be asked: 'in what circumstances is he likely to pose a risk?' A picture of his aggressiveness should be drawn in the context of his mental disorder, his relationships, his environment, and the opportunities for aggression. Next, it can be asked: 'what factors can be changed and how?' For example, admission to hospital may alter relationships, social circumstances and opportunities: it may also provide treatment which will cure or modify his mental disorder. Then, it can be asked: 'how and when can we provide security, supervision, and support such that the risk posed by the man is minimized?' Finally, 'when will the point be reached when the appropriate mixture includes supervision outside of hospital?'

Seen in this way, the question about risk for the individual becomes tolerable. All or none decisions are avoided. Instead, a plan of management is drawn up, risks are modified, and flexibility is ensured with the aim of adjusting the arrangements as need arises. Mr A is no longer either dangerous or not dangerous; he is a man who poses risks in well understood circumstances; he is to be subject to supervision to minimize those risks; he will be continuously monitored; predictions about his behaviour will be based on good information and will be for very short periods (e.g. one appointment to the next).

Justice

A brief word about the philosophy of incapacitating those who are called dangerous may be in order at this point. In the past 'dangerous' individuals suddenly lost all personal power. In contemporary thought, this seems to be going too far. Nowadays, we believe that no one person or one profession ought to be empowered alone and without challenge to restrain and imprison someone on grounds of dangerousness. Whenever restraint is exercised, the individual subject to that restraint should have some possibility of having his (or her) position reassessed periodically and independently.

Some go as far as challenging the principle of protectionism itself, portraying the detention of people deemed dangerous in order to prevent them harming other people as imprisonment for uncommitted crimes!

To examine this, let us return to Peter Cook, the Cambridge Rapist. He committed a series of nasty, violent rapes over a 12-month period, thus terrorizing the female population of a whole city. Suppose that he had been given a purely retributive sentence, with no element of preventive detention. He might have received a sentence which would have meant his discharge from prison in 6 or 7 years. Even if his sexual needs had considerably diminished by then, it would be difficult to argue that he would do no harm at that stage. Just by being about, he would scare and alter the lives of quite a number of women. Women who would claim that they have just as much right to be unharmed as he does. Weighing this up, the judge decided that he should be given life imprisonment. This was almost certainly a protective or preventive sentence. In the British system, this means that Cook may be released on licence at some unspecified future date, perhaps long after the 6 or 7 years he might otherwise have received and, of course, he may never be released at all. Furthermore, even after release he will be limited in his freedom to some extent, and subject to recall to prison. It is this kind of action that some say is punishment for offences not yet committed.

Such action can also be described as redistribution of harm and risks between the offender and the community. This issue is discussed in some detail in Floud and Young (1981). As they put it:

> 'What is the moral choice between the alternative risks: the risk of harm to potential victims or the risk of unnecessarily detaining offenders judged to be dangerous?'

A more psychiatric example might be of a man with a delusion that his wife is being unfaithful. He plans his wife's death because of her supposed unfaithfulness. He is admitted to hospital because of his 'dangerousness'. Unfortunately, his delusion proves unresponsive to treatment and he remains in hospital for many years in spite of the fact that he has never actually done his wife any harm. The argument runs that this man is being detained for offences he has not committed and might never commit. He is actually being detained because doctors and probably his wife are fearful. It could be argued, however, that if his wife disappeared by changing her name and address and withholding them from him, he would no longer present her with a threat. Even if this were the only consideration and it were true, it might also be considered to be unreasonable to expect her to have to take these steps rather than for him to have to remain in hospital. This is what is meant by the redistribution of harm and risk. In these matters of justice, there are no absolutes, only matters of opinion. Opinions vary, change with time, and therefore the professional should always be both flexible and informed.

A View from the United States of America

The concept of risk plays a central role in mental health law in the USA. On the criminal side, for example, the American Bar Association's *Criminal Justice-Mental Health Standards* (1985) specify that a court should commit to a mental hospital a person acquitted of a violent crime by reason of insanity only if the court finds by clear and convincing evidence that the person is currently mentally disordered and, as a result, 'poses a substantial risk of serious bodily harm to others' (Standard 7–7.4).

On the civil side, despite the efforts of some mental health groups in recent years to focus on the more diffuse deteriorations that mental disorder can precipitate, risk of behavioural harm now seems firmly imbedded as a criterion for commitment in modern American law. The *Model State Law on Civil Commitment* (American Psychiatric Association, 1983b), for example, following Roth (1979), explicitly contemplates the commitment of several types of mentally disordered persons, including those 'likely to cause harm to others'. The National Center for State Courts' *Guidelines for Involuntary Civil Commitment* (1986), in this regard, have recently urged that—

> particularly close attention be paid to predictions of future behaviour, especially predictions of violence and assessments of dangerousness. Such predictions have been the bane of clinicians who admit limited competence to offer estimates of the future yet are mandated legally to do so. (However) such predictions will continue to provide a basis for involuntary civil commitment, even amid controversy about the scientific and technological shortcomings and the ethical dilemmas that surround them (Commentary to Guideline G.1).

Risk that the mentally disordered will commit harm, therefore, is now and is likely to remain one of the core issues in American mental health law. Despite substantial differences in mental health systems (the much larger role of lawyers and judges in the American system, for example), risk of harm to others is an important issue in British mental health law as well (Taylor, 1988a). What follows is a brief survey of recent developments in risk assessment research (*see* Monahan, 1988, for a fuller treatment of these issues).

Risk Assessment

In 1981, most of the research literature on clinical risk assessment of violence among patients was conducted on mentally disordered offenders. A previous review reached a number of conclusions (*see also* Monahan, 1984; Halleck, 1986).

1. Of every three disordered persons predicted by psychiatrists or psychologists to be violent, one will be discovered to commit a violent act, and two will not.
2. The best predictors of violence among the mentally disordered are the same demographic factors that are the best predictors of violence among non-disordered offender populations, e.g. age, gender, social class, history of prior violence.
3. The poorest predictors of violence among the mentally disordered are psychological factors such as diagnosis or severity of disorder, or personality traits.

Much of the research published since 1981 has been conducted on civil patient populations and could be seen as challenging each of these conclusions. Klassen and O'Connor (1988), for example, were able to identify a group of mental patients of whom 60%—nearly double previous estimates— were arrested or recommitted for violent acts within 6 months of release (these were patients with ten or more arrests or commitments for violence; *see also* Convit et al., 1988b; Bieber et al., 1988). Several studies have found that demographic factors associated with violence in 'normal' offender populations (e.g. age and social class; *see* Blumstein et al., 1986) were *not* associated with violence among disorderd groups (Cohen et al., 1986; McNiel et al., 1988), and a large number of investigations have reported a relationship between rates of violent offending and specific clinical diagnoses (e.g. Craig, 1982; Tardiff and Sweillam, 1982; Binder and McNiel, 1988).

What is so striking about recent risk assessment research, however, is not that the research challenges existing assumptions. That, at least, would be provocative. Rather, what is striking is that the research is so inconsistent. For every study that reports increases in predictive accuracy, there is another that finds clinical risk assessment no better than chance. Studies concluding that the relationship between demographic factors and violence among the mentally disordered is weak are balanced by equal numbers of investigations finding strong correlations. One set of researchers recently summarized this situation as follows:

> The accumulated results in the literature to date . . . present inconsistent findings on just about every demographic variable that has been studied. The results of our study add to this *cumulative* inconsistency (Rossi et al., 1986).

Of 7 recent studies investigating the effects of diagnosis on violence, 4 reported paranoid schizophrenics to have higher rates of violence than those with other diagnoses, 2 reported paranoid schizophrenics to have lower rates of violence than those with other diagnoses, and one reported no differences (Krakowski et al., 1986). As Taylor (1982) has stated:

> There is no doubt that schizophrenics are capable of violent behaviour and, there, any certainty about the relationship between schizophrenia and violence ends.

If research on the risk of violence posed by the mentally disordered is to advance, it must transcend the methodological failings that have contributed to the chaotic state of the field. Empirical research on the assessment of the violence potential of the mentally disordered is plagued by 4 problems. They have to do with the factors used to forecast whether violence will occur, the factors used to determine whether violence has occurred, the designs used to test risk assessments, and the coordination of research efforts in the field (*see also* Mulvey et al., 1986).

Problem one: impoverished predictor variables

Violent behaviour among any group of people, let alone people who are seriously mentally disordered, is a complex phenomenon that has many types of social, psychological and biological antecedents (on the last, *see* Mednick et al., 1988; Tancredi and Volkow, 1988). Despite this, much of the existing research on risk assessment among the mentally disordered has employed a very narrow range of predictor variables (e.g. the Brief Psychiatric Rating Scale, *or* past history, *or* a psychological test), chosen without regard to any theory of violent behaviour or any theory of mental disorder. Studies are only beginning to include clinical variables derived from basic theories of stress and aggression, such as psychopathy (Williamson et al., 1987) and the ability of the individual to control anger (Novaco, 1986) or impulsivity (Segal et al., 1988). Craig (1982), for example, reported that 34% of schizophrenic patients in one public mental hospital were clinically rated as having significant anger problems, and that these ratings correlated highly with assaultiveness.

In addition, many risk assessment studies have relied on plainly inadequate classifications of patients, often lumping them into 'psychotic' versus 'non-psychotic' groups, or schizophrenia as compared with 'all other diagnoses' (*see* Monahan and Steadman, 1983). Even those studies that do include standard diagnostic information (i.e. DSM-III R diagnoses) among their predictor variables rarely describe the developmental course of the disorder, although such information may have predictive value (Krakowski et al., 1986).

One recurrent suggestion for improving the validity of clinical risk assessments is to take into account predictor variables reflecting the environmental or situational context, in which violent behaviour is likely to occur, in addition to measuring dispositional factors such as diagnosis (e.g. Monahan and Klassen, 1982; Steadman and Ribner, 1982; Mulvey and Lidz, 1984). The few studies that have incorporated situational predictor variables have yielded important and often counterintuitive findings. Klassen and O'Connor (1985) found that the more friends a released person reported having in the community, and the more time he spent with those friends, the more likely he was to commit a violent act. Friends, in this study, seemed to function more as instigators of violence than as sources of 'social support'.

Finally, what may be the most important aspect of the environment of mentally disordered people is one that is routinely neglected in risk assessment research. The extent to which arrangements have been made to provide aftercare to released patients in the community, and the extent to which released patients comply with aftercare recommendations (in particular, the recommendation to continue taking psychotropic medication) may have a profound effect upon their behaviour in the community. For example, Cohen et al. (1986) found that 36% of released insanity acquittees who took their medication regularly were readmitted to the hospital within 5 years of release, compared with 92% of those who did not comply with medication recommendations.

Problem two: weak criterion variables

Among the most frequent criticisms of existing risk assessment studies is that an unknown, but perhaps large portion of the criterion—violent behaviour—goes undetected and, therefore, many persons who act violently are recorded as inaccurate predictions or 'false positives'. The reliance in many studies solely upon arrest data seems clearly inadequate, given that disordered people who act violently may be returned to a hospital rather than arrested. Klassen and O'Connor (1988), for example, found that released schizophrenic patients who acted violently in the community were 50% more likely to be rehospitalized than they were to be arrested for their violent behaviour. Reliance upon any type of official records—arrest or hospitalization—will overlook violence that did not precipitate formal intervention by a government agency. In another study, Klassen and O'Connor (1987) found that including patient self-reports of violence increased predictive accuracy by 27.8%. As they note, 'more than one-quarter of the "false positives" may not, in fact, be false positives if self-reports are a valid measure of violence' (*see also* the inpatient study of Convit et al., 1988a).

Problem three: constricted validation samples

One of two methodologies are typically employed in risk assessment research. One type of study attempts to predict violence *in the hospital* and the other type attempts to predict violence *in the community*.

The obvious difficulty with trying to predict violence in the hospital is that the structured milieu of the institution and the therapeutic (or at least sedative) effects of medication seriously suppress the base-rate of violence. Indeed, several studies have found the occurrence of violence in the hospital to decrease drastically within 2 days after admission (e.g. McNeil and Binder, 1987). As Werner et al. (1983) have stated:

> To the extent that hostile, excited, suspicious, and recent assaultive behaviour is viewed by ward staff as presaging imminent violence, it is the patient manifesting such behaviour who is singled out for special treatment (e.g. additional medications, more psychotherapy); such selection may reduce the likelihood of engaging in violence. Thus, paradoxically, if the patient who 'looks' imminently violent in this setting is given effective treatments that forestall violent behaviour, he will not in fact engage in violence as predicted, and the initial forecast . . . will be shown to be inaccurate.

Different issues are presented when validating risk assessments in the community. One variant of this type of study takes advantage of 'natural experiments' in which patients have been released for legal reasons notwithstanding clinical predictions of violence (e.g. Steadman and Cocozza, 1974; Thornberry and Jacoby, 1979). The methodological difficulty here is that such natural experiments are very rare and likely to involve patients whose degree of risk is in dispute (and, in fact, often has been disputed by a judge; *see* Kozol et al., 1972), or who are otherwise not representative of many of the patients of most policy interest (e.g. patients being considered for commitment in hospital emergency rooms, or patients being considered for release from short-term commitment).

The more common variant of the research employing community validation methods studies patients released from the hospital with staff concurrence (e.g. Klassen and O'Connor, 1988; Krakowski et al., 1988). Since patients predicted to be imminently violent are unlikely to be recommended for release, however, this methodology must rely on a severely truncated sample of patients. This is aptly referred to as 'sample censoring' by Quinsey and Maguire (1986). Essentially, investigators are relegated to trying to find factors actuarially associated with violence among a sample of patients clinically screened for a *lack* of violence potential. Unless one assumes that clinicians have absolutely no ability to predict violence, this clinical screening excludes from the validation sample precisely those patients most likely to validate the predictions. Satisfactory solutions to this methodological conundrum (e.g. releasing patients predicted imminently violent in order to test the predictions) do not appear legally or ethically viable (Monahan, 1977) and second-best methodologies may be all that are attainable (*see* Menzies et al., 1985). For example, while those who cross into the clinically-defined category of 'high risk' are likely to be denied release (and, therefore, unavailable for community follow-up) during the period in which they occupy this status, there may be a great deal of variation in assessed risk among those who fall below the cut-off and who are released. Some patients, at the time of release, may be judged to be extremely unlikely to engage in violence, while others are assessed as presenting at least a moderate risk of violence (although not so high a risk as to deny release). Research could profitably attend to these differences in assessed risk and examine the extent to which they correspond to differences in outcome.

Problem four: unsynchronized research efforts

In many areas, lack of communication among researchers and lack of coordination among research programmes are problems. This problem appears to be particularly acute in research on the risk of violence by the mentally disordered. It is unusual in this field to find two American studies— let alone crossnational comparisons—that have defined clinical predictor variables in the same manner. Given the retrospective nature of much of the research (e.g. Steadman and Cocozza, 1974), investigators have had to rely for predictor variables upon whatever information happened to be in the patient's records. Follow-up periods vary widely. This fragmentation of research efforts has seriously hindered the development of the field. The fact that each research site defines its predictor and criterion variables in idiosyncratic ways and rarely replicates the measures used by others drastically reduces the confidence with which findings can be generalized and impedes the cumulative development of knowledge. It also means that data from several sites cannot be pooled for more powerful statistical analyses that could reveal more subtle findings.

Conclusion

The problems that have so far hobbled the scientific study of violence among the mentally disordered can only be overcome by enriching our predictor variables, strengthening our criterion variables, exploiting natural variation in validation samples and synchronizing our research efforts. If we do this on both sides of the Atlantic, it is possible that the next generation of risk assessment studies will yield results quite different from those to which we have become accustomed.

17
Principles of Treatment for the Mentally Disordered Offender

Edited by
Pamela J. Taylor
John Gunn

Written by
Fred Browne
Gisli Gudjonsson
John Gunn
Gary Rix
Leslie Sohn
Pamela J. Taylor

Most authors have discussed some therapeutic issues at intervals through this text. Why then a separate chapter on treatment? There are two main reasons: first to re-emphasize that treatment is at least as important as any other activity in forensic psychiatry. Without it, other skills are largely redundant. A detailed knowledge of the law in relation to psychiatry, for example, is extremely useful for the psychiatrist, but not so as to make him an amateur lawyer, rather to give him knowledge which he can usefully apply in generating a safe and effective treatment plan for his patient. Second, there are general issues concerning treatment in forensic psychiatry which are usefully brought together, rather than scattered or repeated very frequently. Some treatments, e.g. the chemical suppression of libido, are so specific that they are appropriately dealt with alongside the clinical problem (e.g. p. 562), but some general principles relevant beyond a single condition are reviewed.

General Considerations

The Therapist as Assessor

Prevention, assessment and treatment are interlinked. Assessment, for example, takes time and involves detailed interviews. Interviews are interactions and in themselves may produce changes. Equally, those who treat a patient are in a good position to make or add to an assessment of the patient's condition and progress. This is not to say that assessment can always be left to the therapist. There may be, for example, ethical issues in disclosing information obtained in a therapeutic relationship, or the therapist may not want to be part of any team assessment process, still less of any evaluation that might lead to public, or semi-public reporting for courts or tribunals. Feelings about the patient may also sometimes intrude, feelings usually involve some degree of indentification with the patient. The therapist may choose to focus exclusively on the interactions between himself and the patient and omit or underplay other evidence. This potential difficulty can be offset in most treatment settings by bringing together evidence from *all* those involved with the patient. The risk of over identification, however, should never be underestimated.

The Environment

Patients should be treated in the environment which best suits their needs. This is rarely a penal environment, and it should have the lowest degree of surveillance and physical security that is compatible with the patient's safety and with the safety of other people. Ideally, the environment should be negotiated with the patient, but this may not be possible when the patient has little or no insight, or when it is prescribed by a court. Treatment should be for as long as is required, which may mean many years. Treatment should not be reserved solely for those who are curable or who will make rapid progress. Treatment for chronic disease is central to the whole of medicine. In such cases treatment can prevent deterioration and it can certainly ameliorate distress. It follows that, whenever possible, treatment should be carried out in the community and, even when in hospital, it should be as close as possible to the place which the patient regards as home.

Personality Factors

Only a few psychiatric diseases can be regarded as not affecting a patient's personality. It is partly this profound interaction between disease and personality that makes psychiatry different from much of the rest of medicine. It is this interaction which makes psychiatric disease so frightening. Each of us is alarmed that some terrible fate could befall us which would change our very nature. Diseases such as schizophrenia thus seem frightening and abhorrent, because they do indeed change personality. Schizophrenia is defined in the International Classification of Diseases (ICD-9) as a disorder of personality. Skilled management of personality disorders is the very essence of forensic psychiatry, and partly why so much emphasis is put upon long-term management.

The Politics of Treatment

Clinicians can never escape political issues, much as they would wish to. The politics of forensic psychiatry include the fact that the patients concerned tend to be very unpopular with other psychiatric services as well as with the general public. Some offender patients have done terrible things. Most of them present expensive, long-term problems. Public fantasies of the 'homicidal maniac' are ubiquitous. Just imagine a flag day for 'criminal lunatics'! This unpopularity has profound effects. Forensic psychiatry patients tend to be rejected. In a 'free market' they would command very little health resource. Forensic psychiatrists are treated with a certain amount of ambivalence. They are respected because they deal with difficult cases. They are wanted as specialists who will take difficult cases away. They are feared as specialists who might bring dangerous patients with them. In this setting, those who are going to treat mentally disordered offenders effectively have to take on the political role of 'product champion', someone who will fight for resources on behalf of his patients and persuade other clinicians to accept his work and allow it to be funded. On occasions, the 'product champion' may also have to tackle groups of local frightened lay people who are determined to send all forensic psychiatry patients away from their area on the grounds that they must *ipso facto* be 'dangerous'.

Community Care

As with any branch of psychiatry, community care is the aim of treatment, and should be the longest phase of treatment in most cases. In debates about community care, the 'community' is rarely defined. It seems to mean 'that which is not in hospital'. It thus includes patients' homes, specialized hostels, sheltered workshops, day centres, outpatient clinics, and hostel wards. For a substantial number of mentally disordered people, it also means the street, skid row, sleeping rough, and, if they offend, it must also include the police station, the court and the prison. For the adolescent, children's homes and schools can be added.

Inpatient care depends upon a multidisciplinary team, usually including psychiatrists, nurses, psychologists, occupational therapists and social workers. Community care should involve the same groups, but rarely does so. Nurses and occupational therapists with highly relevant skills are much less in evidence. Given proper resources, both could be used more in the delivery of more appropriate care and treatment in day hospitals, in day centres, in sheltered workshops, and as visiting advisors/therapists to patients' homes. In reality, much nursing, occupational therapy and social work is carried out by cheaper and less well trained staff, sometimes by volunteers.

A few of those patients who have fallen foul of the law may have a slightly advantageous position in respect of some of the services available. In the

UK, those on restriction orders must have a social supervisor and a psychiatrist to care for them before community care is considered. The social supervisor must be trained and employed either as a local authority social worker or as a probation officer. This requirement assists in finding scarce resources for a group who would otherwise have no priority. This is important since it is not only qualities within the patient, for example his improved health, but also the qualities of his environment and his relationship with it that ensure his continuing safety.

Returning to the politics of forensic psychiatry, an increasingly important task for the forensic psychiatrist is the establishment of community care facilities. There are few champions of the mentally disordered offender, and the forensic psychiatrist must play a full part in ensuring comprehensive care. Voluntary bodies can be joined or established as a vehicle for money and ideas. Each such body will probably concentrate on one part of the community jig-saw, but each part is important. Such bodies can innovate and be relatively free of bureaucracy, they can also adapt to changing circumstances. An example is the Effra Trust in Brixton, London. Originally it was established as sheltered accommodation for epileptic men leaving prison. As the specialist demand for such a service declined, it took on a broader group of men with mental disorders who had been in trouble with the law. It provides sheltered accommodation, support given by a group of non-residential staff, extensive art and occupational therapy, and annual holiday trips away from London. The accommodation ranges from traditional single bedrooms in a hostel to independent living in associated flats. Some severely disordered people are accommodated, although not those who require 24-hour supervision, as the staff are non-residential. While this scheme fills a particular niche, it suffers from the lack of associated organizations filling other gaps, for example there is very little local hostelward provision and there is a shortage of cheap residential accommodation for those who require less supervision. The Effra Trust is, however, informally linked to the local Bethlem Maudsley Hospital, so that outpatient supervision is available for most residents, and both nurses and doctors in the forensic psychiatry service have supportive and managerial roles in the organization.

Most general practitioners are, as yet, rather distant from the care of the mentally disordered offender, but this should change as general practice is encouraged to take an increasing interest in psychiatric services. It will always be necessary for forensic psychiatrists to supervise the more difficult and worrying patients, but there is no reason why this cannot be done in tandem with general practitioners and why general practitioners cannot take full responsibility for some of the less dangerous patients, such as persistent shoplifters.

Medical Records

In psychiatry, especially forensic psychiatry, case records are a vital and delicate therapeutic instrument. Like all clinical tools they should be cherished and kept in perfect order. Notes of the patient's life story with clear indications of sources of such information should be filed chronologically. A helpful device may be to put information from different sources on different coloured paper. All correspondence and clear notes of every patient interaction, every telephone call, every piece of advice given, every prescription, should also appear in strict chronological order. Psychologists', nurses' and social workers' notes should be included in the medical record; also notes from teachers and occupational therapists where relevant. Opinions and speculations should be distinct from factual data. The record should be interfaced with summaries, synopses and reports to others to make rapid perusal of the file easier. The construction of legal and other official reports is dealt with in Ch. 21. These should be filed with the material on which they are based; well constructed reports make good summaries.

In Britain, the Access to Health Records Act 1990 extended the rights of patients to see what is being written about them by health professionals. Any manually held record made on or after 1 Nov. 91—the date of implementation of the Act—has become accessible to the patient at the discretion of the health professional principally responsible for the patient's clinical care, and subject to the non-disclosure of information which might cause serious harm or identify third parties. Health records kept on computer were already accessible under the Data Protection Act 1984, and remain so as modified by the Subject Access Modification Order 1987. The Access to Medical Reports Act 1988 covers the rights of access to medical reports made for employers or for insurance purposes. Experience prior to the 1990 legislation of patient access to records and to statutory reports for Mental Health Review Tribunals or the Courts has suggested that informal arrangements in forensic psychiatric practice, allowing patients to view and discuss their records, were generally conducive to very constructive working with the patient (Parrott et al., 1988).

Inpatient Care: Secure but Therapeutic

Nursing Considerations

The social and physical environment for patients who require some degree of security will have an effect on their subsequent behaviour, relationships and aspirations. Paul and Lentz (1977) described this as the principle of expectancy, saying:

> The frequency of occurence of an action, behaviour or response is the function of the expectation communicated at the time. . . .

Weaver et al. (1978a,b), in their reports of disruptive behaviours on a locked ward, also suggested that a number of patient behaviours were a function, in part, of a set of expectations, beliefs and attitudes held by nurses about the people they were nursing. These included the beliefs that the mentally ill are not responsible for their behaviour, that there is little hope of improvement and that people coming to a ward for the disturbed are going to act in a disturbed manner. The crucial challenge, then, for any manager of an environment for patients who have been disruptive or violent is to provide and maintain a set of circumstances where such behaviour is not regarded as the norm, where responsibility is not entirely taken away from the patient, where there is opportunity for growth and learning, and yet safety prevails.

This is no easy task, because the giving of responsibility to patients can run contrary to the requirements of security and safety in locked environments. Simple, mundane decisions can often be taken outside the control of the patient or, indeed, the front line clinical staff, in the name of safety. An example will demonstrate some of the issues.

> Each morning a number of patients get up early, without prompting, to make themselves tea with their own tea, sugar and milk. In order to do this, however, they have to gain access to the kitchen, usually locked, and handle a potentially dangerous weapon—boiling water. This means that a nurse has to be present, to supervise. The arrangement works well until someone comments that it is dangerous for a nurse to do this and thus a reactive rule evolves, passed on by word of mouth rather than debated and written, that the practice should cease. The patients then no longer choose when they should have tea, they no longer provide their own ingredients, choose the strength of their tea or engage in cooperative behaviour, but queue at directed times for a mug of institutional brew.

Thus emerges the conflict of service provision for violent and offender patients. There are those who think that safety is paramount, that patients cannot be trusted to be responsible and that individual choice can be sacrificed for the greater good. Others argue that some patients need the opportunity to take responsibility and that individual choice is important both as a right and as a basis for effective therapy, even if it involves risk. There is a danger that the team will be split. The resolution of the differences has implications for the future direction the unit takes in its treatment programmes. The clinical ward manager has to balance these needs and views.

Absolute safety and absolute security are unobtainable goals. No amount of double checking, locking of doors or building of walls will ensure this. The role of those considering safety and security is thus to minimize the risk.

Whenever possible, security measures should be unobtrusive, tailored to the needs of individuals, and applied to small groups rather than to everybody. This can be achieved by having separate units which allow the transfer of patients between them as the need for supervision, structure and care varies. In environments where there is no physical separation between levels of security, there are extra demands placed on nursing staff to be aware of individual programmes. This can be extremely difficult, as these can change from day to day and even hour to hour. The picture is further complicated as a ward can have some patients who require one to one supervision around the clock, while others spend long amounts of time off the ward, with little supervision. Some may be provoked by a stimulating, populous environment, but others may need a high level of occupation and activity, even seeking pathological stimulation or attention if they do not receive it. This can mean, for example, that a patient who is allowed to use items that are dangerous, e.g. scissors or modelling knives, is living next door to someone who is thought to be too dangerous to be left on their own. Such situations create pressures not only for those supervising, but also for patients themselves, who may not see the reason for such widely different treatment plans. Nurses have to be able to switch flexibly between approaches as they move from interactions that require control and direction of the patient to those where the patient can be allowed to make decisions. These interactions may take place within seconds of each other.

The proper maintenance of the environment is vital when patients are unable to leave the ward at will. For them, the whole round of daily life will be spent in one place. There is a responsibility to ensure that the environment is as pleasant as possible, and that things are not allowed to fall into disrepair and neglect. The main burden of this responsibility falls on the nursing staff. It should be shared with the patient group who would otherwise have no incentive to maintain the environment. The second principle of environmental influence, is, therefore, involvement. Paul and Lentz (1977) described the acquisition and maintenance of new behaviours as a function of the degree of personal participation. Individuals can be involved through groups to exert real power in shaping their environment (Wright, 1986). This requires a special commitment on the part of those who manage the ward to listen to suggestions and complaints, and to take the necessary action to produce change.

The social environment is influenced by the physical environment. The need to lock doors behind patients may set the tone for all nurse patient interactions. There is a school of thought that 'the ideal nurse-patient relationship is not reached until doors are unlocked' (e.g. Mandlebrote, 1958). Despite this inbuilt barrier to communication in secure hospitals, some form of therapeutic alliance must be established by the nurses and other clinical staff. The direction and intensity of this will depend in part on the philosophy and purpose of the unit. Baldwin (1983), in his article on nursing models for special hospitals, commented that there are three dominant models: the medico-legal, the moral-retributional and the educational. The medico-legal model, he suggested, rests on the detection and monitoring of readily identifiable illnesses and syndromes, and focuses very strongly on the individual patient. This carries the danger that some of the total picture, e.g. environmental influences, may be ignored. The 'moral-retributional model' is untutored and often implicit. It focuses on the transgression of social and moral codes on the part of the patient, and the need for sanctions and the protection of society on the part of nurses. There is little emphasis on change or 'therapy'. This contrasts sharply with the 'educational model', which is based on the defined needs of the patients and often requires training programmes to reduce deficits. Nurses become agents of change, who organize such interventions with the patient on an individual or group basis.

Peplau (1952) expressed the belief that the chief function of the nurse is to maintain effective, interpersonal relationships and to transform as many situations as possible into learning occasions. She described four stages through which the nurse and patient pass:

1. *Orientation*, in which patients recognize that they suffer from some form of ill health which requires treatment;
2. *Identification*, when a relationship is established that is mutually goal directed, and in which there is an exploration of the problem and the resources on hand to cope with it;
3. *Exploitation*, the phase in which the patient uses these resources to help himself; and
4. *Resolution*, the final stage in which the dependence and ties between the therapist and the patient are relinquished in order that the patient can be freed to take up a more independent existence.

These are ideal states and problems may arise when a patient is compulsorily detained and so does not seek help (Rix, 1988) or never gets to the point where he recognizes his ill health. Despite such difficulties, however, Peplau offered a framework for nursing which is valid in secure psychiatric settings, with an emphasis on negotiation, consent and education rather than treatment by threat.

The test for any model is whether it is effective. The educational model does seem to work in practice and one of us (Rix, 1988) has detailed some of the evidence. Clack (1963) also discussed this kind of relationship in her study of nurses' reactions to aggressive behaviour. She described first the nurse who reacts by expressing aggressive feelings through 'laying down the law' rather than talking through the situation and offering an opportunity for learning and developing alternative responses. The second type of response is for the nurse to demonstrate general anxiety by becoming helpless, ingratiating to the patient, avoiding him or changing the environment to accommodate his wishes in order to prevent an aggressive outburst. In a third and recommended model, the nurse sits down with the patient in an effort to establish—

> free communication and exploration, mutual reduction of anxiety and a consistent intervention . . . which allowed learning to take place for both individuals.

Nursing staff are not alone in having to battle with counter transference reactions, even psychiatrists who have undergone a personal analysis can react negatively when victimized (Maier, 1990). In a hospital, however, nurses are most consistently in direct contact with the patients, and their reactions may develop more quickly and intensely and have most impact on the environment. In any hospital, including secure hospitals, nurses greatly outnumber staff from other disciplines and this alone can make their attitudes pervasive. Dubin (1989) emphasized the difficulties in recognizing the strength and variety of feelings in response to violence, and lists some which have much in common with Clack's account. They include impulses to rescue, to support, to hurt, to admire, and to identify with and/or accept compliments from the patients; all may interfere not only with treatment *per se*, but also with safety. Extending this argument Reid (1985) said:

> The most pervasive reason for our failure to deal effectively with anti-social behaviour lies in the collective anger that the public and, to some extent, mental health professionals feel toward antisocial people who are often criminals.

In order for therapeutic intervention to take place, all clinical staff need to feel supported by the wider team in their endeavours, particularly when the patient is disturbed. This requires clear, mutually agreed guidance in the form of treatment plans, policies and procedures. This is particularly important in emergencies when there is a need for a confident and consistent response. Leiba (1980) described in some detail how this can be achieved on a locked intensive care ward with multidisciplinary cooperation. He emphasized the importance of discussing the situation with the patient after the emergency has passed and the situation brought under the control of the staff. This is another example of a management intervention initially aimed at security being used for the patient's education.

The impact of the ward environment is difficult to evaluate, but it has been attempted. First there is the evidence of the impact of a poor or hostile environment. Wing and Brown's (1970) demonstration of the debilitating effects of impersonal and poorly stimulating environments is essential reading. The literature which demonstrates that a hostile milieu may induce or exacerbate illness, violence or both is referred to in Ch. 20. Here it is the immediacy of impact that is addressed.

Grassian (1983) described the detailed evaluation of 14 men in a USA state correctional institution who had been very socially isolated there for between 11 days and 10 months. All developed psychiatric symptoms; many became psychotic, 5 developed problems of impulse control, and 3 were self-mutilating. All the prisoners reported diminution of their symptoms on release from the near solitary confinement, usually within a few hours. Lee (1980) gave an anecdotal account of a philosophy of care in special hospitals where nurses assumed that patients would be violent and were quick to supress any such behaviour at its earliest sign.

> Hospital life was degrading, inhuman and unnatural and this produced precisely the situation that they (the nurses) were trying to eradicate.

He went on to maintain that a change in environment, with a concerned, more individualized approach did much to alter patients' behaviour.

The Butler Committee (Home Office DHSS, 1975) similarly reported that conditions found in secure facilities, such as crowding and lack of privacy, could result in disturbed behaviour. Aiken (1984) showed in his data that half the violent incidents in a locked ward were as a result of the frustration of not being able to leave on request. By far the most important evidence for the power of the hostile hospital environment comes from Greenblatt et al. (1955). Their work was at a time when the custodial asylum model of care was under review. They introduced changes in the milieu of a range of private and public hospitals in the USA at a time *before the widespread use of phenothiazines*. At one large public hospital alone, the seclusion hours were reduced, in association with the changes, from 2900 hours in February, 1952 to 26 hours in November, 1952. The patient population changed very little in that time.

Milieu Therapy

The term milieu therapy is often used interchangeably with the concept of therapeutic community, the underlying principle being that patients are encouraged to participate actively in their own treatment and in the management of their ward or unit. Communication is open and direct between staff, and meetings between them as a group—of the whole 'community'—form a cornerstone of the approach. A therapeutic community in the full sense maintains close contact with adjacent and relevant communities outside the therapeutic setting, and usually practices an open door policy with the patients coming and going freely and participating in activities according to a balance of personal choice and group pressures. Secure facilities cannot be therapeutic communities in this full sense, but most of the attributes of milieu therapy can be applied in whole or in part. Widely accepted as an important approach for the treatment of people with primary personality disorders (*see also* p. 748 and Gunn et al., 1978), the role of such an approach has been more controversial among patients with schizophrenia (Van Putten, 1973). Paul and Lentz (1977) concluded their 6-year study of patients, mainly with chronic schizophrenia, comparing milieu and social learning programmes, by saying that the latter was significantly more effective than the former when measured against relative social functioning before and after discharge, discharge rates and length of stay subsequently in the community, but not that the milieu therapy was ineffective. May (1968), in his comparative study of five treatment methods for schizophrenia in general psychiatry services, showed that milieu therapy alone produced significant improvement in 58% of patients compared with 80% who received ECT 'alone' and 96% who received drugs 'alone'. This is often taken as an indictment of milieu therapy, but the reality is that it was the only one of the therapies that was truly given alone. The others were, in effect, adjuncts to milieu therapy.

Weaver et al. (1978a,b) reported that disturbed and disruptive behaviour among patients on a locked ward decreased once staff had attended to:

1. the low level of activity on the ward—by organizing work and occupational therapy;
2. the dependence of patients on staff caused by the regimentation and ritualization of daily routines—by offering opportunities for responsible decision making; and
3. the avoidance of social integration—by increasing social activities between patients and staff.

A more liberal approach to security increased it. Trips and work off the ward were negotiated, for example, and were associated with a decrease in abscondings and window breaking. Wolf (1977), in a review of the literature, concluded that an environment that emphasizes involvement, order, organization, a practical orientation and a reasonable degree of control is most successful at promoting mental health and social behaviour.

Seclusion and Physical Restraint

Seclusion is still widely practised in hospital care. There is common resort to solitary confinement in stripped cells in prisons, a technique which is mainly used with the mentally disturbed. Other forms of physical restraint, such as straps, body belts and restraint garments are still in use, but rarely so. There is no evidence that seclusion *per se* is of any value and some evidence that it may be damaging. Elements in the seclusion process might be adapted to enhance safe care and to serve as a basis for intensifying therapeutic activity.

Soloff (1984) provided an interesting history of the use of seclusion and restraint, noting that the Greeks advocated its minimal use, but that its origins mainly lie in the religious persecution of the Middle Ages when theories of demonic possession were favoured to account for madness. Instrumental restraint became so much the rule that by the late 18th Century even the King of England, George III, was—

> . . . immediately encased in a machine which left no liberty of motion. He was sometimes chained to a stake. He was frequently beaten and starved, and at best, kept in subjugation by menacing and violent language.

By the early 19th century, however, attitudes were shifting. In his evidence to a Parliamentary enquiry, Dr Monro of the Bethlem Hospital, on being questioned about the differential use of restraints said:

> They are fit only for pauper lunatics; if a gentleman was put into irons, he would not like it.

Connolly, expressed the matter more succinctly:

> Restraint and neglect are synonymous. They are substitute for the thousand attentions needed by the disturbed patient (Hunter and MacAlpine, 1963).

The physical restraint of a disturbed patient is a dangerous procedure. In their survey of assaults on staff in a state hospital in the USA, Lion et al. (1981) noted that 53% had occurred while patients were being restrained. A number of techniques have evolved for disengaging violent patients, and immobilizing them, techniques which require demonstration, practical experience and regular retraining for safe and confident practice.

Skills and clear leadership are most important if restraint is to diminish rather than increase the risk of harm. Restraint may have to be effected in an emergency, so the process must be well rehearsed. Lion and Soloff (1984) emphasized the importance of avoiding injury, inflicting pain and minimizing humiliation.

> The staff restraining the patient today will be seeking a therapeutic alliance tomorrow.

They described the essential personal balance—a 'leader' among the staff who will talk and negotiate with the patient as far as possible and be responsible for indicating the point of initiation of force if necessary, a 'monitor' who will be responsible for the environment, clearing the area of other patients, onlookers and physical obstructions, as well as observing the process throughout, and sufficient numbers of staff both to ensure restraint, if it becomes necessary, and to demonstrate the capability of the staff for establishing control of a dangerous situation. The selection of staff for the various roles will depend on a variety of factors, not least training, but as far as possible the leader should be someone who knows the patient and who retains the chance of striking up the rapport that may still prevent the need for physical restraint. Whether or not rapport is established with the patient, the leader should continue to talk to him about what is happening. There should be a clear statement of purpose and a clear, but non-threatening, set of instructions for the patient which allow him choices other than being physically overpowered or held, but brook no other negotiation. The time for that is past and he must, for example, go to the room designated, sit down and take the medication offered. While this is going on, the other staff must position themselves to have access to the patient's extremities. Effective restraint protects staff *and* the patient from injury.

The use of mechanical restraints is almost entirely unresearched. Aside from the humiliation of the patient that this entails, with resultant potential for later retaliation, the greatest dangers are occlusion of major blood vessels or friction injuries at the site of restraint. Physical as well as mental signs must be closely monitored, and the patient/prisoner must not be left alone.

Seclusion can be defined as the containment of a patient alone in a room or other enclosed areas from which that patient has no means of egress

(Royal College of Psychiatrists, 1982), although some definitions include a note to emphasize the forcible element, and a later Royal College of Psychiatrists (1990a) definition incorporated a requirement for supervision and a clear statement of purpose:

> Seclusion is defined as the supervised confinement of a patient specifically placed alone in a locked room for a period at any time of the day or night for the protection of the patient, staff or others from serious harm.

The Bethlem Royal and Maudsley Hospital uses a definition which includes *any* detention of a patient alone in a locked room. In the special (maximum security) hospitals of England, patients are locked in their rooms at night without possibility of egress, a practice not treated as seclusion, and without the attendant recording and monitoring.

Monitoring guidance for England and Wales is set out in the Code of Practice to the Mental Health Act 1983 (Department of Health and Welsh Office, 1990; *see* Appendix 2, p. 999). It says that if continuous seclusion is needed, a nursing review by two nurses should take place every 2 hours, and a medical review every 4 hours. If seclusion continues for more than 8 hours consecutively, or for more than 12 hours intermittently over a period of 48 hours, an independent review should take place by the responsible medical officer, with a team of nurses and other health care professionals who were not directly involved in the care of the patient at the time of the incident which led to the seclusion. The Royal College of Psychiatrists (1990a) emphasized that for good practice, procedural notes are necessary, but are not sufficient in themselves. There is a danger that regular adherence to a set pattern of procedures leads those carrying them out to lose sight of the primary objective, which is to ask whether the seclusion needs to continue. For this task, it is essential that a nurse has adequate contact with the secluded patient. An acceptable seclusion room must be purpose-built to minimize the possibilities of self-harm and to maximize the opportunities for staff observation and communication.

Threatened or actual violence, to self or others, is the principal reason for secluding a patient. There is little doubt that if the room has been properly constructed, violence to others can be contained for the duration of the seclusion. Further control, however, is another matter. One element of this is that with a disruptive patient out of the way, staff will have better control over the rest of the patient group. Mattson and Sacks (1978), however, noted that other patients become nervous and uncomfortable when one of their group is in seclusion, even if they are relieved to have him out of the way. The Boynton Report on use of seclusion at Rampton Hospital (DHSS, 1980) went further. It suggested that seclusion increased a patient's status, and that this may have escalated the seclusion rates among female patients at Rampton, up to 9% of whom were secluded on any one day at that time. Mattson and Sacks (1978) also reported frequent disturbances as patients are released from seclusion. An impression that patients calm quickly in seclusion is not matched by clinical data, the mean duration for seclusion variously being recorded as 4.3 hours (Thompson, 1986) 1.8 hours (Soloff and Turner, 1981) and 15.7 hours (Binder, 1979).

The components of seclusion usually include isolation from stimulation and demand, the giving of special status to patients, forcible and physical containment, uncertainty about the length of containment and increased individualized staff attention. Medication is often given in conjunction with seclusion. Any one or two of these interventions could be offered without the need to resort to seclusion itself. One study (Antoinette et al., 1990) with children under 14 years suggested that 'locked seclusion' may be preferable to 'unlocked seclusion', because the latter was associated with increased regular and emergency use of tranquillizing medications. On the other hand, other studies have shown no inverse relationship between medication and seclusion (Binder, 1979; Schwab and Lahmeyer, 1979). If seclusion is anything other than a means of emergency containment, it is probably the reduction in stimulation and the individualized attention which is beneficial for some patients.

In seclusion, patients are usually deprived of everything except clothes and bedding, and for these specially nondescript, toughened articles may be provided. The walls are bare, lighting is under staff control and the only means of external distraction is staff observation and evaluation. This is close to sensory deprivation, which is well documented as having adverse effects. It is likely that some of the so-called prison psychoses, documented around the turn of the century (Nitsche and Williams, 1913), were secondary to the sensory deprivation of solitary confinement, and Grassian (1983) has documented the onset of similar, apparently environmentally dependent disorders in a latter day American prison. No one any longer expects seclusion to be therapeutic for the mentally normal, or even the neurotic or personality disordered, but there is still debate about a positive effect for people with schizophrenia. Harris (1959) described 'greater tolerance than normal subjects', noting a reduction in hallucinatory experiences. Reitman and Cleveland (1964) described an improvement in body image and boundary, while Mehl and Cromwell (1969) differentiated between two schizophrenic groups. Patients who withdrew from their environment, either physically or verbally through autistic mutterings and failures to converse, often expressed a liking for sensory deprivation. Others tolerated it poorly. Suedfeld and Roy (1975) demonstrated the divergence between non-psychotic inmates in a correctional service who became grossly psychotic on solitary confinement and people with schizophrenia who became less psychotic. Seclusion is not necessary for the reduction of sensory input. The subtleties required in the assessment, down to a particular subgroup of psychosis, are not possible just before seclusion is considered and the evidence is too slight to defend its use in this way. Mattson and Sacks' (1978) view remains the most satisfactory. Seclusion should not be regarded as a treatment in itself, but as a means of providing an environment in which medication and fatigue are the important therapeutic factors. It may also be a way of providing nurses with a respite, or a change of emphasis, so that they can regain a lost therapeutic alliance, and/or tackle other ward problems.

The few studies of seclusion that exist have been principally preoccupied with numbers and rates of seclusion. Gutheil (1984) and Angold (1989) provide reviews. There are one or two pointers which suggest that certain groups of patients may be more vulnerable to seclusion than others. Rampton Hospital was found to seclude proportionately more men than women (DHSS, 1980), and most studies have shown the young, violent, psychotic man to be most at risk (Angold, 1989). Non-patient factors, relating to numbers, change and preoccupation of staff (e.g. with meals or handovers) have also been found to influence rates (e.g. Campbell et al., 1982; Thompson, 1986). There are no data on which to base guidance on timing, length or frequency, and although suggestions that seclusion should be terminated by a gradual reintroduction to the ward environment seems eminently sensible, there is nothing to support these. There is evidence that seclusion is extremely distressing to patients. Wadeson and Carpenter (1976) evaluated patients' experiences through their art work and found that they revealed the fear, anger, resentment and frustration of their experience up to 12 months later (*see also* frontispiece). Soliday (1985) found that over half of patients felt that seclusion was a punishment and humiliating. Chamberlin (1985) wrote a personal account. Staff have more ambivalent attitudes, many feeling disquiet (e.g. Campbell et al., 1982), but most seeing it as a necessary tool (e.g. Soliday, 1985).

Medication

Forensic psychiatrists manage patients with the whole range of psychiatric disorders; in addition, they are particularly concerned with the management of those who present problems of aggression or sexually deviant behaviour. There are several useful reviews of the use of medication in these circumstances, (e.g. Sheard, 1983; Bond and Lader, 1984; Conn and Lion, 1984). It has to be emphasized that medication is only one aspect of patient management and is complementary to psychological and social interventions. The fostering of good staff-patient relationships can decrease the requirement for medication and can improve patient compliance. The use of medication should always be explained to the patient. The legal requirements for consent in the UK are dealt with in Ch. 2.

In treating aggressive patients, treatment should be aimed at the underlying mental disorder (Singhal and Telner, 1983) rather than aggression *per se*—there are many types of aggressive behaviour and no specific anti-aggression drug (Valzelli, 1981). Many treatments take time to become effective, and a substantial measure of active patient cooperation with them is necessary. The danger of violence may be immediate, so although there is no violence specific drug, reduction of arousal using the more sedative neuroleptics is often helpful and necessary during a crisis.

Medication in Psychiatric Emergencies

For many psychiatric emergencies, haloperidol is regarded as very useful, it can be given orally or intramuscularly, and it is highly potent with a low incidence of oversedation and hypotensive reactions (Ayd, 1972; Conn and Lion, 1984). On the basis of a small study, Resnick and Burton (1984) recommended another butyrophenone, droperidol, which compared to haloperidol has a more rapid onset of action, shorter duration of effect, lower incidence of extrapyramidal side-effects and greater sedative effect. Unfortunately, droperidol can also be associated with hypotensive side-effects. It merits a larger study comparing it with haloperidol.

Benzodiazepines are important drugs for the treatment of alcohol withdrawal and intoxication with drugs which have significant anticholinergic effects, such as phencylidine ('angel dust'). Other aspects of the management of withdrawal are dealt with on pp. 444 and 459. Benzodiazepines may also be useful to supplement neuroleptics in acute psychiatric crises for control of violence, indeed some would advocate their use in these circumstances as a means of limiting the dose of neuroleptic at this time. There is a case report of intramuscular lorazepam being found effective in reducing the agitation of a patient with schizophrenia (Ward et al., 1986), but adequate controlled studies are lacking. Benzodiazepines are usually given either orally or intravenously, as most are poorly absorbed when administered intramuscularly.

Not uncommonly, sedative medication for the control of aggression is prescribed 'as necessary', to be used at the discretion of nursing staff instead of, or to supplement, regular medication. Appelbaum et al. (1983) studied the effect of inpatient violence on anti-psychotic medication. In just over 50% of cases following a first act of violence, medication was increased, but generally such patients had been on low doses beforehand. In more than 20% of cases there was a decrease. Contrary to popular fears, and indeed court decisions in the USA setting limits on the use of medication in psychiatric hospitals, there was no evidence that the nature or quality of medication received by violent patients differed significantly from that for the non-violent except in the maintenance doses received at the time of discharge, when the violent tended to be on higher levels. McLaren et al. (1990) studied 150 randomly chosen administrations of 'as necessary' medication given over a 3-month period in a 30-bedded medium secure unit. Sedative medication, including several neuroleptics, sodium amytal and diazepam were given for control or containment of actual or threatened violence in about two-thirds of cases, and for patient distress in the rest. No one drug appeared to have any advantage over the others. Medication was almost never used in isolation, other interventions such as talking to the patient, distracting him, taking him to his room, were also used. A few patients (7%) responded so quickly to the medication that a placebo effect seemed likely, while about 20% did not settle at all. The remainder settled within an hour, most in half an hour, by showing significant behavioural improvement and gaining significant relief from anxiety, agitation and delusional distress. Most treatments (78%) were given orally. The use of 'as necessary' medication had little impact on overall medication regimes.

Routine Medication for Violent Patients

Organic disorders

Aggression can be a feature of many organic brain disorders, particularly because of impaired impulse control. Neuroleptic drugs have been widely used for these conditions (Burns, 1980; De Cuyper et al., 1985; Lynch et al., 1985; Mlele and Wiley, 1986). Beta-adrenoceptor blocking drugs have been particularly advocated for the control of assaultiveness in patients with brain damage (Elliott, 1977; Yudofsky et al., 1981; Greendyke et al., 1984; Mattes, 1985; Polakoff et al., 1986). These case reports need to be interpreted with caution because in many instances beta-blockers were used as an adjunct to neuroleptics, and it has been demonstrated that these two types of drug interact—propranolol increases plasma levels of chlorpromazine (Peet et al., 1981a).

Nevertheless, there are double-blind placebo-controlled cross-over studies of propanolol (Greendyke et al., 1986) and pindolol (Greendyke and Kanter, 1986) in which no concomitant neuroleptic medication was given, and where a significant therapeutic effect from beta-blockers was found in small numbers of severely demented patients. Pindolol has been reported to cause fewer side-effects than propanolol (Greendyke and Kanter, 1986).

Lithium has been used with success in the management of aggressive mentally retarded patients (Dostal and Zvolsky, 1970; Lion et al., 1975; Craft et al., 1987). It has also been favoured in the management of diagnostically heterogeneous aggressive inpatients (Morrison et al., 1973) and prisoners (Tupin et al., 1973), many of whom had indicators of organic abnormality including epilepsy. Schiff et al. (1982), however, reported a case of an aggressive man with a history of severe head injury whose aggression worsened on treatment with lithium. Jus et al. (1973) reported an increase in seizure frequency and aggression in a group of eight patients with temporal lobe epilepsy who were treated with lithium. On the basis of this evidence, lithium should be used cautiously in the brain-damaged, particularly those with epilepsy.

Although the concept of intermittent explosive disorder as an organic abnormality akin to epilepsy (Monroe, 1970) has been discredited (Leicester, 1982; Fenton, 1984) anticonvulsant drugs have been described as effective in controlling unexplained violence in some people. They include chlordiaz-epoxide and/or primidone (Monroe, 1975), carbamazepine (Tunks and Dermer, 1977) and diphenylhydantoin (Maletzky, 1973; Maletzky and Klotter, 1974). All these compounds have sedative effects which may constitute their important quality in the control of aggression.

Childhood attention deficit disorder is often considered to have an organic aetiology. Hyperactivity and aggression in childhood and adolescence can respond to psychostimulant drugs (Allen et al., 1975). Stringer and Josef (1983) found a beneficial response to methylphenidate in two adults with antisocial personality and a history of childhood hyperactivity. Extreme caution, however, is required in the use of amphetamines and related compounds, because of the risk of abuse and their potential for inducing psychosis.

Schizophrenia and related disorders

Neuroleptics are the mainstay of drug treatment for patients suffering from schizophrenia, including those who are aggressive (Itil and Wadud, 1975; Tardiff, 1983a). Aggression as a manifestation of the disease will often respond more rapidly to medication than its other features, such as thought disorder, hallucinations and delusions. If aggression is part of the usual repertoire of social interactions of the patient and his family, it is less likely to respond to medication than when aggression is out of character (Cohen et al., 1968). No single neuroleptic drug has emerged supreme in the manage-ment of aggressive schizophrenic patients. Evidence for claims that clopen-thixol decanoate is particularly suitable for the management of aggressive schizophrenic patients is growing, however, and a rapidly acting parenteral form (the acetate) for use in emergencies has been developed. Its positive effects are said to outlast those of other rapidly acting drugs, such as haloperidol, and to give rise to fewer extra pyramidal effects (Bobon and De Bleeker, 1990; Hebenstreit, 1990). If a patient fails to respond to an adequate trial of one neuroleptic drug, a trial of a drug from another neuroleptic class can be worthwhile. Some authors have advocated the use of high doses of neuroleptic medication in treatment-resistant cases (e.g. Rifkin et al., 1971; Donlon, 1976; McCreadie and MacDonald, 1977; Dencker et al., 1978; Hollister and Kim, 1982). Other authors have found little or no benefit from high doses (Quitkin et al., 1975; McClelland et al., 1976; McCreadie et al., 1979; Bjorndal et al., 1980; Rimon et al., 1981; Zarifian et al., 1982; Modestin et al., 1983; Bollini et al., 1984; Browne et al., 1988). Clinical deterioration at higher doses has been reported (Rifkin et al., 1971; Van Putten et al., 1974; Barnes and Bridges, 1980). In a comprehensive literature review Baldessarini et al. (1988) failed to find support for the use of high dose neuroleptic treatment. Furthermore, at high doses unwanted drug effects increase and these include a small but significant number of fatalities which may be attributable to the medication (Cancro and Wilder, 1970;

Moore and Book, 1970; Peele and Von Loetzen, 1973; Flaherty and Lahmeyer, 1978; Ketai et al., 1979; Modestin et al., 1981; Bollini et al., 1984).

Lithium is increasingly being considered as suitable for the treatment of schizophrenia. In a review of the literature Delva and Letemendia (1982) suggested that between one-third and one-half of schizophrenic patients benefit from lithium. Van Putten and Sanders (1975) have recommended lithium for treatment-resistant patients. It may be particularly valuable as an adjunct to neuroleptic medication in cases where aggression is a feature. For example Altshuler et al. (1977) reported decreased aggression in five out of six deaf schizophrenic patients and Sheard (1984) reported control of combative behaviour in six out of ten aggressive schizophrenic patients.

Beta-blockers have, in the past, been recommended in the treatment of schizophrenia (Yorkston et al., 1977). In a review of patients notes, Sorgi et al. (1986) found a decrease in assaultiveness in six out of seven patients with chronic schizophrenia who were treated with beta-blockers in addition to neuroleptics. In a double-blind placebo-controlled study of propanolol against chlorpromazine and placebo, however, propanolol produced no greater improvement than placebo (Peet et al., 1981a). Furthermore, Peet et al. (1981b) have demonstrated that propanolol increases plasma levels of chlorpromazine. There may, therefore, be little difference between adding a beta-blocker and increasing the dose of neuroleptic. There seems little justification for the use of beta-blockers in the treatment of schizophrenia at present.

As mentioned above, another drug which has been advocated for the management of aggression is carbamazepine. Klein et al. (1984) found haloperidol plus carbamazepine superior to haloperidol alone in the treatment of excited psychotic states, both manic and schizophrenic. Hakola and Laulumaa (1982) and Yassa and Dupont (1983) have reported a reduction in the violence of small numbers of schizophrenic patients treated with carbamazepine. Unfortunately, large, adequately controlled studies are lacking, so that the place of carbamazepine in the management of violent schizophrenic patients remains to be defined. Small numbers of schizophrenic patients have been reported to benefit from tryptophan (Morand et al., 1983) or medroxyprogesterone acetate (O'Connor and Baker, 1983). Further studies are required before either of these drugs can be confidently recommended. ECT may still have an occasional place as an adjunct to neuroleptic medication, especially in speeding recovery from classically schizophrenic symptoms (Taylor, 1990) which may provoke more serious violence.

Clozapine is an antipsychotic of mixed blessings, but one which must be considered for a patient with schizophrenia who seems otherwise treatment-resistant, the more so if the illness is clearly linked with violent behaviour. Fitton and Heel (1990) and the British Journal of Psychiatry (1992) provide comprehensive reviews. It is the only antipsychotic medication to have emerged from double-blind controlled trials as consistently superior to other neuroleptics in the relief of schizophrenic symptoms and the social improvement of patients (Claghorn et al., 1987; Borison et al., 1988; Conley et al., 1988; Kane et al., 1988). Herrera et al. (1988) found a non-significant trend in favour of clozapine. It also has the great advantage that, given its low dopaminergic activity, extra-pyramidal side-effects, including akathisia and tardive dyskinesia, are extremely rare, so many patients tolerate it better than other neuroleptics and may be more compliant with it. It is described as having an immediate calming effect. The principal disadvantage lies in the fact that it poses an exceptional risk of agranulocytosis, with a cumulative incidence of 2% after one year of treatment (Griffith and Saameli, 1975); several patients died in the early years of the drug's use. Other major side-effects include the neuroleptic malignant syndrome, dose-related epilepsy, with about 5% of patients being at risk of fits at doses above 600 mg (Haller and Binder, 1990), and a toxic delirious state, necessitating withdrawal in about 6% of patients (Grohmann et al., 1989).

Patients should not be considered for clozapine unless they have had no significant symptomatic relief and no good period of functioning in the preceding 5 years in spite of at least three periods of treatment in that time with neuroleptic agents from at least two different chemical classes (phenothiazines, butyrophenones, thioxanthines, diphenyl butylpiperidines, substituted benzamides, dibenzodiazepines), at doses equivalent to or greater than 1000 mg of chlorpromazine for at least 6 weeks at a time (Kane et al., 1988), and at least one of the courses of neuroleptic treatment has been given parenterally.

The risk of agranulocytosis, the most feared side-effect, can be minimized if a series of precautions are rigidly followed. No patient with a history of drug-induced neutropaenia, agranulocytosis or a disorder of the bone marrow should be treated with clozapine, and patients should have a normal blood count at the start of therapy. Aside from any legal requirements with respect to consent to treatment, patients must be sufficiently cooperative with treatment to tolerate weekly blood tests for at least 18 weeks and 2-weekly thereafter. All other drugs with a potential for provoking agranulocytosis must be avoided. These include some antibiotics, analgesics, antidepressants and carbamazepine. Depot neuroleptics in particular should *not* be used, because of their slow wash-out time in the event of crisis. The weekly blood tests are essential during the early weeks of peak risk of marrow suppression and, if the white blood cell count falls below 3000 per mm^3 or the neutrophils below 1500 per mm^3, the drug must be stopped at once and close monitoring of the patient's physical state instituted. A further worry at such a point in treatment is that of rebound psychosis, documented by Borison et al. (1988), but potentially having exceptionally serious consequences among patients who have violent propensities. One patient whose psychosis had responded well to the drug, but who developed bone marrow suppression, not only had a resurgence of psychotic symptoms on cessation of the drug, but became very much more violent and self-destructive than she had ever been known to be previously, and for about 1 month required continuous care, including restraint, from not less than three nurses at any one time (Campbell, State Hospital Scotland, personal communication).

Partly because of the requirement for intensive monitoring, the cost of administering clozapine is very high for a psychiatric treatment, although this has to be considered in the context of the overall economic burden of schizophrenia as a disease (Davies and Drummond, 1990). Revicki et al. (1990) have argued that patients treated with clozapine were no more of a financial burden on a health service than those on cheaper medications. Unfortunately, from the point of view of many forensic psychiatry services, the financial advantages are likely to be gained by the general and community psychiatric teams, and the costs are likely to fall on inpatient, especially secure services. The serious *clinical* risks of clozapine have to be balanced against the risks of morbidity, mortality or harm to others if an otherwise treatment-resistant patient is left that way. The long-term consequences of using clozapine are poorly understood. So far patients followed for 7 years and more have shown a high incidence of problems from hypersalivation (78%) through overweight (63%) to EEG abnormalities (37%). Neurological side-effects, however, seem to be few (Schmauss et al., 1989). No depot preparation of clozapine is available, nor likely to become so because of the risk of neutropaenia progressing to agranulocytosis.

Affective disorders

Van Praag (1986) has reviewed the evidence linking affective disorders and disordered aggression through the common pathway of the serotonergic system. Both mania and depression can result in abnormally violent behaviour, although rarely do. Mania does, however, present with disinhibition, irritability and aggression. Drug treatment of mania is generally with lithium and/or neuroleptics. Patients who fail to respond to lithium may benefit from carbamazepine (Ballenger and Post, 1980). Depression is associated with aggressive behaviour both to the self and to others. Useful drug treatments include antidepressants, neuroleptics and lithium. An antidepressant effect has also been claimed for carbamazepine (Post et al., 1986). Electroconvulsive therapy can be of benefit in both manic and depressive conditions. A combination of lithium and carbamazepine has been found to be helpful for treatment-resistant patients, and, with the exception of depression of thyroid hormones, the unwanted effects seem to cancel each other out (Kramlinger and Post, 1989a,b, 1990).

The neuroleptic malignant syndrome (NMS)

Although, the NMS is uncommon (Addonizio et al., 1986), the risk factors discussed below suggest that psychotic patients who find their way into forensic psychiatry inpatient services may be among those at maximum risk.

The condition is important because it has a mortality rate of 15–20% (Caroff, 1980; Levenson, 1985).

Fever, rigidity, autonomic dysfunction and altered consciousness occurring together in a psychotic patient receiving neuroleptic medication should immediately arouse suspicions of NMS. The combination is by no means pathognomonic however, indeed a more likely diagnosis is that the patient has some febrile illness superimposed on either established or unremarked dystonia. Serum creatine phosphokinase—skeletal muscle type—is raised in NMS, since the most serious complication of the syndrome is a breakdown of the muscle. If extensive enough, this can lead to acute renal failure. Although two or three cases have been reported following the withdrawal of dopamine agonists, almost invariably the condition seems to follow the use of neuroleptic medication. Kellam (1987) warned against necessarily attributing the disorder to the drugs, since case reports of not dissimilar conditions were prevalent in the psychiatric literature well before the advent of phenothiazines; however, most cases improve when the medication is stopped. There is some consensus in the current literature that most cases have followed the use of haloperidol or depot fluphenazine, but as it is likely that these are among the most commonly used neuroleptics and as no one has controlled for overall frequency of use, it cannot be said with any confidence that they pose exceptional risk. No antipsychotic agent seems to have been found exempt from precipitating the disorder.

Eighty percent of reported cases have been under 40 years of age and the male:female ratio is 2:1, while underlying organic brain damage is not infrequent (Caroff, 1980). Itoh et al. (1977) suggested that the more disturbed, sicker patients were at special risk, and that in most cases symptoms developed shortly after commencement on or change of neuroleptic medication. Drug combinations may also be important in predisposition (Smego and Durack, 1982). These authors also suggested that there may be a critical time in the predisposition of the patient for the development of the syndrome, since re-exposure to the drug, which had apparently triggered it, does not necessarily result in recurrence.

Whether or not an indistinguishable condition antedated neuroleptic medication, there is no dispute over the rule that, on diagnosis, neuroleptic medication should be stopped. Smego and Durack (1982) observed that improvement can be expected in 5–10 days of discontinuance of oral medication and 10–21 days of depot. Treatment is otherwise chiefly aimed at limiting damage to or supporting bodily functions, with temperature reduction, nutrition and hydration as routine and ventilation or dialysis if indicated. Preventive measures against venous thrombosis may also be important. Dantrolene and bromocriptine have been advocated to reduce muscle tone, but Levenson (1985) reviewed the literature and concluded that these drugs made little difference. Abbott and Loizou (1986) and Levenson (1985) have reviewed existing hypotheses on the pathophysiology of the condition.

Personality disorders and the neuroses

A wide variety of drugs has been advocated for the treatment of personality disorders and the neuroses. Cloninger (1983) produced a classification of antisocial behaviour syndromes and for each behavioural subtype he suggested drugs which he considered were indicated, and others which he considered contraindicated. His recommended drugs including lithium, neuroleptics, benzodiazepines, psychostimulants, antidepressants, anticonvulsants and others. His scheme is of theoretical interest but, as a clinical aid, it is premature and inadequately supported by clinical trials.

Lithium has been reported to be of value in controlling aggression and rage in personality disordered patients. Kerr (1976) reported a case of a personality disordered child abuser whose explosive rages and aggressive behaviour responded to lithium treatment. Panter (1977) described a similar case responding to lithium, although his patient had at one stage been diagnosed as suffering from schizophrenia. Rifkin et al. (1972) reported a double-blind placebo controlled study of lithium in the treatment of emotionally unstable character disorder and found that lithium was significantly superior to placebo in controlling mood swings. Sheard (1975) reported a single-blind placebo controlled trial of lithium in 12 non-psychotic aggressive prisoners and concluded that lithium produced a significant reduction in aggressive affect and behaviour. A further, larger double-blind study again found a significant reduction in aggressive behaviour (Sheard et al., 1976). Sheard (1983) has suggested that lithium is perhaps the closest to being a specific agent for the control of anger and aggressive outbursts in personality disordered patients. It should be remembered, however, that sedation is a side-effect of lithium.

Opinions are divided over the value of neuroleptics in personality disordered patients. Sheard (1983) did not recommend neuroleptics for aggressive behaviour in this group and stated that they are poorly tolerated. Conn and Lion (1984), however, recommended neuroleptics for violent paranoid and borderline patients because of their affective dampening. We would also emphasize the benefits of reducing paranoid ideas and feelings as well as dampening irritability. Brinkley et al. (1979) found small doses of neuroleptics to be of benefit to borderline patients, and they recommended the use of higher potency drugs, particularly those with activating effects. Although the early literature on pericyazine suggested that it was effective in the control of severe personality disorders, Sheard (1983) has suggested that the absence of more recent replication casts doubt on the initial findings. While neuroleptics can be of value in some cases of personality disorder, the possible benefits of treatment should be carefully balanced against the risks of unwanted effects, such as tardive dyskinesia. A further factor to be considered is the diagnostic difficulty in some cases of severe personality disorder of making a clear distinction from a psychotic disorder.

The use of benzodiazepines in the management of personality disordered and neurotic patients has been the subject of considerable discussion and debate because of reports of unwanted disinhibitory effects of benzodiazepines. The subject has been ably reviewed by Hall and Zisook (1981) who have pointed to the lack of adequately defined and controlled trials. They concluded that in the great majority of instances benzodiazepines diminish anxiety, fear, irritability and aggression. Only rarely do they increase anxiety or produce aggression. These rare paradoxical reactions to benzodiazepines tend to be idiosyncratic and unrelated to predictable clinical indicators. They recommend that chlordiazepoxide and diazepam are better suited to patients who have a history of aggression or poor impulse control. Kalina (1964) considered diazepam a most valuable agent in the control of behavioural problems among prisoners, but more recently caution has been urged in its use (Brown, 1978). It is now becoming increasingly apparent that patients can become dependent on benzodiazepines, so that they should be prescribed cautiously and for limited periods of time.

Substance Abuse

Management of substance abuse is discussed on pp. 455–6 (alcohol) and pp. 475–8 (illicit drugs).

Deviant sexual behaviour

Certain individuals can be helped to control their antisocial sexual behaviour through the judicious use of medication. Its administration and the ethical and medico-legal problems in this area are considered on pp. 557 and 561–5.

Behaviour Therapy

The Basic Principles of Behaviour Therapy

There is no universally accepted definition of behaviour therapy. According to Wolpe (1973), the term was introduced by Skinner and Lindsley (1954) and is used to describe a number of different therapeutic methods which have theoretical ideas in common. These are based on the principles of learning as derived from laboratory experiments, i.e. experimentally derived stimuli can be used to weaken or eliminate unwanted or maladaptive behaviours and initiate and strengthen adaptive ones. The two basic types of learning central to the theoretical conceptions of behaviour therapy are classical and operant conditioning.

Classical conditioning   is confined to reflex reactions within the autonomic nervous system and is particularly important in the development of neurotic disorders, such as anxiety and phobias. Pavlov's (1923) experimental work with animals demonstrated the importance of conditioned responses in basic learning, particularly in connection with the acquisition, generalization and extinction of responses. Watson (1913, 1924) developed the principles of behaviourism, in which there was emphasis on experimental techniques rather than introspection, and the focus of the scientific inquiry was on observable behaviour rather than the mind. Watson and Raynor (1920) demonstrated that it was possible to induce neuroses, in particular phobias, experimentally in human beings by using Pavlov's basic paradigm of conditioning.

Operant conditioning   differs from classical conditioning primarily in that it is concerned with voluntary actions rather than involuntary behaviour. The principles of operant conditioning owe much to the work of Skinner (1938, 1953) which, in turn, was influenced by Thorndike's (1911) Law of Effect principle:

> Any act which in a given situation produces satisfaction becomes associated with that situation, so that when the situation recurs the act is more likely than before to recur also. Conversely, any act which, in a given situation, produces discomfort becomes dissociated from that situation, so that when the situation recurs the act is less likely than before to recur.

Stated more simply, behaviour is affected by its consequences, so that behaviour which is rewarded or reinforced is more likely to be repeated, whereas behaviour which is punished is not. The two basic principles of reinforcement are differential reinforcement (i.e. reinforcement is only given when the desired response has occurred) and schedules of reinforcement (i.e. the frequency and timing of the consequences are carefully worked out).

Social learning theory   is an extension of operant conditioning. It states that behaviour is predominantly environmentally caused. Within social learning theory, however, people are neither considered to be driven by inner forces nor helplessly responding to environmental influences. Rather, behaviour is best construed in terms of continuous interaction between behaviour and its controlling conditions (Bandura, 1973). Stumphauzer (1986) has applied social learning theory to delinquent behaviour stating:

> Delinquent behaviour is acquired through psychological learning principles in a social context, and changing delinquent behaviour requires application and variation of the same principles—also in a social context.

Stumphauzer discusses four main social learning theory principles for modifying delinquent behaviour. The first two principles, positive reinforcement and modelling, aim to increase desirable behaviour, whilst the remaining two principles, punishment and extinction, deal with decreasing undesirable behaviour. The principle of modelling is very important in the development and modification of antisocial and delinquent behaviour. It states that behaviour may be learned and modified by the observation of the behaviour of a model and by observing the consequences of a model's behaviour (Bandura, 1973; Stumphauzer, 1986).

Target behaviour refers to the behaviour that requires modification. As offenders may have a range of psychological or behavioural problems, it may be necessary to concentrate on more than one target behaviour. Further, the extinction of an unwanted behaviour may simply leave the patient with a vaccuum to be filled by other maladaptive responses, so it may be important to attempt to increase desirable behaviour simultaneously with reducing undesirable or inappropriate behaviour. In clinical practice, it is rare to focus exclusively on the offending behaviour itself, although one might do so in the case of some sex offenders (Maletzky, 1991). Lundman (1984) has discussed the main intervention points.

Convenience behaviour. The emphasis in psychological treatment in institutional settings for offenders is most commonly on 'convenience behaviour', that is activities that enable the patient to be managed within a relatively closed social community. Gudjonsson and Drinkwater (1986) drew a distinction between 'traditional' and 'psychological' techniques. The former include management strategies, such as seclusion or restraint, already discussed, or exclusion, when a patient is prevented from entering a unit, ward, part of a ward or a specified activity. They are not treatments in themselves, but focusing on convenience behaviours is sometimes a useful therapeutic objective, since it may be that behavioural problems within such a setting are the limiting factors in admitting or transferring patients to open psychiatric wards, to a hostel or even back to their family and neighbours. Problems related more specifically to behaviour which is sometimes precipitated by long stay in an institution, such as a prison or hospital, are also encountered. Since they have arisen in part through fortuitous and malign conditioning, it follows that planned, positively structured behavioural programmes and influences on the overall regime may not only remedy maladaptive learning in these circumstances, but also play a part in its prevention.

The importance of the treatment setting

Whilst institutional and residential settings facilitate access to patients, many institutional settings give little opportunity for those patients to practice the full range of skills taught in behaviour therapy. Among outpatients, however, treatment objectives may be hampered by repeated failure to keep appointments, to carry out prescribed homework, or unwillingness to apply the skills that they have been taught.

Examples of Behaviour Therapy

Aversion techniques

The primary purpose of any aversive technique is the removal of an unwanted response from the person's behavioural repertoire. Such techniques comprise two different types of sanctions. First, rewards and privileges may be withdrawn. This sanction is commonly seen in clinical and institutional settings where inappropriate behaviour results in removal from positive reinforcement or time-out from reinforcement or loss of privileges. Secondly, an aversive stimulus or punishment may be presented immediately following an undesirable thought or behaviour. There may be special disadvantages in using such a technique among offender patients, which have not been thoroughly explored. Many offenders have come from harsh, punitive backgrounds and in many cases, particularly of sex offending, the deviant behaviour appears to have followed aversive or painful stimuli in childhood or adolescence (e.g. Burgess et al., 1987). Further, most offender patients are undergoing treatment either in the context of more general punitive sanctions—such as imprisonment—or as explicit alternatives to these. There is a danger that an aversive stimulus introduced as part of treatment will do more to reinforce the association between punishment and treatment than between the target behaviour and pain. Another serious problem is the potential for crossover between behavioural techniques. The impact of modelling on the behaviour of the observer is still widely acknowledged and may be a factor in the development of deviant behaviour arising in the punitive backgrounds just referred to. Similar behaviour on the part of a 'therapist' could do more to reinforce or extend deviancy than suppress it.

Aversion therapy. Aversion therapy techniques involve the pairing of an aversive stimulus (e.g. electric shock, nausea-inducing drug) with the unwanted fantasy, thought, feeling or activity that is subject to modification. Aversion therapy can be conceptualized as falling within either classical or operant conditioning paradigms. It can produce conditioned anxiety to previously pleasurable behaviour through classical conditioning principles, whereas from an operant conditioning perspective, the undesirable behaviour is punished by the aversive stimulus. Aversion therapy has been applied to a range of offending or offence-linked problems, including excessive alcohol consumption and sexual deviations (Hallam and Rachman, 1976). Evidence for its immediate efficacy, however, is modest, and evidence that any gains are generalized beyond the therapeutic situation slight. These issues, together with concerns about the ethical paradox of inflicting pain to teach control of the infliction of pain, have led to the aversion therapies based on an electric shock falling largely into disuse.

Covert sensitization. Covert sensitization is used as an acceptable variant of aversion therapy, particularly for sex offenders (Cautela and Wisocki, 1971; Maletzky, 1991) and delinquency (Cautela, 1967). It involves subjects being able to create a vivid imagery of themselves offending; once this has been achieved, they are instructed to imagine a scene or event which is unpleasant for them (e.g. nausea, vomiting, being caught). In theory, this will become inextricably associated with the unwanted behaviour and inhibit it. By their nature, covert sensitization techniques are more flexible in their application than physically aversive stimuli, such as electric shocks, in that they can be practised and implemented outside the treatment session. The main disadvantage is that their success depends not only upon the motivation and cooperation of the subject, but also on the possession of rather specific skills, in particular the capacity to create mental imagery.

Time-out. Time-out is the contingent withdrawal of access to positive reinforcement and this is most commonly achieved by isolating the individual in a non-reinforcing environment, such as in a small room that is bare of furniture. If there is nothing in the time-out room to entertain the individual, then the procedure may effectively eliminate all sources of reinforcement. The period spent in time-out is usually short, generally not more than a few minutes. Longer periods are no more effective. Time-out differs from seclusion in several respects. It is a preplanned programme which is carefully defined, constructed and implemented, and it is based on a sound social learning principle. One major problem with the use of time-out programmes in psychiatric hospitals is that if the patients do not cooperate fully with the programme, for example by refusing to go into the time-out room after exhibiting the target behaviour, either the programme breaks down and the treatment fails or they have to be physically removed to the time-out area. The latter may result in violence, and thus be counter-productive to the programme, which may have been designed to control violence. If the use of time-out has to be prolonged or repeated, it may, in some conditions, become a positive reinforcer, while in others there are dangers of moving into sensory deprivation. Programmes have to be very carefully designed and tailored to each individual to take account of all these possibilities (Gudjonsson and Drinkwater, 1986).

Neutralizing maladaptive reinforcers

Extinction. The objective of extinction techniques is to eliminate reinforcers that maintain the occurrence of the undesirable behaviour. If the undesirable behaviour has been positively reinforced in the past, then completely ceasing to reinforce the behaviour should cause it to decrease in frequency. In institutions, undesirable behaviour, such as temper tantrums or helplessness, may be reinforced when patients are given special attention as these problems arise but are ignored when doing well.

Overcorrection. The general principle of overcorrection is that people learn to accept responsibility for their undesirable behaviour by performing prosocial responses that are relevant to their undesirable behaviour. The technique comprises two separate components, labelled positive practice and restitution (Azrin and Foxx, 1971). The two components are sometimes combined into one procedure, but commonly only positive practice is used. Positive practice means that the person is required to repeat over and over again a desirable behaviour that is incompatible with the undesirable behaviour. One very self- and property-destructive girl, for example, who repeatedly shredded her clothes, was engaged in an intensive sewing programme under close supervision, most of the items she was asked to sew being her own clothes. Restitution consists of the correcting of whatever in the environment has been disrupted by the undesirable behaviour, sometimes even through scaled financial contribution to repair the damage. The results compare favourably with other behavioural approaches in suppressing aggressive and disruptive behaviour (Foxx and Bechtel, 1982).

Positive Reinforcement Techniques

The provision of incentives or rewards for offenders when they engage in prosocial behaviour or when they are not engaged in antisocial behaviour is one of the most effective ways of modifying behaviour (Stumphauzer, 1986). Either way, the basic principle of positive reinforcement is the increase in the strength or frequency of desired behaviours at the expense of undesired.

Although there are in theory fewer ethical problems with the use of positive reinforcement techniques than aversive techniques, the dividing line between failure to earn positive reinforcers and time-out from positive reinforcement is fine indeed. Sometimes positive reinforcement is explicitly used in conjunction with other techniques, such as time-out, extinction procedures, and aversive-conditioning.

Within institutional settings, techniques based on positive reinforcement principles can be either individually or group-based. The latter often involve 'token economy' procedures (Ayllon and Milan, 1979), which have three central characteristics:

1. objectively defined goals and target behaviours;
2. tokens (which act as conditioned reinforcers); and
3. back-up reinforcers for which the tokens can be exchanged.

Cognitive Therapy

Cognitive-behavioural therapies grew out of traditional behaviour therapy and are based on the fundamental assumption that cognitive events (i.e.

thinking, interpretations, assumptions, and strategies of responding) are important mediating variables for behavioural change (Kazdin, 1978). Dobson and Block (1988) have provided a useful chronology of cognitive-behavioural therapies, comprising *cognitive restructuring, coping-skills therapies,* and *problem-solving therapies.* The basic assumption of cognitive restructuring is that emotional distress is the result of maladaptive thoughts. Through clinical intervention, more adaptive thought patterns can be developed. Coping-skills procedures focus on patients developing a repertoire of skills that helps them to cope with stress. Problem-solving, which often comprises a combination of cognitive restructuring and coping-skills procedures, focuses on the development of general strategies for coping. Cognitive therapy has been found to be particularly effective with some types of depression and panic disorders (De Rubeis and Beck, 1988).

There is growing evidence that cognitive-behavioural techniques are, by and large, more effective in reducing delinquency and adult offending than other psychological techniques (Garrett, 1985; Ross and Fabiano, 1985). Ross and Fabiano presented an important conceptual model for delinquency and rehabilitation programmes. It is postulated that criminal behaviour is associated with delayed or impaired cognitive development, and that the enhancement of cognitive skills decreases criminal behaviour, because cognitive skills insulate people from personal, social and environmental pressures towards criminal behaviour.

Anger management

In spite of the efforts of a number of authors, e.g. Rothenberg (1971) and Novaco (1976), anger is still not often considered as a separate affect with potential for disorder and hence treatment. Depression and anxiety are much better established in this respect, yet anger plays a prominent role in the genesis of much antisocial behaviour, especially in mentally disordered people. An excellent exposition of the clinical problem of anger put in a historical context is given by Novaco and Welsh (1989). They emphasized the cognitive influences in the production and prolongation of anger, and try to draw away from the simpler, older notion that anger is a passion that seizes an individual and makes him irrational. They suggested five biases in the development of anger:

1. attentional cueing (in order to get angry about something an individual must first pay attention to it);
2. perceptual matching (previous exposure to aggression will increase a readiness to perceive aggression);
3. attribution error (believing that people do what they do because of what they are rather than because of current circumstances);
4. false consensus (imagining that others behave as oneself does);
5. anchoring effects (initial judgements become resistant to change).

Novaco (1975, 1978) has extended Meichenbaum's (1975) stress inoculation training model as a treatment for anger. Anger management procedures involve cognitive restructuring and skill training. Novaco emphasized the interactions between anger and other affects. This must imply that adjunctive pharmacological treatments for depression, anxiety and mania are an integral part of anger management where indicated.

Novaco (1975) suggested that the first step in the treatment of anger is a detailed assessment and he begins with his own Novaco Provocation Inventory. This should be followed by a detailed clinical interview aimed at assessing the patient's thought processes and his problem-solving strategies. The cognitive phase of the treatment is concerned with identifying the persons and situations that trigger anger. This is followed by fostering the recognition of the difference between anger and aggression. The patient is then encouraged to analyse the thoughts and bodily feelings that lead to anger and to discriminate between justified and unstified anger. He is taught to recognize the signs of tension and arousal that begin early in the provocation sequence. In skills acquisition, the patient is taught to change his perceptions of provocative stimuli and to reduce the importance in his thinking of such provocations. The patient is also taught how to relax and to develop humour as an alternative to anger. The aim of all this is to enable patients to recognize how anger develops, and then communicate that anger in a non-hostile form. Howells (1987) has provided a detailed review of the effectiveness of anger-management. The results from various studies provide evidence for the effectiveness of the procedures in treating anger related problems. Anger-management techniques may be difficult, however, to apply to some mentally abnormal offenders, because of the amount of cooperation and motivation required for anger control training (Alves, 1985).

Applying the Treatments

Behavioural approaches to treatment require not only some preliminary motivation on the part of the patient, but also prolonged commitment, and, in some cases, other skills, such as imagining to order. Focus on the patient's motivation should not, however, obscure the vital impact of the patient's environment, including family, friends and fellow clinicians or the key worker. Many elements in the patient's surroundings will have been behaviour-maintaining, and the behaviour therapy intervention will often be in competition with these for impact. If the behavioural regime seems in any way harsh, there is likely to be dissent among other clinicians, nursing staff in particular, who may be expected to play a key role in applying the negative or positive reinforcement, which sooner or later will show in failures of consistency on the part of staff, or even direct sabotage. This is a particular problem in an inpatient setting. Failure to respond to or comply with behaviour therapy should be addressed by as vigorous a re-evaluation of factors outside the patient as well as the patient himself.

Psychotherapy

Some Principles of Practice

All psychiatrists, and indeed any practitioner who works directly with patients/clients, engage in a dynamic relationship which in itself holds assessment potential, therapeutic possibilities and dangers. Many practitioners deliberately restrict the developmental or existential qualities in any therapeutic relationship, while using some of its psychoactive properties, such as 'doctor knows best', to try and ensure treatment or supervision compliance and to enhance the non-specific, or placebo effects of treatment. Limiting the use of the treatment possibilities of a professional-patient relationship may be focused on hostility to this mode of working, but perhaps also on an only partly recognized fear of its potential for eliciting strong, if not necessarily positive reactions. While many remain unconvinced of the effectiveness of dynamic psychotherapy *per se*, the dangers of failing to recognize crucial qualities in relationships between patients and key others must be addressed, and those trained in dynamic psychotherapy can make an important contribution to this.

Forensic psychiatry, perhaps more than all other branches of psychiatry, requires an understanding of a patient's actions in terms of his mental state and relationships. It is fundamental to an adequate response to questions posed by the courts and other lay bodies, it is vital to the safe care of the patient and is potentially protective of future victims who could include fellow patients or prisoners and staff. Whether encouraged to do so or not, most patients/clients will bring elements of their past experience into their new relationships. Only some groups, such as the narcissistic personality disordered, perhaps peculiar to forensic psychiatry in their most extreme forms, may prove difficult to engage, because of their lack of curiosity about relationships, about anything other than their image of themselves. Here perhaps emphasis on novelty of imagery and fresh metaphors for reported experience have most to offer (Cox and Theilgaard, 1987). It is in the successful management of professional, therapeutic relationships that possibilities for positive change emerge—whether treatment is primarily supportive, behavioural or primarily analytic—and in the failure to recognize and contain hostile developments that dangers for the therapists and others may ensue.

An assumption central to the psychotherapy of offenders is that many assaults or abuses of others are expressions in action of a mental state which, if not remembered and understood, will repeat itself in further similar actions. The psychotherapeutic intentions in such cases would, therefore, be directed to helping the patient to 'remember and recall' the relevant mental states. These must be revived and fully understood by the patient, so as to interfere with any future forgettings and therefore actions. For some patients the converse holds, they recall only too easily the states that are associated with action, and for them understanding and reintegration of the material are the tasks.

The next assumption is that the psychotherapeutic sessions are the areas in which such rememberings or reworkings should occur and recur, and that it is the clinical responsibility of the therapist to share with the patient the meanings of these rememberings. They will not present themselves as exact replicas of previous mental states, but it is the work of the therapist to recognize similarities between the material presented with its meanings and the underlying mental states. Gradually a comprehensive understanding of mental state and meanings can be built up with the patient. Freud (1905b) wrote:

> What are transferences? They are new editions or facsimiles of the impulses and phantasies which are aroused during the progress of the analysis but they have this peculiarity, which is characteristic for their species, that they replace some earlier person by the person of the physician. To put it another way, a whole series of psychological experiences are revived, not as belonging to the past but as applying to the person of the physician at the present moment.

The reference to transference to an 'earlier person' must, however, surely limit both the use and understanding of the transference. Must transference occur only from an earlier real person to the person of the therapist, or can whole situations from the past be transferred?

Strachey (1934) suggested that what is being transferred is not primarily an external object (albeit an important one) of the child's past, but what has come to be called the internal object. The knowledge of the ways in which such internal objects are constructed, and therefore affect the character structure of the individual, also helps to understand how such transferences colour the patient-therapist relationship.

In her paper on *The Origins of Transference*, Klein (1952) wrote:

> Transference originates in the same processes which in the earliest stages determine object relations. Therefore, we have to go back again and again in analysis to fluctuations between objects, loved and hated, external and internal, which dominate early infancy . . . (we can) . . . fully appreciate the interconnection between positive and negative transference only if we explore the early interplay between love and hate, and the vicious circle of aggression, anxieties, feelings of guilt and increased aggression, as well as the various aspects of objects towards whom these conflicting emotions and anxieties, are directed . . . it is the analysis of the negative transference which is a pre-condition for analysing the deeper layers of the mind.

Following Klein's (1946) understanding of the mechanisms, anxieties and defences which operate in earliest infancy, the path was clear for later analysts to see that a person with schizophrenia could form transferences, and therefore be capable of being analysed. She ended her 1952 paper by pointing out two important additions to earlier views. First, she made it clear that it is essential to think of transference in terms of total situations transferred from the past and, secondly, that the transference does not depend on direct references to the analyst in patients' material. From this, it already seems that transference should be regarded as a broad concept, but further development in the understanding and utilization of transference as a therapeutic tool lies in the concept of projective identification, and the concept of the psychotic and the non-psychotic parts of the mind.

The term projective identification was introduced by Klein (1946). Rycroft (1968) described this as:

> The process by which a person imagines himself to be inside some object external to himself . . . it creates the illusion of control over the object and enables the subject to deny his powerlessness over it.

Bion (1957) in discussing the transference in the analysis of the patient with schizophrenia said:

> The relationship with the analyst is premature, precipitate and intensely dependent; when under pressure of his life and death instincts, the patient broadens the contact, two concurrent streams of phenomena become manifest. First, splitting of his personality, and projection of the fragments into the analyst i.e. projective identification becomes overactive with consequent confusional states such as Rosenfeld (1952) has described.

One of us (L.S.), with extensive experience in the treatment of such patients, has found that such processes are not restricted to patients with schizophrenia. Personality disordered patients, who are nevertheless dominated by psychotic defence mechanisms, and those with non-schizophrenic psychotic illnesses are capable of identical transference experiences. Psychotic, as well as neurotic patients, are capable of having a fantasy about the analyst which needs to be analysed. These patients develop a feeling that the analyst contains within his personality elements readily recognizable as existing originally within their own mental make-up—and they maintain that it emanates solely from the therapist. A less extreme variation takes the form of the patient feeling confused by such feelings and beliefs. Whilst the mad part of the patient's mind is dominated by the conviction that the therapist, for example, harbours murderous intent towards him, the sane part, usually less evident, feels overwhelmed by such convincing propaganda coming from the mad part of the mind, but still retains a tenuous hold on reality. This dominating character of the psychotic part of the mind is the basis for the introduction of a further element in the transference—that of the crime itself.

Some Case Material

The treatment of a psychiatric patient who has assaulted or abused another person cannot occur without the recognition of the crime/or crimes in the transference. It will appear sometimes directly, overtly, but more usually in disguised form as a distinct part of the transference. Failure to recognize this essential part of the transference will leave the patient untreated and, therefore, exposed to further acting out, and maybe destructive acting out. An example illustrates how the criminal offence may be introduced into the therapy.

> A young man had been hospitalized for several years after attacking a young boy and holding him hostage. He was later arrested after stopping two other boys, acting oddly and talking to them with great intensity. He was convinced that he came from another world and that he had been sent to Earth to investigate its culture, along with a small group of others. The first boy had been part of his scientific inquiries, and the other two were messengers from his world. He had adopted a complex and consistent story to account not only for his extraterrestrial origins, but also for his apparently human presentation. Hostage taking had been a new departure for him, but he was known to have engaged in related activities, construed by his victims as threatening, on a number of other occasions.
>
> In a key session he complained he felt that there was a peculiar atmosphere in the room, and that the therapist was only seeing him to steal all his superior secrets—to share them with the therapist's ignorant colleagues. The patient felt he was being accused of interfering with 'somebody from his own side' (the two 'messenger boys'), while he was experiencing total innocence of this. At the same time, he felt himself to be the victim of invasive, prurient curiosity and held for this reason, as if a hostage, by the therapist.
>
> This situation clearly mirrored the crime and related events which led to his arrest and hospitalization—only he had split off the criminal intent and projected it into the therapist. Thus, the crime emerged in the transference. Transiently, he was able to recognize this, but he soon returned to his former 'innocence'. It became the duty of the therapist constantly to return to this constellation, or look for it in other material. Otherwise the potentially dangerous form of acting out in this unfortunate young man, who seeks to establish an idealized version of himself, ceaselessly and madly, would persist.

This young man's therapy was an important avenue to improved understanding of his condition. Unfortunately, his very early deprivation and developmental failures meant that his progress to health was slight, and the intensive work was of more value in confirming the continuing risks that he posed than in alleviating his problems.

A woman from a more stable background who had advanced to a higher level of adjustment before becoming psychotic provides a picture of the more conventionally therapeutic possibilities for psychotherapy, even among people with a psychotic illness who have engaged in the extremes of violent behaviour.

> The patient suddenly experienced a psychotic breakdown during her first job away from the parental home. She returned home. Independently acquired accounts called into question the reality of the suddenness of the onset of this illness, but the subjective reality of the flip from sanity to madness for the patient emerged in therapy as one of the most real and imperative anxieties of her life: that something horrible could still happen to her without anyone, least of all herself, noticing any dangers.
>
> During the course of a third breakdown, she killed her cohabitee. She said she was driven to it by a conspiracy among political extremists and hallucinated voices that told her that the only alternative was that they would destroy her. The preface to the relationship, and indeed

the killing, however, was serious—prolonged ideological conflict with her successful, well-adjusted and tenderly concerned sister, and her flight from the family home after thrusting a knife into the sister's locked bedroom door.

A diagnosis of schizophrenia was made and her psychotic symptoms were suppressed by substantial doses of neuroleptic medication. Although the offence was almost certainly delusionally driven, the fact of the psychosis did not in itself seem an adequate explanation for the murderous hostility to her sister or the eventual victim. In therapy, elements kept recurring. In her family, academic and material success coupled with genteel behaviour were the only things that brought reward and recognition. Her vulnerabilities were unrecognized or ignored by all but her sister and the woman she had killed, the latter having similar insecurities, but responding by heavy drinking. The psychotherapy sessions threatened to become a forum for a 'terribly nice', polite relationship with a 'nice' younger woman (the therapist) who was subjected to hints of anxieties, then rapidly reassured and then entertained with affectless accounts of past madness. An unwary therapist would have been reassured by the patient's 'insight', current freedom from symptoms and sensitivity to the therapist's feelings.

The sessions, however, were directed towards a development of an environment which could recognize her mad, murderous potential and the tracing of its origins, instead of colluding with the politeness and side-stepping or ignoring the turmoil. An example to illustrate this occurred after she had spent a day at a hostel, which was, as she wished, away from the rigours and violence of inner city life. In her session, she reported that she had been sleepless, but very quickly played down this fact. It was known to both patient and therapist that sleeplessness frightened her, and the fact that she had minimized her own and what she felt to be the therapist's anxiety about such a fact was pointed out to her, but without much manifest effect. She kept describing, however, in the session, two pet animals at the hostel, complaining that she could not understand why the people in the hostel seemed to ignore them and that if and when she went there herself, she would undertake to look after them and feed them. Throughout this telling, she seemed restless and kept mentioning that the hostel seemed to be in a very isolated part of this small town, and that it was really very far away. It was understood by the therapist that the 'far-awayness' referred to far away from the safety of 'here', where the session was taking place, and the isolation was reminiscent of her feelings when her control broke and she killed. Soon, however, she was talking animatedly about the women with whom she would be sharing a room and how she would fit her things in and make some cushions to make it look nice and make herself a nice home with nice new friends.

The therapist did not accept these reassurances, but rather took up her identification with the hostel's pets. The atmosphere changed. The patient cried, punctuating her crying with loud apologies. The therapist suggested that she felt that she, the therapist, and other clinicians were abandoning her and ignoring her need for protection. The patient said that she was suddenly reminded of her anxieties as an adolescent girl, when she had had to leave home feeling unprotected, whilst she had to be so reassuringly calm because it was 'the right thing to do' and her family expected it. This was a very moving admission from this patient, in the first place because it was unaccompanied by any camouflaging gentility, and secondly because it led to her suggestion that maybe already then the seeds of her illness had been present. The description may appear somewhat banal in the re-telling. The fact, however, is that it lead to a situation in which the patient began to use the sessions honestly, and to be herself without being a 'lady' corseted by hypocritical well-being.

The interesting facts in her treatment include two elements. Despite the manifest absence of apparent psychotic symptoms, which we assume are due to medication, her mind until the stage described needed a secure envelope both in the sense of the secure institution and of her 'socialized' containment of her anxiety. By contrast, despite the underlying psychosis, she was able to engage in therapy, use insights and learn about her emotional vulnerabilities as well as more healthy, adaptive ways of living with them. She progressed to more-or-less independent living, developed a healthier relationship with her sister and survived a change of therapist, all without psychotic or violent relapse. She could recognize and acknowledge her capacity for murderousness, not only in the very tragic, concrete sense, but in the related capacity of her mind to murder some of its own contents.

In spite, of much vociferous resistance from many psychiatrists to the admission and treatment of patients with psychopathic disorder (*see* Ch. 9), they are still occasionally compulsorily admitted to secure hospitals and successfully engaged in treatment. The difficulties in engagement should, however, not be underestimated and the boundaries between personality disorder and psychosis in some of these cases often seem slight.

> A young woman killed her six-month-old baby within weeks of beginning a very hostile outpatient relationship with a psychiatrist. She was admitted to a secure hospital after the killing, but showed the same capacity to irritate and frustrate her new therapist as she had the original psychiatrist. Initially, she had the capacity to provoke anger in everyone in her environment, leading to peculiar arguments in which she was invariably treated as if she possessed a totally rational mental apparatus. As these increased in frequency, staff expressed growing doubts about whether she was 'ill' and, therefore, whether she should be in hospital and whether she merited treatment. The psychotherapy supervisor had grave doubts about the rationality of her arguments, but they did produce, even in him, a dangerous admiration of her capacity not only to create such arguments, but also to give the impression that she was a sensible, logical woman. She projected into her therapist her internal irrationality and then mothered the situation going on in the therapist's mind as if she were a good, kind, sensible mothering person, who would modify and mollify any anger or needs. This was not a very promising situation with a woman who had murdered her own infant!
>
> She had been taken into care as a young child, due to her mother's illness and to the death or desertion of her father, a shadowy figure. At the age of 16, allegedly after being raped by two strangers, she was admitted to a mental hospital with paralysis and inability to speak. The symptoms cleared and she was discharged, but then she embarked on a series of relationships with violent and bullying men. At the time of the killing, she was estranged from the father of the child and said that she had feared he would claim it. She thought that she might have killed the child to forestall its loss.
>
> During a year of psychotherapy, she claimed complete amnesia for the killing, but reported her alleged dreams of it frequently and in detail to anyone who would listen. It is difficult to know how far these accurate reports represented actual recall, and how far the learning of material detailed in the evidence supplied to the court, which she had read, but her attachment to the accounts was undoubted, while she maintained an apparent dissociation, distancing and moral puzzlement at what had happened.
>
> The hypothesis to account for her position was that she was replicating her childhood experiences. In childhood, she was forced to adopt both the position of the good child to gain any kind of care, and, in the absence of an effective mother, simultaneously that of a pathologically idealized mother. Her identification with her baby as a needy infant deserted by its father and the consequent competition with it from her good child self for the attention of her idealized mother self was too great for this fragile dissociation to bear. She killed the child as an act of killing her awareness of her own needs and, therefore, must have been not only close to madness at the time, but continuing in such a state to maintain her belief in her self-sufficiency and idealized mother role.
>
> The therapist continues in his attempts to help her recognize and work through these issues, while she continues to infantilize him and 'murder' his efforts all the time, tending to confirm the hypothesis. Outside the sessions, well nurtured in the hospital environment and unchallenged by others, she developed a rational, nurse's main helper role. She could pass equally well as the model patient or good mother, and the psychotherapy sessions remain a most important window on the continuing underlying psychopathology.

The Flexibility of Psychotherapy

The three cases have been described in some detail to enable illustration of certain key features of psychotherapy with severely mentally disordered offenders. The particular school of psychotherapy matters little, sessional details matter little, the only rules are that a professional relationship is the tool of treatment, the therapist is attentive and rigorous in the questioning of his understanding of process and that the standard, discriminatory criteria for such treatment may be abandoned.

Selection of patients

No characteristic such as gravity of illness, seriousness of presenting behaviour or evidence of low intellectual performance would in itself be a bar to psychotherapy. We have been repeatedly surprised to see how seriously and psychotically ill patients can bring themselves into the process of treatment, and equally disappointed by those who ask for treatment and then truant and lose interest or act violently and are lost. At least within a secure environment, nothing seems to be lost in commencing treatment and seeing what happens. In spite of a possible but probably small risk of violent acting out, this is probably also true in an outpatient setting.

Change or support?

However broad, a single criterion for outcome of psychotherapy for the mentally abnormal offender is too limiting. In particular, many patients are simply too ill for the prospect of substantial change or cure to be realistic, but they can none the less benefit from psychotherapy. Masserman (1953), although not specifically referring to forensic psychiatric practice, captured something of the misunderstandings that may arise over goals and expectations of psychotherapy:

> Psychotherapy has been limited to 'any process that leads to the establishment of insight in the patient'—insight, of course, representing that mutually happy state in which the patient professes acceptance of the current formulations of his therapist . . .
> Unfortunately, the melee has been rendered all the more confusing by the disquieting paradox of patients who had supposedly achieved the various brands of dazzling understanding, yet were pathetically unable to apply this wisdom to the solution of their personal problems . . .
> I defined psychotherapy as *any* procedure available to the ethical practitioner that helps the patient become happier, more creative, and better adjusted in his familial and social milieu.

This does not rule out the successful demonstration of links between past and present, or the acquisition of working insights—in our second case positive results of this kind were attained—but it does not over-emphasize these as goals, and widens the scope for activity considerably.

Cox has long experience of working with such severely psychotic and personality disordered patients, held for years in maximum security as a result of the seriousness of their offences. With a Danish colleague (Cox and Theilgaard, 1987), he described a modification of dynamic psychotherapy, which he calls the Aeolian Mode, peculiarly appropriate to the vulnerable, extremely damaged and pathologically defended individuals that are so common in forensic psychiatric practice. This depends on the therapist's capacity to recognize a moment of incipient dynamic instability in which the patient is optimally receptive to an initiative from the therapist. In this the therapist must bring a new experience or association to the patient's attention, something which was not there before, but which gives the therapist an insistent, imperative appreciation of the rightness of a pattern of connection between immediate state or statement and overall predicament. Crudely, that which needs to be said could not be expressed in any other way (Cox 1978). It rests on attentiveness, accurate empathy and the creative use of fresh imagery and metaphor. Emphasis may be on transference interpretation or supportive work, depending on the patient's individual needs, but the thrust is towards change and integration with the facilitation of endopsychic change as one goal, but the consolidation of effective defences as appropriate.

Thus, one legitimate goal for therapy is improvement of the patient to the point at which he can comfortably look both backwards and forwards in his life, and safely move on from enclosed treatment to more ordinary living outside hospital, prison or restrictions of any kind. An equally important goal is that the patient can simply be 'held' (Cox, 1986), i.e. enabled to contain his conflicts with a modicum of comfort and to accept the shelter of a closed environment and—

> retain hope in the indeterminacy of relationships which have not been chosen and yet cannot be readily relinquished.

Confidentiality

If during treatment the patient's understanding of his mental mechanisms remains deficient, the therapist's understanding and, in turn, that of other key figures in the patient's environment may improve. This can only occur with accurate empathy, supervision, and sharing of the psychotherapeutic work. There remain differences between therapists in the matter of how much information arising in the therapeutic relationship should be shared with the whole clinical team. There are those therapists even in forensic psychiatric practice who would argue that the psychotherapeutic relationship should remain sacrosanct in its privacy. We have not adhered to this view, and believe that the openness practised has had distinct benefits.

Before commencing treatment, the patients are informed that the therapist will be having regular supervision sessions with a supervisor. It is also made clear that the therapist and supervisor will have a discretionary right to act upon any information received during the sessions should they become anxious about either of two features: the actual illness prevailing, and security. To date, this process does not seem to have interfered adversely with the progress of treatment. This awareness of facts and the sharing of them can also, with the patient's knowledge, be extended so that, as part of the overall treatment plan, the patient is reminded of the openness and each member of the care team will feel free to communicate with each other as freely as seems appropriate for the patient's benefit. Considering the world in which so many patients have been living, including the intrinsic secretiveness and dishonesty implicit in their mental states, it has often seemed that, despite some complaints, the patients have felt protected by this statement of openness and its implications.

Staff support

Cox (1986) argued that it is possible that—

> it is within the 'inner world' of the hospital itself that a psychotherapist may, in the long run, assume his most important role.

He regarded the 'holding' of staff as being as important as the holding of the patient, enabling them to leave aside defences that might otherwise render them therapeutically ineffective, even damaged. In an analogy with Winnicott's (1965) description of the potential terrors of an infant: 'a slight failure of holding . . . brings . . . a sensation of infinite falling', he highlighted the dangers for staff in coping with the projections of the violent offender-patient. Without ensured support, they too may experience a plunge into an infinity of terror or hostility. They may merely become another statistic in Reid's (1985) collective:

> The most pervasive reason for our failure to deal effectively with antisocial behaviour lies in the collective anger that the public and, to some extent, mental health professionals feel towards antisocial people, who are often criminals.

Linking the issues of openness and support further, there is the practical reality of ensuring the physical safety of the patient and his contacts. Patients who have killed or maimed—sometimes even within secure institutions—have a demonstrable capacity for inflicting exceptional harm. Is a psychotherapeutic relationship ethical if it denies fellow treaters vital information, in the name of confidentiality, about an overt or covert threat of suicide or assault?

Psychotherapy or Sociotherapy?

Even an individual psychotherapeutic relationship is a form of social relationship, with its potential for learning and improving social behaviour. Whiteley (1986), however, made the following practical distinction:

> Psychotherapy is primarily a listening process, with understanding coming from the therapist's interpretation of the individual's communications and facilitating the development of a more stable emotional life. Sociotherapy is a more active process, with behavioural change coming from the experience of new and more satisfactory ways of coping with interpersonal interactions.

Early concepts of a therapeutic community placed the emphasis on sociotherapy as the principal instrument of change (Jones, 1956). Now it is easily accepted that the two approaches, in so far as they differ, fit comfortably together, and Rapoport (1960) emphasized that the patients/clients in such a setting who improved were those individuals who could make a relationship with a key staff member. Nevertheless, it has often been argued that the involvement of a peer group in the treatment of those with antisocial behaviour problems is vital. Whiteley (1986) presented the crucial issue:

> . . . the personality disordered individual . . . is most influenced by his peers, and the staff need to stand back and let them deal with him. He knows only too well where he stands with staff, parent or authority figures with whom he has been in set manoeuvres all his life. Thus, a co-therapist with a staff member in the new residents' group at Henderson will be a representative from the residents' community with whom he feels an *affinity*. Secondly, he has to be *affiliated* . . . feel accepted and able to join and be one of the group.

Efficacy

Psychotherapy is a daunting treatment for patients, practitioners and those who would and must evaluate it. It makes considerable practical and emotional demands on patients and therapists alike, often for long periods. The demands on the psychotherapists are acknowledged as sufficiently high that a prerequisite to becoming a therapist in the dynamic schools is a personal analysis, in whole or in part preceding a training analysis. Few patients are that well equipped! For researchers the problems are immense. The modes of psychotherapy are legion. Even when a named, specific school or technique of psychotherapy is being applied—and there are plenty of these—the person of the therapist and the quality of the relationship established between patient and therapist remain the fundamental tools of treatment, and, in turn, unique variables to each case, which complicate the evaluation of its efficacy. It has to be conceded that the psychotherapeutic process itself is only one of many psychological influences impinging on the patient at any one time and over his whole life, and that the number and range of internal and external influences as variables will, in turn, be multiples of the numbers of patients under study. How is it possible to select appropriate subjects for study? How is it possible to select controls? How is it possible to select relevant components of the psychotherapy—to ask in general terms whether psychotherapy works is probably almost as meaningless as to ask whether medical treatment works. How should outcome criteria be selected? Is conventional scientific methodology even appropriate to the task?

The American Psychiatric Association Commission on Psychotherapies (1982) provided a full review of the problems, solutions and research work to that time, mainly in non-offender populations. In spite of the problems, there have been many attempts to evaluate psychotherapy, perhaps the most elegant subsequent study which bears relevance to the field of forensic psychiatry being the comparative study of insight-oriented psychotherapy with reality-adaptive, supportive psychotherapy for schizophrenia (Stanton et al., 1984). In this study, the nature of the intervention is tightly defined, and the therapists nearly so, all being trained and experienced. The process of therapy was tightly monitored. The environment and context of the treatment similarly received close attention, the psychotherapy deliberately being an adjunct to other forms of treatment and therapeutic environment. Patients were selected by clearly described criteria, and then further defined, one key aspect being that all had 'middle prognosis' schizophrenia. The drop-out rate from therapy was high, however, so unsought biases in selection nevertheless operated, although the sample size of 95 remains substantial. A multiplicity of measures were used and described in detail. The companion paper of the study by Gunderson et al. (1984) reported on patients who completed at least 6 months of psychotherapy over 2 years. It comfirmed the complexity of the interaction between the type of psychotherapy provided, the context of the therapy and the nature of the effect. Overall, the insight-oriented group had a small advantage in areas of ego functioning and cognition, for example paranoid and primary process-thinking was significantly improved at 12 months in this group, while the reality-adaptive supportive group did best in some aspects of social functioning and was less likely to relapse. The chief importance of the study, however, was in showing the quality of evaluation that can be achieved and the extent to which independent variables may modify outcome. The overall results, for example, masked the fact that the treatment had opposite effects on social functioning in different settings—the one showing an advantage in two of the hospitals, but the other in one of them.

Although in a hospital setting most offender patients have a psychotic illness, usually schizophrenia, most of the studies of psychotherapy in relation to delinquents or offenders have been done with the personality disordered. All relate to a style of working which has more in common with a therapeutic community than a hospital. Almost all refer to specialist units, some free standing with health service affiliations, some as part of the penal system.

Common to almost all studies of psychotherapeutic interventions is the high drop-out rate. In the hospital-based study of psychotherapy for schizophrenia just described (Stanton et al., 1984), for example, 164 of 186 suitable patients consented to participate, but a further 69 (42%) dropped out before completing the minimum 6 months in their assigned treatment, and attrition continued such that by 2 years after commencement of therapy, only one-third of the initial sample remained in treatment. In the Henderson Hospital (in the South of England), designed for the personality disordered, 20–30% of a series of those accepted as suitable for starting treatment had dropped out within 3–4 weeks of commencing (Whiteley, 1970; Copas and Whiteley, 1976). In the only psychiatric prison in Britain—Grendon—it was found that a very similar proportion of men selected for treatment returned to ordinary locations in other prisons within about the same timescale (Gunn et al., 1978), although in both the hospital and prison personality disordered groups the subsequent attrition rate was less marked than in the schizophrenia group. Once bonding to the community had taken place at Henderson or Grendon, it did seem more durable.

If the evaluation of psychotherapy for non-offender patients has proved difficult, how much more has this been true of the offender groups. One of the most constraining factors has been preoccupation with offending and re-offending as an outcome criterion. This is for two reasons. First, as a relatively expensive form of treatment, it tends to be specially funded for this group, and funders want evidence of cost effectiveness that is crudely practical. This has also led to a tendency to evaluate the impact of institutions rather than the efficacy of a defined treatment for defined patients. Jessen and Roosenburg (1971) stressed the mistake of focusing on comparisons between institutions. Secondly, where long-term follow-up is attempted, re-offending, mortality and hospital re-admission information is among the data most consistently available through the criminal records office, the office of population statistics and the mental health index records. Robertson (1989) has reviewed the limitations of this approach, which is also discussed on pp. 750–1. Here, it is perhaps worth emphasizing that no one would take the criminal record as a measure of neuroleptic drug efficacy, although the other two measures may be at least partially appropriate.

Copas and Whiteley (1976) identified clusters of patients on dimensions between high and low anxiety and intra- and extra-punitiveness. The clusters were of assistance in predicting outcome for treatment at the Henderson Hospital. Among those completing treatment and having previously committed criminal offences, 40% were not convicted over 2 years of follow-up and about 60% of those with previous psychiatric hospital admissions avoided re-hospitalization. No control group was presented, so it is impossible to be sure whether it was the hospital, or some element of its provision, that influenced these overall improvements.

The Institute of Psychiatry study of Grendon prison (Gunn et al., 1978) took a more comprehensive view showing significant improvements in mental state and changes in attitude, as well as improvements in social behaviour during the time in Grendon for those completing treatment. A substantial proportion of the men had been previously violent, within institutions as well as without, but there was no violence in the therapeutic community among those who stayed, and very little among those leaving in the first month while they did remain in Grendon. Outcome measures on leaving the prison were reduced to the usual, unsatisfactory ones of criminal recidivism or death, and this was the principal source of comparison between Grendon men and those completing conventional imprisonment. It was no surprise that the Grendon men differed little from the control group in the early stages of release.

In Geneva, de Montmollin et al. (1986) evaluated the effect of a therapeutic community modelled on Grendon prison within a prison of young adult male serious offenders. The unit requires both social cooperation on practical matters and participation in psychotherapeutic groups. The authors noted improvement in behaviour while in the community and, like M. Cox in special hospitals, noted the 'maintenance of hope' and dignity during a long sentence as a key goal of such work, satisfactorily met. Again, however, their only measure of outcome beyond the unit was criminal recidivism. Within 2 years, twelve men were already lost to information gathering and one was dead. Barely half of the remainder had remained offence free (*see also* pp. 753–4). In an intermediate unit, neither prison nor hospital, in the Netherlands—Mesdag—physical security is high, but the unit is therapeutic, with only about one-quarter of a staff of 200 being security officers. With a thoroughly eclectic approach including education, social clubs, family work and occupation as appropriate, about 40% of the inmates also receive individual psychotherapy for up to five times a week. On release, about 30% committed crimes as/or more serious than the one for which they were originally sentenced, and 15% killed after discharge (Smith, 1984). The most highly dangerous and unstable offenders, however, tend to be selected for this institution, the overall re-offending rate for ex-prisoners in ordinary penal institutions in the country being about 66%. Other aspects of the quality of life and treatment in this setting were not described, but at a forensic mental hospital in the Netherlands, in which over 80% of the patients had committed at least one seriously violent crime, Feldbrugge (1986) focused almost exclusively on the psychotherapeutic possibilities, processes and blocks within the institution and emphasized the staff reactions and problems in treatment as well as those of the offender patients.

The longer the follow-up of offender patients/prisoners who have been in psychotherapy, sociotherapy or both, the more dependence there is on criminal recidivism and death as the outcome measures. In the Grendon study it was found that 6 months after release the response rate to questionnaires had fallen to 41%, and by 12 months it was in single percentage figures in spite of regular personal correspondence, including birthday cards (Robertson and Gunn, 1987). New follow-up techniques are needed. McCord (1978) found that 30 years after counselling a group of predelinquents did less well in criminal reconviction rates than other predelinquents who were not counselled! McCord and Sanchez (1982), in an entirely different sample, obtained a similar result, even demonstrating a crossover from an initial advantage for a group of delinquents treated in a therapeutic community type of institution compared with a more conventionally managed group such that, at 25 years, the former seemed less well adjusted. They speculated that the longer term disadvantage might be real, and might reflect the side-effects of the more socializing components of the community. Perhaps the boys used some social skills which marked them out as different or rendered them less functional in their communities of origin. How possible is it to make sense of any outcome measures at all at 10, 25 or 30 years following an intervention which was short and trivial if taken in the context of an offender's total experience at the time of the treatment, let alone in the context of his whole life. How many other factors are influencing criminal behaviour? Almost certainly the arbitrarily derived and inaccurate measure of re-offending is not an adequate indication of any progress.

Motivation and Maintenance

Two issues remain to be addressed. First there is the problem of motivation for change. It is possible, but there is almost no evidence either way, that it is this quality above all that is crucial to the prevention of recidivism and promotion of genuine health and well-being (Robertson and Gunn, 1987). In the Grendon study, those with a more positive attitude to psychiatry and rated as more motivated by the researchers were less likely to have further court appearances during the 10 years after leaving Grendon. Is a positive attitude to the prospect of change something that can be brought about? Is the success of so much other treatment, physical or psychological, dependent on positive motivation for change? A treatment which is not attractive enough to be taken up by those to whom it is offered is a failure.

The second issue relates to treatment maintenance. Most of the studies of psychological treatments, and psychotherapy especially, seem to be based on the assumption that they ought to be curative, given the apparent expectation that any improvement observed will persist after treatment has ceased. Quite apart from the fact that there is no guide as to how long treatment should be, or what the indicators of stable change are, this tendency sets psychotherapy apart in its evaluation from other treatments. Maintenance therapy with neuroleptic medication for schizophrenia, or lithium for the manic-depressive illnesses is expected, and accepted as necessary for the majority of cases. Maintenance of the psychotherapeutic and sociotherapeutic environment, or at least those aspects of them that fit well and positively with the patient's needs, may be as important, and perhaps should be a focus of much more rigorous attention than it has been to date. In clinical practice, it may be more efficient and effective to devote most of the limited resources available to long-term aspects of care such as support, long-term psychotherapy, community nursing, depot clinics, day centres or sheltered workshops.

18

Forensic Psychiatry in the National Health Service of England and Wales

With commentary on Scotland and Other Countries

Edited by

Pamela J. Taylor

Written by

Adrian Grounds

Pete Snowden

Pamela J. Taylor

With contributions from

John Basson and John Gunn

Historical Context

The care of the insane has a long history with some significant pioneer developments well before the 19th century (Allderidge, 1979). Nevertheless, as Porter (1991) has pointed out, there are very few substantial texts on the history of British psychiatry. He recommends Lewis (1955), Leigh (1961), Parry-Jones (1971), Jones (1972) and the three volumes by Bynum et al. (1985a,b, 1988). Ackerknecht (1959) widens the perspective into the rest of Europe. Allderidge (1979) herself gives a brief but fascinating overview, suggesting that few of the ideas prevalent in present-day psychiatry are new. She suggests that at least as early as the 15th century some hospital provision was made, in Britain, for the insane. The Priory of St Mary of Bethlehem was founded by Simon Fitzmary in 1247 in Bishopsgate. By 1403, six insane men were included amongst other sick people—perhaps making the equivalent of the first general hospital psychiatric unit? Such mixing of diseases did not last long. The new Priory soon specialized in cases of insanity. Patients were kept there largely at the behest of friends and relatives. Allderidge cites Dalton (an early legal textbook) as saying in 1581:

> Every man may also take his kinsman that is mad, and may put him in a house, and bind him and beat him with rods without breach of the Peace.

The general community seemed rejecting too—almshouses, for example at Croydon, Ewelme and Coventry, prohibited the admission of the insane.

Allderidge cites an extract from William Gregory's chronicle of the early 15th century which implies an understanding of the longevity of mental illness:

> . . . Bedlam. And yn that place ben founde many men that ben fallyn owte of hyr wytte . . . and sum ben restoryde unto hyr wytte and helthe a-gayne. And sum ben abyding there yn for evyr, for they ben falle soo moche owte of hem selfe that hyt ys uncurerabylle unto man.

By the 17th century, however, the new Bethlem set a ceiling of 12 months on admissions. Patients were either cured, or discharged as incurable at that point, which suggests that debates about length of stay and treatability are not new. The 'private sector' has been previously employed to help the insane, indeed private 'mad houses' constituted the main provision outside the home for the floridly mad from the late 17th century until the reforming Acts and public asylum building programme of the late 18th and 19th centuries. The second half of the 18th century did see the establishment of public subscription hospitals, but this movement tended to exclude the insane.

The asylums which were built in every county resulted from the 1807 Select Committee appointed to enquire into the state of criminal and pauper lunatics. The Committee observed that to confine lunatics—

> in a common Gaol is equally destructive of all possibility of the recovery of the insane and of the security and comfort of other prisoners (an observation that is still relevant see Gunn et al., 1991b).

By the late 18th and early 19th century, lunacy commissioners were established to inspect hospitals offering care to the mad. Is the establishment of the Mental Health Act Commission in the late 20th century a revivification?

What might be taken as an early phase of modern *forensic* psychiatry also has modern overtones. In the 18th century, there was no special provision for criminal lunatics, who were scattered throughout prisons and workhouses. A few were in the Bethlem Royal Hospital. The attempted assassination of George III by James Hadfield stimulated the introduction of the 1800 'Act for the safe custody of insane persons charged with offences'. Lunatics whether unfit to plead or not guilty by reason of insanity, were to be kept in 'safe custody' in some suitable place. As there was no suitable place, Hadfield was sent to Bethlem from which he escaped in 1802. He was recaptured, sent to Newgate, but not readmitted to Bethlem until 1816 (Allderidge, 1974). The government provided the Governors of Bethlem, which was about to be rebuilt, with the capital and revenue for a state criminal lunatic asylum in its new development. This was no doubt an attractive offer to the governors of a private foundation. The new Bethlem opened at St George's Fields in 1815 with two wings set aside for 'criminal lunatics'. There were places for 45 men and 15 women. There was no contact between the criminal patients and those in the main hospital and any movement from the wards required the Home Secretary's permission. The wards quickly filled and became overcrowded, and the wings were enlarged, but could never keep up with the demand. In 1857, 40 of the 'better class' of criminal patients were transferred to an ordinary ward of the hospital which had had a security upgrade. The government was forced to make better provision and so a new, separate, secure hospital was built in Windsor Forest at Broadmoor to house 500 patients. During 1863 and 1864 all the 'criminal lunatics' were transferred to the new hospital, the old criminal lunatic wings at Bethlem were knocked down, and the Treasury paid for the demolition! (Allderidge, 1974). Thus the first security units for mentally disordered offenders led to the progressive rejection of criminal patients from mainstream psychiatry.

The range of facilities, concepts and laws inherited from this chequered history should by now ensure a facility to match the needs of almost any patient, but this is not so. 'Treatability' as a concept most recently introduced in the Mental Health Act 1983, has been much misused (*see* pp. 401–4). A 'new' gap in provision has been identified—that of provision for those patients requiring long-term hospitalization in medium security. The need for a Thomas Guy, who founded his hospital for people excluded from other hospitals as incurable, is as great as ever.

Current Structures, Ideologies and Practice

In the 1950s, with the introduction of phenothiazines and antidepressant medications, there was recognition that many psychiatric patients could be safely treated outside hospital. With the simultaneously growing financial benefits available in the welfare system, the need for large hospitals exclusively for the mentally sick was questioned. The MHA 1959 for England and Wales reinforced the move towards general hospital and community-based district mental health services, and by 1962 the goal for phasing out the mental hospitals was formally outlined by the then Health Minister, Enoch Powell. There was a substantial decline in mental hospital population over that time. The peak for the number of patients in psychiatric hospitals in England and Wales was about 150 000 in 1954. By 1974 this figure was 95 000, despite an increase in the general population and a large rise in psychiatric admissions during the same period—from 72 000 to over 180 000 (Eason and Grimes, 1976). Almost all provision was for voluntary patients and was 'open'. Almost exactly similar patterns were occurring in the USA (e.g. Bassuk and Gerson, 1978) and in other western countries. In England and Wales, the projected level of demand for mental hospital beds has not fallen to the level extrapolated from these calculations of the 1960s and '70s. Even at the peak of the enthusiasm for decanting the mental hospitals to the community, there were voices calling for a different sort of idealism—for services which incorporated a balanced mixture of provision according to need rather than a more or less unitary polarization, formerly to the asylum, now to the community.

As early as 1961, for England and Wales, the working party on special hospitals (Ministry of Health, 1961) recommended that the then regional health boards should arrange their psychiatric services to ensure the provision of a variety of types of hospital unit, including some secure units and some special diagnostic units for patients requiring security, with transfers being made between them as necessary. By 1973, gaps in hospital provision, particularly secure provision, were being identified both for the disturbed hospital patient (DHSS, 1974—the revised Glancy report) and for the mentally abnormal offender (Home Office/DHSS, 1975—The Butler Report). Gunn (1976), a working group of the World Health Organisation (1978) and The Royal College of Psychiatrists (1980) described similar visions of comprehensive psychiatric service for mentally and behaviourally disturbed patients that would not only provide for each level of requirement, but also ensure free movement of the patients between the various parts of the service. The concept of the integrated system of psychiatric care was established, and was adapted for offender patients (Gunn, 1976). A model of such provision might appear as in Fig. 18.1. In theory, a patient ought to be able to enter the system anywhere, and quickly move to the appropriate level of care.

The importance of such a model was indirectly emphasized in the Audit Commission's Report on Community Care (National Audit Office, 1987). Finding that progress towards community care for the mentally disordered had been 'particularly disappointing', it was, nevertheless, able to identify the qualities of successful projects. Three of the six qualities reflected integration within and between services—local service integration cutting across agency boundaries, a multidisciplinary team approach and a partnership between statutory and voluntary organizations. The other qualities emphasized the importance of local commitment and local community links, with minimum bureaucracy. With the exception of the latter quality, bureaucracy being thrust on forensic psychiatry by the nature of the legal status of many of the patients, these key features for success describe well the principal thrust of forensic psychiatry services in England and Wales. Largely organized on a regional basis, with local commitment, each service has its product champion and, from a multidisciplinary base, does indeed extend to partnership with a range of other professional, statutory and voluntary agencies. The one nationally organized element—the Special Hospitals Service Authority (*see below*)—commits a proportion of its resource to forging links with regional psychiatry services and with national and local statutory and non-statutory bodies.

There remain barriers to full integration. Some are attitudinal. Services, including the psychiatric services outside forensic psychiatry, remain anxious about or hostile to the mentally abnormal offender. Dell's (1980) work on

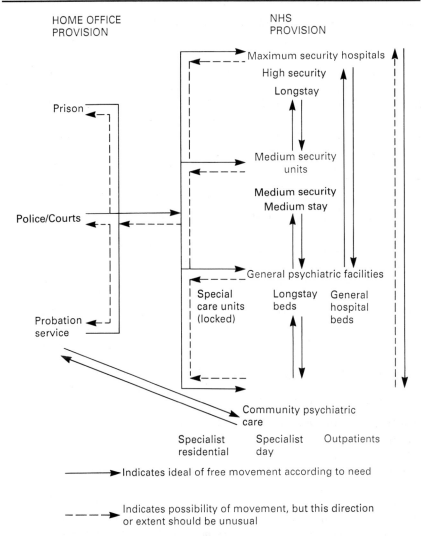

Fig. 18.1   Integrated services for offender patients.

the transfer of special hospital patients to other NHS hospitals amply illustrated some of the problems in showing that the rates of achieving transfer were significantly slower where informal approaches could not be or were not made, or where the local consultant/clinical team did not visit the patient early in the process of transfer negotiations. Some of the barriers are, nevertheless, highly practical. Resources are lacking, or imbalanced. The provision of medium security in England and Wales is still far below the 20 per 100 000 population agreed shortly after the 1975 Butler Report, and this creates a bottle-neck in a system which supports up to 35 patients per 100 000 in maximum security, even allowing for the fact that not all of these will need to pass through a medium security unit. A Department of Health enquiry for the Review of Services for Mentally Disordered Offenders (Department of Health, Home Office, 1992) found that while the number of maximum and medium secure beds had risen slightly over the 5 years 1986–1991 (by about 20 and 100 respectively), there had been a disproportionate continuing fall in locked or lockable inpatient facilities in other parts of the psychiatric services, by nearly half to 639 beds for mental illness and over half to just over 300 in mental handicap. Non-secure beds had also dropped substantially by about 13 000 in each category (to nearly 60 000 and just over 29 000).

Maximum Security Hospitals

The maximum security psychiatric hospitals stand at one extreme of the range of hospital provision for violent and offender patients. Three special hospitals—Ashworth, Broadmoor and Rampton—provide 'conditions of special security' for people in England and Wales who are subject to detention under the MHA 1983 and who are also dangerous (NHS Act 1977). The State Hospital at Carstairs provides a similar service for Scotland.

Special Hospitals for England and Wales

Management in evolution

Broadmoor, the first of the English special hospitals, was an early symbol of the pressures against integrating services for the mentally abnormal offender. It arose out of demands from both hospital and penal systems to provide a separate institution for criminal lunatics. The Lunacy Commissioners held the view that it was 'highly objectionable' that such persons be detained in a general lunatic hospital (Parker, 1985). The Home Office became the purchaser of facilities at Fisherton House in Salisbury in order to house their insane criminals outside prison. The first patients were not admitted to Broadmoor Hospital until 1863, 54 years after a Parliamentary Select Committee recommendation, thus providing a precedent for lengthy delays in provision for the mentally abnormal offender. Direct Home Office management ceased only after the Criminal Justice Act 1948. At this point, the hospital was taken over by the Board of Control, although the Home Office retained control of admissions and discharges. Only after the MHA 1959 did the management of Broadmoor pass to the DHSS. Until that time no civil patient had been admitted.

Rampton hospital was built in 1910 and run by the Home Office, but passed to the Board of Control in 1920 and, in turn, to the Ministry of Health in 1947. Moss Side Hospital, built in 1914, now a part of Ashworth Hospital, was never a Home Office establishment, while Park Lane Hospital,

Ashworth's other constituent, built in 1974, was run directly from the DHSS from its inception. An interesting sidelight is thrown on the development of the special hospitals in the accounts of several former patients ('Warmark', 1931; Allen, 1952; Thompson, 1972; Reeve, 1983; and Harding, 1985).

Funding and management of the special hospitals remains independent of the regional and district health authority structure. A tier of management and accountability more local to the hospitals than the mental health division of the DHSS was recommended on many occasions (House of Commons, 1968; NHS Hospital Advisory Service Report 1988 on Broadmoor Hospital, unpublished, and the Report of the Boynton Committee, DHSS, 1980). The Boynton Committee was set up to review the management and functions of Rampton hospital after allegations in a television documentary of cruelty to patients. It explicitly avoided investigations of assault or criminal behaviour, leaving that to the police over the next 4 years of the hospital's life, and heavily criticized the management structure and regimes. Although there were a number of calls for closure of the hospital (e.g. *Lancet*, 1980), plans for reorganization and revitalization won the day. The Rampton Hospital Board was established by statutory instrument in 1981 to undertake some

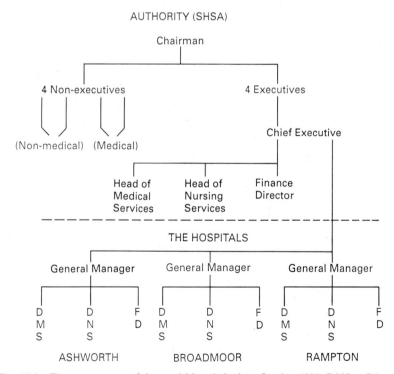

Fig. 18.2 The management of the special hospitals since October 1989. DMS = Director of Medical Services; DNS = Director of Nursing Services; FD = Financial Director.

management functions on behalf of the Secretary of State. Considerable improvements followed at Rampton, but a further HAS report (National Health Service Health Advisory Service, 1988) again attacked the management structure for Broadmoor Hospital. Other important criticism of the conditions in special hospitals include the Biennial Reports of the MHAC (1985, 1987 and 1989) and the more personal views of Chiswick (1982).

A new special health authority, the Special Hospitals Service Authority (SHSA) assumed responsibility for holding the budget for the hospitals, employing all the staff (who had formerly been government employees) and running the service in 1989. The change in management has brought greater parity of function with other parts of the NHS. The structure of the SHSA is shown in Fig. 18.2, the central management structure being reflected at each hospital, applying the principles of general management with responsibilities clearly defined. Each hospital also has the advice and support of a local health advisory committee which also facilitates links with the local community and catchment area services. The work of the SHSA is subject to annual ministerial review at the Department of Health. The potential for the delivery of a high quality service certainly exists, but Chiswick's (1982) warning should remain constantly in sight:

> An institution does not automatically become a hospital because the sign over the door says so.

Admissions policies and practice

The most obvious difference between special hospitals and other hospital provision lies in the physical security of the special hospital. Each makes use of substantial perimeter security. The internal physical security is also high. It is appropriate that the capacity for physical security should be exceptional—homicide, as well as suicide, is not unknown within the special hospitals. The level to which staff are forced to rely on physical security is perhaps less appropriate. Paradoxically, given how far security depends on the skills and numbers of trained staff, staff:patient ratios are lower in the special hospitals than in the medium security units. Partly in order to ensure the balance is safe by day, patients are almost invariably locked in their rooms throughout the night, without the possibility of egress except in a life-threatening situation. There is almost no possibility of therapeutic activity at night, a time when psychiatric patients are not uncommonly distressed and in need of support, although one or two pilot projects to increase night staffing now exist. The use of seclusion in special hospitals is high, compared to anywhere else in the NHS, but the reasons are unclear. Security in another sense is high. Patients tend to spend a long time in special hospital. The average length of stay is about 8½ years, varying according to class of disorder. Patients then almost invariably carry a stigma of some kind, whether they go back to prison, to another hospital or the community. The decision to admit a patient to special hospital thus has very serious consequences for that patient and particularly stringent criteria in the policies and procedures for admission have been adopted.

Each serious candidate for a special hospital bed must be compulsorily detainable in a hospital on grounds of mental disorder as defined in the MHA 1983 *and* pose a grave and immediate danger to the general public. In relation to dangerousness, the factors listed for consideration include evidence of unprovoked or random physical or sexual assaults on members of the public; psychotic symptoms which involve specific people, with or without threats, which could lead to the commission of violent acts; arson; the use of poison or drugs to cause harm to others; the use of firearms, knives, explosive devices, missiles and other weapons; sadistic behaviour; hostage taking; and persistent, scheming or determined absconding in the context of harmful or potentially harmful behaviour. Great emphasis is placed on restricting admission to those who could not possibly be managed anywhere else. Every effort is made not to admit a patient to special hospital solely on the grounds of inadequate provision by his local health authority.

Table 18.1
Special Hospital Catchment Areas by Health Region

Mental handicap

Ashworth Hospital	*Rampton Hospital*
Mersey	East Anglia
N W Thames	N E Thames
North Western	Oxford
Northern	S E Thames
Wales	S W Thames
West Midlands	South Western
	Trent
	Wessex
	Yorkshire

Mental illness and psychopathic disorder

Ashworth Hospital	*Broadmoor Hospital*	*Rampton Hospital*
Mersey	Oxford	East Anglia
N W Thames	S E Thames	N E Thames
North Western	S W Thames	Trent
Northern	South Western	Yorkshire
Wales	Wessex	
W Midlands		

Early in 1989, catchment areas were defined for each of the hospitals, based as far as possible on rational geographical divisions and existing trends in practice. The catchment areas are shown in Table 18.1. This organization has led to the development of improved clinical relations between the special hospitals and 'their own' regional forensic psychiatry services. A consultant psychiatrist from one of the hospitals always assesses a referred patient,

Table 18.2
The Fate of Applications for Admission to Special Hospital

	Referrals	
	Accepted 1984–1988 mean	*Rejected 1984–1988 mean*
Mental illness	138	41
Psychopathic disorder	67	23
Mental impairment	21	20
Severe mental impairment	2	2
Total:	228	86
Total annual referrals	314	

Figures derived from the Annual Patient Statistics, Department of Health, 1989b.

occasionally in conjunction with another member of the clinical team, and provides a report with recommendations about admission, but the decision to admit is that of the hospital's multidisciplinary admissions panel which includes the Director of Medical Services, the Director of Nursing Services and the most senior social worker and psychologist.

The fate of referrals to special hospitals in the last 5 years of a single admission panel at the Deparment of Health is shown in Table 18.2. The majority of patients were accepted, the average for the years being 73%. People with mental illness or psychopathic disorder, however, were much more likely to be admitted once referred (77 and 79% respectively) compared with the mentally impaired groups (50%). Since each hospital has had principal control of its own admissions, there has been a tendency towards fewer admissions, with the personality disordered and the mentally impaired slightly more affected than the mentally ill.

During the last 30 years, there has been an overall decline in admissions to special hospitals. The greatest fall was between 1968 (353) and 1984 (171). After a new peak of 223 in 1986, numbers have again fallen. As shown in Fig. 18.3, similar fluctuations have occurred in the resident population, which fell by over 25% between 1973 and 1982. It may be coincidence, but the medium secure units started to open in the mid-1970s, and were reaching their capacity by the mid-1980s when the special hospital population started to rise again.

In matters of detail, too, there may have been changes. Naismith and Coldwell (1990) compared a series of men admitted to special hospitals in 1987/88 with those admitted in 1970/71 (Tennent et al., 1974). They were comparing admissions to hospitals in different parts of the country, and so multiple community related factors may have been operating. They noted, however, 28% lower admission rates from the courts in the later years, and little use of the new remand provisions in the MHA 1983. They thought that the secure units had had an impact. A higher proportion of the patients had been admitted on transfer from prison, reflecting a more general trend. The

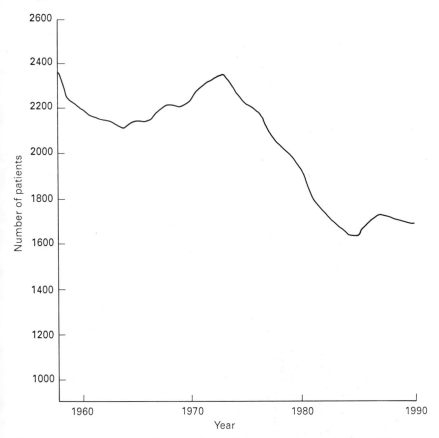

Fig. 18.3   Special hospitals' resident population (31 December each year) 1958–1990.

relatively high proportion of patients from ethnic minority groups (15%) had remained constant over the years.

Inpatient characteristics

Table 18.3 shows the distribution of special hospital inpatients according to the MHA 1983 category of their mental disorder. This is important information in that its recording is consistent across a number of systems, and it is the only consistently recorded data of diagnostic relevance. Its value has been called into question by Dell and Robertson (1988). They claimed that at least in Broadmoor, 17% of a subgroup of men resident in the early 1980s with an MHA 1959 classification of psychopathic disorder were regarded by their consultants as mentally ill, while, in an equivalent group, 8% of men classified as mentally ill were thought not to be suffering from illness. This, nevertheless, implies that over 80% of cases are correctly

Table 18.3
The Mental Health Act 1983 Categories of Disorder for Patients Resident in the Special Hospitals in March 1990

| | Hospital and sex of patients | | | | | |
| | Ashworth | | Broadmoor | | Rampton | |
Mental Health Act classification	M	F	M	F	M	F
Mental illness	338	29	309	79	257	48
Psychopathic disorder	156	46	79	32	105	30
Mental impairment	57	7	2	1	41	19
Severe mental impairment	14	1	–	–	25	33

classified, which is generally regarded as good for any disorder classification system. Further, a number of the patients had in any case been classified under more than one category of disorder. At the time of a 1990 census (Taylor et al., in preparation) 34 men and 14 women had a dual mental illness and psychopathic disorder classification (included under mental illness in Table 18.3) while 59 men and 15 women had a classification of mental impairment in addition to their illness or psychopathic disorder classification.

The majority of patients (68%) were under Home Office restrictions on discharge (S.41 MHA 1983), but an important minority (18%) under civil orders (S.3 MHA 1983), with the remainder being unrestricted offender patients. Most of those who are admitted from the courts have committed offences of violence against the person, a minority have set fires or committed a sexual assault. Men outnumber women by a ratio of 4:1 overall, but this ratio differs according to disorder (Taylor et al., in preparation). Most of the patients (60%), at the time of the census, were under 40, but no less than 95 (6%) were aged 60 or over. Two hundred and ninety six people (17%) had been resident in a special hospital for more than 15 years.

There have been frequent claims from many sources that substantial numbers of special hospital patients do not need the maximum security provided. Dell and Robertson (1988) reported that consultants in Broadmoor thought that less than one-third of the patients studied needed maximum security. As part of the census study at March 1990, consultant staff were asked to rate separately the perimeter and internal security needs of their patients and also their dependency requirements. Although higher than the estimates for the single hospital sample just referred to, still only 41% (703) patients of the total population of the special hospitals at the time were deemed needy of at least one measure of maximum security and only 182 (11%) of both. Maximum dependency need was much less often recorded, for 263 people, two-thirds of whom also had a maximum security requirement. The majority of the rest of the patients (755) were judged to require one element of medium security, but no less than 248 patients (15%) were said to require ordinary general psychiatric inpatient provision or community care. The consultants reported considerable difficulties in their attempts to move patients to more suitable placements, a problem discussed more fully below. It must be stressed again that these estimates of security needs are based entirely on the opinions of the patients' special hospital consultants. They may not represent the full picture, but they are important, because it is the consultants who generally initiate transfer or discharge.

Treatment in special hospitals

Although therapeutic activity and security are by no means incompatible, there are problems in the successful delivery of some treatments in maximum security. Special contracts with patients may be necessary over the sharing of some kinds of information revealed in psychotherapy. The maintenance of freshness in approaches to treatment, and therapeutic optimism can be hard in the day-to-day relationships with patients who will spend 8 years or more in hospital, longer than most psychiatric staff in other settings would expect to have to work with the same patients. The range of treatments offered is, nevertheless, comparable to that in any other psychiatric hospital. The relevance of various specific approaches is dealt with more fully in Ch. 17, but psychotherapy and educative approaches perhaps merit special mention here.

Black (1984) has offered a general overview of treatment in maximum security settings, while Grounds et al. (1987) focused on the more specific, in the form of a unit at Broadmoor specializing in the management of young men with personality disorder. In terms of the number of patients with personality disorder in special hospitals, there has been only one other such unit for men, at Ashworth Hospital, and no comparable unit for women. M. Cox (1976, 1978, 1979, 1982, 1983), from experience in maximum security, has demonstrated the commonality of approach between forensic psychiatry and psychotherapy, with both 'holding' the disturbed. Forensic psychiatry often uses a variety of means including staff numbers and observation skills and often physical security while psychotherapists in the field seek to build a 'holding relationship' (Cox, 1986). The most elegant description of the process of his work, appears in his account with a Danish colleague (Cox and Theilgaard, 1987):

Attend. Witness. Wait.
Discern, formulate, potentiate and reflect mutative metaphoric material.
Attend. Witness. Wait.

The book goes on to elaborate the deceptive simplicity of this advice.

Education is an important therapeutic tool in special hospitals, both in its convential forms in helping people to acquire cognitive and academic skills, and in some of the more specific treatments it has spawned, such as drama therapy and art therapy. Bennett (1989) has reviewed the overall application of education in settings for the mentally disordered over the past 200 years, as well as its use in the special hospitals. He described a remarkable resistance to the introduction of education from John Connolly's time, when

Connolly was forced to abandon a project on grounds of cost, and then the even more pernicious influence of those who argued that since mental disorders were hereditary, education was a waste of effort. Education is now widely accepted as an important and appropriate input for the mentally ill as well as the mentally impaired (Gan and Pullen, 1984). Educational projects have long been well established in the special hospitals, and in 1966 the local education authorities were involved to enhance the range and quantity of provision. Only Broadmoor now relies exclusively on its own educational service. Bennett provides a detailed evaluation of education in Rampton Hospital.

Transfers and discharges from special hospitals

The difficulties in achieving onward movement of patients from special hospital.   The movement of most patients out of a special hospital is still attended by greater bureaucracy than from any other hospital. The justification runs that since the patients were at one time regarded as exceptionally dangerous, then exceptional measures are called for in determining release. In England, the discharge or transfer of the few patients without Home Office restrictions on discharge is generally dealt with entirely by their consultant and clinical team, while the proposals for the nearly 70% of patients detained with such restrictions have to be additionally approved by the SHSA and the Home Office. The process of Home Office approval may be more or less complex according to the perceived degree of dangerousness in each case. In most cases the civil servants of C3 Division of the Home Office (*see* p. 182) provide advice for the minister who takes a decision accordingly. For a few cases, the minister seeks additional advice from the Advisory Board on Restricted Patients. (*see* pp. 185–6.)

Mental health review tribunals (MHRT) may order the discharge of any patient, including restricted cases. MHRTs have also increasingly taken to recommending appropriate levels of security and treatment for the patients remaining in hospital. In 1988, MHRTs discharged 21 restricted patients and 10 unrestricted patients, just 4% of those coming before them in each case (Department of Health, 1989b). A comparison of these figures with those presented in Hamilton (1985) suggests that the increased availability of MHRT hearings since the MHA 1983 has had little practical impact on the fate of special hospital patients. There is empirical support for such caution in that for the 2-year period following special hospital discharges in 1971, consultant/responsible medical officer discharges faired substantially better than MHRT discharges in terms of reconviction rates (Acres, 1975), and this is still borne out in relation to serious reoffending (Home Office, 1990a).

As early as the 1970s, a major concern on the part of special hospital staff and the DHSS was increasing delays in moving patients out of special hospital when they were no longer thought to need maximum security.

DHSS figures show that in May 1976 more than two-thirds of patients for whom transfer had been agreed had been placed within a year, while 4 patients (3% of the group) had had to wait for more than 3 years. A steady deterioration in this position meant that by May 1979 only 40% were placed within 12 months and more than one-fifth (43 patients) were waiting for over 3 years (Dell, 1980). Dell went on to explore the problems in transfer for the 163 patients in 1976 who had been approved for transfer by the DHSS, but were awaiting their move to other locations in the NHS. About one-quarter were still awaiting transfer 2 years later, with the severely mentally handicapped patients facing the most serious delays. The patients under restriction orders and those who had engaged in the most clearly criminal behaviour were most readily placed. Where special hospital staff were able to make informal approaches, the wait was also shorter, and once a visit by an NHS consultant from elsewhere had taken place, the chances of early transfer were considerably improved. The main reason given for refusal of patients included there being no room in the proposed receiving hospital (29%), or various other deficiencies in facilities such as lack of security or closed ward (10%). Catchment area disputes were not infrequently used to delay or block transfer. Patient characteristics accounted for some rejections (20%) and the special problem of patients with the combination of mental illness and mental handicap was noted (7%). Outright staff refusal, patient unseen, accounted for over 10% of refusals. With the 105 patients who were actually transferred, there were few problems during the 2 years of the follow-up part of the study. Seven caused sufficient concern for return to the special hospital to be requested, and all requests were met. Just 3 had committed further serious offences and were removed by police and prosecuted.

No improvement in transfer rates has followed. In 1988, 28% of the patients transferred had waited for more than 2 years, and 6% for more than 6 years (Department of Health, 1989a). In March 1990, the consultant questionnaire census of patients (Taylor et al., in preparation) showed that a formal transfer proposal had been made for 315 of the total of 1708 special hospital patients. Limiting factors in the transfer were noted in a majority of cases (225 or 71%). Lack of provision outside special hospital in one form or another accounted for 79% of the cases of delay in developing or implementing the proposals. Administrative delays in processing the cases were not wholly unimportant, but they were more often than not related to the problem that an adequate external facility was not available.

Measuring outcome of special hospital stay and the success of transfer decisions.   Studies of discharged special hospital patients generally make no distinction between outcome in relation to treatment received there and outcome of the discharge decisions. The lack of distinction, and the heavy focus on offending and reoffending, as indices of outcome, have probably been among the principal factors that have held back therapeutic developments and disproportionately emphasized the custodial properties of the hospitals. Further, the studies do not allow for the impact of the new environment once the patient has left the hospital.

The primary tasks of the special hospitals should be the assessment of mental disorder, the determination of the relevance of that mental disorder to offending or dangerous behaviour for any given patient, the delivery of effective treatment for the disorder and assessment of the interactions between the patient and his environment that may be critical to his relapse, dangerous behaviour or both. If it can be shown that in an individual case the disorder contributed substantially to the offending behaviour, and the patient is cured, then effective treatment should have as great an impact on further offending as on the disorder. Where improvement rather than complete cure is achieved, then treatment maintenance and the qualities of the patient's subsequent environment become progressively more important. Follow-up information about patients will only make sense in the context of data about their ongoing care and social setting. Measures of efficacy should, therefore, be measures of the extent to which the disorder has resolved and whether the environment is conducive to improvement. It is appropriate to measure reoffending, but as a second line outcome criterion, and in context. This should not be taken to imply that good psychiatrists are any less concerned about the safety of their patients than their non-psychiatric colleagues, than their patients' close associates or than the general public would wish them to be. It serves merely to underline the principal expertise and task of a hospital service, special or otherwise. The assessment of dangerousness in the context of mental disease is dealt with more fully in Ch. 16.

Where the offending behaviour is thought to be largely unrelated to the mental disorder, then reoffending is patently a bad measure of outcome. Treatment of the mental disorder would not be expected to have much impact on violent or criminal behaviour in these circumstances, but placement in a special hospital may, nevertheless, have been appropriate. Even the most serious offenders are entitled to treatment if they become disordered, but the nature of their offending behaviour may render it unwise to treat them in conditions other than those of special security. The measures of efficacy of the placement would again primarily be in terms of impact on their disorder, although the safety of the patients and the safety of others during their special hospital stay has also to be monitored. No follow-up study so far has distinguished between patients according to relevance of the mental disorder to offending.

Within the limits imposed by their selection and choice of outcome criteria, what have the follow-up studies of special hospital patients shown? Black (1982) followed up 125 men leaving Broadmoor Hospital, 42% of whom were classified as psychopathic. His work treated the group as homogeneous for relevance of mental disorder and simply took hospital readmission or reoffending as outcome measures. At one level, his figures were reassuring, and a testimony to special hospital treatment. In 5 years, nearly two-thirds of the discharged patients (76) remained out of the courts and over three-quarters (97) had avoided imprisonment. Perhaps more surprisingly, an even more substantial majority had remained out of hospital. Black went on to show that the best predictor of the reoffending was previous offending, and the best predictor of readmission to hospital was previous admission. The offending and psychiatric careers thus appeared more or less independent, although there is no way of telling from the data how far such individual histories may have achieved nothing more for the patient than the reinforcement of the prejudices of psychiatrists, sentencers or both, such that the subsequent allocation to a health or criminal justice system consequently was more a reflection of observer attitudes than patient behaviour at the time.

Tong and Mackay (1959) and Gathercole et al. (1968) focused on the mentally impaired leaving Rampton and Moss Side (now Ashworth South) hospitals respectively and followed them for not less than 4 years. Remarkably similar proportions of the patients were returned to special hospital (20%) or reconvicted (20–26%). The Aarvold Committee (Aarvold et al., 1973) commissioned a review and Acres (1975) personally studied patients in all MHA 1959 disorder categories from all of the special hospitals, but in both cases only if they had been discharged directly to the community. The former study identified important differences in reoffending between patients discharged without formal conditions and those conditionally discharged, favouring the latter. Acres, on reconviction data, found the same sort of differences, and showed that the mentally ill fared better than the personality disordered. He also found that MHRT discharges were less satisfactory than discharges by or on the direct recommendation of the responsible medical officer. He did, however, employ a range of other outcome criteria including a wider spectrum of evidence of social adjustment, and is the most satisfying in this regard. Tennent and Way (1984), and Dell and Robertson (1988) have reverted to principal reliance on post-hospital offending data. Tennent and Way presented similar results in the sense that they found serious reoffending rare, they also found conditional discharge and mental illness to be associated with better outcome with respect to offending, but Dell and Robertson found no significant difference between mental disorder categories.

Maximum Security in Scotland

The State Hospital at Carstairs is the sole hospital for Scotland for the treatment of legally detained patients who require treatment 'under conditions of special security on account of their dangerous, violent or criminal propensities'. It is also the regional secure unit for Scotland. The population of Scotland is about 5 million. The hospital is provided by the Secretary of State for Scotland under section 90 of the Mental Health (Scotland) Act

(MH(S))A 1984). This Act provides for a State Hospital management committee, which is appointed by the Secretary of State, and oversees the management of the hospital on his behalf. The committee is a multidisciplinary group, including psychiatrists predominantly from general psychiatric services. The day-to-day running of the hospital has been undertaken by a hospital management team comprising leading members of the relevant professional disciplines and, since 1990, led by a general manager. Staffing levels in relation to patient numbers are comparable to those in the special hospitals. Although, like the special hospitals, the State Hospital had become relatively isolated in some respects, this problem has been ameliorated in recent years through the practice not only of including general psychiatrists on the management committee, but also of State Hospital consultants usually having two or three sessions a week working with other health boards.

Most of the patients in the State Hospital are from Scotland, but Northern Ireland, with a population of about 1½ million and in the absence of a maximum secure facility of its own, also refers there almost all of its patients requiring maximum security. At any one time, there are only about 12 of the latter which, even allowing for a few placed in England, reflects a low usage of a maximum secure hospital. In addition, there are from time to time transfers from England or Wales (under section 80 of the MHA 1983) or in the reverse direction (under section 77 MH(S)A 1984). Numbers of inpatients have declined—from 268 in 1983 to a low of 210 in 1987—but there has been a slight rise since. These figures reflect an increase in both admissions and in transfer and discharge rates. At the end of 1990 there were 108 'state' patients, all but two were male, and 114 non-Secretary of State patients (87m, 27f) in residence. Of the state patients, all detained with restrictions on discharge, about 60% had been convicted of a criminal offence in association with mental disorder and transferred under the MH(S)A 1984, the majority of them mentally ill, but 20% had been found insane in bar of trial and 20% had been transferred as sentenced prisoners. In Scotland, patients on interim treatment orders or detained under the Criminal Procedure (Scotland) Act 1975 must be held in the State Hospital unless for special reasons a court directs otherwise. The non-state patients were mostly from other psychiatric hospitals (60%), but about 30% were on unrestricted court orders having been convicted of an offence, while about 10% were remand patients.

Unlike their special hospital counterparts, State Hospital consultants have autonomy in their admission decisions, but none in their discharge decisions. Under Scottish mental health law, even unrestricted cases must pass before the medical subcommittee of the State Hospital management committee, although disagreement is almost unknown. A strong representation of outside psychiatrists in this group is probably a factor in the greater ease of discharge for State Hospital than for special hospital patients. There is a requirement for the State Hospital consultant to carry out a special review of the condition of any patient during the 4th week of his detention, and if he considers it appropriate to recommend discharge. Although it is not a statutory requirement, it is usual practice for unrestricted patients to make an annual appearance before the medical subcommittee just described. In relation to restricted cases, the psychiatric advisor to the Secretary of State, who is *ex officio* a member of the State Hospital management committee and of the medical subcommittee, not only sees all reports on restricted patients, but also sees the patients themselves at least once every 18 months with their RMO. It is difficult to say whether it is this or some other difference between the Scottish and English systems that influences outcome for the State Hospital's restricted patients, but both their fate and the quality of the collated information about them seems better than for their English counterparts. Between January of 1978 and of 1988 there were 116 transfers to other hospitals and 19 conditional discharges (Ratcliff, 1988). 75% were progressing well, 13% were continuing in detention in hospital elsewhere while just 14 patients (12%) were returned to the State Hospital. Four of these were recalled on grounds of relapse of their mental illness, 6 for deteriorating behaviour in the context of personality disorder and only 4, all men, as a result of criminal convictions, 2 against the person. Three of these had been hospital inpatients at the time and only one in the community. All received prison sentences before a return to the State Hospital for reassessment.

State Hospital patients who wish to appeal against detention apply to the Lanarkshire Sheriff's Court, which deals also with all prison transfer appeals, and sits about once every 6 weeks in the hospital. Both patient and hospital are represented by counsel at these hearings.

Maximum Security in Other Parts of the World

Maximum security hospitals are not unique to Britain, nor are their attendant problems. Few of those countries with a maximum security hospital have been without a major scandal or inquiry in relation to care offered there. The nature of the problems have been fairly consistent, but the solutions different. Norway, for example, closed its Reitgjerdet hospital in 1982, after an inquiry (*Rapport om forholdene ved Reitgjerdet sykehus*, Oslo, 31 August 1980) that found that the hospital's treatment was restricted to the use of drugs and seclusion for long periods (Davis, 1980, 1981). Criminal investigations into alleged violence by staff to patients ran in parallel with the inquiry.

In 1987 the Mason committee reported on the restrictive and impoverished treatment of offender patients in hospitals in New Zealand, which included the maximum security hospitals Carrington and Oakley (Mason et al., 1988). The committee recommended the provision of skilled forensic psychiatric services, based on medium and minimum security provision and, above all, extended specialist training programmes. The fate of the maximum security provision would depend on the rate and success of the new developments.

The inquiry into Oak Ridge Hospital at Penetanguishene in Canada, is dealt with in Ch. 20 (pp. 800–2).

Problems arising in the USA have been as various as the states making provision, but themes of restrictive and deprived regimes are not absent. Actual closure of maximum security institutions, however, seems to have occurred as a result of entirely different issues, for example challenges to the legality of the detention of offender patients. A particularly important example was that of Johnnie Baxstrom, a man found insane while serving a prison sentence in New York state and transferred to the state institution for insane criminals. On appeal, he was released, and this set a precedent for others, such that nearly a thousand patients were removed from the institution at a stroke. This experience is often mistakenly cited as evidence that maximum security institutions are unnecessary. The case and the subsequent follow-up studies are dealt with on pp. 626–8.

Medium Secure Units

The Background

The development of medium security in the NHS has been reviewed by Bluglass (1985) and Snowden (1986). It probably started with the Emery Report (Ministry of Health 1961), which recommended such provision by Regional Health Authorities at the level of about 20 beds per million population. Little was achieved until after the publication of the final recommendations of the Committee on Mentally Abnormal Offenders (The Butler Committee; Home Office/DHSS, 1975), which urged 2000 medium secure beds for England and Wales. Delay in achievement, which in many health regions persisted well into the 1980s, was in spite of the intervening Glancy Report (DHSS, 1974) and the interim report of the Butler Committee (Home Office/DHSS, 1974). The Butler Report probably succeeded in stimulating development for three or four reasons. An exceptional pressure on the government to review provision for mentally abnormal offenders followed the charges against Graham Young for murder by poisoning, in circumstances similar to the offences which previously led to his special hospital admission (Holden, 1974). The Butler Committee was announced on the day of his conviction on these charges (House of Commons, 1972). Then there was the growing evidence of need, of mentally abnormal offenders inappropriately placed because of a lack of facilities. Thirdly, there was a small, but growing band of 'product champions', psychiatrists with skills and training in forensic psychiatry, but used to working outside the special hospitals. Seven new posts were established by 1975 on the advice of a Home Office working party (the Gwynne Report: Home Office, 1964), which were jointly funded between the Home Office and the NHS. Finally, and perhaps most importantly, the government earmarked new monies and encouraged each regional health authority (RHA) to develop secure facilities by undertaking to fund centrally the capital costs, and up to one-third of the resultant revenue costs.

Interim Secure Units

The task of converting existing psychiatric hospital wards into secure units was relatively easy. Ten of the 14 RHAs in England eventually opened an interim secure unit (ISU). In most cases, physical security was provided by a double door airlock system, minor modifications to the fabric and furnishings, unbreakable glass and a fenced external exercise area. The early planning teams recognized that the security and safety of staff and patients related to the number and quality of nursing staff as much as to the building, and persuaded the DHSS to accept much higher nurse to patient staffing ratios than on open psychiatric units. The RHAs which involved a forensic psychiatrist in the planning process were first off the mark. The first ISU, which opened in 1976 (Rainhill hospital, Mersey RHA), was followed shortly after by the Prestwich Unit, the latter considerably limited in its operation by pressure from nursing unions. The Knowle Hospital Unit, Hampshire, opened in 1977, but it was 1980 before the next one, the Bethlem Royal Hospital Unit in London. Others then followed. The first four ISUs to open served as models for those that followed, and as a consequence there were many similarities in operational policies.

Unfortunately, the pressure to build permanent secure units was such that in many cases irreversible planning decisions for permanent units were made before the accumulating clinical experience was sophisticated enough to provide reliable advice. Small units of 15–20 beds, providing a forensic psychiatric service to a subregional population worked (Jones and Berry, 1985), but almost every ISU has (or will) close when the permanent unit opens. In most of the geographically large RHAs this means a single regional secure unit (RSU) with 50–100 beds serving a population of at least three million instead of between one and three smaller ISUs relating to a smaller subregional population.

Regional Secure Units

Structure

The delays in developing and opening the regional secure units were widely criticized (*Lancet*, 1976; Parker and Tennent, 1979; Kilroy-Silk, 1982). Stocking's (1985) study, however, demonstrated the complexities in the take-up rate of an innovation in the Health Service, and in each RHA there were many reasons for the delays (Snowden, 1985). Some RHAs, particularly those with a forensic psychiatrist, took account of existing facilities, the population density and size of the region before deciding on a service model, and the location of the permanent unit. The South East Thames RHA (SETRHA) chose a complex model: a 30-bed central secure unit, with four small 15-bed area (secure) clinics in other parts of the region, in order to provide an efficient local service to the communities. Some RHAs opened separate outpatient office accommodation in non-hospital based locations. Others did not consider the extra-unit services and developed a single RSU on inappropriate hospital sites often on the edge of a large region, making it difficult for staff to work outside the unit in a meaningful way. Most of the RSUs were built on extensive hospital sites, although with the closure programmes for larger mental hospitals now coming to fruition, some are under threat. In few, if any, cases will it be safe or therapeutic to run a secure unit in total isolation from other health service facilities.

RSU planning teams were only given general design advice in the DHSS guidelines (DHSS, 1975), the maximum number of beds in each RHA was fixed by the DHSS, using the Glancy figure of 20 beds/million rather than the Butler figure which doubled this estimate, and there was a maximum allowance of 50 sq. metres of floor space/patient. There were a number of architectural problems to consider (Ingham, 1975), in particular how to blend the building into the surroundings to prevent a penal appearance. As with the ISUs, there are nevertheless obvious security features, such as outdoor exercise areas bounded by wire mesh fencing, and an entrance lobby with a double door airlock system under electronic control. Inside the unit, there are locked/lockable doors, windows which are generally unbreakable, and decoration and furniture which has been chosen to be robust enough to withstand damage, but structured also to minimize injury to self or others. Another important consideration has been the engineering (Williams, 1976), of heating systems, ventilation (because of restricted window openings), electrical systems, internal communications, fire and attack alarm systems. Not surprisingly, mistakes were made, particularly by those planning teams who did not adequately involve ward-based nursing staff (Berry, 1987). Nurses need to have confidence in the building design, because of its influence on working practices and operational policies. Unhappiness with the design may make it difficult for them to achieve a reasonable balance between their therapeutic and security roles. Hellman (1988) considered architectural and economic appraisals of secure units in one health region (SETRHA), some 3 years after the purpose-built units were occupied.

The first RSU opened in November 1980. Two of the first units to open suffered from being first, and extensive rebuilding has been necessary to overcome design faults. The development and opening of new units is a continuous process; Table 18.4 summarizes the situation in England and Wales at December 1990. Some of the completed beds are not open for admissions, more usually because of difficulties in staff recruitment than financial considerations, although both apply.

Table 18.4
Permanent Secure Facilities Open in England and Wales by December 1990

Regional Health Area	RSU site (s)	No of beds	Comments
Northern	St Luke's Hospital Middlesbrough	25	This was the first unit to open in November 1980; RSU poorly built and located on edge of large region; extensive rebuilding complete
Yorkshire	Fieldhead Hospital Wakefield	48	Four special care units provide additional back-up facilities around the region
North Western	Prestwich Hospital Manchester	88	The only permanent secure unit for adolescent offenders is sited here
	Whittingham Hospital, Preston	24	
Mersey	Rainhill Hospital Merseyside	50	This small, compact region decided to open a community outpatient base in central Liverpool to complement the RSU located outside the main population centre
West Midlands	Rubery Hill Birmingham	100	This unit opened in 1987 when the two experienced ISUs closed
Trent	Towers Hospital Leicester	45	Located on southern edge of a large region whose main population density is in the north; this RSU has undergone a rebuilding programme
East Anglia	St Andrew's Hospital Norwich	36	This is this region's only service base
North West Thames	St Bernard's Hospital Ealing	40	There may be plans for other secure units; there is already a separate community base
North East Thames	Friern Hospital Hackney	12	The 10-bed ISU at Friern Hospital will close when an RSU for this region eventually opens
	Runwell Hospital	14	
South East Thames	Bethlem Royal Hospital Beckenham	25	The central Bethlem clinic, built for 30, is the most secure facility; two area clinics are threatened by closure of their parent hospitals (C.H. & H.H.)
	Cane Hill Hospital (C.H.) Purley	15	
	Bexley Hospital	15	
	Hellingly Hospital (H.H.) Eastbourne	15	
	Maidstone Hospital	15	

Table 18.4 (cont.)
Permanent Secure Facilities Open in England and Wales by December 1990

Regional Health Area	RSU site (s)	No of beds	Comments
Wessex	Knowle Hospital Fareham	28	This is the only service base in the region; it is also the least physically secure RSU building in the country.
South Western	Langdon Hospital Dawlish	30	This elongated semirural region has two purpose-built RSUs
	Glenside Hospital Bristol	30	

Oxford region has an interim unit at Fairmile Hospital (13 beds) and another at Milton Keynes (12 beds), but the former will close when a proposed RSU opens.

South West Thames has undergone a change in philosophy. Up to now multiple special care units situated in psychiatric hospitals have been supported by the regional forensic psychiatrists. A 10-bed ISU opened in late 1991 at Springfield Hospital and a permanent RSU will follow.

Wales is still formulating plans for permanent RSUs. At present there is a forensic psychiatry facility at Whitchurch Hospital, Cardiff. An interim secure unit was opened in February 1992 at Bridgend Hospital.

Inpatient services

Medical, nursing, psychology, social work, occupational and rehabilitation staff are all involved in the assessment, treatment, discharge and follow-up of patients. Although there are some differences in the way that services have developed, there is now enough information to describe what is generally done.

Admissions.   Data on secure unit admissions have come from two sources. Table 18.5 summarizes the early published material from four ISUs (Higgins, 1981 for Rainhill hospital; Reid et al., 1982, for Prestwich hospital; Gudjonsson and MacKeith, 1983b and Offen and Taylor, 1985 both for the Bethlem Royal hospital; Treasaden and Shepherd, 1983 for Knowle Hospital). Additional comparative information has been presented (Berry, 1986, unpublished) from the first 400 patients admitted to secure units (from 1 March, 1983) in seven health regions. Faulk and Taylor (1986) have added to the account of the Knowle (Wessex) Unit.

At least a quarter of admissions overall have been female, a figure much higher than was expected, but this conceals considerable variation. Following the study reported for the Bethlem Royal hospital, for example, no female patients were admitted at all for periods exceeding a year through lack of suitable referrals. Berry found female admissions to be significantly younger (average age 27.8 years) than males (average age 33.4 years). It is also

Table 18.5

Admission Data from Interim Secure Units and Regional Secure Units Published between 1981–1986

Study	ISU/RSU	Period under study	Total no admissions	Caucasian		Ethnic minority		Total	
				Males (%)	Females (%)	Males (%)	Females (%)	Males (%)	Females (%)
Higgins (1981)	ISU	4 yrs	35	—	—	—	—	21 (60)	14 (40)
Reid et al. (1982)	ISU	4 yrs 5 months	48	—	—	—	—	48 (100)	—
Treasaden and Shepherd (1983)	ISU	4 yrs	87	—	—	—	—	73 (84)	14 (16)
Gudjonsson and MacKeith (1983b)	ISU	2 yrs 2 months	23	—	—	—	—	16 (70)	7 (30)
Offen and Taylor (1985)	ISU	1 yr 8 months	28 (37%)†	—	—	—	—	23 (50)	5 (18)
Berry (unpublished)	10 ISU* 2 RSU	3 yrs	400	238 (78)	85 (90)	68 (22)	9 (10)	306 (81)	94 (19)

* Study of secure facilities in seven health regions.

† Percentage shown is of total referrals during the study period.

interesting to note that around one in five male admissions came from the ethnic minorities, predominantly Afro-Caribbean. Cope and Ndegwa (1991), who also found that Afro-Caribbeans were admitted in numbers in excess of their representation in the local West Midlands population, put forward a number of tentative explanations for this from decision-making by the police and the courts to the lower use of local psychiatry services by Afro-Caribbeans for reasons that may be related to both the perception of these services as racist and coercive and services not meeting the needs of this community. Another factor is nature of disorder. In Berry's (1986 unpublished) series of 400 patients, 84% of those from the ethnic minority groups had a diagnosis of schizophrenia, compared with only 52% of the Caucasian patients.

Patients are referred from a wide variety of sources including the courts, prison medical service, solicitors, police and probation service as well as other psychiatrists. A small number of patients are 'directed' admissions from the RHA. Transfers between secure units, and even self-referral, make up another small group, but over 80% of all admissions have come from the courts, prisons, special and NHS hospitals. The balance between admissions from prison and other sources varies between units. The explanation for this is not yet clear, but the kind of relationship that each service has developed with the referral agencies is particularly important. In the north west of England, for example, the relationship between the prison medical service and forensic psychiatry services has been particularly successful (House of Commons, 1986b).

Legislative changes have influenced the quality and quantity of the input provided to prisons by forensic psychiatrists. Prior to the MHA 1983, the two most common methods of transferring a remand prisoner to hospital were either utilizing section 73 of the MHA 1959 (transfer for 'urgent' treatment order) or bail with a condition of hospital residence. The remand to hospital legislation under the MHA 1983 is probably leading to more admissions from remand prisons. In 1984 (Home Office, personal communication) 27 patients were admitted under S.35 (remand to hospital for report on mental condition) and 6 patients under S.36 (remand to hospital for treatment) of the MHA 1983. Most of these patients would have been admitted to secure units (although a breakdown of these figures is unavailable). In 1985, the respective numbers were 159 and 34. The other remand provisions have not fallen into disuse, and there is an impression of a considerable increase in remand work. Furthermore, it does not only affect psychiatrists. Over a 9-month period from December 1986, over 400 hours of nursing time was required to escort 39 patients from the RSU at Prestwich Hospital, Manchester, to various courts within the North Western health region.

Around one-quarter of secure unit admissions come from NHS hospitals. Although most are technically non-offender patients, they tend to form an exceptionally difficult group, already having proved themselves dangerously out of control in less specialist hospital settings. Some progress fairly rapidly to special hospital. The special hospital patients, who are either admitted for assessment in less secure surroundings or as part of a formal rehabilitation plan, create different problems, not only because of the generally very serious nature of their offences, but also because of their lengthy periods of previous hospitalization, which may handicap rehabilitative efforts. The close juxtaposition of acutely disturbed patients and patients with rehabilitation needs in the same unit poses a particular challenge for the smaller units in balancing the nature of care.

Treasaden's review (1985) of four ISUs found the main behaviour problem leading to admission to be personal violence (range 67—83%). Fire-raising (range 9—14%) and sexual misbehaviour (range 3—10%) were the next largest groups. Offen and Taylor (1985) found that violence was a precipitant to the referral in all but 13 (18%) of cases in their series, and that the more serious the index violence, the more likely it was that a bed would be made available. Just over one-third of the very violent group was turned away (usually as too violent for the unit to cope) compared with nearly half in the moderately violent group and two-thirds of the tiny, minimally violent group, thought to be safely manageable elsewhere. The longer-term violence history was less important, with only a non-significant tendency to accept the most violent. Berry's (1986, unpublished) account of the reasons for admission in this cohort of 400 admissions does not allow easy comparison with earlier studies. He does, however, suggest that a small number of patients are admitted to secure units for danger to self, administrative reasons, management problems other than dangerousness, and breakdown in the community.

Referral and assessment process. Although most of the studies just reviewed do not give a complete picture of clinical practice, as they do not describe rejected referrals, it is possible to make some generalizations about admission criteria for secure units:

1. Most patients will have clear evidence of mental disorder, and will meet MHA 1983 criteria for compulsory detention, however, a very small number of patients are admitted informally;
2. The type of presenting behaviour (often violence to others) is such that the security and facilities of the unit are appropriate for assessment or treatment;
3. There are good prospects of discharging the patient within 18 months to 2 years. This criterion, now much criticized, was advocated by the Glancy Committee (DHSS, 1974), mainly to prevent beds becoming blocked.

Each referral is usually seen by a psychiatrist and a nurse, but other disciplines may be involved. The patient is interviewed, discussion is usually held with staff from the referring unit and all relevant documents are

Table 18.6

Referrals Rejected and Accepted from NHS Hospitals, Prisons and Special Hospitals to the RSU, North Western Regional Health Authority between January 1983–August 1986

	NHS hospitals	Prison	Special hospitals
Number accepted (%)	55 (32%)	59 (78%)	24 (56%)
Number rejected (%)	115 (68%)	16 (22%)	19 (44%)
Total	170 (100%)	75 (100%)	43 (100%)

carefully studied. In the Manchester (adult) RSU, between January 1983–August 1986, a total of 288 patients were referred from NHS hospitals, prisons or the courts for admission or advice.

Table 18.6 illustrates the pattern of admissions and rejections by referral source. The total number of prison referrals is increasing, and during the 4-year period, 78% were accepted (out of 75 referrals). For NHS hospital referrals the opposite is found. Of the 170 referrals during the same period less than one-third were finally accepted. These findings are similar to Mersey ISU (Higgins, 1981) where only one-third of NHS hospital referrals were admitted over a 4-year period. Such patients were refused admission because dangerousness had been exaggerated, or staffing, morale or service difficulties had magnified management problems. Bond (1989) followed-up 32 patients refused admission to an RSU from a variety of sources. He found that the majority of mentally ill remand prisoners refused RSU admission found hospital placements in local hospitals. The group of difficult, uncooperative, uncontrolled or asocial patients in psychiatric hospitals who were not accepted proved to be manageable with changes to the treatment regimes. The most common reason for a special hospital patient being rejected was the view that rehabilitation would take too long and that further work could be done in the special hospital.

Great thoroughness must attend all assessments, and original documentation of all key incidents together with independent or observer accounts of the patient must be sought. There is usually a mountain of documentation including the clinical notes, previous and other current psychiatric, social work or probation reports, police documents and witness statements. The importance of studying originals lies in the problem that inaccuracies may find their way into a report and simply be repeated over the years. A recent enquiry into a homicide by a patient transferred to an RSU from a special hospital highlighted the importance of coming to a properly informed judgement at initial assessment (Mersey RHA, 1987). An assessment based on inadequate or incomplete information can make each further decision flawed and possibly dangerous.

Treatment.　Some units have set up a graduated system of inpatient management with admission, treatment and predischarge wards. Others have divided patient areas between clinical teams which admit all the patients coming from a particular subregional catchment population. Some are too small for this level of organization. Whatever the system, conventional treatments are given which, depending on the ethos of the unit, may have an eclectic, behavioural or predominantly psychodynamic approach. Each patient is assessed by the clinical team, attempts are made to establish the relationship between problem behaviour and mental disorder and an individual treatment programme is implemented. It may be necessary to use one or two nurses to provide 24 hour close and intrusive monitoring of a patient (specialling). Another technique is 'time out', which does not necessarily mean moving the patient to a special room, but must ensure that the patient has relief from the environment or elements in the environment that seem to be stimulating or reinforcing his behaviour. Occasionally, seclusion may be needed. Each secure unit has a specially designed secure room, the bigger ones more, and strict guidelines to safeguard both patients and staff if the forcible locking up of a patient is required (*see also* Ch. 17).

It is generally essential for a patient to be assessed outside the unit before he can be placed elsewhere. The treatment programme is then extended to include periods of leave away from the ward. It is usual for each patient to be granted leave in a graduated manner so that progress can be carefully monitored. Escorted leave is the first stage, with unescorted trips outside the unit following, first within and then outside the hospital grounds in which the unit is located. Debriefing of patients on their return from unescorted leave, and clear documentation is very important, particularly in relation to restricted patients who require the permission of the Home Office for any leave outside the hospital grounds. A great deal of administrative time is spent liaising with C3 Division of the Home Office on planning rehabilitation for this group.

Specialist Secure Units

Mental handicap units

Among the mentally disordered, the mentally handicapped are relatively rarely involved in offending, and when they are the majority can be managed in the community (*see also* Ch. 7). A few, nevertheless, require secure provision. The proportion and numbers in special hospitals have declined over the last decade, but 200 remain, constituting 12% of the special hospital population. Many of these need not be there if medium secure provision were available.

The Department of Psychiatry in Oxford (Gath and Orly, 1976; Gath, 1978) carried out its own survey of medium secure needs for the Oxford health region. They identified 41 people in a suitable level of care, and 125 not so placed. Just 63 of these were thought to require a hospital placement with security, and the majority of these (37) were mentally handicapped.

The need for some specialist secure provision for the mentally handicapped is increasingly recognized (e.g. Spencer, 1989), but actual developments have had to rely on 'product champions' and their use of existing facilities. North West Thames RHA has developed a unit along very similar lines to the Yorkshire model described by Spencer, in the grounds of the large mental handicap hospital, while SETRHA has developed a unit in a general psychiatric hospital, which is rarely locked, but has the same staff/patient ratios as the nearby regional medium secure unit, and which does make use of its seclusion room from time to time. Perhaps the best described approach to an effective secure environment with treatment for the mentally handicapped, albeit explicitly not a medium secure unit, is that of the Northumberland Unit (Day, 1988). Spencer (1989) refers to the Yorkshire mental handicap unit as a 'difficult to place patients unit', but it is closely associated with the regional secure unit for mental illness. Another approach is to develop secure provision for the mentally handicapped from within the forensic psychiatry rather than mental handicap specialist services. The Leander unit, in Langdon Hospital, Dawlish, is a good example of this model.

Adolescent units in the NHS

Severely disturbed adolescents almost invariably have an important medical component to their problems, including pervasive developmental disorders with both neurological and behavioural correlates, and self-injurious behaviours. Their needs range from the medical, psychiatric and psychological to the social and educational, but there is a relatively small group for whom diagnoses such as schizophrenia, manic depressive psychosis or anorexia nervosa apply. A disease model is thus regarded by some as inappropriate for adolescent care. This deprives many adolescents of psychiatric or psychological input altogether, as many special boarding schools or assessment centres lack psychiatric or even psychological input. The problem is particularly severe for the psychiatrically disordered adolescent offender. The attempt to avoid institutionalization for adolescents has meant that NHS inpatient facilities for them are rare indeed. About ten places are available in one of the special hospitals, but the service there is still far from adequate. There is just one NHS adolescent forensic psychiatry service with a secure unit for the whole of England and Wales—the Gardener Unit in Manchester. This unit (Bailey et al., in preparation) has recently analysed the first 100 admissions. Mental Health legislation was used in one-quarter of the cases, the rest were admitted using Child Care legislation. The mean age of the 79 males and 21 females was 15.3, with the youngest as low as 11 years. A diagnosis of conduct disorder was made in 53%, mixed disorder of conduct and emotion in 31%, and 13% had a diagnosis of psychosis. The largest group by offence were sex offenders (34%), next came arsonists, and then serious violent offenders. As a group, all showed high levels of disruption and disadvantage in their backgrounds. Other, mainly non-medical secure facilities are described in Ch. 5.

Dilemmas and Remaining Challenges

Neither size nor site of the purpose-built secure units was always determined by ideology. There was an initial intention in South East Thames to build a single unit of about 90 beds on the Bethlem Royal Hospital site, a plan which was firmly rejected by local residents and staff alike (Gunn, 1976). The consequent plans for the distribution of the beds across five units were quickly embraced among health care staff as more ideologically sound, with the theoretical opportunity to manage patients closer to their communities of origin. The model is of undoubted advantage in these terms, in spite of some still quite large distances to be travelled, and also for the fact that close teamwork is possible and the network of units mutually supportive, but the pattern has also shown disadvantages. The costs of running the service are slightly higher than for a single unit with a comparable size service. The most important problem arising is that as the parent mental hospitals are run down and closed, the secure units face either serious isolation which can be dangerous, or the disruption and cost of moving to a new site. The latter is likely to be part of a district general hospital, which may be less suitable if space or options for therapeutic activities are thereby very limited.

By contrast, the 100-bed unit of the West Midlands health region, a single site unit for the largest health region in the country, arose because of objections to a three-unit model. It now looks more viable as a self-contained unit as the other health service facilities on the site close. Nevertheless, the extent to which it is forced to increase its already considerable self-sufficiency may increase the risks of institutionalization, and force it along the pathway of an increasingly parallel service pattern.

In other areas, geography remains the limiting factor. The area of the South Western health region, which is large by English standards, is served by two units, 110 miles apart. This distance has prevented significant mutual working, training or security back-up one for the other, although rotation of the psychiatrist trainees is being attempted. Community outreach work and liaison with other NHS catchment areas is theoretically easier in more densely populated urban areas, but often deprivation in these areas threatens the community prospects for rehabilitation. Just one unit is sited in an inner city area, with the additional disadvantage of limitations of physical space in and around the unit itself.

Lower Levels of Security in Scotland

There are no regional secure units in Scotland. The State Hospital explicitly offers some service in this regard, in contrast to the special hospitals for England and Wales which do not accept patients on these grounds, but provide by default a certain amount of care for existing patients who have progressed beyond the stage of needing maximum security, but are likely to need medium security for the long term. The care of other mentally disordered offenders needing less than maximum security in Scotland is provided by forensic psychiatry intensive care units (Woodside et al., 1976; Basson and Woodside, 1981). They have a very small number of patients, of either gender (usually about 12) and relatively high nursing staff levels (5 by day and 3 at night). Although generally locked, the physical security is otherwise low. The turnover can be very high, for example 400 admissions in 3 years to the 13-bedded Edinburgh unit (Basson and Woodside, 1981).

Comprehensive Forensic Psychiatry Services

Everybody is in favour of comprehensive services, the term is a warm cliche with a halo. It is difficult, however, to move from the concept to provision. The elements of a comprehensive service are increasingly well understood, but how are they best listed? Does such a service deskill or enhance other services, such as probation work or general psychiatry? How far does a comprehensive forensic psychiatry service embrace prison work and court work as well as hospital work? It is probably unwise to be too prescriptive about these matters. General principles will help administrators and others provide particular services according to changing circumstances, ensuring that gaps are plugged and connections are made. The main principle of comprehensive forensic psychiatry is that an appropriate medical service is available in each and every setting that the patient encounters, the service is aimed at the long term rather than the short term and the service embraces other professions such as nursing, social work, psychology and occupational therapy. An 'appropriate' medical service is one designed to tackle the problem encountered. It is, for example, inappropriate to ask district general hospital units to take on all forms of psychiatric care.

This concluding section considers just a few topics which are sometimes neglected in order to stress their importance for a fully comprehensive service. A number of elements crucial to a comprehensive service are discussed elsewhere and can be considered slightly outside the Health Service, e.g. prison psychiatry (pp. 741–2), court liaison schemes (p. 728), civil work (pp. 102–7).

Special Care Units

Bowden (1978b) noted the importance of the availability of a locked facility if psychiatric hospitals and units were to accept offender patients for treatment. It is accepted that there is a bottle-neck between maximum secure facilities, provided at the rate of 35 beds per million population, and medium secure facilities, at the rate of 20 beds per million population. No one knows precisely how many locked or lockable special care facilities exist in England and Wales for the short-term management of the very acutely disturbed or for the longer-term management of the more chronically behaviourally disordered—two very different tasks, but an estimate by the DOH for the Review of Services for Mentally Disordered Offenders 1991–92 of locked or lockable psychiatric facilities overall in the NHS (including psychogeriatric places) suggested a substantial decline in availability to a figure only about 200 greater than the number of medium secure beds (DoH, Home Office, 1992).

One health region (South West Thames) had until 1991 based its care on the provision of a number of small special care units in the absence of a purpose-built medium secure unit, but the presence of a forensic psychiatry service. One measure of the efficacy of regional secure provision lies in its relative quest for maximum secure hospital places. In 1987, this region had the second highest referral rate to special hospitals per million population, ahead of the two regions without either secure units or truly developed forensic psychiatry services at that time. The relatively high referral rate would imply at least recognition of the problems of offender patients. The fact that this region also had by far the highest rejection rate for referrals to special hospital may imply that the absence of a full range of secure facilities in the region was indeed a key factor in many of the referrals (Department of Health, 1989b). Locked wards are a necessary, but not sufficient provision in the range of services for the mentally abnormal offender and behaviourally disturbed patients. The referral and acceptance rates for 1991 were more closely in the balance (SHSA, 1992).

Open Inpatient Care for Offender Patients

In recognition of the fact that offender patients need a full range of specialist provision, many forensic psychiatry services have found ways of providing open care, a stage of responsibility beyond the relatively free access to the outside world by patients enjoying full parole rights from a secure building. Most, not having had specialist services prior to the development of regional forensic psychiatry, have set aside open areas in the only place they can—the secure unit. Some have gone so far as to develop a tiny, independent living facility, so that there are two or three beds that function as a hostel ward or flat. Such developments have usually required physical modification to the original building, as the need for such care was not fully appreciated until the services were running. The Maudsley Hospital had separate inpatient provision of six beds prior to the establishment of its secure unit at the Bethlem Royal Hospital, and now has twelve. These are to serve both local and national demand. Security exists on such units, but ensured by the skills and balance of staff, with physical constraints at a minimum.

Most open provison for mentally abnormal offenders and the behaviourally disturbed must be provided from within general psychiatry, unless there is to be a major expansion of forensic psychiatry. Mental disorders probably do carry an increased risk for coming before the courts, but much of this behaviour is of nuisance value rather than being dangerous. Even much of minor to moderate violence can be safely managed in general psychiatric facilities, because it is largely driven by a disease which is treatment responsive. It is the patients who trespass, beg, thieve or deceive in minor ways, or break windows, but who are either poorly compliant with treatment, poorly responsive to it or both, who are most disadvantaged. If they drink alcohol or abuse non-prescribed drugs as well, then the health care system seems totally unable to cope. It is said of such patients that they have a right to choose their course, or that in the absence of motivation treatment will be impossible, or that if they take cannabis their psychosis is mainly drug-induced and that this does not justify hospitalization. In reality, most of these patients simply demand too much of their local housing, social and health authorities alike, as they are presently resourced, and, they consequently, are denied basic care. They are not dangerous, and are therefore usually denied specialist forensic psychiatric services as well.

Community Management of Offender Patients: General Principles

The key to successful management in the community is the development of a sense of security, founded in reality, for patient and support staff alike. For the patient to feel secure, he will need satisfactory accommodation, adequate finance for basic needs and the skills to manage his monies, the sense that even if he is symptomatic, his symptoms are not intrusive and that he can control them, the knowledge that if he reaches a crisis, there are people he can turn to for immediate help, and the mastery of the system for getting to them. If all these elements are in place, the psychiatrist and coworkers will also feel secure; however, they will also want to see the patient regularly to satisfy themselves that the conditions continue to hold true, to be confident that the patient will seek help by the conventional route of asking for it rather than acting out in some way and, for a number of cases, they will need systems of support and advice for themselves. Some patients will remain extremely dependent and demanding in spite of all efforts to wean them away from intensive care. The sharing of the work among the team, and an occasional independent review of the management, are essential. Staff also need reassurances that their efforts are worthwhile; patient stability is an important objective, and this should be made explicit to staff. Treatment remains possible even when cure is elusive or impossible. Some patients remain potentially dangerous, and it is good practice to have more than one person monitoring mental state and behaviour. Other patients may become dangerous to the staff themselves as their dependency, and their anxiety about their dependency increases, or as they develop powerful transferences, whether or not the latter are encouraged in therapy. The availability of advice from someone with training in the psychodynamic understanding of relationships is essential. The complexity of patient-therapist relationships, and the importance of providing a full range of appropriate supports for a key worker, with the flexibility to be able to change that key worker if necessary, were seen in the case of Sharon Campbell, who killed her social worker. The event and subsequent inquiry (DHSS, 1988b) prompted the Royal College of Psychiatrists to draft guidelines on the after-care and community management of patients in any part of the psychiatric services (Royal College of Psychiatrists, 1991). The Department of Health has offered circulars on hospital discharges (HC (89) 5) and, jointly with the Department of Social Services on *The Care Programme Approach* (HC (90) 23/LASSL (90) 11).

It is important that systems for providing community care are devised jointly by patients and staff. Unless the patient has some sense of ownership of the plan, his compliance will always be in jeopardy. If he does not like his accommodation he will not stay. If he does not relate well to the people with whom he must share that accommodation, he may resort to aggression to resolve his problems. His financial situation is likely to be precarious at best. He may, at least initially, find it easier to cope if he contracts for money to be paid directly in lieu of rent, electricity or gas, and he may use a bus pass more responsibly than cash for fares. If, however, he is not a willing partner in these contracts, fights may ensue with social security officials. Lack of occupation may be both damaging and give an opportunity for deviant behaviour to re-emerge, but work or a day centre which is unattractive to the patient will be a source of provocation, and may become a focus of battles for control. People offering help must actually provide it, when it is needed. The necessary trust for safe management is a two-way process.

In England and Wales, there are provisions in law which may assist community management. Section 117 of the MHA 1983, requires that health authorities and local authorities must provide for the after-care of previously compulsorily detained patients. Other sections in the Act provide a legal framework for a structure which may bind patient and psychiatrist and patient and social supervisor alike into safe therapeutic practices. It is possible for patients on treatment or hospital orders to go out of hospital on trial leave (for up to 6 months if their departure follows at an early stage from renewal of detention). For civil patients, Sensky et al. (1991) showed that across a small group (35), various in their characteristics and clinical supervisors, for whom such an arrangement had been tried, treatment compliance was improved and both time spent in hospital and levels of dangerousness reduced. It is not possible for this arrangement to continue, however, without readmission to hospital, and readmission solely for the purpose of renewing the detention order is now explicitly illegal (*Hallstrom* and *Gardiner*).

Guardianship (section 7 MHA 1983) remains an option for the legal enhancement of control for unrestricted offender patients as they return to the community (*see also* pp. 39 and 191). It is not much used, but does provide for required residence at a specified place, required attendance at hospital and required access to the patient as necessary. It allows for all but actual compulsory treatment with drugs (or other physical treatments) and, if local social services can be persuaded to assist in the event of a patient being eligible, thus has most of the qualities that might be sought in a community treatment order. The kind of community treatment order which was proposed by the Royal College of Psychiatrists (1987) envisaged very little more. It did not include physically enforcing physical treatments outside hospital. Home Office restrictions have much the same effect, except that the controls are maintained over the medical and social supervisors as well as over the patients and are usually unlimited in time. Conditions of discharge may be specified in even greater detail, there is no legal bar, even, to specific treatments being named as conditions of discharge. Most psychiatrists, however, would properly resist this. In 1987, the Home Office and then Department of Health and Social Security jointly issued three extremely helpful booklets in relation to the supervision and after-care of conditionally discharged restricted patients, one being notes of guidance for the supervising psychiatrist (*see* Appendix 3 p. 1011), one for the hospitals preparing for the conditional discharge of the patients, and one for the guidance of social supervisors.

Other countries, such as the USA and some states in Australia, have gone much further than Britain in legally enforcing treatment in the community. In some respects, such orders follow on naturally from policies of deinstitutionalization (Bottomley, 1987). Some places, such as Queensland, Australia, merely allow indefinite extension of leave from hospital (Westmore, 1988). Examples in the USA (Bursten, 1986) include Tennessee, which has introduced new provisions which start at the time of discharge from hospital and Oregon, which uses the criminal statute to ensure community care for offender patients (*see also* Cham, 1982). The specially instituted provisions tend to be stringent in the requirements for evidence of previous non-adherence to follow-up treatment plans and previous repeated dangerous incidents. Mulvey et al. (1987) discussed the continuing dilemma in such arrangements, while Bursten (1986) opined that although patients in mandatory outpatient care in Tennessee showed a reduction in readmission rates compared with controls, his research failed to support the hypothesis that this reduction was due to the compulsory treatment law.

Community Forensic Psychiatry Services

Medical, psychology and social work staff based in medium secure units, often together with linked community psychiatric nurses, have developed specialist community services in each health region for mentally abnormal offenders. Some patients discharged from a secure unit are not referred back to local general psychiatric services (integrated patients), but are followed up in a 'parallel' manner by the forensic psychiatry team (Gunn, 1976). This small group of 'forensic psychiatry patients' are chosen and closely monitored on the basis of the balance between the nature of their disorders, the assessment of dangerousness, previous criminal career, and whether or not Home Office supervision is necessary. Most general and forensic psychiatric outpatient services simply see a range of patients in a designated outpatient building. This is as true for patients discharged from specialist inpatient care as well as those newly referred by the courts, lawyers, the probation service, hospital service, general practitioners or even the patients themselves. Cooke (1991) has described one aspect of such services at one centre in Scotland (the Douglas Inch Clinic, Glasgow). The special problems experienced and posed by disruptive or offender patients sometimes lead to optimal provision being made through sessions that are highly specialized, either by the nature of the disorder, the nature of the setting or both.

Clinics for specified disorders

In the 1960s, Lion and his colleagues, in Baltimore, USA, began running a specialist service for violent and potentially violent patients (Lion et al., 1969; Lion, 1975). Most of these patients had already been violent, some had criminal histories. The aims of the clinic were principally twofold. First, emergency care was provided, with immediate support and referral on to another appropriate facility, which was for inpatient care in about one-third of a series studied. The second aim was to reinforce the patients in their quest for psychiatric help when they felt violent. Over a 9-month period two-thirds of the patients made repeated visits in crisis.

Sex offenders continue to pose a particular challenge to services, because of the reluctance of many courts to pass down non-custodial sentences and the concomitant reluctance of hospitals to offer inpatient care. Part of the reluctance in England and Wales derives from the MHA 1983, which states that no one shall have compulsory care for 'promiscuity or other immoral conduct', or for 'sexual deviancy' alone (S.1 (3)). This clause is widely misinterpreted. As discussed on pp. 26 and 522, the Act does not set out to deny treatment to patients with sexual disorders. Probation orders, with or without a condition of treatment, offer perhaps the best model for ensuring not only engagement, but also continuing compliance with treatment, and a number of centres have now taken advantage of this to provide clinics or groups for such men (e.g. Mendelson, 1988). The Avon Probation Service has recently completed 10 years' experience of such work by two probation officers, for which they have had regular input and supervision from a consultant psychiatrist (Cook et al., 1991). Only about half of the men offered the experience completed therapy, but they showed a significant advantage over the others in terms of avoiding reoffending. Mezey (1991) has reported an experiment along similar lines in London, with two probation officers and two psychiatrists conducting group work with men on a condition of their probation order. Considerable concern has from time to time been expressed about the possibility that group work for sex offenders may foster unwanted side-effects, such as creating contact groups for passing on information about potential victims. There is no evidence that this has been a problem in practice.

Clinics in special places

Those in forensic psychiatric practice rapidly become familiar with the problem that not all those who have psychiatric problems are willing to identify themselves publicly as such, or are able to make the commitment or effort necessary to reach the psychiatric outpatient department. Accordingly, some practitioners are ready to leave their office to deliver services outside hospitals.

Forensic psychiatrists take up sessional work in prisons. More often than not, the time is taken by assessment work, but occasionally arrangements have been made to offer specialist services, such as psychotherapy, in prison. Many mentally abnormal offenders go to prison only because they are homeless. Aside from the fact that some of their offences may have been dictated by this plight, the decision to remand in custody or not in the event of a criminal charge depends very heavily on whether the court can be convinced that an offender will return to court or comply with requests for medical reports. If the accused has no fixed address, this is unlikely (Gibbens et al., 1977). The Probation Service and the Crown Prosecution Service have made attempts to divert from custody some of those in this group charged with offences. Joseph has taken a leading role, as a psychiatrist, both in holding clinics for the homeless in a primary care setting (Joseph, 1990a) and in specially targeting the offender subgroup with a service provided directly to the courts (Joseph, 1990b).

The holding of clinics outside a hospital may not always raise the direct contact rate between patient-clients and psychiatrists, but may foster other potentially valuable functions. Bowden (1978a) explored the possibility of a psychiatric clinic in a probation office. The referral and take-up rates by prospective patients were low, but the opportunity for liaison and advice on cases for probation officers was well used. A number of forensic psychiatrists now follow such a consult-liaison model with one or more probation offices. One of the authors has had experience of this at an Inner London office, run as a monthly seminar. Presentations of difficult cases resulted in the referral of some clients to various psychiatric services, but frequently the seminar was simply a forum for explaining mental disorder, and offering support and advice. Another of the authors runs clinics in Manchester probation offices and offers a new assessment and follow-up service for clients referred by probation officers as well as support, advice and supervision of selected cases for probation officers on an individual basis. In both service models, the discussion of case management with probation officers often becomes a form of informal audit. Review of action in a case is invariably coupled with educational input. Probation officers find such arrangements useful, the reciprocal learning opportunities for the psychiatrist are also considerable.

Academic Forensic Psychiatry

The Health Service is incomplete without academic services—they provide the knowledge base, knowledge development and the exchange and transfer of knowledge from one generation to another. Although as a relatively new speciality, clinical growth in forensic psychiatry has tended to outstrip academic growth, few English centres are now without specialist training schemes for forensic psychiatrists, and other schemes are developing for the clinical disciplines related to forensic psychiatry. The British insistence on research as an integral part of higher training in medical disciplines, including forensic psychiatry, has fostered a basic interest in research at most of the training centres. Our principal experience is of the training of doctors and psychiatrists, albeit in collaboration with other disciplines, so we will only risk more detailed comments on the medical aspects of education in forensic psychiatry. However, the principles of medical training, based as it is on an apprenticeship plus lectures, seminars and private study giving a wide range of practical experience under supervision, form a useful template for the development of any health or social service discipline.

The embryo forensic psychiatrist in Britain ideally follows general medical training with a broad training in general psychiatry embracing the recognized subspecialities of psychiatry, i.e. general psychiatry, mental handicap psychiatry, child and adolescent psychiatry, psychotherapy and forensic psychiatry. Entry into an approved registrar rotational training scheme should offer the possibility of such a mix, but in reality these subspecialities, especially forensic psychiatry, are not always available. Experience in other important branches of psychiatry, such as the psychiatry of addictions, is also available in some schemes. A minimum of 3 years in such a scheme renders the doctor eligible for the Royal College of Psychiatrists' Membership examination. Success in this is the passport to higher psychiatric training.

Entry into higher training is usually the point of specialist commitment for most psychiatrists, meaning a recommended further 4 years of training, again based on the principles of apprenticeship and theoretical study, but with the assumption of gradually increasing responsibility such that, appointments committees aside, the transition to fully qualified specialist is almost imperceptible. In the British NHS, there are important roles for both full specialist forensic psychiatrists and psychiatrists who have trained equally, or mainly in another of the psychiatry specialities, but have spent not less than one year training in forensic psychiatry. The most usual combination is general psychiatry with forensic psychiatry, but there is unmet demand too for specialists in mental handicap, child and adolescent psychiatry, and psychotherapy with forensic psychiatry experience.

Full specialist training means that trainees must have experience of working in maximum, medium and low security hospitals, in prisons, within the community, and with probation officers. The development of skills in the psychotherapy of offenders and violent patients, in criminal and civil assessment and report work, and in the management of services, indeed in all the skills of forensic psychiatry listed in the Introduction (p. 29) should be developed this way.

The training schemes themselves are scrutinized by peer review. Pre-'membership' general (registrar) training is overseen by a subcommittee of the Royal College of Psychiatrists' Court of Electors, which undertakes regular visits to each scheme, and recommends changes, approval, or disapproval. Only candidates who have undertaken approved training can take the membership examination, although there is scope for approval of individual training packages if, say, part of the experience has been gained abroad. The same principles apply to higher (senior registrar) training, but this time the approval visits are undertaken by the speciality advisory subcommittee for forensic psychiatry of the Joint Committee on Higher Psychiatric Training (JCHPT). The latter committee is joint between the Royal College of Psychiatrists and the Association of University Teachers of Psychiatry. For further discussion of the principles of such education *see* Gunn (1986a); for details of the specific training requirements *see* Joint Committee on Higher Psychiatric Training (1990).

Research, the lifeblood of any speciality, is still in short supply in forensic psychiatry. Every senior registrar is expected to undertake some as part of training. In reality, few conduct substantial projects, very often because there are too few research supervisors. Academic medicine ultimately depends on a nucleus of academic doctors, not only with the relevant training and expertise, but also with designated time for such research. Further, in no branch of medicine can the doctors function in isolation. Forensic psychiatry, like general psychiatry, requires interaction between other non-medical clinical disciplines and basic scientists, and it also requires liaison with criminologists, lawyers, philosophers, and sociologists in its academic life. No university in the UK provides this kind of combination. The largest university centre for the subject, and the only university-funded Department of Forensic Psychiatry, is at the Institute of Psychiatry (the Maudsley) in London; it has a professor of forensic psychiatry, a non-medical clinical lecturer and a secretary paid by the university; everybody else in the department is paid for by the NHS, or a research grant. Clinical psychology, social work, nursing, statistics, and neurosciences, are well represented in that setting, liaison with lawyers and criminologists is fostered through inter-university links. In the rest of the UK, only Edinburgh and Cambridge have university-funded posts (one for each) in forensic psychiatry. A senior psychiatrist has a personal chair in forensic psychiatry in the University of Birmingham and is developing an academic department there in association with a university department of forensic psychology. In Cambridge, the senior academic forensic psychiatry post is centred in the university depart-ment of criminology as well as of psychiatry. Two London medical schools have developed small subdepartments of forensic psychiatry with NHS funds. Plans to develop academic departments and units elsewhere in the UK will depend not only on immediate funding, but also on the training and motivation of new staff, particularly medical staff to develop this aspect of services. It is our impression that academic forensic psychiatry is at a similar or even earlier stage of development in other countries.

Textbooks cannot really be prescriptive. Guidance to further thinking is the best they can provide, yet there is one clear certainty for forensic psychiatry—patient services will not develop adequately without the devel-opment of academic services, so the clinician or planner concerned with development of services must include academic services.

19

The Mentally Disordered Offender in Non-medical Settings

Edited by Pamela J. Taylor	*Written by* Maureen Barry Gisli Gudjonsson John Gunn David Hall Paul d'Orbán Stephen Stanley Pamela J. Taylor

With contributions from

Enda Dooley

All psychiatrists will sometimes work in non-medical settings or in close conjunction with colleagues who have a completely different orientation or specialist training. Most usual contacts are with lawyers, police, prison staff, probation officers and voluntary workers. Not all have professional bodies in the same sense as doctors, and voluntary workers. Although individually working to high personal and ethical standards, they cannot be expected to share professional standards as such. The scope for misunderstanding is considerable. Each group must understand the strengths, limitations and aims of the other to ensure effective and ethical practice. The relationship between a doctor and a probation officer under a probation order with condition of treatment is unique in its formal contractual obligations between practitioners. In common with probation officers, forensic psychiatrists regularly work to the courts (*see* Chs. 2 and 4), in prisons and with voluntary organizations. Whether offender or victim, however, the prospective patient's first contact with non-medical systems is generally with the police.

Working with the Police

Apart from their large responsibilities in traffic and other types of social control, the police in Britain are concerned with preventing crime, detecting and arresting suspects, collecting evidence and bringing suspects to court. They may have a custody role during the remand period, but the police are not concerned with punishment. Busuttil and Wallace (1990) have described the considerable responsibility police officers accrue in the medical supervision of their custodial charges, most of whom, in their Edinburgh survey, were taking medication. Psychiatric and other medical advice is thus sometimes essential. Psychologists may be called into similar relationships, which raise further special issues (Ainsworth and Pease, 1987).

Psychiatrist-led Collaboration

The guiding principle for the psychiatrist is the Declaration of Geneva (p. 1015). Very exceptionally, other people's interests have to over-ride the interests of the patient. It is unusual that mentally disturbed people put others at serious risk, but it is never in the best interests of a patient to allow him to carry through dangerous behaviour. Taking no action in respect of continuing suspected offences would be bad psychiatric practice. Not the least of the functions of psychiatry is to prevent the mentally abnormal offender from harming himself through harming others. The doctor-patient relationship requires, however, that any reporting to the police of serious, imminent threat is done with the utmost sensitivity and concern for the continuing welfare of the patient. It should only be done after consultation with the patient, unless the patient is genuinely unreachable. If the patient has a friend or family member that he trusts, it is generally best to consult them too, providing the patient consents. During the course of the discussion, the purpose of the report to the police should be made clear. As with all crisis management in forensic psychiatry, the aim is to bring about sufficient change in the balance of relations between the patient, the environment and his potential victims that safety is restored. One possible outcome of police involvement is that allegations of dangerous behaviour can be thoroughly investigated and documented in ways beyond the skills or resource of psychiatry. Another is that, if the evidence supports concerns or allegations about dangerousness, legal steps can be taken to change the status of the potential victims where these are few and known, perhaps through legal injunction to bar the patient from access. The status of the patient may be changed in some way, such that if a case is proven against him in court, for example, he may be bound into a treatment or supervision contract, or be required to receive treatment in hospital. For those patients who retain some control over their behaviour, confirmation from the police and the court that they must accept some responsibility for it may be a catalyst for improvement in therapy.

All citizens have responsibilities to assist the police with relevant information when it is reasonable to suspect that a crime may have been committed. Patients, however, may disclose to a doctor that they have committed an offence and expect him to honour this confidence. Whether this is possible depends on a variety of subtle factors. Honouring such confidence is not in itself a criminal offence (Finch, 1984), whereas obstructing police enquiries could be. In court, the doctor may be forced to disclose information. It is worth noting that hearsay from a patient does not constitute evidence. It is not the same as a sworn statement made within the Judges' Rules.

The first step for the doctor after a patient's disclosure of offending is to assess the likely truth of the statement in the context of the patient's clinical state. It may be a conscious lie on the part of the patient to gain attention or defend against a sense of inadequacy, it may be fantasy or even a delusion. Debate with a colleague or peer group about whether the disclosure should be further shared may be very valuable. The debate should examine not only the likely truthfulness of the disclosure, but also its relevance to the current problem, and its potential for being repeated. Medical defence organizations are always prepared to offer further support or advice for doctors in such circumstances.

Other formal responsibilities include informing the local police and the Home Office (or other appropriate government department) when a patient on a restriction order under the Mental Health Act 1983, life licence or parole fails to report as agreed, or 'gives cause for concern'. Statutory reporting in relation to substance abuse is dealt with elsewhere (Ch. 11).

If a case is reported to the police, contact should be made with the most senior police officer available and the continuing interest of the psychiatrist made clear to that policeman. At first, the police may be highly sceptical and require some corroborative evidence that it is worth spending resources to pursue the case further. It is important for the psychiatrist to assist the patient to obtain a legal adviser if he does not already have one, and to liaise carefully with that legal adviser during the period in which the police are making enquiries. If the patient should be remanded in custody, one or more visits to the patient during that period are valuable in helping the patient to understand that he has not been abandoned, and in gathering further information for reports that may be required by the solicitor or the court.

CASE 1
A man under treatment for some years for persistent firesetting had been coping quite well, and resisting the firesetting until his girlfriend left him. At that point he destroyed five separate properties by fire within a day or two, allegedly harming no one. Two days later he came for his routine outpatient appointment and told a junior psychiatrist about his activities. The consultant was contacted immediately, and came to see the patient. After discussion, the patient agreed that the police had to be informed. This was done in the presence of the patient in the hospital consulting room. The police asked for the man to go back to his home address, they interviewed him shortly afterwards and charged him with arson. The patient was seen regularly during the remand period. He was found guilty of setting the five fires, sentence being set aside in favour of a hospital order with restrictions.

CASE 2
A young man with several criminal convictions for serious violence sought help for his

aggression, but also bragged about it. On one occasion he came drunk to his outpatient appointment, which was unusual. He suddenly threatened to kill his doctor, he stood up apparently to do so, but displaced his aggression on to a nurse who had just arrived to assist. The nurse was knocked to the ground and sustained a minor scalp wound. The man then turned his attention to the wall, beating it so savagely that he broke two carpal bones in his hand before accepting sufficient medication to sedate and calm him. He was admitted to hospital for 48 hours. The nurse wished to press charges. This did not seem to be against the long-term interests of the patient who no longer needed to stay in the hospital. The consultant then discussed the situation further with the patient and explained the decision to encourage the police to interview him, and that charges might follow. At the same time the patient was reassured that he would receive all support through the court proceedings.

The police were initially reluctant to pursue the case, but after a report and discussion did so. The man was given both the report to the police and the report to the court to read for himself. The magistrate responded almost as part of the clinical team. The man was convicted, a small fine imposed and a small compensation order made, both of which he was allowed to pay in instalments. The patient was relieved: 'I know where I am this time', and during further treatment began to express interest in what had happened to the nurse and whether he was definitely receiving the compensation monies. This was the first indication of concern that he had ever shown for one of his victims.

Any hospital will have issues which will require routine discussion with the police from time to time. These may include the level and management of violence in the hospital, policies on theft and policies on absconding patients. There should be no hesitation about this on the part of the hospital authorities and the medical profession. The police are uniquely well placed to advise on many aspects of crime and violence prevention. In exceptional circumstances, they may provide emergency assistance within the hospital if requested to do so.

Police-led Collaboration

The police, in turn, may call upon the services of psychiatrists, either requesting assistance with difficult individuals in the police station, or bringing patients to a hospital for care and attention. In England and Wales, S.136 of the MHA 1983 allows a police constable to take someone he regards as mentally disordered and in need of protection, or who is likely to harm others, from a public place to a place of safety for a period up to 72 hours, for assessment by a doctor and a social worker. It is to everyone's advantage to have clear, agreed local policies about the procedure in such cases.

Policemen are familiar with and good at recognizing severe mental abnormality. Sims and Symonds (1975), for example, found that in a series of 252 such police referrals over 12 months in Birmingham only 46 did not result in admission to hospital. Fifty-seven percent of the patients were psychotic. Kelleher and Copeland's (1972) findings in London were of the same order, although it has subsequently been shown that in London (Szmukler et al., 1981), in other urban and more rural settings (Fahy et al., 1987) such patients are less likely to continue in treatment than other patients. It is worth considering that resistance to helping these patients on the part of psychiatric staff may be a factor in their premature discharge.

Failure to receive them may result in their being taken to prison, or, worse, their acting through suicidal or otherwise dangerous behaviour. The Butler Committee (Home Office/DHSS, 1975) recommended that these police powers should be used extensively and this is still good advice. Dunn and Fahy (1987) studied the police perception of the problem from a 23% sample of London police stations. Fifty-six percent of these police stations thought that the mental hospitals in their area provided inadequate support for the police in their dealings with the mentally ill, and 71% thought that medical and social work back-up in police order cases was inadequate. Consistent with this, two-thirds thought that they would not have had to use the police order at all if medical and social services had been more efficient. In spite of their good record at identifying mental disorder, as many as 61% at the stations recorded that the police felt that they had had insufficient training to deal with the problems caused by the mentally disordered.

Rogers and Faulkner (1987) examined the case records of people referred by the police to three places of safety in the Greater London area. During two years, 273 people were referred on a total of 326 occasions. The profile tended to be young and male from social classes 4 and 5. The majority were unemployed and many were homeless. 'Afro-caribbeans' were overrepresented. The findings suggested that the extent of police involvement in making referrals to the psychiatric services in London is much greater than is suggested by official figures, which record only removals to hospital. The authors concluded that the—

> large number of referrals . . . suggests that the police are currently acting as a major source of referral to the psychiatric services. Social workers were rarely involved in referrals under section 136 of the MHA 1983. Referrals to hospital were more likely to be admitted for the full three days allowed under section 136 than those at the other two places of safety (a police station, and the emergency and assessment unit at the Maudsley hospital).

Social Worker-led Collaboration

Another point of contact between police and psychiatrist lies in case conferences called by social services departments to review the progress of children at risk as victims of domestic violence. The doctors who attend these conferences are frequently general practitioners, but they may be psychiatrists treating either the potential victim or the potential aggressor. There is a good deal of sensitivity, indeed resistance, concerning the transfer of information about behaviour between professionals in different disciplines in such case conferences (*see* Martin, 1978 for a discussion). Even though there is a genuine risk of information being mishandled on occasions, the need for everybody to be fully informed in such a dangerous area is paramount, and professional scruples about disclosure have to be put into the scales against the risks to a child's life. Nevertheless, every disclosure should be very carefully considered; half-baked theories or interpretations may be taken by others as established facts simply because they come with professional authority.

Contractual Work

In Britain, there are no psychiatrists working full time for the police. There are three main types of part-time contractual work that may be sought by the police in Britain: attendance at sieges, contribution to training, and general or specific advice to the CID. Fees are often negotiated for these tasks, but not always.

Sieges

Siege work is unlikely to figure prominently in the life of any psychiatrist, but it arouses great public and professional interest. This interest often arises because of a misunderstanding of the extent of the psychiatrist's role. The police remain fully responsible for the organization of the operation, and negotiations are conducted by specially trained senior police officers. Psychiatrists may be asked by the negotiators for an evaluation of the state of mind of the hostage taker. Simple, clear clinical comment may be helpful. In a situation where everyone is hungry for information, it is very tempting to go beyond the data and speculate—a temptation that must be resisted. A myth is that anyone beginning a siege must be 'mad', and therefore a psychiatrist is needed to assist the police in understanding his behaviour. Paradoxically, sieges by mentally disturbed people do not, in practice, usually involve a psychiatrist. They are usually conducted by a lone perpetrator, are not invariably associated with the taking of a hostage, and generally last less than 24 hours. Police forces are used to these incidents, and they are generally able to manage them alone or with simple advice by phone. Psychiatrists are normally reserved for incidents which last much more than 24 hours. These are likely to be where more than one perpetrator is involved, and therefore much less likely to be carried out by mentally disturbed individuals.

The psychiatrist is extremely busy at such a siege. He will be called upon by the police to deal with the medical problems that arise. These problems can arise with any of the actors—hostages, perpetrators, policemen or the wider circle of people who further surround these. The hostages, unprepared for their role, are the most vulnerable. Some of them may have had medical problems before capture, and these must receive attention as rapidly as possible. Some may have been injured in the take-over. Negotiations will include attempts to persuade the perpetrators to release sick hostages and sometimes to implement medical advice, for example managing diabetes. The psychiatrist may need a general practitioner (police surgeon) available.

Some hostages will rapidly develop symptoms because of the stresses induced by the terror under which they are placed. The symptoms vary widely from the more obvious effects of panic, such as weeping and aggressive behaviour, to somatic symptoms such as vomiting, diarrhoea, heavy painful menstruation, pains in the chest, overbreathing. Perpetrators may require simple medical advice for the hostages, but every attempt should be made to bring forward their release. Attention must also be given to matters such as maintaining hygiene, nutrition and simple first aid remedies within the stronghold. Doctors should never go into the stronghold and risk being taken hostage themselves. Medicines should not usually be sent in, as there is no control over how and to whom they are administered, and many drugs have potential for misuse in a way that could dangerously destabilize the situation. One absolute rule is that no attempt whatever should be made to administer drugs to anyone surreptitiously. Sedatives in drinks are for story books, not real life.

The stress of the incident, especially through lack of sleep, and perhaps injury too, will also create problems for the hostage takers. Part of the role of the psychiatrist is to assist the police in reducing that stress, and make everyone as comfortable and rested as possible within the stronghold, so that rational discussion can take place. Attempts to find objective measures of stress that may assist in the prediction of risk (Gunn and Gudjonsson, 1988) are so far too embryonic and cumbersome to be of much practical assistance. Even the policemen at the incident will come under enormous pressure and may show symptoms of stress themselves, such as sleeplessness, heavy smoking or drinking too much when off duty. During the course of the siege, they may need counselling, or advice about sleep, and extra rest days. Two problems which have to be particularly looked for in any of the participants are stress-induced paranoid reactions and hypomanic reactions.

There is an aftermath for all those involved in a siege, and the psychiatrist has an obligation to ensure that, as far as possible, the participants are aware of this, and that help is facilitated if required. Some of these issues are dealt with more fully in Ch. 23.

Training

Psychiatrists may be asked to assist with police training. Specific training is, for example, given to potential negotiators from all over the country on a course in London. Each course includes a half day with a psychiatrist who discusses the medical problems at a siege and also gives guidance about the kinds of mental disturbance, which may induce an individual to take a hostage. Other forms of training include general instruction in basic psychiatry, specialized discussions about drug problems, and advice to senior officers undertaking private study or theses as part of their advanced training. In practice, in Britain, psychiatrists undertake very little training of police officers and, as illustrated in Dunn and Fahy's (1987) survey, more resource is needed for such work, which would be to the mutual advantage of both professions, and ultimately of patients.

Police Interviews as Evidence

Some defendants challenge police evidence on the grounds that a confession statement was incorrectly obtained by police officers, possibly because it was obtained under duress. It is also clear that some false confessions are made because of abnormal mental states (Gudjonsson and MacKeith, 1982). Assessment by a psychiatrist or psychologist may be requested.

A case which has influenced interviewing practice in England is the Confait case. Three youths (one of them mentally handicapped) were convicted, on their own confession, of killing Mr Maxwell Confait. Two years later the convictions were quashed and the Home Secretary set up a judicial enquiry (Fisher, 1977). Fisher concluded that the confession statements were unreliable because the police had questioned the men in breach of the Judges' Rules about police interviews, which have been used since 1912 and were revised in 1964. These constitute a code of practice which does not have the force of law, but which the police are expected to follow. Two of the breaches in the Confait case were that two young men under 17 were interviewed without an independent adult being present, and the mentally handicapped man was 'prompted' by the police officers.

Matters of police interrogation were among the things referred to the Royal Commission on Criminal Procedure (1981). In a study conducted for the Royal Commission, Irving and Hilgendorf (1980) estimated that less than half of suspects have a normal mental state at interview. Table 19.1 lists their judgements of the suspects' mental state in 60 cases which they observed.

Table 19.1
Suspects' Mental State

	No.	%
Affected by drink or drugs	11	18
Mentally handicapped	1	2
Mentally ill	5	8
Frightened	8	13
Withdrawn	5	8
Aggressive	7	12
Friendly	9	15
Nothing noted	14	23
	60	100

From Irving and Hilgendorf (1980).

The types of mental illness were not specified. As the authors explain, the police officers tended to over-react to obviously mad states and under-react to depression and anxiety. Their view was that the practical instruction received by policemen on psychiatric matters is inadequate.

One important effect of the Royal Commission has been the Police and Criminal Evidence Act 1984 (PACE). This was implemented in 1986 and gives force of law to the Judges' Rule that anyone who is thought to be mentally ill or mentally handicapped must have an appropriate adult with him or her during any interview; an appropriate adult may be a relative, but others are also eligible, including psychiatrists. In any case in which the defendant is incoherent other than through drunkenness alone, the custody officer must summon a doctor.

If a doctor is involved in this procedure, his tasks are to make sure that the interview is carried out in a reasonable manner, given the accused's mental state, and to advise the police officers when mental abnormalities such as delusions, thought disorder or amnesia are making the interview grossly unreliable. One feature which a frightened or abnormal suspect may exhibit is suggestibility, with the effect of agreeing too readily with leading questions. If this is an issue before, during or after an interview, a separate psychological opinion should be sought. Gudjonsson (1984a) has developed a scale of interrogative suggestibility which can improve objectivity in distinguishing between false confessors and deniers (Gudjonsson 1984b).

Psychiatrist to the Police Officer

Police officers may be referred as patients, by their internal medical services or through ordinary NHS arrangements. There are special points to be considered. First there is the 'macho' image which a largely male and 'tough' profession gives itself. This means that it is especially courageous for a policeman to seek psychiatric help, many who need it fail to seek it, and those who do may put their job in jeopardy because of the attitudes of their colleagues. To many in the police force, psychiatric disturbance is equivalent to weakness and unreliability, yet police work is stressful (Ainsworth and Pease, 1987). Officers may be overworked, have to deal with ghoulish, frightening or psychologically disturbing events. They are sometimes attacked, injured, captured, or see a colleague die and, as a result, are prone to develop post-traumatic stress disorders. Untreated, these disorders can lead to inefficiency, time off work for somatic symptoms and, on occasions, to strange, damaging and even criminal behaviour.

Senior officers may expect reports about policemen patients. Whether it is right to provide such reports should be discussed with the patient; the nature of the referral will determine the correct response in most cases. Difficult psychiatric decisions will include advising an officer to change his work, either within the police force, or away from it. Usually, however, and senior staff need to be educated to this fact, a responsible, effective policeman can be restored to health and work even if he requires sick leave and treatment for an affective illness, or an anxiety state. The more crippling psychiatric disorders such as schizophrenia, severe personality disorder and dementia are not compatible with police work.

Mentally Disordered Offenders in Prison

The Prison Health Service in England and Wales

In 1774 an Act was passed in England and Wales 'for preserving the health of prisoners in gaol' and under that Act local justices were obliged 'to appoint an experienced surgeon or apothecary'. The surgeon or apothecary was also required to be resident and have no practice outside the prison. Thus began the English Prison Medical Service, in response to a typhus epidemic which was spreading from the prisons to surrounding communities. This gradually evolved into a service attempting to provide health care for all prisoners, a rapid medical reporting service to the courts, and psychiatric help, including specialized psychiatric facilities such as the therapeutic community at Grendon prison. The history of the Prison Medical Service is covered in more detail in *Psychiatric Aspects of Imprisonment* (Gunn et al., 1978).

The Prison Medical Service has been subject to much criticism. In an attempt to effect improvements, a number of reviews have been undertaken, all have suggested modifications to the service (Smith, 1984; Gunn, 1985a). An extensive re-evaluation of the service was completed by the House of Commons Social Services Committee (House of Commons, 1986b). The Royal College of Physicians (1990b) established a working party to focus on recruitment and training of doctors for the service. In 1990 an internal 'efficiency scrutiny' recommended a new management structure, a change of name to the Prison Health Service—and the buying in of all psychiatric and other medical services, mainly from the National Health Service (NHS), on a contract basis (Home Office, 1990b). The Home Office has accepted the recommendations, but actual change is slow.

Most large local prisons with a sizeable remand population have at least one, sometimes two or three full-time prison doctors and some part-time doctors providing primary care. Some of the bigger institutions also employ part-time specialists. These are most commonly psychiatrists who visit for one or two sessions a week, but physicians, venereologists and gynaecologists may also visit regularly. Some prisons even have operating theatres for visiting surgeons. Dentists, opticians, physiotherapists, speech therapists and occupational therapists may also have contracts at prisons.

In a typical year, prisons in England and Wales will supply 7000–10 000 reports to courts, mainly psychiatric reports. In addition, reports are required by the local review committees and the Parole Board (*see* p. 186), and a few reports concerning allocation or management of difficult prisoners may also have to be prepared. All inmates must, in theory, receive a general examination on reception and on discharge from prison. At Brixton, the largest of the remand prisons, this may mean 100 examinations per day. Further, there will be up to two million occasions a year when inmates report sick. A survey at one local prison (Bedford) suggested that prisoners have a higher rate of consulting doctors than is usual in general practice (Martin, E. 1984; Martin et al., 1984). This may, however, be as much a commentary on institutional life as the general health of the inmates. Prisoners are not entitled to stay in bed for a cold, nor even to have an aspirin without official permission. Much of the illness reported in the Bedford study could have been dealt with in the community without recourse to doctors. There are, too, men who report sick frequently in response to their misery at being in prison, or as a means of obtaining some small degree of social interaction with other prisoners and with the hospital staff.

Hospital services are provided for men almost exclusively by prison officers who have had a 24-week training in nursing as part of their 18 months of combined officer training. About a thousand of these hospital officers are employed. A few of them are also trained nurses and it is now Prison Department policy to recruit many more such men, in line with the service to female prison hospitals which is supplied almost exclusively by fully trained female nurses.

Remands in Custody

After someone is charged with an offence, there is a period of police and defence enquiry, and a wait for a place in the courtroom for the hearing. Usually, the more serious the charge the longer is the wait, and it can be a year or more. During the waiting or remand period, there are occasional court appearances to check and justify the wait. The remand need not be spent in custody; bail, with or without conditions, or remand under one of the MHA 1983 provisions are all possibilities in England or Wales (pp. 33 and 73). The prison may be crucial in assisting the court in such decisions about remand. Many alleged offenders, even those who have not committed an imprisonable offence (Gibbens et al., 1977), are sent to prison expressly for prison doctors to prepare a psychiatric report. This is an unsatisfactory system, still in operation despite a Home Office directive (Home Office Circular 66/90) that—

> a mentally disordered person should never be remanded to prison simply to receive medical treatment or assessment.

Full-time prison doctors do not have ready access to NHS facilities. The medical remand system is also inefficient. In 1973, Bowden (1978b) examined this process at the largest remand prison in England, Brixton prison. Over a 3-month period, 634 men were remanded into custody at Brixton for medical reports. Only 87 received recommendations for psychiatric treatment and 82 were referred to hospital. Men were more likely to receive a treatment recommendation if they were acutely mentally ill, potentially violent, or had a past history of psychiatric treatment. They were less likely to get a treatment recommendation if they had a history of excessive drinking, extensive criminal behaviour or a diagnosis of psychopathic disorder. Two of us (Taylor and Gunn, 1984) confirmed the latter in their larger survey at the same prison. The poverty of psychiatric assistance for such people is dictated by both attitude and resource. Ordinary NHS hospitals no longer expect to ensure that their patients cannot run away. Indeed, Bowden (1978b) showed that even though patients from his series were rarely placed in locked facilities, hospitals without any such possibility were maximally rejecting. Purpose-built secure beds did not then exist, except in the maximum security hospitals, and are still too few in number.

The inefficient and uneconomic process of custodial remand is probably at its worst in London, although it also occurs in other big cities. Gibbens et al. (1977) compared the medical remand process in London and Wessex and found that courts in the rural area asked for fewer medical reports, but made a medical disposal in a higher proportion, especially probation orders with a condition of treatment. Two reasons were suggested for this: first, pretrial reports by probation officers were almost routine at the time in Wessex, and secondly a higher proportion of offenders were remanded on bail in Wessex, and thus seen first by NHS consultants rather than prison doctors. In a survey of men and women remanded to one of three English prisons (Brixton, Holloway or Risley) Dell et al. (1991) confirmed the continuing inefficiency of custodial remands. Few of the mentally disordered were so remanded because of the nature of their offences. Usually, it was because these alleged offenders were viewed by the courts as probably in need of social or psychiatric help. Unfortunately, consequent referral for an outside medical assessment generally lengthened the time that the individual spent on remand, while those people who were judged sufficiently ill to require detention in hospital remained in prison for longer than those not accepted for hospital.

Offenders awaiting trial or sentence in custody are much more likely to exhibit serious mental disorder than the general population (Taylor and Gunn, 1984; *see also* p. 334), or indeed than sentenced prisoners. Further, any underlying illness, such as schizophrenia or depression, may be exacerbated, the prisoner may exhibit disturbed behaviour, suicidal ideas and/or actions may become prominent and even eating may present difficulties. Prison hospitals are not designated hospitals under the British mental health acts, therefore patients cannot be compulsorily treated there except in an extreme emergency, in which case the prison doctor has a common law duty to act to protect the patient/and or others. The result is that psychotic prisoners who refuse medication often deteriorate. Prison doctors can and do seek NHS opinions on such seriously disturbed patients, and there is power in British mental health legislation (*see* pp. 33 and 35) to transfer a remanded prisoner to a psychiatric hospital. The Home Office is encouraging doctors in England and Wales to use this more extensively. If the individual requires inpatient hospital treatment this would be taken by the Secretary of State to constitute urgent grounds for transfer.

Sentenced Prisoners in England and Wales

The clientele

Once a man or woman is sentenced to prison in the UK, their medical care is the exclusive province of the prison authorities. Prisoners have no right to call in a doctor of their own choice, no right to change their medical officer if they do not get on with him and no right to a second opinion. Occasionally, attempts are made to pacify dissatisfied prisoners by allowing them these choices.

A substantial minority of those with mental disease are sentenced to imprisonment. In the survey of Brixton prisoners (Taylor and Gunn, 1984), for example, rather more than 20% of the men with a psychotic illness were sentenced to imprisonment, and just over 40% of those who had been identified as having some other mental disturbance. Among more serious offenders, it is well recognized that mental disorder is an important factor in the imposition of a life sentence (Thomas, 1979). There are no hard data available which indicate that mental health necessarily deteriorates during imprisonment (p. 78), yet, on common-sense grounds, it is likely that some people will react badly. The stresses of imprisonment include loss of or separation from home and loved ones, overcrowding, lack of exercise, boredom, loss of purpose. A few individuals may be helped by imprisonment because of the provision of shelter and proper food, the removal of unbearable responsibilities and the provision of a certain kind of daily structure. Nevertheless, prisoners are at a greater risk of serious suicide attempts and actual suicides than are members of the general population. Other self-destructive behaviour, such as self-mutilation or swallowing foreign bodies, is also well known (pp. 816–18). Further, there are prisoners who develop psychoses (best *not* called prison psychoses to avoid confusion with the Ganser-like states, pp. 424–6, which are reputed to occur in prison but which are hardly ever seen in Britain). These psychoses may respond to removal from prison to hospital. Clinicians in prison must, therefore, maintain vigilance for depression, suicidal ideas (especially early in imprisonment) and psychosis.

The number of psychiatric cases in prison is a contentious issue. The English Prison Health Service is consistent in its view that too many mentally disordered offenders are sent to prison. A difficulty in determining the number arises through disagreement about what constitutes 'a case'. One important factor is the number and severity of symptoms. Another, in psychiatry, is motivation for treatment. In the community a patient, A, with neurotic problems may not seek help, whereas his identical twin brother with identical symptoms does and thus becomes a case. If A is sent to prison, he too may seek help. Other people may refuse help in prison even though they would accept it outside. After trying to take all these factors into account, an Institute of Psychiatry survey in 1972 (Gunn et al., 1978) estimated that about one-third of all sentenced prisoners could reasonably be regarded as psychiatric cases. Only very few of the sample could be interviewed, but the interviews suggested that the commonest problems were alcoholism and personality disorder, with schizophrenia and affective disorder afflicting only 1% each of the prison population.

The only fully comprehensive survey of the mental health of sentenced prisoners was conducted by the Institute of Psychiatry in 1988–90 (Gunn et al., 1991b). A representative sample of 2054 men, boys and women was interviewed by psychiatrists. Table 19.2 shows the pathology discovered in percentage terms. The diagnoses were made using ICD-9 criteria (WHO, 1978). It is acknowledged in the study that the personality disorder category must be an underestimate of the number expected; with more time, more information would have been available and diagnoses of less gross cases possible.

Table 19.2
Prevalence of Psychiatric Disorder in Sentenced Prisoners

	Adult males % n = 1365	Male youths % n = 404	Females % n = 273
Schizophrenia	1.5	0.2	1.1
Affective disorders	0.5	0	0
Paranoid disorders	0.4	0	0
Neuroses	3.6	3.0	7.7
Adjustment disorders	1.6	1.5	5.5
Personality disorders	7.3	11.4	8.4
Sexual deviation	2.4	0.2	0
Alcohol abuse	8.6	8.7	4.4
Drug abuse	10.1	6.2	24.2
Epilepsy/organic	0.5	0.2	0.4
Mental retardation	0.4	0.2	2.2
Diagnosis uncertain	1.3	0.5	1.8

The survey also estimated the treatment needs of these prisoners, and rated them in the following categories:

'outpatient' supportive care (in prison);
a therapeutic community (such as Grendon prison);
transfer to the NHS as an inpatient; and
further assessment (in prison).

Table 19.3
Treatment Needs of Sentenced Prisoners

	Adult males %	Male youths %	Females %
Outpatient in prison	10.2	9.2	22.3
Ther. Community	5.9	4.0	7.3
Inpatient NHS	3.5	1.0	4.0
Further Assessment	5.0	5.4	9.2

From Gunn et al. (1991a).

Table 19.3 indicates that there is a substantial unmet treatment need in English prisons. At the time of the survey approximately 1000 prisoners should have been transferred to the NHS and approximately 2000 prisoners needed a therapeutic community. Over 4000 prisoners were requiring 'outpatient' psychiatric care in prisons, whilst about 2000 needed further psychiatric investigation, a heavy burden indeed for forensic psychiatric, prison medical and related services.

The range of psychiatric care needed in prisons

The Institute of Psychiatry survey looked at the facilities provided by English prisons at the end of the 1980s and recommended changes. It examined facilities for different diagnostic groups.

Psychotic prisoners are usually known to prison staff and allocated to prisons which have full-time cover from a doctor. A particular problem for this group of patients was that their fate depended upon the expertise of those prison doctors, which was very variable. One or two prisons (eg. Grendon, Parkhurst), take a special interest in psychiatric matters and in these, in spite of the difficulties, diagnosis and treatment is of a high standard. Relationships between prison and NHS services varied from the adequate to the 'strained'. Some of the prisoners stayed in 'prison hospitals', something of a misnomer for collections of cells and dormitories pressed into a service for which they are unsuitable, often staffed only by hospital officers, rather than by trained nurses; 'sick bay' would be a more appropriate term. It must be stressed again that such places are not recognized as hospitals under the MHA 1983, treatment cannot be enforced and there is no safeguard of inspection by the Mental Health Act Commission. It is possible to see an acutely psychotic prisoner locked, on his own, in a cell for the whole day. He may be clad only in a canvas shift with no possessions or furniture other than a mattress, possibly soaked in urine or soiled with faeces.

Many psychotic prisoners stay inappropriately in prison, because NHS facilities are either not offered or not available. This is due to a shortage of longer-term medium security beds in the NHS and low tolerance on the part of NHS staff for 'difficult' behaviour. Such problems are compounded by returning so-called 'treated' patients to prison on large doses of medication. In prison, refusal of medication is common and relapse is certain.

Mentally handicapped prisoners   find it difficult to live in ordinary prison locations without becoming a target for bullying or exploitation. Such prisoners frequently find themselves in the prison 'hospital', the segregation unit or special vulnerable prisoner units. Prison officers more often than not believe that such people do not belong in prison, certainly they have no special training in managing them. Education services for many of these prisoners are simply non-existent. Prison doctors, like NHS doctors, take little interest in this group of prisoners.

Neurotic patients   outside prison cope with a mixture of support, ranging from GP prescriptions for tranquillizers to counselling from nurses, support from friends, tobacco, cannabis and alcohol. Most of these are withdrawn by admission to prison. Prison doctors are very parsimonious with tranquillizers and marketed drugs (tobacco, alcohol, and cannabis) are in very short supply. There is considerable scope in prisons for the development of supportive counselling, and psychotherapeutic services for these prisoners. Group psychotherapy is probably the most effective form of such treatment (Gunn et al., 1978).

Personality disorder   is one of the two largest categories of pathology found in prison. Prisoners in this category are often ignored but, if their problems come to notice, they may find themselves frequently moved from prison to prison, punished or in segregation. A privileged few will receive some form of psychotherapy, a very few going either to the Wormwood Scrubs annexe (*see* p. 565) or to Grendon prison (*see*. pp. 688–90 and below), which are therapeutic communities. Improved NHS facilities for this group of patients would ease the burden of imprisonment for all staff and all prisoners alike, because a small proportion of highly disruptive prisoners, inadequately managed, can create widespread misery (see also *Criminal Behaviour and Mental Health*, vol. 2, no. 2, 1992).

Sexual deviations   constitute another prominent problem among prisoners for which little facility is provided. The male sentenced prison population in England and Wales increased by 8% between 1979 and 1988. Over the same period the number of men serving sentences for rape increased from 579 to 1069 (85%) and for other sexual offences from 1105 to 1608 (46%) (Home Office, 1989c). Not all sex offenders can be assumed to be suffering from a sexual disorder, but there is an accumulation of such patients within the sentenced prison population.

As for those with other personality problems, therapeutic communities and group psychotherapy are badly needed for this group, but are in very short supply. The Institute of Psychiatry survey found that the majority of sex offenders pass through the prison system without full assessment. Clinical psychologists could and should be involved in such assessments, and in the provision of specific treatment, such as behavioural therapy, cognitive therapy and sex education.

Prison doctors, understandably, feel that referral to the NHS in these cases is a waste of time, so few opportunities are provided for such patients. Special hospitals can and do treat sexual deviations quite well, but rarely on transfer from prison. Once again, considerable NHS growth is required for this group of patients.

Drug dependency   is the commonest psychiatric problem among sentenced prisoners. Cannabis has replaced tobacco as prison currency. A small number of drug dependent men are treated in Wormwood Scrubs annexe and at Grendon prison and such therapeutic communities are highly suitable for those drug abusers who see their disorder as arising from personality problems. Holloway prison has established a pilot scheme for women which is very successful. It includes a brief standard withdrawal from opiates, using methadone for women who show withdrawal symptoms. Further treatment is based on educational groups often involving visitors from outside agencies. The arrangement is seen as helpful by prisoners, provides an incentive to reveal their drug problems, and helps to establish a positive relationship with prison staff, including doctors.

Treatment in other English prisons is haphazard. Probation officers may play a leading role, although prison officers and psychologists are involved in some prisons. Narcotics Anonymous (NA) sometimes runs groups for prisoners. Prison doctors, by and large, do not see the treatment of drug dependency as part of their work, and a few are actually hostile to drug abusers as the number of drug abusers sent to prison increases and as the fears of HIV infection by needle cross-contamination grow. Just one or two prisons have regular sessions provided by a specialist in substance abuse. This must surely be the way forward and will be easier with the reorganized Health Care Service for Prisoners.

Alcohol dependency   presents similar problems to the prison service, although, these days, it has a lower profile than other forms of drug dependency because alcohol is not taken parenterally. All young offender institutions and most adult prisons in England and Wales offer some form of treatment for alcohol abuse. At its best, such treatment is a coordinated package between probation, psychiatry, psychology, discipline and education staff. Groups for alcohol abusers have a strong educational orientation. The underlying principle is to encourage people to become aware of their alcohol intake and set limits. At some prisons, the level of service is little more than handing out educational leaflets. One local prison has regular seminars by a psychiatrist working in NHS addictions services. His major frustration is the general lack of treatment facilities outside prison.

Therapeutic communities

The concept of a 'psychiatric prison' has been around for a long time. The Commissioners of Prisons (1921) were impressed by the apparent connection between some cases of battle trauma and aberrant behaviour. They were also aware of a growing understanding that 'mental defectives' who offended responded better to treatment than punishment. In their report for 1919–20 they said:

> The opinion has been growing in intensity for some years that mental and physical disabilities may largely contribute to the commission of crime, and that it is the duty of the community to investigate thoroughly such causes.

Following this, part of Birmingham prison hospital was set aside for the 'reception of persons on remand whose mental condition appears such as to warrant careful investigation'. A full-time prison doctor, Hamblin Smith, was appointed to carry out this work. In his books (e.g. Smith, 1922), he expanded on the theme of treatment rather than punishment, especially for recidivist prisoners, arguing the case partly on humanitarian grounds and partly on economic ones. He was frustrated, however, by a near total lack of facilities. He argued for special institutions to be established and set up a medical postgraduate course at Birmingham University on *The Medical Aspects of Crime and Punishment* (Commissioners of Prisons, 1924).

The claims of psychological medicine to cure crime were examined by the 1931–2 Departmental Committee on Persistent Offenders (Home Office, 1932), but they were sceptical and so recommended 'a systematic follow-up of the cases dealt with'. Nevertheless, Hubert was appointed as the first psychotherapist to Wormwood Scrubs in 1933, and published a report written jointly with East, a Prison Commissioner, later to be the first lecturer in forensic psychiatry at the Institute of Psychiatry (East and Hubert, 1939). This recommended 'the creation of a penal institution of a special kind', as a clinic and hospital, as a criminological research centre, as a prison for training and treatment, and as a colony for those who did not respond to treatment. East and Hubert rejected the view, by then firmly espoused by Smith (1934), that mentally abnormal offenders should be transferred out of the prisons. They believed that the prison medical service had the expertise that made them *more* suitable than others to treat the 'non-sane non-insane' (as East called them). They also defined the main purpose of prison psychiatry as the prevention of recidivism, a bogey which even now cannot be shaken off (*see* Gunn et al., 1978, for a fuller account).

Grendon Prison. The Second World War delayed the implementation of the East-Hubert report and it was not until 1962 that Grendon prison first opened its doors to prisoners. It rapidly established itself as a therapeutic community. When it was investigated in the mid-seventies (Gunn et al., 1978), it had five operational wings, three for adult men and two for young male offenders, each with a heavy emphasis on group psychotherapy, and an absence of medication. Men had to volunteer to go. Each inmate joined a wing which provided an environment in which everything was questioned and discussed. The hierarchy between officers and men was lowered and first name relationships developed. The prisoners were given some opportunities for democratic self-government (within security rules). Each man was assigned to a small group for regular treatment sessions, these usually run by prison officers. Regular complete wing meetings were also held. No one could visit Grendon and fail to notice the difference between it and almost every other British prison in terms of atmosphere. Grendon had a sense of purpose.

All prisoners at Grendon had the right to return to an ordinary prison if they felt unable to cope with the regime, and some deemed as too disruptive, too violent or too ill were also transferred out. A consecutive sample of admissions (107) was studied between June, 1971 and May, 1972—27 left prematurely on one of these grounds and 80 men remained for detailed study (Gunn et al., 1978; Gunn and Robertson, 1982). At the beginning of treatment, the prisoners were neurotic, lacking in social self-confidence and antagonistic to authority figures. All these features improved markedly with a few months' treatment at Grendon, yet such good results are scarcely regarded. So much emphasis was and still is placed on reconviction rates. The model in reality was that prisoners were taken out of the criminal world for a few months, given a dose of psychotherapy, then put back into the criminal world with the expectation of all 'criminal tendencies' being 'cured'. The latter is a naive view of human nature and motivation, which takes no account of the impact of the environment. It is interesting that Hamblin Smith understood this well enough back in 1922:

> Even were all our institutions perfect, they could do no more than prepare an inmate for the real test, which comes when he leaves the institution. It is as well to remember this, for often people talk as though some special form of institution was able to reform by itself. . . . We cannot do more than attempt to enable our patient to adapt himself to reality.

It is no surprise that in a 10-year follow-up study of these Grendon men (Robertson and Gunn, 1987), there were few differences between those men and a group of matched controls in terms of the frequency or severity of postdischarge convictions. It is no surprise, because no attention was given to their transitional- or after-care; no supports, no psychotherapy, no gradual rehabilitation, no resettlement was offered to any of the sample—they were simply discharged, or returned to ordinary location in other prisons.

Grendon has unique values which it gives to psychiatry and prison medicine. Then it provided a model therapeutic community, one that has been copied at home and abroad. It showed that non-medical staff, particularly prison officers can be trained as therapists. It provided a system of effective management for dangerous and disruptive prisoners. It is a curious paradox that whilst the Grendon model is frequently criticized, it is also imitated.

As a result of a review (Home Office, 1985d) Grendon was changed. A later study of Grendon (Genders and Player, 1989) described the changed features. Grendon has now become a multifunctional establishment, providing a general assessment psychiatric unit as well as one with potential for group therapy. The therapeutic community is just one aspect of its work, and necessarily taking fewer men. By 1989 only 88 men were in such treatment, a very small contribution to the total prison need for such a facility. The entry into and persistence within the therapeutic community must be voluntary; no prisoner may be sent directly by a court and category A prisoners are not eligible on security grounds. Prison doctors select by Home Office criteria for admission to the treatment, which include motivation to partake in the group process and the ability to 'learn to communicate openly within a group without recourse to physical violence'. The diagnostic group 'best suited' for the treatment is personality disorder, and inmates should have at least 12 months to serve when they go to Grendon. Very few black or prisoners from Asian backgrounds get referred to Grendon; this may be because they are less likely to manifest personality disorder than their white peers, as seems likely among lifers (Taylor, 1986) and probably remanded prisoners (Taylor, 1987, 1988b). Drug abusers, and men over 40 are considered unsuitable. Grendon is said to have expertise in treating explosive, aggressive individuals, arsonists, sex offenders, unusual murderers, those who deliberately self-mutilate and 'the isolated and hostile individuals who prove difficult in other prisons'.

In the 15 years between the two main studies, the mean age of the inmates had gone up to 31 years, and yet fewer had served previous prison sentences (Genders and Player, 1989). Virtually all the 1987/88 sample were serving sentences of 3 or more years, 81% of them for an offence against the person (violence or sex). The earlier population had been, in the main, recidivist property offenders, although over half of them had committed violence at some stage in their criminal career.

Genders and Player (1989) found that the basic principles of treatment at Grendon have changed little since the earlier research. There are three adult wings, each having 8 officers for 35–40 prisoners. Each wing has two therapeutic forums, the small groups consisting of 6–8 inmates who meet three times a week for an hour, and the wing or community meetings which occupy 1 hour twice weekly. The small groups are of a slow-open type, in that membership gradually changes as individuals leave and are replaced by others. The wing meetings are attended by all inmates and as many staff as possible and they are chaired by an elected inmate. Staff meetings are also held on the wings three times each week; two of these meetings are set aside for 'business', the third is a 'sensitivity' group during which staff talk about their own problems in the work.

Like the previous research team, Genders and Player have recommended the development of this system of management and treatment in other parts of the prison system. This seems no more likely after the second report than after the first.

Wormwood Scrubs annexe.   The therapeutic annexe at Wormwood Scrubs prison was an attempt to extend the Grendon concept into other prisons. When it is operational, it is a self-contained wing in the prison, under the direction of prison doctors, modelled on the therapeutic community of Grendon. At different times, it has put an emphasis on the treatment of alcohol abusers, other drug abusers, and sex offenders. It is subject to the pressures of being a small medical unit in a much larger closed community (the prison) and, therefore, to severe manpower and crowding pressures. From time to time, it is closed.

Responses to disruptive and exceptionally dangerous prisoners

Barlinnie Special Unit, Glasgow.   In the late 1960s, Scotland ran into severe problems in managing some of its disruptive and violent prisoners, a number of whom came from the Glasgow street gangs of that time. In October 1966, Inverness prison opened a small segregation unit for prisoners deemed to be 'violent, subversive, or recalcitrant'. The regime within the unit was deliberately spartan, but prison officers complained that prisoners were having too many privileges (Coyle, 1987). An internal investigation prompted changes such that prisoners were more separated from staff by a 'grilled corridor'. The revised unit was opened in April, 1971. In December 1972, 4 prisoners seriously attacked prison officers during an evening recreation period.

> They were subdued only after a battle in which one officer lost an eye, others sustained stab wounds and two of the prisoners were injured (Coyle, 1987).

To some extent this terrible incident had been predicted. In 1970 a working party, established by the Scottish Home and Health Department, had been set up to make recommendations about the treatment of potentially violent prisoners, because there were 14 attacks on prison officers involving weapons and 34 prisoner/prisoner assaults (16 with weapons) between 1968 and 1970 (Whatmore, 1987). The working party visited Grendon and Parkhurst prisons, Broadmoor Hospital and the State Hospital at Carstairs, and establishments in Denmark. Finally, a special unit was set up in a separate wing in Barlinnie prison, Glasgow, with its own governor, a visiting psychiatrist, and places for 10 prisoners. The traditional officer-inmate relationship was to be modified into a therapist-patient relationship. To do this, the original staff were sent on an 11-week course which included 2 weeks at Grendon, 2 weeks at Broadmoor and 2 weeks at Carstairs. Each prisoner was to be involved in decision-making and answerable to the whole community in a weekly community meeting. In addition, crisis meetings could be called urgently. The staff were supported by the psychiatrist at a weekly staff meeting. The first prisoners were three of those involved in the mini-riot at Inverness. One of them has written his account of these events, the unit and his successful rehabilitation (Boyle, 1977). Rules for the unit now include that all staff (except the Governor) are volunteers, and for prisoners 'once out, never back', no violence or drug abuse, and open visiting. The selection of prisoners is by 3 senior unit prison staff, together with the unit psychiatrist and a clinical psychologist. This team must be convinced that the prisoner presents problems which cannot be dealt with in any other Scottish secure facility *and* that the prisoner wants to come and has some motivation towards positive change. Inevitably, the unit has been criticized as 'expensive', 'too soft', or 'encourages men to misbehave to get there', but the 2–3 dozen inmates dealt with in the first years have largely been managed successfully. Three-quarters had killed or attempted to kill, and all had been very violent. Only 3 had sentences of less than 10 years' imprisonment and over two-thirds had received additional sentences for offences while in prison. Eighty per cent had a category A security rating. Five men were removed from the unit, two asked to leave, and one killed himself. The longest stay in the unit for prisoners was 7½ years, 3½ for governors (Whatmore, 1987). Cooke (1989) studied the 25 prisoners who had been through the unit up to November, 1986. Only two assaults occurred on the unit, during a mean length of stay of 3½ years, compared with the expected frequency of 105, and there were only eight serious incidents, including barricading or smashing up the cell or roof top demonstration. The expected frequency was 49, the expected rates taking account of the observed number of assaults before transfer and the length of time before transfer and on the unit. After leaving the special unit to return to other prisons this improvement was largely maintained, the rates were 10 and 17 respectively.

La Paquerette Sociotherapeutic Centre, Geneva.   Champ-Dollon prison in Geneva is primarily a remand prison for French-speaking Switzerland. It is serviced by doctors from the Institute of Legal Medicine in Geneva. Medicine practised within the prisons in this canton has been independent of prison administration since the early 1960s. The doctors have to write reports on prisoners and recommend treatment. As in most jurisdictions, hospitals have been and are more willing to take patients with psychosis and less willing to take those with personality disorder, yet a lot of the latter group come before the courts, fail to adapt to the ordinary prison system and clearly need treatment. The Director of the Institute of Legal Medicine (then Professor Bernheim,) drew up plans for a therapeutic community within the prison, after visiting the Netherlands, the USA, and spending 6 months as a participant observer at Grendon, in England. Potential inmates are assessed much as for the latter, and have to be able to make a free, informed choice about entry.

Half the unit—*La Paquerette*—opened on a day care basis in 1979, but it became fully operational in 1986. In 1990 10 men were serving sentences varying from 1.5 years to life imprisonment (Gunn, 1990). Most were suffering from severe personality disorders, with sociopathic traits, but one man had a psychosis well controlled by medication. The unit was run by a non-medical female sociotherapist and administrator (de Montmollin et al., 1986). Each week was structured, with every man belonging to a small group of 5 inmates for twice weekly meetings, and participating in whole community meetings three times a week as well as work. Prisoners were elected to special responsibilities (such as preparing all the meals), and were the subject of regular audit on their progress. Crisis meetings could be called. Unlike Grendon, *La Paquerette* staff had a role in the rehabilitation, resettlement and follow-up of some of their prisoners. Between 1st August, 1979 and 31st March, 1987, 113 men had been through the unit, 58 remaining more than 4 months. Outcome bore a close resemblance to the Grendon findings (Gunn et al., 1978), with positive changes in psychological state and attitudes, but recidivism for offending in 15 of the 38 cases (39%) who had been released and for whom data were available (de Montmollin et al., 1986).

Small units in English prisons.   All substantial prison systems have the problems just described in the Scottish and Swiss systems of a significant number of disruptive and dangerous prisoners who invite segregation, sometimes on a long-term basis. They also contain quite large numbers of prisoners with severe personality disorders. Grendon is a partial response to the problem; C Wing at Parkhurst prison was a further, even more medical response, in the 1970s. It was yet another therapeutic community partly inspired by Grendon but, in this case, it was more directly supervised by an experienced prison psychiatrist, more emphasis was given to individual treatment, men with psychoses were accepted, and drug treatments were acceptable. Unfortunately, the wing had to close in 1979 when riots caused an acute accommodation crisis in the rest of the prison and the wing was taken over for ordinary prisoners.

The influence of Barlinnie and C Wing (and therefore, indirectly, Grendon) emerged more obviously in the 1980s. A committee was set up by the Home Secretary in 1983 'to review the maintenance of control in the prison system'. It looked at existing systems in Canada, the USA and West Germany, as well as the UK. It produced an imaginative report in 1984 with wide ranging recommendations, including a better overall system for long termers, a series of specialized small units and particularly noted that a revitalized Parkhurst C Wing and a developed Grendon regime would have much to offer (Home Office, 1984a). A direct result of this report was the establishment of a Research and Advisory Group on the Long Term Prison System, which like the review group, included outside academics. C Wing at Parkhurst was reopened and two similar small units established in other prisons (Lincoln and Hull), the latter depending more on psychology than medical input (Home Office, 1987f).

The new C Wing is much less under medical control than the old one, but it still has a strong psychiatric bias. Governors refer prisoners for consideration. The men have to meet the following criteria:

1. high security category (A or B);
2. a history or symptoms of mental disorder;
3. a recent history of one or more of the following:
   a. violence to others;
   b. offences resulting in formal reports;
   c. damage to property;
   d. dangerousness or disruptive behaviour.

The aim is to get men who have spent long periods of segregation into a relaxed and safe environment. The heart of the C Wing regime is the personal officer scheme.

> It is the responsibility of the Personal Officer (and his deputy) to develop a close knowledge of his inmate, to monitor and record his behaviour and progress, and to build up a relationship with him. The Personal Officer is the inmate's first point of contact within the unit and nothing should happen to the inmate (except in an emergency) without his Personal Officer's knowledge (Home Office, 1987e).

Prison officers each have a small case load of prisoners for whom they have special responsibility. The prisoner deals with the prison management via his personal officer. The officer advocates his prisoner's needs and desires (Evershed, 1987, gives a fuller account). A prison doctor visits two or three times a week, and a psychologist provides counselling for inmates, social skills training and staff support groups. The regime is different from Barlinnie and Grendon in that prisoners do not have an automatic right to leave the unit on request, and they play no part in management decisions.

The number of men in the unit at any one time is about 18. Preliminary research (Coid et al., 1991) has shown that all these difficult men have multiple psychiatric problems, all have major difficulties in forming and establishing relationships with other people, half of them have experienced either a schizophrenic or paranoid illness and 70% have had a depressive illness. The three prominent features in the group are extreme suspiciousness of others, long-term irritability, and bouts of mounting tension, irritability and dysphoria leading to aggression. It is of interest that the men perceived these problems as internal and independent of the stresses of imprisonment.

Transfers between Prison and Hospital under the Mental Health Acts

The UK MHAs allow two doctors to propose a transfer from prison to hospital, and the Secretary of State to direct accordingly. Sentenced prisoners who suffer from any of the categories of mental disorder identified in the Acts may be thus transferred, in contrast to remanded prisoners for whom the conditions are limited to mental illness and severe mental impairment. Such prisoners usually have a restriction order applied to them, so that they cannot be discharged from hospital, without the consent of the Secretary of State, before their earliest date of release. In the early years after the MHA 1959, the transfer process seemed both effective and efficient (Walker and McCabe, 1973). There was, however, a steady decline in such transfers in England and Wales throughout the 1960s and 70s (Robertson and Gibbens, 1980). By 1975, only 75% of applications were successful, compared with 94% in 1966/67. Parker and Tennent (1979) noted that between 1962/4 and 1972/4 the average daily prison population had risen by 22%, but the number of transferred prisoners had fallen by 30%. Paradoxically, at about this time, the Butler Committee (Home Office/DHSS, 1975) had even recommended an extension of the application of transfer orders under the MHA 1959 to people outside the defined mental disorder categories, to include sexual deviation, alcoholism and drug dependency where NHS units were available for their treatment. By 1979, only 25% of sentenced prisoners who had been diagnosed as 'mentally ill' by prison doctors were recommended for transfer to hospital, and just 53% of these were actually transferred under the MHA 1959 (Cheadle and Ditchfield, 1982). Following these findings, the Prison Department urged prison doctors to increase their efforts to obtain places, and the number of transfers rose again. By the 1980s, prison doctors in England and Wales were managing to transfer up to 150 cases each year, but since 1984 numbers have declined again (Home Office/DHSS, 1987).

Robertson and Gibbens (1980) concluded that, in England and Wales, the patients most likely to be transferred to hospital are those who are less criminally experienced, and those suffering from 'mental illness', usually schizophrenia. Only 2% of transfers receive the label 'psychopathic disorder'; very few mentally impaired prisoners were transferred. Cheadle and Ditchfield (1982) showed that even within the mentally ill prisoner population further discrimination occurred:

> The most striking influence of psychiatric history on admission policy was whether or not the disorder was chronic. Only six of the psychiatrists (out of 39) said they were willing to provide care in the long term.

The problems created by chronicity of disorder were also emphasized in a later study (Coid, 1988). It showed that 1 in 5 prisoners on remand was rejected by NHS consultant psychiatrists. Those with mental handicap, organic brain damage or a chronic psychotic illness rendering them unable to cope independently in the community were most likely to fall into this group and be sentenced to imprisonment as a consequence.

Similar problems pertain in the USA. Gearing et al. (1980) and Halleck (1966) reported that referrals for transfer from prison to hospital were 'appropriate' in that such patients tended to have a history of mental hospitalization or identified disorder before sentencing. Monahan et al. (1983), however, emphasized that while these studies may provide reassurance that there are not too many prison to hospital transfers, they do not consider the possibility of too few. Hartstone et al. (1984) found that in six states, half of the prison staff said that too few inmates were transferred to mental hospitals, often because their behaviour was insufficiently visible, annoying or disruptive.

Prison to hospital transfer provisions, although underused, remain an important safeguard in any mental health care system, designed to ensure that if severely mentally disordered people are not identified at trial or sentencing, then there is a way of getting them to the right place. Similarly, if prisoners develop a mental disorder during, or as a result of, imprisonment, they can be removed and treated in hospital. It is the responsibility of hospitals to provide appropriate treatment and security for these patients.

In the UK, once a prisoner is transferred, he may serve the rest of the sentence in hospital, and be discharged to the community from there. A recovered patient can also be returned to prison, however, and it is sometimes difficult to ascertain what will be in the patient's best interests. While in hospital, prisoners may apply for a Mental Health Review Tribunal, but its maximum power is to release from the hospital order, thus the individual becomes immediately liable to be returned to prison. While it is possible to translate a life-sentenced prisoner into a 'technical-lifer', which effectively means that the lifer becomes a patient under Home Office restrictions on discharge, even this scarcely used adjustment is not open to the man with a fixed term sentence. A prisoner patient in hospital may not be released before his EDR, and his rehabilitation, should this include any leave outside the hospital, is similarly suspended until within 2 or 3 months—literally—of his EDR. Information about the longer-term fate of transferred prisoners is sparse. In the 1960s, the vast majority of cases went to ordinary psychiatric hospitals (about 70%), but numbers have since fallen. Transfer to special (maximum security) hospitals now accounts for a greater proportion of the prisoner patient group. Grounds (1991) studied the records of 380 cases transferred to Broadmoor Hospital between 1960 and 1983, constituting 15% of the hospital's admissions over that time, and just over half of the total group of prisoners transferred to special hospitals. Nearly 30% were under a life sentence, and significantly more likely to be mentally ill (82%) than their peers under determinate sentences (67%). During the 23-year period studied, 317 cases left Broadmoor, the largest group (50%) going to the community, often via an open hospital first, and just over one-fifth returning to prison. Concern was expressed that over time there had been a significant trend towards transferring prisoners later in their sentences, and that, in turn, this was correlated with longer stays in hospital.

There is a view (*see* pp. 401–4) that serious offenders with some mental disorders, especially psychopathic disorder, should not, as a deliberate policy, be offered hospital care at the sentencing stage. Instead, they should be sentenced to imprisonment, and then moved to hospital on a transfer order as appropriate. This advice must, however, be tempered by the finding of a major decline in use of prison transfers for the psychopathically disordered group (Grounds, 1991). They are unusual. Such offenders remain disadvantaged. The following case even included some manipulation of clinical dignosis to best fit the legal category which would facilitate rejection. The disadvantage to the patient was only partly remedied by the transfer process.

> At 35, a man of previously stable background started drinking heavily. Five years later he burnt out a number of empty buildings. Soon after arrest, the prison doctor recorded:
>
> 'He told me how he knew that his wife was unfaithful because she exhaled in a certain way. He realised also that there were certain conspiracies against him.'
>
> He had auditory hallucinations, passivity phenomena, delusions of persecution and ideas of self-destruction. Some 6 months later he was again found to be 'grossly psychotic' and he was started on neuroleptic medication to which he made a good response, but he refused to continue with it.
>
> A psychiatrist was called in to provide the reports to the courts:
>
> 'I am most concerned at the fanatically controlling and morbidly jealous aspects of the prisoner's behaviour. Almost the whole of the relationship to his wife centres on the assertion she is unfaithful. . . . In summary he has a severe disorder of personality . . . I do not believe these disorders are treatable and I can find nothing to suggest that a hospital order is indicated.'
>
> The trial judge responded in the only way he could, given serious offending and identified psychiatric disorder without a medical recommendation. He imposed a life sentence. Less than 2 months later the man, constantly talking, shouting and restless, broke the windows of his cell and was found digging up the walls 'searching for the wires of the intercom that is winding me up'. All this upset fellow prisoners so much that he had to be moved into isolation for his protection. He attempted to hang himself from the bars of the isolation cell.

Fortunately the possibility of transfer enabled this man to reach a secure hospital at last, and there he remained, albeit much improved, for the 6 years. The report of the psychiatrist safeguarded the local psychiatric services from having to provide care, but put the man's life at risk and, in spite of the transfer provision, left him a life sentenced prisoner and impaired his short and medium-term prospects for rehabilitation.

Self-destructive Behaviour

Suicide and parasuicide

The death rate of people in prisons in England and Wales is about 1–2 per thousand inmates per year. In 1987, there was a dramatic rise in self-inflicted deaths, from 21 in the previous year to 46 (42 of whom received a Coroner's verdict of suicide (CVS)). In 1988, there was a slight fall, to 37 (CVS 30) at a time when the daily prison population was 49 000 and the annual throughput 300 000. Self-inflicted deaths have continued to rise since (HM Chief Inspector of Prisons for England and Wales, 1990). This report also discusses strategies for the prevention of self-harm.

There is less definitive information about parasuicide and other self-destructive behaviour, although most observers would agree that such behaviour is particularly common in prisons. Indeed, some prisons have museums of objects with which inmates have harmed themselves, such as lavatory chains and bed springs found in stomachs.

Suicidal behaviour in prisons is discussed in more detail elsewhere (pp. 313–16). It is a problem for which the prison doctor must be especially alert.

Hunger strikes

A special problem which may arise in prison (although it can also occur in other settings) is protest by hunger strike. Such action poses serious ethical, psychiatric and physical problems for any attending doctor. Little or no research has been done on the subject.

Hunger strikes have a long and notorious history. In Britain, they have been particularly associated with suffragettes in the early part of the century and more recently with the IRA (Beresford, 1987), although O'Connor and Johnson-Sabine (1988) claim that most hunger strikes represent individual protests or pathology and are not politically motivated. Their sample was mainly of remanded prisoners in England, in a few cases transferred to hospital. In South Africa, the experience with political hunger strikes has been exceptional, with over 800 cases in early 1989 alone. These protests followed detention without trial, even without charge, and the courageous response of some doctors is well documented (Kalk and Veriava, 1991).

The current British legal position has evolved this century (*British Medical Journal* Legal Correspondent, 1974). A suffragette brought an action for assault in 1909 against a prison official, but the action was dismissed on the grounds that it was the duty of prison officials to preserve her health. This case formed the basis of the legal justification for forced feeding. The medical evidence called in the case included that from Dr Craig, a senior physician at the Bethlem Royal Hospital who said he had carried out forced feeding thousands of times and it had never caused injury! In cross-examination he said he had known patients who were continuously force fed for 2½ years! Later, deaths were reported from inhalation pneumonia or syncope. In 1974, the Price sisters, of the IRA, went on hunger strike in Brixton prison. They were force fed, but complained that they should not be. The Home Secretary reviewed the situation and said that—

> if a prisoner persisted in refusing to accept any form of nourishment the prison medical officer should first satisfy himself that the prisoner's capacity for rational judgement was unimpaired by illness, mental or physical. If so satisfied the

medical officer should seek confirmation of his opinion from an outside consultant, and, if the consultant confirmed the medical officer's opinion, the prisoner should be told that he would continue to receive medical supervision and advice and that food would be made available. He should be informed that he would be removed to the prison hospital if and when it was considered appropriate and it should be made clear to him that there was no rule of prison practice which required the medical officer to resort to artificial feeding, whether by tube or intravenously. The prisoner should be plainly and categorically warned that the consequence and inevitable deterioration in his health might be allowed to continue without medical intervention unless he specifically requested it.

It was also announced that this policy would apply to the whole of the United Kingdom (*British Medical Journal* Notes and News, 1974a).

The Central Ethical Committee of the British Medical Association (1974) issued a statement relaying the view of the President of the General Medical Council that the participation by a doctor in procedures to feed artificially a prisoner against his wishes would not be regarded as serious professional misconduct, provided that such procedures were lawful and designed to preserve a prisoner's health. Equally, if a doctor thought it was ethically repugnant to participate in the artificial feeding of a prisoner against his wishes, a refusal by the doctor to take part in such procedures would not be regarded as serious professional misconduct. The British Medical Association believed that applicants for prison doctor posts should be made aware that they may have to deal with hunger strikers (*British Medical Journal* Notes and News, 1974b).

Life-Sentenced Prisoners in the UK

Life imprisonment is the mandatory sentence in the UK for murder committed by a person of 21 years or over. It is also the maximum sentence for a range of other serious offences including manslaughter, rape and arson. A person serving such a sentence, commonly known as a 'lifer', is in a different category from other prisoners because the psychology of an indeterminate sentence is different from that of every other sentence, because special administrative and other procedures are set up to deal with lifers (*see* pp. 186–7, 778–82) and because it is likely that life-sentenced prisoners include a disproportionately high number of mentally abnormal people.

Until the abolition of capital punishment, there were very few lifers. The Gowers Report (Royal Commission on Capital Punishment, 1953) made brief reference to the prevailing view, that the lifer should be encouraged to make a fresh start by his own unaided efforts. Between 1957—the year of the Homicide Act—and 1964—the last year before abolition of capital punishment—the population of lifers had risen from 122 to 365. Ten years later numbers had nearly doubled, and by 1984 there were nearly 2000 lifers in total in England and Wales. Policies, and guidance on through-care and supervision (Home Office, 1984c) had become essential (*see* p. 776). The Home Office (1988e) has also issued a useful little booklet for lifers.

> Immediately after you have been sentenced your trial judge will write to the Home Secretary . . . giving his view on the length of detention necessary to mark the seriousness of the offence. The Lord Chief Justice will add his own view and, in the light of this, the Home Secretary will set the date on which your case will be referred to the local review committee (LRC). . . . This date will normally be 3 years before the expiry of the period . . . to mark the seriousness of the offence . . . murderers of police and prison officers, terrorist murderers, those convicted of sexual or sadistic murder of children and . . . by firearm in the course of a robbery should normally expect to be detained *at least* 20 years in custody. . . . It should be noted that the date set for the first LRC review . . . does not take accout of risk which . . . will be the overriding factor . . .

Lifers and psychiatric disorder

There is a positive correlation between serious violence, especially homicidal violence, and mental disorder (*see also* Chs. 8 and 12) and it is sentencing policy in England and Wales to use the life sentence as a means of—

> providing indefinite preventive confinement for offenders who are potentially dangerous as a result of mental disturbance or irritability (Thomas, 1979).

In this context, it is hardly surprising that high levels of mental disorder have been identified among lifers in England and Wales, but this is a finding echoed in other countries too. Rasch (1981) studied half of a population of lifers in Germany (the others refused). He found nearly half of the study group to be 'highly disturbed', the majority of them being depressed. Sapsford (1983) pointed out that a number of the most seriously disturbed men in his series had been transferred to hospital under the MHA 1959, but still two-thirds of both reception and mid-term men showed anxiety on his scale, while 46 and 38% respectively were depressed. The long time servers were almost by definition mentally abnormal or sexually deviant. In Scotland, Heather (1977) found that 56% of indefinite prisoners were 'dysthymic', on the Delusions Symptoms State Inventory, and 20% were psychotic, rates much higher than those found in normal populations, but similar to psychiatric outpatient groups. One of us (Taylor, 1986) surveyed all probation officers in the Inner London Probation Service for information about their lifers. Diagnoses were based on medical reports. Not less than 10% of the men had a diagnosis of schizophrenia, 12% of the men and the women diagnoses of depression, and one-third of both had well substantiated personality disorders. If serious substance abuse and epilepsy were added to these diagnoses, only one-third of the lifers were without a psychiatric diagnosis. The receipt of treatment seemed more a matter of chance than design.

Women in Prison

At any one time between 3 and 4% of prisoners held in England and Wales are women. Until about 1970, the numbers were very small indeed, considerably less than 1000, but have been steadily rising since, to about 1800 in 1988. Since the genders are strictly segregated in prison, this inevitably means that there is not the same range of facilities available to women as to men. This becomes a particular problem for the life-sentenced prisoners (less than 20 women), and the category A prisoners (also less than 20, in an overlapping group). There are 12 establishments for female prisoners in England and Wales, and only one maximum security block. The stresses of being in a small and constant, but unchosen, peer group are considerable in themselves, but the isolation of the prisons from the homes of most of the women ensures that almost all community ties are completely severed. This is a particular problem for those women who have children. There is one prison for women in Scotland. Self-injury, firesetting, barricading and property destruction are disproportionately common among women prisoners compared with men and disciplinary offences run at twice the rate. Mandaraka-Sheppard (1986) was inclined to emphasize the importance of environmental factors in precipitating these behaviours, but it may also be that female prisoners have a higher rate of primary pathology. The characteristics of female prisoners, and their special problems are dealt with more fully elsewhere (Ch. 15).

Juveniles in Prison

Prisons and other non-NHS secure facilities for young offenders are dealt with in Ch. 5.

A Note on Irish Prisons

All persons remanded in custody in the Republic of Ireland undergo a screening physical examination on reception into prison. General medical services are provided in Irish prisons by part-time medical officers. They are assisted by prison medical orderlies, who are specially selected prison officers, usually with a knowledge of nursing and first-aid. There are no nurses employed in the prison service.

If psychiatric illness is queried on reception or while the individual is on remand, an opinion is generally obtained from the visiting psychiatrist to the prison. In the Dublin area, this service is provided by psychiatrists from the Central Mental Hospital (CMH) in Dundrum. Outside the Dublin area, local general psychiatrists provide this service. As no Irish prison has a hospital wing, treatment of mentally disordered offenders must take place on general location. Treatment cannot be imposed on a prisoner against his or her will.

If it is considered necessary to admit an inmate to hospital for psychiatric treatment, then arrangements can be made to transfer the individual to the CMH in Dundrum, either by means of a hospital order under section 17(6) of the Criminal Justice Administration Act 1914, in which case the person may return to prison at will, or by Ministerial Order under the Central Criminal Lunatic Asylum (Ireland) Act 1845. The latter allows for compulsory treatment after transfer of a prisoner who requires 'treatment which cannot be properly given in prison'. The order can only be terminated if two doctors sign a form to the effect that the individual is fit to return to prison and arrangements can be made, if necessary, for further treatment in prison. A patient transferred to the CMH on a hospital order cannot be detained there after the expiration of his sentence. He must either be released, or arrangements made for transfer to a local, area psychiatric hospital (under a section of the Mental Treatment Act, 1945). O'Connor (1990) has described the characteristics of transferred prisoners between 1983 and 1988. Perhaps not surprisingly, since the CMH is the only hospital able to receive prison transfers, the majority of index offences were trivial. Even though the largest diagnostic categories were schizophrenia (31%) and personality disorder (25%), the length of stay was generally brief—with the average length a few weeks regardless of diagnostic category or proportion of remanded prisoners in the group.

The difficulties which prison doctors can get into simply because of the politics of imprisonment is exemplified by a prison medical footnote to Irish history. During the late 19th century, Irish prison doctors served under a centralized General Prisons Board charged with establishing a uniform penal system. That system housed not only ordinary prisoners, but also political prisoners like Fenians who demanded a special status. The Government insisted they be given no special status, and they were not, yet it was known that prison doctors could exempt any prisoner from the ordinary regime, so nationalists attacked the doctors' reputations and boycotted their practices. If the doctors gave in to this pressure, then the Government could remove them from their prison posts and deny them other positions.

Improving the Quality of Prison Life: Some other European Experiences

A recent digest of criminal justice information (Home Office, 1990c) gives international comparisons for the size of prison populations. The UK has the highest prison population per 100 000 population (rates for Northern Ireland, England and Wales and Scotland are very similar), of a group of European Countries including West Germany, Turkey, Netherlands, Sweden and Spain. By comparison, the prison population per 100 000 recorded crimes is about the same for England and Wales as for West Germany, Greece and France, but almost double the rate for Scotland.

The Dutch experience

Penal reformers still travel to the Netherlands for inspiration, John Howard having started the trail in the 1770s. The Dutch imprison far fewer of their population than the British. For every 100 000 of the population about 100 people in Britain are in prison compared with 30 in the Netherlands, half of the latter being foreign nationals. Proportionately more of the prisoners are on remand in the Netherlands. Remand prisoners may be quite isolated as visits from outside are restricted. Virtually 100% are convicted, however, and they are then often deemed to have served their sentence, or much of it, on remand (Smith, 1984). The gap between Britain and the Netherlands in terms of numbers of people in prison has been widening, largely because prison sentences in Britain have been getting longer, while they had been getting shorter in the Netherlands until the 1980s. Since then, there has been a trend towards longer sentences for more serious offenders, but community alternatives where a short sentence would have been given, particularly to juveniles (Frans Derks, Personal Communication 1990). Much of the difference is attributed to better judicial education in the Netherlands (Downes, 1982), although it also has to be noted that serious crime rates have not risen sharply in the Netherlands, as they have in Britain. The Dutch prison budget is very similar to the British (Smith, 1984), in spite of the smaller prison population (about 7600 adults and 760 juveniles) and this at least partly explains the relatively humane conditions in the prisons. In the Netherlands, each prisoner has a single cell by law, prisoners wear their own clothes, may send and receive uncensored mail and often make phone calls. Prison riots are almost unknown in the Netherlands. Suicide rates, however, are several times higher than expected in the community (Smith, 1984).

Most medical work in Dutch prisons is conducted by general practitioners, contracted on a sessional basis. Apart from routine medical examinations, they respond to requests for consultation, and must see prisoners who are undergoing punishment, to maintain a check on their health. They have no part to play, however, before punishment is ordered, and they take no part in intimate security searches or anything which might be construed as being in the greater interest of the institution than the prisoner. Specialist psychiatric assessments may be called in. The most usual route for psychiatric assessment for the courts is through the Pieter Baan Centre in Utrecht, which admits people for a 7-week multidisciplinary assessment before presenting a full report to the courts.

Offenders may be diverted into the mental health care system, as appropriate, and a decision to discontinue criminal procedures is based on very similar criteria to those in Britain, including the nature and seriousness of offence, dangerousness of offender and degree of mental illness. There is, in addition, a system of eight clinics with nearly 500 places which are neither hospitals nor prisons, although funded by the Ministry of Justice. All are run according to psychological philosophies, but each differs in model. They are known as TBS Clinics because the inmates are 'Ter Beschikkingstelling', which means that they are placed at the disposal of the government in order to be admitted to a secure clinic for treatment. This is an order which is governed by the Dutch Criminal Code and the Psychopaths Act of 1928, reformed in 1988. Candidates are those thought to have been not fully responsible for their crime, and who have committed a dangerous offence like rape or arson thought susceptible to repetition. It is a potentially indefinite order, but reviewable by a court after the first 2 years at 1 or 2-year intervals. The average period served is 4½ years. Although people with psychosis are increasingly being admitted to these clinics, the majority of patients have a personality disorder. Unfortunately, much of the research on post-treatment outcome has been based exclusively on recidivism rates. Half the former clients were reconvicted of an offence within 2 years, and 30% were sent to prison again, but it must be emphasized that offenders referred to the TBS Clinics have been highly selected for their dangerousness, and there is no way of knowing what would have happened if they had not been sent to these clinics.

Sweden and Denmark

The emphasis in prison provision in Sweden and Denmark is on normalization of prisoners' lives to the maximum level possible within the bounds of security. There are far fewer prisoners per head of population than in Britain, but rather more than in the Netherlands. In Sweden, most medical care is provided independently of the prison service with just three full-time prison doctors. In Denmark, prison medical staff are still employed by the prison service and even in Herstedvester Special Institution, the primary goal is the protection of society and the provision of psychiatric treatment is secondary. Thus, although this prison has been granted the status of a mental hospital to enable compulsory treatment, the psychiatrists have remained sensitive to its real nature and the ethical dilemmas this poses in treatment. Psychotic patients would generally be transferred out to the health care system. In both countries, there is great emphasis on work or study, prisoners in Swedish prisons, for example, generally being expected to complete 40 hours a week, and all prisoners within Denmark being required to include work or education as part of their programme. Social normalization is emphasized too, and families may not only visit, but in some cases, they may stay overnight or for a weekend. It is perhaps this emphasis on normal social values within the prisons that creates most interest, and from which other countries have most to learn.

Prison Health Care : Setting Standards

The Home Office (1982) has outlined the tasks of the prison doctor as the examination of all inmates on admission and discharge, the provision of reports to court and to the Parole Board, the regular review of prisoners serving life imprisonment, the examination of prisoners charged with offences, the hygiene of the establishment as a whole, and the total well-being of its inmates. One of us (Gunn, 1985a) has largely agreed with this perspective and emphasized that, in addition, it is useful for the prison doctor and the prison psychiatrist to influence the general milieu of prisons:

> In prisons doctors can use their knowledge of group psychotherapy, therapeutic communities, and the consequences of stress to give advice about better management. . . . Indeed ultimately such a preventive role could be developed into the most important psychiatric role of all within prisons.

A similar view was expressed by Suarez (1972):

> (p)sychiatry would do better to spend its time treating the institution itself rather than the individual inmates within it.

However, Roth (1980) warned against such sentiments because they can lead to the view that prisons can become transformed into places of treatment. Staff and inmates alike recognize that prisons do not and cannot exist primarily for purposes of treatment. They are primarily places of protective custody where men and women endure punishment imposed by the courts. Anyone in any doubt should read in full the Home Office (1988e) booklet for lifers (*see also* p. 761).

The American Psychiatric Association (APA) (1989a) Position Statement on psychiatric services in jails and prisons takes its cue from equal opportunities legislation. Not only is discrimination on grounds of sex, religion and race outlawed, but also that on grounds of low public and political status. Prisoners generally fall into these latter groups and the APA argues firmly that:

> the fundamental goal of a mental health service should be to provide the same level of care to patients in the criminal justice process that is available in the community.

So far, in Britain, minimum levels of care for prisoners have not been established in law, but in the USA the courts have endorsed the sentiments of the evolving APA position (Connors, 1979; Wilson, 1980). Two cases (*Bowring* and *Estelle*) led to the setting of a 'deliberate indifference' standard, for which the key factor in determining whether a system for providing psychological or psychiatric care is constitutionally adequate is whether inmates with serious disturbances are provided 'reasonable access' to medical personnel qualified to diagnose and treat such disturbances. Further, 'lack of funds is not an acceptable excuse for unconstitutional conditions of incarceration' (*Finney*). A later, key judicial opinion held that mental health care in jails should be held to the same standard as care for physical ailments (*Inmates* v *Pierce*) and that—

> the jail is not a mental health facility, nor do administrators intend that it should become one. It must, however, be staffed and organized to meet emergency situations, to make appropriate referrals, and to carefully care for and protect those who must be housed in the jail for whatever reasons despite their mental illness.

Whether such rulings have led to commensurate widespread improvements in practice is another matter.

Steadman and colleagues (1989) conducted a survey of jails in 42 communities in 26 states of the USA. They were drawn about equally from each of the four major regions of the country, although over 75% of all jails are clustered in the southern and north central states. The prisons were chosen for their interest in health care provision. Data were collected from site visits as well as wide ranging paper questionnaires and telephone interviews. They were able to draw five principles for service planning from this experience, together with a set of guidelines for setting standards, which could with benefit be adopted in Britain.

1. 'The mentally disturbed jail inmate must be viewed as a community issue.' The time spent in jail by most inmates at any one time is short, they come from the community and will go back to it and are likely to need continuity of care.
2. 'The jail is and should remain primarily a correctional facility.' Nevertheless—
3. 'Serious mental health needs among inmates require limited but high quality professional services in every jail.'
4. 'Correctional administrators should concentrate on developing mental health services in the areas of identification, crisis intervention and case management at release.'
5. 'There is no one best way to organize a jail mental health program.'

The associated definitions of nine essential services to be provided by a prison mental health service provide a good basis for generating standards of service delivery.

1. *Intake screening* should prevent newly arrived prisoners who pose a health or safety threat to themselves or others from being admitted to the prison's general population and get them rapid access to medical care. A jail was considered to operate screening if:
   (a) new inmates were routinely asked questions pertaining to their mental health,
   (b) the questions were printed on a standard form; and
   (c) the screening form was completed at intake.
2. *Psychological evaluations* were defined as assessments by clinical inter-

view, performed by mental health professionals. In order to be credited with this service, the jail must be initiating the evaluation as part of its service programme and not merely responding to demands from the courts.

3. *Assessment and provision of reports for the courts.*

4. *Use of psychotropic medication.* Here the standard was simply use, and would bear further definition.

5. *Substance abuse counselling.* The therapy had to have a clear psychological orientation and be for assistance with overcoming a drug or alcohol problem, be available to all inmates in need of it, or a defined subgroup, and if not done in the jail, correctional officials had to provide the necessary transport to prearranged sessions. Provision of contact names and addresses was not sufficient.

6. *Psychological therapy.* The therapy had to be properly scheduled and a session consist of a clinical interaction, oriented towards assisting improvement in behaviour, between an inmate and a mental health professional, the latter with at least a master's degree.

7. *Inpatient care.* Emphasis was placed on the notion that a prison provides 'infirmary' rather than hospital care. 'An infirmary is an area established within the correctional facility in which organized bed care facilities and services are maintained and operated to accommodate two or more inmates for a period of 24 h or more and which is operated for the expressed or implied purpose of providing skilled nursing care for persons who are not in need of hospitalization' (American Medical Association, 1981).

8. *External hospitalization.* Credit was given for this service if seriously disturbed inmates were transferred to a local hospital or specialist forensic psychiatry unit.

9. *Case management.* This meant that formal referrals to outside mental health agencies were made for prisoners as necessary, and appointments were arranged as appropriate.

These nine services were regarded by Steadman and colleagues (1989) as basic. Larger prisons, it was emphasized, would have the opportunity to develop wider or more specialist services. Training, staff support and research would also have to be addressed. At a time when in Britain voices are beginning to be raised in favour of establishing and recognizing hospitals in prisons, it is worth re-emphasizing the strong stand against this advocated by Steadman and his group, and Roth (1980). They argue that the ability of psychiatrists to influence the milieu and to communicate with prisoners is notable only when they (the psychiatrists) are willing to admit that treatment is not the sole or even the major purpose of incarceration, and by inference that their role is limited. Doctors in prisons should seek to maintain health, otherwise their task is to make links with the ordinary, non-penal health services as appropriate.

The Probation Service in England and Wales

A Historical Perspective

The probation service in England and Wales had its origins in voluntary pioneering, when, in 1876, the Church of England Temperance Society appointed missionaries to the Metropolitan Courts. An earlier American model was the basis of much that followed (Bochel, 1976). The English task became clearer under the Summary Jurisdiction Act 1879, and the Probation of First Offenders Act 1887, but it was not until the Probation of Offenders Act 1907 that this supervision was anything but informal. After 1907, justices could appoint probation officers, and require local authorities to pay for them. In 1925, the Criminal Justice Act of that year made it mandatory for judges to appoint probation officers for every probation area, the expense then to be met half by the local authority and half by the exchequer. The range of tasks for the probation service expanded with the growing recognition that the circumstances of an offender may be relevant not only to his culpability, but also in the way in which he may be expected to respond to the various methods of dealing with him which are available to the court, and his capacity to meet fines, compensation, or other financial orders. Responsibility for aftercare of prisoners became an important feature of work. Trends in supervision have been towards more formalization of conditions, but role expansion has brought selectivity in, say, routine reporting and, in turn, guidance on safeguarding particular groups. Young offenders have been explicitly and particularly targeted for comprehensive social enquiry reports. The Criminal Justice Act 1991 sets the framework of a justice model of sentencing within which the probation service will supervise offenders and prepare reports (*see* Home Office, 1992a, b).

In addition to criminal work, the probation service has long had a high profile in matrimonial considerations, again initially voluntarily, but with statutory authority following the Summary Procedure (Domestic Proceedings) Act 1937, and the superseding Magistrates' Court Act 1952. Since 1950, under the Matrimonial Causes Act of that year, probation officers have served as welfare officers in the divorce courts, reporting in respect of custodial, maintenance or educational decisions to be taken by the court. Reports may similarly be required to magistrates' courts under the Matrimonial Proceedings (Magistrates' Courts) Act 1960. Under the Matrimonial Causes Act 1973, the High or County Court judges must be satisfied that proper arrangements have been made for the future of any child before the decree absolute can be granted. Probation officers have taken a leading role in conciliation work.

The development of the work of the probation service, together with the attendant legislation, is dealt with in greater detail in Bochel (1976).

The Size of the Task

In the late 1980s the prison population stood at something in excess of 45 000 at any one time, reaching a peak of nearly 50 000 in 1988, with something approaching 120 000 imprisoned in any one year. Only a bare majority of these (64 000 in 1989) were serving immediate custodial sentences; an estimated 35 000 were remanded in custody awaiting trial or sentence (but not receiving a custodial sentence if they were sentenced); approximately 1700 offenders were committed for non-payment of fines (Home Office, 1990e, 1991).

A large part of probation work has inevitably been with after-care and, in 1989, 51 000 new after-care cases were recorded by the probation service. These included 12 000 adults released on parole, 16 000 offenders beginning after-care from a sentence of detention in a young offender institution, 400 commencing supervision on various indefinite arrangements (including life licence, section 53 of the Children and Young Persons Act 1933 and conditional discharge of restricted patients under the MHA 1983). No less than 27 000 offenders sought help under voluntary after-care arrangements (Home Office, 1990e.) Much probation effort was also, however, directed at assessment with over 200 000 social inquiry reports prepared in 1989. At the end of that year over 82 000 offenders were on some form of community supervision, including 4000 juveniles under the Children and Young Persons Act 1969. Of the 52 000 on a probation order, less than 2% had a condition of psychiatric treatment attached (Barker, 1988, Home Office, 1990d).

For these tasks, there are 55 probation areas in England and Wales, fielding about 7000 professionally qualified probation officers, about 9000 support staff (Home Office, 1990d) and about 7000 voluntary associates, the latter men and women usually with no relevant qualifications, but able to comply with the 'befriending' element of the roles of the probation service.

The Home Office fully funds probation work in prisons and statutory hostels, and also provides fully for student training. For all other activities, the Home Office provides most of the budget, but Local Authorities contribute 20%. The allocation of grants is, however, under review by the Home Office, with the introduction of cash limits in 1992.

The Roles of the Probation Service

The principal roles of the probation service are the provision of information and advice to the courts and the supervision of offenders in the community (*see also* Ch. 4). Although these themes have been elaborated and diversified, particularly with the introduction and development of aftercare supervision, they have remained the core of probation work. The probation service has become established as a professional social work agency. This was not necessarily a foregone conclusion, despite the reimportation of case work ideas into British practice (McWilliams, 1986). Bochel (1976) has shown how the Probation of Offenders Act 1907 could have led probation officers to be more firmly correctional—that is to say more specifically concerned with the enforcement of the law and less with judgments about the best interests of individual offenders. The White Paper *Crime, Justice and Protecting the Public* (Home Office, 1990a) emphasized the controlling aspects of the Service's role. Consequently the 1991 Criminal Justice Act sets the court's decision to make a supervisory order firmly within a justice model of sentencing, while supervision on release from custody is also linked more strongly than before to the length of sentence imposed by the courts. Within supervisory orders ('community sentences' in the wording of the Act), a distinction is articulated between the severity or onerousness of the order, its length and formal conditions, which are a part of the punishment, and its content, which may be individualized, should be designed to tackle offending behaviour and can be seen as rehabilitative in intent. This distinction specified, but does not resolve, an undoubted tension between the two aspects of probation service work—care and control.

The supervision of psychiatric orders and licences is a dyadic task, where the primary responsibility for the probation officer is to ensure that the subject keeps to the conditions of the order or licence, and to enable a recall decision or breach proceedings, if these become necessary. Case work with such clients is regarded as secondary to these tasks. Reality and practice, however, are less stark. The distinction that is drawn between control and care is unlikely to be so marked, perhaps particularly with offender patients. First, in supervising patients conditionally discharged from psychiatric hospital, probation officers can only make realistic reports on the basis of close knowledge of the patient. The guidelines for social supervisors, prepared by the Home Office and the then DHSS, recognize this in requiring frequent and regular contact between supervisor and patient. Norris (1984), in her study of patients discharged from Broadmoor hospital, commented on the tendency of supervisors who were not in regular contact to regard no news as good news, and so be in some cases falsely optimistic about the progress of patients. Secondly, the resettlement of discharged patients into the community is likely to affect their future behaviour and prospects for recall; the probation officer, as social supervisor, is likely to be a key resource in enabling successful resettlement. Further, the supervision of clients receiving outpatient treatment as a condition of a probation order is likely to be linked to their successful completion of treatment. Overall, it is unlikely that there will be a complete schism between the offender's response to treatment as a patient, and his response to supervision as a client of the probation service.

Reports for the Courts

The Morrison Report (Home Office, Scottish Home Department 1962) defines a probation officer as 'a social case worker who is an officer of the court'. Nowhere is the dilemma that this poses more apparent than in the preparation of the social enquiry or pre-sentence report for the criminal courts. This is dealt with more fully elsewhere (Ch. 4). Such work has much in common with that of the psychiatrist. There are, however, important differences. The probation officer, as a court officer, reports directly to the court and for the court and not primarily for the client. This lack of balance in an adversarial legal system concerns many officers, even though their aim would be to provide objective reports regardless of the commissioning agency. They believe themselves to be just as susceptible as anyone else in the court process to the pressure to 'get a result', and various strategies in achieving this through the social enquiry report have been identified (Pearce and Wareham, 1977; Carlen and Powell, 1979). Probation officers thus have usually resisted providing a social enquiry report except where a guilty plea has been entered or a finding of guilt established.

Officers to the Crown Prosecution Service

The Prosecution of Offences Act 1985 created a new, national agency of prosecuting lawyers—the Crown Prosecution Service (CPS) (*see also* Ch. 4)—and, in turn, new points of intervention by the probation service. The CPS must balance two principal factors in determining the strength of any case and in deciding to proceed. The first is the quality of the evidence against any given individual—mainly addressed by the police—and the second lies in the broader circumstances of the defendant in the case, and whether the prosecution is 'in the public interest'. On the latter criterion, the probation service has a potentially important role. Two major schemes have developed in several pilot areas in response to the challenge: the Bail Information Schemes and Public Interest Case Assessment.

Bail information schemes

The Bail Act 1976 established a general right to bail, while listing certain exceptions. It directs the court to come to a decision on the basis of information which includes the nature and seriousness of the offence, the strength of the evidence, the character, antecedents, associations and community ties of the defendant, but makes no provision for ensuring that this range of crucial information is available. The probation service have provided relevant social information where possible to the courts on an *ad hoc* basis. After the creation of the CPS, the service also became the focal point for the provision of bail information to the courts. In 1987, the Association of Chief Officers of Probation sponsored eight pilot bail information schemes, which sought to provide *verified* information about the defendant to the CPS on a regular basis, targeting, in particular, cases where police objection to bail had been raised.

Under the pilot schemes, a bail information sheet is prepared. It is not submitted to the court, but considered, in conjunction with police objections, by the Crown Prosecution Service. Because the schemes dealt with cases before their first appearance in magistrates' courts, or at the latest before their second, defendants had generally not entered a plea and were often not even legally represented. Participation in the scheme, therefore, required the consent of the defendant. For consenting clients, the presentation of information had to be in writing, an exact copy subsequently being presented to any solicitors employed for their defence. No mention of the offence, no opinion about the defendant, and no recommendation or suggestion on outcome could be made. The schemes were intended as purely information services.

The Vera Institute of Justice, a USA based organization, cooperated with the probation service in England and Wales to evaluate the impact of the pilot bail schemes (Stone, 1988). It seemed unlikely that the Bail Information Service was applied randomly to clients, so testing of its impact required carefully considered approaches. Prediction scores were generated for each of the eight participating courts, all outside London, taking into account the five or six items, like the nature of current allegations, previous convictions, previous breaches of bail, nature of defendant's stress, that were most likely to predict bail for that court. Bail rates were compared with prediction scores for cases appearing in these courts before, during, and in some cases after the pilot schemes. Of 1367 cases for which information was available by the second court appearance, during the operation of the schemes in 1987, the information seems to have been crucial in nearly 400 bail decisions. The defendants bailed as a result of the extra information seemed neither more nor less likely to breach conditions of bail than those bailed without extra information. No complaints about decisions in these cases were recorded from the police. The success of the pilot schemes led to further expansion, including in 1989 the setting up of the Greater London Bail Information Scheme. This covers, at the time of writing, six courts and two custodial institutions and arose from the cooperation of the five London Probation Services. This has enabled the provision of bail information to be tested in the pressured and complex environment of London courts and institutions.

Discontinuance

Discontinuance is a different development which has similarly followed the inauguration of the CPS and rests on many of the same principles as a bail information scheme. The subject is at the same stage of the prosecution process, has to be consenting, there is no focus on the alleged offence, and the report is addressed to the CPS. The information is verified, the sources are made clear, and is selected to be relevant to the Code for Crown Prosecutors 1986, a public document prepared by the CPS, but with additional guidelines not available to the public. The Code requires Crown

Prosecutors to assess the evidence to determine whether it presents a realistic prospect of conviction and lists factors which should be addressed in determining 'whether the public interest requires a prosecution'. These include likely costs of the case set against likely penalty, the likelihood of 'irreparable harm', particularly for the very young or the very old offender or the mentally disordered. A pilot study—the Public Interest Case Assessment Project—reviewed the activity of the probation service in relation to the work of one court (Horseferry Road, London), the response of prosecutors and the impact on discontinuance of prosecution (Stone, 1989). In 18% of cases, the enquiry was regarded as crucial to discontinuance, and in only one-third was it found 'not helpful'. Before the experiment just 1% of cases (totalling 105) had been discontinued, rising to 4% (553) for the larger group studied during the control period, and 7% (575) during the experimental period. After the intervention period, discontinuence fell to around pre-experimental levels (2% or 152 cases).

The Work of the Court Welfare Officer

Probation officers act as court welfare officers for both the High Court and county courts in England and Wales, their main duties being to report on children involved in divorce or wardship cases and to provide the opportunity for conciliation for the distressed families in resolving their practical difficulties. Once a judge or registrar has made a direction for a welfare officer's report, the officer must arrange to visit all parties involved, including the children, the parents, and any other people who are directly concerned with looking after the children or who have been cited as willing to do so. If a child is in care, whether voluntarily or under a care order, contact must also be made with the local authority social services department, with a request for a report from them. From time to time a child in question may be abroad, and a report must then be requested from the relevant foreign agencies. Where a child has a serious illness, disability, or behaviour problem, medical reports may also be required.

The welfare officer's report collates all this information and is filed in the Divorce Registry where, for a small fee, copies are available to all interested parties and their legal representatives. Under the provision of successive Acts, for example the Matrimonial Proceedings (Magistrates' Courts) Act 1960, the Matrimonial Proceedings (Children) Act 1958, the court may make a child subject to a custody order under the supervision of a probation officer. The probation officer may also act as a *guardian ad litem* in applications before the county courts or juvenile courts, particularly where the local authority is the placing agency or interested party in adoption. In addition, welfare officers may be required to keep in touch with the children or other parties pending further hearings, without any supervision order being made.

The late 1980s have also seen a growth in conciliation work in civil cases as an alternative to the adversarial form of proceedings on which the requirement to prepare reports was originally based. Probation officers deal with around 10 000 conciliation cases a year, of which the great majority (nearly three-quarters in 1989) are completed in court, while the remainder (around 3000 in 1989) are adjourned (Home Office, 1990d). Conciliation is distinct from the preparation of reports. Information provided by parties to conciliation is privileged and may not be transported into a report if the parties fail to agree. Practice in civil work generally has also developed in the direction of conciliation and on enabling the parties concerned to resolve their disputes in a constructive way.

The Welfare of Prisoners

In 1953, the Maxwell Committee (Home Office, 1953) recommended the appointment of prison welfare officers in local prisons, who would be qualified social workers to help prisoners with personal and domestic problems, to identify those likely to benefit from friendship and assistance when released, and to prepare case histories and constructive plans for discharge. Ten years later the probation and after-care service was formally given responsibility for the service on the recommendation of the Report of the Advisory Council on the Treatment of Offenders (Home Office, 1963). Existing prison welfare officers were integrated into the probation and after-care service, becoming probation officers seconded to prisons. Stone (1985) expressed the concern that probation officers working in prisons are in danger of giving legitimacy to existing regimes. Individual care can only be provided within strict limits and the balance of work, he argued, may divert concern from the unacceptable state of the institutions through focusing on the individuals. As partial evidence he cited a 1984 unpublished Home Office Statement of National Objectives and Priorities:

> Sufficient resources should be allocated to through-care to enable the service's statutory obligations to be discharged . . . Beyond that, social work for offenders released from custody, though important in itself, can only command the priority which is consistent with the main objective of implementing non-custodial measures.

Following the Criminal Justice Act 1982, and a subsequent change in probation rules, the probation and aftercare services dropped the 'after-care' component of their title. In the late 1980s, with increasing pressure on all public service providers towards 'efficiency' and 'accountability', voluntary after-care, a natural extension of statutory supervision, or a partial substitute where no such arrangement was open to the offender, has been eroded almost to the point of being as voluntary to the probation officer as to the client. The Criminal Justice Act 1991 provides for voluntary aftercare only for prisoners serving short sentences and not subject to supervision under licence on release.

Through-care

'Through-care' is a concept of working with prisoners, such that social work intervention is available to them throughout their sentence whether on a statutory or voluntary basis. Jarvis (Weston, 1987) listed the objectives of through-care as an attempt to limit the harmful effect of a custodial sentence on the individual and his family, the provision of support and help towards a more satisfactory level of social functioning, and the provision of supervision in relevant cases.

In its review of through-care, the Inner London Probation Service (ILPS, 1988) suggested that—

> probation officers should offer a full through-care service to all prisoners sentenced to 6 months or longer and to all prisoners subject to statutory after-care.

This important recommendation was, however, accompanied by a shift from the Jarvis principles to a primary objective of reducing a client's offending. It is important to demonstrate the efficacy of costly services and McCord's (1978) work has clearly demonstrated the logic of being suspicious of accepting subjective impressions of benefit recorded by counsellor or client. Criminal records, providing information about reoffending, provide an easy, objective and readily available marker of one sort. They are, however, far from adequate as a measure of social safety and reintegration. Much offending behaviour never reaches the attention of the criminal justice system, but is, none the less, a threat to society. People may be a major drain on society for other reasons, for example in their inability to work. Former prisoners remain a terrible risk to themselves, with a far higher mortality rate than the general population, mainly through suicide, accident or behaviour leading to an open verdict in the coroner's court (Robertson and Gunn, 1987). All these issues are measurable and important too.

Parole

Anyone serving a determinate prison sentence of more than 6 months in the UK, imposed before 1 October 1992, may have the final third set aside, providing they behave themselves in prison. Such remission has been a right for every prisoner, and because loss of remission only occurred as a punishment following adjudication arising out of alleged bad behaviour, it was seen as a means of maintaining discipline within the prison. Parole was, by contrast, a privilege, afforded to a highly selected minority of prisoners, which allowed them the possibility of serving up to a further one-third of their sentence under licence in the community rather than in custody. It was first introduced to England and Wales in the Criminal Justice Act 1967, although it was hardly a new concept as it was by then already widespread in the USA. The development of the procedures is reviewed in Stanley and Baginsky (1984). In brief, two levels of multidisciplinary committees were set up, each of which included the judiciary, magistrates, the probation service, and some medical advice, the local review committees being attached to the local prison and the central committee being known as the Parole Board (*see also* Ch. 4). In addition, the Home Secretary has a supporting civil service department in the Home Office.

The Criminal Justice Act 1991 abolished remission and changed the parole system for offenders sentenced to custody after 30 September, 1992. Offenders sentenced to under four years will be released automatically after serving half their sentence, provided they did not misbehave in prison; those serving between one and four years will be subject to supervision on licence up to the three-quarters point of the sentence and subject to recall to serve the balance of the sentence if they commit an imprisonable offence. An offender sentenced to four years or more will be subject to discretionary release at the recommendation of the Parole Board between the half-way and two-thirds points of their sentence; all who are not released on parole will be released automatically on licence at the two-thirds point. All licences will last until three-quarters of the original sentence has passed.

There are special provisons to allow for sex offenders, at the direction of the sentencing judge, to be supervised on licence until the end of their sentence. The probation service has a key role in the preparation of reports for consideration for parole, which will often be presented by both the prison-based officer and the community-based officer, the latter having a principal responsibility for supervision if the parole or licence is granted. Issues which must be addressed include 'progress' and behaviour in prison, social networks and the patterns and context of offending prior to imprisonment, with a commentary on how far the context may have changed, victim typology and the relevance of alcohol or drugs.

The parole system will deal only with long-sentence prisoners, with local review committees being phased out. Concerns over the secrecy of the previous parole system have been met by a commitment to greater openness in decision making, including the disclosure to prisoners of information in reports.

In 1981, the ILPS undertook a small scale study of one office specializing in the supervision of parolees. Twenty-four clients were involved in the project, with offences including manslaughter, rape, indecent assault, other assaults and robberies. The results of the study (Maitland et al., 1983) showed that, contrary to an impression given by Morris and Beverly (1972), parolees' problems were not purely practical ones, but included difficulties in social readjustment after release to the community. There was not a clear distinction between practical problems (which included housing, work, money), emotional difficulties and issues arising from the original offence, including a concern that the client might reoffend. The study drew two important conclusions about the supervision of parolees, which may also be related to the management of conditionally discharged patients. The first is the importance of the compulsory nature of supervision, and the sanction of recall to prison which is clearly seen to back this up; the second is the importance of the supervisor focusing on the parolee, rather than his family or other contacts, to enable a degree of confidence in the relationship:

> The existence of the compulsory elements somehow provide the impetus for both client and officer to face up to and deal with problems arising. If the parolee is obliged to attend regularly, then issues cannot seriously be ignored, or good intentions fade into inaction. . . .
>
> What seems to happen is that if the parolee perceives the probation officer as the family's and if the family should have (a social worker), he (sic) will not think it appropriate, or will not feel able, to bring his (sic) problems to the probation officer. . . .

A further implicit theme of the parole study, which recurs in other studies (e.g. Goldberg and Stanley, 1985), is the importance to outcome of the personality style of the probation officer, as well as of the model of work adopted. Norris (1984), in her study of released Broadmoor hospital patients, found evidence of a distinction between the person and role of the social supervisor. Social supervisors were seen as least like patients' selves, but were more likely to be nominated 'first choice helper' by discharged patients than were doctors, nurses, friends or family. Day (1981) found that positive attitudes by clients towards probation officers were associated with the perception of the probation officer as someone who 'understands'. The highly structured form of supervision with 'treatment plans', regular and frequent interviews with the client, and regular reports to the Home Office, is important for the protection of the public and the ex-offender or ex-patient, but not necessarily optimal, or even sufficient without considering the quality of relationship between superviser and supervised.

Life sentence

The life sentence (*see also* pp. 75–7, 760–1) is the ultimate occasion for through-care and regular reporting. A Home Office circular (55/1984) sets out the tasks for the probation service in some detail. It construes the lifer's career in four phases:

1. from the first court appearance to immediately postsentence, during which time a probation officer from the prisoner's home area should be in regular communication with the remand prison probation officer;
2. the prison career, in which social works rests largely with the prison-based officer, aided by support for the family from the home area team;
3. preparation for release, shared by the prison probation officers and those in the receiving area; and
4. the postrelease phase, resting principally with the receiving area officer.

The value of having a second probation officer from the home area involved in the case is something that everyone working with extremely difficult and challenging offenders might consider, including psychiatrists. Such a pairing system has been operated to advantage by psychiatrists in some parts of the special hospital system, but it is rarely operated between senior psychiatrists working with offender patients in the community. A true partnership between disciplines may provide effective checks and supports, but intradisciplinary partnership can bring special additional advantages in some cases.

The tasks set out for probation officers by the 1984 Home Office circular could apply, with benefit, to other disciplines, for example prison medical staff, involved at comparable stages of a prisoner's career. They could also be applied with advantage to someone starting a long period of hospitalization after an offence. The requirements for the period immediately postsentence, and those for the prison career are set out in Tables 19.4 and 19.5 respectively (*see also* Ch. 4).

The Pre-release Employment Scheme

Many lifers are released via a period of approximately 6 months on the pre-release employment scheme (PRES). They live in a PRES hostel, which is a place attached to a prison, and the period spent there is regarded as part of their imprisonment. The difference between being in a PRES hostel and actual imprisonment is the requirement to take ordinary paid employment

Table 19.4
Preparing a Postsentence Report on a Life Sentenced Prisoner: The Questions

1. Who are the significant persons whose relationships with the prisoner are affected by the crime and sentence?
2. In respect of these, what changes are apparent in their attitudes to the offender? How are these related to the offence of which he is now convicted?
3. Realistically, what are the chances of sustaining the relationship in a helpful way over a longish period?
4. What are the practical problems at home, e.g. debts, house ownership, loss of the offender's personal contributions both in money and in effort around the house?
5. Who can visit and with what degree of difficulty? Who cannot visit and who will not visit?
6. What other consequences have flowed from events, e.g. if a man or woman has killed a partner, who is now looking after the children?
7. What hostility will he still have to face, e.g. family rejection, local feeling?
8. What hostility do his relatives have to face from neighbours, relatives of victim, etc?
9. How can the family together or individually be helped with their feelings about the offence, the offender, the sentence?
10. What advice can be offered to those dealing with the offender?
11. Is there anything of significance in the offender's medical history?
12. Particularly for younger lifers, what are their educational attainments and aspirations?

Information from Home Office Circular No. 55/1984. *Through Care and Supervision of Life Sentenced Prisoners.* Prison Department Circular Instruction No. 37/1984. (Home Office, 1984c)

Table 19.5
Career Planning for the Life Sentenced Prisoner

The management of the life sentence (including Career Planning, Review Boards as set out in Prison Department Circular Instruction 1/1982);

Common reactions and experiences of life sentence prisoners;

Analysis of information and recognition of change over protracted time scales;

Distinction between life licence and parole to be considered in reporting to the local review committee;

The concept of dangerousness, patterns of behaviour and assessment of risk;

Management of denial, disappointment, frustration and tension;

Pre-release initiatives;

Recording and preparation of information for the future supervisors;

Preparation of the future licensee to ensure understanding of the need for close supervision and the limits of confidentiality.

Information drawn from Home Office Circular No. 55/1984. *Through Care and Supervision of Life Sentenced Prisoners.* Prison Department Circular Instruction No. 37/1984.

in the community by day and return to the hostel by night. Ironically, it is often the most vulnerable and disadvantaged that are excluded from such programmes. In a joint study between the Institute of Psychiatry and the ILPS of all life licensees released to the London or Home Counties probation areas in 1984, those excluded from PRES were significantly more likely to be older or to have alcohol problems (Grounds, Davies, Taylor unpublished data). Even those accepted still faced considerable difficulties.

One man, referred for psychiatric help after his release because he had a disabling adjustment reaction, described some of the issues most eloquently:

> When 18 months before my release I was told that a date had been set for my freedom I felt elated. I kept thinking about being able to work for a living again, of being anonymous, of being independent. I sent off for jobs, to get no replies. I was placed on a pre-release scheme and finally my boss gave me the start, fully aware that I had been in jail for murder. I started on £95 per week. That is £12 less than the job was advertised for. He knew the score and he knew that I had no alternative but to accept the terms. During week-end furloughs I would stay at friends or with parents. I met a woman and had high hopes of things working out, but a few weeks before my release that relationship folded. It was my fault. I spoke to her and treated her like a fellow con. We were distant and cold. Now I am beyond the pre-release scheme. I am on the dole, in lodgings, no job, no money, no friends. It took me ten years to come to this nothingness. Reports are made to the Home Office regularly. I am 'getting on OK'.

Life Licence

Over the last three decades the number of lifers in England and Wales has been steadily increasing, and, until 1983, the number released on licence each year was increasing too. In 1983, 96 were released on licence but, in 1984, the year after the Home Secretary announced major changes in the rules and procedures for release, only 68 were released, and numbers have remained lower. The procedure for determining licence is similar to that described for parole, but the Home Secretary has to consult with the Lord Chief Justice and, if available, the trial judge as well. In 1983, the Home Secretary set further limits, such as setting arbitrary minimum periods of 20 years in jail for lifers convicted of certain offences, for example killing a police officer. Of 853 life sentence prisoners released into the community between 1971 and 1983, less than 5% had committed a further serious crime, most within 5 years, but 78% had committed no further offence of any kind (Coker and Martin, 1985).

Coker and Martin (1985) also studied other aspects of the social adjustment of 239 released male lifers, drawn from two periods (1960–64 and 1970–74), before and after both abolition of the death penalty and the establishment of the local review committees and the parole board. There were few differences in adjustment between the two groups. On balance, although less likely to offend than before their life sentence, the men showed very similar levels of adjustment to their pre-life sentence status. Most of those who had had their own home prior to the offence again found a home for themselves after release, while the minority who had been dependent on lodgings before tended to go back to lodgings again. Levels of employment were also very similar, with just over 60% managing to find work. Further, there was very little downgrading in the nature of the work.

Ninety-two per cent of the men in the sample had killed, and 70% of these in a domestic setting. Therefore, as Coker and Martin so neatly put it, the lifers had 'a problem qualitatively different from that of most people entering close personal relationships'. Most of the relationships that they had at the time of their life sentence were broken by the sentence, if not by the offence itself. Proportionately more of the men, however, developed stable marital-type relationships after release than had achieved them before. About 63% of them were in marriages or stable cohabitation when they were released on licence, compared with just under half previously. Although this may have been partly a reflection of their increased age, some having been very young when they received their life sentence, it would also suggest a capacity for coping better with closeness to others.

Despite their generally optimistic findings, however, Coker and Martin found a hard core of men who did seem disturbed. They found, for example, that some element of change in work or in accommodation was inevitable, but that 28 men (14% of the sample) changed accommodation six times or more during the study (5 years). A similar pattern was found in relation to employment. These men were very much more likely to continue supervision beyond the usual 5-year period, and also had a much higher reconviction rate than the other men. A series of case histories presented suggested frank psychiatric disorder in a number of them.

In 1982, 238 life sentenced men and women were known to the ILPS, and a sample of 183 studied through their probation officers (Taylor, 1986); only eight were women. Nearly three-quarters had been convicted of murder. By the time of the study, 54 had been on licence in the community at some stage. The only difference between the detained and released lifers in their psychiatric diagnoses or previous treatment was that those with a personality disorder were significantly less likely ever to have been on licence. Sixteen men and one of the three women who had been released had also been recalled at some time, in two cases on more than one occasion. Only three of those recalled sustained further violent charges or convictions, and a further four convictions for non-violent offences. In only one case was a reoffence the trigger for recall, although in two others violence had been committed and one man had resumed indecently assaulting young males. Offending behaviour was, thus, an unusual reason for recall. Lifers who had been recalled at some stage were significantly more likely to have had a depressive illness than those remaining in the community.

A more detailed, prospective study followed all lifers released into the London and Home Counties probation areas between 1983 and 1984. There were 29, but just 21 participated in the full study. One of the refusers had a psychotic illness and was soon returned to prison. Among the men and one woman interviewed, there was good social adjustment in terms of accommodation. Four, however, were identified as psychiatric cases, while severe or moderately severe social problems were identified for half of the men. These included disturbances in family relationships, severe difficulties in interpersonal relationships beyond the family and alcohol abuse (Grounds, Davies, Taylor, unpublished data).

Statutory Supervision of Restricted Patients

Patients with Home Office restrictions on discharge from hospital must be supervised by a psychiatrist and a social worker as a condition of any release. In up to half of cases the social supervision is provided by a probation officer. Conditional discharge, its supervision and outcome are dealt with more fully in Chs. 2 and 4.

The Probation Order

Since the 1907 Probation of Offenders Act, probation has been available to the magistrates' courts for dealing with offenders convicted of any offence, and to the Crown Courts for those convicted of an imprisonable offence. It was based on a model established in Massachusetts, USA, in 1869 (Bochel, 1976). In 1959, the Departmental Committee on the Probation Service defined probation as:

> The submission of an offender while at liberty to a specified period of supervision by a social case worker who is an officer of the Court, during which period the offender remains liable if not of good conduct to be otherwise dealt with by the Court.

In law, the probation order had much in common with mental health legislation in relation to offenders in that sentence was set aside in favour of a probation order to allow for offenders to demonstrate their ability for change—or reform—and to provide them with help to do so. It differed from mental health legislation in that offenders can only submit to probation voluntarily and, if they broke any of the conditions, they were liable to be returned to court for sentencing for the original offence, and possible further penalties for breach of probation. The Criminal Justice Act 1991, made the probation order a sentence of the court, restricting an offender's liberty in proportion to the seriousness of the offence.

When a court makes a probation order, the standard requirement is that the probationer must be of good behaviour, must report as directed by the probation officer, receive visits at home as required and keep the probation officer informed of life changes, such as change of address. Treatment requirements became available to the courts under the Powers of the Criminal Courts Act 1973.

The Criminal Justice Act 1991 groups requirements into five types:

1. requirements as to residence;
2. requirements to receive treatment for a mental condition;
3. requirements to receive treatment for drug or alcohol dependency;
4. requirements to participate or refrain from participating in specific activities;
5. requirements to attend a probation centre (formerly day centre or day training centre).

The restriction on liberty imposed by any additional requirement should be commensurate with the seriousness of the offence for which it is imposed. Probation orders are set for a minimum of 6 months and a maximum of 3 years, although they may be terminated early either for exceptionally good or bad performance, in the latter case with alternative sanctions likely to be imposed on return to court.

Probation orders accounted in 1989 for 10% of all disposals for indictable offences handed down by English courts (Home Office, 1990d). Annually, between 45 000 and 50 000 probation and supervision orders are made (three-quarters for indictable offences) and the number being supervised at any one time is nearly 60 000.

The number of offenders receiving a probation order has changed relatively little in the late 1980s, generally lying between 40 000 and 42 000. The contribution of the psychiatric condition has shown an overall trend towards disuse (*see* Fig. 19.1). This may have to do with a gloomy medical view of probation, Gibbens et al. (1981), citing psychiatrists as estimating that only 5% of patients treated under a psychiatric condition in the probation order were 'much improved'.

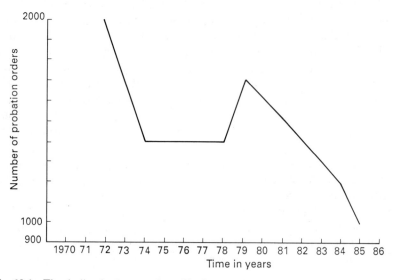

Fig. 19.1   The decline in the use of psychiatric probation orders over time in England and Wales.

It does not appear that the medical criteria for deciding on commitment to a psychiatric probation order are at all clear, or have been tested. There is a sense in which psychiatrists seem merely to be operating another form of rejection of offenders. Lipton et al. (1975), and Brody (1976), American and UK perspectives respectively, concluded that no form of 'treatment' was demonstrably successful in relation to reconviction rates. Unfortunately, such a limited way of evaluating outcome remains the mainstay of such work. Palmer (1975) took a further and more critical appraisal of the findings. He highlighted the problems of small sample size in many of the studies that suggested successful outcomes, biasing against significant finding of success. In particular, however, he targeted the misleading effect in the majority of studies of accepting efficacy only in terms of general outcome for the group, when an 'interaction effect' seemed important—that is that some projects seem to work for some people and not others, and that some workers obtained different results from others with specified client groups. An example of this was given by Folkard et al. (1974, 1976), who evaluated the effects of 'intensive' and 'ordinary' probation suspervision for 'high risk cases'. There was no overall difference in efficacy, but a sort of matching did emerge. Those with extensive criminal careers, but few personal problems, did best with ordinary supervision, while those with more personal problems responded more to the intensive work.

A 6-year follow-up study of a cohort of offenders given a range of sentences in November, 1971 (Philpotts and Lancucki, 1979) found that there was no association between nature of sentence and subsequent reconvictions, the best predictor of further offending being previous offending. Walker et al. (1981), however, reanalysed the data. In spite of difficulties because of the relatively small numbers of offenders in some categories, they examined outcome in relation to sentence, while holding the number of previous convictions and the nature of the index offence constant. For adult males, probation was found to be less effective than imprisonment for a first offence, more effective than imprisonment for those with 2–4 previous convictions and as ineffective as imprisonment for those with 5 previous convictions or more. Stanley and Baginsky (1984) observed that imprisonment is sufficiently unusual for adult male first offenders that the apparent efficacy of imprisonment for them is more likely to relate to their being 'special cases' than a tribute to the deterrent effect of imprisonment.

Although the probation order is, in theory, as voluntary for the client as for the supervisor, concern has been expressed about the potential for coercion of clients into social treatment of unproven efficacy, medical treatment or both (Bottoms and McWilliams, 1979). Failure, however, to offer such an option principally on grounds of concern that a potential client who might face a prison sentence cannot make a free choice is to deprive him of choice altogether. The response to the risks of pressures must be impeccable practice in enhancing the choices and the freedom of choice as far as possible.

The roles and expectations of each participant in the probation contract should be very clear to each before an order is made, each potential client should be entitled to read all the probation and medical reports material to the decision, and to question the conclusions without prejudicing the support of the probation officer or psychiatrist. It is important for the psychiatrist writing such a report to be aware that it may be shown to the patient/client by the probation officer (or lawyer). If there is any risk that disclosure of the report, or any part of it, maybe harmful, or may interfere with therapeutic rapport with a patient whom the psychiatrist is proposing to treat, then the psychiatrist should discuss any such problems beforehand with the probation officer. It is essential in any case that the psychiatrist and the probation officer should discuss in advance any proposal for joint work.

The Community Service Order

The community service order was introduced in the Powers of the Criminal Courts Act 1973, with a three-pronged philosophy behind it. As an alternative to custody, it would, nevertheless, retain a retributive element by depriving the offender of free time in the community. It would also allow him to make reparation to that community. Often, through offering new experiences to him, it would both minimize further alienation from society, and be a potential vehicle for rehabilitation.

The order may be imposed by a court for any imprisonable offence, if the offender is assessed as able to perform the order. Judge Goldstone (1982) recommended a tariff of equivalence between fines, imprisonment and community service. On his scale 200 hours of community service would be the equivalent of £300 fine or nine months' imprisonment. As for a probation order, the offender must consent to the order, with the sanction of a return to court for alternative sentencing in the event of reoffending or major problems. The court determines the length of the order, but the probation officer, in consultation with the offender, determines the nature of the work, in turn supervised by a relevant paid worker, generally skilled at the task in hand. Community service is unpaid, but should not interfere with paid employment if the offender has a job. The minimum length is 40 hours and the maximum 240 hours, the latter amounting to one full day a week for about 12 months.

By 1982, only a slightly lower proportion of offenders received community service orders rather than probation orders, with nearly 31 000 starting community service orders (Home Office 1984b). Pease (1981) showed that, as with a probation order, 75–80% of offenders completed the order successfully, 9–10% reoffending during the order and the remainder not complying with the terms of the order in some other way, for example absconding or not working satisfactorily. Using longer term recidivism as the index of outcome, the community service order is unremarkable in its effects, although Pease points out the balancing qualities. Such orders are much less expensive to run than imprisonment, have fewer social costs and offer the advantage that useful work is completed.

Deferred Sentence

Deferred sentences were introduced to England and Wales in the Criminal Justice Act 1972. Deferment can be for up to 6 months and provides an opportunity for the court to take account of behaviour after conviction and the offender to capitalize on such possibilities as a job offer, demonstration of his capacity for change and sometimes compensation for the victim. Few people are involved and the numbers vary only slightly from year to year. In 1983, for example, about 1–2% of people convicted of indictable offences in magistrates' or Crown Courts were sentenced after deferment of sentence. About 13% of those returning to magistrates' court and 35% of those to Crown Court received immediate or suspended prison sentences.

The Suspended Sentence and Suspended Sentence Supervision Order

Since 1968, English courts have had the power (under the Criminal Justice Act 1967) to suspend the implementation of a prison sentence of up to 2 years, such that, if the individual is not convicted of any further offence within a stated period, then he will remain free. This was mandatory for sentences of 6 months or less until the Criminal Justice Act 1972. The Criminal Law Act 1977 created a new power, that of partial suspension of sentence, implemented in 1982. Under this, the offender served only the first part of a prison sentence in jail. The latter is very rarely used (less than 1% of adult male offenders). The use of full suspension has been more or less steady over the last decade, affecting slightly over 10% of adult men convicted of indictable offences, even though the length of the sentence that can currently be suspended has made it, effectively, a Crown Court disposal. Under the Criminal Justice Act 1982, the option of suspended sentences was abolished for young people (aged 17–20).

The Criminal Justice Act 1982 empowered the courts to add a supervision order to a suspended sentence with the proviso that the length of the order should not exceed the period of suspension. This bears similarities to a probation order, but the probation order requires the offender's consent to supervision, while the supervision order does not, and the sanction of imprisonment is explicit. The order is added in only a tiny minority of cases (5% in 1982; Home Office, 1984b) and it is far from clear that it adds an important dimension to sentencing.

On the introduction of suspended sentences there was a very slight fall in the number of people imprisoned (Haxby, 1978), but a more substantial increase in the number of people liable to imprisonment. About one-third of suspended sentences are activated, by no means all for offences that would otherwise have attracted imprisonment, and thus, over time, it seems likely that more people have actually been imprisoned as a result of the provision, than without it.

Hostels

Homelessness is an important problem for many offenders at some stage in their career. A range of accommodation can be made available through the probation service as an important part of settlement or resettlement. This includes some purpose built and run probation hostels. The probation service has statutory powers for the management of hostels for offenders and of bail hostels. They may only be operated under the jurisdiction of the probation service, although the probation service has the power to commission others to run hostels on its behalf. Most such hostels were set up with the notion of providing not just a home, but also the basis of a 'treatment regime', with a rota for hostel tasks, social skills, training and other group attitudes. Sinclair and Clarke (1981) called the value of these more therapeutic hostels into question, saying that they could find no evidence that they influenced the recidivism rate, and adding that social skills and attitudes developed within the hostel were not necessarily transferred into the outside world. Using a rather different approach in Inner London, however, Maitland and Woodward (1983) emphasized the value that clients placed on support, and a certain amount of regulation of their activities.

Special Schemes

Day training centres and voluntary day centres

Another provision in the Powers of the Criminal Courts Act 1973 was to allow attendance at specified day centres for up to 60 days to be a part of a condition for probation. Four experimental centres were set up, with 100% funding from the Home Office, in London, Sheffield, Liverpool and Pontypridd. Although each developed their own style of working, all provided full-time, non-residential training in social skills, particularly directed at inadequate offenders who might otherwise have served a succession of short custodial sentences, and who were becoming at risk of a longer one. The service was said to cost as much per head as imprisonment (Shaw, 1980), and was not more widely adopted.

A number of other day centres did emerge, many run by voluntary bodies and in metropolitan areas. They target principally the young, unemployed offender. The emphasis is on work or technical activities, and, where appropriate and available, literacy or other educational skills, group work, social skills, role play and drama. Until the Criminal Justice Act 1982, attendance at such centres had to be entirely voluntary. Since 1982, it has been possible for a condition of attendance to be added to a probation order, and the distinction has become blurred between the original day training centres, now only 80% funded by the Home Office, and some voluntary centres which have developed similar programmes and staff client ratios (For a fuller discussion *see* Mair, 1988). The Criminal Justice Act 1991 classes them as probation centres.

The motor project

A special project for young people, many under age for driving on public highways, who persistently steal cars, has been running in London for a number of years. (*See* p. 580).

Social Work Provision for Offenders outside England and Wales

Scotland has no distinct probation service. Many of the provisions and activities just described are in place, but depend for their execution on generic social workers. Northern Ireland does have a separate probation service. Paradoxically, in view of its very high imprisonment rate, the concepts of probation and probation officers, as well as many subsequent innovative schemes, have been imported from the USA. Stanley and Baginsky (1984), as British writers, illustrate some of the schemes transferred, chiefly from the standpoint of models for alternatives to custody, while Clear and O'Leary (1983), as Americans, construe the primary purpose of community supervision as 'risk control'. The USA continues to have a considerable influence on English policy in the sense that ideas on bail information schemes, discontinuance and privatization of services are all imports from there.

The Scope of Voluntary Organizations in England and Wales

Voluntary organizations are the main providers of residential accommodation for forensic psychiatric patients discharged from prison or hospital into the community. Their role in after-care, and in preventing admission to hospital, or custody, is crucial. In addition to residential accommodation, these organizations also provide a range of other services.

Organizations Principally Serving the Mentally Disordered

The leading organization serving people with a disturbed mental state in Britain is MIND (The National Association for Mental Health), which provides advice and information on a large number of mental health issues; these include treatments, welfare benefits, housing, unemployment and legal problems. It also campaigns actively on behalf of patients, and a network of local mental health associations affiliated to MIND serves to implement local initiatives. A variety of other organizations exists, focusing upon sufferers from specific forms of disorder, e.g. National Schizophrenia Fellowship, Depressives Anonymous, The Phobics Society and organizations such as Release, dealing with drug abuse, or the Effra Trust, dealing with epileptic and mentally or physically disabled offenders. Still others provide a specific form of service, whatever the diagnosis—including sheltered accommodation or support to relatives. In Britain, individuals who have a mental handicap, and their families, would normally turn to the main organization for their special needs: MENCAP.

Organizations Principally Serving Offenders

The largest organization for offenders and ex-offenders in England and Wales is NACRO, The National Association for the Care and Resettlement of Offenders. NACRO aims to involve the community in crime prevention by assisting with the provision of housing, employment, youth training and education, and it offers advice and projects for offenders and people at risk.

There are also voluntary organizations for helping ex-offenders in more specific areas, such as the Stanton Foundation or the Carr Gomm Society which focus on the provision of accommodation, while still others principally offer a befriending service to ex-offenders (such as the Society of Voluntary Associates—SOVA—and the New Bridge Society, a London-based organization whose services are also available for offenders in prisons all over the country and may include employment advice). Project Full-Employ, although not specifically for ex-offenders, offers retraining programmes for young people, while the Prince's Trust may similarly offer grants for projects. Organizations which target young offenders include the National Children's Home, the Rainer Foundation and Community Service Volunteers.

A number of voluntary organizations exist specifically to provide advice and support to relatives of prisoners. Others, while offering assistance to individual offenders and their dependents, are better known for their campaigning activities, such as for more humane prison conditions, a decrease in the use of prison for petty offenders, and a more equitable criminal justice system. The Howard League, the Prison Reform Trust, and The Institute for the Study and Treatment of Delinquency are important in this field, while smaller agencies have grown up to target the special issues in imprisoning some subgroups, such as Women in Prison. The National Council for the Welfare of Prisoners Abroad provides assistance for those who may be imprisoned in other countries, and their families where possible, while they are abroad, and arranging facilities appropriate to their needs on their return. In addition to the national bodies, a number of organizations deal with local issues connected with offending. They are known as the Local Volunteer Bureaux.

Coordinating Activities

Voluntary services may be provided within the context of statutory supervision, and even statutory partnerships (other statutory requirements are to do with underpinning standards, for example the Registered Homes Act 1984). Less formal, but very important, partnerships between the various agencies—the probation service, local statutory organizations and the voluntary and private sector—are now explicitly encouraged. The offender accommodation forums, which exist in every probation area, constitute one example. They are covered by the probation service and include representatives of local and national housing associations, the local authority and the police. They devise overall policy for the needs of offenders, oversee the standards of practice of existing projects and advise the Chief Probation Officer on new ones.

Planned After-care

Section 117 of the MHA 1983 confers a joint duty upon—

the District Health Authority and the local social services authority to provide, *in co-operation with relevant voluntary agencies*, after-care services for any person to whom this section applies . . . until . . . no longer in need of such services—(our italics).

These include those detained under section 3 (for treatment), section 37 (hospital or guardianship order) and section 47 or 48 (removal to hospital of prisoners). Department of Health procedures require the health and local authorities to devise care plans for all detained patients on the point of discharge. If it is intended to use voluntary organizations as part of planned after-care arrangements, then it is essential that these organizations be closely consulted and involved before discharge actually occurs—in fact, this should apply whatever the legal status of the patient. Such organizations are likely to be involved in ensuring, as appropriate, that their client receives proper day care, employment and recreational pursuits, attends hospital outpatient appointments, and keeps in touch with the social supervisor. They may well be the first to report any significant deterioration in the patient's behaviour. It is, therefore, vital that the voluntary organizations, and the supervisor, be informed of any predisposing factors or warning signs suggestive of an imminent breakdown in the patient's mental health. Regular monitoring and supervision can help greatly to prevent such an occurrence.

Management of Voluntary Organizations

The larger national organizations are usually managed by a professional director, who is usually a member of an executive committee which is itself accountable to a management committee or other governing body, sometimes a limited company. Members of management committees volunteer their services and are chosen either for their professional expertise, for example, a treasurer who is a bank manager, or for their interest in the community or in the aims of the organization. The latter may include representatives of criminal justice agencies, industry, the church or members of parliament. Organizations which have charitable status or are a limited company (which enables them to raise funds) must have a constitution which lays down rules for the election of officers, conduct of the organization's business and the overall aims and objectives.

Local and national organizations, which receive Home Office funding, will usually be expected to have a Home Office representative on their management committee. This task often falls to a probation officer, who is expected to ensure that proper standards of care are maintained and that there is an adequate level of 'take-up' of the accommodation. Voluntary organizations for offenders frequently appoint a probation officer or social worker (not on the management committee) who will act as a liaison officer between that organization and the probation or social services. This is intended to ensure that the policies and practices of both organizations are mutually understood, and that individual clients are receiving adequate and appropriate supervision. Adequate preparation and continuing support and supervision for volunteers is necessary, not least to demonstrate an organization's competence. The risk of dangerousness is an ever present factor for voluntary and statutory organizations, particularly the residential ones, and reported incidents are on the increase. It is, therefore, important for organizations to issue guidelines for helping staff deal with dangerous and unpredictable situations, and training in dealing with violent clients.

A psychiatric input in terms of serving on the management committee, or providing a liaison service is usually welcomed. A psychiatrist can advise about admission policies, dangerous clients, mentally disordered clients and problems with substance abuse. Close liaison between a psychiatric service and a voluntary body can be of great mutual benefit to both services.

Funding

Many organizations termed 'voluntary' should more accurately be described as 'non-statutory', since they may be in receipt of considerable amounts of government funding. Those in receipt of government grants for accommodation for homeless people generally operate on deficit funding and are required either by the Home Office or the DSS to maintain a certain occupancy level in order to qualify for that grant. Non-residential organizations also obtain government funding, but look to other sources of income, such as charitable trusts, local authority grants, inner city partnerships, or urban aid. The Department of Employment is also a source of funding. Changes in local and central government policy can affect the lives of voluntary organizations, and sometimes their original focus of operation will alter in order to establish projects which will qualify them for government funds.

The movement towards the closure of psychiatric hospitals and the concomitant emphasis upon care in the community is having major implications for voluntary organizations. This trend is welcome in so far as it provides, in reality, improved individual care in a less stigmatizing environment. Further pressures arise from overcrowding in prisons and the drive to find community alternatives. Voluntary organizations are very apprehensive that, dependent as they often are upon charitable income, and on unpaid or low-paid staff, they will be unable to increase their resources in parallel with increasing demand. Financial constraints on public sector spending also mean that in some areas local authority sponsorships to place mentally ill people with voluntary associations are curtailed, giving rise to further financial difficulties for those associations. The government response is set out in a document *Partnership in the Community* (Department of Health, 1990), an important concept which does not obviate the need for government funding, preferably ring-fenced funding.

20
Secure Institutions:
their Characteristics and Problems

Edited by
John Gunn

Written by
Adrian Grounds
John Gunn
Paul Mullen
Pamela J. Taylor

With additional material from

Enda Dooley

The changing pattern of psychiatric care, away from long-term institutional containment towards community management, is making knowledge and understanding of health and penal institutions relatively uncommon and thus of special importance for the forensic psychiatrist.

In their valuable critical survey of some of the key literature on institutions, Jones and Fowles (1984) noted that sociologists use the term 'institution' in three ways:

1. in reference to generalized social responses, such as marriage and the family;
2. in reference to more specific social responses, for example, the police;
3. to refer to residential establishments.

A key problem with many of the patients presenting to forensic psychiatry is that they have proved incapable of coping with the first category of institution—generally accepted social responses. Society regards this as deviant, particularly when failure to cope involves violent or other criminal activity. Society is scarcely more tolerant if the deviation is exclusively one of mental disorder, and it often seeks to limit the deviance by surrounding each individual concerned with prescribed, even legally enforced institutions of the second and third kinds. This chapter considers the issues that arise for the patient confined to residential institutions.

Parker (1985) has given a good account of the development of secure provision for patients in England and Wales. She identified four elements which make a hospital secure:

1. the physical security, i.e. the architecture, the locks, mechanical constraints;
2. the type and quality of nursing care, i.e. staff ratios, techniques of observation, counselling, and restraint;
3. patient control using medical and psychological treatments;
4. patient motivation which determined the levels and type of 1, 2, and 3 required, noting that motivation fluctuates and can be changed by management.

The history of imprisonment is more complex and is bound up in the history of ideas of punishment and harm (*see*, for example, Heath, 1963). Incarceration is now the worst type of punishment applied to Western Europeans, but still involves elements of transportation and banishment. Other countries such as the USA still kill offenders. No simple account of the history of imprisonment is available, there is instead a vast literature on the development of different aspects of imprisonment. Hinde (1951) provided a useful introduction. McConville (1981) provided a scholarly account of the beginnings of imprisonment in modern England. Williams (1970) gave a useful overview of developments. An illustrated volume is Walker (1972).

The term 'total institution', which is associated with the work of Goffman (1961), deserves comment. Goffman distinguished four key features of the total institution. First, all aspects of life are conducted in the same place and under the same single authority. Second, each phase of the member's daily activity is carried on in the immediate company of a large batch of others, all of whom are treated alike and required to do the same thing together. Third, all phases of the day's activities are tightly scheduled, with one activity leading at a prearranged time into the next, the whole sequence of activities being imposed from above by a system of explicit formal rulings and a body of officials. Finally, the various enforced activities are brought together into a single rational plan purportedly designed to fulfil the official aims of the institution. Goffman stated:

> In total institutions there is a basic split between a large managed group, conveniently called inmates, and a small supervisory staff. Inmates typically live in the institution and have restricted contact with the world outside the walls; staff often operate on an 8-hour day and are socially integrated into the outside world.

Critiques of Hospitals as Institutions

The literature of institutional care can be considered under four broad headings: sociological studies, psychiatric and psychological research, official inquiries and reports, and published narratives.

Goffman's approach in *Asylums* (Goffman, 1961) was ethnographic, and his work was important in articulating the experience and dynamics of the social world of the institution, although the account is a selective and partial one. He spent a year at St Elizabeth's Hospital, Washington DC, which housed at that time some 7000 patients, and functioned almost as a small town. He made observations of patients, noting for example the degree of social withdrawal; he studied institutional ceremonies such as the annual Christmas play, he noted the power structures and, in particular, the need for patients to submit and obey. He was not able to tease out which elements of behaviour were due to mental abnormality and which due to the social structure. His book is sometimes taken as a condemnation of hospital life. It was not that, nor can the experiences of St Elizabeth's be extrapolated to all other mental hospitals of whatever size, however funded. Goffman's somewhat prophetic conclusion is worth citing nevertheless:

> Mental hospitals are not found in our society because supervisors, psychiatrists, and attendants want jobs, mental hospitals are found because there is a market for them. If all the mental hospitals in a given region were emptied and closed down today, tomorrow, relatives, police and judges would raise a clamour for new ones, and these true clients of the mental hospital would demand an institution to satisfy their needs.

Foucault's *Histoire de la Folie*—translated as *Madness and Civilisation* (1967)—was written as a history of 'unreason' (which has a wider meaning than 'madness') from the middle ages until the 19th century. Foucault traced the development of confinement, and he claimed among other things that the asylum was concerned with the inculcation of fear and the imposition of moral judgements. As Jones and Fowles (1984) noted, even though he was more of an image maker than a historian, Foucault's recognition of the fundamental importance of authority and power relations in institutions was an important contribution. Goffman argued that although psychiatrists and nurses try to treat all behaviour as symptomatic of pathology just like physical symptoms and morally neutral, such a position is impossible to sustain. In every other setting, aberrant behaviour is criticized and/or punished—social order depends on it. So such mechanisms also creep into hospital life, and into psychiatric treatment.

Barton (1959) considered that long-stay patients suffered from at least two diseases, the one which triggered their admission and a secondary one, 'institutional neurosis'. He claimed that such a neurosis also occurred in prisoner of war camps, other prisons, orphanages, and tuberculosis sanatoria.* The clinical characteristics of the disorder were apathy, lack of initiative and individuality, loss of interest, submissiveness, inability to plan for the future. Wing (1962) gave further credence to the concept when he studied male patients in two mental hospitals. He found a progressive increase with length of stay in the proportion of patients who appear apathetic about life outside hospital. In the later 'three hospital study' (Wing and Brown, 1970), it was shown that the severity of impairments was closely associated with the degree of environmental understimulation. This study argued for the provision of more stimulating environments in order to avoid much of what Wing

---

* The *Magic Mountain* by Thomas Mann (1924) is an evocative exposition of this concept.

called 'institutionalism'. The major conclusion drawn by Wing and Brown was that:

> A substantial proportion, though by no means all, of the morbidity shown by long-stay schizophrenic patients in mental hospitals is a product of their environment.

Wing has since, however, re-emphasized that the debilitating effects are to do with levels of stimulation rather than being in hospital *per se* (Wing, 1990). Indeed, Brown et al. (1966) found no significant differences in adjustment between a sample of patients returned to the community early and a sample returned late.

The most important critiques of psychiatric hospitals during the last 20 years have been official inquiries, which have often arisen from public allegations of brutality or neglect. They are important for two reasons: first, they have played a part in achieving reform through defining some of the basic determinants of good practice; and second, they have enabled a better understanding of the complex reasons why institutions intended to provide care can allow neglect and inhumanity. It should not be forgotten, however, that:

> Yesterday's 'scandals' of the institution have already been replaced by today's 'scandals' of the community (Rose, 1986).

J. P. Martin (1984) highlighted factors from such reports including geographical isolation of the hospitals and intellectual/professional isolation within them; patients lacking support from people outside; failures to take remedial action locally despite internal knowledge of unsatisfactory standards; failures of leadership and management; severe shortages of staff and resources; inadequacies of training; personal failings; and 'corruption of care', which occurs when—

> the primary aims of care—the cure or alleviation of suffering—have become subordinate to what are essentially secondary aims such as the creation and preservation of order, quiet and cleanliness.

In his general conclusions, Martin noted that failures of care result from complex chains of interconnected events, and inquiries have often had to pay more attention to the context in which care is provided than the individuals involved. The power of a group of workers is of central importance in setting standards. It can be exercised to maintain professional standards in the face of pressures, but it can also operate so as to subvert therapeutic aims, and isolate and discredit justifiable criticism. Beardshaw (1981) set out many of the group pressures which make staff stand together or at least keep silent about poor standards and frank malpractice. There is the fear of not being believed, there is the strong loyalty to an intimate peer group, there is the ignorance/uncertainty that a complaint is justified, there is lack of confidence that, even if proved, the complaint will lead to improvement, and fear that it may lead to reprisals from colleagues.

Accessible channels for complaint are, therefore, important, using both internal complaints procedures and, on occasions, independent external scrutiny.

The needs and training of staff are fundamental when considering preventive and corrective remedies. Martin noted:

> In the last analysis, there is no more effective remedy than staff development.

He pointed out the subtle ways in which staff can deny cruel and inhumane practices by processes of rationalization, such as denial that hurt is experienced; and he quoted Matza's comment in relation to maintaining proper standards of care: 'Norms may be violated without surrendering allegiance to them' (Matza, 1964).

Menzies (1960) attempted to understand psychodynamically the problems faced by nursing staff at a London teaching hospital. The high level of known distress and anxiety among nurses frequently led to withdrawal, with one-third of trainees leaving before completing their training, and high rates of sickness. The anxiety seemed to be precipitated by constant reminders of death, illness and disability, which trigger primitive universal fears. Defences to the anxiety develop, she suggests, as follows: splitting the nurse-patient relationship so that no one relationship becomes very important, depersonalization and denial of the significance of the individual, detachment and denial of feelings, ritual performance of tasks, social redistribution of responsibility and irresponsibility, 'delegation' of responsibility to superiors and avoidance of change.

Legal rights also require some emphasis (Gostin, 1985; Hoggett, 1985). Bean (1985) notes, clinicians are inevitably 'more interested in welfare than legal norms' and tension between therapeutic aims and legal restraints protecting patients' fundamental liberties is as unavoidable as it is necessary (Grounds, 1986). Rose (1985, 1986) has drawn attention to the limitations of 'rights–based strategies', particularly their inability to deliver the social resources and services they promise. Nevertheless, there have been cases in which, for example, alleged breaches of the European Convention of Human Rights have been upheld against the UK, resulting in new safeguards concerning standards of care and reviews of detention (*A v United Kingdom*; *X v United Kingdom*).

Rampton Hospital, England

In May 1979, Yorkshire Television made a film about Rampton special hospital called 'The Secret Hospital' which contained serious allegations of ill-treatment of patients by staff. An enquiry was established which reported a year later (Department of Health & Social Security, 1980). In the report (often known as the Boynton Report), the hospital was described as a backwater. They particularly criticized the hospital for including punitive practices as well as treatment. They found a lack of professional leadership, and leadership instead by a trade union, the Prison Officers' Association. They noted a very poor quality of life for patients. The *Lancet* (1980) said:

> The description of the patient's day is particularly chilling. On the male block wards patients spend eleven hours locked in their rooms with no personal belongings, not even a radio. At about 8.00 a.m. they are woken, their beds are stripped and searched, and they proceed in a single file to the sluice with their chamber-pots. They then collect a set of day clothes from a store and change in the main corridor, under observation, handing their night clothes into the store . . . meals are eaten in silence. At lunchtime patients are allowed to watch television, but anyone wishing to smoke has to leave the lounge to light his cigarette on a wall lighter in the corridor. Having lit his cigarette the patient waits on the threshold of the room and says 'Please may I come in Sir?'.

The Boynton Committee made 205 recommendations, including the setting-up of a body to inspect and monitor all institutions holding detained patients, a reduction in the number of patients at Rampton, properly designed individual treatment programmes for each patient, and management by a hospital management team consisting of a medical director, a chief nursing officer and an administrator. *See also* pp. 658, 697.

The *Lancet* (1980) was critical of the recommendations suggesting that they were 'bland' and that the review body had missed an opportunity to close an awful hospital, had failed to look behind the problems, and had not examined the American experience, which suggested that the only really effective way of improving big old hospitals is to provide them with academic linkages (Knesper, 1978).

Broadmoor Hospital, England

Soon after the Rampton scandal its sister hospital in Berkshire had its own problems. On 6 July 1984, Mr Michael Martin, a patient at Broadmoor, was found dead in his room. The following October an inquest returned a verdict of 'accidental death aggravated by lack of care'. Two months later the Minister of Health appointed Miss Shirley Ritchie QC to enquire into the death of Mr Martin. He died because he aspirated his vomit (mainly confectionery). She concluded that, when he was agitated, he was man-handled incorrectly, that he should not have been given '5 & 2' following a lot of food and without medical authority (5 & 2 is 500 mg sodium amytal and 200 mg promazine intramuscularly), and that he should have been monitored in seclusion more effectively. She recommended that more staff were needed in the special care unit, proper training in control and restraint should be given, heavy sedatives should only be prescribed by doctors, and heavily sedated patients should be constantly observed (Ritchie, 1985). Ministers thanked Miss Ritchie and accepted her recommendations apart from the one suggesting that only doctors should prescribe heavy sedatives. They argued that writing advance prescriptions to be given at the discretion of nurses 'is regarded professionally as an acceptable clinical practice'. This point raised eyebrows in the House of Commons and caused an adjournment debate (House of Commons, 1986b). The Department of Health stuck to its guns saying that psychiatrists and nurses agreed with its position.

A wide-ranging evaluation of Broadmoor Hospital was conducted by the Health Advisory Service in 1988 (National Health Service Health Advisory Service DHSS Social Services Inspectorate 1988), the second such review. The report was very critical but, unlike the Rampton enquiry, just described, the report was the product of a routine HAS visit and not produced in the wake of a crisis. The visitors noted the—

> surface characteristics of a penal institution: high external walls, barred windows, uniformed staff, security practices and keys worn openly everywhere.

They noted two main treatment methods, psychotropic medication and milieu therapy (undefined), but no evaluation of the efficacy of these treatments. They further noted that the usual collaborative approach between patient and therapist was missing, and they commented adversely on the strict segregation of male and female patients, apart from occasional recreational activities.* A further criticism was the long periods of seclusion suffered by some patients to the point where 'some patients become psychologically dependent upon seclusion'. Few aspects of the hospitals escaped attack, e.g:

> Credible leadership is not obvious. Organizational philosophy and style are not shared. Most management activity is conducted at too high a level.

Even the Mental Health Act Commission came under fire for listing too many minor matters as:

> This can distract attention and impact from the major issues.

The report advised, among other things, more effective management including the appointment of a general manager, a restriction on size, managers for every ward, an integrated patient day, the establishment of a predischarge hostel, greater integration of male and female patients, educational opportunities for understanding the issues concerning sexuality in institutions, the monitoring of control and restraint procedures, minimal use of seclusion, outsiders to advise on patient care, the employment of one or two occupational therapists, a complaints procedure, additional consultants, and nurse promotion based on qualifications and merit rather than experience.

A major management reorganization took place in 1989 (*see* pp. 696–707).

Oak Ridge, Penetanguishene, Ontario, Canada

Ontario has one maximum security hospital. It was constructed, in the 1930s, to be rather like a prison. The hospital became famous in the 1960s

---

* Dickens (1868) described the social life in such an institution, the Boston State Hospital, in his American Notes.

and '70s because of its 'social therapy program'. This was a brave attempt to get round the severe shortage of staff at the hospital, and to include a therapeutic community. There were four wards in a hierarchy. On the admission ward, new patients studied papers on groups and interpersonal interaction. Study groups were run by 'patient-teachers' (i.e. patients who had graduated to this special status). The next ward was run by patient committees and emphasized personal responsibility. Ward 3 included a 'total encounter capsule' in which patients were placed for hours, sometimes days at a time; they were monitored by television in case violence boke out, otherwise they had no connection with the outside world, apart from meals which were passed in at regular intervals. The fourth ward was the privileged area and included work programmes and freedom of movement. Psychotic patients were not usually given anti-psychotic medication, but various psychoactive drugs were used on selected 'volunteer' patients as psychotherapy adjuncts. These included LSD, scopolamine, amphetamine, and alcohol. One of us watched, on one occasion, a patient being given scopolamine until he was delirious. He was then nursed back to normal health by other patients. The rationale for this was explained as regression to infancy followed by more loving parenting than he had previously received. His offences were mainly persistent thefts of money from his mother.

In 1976, the Office of the Ontario Ombudsman enquired into this programme and reported on it favourably (*see* Hucker et al., 1986), but in 1978 there was a lock-out of professional staff by attendants. In 1982 two patients made complaints alleging that the Social Adaptation Treatment Program infringed their personal rights and freedoms. The allegations were investigated the following year by a forensic psychiatrist at the request of the Ministry of Health. A full enquiry under the chairmanship of Dr Stephen Hucker was established the following year. This account draws heavily on this unpublished report.

The Hucker Report was very critical of the hospital and made 89 recommendations. Its most radical suggestion was that Oak Ridge should be closed and replaced by two smaller units, one near the same site at Penetanguishene and one 'near a large urban centre' (i.e. Toronto). The list of other recommendations included abandoning the role of 'attendants' and employing more nurses instead, increasing the number of staff, much greater emphasis to be placed on education, improvement of occupation therapy facilities, behaviour therapy programmes to be individually tailored, seclusion to be limited to 24 hours unless agreed by the medical director, more female staff to be employed, no excessive deprivation of the basic necessities of civilized life, psychological tests to be administered by psychologists, the silence rule to be rescinded, the cuffing of patients to be discontinued, water supplies to patients' rooms to be interrupted only in exceptional circumstances which are clearly documented, clear policies to be developed for the use of electroconvulsive therapy, the number of trained forensic psychiatrists to be increased, ward supervisors to be registered nurses, the use of patient-teachers to be restricted and always to be supervised by staff, the development of a formal seclusion policy, conjugal visits to be allowed for suitable patients, and patients to be allowed greater access to pay phones.

This selection of adverse reports is given to illustrate the generality of problems faced by big security hospitals. Questions about leadership, the number and training of staff, policies for seclusion, the management of violence, monitoring the quality of life for patients, individual patient care plans, complaints procedures, are common to all. It is strange that few critics focus on the issue of academic linkages. Knesper (1978) showed that the quality and quantity of recruitment to large mental hospitals is improved by such linkages. These linkages would also provide training, continuing evaluation, a steady flow of outside visitors, and, above all, continuous informed debate.

Critiques of Prisons as Institutions

There is a tradition of sociological research in prisons. Morris and Morris (1963), for example, studied the culture of Pentonville prison, and Cohen and Taylor (1981) attempted to work alongside a group of prisoners in order to study their subjective experience of long-term imprisonment. Priestley's *Jail Journeys* (1989) is a harrowing anthology of English prison life during this century, and Parker's *The Frying Pan* (1970) is another celebrated set of narratives about Grendon Prison. Recent analyses of the prison system in Britain have been produced by Rutherford (1986b) and Stern (1989), and of the medical care for prisoners by Smith (1984). The work of the Prison Medical Service was examined by the House of Commons (1986c) Social Services Select Committee.

The prison population in England and Wales had been expanding until the end of the 1980s. Efforts to reduce overcrowding by a new prison building programme failed, and many prisoners continue to endure squalid conditions. The rise in prison population would seem to be an obvious potential cause of morbidity. D'Atri et al. (1981) have shown that prisoners' blood pressure levels and death rates are related to spatial density. Major prison expansion has also occurred in the USA and several other Western European countries. Rutherford (1986b) argued:

> The crucial factor in understanding changes in prison population is less the level of recorded crime or known offenders but, more significant, the responses to crime by officials engaged throughout the criminal justice process.

He urged the need for a coordinated policy to reduce the prison population and suggests reducing the capacity of the prison system, enacting legally enforceable minimum standards for prison conditions, introducing new early release mechanisms, and widening the range of non-imprisonable offences.

Stern (1989) analysed the late 20th century crisis in British prisons. In 1987, the UK locked up proportionately more members of its population than any other European country except Turkey and Austria, some 95 people per 100 000. If Scotland and Northern Ireland were considered separately, they topped the European league at 106 and 119 per 100 000 respectively.

The Home Office (Barclay et al., 1991) pointed out, however, that international comparisons are difficult because crime rates are so variable between countries. They maintain that part of the explanation of the high British lock-up rate is the high level of criminal behaviour in Britain. In 1985, England and Wales had a lower prison population per 100 000 recorded crimes than Greece, Germany, Austria, or Italy at about 1500 prisoners/100 000 recorded crimes. The rate for the USA is estimated to have been about 5000 prisoners/100 000 recorded crimes in the same year.

Stern emphasized that the conditions for both the 29 000 prison staff and 50 000 inmates would be improved if staff needs were met by an improved working environment. She also recommended dividing each prison into smaller self-contained units. She quoted the Control Review Committee (Home Office, 1984a):

> Prisons cannot be run by coercion . . . it is most important that both staff and inmates should feel that they are getting a fair deal, and that all who live and work in a prison should have a stake in perceiving its orderly management . . . prisons function on humane personal relations between staff and inmates.

Her main recommendations were that a national penal policy should be developed, the building of prisons in out of the way places should be stopped, old city prisons should be refurbished, a code of minimum standards for prisoners should be established, prison officers should have more extensive training, and prison rules should become legally enforceable.

The expanding prison population has been associated with a growth in the number of long-term prisoners. Since the passing of the Homicide Act 1957, the population of life sentence prisoners in England and Wales increased from 140 in 1957 to over 2500 in 1990. There is evidence that the prevalence of mental disorder amongst life-sentenced prisoners is high (Taylor, 1986).

The very limited amount of research that has been carried out on the psychological effects of long-term imprisonment generally suggests that the disruption of social relationships experienced by prisoners is a more significant problem than objective psychological deterioration (*see*, for example, Walker, 1987). Sapsford (1978) studied men serving sentences for homicide offences in a maximum security prison, and found evidence for an increase in introversion and a tendency for some men to become more dependent on routine and staff support as the sentence progressed. Outside social contacts diminished considerably, and wives and girlfriends had nearly all lost contact with the men by the end of the fifth year of sentence. Over half had no contact at all after conviction except to serve divorce papers. Bolton et al. (1976) who have conducted the longest follow-up study of prisoners available

(19 months) showed there was no evidence of psychological deterioration over this period and there was even improvement on some measures! Richards (1978) found that long-term prisoners tended to rate deprivation of outside relationships as a more severe source of psychological stress than the privations of prison life. The fears of a particular group of long-term prisoners in a maximum security wing and their strategies for 'psychological survival' were described in more detail by Cohen and Taylor (1981). Coker and Martin (1985) also noted that, whilst long-term prisoners may fear psychological deterioration, such deterioration is unlikely, although their contacts with the outside world may be lost. Coker and Martin noted:

> Considerable personal resources are needed to cope with institutional regimes whose destructiveness may lie more in their power to isolate than injure, for men are cut off from their families and the community.

The consequences of imprisonment for the children were studied by Shaw (1987) who estimated that the number of children affected by the imprisonment of their fathers may be at least 100 000 annually in England and Wales. He painted a picture of the extensive suffering inflicted on families as a hidden consequence of imprisoning offenders.

Problems Arising in Institutions

Violence and its control in an institution depend on an interplay between the nature of the individuals in the institution and the nature of the institution itself. Hospitals have some choice over admitting violent individuals, prisons do not. For both sorts of institution, the incidence of violence is much higher on reception than later on.

It is unclear whether those who commit violence in the institutional setting are generally the same people who engage in this behaviour outside the institution or whether they form a subgroup of people who are provoked by the institutional setting. Longitudinal studies are required.

In a US Veterans Administration hospital, Rofman et al. (1980) studied the records of all 59 compulsory, emergency admissions over the 12 months from January 1977, which had arisen following physical harm. They compared them with 59 records of admissions for other reasons. During the first 10 days only was there a difference between the groups in inpatient violence, 24 of the first group carrying out 39 acts and 5 controls carring out 8. Further analysis suggested that actual preadmission violence did not predict inpatient violence. Among the compulsorily admitted patients, 13 (43%) of those who had previously been violent continued to be so in hospital, while 9 (39%) of those merely threatening carried out a violent act as an inpatient. Over a similar time scale, Werner et al. (1983) found a low correlation (0.3) between preadmission and inpatient violence among 40 male patients, significantly lower than physicians had predicted. Krakowski et al. (1988) followed 44 psychotic patients admitted to a special unit for which the criteria for admission included two acts of violence within the previous month which had failed to respond to 'standard interventions'. Violence was recorded by observation and reduced to negligible levels over the 8 weeks of the study. The reduction was significantly correlated initially with reduction in symptomatology and later with improvement in social functioning.

An evaluation of the progress of over 300 patients in English special hospitals and regional secure units (Roscoe, 1988) suggested that the strongest association between preadmission and inpatient problems is the *number* of behavioural problems, but in general, the behaviour prior to admission seemed to bear only a limited relationship to the behaviour in hospital.

Violence in Hospitals

Almost all that is known about violence amongst patients presenting for psychiatric hospital admission comes from American studies. Lagos et al. (1977) randomly selected the records of 400 patients admitted to hospitals in New Jersey in 1974. Twenty per cent of the sample had been physically violent towards persons or objects, and another 11% were described as 'acting violently'. Among 321 patients with mental illness, 18% had merely threatened violence, but 18% had been physically violent, most against people rather than property. Tardiff and Sweillam (1980) examined records of 9365 patients admitted to public hospitals in New York State, and found 10% had shown violence against others and 11% exclusively self-inflicted violence. Among clinical characteristics, the primary diagnosis was the most important correlate of violence prior to admission. Patients with alcoholism or drug dependency were less likely to present assaultive or suicidal problems, but those with schizophrenia had the highest rates.

In England, Johnstone et al. (1986) studied 253 people presenting with a first episode of schizophrenia between August 1979 and December 1981. The police had been involved in the events leading to admission in 22% of cases. When the patients' histories of disturbed behaviour were examined in more detail, 13% had shown behaviour potentially threatening to the lives of others at least once or twice, and a further 6% repeatedly so.

This English sample was not strictly comparable with the American one, but it raises the question as to whether the increasing trend towards avoiding hospital admission for the mentally disordered has been associated with an increase in the violence of patients who do present for admission. In 1978, Sosowsky reported on the follow-up of 301 patients, all but 16 of whom had been admitted to Californian state mental hospitals from one county in 1972/3. He found that arrest rates for violence involving bodily harm had more than tripled following the liberalization of health care provision. Steadman

(1985) conducted a study over a wider base: 6273 mental patients and prisoners in six states of the USA. He found substantial differences between the admission samples of 1968 and of 1978, again across the 'liberalization divide'. Former mental hospital patients were being imprisoned more frequently, although there was little evidence that mental hospital bed closure was a significant factor in the increase in the prison populations during that time. Those admitted to mental hospitals in 1978 were much more likely to have been involved with the criminal justice system than in 1968. Furthermore, there was an increase in the proportion of violent offending.

Most research on violence within psychiatric hospitals has been based on analyses of official violent incident forms, which can be unreliable. Lion et al. (1981), in a Maryland state hospital of 1500 beds, showed a wide discrepancy between levels of assaults noted in the daily ward records and those formally reported within the hospital system, a situation which may also occur elsewhere. In one year there were 203 official reports of violence, but five times as many (1108) were noted in ward records. Nevertheless, the characteristics of assaultive people in hospital, reported by whatever means, showed remarkable consistency; a small number of patients accounted for a large number of assaults and admission units were particularly vulnerable. A further important finding was that although up to half of the staff on one admission unit had been assaulted, 14% became victims on three or more occasions.

Tardiff (1983b) studied 5164 patients, resident for at least 3 months in 1979 in the adult general psychiatric wards of two large New York state hospitals. A team of trained investigators, drawn from hospital staff, interviewed patients and relevant staff on any wards except those where they usually worked. Important differences emerged between the characteristics of Tardiff's assaultive inpatient group and his admission group, described above (Tardiff and Sweillam, 1980). The predominance of males in the admission sample was not apparent in the inpatient series. This compares with Fottrell's (1980) English study of hospital inpatients, among whom assaults by women were more common than assaults by men. In Tardiff's inpatient sample, in contrast to the admission sample, non-paranoid schizophrenia, mental retardation and seizure disorders were all associated with higher assault rates, but paranoid schizophrenia with a lower assault rate. People with organic brain syndromes associated with psychosis were prominent in both. These findings raised a number of questions. Is institutional separation from the usual social milieu particularly helpful for people with paranoid schizophrenia and particularly oppressive for those with non-paranoid schizophrenia? Are organic brain syndromes particularly resistant to treatment of any kind? There was extensive use of neuroleptic medication in the inpatient sample. Did this contribute to the association between assaultiveness and seizure disorder amongst the inpatients? Does institutional residence affect self-image?

Fottrell's (1980) study in England, which depended heavily on staff recording of violent incidents, found that most incidents were petty, and a small group of patients accounted for the majority. Although patient turnover figures are not given, it is perhaps of interest that in the two mental hospitals with similar bed numbers, the one admitting from an urban area had many more violent incidents (353 in 12 months) than the one with a rural catchment area (54 in 4 months).

In contrast to the situation in prisons described by Davies (1982) and in the RAG report (Research and Advisory Group on the Long Term Prison System, 1987), Fottrell's work suggested that, in hospitals, staff are generally the most likely people to be victims of assault. Lion at al. (1981) noted that most assaults took place when patients were being restrained. Are staff in hospitals more interventionist than prison staff? Rix and Seymour (1988) studied a secure unit with relatively high staffing levels and high intensity therapeutic programmes throughout the day, and found that violent incidents were evenly distributed throughout the period 7.00 a.m.–11.00 p.m., and were especially directed at the staff in most contact with the patients. Other hospital studies have shown a peak occurrence in the early morning, coinciding with peak demands by staff on patients. In this regard, it may be of interest that in an American study of assaults in a maximum security hospital (Dietz and Rada, 1982), the ratio between patient and staff victims was much closer to figures cited for prisons. In this hospital, correctional officers far outnumbered nurses and other health care professionals, and were the most likely victims.

Though the risks of physical violence in penal institutions and hospitals are not insignificant, only a few incidents result in serious harm. Ekblom (1970) has calculated the real risks from psychiatric inpatients, allowing for length of exposure. In all the psychiatric hospitals in Sweden over the 10 years between 1955 and 1964, there were just 17 cases of serious injury resulting from assaults, and 8 deaths. On this basis, the risk of death for members of staff was one in 250 million working hours, and for other patients, one in 350 million inpatient hours. This study was conducted before 1970 and only dealt with the most serious forms of violence. Has the risk of institutional violence increased? English prison statistics suggest a rise in the absolute numbers of assaults during the 1980s, but that was a period when the prison population rose and the yearly *rates* for assaults showed little fluctuation. Figures for the British health service are less clear. Certainly the risks are not confined to psychiatric hospitals and prison staff. In a survey carried out in 1985 for the Health and Safety Commission (Health Services Advisory Committee, 1987) on a 0.5% sample of the one million employees of the National Health Service in a wide range of posts, about one-third had experienced significant abuse by patients or their associates. Nearly 5% had been threatened with a weapon, 11% had sustained minor injuries and 0.5% serious injuries. These rates are much higher than the rates of either serious assaults (1 in 5300 for males and 1 in 2500 for females) or more minor assaults (1 in 310 and 1 in 880 respectively) reported to police by the general public (Walmsley, 1986).

The most disturbing problem is that too little is known about the 'assaulter-environment' combination which poses the greatest risk. English and American prison studies differ in the role they attribute to crowding in institutions. Dietz and Rada (1982) showed that social density (the level of patient-to-patient interaction) was a more important trigger to violence than physical density (the square footage of space available per patient). Some settings, where social density is high but structured, however, such as the psychiatric prison at Grendon, seem to be associated with less violence than more conventional prisons, where the physical density is relatively high, but the social densities relatively low.

On the individual level, not only violence history but also psychiatric disorder consistently emerge as risk factors. In hospital and some prison samples, psychosis seems to carry the greatest risk, and furthermore, staff regard violence from this group as largely unpredictable. In one study of women in a locked intensive care ward (Cooper et al., 1983), only 3% of the incidents were said to have been predictable; and even in a maximum security setting, where presumably staff were highly trained to anticipate violence, only 77% of the 221 batterings were predicted (Dietz and Rada, 1982). Davies (1982) claimed that systems developed in English prisons to predict unrest and riot (e.g. Zeeman et al., 1976) have proved highly reliable, but nevertheless have not enabled preventive action. This would not be surprising at a time when a crisis is imminent. Grendon prison (Gunn et al., 1978) and the Special Unit at Barlinnie prison (Cooke, 1989) stand as testimony that things can be done to minimize violence in institutions. The RAG report (*see* above) described imaginative developments for the future which borrow from these more positive experiences.

All organizations that deal with seriously disordered people need to be prepared for physical violence. Policies appropriate to each setting whether it be the outpatient department, the ward, the corridors, or the home, should be developed. Managers of health authorities, hospitals, prisons, should all develop policies for handling violent people (*see* e.g., Gunn, 1986b).

Violence in Prisons

Davies (1982) provided a review of the nature, frequency and aetiology of violence in prison. His own research studied day-to-day violence in Birmingham Prison, between July 1977 and June 1979, and demonstrated the difficulties of establishing a true figure. The number of deliberate injuries reported by prison hospital staff did not match numbers of disciplinary reports. Nevertheless, both systems of recording showed similar patterns, for example, with violence virtually ceasing during the night. About two-thirds of incidents were between inmates only. Tension between cell mates and 'odd' behaviour (i.e. which needed observation in the prison hospital) together accounted for 38% of the violence on disciplinary reports for which a cause was established.

Other studies are more definite about the role of psychiatric disorder in precipitating violence. Bach-y-Rita and Veno (1974), studied 62 men in a special unit for the habitually violent in a Californian prison. By prison policy, psychotic men were excluded, but research interviews revealed that about a third of these inmates had psychotic symptoms, and that at least 13 had paranoid schizophrenia.

The RAG report (above) noted that 22% of the 'difficult', mainly violent, prisoners in England and Wales had a previous psychiatric history, compared with 9% of others. The 'difficult' also had twice the rate of self-injury. Fifty-two per cent were serving life sentences, nearly twice the proportion in the other group. Other studies of English lifers give some indication of the relative importance of different types of disorder. Sapsford (1983) noted that the majority have some neurotic complaints; estimates of psychosis range from 10% (Taylor, 1986) to 20% (Heather, 1977), while at least one-third have a personality disorder (Taylor, 1986). In the latter series, those with personality disorder were significantly more likely than the other lifers to have been violent during the custodial part of their sentence.

Elements of the prison environment, especially overcrowding, are often cited as precipitants of violence. However, Davies (1982) described a period of industrial action within the English prison service, when the Birmingham prison population fell from about 1000 to 600. During this time, he found no reduction in measures of prisoners' unrest. At the higher residence figures, there were 2–3 prisoners in most cells and 50 prisoners per toilet recess. Speed (1973) showed that the incidence of recorded violence in some English prisons fell during one phase of *increasing* population. She suggested that the consequent reduction of isolation in cells was the principal mediator of improvement.

The picture in Britain is complex and always changing. Woolf and Tumin (1991) reported on 'the worst series of prison riots in the history of the British penal system'. They occurred during the first 25 days of April 1990 and involved prisons at Manchester, Glen Parva, Dartmoor, Cardiff, Bristol and Pucklechurch. The worst riot was at Manchester. Manchester (Strangeways) was the largest prison in England and Wales. It was a local prison. It was built in 1868 with radial design having a central rotunda and six radiating wings. At the time of the riot, it was grossly overcrowded. Its 'certified normal accommodation' was for 970 men, but it contained 1647 men. Woolf and Tumin described the living conditions as 'insanitary and degrading'.

The inquiry opined that the riots could not be dismissed as one-off events, or as local disasters, or a run of bad luck. They thought that the riots were symptomatic of serious underlying difficulties in the prison system. The

Woolf Report (as it has come to be known) made twelve 'central recommendations':

1. closer cooperation between the different parts of the criminal justice system and a national forum should be established;
2. more visible leadership of the Prison Service by a director general;
3. increased delegation of responsibility to governors of establishments;
4. an enhanced role for prison officers;
5. a 'compact' or 'contract' for each prisoner;
6. a national system of accredited standards;
7. a new prison rule that no establishment should hold more prisoners than is provided for in its certified normal level of accommodation;
8. access to sanitation for all inmates;
9. more visits and home leaves and location in community prisons as near to the prisoner's home as possible;
10. a division of prison establishments into small secure units;
11. a separate statement of purpose and separate conditions for remand prisoners;
12. improved standards of justice within prisons involving the giving of reasons to a prisoner for any decision which materially affects him.

It is not clear how large a part mentally disordered prisoners played in the riots. It is clear, however, from the Woolf Report that at Manchester they had some significance. In the week preceding the riot, the governor was asking for a psychologist to advise him how to manage his population. The Chief Probation Officer for Manchester said that he regarded the mix of prisoners as 'highly inappropriate'. He said the mix included mentally disordered offenders (some of whom at times had experienced psychotic episodes), sex offenders, remand prisoners, and 'volatile and disturbed' lifers.

The report noted the importance of trying to divert mentally disordered people away from the prison system, whilst acknowledging that—

> there will remain for the foreseeable future, a significant problem for the Prison Service in accommodating mentally disordered offenders.

The Report paid special attention to those who under English Prison Rule 43 are segregated for their own protection, either in separate cells where they remain without release for long periods or in vulnerable prisoner units. Such prisoners are usually sex offenders. Intense victimization of sex offenders by other prisoners is the norm in British prisons. It also occurs in the USA and Canada, but the only continental European country in which it occurs is France. The enquiry commented that sex offenders are absorbed successfully into the prison community at Grendon prison. At the time of the riots, some 8% of English prisoners were held in segregation under Rule 43, or its young prisoners equivalent Rule 46, the growth in numbers of such prisoners being substantially faster than the growth in the overall prison population. Woolf and Tumin accepted that sex offenders need protection, but regarded Rule 43 as inappropriate. They recommended a new prison rule which would ensure protection for the sex offender and yet provide association and a regime equivalent to that of other prisoners (as happens in some vulnerable prisoner units). They also endorsed the proposal from the Institute of Psychiatry (Department of Forensic Psychiatry, 1992) that the Prison Department should build a second Grendon, and went further in suggesting that Grendon prison could be used as a training ground for prisoner management.

A final focus on mentally disordered prisoners in the Woolf Report was on drug abusers. They noted the high prevalence of drug abuse (Gunn et al., 1991b) and endorsed the proposals in that Institute of Psychiatry report, particularly the need for specialized training for all prison staff, greater efforts to coordinate and improve practice, standard opiate withdrawal regimes similar to those offered at Holloway prison, therapeutic community treatment for drug abusers and alcohol abusers, based preferably on the Grendon model, liaison with treatment agencies in the community, and the appointment of an individual responsible for coordinating the services available to drug abusers.

Although evidence arising from the effects of unplanned changes to the prison environment is mixed, and inferences cannot be generalized in view of the heterogeneity of the populations concerned, evidence that planned changes can be beneficial is provided by an English study. Men consecutively received into two prisons, Grendon (107 men) and Wormwood Scrubs (35) were compared (Gunn et al., 1978). One-third of each group had previously endangered the life of another, and 60% of each had been involved in some kind of violence. Of Grendon's men, 27 were transferred away from the prison prematurely, but only three for involvement in violence. Researchers, independent of the prison system, asked the prisoners about their violence. Of the Grendon men interviewed, 5% said that they had been involved in fighting in the prison, in contrast to 26% of the Wormwood Scrubs men, a significant difference. The Grendon men were managed in a therapeutic community, whereas the Wormwood Scrubs prisoners were in ordinary location receiving psychotherapy—usually weekly.

Suicide in Hospitals

Every year over 100 people in England and Wales intentionally kill themselves while they are inpatients in a psychiatric hospital (Crammer, 1983). They represent about 5% of all suicides. Other studies (Copas and Robin, 1982; Evanson at al., 1982) have indicated that there are particular factors associated with increased risk. Among these are a diagnosis of major affective disorder, being male, and the first week of admission. Inpatients with a diagnosis of affective illness who kill themselves may have a history of previous attempts, but Roy (1985) commented that there is little evidence that this is the case in schizophrenia.

The psychiatric inpatient suicide rate in England is approximately five times that of the general population. During the first week in hospital, the rate of suicide is between 15 and 60 times greater than that for comparable sex and age groups in the general population (Copas and Robin, 1982; Fernando and Storm, 1984). Evanson's study (1982) in the USA indicated that a history of inpatient treatment increased the risk of suicide to a greater degree for women than men.

Because the drive to commit suicide is often state dependent—in that it varies with such factors as the severity of illness and exposure to psychosocial stresses—it is probably more useful to look at periods of increased vulnerability rather than to attempt relating risk to individual factors such as sex, age and diagnosis. A patient's desire to kill himself is rarely consistent over a long period of time. Sometimes a patient's suicidal urge may be directed to specific methods, and if these happen to be available then the risk is increased.

In assessing the risk of suicide amongst psychiatric inpatients, certain indicators of increased risk have been noted (Morgan and Priest, 1984). Patients may communicate the idea, often covertly, but sometimes overtly to the extent of saying how they will carry out the act. Patients may show ambivalence towards committing suicide, and this may be reflected in assurances that they feel better, which are not intended to deceive. Temporary improvement within the supportive atmosphere of a hospital ward, with a decreased desire to die, may be misleading for assessing longer-term risk. Goh et al., (1989) noted that half of their series of hospital suicides were thought to be improving at the time of death. Though depression is associated with inward aggression, Morgan and Priest (1984) noted that a number of patients who committed suicide had been aggressive towards others. This may reflect a process of 'malignant alienation' whereby depressed patients provoke rejection and a loss of support from staff and from their family. This alienation accelerates as the patient proceeds towards the fatal act.

In looking at suicide amongst hospital inpatients, it is necessary not only to examine risk factors pertaining to the patient, but also to examine factors within the structure and staffing of the ward environment that may be relevant (Crammer, 1984). Over half of inpatient suicides occur when patients are outside the hospital, either on leave at home, or having absconded. Though suicide within hospital is uncommon, nevertheless, when it occurs, it produces great guilt in the medical and nursing staff caring for the patient. Crammer (1984) suggested two features of ward atmosphere which might decrease suicidal drive in patients. First, a calm routine, and staff who are themselves calm and unruffled, may have a settling effect on a distressed patient. Second, a patient's personal relationships with others on the ward may be important.

A further factor which may exacerbate a pre-existing risk is poor design of a ward, hampering unobtrusive observation. Inadequate staffing, especially when staff are inexperienced or do not know the patients on a ward, contribute to low morale. Langley and Bayatti (1984) in a study of patient suicides in an English hospital over a 10-year period found that a disproportionate number of the deaths occurred when the principal consultant was on leave, and the authors supported Coser's (1979) suggestion that the destruction of social systems (in this case within the hospital) promoted suicide. Petrie et al. (1988) noted that helplessness and poor self esteem were the best predictors of repeated suicidal behaviour. As well as noting factors in the patients' backgrounds combined with acute stresses, they commented on the additional factors of suggestibility (e.g., media, peer group) and availability of a suitable method.

With the increasing trend towards the management of more vulnerable and disturbed patients in the community, plans for the discharge or rehabilitation of long-stay patients may disrupt long-established routines and social systems. The ensuing uncertainty and lack of support may lead to a situation of helplessness and despair, following on to suicide. Suicide occurring in psychiatric patients, both in- and outpatients, is likely to have increasing medico-legal ramifications in terms of issues relating to the responsibility of hospitals and their staff to protect the patient from the consequences of his own actions (Brown et al., 1986).

Suicide in Prisons

The suicide rate in prisons in England and Wales rose in the late 1980s to approximately 90–100 per 100 000 of the average daily population (Her Majesty's Chief Inspector of Prisons for England and Wales, 1990). This is about eight times greater than the rate for males in the general population, which in 1984 was 11.8 per 100 000 (McClure, 1987). In the USA, although the suicide rate (for males) in state and federal prisons is only about 1½ times that in the general population (Lester, 1982), the rate in local jails is 16 times greater than in the general population (Hayes, 1983). It has been commented upon that local jails in the USA (which serve as a short-term or remand facility) test the suicide potential of a suicide-prone group and so tend to filter out from the prison system those who are most prone to commit suicide (Stone, 1984). Reports from other countries (Burtch, 1979; Tournier, 1983) appear to indicate that the suicide rate in English prisons lies at the lower end of the international range.

A number of studies (Faulk, 1976; Gunn et al., 1978; Topp, 1979; Home Office, 1986c; Dooley, 1990) indicate that the prison population has an excess of known risk factors for suicide. Prisoners are more often male, single, have a history of psychiatric illness or alcohol abuse, and are in an acute state of uncertainty regarding the future (if on remand) with the consequent disruption of social ties. Therefore, it is not surprising that the prison suicide rate is greater than that of the general population. Nevertheless, in committing an offender to prison, the onus of care is placed on the prison authorities, and, regardless of the possible cause, the fact that suicide occurs more frequently in prison compared to the general population is a source of serious concern (Home Office 1986c; Her Majesty's Chief Inspector of Prisons, 1984, 1990; Smith, 1991).

What features are particular to suicide in prison? The fact that suicide in prison predominantly involves males in younger age groups reflects the nature of the population, though prison suicides are significantly older than the mean age of prisoners (Dooley, 1990). It may be that females are underrepresented, though in view of the small proportion of females in the prison population this is difficult to assess. Successful suicides tend to have a more frequent history of psychiatric treatment, both in prison and on the outside. Alcohol abuse is more prevalent among prison suicides compared to the general prison population, as is a history of previous suicide attempts. Compared to other prisoners, those committing suicide are more likely to be single, though less likely to be divorced, separated, or widowed (Home Office, 1978c). With regard to stage of custody, suicide is up to four times more likely in prisoners who are on remand or who have been recently sentenced compared to the prison population as a whole. Indeed, the proportion of suicides who are unconvicted or unsentenced is increasing (Her Majesty's Chief Inspector of Prisons for England and Wales, 1990). Phillips (1986) in a study of a remand population found that those charged with crimes of violence had an increased rate of suicide, a finding confirmed by Dooley (1990). Burtch (1979), however, in his study of a Canadian penitentiary population found no association between violent crime and suicide. English prisoners serving a life sentence also have a greatly increased risk compared to the general prison population.

Approximately 90% of suicides in prison in England occur by hanging, as this is the most ready and efficient method available. Prison suicide occurs more commonly between midnight and 8.00 a.m. (Dooley, 1990). Almost all suicides occur in a single room or cell.

Due to its relative rarity, the accurate prediction of suicide in a particular individual is dogged by the problems of false-positive and false-negative prediction. It is likely that efforts to improve the training of staff and the regimes within prisons will have more effect than trying to identify particular individuals who will commit suicide (Correctional Service of Canada, 1981; Home Office, 1986c; Her Majesty's Chief Inspector of Prisons for England and Wales, 1990). A report from the USA (Charle, 1981) identified five requirements for a successful prison suicide prevention programme:

1. proper training of officers and staff to recognize and respond to potentially suicidal inmates;
2. the creation of systems within the prison that identify inmates needing special attention;

3. medical and psychological programmes that allow the staff to have quick and easy access to their patients;
4. interior gaol design that does not lend itself to easy suicides;
5. formal investigation of all suicides—not only to make staff accountable for lapses, but also to provide support and a forum to identify flaws in the system.

More recently, an enquiry by Her Majesty's Chief Inspector of Prisons for England and Wales (1990) recommended a whole series of steps designed to reduce the number of suicides, and suggested that the main responsibility for individual prevention should be shouldered by prison medical officers. The inspectorate believed that the main role of non-medical staff is to refer potentially suicidal patients to the prison doctor, and that hospital officers should have a special role in identifying those with mental disorder, drug abuse, alcoholism, and suicide risk. The kind of things non-medical staff should look for include substantial changes in behaviour, changes in mood (including rapid improvements in mood), and refusal of food. Preventive measures could include location in a special place (hospital dormitories being best) special 15-minute watches, restriction of work and/or tools, referral to an outside psychiatrist, referral to the chaplain or probation officer, the provision of medication and/or psychotherapy. As the inspectorate put it, however:

> The visits we made to penal establishments revealed that most prison staff have had very little education or training in the subject of suicide. . . . If hospital officers are to be assigned the task of screening receptions for suicide risk . . . they . . . must be given adequate training.

In 1984, the English Home Office issued new guidelines for the prevention of suicide (circular Instruction No. 20/1989). On reception, an inmate has to be assessed by a hospital officer and a doctor to determine his/her level of suicide risk. This is to be done partly by filling in a questionnaire which asks about previous suicidal behaviour, previous psychiatric disorder, a history of drug or alcohol abuse, police or probation service warnings, high risk convictions (homicide, sexual offences, offences against children), level of social support. The questionnaire also requires a mental state examination. Following this the prisoner is classified as:

1. a positive risk; or
2. no immediate risk, but requiring further assessment; or
3. no risk.

Those classified as (1) should be put in the prison hospital overnight, then later either in specially supervised (perhaps stripped) accommodation, or in shared accommodation. Those classified as (2) need not be admitted to the hospital, but shared or supervised accommodation should be provided.

Danto (1973) edited a series of papers from the USA describing suicidal behaviour in two or three US jails (short-term prisons). In that book, Hoff

(1965) showed that there is an increased risk of suicide for individuals sent to prison in several countries and that this risk is greatest for the pretrial prisoner. Johnson (1973) pointed out that prisons are peculiarly deficient in the emotional supports which we all seek when under stress. He linked the behaviour to other forms of self-damage.

Scotland too has had its difficulties. Between October 1981 and April 1985 there were seven suicides at the Young Offenders Institution at Glenochil. An enquiry was instituted after the first five of these, under the chairmanship of Dr Derek Chiswick (Scottish Home & Health Department, 1985). A series of recommendations included identifying those boys at special risk by carefully looking for adverse home factors, recent bereavement, prerelease anxiety, uncertainty about the date of release, alterations in mood or energy, loss of interest, and comments which indicate despair. They went on to propose three levels of care for those identified as at special risk. 'Extra care' should alert the staff to the need to be vigilant and should provide accessibility for the inmate to staff day or night. Normally, such extra care should not be necessary for more than a week. If it is, or if the inmate is of more serious risk, then 'close care' should be applied which means transferring the inmate to the prison hospital where he can be nursed in company and where a designated member of the nursing staff knows the boy's whereabouts at all times. For boys perceived to be at the greatest risk of suicide, 'special care' should be instituted. Again this would be in hospital, but this time the boy should be permanently in sight of a designated nurse, even when washing and toiletting. Nurses should swap this duty every hour, but even so be encouraged to develop a friendly confiding relationship with the boy. Education should be continued for those on 'close' or 'special' care. It was also recommended that Glenochil should employ both a consultant forensic psychiatrist and a consultant adolescent psychiatrist, a personal officer scheme be developed for the institution as a whole, and female as well as male staff should be recruited.

A point which does not emerge from the literature on the prevention of suicide in institutions, but which we want to emphasize here, is that just as the real issue in tackling externally directed violence in prisons is a radical reform of the regime, so something similar must follow to reduce effectively suicide rates in institutions. It is not enough to identify high risk individuals and to have observational policies (although these are crucial), it is also important to allow tensions, grievances, and despair to be verbalized and to be heard. Prison environments should be designed with violence prevention (both externally and self-directed) in mind. Psychiatrists should contribute to the design of such healthier environments.

Self-mutilation

Self-mutilation is a serious behavioural problem which is akin to suicidal behaviour and which is particularly likely in institutions, although it happens in other settings too. The whole range of self-mutilation behaviour will not be considered here as it is outside the scope of this book. For example, some particularly horrific self-mutilations follow from the delusional ideas of schizophrenia, e.g., the removal of eyes, the destruction of testes, the amputation of fingers. These are not especially related to institutions, although they tend to occur more often in hospital or prison for other reasons (Shore et al., 1978; Shore, 1979).

The classic description of the self-mutilator is a young attractive female, a nurse or paramedic, who has a history of sexual or physical abuse in childhood, trauma at school and trouble with the police, an individual of low self-esteem with a dislike of her own body (Simpson, 1976). Yet this is not the complete picture familiar to the prison governor who will often have a museum of foreign bodies swallowed by men. In South Carolina, Johnson (1973) surveyed 291 male prisoners who injured themselves. These men were more likely to be first offenders, the commonest injury was a self-inflicted cut from a razor blade, or other sharp object (often specially fashioned), some put noxious substances on the wounds, some burnt themselves, ripped open old wounds, or threw themselves to the ground.

An individual finding relief from tension by self-mutilation is a very frequent feature. Typically, the patient describes the skin as anaesthetic at the time of the cut. The damage relieves feelings of unbearable tension and returns feeling to the skin. Coid et al. (1983) found raised plasma metenkephalin levels in patients who habitually mutilated themselves.

The reasons that the behaviour appears to occur more commonly in institutions than in the community are not entirely clear. No doubt institutions selectively collect individuals with a range of behavioural problems. However, imprisonment itself, the feeling of being trapped, or some other aspect of institutional life may play an additional role. Jones (1988) has noted self-mutilation behaviour in macaque monkeys. This occurs when the animal (a highly social animal) is isolated and is more likely to occur in an animal that has been previously isolated, particularly if that isolation occurred soon after weaning. It occurs, too, when the animal is frustrated and appears angry, e.g., when his food is denied.

A man known as 'Flush' who swallowed many foreign bodies describes his thoughts:

> I wanted an enquiry into the running of the prison, so I decided to swallow some articles. I thought I would be sent to hospital to have them removed, and some high-up would say 'There's something wrong here, he's never done this before', then I could tell him all about what was going on in the prison. So one day, in the cell, I broke the mouth-piece off a spoon, and swallowed the handle. Then I broke some pieces of wire from the bed-spring and swallowed those, then some fittings from an electric bell and part of an electric light bulb. As you swallow each article you have a drink of water. You're sick, perhaps a dozen times, and it may be half an hour before you can get it down, but I always seemed to have the perseverance to keep at it. I never felt any pain, except once when I swallowed the chain from a sink-plug in the bathroom. It was about 18 inches long and seemed to wrap itself round my spine.

Eventually 'Flush' or Harry died. He swallowed five open safety pins, went to hospital and demanded to have them removed. However, he died before any surgery was undertaken, four of the pins settled in his stomach, the fifth pierced his oesophagus and his heart. He refused a blood transfusion. (*Portrait of a Psychopath*, Lloyd and Williamson, 1968). (*See also* pp. 404–5.)

No one should doubt the difficulty of managing patients such as Harry, nor the fury they engender in their carers. Faulk (1988) recommended anxiolytics to reduce the tension which induces the behaviour plus a structured behavioural-based nursing approach using warmth and concern, taking care not to allow the programme to be driven by an underlying repressive urge in response to the anger induced by the patient.

Infection Control (with an emphasis on HIV)

Institutions pose special hazards in respect of infections because of the high population density, and the relatively slow population turnover. Hospital and prison administrators have, therefore, to concern themselves with the hazards of such potentially lethal diseases as salmonella poisoning. Indeed the Prison Medical Service arose from an 18th century fear that typhus, then endemic in prisons, would spread to the surrounding population (Gunn et al., 1978).

Many infections still threaten and occasionally attack prisons and hospitals, e.g. food poisoning and Legionnaire's Disease. For a proper understanding of these problems, the reader is referred to textbooks on public health and the literature on infectious diseases, however, it may be worth mentioning briefly here the relatively new, but very considerable problems of hepatitis B and AIDS (acquired immuno-deficiency syndrome). Both are caused by viruses which are transmitted by bodily fluids, both have very high mortality rates, neither is curable. In some ways, hepatitis B is a more serious problem because not only is it transmitted by bodily fluids, especially blood, but it may also be transmitted by mouth. The AIDS (HIV—human immunodeficiency) virus, however, usually evokes more emotion, possibly because death rates have risen faster, possibly because it is more closely linked with sexual activity, possibly because prophylactic immunization against hepatitis B is available (British Medical Association, 1987), whereas there is no such prevention for AIDS. Both viruses can be transmitted by sexual intercourse, vaginal or anal.

The general principles for protection against these diseases include vaccination for all health workers against hepatitis B, a policy for handling blood and other bodily fluids in a uniform and scrupulously hygienic manner, the avoidance of needles and other sharps as far as possible, sterilization of instruments, needles, dressings and surgical clothing to the highest known standards and the safe disposal of contaminated waste (UK Health Departments, 1990; Advisory Committee on Dangerous Pathogens, 1990).

Apart from the straightforward hygienic measures referred to in the documents above, there is a further problem within institutions and that arises because these viruses depend for their spread on particular forms of human behaviour. The target behaviours for prevention are self-injection and sexual intercourse. Institutions, such as prisons and hospitals, will have a considerable number of individuals who indulge in such activities. Of course, such behaviours are generally proscribed in such institutions and that may well reduce the level of such behaviour, but it does not prevent it entirely. Reference has been made to the needle sharing problem of drug abusers in Ch. 11. Dye and Isaacs (1991) found that of 43 intravenous drug users in a Scottish prison, 42 had injected outside of the prison and 22 (76%) shared needles inside the prison. This level of problem in Scotland was confirmed by a community survey in Glasgow (Kennedy et al., 1991). Strang (personal communication) is hopeful that the availability of detoxification treatment in prisons will reduce needle swapping, since it could be that drug abusers prefer to run the risk of cross-infection rather than endure untreated withdrawal symptoms. Strang also points out that in San Francisco and in Melbourne prisoners are provided with bleach and told how to clean their needles. Harding (1987) carried out a survey of 17 countries on behalf of the Council of Europe to discover how prison doctors and administrators have responded to the AIDS epidemic. He argues that AIDS among prisoners is especially significant for the European community as a whole. For some reason, HIV infection is very much commoner among homosexual men than among heterosexual people in Europe. It is commoner among heterosexuals in parts of Africa. Homosexual activity takes place in prison among men who are heterosexual outside of prison. Prison thus provides an ideal bridge for the European HIV to move from the homosexual population to the heterosexual population.

All the countries surveyed by Harding had a policy for testing prisoners' HIV status, 12 countries (including the UK) offered testing on a voluntary basis especially to high risk groups. Three countries simply waited for a prisoner to ask for a test, two countries (Luxembourg and Portugal) tested all their prisoners. Seropositive prisoners were not subject to restrictions of any kind. Violent seropositive prisoners were segregated in Norway. In three countries seropositive prisoners were kept in single cells, one of these, Ireland, prevented seropositive men having access to the workshops. The UK has a policy of separating identified seropositive prisoners 'for managerial reasons'. Portugal places all such prisoners in strict isolation.

The information given to prisoners varied. In Austria, doctors have a legal duty to inform prisoners of a seropositive test and its implications under the Austrian AIDS Act. In Spain, seropositive prisoners receive advice and condoms if requested. Written information is distributed to all new prisoners in five countries. In some European countries (e.g. Spain and Switzerland) condoms are available to prisoners. France and the UK have taken a policy stand against the issuing of condoms on the grounds that it would imply condoning or encouraging homosexual behaviour in a public institution and it might even increase the amount of risky behaviour which takes place in prison. Since the Harding (1987) paper, the Prison Medical Service of England and Wales has introduced a videotape on AIDS and its prevention for all new prisoners to see.

The Woolf Report on prison disturbances, mentioned above, p. 810 (Woolf and Tumin, 1991) commented on the English HIV policy of placing all seropositive prisoners under 'viral infectivity restrictions' (VIR). This means the prisoners have single accommodation, and are excluded from the kitchens or work which risks blood spillage; many were, in fact, kept in prison hospitals or on a special wing:

> The Inquiry visited a small, dingy and airless basement unit at Wandsworth Prison which contained a number of inmates who were either HIV positive or were awaiting the results of HIV tests. Apart from an hour's exercise, visits to the library, and some classes, they were confined to this small area. . . . It is hardly any wonder that given the prospect of such conditions, prisoners who may be concerned about the possibility of having the AIDS virus, may be reluctant to express that concern to the prison authorities. . . . The conditions were a travesty of justice.

They could see no justification for VIR. The inquiry was more impressed with the approach used in the Scottish system at Edinburgh in which every new recruit, staff and inmates, received AIDS education. They urged that a new policy should be devised by the English Prison Service. Farrell and Strang (1991) highlighted the dangers of the present policy which implies that those who are not identified are not infected! Yet it is known, for example, that at least 10% of English prisoners are serious drug users (Maden et al., 1991).

Every institution needs a series of policies to deal with infectious diseases. Every institution needs an infectious diseases committee which can revise and monitor policies as knowledge develops. Every policy should be tempered by ethical considerations. It is a frightful fate to develop AIDS, such a fate should not be exacerbated by further victimization. Every policy should be informed from up-to-date literature and from visits to other centres, especially abroad.

Sexual Behaviour

Sexual behaviour does not cease simply because people are admitted to an institution. Undoubtedly, it changes because of the constraints of the institution. One prominent feature of institutional life is the wish by those running the institution to control the behaviour of those in it. Sexual behaviour is always difficult for others to control, this is no less true in an institution. Curiously, however, this is rarely acknowledged. There is, in Britain at least, a deep embarrassment about sexual behaviour, this is coupled with the clear management principle that illegal behaviour shall never be 'condoned' in an institution. As mentioned above, the English Prison Department ruled out the possibility of issuing condoms (which might reduce the level of HIV cross-infection amongst prisoners) partly on the grounds that to do so would be tantamount to condoning buggery in a 'public' place, which is illegal.

Heterosexual behaviour is not absolutely unknown in prisons, but it is very uncommon, because prisons are rarely mixed sex institutions in terms of staff or inmates. Homosexual behaviour on the other hand is said to be quite common (e.g. Prison Reform Trust, 1991). Men and women deprived of most pleasures in life are herded together, frequently sleeping two or three to a cell. Homosexual love and activity inevitably develops, not just between those who were homosexual before they arrived at the prison, but also among others whose need for love and sex are strong enough to turn them to homosexual activity at least for the duration of the incarceration. Sexual activity may bring cross-infection. Love also usually brings emotional pain. It brings pain to people who are ill equipped to bear it. Many, for example, are in trouble because they have difficulties with interpersonal relationships, many men are sex offenders. The anguish of unrequited love, of enforced separation, of intense jealousy is no less because it occurs in an institution. Indeed, some prison assaults and occasionally homicides are the direct consequence of homosexual liaisons.

Neither prisons nor most hospitals in Britain have policies for the management of sexual behaviour. The official view is that sexual activity is not allowed and, therefore, cannot be discussed. In some institutions, individuals caught in sexual acts may be punished, and attempts to break up sexual liaisons by separation are also commonplace. In the special hospitals, considerable effort is expended on the prevention of heterosexual activity ostensibly because of concerns about pregnancies, and it is widely acknowledged that a blind eye is turned to homosexual activity. Patients find this discrepancy in approach confusing and unjust. In neither case do they receive help if their relationships become complicated because, to repeat, officially, sexual relationships do not occur. Contrary to popular expectation, the one mixed sex ward in the special hospitals has not led to promiscuity. It has highlighted instead more fundamental problems, often terror of sexual activity in both men and women, terror which is presumably related to childhood or early adult experience of sexual abuse.

Gordon (to be published) has reviewed the small amount of literature which relates to the sexual behaviour of patients in hospital. It is notable for the absence of references to homosexual behaviour. Gordon quoted Akhtar et al. (1977) as studying in a general psychiatric hospital patients who had displayed overt sexual activity. The patients tended to be younger, single, duller, and more character-disordered than other patients. Most of the sexual behaviour noted was heterosexual, but short of sexual intercourse. Akhtar et al. said that the nurses usually reacted with anger, disbelief or denial. The authors said:

> The double bind of inpatient psychiatric treatment is that in the actual management of patients ideas of proper conduct must be held up as desirable, and patients treated as responsible persons, capable and motivated to normalise their interpersonal and social relationships. However when patients attempt to meet normal sexual needs we find ourselves at a loss as to what our response should be.

Gordon also quoted an English study (Morgan and Rogers, 1971) of single sex rehabilitation wards in the 1960s. Ninety-three patients made 52 couples. Of these, 30 of the couples had broken off the relationship by the time of discharge and in one of these the male patient killed the female patient. Four of the couples married after discharge. Gordon ends his review suggesting that institutions need to ensure that opportunities for emotional development can occur within those institutions. To this end, he suggests that comprehensive sex education needs to be made available, staff need to be trained in emotional and sexual counselling, facilities need to be considered for patients to have sexual privacy.

On the whole hospitals do not have policies about heterosexual behaviour. Broadmoor is an exception and has an interesting document which puts some emphasis on integration of the sexes at both patient and staff levels in spite of the fact that the hospital has no mixed sex wards. It would be interesting to study why the special hospitals are so reluctant to follow this route in spite of official policies. The Broadmoor policy says:

> Segregation of the sexes should occur only where this is clinically indicated or otherwise unavoidable. . . . A number of wards which are integrated for patients and staff should be available.

It is accepted that patients will develop emotional and sexual needs towards fellow patients and visitors but—

> within the hospital generally, close emotional and sexual activity, particularly involving sexual intercourse, will not be allowed, whether of a heterosexual or homosexual nature.

Relationships between staff and patients are not just discouraged, they are prohibited. Pornography which is available in newsagents is to be allowed, but not 'the harder core pornography'.

Marriages in Institutions

Homosexual liaisons in institutions have the advantage that they do not pose the potentially very tricky problem of marriage. In England, Wales and Northern Ireland current marriage law is governed by the Marriage Act 1949, the Nullity of Marriage Act 1971, the Matrimonial Causes Act 1973, and the Marriage Act 1983. The Marriage Act 1983 was specifically designed to facilitate marriage for prisoners, those who are housebound, bedridden and in detention (e.g. in hospital). A DHSS circular (HC(84)12) was issued in 1984 to explain the position. The Marriage Act 1983 was the result of a ruling of the European Court of Human Rights concerned with the delays which prisoners in England and Wales were experiencing before being able to marry. Article 12 of the European Convention on Human Rights says:

> Men and women of marriageable age have the right to marry and found a family according to the national laws governing the exercise of this right.

The reference to 'founding a family' has been interpreted simply as the right to be legally married, not to any right to consummate the marriage and rear children, much to the relief of special hospital managers and prison governors, although whether that is all that was originally intended by that phrase is not clear.

The changes introduced by the Marriage Act 1983 relate only to the location of a marriage ceremony. It allows the Registrar General to issue a special licence for a particular marriage to be conducted in a particular home, hospital or prison under special circumstances. It does not alter the basic requirement for anyone entering marriage to be capable of understanding the nature and purport of marriage and to be capable of consenting to it. It is thus open to anyone to object to the marriage of a patient in hospital on grounds of competence by lodging a caveat with the Registrar, but the level of competence required is very low. He will give the person who gave notice of marriage an opportunity to answer the objection. There is a right of appeal to the Registrar General should the local Registrar uphold the objection (*see also* pp. 108–9).

Broadmoor Hospital also has a policy document concerning patients' marriages. First, every patient who wishes to marry is counselled about the proposal. The patient and the prospective spouse are counselled separately and together. The policy document does not say what this counselling should include, but its goal is to ensure that both parties understand the nature of the contract, and that the marriage will not alter their special hospital lifestyle, especially their enforced celibacy; the counselling should also ensure a full exchange of personal details between the couple. The document deals with the entering of a caveat against the marriage on grounds of competence. It urges full consultation with the whole clinical team before this is done, plus the patient's family, the hospital chaplain, and the managers of the hospital.

Consummation of such marriages is a particularly difficult issue. In practice, married special hospital patients are not allowed to consummate their marriages. The policy document says that they can apply for conjugal arrangements, but in practice they are refused. There are two arguments used for the refusal, the first is that as other patients are not allowed to have sexual intercourse, married patients must have no extra privileges, the second is related to suggesting that, if married patients were allowed sexual intercourse, then there would be a flood of requests for marriage. The inability of Broadmoor patients to consummate their marriage has given the hospital chaplain a special dilemma. He does not believe that a person can take a Christian marriage vow if they know they cannot consummate their marriage and thus he will not conduct such a wedding ceremony, it has to be a civil one, although he will give a church blessing to the civil arrangement.

By policy then, marriage in a special hospital confers no advantages. Some married patients claim that it confers disadvantages. They believe that they are more heavily chaperoned than other patients and point out that quite a lot of sexual intercourse, in a clandestine fashion, both heterosexual and homosexual, takes place in any big institution.

Institutional Quality Control

'Performance indicators' are a buzz concept at the end of the 20th century. The concept could be harnessed to make secure institutions more effective. Such indicators could also become a tool for enhancing knowledge about how institutions work and how wider social systems work. Distinctions would have to be made between different types of institutions, e.g. prisons and secure hospitals have different objectives, but similar methods could usefully be applied across these differences.

What are the standards by which a secure institution should be judged. Security must come first, but what is that? Presumably, it means that those who are designated as patients or inmates remain within the institution and/ or under control. No doubt, this objective explains the walls, bars, dogs, truncheons, uniforms, keys and other paraphernalia which so dominate some institutions. No doubt, one measure of quality control must be the number of escapes and abscondings. Security training, systems of handling potentially dangerous tools and objects, and external physical barriers are all important in this respect; so too are lines of communication between inmates/ patients and staff—it is important to know who is disgruntled, and what the relationships are between various individuals, it is even more important that grievances are identified and settled.

Security also means internal security, the prevention of violence and disorder. This is a task related to escapes, but even more difficult. A 'good' prison or secure hospital is, in part, one that has few disturbances or assaults. As this chapter has indicated (albeit very briefly), there is information available about the prevention of violence in institutions whether that is outwardly directed or inwardly directed violence. To oversimplify and put very crudely, prisons like Grendon are less violent than prisons like pre-riot Manchester. Prison systems like the one in the Netherlands are less violent than those like the ones in France or the UK. This is not a textbook of social theory, so it has no discussion about the underlying reasons for this, but an important factor may be the distribution of power within any social system (Gunn, 1991d). The argument is that violence and disorder occur when a social hierarchy is unbalanced in terms of its power distribution. If individuals within the social system either feel intense powerlessness or find that ways of adjusting their social status by non-violent means are absent or blocked, then violence may result. The proposal from this argument is that every effort should be made, in any social system, to distribute power optimally so that every individual has some, and has ways of acquiring more without recourse to violence. 'Good' prisons will thus include effective staff inmate communications, attention to grievances and despair, and some degree of prisoner autonomy and democracy.

Security is not the only objective of a secure institution. Most inmates/patients will be looking to the exit and thinking of life afterwards. The best institutions will assist in this task. If patients and prisoners are to resume their places in wider society, then they should be subject to norms inside the institution which reflect the norms of healthy society outside. Herein lies a major problem for the manager of any closed institution. It is very difficult to run a large closed establishment and simultaneously achieve ordinary societal norms. Sexual activity and marriage illustrate this point well.

In order to approach such an ideal, the special stresses of institutional life need to be more clearly identified and acknowledged. Every deviation from ordinary norms (e.g. every restriction of freedom) needs to be justified in ways that can be argued coherently. Every patient and prisoner requires individual attention. The inevitable development of friendships, enmities and sexual liaisons should be acknowledged, and assistance offered to those who ask for it or appear to need it.

Staff too are members of the institution. They too will be affected by the regime. They should be encouraged to try and adjust this to make it as close to the free world as is possible within the limitations of security. This should be done for the health of staff and inmates alike. Above all, there should be effective and frequent opportunities for staff and inmates to discuss all rules and regulations, and there should be counselling available to both staff and inmates for serious personal problems.

The quality of an institution can then be measured by fairly crude indicators such as the number of escapes, the number of disturbances, and the number of assaults or suicides. It may also be possible to measure quality by more subtle measures which would need to be developed specially for the task. These measures would indicate how power is distributed within the institution, the ways in which individuals communicate, and levels of psychological distress. It would be for empirical research to test whether the cruder measures correlate with the more subtle ones, as is expected.

21
Psychiatric Reports for Legal Purposes in the United Kingdom

Edited by
Adrian Grounds

Written by
David Carson
Nigel Eastman
Gisli Gudjonsson
John Gunn

The Forum of the Court: Theoretical Aspects

Forensic psychiatry is the meeting place between law and psychiatry. But they do not always meet as friends or supportive acquaintances (Fennell, 1986). At times there may be mutual suspicion. This introductory section will suggest possible reasons. Two large professions will clearly each embrace a wide range of opinion, but there seem to be core concepts which differ between the professions. These are presented here as a polemic, as an educational exercise. In practice, the principles discussed may be of use in understanding medico-legal conflict if applied with allowances for the individual case being made.

Epistemological Differences

Lawyers, particularly in the UK, tend to be positivists. They see facts existing independent of observation. There may be problems in establishing what happened, but, for lawyers, those problems are in the witness and not in the process of observing and witnessing. The complaint from others is not just that, for example, lawyers regularly expect witnesses to recall reliably, in stressful proceedings, detailed incidents observed under stress that took place at least many months previously; the complaint is that lawyers have inappropriately embodied their theory of knowledge into the law.

Witnesses before UK courts are either witnesses to facts or expert witnesses, like psychiatrists, who are allowed to express opinions on matters within their specialty. So evidence, for lawyers, is either fact or opinion. Lawyers also use this distinction in their cross-examination techniques.

Witnesses stating facts are reported as being more certain; witnesses express-ing opinions can, much more easily, be made to change their evidence (Evans, 1983; Napley, 1983). This either fact or opinion distinction seems false. Witnesses in courts must use words. In doing so, they must form an opinion about which words are the most appropriate to describe the 'facts'. There are even opinions about the meanings of particular words. Sometimes, judges will declare that a word or phrase has its ordinary or natural meaning as used by ordinary English language users. The problems in discovering such people are not alluded to and this has enabled judges to go on to declare what ordinary people mean by such terms as 'mental illness' (*W.v.L.*), ignoring psychiatrists' skills.

Lawyers are also positivists in that they take law and justice as given. The law is there in the statutes and precedent reports. That is where they research, not in the behaviour of the police, judges or other law enforcers. In contrast, an interpretativist approach would argue that the law is what happens in practice rather than what might or should happen.

Many psychiatrists may also be positivists seeing mental disorder as entirely in the patient, at a biochemical or physiological level. Certainly this is the basis of Ingleby's (1981) criticism of psychiatry. A positivist approach may often be appropriate and produce relief for the patient. But diagnosing in order to isolate the mentally disordered patient involves interpreting behaviour, acts and words, and making judgments. Indeed, psychiatrists are required to do this when compulsorily detaining patients under UK mental health legislation.

Psychiatrists, however, are usually aware that their knowledge of patients, generally and individually, is dependent upon interpretation, upon under-standing cultural and other differences, upon the nature and quality of the relationships they have with their patients, and upon empathy with certain experiences.

Reasoning Differences

Lawyers are in practice required to be positivists whilst psychiatrists recognize that their knowledge is often, if not always, dependent upon observation and interpretation. This is the key to other differences between legal and psychiatric modes of thought and the difficulties psychiatrists can have as expert witnesses. Aubert (1963) outlined six ways in which legal thought differed from social scientific thought, differences which also apply to psychiatric modes of thought which are essentially interpretative.

1. Lawyers tend to dichotomize; you are guilty or not guilty, depressed or not depressed, it was reasonable or unreasonable, one or the other.
2. Lawyers try to match events and words. The object is to fit an event or person into a formula, a defendant into the diminished responsibility

defence. For lawyers, the issue is not the totality or essence of the event or person's problems, but whether enough facts match a verbal formula, because that justifies a particular response. In contrast, psychiatrists should respond to the whole person and not just the parts that fit into a disorder.

3. Although courts make decisions for the future, for example, concerning punishments, they also decide upon the past. What a defendant did justifies and explains, for a lawyer, the decision taken as to his or her future. But for psychiatrists the decision for the future needs to take account of what is and will be available.

4. Psychiatrists aim to be able to make increasingly general statements that will encompass more people, more situations, more treatments. This will not always be possible, but it is an implicit objective. They wish to encompass as much as possible within a statement. The difference between legal and psychiatric thought is that for the lawyer there is no such generalizing objective. Arguing that a client's problems arise from being a council tenant, a man, a woman, an employee, black or whatever, are of no legal relevance in itself, however powerful that identifying feature may be as a historical, sociological or political explanation. In trying to fit within certain precedents, whilst avoiding others, the lawyer will emphasize unique rather than general features of the client's case, for example that the defect of reason was due to epilepsy so that the McNaughton Rules should not be applied (*Sullivan*), (*see* pp. 57–8).

5. Law is not probabilistic in a scientific sense. Certainly, concepts of probability are used in court; generally the prosecution must prove the defendant guilty beyond reasonable doubt, and, in civil cases, the plaintiff must prove his or her case on a balance of probabilities. Percentages are sometimes used to explain these concepts, but are otherwise rarely used. There is controversy over adopting probability theories (Eggleston, 1983; Cross and Tapper, 1985; Hodgkinson, 1990). Psychiatrists will use probability theory and tests much more readily, for example in assessing the likelihood of a drug reaction.

6. Law is not causal. Certainly, it decides what happened in disputed incidents, but it does so according to legal rules of causal relationships. For example, someone will only be treated as having caused something by omission if he or she had a special relationship with, or duty of care to, the victim (Hart and Honore, 1983). Psychiatrists are not restricted in their recognition of causes, although they may invoke certain causes, biochemical rather than social, because of preference. They are concerned with scientifically demonstrable or falsified causes. Legal rules of causation cannot be falsified, only overruled.

Value Differences

Lawyers and psychiatrists are likely to hold different values. For example, lawyers will emphasize free-will more than determinism. This is reinforced by the content of the law and court procedures. It is difficult, for example, to be unfit to plead. Likewise, the McNaughton Rules do not help the person who only has an inability to control his or her behaviour.

Lawyers are more likely to value explicit and certain outcomes. Imprisonment for a fixed or recommended time will often be seen as better than detention in a hospital for an indeterminate period. Explicitness and predictability are highly valued by lawyers. Freedom from interference, for example, the right to die 'with your rights on' is valued. Lawyers value the right to make decisions for oneself and, indeed, would see that as a major constituent of individuality (Gostin, 1983b). Psychiatrists are more likely to interpret the experience of their patients, their personal or social distress, and justify intervention to reduce pain because the experience is the primary issue rather than ascribed rights.

Arguing Differences

Lawyers frequently reify. They create explanatory concepts and then treat them as if they really exist. The effect is seductive. Concepts of rights, of the rule of law, of property and personality have an appeal for us. Often these are based upon a natural law theory that argues that these concepts exist and adhere to us simply because of our human or social nature. As shorthand descriptions of values they are unobjectionable, but they become more than habits of thought. Many people prefer the rule of law to rule by people without appreciating that the former is only the latter by very successful people. Social values, opinions or standards are also reified so that differences and plurality are minimized. The process also exaggerates the effects of lawyers' tendency to classify. When a defendant is found guilty by a court, all the decisions taken in consequence of that decision will ignore the controversy. There is no reduction in sentence, for example, for uncertainty about conviction or evidence that was, or could not be, admitted.

A favourite way of arguing for lawyers is to declare. Emphasis is upon persuasion, rhetoric (Perelman, 1963). H. L. A. Hart, when Professor of Jurisprudence at Oxford University, wrote:

> Legal reasoning characteristically depends on precedent and analogy, and makes an appeal less to universal logical principles than to certain basic assumptions peculiar to the lawyer; . . . (Hart, 1963).

Extensive appeal is made to commonsense; whether it is common or makes sense is rarely investigated. Frequent use is made of 'reasonable', 'sensible', 'fair' and similar words, so that a declaration, by lawyer or judge, that something is 'reasonable' tends to be accepted both for itself and by disarming others who do not wish to be regarded as unreasonable.

All this leads Campbell (1974) to write:

> The point that the law is merely one scheme of interpretation, that it construes reality in particular ways and that there are no correspondents in the real worlds to these concepts is forgotten or never realised.

Campbell argued that these distinctive features of lawyers' reasoning and arguing are the product of court work being the paradigm form of legal work and reasoning. They flow from the practical requirements of obtaining decisions in courts. Particularly in the adversary system of the common law world, judges have to choose from the two (or more) versions put before them. They have to deal with the particular case and cannot refuse to decide. Every decision needs to be justified. By being able to choose and state the facts found, the judge is able to minimize any controversy there may have been and which might otherwise continue.

The Forum

It may well be then that the needs of the courts are the principal source of the difficulties between lawyers and psychiatrists. More than most specialties in medicine, psychiatry is dependent upon interpretation and opinion. Kenny (1983) suggested that psychiatry, as represented in the courts, appears unscientific because of the difficulty of distinguishing fact and value. Chiswick (1985) described how, in preparing reports for particular sides in the court process, psychiatrists may be breaching their ethical duties to their patient. Courts, unfortunately, provide a seductive forum for publicity and intellectual sparring; a 'heady atmosphere' is Chiswick's phrase.

But courts are not, and need not be, the focus and determinant of the relationships between psychiatry and law. The cases which attract attention and give concern to psychiatrists and/or lawyers are relatively few and atypical. Much more common than the aggressive cross-examination will be the letter or report, by a psychiatrist or general practitioner, for which the court will be profoundly grateful. The medical report will often provide the court with an easy solution to its dilemma. Here there will be few problems. Perhaps we should be more concerned about the potential for collusion in the 'easy' cases.

The potential for a cooperative relationship has been marred by this preoccupation with courts as the locus of interaction and with the psychiatrist's role in legal contexts only as an expert witness. Stone (1982) has vigorously condemned legal interventions in psychiatry. But his strictures relate to a few court decisions and legislative inventions. His concern is at the grand level of the few court cases that excite controversy and the impact of new legislation.

Rose (1986) also argued that the differences between law and psychiatry have been exaggerated. Like M. Moore (1984) he argued that they hold a similar theory of human nature. Rose noted that the antagonism is most acute in courts, but he did not see that as an explanation. He demonstrated that both law and psychiatry are inherently interpretative and subjective. He believed that the criticism of psychiatry for not being objective is misguided, for—

> all clinical medicine involves the application of socially, historically and culturally variable norms of health and sickness to particular cases (Rose, 1986).

Diagnosis involves much more than checking the patient's symptoms against a checklist.

Common Ground

This analysis has stressed that the problems between law and psychiatry are the result of an overemphasis on the dialogues taking place in court. The incentive to appear in courts may be powerful, but, psychiatrists, as expert witnesses, can overstep their expertise when generalizing or predicting in a desire to utilize their special experience and ability to effect changes in some individuals.

If lawyers and psychiatrists are to have a productive future then, it is suggested, both should concede the limits of their roles and claims to knowledge. Lawyers could become more genuine advocates looking to the broader social, political and civil interests of their clients, instead of only providing solutions where a problem fits a legal category. This would not produce a cosy consensus, but could continue to challenge psychiatry, for example, in the use of diagnostic statements about people with problems in ordinary living.

More work could be done at the pretrial stage in testing the alternatives proposed. Lawyers could be involved in preparing risk-taking guidelines to encourage the taking of risks and to challenge psychiatric paternalism. They could, in individual cases or generally, prepare standards of treatment, care and rehabilitation. They could draw out the desirable meaning of 'informed consent', give practical effect to concepts of dignity and self-determination.

Psychiatrists could issue self-denying ordinances. For example, they could collectively announce that they will refuse to give evidence on whether their patient's 'mental responsibility for his act', within the diminished responsibility defence, was 'substantially impaired' on the basis that such a judgement involves moral rather than psychiatric concepts. They could give some practical reality to team work by encouraging other professions to give evidence. They could issue guidance, as a profession, about the strengths and weaknesses of their evidence for the benefit of lawyers. That could encourage more appropriate questions and they could challenge lawyers' causal assumptions and rules. Psychiatry, on occasions, seeks legitimacy through involvement with courts, but courts also need a legitimacy and objectivity through association with being scientific.

Lawyers and courts have important social and political roles to play, but they are not above question. The same is true of psychiatrists. Perhaps psychiatrists should not be so keen to play the lawyers' games.

Preliminary Matters

When asked to provide a psychiatric report, the first question the psychiatrist has to address is whether it is appropriate to take the case. In particular, is it within the role of his expertise? For example, does it truly concern a psychiatric matter, and, if so, might it require more specialist psychiatric expertise (for example neuropsychiatry)? Apart from technical qualifications, practical questions should also be considered, such as whether the catchment area psychiatrist would be a better choice if outpatient care or hospital admission could ultimately be required. If it *is* appropriate to take the referral, it is important next to consider the type of *role* expected. Is the request (as in the majority of cases) for an expert opinion which is going to be available to the court, or is the request one which will result only in 'advice to counsel' (or solicitors), in which case the involvement is not independent, except in the obvious respect that a medical opinion will always be a responsible professional one. In making this distinction, it is important to note that, in many cases, it is common for psychiatrists called to give oral evidence in criminal or civil cases to adopt both roles, consecutively, so that an 'independent expert opinion' is given to the court through a report and in the witness box, but the psychiatrist also gives 'advice to counsel' regarding psychiatric matters in the hearing, for example, in relation to the evidence of another expert. Some psychiatrists eschew such an 'adviser' role and see it as inconsistent with the role of independent expert to the court; however, most accept it as necessary and ethically valid so long as clear demarcation between essentially different roles is maintained.

Next, it is essential to be clear about the *issues* that are to be addressed and, in particular, to distinguish clearly between legal and medical issues. Clarification of this will facilitate relevant thought as well as ensure that medical role boundaries are maintained, and that opinion and advice is restricted to medical issues (as they relate to particular legal questions).

It is important to be aware of the potential for in-built bias which can arise where the request derives from one side or the other (that is, not from the court itself). Such bias can occur simply by virtue of the particular issues and questions raised in the referral, since other potentially relevant questions may be omitted. In these circumstances the psychiatrist must decide whether to respond in the report only to those questions asked (as most do), or whether to anticipate other issues where they are sufficiently obvious.

It is important to be aware of the specific forum in which the case will be heard, since procedures and rules vary between different settings and this may affect the presentation of psychiatric information and the range of recommendations that may be available.

Having described ways in which legal factors impinge upon the writing of reports, it is essential to emphasize that the preparation of such reports should always be founded upon ordinary good general psychiatric practice, uninfluenced by the legal setting. The practice of providing psychiatric reports for courts involves making ordinary diagnoses and prognoses, albeit based upon a somewhat differently focused enquiry and presented in a way which acknowledges the court's needs.

Special Ethical Considerations

There are ethical differences between ordinary clinical psychiatric practice and preparing psychiatric court reports. The expectations which are an integral part of a normal clinical interview may be modified. The person interviewed is, therefore, not only a 'patient' (even if he happens to have been the psychiatrist's patient beforehand), but also a lawyer's 'client'. This means that issues of confidentiality will be different from the simple doctor/ patient ones (*see below*).

There are other more general ethical matters which arise repeatedly in legal psychiatric practice, most of which derive from the relationship and boundaries between law and psychiatry. Psychiatrists differ in the strictness with which they interpret and operate their role boundary and they must make their own decisions. The understandable expectation that the courts will correctly define the boundary is not always borne out. Judges can rule wrongly in regard to such specific matters as psychiatric evidence. They may, for example, order a psychiatrist to express an opinion about the responsibility or otherwise (i.e. the guilt or otherwise) of a defendant's actions, a matter which is clearly moral, not psychiatric. In the majority of cases which occur in lower courts, it is usually up to the psychiatrist to be boundary vigilant.

The Forums in England and Wales

A psychiatrist in England and Wales may be asked to provide reports for any of the following legal and quasi-legal forums shown in Table 21.1.

Different forums use different procedures and rules of evidence. For example, courts impose stricter rules of procedure than tribunals, and, in general, criminal courts operate stricter rules of evidence than, for example, courts concerned with child care. The boundaries of expertise may also be set differently between courts, 'softer' evidence being permitted in child care

Table 21.1

Criminal Courts

    Magistrates' courts
    Crown Court
        (including the Central Criminal Court)
    Court of Appeal (Criminal Division)
    House of Lords

Civil courts

    County courts
    High Court
    Court of Appeal
    House of Lords

Juvenile courts

Coroners' courts

Mental Health Review Tribunal

courts, for example, than in courts determining criminal liability (Betts, 1988; Wolkind, 1988).

Constructing a Report

Case Preparation

Providing a psychiatric report does not begin with interviewing the patient. Preparatory work is necessary and this is emphasized in major cases by the awareness that what is done (or not done) may be explored in cross-examination. Similar standards of investigation should apply to minor cases, even though such public exposure is less likely.

First of all, it is necessary to ensure that the instructions from the referring source are adequate and make clear what issues the lawyers wish addressed. If the instructions do not ask clear questions, then clarification can be requested before going further. It may be unwise to respond to a request that says merely 'please provide a psychiatric report'. On the other hand, the lawyer may be seeking guidance about a puzzling case. He may be unaware of treatment which is available for his client. He may be unaware of all the pros and cons of pursuing a psychiatric approach. A preliminary discussion will help to clarify and inform.

It may be helpful to list the legal and medical issues which appear to be the crux of the case. It is also important to ensure that all relevant documents concerning the case, such as the depositions, social enquiry reports, previous convictions, previous or current psychiatric reports, postmortem or other pathology reports, and police interview transcripts, are available.

Interviewing the Defendant

Practical matters

1. *Location*: this will be in outpatients (if on bail); in prison (if in custody); possibly in a police cell or in hospital (if remanded by the court or transferred from custody). It is important to determine that adequate assessment can be made in the place available.
2. *Time*: allow sufficient time before the hearing for further investigations to be conducted should they prove necessary. Also, allow sufficient time for each interview, especially bearing in mind prison restrictions on hours, which are strictly maintained. Several interviews are also better than one, and may be essential in a difficult case, although resources will frequently only permit one.

Ethical matters

It is important to ensure that both doctor and patient have correct perceptions and expectations. The difference from the normal professional role of the psychiatrist should be explained to the interviewee. The matter of confidentiality most obviously reflects the distinction between the report situation and an ordinary doctor/patient relationship. This arises because third parties are automatically involved, and because a single piece of information may have both psychiatric and legal significance. Hence a doctor may be obliged for medical reasons to include information which has direct legal impact, perhaps even on the verdict. Even if the information is of legal relevance only (and therefore is not included in a report), there is no right of privilege over such information and, if the psychiatrist were giving oral evidence, the court could insist on its divulgence (even though this is extremely rare). As a result, it is good practice to explain clearly the nature of the professional interaction and its purpose, including that of preparing a report for defence lawyers or the court.

The setting of the interview may have coercive significance and the psychiatrist should be aware of this. Where access to previous psychiatric records is needed, specific patient consent should be gained (if he is competent). The issue of explicit discussion of the offence charged is dealt with below, but here we note that, if the defendant denies the alleged offence or is inconsistent, the psychiatrist must decide whether questioning is really necessary for psychiatric assessment. In general, it is probably good practice to err on the side of exclusion of legally relevant material in a disputed verdict case. However, where the mental state and the supposed criminal act are intimately linked, this advice may be hard to follow. In any case, it is important to get the accused person's view on why he has been charged with the offence.

Clinical interview

Once the purpose and context of the interview has been explained, the interview proceeds like any other assessment interview, although the relevant clinico-legal issues will affect the weight given to various aspects of the interview.

It is probably sensible not to discuss the offence right at the beginning of the interview, but time must be allowed for the defendant to give his version of events, and his explanations. Pain, repression, and embarrassment may all interfere with this, so a high degree of sensitivity and tact is needed.

Questioning about family history, personal history and social history should be weighted according to their relevance to diagnosis, prognosis and the legal issues. Too much time spent on mundane irrelevances may squeeze out crucial questions. The previous medical history and previous psychiatric history will always be of importance, and the psychosexual history may be emphasized where a sexual offence is concerned. There should always be enquiries about substance abuse. It is usually helpful to get the patient to describe recent psychiatric symptoms (both pre- and postarrest) and this may then lead into a discussion of the offence. Reference to the offence should concentrate on psychiatric aspects, with particular reference (where possible) to the mental state at the time, as well as possible mental mechanisms. Eliciting and recording the current mental state is, of course, important, not only in pointing to the possible mental state at the time of the offence, but in determining disposal recommendations

At the end, it may be helpful to reorganize the clinical information in terms of the important legal issues concerning verdict and disposal, and to review what further information and/or investigations may be necessary.

Further investigations

It is good practice to gain further information about a patient from relatives, friends, previous social enquiry forms, the criminal record, and from depositions relating to the case. Obtaining previous medical and psychiatric records will be important (subject to consent), including the prison hospital case papers ('inmate medical record'), if a defendant is on remand in custody.

Further specific clinical investigations most commonly involve psychometry. This may be in the form of intelligence tests, tests of memory, and tests aimed at eliciting generalized or focal neuropsychological deficits. Occasionally, the issues of suggestibility and compliance arise. All these matters require specialist psychological assessment, and the lawyers should be so advised. It is not appropriate for psychiatrists to play at being amateur psychologists. Where indicated, physical and neurological investigations may be arranged, but no attempt should be made to stray very far into the fields of general medicine and neurology, and a separate opinion should also be advised for these fields.

Other psychiatric experts

When an opinion has been formed it may be sensible to contact other 'experts' who have also seen the patient. It is courteous to inform the instructing solicitor before this is done. In general, such contact is to be encouraged, since it ensures that any differences of opinion are not based on different data bases, and it also often focuses any differences of opinion in advance of the hearing. In court it is useful to reduce the differences between apparently competing experts by explaining to the court how much is agreed upon and why there are differences on specific points. In minor cases, it is uncommon for more than one psychiatrist to be involved.

The Structure of the Written Report

Psychiatrists vary greatly in how they prefer to present information in reports. One suggested broad framework and a few guidelines are given below. For further reading on reports *see* Scott (1953), Gibbens (1974), Grounds (1985), and Carson (1990b).

A few general points in regard to court reports are in order.

1. A court report is not a 'formulation' or 'case presentation'; rather, it is the presentation of psychiatric information for a non-psychiatric purpose.
2. Clarity is crucial.
3. Avoidance of over inclusiveness and pursuit of legal relevance should be an aim.
4. Technical terms should be avoided wherever possible; if it is considered appropriate to include them, then definitions and explanations must also be offered.
5. Only facts and opinions that can be sustained under cross-examination should be included in a report; always indicate the source of those facts.
6. The defendant may see the report, so avoid giving personal information of which he is unaware (for example, adoptive status or illegitimacy).
7. The report is about the defendant so avoid disclosing privileged information about others.

8. Write with conscious reference to the limits of the psychiatric role.
9. Remember that others might use the report during subsequent hospital treatment or sentence.
10. Once a report has been presented in court, it ceases to be a confidential document. Some confidentiality can be preserved in some cases by asking a judge or magistrate to avoid reading out loud sensitive parts of the report. They will usually respect the request. Even if a report is not presented in court, confidentiality cannot be guaranteed once it leaves the hands of the writer.
11. Avoid value laden statements.
12. Be specific and avoid general terms.
13. Give reasons for conclusions.
14. Exclude psychiatric information not directly relevant to the court's purposes.

A report should be as long, and no longer, than is necessary for its legal purpose. As a result, the forum will, to some extent, influence the report. Magistrates have little time to read reports, often doing so in front of the defendant, and will welcome brevity. Judges in the Crown Court and the High Court will have time to deliberate on reports and, in more major cases, issues are often not only more weighty, but more complex medico-legally. As a further general rule, it is probably wise to include only limited background information, being selected on the basis that it supports and makes more comprehensible the legally definitive aspects of the report.

The problem of hearsay

Psychiatrists frequently rely upon information provided by others, i.e. 'hearsay' from a legal point of view. No problem usually arises except where such information might be given in oral evidence. Judges generally do not require separate 'proof' of such information (by requiring informants to give evidence in court). However, the psychiatrist should be aware of the distinction between quoting statements of informants as explanatory and justificatory of a psychiatric opinion as opposed to being evidence of the factual truth of those statements (which the jury might rely upon). It is specifically important to avoid re-statement, even in the written report, of allegations by others (or other legally relevant hearsay). It is good practice to indicate the source of information: 'From his mother I learned that . . .' or 'The police file indicates . . .', or to indicate sources generally by subheadings e.g. 'Family History (from the patient)'. It is worth noting too that it may be inadvisable to say: 'The patient says . . .', as this could indicate to some lawyers that the writer does not believe his informant, which may not be the case at all.

The structure of a report may be considered under conventional clinical headings, although they may sometimes be appropriately amalgamated for report purposes.

Introduction

It is essential to list exactly the sources of information (including clinical interviews and tests) on which the opinion is based. This should include listing of all types of documents seen and particular informants interviewed, as well as past medical and psychiatric notes read. Where, ideally, access to other information would have been helpful, note its non-availability.

Background history

Since most family, personal and social history, is not usually of direct legal relevance, it may be helpful to use a composite heading which lays a simple backcloth for the court, perhaps highlighting matters that may be of explanatory help in regard to the opinion and recommendations to be made in the report. If it is absolutely essential to make reference to the disorders or the behaviour of identifiable others then their permission should be sought wherever possible.

Psychosexual history

The psychosexual history may be appropriately incorporated into the background history in many cases, but if it is of direct and major relevance to the court (for example, in the case of an alleged sexual offence) a separate heading is probably helpful.

Substance abuse

There should always be enquiries about alcohol and other drugs which influence mental activity and, where relevant, appropriate comments should be included in the report.

Previous medical histroy

Only information relevant to the ultimate opinion and recommendations need be included under the previous medical history.

Previous psychiatric history

The previous psychiatric history will be of major importance, and some detail should be offered of previous episodes of mental disorder, treatment and outcome, including on what legal basis (formal or informal) treatment occurred. Technical terms should be avoided as far as possible or clearly explained, so that the court can use the information correctly.

Alleged offence(s)

Where it is appropriate to refer to the alleged offence, it is wise to apply the general rule of restricting reference to the defendant's account solely to those aspects which help to define his concurrent mental state or to those which are psychiatrically relevant in some other way. For example, where a defendant retells the story of his killing of a victim in terms that are delusional or hallucinatory it may be necessary to quote him verbatim (whilst not necessarily implying his 'confession' is valid).

To reiterate, the alleged offence should not be referred to in a pretrial case where the defendant denies committing it, unless there is some over-riding reason to make such reference (e.g. the description of the mental state would be seriously incomplete without it).

Opinion

This section can be written in terms of answers to specific legally relevant questions. For example, each question could be individually stated, followed by an answer that states the psychiatric opinion and then relates it to the particular legal question. Alternatively, a paragraph or two setting out the medical data and the opinion in the context of the legal questions may also be satisfactory.

Opinions should always be expressed with reference to any measure of doubt there may be. Yet firm conclusions are required. If introduced by 'In my opinion', it is clear that the possibility of other views is accepted. It may be helpful to give reasons for coming, on balance, to one view rather than another.

Where the opinion concerns questions relevant to the verdict, there may be a request to deal with possible links between a mental disorder and the illegal act. Although the link is sometimes apparently obvious, it is wise to acknowledge that perceived connections are often little more than hypotheses. In some cases, it is better to restrict opinion to coincidental description of the mental state and the alleged crime, without explicitly presuming causality. It is perhaps not surprising that psychodynamically oriented opinions are less restrained in this respect, but such opinions may be open to easy attack on cross-examination. In general, description is more reliable and robust than explanation. On the other hand, the court does want an opinion not just a reiteration of facts, and a report that is hedged with too much doubt may be completely disregarded. Thus a balance has to be struck which acknowledges uncertainty, but which also gives an authoritative view. Whatever style the opinion is written in, it should always include somewhere a clear medical statement about the patient's condition. If a mental disorder is discovered, then this should be stated and labelled medically. If several are discovered, they should all be listed. Equally, the report should also refer to prognosis and give some indication of what treatment is required. These medical views can be used to answer or illuminate the legal questions posed. As indicated previously, in answering the legal questions care should be taken to avoid straying beyond medicine into law or morals.

Where other types of expert have seen the defendant, especially psychologists, it is important to encourage submission of a separate report to the court, although a summary of that report may be included in the psychiatric report.

Recommendations

Recommendations are usually concerned with disposal, and are dealt with below in 'Issues at the Sentencing Stage' p. 849. Clarity of argument is vital, with clear reasons given for any suggested disposal. Recommendations should be restricted to those that relate to psychiatric care. No patient should be recommended for a punitive disposal such as imprisonment, even by implication, though it is appropriate to spell out the consequences of imprisonment as courts must consider its effects under the Criminal Justice Act 1991.

A signature is not an ego trip but simply a clear description of the strictly relevant qualifications and post held. Doctors in junior and training posts should indicate somewhere, preferably in the signature, the name of the consultant who is ultimately responsible for the case.

The Use of Reports in Criminal Proceedings

In England and Wales all criminal cases begin in a magistrates' court, whether it be in relation to a charge of a minor motoring offence or a charge of murder. The vast majority of cases remain, and can only be dealt with, in a magistrates' court, the rest progress to the local Crown Court or, unusually, to the Central Criminal Court in London (the 'Old Bailey').

Legal issues, and therefore psychiatric matters which potentially relate to those issues, can be categorized most simply according to legal 'stages'.

Pretrial Stage

At the initial magistrates' court hearing, if the case is not dealt with immediately, the defendant will be remanded, either in custody or on bail (and, therefore, at restricted liberty), to a further hearing. Such remands can be repeated until such time as the case is either dealt with by a magistrates' court or, alternatively, is 'committed' (after a committal hearing) to the Crown Court. At the defendant's appearance for trial (either at a magistrates' court or the Crown Court) the immediate issue (although usually not formally addressed) is that of the defendant's 'fitness to plead'. The whole of the period up to the presumption or determination of the defendant's fitness to plead may be termed the 'pretrial stage'.

A defendant may be referred by the court for a psychiatric report through one of a number of mechanisms during the pretrial stage. These reports will address issues specific to the pretrial stage itself, but may also commonly consider trial and disposal issues since, in the majority of minor cases, the psychiatric report does not influence the verdict, but only the disposal. The mechanisms of referral are as follows.

1. A magistrates' court or the Crown Court may remand a defendant to hospital for reports under section 35 of the Mental Health Act 1983 (MHA 1983). This allows assessment, but in itself does not provide for compulsory treatment of the defendant, although this may be justified on common law grounds, for example in an emergency, and can, also, be arranged by the addition of a treatment order under section 3 of the Act (*see* Code of Practice—Appendix 2). Such a remand order can be made in favour of any type of psychiatric hospital or ward (secure, locked or open) and the defendant then becomes a patient detained under the MHA 1983.

2. The Crown Court may remand to hospital for treatment under section 36 of the MHA 1983.

3. The court may remand the defendant on bail, but with a condition that he reside in a particular hospital ward. This may also be a route, therefore, to achieving a 'remand psychiatric report'; however, the defendant is, of course, not a patient detained under the MHA 1983.

4. If the court does not consider it necessary for the defendant to be either in custody or an inpatient, then it can remand on bail with ordinary conditions of residence (for example, at home or in a bail hostel) and require at the same time that an outpatient psychiatric assessment and report be carried out.

5. The court may remand the defendant in custody and, at the same time, request of the prison medical staff that a psychiatric report be provided. This might be completed by a prison medical officer or by a visiting psychiatrist who attends the prison. Such reports may be further supplemented by information derived from a catchment area psychiatrist or regional forensic psychiatrist who has been asked by the prison medical officer to attend the prison in order to give an opinion.

The ways in which courts obtain psychiatric reports vary. The court can ask directly, for example by a request to the prison in the case of a defendant remanded in custody, or, alternatively, it can do so through either the probation service or the defence solicitors, who would then make the referral to the psychiatrist. This latter mechanism arises more often where the defendant is not remanded in custody.

If the court has not requested a psychiatric report, then such a report may be provided in any event via one of a number of other routes.

1. Whilst on remand, either in custody or bail, defence solicitors (or the probation service) may independently request an opinion. It is the duty of the defence solicitors to do so if they suspect the defendant may be mentally disordered.
2. Whilst on remand in custody, a prison medical officer may consider that the defendant suffers from a mental disorder and he may, therefore, offer a 'voluntary report' to the court, which the court may, of course, choose to acknowledge or reject.
3. The Prison Health Service has a policy whereby certain types of criminal charge, by virtue of their nature, automatically merit a psychiatric report (a 'nature of charge' report), for example in cases of murder.

Any report prepared at the pretrial stage should address the issue of fitness to plead (*see* pp. 43 and 125), although unfitness is a rarity in practice, and the issues addressed by most remand reports are concerned with trial or sentence.

Trial Stage

Reliability of evidence

The reliability of evidence has two components. The first component is the person's ability to report observed events or experiences accurately and completely. This is the cognitive side to reliability and is dependent upon the person's intellectual and memory functioning, and general susceptibility to suggestive influences, in addition to the factors which influence the acquisition, retention and retrieval of information.

The second component to the reliability of evidence is the willingness to tell the truth, or to cooperate with the assessment. Here, the expert is beginning to trespass into the area reserved for the jury, so in Britain experts are not allowed to give evidence on general psychological factors which are likely to affect the reliability of evidence given by the ordinary member of the public. For this reason, psychological evidence regarding eyewitness testimony is not allowed. Indeed, one has to be able to demonstrate that the defendant, victim, or witness, possesses some abnormal characteristics which makes him especially vulnerable to giving erroneous testimony. There are two kinds of circumstances where mental health professionals are likely to be asked to give expert evidence on reliability issues in criminal trials. First, they may be asked to give an opinion on the likely reliability of evidence of mentally handicapped witnesses or victims. Second, they may be asked to act as expert witnesses in cases where people have retracted self-incriminating confessions made to the police during interrogation (*see also* section on Provocation below, p. 848).

Competence and reliability of a witness in court

In court, the competence and reliability of a witness are dealt with as separate matters. Competence is a matter for the judge, reliability is a matter for the jury. In a previously reported case (Gudjonsson and Gunn, 1982), a woman suffering from mental subnormality alleged that she had been raped. The prosecution challenged both her competence and reliability as a witness. She was asked to undergo a combined psychiatric and psychological examination. In the absence of the jury, expert evidence was given about her ability to understand the truth, her concept of God, and her understanding of contempt of court. The judge also asked her questions on these points and satisfied himself that she was sufficiently competent to be a witness. In front of the jury, further expert evidence, mainly psychological, testified to her suggestibility, in particular whether she was thought to claim perceptions that had no objective basis, and whether she could be easily persuaded to give expected or suggested answers to questions. Special tests were devised for this.

False confessions

Defendants may retract confessions they had previously made to the police and where the principal evidence against them is their own confession. How many of these retracted confessions are actually false confessions is not known. However, a sufficiently large number of false confession cases have been documented in the literature to warrant the attention of mental health professionals (Gudjonsson and MacKeith, 1988).

With the introduction of the Police and Criminal Evidence Act 1984, the two specific elements to the exclusionary rule of confession statements are 'oppression' and 'reliability'. The Codes of Practice for Police Officers (Home Office, 1985e) give provisions relating to the interviewing of mentally ill and mentally handicapped persons. Incidental breaches of the Codes will support arguments as to unreliability under section 76(2)b. The relevance and admissibility of a confession are a matter of law and are dealt with by the judge, whereas the question of weight is a matter for the jury. The expert witness may give evidence twice, once during a 'trial within a trial' (where the judge decides on the admissibility of the self-incriminating statements) and, subsequently, during the trial proper, and in front of the jury, if the judge allows the statements in evidence.

Kassin and Wrightsman (1985) have suggested three psychological types of false confession.

1. *The voluntary confession*, where the confession is made in the absence of any form of external pressure or elicitation.
2. *The coerced-compliant confession*, where defendants falsely confess for some instrumental gain (e.g. in order to get out of the police station) whilst under police pressure, knowing full well that they did not commit the crime they have confessed to.

3. *The coerced-internalized confession*, where defendants become subtly persuaded during police questioning that they committed the crime of which they are accused. The coerced-compliant confession is most commonly reported in the literature.

Retracted confessions involve varied and complicated phenomena. Persistent personality characteristics such as phobic symptoms, memory problems, intellectual deficits, suggestibility and compliance are often relevant, in addition to the mental state of the defendant at the time of questioning (Gudjonsson and MacKeith, 1988). Further issues to be considered include the interrogation technique used by the police, the length of time kept in custody and interrogated, the degree of access to a solicitor, family and friends, and the amount of sleep and food taken.

Suggestibility

Interrogative suggestibility was defined by Gudjonsson and Clark (1986) as:

The extent to which, within a closed social interaction, people come to accept messages communicated during formal questioning, as the result of which their subsequent behavioural response is affected.

These authors provided a detailed theoretical model for understanding the process and outcome of interrogations. According to the model, interrogative suggestibility is dependent upon the coping strategies that people can generate and implement when dealing with the uncertainty and expectations of the interrogation. Empirical support for the model is provided by Gudjonsson (1988b). This type of suggestibility can be measured by the Gudjonsson Suggestibility Scale which has two parallel forms (Gudjonsson, 1987b).

Related to interrogative suggestibility is *compliance*, which refers to the—

tendency of the individual to go uncritically along with requests made by people perceived to be in authority, even though the person does not necessarily agree with the request (Gudjonsson, 1989).

It differs from suggestibility in that there is no personal acceptance of the request or suggestion even though the person goes along with it. Both suggestibility and compliance are important in the assessment of retracted confession statements, but, to reiterate, they are psychological variables whose relevance depends on the circumstances and nature of the individual case, and must therefore be assessed in that context.

Intent

To recap from Ch. 2, to be guilty of an offence (except in cases of absolute liability, usually quite minor offences) a defendant must be shown to have committed the *actus reus* ('guilty act') whilst having *mens rea* (the relevant 'guilty mind').

Intention is not a psychiatric concept, however, the capacity to form any particular intention may be related to medical or psychiatric disorder. Some crimes are designated as requiring 'specific intent', and it may be possible, therefore, to argue in a psychiatric report and in court that a particular medical or psychiatric disorder removed the relevant capacity. But, to give an opinion as to the fact and nature of (legal) intent is to speak to the 'ultimate issue' that the jury must address and, in law, not even an expert witness may give an opinion as to the ultimate issue. Hence, it may be appropriate to describe in detail a defendant's mental state at the time of the *actus*, as it can sometimes be reconstructed retrospectively, and to do so in such a fashion that the court can, if it so wishes, draw an inference as to the nature of the defendant's (legal) intent. But any report or oral evidence should fall short of an opinion as to what the intention was. Some psychiatrists appear to take a different stance on this issue and to be prepared to address to the fact or quality of the intention itself. Such a view fails to distinguish between the description of the quality of the mental state and the quality of intention. Even courts themselves will, on occasions, fail to draw the relevant distinction clearly, but the psychiatrist should, at the very least, be aware of it and of the way in which it relates to the proper demarcation of role boundaries, so as to be prepared to resist admonitions to behave otherwise from less scrupulous or less well informed judges.

Psychiatric defences

The substantive law relating to psychiatric defences is dealt with in Ch. 2, and this section will consider only matters which concern the application of such defences in the practice of writing opinions and giving oral evidence.

The importance of understanding and being limited by different role boundaries is nowhere better illustrated than in giving opinions in regard to various psychiatric defences.

Diminished responsibility.   The diminished responsibility defence to homicide in England and Wales has almost entirely replaced, in usage, that of insanity under the McNaughton Rules.

Role boundaries strictly interpreted would imply that expert psychiatric opinion should go no further than stating the nature of the diagnosis and (possibly) the fact that such a diagnosis amounted to 'abnormality of mind' within the terms of section 2 of the Homicide Act 1957. Hence, strictly, no report should address the question of whether the effect of any 'abnormality of mind' was such as to 'substantially (impair) . . . mental responsibility'. This latter element of section 2 appears clearly to address a moral and not a psychiatric matter and, as such, should not be the subject of psychiatric opinion. However, it is a frequent practice of defence lawyers (and prosecution also) to request a psychiatric opinion as to whether the defendant is 'diminished', and it is even common judicial practice to allow, request, or even demand that the psychiatrist address the issue of 'substantial impairment of mental responsibility'. Probably the most diplomatic approach is to fall short of making any clear statement on the legal moral question, but to describe, in psychiatric terms, the impact of the psychiatric disorder on the quality of judgement and normal resistance to offending and to leave the court to take the final step of drawing a moral implication as to whether the defendant's quality of judgement was affected sufficiently to find 'substantial impairment of mental responsibility'.

Where the psychiatric diagnosis as it can be reconstructed at the time of the *actus* is a psychotic one, there will often be little difficulty in offering an opinion as regards the effect of the disorder on judgment. In cases of personality disorder, there may be much greater difficulty and this is reflected in differing general professional approaches adopted by psychiatrists.

A further problem arises in relation to transiently abnormal mental states. Hence, where a defendant has a personality which is of a type which, whilst falling short of being disordered, predisposes him to an episode of acute mental disturbance which then 'causes' a homicide, it has to be considered whether this can reasonably be argued in expert evidence to be a legal 'abnormality of mind'. The question may become further complicated by the fact that behaviour on the part of the victim may have partially precipitated the defendant's mental decompensation. Ultimately, it is for the court to determine whether such a constellation can amount to 'abnormality of mind', and psychiatrists might do well to restrict their expert opinion to a description of the mental phenomena so that the court may draw its own legal implication.

In circumstances where, concurrent with any possible 'inherent' abnormality of mind, there is ingestion of alcohol or drugs, the psychiatrist will have to determine whether (given the usual non-availability of self-induced intoxication as a defence) the inherent aspects were sufficient alone to describe the 'abnormality of mind' required by section 2. This may be a difficult or impossible question to answer.

Where drug or alcohol ingestion (or withdrawal) results in a psychosis understood psychiatrically as separate from 'ordinary' intoxication, then that might, of course, amount to 'abnormality of mind' as well as perhaps amounting also to a 'disease of the mind' and insanity.

To the extent that any change has occurred in the defendant's mental state between the time of the *actus* and any psychiatric assessment, there will always be a need to reconstruct the defendant's mental state as it most likely was at the relevant time. This will be based partly on what the defendant recalls of the period, upon evidence from depositions, inference from previous observations of the defendant as they emerge from his previous psychiatric history and, where available, evidence from the defendant's family and friends. Such reconstruction is always open to criticism, as it relies partly on the defendant's own recollection. Courts have, on occasion, chosen to cast doubt on the skill of psychiatrists in determining whether alleged abnormal mental phenomena at the time of the *actus* have been validly elicited from the defendant. Corroborative evidence is, therefore, of great importance.

Insanity.   The defence of insanity is little used in practice today, (*see* p. 47 for more details). In writing a report which addresses insanity, it is important to understand the relatively narrow criteria which are implied by the definition and, in particular, to appreciate its essentially 'cognitive' basis; that is, it is a defence to do with 'knowing' rather than 'feeling'. It is likely to be restricted to abnormal mental states where there is serious cognitive impairment, for example, organic psychoses, or disturbances of consciousness.

Provocation.   The defence of provocation is not strictly a psychiatric defence, and some would argue that, as it is a defence which is built on the concept of 'the reasonable man' and, therefore, one without psychiatric disorder, it is a defence which never concerns psychiatrists. However, there have been occasional attempts to introduce mental characteristics as implying unusual susceptibility to a particular quality of provocation, and English law has now moved very close to the New Zealand position in which under the New Zealand Crimes Act 1961, section 169 defines anything as provocation if it was:

> Sufficient to deprive a person having the power of self-control of an ordinary person, but otherwise having the characteristics of the offender, of the power of self-control.

Following *Camplin*, as Smith and Hogan (1988) pointed out:

> The reasonable man must now be considered by the jury with the age, sex and *other personal characteristics* of the accused (our italics).

The judge must explain what type of reasonable man the jury should look for, but it is for the jury to decide how the characteristics (say age) should actually be taken into account in assessing the level of provocation. Smith and Hogan pointed out that the jury are not to give weight to characteristics such as unusual excitability, pugnacity, bad temper, or transitory depression, but this clearly leaves scope for the relevant reasonable man in a specific case to have say, impotence, or mental illness, or mental handicap. It might, therefore, be appropriate in some cases for a psychiatrist to give evidence as to whether the accused does or does not have characteristics that could be relevant. What the psychiatrist cannot do is to determine whether the reasonable man with such characteristics would have been provoked to the alleged criminal act in the circumstances, that is for the jury. This is clearly also an area where psychology might become increasingly important to determine the presence or absence of relevant characteristics, e.g. intelligence, suggestibility. If the case for provocation is strong, psychiatric defences are usually inappropriate.

Infanticide. At one time, it seemed that virtually any woman who killed her child within the statutory limit of time was charged with infanticide and not murder. Hence, psychiatrists were rarely required to determine whether the defendant's 'balance of mind was disturbed' as a result of 'not having fully recovered from the effect of giving birth to a child or by reason of the effect of lactation consequent upon the birth of the child'. More recently, it is increasingly common for women to be charged initially with murder. It is then for the defence to decide whether to argue for infanticide or diminished responsibility. Strictly, if no specific causality can be attributed to the birth or subsequent lactation, then the psychiatric report should not argue that the case was of infanticide, but potentially one of 'diminished responsibility' where there is no causal restriction (*see* pp. 49–50, 50–3).

Issues at the Sentencing Stage

In the great majority of cases, a psychiatric report will have its legal impact not on the verdict, but rather on disposal. Most cases do not involve homicide or some other charge where a psychiatric defence is likely to be pleaded. Hence recommendations about disposal are often the nub of a report, particularly so far as the court is concerned.

A court may use any psychiatric report either specifically in relation to recommendations for some form of medical disposal or more generally in sentence mitigation.

Psychiatric reports in mitigation

Although the law allows in various ways for the negating of *mens rea* on the basis of psychiatric disorder, in practice most mentally disordered defendants who have committed the *actus reus* are found guilty of the offence, even where there may have been a direct relationship between the disorder and the *actus*. However, the court may then take account of such disorder by way of mitigation through a reduction of the sentence. The psychiatrist should bear in mind that sentencing is largely at the court's discretion (except where it goes beyond any statutory maxima and where there is a mandatory sentence, as in murder) and advice should, therefore, be tendered tactfully, as well as in terms which restrict commentary to medical matters. It is quite inappropriate to recommend or imply that punishment would be suitable in a particular case. Punishing people is not the province of psychiatry. The nearest a medical report should come to that issue is to explain the deleterious effects which different types of punishment might have. If the witness is pressed to express a view on the learning aspects of punishments, then he should explain that there are few data to go on, and a criminological opinion would be required to interpret them, also that learning by punishment in behavioural treatment is an entirely different process. Courts will often take note of sensitively worded reports which clarify the link between the disorder and the *actus*, or which make sensible suggestions as to the likelihood of further mentally disordered offending in regard to different possible penal disposals. Some would argue that it may also be helpful to place on record a view that some particular kind of help should be provided during (or perhaps immediately after) the serving of any sentence. Even here, there are special difficulties. A man with a personality disorder may be expected to benefit from Grendon prison (*see* pp. 688–749). If a comment about this is omitted from a psychiatric report, he may be sent to prison and his case ignored. If, however, a comment is made, the judge may seize the opportunity to send the man to prison 'for psychiatric treatment'. Worse, a judge may sentence a defendant to a longer sentence in a vain attempt to ensure that he gets to Grendon and has sufficient time there! In fact, a court has no control over a prisoner's management during a prison sentence, and a better solution is to indicate the man's need for treatment, note the hospital that has been approached and thus show that treatment is not available. If a prison sentence is then given, it can be followed up by a letter to the receiving prison with a copy to Grendon prison, making a clear and well argued case for treatment at Grendon.

Medical disposal

Any medical recommendation must be practical and within the court's power. To this end, it is essential to hold discussions with any other people who would be involved in the recommended disposal. For example, if a hospital order or an interim hospital order is to be recommended and the relevant bed is under a different (catchment area) psychiatrist, then this should be discussed with that psychiatrist. If possible, the latter should have assessed the defendant by the time of the hearing, and agreed to provide a bed, since no order can be made without a statement of bed availability, and the court will often be concerned to avoid a further period of remand, especially in custody. Where in England and Wales a recommendation of placement in a special hospital is being made, this will require the support of the admissions panel of the special hospital concerned. Similarly, if a probation order with a condition of outpatient psychiatric treatment is recommended, it will be necessary to gain the relevant probation officer's agreement that a probation order is appropriate.

In recommending any medical disposal, there should be cogent and coherent argument offered in its favour. No court should be expected to make an order just because a psychiatrist says that it is appropriate. If more than one option is to be offered, then it may be helpful to the court for the arguments in favour and against each to be rehearsed briefly in the report. It is frequently the case that, where outpatient treatment is being considered, patient motivation is a crucial element in prognosis, for example, in relation to sexual offending or substance abuse. It will be important, therefore, both to address that motivation specifically, and to argue clearly as to which disposal type best matches the degree of motivation.

Some psychiatrists would argue that for a medical disposal to be appropriate, especially a hospital order, there must have been a connection between the mental disorder and the *actus*. Strictly, this is not necessary and only the defendant's mental state at the time of disposal is relevant.

If a hospital order is recommended, either the report must be accompanied by the relevant form duly completed or, alternatively, the 'recommendations' section of the report must include one of the forms of words required by the relevant section of the Act to justify detention in hospital. Additonally, there must, of course, be a further medical opinion, and it is wise to ensure this is available to the court simultaneously.

It may be appropriate to address the issue of the addition of a restriction order to a hospital order. The reader should refer to Chs. 2 & 16 for discussions of dangerousness and the criteria required for the order. In practical terms, the making of such an order may hamper the freedom of the clinician in his management when the patient is an inpatient, but may aid outpatient treatment of a patient who is unwilling or inconsistent in his attitude to medication.

Reports for Other Purposes

Psychiatric reports may be required in non-criminal forums, most notably for mental health review tribunals (MHRTs *see* p. 188) and civil courts in regard to a variety of civil litigation matters. The principles which should apply to providing these reports are similar to those already enunciated in this chapter, although the different types of issues and forums may give rise to some variation in particular practices.

Reviews of Detention in Hospital

Psychiatrists provide reports for MHRTs in relation to detention, either in their capacity as responsible medical officer or as a psychiatrist acting independently and instructed by the patient or his legal representative.

When reports are prepared at the request of the patient's legal representative, the lawyer will decide whether or not to use the report. In addition, it is improper for the psychiatrist to disclose the report to anyone else without the consent of the legal representative. However, the High Court has held that a doctor's duty of confidence to a patient detained in a secure hospital for reasons of public safety could be subordinate to a public duty of disclosure, if the doctor considered such disclosure necessary to ensure that the hospital (or the Home Secretary and the MHRT) were fully informed about the patient's condition. (*Egdell*).

It should be noted that MHRTs are not courts and do not apply strict rules of procedure or evidence. The process is rather more one of 'investigation' than 'trial'. Indeed, this has given rise to criticism that patients' rights of appeal are, therefore, largely illusory since the tribunal hearing often functions more as a 'case conference' than as a testing of the psychiatric and legal bases for detention (Peay, 1989).

A report to an MHRT should be based not only upon recent interviewing of the patient and clinical staff caring for him, but also upon a detailed review of the previous psychiatric history and records. Its conclusion should be addressed to the key issues which concern the MHRT and which relate to the MHRT's powers. Hence, it may be appropriate for the 'opinion' to express a well argued view as to the current presence or absence of mental disorder, as defined in the relevant section of the MHA 1983. It should go on explicitly to express the question of the, again current, need to be in hospital either for the health or safety of the patient or for the protection of others. Finally, in England, it should address the question of treatability where the psychiatric basis for detention is either 'psychopathic disorder' or 'mental impairment' (*see also* pp. 401–4). Any 'recommendations' should be written in the knowlege that, for example, where there is no current mental disorder in terms of the Act, the MHRT *must* discharge the patient, however dangerous to self or others. However, the recommendation may not favour immediate discharge, and so it may be appropriate to recommend deferred discharge in order to allow necessary arrangements to be made. It may also be useful to make a recommendation even though the MHRT has no power to implement it, for example, a move to a less secure hospital setting, whilst still detained in hospital under the Act, because the MHRT can include such a suggestion in its report, even though the suggestion does not carry the force of law.

Other Civil Matters

Civil courts differ from criminal ones both in the 'sides' to the dispute and the 'level' of required proof, in that the level of proof is not one of 'beyond reasonable doubt', but of 'on the balance of probabilities' (*see* Ch. 2)

There is a variety of types of proceedings in which a psychiatrist may become involved. Some involve psychiatric patients, or persons putatively suffering from mental disorder (for example, in relation to various types of civil capacity); others concern alleged 'psychological damage' (in negligence actions); another group involves not patients but doctors, where the instructed psychiatrist gives an opinion on the quality of psychiatric care offered to a patient by another psychiatrist (again in negligence actions). The psychiatrist will most usually write a psychiatric report for the court, but might in some cases simply write advice to counsel (or solicitors) after reading the papers relating to the case.

Civil Capacity

The law applies an 'action specific' concept of competence. Hence, a person may be competent to marry or to make a contract, yet be lacking testamentary capacity. Similarly, the patient may even be competent to manage his affairs (currently) and yet not possess legal testamentary capacity. The role of a psychiatrist in such issues must be solely within the terms of the legal criteria which apply to the particular capacity at issue. There is no such thing as 'general mental capacity' in law. Details of previous psychiatric history and background history are relevant only to the extent that they assist in determining capacity. The report should concentrate on the mental state and the ways in which its details relate to the legal criteria of the specific capacity at issue. As an example, testamentary capacity requires that the person is able to know the extent of his estate and those who might have a call upon it, so as to be able to decide how to distribute that estate. The arguing of incapacity must be written such that it can be seen to arise clearly from psychiatric and/or medical phenomena observed. Of course, in this particular example, it is usual for the issue to arise only after the subject has died, and so medical evidence must rely on past knowledge of the testator (concurrent with the making of the will) or (less reliably) reconstruction of his capacity from documentary and other evidence, such as interviewing friends and relatives. Other common 'capacity issues' include the capacity (1) to marry; (2) to contract; (3) to care adequately for a child (in child care proceedings) and (4) to deal with personal financial affairs, as defined in relation to referral to the Court of Protection.

Psychological Damages (Compensation)

Psychiatrists are sometimes called upon to give evidence as to psychological sequelae of some event of legal significance. The law relating to 'nervous shock' is dealt with on pp. 102–7. Here it is important to note that the psychiatric report should be detailed and include, where possible, evidence from third parties. Basically, it should have a structure akin to the structure outlined for criminal cases above, but with a different emphasis. In particular, the reader should be able to see from the report the mental health of the patient before the accident, the mental health immediately after the accident and the mental health at the time of the examination. It should outline the patient's life history, personality development and previous psychiatric history. The report should give the patient's version of the accident or incident and his subsequent history. A detailed mental state examination should be made, preferably on more than one occasion and listed fully. Every effort should be made to obtain previous psychiatric data, including other contemporary opinions. The opinion should include an argued view as to whether the incident has caused psychological damage. If the opinion is that it has, then a diagnosis or diagnoses should be listed with evidence in the report. Each diagnosis should include a view on prognosis. This is essential as the quantum of damages will partly turn on the projected duration of the disorder(s). Diagnoses should be reasonably standard, but may include post-traumatic stress disorder, pathological grief and substance abuse. A further opinion should also be given about 'loss of amenity'. This is a description of the dysfunctions resulting from the psychiatric disorders. It may include an inability to work, marital disruption, a restricted social life, loss of promotion prospects and so on. The list of headings for the report could be as follows:

Introduction—including sources of information
Family history
Personal history—from birth to accident
Sexual and marital history—from birth to accident
Previous medical and psychiatric history—up to the accident
The accident—a detailed account of what happened to the patient
Immediate aftermath—an account of the patient's life and health for, say,
    1 month after the accident; this should include any impulsive or self-
    destructive behaviour, substance abuse (including tobacco), and
    deterioration of personal relationships
Subsequent progress—bringing the story up to the date of examination
Examination—a *detailed* mental state evaluation
Opinion—*all* psychiatric diagnoses, their severity, prognosis and relation-
    ship to the accident plus an account of any loss of amenity; the
    relationships between psychiatric disease and physical disease (e.g.
    anxiety leading to excess smoking leading to a physical threat) should
    also be mentioned.

Psychiatric Negligence Actions

Psychiatrists are sometimes called to give advice to counsel or opinions in court concerning the quality of professional care offered to a patient by another psychiatrist. The court will not be concerned with a standard of 'whether the advising psychiatrist would have treated the patient in a similar fashion', but rather with 'whether the treatment fell within a range of competent treatment such as could be expected from a clinician of that particular grade and level of experience'. Hence, the advising psychiatrist should refrain from giving an opinion in the vein of 'I would not have treated the patient in that way'. The report will have to be constructed according to the issues involved, but it should include where possible an examination of the patient, an examination of the relevant medical notes, and a discussion of the treatment in the context of the appropriate literature. It is clear, therefore, that this type of report is better undertaken by an expert in the field in question rather than by a forensic psychiatrist, since the predominant skill required is knowledge of particular medical techniques rather than the art of writing reports. However, forensic psychiatrists are sometimes instructed because of their familiarity with medico-legal matters.

Appearance as a Witness

Most of the discussion in this chapter concerns the preparation of *written* reports. With careful planning and consultation, the majority of medico-legal work can be conducted on a written basis. It is imperative that it should; the limited psychiatric resource available to any given community, must be husbanded very carefully. However, most psychiatrists will have to appear in court on occasions, e.g. in Britain a court cannot send a patient to hospital with a restriction order unless *oral* evidence has been given by a psychiatrist.

Standing in a witness box, even with the cloak of 'expert' about one's shoulders, is a daunting business. It is especially difficult when there is cross-examination. An appearance in the sentencing stage of a criminal hearing, so that a judge can inform himself better before he decides on a sentence, usually amounts to a congenial three-way conversation between the expert, the defence counsel and the judge. An appearance on behalf of a patient claiming damages from a wealthy industrialist following an accident is quite a different matter. Large sums of money may be at stake, and the company will employ an experienced counsel to discredit, as far as possible, the medical evidence given on behalf of the claimant, so the cross-examination can be hostile and full of traps for the unwary. In a criminal trial, which is highly publicized, the Crown counsel may wish to discredit the psychiatrist appearing for the defence as part of his strategy to obtain a conviction, or the most serious conviction possible (e.g. the Sutcliffe trial pp. 54–5). An Australian lawyer has written:

> Looking back over my years of legal practice, I have little doubt that the cross-examination of psychiatrists offered me the greatest forensic challenge. It was a kind of blood sport . . . I rarely had any logistic problems in convincing a jury—or even a judge—that the accused was, or was not, insane, schizophrenic or not schizophrenic, potentially violent or not, the result depending merely which side I was on. This is not to imply that I had any special talents, but rather that psychiatrists lacked them. . . . In the real world of court battles, I have had psychiatrists under cross-examination for up to three days—much to their annoyance when they (i) did not expect their judgement to be questioned, and (ii) cancelled only one patient in between a busy consulting practice (Gerber, 1984).

Now things are rarely as bad as this, but these views, which are hair-raising when read *in extensio*, indicate that, on those occasions when psychiatrists feel obliged to go into the witness box, they should be well prepared. Gee and Mason (1990) give good practical advice written from the perspective of experienced medical witnesses. Carson (1990c) gives lots of wrinkles from a lawyer's perspective. Both are cheap and easy to read in the train or taxi on the way to court, although some of their basic advice will be too late by then, because they urge preparation and anticipation. They include, however, practical advice on presenting evidence and avoiding pitfalls in cross-examination. Gee and Mason particularly deprecate the American practice of coaching witnesses before a court appearance, but acknowledge that presentation may be nearly as important as content in giving oral evidence.

In the USA, studies have been undertaken to determine, for example, the factors which affect assessments of witness credibility. However, these studies are not likely to help the novice a great deal. For example, Miller and Burgoon (1982) concluded that there are certain patterns of non-verbal and vocal cues which are associated with deceptive communication, e.g. reticence, withdrawal, vagueness, uncertainty, incongruous responses, *but* observers are not notably successful in detecting deception perpetrated by relative strangers—observers guessed liars correctly about half the time.

The firmest advice that can be given to the putative expert witness in the space available here is—know your case, understand the background concepts you are going to use, discuss your evidence with the lawyer calling you, be confident in the witness box, and use plenty of eye contact with lawyers, judge and jurymen. If your evidence is discredited, do not take it to heart, courts are arenas, theatres, which pursue a legal purpose often unrelated to psychiatry.

22
Ethics in Forensic Psychiatry

Written by
John Gunn
Pamela J. Taylor

Codes and Principles

Ethics is often used as a word meaning moral values, but ethics should not simply be equated with a set of rules or a code. Ethics is a branch of philosophy. It is the study of how moral ideas develop, how they interact, how they relate to other aspects of human learning and how they may be applied in practice. Medical ethics should be a systematic study of how moral principles can be applied to the practice of medicine. This chapter reflects the bias of this book and focuses on medical ethics, but many of the issues considered have relevance for other professions as well.

Medicine is a highly value laden subject. The very definitions of disease and the attending on sick people are based on moral assumptions. These moral assumptions have changed with time, but they have always to be in step with the broader morality of the society in which they are placed, and they have to be tested within the peer group of other doctors.

Morality so pervades psychiatry that every chapter in a psychiatric textbook will embrace moral issues either implicitly or explicitly. To give an example, the discussion that takes place in more than one place in this book about the suitability of retaining and treating mentally disordered people in prison is in large part a moral one. Scientific information about the efficacy of treatment in prison will influence the argument, but such scientific knowledge is unlikely ever to override completely the moral debate.

Given that moral issues are dealt with throughout this book, why is a special chapter on ethics required? It is needed to do three things, first to draw attention to the codes of practice which the medical profession has agreed upon or is likely to agree upon. All doctors are now expected to conform to internationally agreed rules of practice. This fits with the growth of what might be called 'international moralism' of the 20th century, e.g. the United Nations charter, and codes of practice for every human activity, even warfare. Second, the chapter highlights one or two moral issues which are specific to or more frequently encountered in forensic psychiatry. Third, the chapter indicates to the reader further avenues of exploration. Moral issues always generate discussion, the references given here will lead into a larger literature. It is a chapter more for raising questions than for providing answers.

A discourse on ethics frequently starts with the Greeks and the Hippocratic Oath, or with Hammurabi and the Babylonians. Musto (1991) takes the reader from Greece and Rome to the religions of the middle ages, up to the French Revolution, and into 19th-century Britain. In 1803, Thomas Percival published his famous *Medical Ethics*. It is even now of interest and resonant with some modern values, but it shows that ethics are related to time and culture and some elements are subject to change. Percival told us for example:

> The law justifies the beating of a lunatic in such manner as the circumstances may require. But a physician, who attends an asylum for insanity is under an obligation of honour as well as of humanity, to secure to the unhappy sufferers, committed to his charge, all the tenderness and indulgence compatible with the steady and effectual government. And the strait waistcoat, with other improvements in modern practice, now preclude the necessity of coercion by corporal punishment.

Percival also noted:

> It is a complaint made by coroners, magistrates, and judges, that medical gentlemen are often reluctant in the performance of the offices, required from them as citizens qualified by professional knowledge to aid the execution of public justice. These offices, it must be confessed, are generally painful, always inconvenient, and occasionally an interruption to business of a nature not to be easily appreciated or compensated.

He went on to suggest that 'as they admit of no substitution, they are to be regarded as appropriate debts to the community'. Fewer doctors are, these days, reluctant to go to court and few of them would regard themselves as paying a debt to the community when they did so. In almost 200 years, the balance of duty to the community has altered, so that now a modern Percival should be urging the doctor to attend less to the attractions of court work and more to the treatment needs of patients. Some of his advice does, however, stand the test of time.

> When a physician or surgeon is called to give evidence he should avoid, as much as possible, all obscure and technical terms, and the unnecessary display of medical erudition. . . . When two or more gentlemen of the faculty are to offer their opinions or testimony, it would sometimes tend to obviate contrariety, if they were to confer freely with each other, before their public examination.

Percival quoted a trial about industrial pollution turning on scientific evidence: 'two physicians of eminence were summoned to the assizes. . . . The evidence they offered was entirely contradictory.' One physician had done experiments and presented scientific data, the other made general assertions about the pollutants, the latter evidence prevailed over the former 'from the authority of the physician who delivered it'—*plus ça change*!

Percival's book influenced the first code of ethics of the American Medical

Association drafted in 1847 (Musto, 1991). Much has happened since then, and a whole range of codes have been written. The most important for psychiatrists are the Declaration of Geneva (1948, amended 1968 and 1983), the International Code of Medical Ethics (1949, amended 1968 and 1983), the Declaration of Helsinki (1964, revised 1975, 1983 and 1989), and the Declaration of Hawaii (1977, revised 1983). The American Psychiatric Association's (1989b) annotations to the American Medical Association's Principles are also worth study by other nationals. These are all listed in Appendix 4. Study of these will give initial guidance to the psychiatrist for most moral questions.

Internationalism

A good deal of international concern has been expressed about the plight of mental hospital patients in a number of countries. There have been persistent allegations that political dissidents in the Soviet Union have been locked up as mentally abnormal and 'treated' with psychotropic drugs in order to change their opinions (Bloch and Reddaway, 1977; Lader, 1977). The Soviet Union was forced to resign from the World Psychiatric Association for a few years because of this pressure. Eventually the Soviet Government allowed western observers to inspect their hospitals. The United States sent an official delegation in 1989. They mainly visited the Special Psychiatric Hospitals (maximum security hospitals) and concluded that conditions within them were unduly harsh and restrictive, patients being denied basic rights, punished with medication, and abused by staff. Patients were not allowed to participate in decisions about their own treatment (US Delegation to Assess Recent Changes in Soviet Psychiatry, 1989). A further visit was conducted in 1991 on behalf of the World Psychiatric Association. This team (chaired by James Birley from the UK also included Loren Roth, medical leader of the previous US delegation) concluded that whilst at that time there was no evidence of new cases of the political abuse of psychiatry, this was more due to changes in the law than to changes in psychiatric practice. The All Union Society of Psychiatrists and Neurologists remained controlled by the State as an agent of the State (World Psychiatric Association Team, 1991).

Different concerns led to pressure on the Japanese Government (Totsuka et al., 1986; Harding; 1991). In Japan, there is a rich and powerful private mental hospital association and very large numbers of people have not only been kept in such hospitals, but under compulsory detention. Totsuka calculated that 250 out of every 100 000 Japanese were detained in mental hospitals compared with the WHO standard of 5 per 100 000 (Lancet Correspondent, 1987). From 1968 onwards, reports of violence to patients, including patient deaths, began to emerge. In 1984, the director of a hospital was sent to prison for putting profits before patient care, and in 1986 another director of a hospital was caught bribing welfare staff to send patients to his hospital. Totsuka, a lawyer, formed a group which founded the Japanese Fund for Mental Health and Human Rights. Nakayama (reported in Harding, 1991) surveyed 'refractory patients' in Japanese hospitals and found extreme overcrowding, a lack of therapeutic activities, widespread use of seclusion and heavy doses of neuroleptic drugs. Totsuka and his group campaigned via the United Nations Commission on Human Rights and in 1988 a new mental health act became law. The new law introduced the new (to Japan) concept of voluntary hospitalization and set up psychiatric review boards for each prefecture.

The work of Totsuka and his colleagues led not only to a new mental health act in Japan, but also to UN Principles for the Protection of Persons with Mental Illness and for the Improvement of Mental Health Care. The first principle sets out a list of basic rights including the right to the best available mental health care and a right to exercise all civil, political, economic and cultural rights without discrimination. Principle 3 says that every person with a mental illness shall have the right to live and work, as far as possible, in the community. Principle 9 says that every patient shall have the right to be treated in the least restrictive environment, the treatment and care of every patient being based on an individually prescribed plan. Principle 10 says that medication shall never be administered as a punishment. Principle 11 requires informed consent before the administration of any treatment unless proper procedures have been applied to detain the patient in hospital and determine that he lacks the necessary capacity to give consent, when an independent authority should check the proposed plan of treatment. Psychosurgery, under this principle, should never be given to an involuntary patient, nor without informed consent, nor without an independent check. Principle 14 urges adequate resources for mental health care. Principle 17 requires a judicial review body to oversee the compulsory admission of patients to hospital, with, if necessary, representation to the review body by counsel appointed by a patient (Principle 18). Prisoners, too, should receive the best available mental health care (Principle 20).

The Council of Europe established, in 1989, a mechanism to reduce the possibility of torture or degrading treatment of detained people, including mental hospital patients, within its member states (Harding, 1989b). Visits to psychiatric hospitals and prisons are to take place. The visitors will have 'unlimited access' to such places and they will make a report, including recommendations, to the government concerned. Only if the government does not cooperate or refuses to implement the recommendations will the report be made public.

Competing Interests in the Psychiatric Care of the Mentally Abnormal Offender

The relationship of man to his society is highly complex. Personal integrity depends on limits on intrusions by others; it is not uncommon for the needs of one person to conflict with those of another. When ill health gives rise to such conflict, doctors are sometimes expected to be the means of arbitration. If, for example, a person presents with one of a list of specific infections, the doctor has a duty to the patient to provide treatment, but in many countries he also has a legal obligation to society to take steps to prevent the individual from spreading his disease. Some of the ordinary rules of confidentiality can no longer apply, and the doctor must notify the relevant authorities of the patient's disorder, whether the patient wishes him to do so or not. Psychiatrists also have a special role in medicine with their powers for compulsory detention. Where an individual may act dangerously the psychiatrist may, even without the patient's consent, have a duty to warn relevant people or authorities (*see below*).

Each psychiatrist comes to the role of arbiter with at least three interacting identities: as an individual, as a member of society, and as an agent of someone. He may represent the patient directly, or indirectly through the patient's representative, or he may be a representative of society. Society is not synonymous with the state but, in practice, it is commonly the state that purports to represent society—in England via bureaucracies such as the Crown Prosecution Service, the Home Office or the Department of Health. Less commonly, the psychiatrist acts for the police, or for a pressure group. The demands of these different agencies may conflict. The psychiatrist will not feel entirely free of obligations to other agencies, even when he is expressly acting for one of them.

The Psychiatrist as an Individual and as a Member of Society

The most influential factor in attempting to balance the needs of a patient and the needs of society must be knowledge. This will include factual knowledge of the nature and course of mental disorder, of the kinds of risks it may entail, and, in forensic psychiatry, knowledge of criminology. Detailed, accurate knowledge of the patient is also essential. Ignorance, where knowledge is available, is unethical.

Sometimes, however, the body of knowledge is poor. Personality disorder is a condition for which knowledge is limited (*see* Ch. 9). The limits to knowledge lead to arbitrary behaviour by psychiatrists. At one extreme, people with personality disorders may be denied treatment. The treatment of such patients under compulsion is declining (Robertson, 1982), while their voluntary treatment forms a tiny part of the average psychiatrist's work (e.g. Pomeroy and Ricketts, 1985). Although most forensic psychiatrists do have such patients among their clientele, one regional health authority in England has barred their admission to one secure unit. By contrast, the prison populations have a large proportion of such patients (Taylor and Gunn 1984; Gunn et al., 1991b), and around 50% of life sentenced prisoners (Taylor, 1986) suffer from sociopathic disorder. There is only a small chance that such prisoners will receive treatment even if they request it (Gunn et al., 1991a,b). Is prison the right place for people with a recognized mental disorder? What happens to the handful of patients who do go to hospital? Dell et al. (1987), examining records of patients in one special hospital, commented that for patients admitted under the Mental Health Act 1983 as 'mentally ill' there appeared to be no statistical correlation between length of stay and admission offence, and suggested that discharge decisions were, therefore, being taken primarily in relation to the progress of mental state. For those in the MHA 1983 'psychopathic disorder' category, the factor they found that best correlated with length of stay was the gravity of the admission offence. In 1984, there were just four admissions to Broadmoor special hospital on grounds of 'psychopathic disorder'. Which is the greater immorality, the failure to offer psychiatric services to such patients or their length of stay being related to the gravity of their index offence?

In an individual case, the psychiatrist will have a great deal more information than simply a diagnosis of disorder and the type of offence or threat. When considering the balance of individual and societal needs, interviews with the patient must be supplemented by independent accounts of mental state and behaviour. Yet it has to be remembered that independent data is no less susceptible to deviation from 'the truth' than the patient's own account. In a recent example of a child abuse case, there seemed no single account from anyone that was wholly reliable. The patient faced a long prison sentence if found guilty; some of the patient's family had long been recognized as abusers of the patient, and expressed no sympathy for her plight; the authorities involved in the case; from the hospital and social work staff to the police; could all have been accused of neglect had they not assured the court that up to the point of the index offence there had only been evidence of good parenting. Lewis et al. (1988) set out almost identical problems for 12 of 14 juveniles sentenced to death in the USA. Relatives and others minimized relevant histories of abuse, in some cases even testifying against the accused.

The obtaining of accurate detailed knowledge may thus be time-consuming and difficult, but the making of decisions with major consequences in its absence is unethical. The principal problem arising from lack of knowledge is that personal prejudices, more or less influenced by general social prejudices, are likely to have more influence than when knowledge is abundant.

The Psychiatrist as the Agent of the Patient

In most doctor/patient relationships, there is an expectation that the doctor's first concern is with the individual patient, yet wider social concerns can never be ignored, the doctor may have over-riding legal obligations or issues of public safety may arise.

Confidentiality

The UK General Medical Council (GMC) (1987) booklet on professional conduct and discipline includes guidelines on professional confidence which require that, in general, the doctor must not divulge outside a professional relationship information which he has gained within it, unless he has the permission of the patient to do so—this includes non-clinical duties, such as administration and medico-legal work. However, no UK patient has an absolute legal right to medical confidentiality, as exists in some states of America under the Privilege Statutes (Group for the Advancement of Psychiatry, 1960). The GMC document lists a number of exemptions, e.g. a breach of confidentiality may be thought to be in the patient's own interest, although this may need to be fully justified subsequently, or the doctor may have an overarching social obligation in the case of a highly dangerous condition, such as a duty to report the name of a patient with epilepsy to a driving authority. It is even possible under GMC guidelines to widen the notion of 'public interest' so that a doctor may be allowed to help the police to arrest his patient if he is confident that the patient has committed a serious crime. Some have argued though (e.g. Seighart, 1982; Lock, 1984; Macara, 1984) that these established principles are outdated.

Medical records, their accessibility and ownership is a continuing area of confusion (Kenny, 1982). It is generally in the interests of patients that full and accurate records are kept, but while the ownership of the record falls to the employing authority, the ownership of the data within is less clear. Modern psychiatric care is multi-professional. The effective involvement of others requires sharing of information. Not all colleagues are employed by health authorities or subscribe to professional bodies with disciplinary powers, such as the GMC, nor do they necessarily share the same ethical principles. Social workers have found difficulties with the requirement in some parts of England that clients' records be subject to local government scrutiny. An attempt to provide a patient with suitable treatment and facilities may thus endanger confidentiality. Does this make some disclosures to social workers unethical? Can safeguards against important breaches of security be devised? Surely the patient should know what is likely to happen to information given to the doctor?

Patients may request reports about their health for an employer, an employment agency, the Department of Social Services, an insurance company or a housing authority. It is recommended that such material be marked 'in confidence' and exclusively for the attention of the person or body to whom it is addressed, but such marking is not legally binding. Privileged information passed to other people is out of the patient's and the doctor's control. Doctors should set personal codes about the exchange of information. Information should not be passed to a third party without the express (usually written) permission of the patient or informant. Unless required in law, case notes, which include data from a variety of sources, should not be handed over in their entirety unless permission has been gained from each source. Where this has not been possible, the name of each informant may be given to the third party for consultation.

If patients are under legal restraint (e.g. on a restriction order), they lose most of their rights to confidentiality; civil servants and others require to be fully informed about such patients by the doctor. Employers, landlords, future spouses/companions, may all have a right to know something of a patient's history. When a patient refuses permission for even limited data transfer, then this fact and its consequences has to be made clear to all parties concerned. Patients' general rights to confidentiality do not override a potential victim's rights to be forewarned. Nevertheless, only the minimum information necessary to comply with reasonable safety should be issued. These matters are discussed more fully in a Royal College of Psychiatrists document (1990b) which contains an appendix on *Confidentiality and Forensic Psychiatry*. The APA has also published *Guidelines on Confidentiality* (American Psychiatric Association, 1987b), and the APA ethical annotations given in Appendix 4, spell out some strict principles, for example:

> Confidentiality is essential to psychiatric treatment
> A psychiatrist may release confidential information only with the authorization of the patient or under proper legal compulsion and
> Ethically the psychiatrist may disclose only that information which is relevant to a given situation. He/she should avoid offering speculation as fact. Sensitive information such as an individual's sexual orientation or fantasy material is usually unnecessary.

The interests of other people in addition to the interests of the patient were brought forcibly to the attention of doctors in the USA by the complex and far reaching *Tarasoff* decision.

> In brief, when a student at the University of California, who was in psychotherapy, became violently jealous of a fellow student, Tatiana Tarasoff, the therapist warned the police. The police interviewed the man and decided to take no action. Subsequently, the man left treatment and sometime after that killed Ms. Tarasoff. The woman's family sued the University for damages, lost the suit initially, but won it on appeal on the grounds that therapists have a duty to warn potential victims. This was modified in a further special appeal that therapists have a duty to *protect* potential victims. This could be done by warning the potential victim, talking to the police, or admitting the patient to hospital.

Dyer, A. R. (1988) provides a more comprehensive account. Appelbaum et al. (1989) discuss the impact that this Californian case has had on the rest of the USA, including new laws in other states, the large amounts of compensation being awarded in a few cases, and the general anxiety among psychiatrists. The American Psychiatric Association has drafted a model statute on the physician's duty to take precautions against patient violence. The essence of it is an attempt to limit the liability of therapists to those cases where there is clear evidence of potential violence and to limit the physician's duties to practical steps such as those suggested in *Tarasoff*. Gagné (1989), a Canadian psychiatrist, mused that the responsibility for wrongdoing has gradually shifted over time from the doer, to the devil, to insanity, and now to the psychiatrist.* An over-reaction perhaps, but the Tarasoff case does illustrate that the public perception of morality in medicine is changing and, to some extent, the doctor has to take this changing perception into account. Weinstock (1988b) has suggested that the Tarasoff decision has meant that standards of confidentiality have increasingly yielded to a perceived duty to protect third parties. He recommended that ethical behaviour for psychotherapists must include the willingness to take some reasonable risk to preserve patients' confidentiality if they judge that there is little real danger to the potential victim.

Langton and Torpy (1988) gave a good example of a practical dilemma involving these principles.

> A 23-year-old man with sadistic sexual fantasies asked for help. He said he had embarked on attempted sexual assaults on several women. Among other things, he indulged in homosexual sadomasochism and his genitals and nipples were pierced with metal rings and bars. He had a collection of knives. His masturbatory fantasy was to imagine following a woman, attacking her with a knife and then forcing her back to his bedsit where he would tie her up, stab her to death and masturbate beside her body. He insisted on strict confidentiality. Compulsory admission under the MHA was considered, but rejected on the grounds that he would then refuse to cooperate with treatment. Reporting to the police was considered, but rejected on the grounds that he would not talk to them, further how could they protect a potential victim when none had been identified? Instead, he was seen regularly for outpatient psychotherapy. Antilibidinal drugs were tried without success. After 14 months he removed his genital piercings, became more self-confident, disposed of his weapons and his books on sadism, found work and stopped attending. At 20 months, he sought further treatment because he was in a difficult homosexual relationship.

Did the therapists take the right decisions? Opinions will divide. The one weakness in this story is the lack of mention of peer group discussion, a procedure which is always illuminating and often reassuring.

What to tell the patient

Often the patient knows less about his own case than do his advisers. This may be justifiable if the patient's capacity or his mental state will not allow full disclosure (*see below*) or comprehension, but such a situation should not be routine or arise without deliberation.

In Britain, the Access to Health Records Act 1990† gives patients the right of access, subject to certain exemptions, to recorded information about

---

* Perhaps the film *The Silence of the Lambs* is the apogee of that process!
† The NHS Management Executive has issued guidelines to the Act (HSG(91)6) obtainable from DOH Store, Heywood OL10 2PZ.

themselves made since November 1991, which is not already covered by rights of access to computerized records under the Data Protection Act 1984, The Access to Personal Files Act 1987 or The Access to Medical Reports Act 1988. The 1990 Act allows the patient or his representative to inspect the patient's medical record. Partial exclusions from the file may be made if the information is 'likely to cause serious harm to the physical or mental health of the patient or any other individual', or if it is 'relating to or provided by an individual other than the patient, who could be identified from that information'; those partial exclusions may be made without telling the patient they have been made. The patient may have incorrect information corrected, and his refutation of any other recorded material documented.

The effect of the Act is to extend the principles and procedures of the Data Protection Act to cover all health records. One problem for the psychiatrist is that, traditionally, little effort has been made to separate information according to its sources. Probably always good practice, this should now be regarded as very important. It is certainly always wise, in any official document, to indicate the source of any alleged 'fact'. Opinions, particularly opinions of the doctor, should also be kept separate, so that they are not given as facts. Opinions embrace everything from a differential diagnosis to jottings concerning possible interpretations during the course of psychotherapy.

Sergeant (1986) reviewed a consecutive sample of 100 of his own case notes and found that 90% of the records contained sensitive items about the patients themselves, their friends or relatives, including unintelligible notes, alarming comments or insulting comments. Problems of this kind in note keeping ought to be remediable with improved practice. Comments about the feelings of relatives, for example fear, will remain pertinent and sensitive. In no less than 18 cases, Sergeant believed that access to the full record could have provoked a serious reaction, such as a suicide attempt or violent outburst. Many interviewees had given the data in strict confidence, they might be less frank in future. Atkinson (1989) pointed out that some patients with schizophrenia have hitherto not been told their diagnosis (although their relatives may have been) on the grounds that it might harm them, yet there is no research to support this hypothesis. Soskis (1978) found that a sample of patients with schizophrenia knew little about their diagnosis and almost nothing about the benefits of drug treatment, but were extremely well informed about the risks and side-effects of such treatment. The converse was true for medical patients. Parrott et al. (1988) have addressed the issue of patient access to records specifically for the patient in a forensic psychiatry service and found it surprisingly problem free.

For the forensic psychiatrist, there is the longer-standing problem of how much access to give a patient to reports about him. Technically all reports submitted to a court are 'public' documents, so a patient could have access from that source if he insisted. In practice, if reports have been commissioned by a solicitor, the patient will usually be given access. A more serious worry is the extent to which sensitive information could be made really public. In Britain, reports are handled fairly confidentially, and judges and magistrates can often be persuaded to keep all or part of the report silent. Something similar happens at mental health review tribunals. Here, two copies of the report are prepared on some patients; a shorter version omitting sensitive material which the doctor believes the patient should not see. The shorter version is handed to the patient, while the full version is handed to the members of the tribunal and to the patient's legal adviser.

We believe it is good practice in nearly all cases to let the patient see all reports about him; whenever possible they should also be discussed with him by the writer. Possible exceptions to this rule include paranoid patients and those with severe mental handicap, but even patients from these groups should not routinely be excluded from such practice. The patients should be advised to return the report, since few can adequately maintain confidentiality. This process can be more than informative, it can also be therapeutic.

Informal and civil advocacy or guardianship

A patient may choose or have chosen for him some person to act as an intermediary or advocate for him with the doctor. At the simplest level a spouse or other relative is asked by the patient to accompany him when seeing the doctor, to ask some of the questions or share some of the decisions. Where the patient is under age, there is an expectation that parents or a guardian will generally be involved. Sometimes, particularly if a patient is in hospital, a primary nurse or a key worker may act on behalf of the patient. For people with a mental handicap, a system of patient advocacy is developing in which a lay person volunteers to work with such people and act on their behalf in certain situations. At a much more formal level, professionals, usually from within social services, may become guardians in respect of children, or of the adult mentally disordered. Rarely, if ever, are professionals or volunteer advocates chosen by the patient, and occasionally a relative may be imposed rather than chosen. Except where a social worker has been appointed as guardian, or has a statutory mental health role, none of the people mentioned has any legal powers in relation to medical decision-making.

An Institute of Medical Ethics Working Group (Nicholson, 1986) explored many of the delicate issues in relation to medical communication and decision-making with children. Although their principal concern was with research, their evidence and recommendations are of value in considering any patient group likely to be less than fully competent in a much wider range of circumstances. Although, therefore, openness about the patient's state and treatment, and assistance in decision-making where the patient may seem marginally competent to decide for himself, may seem protective of the patient, this openness and sharing should only take place to the limits that the patient himself wishes to impose. Not infrequently, patients are adamant about wishing to exclude even their next of kin from some matters. When necessary, they may prefer to involve a wholly independent person in difficult decision-making.

The Psychiatrist as Agent of the Patient's Lawyer

A familiar situation for the forensic psychiatrist is to act wholly or in part as the agent of the patient's lawyer. The lawyer is expected in the very crudest terms to take instructions from his client, and will, in turn, issue instructions on this basis. Within a restricted area, therefore, the lawyer is committed to acting more nearly for the patient than does anyone else; he becomes his mouthpiece for the moment. This is not necessarily the same thing as acting for the patient in his best interests, although lawyers who are also familiar with mental health work often do manage to combine both sorts of advocacy.

In working with any lawyer there are various shifts in the balance of interaction and care that must be recognized. The quality of confidentiality changes with the involvement of a lawyer. Most doctors are familiar with the near automatic transfer of the psychiatric report, prepared at the request of a solicitor, from the lawyer to the patient, often without enquiry about the likely effect on the patient, or about the patient's capacity to maintain the confidentiality of his own report. The psychiatrist must be prepared to take the initiative in advising about this.

Whenever medico-legal work is to be undertaken, the implications of this should be explained to the patient. He should know that information given to the doctor will be given to the instructing lawyer, will probably be given to the court and may end up on a prison or other case file. Lawyers may choose to withhold information that a doctor might regard as in the best interests of the patient.

> One example is of a woman in her early twenties who had developed grandiose and destructive religious ideas. It says in St Matthew's Gospel (5.3): 'If thy right hand offend thee, cut it off, . . .'. It had, and she nearly did. At the time of assessment, she was charged in connection with serious harm to a woman she had been trying to help according to her religious tenets. It seemed likely that having spent a period of time in hospital for treatment of depression, following the near amputation of her hand, and having given up good career prospects to follow a progressively more itinerant, detached and chaotic lifestyle over the previous 3 years, that she might have been developing a schizophrenic illness. The patient's lawyer chose to suppress the psychiatric report and to ignore the offer of a psychiatric hospital bed in open conditions because the woman herself wanted to run a religious defence and go free. In the event she was found guilty. The judge expressed sympathy for the woman's good intentions, but considered her dangerous and passed a sentence of imprisonment, unaware of the psychiatric background. The woman quickly became overtly psychotic and threatening in prison, was transferred to a maximum security hospital and has remained there for the last 10 years. The disparate interests of the patient conflicted to her disadvantage.

This example demonstrates a range of the potential difficulties in doctor-lawyer-patient relations. The patient wished to expound on her motives and be exonerated of guilty intent. She neither believed she was insane nor wished to be labelled so. The doctor, too, doubted the guilty intent, but argued probable mental disorder and tried to secure appropriate care. The lawyer chose to exercise selective control on the information available to the court. Treatment priorities were totally disregarded. In a future such case in England, it might be possible to submit the psychiatric report to the court anyway following the *Edgell* decision (*see also* McHale, 1991).

In presenting data to the court or other public body, no vestige of confidentiality of the information given can be guaranteed. While it is true that requests to a court for particularly sensitive material not to be read out in open court are often respected, once evidence is contested, then any data from the patient that the doctor or psychiatrist has included in the report are vulnerable. Particular caution is required with respect to data about other people who are significant in the patient's life, such as a relative with similar illness, or his victim. The patient's permission for a report about him to go before a court cannot be taken to imply permission to present material about other people. Where data must be included because of its relevance to arguments in the case, every effort must be taken either to protect the precise identity of the individuals referred to, or to gain their permission to discuss aspects of their life.

The Psychiatrist as Agent of Society

Actions breaching confidentiality to protect the public can be partly justified on the grounds that they are also in the best interests of the patient. It is of no value to a patient to harm someone else. On the other hand, society's use of the psychiatrist can be more blatant and less therapeutic in the courts and the penal system. Psychiatry can, for example, be discredited in order to secure a conviction, only to be restored to credibility for the sake of imposing a punitive sentence.

In the USA doctors may be asked to testify that a convicted criminal is fit to die or even too dangerous to be allowed to live (*see below*). It is difficult to resist pressures to do these things when they come with the majesty of the law, although familiarity with the process of giving evidence in court (Carson, 1990c) may offer considerable protection in this regard. Veiled threats concerning status and job prospects may pose another threat to ethical practice. The argument that the doctor should be involved in the prevention of violence to others is understandable, but medical ethics demand that this should be done with minimal violence and damage to the patient.

In spite of a remarkable submission by the Home Office that there are no special ethical problems for the prison doctor (*Freeman*), there are, in fact, especially complicated problems for doctors working in institutions which are established by the State expressly to control the behaviour of individuals.

The services of particular interest in this respect are the security hospital services, the prison service and the police. The complications arise from juxtaposing the Geneva Declaration tenet, 'The health of my patient will be my first consideration' (*see* Appendix 4), with the old dictum that nobody can serve two masters simultaneously. Even within the Geneva Declaration, the loyalty to one's patient is third on the list. Top, and maybe overriding all the others, comes a pledge 'to consecrate my life to the service of humanity'. There are occasions when practitioners will have to agonize over the relative weight to be given to humanity in general against the interests of any particular patient. We believe that whenever there is tension between patient and community, the doctor should not only debate the matter within himself, but also with other practitioners and, having arrived at a decision, he should write that down, with evidence for the arguments that led to the decision.

Security hospitals

Security and treatment are not incompatible, indeed effective treatment requires that both staff and patients feel secure. Conflict is mainly confined to a few areas in which the responsible doctor believes that the therapeutic need for security is over, whilst political authorities, such as the Home Office, disagree. In such cases, it is sensible for the doctor to seek at least one other opinion, to discuss the matter with the patient's lawyer, but above all to discuss the matter in detail with the retaining authority. Such a process will usually bring compromise, and new therapeutic ideas which will enable the patient to continue to make progress.

Prison service

Three categories of doctors practice in British prisons, full-time prison doctors, part-time prison doctors, and outside doctors called in for particular purposes, usually a report. Bowden (1976) has argued that as far as the work of the full-time prison medical officer is concerned, his dual allegiance to the State and to his patients creates such difficulties that it results in activities which favour the State. Certainly the tensions for prison doctors are much greater than for those working in a health care system. In prisons, an important objective of the institution is to punish, this has to be contrary to any medical objective. Doctors can and do temper the harshness of prison by looking after the needs of individual patients and by protecting them as far as possible, but they are in a difficult position if the prison governor expects one thing and a patient's health requires another. The conflict can be alleviated to some extent by calling in doctors who are not in the employ of the prison authorities, a practice which should be extended at least in England and Wales as the Prison Medical (Health) Service becomes a predominantly purchasing agency.

Even relatively simple medical duties can create conflicts for a prison doctor. He may be asked to certify someone as fit for punishment. At one level, this is reasonable, as it offers the doctor an opportunity to protect patients with disabilities from punishment, but, unfortunately, it also has the effect of the doctor colluding with punishment of healthy people, which may be detrimental to their health. The prison doctor also knows that the incentives to fabricate illness are greater in these circumstances than in other situations. An approach which could be adopted by prison doctors, but has not been so far, is to decline to examine anyone about to be punished. This would prevent the doctor's conflict and indicate more clearly who is responsible for what.

Purchaser/provider arrangements for health care in prisons will give a new set of conflicts, but also opportunities to improve standards. For example, is it ethical for a health authority or an individual doctor to undertake a contract to provide medical services to a prison if basic health care facilities within that prison are inadequate? Would it be reasonable to provide medical services to a prison that had an inadequate supply of nurses, or in which pharmacy budgets are too low? Should a doctor working on the purchaser side of the contract, i.e. for the prison itself, continue to do so if he has little or no control over the level of finance allocated to medical requirement?

Police service

A previous paper discussed some of the ethical issues relating to psychiatric work within the police service (Ochberg and Gunn, 1980). In principle, the same dilemmas arise as with the prison service, but they are usually less intense. No psychiatrist works full-time for the police service, and the police are not usually responsible for the day-to-day care of prisoners. In situations where they are, however, such as when police stations are used as temporary remand centres because of overcrowding, then the same issues arise in police work as in prison work.

As with other areas of conflict over medical work, working with policemen necessitates a clear understanding of psychiatric objectives and a deliberate decision on each occasion, balancing the needs of the patient, or potential patient, the needs of other people, and the needs of the police service itself. There is not much dilemma, for example, in the use of medical knowledge to assist the police to release a person taken hostage by a terrorist, provided the police make every effort also to arrest the terrorist unharmed. Further-more, it is probably not the business of doctors to act as moral advisers to the police in their own dilemma of balancing risk to terrorist against risk to hostage. If that balance was to go significantly against the doctor's personal moral code, then he should resign his police work, maybe protest as a citizen, but still not confuse his medical role with his general citizen's responsibility.

Some areas of police work are more problematic. A police surgeon, for example, may declare that an individual has excess alcohol in his veins, knowing that this will result in the suspect's prosecution and this may not be of benefit to the individual. In practice, the police surgeon will have decided to undertake this type of work before he meets any particular patient. An especially onerous responsibility of this kind arises when a doctor is called to a police station to decide whether an individual is fit to be detained or fit to be interviewed. A mistake here may result in, for example, a death by suicide in prison, or a false confession. As with other ethical dilemmas, it is not only a wise judgement between the needs of the individual and the needs of the community which is required, but also a high degree of psychiatric knowledge and skill.

The paper drew attention to five important issues in multiprofessional working—professional identity, health ethics, transfer of information, peer review, and education in deontology (ethics).

1. Psychiatrists should never lose their distinctive role; they are not policemen, prison officers, social workers, nurses or anything else at all. For a psychiatrist, the tenets of psychiatry must come first. Nevertheless, interdisciplinary discussion is essential.

2. WHO distinguishes medical ethics, the ethics of person-to-person relationships, from health ethics, defined as the accountability of governments to their populations in regard to health matters (World Health Organisation, 1975). Unfortunately, what constitutes health ethics is left very vague as 'the attainment by all peoples of the highest possible level of health'. They do probably mean, however, that any member state of the United Nations has the responsibility to see that the services it provides, and these services include the police force and the prison service, should be compatible with high levels of health for all citizens. It would, therefore, be unethical in WHO terms for a doctor to collude with police or prison department policies that endangered the health of citizens. Health ethics need codification.

3. Transfer of information is dealt with in more general terms below.

4. Peer review has been stressed repeatedly throughout this chapter.

5. Education in deontology should be fundamental to all medical education; that such education is deficient in Britain is a cause for concern and possibly the root of some ethical lapses.

The Right to Treatment

One difficulty in discussing ethical practice is that moral issues get tangled up with legal ones. Moral values in a society metamorphose into laws. 'Rights' can, therefore, be legal protections under perhaps a bill of rights, or simply moral imperatives as agreed by a professional group or society at large. Discussions on 'rights' will be different in different places at different times. Legalistic societies, such as the USA, will emphasize the law and its complexities. Britain, which has no bill of rights, will rely more on social pressure and parliamentary debate, although this may not always be effective. Mentally abnormal people, especially those with antisocial propensities are not generally regarded with much sympathy (Hill, 1982).

An important right that is relatively neglected, at least in Britain, is the right to treatment. This seems to be a fairly fundamental precept for medical practice in an affluent society. The British National Health Service was based on the idea that all citizens should be able to get necessary medical treatment no matter what their income. Income is not the only obstacle though, provision of services and incarceration also influence treatment opportunities. It was these latter factors that induced an American court in 1966 (*Rouse*) to spell out two new rules:

> 'The purpose of involuntary hospitalization is treatment not punishment.' and
> 'Absent (i.e. without) treatment, the hospital is transform(ed) . . . into a penitentiary where one could be held indefinitely.' (Cameron, 1969)

The judge went further in his writings after the case (Bazelon, 1969), saying:

> Ideally, we should be able to ensure that each involuntarily committed patient receives the best and most appropriate treatment. But if psychiatrists cannot agree what this might be in the individual case, it is nevertheless essential to ensure that the patient confined for treatment receives some form of therapy that a respectable sector of the psychiatric profession regards as appropriate.

Note that, as elsewhere, the peer group is the reference point.

This judgment had an effect on US thinking about mental hospitals and the patients locked up in them. Rachlin (1974) pressed further:

> The paramount civil right of the patient should be that of adequate treatment.

and—

> the most important civil liberty which can be granted to the seriously ill patient—freedom from psychosis—

He suggested that freedom to wander the streets in terror of paranoid delusions is not freedom at all. A further principle that has developed from this is that treatment should be provided in the least restrictive environment possible. In the USA, several class action suits on behalf of patients have been successful, although Nordwind (1982) is not impressed that they have had much general impact. Whilst patients detained against their wishes thereby have a right to treatment, voluntary patients do not. She has urged new developments in the right to treatment law which will—

> compel creation or remediation of community care services and programs for chronically mentally disabled persons in their communities.

If it were fully accepted that anybody who is diagnosed as a psychiatric patient using agreed criteria (say the ICD–9) should have the *right* to psychiatric treatment if they so wish, and treatment is defined in terms of appropriate medicines, nursing, psychological treatments and community support, then this doctrine would have a profound impact on international psychiatry. Medical attitudes would have to change, new resources would have to be found, prisons would have to change, and many prisoners would have to be moved out of prison into health facilities. It is the attitudinal change which is perhaps the toughest. Laws and moral values ultimately depend upon peer group reference. If, as seems the case, doctors are as hostile to troublesome and offensive patients as everyone else, then such patients will always get a raw deal. The English mental health legislation says that patients in the legal categories of psychopathic disorder and of mental impairment (*see* pp. 13–15) are subject to different rules of admission from other patients, and this tends to exclude some patients from treatment. Although the rules are actually concerned with *compulsory* admission and treatment, they reinforce negative attitudes to treatment in a wider sense and thus also indirectly affect voluntary treatment for such patients.

Consent to Treatment

A patient's 'right' which has had far more attention than the right to treatment is the right *not* to have treatment. The first and fundamental point that is now widely agreed and incorporated into the law in most countries is that, when patients embark upon treatment, they should either know what they are letting themselves in for, and agree to it (i.e. give 'informed' consent) or, if for some reason that is not possible, they should have their interests safeguarded by others, through laws and agreed procedures.

The British law covering consent to treatment is set out in Ch. 2. One or two points in that legislation are worth emphasizing here. One is that the first criterion for compulsory admission of a patient to hospital is that it is necessary for his health. Considerations of his safety logically follow, and the question of the protection of others is raised. Another is the introduction of legislation establishing consent to treatment, or for overriding refusal, once a patient is detained involuntarily under one of the mental health acts. The procedures are different for different types of treatment, so they are less stringent for psychotropic medication, more stringent for ECT, and most stringent of all for psychosurgery and hormonal implants.

The law is strangely silent when mental ill health threatens physical health. For example, one patient had bilateral cateracts causing severe loss of vision. He declined surgery not because of any aversion to surgery *per se*, but on the grounds that it would do no good as only the removal of his enemies' ray machines would help. His beliefs did not abate with psychotropic medication. His quality of life would have been substantially improved with surgery. Further, it could be expected that his mental state would improve if his sight improved, but it is hard to argue eye surgery as a treatment for psychosis! As usual, the doctor may be greatly helped in his efforts to ensure the best for the patient by peer review and support, and may be protected in extreme cases by judicial review, but even case law in this area is scanty. Some guidance has been given by *Re F*, a case which concerned the sterilization of a severely mentally handicapped woman.

Problems are also raised by the obtaining of consent for investigative procedures. Some are physically invasive, some (e.g. HIV serum testing) are socially or psychologically intrusive. The World Health Organisation (1987b), the British Medical Association (1988), the General Medical Council (1988) and the Royal College of Psychiatrists (Catalan et al., 1989) have all published helpful, widely agreed guidelines on HIV testing, which may serve as models in some other contentious areas too, such as screening for illicit drugs or alcohol.

Competence

There is always an underlying question in psychiatry about the patient's capacity for decision making, and there is no absolute standard of such competence. A patient may be deemed not competent to consent to be admitted to hospital, but competent to decide whether or not to have medication once there. Tests of competence have to be designed specifically for the task in hand. A clinical example may illustrate. A potential witness may believe that God has been killed by the Devil and that this catastrophe can be managed only by brave lying to throw him off the scent. Such a person is not competent to be a witness, yet the same person may understand that a period in a psychiatric hospital is both desirable and likely to be beneficial, and thus be competent to agree to be admitted as a voluntary patient.

The moral/ethical matters to be considered in assessing competency have been well set out in Appelbaum and Roth (1981). They argued that in evaluating any patient's competence five issues must be considered.

1. Psychodynamic factors, for decisions are not made in an emotional vacuum: 'The seemingly neutral words of the informed consent form or doctor-patient consent interview can, in fact, be highly charged for the patient.
2. The accuracy of the historical information conveyed by the patient. The patient's history should be checked with informants.
3. The accuracy and completeness of the information disclosed to the patient. In Britain, it is legal doctrine that what information is given to a patient is a matter for medical judgement (*see below*). Appelbaum and Roth rightly suggest that the doctor should always check back on how much the patient has actually understood.
4. The patient's mental state. Competency may fluctuate as mental state

fluctuates. Unless there is an emergency, the patient's competency should be evaluated on more than one occasion.

5. The effect of the setting in which the consent is obtained. The patient may dislike a particular hospital or a particular nurse or doctor, this must be taken into account.

They conclude:

> The clinician . . . knows that what the law calls competency is, in fact, a set of deductions from a variety of clinical data. . . . False positive findings of incompetency will provoke unnecessary court procedures . . . and . . . substantial injury to . . . sense of self. False negative findings of competency leave patients who have inadequate decision-making powers without the protections afforded by substitute decision makers.

And finally:

> *Clinicians who would be loathe to offer a diagnosis and dynamic formulation for an outpatient after one visit are often surprisingly willing to declare a patient competent or incompetent on the basis of a single brief interaction* (italics added).

The Appelbaum and Roth conclusion implies that second opinion doctors should be very careful, and take a lot of time, before disagreeing with a clinical team which has evaluated a patient with some thoroughness. Perhaps one important role for the second opinion doctor is to ascertain that the clinical team has indeed evaluated the situation with thoroughness.

Information

An integral part of competency consideration is the nature and quality of information available to the patient. How much has been acquired and how much comprehended? 'Informed' consent is an American doctrine that is central to legal regulations there. The term used in Britain is 'real consent' and some of its principles arise from a difficult case concerning the Maudsley Hospital (*Sidaway*). In that case, Lord Templeman said:

> A patient may make an unbalanced judgement because he is deprived of adequate information. A patient may also make an unbalanced judgement if he is provided with too much information and is made aware of possibilities which he is not capable of assessing because of his lack of medical training, his prejudices, or his personality.

As the judgment later explains, this puts the responsibility for deciding what information the patient shall have squarely on the shoulders of the doctor.

An excellent study of the use of information in the consent process has been made by Lidz et al. (1984). The informed consent procedure ought to be a fundamental reordering of the doctor-patient relationship along egalitarian-participatory lines. The goals of the informed consent doctrine are (1) to promote individual autonomy and (2) to encourage rational decision-making.

In practice, it may simply amount to getting a patient to sign a piece of paper describing a forthcoming treatment. After 4 years of studying the way informed consent was handled in an evaluation centre, a research ward, and an outpatient clinic, the authors concluded:

> Informed consent of the pristine form envisioned by law and by ethicists was only rarely, if ever, to be found in the hospital.

More fundamentally, they saw no evidence that informed consent had beneficial effects. It did not improve staff-patient communication, improve patients' cooperation with treatment, lead to better patient understanding, or lead to greater patient autonomy. Patients did not refuse treatment in large numbers nor was there great patient anxiety about the risks of treatment. The worst feature of the procedure was the staff cynicism about it. The broad conclusion that can be drawn from this thorough study is that improvements in medical standards are more likely to come from internal educational processes than external legal contraints. The American experiment of complex legal forms is not one to be followed. This is not to say, however, that the notion of 'consent' should be devalued or abandoned. The same group also showed (Roth et al., 1982) that real retention of information about a procedure, best ensured through interview, was significantly associated with treatment compliance.

The British doctrine of 'real consent' needs more research, yet it would seem indisputable that the way to impart information to patients is by discussion. A discussion within the bounds of the patient's competence can lead to questions and the clarification of the important issues for that particular patient. Appelbaum and Roth (1984) suggested that a series of discussions would make the whole process alive and meaningful. Is not that part of psychotherapy anyway?

One of us (Taylor, 1983) has presented a simple aide-memoire based on the word INFORM for the negotiation of valid consent to treatment or, indeed, assessment procedures or research. The requirements for real consent are:

an *I*nformed psychiatrist
*N*on-technical presentation to patient
*F*amiliarity with patient
*O*ther informants (e.g. family, primary nurse)
*R*epetition of information
*M*oral obligation (no threats!)

Consent forms may from time-to-time have to be used, but these should be simple documents in which the patient confirms that he has been informed to his satisfaction about what is proposed and is willing to go ahead. It should be remembered that most consent forms are for the protection of the doctor, not the patient. In one study we conducted, more than one paranoid patient refused to sign the consent form, but was entirely happy to continue with the research interview.

It should never be assumed that consent is for ever. The patient may choose to withdraw it when he has had experience of what the treatment is really like. Further discussion should follow. Even if at some point compulsion is used to ensure that a patient receives appropriate treatment, the process of communication about his condition and its treatment should continue. Someone who is too disordered to make appropriate decisions is rarely too disordered to be frightened and to benefit from appropriate reassurance and is never too disordered to disqualify themselves from ordinary human courtesy.

Research in Forensic Psychiatry

The problem of the negative emotions which surround 'research' in general psychiatry also apply to forensic psychiatry research. Thus many people are suspicious of the very word 'research', imagining harm being inflicted on patients with no prospect of benefit to them personally. Rarely are the positive aspects of research emphasized. In fact, research subjects get a lot of attention which they enjoy and from which they may benefit, and they get a sense of satisfaction in being able to do something for others. Treatment must be based on sound knowledge derived from research, and clinical styles and methods are improved by the importing of research methods of inquiry and scepticism. For these treatment reasons, research is inherently ethical unless it can be shown to be flawed. A set of principles for biomedical research was annunciated by the World Medical Association in 1964 (the Declaration of Helsinki), amended in 1975, 1983, 1989, and is given in Appendix 4. The frequency of updating gives a clue to the difficulties and the rate of change in this area. Although not designed with psychiatric patients specifically in mind, they do form a useful guide for all research with patients.

Research ethics committees are now common in most western countries. They function as gatekeepers allowing approved, i.e. morally approved projects to pass and rejecting others. In the best ethics committees, scientific rigour is also examined, because a project which cannot have a useful scientific outcome is morally dubious. Herein lies a problem, ethics committees themselves vary in composition, skill, knowledge and use varying moral criteria (Lock, 1990). The Department of Health (1991) has issued useful guidelines for the establishment of ethics committees to offer advice on research on NHS patients or their records and/or by NHS staff. It is rare for one ethics committee to accept on trust the opinion of other ethics committees.

The most serious weakness in the current system of testing the morality of research is that there is no organization anywhere looking at the morality of *not* doing research. Unanswered questions can and do leave patients in pain or with shortened life spans. Rarely, if ever, does the morality of turning a project down get an airing. A review by Eichelman et al. (1984) is an exception.

Competence to consent is, of course, relevant to a discussion on research. The mentally incapacitated patient may not be able to provide consent in the same degree as the fully competent patient, although it is our experience that many frankly psychotic patients are capable of discussing their consent in meaningful terms. Several deluded and hallucinated patients have volunteered for research programmes understanding that they were being invited to act as 'guinea pigs' and have engaged in sophisticated debate about that, while others have made clear that they wish to be reconsulted on a regular basis. The intriguing difficulty of the response of paranoid patients to a written consent form has been mentioned already.

Should psychotic patients be excluded from a study? Will not that invalidate the results? (Edlund et al., 1985). If all mentally handicapped patients and all seriously deluded patients are excluded from research, will not that further disadvantage people already seriously disadvantaged? Treatment can, ultimately, only be tested adequately in those for whom it is intended. While severely disabled patients should never be disadvantaged by being submitted to unsound or damaging research, neither should they be deprived of taking part in research into their condition. Where there is doubt about competence, consent for the proposed research should be obtained if possible by proxy using close friends, relatives, or nurses and doctors *caring for* (as opposed to researching into) the patient, even though this has no legal standing (Nicholson, 1986, has relevant material). Ethics committees should assist in determining the appropriate level of consent, and soundings about 'consent' from the patient should be taken constantly. Even with an incompetent patient, it is not difficult to discern whether the procedure itself (e.g. interview, X-ray, blood test) is causing distress or harm. If it does, it should be modified, postponed or abandoned.

Incarcerated Patients

Research on prisoners and compulsorily detained patients has a bad name, because there was a phase in the USA when such people were bribed to undertake dangerous research (e.g. becoming dependent on opiates) by offers of earlier release. Such practices have been stopped, can be easily prevented, and should not now be used as a reason to prevent studies on patients in secure institutions. The majority of such patients are able to give real consent to things like treatment. Patients should be encouraged to take, in safety, as full a part as possible in the life of their community, and that includes research.

Offenders and Prisoners

Offenders, whether in prison or not, are free to decline to see doctors or partake in research. All studies on offenders report a refusal rate. Some prison interview studies report a low refusal rate, this is because most prisoners actually enjoy talking to outside researchers, they queue up and may want to know why they are not in the sample! Far from harming prisoners, the attention and discussion which it brings may actually benefit them. On the other hand, it should be made clear to prisoners that no linkage is ever made, however distant, between special privileges or earlier release and participation in a research project.

A more difficult problem with prison research, although it is a problem in all research, is safety of information. Whether on remand or being considered for parole, an inmate could give information to a researcher which could be damaging to his case if fed into the administrative system, e.g. an offender might reveal hitherto undetected offences. Scrupulous attention has, therefore, to be given to confidentiality and the real limits of that confidentiality must be clearly understood by both researcher and subject. It is sometimes feared that courts could demand a researcher's confidential record. This is most unlikely, if only because information on the record would be hearsay and of no use in court. It has never happened in Britain, and the Director of Public Prosecutions confirmed in an answer to a query about one of our research projects on remanded prisoners that he would not take such a step. Another fear is the subpoena-happy defence lawyer who believes that confidential research records could help his client, but we have never encountered this. The few solicitors that have enquired about such information have always respected their client's privacy when matters are explained. Nevertheless, the research psychiatrist is under the same obligation as other medical practitioners to consider a breach of the general confidentiality rules if, in his judgement, there is a serious risk to the future health and safety of the subject or identifiable future victims. We have always chosen to make this explicit in the initial discussion with the individual subject.

The Psychiatrist in Court

Weinstock (1988a) surveyed 102 members of the psychiatry and behavioural section of the American Academy of Forensic Sciences and found that the work most often quoted as giving rise to ethical problems was testifying in court. The principal concerns were being a 'hired-gun', withholding part of the truth to endorse a particular legal position, and giving sworn testimony without adequate knowledge. One of us has elsewhere (Gunn, 1991a) argued that it is wrong to devote too much time to court work when skilled professional services are in such short supply. Long wrangles in court may be entertaining, but often they have little impact on the patient's future and they can divert the doctor away from treatment.

One point sometimes made in the USA (e.g. Sadoff, 1988) is that it is unwise for a treating psychiatrist to testify about his patient—

> even though lawyers and judges may believe that his testimony is the most effective because he knows the patient best.

The argument is that the treating doctor is bound to be biased in favour of his patient. We would argue, on the contrary, that in an adversarial system this is no disadvantage and is well understood. The ethical obligation is to try to be objective, as far as possible, to tell the truth, the whole truth and nothing but the truth, but to realize that *every* observer is biased and note the direction of one's own bias.

The general view in Britain is that the most satisfactory recommendations to courts are likely to come from the service provider, since he knows best the likely fit between the prospective patient and his services. Medical recommendations from a doctor who is prepared not only to recommend. treatment, but to provide it, are going to be more relevant than those written in the abstract. In any case, British law requires evidence that there is a doctor willing to treat in a specified hospital before a hospital order can be made.

An important issue in the writing of reports is the power of the negative comment. It is much easier to persuade a court that someone is dangerous, or bad, or in need of long-term incarceration than any of the opposites. One reason is that societal bias against the mentally abnormal offender is generally negative (Hill, 1982), and negative comments are likely to be flowing with the general attitudinal current. Negative comments may be necessary (at least the non-moral ones about prognosis may be), but they should be set in the context of a positive background (e.g. the treatment which is appropriate), and should never be made without strong evidence. A negative comment in a negative background (e.g. this man is an untreatable psychopath) is unlikely to be challenged and is tantamount to fixing for the accused a long prison sentence—not the business of psychiatry. The psychiatrist should also be scrupulous about never crossing the medical threshold in making non-medical recommendations for disposal; this is peculiarly inappropriate if the accused is suffering from a mental disorder, but just as unacceptable for those who are not. The court may invite or press for such recommendations, but the psychiatrist should resist. Such comments would be irrelevant and incompetent and such an invitation is highly unlikely to be for the benefit of the offender. It is our belief that it is incompatible with the work of any of the caring professions to recommend imprisonment. Such a recommendation from doctors is certainly unsound.

The word dangerousness (dealt with in Ch. 16) merits a special mention. It should not be used in court, in other legal forums, or in legal documents. It is perfectly possible to discuss the prognosis of a patient's condition, the type of treatment required or still required, and the risks of any course of action without involving the use of a word which brings a great deal of negative emotional baggage with it, baggage which may well render objective discussion impossible.

The Death Penalty

The whole process of capital punishment distorts the work of the forensic psychiatrist. When a man or woman is charged with homicide in Britain, it is not too difficult to assess honestly and objectively the presence or otherwise of mental disorder in that individual and to apply the various legal tests for recommendations to the court or penal authorities. If capital punishment lurks in the background, then the doctor is in an immediate state of conflict for his medical instincts and attitudes will drive him to find any reason, however flimsy, to argue that the prisoner should not be killed. It can be argued that he is duty bound to do this. A primary role for a doctor is to preserve life. Worse is to come after a sentence of death has been passed, because the prison doctor may then be expected to certify that the condemned man is 'fit to die'. It is one of the curious perversities of human thinking to designate the judicial killing of the sick as unjust, but the judicial killing of the healthy as just in specific circumstances. In the days when capital punishment existed in Britain, murderers were sometimes saved from the gallows by illnesses such as tuberculosis. A monstrous question for the prison doctor was whether or not it was reasonable in medical terms to treat a condemned person's illness, to make them become fit enough to be killed. Refusing to treat could save the patient's life, a paradox indeed. Some (e.g. Mossman, 1987) still think it is legitimate for doctors to participate in this ghoulish social travesty. We would commend the considered view of an American forensic psychiatrist (Pollack, 1980).

> Following my testimony in the trial of Sirhan Sirhan for the murder of Senator Robert F. Kennedy, I have regularly refused requests from the courts and prosecuting attorneys for psychiatric opinions on criminal responsibility in certain cases. Earlier, though personally opposed to capital punishment, I had recognized it as an accepted part of the criminal law, and thus I felt it was not unethical for forensic psychiatrists to participate in capital cases for the prosecution if they were able to accept this principle of criminal justice. I no longer can do so.

We go even further and commend the resolution passed by the Third World Congress on Prison Health Care in Bristol 1988 which stated that the Congress:

> Opposes any and all participation by health professionals in any action which could be interpreted as cooperating with the execution of the death penalty.

This was ratified by the World Psychiatric Association in 1989 in the following terms:

The WPA declares that the participation of psychiatrists in any such action (executions) is a violation of professional ethics.

This echoed the AMA (APA) Principles of Medical Ethics, Section 1, 4 (Appendix 4), and a 1981 World Medical Association resolution:

> It is unethical for physicians to participate in capital punishment, although this does not preclude physicians certifying death (Kastrup, 1988).

To grasp the full significance of the death penalty, it is important to know which people are finally selected for execution by a complex legal system. Lewis and her colleagues in New York examined two series of death row inmates in the USA. Lewis et al. (1986) evaluated 15 people (13 men and 2 women) sentenced to death in five different States. The condemned people had exhausted all avenues of appeal and were close to death. All had histories of severe head injury, five had major neurological impairment, seven had mild neurological problems, six had schizophreniform psychoses antedating imprisonment and two others were manic-depressive. Naturally, the team asked themselves how such serious disorders were not previously identified. They thought that—

> probably, nobody suspected their existence and hence nobody looked for them. Moreover, contrary to the popular notion that murderers are simply sociopaths who will feign illness to 'get off', most of the subjects did not consider themselves sick or impaired and did not request specialized evaluations.

A later paper (Lewis et al., 1988) evaluated 14 condemned boys under the age of 18 in four States. Nine had major neurological impairment, seven suffered psychotic disorders antedating imprisonment, seven showed significant organic dysfunction on testing, and only two had full scale IQs above 90. Twelve had been brutally physically abused and five had been sodomized by relatives. As with the adults, the juveniles tried to hide evidence of cognitive defects and psychotic symptoms. Similarly, the boys were ashamed of their parents' brutality towards them and tried to conceal or minimize it.

> The very factors that led to the juveniles' aggression in the first place also contributed to an inadequate defence during the sentencing phase of their trials. Brain damage, paranoid ideation, physical abuse, and sexual abuse, were either overlooked or deliberately concealed.

As Lewis et al. (1986) pointed out:

> The question remains whether death row inmates differ clinically or in other ways from similarly violent individuals who receive less harsh sentence.

To complete any deficient education on the death penalty and the role expected of the medical profession in it, we would also commend an article by Jones (1990) in which he described the history and development of the electric chair in the USA, and the use of necropsy 'to complete the killing'. In many jurisdictions, the death penalty cannot take place without the presence of a doctor. If all doctors adhered to the WPA ruling (above), executions in those places would stop.

Teaching of Ethics

Whilst the introduction of sanctions against unethical practitioners is one way to control doctors' behaviour and thus safeguard patients, another is to provide them with better and more detailed education. Most British medical education does not include courses on ethics and philosophy as basic subjects. In 1980, the GMC recommended that ethics should be taught to all medical students. In Belfast, all students have a compulsory fourth year 3-week course which includes the following topics: autonomy, consent, telling the truth, confidentiality, allocation of resources, limitation of treatment, resuscitation, euthanasia, defining death, autonomy of the child, management of the handicapped, child abuse, research ethics, prenatal fetal diagnosis, impaired autonomy and paternalism (Irwin et al., 1988). In Heidelberg, an ethics course was changed because of increasing student concerns; these included how to respond to patients' questions when their consultants had already deceived them, and worries about inflicting pain on patients. The authors (Osbourne and Martin, 1989) advocated a small group tutorial seminar based on case studies for this work.

23
Victims and Survivors

Written and Edited by
Pamela J. Taylor

with contributions from

John Gunn and Gillian Mezey

On Becoming a Victim

> A victim is a living being sacrificed . . . in performance of a religious rite: a
> person or thing, injured or destroyed in the pursuit of an object, in gratification of
> a passion, or as a result of an event or circumstance.

The Oxford English Dictionary sets the scene without emotion. Few people
are now overtly sacrificed in the name of religion, although the mass 'suicide'
in Jamestown, Guyana, was as recent as 1978, 'holy wars' continue and
sacrifices in civil strife, political struggles and war remain commonplace
around the world. Huge natural disasters and major accidents seem to occur
with increasing regularity; accidents with one or two fatalities or serious
injuries are now so frequent that they rarely merit publicity beyond the
immediate family or community affected.

Recognition of the psychological effects of becoming a victim is growing.
With this, demand arises for more than occasional support from family and
friends, but also the informed efforts of lay counsellors and advisers and
treatment from mental health specialists. Further, expert psychiatric and
psychological reports to civil courts in the pursuit of compensation or to
such bodies as the (English) Criminal Injuries Compensation Board may be
required. In the criminal courts in England and Wales, the victim's place
remains anomalous, his role at its strongest being as a witness for the
prosecution. While the defendant has the benefit of full legal advice and
support, the victim does not. While the defendant may seek to introduce
evidence of good character and mitigating psychological explanations for his
behaviour, the witness may be subjected to challenge of good character, or
of their competence as a witness by reason of psychological disorder. Thus,
the event or act which first victimizes a person not uncommonly sets in chain
a series of further traumas. One victim of sexual assault regarded her
experience in the criminal court as worse than the rape itself, and kept

asking to withdraw from the long drawn-out compensation procedure to try and avoid what she felt was the public repetition of her rape. Those subject to massive publicity of their case, and the relentless pursuit of journalists generally suffer additional significant trauma. All of this is over and above the more fortuitous triggers of renewed distress in the routine of everyday life.

Reaction Forms

Terminology and Diagnostic Categories

The possibility of a relationship between trauma and impaired psychosocial functioning has been recognized for centuries. Shakespeare provided fictional accounts—for example in Hamlet's 'unmanly grief' following his father's murder. Pepys described his own experiences following the great fire of London in 1666, as well as the reactions of others, all summarized by Daly (1983). War has supplied the richest variety of terms and descriptions, for example 'Soldier's Heart', 'Da Costa's syndrome', 'nervous exhaustion', 'effort syndrome', and 'neurocirculatory asthenia' of the American Civil War, 'shell shock' of the First World War (WW1) and 'flying stress' and 'combat exhaustion' of the Second World War (WW2), followed by the 'combat neuroses' of subsequent hostilities. The status of such disorders has fluctuated considerably. There now seems little doubt that failure to recognize such disorders following the appalling trauma in the WW1 trenches led to men being shot as cowards, some having left their posts in an obvious state of disorientation (Babington, 1985). Nevertheless, many men were recognized as suffering from shell shock, one estimate being of up to 40% of casualties, and over twenty army hospitals in the UK were set up to deal specifically with them.

Major disasters have generated an increasing literature since 1944, when Lindemann published his classic paper on 'acute grief' following the Coconut Grove fire disaster. Such disorders have been incorporated in the International Classification of Diseases, although in the 9th version ICD–9 the operational definitions of acute reaction to stress (308) and adjustment reactions (309) seem crude in terms of what we now know about the range and duration of symptoms. The American diagnostic and statistical manual (DSM-III-R) includes post-traumatic stress disorder (PTSD) as an anxiety disorder, while ICD-10 will incorporate it as an adjustment disorder (World Health Organization, 1992).

Post-Traumatic Stress Disorder (PTSD)

Definition

The DSM-III-R definition of PTSD is operational, but strict. It requires a trauma 'outside the range of usual human experience' and, while giving PTSD the full status of mental disease, shifts the burden of abnormality on to the event—'an event . . . that would be mentally distressing to almost anyone'. ICD-10 has followed suit in this regard. It is in marked contrast to the emphasis, in the diagnostic criteria for adjustment disorder. Here the stressor may be more commonplace, but the—

> *maladaptive nature of the reaction* is indicated by either impairment in occupational or social function or *symptoms that are in excess of a normal and expectable reaction to the stressor* (our italics).

To qualify for PTSD under the American system a person must have had:

not less than 1 month with at least one intrusive repetitive phenomenon— such as recollection of the event, flashbacks or dreams; *and*

at least three indications of avoidance—be that of ordinary experiences or activities, activities reminiscent in whole or in part of the event, or avoidance of recall of the events; *and*

at least two indicators of increased arousal—such as poor sleep, poor concentration, irritability.

It is also noted that onset is usually, but not invariably, within 6 months, and that other features may be associated, such as depression or guilt, sometimes sufficiently for more than one diagnosis to be appropriate.

A most surprising omission in this definition is the lack of mention of feelings of loss of control over the environment, others, self and the future. A sense of personal powerlessness is common, and often accompanied by an observable increase in dependancy behaviours.

Although the DSM-III-R incorporates a statement of invariable aetiology into the definition of PTSD, and there is face validity in doing so, associations between trauma and disease are far from clear. Evidence that external events may have psychological impact, and result in mental disorder, is long-standing (e.g. Paykel, 1974); however, the extent to which it is the event *per se* that is associated with the disorder has been subject to repeated challenge (e.g. Fergusson and Horwood, 1987). There is no evidence that traumatic events are associated exclusively with the cluster of symptoms defining PTSD, quite the contrary. There is equally no evidence that noxious events, even those generally accepted as outside the range of usual human experience, invariably lead to such a disorder. A further problem lies in the threshold for 'usual human experience'. Can there be a universal standard? 'Simple bereavement' is denoted a common experience, but within any one lifetime the loss through death of a parent is an unusual event. Burstein (1989) mused on the specific diagnostic conundrum raised by motor accident victims. In his series of 70, all met symptomatic criteria for PTSD, criteria which simultaneously ruled out an adjustment disorder. The 70 people, however, constituted a mere handful of the 15.5 million in such accidents in the USA in 1984. In DSM-III R terms, then, do these people have no diagnosis by virtue of the precipitant being commonplace?

The introduction of standardized methods of assessment may diminish the problem of variable threshold for symptoms of disorder. Demonstration of a link between trauma and disease is a more difficult task, important both for clinical assessment, whether or not for the courts, and research. Assessors generally start work only after the traumatic event, by which time peoples' perceptions of their state or that of others may be profoundly distorted by an assumption that all was well before the disaster and all was not well afterwards. There are two studies that have contemporaneous data from before and after trauma. Both refer to children, and results may not apply to adults. Milgram and Milgram (1976) studied a group of children who had completed an anxiety rating scale in May 1973, just before the Yom Kippur War in October 1973, and then again in December 1973 just after it. Average anxiety levels for all the children increased significantly. Burke et al. (1982) had screening data from parents, teachers and the children themselves on a group of 81 preschool children who had participated in a Head Start programme. Six months later the area was hit by a severe blizzard and flood, immobilizing and damaging the city, forcing many evacuations. They repeated the assessments 5 months after the event. The parents tended to deny problems in their children, but significant problems emerged, including higher scores on the anxiety scale for the boys and an increase in aggressive conduct among those already identified as having special educational needs.

Assessment

There are major pitfalls in the clinical assessment of PTSD. First, patients sometimes present years after significant trauma. Data collection is thus of necessity retrospective, and often not any longer subject to independent corroboration. Intervening events may colour the patient's perceptions, memory and interpretations of the alleged event. Then, there is denial on the part of the patient and failure to enquire on the part of the physician. In one inpatient hospital survey of 105 women (Craine et al., 1988), for 56% of the 53 who claimed sexual abuse in childhood, the history had not been previously identified; 66% of these women met diagnostic criteria for PTSD, but none had been clinically recognized as suffering from it; 80% believed that they had been inadequately treated for problems associated with the abuse. It is not possible from the report to estimate the risk of false positives in this series, but it seems likely that the results indicate a real underidentification of PTSD through under enquiry.

Instruments to assist in the assessment and definition of PTSD are being developed. Keane et al. (1988), for example, developed a 35-item self-rating scale for combat survivors, while a related group (Keane et al., 1987) reviewed methods of psychological assessment and presented a reliable and valid multiaxial approach for the assessment of PTSD. Pitman et al. (1987) refined a psychophysiological approach to supplement clinical interviewing.

Physical correlates of psychological signs and symptoms. Several reviews have appeared recently summarizing links between the psychological manifestations of PTSD and physical change, each with a slightly different emphasis. Calabrese et al. (1987) discussed the impact of stress, bereavement and depression on immune function. Their data are equivocal, although a consistent finding is that lymphocytes taken from a person subjected to severe psychological stress do not reproduce well *in vitro* when challenged by an antigen. The possibility that immunotransmitters may, in their turn, possess mood altering powers was also discussed. The relative impact of stress, bereavement and depression on immune function does not appear to be distinctive.

Friedman (1988) emphasized sympathetic arousal and neuroendocrine change. He presented considerable evidence to support the hypothesis that PTSD is a hyperarousal state, characterized by excessive sympathetic activity. He argued that the differences between people with PTSD and those with other disorders, such as depression, are partly of degree, but not exclusively so. Aside from higher readings on such measures as baseline heart rate, systolic blood pressure and forehead electromyogram, together with higher urinary norepinephrine/cortisol ratios, the patterns of sleep and dreaming appear specific. All stages of sleep may be affected, perhaps in characteristic combinations, but the interesting additional findings included the increased physiological reactivity to non-specific auditory stimuli found during sleep (Kinney and Kramer, 1985) and the fact that the traumatic nightmares appear not to be confined to REM sleep alone (van der Kolk et al., 1985).

Reaction Development over Time: is there a Pattern?

Lindemann (1944), describing the aftermath of a disaster in which many people were burnt to death, focused on the elements of grief. He described somatic distress, preoccupation with the image of the deceased, guilt, hostile reactions and loss of previous patterns of conduct. The process of recovery, he said, was the task of working through from bondage to the deceased to emancipation. He saw the pattern of response as a phasic alternation between intrusive reliving of the experience, with hyperarousal, and numbing, with withdrawal. Horowitz and Wilner (1976) listed the phases as outcry, denial, intrusiveness, working through and completion, while stressing that an individual may enter the sequence at any point and go through in any order. Others emphasize the extremes that the denial and withdrawal may take, for example into dissociative states (e.g. Spiegel et al., 1988).

Parkes (1972), dealing with 'simple' bereavement as the key trauma, described a less vacillating ordering of stages—from alarm, numbness, pining or searching through depression to recovery. The cycle is neat, and attractive, especially with the final state of recovery apparently clear. There have been attempts to delineate such phases in response to trauma of other kinds, for example, Wallace, 1956 (cited in Weil, 1973) wrote of the four succeeding elements of shock, suggestibility, euphoria and ambivalence following experience of a natural disaster. Symonds (1975) also described four stages with only slight variation: shock and denial, followed by fright and clinging behaviour, and the third stage of apathy, with both inwardly and outwardly directed recrimination and rage. This third stage, she suggested, is particularly likely to be lengthy, so much so that in some individuals the fourth stage, of resolution, is never reached. The phases do make some clinical and even survival sense, and may help account for some phenomena which initially seemed puzzling. Immediately after some personal or major disaster, people do tend to wander aimlessly, perhaps perform inconsequential tasks and may show little awareness of the situation. Wallace suggested that this stage, although variable, is often quite brief and merges into the suggestibility stage, giving a potential survival advantage, since the survivors may thus be more compliant with rescuers. The so-called euphoric state, said to follow, is less one of elation than of profound restlessness, irritability, overestimation of capacity for putting things right and altruism, perhaps coupled with immediate relief at survival. Reality then impinges more as the injuries, horrors, fears or other consequences of the disaster come into focus. Survival guilt, a sense of helplessness, perhaps translated into irritation with the apparently more controlled and controlling helpers and authorities pervade a more ambivalent phase to personal survival and the surviving, but perhaps changed, environment. Masserman (1953) discussed the wish to flee from the site of a disaster, merging into uncertainty whether to run or stay. Among victims of criminal assault, too, a restlessness is apparent, for example in moving house, changing jobs or making and breaking supportive contacts. Also recorded is a falling away of initial satisfaction with probably the most common group of initial helpers—the police (Shapland et al., 1985). One explanation for this could be that the relationship between victim and police does change objectively, for example as the police challenge victim witness statements, but an alternative is that the survivor's internal world is changing.

Factors Influencing Development of Post-Traumatic Reactions

Victim centred

Age.   People of any age may develop profound and durable psychological reactions to trauma. Aside from natural disaster, however, traumatic events tend to be selective by age. Active armed combat and crime involve younger people both as perpetrators and victims. In the British Crime Survey, for example, it was established that, even when figures were corrected for exposure, the proportion of men between 16 and 30 who became victims of street crime was still over twelve times higher than for men of over 60. The proportions fearful of becoming victims of crime were almost reversed (Hough and Mayhew, 1983; Clarke et al., 1985).

Age has rarely been considered as an influencing variable in reactions to trauma other than bereavement, where the intensity of the reaction has been said to be greater in young adults rather than in children or the elderly (Parkes, 1965). It remains unclear whether particular age groups are more or less susceptible to developing PTSD. The point is sometimes made that children may find it much more difficult than adults to report their problems, and may more commonly refuse to discuss the trauma, or even become mute. There is no hard evidence on this point, although a history of physical or sexual abuse in childhood closely guarded until well into adult life certainly appears common. Much of this silence may be better attributed to the significant adults in the child's life who, even after such events as natural disaster, deny problems in their children (e.g. Silber et al., 1957). McFarlane et al. (1987) found schools that refused to cooperate in their long-term follow-up of children caught up in a bush fire, because the teachers could not see the need for such continued research. Terr (1981) reported an even more potentially destructive pattern of denial. A mental health centre physician confidently predicted to parents and children that only 1 in 26 of the children, kidnapped in their school bus, would develop symptoms. All did, but there was a considerable reluctance among the parents to admit that their child was 'the one', and to seek help. Terr went on to emphasize the lack of amnesia, haziness or denial for the event among the children themselves compared with the adults, although the children did tend to deny symptoms. The children she studied were aged between 5 and 14 and she observed that their reactions were remarkably similar, regardless of their stage of psychological development. Sugar (1989) also emphasized that treating the parents and allaying their anxiety is important, but not sufficient for the children.

Terr (1991) has subsequently distinguished between two types of trauma in children with characteristic symptom presentation, although cross-over is possible. The single-blow traumas, like the school bus kidnap, are particularly likely to be followed by full, detailed memories, attachment to omens and misperceptions, including misidentifications, visual hallucinations and peculiar time distortions such as the inability to conceive of a future. These features are rarely present among children from the other group—those subjected to variable, multiple or long-standing traumas. Conversely, among these, characteristics generally absent in the single-blow group are frequently observed. They include denial and psychic numbing, self-hypnosis and dissociation and rage. Where a single-blow results in an enduring loss, such as the death of a parent, or prolonged disability or disfigurement, the child may show elements of both presentations and often, too, of withdrawal, perpetual mourning or depression. Even following a single-blow trauma, symptoms tend to endure. The children in the school bus kidnap, for example, had symptoms that persisted for at least 4 years (Terr, 1983b).

Sex.   Some traumatic experiences tend to have been sex specific, such as combat. According to the British Crime Survey (Hough and Mayhew, 1983), even victims of personal violence in every-day life are much more likely to be male than female, although attention to the problems of victims of sexual assault has focused almost exclusively on women, and the British Crime Survey exclusively questioned women about this particular experience. Groth and Burgess (1980) and Mezey and King (1989) have redressed the balance a little in reporting on sexual assault among males.

Reactions of men and women to the experience of becoming a victim seem to be remarkably similar in many respects. The experience of sex neutral events—such as burglary, non-sexual assault or disaster should provide definitive evidence in this area, but the information is slight. Maguire and Bennett (1982) suggested differential effects between 163 men and 159 women following burglary. Initially, the men were much more likely to express anger and the women shock, upset, tears or confusion. Four to ten weeks after the event most of the worst affected were women. Furthermore, one of the most disturbing long-term effects was experienced almost exclusively by women—the sense of 'pollution' or 'violation'. Some had felt impelled to 'clean the house from top to bottom'. Two of the women had decided to move house to escape the feelings, and five had burnt furniture.

Other hints of differences come from Milgram and Milgram's (1976) work with children before and after war. Average anxiety levels increased significantly after the war for all of them but, while girls had shown higher baseline levels, the boys showed significantly higher levels than the girls after the war, regardless of self-concept or level of involvement in the war. The findings of Burke et al. (1982) were very similar (*see* above).

Cultural background.   Very little is known about the effects of cultural background on response to a traumatic event, and yet it would be surprising if there were none. Zborowski (1952) found differences in response to the specific trauma of physical pain according to ethnic origin.

It may be that Western society is relatively indifferent to the problems of other cultural groups who have been traumatized, sometimes as a result of their political or religious views. Mollica et al. (1987) made the point that, at the time of their writing, more than 700 000 refugees from Indo-China had settled in the USA since 1975, and yet there was no epidemiological study and little other work examining their problems. The act of enforced and often precipitous departure from one's native land, without prospect of safe return, might in itself be construed as a traumatic event. In their sample of fifty-two people, each had been through additional terrible stresses including a mean of ten traumatic events and two torture experiences. Most had major psychiatric disorder, with nightmares and sleep disturbance as the most treatment resistant. There did appear to be some differences in response to treatment between national subgroups (Mollica et al., 1990). While it is obvious that no cultural group is immune to serious psychological disorder following trauma, it would be useful to know if any particular style of coping were to offer any advantage.

Some subcultural groups, such as young, heavy drinking males (Hough and Mayhew, 1983) may be more vulnerable to becoming victims. Others, including the mentally or physically ill are discussed more fully below.

Experience of previous traumatic events. While there may be a core psychological symptomatology common to the experience of severe trauma, it would seem likely that the details of content and the depth and duration of suffering would be determined in part by the individual's previous characteristics and previous experiences. McFarlane's data (1988a) on 469 fire-fighters exposed to an extreme level of danger in an Australian bush fire supported his contention that the fire was a necessary, but not sufficient explanation of the onset and pattern of the subsequent psychological disorders. Previous experience of adverse events before the fire was particularly likely to be associated with chronicity of symptomatology. Solomon et al. (1988) noted that even indirect experience could be powerful. Ninety-six Israeli casualties of the 1982 Lebanon war, whose parents had survived the Nazi holocaust, were compared over a 3-year period with casualties without such histories. Apparently healthy before the war, the second generation survivors of the holocaust reported a greater number of PTSD symptoms than their non-holocaust peers, and their symptoms persisted for longer.

Most victims experience a particular trauma once only, but Gottfredson (1984) found that, in a representative sample of people of 16 and over (from the British Crime Survey), 14% had been victims of crime on more than one occasion, and 2% had been repeatedly involved in personal contact offences. Taking the victims as a subgroup, this meant that nearly half had suffered repeated victimization, including nearly one-third of those suffering personal assault, an estimate very similar to that of Shapland et al. (1985) for crime reported to the police. Gottfredson did not comment on the emotional impact of such repetition. Shapland and her group similarly were not focusing particularly on the psychiatric problems, but they noted that emotional disorder tended to persist and to become more prevalent with time, and that cumulative experience may deter reporting. Whether this followed from simple dissatisfaction with the criminal justice system, or evolving disorder is less clear.

It has been argued that repeated negative experiences tend to lead to pathological behaviour, which may include the inability to resist or avoid further events of a negative kind. Seligman and his co-workers (e.g. Seligman and Maier, 1967) coined the term 'learned helplessness', having studied animal models in which electric shocks were delivered to dogs denied the opportunity of escape. After a while, some of the dogs gave up trying to escape from the shock. This may be a valid model for a partial understanding of the behaviour of some victims, and perhaps particularly victims of domestic violence. In Gayford's (1975a, b) sample of battered women, for example, who were subject to repeated and demonstrable physical injury from their marital partner, the majority had left home at some point prior to the survey, 36 had fled more than four times (and some ten or twenty times), returning home as often. Less than half of the women described their childhood as happy and aggression by one or both parents figures prominently for more than half, with regular violence being a problem for over a fifth of women. Nearly three-quarters of the women had attended doctors with symptoms that resulted in the prescription of antidepressants or tranquillizers. Forty-two had made suicidal attempts or gestures, although only 16 said that they had really wanted to die. Could the failure to sustain effective escape behaviours be a form of 'learned helplessness'?

Ruch et al. (1980) and Kilpatrick et al. (1984) commented on more immediate life events. Both groups of workers studied rape victims and found that those who had experienced a moderate amount of disruption in their lives (in terms of job change, moving home, bereavement, etc.) in the year before the attack fared better than either those with no disruption or those with a great deal of disruption in that year. In the Kilpatrick group, those who adjusted better and more quickly had had significantly fewer negative life events over the period under study. The Maudsley study of rape victims (Mezey and Taylor, 1988) drew attention to the contrast between women whose rape appeared to be a relatively isolated negative event in the context of a generally satisfying lifestyle and women who had been assaulted, often at home and in the context of previous assaults. The former, although in some cases intensely symptomatic, reported their assault to the police and were prepared to talk about their problems and seek help. The latter were reluctant research subjects, generally transient in treatment, and all avoided the police.

Previous morbidity. Two key issues again emerge in the context of the effect of previous morbidity on traumatic reactions—the extent to which it predisposes the individual to becoming a victim, as well as the extent to which it contributes to the reaction itself.

It has already been noted that older age, often associated with some physical vulnerability, carries a low risk of becoming a victim of crime, whether or not the figures are adjusted for exposure (p. 891). Children, however, may have special problems in this regard. Lynch (1975), for example, compared 25 violently-abused children with their non-abused siblings and found that, although parental factors were relevant, a most important factor lay in illness of the child during its first year of life. Elmer and Gregg (1967) also emphasized the importance of low birth weight, congenital abnormalities and serious illness in predisposing to the abuse of the child concerned.

In relation to psychiatric disorder Ekblom (1970) showed a definite, but tiny, risk of serious injury among hospital inpatients from other disordered patients. Lehman and Linn (1984) studied outpatients. Of 274 randomly selected psychiatrically disabled residents of board and care homes in Los Angeles, one-third had been victims of crime in the preceding year, compared with 3.5% of the general population and 23% of the general population living in similar housing conditions. The victims of violence among the psychiatric patients tended to be more socially active than other victims or their non-victimized peers, but also reported more psychopathology and less life satisfaction.

Burgess and Holmstrom (1974 a, b) were among the first to argue that under severe stress—in this case rape—previous disorder may re-emerge. They identified a subgroup of women in their series who had described preassault physical or psychiatric morbidity which tended to reappear or intensify, in addition to any PTSD symptoms. Frank et al. (1981) found that victims with previous psychiatric disorder tended to show a poorer initial adjustment to rape than those without. Atkeson et al. (1982) found that post-rape depression was commoner among women who had previously been anxious or physically ill, but Kilpatrick et al. (1984) found previous disturbance irrelevant, again among rape victims. Among soldiers, an association between premilitary adjustment and development of PTSD is often not found (e.g. Foy et al., 1984). McFarlane (1988 a, b), described fire-fighters (1988b) as of 'above average psychological adjustment for their communities', but, nevertheless, showed that those with the more chronic forms of disorder scored significantly higher on trait neuroticism measures than the others (1988a) and were significantly more likely to have a family history of psychiatric disorder (1988b). There are hints of inherited vulnerability in relation to military experiences too. Davidson et al. (1985), for example, found particularly high rates of family psychopathology, especially alcoholism, depression or anxiety, among disturbed veterans.

Could pre-existing or coexisting psychiatric disease ever protect a person from the full impact of psychological trauma? In most cases it seems that, if anything, psychiatric disease prevents psychiatric staff from identifying abuse and some of its direct consequences. Craine et al. (1988) showed this in relation to reported sexual and physical abuse, as described above (p. 888). The only hint of a truly protective effect of preassault disorder comes from personal clinical experience. A young woman with a full scale score on the Wechsler Adult Intelligence Scale (WAIS) of 60 was raped by one of the workers involved in her care. Although she had a full range of symptoms of sufficient intensity to invoke a diagnosis of PTSD, and of 12 months' duration when first seen, she seemed at no time to have experienced the self-blame almost invariably reported by other such victims. Perhaps her more than averagely concrete appraisal of her situation offered her this small protection.

Event/assault centred influences on the victim

Although it is believed that certain characteristics of traumatic events, such as an associated death threat or long duration of uncertainty, may predispose to exceptional problems, it is often the case that several of these factors are operating in any one incident. No one has sytematically attempted the task of establishing whether, when multiple-event-centred factors operate, the effects are additive or compound, or whether once past a critical threshold of stress, it matters not what extra trauma is thrown at the victim.

Threat of extinction/near death experiences.   When an overwhelming threat presents to people who are unprepared for it, whatever the nature of that threat, it seems that only a minority remain calm and fully collected (10–15%), the majority show submission or 'frozen paralysis', while a further minority show uncontrollable emotions, confusion or disorientation (10–25%) (e.g. Tyhurst, 1951; Symonds, 1975).

McFarlane (1988 a, b) specifically enquired about perceived threat of death among fire-fighters facing a bush fire; 44% believed that they were close to death at some stage. Intensity of exposure and perceived threat were not predictors of PTSD and/or severe prolonged reactions of any kind. Figley (1978) made similar observations in relation to professional combat and PTSD, as did Bell et al. (1988) in relation to civilian trauma.

Facing death, even when there is no personal threat, has also been shown to be associated with significant distress, although not necessarily PTSD. Jones (1985) described the effect on rescuers of recovering and identifying human remains after the mass suicide of religious cult members in Jonestown, Guyana, in 1978. The response rate to questionnaires was low, perhaps itself a form of denial. One-third of the helpers group had dysphoric symptoms for up to 3 months compared with 9% of a control group. Davidson (1979), studying police officers involved in the aftermath of a fatal aircrash, found that one-fifth of them needed psychological treatment for PTSD. Symptomatology is sufficiently common after a violent experience or one involving death or threats to life, that in any psychiatric interview, a routine question to check for such experiences is a useful screening device. An affirmative answer should alert the questioner to the possibility of PTSD (Kolb, 1989).

Extent of physical damage.   Physical injury does not consistently seem to exacerbate post-traumatic reactions, indeed it may even be associated with enhanced psychological recovery. It is difficult, however, to draw firm conclusions from reported research. Sampling is a problem for almost all studies of victims. Ellis (1983), for example, summarizing research with 118 rape victims pointed out that this substantial group constituted only about one-tenth of the rape victim population in Georgia, and that it was the victims of the most violent and injurious assaults that were least likely to participate in the study. Within these limits, Frank et al. (1980) did not observe physical injury to have any bearing on psychological outcome, while Norris and Feldman-Summers (1981) found that severity of assault among rape victims was associated with subsequent psychosomatic symptoms.

Rape is a solitary, individual experience. Comparisons between the injured and the non-injured may mean more after collective trauma. Neither McFarlane (1988a) nor the Patricks (1981) found a relationship between degree of personal loss or injury and patterns of symptom development after disaster. Green et al. (1985), by contrast, studying survivors of a fatal supper club fire, found that the variables contributing most to the presence of symptoms up to 2 years afterwards were the experiences of the fire, including bereavement and personal injury. Evidence from combat studies is even more mixed. Foy et al. (1984), for example, demonstrated that combat experience and especially wounding was much more important in terms of subsequent development of PTSD than premilitary adjustment. Hoiberg and McCaughey (1984), by contrast, found the seriously injured less psychologically disabled than uninjured men surviving a naval collision. The former, however, were hospitalized together and, fortuitously, formed a strong peer support group, while the uninjured had been scattered and were without such support. Focus on a single, simple variable can be misleading.

Duration of exposure to event. Trauma may be brief, prolonged or repeated. The crucial psychological variable seems to be prolongation of uncertainty about the final extent of damage to be inflicted, but cruder physical factors, such as malnourishment or repeated injury, must never be neglected as being themselves powerful contributors to long-term problems. Krystal and Niederland (1968) described how the chronic malnourishment and ill health during concentration camp detention, when coupled with the survival value of apparent health, led to subsequent somatization. Speed et al. (1989) also showed that, among prisoners of war, torture and proportionate loss of body weight were the strongest predictors of PTSD, and particularly chronic PTSD, persisting up to 40 years. Tennant et al. (1986) eliminated organic factors and over a similar follow-up period established that prisoners of war of the Japanese were significantly more likely to have depression or anxiety neuroses than their peers in combat. They attributed this to duration of stress.

Repeated short exposure to lesser trauma, or even repeated threats, may be particularly likely to lead to atypical or prolonged disturbance. Schottenfeld and Cullen (1985) studied a small series of patients who had suffered exposure to industrial toxins. Three of them had typical PTSD. They had experienced acute, life-threatening occupational injury or exposure. Twelve had atypical PTSD, of whom 10 had suffered chronic or repeated exposure for between 1 and 4 years. The symptoms were almost exclusively somatic, with recurrent physical symptoms such as lightheadedness, headache, chest pain rather than nightmares or intrusive thoughts. Women living in the vicinity of the Three Mile Island nuclear power reactor had had post-traumatic psychological symptoms which had been resolving over the 6 years following the disaster (Dew et al. 1987). The symptoms returned when the reactor was restarted. Further physical disaster was unnecessary to rekindle symptoms.

Victim isolation.   Each person's experience of a major trauma is individual, but some can be more isolated than others by the nature of the event. Most victims of criminal assault, and some in road accidents, differ from their counterparts in war, natural or man-made disasters in being alone with their assailant or assailants. It is doubtful whether the sharing *per se* of a specific traumatic experience assists subsequent adjustment, but the capacity to relate afterwards to a peer group defined by the common experience is probably helpful. Group cohesion, however, does not, indeed cannot necessarily follow from a group experience. Weisaeth (1989) has spoken of three distinct groupings in relation to such shared experiences—the community, the company and the communicational or fortuitous grouping.

Community grouping implies a group that lives and works together, such as an army unit. Such communities are generally small and the most vulnerable to serious trauma but, by the same token, have the greatest capacity for working through the experience. Weisaeth described a platoon of Norwegian soldiers caught in an avalanche. Sixteen were killed. This constituted half the community; further, four of the survivors were high risk men in terms of pretrauma or family history, which meant that the overall potential for the incidence of PTSD in the group was very high. The men were kept together and some early supportive interventions offered. None developed PTSD. Most communities are defined simply by geographical proximity and little else until hit by a similar kind of natural disaster or war. Nevertheless, the 'common enemy' can facilitate bonding and, in turn psychological survival, if the community can remain together.

The *company* is a much more complex social grouping. It is defined by substantial shared experience such as work, but is often scattered geographically. The potential for the value of the 'company' grouping, which was lost through geographical separation, has been highlighted in the Hoiberg and McCaughey (1984) study.

Weisaeth's third, *communicational*, group is artificially united by the common experience of trauma, such as survivors and their relatives of a major transport disaster. The risks of subsequent isolation for such a group are considerable, as people may live in widely different places. Survivors' reactions in these circumstances are mixed, and largely anecdotal. After the P & O ferry disaster at Zeebrugge (*see* pp. 103–4), affecting hundreds of families in England, one man talked of the intensity of relationships formed with complete strangers at the disaster site, of the immediate relief, but of the avoidance of further contact with such a group in order to avoid re-exposure to the painful feelings. Others talked of the importance of the possibility of contact through a newsletter or of memorial events, which enabled reunions with the only people who could now understand them. Relatives and friends not directly touched had grown tired of hearing of the disaster and expected them to have put it behind them.

Knowledge of the assailant.   Historically, the personalization of fate into humanoid gods may be evidence for man's need to identify the source of his ills in rather concrete terms. One man who survived the P & O ferry disaster named the sea as a murderer until it became clear that a rather more conventional target of employees of the shipping company might be identi-fied as unlawful killers. The survivor of a criminal assault is often concerned above all that their assailant be identified and found. Until that time, most remain haunted by the horrible possibility that any individual of similar age, sex or shape might pose a threat to them. The unseen or masked assailant seems to leave the individual proportionately more anxious. Just as knowl-edge can be reassuring, however, it may also prove alarming. For some, a discovery that their assailant is about to be released from prison can precipitate a recurrence of symptoms. In general, however, victims prefer to be informed, and, in criminal cases express great frustration and anger with the criminal justice system when this is not so (Shapland et al., 1985).

It is widely accepted that it is not uncommon for assailants to be known to their victims, but it is extremely difficult to gauge how common. Figures are usually calculated on the basis of recorded crime. It might be expected that people are much more reluctant to report offences or assaults committed by people known to them, and there is some evidence to support this (Mezey and Taylor, 1988). The most reliable figures are likely to emerge from details of offences with a high clear-up rate, like homicide, or from studies which do not depend on the reporting of crime to the police, such as the British Crime Survey. The general principles which emerge are that property offences, especially theft, are almost always committed by strangers, but that incidents of assaultive violence often follow from previous acquaintance (Gottfredson, 1984). Studies consistently report that, in the majority of homicide cases, the victim is known to the offender, although the closeness of the relationship seems to vary enormously from community to community (West, 1968). Even for rape, when some behaviours such as forcible sexual intercourse by the spouse have been excluded on technical grounds, there seems to be general agreement that about one-third of women know their assailant (Amir, 1971; Macdonald, 1971).

It is not known whether the psychological effects of a major trauma truly differ when assailants can be identified compared with when they cannot, or when they are well known rather than strangers. Reluctance to report known assailants and the probably higher risk of such assaults being repeated, suggest that more than family loyalty is triggered by such violence. Elmer's (1977) work, however, is interesting in this context, although highly specific. She compared accidentally injured with abused infants. The children had been virtually indistinguishable at birth, but the abused children had significantly more health problems and neurological signs for up to a year after the injury. Thereafter, no significant difference could be found.

Specificity of the event or its elements.   Taking all the trauma literature together, it is hard to make a case for a particular form of trauma being consistently associated with its own typical pattern of symptom production, or even duration. The content of symptoms, as opposed to their form and clustering, does seem strongly influenced by the nature of the trauma. That some of the repetitive phenomena, such as nightmare and flashbacks, are simply repeated or reconstituted images of the incident is hardly surprising. The specificity of content of some of the phobic states has also been frequently remarked. After a prolonged siege in which two hostages died, for example, one survivor found himself vulnerable to the smell of a particular brand of aftershave. One of the terrorists had used it and subsequent exposure provoked anxiety. A survivor of the P & O ferry disaster found that his lifestyle was increasingly restricted because he had to avoid proximity to plate glass, which triggered panic. This even prevented him from going shopping. On the boat, he had watched fellow passengers plunge screaming through plate glass to their deaths.

Environmental issues

The high risk environment.   Crime does not occur randomly, and much of the philosophy behind newer police initiatives in Britain, such as those involving neighbourhood watch schemes, is based on this assumption. This could also be said of many largely man-made disasters, such as the Buffalo Creek disaster in West Virginia in 1972, the Regency Hotel skywalk disaster in Kansas City in 1981 and the P & O ferry disaster off the Belgian Coast in 1987. Action may be taken both to minimize the occurrence of such incidents and the occurrence of their potential consequences. Constructions over the San Andreas fault on the west coast of North America, for example, are designed to minimize the effects of earthquakes, while emergency services are preplanned. The contrast between the physical impact of earthquakes of similar severity in Armenia in 1988 and in California in 1989 was very striking, in terms of both immediate damage inflicted and physical recovery.

Ziegenhagen (1976) pointed out the differential effects of economic status on becoming a victim of crime. People subjected to repeated victimization were of lower income status than single incident victims. The relative effects of environment on psychological consequences of assault, rather than on the incidence of assault itself, are harder to determine, but seem to be reflected in areas like attitudes to police intervention and concern about future risk.

In Ziegenhagen's study, in contrast to the single incident victims, the repeated victims reported feeling unsafe; worse, they reported expecting better treatment from the police as suspects of crime than as victims.

One important environmental issue is gun control, where it is clear that psychological factors are important in bringing about changes. Targeted communities respond to a combination of information and tough negative reinforcement against possession. They do not respond to information alone, or even to gun control laws alone. The data to support control arguments are impressive. A study of two North American west coast cities, one on each side of the USA—Canadian border, for example, showed differences in crime patterns associated with different policies (Sloan et al., 1988). Rates of burglary, robbery and assault were similar, but the rate of firearms assaults seven times greater in Seattle than Vancouver. The risk of homicide, usually by hand gun, was also higher in Seattle, where the gun control laws are less strict. Where controls have been introduced, efficacy seems to depend on the size of the penalty for breaking the law, and an appreciation by legislators that if the weapons are available at all, they will be used. The safest environment is the one in which the ban on firearms has been extended to the home. Where the law is only against carrying them outside the home, the impact on firearm use in crime is small (Jung and Jason, 1988). A heavy and specifically identifiable penalty for carrying guns seemed to have an impact on domestic killings in Washington DC, but a sentence for firearm possession in Michigan which was significantly less than that for the offence with which it was associated, and to run concurrently, produced no effect.

Hospitals and other institutions which contain disturbed or violent individuals are environments which carry their own special risks. Within such hospital settings, although there may be a large number of violent incidents, these tend to involve a small number of patients who are repetitively assaultive. Drummond et al. (1989) described a very significant decline (92%) in violent incidents in an Oregon hospital after such patients had been identified, and computer flagged wherever they were in the hospital. Appropriate advice was thus made immediately available to all staff with whom they were likely to come in contact, for example that patients should be searched for weapons or hospital/security asked to be on standby.

Contamination of environment. An important factor in the development of psychological symptoms appears to be the sense of the victim that their environment has been soiled (e.g. Maguire and Bennett, 1982), damaged or rendered unsafe. Some respond by attempting to increase their personal or domestic security, for example, by changing their personal appearance, wearing running shoes, carrying alarms, or adding locks and alarms to their homes. Others become almost itinerant in their attempts to move away from the area of threat, changing jobs, home and even sometimes cutting themselves off from family and past friends (e.g. Mezey and Taylor, 1988).

Prognosis of Post-Traumatic Reactions

Victims of some forms of trauma are notoriously avoidant of continuing contact with services (e.g. Rounsaville, 1978; Katz and Mazur, 1979). Although most of the reports of this problem relate to the experience of personal violence, clinical experience suggests that this pattern may follow other traumas. Such follow-up studies as there are may, therefore, not be of representative people. Some studies report simply the evolution of psychiatric symptoms following unpleasant events, while others attempt to focus on people with a specific syndrome or disease, usually PTSD. A case for two forms of disorder has been argued, one of early onset and one of late.

Fairly immediate onset of symptoms of short duration is not infrequently observed. Most of the women in the Maudsley study of rape victims (Mezey and Taylor, 1988) may have fallen into this category, described earlier in the USA (e.g. Sutherland and Scherl, 1970) with observed resolution of symptoms in 3–4 months. Longer term follow-up remains essential to explore the possibility that the recovery from such quickly rising and falling symptoms is unstable. Many victims of offences such as rape go on to much longer-term psychiatric disorders (e.g. Kilpatrick et al. 1981; Nadelson et al. 1982). Furthermore, there is evidence to suggest that even if early relief from specific classical symptoms, such as intrusive thoughts and depression, occurs, there may be other more persistent changes, such as lowered self-esteem (Mezey and Taylor, 1988). The risk of behavioural and social problems may also be longer standing, including increased alcoholism rates and mortality by suicide or motor accident (Hearst et al., 1986).

The second form of disorder described may have a slower, or delayed onset of symptoms, for which various explanations have been offered, such as early repression of emotions. McFarlane et al. (1987) noted that, after a bush fire which killed 14 people, thousands of livestock and destroyed many houses, prevalence of behavioural and emotional problems 2 months after the fire was less among children exposed to the fire than in a comparison group. By 8 months after the fire, however, the prevalence of psychiatric morbidity was significantly greater in the fire group, and this persisted through the 26 months of follow-up. Work with adults involved in the fire, the fire-fighters, showed a similar delay in onset of PTSD. After a cyclone in Sri Lanka, less than 5% in unaffected villages developed symptoms compared with nearly 80% in affected villages. Symptom development fell into two clusters—'early' and 'late', the latter emerging after a lag of at least 4 weeks. Timing was not, however, predictive of outcome in terms of nature or length of response (Patrick and Patrick, 1981).

Watson et al. (1988) seemed to confirm the lack of prognostic value in the early-late distinctions. They compared Vietnam veterans reporting within 6 months with those with delayed symptom onset. The groups did not differ significantly in the number or severity of their symptoms, nor was there any difference between them in observer judgement of the severity of their trauma or their history of previous stress.

It is tempting to sum up simply by saying that symptoms can last at least as long as the period of follow-up. Almost all late studies of survivors of any of the major traumas under discussion suggest that at least a sizeable proportion of the subjects will be symptomatic years later. The longest follow-up studies in relation to criminal behaviour tend to be of adults who were violently or sexually abused as children. If the target group for study is formed by adults with mental illness, then the alleged rates of abuse are extraordinarily high for men and women (e.g. Jacobson and Richardson, 1987) and in one study the majority of those with a history of abuse could be described specifically as still meeting the criteria for PTSD (Craine et al., 1988). Studies which have less potential for sampling bias confirm an association between adult symptomatology and childhood abuse (e.g. Mullen et al., 1988). Studies of combat veterans, prisoners of war (POWs) and survivors of concentration camps provide the other main pool of evidence for the persistence of disorder. Speed et al. (1989) showed that 29% of a group of WW2 POWs still satisfied PTSD criteria 40 years after their experience. The men were selected only to the extent that they had responded to an offer of complete medical examination by the USA Veterans Administration. The psychiatric examination had been performed with a random subsample. A questionnaire study of a larger sample, albeit with a less than 50% return rate, put the prevalence of persistent symptoms even higher—at 56% (Zeiss and Dickman, 1989). The durability of disorder among many who were the primary victims of concentration camps is not in doubt (e.g. Krystal, 1968; Horowitz, 1976), but more recent work has opened up the question beyond duration of personal disorder to intergenerational transfer. Solomon et al. (1988) found evidence that Israeli combat soldiers were at greater risk for PTSD if one or both of their parents were holocaust survivors than if they were not. Sigal et al. (1988) studied the grandchildren of survivors, in this case children who had suffered no additional major traumas, and found them indistinguishable from other children in mood, behaviour or personality measures chosen. Their relative vulnerability if subject to major stress in future remains an open question.

Epidemiology

The Epidemiology of Victimization

In spite of the range of traumatic external hazards that confront human beings, the personal chance of becoming a victim is relatively small. Full scale war which involves civilian bombardment or planned genocide are exceptions to this rule but, even in times of war when the combat takes place away from the parent community, the real threat of exposure is quite small.

Of the 250 million population of the USA, for example, four million served in Indo China sometime during the Vietnam war, but just 800 000 were assigned to combat. Even among draft eligible men, 75% did not enter the armed forces. Of the 5.2 million men born in the USA between 1950 and 1952, 4142 died in the war, i.e. 0.08% of the group at highest risk (Lipkin et al., 1982; Hearst et al., 1986). Morbidity and mortality indirectly related to combat, and particularly postwar psychosocial problems were, however, of a different order altogether.

Civilian accidents, unless involving large numbers of people simultaneously as when a plane crashes, rarely merit much attention in the media, and, as the latter might also imply, they are relatively common compared with other traumatic events. Nevertheless, a small minority of exposed people, even over a lifetime, suffer significant physical injury as a direct result of an accident. Becoming a victim of crime which, by contrast, receives a great deal of media attention, is a rare phenomenon. From the British Crime Survey data, collected in 1981 (Hough and Mayhew, 1983), it was calculated that a 'statistically average' person aged 16 or over could expect:

a robbery once every 5 centuries;
an assault resulting in an injury once every century;
the family car to be stolen or taken by joyriders once every 60 years; and
a burglary in the home once every 40 years.

The Epidemiology of Psychological Disorder following Victimization

Determination of the real prevalence of psychological disorder after becoming a victim is made extremely difficult in part by the nature of those disorders. Victims are commonly reluctant to come forward and describe what they have been through and what they feel about it (e.g., Ellis, 1983, *see* p. 896). The attrition rate in longitudinal studies is notorious (e.g. Mezey and Taylor, 1988).

Helzer et al. (1987) studied over 3000 people, in one of the survey sites for the US Epidemiologic Catchment Area Study of psychiatric disorders. The subjects had been selected to be representative of the state of Missouri and of the nation as a whole. They found that some symptoms of PTSD, such as hyperalertness and sleep disturbances, occurred commonly in the general population. Furthermore, for nearly half of the symptomatic, the symptoms did not persist for 6 months. PTSD, as defined in DSM-III-R was present in about 1% of the sample. Exposure to external trauma was generally a prerequisite to symptomatology. Although women described the discovery of a spouse's affair, being poisoned, and having a miscarriage as significant stressors, the most common precipitating event for a woman was being attacked while, for a man, combat or seeing someone hurt or die were the critical events; 3.5% of the population who had been exposed to physical attack or were Vietnam veterans who had not been wounded suffered PTSD compared with 20% of wounded veterans. Overall 49% of the symptomatic found that their symptoms lasted less than 6 months, while a third complained that the symptoms lasted for more than 3 years, the combat veterans showing the highest rate of such persistence (53%). People with PTSD were twice as likely to have another psychiatric disorder as defined by DSM-III-R than were those without it, the most likely being obsessive-compulsive disorder, dysthymia and manic-depressive disorder. Alcohol and drug abuse was also high. Childhood behaviour problems were associated both with a greater adult experience of personal attack and of subsequent PTSD.

Thus, on the basis of the findings of this study, PTSD in the general population occurs with about the same frequency as schizophrenia or diabetes, regarded as fairly common diseases. The study has, however, been heavily criticized, not least for its reliance on the Diagnostic Interview Schedule (DIS) (Haber-Schaim et al., 1988; Keane and Penk, 1988; Kulka et al., 1988). Furthermore, the subsamples of Vietnam veterans were very small. The concern is principally that Helzer et al. (1987) considerably underestimated the occurrence of PTSD. Larger studies of Vietnam veterans have put the rates of PTSD at higher levels, for example Centers for Disease Control (1988). In this study, nearly 8000 Vietnam veterans and over 7000 non-Vietnam veterans were compared on telephone interview, and sub-samples of 2490 on more extensive examination, albeit also using the DIS. Fifteen per cent of Vietnam veterans experienced combat-related PTSD at some time during or after military service, 4.5% depression, 4.9% anxiety and nearly 14% alcohol abuse or dependence. Hearst et al. (1986) emphasized the postservice mortality rates. Total deaths among draft-eligible men in California and Pennsylvania were 4% higher than expected, the excess being entirely accounted for by suicide and road accidents. Those who had actually entered military service were 65% and 49% more likely to die from subsequent suicide or road accidents respectively.

There were no cases of trauma by natural disaster in the study of Helzer et al. (1987). The published material mainly consists of descriptive accounts of highly selected samples. Among the more systematic studies, Patrick and Patrick (1981) reported that between 20 and 80% (variance between villages) of the surviving population at the centre of destruction by cyclone in Sri Lanka reported symptoms of psychiatric illness, compared with up to 4% in unaffected villages. For 75% of the symptomatic, the illness persisted for 6 months. McFarlane (1988a) studied what proved to be a representative sample of 469 fire-fighters attending a bush fire in Australia. Thirty per cent were designated 'psychiatric cases' on General Health Questionnaire (GHQ) (Goldberg, 1972) ratings. GHQ score at 4 months predicted subsequent confirmation of PTSD at 8 months (McFarlane, 1988b). Physical health may also be affected. In a 1-year follow-up study of the population of Bristol,

England, after serious flooding of shops and houses, there was a 50% increase in mortality (Bennet, 1970). Reports of increased leukaemia and spontaneous abortion followed a not dissimilar episode of flooding in New York (Janerich et al., 1981). These reports may well be compatible with the immunological incompetence model for disorder development (pp. 931, 933).

The Epidemiology of Fear of Victimization

One of the greatest problems for a victim is fear of further trauma, and for many this includes the reliving of the experience in imagination and a consequent tendency to avoid conscious recall of the memories. It is apparent from the work of the British Crime Survey (Hough and Mayhew, 1983) that many become surrogate victims through media exposure. In answer, for example, to the query 'How safe do you feel walking in this area alone after dark?', 60% of women over 60 living in inner city areas said that they felt very unsafe, as did 29% living outside cities. Nearly 30% of inner city men over 60 were similarly concerned, yet only just over 1% of women and half as many men in these age groups actually become victims of crime. Some 58% of the older women said that they sometimes avoided going out after dark for fear of crime; however not more than 5% of men made a similar claim and only 8% of all respondents said that they never went out alone at night. It seems, then, that fear of crime is disproportionate to risk, at least in Britain. Only in the nature of crimes feared did there appear to be some semblance of rationality. Fourteen per cent of people said that they worried most about burglary. This is indeed one of the more common crimes, but only 1% worried about vehicle theft, next in the frequency league. Thirty-four per cent, mostly manual workers and women, were worried most about mugging and 23% about sexual attacks. Age in part determined the nature of the fear, the younger women being most worried about sexual attacks.

Victim Groups of Special Importance

Accident, with Particular Reference to Head Injury

Miller (1961) described 'personal experience of about 4000 patients examined for medico-legal assessment during a dozen years of consultant practice', and gave a more detailed account of 200 consecutive cases of accidental head injury, 50 followed for 3 years. He promulgated the view that occupational difficulties, persistent headaches and neurotic symptoms following such injury is a 'compensation neurosis', which clears on settlement of the claim. In only 2 of the 50 cases, he claimed, did symptoms persist once this had happened. In a later report, he asserted that postconcussional symptoms are rare after injuries at sport or in the home, where compensation is not payable (Miller, 1969). He also detailed his attendant personal philosophies:

> There are many middle-class patients who sustained physical injuries under conditions which would thoroughly justify compensation, but who flatly refused to claim . . .
> The average industrial worker . . .
> Unconvinced that a wider distribution of consumer goods has changed the basic structure of society, he continues to nourish a strong awareness of the antithesis between 'us' and 'them' . . .
> This, then, is the social setting in which accident neurosis flourishes . . .

Lishman (1987), in his review of the field, noted that pertinent factors additional to the accident *per se* in the development of post-traumatic neurotic symptoms included marked emotional reaction at the time of the injury (Brenner et al., 1944), its occurrence in an emotionally laden setting (Guttman, 1946) and the absence of post-traumatic amnesia, which would have obliterated the memory of the trauma (Denny-Brown, 1945). Lishman discussed in more detail the interplay between physical damage and post-traumatic psychological adjustment. Fatigue, irritability and sensitivity to noise, together with more specific somatic complaints such as headache and dizziness, are the commonest supplements to anxiety features. Ota (1969) suggested that these neurotic disorders outnumber all other forms of disability following head injury.

Subsequent writers have shown no association between symptom development or persistence and compensation. Kelly (1975) studied prospectively 110 patients with an outstanding claim for compensation (62 from professional or managerial groups) and 34 comparable patients without). A majority of those head injured in circumstances that did not involve a claim developed symptoms generally indistinguishable from those in patients with outstanding bids. Among the latter, in spite of persisting symptoms, 76% appeared to resist accepting their disability to the extent that they returned to work before any settlement was made. There was no association between severity of injury, and the subsequent development of post-traumatic symptoms. In a second series of 106 patients with compensation claims, simultaneously reported, only 30 had received any treatment. Twenty-five of these recovered and returned to work. Of the other 76, just 11 returned to work before settlement. Only 13 of them had refused treatment. In 44 cases, no treatment was suggested, or it was inadequately pursued. In as many as 19 cases, doctors positively refused treatment on the basis that the symptoms were imaginary or of 'compensationitis' and that those presenting just needed to snap out of it!

Kelly and Smith (1981) then studied 50 patients who had not returned to work at the time of last psychiatric evaluation before compensation. After settlement, 4 had died of unrelated causes without returning to work, 16 returned around the time of settlement, only 1 at pretrauma level, and 3 had subsequently taken part-time work. Thus nearly half the sample were still out of work, on average nearly 3 years after settlement. They tended to be older, and to have been in more dangerous occupations. Only 4 people in total expressed dissatisfaction with the compensation.

Burstein (1989) emphasized the importance of direct questioning of patients about their symptoms, since he found that an appearance of normality often masked significant impairments, including restricted sexual activity, decreased assertiveness and conflict avoidance. He, too, found that the possibilities of financial compensation did not significantly affect the course of symptoms.

Thus, while Miller correctly identified an increase in neurotic symptoms following accidental head injury, which seem to have much in common with the symptoms following other types of trauma, subsequent findings suggest that they are largely unrelated to issues of compensation. 'Compensation neurosis' is a misnomer in most cases, and there is certainly no excuse for either pejoritive judgments of patients or failure to offer appropriate treatment.

Crime

Burglary

Many local victim support schemes in Britain started out by delivering services primarily to victims of burglary, who, indeed, probably still form the majority of the average case load. The pioneering victims' support scheme in Bristol (cited in Maguire and Bennett, 1982) reported that of the 315 people they saw during the first 6 months of operation, 97% had experienced theft or burglary. About one-third had been 'upset to a degree that called for some help in restoring normal coping ability' and 7% had suffered 'a severe and long-lasting impact, affecting their lifestyle'. A Canadian study (Waller and Okihiro, 1978) reported broadly similar findings. Maguire and Bennett's (1982) study dealt mainly with the burglars. They also, however, interviewed 163 men and 159 women who had been burgled in Banbury or Reading, areas of England with a higher than average proportion of middle income people. The majority felt surprise and an initial resistance to accepting the fact of burglary; twice as many men (41%) as women felt anger, but three times as many women (29%) complained of shock. Four to ten weeks after the event, 65% of those interviewed said that the burglary was still having some effect on their lives, usually feelings of insecurity and a tendency to keep thinking about the burglary. Fifteen per cent (48) experienced fear, in many cases of the burglar returning; 11 of the 322 interviewed were burgled again during the year of the study; 6% said that their physical health had suffered and smaller numbers had more profound psychological disturbances. Many, for example, developed a suspiciousness of people following the incident, but 3 developed frank paranoia. Women, almost exclusively, tended to suffer from a sense of violation or pollution as a result of their experience, and some even made an explicit analogy with sexual assault.

Effects that were even more lasting ranged from the immensely practical, such as increasing insurance cover or physical security of the house, to the emotional. Women were more likely to experience serious lasting effects. In general, the characteristics of the burglary, such as time of day discovered or amount stolen, had no impact on reactions, the one exception being where property had been strewn about, fouled or seriously damaged.

About 80% of people had contacted the police immediately, probably a higher proportion than for other crimes. The fact that most people were satisfied with the police had more to do with the nature of police response than its consequences, as the burglars were rarely caught. Class differences, however, seemed to have a powerful effect on the police, not wholly explained by the value of the property stolen. Fingerprints, for example, were taken in 77% of cases with a middle-class background but 56% of those with a working class; 23% of the former received three or more visits in connection with the burglary, but only 10% of the latter. It is striking to contrast this relative effort on the part of the police with the fact that female working-class victims were the most likely to suffer serious after-effects. The subgroup of victims who had been most seriously upset were also most likely to take a very punitive attitude towards the offender, but even so, only 21% considered that measures such as personal revenge or corporal punishment would be appropriate. Despite seeing a burglary as a serious offence, few thought custody appropriate for the burglar, and most were preoccupied with the notion that the offender should repay his 'debt' in a useful way and that, if he could be reformed, other households would be spared the same experience. By contrast, although being somewhat lenient towards 'their own burglar', people tended to prefer much tougher, more purely punitive measures for the hypothetical burglar.

Violence

Violence against the person.   As just described, any crime may seem a violent assault on those who have suffered it, but physical contact crimes have been studied separately. Shapland et al. (1985) interviewed and collected data on 276 people in the Coventry and Northampton areas who had been defined by the police as victims. Nearly one-third of them had been victims of sexual assault, these exclusively women, and the remainder, men and women, of physical assault or robbery. Less than 40% had reported to the police themselves, with most of the rest being reported by friends, relatives or bystanders. About 40% had at some stage been against the idea of prosecuting their assailant. This was considerably influenced by whether the assailant was known to them, as in 50% of the less serious assaults and five of the six rapes.

At the initial research interview, usually within days of the offence being reported to the police, only 24 (9%) of the victims said that they had suffered no mental, physical of social effects as a result of the assault, while at the final outcome interview, up to 2½ years later, 75% still mentioned some problems. The financial consequences tended to be of a low level and, even though nearly 40% lost time from work, they were said to have resolved by the time of the final interview. Nearly 70% of the victims had had need of immediate attention from a doctor, usually in a hospital casualty department: 19% of them admitted as inpatients. A majority suffered some kind of emotional effect, which often led to changes in behaviour and social life. The physical, psychological and social effects were increasing in prevalence at around the 18-month stage. The victims of simple physical assault were least likely to report such problems, but even so a majority (60%) reported persistent symptoms at the third and fourth interview. This group included police officers, who were significantly less likely to complain of medico-social problems than others, while work-related assaults among the latter, such as bus drivers and shopkeepers, resulted in some of the most serious effects. Often such people were unable to get back to work and guilt about this seemed to compound their problems. Active support from employers and colleagues helped. There was no gender difference in the severity of reactions to the more purely violent offences and robbery. The victims of sexual assault, all women, were more likely to feel guilty; they also more commonly attributed anger to male relatives.

Family violence.   Much violence in society goes undetected or unreported and this is particularly true of family violence. Empirical data support the view that, overall, the family may be the most dangerous place in society (Stanko, 1990). Societal ambivalence to violence at home has meant that attempts at offering protection to the vulnerable are relatively recent.

The Romans and Greeks positively encouraged infanticide to keep the nation strong and virile. Prevailing views for centuries encouraged beatings of wives, children and servants, not only in the interests of ensuring earthly obedience, but also for saving the immortal soul! People with epilepsy were flogged, to drive out the devil causing the fits. A good deal of abuse, however, was far less altruistic. Children in the 19th century were sometimes starved or ill-used so that parents could profit from burial clubs, or they were mutilated so that they could be more effective beggars. Fontana (1976) reports one particularly telling 19th century American story. Mary Ellen was being maltreated by her adoptive parents. No action could be legally taken against them. Local church workers, therefore, appealed to The Society for the Prevention for Cruelty to Animals and finally succeeded in rescuing her on the grounds that, as a member of the animal kingdom, she was entitled to protection under the law against animal cruelty. The Society for Prevention of Cruelty to Children was founded soon after in New York City, in 1871.

In Britain, the first official government enquiry into conjugal violence took place in 1875, it was followed by the Matrimonial Causes Act 1878. The first British legislation on behalf of children was the Prevention of Cruelty to Children Act 1889, the (British) National Society for Prevention of Cruelty to Children following in 1899. Tardieu, a professor of legal medicine in Paris, has been credited with being the first, in 1868, to recognize multiple injuries in a child as the product of domestic violence, but in the same year a London surgeon confidently attributed similar observations to rickets. It was not until 1946 that Caffey published observations of the common association of subdural haematoma and abnormal X-ray changes in the long bones and a further 7 years before this was further associated with wilful damage (Wooley and Evans, 1955). In 1962, Kempe and colleagues pressed the term 'battered child syndrome', and interest finally began to give rise to more active intervention and management. In 1971, Chiswick Women's Aid became the first organization in Britain to offer refuge to women and their children suffering in violent families (Pizzey and Shapiro, 1982) and then, in 1975, the House of Commons set up a Select Committee to consider violence in marriage, which a year later extended itself to consider violence in the family more generally (House of Commons, 1975b). In 1974, there was a Royal College of Nursing appeal for investigation into the problem of violence towards the elderly. In many parts of North America there are now statutory requirements to notify authorities of suspected cases. It is estimated that up to 5% of the elderly are being abused. Homer and Gilleard (1990) reported that no less than 45% of carers admitted to some form of abuse, all of them living with the elderly person and many with a long-standing history of poor relationships and mutual abuse. Alcohol consumption by the carer was a very significant risk factor.

A full and useful historical perspective on violence in the family is provided by May in Martin's (1978) comprehensive volume on *Violence in the Family*. More recently Dale and his colleagues (1986a) have contributed a less academic, but extremely practical, introduction to the field with chapters on the legal context of child abuse as well as the key issues in intervention.

The true extent of the problem of family violence remains unknown, but various estimates have been attempted. McClintock (1978) in an English survey of violence in urban areas found that about 15% of indictable crimes of violence against the person were committed within the family, a proportion which had remained constant between the 1950s and the 1970s. In 1970, 1527 indictable violent crimes committed within the family were known to police. It is thought that domestic crime is least likely of all crimes to be reported. This figure represents the very minimum estimate of serious crime, and excludes all cases designated as minor, such as 'common assault', generally dealt with in the magistrates' courts. Figures specifically for child abuse at that time were estimated at 6 per 1000 in the USA (Kempe, 1971), amounting to about 40 000 known cases annually. In the UK about 3000 per year were recognized (Lancet, 1971). Estimates of national mortality from child abuse were 1.3% in the UK (National Society for the Prevention of Cruelty to Children, NSPCC, 1969) and remarkably similar at 1.4% in the USA (Gil, 1969). Since then, it would appear that rates of abuse have been rising, but it is unclear how far these represent a real rise, and how far the figures reflect improved identification of problems. In one year, for example, in which 7000 reports of child abuse had been recorded in the USA, Kempe and Kempe (1978) estimated that in reality there had been between 2.5 and 4.1 million. In 1989, in Britain, the NSPCC reported helping 54 000 children who were victims of physical, sexual and emotional abuse or neglect, a 12.5% increase over the previous year (NSPCC, 1989). Most referrals (86%) were from non-statutory or unofficial sources. Just over one-third of the children were under 5, and nearly two-thirds under 10. Physical abuse remained the most serious problem numerically (5204 cases), with neglect (4532) and being left alone (3678) close behind, and sexual abuse accounting for 3680 cases.

Physical injuries range from the trivial to the very serious, but it is salutory to note that Birrell and Birrell (1968) and Oliver et al. (1974) estimated that at least one-quarter of children subjected to serious attacks suffered permanent intellectual damage, with the 0–4-year-olds at most risk. MacKeith (1975) estimated that there would be 600 new cases of mental handicap a year as a result of battering, at that time.

On a more optimistic note, in one city in the USA, Denver, a change in policies in the reporting of child abuse figures resulted, between 1960 and 1975, in an apparently dramatic increase in reported abuse, but a fall in mortality, from 20 to 1 (Kempe and Kempe, 1978).

Most studies focus on the nature and effects of the more or less deliberate infliction of physical harm against another person. It is a form of violence most easily defined and least difficult to measure, but it represents only one end of the spectrum. Violent feelings between family members may also be expressed in passive aggression, they may sometimes even take the form of suicidal behaviours, be displaced to property, or to people outside the family. Sexual abuse may also be primarily a violent act, and this is dealt with more fully below. A more rare and recently identified form of abuse is that of Munchhausen by proxy (Meadow, 1977, 1982, 1989) in which a parent, usually the mother, induces some non-specific symptomatology in her child—like a high temperature—and presents repeatedly with the child to hospitals for investigation.

Researchers have attempted to understand the conditions that may predispose to family violence. In one examination of the basic information recorded by police in over 1500 reported cases of family violence in 1970, the following characteristics emerged (McClintock, 1978):

1. The majority of the victims were female, but 25% of the victims were husbands battered by their wives or fathers battered by their sons. This high proportion of female victims fits with the analysis of trends

in crimes of violence in England and Wales which shows that more than 50% of assaults against women are domestic compared with only 8% of assaults against men (Davidoff and Dowds, 1989). No age group was immune from violence, but peaks for being assaulted occurred in the late twenties, the late thirties and the early forties;

2. In over two-thirds of cases the conflict was between spouses or cohabitees. The next largest groups in rank order involved attacks by a parent upon a child, a child attacking a parent or siblings attacking each other;

3. The majority of violent crimes were identified in socio-economically deprived areas, more than 85% of the families having a bread-winner as a manual, casual, or semi-skilled worker. Seventy-five percent of the families were from the indigenous white population; there was some evidence to suggest that the ethnic minorities were less likely to report crimes of domestic violence to the police than the white population;

4. The situations leading to the outbreak of violence in the home were variable. In nearly 82% of offences there was no indication of alcohol having been taken by either the offender or the victim immediately prior to the offence. This contrasts with findings in samples identified in other ways, for example on entry to a women's refuge (e.g. Gayford, 1975a, b), which report much higher rates of alochol use. Most of the offences occurred during a weekend, and invariably the evening hours were the most vulnerable times. Weapons were used in less than half the cases and on the majority of occasions (60%) the injuries were fairly trivial. Fifteen per cent of victims, however, sustained multiple internal injuries and 4% died.

Battering parents are dealt with more fully elsewhere (pp. 502–7). Here it suffices to re-emphasize the fact that many seriously battering parents or spouses have experienced inadequate or hostile relationships with parent-figures in childhood. There are animal (Harlow and Harlow, 1962, 1969) as well as human models for this. Oliver et al. (1974), studied all cases of severe physical abuse among preschool children in one defined area of England, and found that the parents actually abusing a child differed from their spouses in being more likely to have been childhood victims of serious abuse or neglect themselves. A range of other problems have been identified among growing children who have been abused. Morse et al. (1970) followed such children for 3 years and found that 70% were outside the normal range for intellectual, emotional, social and motor development. A serious problem with this study, as with most others of its kind, is that comparable preabuse data is not available. One-third of the children in the sample became victims of serious abuse again during the 3 years. Green (1978) emphasized the significantly higher rates of suicide and self-mutilating behaviours in a group of abused and neglected children, compared with their normal peers. A particularly useful study showing that the effects of physical abuse in childhood, often including sexual abuse, are persistent to adult life was that of Mullen et al. (1988).

Observing violence.   The relative effects of observing 'violence' rather than receiving physical blows is still a matter of debate. There are two main hypotheses. First, it is suggested that real, extremely harrowing scenes of death, injury or destruction, be these in the person's immediate experience or through the medium of television or film, can cause psychological trauma. It has been shown repeatedly that personal physical injury is not a prerequisite of PTSD, in fact one of the commonest precipitating events for PTSD among men has been shown to be seeing someone hurt or die (Helzer et al., 1987). Even in law, in Britain, it has now been acknowledged that in certain circumstances the witnessing of a personally relevant traumatic incident in reality or in film may result in subsequent symptomatology sufficient to constitute compensable disorder. Although it is not generally possible to quantify the relative effects of witnessing rather than receiving some form of violence, some research among child victims of family violence suggests that those who witness violence experience disturbance at levels intermediate to those among directly abused children and to those who have suffered no form of abuse at all (Hughes, 1988).

The second hypothesis is much more contentious—that fictional violence, aggressive or deviant sex in books, films or TV programmes increases the likelihood of a viewer committing violence or deviant sexual acts or both. The evidence, taken overall, remains equivocal unless the circumstances of viewing are highly qualified (*see also* pp. 496–9).

Sexual crimes

Witnessing indecent exposure.   Most of the literature on becoming a victim of imposed sexual behaviour focuses on the more serious crimes. Nevertheless, in Britain at least, indecent exposure is numerically the fourth most important sexual crime with over 2000 convictions a year recorded. It is highly likely, given its low status as a crime, that this represents a disproportionate underrecording. It is almost certainly the commonest experience of sexual abuse (Gagnon, 1965).

The only researchers clearly to have separated the consequences of indecent exposure from the consequences of other sexual crimes are Gittleson et al. (1978). They surveyed 100 female nurses at a psychiatric hospital and found that 44% had been victims of indecent exposure, one-third of these on two or more occasions. Just two-thirds of the incidents were disclosed to others, and only 18% to the police. Long-term distress was most unusual, 77% of the women reporting that they felt fine within a week of the incident, and only two claiming to be upset years later. Nevertheless, despite the mean time difference between the offence and interview of nearly 15 years, the incident was recalled in detail in all cases, and the subjects said that they welcomed the opportunity to talk about it. One of the most striking findings was that in 1 in 5 cases the reaction of the family and friends had been more distressing than the incident itself.

Rape victims.   According to the Sexual Offences (Amendment) Act 1976, a man commits rape if he has sexual intercourse with a woman who at the time of the intercourse does not consent to it and, at that time, he knows that she does not consent to the intercourse or is reckless whether she consents to it.

Until March 1991, a husband in the UK could not be accused of raping his wife unless legally separated, but then in *R* v *R*, a conviction for rape of a woman by her husband was upheld on the grounds that '. . . a rapist remained a rapist subject to the Criminal law irrespective of his relationship with his victim'. Remaining anomolies within British law include the facts that boys under the age of 14 years cannot be convicted of rape, and forced oral or anal penetration of a woman, or forced vaginal penetration by any instrument except a penis, is not legally recognized as rape. The rape victim is, by definition, a female, as vaginal penetration is specified. Ejaculation need not necessarily occur. In spite of this, the presence of sperm on forensic testing is generally required as corroborative evidence of the rape. The popular myth of the fictitious claim or the 'vengeful woman' persists, even though in reality under-reporting is a far more serious and well-documented problem.

Although rape victims are often depicted as young, attractive and sexually provocative females, there is no typical victim profile. Children, teenagers, women in their eighties and pregnant women have all been raped. The likelihood of a woman being raped is related to her risk of becoming a victim of any type of crime rather than her conventional sexual attractiveness. The concept of the young white victim and black stranger-rapist is also a product of reporting bias. There are undoubtedly certain behaviours and lifestyles, for example prostitution, that increase the risk of rape, but such circumstances do not convey guilt. They should not be used as mitigation for the rapist's actions, although in many cases this is what happens.

Rape can be a life-threatening crime, as often an expression of anger and aggression as of sexual passion (Groth et al., 1977). In sadistic rape, it is the victim's fear and humiliation that is sexually exciting to the rapist and a number of these cases end in the victim's death (Ressler et al., 1983). In so-called power rape, the attacker generally uses no more force than is necessary to get the victim to submit. Some genuine differences in the assailant's motivation in the offence may partly account for the contradictory advice offered to women on self-protection. A woman's decision not to fight is sometimes misinterpreted, by the police, courts, friends and family alike. Although some recommend fighting approaches and training in physical combat, there is some evidence that passive resistance and an attempt to talk to the assailant may be safer than counter-attacks, which may only escalate the attacker's violence (Bart, 1981).

The reaction of women to rape was first described by two Americans as the rape trauma syndrome (Burgess and Holmstrom 1974 a,b; 1979). Several other American groups have added to knowledge about the patterns of reaction (e.g. Becker et al., 1979; Kilpatrick et al., 1981, 1985; Ellis et al., 1981; Ellis, 1983; Atkeson et al., 1982; Nadelson et al., 1982; Carmen et al., 1984), with Gise and Paddison (1988) providing a particularly useful review, together with a note of optimism on reduction of the problem through education. Postrape reactions have also been described in a group of British women (Mezey and Taylor, 1988). Rape trauma syndrome has psychological, behavioural and somatic components and shares many features with PTSD and acute stress reaction. It is perhaps unique, however, among crimes in the enforced intimacy of contact between victim and offender, and the deep shame experienced by the victim, often with a remarkable lack of anger towards the offender (Mezey and Taylor, 1988). A voyeuristic response by social networks and the media to the rape victim makes it difficult for her to shake off this label in the same way as a burglary victim might, and creates a damaging secondary victimization process (Williams and Holmes, 1981). Punitive judgments and dismissive remarks about the victim's culpability do little to aid recovery. Nevertheless, symptoms are said by some authors to resolve within 4–6 months in the majority of women (e.g. Sutherland and Scherl, 1970), but by others to be more enduring (Ellis et al., 1981). The features resolving may only be the more acute and florid symptoms of anxiety, depression and repetitive phenomena (Mezey and Taylor, 1988), while other problems, including guilt, low self-esteem, vulnerability and emotional distancing, sexual dysfunction and assault-related phobia are more persistent. This clustering seems to be as evident in men who have undergone similar experiences (Mezey and King, 1989).

Adult male victims of sexual assault.   Forcible anal penetration of men by men is a recognized problem of institutional life (Sagarin, 1976). The fact that men, both homosexual and heterosexual, can be sexually assaulted in the community is less well known, and there has only been one study carried out in Britain on this problem (Mezey and King, 1989). In Britain, male sexual assault is not recognized legally as rape and receives lesser penalties in law, with a maximum of 10 years' imprisonment possible, compared with life imprisonment for rape. The offence of buggery fails to distinguish between consensual and non-consensual acts or the gender of the victim. There is some evidence that the number of male victims is increasing, particularly in the USA, where a number of States have changed the definition of rape to include men (Kaufman et al., 1980).

Some American research has suggested that male victims of sexual assault are more likely to be physically injured than female rape victims, and are more likely to be victims of multiple assailants (Groth and Burgess, 1980;

Kaufman et al., 1980). The little research in this area suggests that the reactions of men following sexual assault are very similar to those of women who have been raped, although the sense of stigmatization and shame experienced may be even greater than for women victims, often centring around conflicts of gender identity and sexual orientation (Mezey and King, 1989). There are also reports that male victims may express more overt anger after sexual assault (Carmen et al., 1984; Goyer and Eddleman, 1984).

Child victims of sexual abuse. Sexual abuse of children may be defined as the involvement of dependent, developmentally immature children and adolescents in sexual activities which they do not truly comprehend, to which they are unable to give informed consent, or that violate the social taboos of family roles (Kempe and Kempe, 1978). This definition is broad and covers both incestuous and extrafamilial cases, and intrusions at all levels of seriousness on a child. The considerable range of definitions employed is just one of the difficulties recognized in reviewing research on the extent of the problem (Markowe, 1988). In addition, most studies are based on the unverified reports of the alleged victim. Fortunately, it seems likely that the majority of accounts are reliable (Herman and Schatzow, 1987). They found that even when recollections of such experiences were first produced in the course of therapy, 74% of them could be independently confirmed and a further 9% were indirectly supported.

The estimation of prevalence of abuse in childhood is also difficult because of sampling problems. Where samples of the general population have been questioned about sexual attention from an adult when they were a child, rates of 20–25% are fairly consistent (e.g. Gagnon, 1965; Harter et al., 1988), with females more than twice as likely as males to become such victims (Finkelhor, 1979). In Britain, 2019 people of 15 and over were interviewed, about a range of issues, including sexual experience, as part of a MORI (Market and Opinion Research International) random survey, thought to yield a nationally representative sample (Baker and Duncan, 1985). Twelve per cent of women and 8% of men said they had been sexually abused before the age of 16. The survey may also give one of the best indications of changing patterns of abuse: 13% of 15–24-year-olds reported sexual abuse as children, compared with 3% of those over 64, a significant difference. Estimates of childhood abuse in the USA may be as high as 62% among females (Wyatt, 1985) and 30% for males (Landis, 1956). A study (Russell, 1986) on the west coast of the USA of 930 women unselected for adult pathology, and explicitly not patients at the time of the study, found that 38% had experienced at least one episode of sexual abuse before their 18th birthday, 16% reported at least one incestuous experience by then and 5% sexual experience with their father.

The prevalence of incest is least clear. There have been increased reports in recent years, perhaps as the taboo on disclosing lessens. Overall about ten times as many females as males report incest. Male victims tend to be slightly older than female ones, to experience more physical injury and to be very much more likely to be the victims of homosexual abuse. A child's vulnerablity to sexual abuse relates to factors in the child, in the offender, in the family and in the community in which that family functions. Some communities tolerate sexual activity between children and adults and in such societies no significant ill-effects on the child have been reported (Ford and Beach, 1952; Currier, 1981). Incestuous families in western society tend to be isolated and socially chaotic, with loose inter-generational boundaries (Finkelhor, 1979; Herman and Hirschman, 1981).

Children who become victims of sexual abuse are not infrequently described as being attractive and seductive, their behaviour being construed as provocative and collusive (Gibbens and Prince, 1963; Yates, 1982) and there is increasing challenge to the concept of the 'sexual innocence' of children (Constantine and Martinson, 1981). Physical harm to a child is relatively unusual, but physical injury is not the only form of harm that may ensue. It is accepted that, in western society, any apparent encouragement on the part of a child, in the context of his or her immature emotional and cognitive functioning, and perhaps learning behaviours, does not constitute valid consent. Such an interpretation would be an abuse of power and trust.

An uncertainty in assessing the impact of sexual abuse on children lies in deciding whether any associated disturbance arises out of the abuse, whether it follows from predisposing factors that made the child vulnerable in the first place, or whether subsequent attitudes to the child, such as panic, horror or condemnation of the act, are themselves harmful. There is evidence that cases brought to court, with the attendant stressful physical examinations and questioning, produce more severe and lasting ill-effects than those that are not (Gagnon, 1965).

Studies looking at the proximate and the long-term effects have been carried out. In the short term, behavioural, emotional and somatic disturbances have been described, the persistence of which relate to the child's developmental level and prior history as well as to the type and chronicity of the abuse (Lewis and Sarrel, 1969; MacVicar, 1979; Adams-Tucker, 1982). In the longer term, some studies have suggested no serious effects for the majority of victims. Gagnon (1965), for example, found that only 5% of women who had experienced sexual advances as children reported maladjustment as adults. Nash and West (1985), however, found a much higher prevalence. Others have found links with psychiatric illness (Lukianowicz, 1972; Herman, 1981), suicide (Goodwin, 1981), delinquency (Weiss et al., 1955), subsequent law-breaking (Groth and Birnbaum, 1979), delinquency, drug abuse and crime (Burgess et al., 1987), prostitution (James and Meyerding, 1977; Silbert and Pines, 1982), distortions of personality development (Bender and Grugett, 1952) and sexual dysfunction (Burgess et al., 1987). Contrary to popular belief, adult homosexuality does not seem to be a consequence of adult male abuse in boys. Most committed adult homosexuals who can recall experience with an adult male in childhood report that their homosexual interests had already developed (Bell et al., 1981). For many victims, however, the abuse affects the quality of their personal relationships in later life and their personal adjustment (Tsai and Wagner, 1978). A very long lasting sense of guilt is frequently described over having kept the abuse secret (Fritz et al., 1981) and sometimes over the events following disclosure. There is anger towards the abuser, and often resentment towards the mother for having failed to protect them. Some authors have suggested that it is the involvement of the criminal justice system which may give rise to the most severe post-traumatic symptoms (e.g. Goldstein et al., 1979; Wald, 1982), but Runyan et al. (1988) offered a balancing view that, if handled appropriately, a court appearance may be therapeutic. Long delays in resolution adversely affected the children. Other consequences of reporting may also be very disruptive. One British study showed that 13% of reported cases ended with the child being taken into care (Mrazek et al., 1983). Other countries seem to adopt a less punitive approach to the problem. In the Netherlands, child sexual abuse is handled by a confidential doctor's service (Doek, 1978) and in Canada by child protection services (Cormier and Cooper, 1982b). Hall and Harris (1988) described developments in effective response in one inner city district in England.

An important area of consistency in the literature relating to child sexual abuse is the finding that adult problems with adjustment are far commoner when the biological relationship between the child and the adult perpetrator is close (e.g. Harter et al., 1988). A further disproportionate risk in these circumstances is that of consanguinous pregnancy, with its attendant disadvantages. Seemanova (1971) found that 14% of 161 children of incestuous liaisons died, compared with 5% of 95 children born to the same mothers by unrelated partners. Two-fifths of the survivors among the probands had major physical abnormalities compared with just 1 in 20 controls.

Victim precipitation

Many victims become so fortuitiously. Some, whether consciously or unconsciously, contribute to their own victimization. This is an area which is difficult to examine dispassionately. In some cases, the contribution is totally without the control of the victims, for example, the congenital abnormalities or low birth weight of babies particularly at risk for abuse (Lynch, 1975). The role in precipitation is never, however, simple. Wolfgang (1958a) studied all criminal homicides in Philadelphia between 1948 and 1952. The victim was the first person during the incident to show a weapon or to use force against the subsequent killer in 150 cases (26%). The victims, however, could not tell their own story and 'survivor bias' may have been a factor in this evidence. Several other characteristics were significantly associated with these 'victim precipitated' homicides. The victims were male, often spouses, and the offenders female. The victims had been stabbed, had had alcohol, and in an examination of previous arrest records of victims and offenders, the victims were significantly more likely to have had a record, particularly for assault. Voss and Hepburn's (1968) study of 394 criminal homicide victims in Chicago in 1965 found as many as 50% of non-white male homicides were said to be victim precipitated, compared with one-fifth of white male and non-white female, but less white female homicides. Pizzey and Shapiro (1982), on the basis of their very extensive and intimate experience with women entering a refuge to escape from domestic violence, identified a subgroup of women that they described as 'violence prone'.

A question as often debated is victim 'exacerbation', whether physical resistance against the offender may be more harmful than helpful. Block (1981) highlighted variation in sampling as one reason for the very confusing messages given in the literature. He noted the very different results obtained between cases reported to the police, and cases not reported. In a group who had reported to the police, victim resistance had slightly decreased the proportion of successful robberies from 98 to 78%, but greatly increased the probability of victim injury. In a substantial community survey, by contrast, just 40% of the robberies had been completed with victim resistance compared with 90% without. Again the resisting victim was more likely to be injured, although evasive resistance seemed less likely to be associated with damage than confrontational resistance.

The position is even more confused in respect of rape. Block (1981) described a study of police records presented by Griffin and Griffin in 1978 as advising women to resist their assailants with all means at their disposal, because 86% will remain free of serious physical injury whatever method of resistance is employed. Bart (1981) had less confidence in confrontational resistance, and advocated passive resistance including attempts to talk down the potential rapist as both safer and more effective in preventing completion.

The recidivist victim

The British Crime Survey findings, based on a one in 11 000 household survey in England and Wales, suggested that, overall, repeated personal assault was rare (2%), (Gottfredson, 1984), but that a subgroup of such victims was vulnerable. Among victims of violent crime, 28% had suffered similar experiences previously. Rates in New York seem similar (Ziegenhagen, 1976), but interviews by Shapland et al. (1985), in two English towns, with people at the point when an act of violence against them had been recorded by the police as a crime, suggested that only a minority were presenting as first time victims. One-third said that they had been before the courts previously as victims of similar offences, but a further third said that they had suffered similar assaults without reporting them.

The place where people are most likely to become repeated victims to personal abuse is in the home, their assailant generally being known to them (Stanko, 1990). Battered wives may find it morally, or financially, impossible to leave husbands, even if they have given up hope of reform, although in at least one survey of battered women (Gayford, 1975a, b) as many as 25% had chosen to marry in spite of having been previously violently abused by the men who became their husbands. Children of violent or incestuous families are even more powerless in their ability to leave. These issues apart, the factors in recidivism among victims seem similar to those associated with recidivism among the perpetrators of crime, both, for example, being more likely to come from low income groups and large or unstable families. Recidivist crime victims also seem disproportionately likely to report repeated victim experiences of other kinds, such as traffic accidents, household accidents or fires (Gottfredson, 1984).

Secondary victims

Families, friends or associates of the principal victim may also be traumatized, but this is even less well recognized. Some reference has already been made to the problems of rescuers in the face of a massive trauma (Jones, 1985). Many of the studies of victims of sexual abuse note that the victims felt as much if not more distress at the reactions of their relatives or confidants as at the offence itself (e.g. Gittleson et al., 1978), while Shapland et al. (1985) were specific about the anger among male relatives reported by female victims. One or two centres now offer support specially for the partners of sexual assault survivors, but reports of their work is largely anecdotal (e.g. Cohen, 1988).

The families of victims of crime.   When a relative has been killed the trauma is likely to be particularly great. Masters et al. (1988) reported on a series of 1182 families of Brooklyn, New York homicide victims who were receiving outreach counselling following the event, drawing attention to the series of losses abruptly thrust on such people. These include loss of loved ones, loss of illusions of safety and invulnerability, and a loss of sense of trust in the surrounding community. They, nevertheless, emphasized symptoms in terms of PTSD rather than uncomplicated grief, and suggested that recovery was delayed either by the knowledge that the killer was usually still alive, and in some cases unpunished, or by repeated confrontations with the criminal justice system. In Britain, the National Association of Victims' Support Schemes has taken a leading role in offering practical help to such families, while a number of families have been active in generating self-help groups (Evans, 1986). The very special problems of children whose mother has been killed by their father have been addressed by Black and Kaplan (1988), with a recommendation that all such children should be seen in a child psychiatric department.

There is now considerable evidence that the impact of prolonged victimization may have intergenerational consequences. Recognition of this has received comment in relation to the concept of cycles of disadvantage (Rutter and Madge, 1976), with particular reference to children of abusers who may, in turn, become abusers themselves. More recently, it has been observed that grandchildren of the survivors of the Holocaust are more prone to subjective symptoms and high arousal under stress than those with no connection (e.g. Sigal et al., 1988).

The offender as victim

The offender may himself be a victim—either in relation to his experiences prior to his offending or following his identification as an offender. Some of the evidence for previous victimization has already been cited above. Childhood receipt of violence (Oliver and Cox, 1973), sexual abuse (e.g. Earls et al., 1984) or both (Burgess et al., 1987) seeming particularly likely to lead to comparable behaviour in adolescence or adulthood, especially amongst males. Further victimization subsequent to the offending is also not unlikely, sex offenders being especially vulnerable to violent attack, or to sexual assault (Sagarin, 1976): many request placement in solitary confinement or special wings within prisons. The offender's family is also vulnerable. They acquire the stigma of the offence, they may lose their breadwinner and they suffer social rejection (Morris, 1965; Matthews, 1983).

Disasters

Kinston and Rosser (1974) define disaster as a situation of massive collective stress. Its relative unexpectedness may separate it from other collective experiences, such as war, at least in the minds of the victims, but such distinctions are not sharp. Kinston and Rosser highlight the resistance to acknowledging psychological consequences—both on the part of the victims and of the relief workers—and the consequent difficulties in identifying real need and delivering appropriate care. It was 17 years, for example, before there was systematic study of the psychosocial consequences of the nuclear bombing of Hiroshima. Even in simulated disasters, it was noted that rescuers became confused and disturbed by the sight of massive injuries to an extent that impaired their work (Menczer, 1968), but there was no attempt to elucidate further. It was not until the early 1970s in the USA (Stern, 1976) and the early 1980s in Britain (*McLoughlin*) that the principle of legal compensation for psychological damage suffered by civilians was accepted. The principle of compensation for physical damage had by that time long been established and, indeed, it may reflect prejudices towards psychiatric disorder that initially neurologists were still being called upon to assess the patients when the issue at law was of 'psychic impairment' (Stern, 1976). As recently as 1987, McFarlane et al. reported that long-term follow-up of children exposed to a bush fire was prevented by their schools, because 'they could not see the need for such continuing research'.

Most studies of disaster have been descriptive accounts following well-publicized incidents. Early examples include Lindemann's (1944) account of the consequences of a nightclub fire and Wallace's (1956) of a tornado in the USA, while among the later ones are a flood and slagheap collapse in West Virginia, USA (Newman, 1976), a cyclone in Ceylon (Patrick and Patrick, 1981), a building collapse in Kansas City in USA (Wilkinson, 1983) and a bush fire in Australia (McFarlane et al., 1987). The evaluation of survivors is usually cross-sectional, or the follow-up very short, and consequently a somewhat artificial picture of prevalence, severity and duration of problems emerges. Where study has been longitudinal, a much more useful picture emerges. McFarlane et al. (1987), for example, were able to show that an absence of early symptoms was not indicative of good prognosis, and that had calculation of prevalence of symptomatology been done at 2 months after the fire, the estimates would have been highly misleading. At that point, the prevalence of behavioural and emotional problems was less in children exposed to the bush fire than those not. Leopold and Dillon (1963) followed 34 survivors of a tanker freighter collision in the Delaware River, USA, for 4½ years, having first seen them between 48 hours and 13 days after the crash and fires. In the USA, seamen under contract to a vessel have an automatic right to 'realistic compensation' if they are injured during service, cause is unimportant. Thus these men received compensation, but none of them was offered any psychiatric treatment. Seventy-one per cent deteriorated over the 4 years or so of follow-up. Only 12 had been able to return to reasonably regular work at sea, although all but 4 had tried to do so.

Kinston and Rosser (1974) formulated a proposal for planning services. They argued that disorders identified subsequent to a disaster are made up of caused illness, precipitated illness, and illness which could have occurred at that time anyway. They calculated that the incidence of depressive illness alone in a disaster-struck community could increase by 350%, and that of unspecified neurotic illness by 110%. They conceded that in the absence of data on the effectiveness of intervention, it is difficult to calculate the manpower requirement to cope with this, but they recommended three general points for action:

1. A psychiatrist should visit all major disaster areas in the first few days after the event and, taking into account normal availability and standards of care in the area, advise on first-aid, intermediate and longer-term treatment needs;
2. A world/nationwide register of disaster-experienced psychiatrists, who could act as consultants, should be set up;
3. Teams of psychiatrists and allied professionals should be available for integration with the general relief response in areas where psychiatric services are non-existent or underdeveloped.

Torture

Although its exact prevalence is not known, torture is widespread, its occurrence verified in 98 countries throughout the world (Amnesty International, 1984). In the 1970s, in Canada, about 7000 Latin American refugees entered the country, about half of them managing to get medico-legal assistance. Allodi and Cowgill (1982) estimated that about 500 of these had definitely been tortured. Both the torture and psychological symptoms are commonly concealed by the sufferer, sometimes because the doctor-patient relationship feels authoritiarian and thus to have parellels with that of torturer and tortured or, occasionally, for fear of giving information so long with-held at such cost (Cienfuegos and Monelli, 1983). An additional difficulty in establishing a therapeutic alliance with torture victims arises from the fact that so many of the survivors speak a different language and are of a different culture from the doctor to whom they present.

Goldfeld et al. (1988) summarized the range of torture techniques known, and some of the physical consequences. They divided the principal psychiatric presentations in survivors into three main clusters:

1. the cognitive, which include disorientation, confusion, memory disturbance and poor concentration;
2. the psychological which include anxiety, depression, irritability and aggression, social withdrawal;
3. the neurovegetative symptoms which include lack of energy, insomnia, nightmares and sexual dysfunction.

Some authors (e.g. Allodi and Cowgill, 1982) have claimed a specific torture syndrome, but the evidence for this is not strong, although there seems to be a particularly high rate of head injury during torture or detention and of subsequent cognitive complaints. None of the studies to date reports full and systematic neuropsychological examinations. The prevalence and clustering of individual symptoms is difficult to estimate, because of the considerable variation in time between torture and presentation—from a few months to several years—even within individual study samples. Further, it is rare that torture is the sole adverse experience. Loss of family, culture, social status and nationality are commonly associated (Mollica et al., 1987). Up to 94% of one sample of 98 survivors of torture (Domovitch et al., 1984) were said to show anxiety features, abut 80% insomnia and nightmares and around two-thirds claimed poor concentration, depression, irritability, social withdrawal or sexual dysfunction. The Danish figures (Rasmussen and Lunde, 1980) were rather lower, but still nearly half of a sample of 135 complained of memory disturbances and/or poor concentration and 20–30% had anxiety, depression or irritability.

During WW2, many prisoners of the Japanese were virtually tortured by being subjected to severe abuse, deprivation of food, shelter, clothing and medical care for up to 3½ years. Kluznik et al. (1986) cite Cohen and

Cooper (1954) as showing a marked excess of 'psychoneurosis' and 'psychosis' among Pacific prisoners of war, but no such excess among those imprisoned in Europe in a total sample of 3654 men followed for 6 years. In a study which also included survivors of the Korean war, Beebe (1975) found a higher morbidity, maladjustment and disability among 2543 prisoners of war than among a combat sample. Kluznik et al. (1986) conducted structured psychiatric examinations with former prisoners of war, 135 held in Europe and 35 in the Pacific, 40 years after their experience, and already in receipt of compensation. It was the impression of the assessors, and of independent informants, that the men played down their symptoms. Sixty-seven per cent had a lifetime diagnosis of PTSD, of whom 29% had fully recovered by the time of interview. Thirty-nine per cent still reported mild symptoms, 24% moderate and 8% had made no improvement or had deteriorated. Alcohol consumption was consistently reported as heavy shortly after their return to the USA, but as a short-lived problem for 75%. Nevertheless, this meant that for just over a quarter of the men interviewed, a clinical diagnosis of alcohol abuse or dependency could be made at some stage in their lives. Levels of general disturbance were thus higher than those found in the epidemiological surveys of Vietnam veterans (e.g. Centers for Disease Control, 1988 but high rates of psychosis were not found (Cohen and Cooper, 1954; Beebe, 1975), nor was a high rate of psychopathy (Wolf and Ripley, 1947). The high mortality rates for these disorders may explain their absence in a 40-year follow-up sample, while the more detailed information gathering, including interview, might account for apparently higher overall symptomatology.

British prisoners of war from Japan have been studied by Khan (1987). He found that more than 30 years after release ex-prisoners of war were psychologically more maladjusted with higher psychiatric morbidity than surviving compatriots who also fought in Burma, but who were not captured. Thirty-seven per cent of the ex-POWs were diagnosed as suffering from a recognizable psychiatric disorder such as depression or chronic anxiety. In retrospect, it seems that symptoms had fluctuated in these men, middle life being the least troublesome with the stresses of later life increasing the level of pathology.

The survivors of concentration and extermination camps were subjected to the most extreme brutality that one man could inflict on another. Krystal and Niederland (1968) reported on 20 years of experience of working with survivors of such camps, who came to their attention for psychiatric evaluation as required by German restitution laws. People with the most severe mental disorders such as schizophrenia, or with self-destructive behaviours, had been quickly killed. The hyperalert, the pliable and adjustable, it was suggested, seemed to have a better chance of survival, and thus in one sense survivor groups would simultaneously be biased towards identifying people with hyperarousal states, but otherwise the most healthy.

Krystal and Niederland reviewed in detail 149 randomly selected records from among their patients, and found evidence of many of the symptoms now recognized as classically post-traumatic—such as sleep disturbances and nightmares. Ninety-seven per cent of the sample had chronic anxiety symptoms, with multiple phobias. The content of the symptoms, rather than their nature, was specific to the experience. Ninety-two per cent of the people studied had survivor guilt, and 79% showed masochistic personality traits which appeared to correlate with it. Survivor guilt was especially high both in incidence and severity among those who had lost one or more children, while the loss of an only child, or of all children where none were born after liberation, was associated with the most severe depression, in several cases this being psychotic. In spite of the near universal experience of severe, and sometimes disabling symptomatology, only eight people in the series had had a family or previous personal history of significant emotional problems. Mild problems before capture were associated with severe mental illness following the experience of the camps.

The authors remarked on the particularly high rate of somatization in the survivors, ranging from physical tension and headache to peptic ulceration and arthritis. These occurred particularly in the 15–30 age group (60%). A partial explanation was the strong association of these symptoms with overwhelming rage and despair under enforced complete passivity. The symptoms were less severe in those who were able to be more active and among those naturally adjusted to relatively passive relationships, for example children and much older people. Much later, Mollica et al. (1990) reported similar emphasis on somatic symptoms in Southeast Asian refugee survivors of mass violence and torture. While the overtly psychological symptoms improved with treatment, they found that the somatic symptoms tended to worsen.

One of the most important aspects of the book is that Krystal and Niederland (1968) looked critically at their own work. They suggested that the pressure on forensic psychiatry to categorize such people, forcing them into pre-existing nosological categories in order to be able to support their applications for pensions or compensation was highly unsatisfactory in terms of understanding their problems. The effects of conventional examinations and adversarial positions were particularly instructive in this regard. They suggested that a rather rigid question and answer style is in these circumstances too like 'the style of a Prussian non-commissioned officer', and would be highly likely to give rise to misleading replies. In possible support of this point, they cited a German-speaking researcher as finding that the survivors of Nazi persecution had a lower rate of all mental illness except hysteria than the native-speaking population of New York. Even allowing for the psychological strength that may have predisposed to survivor status, this seems too much like suggesting that mental health may be improved by persecution! An earlier German view that hysteria is essentially a fraud designed to get a pension was also cited (as Hoche, 1929) to complete the picture. The Krystal and Niederland understanding of the almost invariable hypochondriasis in this group, but not an uncommon accompaniment of PTSD of any origin, was that it could only be tackled in treatment by acknowledging its specific origin. This they construed as having been the hypercathexis of the body image, produced by dependence on the quality of the body's function and appearance in order to avoid selection for the gas chamber.

Hostages and Kidnap Victims

Most hostages and kidnap victims are frightened for their lives over extended periods (days, months, and sometimes years), and suffer extreme levels of arousal. Some attention has been paid to their behaviour during a siege or kidnap because it is unpredictable, and police or professional rescuers, therefore, never rely on hostages to assist them in securing their release. The so-called 'Stockholm Syndrome' was a term that came into fashion after a bank raid in Stockholm in 1974 went wrong and turned into a siege (Gunn, 1985b) and is often cited as evidence for possible hostage collaboration. One of the female victims not only had sexual relations with one of the robbers, but, after the incident was over, continued to visit him in prison. The sudden development of strong, positive, affectionate bonds between strangers may certainly happen when people are thrown together in highly emotional, especially life-threatening circumstances, and it is not surprising that from time to time such bonding occurs with an aggressor. Perhaps it even has survival value. Another well-known case was of Pattie Hearst, a millionaire's daughter who was captured by the Symbionese Liberation Army and who, after a few weeks, was seen assisting the group to rob banks. After her release from this group, she was surrounded by bodyguards and subsequently married one of them. Political and religious conversions under emotional circumstances have been described from biblical times onwards (Sargant, 1957). Among the personal descriptive accounts of the ordeal of being taken hostage (e.g. Jackson, 1973; Cramer and Harris, 1982) are indications that positive bonds between captor and captive are not invariable or even usual. In the case of the Iranian Embassy Siege (Cramer and Harris, 1982, Sunday Times Insight Team, 1980), it was possibly strong negative feelings between the terrorists and some of their hostages that led to a violent denouement.

After release, hostages suffer the same types of symptoms as other victims who have endured life-threatening experiences and may develop PTSD and/ or affective illnesses. Like other victims, they too are unlikely to seek help for these diseases. As with others, this may be because of guilt feelings, fear of the pain of rehearsal of the event or, particularly in this group, a fear of losing some or all self-control. Flashback symptoms, terrifying dreams, and phobias were described in 14 correctional officers held hostage during a prison riot in New Mexico (Hillman, 1981). Hillman postulated that it is the intensity of the hostage experience rather than its duration which determines the development of later illness, but it seems unlikely that intensity or duration would be unequivocally paramount in most cases. The vulnerability of children was demonstrated by a 4-year follow-up of 25 school children who were kidnapped for 27 hours. All the children developed post-traumatic symptoms which persisted at least for 4 years (Terr, 1983b). Brief psychiatric intervention 5–13 months after the trauma did little to relieve symptoms.

War

Victims of war, whether civilians or soldiers, suffer high levels of associated psychosocial disability, although most of the research has followed combatants. War was the precipitant of most of the earlier accounts of post-traumatic disorders. Few would now argue against the proposition that it is the symptom content, rather than their type or pattern, that appears relatively specific. Thus the flashbacks and nightmares in the veterans of war are exclusive only in the sense of being of the combat experience, and increased arousal follows from exposure to stimuli, suggested or real, which are reminiscent of the original exposure in war (e.g. Dobbs and Wilson, 1960; Blanchard et al., 1983).

The Centers for Disease Control (1988) examined the health of Vietnam veterans up to 20 years after returning from combat. Fifteen per cent had met diagnostic interview schedule criteria for combat-related PTSD at some time during or after service. In the month before examination, 21% had one or more symptoms, and 2% still met full diagnostic criteria, a figure twice as high as the alleged 1% prevalence in the general population (Helzer et al., 1987). Nevertheless, the national Vietnam veterans readjustment study (Kulka et al., 1988 as cited in Kolb, 1989) put the current rate of PTSD much higher, at 15% for men and 9% for women. Those exposed to active combat in the heart of the war zone had rates of PTSD three to five times higher than those in moderate or low exposure zones.

PTSD, however, accounted for only a small fraction of the problems among war veterans. The Centers for Disease Control (1988) study found suicide, violence against others, alcoholism, divorce and unemployment rates were all high, and that this was a finding consistent with other studies. Hearst et al. (1986) made a comparison of mortality rates between men drafted for military service in Vietnam up to 10 years after this draft, and those remaining at home. The Vietnam veterans had a significantly higher mortality rate, the principal causes of death being suicide and motor accidents. There is still controversy, however, about whether men suffering PTSD in relation to war are subsequently more violent or crime-prone than their peers who have escaped the disorder. Shaw et al. (1987) found that the prevalence of PTSD among Vietnam veterans in prison for criminal behaviours of various kinds (39%) was very similar to that among law-abiding citizens in the community. They were unable to show any direct relationship between PTSD and the crime leading to imprisonment. A significantly greater proportion of the imprisoned veterans than the community controls had shown evidence of antisocial personality disorder and high use of drugs and alcohol prior to service. This is the exception. Other studies have found a relationship between PTSD and violent or criminal behaviour in combat veterans who were previously non-violent (Wilson and Zigelbaum, 1983; Solursh, 1988), although not necessarily leading to arrest (McFall et al., 1991).

The possibility that some of the postcombat disorder seen could be secondary not only to psychological stress, but also to organic brain damage also has to be considered. Following the Vietnam war, for example, Levy (1988) in a double blind controlled trial found that those soldiers exposed to the herbicide agent orange were significantly more likely to show both PTSD and organic psychological deficits.

Understanding the Disorder: Models of Disorder Development

Concepts of Stress

The word stress is in common usage, and has a wide range of meanings. In medicine, stress is probably best understood as a distortion of the normal equilibrium between an organism and its environment such that the organism is damaged or threatened. Cox, T. (1978), for example, regarded stress as a phenomenon arising from the imbalance between the demand on the person and his ability to cope. A 1958 congress on the relationship between stress and mental illness (Lancet, 1958) came to the view that stress is a subcategory of 'challenge', stress being a challenge which poses problems to the organism which cannot be met at all, or can only be met by varying degrees of adaptation. The congress agreed that, under stress, organisms may change in four ways, each temporarily or permanently. An organism will change in its emotional systems, behaviourally, in its physiology and structurally. These four types of change are not necessarily correlated, and in some cases one or two may be absent altogether. They still represent four areas of examination appropriate to the assessment of the effects of stress.

Psychological Models

Conditioning and sensitization

When faced with a stressful stimulus all animals, including man, experience a rise in physiological arousal, associated avoidance behaviours including flight, withdrawal or aggression. As this is occurring, all kinds of stimuli, directly or indirectly related to the threat, may become associated with the changed state of arousal and subsequently rekindle the associated distress. Where the stress is prolonged, an increasing range of experience becomes open to this association or conditioning. Furthermore, in the context of a particularly intense or prolonged stress, or in constitutionally vulnerable individuals, arousal may become so generally heightened that almost any stimulus, internal or external, will produce responsive or anticipatory fear, dysphoria or both. Among authors who have advanced models for the understanding of PTSD, Kolb (1987) is particularly effective in setting his own work with Vietnam combat veterans and the work of others with animals in the context of conditioning theory. His model provides an important link between psychological and physiological symptoms.

Inescapable shock

The animal model of 'learned helplessness' (Seligman and Maier, 1967), concerned with the response to severe physical distress such as continuous electric shock, loud noise or submersion in cold water from which there was no escape, seems to fit many trauma situations in both the nature of the stimulus and the response. They demonstrated, in controlled trials, that the trauma *per se* was a necessary, but not sufficient, condition for the syndrome, the lack of individual control in terminating the stress being the other significant factor. Three crucial elements were observed, namely of chronic distress, decrease in motivation for learning new contingencies and actual deficits in learning to escape from novel aversive situations.

Originally used as a model for understanding depression, van der Kolk et al. (1985) adapted the model as the 'inescapable shock' explanation of the trauma reaction. Applied to humans, it may help to explain the failure or reluctance to engage in therapy and a failure to cope with work or social responsibilities. Some of the more maladaptive behaviours which follow early trauma in some people, such as physically abused girls marrying violent husbands, or sexually abused boys and girls becoming abusers or prostitutes, may also be explicable in these terms.

The challenge to self-control

Survivors often complain that one of the worst elements of their experience was the sense of being out of control over their destiny. Among Terr's series (1983b) of 25 kidnapped children, even at 4 years after the incident 23 of the children were unable to envisage or plan for a future. The importance of the experience of being unable to control pain or distress has already been described (Seligman and Maier, 1967; Maier and Seligman, 1976). A sense of control may be important in other ways too. Rotter (1966) developed the concept of locus of control, and an instrument for measuring it. He described people as tending towards one of two poles in this regard—those who have an internal locus of control, with a strong sense of being able to control what happens to them, and those with an external, who feel themselves subject principally to the influences of others or the vicissitudes of fate. He showed that prolonged adverse experiences of some kinds, for example, low socio-economic status, appeared to be associated with high externality. Kilpatrick et al. (1972) found that a high sense of internal locus of control was one of the factors associated with long-term survival in a group of dialysis patients, another being relative indifference to fellow patients, which, in essence, meant a lack of survivor guilt. Breier et al. (1987) tested 10 healthy volunteers on psychological and physiological measures after exposure to a loud noise which in one trial was controllable and in the other not so. The uncontrollable stress made the greater impact.

Immunological incompetence as a psychological mechanism

Immunological compromise as a physical problem is now well recognized in association with severe stress, probably as a conditioned response (Laudenslager et al., 1983). The concept has also been applied to the development of psychological responses (Garb et al., 1987), and leads naturally to a potentially useful means of relief of symptoms and even, in some circumstances, prevention. The approach is known as stress inoculation training (Meichenbaum, 1985).

Denial and dissociation

Denial in some degree is a common mechanism for reducing anxiety, but it may be associated with debilitating, even damaging behaviours, and may be one of the most destructive factors to treatment and resolution. Horowitz (1976) decribed it as characterized by inattention, avoidance, amnesia, constriction of thought processing and emotional numbing. It is difficult to know how far failure to disclose correlates with denial; Rosenfeld (1979) recorded that of 18 patients in psychotherapy, 6 had been incest victims, but only 1 offered the information spontaneously. Nash and West (1985) noted that of 94 women who had reported sexual abuse in their randomly selected sample of 452, 55% had never previously disclosed their abuse. Even nurses, in one study, failed to acknowledge an emotional response to physical assault (Lanza, 1983), although 45% had lost time from work as a result of the incident, and 65% admitted to taking up to a year to recover fully from the effects. At interview, they revealed a fear of being overwhelmed and unable to function if they acknowledged the feelings, while others believed that being assaulted could be construed as part of their job and they ought not to react emotionally.

Dissociation suggests a complete splitting of the painful affects from consciousness, sometimes with the substitution of other symptoms. There have been a number of reports of experiences that appeared dissociative in nature following trauma or near-death experiences (for example Van Putten and Emory, 1973; Greyson, 1985; Mueser and Butler, 1987). Brett and Ostroff's (1985) review of imagery and PTSD is also useful in this context. There has, however, been little empirical study, although Spiegel et al. (1988) have shown that hypnotizability, which they construe as the capacity to experience dissociation in a structured setting, may be associated with PTSD. Similarly, Stutman and Bliss (1985) compared combat veterans who had symptoms of PTSD with those who did not and found the latter to have significantly lower hypnotizability scores. Neither study resolves the further question, whether the experience of trauma enhances hypnotizability, or whether highly suggestible/hypnotizable individuals are more likely to develop post-traumatic reactions.

Physical Models of Understanding Post-Traumatic Reactions

Kardiner (1941) is often credited with being first not only to describe the full syndrome of PTSD, but also to link it to organic change, referring to it as a 'physio-neurosis'. There is now general agreement on an association between measurable physiological arousal and PTSD (e.g. Kolb, 1987; Friedman, 1988). Kolb went on to consider whether the changes may become permanent, through changes in synaptic function or even neuronal death. As an analogy for the latter, he pointed out that loud noise may lead to permanent deafness. Brende (1982), investigating electrodermal responses in Vietnam veterans found that some cortical changes did appear permanent.

Friedman (1988) specified sympathetic overarousal accompanied by neuroendocrine changes and sleep disturbance. Ross et al. (1989) have argued convincingly from the growing number of sleep studies that a disorder of REM sleep mechanism may be pathognomic of PTSD, and relevant even to such apparently wakeful experiences within that context of flashbacks or startle responses.

Although there has been some interest in trying to identify biological markers for PTSD (e.g. Lerer et al., 1987), much of the work on biochemical changes has focused on neurotransmitters (e.g. van der Kolk et al., 1985). In animals, exposure to inescapable shock has been shown to be associated with increased noradrenalin turnover, increased plasma catecholamine levels and depleted brain noradrenalin, dopamine and serotonin with increased acetylcholine (Schildkraut and Kety 1967; Anisman 1978; Anisman et al., 1981). Anisman et al. (1981) also showed that, while the delivery of electric shocks had no mean effects on naive mice, noradrenalin depletion followed in those previously subjected to inescapable shock.

Burges-Watson et al. (1988) reviewed the evidence for the inter-relationship between stress and encephalins and endorphins. These include studies of postoperative states (Cohen et al., 1982) and self-mutilators (Coid et al., 1983). Opioid exhaustion, they suggest, may result in the failure of an effective inhibition of locus coeruleus neurones, resulting, in turn, in noradrenalin release followed by catecholamine excess. Certainly the locus coeruleus plays a crucial role in sleep regulation, which may link their hypothesis to the sleep work just described.

Animal models also suggest the possibility of immuno-compromise following severe trauma. In rats, Laudenslager et al. (1983) demonstrated immunosuppression and Visintainer et al. (1982) an increased incidence of tumour genesis. Reference has already been made to an increased mortality and rates of leukaemia and spontaneous abortions in human populations after natural disasters (Bennet, 1970; Janerich et al., 1981). Calabrese et al. (1987), in an excellent review of human work, found only one absolutely consistent result, that lymphocytes do not reproduce as well *in vitro* when challenged by an antigen when they have been taken from a person who has been subjected to stress. Dorian and Garfinkel (1987) have, however, commented on the widespread immunological change found under some conditions of stress, including bereavement.

From Victim to Survivor: Help and Treatment

Recovery from psychological trauma is more than simple relief from the intrusive distress of nightmares, flashbacks, panic attacks, depression and the like. Such relief may be important, but it may be achieved principally through the medium of avoiding recall of the event and contact with known triggers of distress. Horowitz (1976) described recovery as the capacity to recall the trauma at will, while being equally capable of turning one's mind to other matters.

Attitudes to Victims

Within the voluntary sector, there is an increasing movement away from the use of the term 'victim' in favour of the term 'survivor'. The goal is to encourage both the victim and the surrounding community to respond more positively to their plight. There is a sense of some hopelessness or permanence in the term 'victim', but while 'survivors' may need treatment and support, they will live, and maybe recover.

There is tremendous ambivalence in society to victims. Since private prosecutions have become a rarity, the law has given no well-defined role to the victim in the criminal justice system (Shapland et al., 1985), the victim at most having a part to play as witness to a crime and even here, unlike the offender, without the benefit of personal legal support or advice. There is some curiosity about the experience of victimization, carried to unacceptably intrusive extremes by some elements in the press, but there is also a reluctance to becoming involved to the point that bystanders will actually withhold immediate help from, for example, victims of crime (Mawby,

1984). An extreme example is a case known to one of us in which a naked psychotic man raped and strangled to death a woman in the public hallway of a group of flats. Two neighbours separately witnessed this, but decided not to intervene or seek help as it was 'obviously a lover's quarrel'.

While a victim may attract sympathy, evidence of survival skills may arouse something akin to jealousy and hostility. One man who had survived the P & O ferry disaster (*see* pp. 103–4), for example, had steadfastly turned away all press inquiries for several months. Finally, perhaps as his recall of events also became more bearable, he agreed to talk to a local journalist, thinking that if he did so the press would have what they wanted and leave him alone. He described his narrow survival and the strange sense of intense energy immediately afterwards when he was able to assist nine or ten people to safety. On arrival at work the next day several greeted him with sarcastic comments, 'quite the hero now aren't we'. Another survivor who similarly allowed an interview by a persistent and intrusive reporter received poison pen letters. Others reported envious remarks from neighbours if they bought anything new, 'Oh! the compensation has come through then has it?' Even among professionals attitudes are hardly better. Kelly (1975) described the failure of the medical profession to offer treatment for psychological problems to accident survivors, coupled with exhortations to them to pull themselves together. The term 'compensation neurosis' (*see* pp. 415, 906) is hardly value free.

Immediate Psychological Intervention : Expendable or Essential?

Lindemann (1944) was very clear in his views about the immediacy of need for help for the survivors of trauma.

> Since it is obvious that not all . . . can have the benefit of expert psychiatric help, much of this knowledge will have to be passed on to auxiliary workers. Social Workers and Ministers will have to be on the look-out for the more ominous pictures . . . while assisting the more normal reactions themselves.
>
> Proper psychiatric management of grief reactions may prevent prolonged and serious alterations in the patient's social adjustment as well as potential medical disease.

Following Lindemann's exhortations, immediate or early 'crisis intervention' came to be seen as the mainstay of work with victims and survivors. He emphasized that this did not mean comfort alone, but also the provision of adequate assistance for the grief work, the coming to terms with changed circumstances which inevitably mean serious loss, sometimes including actual bereavement. Lindemann advocated eight to ten interviews, few seem to have postulated more than 2–3 months' work, but those working with victim support schemes have generally argued that longer-term support can be required (e.g. Gay et al., 1975). The principal goal is restoration of function to the pre-crisis level. Sifneos (1967) suggested that people with poor pre-crisis adjustment, or pre-existing difficulties in interpersonal relationships, might only be able to cope with 'crisis support' and not the full crisis intervention, the latter implying some challenge to defences with some raising of anxiety. Jacobson (1979) suggested that predominantly supportive work, supplemented as appropriate with practical help or environmental intervention, would be within the scope of concerned individuals who have received no more than task-oriented training. Individual work which takes into account the individual's personality, previous experience and coping styles may amount to short-term dynamic psychotherapy and requires a much higher level of training and experience.

A serious difficulty in evaluating such work is that if interventions are made early, they are being made at a time when most people are undergoing a period of maximum change in their symptomatology. The fact that acute symptoms may have resolved within the 2–3 months of therapy may mean nothing more than that the disorder is following its natural course. Nevertheless, one of the key elements of crisis work, the ventilation of painful affect, has been shown to be effective in short-term well-being. In an ingenious but simple study, Pennebaker et al. (1988) randomly assigned 50 allegedly healthy undergraduates to write about either traumatic experiences or neutral, superficial experiences, each over 4 consecutive days. Self-report and objective data were evaluated blind, and showed clear health advantages for the group ventilating their traumatic experiences.

Although the value of early crisis intervention for the gravely traumatized for preventing more serious disorder is unproved, this is no argument against its provision, for controlled trials may yet show benefits. Even if they do not, supporting distressed people is a humane activity, and it could be that treatment in the longer term for those who develop chronic disorder is enabled by the establishment of contacts and relationships in the acute phase.

There are significant problems in both early and longer-term counselling, which should lead to a requirement that every counsellor, including the lay ones, should not only have basic training in survivor counselling, but also some supervision and support immediately available to them. After a violent experience, one of the major responses is anger. If the therapeutic relationship is at all effective, much of that anger will be directed towards the counsellor. Many patients/clients will be aware of their hostility, and guilt ridden about it, tending to avoid further interviews. The problem may be compounded if the psychiatrist or counsellor is unprepared for the anger and the guilt. Either they may respond with a hostile countertransference, or feel diminished and drained by the hostility which, in turn, may lead to 'burn out' (Freudenberger, 1974), and the inability to continue in such work.

Voluntary Support and Self-Help

Mawby and Gill (1987) reviewed the development of volunteer services for victims, and their interaction with statutory provision. In Britain, a pilot scheme for victim support was first set up in Bristol in 1971. The National Association of Victims' Support Schemes was founded in 1979, followed by a rapid rise in referrals, and growth of schemes registered with them. In 1980 there were 67 schemes with approximately 14 000 referrals but, by March 1986, 293 schemes were in existence, with 185 000 referrals. Hough and Mayhew (1985), nevertheless, found that only about 1% of people who report crime to the police are ever referred to such a scheme. They tend to be selected by police as belonging to one of the groups traditionally regarded as vulnerable—women, the elderly or those living alone (Williams, 1983). The case for such selection is unresearched.

An important characteristic of the victim support schemes is that they offer services immediately, contacting the individual at home by letter, telephone call or personal visit, and not relying on the victim to take the first initiative in seeking help. They may provide practical support, such as assisting their clients, where they wish it, to make insurance claims or to increase security, to get medical help if relevant and to contact relatives, friends or other support agencies. Chapman and Gates (1978) found that this kind of mixed approach seems to reflect demand. Of 147 victims in their series contacting a rape crisis centre, 71% said they needed to talk to someone, 46% wanted information about the criminal justice system, 35% wanted someone to go with them to the hospital and another 25% wanted other medical advice. In Britain, some schemes will limit their visits to two or three in number, others have a more open-ended policy, but the goal of all is to be primarily available for immediate and short-term help.

Professional Treatment

Pharmacological treatments

Friedman (1988) pointed out that most drugs that seem to have some value in PTSD are effective in *both* depression *and* panic disorder. He concluded his useful review of the field by pointing out that there is no definitive pharmacological treatment for PTSD and, furthermore, that drug therapy alone is never sufficient to alleviate suffering. Kolb (1989) commented that 'the basic symptoms of PTSD are beyond modification by any of the social or psychotherapeutic approaches. Such efforts assist . . .', and advocates drugs, particularly those which attenuate discharge of the locus coeruleus as necessary adjuncts. Bleich et al. (1986), reviewing the treatment of 25 patients in a special unit for PTSD, found that pharmacotherapy appeared to have a positive impact on psychotherapy in 70% of cases.

Monoamine oxidase inhibitors (MAOIs) seem to have enjoyed particular favour initially. Hogben and Cornfield (1981) reported five successfully treated cases, a number of others followed, but with even smaller series. Although the efficacy of the MAOIs in the treatment of depression has been disputed (Greenblatt et al., 1964; Medical Research Council, 1965) they are powerful inhibitors of REM sleep. Nevertheless, the one double blind controlled trial for PTSD has failed to show an advantage (Shestatsky et al., 1988). Friedman (1988) drew attention to their potential dangers among post-traumatic survivors, given the high rates of alcohol and other drug abuse or dependency among them.

Benzodiazepines have been shown to be effective (van der Kolk, 1983) in the palliation of symptoms. In line with the view that those drugs which appear to combine anxiolytic and antidepressant properties are likely to be most effective, alprazolam, a long-acting variant, was proposed as of particular benefit (Feighner et al., 1983), but has since fallen into disfavour as being among the more likely to induce dependency. Adrenergic blockers are, perhaps, logical alternatives for which there is some evidence of efficacy (Kolb et al., 1984). A systematic attempt to study the effects of propranolol in a small sample of children showed significant symptom reduction for some (Famularo et al., 1988).

Several studies have suggested that tricyclic antidepressants, especially imipramine, may be of value in suppressing flashbacks, reducing nightmares, dampening arousal and averting panic, as well as specifically tackling any depression (e.g. Friedman 1981; Burstein, 1982; Bleich et al., 1986). It has even been argued that the tricyclics may exert their effect through enhancement of endogenous opioid production (Malseed and Goldstein, 1979). In spite of Kolb's (1986) advocacy of chemical attenuation of locus coeruleus discharge, which this would facilitate, he is very sceptical of the hypothesis which likens PTSD to the addictive state, generating a need for opioid generation (van der Kolk and Greenberg, 1987). Again, properly controlled studies are lacking.

Of other drugs, lithium is the only one that has been specifically advocated (van der Kolk, 1983; Kitchner and Greenstein, 1985). Friedman (1988) argued that antipsychotic drugs have no place in the routine treatment of PTSD, with even the paranoid and hallucinatory symptoms responding better to reduction in the levels of arousal by other means. Bleich et al. (1986) provided confirmation for this view in their small study. Only in those rare cases of frank psychotic illness or overwhelming aggression, self or other directed, may there be a place for neuroleptics in post-traumatic states.

Psychological treatments

Behavioural approaches. Work with victims and survivors is fairly typical of work with other groups of people with marked arousal and secondary maladaptive behaviours. The face value of a behavioural approach is high, but the experimental evidence for efficacy low, often depending primarily on individual case studies (e.g. Blanchard and Abel, 1976; Forman, 1980). A further problem among victim groups may be their difficulty in engaging with consistency, but Veronen and Kilpatrick (1983) made the additional observation that one behavioural treatment offered in their study—desensitization—had not even proved initially attractive enough to be chosen by sufficient rape victims to permit a trial. Peer group counselling suffered a similar fate.

One potentially important behavioural approach is to tackle the avoidance of acceptance of loss and of unpleasant affects so often associated with unresolved post-traumatic states. Following earlier, promising descriptions of behavioural treatment for morbid grief (e.g. Ramsey, 1977, Gauthier and Pye, 1979), Mawson et al. (1981) randomly assigned 12 patients to a guided mourning group or a control group. After a waiting period of 2 weeks, the former group was required to write at least one page daily about the deceased, to look at a photo of them each day and to think as often as possible about the person, while in the treatment sessions (three times weekly for 2 weeks), also being encouraged to say goodbye out loud to the deceased. The control group were encouraged to avoid thought of the deceased and given distraction techniques. Patients in the guided mourning group improved significantly more than the others, and maintained that improvement through the 10–28 weeks of follow-up, the control patients still showing no trend towards improvement. Modifications of this technique to apply to the variety of losses and specific fears experienced after a range of traumas could be of benefit.

Stress inoculation training.   When Veronen and Kilpatrick (1983) presented women who were symptomatic 3 months after rape with a choice of treatment options, most opted for stress inoculation training. This is a collective term for a conglomerate of techniques, aimed at stress prevention as well as stress relief, which, according to its principal protagonist (Meichenbaum, 1985) was born out of dissatisfaction with behaviour therapy procedures. The emphasis is on training, employing a mixture of directive and socratic techniques, with the goal of each patient or participant passing through three phases, which overlap.

1. *The education or conceptualization phase.* Here a subject learns to self-monitor maladaptive thoughts, images, feelings and actions and observes problem-solving techniques.
2. *The skills acquisition and rehearsal phase.* Coping skills are modelled or taught and the maladaptive behaviours linked as triggers to implement the new repertoire. Rehearsal in imagination is encouraged.
3. *The application and follow-through phase,* during which skills are consolidated and extended, with booster sessions as necessary.

In Veronen and Kilpatrick's adaptation, rape victims were taught that anxiety is an unavoidable aspect of life and must be managed; they explained its origins. They taught coping skills for the various elements including covert modelling and role play for the enacted elements, techniques such as thought stopping and guided self-dialogue for the cognitive elements and relaxation, and breath control for the autonomic elements. Preliminary results were promising. Meichenbaum (1985) summarized the diversity of applications, which include its use by professional groups preparing to face potentially stressful tasks.

Individual psychotherapy.   Some of the earlier and detailed accounts of individual therapy for the survivors of the Holocaust are invaluable for the picture they give of traumatic and defensive reactions to the severest of traumas (Krystal, 1968). The commitment was to long-term dynamic treatment, a resource not readily available to most patients. Briefer forms of psychotherapy have been studied more systematically. Marmar et al. (1988) explored the relative effects of individual and group therapies for 61 women with unresolved grief and stress symptoms following the death of their husbands between 4 months and 3 years previously. They were randomly assigned to either 12 weekly sessions of individual dynamic psychotherapy from experienced psychotherapists or to one of five mutual self-help groups, run by women who had resolved their own grief reactions after losing their husbands on average 8 years previously. When treatments actually received were compared, they were found to be equally effective, but significantly fewer of the women in the self-help groups completed the treatment. Overall, therefore, there was a greater decline in pathology among the women in individual dynamic psychotherapy.

Group psychotherapy.   Groups are often regarded as the optimal approach for the treatment of reactions to trauma. Sprei and Goodwin (1983) described a rape survivors' group, advocating open membership with people choosing when they would enter, and when they would leave. The group function in such circumstances they saw as largely information-sharing and support. The emphasis on group work that is largely peer led and executed arises from an often cited view that victims only feel comfortable talking to other victims. Veronen and Kilpatrick's (1983) finding that when offered therapeutic alternatives, women who had been raped rarely chose the peer group option, taken together with the study of bereaved women just described, suggests that the view may not only be mistaken, but may lead to therapeutic disadvantage.

An impressive study of group work in this field is that of Roth and colleagues (1988). The exposition of the difficulties and limits to the study is worth reading in itself. Seventy-two women with long-standing symptoms following sexual assault responded to a written questionnaire study; 29 agreed to further interview assessment and 9 agreed to enter group therapy, having had symptoms for 8 years. Seven completed the treatment, while among 13 control women only 6 did so. The group therapy was not conducted in isolation. Apart from any random influences, 5 of the 7 women completing therapy were also in individual therapy throughout, and the other 2 started such treatment work. The authors suggested that such serious group work may not be safely attempted without the adjunct of individual psychotherapy. In neither of the two subsamples were depressive symptoms fully resolved, but both intrusive fears and depressive scores improved significantly more in those receiving group therapy than in the controls.

Environmental Manipulation and Prevention of Trauma

The influence of a therapist compared to the influence of relatives, friends and other features in the individual's environment is likely to be small. For some, an important part of the solution to problems is removal from the dangerous environment. Rarely is it possible to increase the comfort and safety of the environment by removing one key perpetrator of abuse. The women's aid organizations arose to offer a safe haven where this was otherwise impossible, and thus to extend the choice for change to women and children in a threatening domestic environment. Sometimes the vulnerable in this setting can be further protected by law, for example by the use of injunctions. Potential victims will find victim support schemes, citizens' advice bureaux or the police helpful in guiding them to some such appropriate arrangement. An injunction is far from complete protection, since the persecutors may choose to disregard the sanction, but for many victims it is an important step in acknowledging and defining a threat and beginning to restore their safety.

For children there is, in theory, a much more effective safety net of legislation although, in practice, the balance between damage to the child by leaving him in his home environment and damage from removing him, with all the attendant traumas of separation and the insecurities of surrogate care, is often difficult to determine. In England and Wales, legislation places the burden of intervention, once a case of child abuse is suspected, on the local authority 'to cause inquiries to be made' in consideration of grounds for bringing care proceedings, although the police or NSPCC may initiate them. A number of models of good practice in the investigation and management of alleged abuse have been advocated (e.g. Giaretto, 1982; Dale et al., 1986a; Hall and Harris, 1988). The legal provisions, with their implications, are discussed on pp. 102, 243.

Helping the Helpers

A number of publications have now highlighted the risks of stress symptoms encountered by professional and volunteer helpers of the traumatized—in the acute situation (e.g. Jones, 1985), in the medium term (e.g. Mezey and Taylor, 1988) and in the longer term with the problem of 'burn out' (e.g. Freudenberger, 1974). Others have emphasized the destructive effect for the patients or clients of unresolved affects and defences among therapists (e.g. Dale et al., 1986b). Nevertheless, although there is increasing agreement that anyone undertaking trauma work will have need of 'adequate supervision and support', there is no standard as to what this might be. We have found regular peer group support and access to at least occasional advice or supervision from a psychodynamically trained psychotherapist invaluable.

Legal Issues

The Victim in the Criminal Justice System

Several authors have reviewed the diminishing place of the victim in the criminal justice system (Schafer, 1960; Shapland et al., 1985; Mawby and Gill, 1987). Anyone in Britain may still bring a private prosecution against another but, in practice, this is extremely rare and usually the state takes over. From that point, victims have only a 'bit part', at most participating as a witness of the crime under trial, but often receiving no further information about what happens to their case. As a witness in court, they may generally expect anything from indifference to hostility. The main purpose of the criminal court is not the well-being of the victim, but the trial and, if convicted, the sentencing of the offender.

Shapland et al. (1985) called for several improvements in conditions which would require little more than the will to institute. First, they suggested that victims should be more informed through widely available booklets or pamphlets about procedures and support available. In individual cases, a specially designated liaison officer at each divisional or subdivisional police station should ensure delivery of such news as whether their assailant has been caught, where remanded, the date of court appearances and the final outcome of 'their' case. Second, the processes of investigation and prosecution should be more sensitive. All early contacts, from emergency call controllers to scene of crime officers, must understand that people under stress may find it difficult at first to give more than fragmented information. Victim safety and medical care must take priority over investigation.

Statements and investigative tests should, as far as possible, be arranged at the convenience of the victim witness. At court, adequate facilities should be available for waiting, in particular the victim witness should not be obliged to wait in the same area as the other witnesses or defendant, or in the public gallery.

The victim in the criminal courts

Victim witness competence.   There are some circumstances in which the competence of witnesses may be called into question. The impugning of the character or morals of the victim witness tends to be predominantly a feature of rape cases. Other issues in relation to adult victim competence, for example cognitive abilities, are dealt with on p. 844. These are important areas where psychiatrists may be asked to give evidence in court.

There are now several studies which have examined competence of children in the reporting of sexual abuse, the area in which there is likely to be simultaneously most dependence on their testimony in court and most concern about it. Dent and Stephenson (1979) demonstrated the extreme importance among child witnesses of avoiding leading questions at all times during the investigation as well as during the legal process. Wehrspann et al. (1987) reviewed the criteria said to distinguish between true and false allegations. Collection of data is taken from each of three sorts of inter-views:—investigative, validating and therapeutic—the latter also potentially a source of validation. Physical findings such as the presence of sperm or venereal disease may provide overwhelming corroberation of the child's evidence, but, where not, various elements in the interviews have consistently been identified as supportive of credibility (Undeutsch, 1982; Faller, 1984; Nurcombe, 1986). These elements are spontaneity, repetitions, internal consistency, external consistency, embedded responses, amount and quality of detail, that the story is told from a child's viewpoint, emotional state consistent with disclosure, consistency in the face of challenge, lack of suggestibility, sexually specific symptoms or behaviours and apparent motivation for disclosure. It is suggested that a well prepared report will give evidence of evaluation of the interview under each of these headings. The controversial area of the scientific reliability of evidence based on play with anatomically correct dolls was debated by Yates (1988), who supported the principle of their use while calling for guidelines, and Terr (1988), opposed to their use in expert testimony, but supportive of further research.

Jones and McGraw (1987), studying all 576 reports of child sexual abuse made to the Social Services Department of Denver in 1983, of which 47% proved unfounded, found that just 8 (1%) made by a child appeared to be fictitious, although a further 25 (4%) were 'recanted'. Twenty-six (5%) adults had apparently fabricated an abuse story on behalf of the child. Among 17 girls and 4 boys, where accounts proved to be fictitious, 5 were made by the child alone, 7 in conjunction with an adult and 9 by the adults alone. These children gave their accounts with little accompanying emotion and under minimal pressure, they were inclined to be vague, but 4 of them had definitely been previously traumatized and were probably suffering from PTSD. In 7 cases where allegations were jointly made by an adult and child, it was not clear who had initiated the process, and parental distress or disturbance was often apparent. The mother of one child had herself been sexually victimized, and overidentified with her child; another mother was psychiatrically disturbed; in other cases there were ongoing custody or access disputes. Klajner-Diamond et al. (1987) noted similar issues in relation to false reporting, and added occasional problems arising from an overconcerned, overcommitted professional. Awad (1987) extended the discussion of sexual abuse allegations in the context of custody and access disputes.

Everyone may have difficulty in the conscious recall of the details of a highly charged event, or of a fairly ordinary event in a highly charged or stressful situation, such as police interrogation or giving evidence in court (e.g. Clifford and Bull, 1978). Some have advocated the use of psychological techniques, such as hypnosis, to facilitate accurate recall, but independent reviewers and commentators (e.g. Wagstaff, 1982; Waxman, 1983) have expressed great caution about its use.

Victim witness schemes.   In the USA, there has been concern that victims are not only distressed, but are often also treated badly by the criminal justice system, and that this could have implications for the victim's readiness to cooperate with the system. Consequently, a number of projects and programmes were funded by the Law Enforcement Assistance Administration. The victim witness programmes (Schneider and Schneider, 1981) have something in common with the work of the victim support schemes in Britain. They help witnesses to be kept informed of the progress of their case in the courts, and they negotiate on behalf of victims who want or need to attend when dates are inconvenient. Other tasks may include attending court with the victim and working to improve overall facilities and information.

A more intensely victim-oriented approach is that of victim advocacy (Du Bow and Becker, 1976). Here the interests of the victims are explicitly held to the fore, either through the mobilization of voluntary supporters—they gave an example of over 40 neighbours attending court hearings to make their presence felt in a case including gang intimidation—or through legal representative for the victim. A system of 'victim impact statements' is in operation in many states in which the victim completes a form describing the impact of the crime. In some, it merely is a right of the victim to complete such a statement, and assistance may be offered to do so; in others, victims are encouraged to complete the forms, and in others it is mandatory. Some states even allow victims to include a recommendation on sentence.

Delivering to the Victim: Recovery of Losses, Compensation and Reparation

There are at least three concepts of ways in which some measure of return may be made to the victim of crime or disaster. Restitution means that that which has been taken from the victim is returned to him, or an exact monetary equivalent substituted for it. This approach is largely limited to situations of material loss. In compensation, by contrast, all aspects of the injury or loss, including pain or 'nervous shock', may be taken into account and coupled with predictions of likely ongoing losses and needs. A financial award may be made accordingly. The procedures by which restitution and compensation are made, and the pitfalls in psychiatric reporting, are dealt with on pp. 102–7, 853–4.

Reconciliation, mediation and reparation, as legal concepts, apply only to the results of established crime and require the offender to make personal moves to repair the damage to their victim or to society. The growing awareness of the tendency to exclude the victim from the criminal process was probably the chief impetus behind the development of schemes in which victims and offenders might be brought together, face to face, in the presence of a trained mediator to resolve their conflict. Mawby and Gill (1987) point out that early developments were not without their religious influence, in that Mennonite probation officers in the USA took a leading role. Galaway (1984) and Wright (1984) are among those who have written about their experience with such schemes in the USA and UK respectively. Such schemes depend on conviction of a named offender and then agreement by both offender and victim to participate. In a later paper reported in Mawby and Gill (1987), Galaway noted that, in spite of careful preparation, in one scheme in Minnesota, USA, 34% of referrals were lost by offender refusal and 29% of the remainder by victim refusal to participate. Nevertheless, where victims did participate, they generally reported satisfactory outcome and confirmed reconciliation or mediation as a desirable option.

Reparation, while it may be an arrangement between the victim and his own assailant, may, in addition or as an alternative, require the offender to compensate, or perform some service for another victim, group of victims or the disadvantaged more generally. In Britain such schemes have been incorporated into the justice process at three principal stages: prior to prosecution, prior to sentence or as part of a sentence (Marshall and Walpole, 1985). In the first category, schemes have tended to be principally for juvenile offenders. Davis et al. (1988) warned that, although the schemes may have been started primarily with the aim of advancing the cause of victims, increasingly, because of their association with decisions about the disposal of the offender, they are becoming arrangements which are used more as useful opportunities for diversion of the offender from custody or prosecution than for benefiting victims. The battle to keep the victim centre stage and a focus for concern is never won.

Appendix 1
The Mental Health Legislation of the United Kingdom

For the convenience of readers we have reprinted **some** of the significant elements of mental health law from the three main pieces of legislation in the United Kingdom; the Mental Health Act 1983, the Mental Health (Scotland) Act 1984, and the Mental Health (Northern Ireland) Order 1986. This material is Crown copyright and is reproduced with the permission of the Controller of Her Majesty's Stationery Office.

Although we have tried to reproduce the selected elements exactly, there is no guarantee that we have succeeded, and we have deliberately omitted qualifying sections or articles in order to save space. This appendix therefore must *not* be regarded as any kind of legal authority. **A reader who wishes to check the law for professional reasons should consult the relevant statute.** It should also be noted that sometimes the extracts reprinted here refer to sections or articles which are not reprinted; for these, the full Act or Order must be consulted.

We hope the selected elements printed here will help the reader, particularly the non-British reader, to understand some of the text more clearly. We hope, too, that British readers will dip into the legislation with which they are not familiar. Putting the three pieces of legislation side by side should highlight the similarities and differences between them.

The Scottish Act illustrates the central importance of the sheriff. The Northern Ireland Order is in many ways closer to the English Act. All three instruments include the innovative consent to treatment legislation which is discussed on pp. 33–40, but only that from the Mental Health Act 1983 has been reproduced because of the close similarity between all three. Both England and Northern Ireland have a mental health commission, but Scotland uses an older body, the Mental Welfare Commission, appropriately modified. Only England and Wales make explicit provision for a group of troublesome patients defined in law as suffering from 'psychopathic disorder', Scotland includes such patients under 'mental illness' and N. Ireland excludes patients suffering from personality disorder. The MH(NI)O 1986 incorporates unfitness to plead and insanity legislation.

Mental Health Act 1983

Part 1

APPLICATION OF ACT

1.—(1) The provisions of this Act shall have effect with respect to the reception, care and treatment of mentally disordered patients, the management of their property and other related matters.

(2) In this Act—

'mental disorder' means mental illness, arrested or incomplete development of mind, psychopathic disorder and any other disorder or disability of mind and 'mentally disordered' shall be construed accordingly;

'severe mental impairment' means a state of arrested or incomplete development of mind which includes severe impairment of intelligence and social functioning and is associated wtih abnormally aggressive or seriously irresponsible conduct on the part of the person concerned and 'severely mentally impaired' shall be construed accordingly;

'mental impairment' means a state of arrested or incomplete development of mind (not amounting to severe mental impairment) which includes significant impairment of intelligence and social functioning and is associated with abnormally aggressive or seriously irresponsible conduct on the part of the person concerned and 'mentally impaired' shall be construed accordingly;

'psychopathic disorder' means a persistent disorder or disability of mind (whether or not including significant impairment of intelligence) which results in abnormally aggressive or seriously irresponsible conduct on the part of the person concerned;

and other expressions shall have the meanings assigned to them in section 145 below.

(3) Nothing in subsection (2) above shall be construed as implying that a person may be dealt with under this Act as suffering from mental disorder, or from any form of mental disorder described in this section, by reason only of promiscuity or other immoral conduct, sexual deviancy or dependence on alcohol or drugs.

Part II

COMPULSORY ADMISSION TO HOSPITAL AND GUARDIANSHIP

Procedure for hospital admission

2.—(1) A patient may be admitted to a hospital and detained there for the period allowed by subsection (4) below in pursuance of an application (in this Act referred to as 'an application for admission for assessment') made in accordance with subsections (2) and (3) below.

(2) An application for admission for assessment may be made in respect of a patient on the grounds that—

    (*a*) he is suffering from mental disorder of a nature or degree which warrants the detention of the patient in a hospital for assessment (or for assessment followed by medical treatment) for at least a limited period; and

    (*b*) he ought to be so detained in the interests of his own health or safety or with a view to the protection of other persons.

(3) An application for admission for assessment shall be founded on the written recommendations in the prescribed form of two registered medical practitioners, including in each case a statement that in the opinion of the practitioner the conditions set out in subsection (2) above are complied with.

(4) Subject to the provisions of section 29(4) below, a patient admitted to hospital in pursuance of an application for admission for assessment may be detained for a period not exceeding 28 days beginning with the day on which he is admitted, but shall not be detained after the expiration of that period unless before it has expired he has become liable to be detained by virtue of a subsequent application, order or direction under the following provisions of this Act.

3.—(1) A patient may be admitted to a hospital and detained there for the period allowed by the following provisions of this Act in pursuance of an application (in this Act referred to as 'an application for admission for treatment') made in accordance with this section.

(2) An application for admission for treatment may be made in respect of a patient on the grounds that—

    (*a*) he is suffering from mental illness, severe mental impairment, psychopathic disorder or mental impairment and his mental disorder is of a nature or degree which makes it appropriate for him to receive medical treatment in a hospital; and

    (*b*) in the case of psychopathic disorder or mental impairment, such treatment is likely to alleviate or prevent a deterioration of his condition; and

    (*c*) it is necessary for the health or safety of the patient or for the protection of other persons that he should receive such treatment and it cannot be provided unless he is detained under this section.

(3) An application for admission for treatment shall be founded on the written recommendations in the prescribed form of two registered medical practitioners, including in each case a statement that in the opinion of the practitioner the conditions set out in subsection (2) above are complied with; and each such recommendation shall include—

    (*a*) such particulars as may be prescribed of the grounds for that opinion so far as it relates to the conditions set out in paragraphs (*a*) and (*b*) of that subsection; and

    (*b*) a statement of the reasons for that opinion so far as it relates to the conditions set out in paragraph (*c*) of that subsection, specifying whether other methods of dealing with the patient are available and, if so, why they are not appropriate.

4.—(1) In any case of urgent necessity, an application for admission for assessment may be made in respect of a patient in accordance with the following provisions of this section, and any application so made is in this Act referred to as 'an emergency application'.

(2) An emergency application may be made either by an approved social worker or by the nearest relative of the patient; and every such application shall include a statement that it is of urgent necessity for the patient to be admitted and detained under section 2 above, and that compliance with the provisions of this Part of this Act relating to applications under that section would involve undesirable delay.

(3) An emergency application shall be sufficient in the first instance if founded on one of the medical recommendations required by section 2 above, given, if practicable, by a practitioner who has previous acquaintance with the patient and otherwise complying with the requirements of section 12 below so far as applicable to a single recommendation, and verifying the statement referred to in subsection (2) above.

(4) An emergency application shall cease to have effect on the expiration of a period of 72 hours from the time when the patient is admitted to the hospital unless—

(a) the second medical recommendation required by section 2 above is given and received by the managers within that period; and
(b) that recommendation and the recommendation referred to in subsection (3) above together comply with all the requirements of section 12 below (other than the requirement as to the time of signature of the second recommendation).

(5) In relation to an emergency application, section 11 below shall have effect as if in subsection (5) of that section for the words 'the period of 14 days ending with the date of the application' there were substituted the words 'the previous 24 hours'.

5.—(1) An application for the admission of a patient to a hospital may be made under this Part of this Act notwithstanding that the patient is already an in-patient in that hospital or, in the case of an application for admission for treatment that the patient is for the time being liable to be detained in the hospital in pursuance of an application for admission for assessment; and where an application is so made the patient shall be treated for the purposes of this Part of this Act as if he had been admitted to the hospital at the time when that application was received by the managers.

(2) If, in the case of a patient who is an inpatient in a hospital, it appears to the registered medical practitioner in charge of the treatment of the patient that an application ought to be made under this Part of this Act for the admission of the patient to hospital, he may furnish to the managers a report in writing to that effect; and in any such case the patient may be detained in the hospital for a period of 72 hours from the time when the report is so furnished.

(3) The registered medical practitioner in charge of the treatment of a patient in a hospital may nominate one (but not more than one) other registered medical practitioner on the staff of that hospital to act for him under subsection (2) above in his absence.

(4) If, in the case of a patient who is receiving treatment for mental disorder as an inpatient in a hospital, it appears to a nurse of the prescribed class—

(a) that the patient is suffering from mental disorder to such a degree that it is necessary for his health or safety or for the protection of others for him to be immediately restrained from leaving the hospital; and
(b) that it is not practicable to secure the immediate attendance of a practitioner for the purpose of furnishing a report under subsection (2) above,

the nurse may record that fact in writing; and in that event the patient may be detained in the hospital for a period of 6 hours from the time when that fact is so recorded or until the earlier arrival at the place where the patient is detained of a practitioner having power to furnish a report under that subsection.

(5) A record made under subsection (4) above shall be delivered by the nurse (or by a person authorized by the nurse in that behalf) to the managers of the hospital as soon as possible after it is made; and where a record is made under that subsection the period mentioned in subsection (2) above shall begin at the time when it is made.

(6) The reference in subsection (1) above to an in-patient does not include an in-patient who is liable to be detained in pursuance of an application under this Part of this Act and the references in subsections (2) and (4) above do not include an in-patient who is liable to be detained in a hospital under this Part of this Act.

(7) In subsection (4) above 'prescribed' means prescribed by an order made by the Secretary of State.

Guardianship

7.—(1) A patient who has attained the age of 16 years may be received into guardianship, for the period allowed by the following provisions of this Act, in pursuance of an application (in this Act referred to as 'a guardianship application') made in accordance with this section.

(2) A guardianship application may be made in respect of a patient on the grounds that—

(*a*) he is suffering from mental disorder, being mental illness, severe mental impairment, psychopathic disorder or mental impairment and his mental disorder is of a nature or degree which warrants his reception into guardianship under this section; and

(*b*) it is necessary in the interests of the welfare of the patient or for the protection of other persons that the patient should be so received.

(3) A guardianship application shall be founded on the written recommendations in the prescribed form of two registered medical practitioners, including in each case a statement that in the opinion of the practitioner the conditions set out in subsection (2) above are complied with; and each such recommendation shall include—

(*a*) such particulars as may be prescribed of the grounds for that opinion so far as it relates to the conditions set out in paragraph (*a*) of that subsection; and

(*b*) a statement of the reasons for that opinion so far as it relates to the conditions set out in paragraph (*b*) of that subsection.

(4) A guardianship application shall state the age of the patient or, if his exact age is not known to the applicant, shall state (if it be the fact) that the patient is believed to have attained the age of 16 years.

(5) The person named as guardian in a guardianship application may be either a local social services authority or any other person (including the applicant himself); but a guardianship application in which a person other than a local social services authority is named as guardian shall be of no effect unless it is accepted on behalf of that person by the local social services authority for the area in which he resides, and shall be accompanied by a statement in writing by that person that he is willing to act as guardian.

8.—(1) Where a guardianship application, duly made under the provisions of this Part of this Act and forwarded to the local social services authority within the period allowed by subsection (2) below is accepted by that authority, the application shall, subject to regulations made by the Secretary of State, confer on the authority or person named in the application as guardian, to the exclusion of any other person—

(*a*) the power to require the patient to reside at a place specified by the authority or person named as guardian;

(*b*) the power to require the patient to attend at places and times so specified for the purpose of medical treatment, occupation, education or training;

(*c*) the power to require access to the patient to be given, at any place where the patient is residing, to any registered medical practitioner, approved social worker or other person so specified.

(2) The period within which a guardianship application is required for the purposes of this section to be forwarded to the local social services authority is the period of 14 days beginning with the date on which the patient was last examined by a registered medical practitioner before giving a medical recommendation for the purposes of the application.

(3) A guardianship application which appears to be duly made and to be founded on the necessary medical recommendations may be acted upon without further proof of the signature

or qualification of the person by whom the application or any such medical recommendation is made or given, or of any matter of fact or opinion stated in the application.

(4) If within the period of 14 days beginning with the day on which a guardianship application has been accepted by the local social services authority the appliction, or any medical recommendation given for the purposes of the application, is found to be in any respect incorrect or defective, the application or recommendation may, within that period and with the consent of that authority, be amended by the person by whom it was signed; and upon such amendment being made the application or recommendation shall have effect and shall be deemed to have had effect as if it had been originally made as so amended.

(5) Where a patient is received into guardianship in pursuance of a guardianship application, any previous application under this Part of this Act by virtue of which he was subject to guardianship or liable to be detained in a hospital shall cease to have effect.

12.—(1) The recommendations required for the purposes of an application for the admission of a patient under this Part of this Act (in this Act referred to as 'medical recommendations') shall be signed on or before the date of the application, and shall be given by practitioners who have personally examined the patient either together or separately, but where they have examined the patient separately not more than 5 days must have elapsed between the days on which the separate examinations took place.

(2) Of the medical recommendations given for the purposes of any such application, one shall be given by a practitioner approved for the purposes of this section by the Secretary of State as having special experience in the diagnosis or treatment of mental disorder; and unless that practitioner has previous acquaintance with the patient, the other such recommendation shall, if practicable, be given by a registered medical practitioner who has such previous acquaintance.

(3) Subject to subsection (4) below, where the application is for the admission of the patient to a hospital which is not a mental nursing home, one (but not more than one) of the medical recommendations may be given by a practitioner on the staff of that hospital, except where the patient is proposed to be accommodated under sections 65 or 66 of the National Health Service Act 1977 (which relate to accommodation for private patients).

(4) Subsection (3) above shall not preclude both the medical recommendations being given by practitioners on the staff of the hospital in question if—

(a) compliance with that subsection would result in delay involving serious risk to the health or safety of the patient; and

(b) one of the practitioners giving the recommendations works at the hospital for less than half of the time which he is bound by contract to devote to work in the health service; and

(c) where one of those practitioners is a consultant, the other does not work (whether at the hospital or elsewhere) in a grade in which he is under that consultant's directions.

(5) A medical recommendation for the purposes of an application for the admission of a patient under this Part of this Act shall not be given by—

(a) the applicant;

(b) a partner of the applicant or of a practitioner by whom another medical recommendation is given for the purposes of the same application;

(c) a person employed as an assistant by the applicant or by any such practitioner;

(d) a person who receives or has an interest in the receipt of any payments made on account of the maintenance of the patient; or

(e) except as provided by subsection (3) or (4) above, a practitioner on the staff of the hospital to which the patient is to be admitted,

or by the husband, wife, father, father-in-law, mother, mother-in-law, son, son-in-law, daughter, daughter-in-law, brother, brother-in-law, sister or sister-in-law of the patient, or of any person mentioned in paragraphs (a) to (e) above, or of a practitioner by whom another medical recommendation is given for the purposes of the same application.

(6) A general practitioner who is employed part-time in a hospital shall not for the purposes of this section be regarded as a practitioner on its staff.

(7) Subsections (1), (2) and (5) above shall apply to applications for guardianship as they apply to applications for admission but with the substitution for paragraph (*e*) of subsection (5) above of the following paragraph—

'(*e*) the person named as guardian in the application'.

13.—(1) It shall be the duty of an approved social worker to make an application for admission to hospital or a guardianship application in respect of a patient within the area of the local social services authority by which that officer is appointed in any case where he is satisfied that such an application ought to be made and is of the opinion, having regard to any wishes expressed by relatives of the patient or any other relevant circumstances, that it is necessary or proper for the application to be made by him.

(2) Before making an application for the admission of a patient to hospital an approved social worker shall interview the patient in a suitable manner and satisfy himself that detention in a hospital is in all the circumstances of the case the most appropriate way of providing the care and medical treatment of which the patient stands in need.

(3) An application under this section by an approved social worker may be made outside the area of the local social services authority by which he is appointed.

(4) It shall be the duty of a local social services authority, if so required by the nearest relative of a patient residing in their area, to direct an approved social worker as soon as practicable to take the patient's case into consideration under subsection (1) above with a view to making an application for his admission to hospital; and if in any such case that approved social worker decides not to make an application he shall inform the nearest relative of his reasons in writing.

(5) Nothing in this section shall be construed as authorizing or requiring an application to be made by an approved social worker in contravention of the provisions of section 11(4) above, or as restricting the power of an approved social worker to make any application under this Act.

14. Where a patient is admitted to a hospital in pursuance of an application (other than an emergency application) made under this Part of this Act by his nearest relative, the managers of the hospital shall as soon as practicable give notice of that fact to the local social services authority for the area in which the patient resided immediately before his admission; and that authority shall as soon as practicable arrange for a social worker of their social services department to interview the patient and provide the managers with a report on his social circumstances.

Duration of detention or guardianship and discharge

20.—(1) Subject to the following provisions of this Part of this Act, a patient admitted to hospital in pursuance of an application for admission for treatment, and a patient placed under guardianship in pursuance of a guardianship application, may be detained in a hospital or kept under guardianship for a period not exceeding 6 months beginning with the day on which he was so admitted, or the day on which the guardianship application was accepted, as the case may be, but shall not be so detained or kept for any longer period unless the authority for his detention or guardianship is renewed under this section.

(2) Authority for the detention or guardianship of a patient may, unless the patient has previously been discharged, be renewed—

(*a*) from the expiration of the period referred to in subsection (1) above, for a further period of 6 months;

(*b*) from the expiration of any period of renewal under paragraph (*a*) above, for a further period of 1 year,

and so on for periods of 1 year at a time.

(3) Within the period of 2 months ending on the day on which a patient who is liable to be detained in pursuance of an application for admission for treatment would cease under this section to be so liable in default of the renewal of the authority for his detention, it shall be the duty of the responsible medical officer—

(*a*) to examine the patient; and

(*b*) if it appears to him that the conditions set out in sub-section (4) below are satisfied, to furnish to the managers of the hospital where the patient is detained a report to that effect in the prescribed form;

and where such a report is furnished in respect of a patient the managers shall, unless they discharge the patient, cause him to be informed.

(4) The conditions referred to in subsection (3) above are that—

(*a*) the patient is suffering from mental illness, severe mental impairment, psychopathic disorder or mental impairment, and his mental disorder is of a nature or degree which makes it appropriate for him to receive medical treatment in a hospital; and

(*b*) such treatment is likely to alleviate or prevent a deterioration of his condition; and

(*c*) it is necessary for the health or safety of the patient or for the protection of other persons that he should receive such treatment and that it cannot be provided unless he continues to be detained;

but, in the case of mental illness or severe mental impairment, it shall be an alternative to the condition specified in paragraph (*b*) above that the patient, if discharged, is unlikely to be able to care for himself, to obtain the care which he needs or to guard himself against serious exploitation.

(5) Before furnishing a report under subsection (3) above the responsible medical officer shall consult one or more other persons who have been professionally concerned with the patient's medical treatment.

(6) Within the period of 2 months ending with the day on which a patient who is subject to guardianship under this Part of this Act would cease under this section to be so liable in default of the renewal of the authority for his guardianship, it shall be the duty of the appropriate medical officer—

(*a*) to examine the patient; and

(*b*) if it appears to him that the conditions set out in sub-section (7) below are satisfied, to furnish to the guardian and, where the guardian is a person other than a local social services authority, to the responsible local social services authority a report to that effect in the prescribed form;

and where such a report is furnished in respect of a patient, the local social services authority shall, unless they discharge the patient, cause him to be informed.

(7) The conditions referred to in subsection (6) above are that—

(*a*) the patient is suffering from mental illness, severe mental impairment, psychopathic disorder or mental impairment and his mental disorder is of a nature or degree which warrants his reception into guardianship; and

(*b*) it is necessary in the interests of the welfare of the patient or for the protection of other persons that the patient should remain under guardianship.

(8) Where a report is duly furnished under subsection (3) or (6) above, the authority for the detention or guardianship of the patient shall be thereby renewed for the period prescribed in that case by subsection (2) above.

(9) Where the form of mental disorder specified in a report furnished under subsection (3) or (6) above is a form of disorder other than that specified in the application for admission for treatment or, as the case may be, in the guardianship application, that application shall have effect as if that other form of mental disorder were specified in it; and where on any occasion a report specifying such a form of mental disorder is furnished under either of those subsections the appropriate medical officer need not on that occasion furnish a report under section 16 above.

(10) In this section 'appropriate medical officer' has the same meaning as in section 16(5) above.

25.—(1) An order for the discharge of a patient who is liable to be detained in a hospital shall not be made by his nearest relative except after giving not less than 72 hours' notice in writing to the managers of the hospital; and if, within 72 hours after such notice has been given, the responsible medical officer furnishes to the managers a report certifying that in the opinion of that officer the patient, if discharged, would be likely to act in a manner dangerous to other persons or to himself—

 (*a*) any order for the discharge of the patient made by that relative in pursuance of the notice shall be of no effect; and

 (*b*) no further order for the discharge of the patient shall be made by that relative during the period of 6 months beginning with the date of the report.

(2) In any case where a report under subsection (1) above is furnished in respect of a patient who is liable to be detained in pursuance of an application for admission for treatment the managers shall cause the nearest relative of the patient to be informed.

Functions of relatives of patients

26.—(1) In this Part of this Act 'relative' means any of the following persons:—

 (*a*) husband or wife;
 (*b*) son or daughter;
 (*c*) father or mother;
 (*d*) brother or sister;
 (*e*) grandparent;
 (*f*) grandchild;
 (*g*) uncle or aunt;
 (*h*) nephew or niece.

(2) In deducing relationships for the purposes of this section, any relationship of the half-blood shall be treated as a relationship of the whole blood, and an illegitimate person shall be treated as the legitimate child of his mother.

(3) In this Part of this Act, subject to the provisions of this section and to the following provisions of this Part of this Act the 'nearest relative' means the person first described in subsection (1) above who is for the time being surviving, relatives of the whole blood being preferred to relatives of the same description of the half-blood and the elder or eldest of two or more relatives described in any paragraph of that subsection being preferred to the other or others of those relatives, regardless of sex.

(4) Subject to the provisions of this section and to the following provisions of this Part of this Act, where the patient ordinarily resides with or is cared for by one or more of his relatives (or, if he is for the time being an in-patient in a hospital, he last ordinarily resided with or was cared for by one or more of his relatives) his nearest relative shall be determined—

 (*a*) by giving preference to that relative or those relatives over the other or others; and

 (*b*) as between two or more such relatives, in accordance with subsection (3) above.

(5) Where the person who, under subsection (3) or (4) above, would be the nearest relative of a patient—

 (*a*) in the case of a patient ordinarily resident in the United Kingdom, the Channel Islands or the Isle of Man, is not so resident; or

 (*b*) is the husband or wife of the patient, but is permanently separated from the patient, either by agreement or under an order of a court, or has deserted or has been deserted by the patient for a period which has not come to an end; or

 (*c*) is a person other than the husband, wife, father or mother of the patient, and is for the time being under 18 years of age; or

 (*d*) is a person against whom an order divesting him of authority over the patient has been made under section 38 of the Sexual Offences Act 1956 (which relates to incest with a person under 18) and has not been rescinded,

the nearest relative of the patient shall be ascertained as if that person were dead.

(6) In this section 'husband' and 'wife' include a person who is living with the patient as the patient's husband or wife, as the case may be (or, if the patient is for the time being an inpatient in a hospital, was so living until the patient was admitted), and has been or had been so living for a period of not less than 6 months; but a person shall not be treated by virtue of this subsection as the nearest relative of a married patient unless the husband or wife of the patient is disregarded by virtue of paragraph (*b*) of subsection (5) above.

(7) A person, other than a relative, with whom the patient ordinarily resides (or, if the patient is for the time being an inpatient in a hospital, last ordinarily resided before he was admitted), and with whom he has or had been ordinarily residing for a period of not less than 5 years, shall be treated for the purposes of this Part of this Act as if he were a relative but—

    (a) shall be treated for the purposes of subsection (3) above as if mentioned last in subsection (1) above; and

    (b) shall not be treated by virtue of this subsection as the nearest relative of a married patient unless the husband or wife of the patient is disregarded by virtue of paragraph (b) of subsection (5) above.

27. In any case where the rights and powers of a parent of a patient, being a child or young person, are vested in a local authority or other person by virtue of—

    (a) section 3 of the Child Care Act 1980 (which relates to the assumption by a local authority of parental rights and duties in relation to a child in their care);

    (b) section 10 of that Act (which relates to the powers and duties of local authorities with respect to persons committed to their care under the Children and Young Persons Act 1969); or

    (c) section 17 of the Social Work (Scotland) Act 1968 (which makes corresponding provision for Scotland),

that authority or person shall be deemed to be the nearest relative of the patient in preference to any person except the patient's husband or wife (if any) and except, in a case where the said rights and powers are vested in a local authority by virtue of subsection (1) of the said section 3, any parent of the patient not being the person on whose account the resolution mentioned in that subsection was passed.

Part III

PATIENTS CONCERNED IN CRIMINAL PROCEEDINGS OR UNDER SENTENCE

Remands to hospital

35.—(1) Subject to the provisions of this section, the Crown Court or a magistrates' court may remand an accused person to a hospital specified by the court for a report on his mental condition.

    (2) For the purposes of this section an accused person is—

    (a) in relation to the Crown Court, any person who is awaiting trial before the court for an offence punishable with imprisonment or who has been arraigned before the court for such an offence and has not yet been sentenced or otherwise dealt with for the offence on which he has been arraigned;

    (b) in relation to a magistrates' court, any person who has been convicted by the court of an offence punishable on summary conviction with imprisonment and any person charged with such an offence if the court is satisfied that he did the act or made the omission charged or he has consented to the exercise by the court of the powers conferred by this section.

    (3) Subject to subsection (4) below, the powers conferred by this section may be exercised if—

    (a) the court is satisfied, on the written or oral evidence of a registered medical practitioner, that there is reason to suspect that the accused person is suffering from mental illness, psychopathic disorder, severe mental impairment or mental impairment; and

    (b) the court is of the opinion that it would be impracticable for a report on his mental condition to be made if he were remanded on bail;

but those powers shall not be exercised by the Crown Court in respect of a person who has been convicted before the court if the sentence for the offence of which he has been convicted is fixed by law.

    (4) The court shall not remand an accused person to a hospital under this section unless satisfied, on the written or oral evidence of the registered medical practitioner who would be responsible for making the report or of some other person representing the managers of the hospital, that arrangements have been made for his admission to that hospital and for his

admission to it within the period of 7 days beginning with the date of the remand; and if the court is so satisfied it may, pending his admission, give directions for his conveyance to and detention in a place of safety.

(5) Where a court has remanded an accused person under this section it may further remand him if it appears to the court, on the written or oral evidence of the registered medical practitioner responsible for making the report, that a further remand is necessary for completing the assessment of the accused person's mental condition.

(6) The power of further remanding an accused person under this section may be exercised by the court without his being brought before the court if he is represented by counsel or a solicitor and his counsel or solicitor is given an opportunity of being heard.

(7) An accused person shall not be remanded or further remanded under this section for more than 28 days at a time or for more than 12 weeks in all; and the court may at any time terminate the remand if it appears to the court that it is appropriate to do so.

(8) An accused person remanded to hospital under this section shall be entitled to obtain at his own expense an independent report on his mental condition from a registered medical practitioner chosen by him and to apply to the court on the basis of it for his remand to be terminated under subsection (7) above.

(9) Where an accused person is remanded under this section—
(a) a constable or any other person directed to do so by the court shall convey the accused person to the hospital specified by the court within the period mentioned in subsection (4) above; and
(b) the managers of the hospital shall admit him within that period and thereafter detain him in accordance with the provisions of this section.

(10) If an accused person absconds from a hospital to which he has been remanded under this section, or while being conveyed to or from that hospital, he may be arrested without warrant by any constable and shall, after being arrested, be brought as soon as practicable before the court that remanded him; and the court may thereupon terminate the remand and deal with him in any way in which it could have dealt with him if he had not been remanded under this section.

36.—(1) Subject to the provisions of this section, the Crown Court may, instead of remanding an accused person in custody, remand him to a hospital specified by the court if satisfied, on the written or oral evidence of two registered medical practitioners, that he is suffering from mental illness or severe mental impairment of a nature or degree which makes it appropriate for him to be detained in a hospital for medical treatment.

(2) For the purposes of this section an accused person is any person who is in custody awaiting trial before the Crown Court for an offence punishable with imprisonment (other than an offence the sentence for which is fixed by law) or who at any time before sentence is in custody in the course of a trial before that court for such an offence.

(3) The court shall not remand an accused person under this section to a hospital unless it is satisfied, on the written or oral evidence of the registered medical practitioner who would be in charge of his treatment or of some other person representing the managers of the hospital, that arrangements have been made for his admission to that hospital and for his admission to it within the period of 7 days beginning with the date of the remand; and if the court is so satisfied it may, pending his admission, give directions for his conveyance to and detention in a place of safety.

(4) Where a court has remanded an accused person under this section it may further remand him if it appears to the court, on the written or oral evidence of the responsible medical officer, that a further remand is warranted.

(5) The power of further remanding an accused person under this section may be exercised by the court without his being brought before the court if he is represented by counsel or a solicitor and his counsel or solicitor is given an opportunity of being heard.

(6) An accused person shall not be remanded or further remanded under this section for more than 28 days at a time or for more than 12 weeks in all; and the court may at any time terminate the remand if it appears to the court that it is appropriate to do so.

(7) An accused person remanded to hospital under this section shall be entitled to obtain at his own expense an independent report on his mental condition from a registered medical practitioner chosen by him and to apply to the court on the basis of it for his remand to be terminated under subsection (6) above.

(8) Subsections (9) and (10) of section 35 above shall have effect in relation to a remand under this section as they have effect in relation to a remand under that section.

Hospital and guardianship orders

37.—(1) Where a person is convicted before the Crown Court of an offence punishable with imprisonment other than an offence the sentence for which is fixed by law, or is convicted by a magistrates' court of an offence punishable on summary conviction with imprisonment, and the conditions mentioned in subsection (2) below are satisfied, the court may by order authorize his admission to and detention in such hospital as may be specified in the order or, as the case may be, place him under the guardianship of a local social services authority or of such other person approved by as local social services authority as may be so specified.

(2) The conditions referred to in subsection (1) above are that—

(*a*) the court is satisfied, on the written or oral evidence of two registered medical practitioners, that the offender is suffering from mental illness, psychopathic disorder, severe mental impairment or mental impairment and that either—
  (i) the mental disorder from which the offender is suffering is of a nature or degree which makes it appropriate for him to be detained in a hospital for medical treatment and, in the case of psychopathic disorder or mental impairment, that such treatment is likely to alleviate or prevent a deterioration of his condition; or
  (ii) in the case of an offender who has attained the age of 16 years, the mental disorder is of a nature or degree which warrants his reception into guardianship under this Act; and

(*b*) the court is of the opinion, having regard to all the circumstances including the nature of the offence and the character and antecedents of the offender, and to the other available methods of dealing with him, that the most suitable method of disposing of the case is by means of an order under this section.

(3) Where a person is charged before a magistrates' court with any act or omission as an offence and the court would have power, on convicting him of that offence, to make an order under subsection (1) above in his case as being a person suffering from mental illness or severe mental impairment, then, if the court is satisfied that the accused did the act or made the omission charged, the court may, if it thinks fit, make such an order without convicting him.

(4) An order for the admission of an offender to a hospital (in this Act referred to as 'a hospital order') shall not be made under this section unless the court is satisfied on the written or oral evidence of the registered medical practitioner who would be in charge of his treatment or of some other person representing the managers of the hospital that arrangements have been made for his admission to that hospital in the event of such an order being made by the court, and for his admission to it within the period of 28 days beginning with the date of the making of such an order; and the court may, pending his admission within that period, give such directions as it thinks fit for his conveyance to and detention in a place of safety.

(5) If within the said period of 28 days it appears to the Secretary of State that by reason of an emergency or other special circumstances it is not practicable for the patient to be received into the hospital specified in the order, he may give directions for the admission of the patient to such other hospital as appears to be appropriate instead of the hospital so specified; and where such directions are given—

(*a*) the Secretary of State shall cause the person having the custody of the patient to be informed, and

(*b*) the hospital order shall have effect as if the hospital specified in the directions were substituted for the hospital specified in the order.

(6) An order placing an offender under the guardianship of a local social services authority or of any other person (in this Act referred to as 'a guardianship order') shall not be made under this section unless the court is satisfied that that authority or person is willing to receive the offender into guardianship.

(7) A hospital order or guardianship order shall specify the form or forms of mental disorder referred to in subsection (2)(a) above from which, upon the evidence taken into account under that subsection, the offender is found by the court to be suffering; and no such order shall be made unless the offender is described by each of the practitioners whose evidence is taken into account under that subsection as suffering from the same one of those forms of mental disorder, whether or not he is also described by either of them as suffering from another of them.

(8) Where an order is made under this section, the court shall not pass sentence of imprisonment or impose a fine or make a probation order in respect of the offence or make any such order as is mentioned in paragraph (b) or (c) of section 7(7) of the Children and Young Persons Act 1969 in respect of the offender, but may make any other order which the court has power to make apart from this section; and for the purposes of this subsection 'sentence of imprisonment' includes any sentence or order for detention.

38.—(1) Where a person is convicted before the Crown Court of an offence punishable with imprisonment (other than an offence the sentence for which is fixed by law) or is convicted by a magistrates' court of an offence punishable on summary conviction with imprisonment and the court before or by which he is convincted is satisfied, on the written or oral evidence of two registered medical practitioners—

(a) that the offender is suffering from mental illness, psychopathic disorder, severe mental impairment or mental impairment; and

(b) that there is reason to suppose that the mental disorder from which the offender is suffering is such that it may be appropriate for a hospital order to be made in his case,

the court may, before making a hospital order or dealing with him in some other way, make an order (in this Act referred to as 'an interim hospital order') authorizing his admission to such hospital as may be specified in the order and his detention there in accordance with this section.

(2) In the case of an offender who is subject to an interim hospital order the court may make a hospital order without his being brought before the court if he is represented by counsel or a solicitor and his counsel or solicitor is given an opportunity of being heard.

(3) At least one of the registered medical practitioners whose evidence is taken into account under subsection (1) above shall be employed at the hospital which is to be specified in the order.

(4) An interim hospital order shall not be made for the admission of an offender to a hospital unless the court is satisfied, on the written or oral evidence of the registered medical practitioner who would be in charge of his treatment or of some other person representing the managers of the hospital, that arrangements have been made for his admission to that hospital and for his admission to it within the period of 28 days beginning with the date of the order; and if the court is so satisfied the court may, pending his admission, give directions for his conveyance to and detention in a place of safety.

(5) An interim hospital order—

(a) shall be in force for such period, not exceeding 12 weeks, as the court may specify when making the order; but

(b) may be renewed for further periods of not more than 28 days at a time if it appears to the court, on the written or oral evidence of the responsible medical officer, that the continuation of the order is warranted;

but no such order shall continue in force for more than 6 months in all and the court shall terminate the order if it makes a hospital order in respect of the offender or decides after considering the written or oral evidence of the responsible medical officer to deal with the offender in some other way.

(6) The power of renewing an interim hospital order may be exercised without the offender being brought before the court if he is represented by counsel or a solicitor and his counsel or solicitor is given an opportunity of being heard.

(7) If an offender absconds from a hospital in which he is detained in pursuance of an interim hospital order, or while being conveyed to or from such a hospital, he may be arrested without warrant by a constable and shall, after being arrested, be brought as soon as practicable before the court that made the order; and the court may thereupon terminate the order and deal with him in any way in which it could have dealt with him if no such order had been made.

39.—(1) Where a court is minded to make a hospital order or interim hospital order in respect of any person it may request—

(a) the Regional Health Authority for the region in which that person resides or last resided; or

(b) any other Regional Health Authority that appears to the court to be appropriate,

to furnish the court with such information as that Authority has or can reasonably obtain with respect to the hospital or hospitals (if any) in its region or elsewhere at which arrangements could be made for the admission of that person in pursuance of the order, and that Authority shall comply with any such request.

(2) In its application to Wales subsection (1) above shall have effect as if for any reference to any such Authority as is mentioned in paragraph (a) or (b) of that subsection there were substituted a reference to the Secretary of State, and as if for the words 'in its region or elsewhere' there were substituted the words 'in Wales'.

Restriction orders

41.—(1) Where a hospital order is made in respect of an offender by the Crown Court, and it appears to the court, having regard to the nature of the offence, the antecedents of the offender and the risk of his committing further offences if set at large, that it is necessary for the protection of the public from serious harm so to do, the court may, subject to the provisions of this section, further order that the offender shall be subject to the special restrictions set out in this section, either without limit of time or during such period as may be specified in the order; and an order under this section shall be known as 'a restriction order'.

(2) A restriction order shall not be made in the case of any person unless at least one of the registered medical practitioners whose evidence is taken into account by the court under section 37(2)(a) above has given evidence orally before the court.

(3) The special restrictions applicable to a patient in respect of whom a restriction order is in force are as follows—

(a) none of the provisions of Part II of this Act relating to the duration, renewal and expiration of authority for the detention of patients shall apply, and the patient shall continue to be liable to be detained by virtue of the relevant hospital order until he is duly discharged under the said Part II or absolutely discharged under section 42, 73, 74 or 75 below;

(b) no application shall be made to a Mental Health Review Tribunal in respect of a patient under section 66 or 69(1) below;

(c) the following powers shall be exercisable only with the consent of the Secretary of State, namely—

(i) power to grant leave of absence to the patient under section 17 above;

(ii) power to transfer the patient in pursuance of regulations under section 19 above; and

(iii) power to order the discharge of the patient under section 23 above;

and if leave of absence is granted under the said section 17 power to recall the patient under that section shall vest in the Secretary of State as well as the responsible medical officer; and

(d) the power of the Secretary of State to recall the patient under the said section 17 and power to take the patient into custody and return him under section 18 above may be exercised at any time;

and in relation to any such patient section 40(4) above shall have effect as if it referred to Part II of Schedule 1 to this Act instead of Part I of that Schedule.

(4) A hospital order shall not cease to have effect under section 40(5) above if a restriction order in respect of the patient is in force at the material time.

(5) Where a restriction order in respect of a patient ceases to have effect while the relevant hospital order continues in force, the provisions of section 40 above and Part I of Schedule 1 to this Act shall apply to the patient as if he had been admitted to the hospital in pursuance of a hospital order (without a restriction order) made on the date on which the restriction order ceased to have effect.

(6) While a person is subject to a restriction order the responsible medical officer shall at such intervals (not exceeding 1 year) as the Secretary of State may direct examine and report to the Secretary of State on that person; and every report shall contain such particulars as the Secretary of State may require.

42.—(1) If the Secretary of State is satisfied that in the case of any patient a restriction order is no longer required for the protection of the public from serious harm, he may direct that the patient shall cease to be subject to the special restrictions set out in section 41(3) above; and where the Secretary of State so directs, the restriction order shall cease to have effect, and section 41(5) above shall apply accordingly.

(2) At any time while a restriction order is in force in respect of a patient, the Secretary of State may, if he thinks fit, by warrant discharge the patient from hospital, either absolutely or subject to conditions; and where a person is absolutely discharged under this subsection, he shall thereupon cease to be liable to be detained by virtue of the relevant hospital order, and the restriction order shall cease to have effect accordingly.

(3) The Secretary of State may at any time during the continuance in force of a restriction order in respect of a patient who has been conditionally discharged under subsection (2) above by warrant recall the patient to such hospital as may be specified in the warrant.

(4) Where a patient is recalled as mentioned in subsection (3) above—

(a) if the hospital specified in the warrant is not the hospital from which the patient was conditionally discharged, the hospital order and the restriction order shall have effect as if the hospital specified in the warrant were substituted for the hospital specified in the hospital order;

(b) in any case, the patient shall be treated for the purposes of section 18 above as if he had absented himself without leave from the hospital specified in the warrant, and, if the restriction order was made for a specified period, that period shall not in any event expire until the patient returns to the hospital or is returned to the hospital under that section.

(5) If a restriction order in respect of a patient ceases to have effect after the patient has been conditionally discharged under this section, the patient shall, unless previously recalled under subsection (3) above, be deemed to be absolutely discharged on the date when the order ceases to have effect, and shall cease to be liable to be detained by virtue of the relevant hospital order accordingly.

(6) The Secretary of State may, if satisfied that the attendance at any place in Great Britain of a patient who is subject to a restriction order is desirable in the interests of justice or for the purposes of any public inquiry, direct him to be taken to that place; and where a patient is directed under this subsection to be taken to any place he shall, unless the Secretary of State otherwise directs, be kept in custody while being so taken, while at that place and while being taken back to the hospital in which he is liable to be detained.

Transfer to hospital of prisoners, etc.

47.—(1) If in the case of a person serving a sentence of imprisonment the Secretary of State is satisfied, by reports from at least two registered medical practitioners—

(a) that the said person is suffering from mental illness, psychopathic disorder, severe mental impairment or mental impairment; and

(b) that the mental disorder from which that person is suffering is of a nature or degree which makes it appropriate for him to be detained in a hospital for medical treatment and, in the case of psychopathic disorder or mental impairment, that such treatment is likely to alleviate or prevent a deterioration of his condition;

the Secretary of State may, if he is of the opinion having regard to the public interest and all the circumstances that it is expedient so to do, by warrant direct that that person be removed to and detained in such hospital (not being a mental nursing home) as may be specified in the direction; and a direction under this section shall be known as 'a transfer direction'.

(2) A transfer direction shall cease to have effect at the expiration of the period of 14 days beginning with the date on which it is given unless within that period the person with respect to whom it was given has been received into the hospital specified in the direction.

(3) A transfer direction with respect to any person shall have the same effect as a hospital order made in his case.

48.—(1) If in the case of a person to whom this section applies the Secretary of State is satisfied by the same reports as are required for the purposes of section 47 above that that person is suffering from mental illness or severe mental impairment of a nature or degree which makes it appropriate for him to be detained in a hospital for medical treatment and that he is in urgent need of such treatment, the Secretary of State shall have the same power of giving a transfer direction in respect of him under that section as if he were serving a sentence of imprisonment.

(2) This section applies to the following persons, that is to say—

(a) persons detained in a prison or remand centre, not being persons serving a sentence of imprisonment or persons falling within the following paragraphs of this subsection;
(b) persons remanded in custody by a magistrates' court;
(c) civil prisoners, that is to say, persons committed by a court to prison for a limited term (including persons committed to prison in pursuance of a writ of attachment), who are not persons falling to be dealt with under section 47 above;
(d) persons detained under the Immigration Act 1971.

(3) Subsections (2) to (4) of section 47 above shall apply for the purposes of this section and of any transfer direction given by virtue of this section as they apply for the purposes of that section and of any transfer direction under that section.

49.—(1) Where a transfer direction is given in respect of any person, the Secretary of State, if he thinks fit, may by warrant further direct that that person shall be subject to the special restrictions set out in section 41 above; and where the Secretary of State gives a transfer direction in respect of any such person as is described in paragraph (a) or (b) of section 48(2) above, he shall also give a direction under this section applying those restrictions to him.

(2) A direction under this section shall have the same effect as a restriction order made under section 41 above and shall be known as 'a restriction direction'.

(3) While a person is subject to a restriction direction the responsible medical officer shall at such intervals (not exceeding one year) as the Secretary of State may direct examine and report to the Secretary of State on that person; and every report shall contain such particulars as the Secretary of State may require.

Part IV

CONSENT TO TREATMENT

56.—(1) This Part of this Act applies to any patient liable to be detained under this Act except—

(a) a patient who is liable to be detained by virtue of an emergency application and in respect of whom the second medical recommendation referred to in section 4(4)(a) above has not been given and received;
(b) a patient who is liable to be detained by virtue of section 5(2) or (4) or 35 above or section 135 or 136 below or by virtue of a direction under section 37(4) above; and
(c) a patient who has been conditionally discharged under section 42(2) above or section 73 or 74 below and has not been recalled to hospital.

(2) Section 57 and, so far as relevant to that section, sections 59, 60 and 62 below, apply also to any patient who is not liable to be detained under this Act.

57.—(1) This section applies to the following forms of medical treatment for mental disorder—

  (*a*) any surgical operation for destroying brain tissue or for destroying the functioning of brain tissue; and
  (*b*) such other forms of treatment as may be specified for the purposes of this section by regulations made by the Secretary of State.

(2) Subject to section 62 below, a patient shall not be given any form of treatment to which this section applies unless he has consented to it and—

  (*a*) a registered medical practitioner appointed for the purposes of this Part of this Act by the Secretary of State (not being the responsible medical officer) and two other persons appointed for the purposes of this paragraph by the Secretary of State (not being registered medical practitioners) have certified in writing that the patient is capable of understanding the nature, purpose and likely effects of the treatment in question and has consented to it; and
  (*b*) the registered medical practitioner referred to in paragraph (*a*) above has certified in writing that, having regard to the likelihood of the treatment alleviating or preventing a deterioration of the patient's condition, the treatment should be given.

(3) Before giving a certificate under subsection (2)(*b*) above the registered medical practitioner concerned shall consult two other persons who have been professionally concerned with the patient's medical treatment, and of those persons one shall be a nurse and the other shall be neither a nurse nor a registered medical practitioner.

(4) Before making any regulations for the purpose of this section the Secretary of State shall consult such bodies as appear to him to be concerned.

58.—(1) This section applies to the following forms of medical treatment for mental disorder—

  (*a*) such forms of treatment as may be specified for the purposes of this section by regulations made by the Secretary of State;
  (*b*) the administration of medicine to a patient by any means (not being a form of treatment specified under paragraph (*a*) above or section 57 above) at any time during a period for which he is liable to be detained as a patient to whom this Part of this Act applies if 3 months or more have elapsed since the first occasion in that period when medicine was administered to him by any means for his mental disorder.

(2) The Secretary of State may by order vary the length of the period mentioned in subsection (1)(*b*) above.

(3) Subject to section 62 below, a patient shall not be given any form of treatment to which this section applies unless—

  (*a*) he has consented to that treatment and either the responsible medical officer or a registered medical practitioner appointed for the purposes of this Part of this Act by the Secretary of State has certified in writing that the patient is capable of understanding its nature, purpose and likely effects and has consented to it; or
  (*b*) a registered medical practitioner appointed as aforesaid (not being the responsible medical officer) has certified in writing that the patient is not capable of understanding the nature, purpose and likely effects of that treatment or has not consented to it but that, having regard to the likelihood of its alleviating or preventing a deterioration of his condition, the treatment should be given.

(4) Before giving a certificate under subsection (3)(*b*) above the registered medical practitioner concerned shall consult two other persons who have been professionally concerned with the patient's medical treatment, and of those persons one shall be a nurse and the other shall be neither a nurse nor a registered medical practitioner.

(5) Before making any regulations for the purposes of this section the Secretary of State shall consult such bodies as appear to him to be concerned.

59. Any consent or certificate under section 57 or 58 above may relate to a plan of treatment under which the patient is to be given (whether within a specified period or otherwise) one or more of the forms of treatment to which that section applies.

60.—(1) Where the consent of a patient to any treatment has been given for the purposes of section 57 or 58 above, the patient may, subject to section 62 below, at any time before the completion of the treatment withdraw his consent, and those sections shall then apply as if the remainder of the treatment were a separate form of treatment.

(2) Without prejudice to the application of subsection (1) above to any treatment given under the plan of treatment to which a patient has consented, a patient who has consented to such a plan may, subject to section 62 below, at any time withdraw his consent to further treatment, or to further treatment of any description, under the plan.

61.—(1) Where a patient is given treatment in accordance with section 57(2) or 58(3)(*b*) above a report on the treatment and the patient's condition shall be given by the responsible medical officer to the Secretary of State—

(*a*) on the next occasion on which the responsible medical officer furnishes a report in respect of the patient under section 20(3) above; and

(*b*) at any other time if so required by the Secretary of State.

(2) In relation to a patient who is subject to a restriction order or restriction direction subsection (1) above shall have effect as if paragraph (*a*) required the report to be made—

(*a*) in the case of treatment in the period of 6 months beginning with the date of the order or direction, at the end of that period;

(*b*) in the case of treatment at any subsequent time, on the next occasion on which the responsible medical officer makes a report in respect of the patient under section 41(6) or 49(3) above.

(3) The Secretary of State may at any time give notice to the responsible medical officer directing that, subject to section 62 below, a certificate given in respect of a patient under section 57(2) or 58(3)(*b*) above shall not apply to treatment given to him after a date specified in the notice and sections 57 and 58 above shall then apply to any such treatment as if that certificate had not been given.

62.—(1) Sections 57 and 58 above shall not apply to any treatment—

(*a*) which is immediately necessary to save the patient's life; or

(*b*) which (not being irreversible) is immediately necessary to prevent a serious deterioration of his condition; or

(*c*) which (not being irreversible or hazardous) is immediately necessary to alleviate serious suffering by the patient; or

(*d*) which (not being irreversible or hazardous) is immediately necessary and represents the minimum interference necessary to prevent the patient from behaving violently or being a danger to himself or to others.

(2) Sections 60 and 61(3) above shall not preclude the continuation of any treatment or of treatment under any plan pending compliance with section 57 or 58 above if the responsible medical officer considers that the discontinuance of the treatment or of treatment under the plan would cause serious suffering to the patient.

(3) For the purposes of this section treatment is irreversible if it has unfavourable irreversible physical or psychological consequences and hazardous if it entails significant physical hazard.

63. The consent of a patient shall not be required for any medical treatment given to him for the mental disorder from which he is suffering, not being treatment falling within section 57 or 58 above, if the treatment is given by or under the direction of the responsible medical officer.

64.—(1) In this Part of this Act 'the responsible medical officer' means the registered medical practitioner in charge of the treatment of the patient in question and 'hospital' includes a mental nursing home.

Part V

MENTAL HEALTH REVIEW TRIBUNALS

Discharge of patients

72.—(1) Where application is made to a Mental Health Review Tribunal by or in respect of a patient who is liable to be detained under this Act, the tribunal may in any case direct that the patient be discharged, and—

(*a*) the tribunal shall direct the discharge of a patient liable to be detained under section 2 above if they are satisfied—

(i) that he is not then suffering from mental disorder or from mental disorder of a nature or degree which warrants his detention in a hospital for assessment (or for assessment followed by medical treatment) for at least a limited period; or

(ii) that his detention as aforesaid is not justified in the interests of his own health or safety or with a view to the protection of other persons;

(*b*) the tribunal shall direct the discharge of a patient liable to be detained otherwise than under section 2 above if they are satisfied—

(i) that he is not then suffering from mental illness, psychopathic disorder, severe mental impairment or mental impairment or from any of those forms of disorder of a nature or degree which makes it appropriate for him to be liable to be detained in a hospital for medical treatment; or

(ii) that it is not necessary for the health or safety of the patient or for the protection of other persons that he should receive such treatment; or

(iii) in the case of an application by virtue of paragraph (*g*) of section 66(1) above, that the patient, if released, would not be likely to act in a manner dangerous to other persons or to himself.

(2) In determining whether to direct the discharge of a patient detained otherwise than under section 2 above in a case not falling within paragraph (*b*) of subsection (1) above, the tribunal shall have regard—

(*a*) to the likelihood of medical treatment alleviating or preventing a deterioration of the patient's condition; and

(*b*) in the case of a patient suffering from mental illness or severe mental impairment, to the likelihood of the patient, if discharged, being able to care for himself, to obtain the care he needs or to guard himself against serious exploitation.

(3) A tribunal may under subsection (1) above direct the discharge of a patient on a future date specified in the direction; and where a tribunal do not direct the discharge of a patient under that subsection the tribunal may—

(*a*) with a view to facilitating his discharge on a future date, recommend that he be granted leave of absence or transferred to another hospital or into guardianship; and

(*b*) further consider his case in the event of any such recommendation not being complied with.

(4) Where application is made to a Mental Health Review Tribunal by or in respect of a patient who is subject to guardianship under this Act, the tribunal may in any case direct that the patient be discharged, and shall so direct if they are satisfied—

(*a*) that he is not then suffering from mental illness, psychopathic disorder, severe mental impairment or mental impairment; or

(*b*) that it is not necessary in the interests of the welfare of the patient, or for the protection of other persons, that the patient should remain under such guardianship.

(5) Where application is made to a Mental Health Review Tribunal under any provision of this Act by or in respect of a patient and the tribunal do not direct that the patient be discharged, the tribunal may, if satisfied that the patient is suffering from a form of mental disorder other than the form specified in the application, order or direction relating to him,

direct that that application, order or direction be amended by substituting for the form of mental disorder specified in it such other form of mental disorder as appears to the tribunal to be appropriate.

(7) Subsection (1) above shall not apply in the case of a restricted patient except as provided in sections 73 and 74 below.

73.—(1) Where an application to a Mental Health Review Tribunal is made by a restricted patient who is subject to a restriction order, or where the case of such a patient is referred to such a tribunal, the tribunal shall direct the absolute discharge of the patient if satisfied—

(a) as to the matters mentioned in paragraph (b)(i) or (ii) of section 72(1) above; and

(b) that it is not appropriate for the patient to remain liable to be recalled to hospital for further treatment.

(2) Where in the case of any such patient as is mentioned in subsection (1) above the tribunal are satisfied as to the matters referred to in paragraph (a) of that subsection but not as to the matter referred to in paragraph (b) of that subsection the tribunal shall direct the conditional discharge of the patient.

(3) Where a patient is absolutely discharged under this section he shall thereupon cease to be liable to be detained by virtue of the relevant hospital order, and the restriction order shall cease to have effect accordingly.

(4) Where a patient is conditionally discharged under this section—

(a) he may be recalled by the Secretary of State under subsection (3) of section 42 above as if he had been conditionally discharged under subsection (2) of that section; and

(b) the patient shall comply with such conditions (if any) as may be imposed at the time of discharge by the tribunal or at any subsequent time by the Secretary of State.

(5) The Secretary of State may from time to time vary any condition imposed (whether by the tribunal or by him) under subsection (4) above.

(6) Where a restriction order in respect of a patient ceases to have effect after he has been conditionally discharged under this section the patient shall, unless previously recalled, be deemed to be absolutely discharged on the date when the order ceases to have effect and shall cease to be liable to be detained by virtue of the relevant hospital order.

(7) A tribunal may defer a direction for the conditional discharge of a patient until such arrangements as appear to the tribunal to be necessary for that purpose have been made to their satisfaction; and where by virtue of any such deferment no direction has been given on an application or reference before the time when the patient's case comes before the tribunal on a subsequent application or reference, the previous application or reference shall be treated as one on which no direction under this section can be given.

(8) This section is without prejudice to section 42 above.

Part VIII

MISCELLANEOUS FUNCTIONS OF LOCAL AUTHORITIES AND THE SECRETARY OF STATE

After-care

117.—(1) This section applies to persons who are detained under section 3 above, or admitted to a hospital in pursuance of a hospital order made under section 37 above, or transferred to a hospital in pursuance of a transfer direction made under section 47 or 48 above, and then cease to be detained and leave hospital.

(2) It shall be the duty of the District Health Authority and of the local social services authority to provide, in co-operation with relevant voluntary agencies, after-care services for any person to whom this section applies until such time as the District Health Authority and the local social services authority are satisfied that the person concerned is no longer in need of such services.

(3) In this section 'the District Health Authority' means the District Health Authority for the district, and 'the local social services authority' means the local social services authority for

the area in which the person concerned is resident or to which he is sent on discharge by the hospital in which he was detained.

Functions of the Secretary of State

118.—(1) The Secretary of State shall prepare, and from time to time revise, a code of practice—

(a) for the guidance of registered medical practitioners, managers and staff of hospitals and mental nursing homes and approved social workers in relation to the admission of patients to hospitals and mental nursing homes under this Act; and

(b) for the guidance of registered medical practitioners and members of other professions in relation to the medical treatment of patients suffering from mental disorder.

(2) The code shall, in particular, specify forms of medical treatment in addition to any specified by regulations made for the purposes of section 57 above which in the opinion of the Secretary of State give rise to special concern and which should accordingly not be given by a registered medical practitioner unless the patient has consented to the treatment (or to a plan of treatment including that treatment) and a certificate in writing as to the matters mentioned in subsection (2)(a) and (b) of that section has been given by another registered medical practitioner, being a practitioner appointed for the purposes of this section by the Secretary of State.

(3) Before preparing the code or making any alteration in it the Secretary of State shall consult such bodies as appear to him to be concerned.

(4) The Secretary of State shall lay copies of the code and of any alteration in the code before Parliament; and if either House of Parliament passes a resolution requiring the code or any alteration in it to be withdrawn the Secretary of State shall withdraw the code or alteration and, where he withdraws the code, shall prepare a code in substitution for the one which is withdrawn.

(5) No resolution shall be passed by either House of Parliament under subsection (4) above in respect of a code or alteration after the expiration of the period of 40 days beginning with the day on which a copy of the code or alteration was laid before that House; but for the purposes of this subsection no account shall be taken of any time during which Parliament is dissolved or prorogued or during which both Houses are adjourned for more than 4 days.

(6) The Secretary of State shall publish the code as for the time being in force.

121.—(1) Without prejudice to section 126(3) of the National Health Service Act 1977 (power to vary or revoke orders or directions) there shall continue to be a special health authority known as the Mental Health Act Commission established under section 11 of that Act.

(2) Without prejudice to the generality of his powers under section 13 of that Act, the Secretary of State shall direct the Commission to perform on his behalf—

(a) the function of appointing registered medical practitioners for the purposes of Part IV of this Act and section 118 above and of appointing other persons for the purposes of section 57(2)(a) above; and

(b) the functions of the Secretary of State under sections 61 and 120(1) and (4) above.

(3) The registered medical practitioners and other persons appointed for the purposes mentioned in subsection (2)(a) above may include members of the Commission.

(4) The Secretary of State may, at the request of or after consultation with the Commission and after consulting such other bodies as appear to him to be concerned, direct the Commission to keep under review the care and treatment, or any aspect of the care and treatment, in hospitals and mental nursing homes of patients who are not liable to be detained under this Act.

(5) For the purpose of any such review as is mentioned in subsection (4) above any person authorized in that behalf by the Commission may at any reasonable time—

(a) visit and interview and, if he is a registered medical practitioner, examine in private any patient in a mental nursing home; and (*b*) require the production of and inspect any records relating to the treatment of any person who is or has been a patient in a mental nursing home.

(7) The Commission shall review any decision to withhold a postal packet (or anything contained in it) under subsection (1)(*b*) or (2) of section 134 below if an application in that behalf is made—

(*a*) in a case under subsection (1)(*b*), by the patient; or

(*b*) in a case under subsection (2), either by the patient or by the person by whom the postal packet was sent;

and any such application shall be made within 6 months of the receipt by the applicant of the notice referred to in sub-section (6) of that section.

(8) On an application under subsection (7) above the Commission may direct that the postal packet which is the subject of the application (or anything contained in it) shall not be withheld and the managers in question shall comply with any such direction.

(9) The Secretary of State may by regulations make provisions with respect to the making and determination of applications under subsection (7) above, including provision for the production to the Commission of any postal packet which is the subject of such an application.

(10) The Commission shall in the second year after its establishment and subsequently in every second year publish a report on its activities; and copies of every such report shall be sent by the Commission to the Secretary of State who shall lay a copy before each House of Parliament.

Part X

MISCELLANEOUS AND SUPPLEMENTARY

131.—(1) Nothing in this Act shall be construed as preventing a patient who requires treatment for mental disorder from being admitted to any hospital or mental nursing home in pursuance of arrangements made in that behalf and without any application, order or direction rendering him liable to be detained under this Act, or from remaining in any hospital or mental nursing home in pursuance of such arrangements after he has ceased to be so liable to be detained.

136.—(1) If a constable finds in a place to which the public have access a person who appears to him to be suffering from mental disorder and to be in immediate need of care or control, the constable may, if he thinks it necessary to do so in the interests of that person or for the protection of other persons, remove that person to a place of safety within the meaning of section 135 above.

(2) A person removed to a place of safety under this section may be detained there for a period not exceeding 72 hours for the purpose of enabling him to be examined by a registered medical practitioner and to be interviewed by an approved social worker and of making any necessary arrangements for his treatment or care.

139.—(1) No person shall be liable, whether on the ground of want of jurisdiction or on any other ground, to any civil or criminal proceedings to which he would have been liable apart from this section in respect of any act purporting to be done in pursuance of this Act or any regulations or rules made under this Act, or in, or in pursuance of anything done in, the discharge of functions conferred by any other enactment on the authority having jurisdiction under Part VII of this Act, unless the act was done in bad faith or without reasonable care.

(2) No civil proceedings shall be brought against any person in any court in respect of any such act without the leave of the High Court; and no criminal proceedings shall be brought against any person in any court in respect of any such act except by or with the consent of the Director of Public Prosecutions.

(3) This section does not apply to proceedings for an offence under this Act, being proceedings which, under any other provision of this Act, can be instituted only by or with the consent of the Director of Public Prosecutions.

(4) This section does not apply to proceedings against the Secretary of State or against a health authority within the meaning of the National Health Service Act 1977.

141.—(1) Where a member of the House of Commons is authorized to be detained on the ground (however formulated) that he is suffering from mental illness, it shall be the duty of the court, authority or person on whose order or application, and of any registered medical practitioner upon whose recommendation or certificate, the detention was authorized, and of the person in charge of the hospital or other place in which the member is authorized to be detained, to notify the Speaker of the House of Commons that the detention has been authorized.

(2) Where the Speaker receives a notification under subsection (1) above, or is notified by two members of the House of Commons that they are credibly informed that such an authorization has been given, the Speaker shall cause the member to whom the notification relates to be visited and examined by two registered medical practitioners appointed in accordance with subsection (3) below.

(3) The registered medical practitioners to be appointed for the purposes of subsection (2) above shall be appointed by the President of the Royal College of Psychiatrists and shall be practitioners appearing to the President to have special experience in the diagnosis or treatment of mental disorders.

(4) The registered medical practitioners appointed in accordance with subsection (3) above shall report to the Speaker whether the member is suffering from mental illness and is authorized to be detained as such.

(5) If the report is to the effect that the member is suffering from mental illness and authorized to be detained as aforesaid, the Speaker shall at the expiration of 6 months from the date of the report, if the House is then sitting, and otherwise as soon as may be after the House next sits, again cause the member to be visited and examined by two such registered medical practitioners as aforesaid, and the registered medical practitioners shall report as aforesaid.

(6) If the second report is that the member is suffering from mental illness and authorized to be detained as mentioned in subsection (4) above, the Speaker shall forthwith lay both reports before the House of Commons, and thereupon the seat of the member shall become vacant.

(7) Any sums required for the payment of fees and expenses to registered medical practitioners acting in relation to a member of the House of Commons under this section shall be defrayed out of moneys provided by Parliament.

Mental Health (Scotland) Act 1984

Part I

APPLICATION OF ACT

1.—(1) The provisions of this Act shall have effect with respect to the reception, care and treatment of persons suffering, or appearing to be suffering, from mental disorder, to the management of their property and affairs, and to other related matters.

(2) In this Act—

'mental disorder' means mental illness or mental handicap however caused or manifested;
'mental impairment' means a state of arrested or incomplete development of mind not amounting to severe mental impairment which includes significant impairment of intelligence and social functioning and is associated with abnormally aggressive or seriously irresponsible conduct on the part of the person concerned; and cognate expressions shall be construed accordingly;
'severe mental impairment' means a state of arrested or incomplete development of mind which includes severe impairment of intelligence and social functioning and is associated with abnormally aggressive or seriously irresponsible conduct on the part of the person concerned; and cognate expressions shall be construed accordingly;

and other expressions have the meanings assigned to them in section 125 of this Act.

(3) No person shall be treated under this Act as suffering from mental disorder by reason only of promiscuity or other immoral conduct, sexual deviancy or dependence on alcohol or drugs.

Part II

MENTAL WELFARE COMMISSION

2.—(1) There shall continue to be a body called the Mental Welfare Commission for Scotland (in this Act referred to as 'the Mental Welfare Commission') who shall perform the functions assigned to them by or under this Act.

(2) The Mental Welfare Commission shall consist of no fewer than ten commissioners (including at least three women) of whom one shall be chairman, at least three shall be medical practitioners (in this Act referred to as 'medical commissioners'), and one shall be a person who has been for a period of at least 5 years either a member of the Faculty of Advocates or a solicitor.

(3) Five commissioners of whom at least one shall be a medical commissioner shall constitute a quorum of the Mental Welfare Commission.

3.—(1) It shall be the duty of the Mental Welfare Commission generally to exercise protective functions in respect of persons who may, by reason of mental disorder, be incapable of adequately protecting their persons or their interests, and, where those persons are liable to be detained in hospital or subject to guardianship under the following provisions of this Act, their functions as aforesaid shall include, in appropriate cases, the discharge of such patients in accordance with the said provisions.

(2) In the exercise of their functions as aforesaid, it shall be the duty of the Mental Welfare Commission—

(a) to make enquiry into any case where it appears to them that there may be ill-treatment, deficiency in care or treatment, or improper detention of any person who may be suffering from mental disorder, or where the property of any such person may, by reason of his mental disorder, be exposed to loss or damage;

(b) to visit regularly and, subject to paragraph (c) of this subsection, as often as they think appropriate, patients who are liable to be detained in a hospital or who are subject to guardianship and on any such visit to afford an opportunity, on request, for private interview to any such patient or, where the patient is in a hospital, to any other patient in that hospital;

(c) in any case where—
   (i) the authority for the detention of a patient—
      (A) has been renewed for a period of 1 year under section 30 of this Act; and
      (B) is renewed for a further period of 1 year under that section; and
   (ii) the patient has not, during the period referred to in sub-paragraph (i)(A) of this paragraph—
      (A) appealed to the sheriff under section 30(6) of this Act; or
      (B) been visited by the Mental Welfare Commission under paragraph (b) of this subsection,

   to visit the patient before the expiry of the period of 1 year referred to in sub-paragraph (i)(B) of this paragraph, unless the patient has previously been discharged, and on any such visit to afford an opportunity, on request, for private interview to any such patient;

(d) to bring to the attention of the managers of any hospital or of any local authority the facts of any case in which in the opinion of the Mental Welfare Commission it is desirable for the managers or the local authority to exercise any of their functions to secure the welfare of any patient suffering from mental disorder by—
   (i) preventing his ill-treatment;
   (ii) remedying any deficiency in his care or treatment;
   (iii) terminating his improper detention; or
   (iv) preventing or redressing loss or damage to his property;

(e) to advise the Secretary of State, a Health Board or a local authority on any matter arising out of this Act which has been referred to the Commission by the Secretary of State, the Health Board, or the local authority, as the case may be;

(f) to bring to the attention of the Secretary of State, a Health Board, a local authority or any other body any matter concerning the welfare of any persons who are suffering from mental disorder which the Commission consider ought to be brought to his or her attention.

(3) Where, in the course of carrying out any of their functions, the Mental Welfare Commission form the opinion that any patient who is—

(a) liable to be detained in a hospital; and

(b) either a restricted patient within the meaning of section 63 of this Act or a person mentioned in section 67(1) or (2) (persons treated as restricted patients) of this Act,

should be discharged, they shall recommend accordingly to the Secretary of State.

(4) On any visit by the Mental Welfare Commission in pursuance of paragraph (b) or (c) of subsection (2) of this section, the visitor shall be, or the visitors shall include, a medical commissioner or a medical officer of the Commission.

Part V

ADMISSION TO AND DETENTION IN HOSPITAL AND GUARDIANSHIP

Grounds for hospital admission

17.—(1) A person may, in pursuance of an application for admission under section 18(1) of this Act, be admitted to a hospital and there detained on the grounds that—

(a) he is suffering from mental disorder of a nature or degree which makes it appropriate for him to receive medical treatment in a hospital; and

   (i) in the case where the mental disorder from which he suffers is a persistent one manifested only by abnormally aggressive or seriously irresponsible conduct, such treatment is likely to alleviate or prevent a deterioration of his condition; or

   (ii) in the case where the mental disorder from which he suffers is a mental handicap, the handicap comprises mental impairment (where such treatment is likely to alleviate or prevent a deterioration of his condition) or severe mental impairment; and

(b) it is necessary for the health or safety of that person or for the protection of other persons that he should receive such treatment and it cannot be provided unless he is detained under this Part of this Act.

(2) Nothing in this Act shall be construed as preventing a patient who requires treatment for mental disorder from being admitted to any hospital or nursing home for that treatment in pursuance of arrangements made in that behalf without any application, recommendation or order rendering him liable to be detained under this Act, or from remaining in any hospital in pursuance of such arrangements if he has ceased to be so liable to be detained.

Procedure for admission of patients: hospital

18.—(1) A patient may be admitted to a hospital and there detained for the period allowed by this Part of this Act in pursuance of an application in the prescribed form (in this Act referred to as 'an application for admission') approved by the sheriff and made in accordance with this Part of this Act.

(2) An application for admission shall be founded on and accompanied by two medical recommendations which shall be in the prescribed form and each such recommendation shall include the following statements, being statements of opinion, and the grounds on which each statement is based—

(a) a statement of the form of mental disorder from which the patient is suffering, being mental illness or mental handicap or both; and

(b) a statement as to which of the grounds set out in section 17(1) of this Act apply in relation to the patient.

(3) An application for admission shall be of no effect unless the patient is described in each of the medical recommendations as suffering from the same form of mental disorder, whether or not he is described in either of those recommendations as suffering also from the other form.

19.—(1) Subject to the provisions of this section, an application for admission may be made either by the nearest relative of the patient or by a mental health officer; and every such application shall be addressed to the managers of the hospital to which admission is sought.

(2) The nearest relative of the patient shall not make an application for admission unless he has personally seen the patient within the period of 14 days ending with the date on which the proposed application is submitted to the sheriff for his approval.

(3) A local authority shall, if so required by the nearest relative of a patient residing in their area, direct a mental health officer as soon as practicable to take the patient's case into consideration with a view to making an application for admission in respect of the patient; and if in any such case that officer decides not to make an application he shall inform the nearest relative of his reasons in writing.

(4) A mental health officer shall make an application for admission in respect of a patient within the area of the local authority by whom that officer was appointed in any case where he is satisfied that such an application ought to be made and is of the opinion, having regard to any wishes expressed by relatives of the patient and to any other relevant circumstances, that it is necessary or proper for the application to be made by him.

(5) A mental health officer who proposes to make an application for admission shall—

(a) interview the patient within the period of 14 days ending with the date on which the proposed application is submitted to the sheriff for his approval and satisfy himself that detention in a hospital is, in all the circumstances of the case, the most appropriate way of providing the care and medical treatment which the patient needs; and

(b) take such steps as are reasonably practicable to inform the nearest relative of the patient of the proposed application, and of his right to object thereto in accordance with the provisions of section 21 of this Act.

(6) A mental health officer shall make an application for admission in respect of a patient where—

(a) he has received the two medical recommendations required for the purposes of such an application; and

(b) he has been requested to do so by a medical practitioner who gave one of the medical recommendations,

and the application shall include—

(i) a statement of the mental health officer's opinion as to whether or not the application should be granted; and

(ii) a statement of the grounds on which that opinion is based.

(7) An application under this section by a mental health officer may be made outside the area of the local authority by whom he is appointed.

20.—(1) The medical recommendations required for the purposes of an application for admission shall satisfy the following requirements—

(a) such recommendations shall be signed on or before the date of the application and shall be given by medical practitioners (neither being the applicant) who have personally examined the patient separately, in which case not more than 5 days must have elapsed between the days on which the separate examinations took place, or, where no objection has been made by the patient or his nearest relative, together;

(b) one of the recommendations shall be given by a practitioner approved for the purpose of this section by a Health Board as having special experience in the diagnosis or treatment of mental disorder and the other recommendation shall, if practicable, be given by the patient's general medical practitioner or another medical practitioner who has previous acquaintance with him;

(c) neither recommendation shall be given by a practitioner on the staff of the hospital named in the application where the patient is to be accommodated under section 57 or 58 of the

National Health Service (Scotland) Act 1978 (which relates to accommodation for private patients) or in a private hospital and, subject to subsection (2) of this section, where the patient is to be accommodated otherwise one only of the recommendations may be given by such a practitioner;

(d) such recommendations shall contain a statement as to whether the person signing the recommendation is related to the patient and of any pecuniary interest that that person may have in the admission of the patient to hospital.

(2) Notwithstanding the provisions of paragraph (c) of subsection (1) of this section, both medical recommendations may be given by practitioners on the staff of the hospital named in the application where—

(a) compliance with the said paragraph (c) would result in a delay involving serious risk to the health or safety of the patient or to the safety of other persons;

(b) one of the practitioners giving the recommendations works at the hospital for less than half the time which he is bound by contract to devote to work in the health service; and

(c) if one of the practitioners is a consultant, the other does not work (whether at the hospital or elsewhere) in a grade in which he is under that consultant's directions.

(3) For the purposes of this section a general practitioner who is employed part-time in a hospital shall not be regarded as a practitioner on its staff.

21.—(1) An application for admission shall be submitted to a sheriff of the sheriffdom—

(a) within which the patient is resident at the time when the application is submitted; or

(b) where the patient is a resident patient in a hospital at the time when the application is submitted, within which the hospital is situated,

for his approval within 7 days of the last date on which the patient was examined for the purposes of any medical recommendation accompanying the application.

(2) Subject to the following provisions of this section and to section 113 of this Act, the sheriff, in considering an application submitted to him under this section—

(a) may make such inquiries and hear such persons (including the patient) as he think fit; and

(b) where an application is the subject of objection by the nearest relative of the patient, shall afford that relative and any witness that relative may call an opportunity of being heard; and

(c) shall, where a mental health officer makes an application for admission in respect of a patient under section 19(6) of this Act and such application includes a statement of the mental health officer's opinion that the application should not be granted, afford the mental health officer an opportunity of being heard.

(3) The sheriff shall not withhold approval to an application submitted under this section without affording to the applicant and any witness the applicant may call an opportunity of being heard.

(4) Any proceedings under this section shall, where the patient or applicant so desires or the sheriff thinks fit, be conducted in private.

(5) The sheriff in the exercise of the functions conferred on him by this section shall have the like jurisdiction, and the like powers as regards the summoning and examination of witnesses, the administration of oaths, the awarding of expenses, and otherwise, as if he were acting in the exercise of his civil jurisdiction.

24.—(1) In any case of urgent necessity a recommendation (in this Act referred to as 'an emergency recommendation') may be made by a medical practitioner in respect of a patient stating that by reason of mental disorder it is urgently necessary for his health or safety or for the protection of other persons, that he should be admitted to a hospital, but that compliance with the provisions of this Part of this Act relating to an application for admission before the admission of the patient to a hospital would involve undesirable delay.

(2) An emergency recommendation shall not be made unless, where practicable, the consent of a relative or of a mental health officer has been obtained; and the recommendation shall be

accompanied by a statement that such a consent as aforesaid has been obtained or, as the case may be, by a statement of the reasons for the failure to obtain that consent.

(3) An emergency recommendation shall be sufficient authority for the removal of the patient to a hospital at any time within a period of 3 days from the date on which it was made and for his detention therein for a period not exceeding 72 hours from the time of his admission.

(4) An emergency recommendation shall be made only by a medical practitioner who has personally examined the patient on the day on which he signed the recommendation.

(5) Where a patient is admitted to a hospital in pursuance of this section, it shall, where practicable, be the duty of the managers without delay to inform the nearest relative of the patient, the Mental Welfare Commission and, except in the case of a patient referred to in section 25 of this Act, some responsible person residing with the patient.

(6) A patient who has been detained in a hospital under this section shall not be further detained under this section immediately after the expiry of the period of detention.

25.—(1) An application for admission or an emergency recommendation may be made under this Part of this Act notwithstanding that the patient is already in a hospital; and where the application or recommendation is made in such a case the patient shall be treated for the purposes of this Part of this Act as if he had been admitted to the hospital on the date on which the application was forwarded to the managers of the hospital, or, as the case may be, the recommendation was made.

(2) If, in the case of a patient who is already in a hospital receiving treatment for mental disorder and who is not liable to be detained therein under this Part of this Act, it appears to a nurse of the prescribed class—

(a) that the patient is suffering from mental disorder to such a degree that it is necessary for his health or safety or the protection of other persons for him to be immediately restrained from leaving the hospital; and
(b) that it is not practicable to secure the immediate attendance of a medical practitioner for the purpose of making an emergency recommendation,

the patient may be detained in the hospital for a period of 2 hours from the time when he was first so detained or until the earlier arrival at the place where the patient is detained of a medical practitioner having power to make an emergency recommendation.

(3) Where a patient is detained under subsection (2) of this section the nurse shall as soon as possible record in writing—

(a) the facts mentioned in paragraphs (a) and (b) of the said subsection (2);
(b) the fact that the patient has been detained; and
(c) the time at which the patient was first so detained.

(4) A record made by a nurse under subsection (3) of this section shall, as soon as possible after it is made, be delivered by the nurse, or by a person authorized by the nurse in that behalf, to the managers of the hospital; and a copy of the record shall, within 14 days of the date on which the managers received it, be sent to the Mental Welfare Commission.

(5) A patient who has been detained in a hospital under subsection (2) of this section shall not be further detained thereunder immediately after the expiry of that period of detention.

(6) In subsection (2) of this section 'prescribed' means prescribed by an order made by the Secretary of State.

26.—(1) Where a patient is admitted to a hospital in pursuance of section 24 of this Act, he may be detained in that hospital after the expiry of the period of 72 hours referred to in subsection (3) of that section if—

(a) a report on the condition of the patient has been furnished to the managers of the hospital; and
(b) where practicable, consent to the continued detention has been given by the nearest relative of the patient or by a mental health officer.

(2) The report referred to in subsection (1)(a) of this section shall—

(*a*) be given by a medical practitioner approved for the purposes of section 20(1)(*b*) of this Act who has personally examined the patient and shall include a statement that in the opinion of the medical practitioner—

   (i) the patient is suffering from mental disorder of a nature or degree which makes it appropriate for him to be detained in a hospital for at least a limited period; and

   (ii) the patient ought to be so detained in the interests of his own health or safety or with a view to the protection of other persons;

(*b*) include, where consent to the continued detention has not been obtained, a statement of the reasons for not obtaining such consent; and

(*c*) contain a statement as to whether the person signing the report is related to the patient and of any pecuniary interest that that person may have in the admission of the patient to hospital.

(3) Subject to subsection (6) of this section, where a report is duly furnished under subsection (1) of this section the authority for the detention of the patient shall be thereby renewed for a further period of 28 days from the expiry of the period of 72 hours referred to in the said subsection (1).

(4) Where a patient is detained in a hospital in pursuance of this section, the managers of the hospital shall so inform—

(*a*) the Mental Welfare Commission;

(*b*) where practicable, the nearest relative of the patient (except where the nearest relative has consented under subsection (1)(*b*) of this section); and

(*c*) the local authority (except in a case where a mental health officer appointed by that local authority has consented under subsection (1)(*b*) of this section),

not later than 7 days after the patient was detained.

(5) A local authority, on being informed under subsection (4) of this section of the admission of a patient, shall arrange for a mental health officer as soon as practicable and in any event not later than 7 days before the expiry of the period of 28 days referred to in subsection (3) of this section—

(*a*) to interview the patient; and

(*b*) to provide the responsible medical officer and the Mental Welfare Commission with a report on the patient's social circumstances.

(6) Any patient may, within the period for which the authority for his detention is renewed by virtue of a report furnished in respect of him under this section, appeal to the sheriff to order his discharge and the provisions of section 33(2) and (4) of this Act shall apply in relation to such an appeal.

(7) A patient who has been detained in a hospital under this section shall not be further detained under this section nor detained under section 24 of this Act immediately after the expiry of the period of detention under this section.

Discharge of patients: hospital

33.—(1) Subject to the provisions of this and the next following section, a patient who is liable to be detained in a hospital under this Part of this Act shall cease to be so liable if an order in writing discharging him from detention (in this Act referred to as 'an order for discharge') is made in accordance with the following provisions of this section.

(2) An order for discharge may be made in respect of a patient by the responsible medical officer, the Mental Welfare Commission or, where an appeal has been taken under sections 26, 30 or 34 of this Act, by the sheriff:

Provided that such an order shall not be made by the responsible medical officer in respect of a patient detained in a State hospital without the consent of the managers of the hospital.

(3) The responsible medical officer or the Mental Welfare Commission shall make an order for discharge in respect of a patient where he is or they are satisfied that—

(*a*) he is not suffering from mental disorder of a nature or degree which makes it appropriate for him to be liable to be detained in a hospital for medical treatment; or (*b*) it is not necessary for the health or safety of the patient or for the protection of other persons that he should receive such treatment.

(4) Where an appeal is made to the sheriff by a patient under sections 26, 30 or 34 of this Act, the sheriff shall order the discharge of the patient if he is satisfied that—

(*a*) the patient is not at the time of the hearing of the appeal suffering from mental disorder of a nature or degree which makes it appropriate for him to be liable to be detained in a hospital for medical treatment; or
(*b*) it is not necessary for the health or safety of the patient or for the protection of other persons that he should receive such treatment.

(5) Subject to the provisions of this section and section 34 of this Act, an order for discharge in respect of a patient may also be made by the managers of the hospital or by the nearest relative of the patient.

(6) An order for discharge made in respect of a patient by the managers of a hospital shall, with the consent of the responsible medical officer, take effect on the expiration of a period of 7 days from the date on which the order was made, and where the responsible medical officer does not so consent he shall furnish to the managers a report certifying that in his opinion the grounds set out in section 17(1) of this Act apply in relation to the patient.

34.—(1) An order for the discharge of a patient who is liable to be detained in a hospital shall not be made by his nearest relative except after giving not less than 7 days' notice in writing to the managers of the hospital; and if within that period the responsible medical officer furnishes to the managers a report certifying that, in his opinion, the grounds set out in section 17(1) of this Act apply in relation to the patient—

(*a*) any order for the discharge of the patient made by that relative in pursuance of the notice shall be of no effect; and
(*b*) no further order for the discharge of the patient shall be made by that relative during the period of 6 months beginning with the date of the report.

(2) In any case where a report under subsection (1) of this section is furnished in respect of a patient, the managers shall cause the nearest relative of the patient to be informed and that relative may, within the period of 28 days beginning with the day on which he is so informed, appeal to the sheriff to order the discharge of the patient and the provisions of section 33(2) and (4) of this Act shall apply in relation to such an appeal.

(3) An order for discharge in respect of a patient detained in a State hospital shall not be made by his nearest relative.

Appeals: hospital

35.—(1) Where an appeal lies to the sheriff in respect of a report on a patient under any of sections 26, 30 or 34 of this Act, the managers of the hospital where the patient is liable to be detained shall, when intimating that a report has been furnished in pursuance of any of the said sections, inform any person having a right so to appeal, whether the patient or his nearest relative or both, of that right and of the period within which it may be exercised.

(2) An appeal under any of the said sections shall be made by way of summary application to a sheriff of the sheriffdom—

(*a*) within which the patient is resident at the time when the appeal is made; or
(*b*) where the patient is a resident patient in a hospital at the time when the appeal is made, within which the hospital is situated.

(3) For the purpose of advising whether any appeal to the sheriff under any of the said sections should be made by or in respect of a patient who is liable to be detained under this Part of this Act, or of furnishing information as to the condition of a patient for the purposes of such an appeal or of advising the nearest relative of any such patient as to the exercise of any power to order the discharge of the patient, any medical practitioner authorized by or on behalf of the patient or by the nearest relative of the patient, as the case may be, may, at any reasonable time, visit the patient and may examine him in private.

(4) Any medical practitioner authorized for the purposes of subsection (3) of this section to visit and examine a patient may require the production of and inspect any records relating to the detention or treatment of the patient in any hospital.

Grounds for reception into guardianship

36. A person may, in pursuance of an application for reception into guardianship under section 37(1) of this Act, be received into guardianship on the grounds that—

- (*a*) he is suffering from mental disorder of a nature or degree which warrants his reception into guardianship; and
- (*b*) it is necessary in the interests of the welfare of the patient that he should be so received.

Procedure for reception of patients: guardianship

37.—(1) A patient who has attained the age of 16 years may be received into guardianship for the period allowed by this Part of this Act, in pursuance of an application in the prescribed form (in this Act referred to as 'a guardianship application') approved by the sheriff and made in accordance with the provisions of this Part of this Act.

(2) The person named as guardian in a guardianship application may be—

- (*a*) the local authority to whom the application is addressed; or
- (*b*) a person chosen by that authority; or
- (*c*) any other person who has been accepted as a suitable person to act in that behalf by that authority,

and any person chosen or accepted as aforesaid may be a local authority or any other person including the applicant.

(3) A guardianship application shall be founded on and accompanied by two medical recommendations in the prescribed form and a recommendation by a mental health officer in such form; and

- (*a*) each medical recommendation shall include—
    - (i) a statement of the form of mental disorder from which the patient is suffering being mental illness or mental handicap or both; and
    - (ii) a statement that the ground set out in section 36(*a*) of this Act applies in relation to the patient, being statements of opinion, together with the grounds on which those statements are based;
- (*b*) the recommendation by the mental health officer shall include—
    - (i) a statement, being a statement of opinion, that the ground set out in section 36(*b*) of this Act applies in relation to the patient, together with the grounds on which the statement is based; and
    - (ii) a statement as to whether he is related to the patient and of any pecuniary interest that he may have in the reception of the patient into guardianship.

(4) A guardianship application shall be of no effect unless the patient is described in each of the medical recommendations as suffering from the same form of mental disorder, whether or not he is described in either of those recommendations as suffering also from the other form.

38.—(1) Subject to the provisions of this section, a guardianship application may be made either by the nearest relative of the patient or by a mental health officer; and every such application shall be addressed to the local authority for the area in which the patient resides.

(2) The nearest relative of the patient shall not make a guardianship application unless he has personally seen the patient within the period of 14 days ending with the date on which the proposed application is submitted to the sheriff for his approval.

(3) A local authority shall, if so required by the nearest relative of a patient residing in their area, direct a mental health officer as soon as practicable to take the patient's case into consideration with a view to making a guardianship application in respect of the patient; and if in any such case that officer decides not to make an application he shall inform the nearest relative of his reasons in writing.

(4) A mental health officer shall make a guardianship application in respect of a patient within the area of the local authority by whom that officer was appointed in any case where he is satisfied that such an application ought to be made and is of the opinion, having regard to any wishes expressed by relatives of the patient and to any other relevant circumstances, that it is necessary or proper for the application to be made by him.

(5) A mental health officer who proposes to make a guardianship application shall—

(a) interview the patient within the period of 14 days ending with the date on which the proposed application is submitted to the sheriff for his approval; and

(b) take such steps as are reasonably practicable to inform the nearest relative of the patient of the proposed application, and of his right to object thereto in accordance with the provisions of section 40 of this Act.

(6) An application under this section by a mental health officer may be made outside the area of the local authority by whom he is appointed.

39. The medical recommendations required for the purposes of a guardianship application shall satisfy the following requirements—

(a) such recommendations shall be signed on or before the date of the application and shall be given by medical practitioners (neither being the applicant) who have personally examined the patient separately, in which case not more than 5 days must have elapsed between the days on which the separate examinations took place, or, where no objection has been made by the patient or his nearest relative, together;

(b) one of the recommendations shall be given by a practitioner approved for the purposes of this section by a Health Board as having special experience in the diagnosis or treatment of mental disorder and the other recommendation shall, if practicable, be given by the patient's general medical practitioner or another medical practitioner who has previous acquaintance with him;

(c) such recommendations shall contain a statement as to whether the person signing the recommendation is related to the patient and of any pecuniary interest that that person may have in the reception of the patient into guardianship.

40.—(1) A guardianship application shall be submitted to a sheriff of the sheriffdom—

(a) within which the patient is resident at the time when the application is submitted; or

(b) where the patient is a resident patient in a hospital at the time when the application is submitted, within which the hospital is situated,

for his approval within 7 days of the last date on which the patient was examined for the purposes of any medical recommendation accompanying the application, together with a statement of the willingness to act of the guardian named in the application.

(2) Subject to the following provisions of this section and to section 113 of this Act, the sheriff, in considering an application submitted to him under this section may make such inquiries and hear such persons (including the patient) as he thinks fit, and, where an application is the subject of objection by the nearest relative of the patient, shall afford that relative and any witness that relative may call on opportunity of being heard.

(3) The sheriff shall not withhold approval to an application so submitted without affording to the applicant and any witness the applicant may call an opportunity of being heard.

(4) Any proceedings under this section shall, where the patient or applicant so desires or the sheriff thinks fit, be conducted in private.

(5) Every such application shall, after it is approved by the sheriff, be forwarded to the local authority for the area in which the patient resides.

(6) The sheriff in the exercise of the functions conferred on him by this section shall have the like jurisdiction, and the like powers as regards the summoning and examination of witnesses, the administration of oaths, the awarding of expenses, and otherwise, as if he were acting in the exercise of his civil jurisdiction.

41.—(1) Where a patient has been received into guardianship in pursuance of an application under this Part of this Act, the local authority concerned shall notify the Mental Welfare

Commission of that reception together with a copy of the application and recommendations relating to the patient's reception within 7 days of its taking place.

(2) Where a guardianship application has been approved by the sheriff and forwarded to the local authority concerned within a period of 7 days from the date on which the sheriff approved the application, the application shall, subject to the following provisions of this section and to regulations made by the Secretary of State, confer on the authority or person named in the application as guardian, to the exclusion of any other person, the following powers—

(*a*) power to require the patient to reside at a place specified by the authority or person named as guardian;

(*b*) power to require the patient to attend at places and times so specified for the purpose of medical treatment, occupation, education or training;

(*c*) power to require access to the patient to be given, at any place where the patient is residing, to any medical practitioner, mental health officer or other person so specified.

Part VI

DETENTION OF PATIENTS CONCERNED IN CRIMINAL PROCEEDINGS, ETC. AND TRANSFER OF PATIENTS UNDER SENTENCE

Provisions for compulsory detention and guardianship of patients charged with offences, etc.

60.—(1) A hospital order made under section 175 or 376 of the Criminal Procedure (Scotland) Act 1975 shall be sufficient authority—

(*a*) for a constable, a mental health officer, or any other person directed to do so by the court to convey the patient to the hospital specified in the order within a period of 28 days; and

(*b*) for the managers of the hospital to admit him at any time within that period, and thereafter to detain him in accordance with the provisions of this Act.

(2) A patient who is admitted to a hospital in pursuance of a hospital order shall be treated for the purposes of Part V of this Act (other than section 23) as if he had been so admitted on the date of the order in pursuance of an application for admission, except that the power to order the discharge of the patient under section 33 of this Act shall not be exercisable by his nearest relative; and accordingly the provisions of the said Part V specified in Part I of the Second Schedule to this Act shall apply in relation to him, subject to the exceptions and modifications set out in that Part and the remaining provisions of the said Part V shall not apply.

(3) Subject to the provisions of section 178(3) or 379(3) of the said Act of 1975, where a patient is admitted to a hospital in pursuance of a hospital order any previous application or hospital order by virtue of which he was liable to be detained in a hospital shall cease to have effect:

Provided that, if the order first-mentioned or the conviction to which it relates is quashed on appeal, this subsection shall not apply and section 32 of this Act shall have effect as if during any period for which the patient was liable to to be detained under the order he had been detained in custody as mentioned in that section.

(4) If within the period of 28 days referred to in subsection (1) of this section it appears to the Secretary of State that by reason of an emergency or other special circumstances it is not practicable for the patient to be received into the hospital specified in the order, he may give directions for the admission of the patient to such other hospital as appears to be appropriate in lieu of the hospital so specified; and where such directions are given the Secretary of State shall cause the person having the custody of the patient to be informed, and the hospital order shall have effect as if the hospital specified in the directions were substituted for the hospital specified in the order.

61.—(1) A guardianship order made under section 175 or 376 of the Criminal Procedure (Scotland) Act 1975 shall confer on the authority or person therein named as guardian the like powers as a guardianship application effective under Part V of this Act.

(2) A patient who is received into guardianship in pursuance of a guardianship order shall be treated for the purposes of Part V of this Act (other than section 42) as if he had been so

received on the date of the order in pursuance of a guardianship application as aforesaid, except that the power to order the discharge of the patient under section 50 of this Act shall not be exercisable by his nearest relative; and accordingly the provisions of the said Part V specified in Part III of the Second Schedule to this Act shall apply in relation to him subject to the exceptions and modifications set out therein, and the remaining provisions of the said Part V shall not apply.

(3) Where a patient is received into guardianship in pursuance of a guardianship order any previous application or order by virtue of which he was subject to guardianship shall cease to have effect:

Provided that, if the order first-mentioned or the conviction to which it relates is quashed on appeal, this subsection shall not apply and section 49 of this Act shall have effect as if during any period for which the patient was subject to guardianship under the order he had been detained in custody as mentioned in that section.

62.—(1) The special restrictions applicable to a patient in respect of whom a restriction order made under section 178 or 379 of the Criminal Procedure (Scotland) Act 1975 is in force are as follows, that is to say—

(a) none of the provisions of Part V of this Act relating to the duration, renewal and expiration of authority for the detention of patients shall apply, and the patient shall continue to be liable to be detained by virtue of the relevant hospital order until he is absolutely discharged under sections 63 to 68 of this Act;

(b) the following powers shall be exercisable only with the consent of the Secretary of State, that is to say—

(i) power to grant leave of absence to the patient under section 27 of this Act; and

(ii) power to transfer the patient under section 29 of this Act;

and if leave of absence is granted under the said section 27 the power to recall the patient under that section shall be vested in the Secretary of State as well as in the responsible medical officer; and

(c) the power to take the patient into custody and return him under section 28 of this Act may be exercised at any time,

and in relation to any such patient the provisions of the said Part V specified in Part II of the Second Schedule to this Act shall have effect subject to the exceptions and modifications set out in that Part and the remaining provisions of Part V shall not apply.

(2) While a person is a restricted patient within the meaning of section 63 of this Act or a person to whom section 67 (persons treated as restricted patients) of this Act applies, the responsible medical officer shall at such intervals (not exceeding 1 year) as the Secretary of State may direct examine and report to the Secretary of State on that person; and every report shall contain such particulars as the Secretary of State may require.

(3) Without prejudice to the provisions of section 178(3) or 379(3) of the said Act of 1975, where a restriction order in respect of a patient ceases to have effect while the relevant hospital order continues in force, the provisions of section 60 of this Act and Part I of the Second Schedule to this Act shall apply to the patient as if he had been admitted to the hospital in pursuance of a hospital order (without a restriction order) made on the date on which the restriction order ceased to have effect.

63.—(1) In this section and in sections 64 to 67 of this Act—

'restricted patient' means a patient who is subject to a restriction order or to a restriction direction;

'relevant hospital order' and 'relevant transfer direction', in relation to a restricted patient, means the hospital order or transfer direction by virtue of which he is liable to be detained in a hospital.

(2) A restricted patient detained in a hospital may appeal by way of summary application to a sheriff of the sheriffdom within which the hospital in which he is liable to be detained is situated—

(*a*) in the period between the expiration of 6 months and the expiration of 12 months beginning with the date of the relevant hospital order or transfer direction; and

(*b*) in any subsequent period of 12 months,

to order his discharge under section 64 or 65 of this Act.

(3) The provisions of section 35(3) and (4) of this Act shall have effect in relation to an appeal under sections 63 to 67 of this Act as they have in relation to an appeal under Part V of this Act.

64.—(1) Where an appeal to the sheriff is made by a restricted patient who is subject to a restriction order, the sheriff shall direct the absolute discharge of the patient if he is satisfied—

(*a*) that the patient is not, at the time of the hearing of the appeal, suffering from mental disorder of a nature or degree which makes it appropriate for him to be liable to be detained in a hospital for medical treatment; or

(*b*) that it is not necessary for the health or safety of the patient or for the protection of other persons that he should receive such treatment; and (in either case)

(*c*) that it is not appropriate for the patient to remain liable to be recalled to hospital for further treatment.

(2) Where in the case of any such patient as is mentioned in subsection (1) of this section the sheriff is satisfied as to the matters referred to in paragraph (*a*) or (*b*) of that subsection but not as to the matters referred to in paragraph (*c*) of that subsection he shall direct the conditional discharge of the patient.

(3) Where a patient is absolutely discharged under subsection (1) of this section he shall thereupon cease to be liable to be detained by virtue of the relevant hospital order, and the restriction order shall cease to have effect accordingly.

(4) Where a patient is conditionally discharged under subsection (2) of this section—

(*a*) he may be recalled by the Secretary of State under section 68(3) of this Act as if he had been conditionally discharged under subsection (2) of that section; and

(*b*) he shall comply with such conditions (if any) as may be imposed at the time of discharge by the sheriff or at any subsequent time by the Secretary of State.

(5) The Secretary of State may from time to time vary any condition imposed (whether by the sheriff or by him) under subsection (4) of this section.

(6) Where a restriction order in respect of a patient ceases to have effect after he has been conditionally discharged under subsection (2) of this section the patient shall, unless previously recalled, be deemed to be absolutely discharged on the date when the order ceases to have effect and shall cease to be liable to be detained by virtue of the relevant hospital order.

(7) The sheriff may defer a direction for the conditional discharge of a patient until such arrangements as appear to the sheriff to be necessary for that purpose have been made to his satisfaction; and where by virtue of any such deferment no direction has been given on an appeal before the time when the patient's case comes before the sheriff on a subsequent appeal, the previous appeal shall be treated as one on which no direction under this section can be given.

(8) This section is without prejudice to section 68 of this Act.

65.—(1) Where an appeal to the sheriff is made by a restricted patient who is subject to a restriction direction, the sheriff—

(*a*) shall notify the Secretary of State if, in his opinion, the patient would, if subject to a restriction order, be entitled to be absolutely or conditionally discharged under section 64 of this Act; and

(*b*) if he notifies the Secretary of State that the patient would be entitled to be conditionally discharged, may recommend that in the event of the patient's not being released on licence or discharged under supervision under subsection 2(*b*)(ii) of this section he should continue to be detained in a hospital.

(2) If the sheriff notifies the Secretary of State—

(*a*) that the patient would be entitled to be absolutely discharged, the Secretary of State shall—

> (i) by warrant direct that the patient be remitted to any prison or other institution in which he might have been detained if he had not been removed to hospital, there to be dealt with as if he had not been so removed; or
>
> (ii) exercise any power of releasing the patient on licence or discharging the patient under supervision which would have been exercisable if the patient had been remitted to any prison or other institution in which he might have been detained if he had not been removed to hospital;

(*b*) that the patient would be entitled to be conditionally discharged, the Secretary of State may—

> (i) by warrant direct that the patient be remitted to any prison or other institution in which he might have been detained if he had not been removed to hospital, there to be dealt with as if he had not been so removed; or
>
> (ii) exercise any power of releasing the patient on licence or discharging the patient under supervision which would have been exercisable if the patient had been remitted to any prison or other institution in which he might have been detained if he had not been removed to hospital; or
>
> (iii) decide that the patient should continue to be detained in a hospital,

and on his arrival in the prison or other institution or, as the case may be, his release or discharge as aforesaid, the transfer direction and the restriction direction shall cease to have effect.

Transfer to hospital or guardianship of prisoners, etc.

70.—(1) If in the case of a person committed in custody while awaiting trial or sentence it appears to the Secretary of State that the grounds are satisfied upon which an application may be made for his admission to a hospital under Part V of this Act he may apply to the sheriff for an order that that person be removed to and detained in such hospital (not being a private hospital) as may be specified in the order; and the sheriff, if satisfied by reports from two medical practitioners (complying with the provisions of this section) that the grounds are satisfied as aforesaid may make an order accordingly.

(2) An order under this section (in this Act referred to as 'a transfer order') shall cease to have effect at the expiration of the period of 14 days beginning with the date on which it is made, unless within that period the person with respect to whom it was made has been received into the hospital specified therein.

(3) A transfer order with respect to any person shall have the like effect as a hospital order made in his case together with a restriction order in respect of him made without limit of time.

(4) Of the medical practitioners whose reports are taken into account under subsection (1) of this section, at least one shall be a practitioner approved for the purposes of section 20 of this Act by a Health Board as having special experience in the diagnosis or treatment of mental disorder.

(5) A transfer order shall specify the form or forms of mental disorder, being mental illness or mental handicap or both, from which the patient is found by the sheriff to be suffering; and no such order shall be made unless the patient is described by each of the practitioners whose evidence is taken into account as aforesaid as suffering from the same form of mental disorder, whether or not he is also described by either of them as suffering from the other form.

71.—(1) If in the case of a person to whom this section applies the Secretary of State is satisfied by the like reports as are required for the purposes of section 70 of this Act that the grounds are satisfied upon which an application may be made for his admission to a hospital under Part V of this Act the Secretary of State may make a direction (in this Act referred to as 'a transfer direction') in respect of him.

(2) This section applies to the following persons, that is to say—

(*a*) persons serving sentences of imprisonment;

(*b*) civil prisoners, that is to say, persons committed by court to prison in respect of a civil debt;

(*c*) persons detained under the Immigration Act 1971.

(3) Subsections (2), (4) and (5) of section 70 of this Act shall apply for the purposes of this section and of any transfer direction given by virtue of this section as they apply for the purposes of that section and of any transfer order thereunder, with the substitution for any references to the sheriff of a reference to the Secretary of State.

(4) A transfer direction with respect to any person shall have the like effect as a hospital order made in his case.

(5) Where a transfer direction is given in respect of any person that person may, within 1 month of his transfer to a hospital thereunder, appeal to the sheriff to cancel the direction, and the sheriff shall cancel the direction unless he is satisfied that the grounds are satisfied upon which an application may be made for the admission of the person to a hospital under Part V of this Act; and, if a transfer direction is so cancelled, the Secretary of State shall direct that the person be remitted to any prison or other institution in which he might have been detained if he had not been removed to hospital, there to be dealt with as if he had not been so removed.

(6) Subsections (2), (3) and (4) of section 35 of this Act shall apply to an appeal under subsection (5) of this section in like manner as they apply to an appeal referred to in that section.

(7) References in this section to a person serving a sentence of imprisonment include references—

(*a*) to a person detained in pursuance of any sentence or order for detention made by a court in criminal proceedings (other than an order under section 174 or 255 of the Criminal Procedure (Scotland) Act 1975, or under any enactment to which section 69 of this Act applies);

(*b*) to a person committed by a court to a prison or other institution to which the Prisons (Scotland) Act 1952, applies in default of payment of any fine to be paid on his conviction.

72.—(1) Where a transfer direction is given in respect of any person, the Secretary of State, if he thinks fit, may by warrant direct that that person shall be subject to the special restrictions set out in section 62(1) of this Act.

(2) A direction under this section (in this Act referred to as 'a restriction direction') shall have the like effect as a restriction order in respect of the patient made under section 178 or 379 of the Criminal Procedure (Scotland) Act 1975.

73.—(1) Subject to the following provisions of this section any transfer order made in respect of a person under section 70(1) of this Act shall cease to have effect if the proceedings in respect of him are dropped or when his case is disposed of by the court to which he was committed, or by which he was remanded, but without prejudice to any power of that court to make a hospital order or other order under section 174A, 175, 178, 375A, 376 or 379 of the Criminal Procedure (Scotland) Act 1975 in his case.

(2) Where a transfer order has been made in respect of any such person as aforesaid, then, if the Secretary of State is notified by the responsible medical officer at any time before that person is brought before the court to which he was committed, or by which he was remanded, that he no longer requires treatment for mental disorder, the Secretary of State may by warrant direct that he be remitted to any place where he might have been detained if he had not been removed to hospital, there to be dealt with as if he had not been so removed, and on his arrival at the place to which he is so remitted the transfer order shall cease to have effect.

(3) Where a transfer order in respect of any person ceases to have effect under subsection (1) of this section, then unless his case has been disposed of by the court—

(*a*) passing a sentence of imprisonment (within the meaning of section 175(7) or 376(10) of the said Act of 1975) on him; or

(b) making a probation order under section 183, 184, 384 or 385 of the said Act of 1975 in relation to him; or

(c) making a hospital order or guardianship order in his case,

he shall continue to be liable to be detained in the hospital in which he was detained under the transfer order as if he had been admitted thereto, on the date on which that order ceased to have effect, in pursuance of an application for admission made under Part V of this Act, and the provisions of this Act shall apply accordingly.

74.—(1) Where a transfer direction and a restriction direction have been given in respect of a person serving a sentence of imprisonment and the Secretary of State is satisfied—

(a) that the person is not suffering from mental disorder of a nature or degree which makes it appropriate for him to be liable to be detained in a hospital for medical treatment; or

(b) that it is not necessary for the health or safety of the person or for the protection of other persons that he should receive such treatment; and (in either case)

(c) that it is not appropriate for the person to remain liable to be recalled to hospital for further treatment,

he shall—

(i) by warrant direct that the person be remitted to any prison or other institution in which he might have been detained if he had not been removed to hospital, there to be dealt with as if he had not been so removed; or

(ii) exercise any power of releasing the person on licence or discharging the person under supervision, which would have been exercisable if he had been remitted to any prison or other institution in which he might have been detained if he had not been removed to hospital,

and on his arrival in the prison or other institution, or as the case may be, his release or discharge as aforesaid, the transfer direction and the restriction direction shall cease to have effect.

(2) Where in the case of any such person as is mentioned in subsection (1) of this section the Secretary of State is satisfied as to the matter referred to in paragraph (a) or (b) of that subsection but not as to the matters referred to in paragraph (c) of that subsection he may—

(a) by warrant direct that the person be remitted to any prison or other institution in which he might have been detained if he had not been removed to a hospital, there to be dealt with as if he had not been removed; or

(b) exercise any power of releasing the person on licence or discharging the person under supervision, which would have been exercisable if he had been remitted to any prison or other institution in which he might have been detained if he had not been removed to a hospital; or

(c) decide that the person should continue to be detained in a hospital,

and on his arrival in the prison or other institution or, as the case may be, his release or discharge as aforesaid, the transfer direction and the restriction direction shall cease to have effect.

(3) A restriction direction given in respect of a person serving a sentence of imprisonment shall cease to have effect on the expiration of the sentence.

(4) Subject to the following provisions of this section, where a restriction direction ceases to have effect in respect of a person that person shall be discharged unless a report is furnished in respect of him under subsection (5) of this section.

(5) Within a period of 28 days before a restriction direction ceases to have effect in respect of a person, the responsible medical officer shall obtain from another medical practitioner a report on the condition of the patient in the prescribed form and thereafter shall assess the need for the detention of the patient to be continued; and, if it appears to him that it is necessary in the interests of the health or safety of the patient or for the protection of other persons that the patient should continue to be liable to be detained in hospital, he shall furnish to the managers of the hospital where the patient is liable to be detained and to the Mental Welfare Commission a report to that effect in the prescribed form along with the report first mentioned.

(6) Where a report is duly furnished under subsection (5) of this section, the patient shall be treated as if he had been admitted to the hospital in pursuance of a hospital order (without a

restriction order) made on the date on which the restriction direction ceased to have effect, but the provisions of section 30(5) and (6) and of section 35 of this Act shall apply to him in like manner as they apply to a patient the authority for whose detention in hospital has been renewed in pursuance of subsection (4) of the said section 30.

(7) Subject to subsection (8) of this section, references in this section to the expiration of a person's sentence are references to the expiration of the period during which he would have been liable to be detained in a prison or other institution if the transfer direction had not been given and if he had not forfeited remission of any part of the sentence after his removal in pursuance of the direction.

(8) For the purposes of subsection (2) of section 37 of the Prisons (Scotland) Act 1952 (which subsection provides for discounting from the sentence of certain prisoners periods while they are unlawfully at large) a patient who, having been transferred in pursuance of a transfer direction from any such institution as is referred to in that subsection, is at large, in circumstances in which he is liable to be taken into custody under any provision of this Act, shall be treated as unlawfully at large and absent from that institution.

(9) In this section 'prescribed' means prescribed by regulations made by the Secretary of State.

Part VIII

STATE HOSPITALS

90.—(1) The Secretary of State shall provide such hospitals as appear to him to be necessary for persons subject to detention under this Act who require treatment under conditions of special security on account of their dangerous, violent or criminal propensities.

(2) Hospitals provided by the Secretary of State under this section are in this Act referred to as 'State hospitals'.

91.—(1) Subject to the following provisions of this section, the State hospitals shall be under the control and management of the Secretary of State.

(2) The Secretary of State may by order constitute in accordance with the provisions of Schedule 1 to this Act a committee to manage, on his behalf and subject to such directions as he may give, a State hospital; and a committee so constituted shall be called a State Hospital Management Committee.

(3) The Secretary of State may by order dissolve a State Hospital Management Committee and any such order may contain such provision as he considers necessary or expedient in connection with the dissolution of the Committee and the winding up of its affairs including provision for the transfer of employment of staff, property, rights and liabilities.

(4) A State Hospital Management Committee may—

(*a*) pay to its members such remuneration; and
(*b*) make provision for the payment of such pensions, allowances or gratuities to or in respect of its members,

as the Secretary of State may, with the approval of the Treasury, determine; and such determination may make different provision for different cases or different classes of case.

(5) A State Hospital Management Committee may appoint such officers and servants on such terms as to remuneration and conditions of service as the Secretary of State may, with the approval of the Treasury, determine; and such determination may make different provision for different cases or different classes of case.

(6) Section 79(1) of the National Health Service (Scotland) Act 1978 (which enables the Secretary of State to acquire land for the purposes of that Act) shall have effect as if the reference to the purposes of that Act included a reference to the purposes of this Part of this Act and as if the reference to any hospital vested in the Secretary of State included a reference to any State hospital.

Part XI

MISCELLANEOUS AND GENERAL

118.—(1) If a constable finds in a place to which the public have access a person who appears to him to be suffering from mental disorder and to be in immediate need of care or control, the constable may, if he thinks it necessary to do so in the interests of that person or for the protection of other persons, remove that person to a place of safety within the meaning of the last foregoing section.

(2) A person removed to a place of safety under this section may be detained there for a period not exceeding 72 hours for the purpose of enabling him to be examined by a medical practitioner and of making any necessary arrangements for his treatment or care.

(3) Where a patient is removed as aforesaid, it shall, where practicable, be the duty of the constable who has so removed him without delay to inform some responsible person residing with the patient and the nearest relative of the patient of that removal.

The Mental Health (Northern Ireland) Order 1986

Part I

INTRODUCTORY

Definition of 'mental disorder' and related expressions

3.—(1) In this Order—

'mental disorder' means mental illness, mental handicap and any other disorder or disability of mind;

'mental illness' means a state of mind which affects a person's thinking, perceiving, emotion or judgement to the extent that he requires care or medical treatment in his own interests or the interests of other persons;

'mental handicap' means a state of arrested or incomplete development of mind which includes significant impairment of intelligence and social functioning;

'severe mental handicap' means a state of arrested or incomplete development of mind which includes severe impairment of intelligence and social functioning;

'severe mental impairment' means a state of arrested or incomplete development of mind which includes severe impairment of intelligence and social functioning and is associated with abnormally aggressive or seriously irresponsible conduct on the part of the person concerned.

(2) No person shall be treated under this Order as suffering from mental disorder, or from any form of mental disorder, by reason only of personality disorder, promiscuity or other immoral conduct, sexual deviancy or dependence on alcohol or drugs.

Part II

COMPULSORY ADMISSION TO HOSPITAL AND GUARDIANSHIP

Admission to hospital for assessment

Admission for assessment
4.—(1) A patient may be admitted to a hospital for assessment and there detained for the period allowed by Article 9, in pursuance of an application for admission for assessment (in this Order referred to as 'an application for assessment') made in accordance with this Article.

(2) An application for assessment may be made in respect of a patient on the grounds that—

(a) he is suffering from mental disorder of a nature or degree which warrants his detention in a hospital for assessment (or for assessment followed by medical treatment); and

(b) failure to so detain him would create a substantial likelihood of serious physical harm to himself or to other persons.

(3) An application for assessment shall be founded on and accompanied by a medical recommendation given in accordance with Article 6 by a medical practitioner which shall include—

(a) a statement that, in the opinion of the practitioner, the grounds set out in paragraph (2)(a) and (b) apply to the patient;

(b) such particulars as may be prescribed of the grounds for that opinion so far as it relates to the ground set out in paragraph (2)(a);

(c) a statement of the evidence for that opinion so far as it relates to the ground set out in paragraph (2)(b).

(4) An application for assessment shall—

(a) be made in the prescribed form; and

(b) be addressed to the responsible Board.

Person who may make application for assessment
5.—(1) Subject to the following provisions of this Article, an application for assessment may be made by—

(a) the nearest relative of the patient; or

(b) an approved social worker,

and such a person is, in relation to an application for assessment made by him, referred to in this Order as 'the applicant'.

(2) An application for assessment shall not be made by a person unless he has personally seen the patient not more than 2 days before the date on which the application is made.

(3) An application for assessment shall not be made by an approved social worker except after consultation with the person, if any, appearing to be the nearest relative of the patient unless it appears to the approved social worker that in the circumstances such consultation is not reasonably practicable or would involve unreasonable delay.

(4) Where the nearest relative of a patient notifies an approved social worker or the responsible Board that he objects to an application for assessment being made in respect of the patient then—

(a) no application for assessment in respect of the patient shall be made by an approved social worker unless he has consulted another approved social worker; and

(b) if, after such consultation, an approved social worker makes an application for assessment in respect of the patient, he shall record the objection of the nearest relative on the application for assessment.

(5) Where a patient is admitted to a hospital for assessment in pursuance of an application for assessment made by an approved social worker without consulting the person appearing to be the nearest relative of the patient, it shall be the duty of that social worker to inform the nearest relative of the patient to that effect as soon as may be practicable.

(6) Where a patient is admitted to a hospital for assessment in pursuance of an application for assessment made by his nearest relative, the responsible Board shall as soon as practicable arrange for a social worker to interview the patient and provide the responsible medical officer with a report on his social circumstances.

General provisions as to medical recommendation
6.—The medical recommendation required for the purposes of an application for assessment shall be in the prescribed form and shall satisfy the following requirements, namely—

(a) the recommendation shall be given and signed by a medical practitioner who has personally examined the patient not more than 2 days before the date on which he signs the recommendation;

(b) the recommendation shall, if practicable, be given by the patient's medical practitioner or by a medical practitioner who has previous acquaintance with the patient;

(c) the recommendation shall not, except in a case of urgent necessity, be given by a medical practitioner on the staff of the hospital to which admission is sought;

(d) the recommendation shall not be given by any of the persons described in Schedule 1.

Application for assessment in respect of patient already in hospital

7.—(1) An application for assessment may be made under this Part notwithstanding that a patient is already an inpatient in a hospital who is not liable to be detained there under this Order; and where an application is so made the patient shall be treated for the purposes of this Part as if he had been admitted to the hospital at the time when that application was received by the responsible Board.

(2) If, where a patient is an inpatient in a hospital, but is not liable to be detained there under this Order, it appears to a medical practitioner on the staff of the hospital that an application for assessment ought to be made in respect of the patient, he may furnish to the responsible Board a report in the prescribed form to that effect; and where he does so, the patient may be detained in the hospital for a period not exceeding 48 hours from the time when the report is so furnished.

(3) If, where a patient is receiving treatment for mental disorder as an inpatient in a hospital, but is not liable to be detained there under this Order, it appears to a nurse of the prescribed class—

(*a*) that an application for assessment ought to be made in respect of the patient; and
(*b*) that it is not practicable to secure the immediate attendance of a medical practitioner for the purpose of furnishing a report under paragraph (2),

the nurse may record that fact in the prescribed form; and in that event the patient may be detained in the hospital for a period of 6 hours from the time when that fact is so recorded or until the earlier arrival at the place where the patient is detained of a medical practitioner having power to furnish a report under that paragraph.

(4) A record made under paragraph (3) shall be delivered by the nurse to the responsible Board as soon as possible after it is made.

(5) Where a record is made under paragraph (3) the period mentioned in paragraph (2) shall begin at the time when it is made.

(6) A patient who has been detained in a hospital under paragraph (2) or paragraph (3) shall not be further detained under the same paragraph immediately after the expiry of that period of detention.

(7) The responsible Board shall immediately forward to the Commission a copy of any report furnished to the Board under paragraph (2) and of any record delivered to the Board under paragraph (4).

Detention in hospital for treatment

Detention for treatment

12.—(1) Where, during the period for which a patient is detained for assessment by virtue of Article 9(8), he is examined by a medical practitioner appointed for the purposes of this Part by the Commission and that medical practitioner furnishes to the responsible Board in the prescribed form a report of the examination stating—

(*a*) that, in his opinion, the patient is suffering from mental illness or severe mental impairment of a nature or degree which warrants his detention in hospital for medical treatment; and
(*b*) that, in his opinion, failure to so detain the patient would create a substantial likelihood of serious physical harm to himself or to other persons; and
(*c*) such particulars as may be prescribed of the grounds for his opinion so far as it relates to the matters set out in subparagraph (*a*); and
(*d*) the evidence for his opinion so far as it relates to the matters set out in subparagraph (*b*), specifying whether other methods of dealing with the patient are available and, if so, why they are not appropriate,

that report shall be sufficient authority for the responsible Board to detain the patient in the hospital for medical treatment and the patient may, subject to the provisions of this Order, be so detained for a period not exceeding 6 months beginning with the date of admission, but shall not be so detained for any longer period unless the authority for his detention is renewed under Article 13.

(2) A report under paragraph (1) shall not be given by—

(a) the medical practitioner who gave the medical recommendation on which the application for assessment is founded; or

(b) any of the persons described in Schedule 1.

(3) Where a patient is detained in a hospital for treatment by virtue of a report under paragraph (1), any previous application under this part by virtue of which he was subject to guardianship shall cease to have effect.

(4) The responsible Board shall immediately forward to the Commission a copy of any report furnished to the Board under paragraph (1).

(5) In this Order 'detained for treatment', in relation to a patient, means detained in a hospital for medical treatment by virtue of a report under paragraph (1) or by virtue of a report under Article 13(2), (3) or (5).

Renewal of authority for detention
13.—(1) Authority for the detention of a patient for treatment may, unless the patient has previously been discharged, be renewed under this Article—

(a) from the expiration of the period referred to in Article 12(1), for a further period of 6 months if the provisions of paragraph (2) are complied with;

(b) from the expiration of any period of renewal under subparagraph (a), for a further period of 1 year if the provisions of paragraphs (3) and (4) are complied with;

(c) from the expiration of any period of renewal under subparagraph (b) for a further period of 1 year if the provisions of paragraph (5) are complied with, and so on for periods of 1 year at a time if the provisions of paragraph (5) are complied with in each case.

(2) Within the period of 1 month ending with the day on which a patient who is liable to be detained for treatment would cease under Article 12(1) to be so liable in default of the renewal of the authority for his detention, the responsible medical officer shall examine the patient and where that medical officer furnishes to the responsible Board in the prescribed form a report of the examination stating the opinions, particulars and evidence referred to in Article 12(1)(a), (b), (c) and (d), the authority for the detention of the patient shall, by virtue of the report, be renewed for the further period mentioned in paragraph (1)(a).

(3) Within the period of 2 months ending with the day on which a patient who is liable to be detained by virtue of an authority renewed under paragraph (2) would cease to be so liable in default of the further renewal of that authority, the responsible Board shall arrange for the examination of the patient by two medical practitioners in accordance with paragraph (4) and where those practitioners furnish to the responsible Board in the prescribed form a report of the examination stating the opinions, particulars and evidence referred to in Article 12(1)(a), (b), (c) and (d), the authority for the detention of the patient shall, by virtue of the report, be renewed for the further period mentioned in paragraph (1)(b).

(4) Where the Board arranges for the examination of the patient under paragraph (3)—

(a) it shall give the patient and his nearest relative not less than 14 days' notice in writing of the date of the examination;

(b) the two medical practitioners who carry out the examination shall be appointed for the purposes of this Part by the Commission;

(c) one of the medical practitioners who carry out the examination shall be a person who is not on the staff of the hospital in which the patient is detained and who has not given either the medical recommendation on which the application for assessment in relation to the patient was founded or any medical report in relation to the patient under Article 9 or 12(1);

(d) the report of the examination shall consist of a joint report signed by both medical practitioners.

(5) Within the period of 2 months ending with the day on which a patient who is liable to be detained by virtue of an authority for detention renewed under paragraph (3) or this paragraph would cease to be so liable in default of the further renewal of that authority, the responsible medical officer shall examine the patient and where that medical officer furnishes to the responsible Board in the prescribed form a report of the examination stating the opinions,

particulars and evidence referred to in Article 12(1)(*a*), (*b*), (*c*) and (*d*), the authority for the detention of the patient shall, by virtue of the report, be renewed for a further period mentioned in paragraph (1)(*c*).

(6) Where a report under paragraph (2), (3) or (5) is furnished to the responsible Board, it shall, unless it discharges the patient—

(*a*) cause him and his nearest relative to be informed;

(*b*) forward to the Commission a copy of the report.

Discharge of patient from detention
14.—(1) Subject to the following provisions of this Article, a patient who is for the time being liable to be detained under this Part shall cease to be so liable if an order in writing discharging him from detention is made in respect of him by the responsible medical officer, the responsible Board or his nearest relative.

(2) The responsible medical officer shall make an order under paragraph (1) in respect of a patient liable to be detained under this Part where he is satisfied—

(*a*) that the patient is no longer suffering from mental illness or severe mental impairment of a nature or degree which warrants his detention in hospital for medical treatment; or

(*b*) that, having regard to the care which would be available for the patient if he were discharged, the discharge would not create a substantial likelihood of serious physical harm to himself or to other persons.

(3) The responsible medical officer shall not make an order under paragraph (1) in respect of a patient detained in any special accommodation unless the responsible Board consents to the discharge of the patient.

(4) An order under paragraph (1) in respect of a patient who is liable to be detained under this Part shall not be made by his nearest relative except after giving not less than 72 hours' notice in writing to the responsible Board; and if, within 72 hours after such notice has been given, the responsible medical officer furnishes to that Board a report in writing certifying—

(*a*) that, in the opinion of that officer, the patient is suffering from mental illness or severe mental impairment of a nature or degree which warrants his detention in hospital for medical treatment and that the discharge of the patient would create a substantial likelihood of serious physical harm to himself or to other persons; or

(*b*) that that officer is not satisfied that the patient, if discharged, would receive proper care;

then—

(i) any order under paragraph (1) made by that relative in pursuance of the notice shall be of no effect; and

(ii) a further order for the discharge of the patient shall not be made by that relative during the period of 6 months beginning with the date of the report.

Guardianship

Reception of patients into guardianship
18.—(1) A patient who has attained the age of 16 years may be received into guardianship, for the period allowed by the following provisions of this Part, in pursuance of an application (in this Order referred to as 'a guardianship application') made in accordance with this Article.

(2) A guardianship application may be made in respect of a patient on the grounds that—

(*a*) he is suffering from mental illness or severe mental handicap of a nature or degree which warrants his reception into guardianship under this Article; and

(*b*) it is necessary in the interests of the welfare of the patient that he should be so received.

(3) A guardianship application shall be founded on and accompanied by two medical recommendations and a recommendation by an approved social worker and—

(*a*) each medical recommendation shall be given in accordance with Article 20 by a medical practitioner and shall include—

(i) a statement that, in his opinion, the ground set out in paragraph (2)(*a*) applies in relation to the patient; and

(ii) such particulars as may be prescribed of the grounds for that opinion;

(*b*) the recommendation by the approved social worker shall be in the prescribed form and shall include—

   (i) a statement that, in his opinion, the ground set out in paragraph (2)(*b*) applies in relation to the patient;

   (ii) the reasons for that opinion; and

   (iii) a statement as to whether he is related to the patient and of any pecuniary interest that he may have in the reception of the patient into guardianship.

(4) A guardianship application shall—

(*a*) be made in the prescribed form; and

(*b*) be forwarded to the responsible Board.

(5) The person named as guardian in a guardianship application may be either the responsible Board or, subject to paragraph (6), any other person (including the applicant himself).

(6) A guardianship application in which a person other than the responsible Board is named as guardian—

(*a*) shall be accompanied by a statement in writing by that person that he is willing to act as guardian; and

(*b*) shall be of no effect unless it is accepted on behalf of that person by the responsible Board.

(7) A guardianship application and any medical recommendation given for the purposes of such an application may describe the patient as suffering from mental illness or severe mental handicap or in both those ways, but the application shall not be of any effect unless each of the medical recommendations describes the patient as suffering from the same form of mental disorder, whether or not either describes the patient as also suffering from another form.

Person who may make guardianship application
19.—(1) Subject to the following provisions of this Article, a guardianship application may be made by—

(*a*) the nearest relative of the patient; or

(*b*) an approved social worker,

and such a person is, in relation to a guardianship application made by him, referred to in this Order as 'the applicant'.

(2) A guardianship application shall not be made by a person unless he has personally seen the patient not more than 14 days before the date on which the application is made.

(3) A guardianship application shall not be made by an approved social worker except after consultation with the person, if any, appearing to be the nearest relative of the patient unless it appears to the approved social worker that in the circumstances such consultation is not reasonably practicable or would involve unreasonable delay.

(4) A guardianship application shall not be made by an approved social worker if he gave the recommendation under Article 18(3)(*b*) on which the application is founded.

(5) Where the nearest relative of a patient notifies an approved social worker or the responsible Board that he objects to a guardianship application being made in respect of the patient, then—

(*a*) no guardianship application in respect of the patient shall be made by an approved social worker unless he has consulted another approved social worker (not being the social worker who gave the recommendation under Article 18(3)(*b*) on which the application is founded); and

(*b*) if, after such consultation, an approved social worker makes a guardianship application in respect of the patient, he shall record the objection of the nearest relative on the guardianship application.

(6) Where a patient is received into guardianship in pursuance of a guardianship application made by an approved social worker without consulting the person appearing to be the nearest relative of the patient, it shall be the duty of that social worker to inform the nearest relative of the patient to that effect as soon as may be practicable.

General provisions as to medical recommendations

20.—(1) The medical recommendations required for the purposes of a guardianship application shall be in the prescribed form and shall satisfy the following requirements, namely—

    (a) each recommendation shall be given and signed by a medical practitioner who has personally examined the patient not more than 2 days before the date on which he signs the recommendation;

    (b) where the medical practitioners have examined the patient separately, not more than 7 days must have elapsed between the days on which the separate examinations took place;

    (c) one recommendation shall be given by a medical practitioner appointed by the Commission for the purposes of this Part, and the other shall, if practicable, be given by the patient's medical practitioner or by a medical practitioner who has previous acquaintance with the patient;

    (d) neither recommendation shall be given by—

        (i) the person named as guardian in the guardianship application; or

        (ii) any of the persons described in Schedule 1.

(2) A guardianship application shall be sufficient if the medical recommendations on which it is founded are given either as separate recommendations, each signed by a medical practitioner, or as a joint recommendation signed by two medical practitioners.

Effect of guardianship application

22.—(1) Where a guardianship application, duly made in accordance with the provisions of this Part and forwarded to the responsible Board within the period allowed by paragraph (2), is accepted by that Board, the application shall, subject to regulations, confer on the Board or person named in the application as guardian, to the exclusion of any other person—

    (a) the power to require the patient to reside at a place specified by the Board or person named as guardian;

    (b) the power to require the patient to attend at places and times so specified for the purpose of medical treatment, occupation, education or training;

    (c) the power to require access to the patient to be given at any place where the patient is residing to any medical practitioner, approved social worker or other person so specified.

(2) The period within which a guardianship application is required for the purposes of this Article to be forwarded to the responsible Board is the period of 7 days beginning with the date on which the patient was last examined by a medical practitioner before giving a medical recommendation for the purposes of the application.

(3) A patient received into guardianship in pursuance of a guardianship application may, subject to the provisions of this Order, be kept under guardianship for a period not exceeding 6 months beginning with the day on which the guardianship application was accepted, but shall not be so kept for any longer period unless the authority for his guardianship is renewed under Article 23.

(4) Where a patient is received into guardianship in pursuance of a guardianship application—

    (a) any previous application under this Part by virtue of which he was subject to guardianship shall cease to have effect;

    (b) if he was previously liable to be detained for assessment or for treatment under this Part, he shall cease to be so liable.

(5) Where a patient is received into guardianship in pursuance of a guardianship application the responsible Board shall immediately forward to the Commission a copy of the guardianship application and of the medical recommendations and the recommendation by an approved social worker on which it is founded.

Part III

PATIENTS CONCERNED IN CRIMINAL PROCEEDINGS OR UNDER SENTENCE

Remands to hospital

Remand to hospital for report on accused's mental condition
42.—(1) Subject to the provisions of this Article, the Crown Court or a court of summary jurisdiction may remand an accused person into the care of the Department for admission to hospital for a report on his mental condition.

(2) For the purposes of this Article an accused person is—

(a) in relation to the Crown Court, any person who is awaiting trial before the court for an offence punishable with imprisonment or who has been arraigned before the court for such an offence and has not yet been sentenced or otherwise dealt with for the offence on which he has been arraigned;

(b) in relation to a court of summary jurisdiction any person who has been convicted by the court of an offence punishable on summary conviction with imprisonment and any person charged with such an offence if the court is satisfied that he did the act or made the omission charged or if he has consented to the exercise by the court of the powers conferred by this Article.

(3) Subject to paragraph (4), the powers conferred by this Article may be exercised if—

(a) the court is satisfied, on the oral evidence of a medical practitioner appointed for the purposes of Part II by the Commission, that there is reason to suspect that the accused person is suffering from mental illness or severe mental impairment; and

(b) the court is of the opinion that it would be impracticable for a report on his mental condition to be made if he were remanded on bail;

but those powers shall not be exercised by the Crown Court in respect of a person who has been convicted before the court if the sentence for the offence of which he has been convicted is fixed by law.

(4) The court shall not remand an accused person under this Article unless an opportunity has been given to the Department to make representations to the court concerning the remand.

(5) Where a court has remanded an accused person under this Article, it may further remand him if it appears to the court, on the written or oral evidence of the medical practitioner responsible for making the report, that a further remand is necessary for completing the assessment of the accused person's mental condition.

(6) The power of further remanding an accused person under this Article may be exercised by the court without his being brought before the court if he is represented by counsel or a solicitor and his counsel or solicitor is given an opportunity of being heard.

(7) An accused person shall not be remanded or further remanded under this Article for more than 28 days at a time or for more than 12 weeks in all; and the court may at any time terminate the remand if it appears to the court that it is appropriate to do so.

(8) An accused person remanded under this Article shall be entitled to obtain at his own expense an independent report on his mental condition from a medical practitioner chosen by him and to apply to the court on the basis of it for his remand to be terminated under paragraph (7).

(9) Where an accused person is remanded under this Article—

(a) it shall be the duty of the Department to designate the hospital to which the accused person is to be admitted;

(b) the court may, pending his admission to hospital, give directions for his conveyance to and detention in a place of safety;

(c) a constable or any other person directed to do so by the court shall convey the accused person to the hospital designated by the Department within the period of 7 days beginning with the date of the remand; and

(d) the Board administering that hospital shall admit him within that period and thereafter detain him in accordance with the provisions of this Article.

(10) If an accused person absconds from a hospital to which he has been remanded under this Article, or while being conveyed to or from that hospital, he may be arrested without warrant by any constable and shall, after being arrested, be brought as soon as practicable before the court that remanded him; and the court may thereupon terminate the remand and deal with him in any way in which it would have dealt with him if he had not been remanded under this Article.

Remand to hospital for treatment
43.—(1) Subject to the provisions of this Article, the Crown Court may, instead of remanding an accused person in custody, remand him into the care of the Department for admission to hospital if satisfied, on the oral evidence of a medical practitioner appointed for the purposes of Part II by the Commission and on the written or oral evidence of one other medical practitioner, that he is suffering from mental illness or severe mental impairment of a nature or degree which warrants his detention in hospital for medical treatment.

(2) For the purposes of this Article an accused person is any person who is in custody awaiting trial before the Crown Court for an offence punishable with imprisonment other than an offence the sentence for which is fixed by law, or who at any time before sentence is in custody in the course of a trial before that court for such an offence.

(3) The court shall not remand an accused person under this Article unless an opportunity has been given to the Department to make representations to the court concerning the remand.

(4) Where a court has remanded an accused person under this Article, it may further remand him if it appears to the court, on the written or oral evidence of the responsible medical officer, that a further remand is warranted.

(5) Paragraphs (6) to (10) of Article 42 shall have effect in relation to a remand under this Article as they have effect in relation to a remand under that Article.

Hospital and guardianship orders

Powers of courts to order hospital admission or guardianship
44.—(1) Where a person is convicted before the Crown Court of an offence punishable with imprisonment other than an offence the sentence for which is fixed by law, or is convicted by a court of summary jurisdiction of an offence punishable on summary conviction with imprisonment, then—

(a) if the conditions mentioned in paragraph (2) are satisfied, the court may by order (in this Order referred to as a 'hospital order') commit him to the care of the Department for admission to hospital; or
(b) if the conditions mentioned in paragraph (3) are satisfied, the court may by order (in this Order referred to as a 'guardianship order') place him under the guardianship of a Board or of such other person approved by a Board as may be specified in the order.

(2) The conditions referred to in paragraph (1)(a) are that—
(a) the court is satisfied on the oral evidence of a medical practitioner appointed for the purposes of Part II by the Commission and on the written or oral evidence of one other medical practitioner that the offender is suffering from mental illness or severe mental impairment of a nature or degree which warrants his detention in hospital for medical treatment; and
(b) the court is of opinion, having regard to all the circumstances, including the nature of the offence and the character and antecedents of the offender, and to the other available methods of dealing with him, that the most suitable means of dealing with the case is by means of a hospital order.

(3) The conditions referred to in paragraph (1)(b) are that—
(a) the offender has attained the age of 16 years;
(b) the court is satisfied on the oral evidence of a medical practitioner appointed for the purposes of Part II by the Commission and on the written or oral evidence of one other medical practitioner that the offender is suffering from mental illness or severe mental handicap of a nature or degree which warrants his reception into guardianship;
(c) the court is satisfied on the written or oral evidence of an approved social worker that it

is necessary in the interests of the welfare of the patient that he should be received into guardianship; and

(*d*) the court is of opinion, having regard to all the circumstances, including the nature of the offence and the character and antecedents of the offender, and to the other available methods of dealing with him, that the most suitable means of dealing with the case is by means of a guardianship order.

(4) Where a person is charged before a court of summary jurisdiction with any act or omission as an offence and the court would have power, on convicting him of that offence, to make an order under paragraph (1) then, if the court is satisfied that the accused did the act or made the omission charged, the court may, if it thinks fit, make such an order without convicting him.

(5) A hospital order shall not be made under this Article by a court unless an opportunity has been given to the Department to make representations to the court concerning the making of such an order.

(6) A guardianship order placing a patient under the guardianship of any person shall not be made under this Article unless the court is satisfied that that person is willing to receive the patient into guardianship.

(7) A hospital order or guardianship order shall specify the form or forms of mental disorder referred to in subparagraph (*a*) of paragraph (2) or subparagraph (*b*) of paragraph (3) from which, upon the evidence taken into account under that subparagraph, the offender is found by the court to be suffering; and no such order shall be made unless the offender is described by each of the practitioners whose evidence is taken into account under that subparagraph as suffering from the same form of mental disorder, whether or not he is also described by either of them as suffering from another form.

(8) Where an order is made under this Article, the court shall not pass sentence of imprisonment or impose a fine or make a probation order in respect of the offence, but may make any other order which the court has power to make apart from this Article; and for the purposes of this paragraph 'sentence of imprisonment' includes any sentence or order for detention, including an order under section 74(1)(*a*) or (*e*) of the Children and Young Persons Act (Northern Ireland) 1968 sending a person to a training school or committing him to custody in a remand home.

Interim hospital orders
45.—(1) Where a person is convicted before the Crown Court of an offence punishable with imprisonment other than an offence the sentence for which is fixed by law, or is convicted by a court of summary jurisdiction of an offence punishable on summary conviction with imprisonment, and the court before or by which he is convicted is satisfied, on the oral evidence of a medical practitioner appointed for the purposes of Part II by the Commission and on the written or oral evidence of one other medical practitioner—

(*a*) that the offender is suffering from mental illness or severe mental impairment; and
(*b*) that there is reason to suppose that the mental disorder from which the offender is suffering is such that it may warrant a hospital order being made in his case,

the court may, before making a hospital order or dealing with him in some other way, make an order (in this Order referred to as 'an interim hospital order') committing him to the care of the Department for admission to hospital and detention there in accordance with this Article.

(2) In the case of an offender who is subject to an interim hospital order the court may make a hospital order without his being brought before the court if he is represented by counsel or a solicitor and his counsel or solicitor is given an opportunity of being heard.

(3) An interim hospital order shall not be made under this Article by a court unless an opportunity has been given to the Department to make representations to the court concerning the making of such an order.

(4) An interim hospital order—

(*a*) shall be in force for such period, not exceeding 12 weeks, as the court may specify when making the order; but
(*b*) may be renewed for further periods of not more than 28 days at a time if it appears to the

court, on the written or oral evidence of the responsible medical officer, that the continuation of the order is warranted;

but no such order shall continue in force for more than 6 months in all and the court shall terminate the order if it makes a hospital order in respect of the offender or decides after considering the written or oral evidence of the responsible medical officer to deal with the offender in some other way.

(5) The power of renewing an interim hospital order may be exercised without the offender being brought before the court if he is represented by counsel or a solicitor and his counsel or solicitor is given an opportunity of being heard.

(6) If an offender absconds from a hospital in which he is detained in pursuance of an interim hospital order, or while being conveyed to or from such a hospital, he may be arrested without warrant by a constable and shall, after being arrested, be brought as soon as practicable before the court that made the order; and the court may thereupon terminate the order and deal with him in any way in which it could have dealt with him if no such order had been made.

Restriction orders

Powers of court to restrict discharge from hospital
47.—(1) Where—

- (a) a court makes a hospital order in respect of any person; and
- (b) it appears to the court, having regard to the nature of the offence, the antecedents of the person and the risk of his committing further offences if set at large, that it is necessary for the protection of the public from serious harm to do so,

the court may, subject to paragraphs (2) to (5), further order that the person shall be subject to the special restrictions set out in this Article, either without limit of time or during such period as may be specified in the order; and an order under this Article shall be known as 'a restriction order'.

(2) The special restrictions applicable to a patient in respect of whom a restriction order is in force are as follows, that is to say—

- (a) none of the provisions of Part II relating to the duration, renewal and expiration of authority for the detention of patients shall apply, and the patient shall continue to be liable to be detained by virtue of the relevant hospital order until he is absolutely discharged under Article 48, 78, 79 or 80;
- (b) no application or reference shall be made to the Review Tribunal in respect of the patient under Articles 71 to 74;
- (c) the following powers shall be exercisable only with the consent of the Secretary of State, namely—
  - (i) power to grant leave of absence to the patient under Article 15;
  - (ii) power to transfer the patient under Article 28;
    and if leave of absence is granted under Article 15 the power to recall the patient shall be vested in the Secretary of State as well as in the responsible medical officer;
- (d) the power of the Secretary of State to recall the patient under Article 15 and the power to take the patient into custody and return him under Article 29 may be exercised at any time;

and in relation to any such patient Article 46(6)(a) shall have effect as if it referred to Part II of Schedule 2 instead of Part I of that Schedule.

(3) A hospital order shall not cease to have effect under Article 46(7) if a restriction order in respect of the patient is in force at the material time.

(4) Where a restriction order in respect of a patient ceases to have effect while the relevant hospital order continues in force, Article 46 and Part I of Schedule 2 shall apply to the patient as if he had been admitted to the hospital in which he is then liable to be detained in pursuance of a hospital order (without a restriction order) made on the date on which the restriction order ceased to have effect.

(5) While a person is subject to a restriction order the responsible medical officer shall at such intervals (not exceeding 1 year) as the Secretary of State may direct examine and report to the Secretary of State on that person; and every report shall contain such particulars as the Secretary of State may require.

Powers of Secretary of State in respect of patients subject to restriction orders

48.—(1) If the Secretary of State is satisfied that in the case of any patient a restriction order is no longer required for the protection of the public from serious harm he may direct that the patient shall cease to be subject to the special restrictions set out in Article 47(2); and where the Secretary of State so directs, the restriction order shall cease to have effect, and Article 47(4) shall have effect accordingly.

(2) At any time while a restriction order is in force in respect of a patient, the Secretary of State may, if he thinks fit, by warrant discharge the patient from hospital, either absolutely or subject to conditions; and where a patient is absolutely discharged under this paragraph, he shall thereupon cease to be liable to be detained by virtue of the relevant hospital order, and accordingly the restriction order shall cease to have effect.

(3) The Secretary of State may at any time during the continuance in force of a restriction order in respect of a patient who has been conditionally discharged under paragraph (2) by warrant recall the patient to such hospital as may be specified in the warrant; and thereupon—

(*a*) if the hospital so specified is not the hospital from which the patient was conditionally discharged, subparagraph (*b*) of paragraph (2) of Article 46 shall have effect as if the hospital specified in the warrant were substituted for the hospital designated by the Department under subparagraph (*a*) of that paragraph; and

(*b*) in any case, the patient shall be treated for the purposes of Article 29 as if he had absented himself without leave from the hospital specified in the warrant, and if the restriction order was made for a specified period, that period shall in any event be deemed not to have expired until the patient returns to hospital or is returned to hospital under that Article.

(4) If a restriction order in respect of a patient ceases to have effect after the patient has been conditionally discharged under paragraph (2), the patient shall, unless previously recalled under paragraph (3), be deemed to be absolutely discharged on the date when the order ceases to have effect, and accordingly shall cease to be liable to be detained by virtue of the relevant hospital order.

(5) The Secretary of State may, if satisfied that the attendance at any place in Northern Ireland of a patient who is subject to a restriction order is desirable in the interests of justice or for the purposes of any public inquiry, direct him to be taken to that place; and where a patient is directed under this paragraph to be taken to any place he shall, unless the Secretary of State otherwise directs, be kept in custody while being so taken, while at that place and while being taken back to the hospital in which he is liable to be detained.

Procedure during trial on indictment

Procedure in relation to unfitness to be tried

49.—(1) The following provisions of this Article apply where, on the trial of a person charged on indictment with the commission of an offence, the question arises (at the instance of the defence or otherwise) whether the accused is unfit to be tried (in this Article referred to as 'the question of fitness to be tried').

(2) Subject to paragraph (3), the question of fitness to be tried shall be determined as soon as it arises.

(3) If, having regard to the nature of the supposed mental condition of the accused, the court is of opinion that it is expedient so to do and in the interests of the accused, the court may—

(*a*) postpone consideration of the question of fitness to be tried until any time up to the opening of the case for the defence; and

(*b*) if, before the said question falls to be determined, the jury returns a verdict of acquittal on the count or each of the counts on which the accused is being tried, that question shall not be determined.

(4) The question of fitness to be tried shall be determined by a jury; and—

(a) where it falls to be determined on the arraignment of the accused, then if the trial proceeds the accused shall be tried by a jury other than that which determined that question;

(b) where it falls to be determinied at any late time it shall be determined by a separate jury or by the jury by which the accused is being tried, as the court may direct.

(5) Where in accordance with paragraphs (2) to (4) it is determined that the accused is unfit to be tried—

(a) the court shall direct a finding to that effect to be recorded; and

(b) the trial shall not proceed or, as the case may be, proceed further.

(6) Where a court has directed that a finding be recorded in pursuance of paragraph (5)(a), the court shall order that the person to whom the finding relates shall be admitted to hospital.

(7) An order under paragraph (6) shall have the same effect as a hospital order together with a restriction order made without limitation of time.

(8) Where the Secretary of State is notified by the responsible medical officer that a person detained in a hospital by virtue of an order under paragraph (6) no longer requires treatment for mental disorder, the Secretary of State may remit that person to prison or to a remand centre or remand home for trial by the Crown Court at the place where, but for the order, he would have been tried, and on his arrival at the prison, remand centre or remand home the order under paragraph (6) shall cease to have effect.

(9) In this Article and Article 51(6) 'unfit to be tried' includes unfit to plead.

Procedure in relation to finding of insanity
50.—(1) Where upon the trial on indictment of any person charged with the commission of an offence—

(a) evidence is given that the person charged was an insane person at the time the offence was committed; and

(b) the jury finds that although the person charged did the act or made the omission charged, he was an insane person at that time,

the court shall direct a finding to be recorded to the effect that the person is not guilty of the offence charged on the ground of insanity.

(2) Where a court has directed that a finding be recorded in pursuance of paragraph (1), the court shall order that the person to whom the finding relates shall be admitted to hospital.

(3) An order under paragraph (2) shall have the same effect as a hospital order together with a restriction order made without limitation of time.

(4) In this Article 'insane person' and 'insanity' have the meanings assigned by section 1 of the Criminal Justice Act (Northern Ireland) 1966.

Transfer to hospital of prisoners, etc.

Removal to hospital of persons serving sentences of imprisonment, etc.
53.—(1) If in the case of a person serving a sentence of imprisonment, the Secretary of State is satisfied by written reports from at least two medical practitioners, one of whom is a medical practitioner appointed for the purposes of Part II by the Commission—

(a) that the person is suffering from mental illness or severe mental impairment; and

(b) that the mental disorder from which the person is suffering is of a nature or degree which warrants his detention in hospital for medical treatment;

the Secretary of State may, if he is of opinion, having regard to the public interest and all the circumstances, that it is expedient to do so, by warrant direct that that person be admitted to hospital.

(2) A direction under this Article (in this Order referred to as a 'transfer direction') shall cease to have effect at the expiration of the period of 14 days beginning with the date on which it is given, unless within that period the person with respect to whom it was given has been received into hospital.

(3) A transfer direction with respect to any person shall have the same effect as a hospital order made in his case.

(4) A transfer direction shall specify the form or forms of mental disorder referred to in subparagraph (a) of paragraph (1) from which, upon the reports taken into account under that paragraph, the patient is found by the Secretary of State to be suffering; and no such direction shall be given unless the patient is described in each of those reports as suffering from the same form of mental disorder, whether or not he is also described in either of them as suffering from another form.

(5) References in this Part to a person serving a sentence of imprisonment include references—

(a) to a person detained in pursuance of any sentence or order for detention made by a court in criminal proceedings, including an order under section 74(1)(a) or (e) of the Children and Young Persons Act (Northern Ireland) 1968 sending a person to a training school or committing him to custody in a remand home but not including an order under any statutory provision to which Article 52 applies;

(b) to a person committed to custody for failure to comply with an order to enter into a recognizance to keep the peace or to be of good behaviour or both; and

(c) to a person committed by a court to a prison in default of payment of any sum adjudged to be paid on his conviction.

Removal to hospital of other prisoners
54.—(1) If in the case of a person to whom this Article applies the Secretary of State is satisfied by the same reports as are required for the purposes of Article 53—

(a) that the person is suffering from mental illness or severe mental impairment; and

(b) that the mental disorder from which the person is suffering is of a nature or degree which warrants his detention in hospital for medical treatment; and

(c) that the person is in urgent need of such treatment,

the Secretary of State shall have the same power of giving a transfer direction in respect of him under that Article as if he were serving a sentence of imprisonment.

(2) This Article applies to the following persons—

(a) persons detained in a prison or remand centre, not being persons serving a sentence of imprisonment or persons falling within the following subparagraphs of this paragraph;

(b) persons remanded in custody by a magistrates' court;

(c) civil prisoners, that is to say, persons committed by a court to prison for a limited term who are not persons falling to be dealt with under Article 53;

(d) persons detained under the Immigration Act 1971.

(3) Paragraphs (2) to (4) of Article 53 shall apply for the purposes of this Article and of any transfer direction given by virtue of this Article as they apply for the purposes of that Article and of any transfer direction given thereunder.

Restriction on discharge of prisoners removed to hospital
55.—(1) Where a transfer direction is given in respect of any person, the Secretary of State may, if he thinks fit, by warrant further direct that that person shall be subject to the special restrictions set out in Article 47; and where the Secretary of State gives a transfer direction in respect of any such person as is mentioned in subparagraph (a) or (b) of Article 54(2), he shall also give a direction under this Article applying those restrictions to him.

(2) A direction under this Article (in this Order referred to as a 'restriction direction') shall have the same effect as a restriction order made under Article 47.

Part VI

THE MENTAL HEALTH COMMISSION FOR NORTHERN IRELAND

Establishment of Mental Health Commission for Northern Ireland
85.—(1) There shall be established a body to be called the Mental Health Commission for Northern Ireland (in this Order referred to as 'the Commission').

(2) The Commission shall exercise—

(*a*) the functions conferred on it by this Order; and

(*b*) such other functions relating to or connected with mental health as the Department may by order prescribe.

(3) Schedule 4 shall have effect in relation to the Commission.

Functions of the Commission

86.—(1) It shall be the duty of the Commission to keep under review the care and treatment of patients, including (without prejudice to the generality of the foregoing) the exercise of the powers and the discharge of the duties conferred or imposed by this Order.

(2) In the exercise of its functions under paragraph (1) it shall be the duty of the Commission—

(*a*) to make inquiry into any case where it appears to the Commission that there may be ill-treatment, deficiency in care or treatment, or improper detention in hospital or reception into guardianship of any patient, or where the property of any patient may, by reason of his mental disorder, be exposed to loss or damage;

(*b*) as often as the Commission thinks appropriate to visit and interview in private patients who are liable to be detained in hospital under this Order;

(*c*) to bring to the attention of the Department, the Secretary of State, a Board or the person carrying on a private hospital, home for persons in need, voluntary home or nursing home the facts of any case in which in the opinion of the Commission it is desirable for the Department, the Secretary of State, the Board or that person to exercise any of their functions to secure the welfare of any patient by—

   (i) preventing his ill-treatment;

   (ii) remedying any deficiency in his care or treatment

   (iii) terminating his improper detention in hospital or reception into guardianship; or

   (iv) preventing or redressing loss or damage to his property;

(*d*) to advise the Department, the Secretary of State, a Board or any body established under a statutory provision on any matter arising out of this Order which has been referred to the Commission by the Department, the Secretary of State, the Board or the body, as the case may be;

(*e*) to bring to the attention of the Department, the Secretary of State, a Board or any other body or person any matter concerning the welfare of patients which the Commission considers ought to be brought to their attention.

(3) In the exercise of its functions under paragraph (1) the Commission may—

(*a*) where it thinks fit, refer to the Review Tribunal the case of any patient who is liable to be detained in hospital or subject to guardianship under this Order;

(*b*) at any reasonable time visit, interview and medically examine in private any patient in a hospital, private hospital, home for persons in need, voluntary home or nursing home or any person subject to guardianship under this Order;

(*c*) require the production of and inspect any records relating to the detention or treatment of any person who is or has been a patient in a hospital, private hospital, home for persons in need, voluntary home or nursing home or relating to any person who is or has been subject to guardianship under this Order.

(4) Schedule 8 to the Health and Personal Social Services (Northern Ireland) Order 1972 shall have effect in relation to any inquiry under paragraph (2)(*a*) as it has effect in relation to any inquiry under Article 54 of that Order, but with the omission of paragraphs 1, 2 and 6 of that Schedule and the substitution for references to the person appointed to hold the inquiry of references to the Commission.

(5) It shall be the duty of any person carrying on a home for persons in need, a voluntary home or a nursing home and of the guardian of any person subject to guardianship under this Order to afford the Commission all facilities necessary to enable it to carry out its functions in respect of any patient.

(6) Where in the exercise of its functions under this Article the Commission has advised any body or person on any matter or brought any case or matter to the attention of any body or

person, the Commission may by notice in writing addressed to that body or person require that body or person, within such reasonable period as the Commission may specify in the notice, to provide to the Commission such information concerning the steps taken or to be taken by that body or person in relation to that case or matter as the Commission may so specify; and it shall be the duty of every body or person on whom a notice is served under this paragraph to comply with the requirements of that notice.

(7) Paragraph (6) does not apply to the Review Tribunal.

(8) In this Article 'voluntary home' has the meaning assigned to it by secton 126 of the Children and Young Persons Act (Northern Ireland) 1968.

Appendix 2
Code of Practice for the Mental Health Act 1983

This appendix is an edited precis of the Code of Practice for the Mental Health Act 1983 of England and Wales. The text has been changed in places and important sections have been omitted. It is given to illustrate how ethical and technical problems in mental health law might be tackled. The reader is asked to consult it merely for its principles and general thrust. This appendix should *not* be used for legal or administrative purposes. The Code itself should always be consulted at source by practitioners who are uncertain about particular points. The full Code is available from HMSO, London, and enquiries about it can be directed to the Department of Health, PHS5, Wellington House, 133–55 Waterloo Road, London SE1 8UG, UK. Extracts quoted directly are Crown copyright and are reproduced with the permission of the Controller of Her Majesty's Stationery Office.

General Principles

1.1 The Act does not impose a legal duty to comply with the Code, but failure to follow the Code could be referred to in evidence in legal proceedings.

Assessment

2.2 Doctors and approved social workers must recognize that both have specific roles to play in assessment, and should arrive at their own independent decisions.

2.3 The decision *not* to apply for admission under the Act should be clearly thought through, and must be supported, where necessary, by an alternative framework of care and/or treatment.

2.6 In judging whether compulsory admission is appropriate, those concerned must consider not only the health and safety of the patient, but also—

the patient's wishes;
the social circumstances;
the cultural background;
the nature of the disorder;
what may be known by relatives and friends;
other forms of care including informal admission and outpatient treatment;
the needs of the patient's family;
the need to protect others from the patient;
the long-term impact of compulsory admission;
the family burden imposed by not admitting;
the appropriateness of guardianship.

2.7 When the patient is willing to be admitted informally, this should be arranged except that compulsory admission may be considered—

a. where there is a strong likelihood that the patient will change his mind;
b. where the patient, although willing to be admitted, is not willing to accept the treatment proposed.

2.8 In considering 'protection of others', it is essential to take into account—

reliable evidence of risk to others;
any relevant details of patient's medical history;
the degree of risk and its nature;
the willingness and ability of others to cope with the risk.

2.9   The assessment of a patient may legitimately involve consideration of any prognosis of future deterioration of his mental health. Factors to be considered are—

> the reliability of the evidence;
> the views of the patient, his relatives and friends;
> the impact of future deterioration on relatives and friends;
> whether there are other means of coping with the deterioration.

2.10   The approved social worker (ASW) has overall responsibility for co-ordinating the process of assessment and implementation of any decision to compulsorily admit a patient.

2.11   The ASW must interview the patient in a 'suitable manner', i.e. calling on interpreters, or others with the appropriate communication skills where possible (bearing in mind the disadvantages of a relative undertaking an intermediary role). Where the patient is unable or unwilling to speak, then the assessment has to be based on other available information. Where the patient is sedated, the ASW must consult with the doctor and either wait till the effects have abated or, in urgent cases, use all other available information.

2.18   The doctor should—

> a. decide whether the patient is suffering from mental disorder and assess its seriousness;
> b. consider the factors set out in 2.6 and discuss them with the applicant and the other doctor involved;
> c. specifically address the legal criteria for admission;
> d. ensure that a hospital bed is available.

2.25   The second medical recommendation should be provided by a doctor with previous acquaintance of the patient (usually the GP) except in exceptional circumstances.

2.26   Most compulsory admissions require prompt action. However the ASW does have up to 14 days from the date of seeing the patient to make an application for assessment or treatment.

2.27   The ASW must discuss with the patient's nearest relative the reasons for *not* making an application and advise the nearest relative of *his* rights to apply.

2.28   Where disagreements between professionals occur, each should ensure that they set out to each other their view of the salient features of the case and their conclusions.

2.29   Where there is an unresolved dispute about an application for admission, it is essential that the professionals do not abandon the patient and the family. An agreed alternative plan should be recorded in writing.

2.30   The ASW is the preferred applicant.

Part III of the Act

3.1   Everyone subject to criminal proceedings has the same right to psychiatric assessment and treatment as other citizens. Everyone in prison or police custody in need of medical treatment for mental disorder which can only be satisfactorily given in a hospital should be admitted to such a hospital.

3.2   All professionals involved in the operation of Part III of the Act should remember—

> a. the vulnerability of people in custody, especially the risk of self-destructive behaviour;
> b. that a prison hospital is not a hospital within the meaning of the MHA 1983.

3.6 Where a doctor is asked to provide an opinion in relation to a possible admission to hospital under Part III of the Act, the doctor should explain to the patient at whose request he is preparing the report and its implications for confidentiality. If the doctor has previously treated the patient, it may be desirable for him to prepare the report. One of the doctors asked to prepare a report should have access to appropriate hospital beds. The doctor (irrespective of who has instructed him) should always have available social, prison, and other relevant records and reports. If the doctor is not given any of this information, he should state clearly that it is lacking.

3.7 Where possible, the doctor should make contact with independent informants.

3.8 It is desirable for a nurse to accompany the assessing doctor where admission to hospital is likely to be recommended. The doctor should make contact with the social worker or probation officer who is preparing a social enquiry report, especially when psychiatric treatment as a condition of a probation order is suggested.

3.9 The doctor should not in his report anticipate the outcome of proceedings to establish guilt or innocence. It is sometimes appropriate to advise that a further report should be submitted to court in the event of conviction and before sentencing. In any report prepared prior to conviction, the doctor may give advice on the appropriate disposal of the patient in the event that he is convicted.

3.10 When the doctor has concluded that the defendant needs treatment in hospital, but there is no facility available, the task is not complete until—

    a. the details of the type of provision required have been forwarded in writing to the district health authority;
    b. in suitable cases, contact has been made with the local NHS forensic psychiatrist.

3.12 The need for inpatient treatment for a prisoner must be identified and acted on swiftly.

3.13 The transfer of a prisoner to hospital under the MHA 1983 should not be delayed until close to his release date. (All relevant information should be transferred with him, 7.1.)

Private Practice

4.1 Where an individual is to be admitted to a mental nursing home or as a private patient to a hospital, neither medical recommendation can be provided by a doctor on the staff of the hospital or mental nursing home. No medical recommendation can be provided by a doctor who receives or has an interest in the receipt of any payment made on account of the maintenance of the patient.

Section 2 or Section 3?

5.2 Section 2 pointers.

    a. The diagnosis and prognosis of a patient's condition is unclear.
    b. A judgement is needed whether the patient will accept treatment on a voluntary basis following admission.
    c. A judgement is needed about the effectiveness of treatment.
    e. The patient has not previously been admitted to hospital.

5.3 Section 3 pointers.

    a. The patient has previously been admitted, assessed, and treated in the recent past.
    b. The patient is under section 2, needs further treatment, but is unwilling to remain in hospital for it.

5.4 Decisions should *not* be influenced by—

    a. wanting to avoid consulting the nearest relative;
    b. the fact that treatment will last less than 28 days;

    c. the fact that a patient detained under section 2 will get quicker access to a Mental Health Review Tribunal (MHRT) than one detained under section 3.

Section 136

10.1   Good practice depends upon the local social services, the district health authority and the police authority establishing a clear policy.

10.8   Section 136 is not an emergency admission order. It enables an individual to be detained for assessment and for any necessary arrangements for treatment and care to be made; when these have been completed, the authority to detain the patient ceases.

10.14 The person must be seen by *both* the doctor and the ASW.

10.18 Where compulsory admission is indicated, and where a hospital is the place of safety, the person should be admitted either under section 2 or section 3. Persons detained under section 136 should not find that their detention continues under section 5(2) or 5(4).

Guardianship

13.1   The purpose of guardianship is to enable patients to receive community care where it cannot be provided without the use of compulsory powers.

13.2   It should be actively considered as an alternative both to admission to hospital and to continuing hospital care.

13.5   Effective guardianship includes the following components:

    a. a recognition by the patient of 'authority' of the guardian;
    b. the guardian should be willing to 'advocate' on behalf of the patient;
    c. readily available support from the local authority for the guardian;
    d. an appropriate place of residence;
    e. access to necessary day care, education and training facilities.

13.8   Guardianship does not restrict the patient's access to hospital services on a voluntary basis, the guardianship order can also remain in force if the patient is admitted to hospital under sections 2 or 4, but it does not remain in force if the patient is admitted under section 3.

13.10 As a potentially useful alternative to hospital orders, courts are empowered to make guardianship orders under section 37. Guardianship orders may be particularly suitable in helping to meet the needs of mentally impaired offenders.

Information

14.2   Section 132 requires hospital managers to ensure that *all* detained patients are given both specific and particular information about their care, treatment, and legal position, and also give it in writing to the patient's nearest relative (unless the patient objects).

14.12 Particular information:

Consent to treatment. The patient must be informed of the nature, purpose, and likely effects of the treatment proposed. Patients must be advised of their rights to withdraw consent and how a refusal can be over-ridden by the second opinion process.

Renewal of detention. When managers are considering the renewal of a patient's detention order, the patient should be told that he has a right to be heard by them.

Applications to MHRTs. There is a statutory obligation on the managers to tell a detained patient of his right to apply to an MHRT.

Mental Health Act Commission (MHAC). There is a statutory obligation to advise patients about the MHAC. Patients should be made aware of visits made by the Commissioners. The managers should ensure that detained patients know that they have the right to complain to the Commission about their detention and other matters.

Medical Treatment

15.3   For the purpose of the Act, medical treatment includes 'nursing and also includes care, habilitation and rehabilitation under medical supervision'.

15.4–15.6   Treatment plans are essential, should include immediate and long term goals and be discussed with the patient.

15.7   The common law, as it relates to consent to treatment, applies to all patients informal or detained, except where statute specifically overrides it.

15.8   Before an individual can be given medical treatment, his valid consent is required, except where the law provides the authority to treat the patient without consent. Treatment can be given without consent when the patient is incapable of giving consent because he is—

a. an immature child, in which case a parent may consent;
b. unconscious and is in urgent need of treatment to preserve life, health or well-being;
c. suffering from a mental disorder which is causing immediate danger to himself or others;
d. otherwise incapable and in need of medical care.

15.9   'Consent' is the voluntary and continuing permission of the patient to receive a particular treatment, based on an adequate knowledge of the purpose, nature, likely effects and risks of that treatment. The assessment of the patient's ability to make a decision about his own treatment and the nature and extent of the information to be given to him are matters for clinical judgement. Permission given under any unfair pressure is not consent.

15.10   The fact that a person is suffering from a mental disorder does not mean that he is thereby incapable of giving consent. Capacity to consent is variable in mental disorder and varies over time in any one person; not everyone is equally capable of understanding the same explanation of a treatment plan.

15.14   The assessment of a patient's capacity to make a decision about his own medical treatment is a matter for clinical judgement.

15.15   In order to have capacity an individual must be able to understand what the medical treatment is and why he needs it, its principal benefits and risks, and the consequences of not receiving the treatment, and he must have the capacity to make a choice. All assessments should be recorded in the patient's notes.

15.17   The House of Lords has ruled that a doctor may lawfully operate on or give treatment to a person who lacks the capacity to give consent provided that it is in the best interests of the patient (i.e. necessary to save life, prevent deterioration, or ensure improvement in physical or mental health). For sterilization, the approval of the High Court is also required. In every case the doctor must act in accordance with a responsible and competent body of professional opinion.

Medical Treatment and Second Opinions

16.1   Part IV of the Act provides specific statutory authority for forms of medical treatment for mental disorder to be given to most patients liable to be detained without their consent.

16.2   The provisions of Part IV can be summarized as follows:

    a. Treatments requiring the patient's consent *and* a second opinion (section 57) are psychosurgery and the surgical implantation of hormones for the suppression of male sexual drive where it is administered as a medical treatment for mental disorder. These safeguards apply to *all* patients both formal and informal.

    b. Treatment requiring the patient's consent *or* a second opinion (section 58) are the administration of psychotropic medicine beyond 3 months and treatment by ECT at any time.

    c. Treatments that do not require the patient's consent (section 63). These include psychological and social therapies. (Consent should always be *sought*, 16.4.)

    d. Urgent treatment.

16.5   Treatments for physical disorder cannot be given under Part IV of the Act unless it is a physical disorder that gives rise to a mental disorder and it is necessary to treat the physical disorder in order to treat the mental disorder.

16.7   Before the responsible medical officer (RMO) refers a case to the MHAC under section 57, he should have fully assessed the patient as suitable for psychosurgery and satisfied himself that the patient is capable of giving valid consent and has consented. The case should be referred to the Commission prior to his transfer to the neurosurgical centre, in the case of psychosurgery.

16.14   A patient subject to the provisions of Part IV of the Act may withdraw consent at any time. Where the patient withdraws consent, he should be told of the likely consequences of not receiving the treatment, that a second opinion may be sought to authorize treatment and of the doctor's powers under section 62 (urgent treatment). This should all be recorded in the patient's notes.

16.17   Any decision to treat a patient urgently under section 62 of the Act is the responsibility of the patient's RMO, who should bear in mind that treatment can only be given where it is immediately necessary to save the patient's life, or to prevent a serious deterioration, or to alleviate serious suffering or to prevent violence to himself or others. It is insufficient for the proposed treatment to be simply necessary or beneficial. In certain circumstances 'hazardous' or 'irreversible' treatment cannot be administered under this section even if it is immediately necessary. The patient's RMO is responsible for deciding whether treatment falls into either of these categories having regard to mainstream medical opinion. Urgent treatment can only continue for as long as it is immediately necessary to achieve the statutory objectives. Before deciding to give treatment under section 62, the patient's RMO should whenever possible discuss the proposed urgent treatment with others involved in the patient's care.

16.29   If the RMO and the second opinion appointed doctor are unable to reach agreement, the patient's RMO should be informed personally by the second doctor. It is good practice for the second doctor to give reasons for his dissent and every attempt should be made to reach agreement. Neither doctor should allow a disagreement in any way to prejudice the interests of the patient. If agreement cannot be reached, the position should be recorded in the patient's notes by the RMO who will continue to have responsibility for the patient's management. The opinion given by a second opinion appointed doctor is that doctor's personal responsibility.

16.30   If the patient's situation subsequently changes, the RMO may contact the MHAC and request a further second opinion.

16.38   The second doctor should seek other professional opinions about the nature of the patient's disorder and problems. He should give due weight to the opinion, knowledge, experience and skill of those consulted.

Patients Concerned with Criminal Proceedings

17.1   A patient who is remanded to hospital for reports or for treatment is entitled to obtain, at his own expense, an independent report on his medical condition.

17.2   The consent to treatment provisions of the Act do not apply to patients remanded under section 35.

17.3   Where a patient remanded under section 35 is thought to be in need of medical treatment for mental disorder under Part IV of the Act, consideration should be given to referring the patient back to court as soon as possible. If there is delay in securing a court date, and depending on the patient's mental condition, consideration should be given to whether the patient meets the criteria of section 3 of the Act.

Patients Presenting Particular Management Problems

18.3   Behaviour which can give rise to managerial problems can include:

refusal to participate in treatment;
prolonged verbal abuse and threatening behaviour;
destructive behaviour;
self-injurious behaviour;
physical attacks on others.

18.4   In exploring preventive methods, staff should be aware of some possible causes of problem behaviours:

boredom;
too much stimulation, noise, and general disruption;
overcrowding;
antagonism from others;
an unsuitable mix of patients.

18.5   General preventive measures for problem behaviour include:

keeping patients fully informed;
giving each patient a defined personal space and a secure locker;
ensuring access to open space;
the provision of quiet, recreation and visitors' rooms;
ensuring access to a telephone;
the provision of structured activities;
staff training;
quick and fair management of complaints.

18.9   Physical restraint should be used as little as possible and never as a matter of course. It should be used in an emergency when there seems to be a real possibility that significant harm would occur if intervention is withheld.

18.10   The rules of physical restraint include making a visual check for weapons and allocating each member of staff a specific task. The aim should be to restrain arms and legs from behind. Neck holds should be avoided, as should excess weight in any one area. Do not slap, kick or punch.

18.11   The judicious use of medication in order to facilitate other interventions can be an important adjunct. Medication should not be used as an alternative to adequate staffing levels.

18.12   The health authority should appoint a senior manager who should be informed of any patient who is being subjected to any form of restraint that lasts for more than 2 hours.

18.13 Health authorities should have clear written policies on the use of restraint.

18.14 *Seclusion* is the supervised confinement of a patient alone in a room which may be locked for the protection of others from significant harm. It should be used as little as possible and for the shortest possible time. Seclusion should not be used as a punitive measure. It is a last resort. It is not a procedure for the prevention of self-harm.

18.15 Hospitals should have clear written guidelines on the use of seclusion, distinguishing between seclusion and time-out.

18.16 The decision to use seclusion can be made by a doctor, the nurse in charge of the ward, or a nursing officer. Where the decision is taken by a nurse, a doctor should attend immediately.

18.17 A nurse should be readily available within sight and sound of the seclusion room at all times, and present at all times with a patient who has been sedated.

18.18 A documented report on any seclusion must be made every 15 minutes.

18.19 A review of seclusion should take place every 2 hours by two nurses, and every 4 hours by a doctor. If seclusion continues for more than 8 hours consecutively, or for more than 12 hours in 48 hours, an independent review must take place with the RMO, and a team of nurses and other health care professionals not directly involved with the patient at the time of the incident which led to the seclusion.

18.20 Seclusion should be in a safe, secure and properly identified room where the patient cannot harm himself. It should have adequate heating, lighting, ventilation, and seating. The patient should always be clothed.

18.21 The room should offer complete observation from the outside, while also affording the patient privacy from other patients.

18.23 Authorities are responsible for trying to ensure that staffing is adequate to prevent the need for locking patients in wards, or rooms.

18.26 There are some patients who may need varying degrees of security. In such cases, the need for security is a prerequisite for treatment. The RMO should ensure that treatment in secure conditions lasts for the minimum necessary period and that the patient's bed on an open ward is retained at all times.

18.27 Authorities should ensure that there is a specifically designated, appropriately staffed secure area, with written guidelines about the categories of patients, the procedures, and the safeguards applicable.

18.28 Patients should never be deprived of appropriate day-time clothing during the day, with the intention of restricting their freedom of movement.

Psychological Treatments

19.1 Psychological treatments are used widely. Some can interfere with patients' basic rights. This is most obviously so in the case of behaviour modification programmes. Group therapy has the power to unleash powerful pressures. No treatment should deprive a patient of food, shelter, water, warmth, a comfortable environment, confidentiality or reasonable privacy (both physical and in relation to personal feelings and thoughts).

19.3 Any behaviour modification programme should form part of a previously agreed treatment plan. At no time should it be used as a spontaneous reaction to a particular type of behaviour. The patient's consent should always be sought.

19.7   Although such treatments may proceed in the absence of consent, this should only be done in carefully justified circumstances. If consent is not or cannot be given, a locally agreed procedure should be adopted in which the RMO should seek the advice of a suitably qualified person who is not a member of the clinical team.

19.8   It is the RMO's responsibility to ensure that delegated workers have adequate skills and abilities.

19.9   *Time-out* is a technique which removes a patient for a period (lasting no more than 15 minutes) from opportunities to participate in or to obtain positive reinforcers immediately following the occurrence of unacceptable behaviour.

19.10 Hospitals should have clear written policies on the use of time-out.

Leave of Absence

20.3   Leave of absence should be well planned. If relatives/friends are to be involved in the patient's care, but he does not consent to their being consulted, leave should not be granted.

20.4   *Unrestricted patients*. The decision to grant leave to unrestricted patients, rests with the patient's RMO who, after necessary consultation, may impose such conditions as he considers necessary. The aftercare provisions of section 117 apply to a patient on leave of absence.

       Restricted patients. Any proposal to grant leave has to be approved by the Home Secretary.

20.6   A patient's leave can be revoked by his RMO. The RMO must arrange for a notice in writing revoking the leave to be served on the patient or on the person for the time being in charge of the patient. The reasons for recall should be fully explained to the patient and a record of such explanation placed in the patient's case notes. A restricted patient's leave may also be revoked by the Home Secretary.

20.8   A patient granted leave under section 17 of the Act remains 'liable to be detained' and the provisions of Part IV of the Act continue to apply unless the patient is one referred to in section 56(1). If it becomes necessary to administer treatment in the absence of the patient's consent under Part IV, the patient should be recalled to hospital.

20.9   A period of leave cannot last longer than the duration of the authority to detain which was current when leave was granted. If the patient has not been recalled from leave at the end of the period of detention, he ceases to be liable to be detained.

20.10 It is unlawful to recall from leave a patient subject to section 3 of the Act solely in order to renew the authority to detain the patient (*Hallstrom* and *Gardiner*).

Managers' Duties to Review Detention

22.1   A managers' review is the process by which the managers decide whether a patient can still be detained or can be discharged. It is a different procedure from referral to an MHRT.

22.2   Managers should undertake a review at any time at their discretion, but must do so—

       a. when the patient requests it, unless there has recently been a review and there is no evidence of change;
       b. when the RMO makes a report to the managers in accordance with section 20 of the Act;
       c. when the RMO makes a report to the managers in accordance with section 25(1) barring a nearest relative's discharge application.

22.3   The managers should ensure that they have reports from the patient's RMO and other relevant disciplines and they should consult with those professionals concerned where they think it necessary.

22.4   If the patient consents, managers must ensure that the patient's nearest and/or most concerned relatives are informed of the review and asked to comment or to be available for interview.

Complaints

23.1   The Hospital Complaints Procedures Act 1985 places a duty for health authorities to investigate any complaint on the part of a patient.

Duties of the Hospital Managers

24.4   The health authority should appoint a committee to undertake the duties of the managers.

24.5   The managers may delegate to officers many of their statutory tasks, but they cannot delegate the task of deciding whether a detained patient should be discharged. This decision is personal, exercised by three or more hospital managers.

24.6   It is the managers' duty to ensure that the grounds for admitting the patient are valid and reasonable, and that all relevant admission documents are in order. Where a patient is admitted following an application by the nearest relative, the managers should request a social circumstances report.

Personal Searches

25.1   Authorities should ensure that there is an operational policy on the searching of patients and their belongings. Such a policy should be checked with legal advisers.

25.2   There should be no routine searches. If there are grounds for a search, the patient's consent should be sought.

25.3   If the patient does not consent, staff should consult the unit general manager or deputy. Unless urgent necessity dictates otherwise, such a search should be carried out by a staff member of the same sex.

25.4   If items are removed, the patient should be informed where these are being kept.

Aftercare

26.2   Section 117 of the Act requires health authorities and local authorities, in conjunction with voluntary agencies, to provide aftercare for detained patients.

Part III Patients—Concerned with Criminal Proceedings

27.2   If a conditionally discharged restricted patient requires hospital admission, it will not always be necessary for the Home Secretary to recall the patient to hospital. For example, the patient may be willing to accept treatment informally, or it may be appropriate to admit compulsorily under Part II of the Act. Further it may not be necessary to recall the patient to the same hospital from which he was conditionally discharged.

27.3   When a recall is being considered, this should be discussed between the doctor and the social supervisor.

27.4   If a patient is recalled, the RMO or deputy should explain to the patient the reason for his recall and inform him that his case will be referred to an MHRT within 1 month.

27.5   The RMO should ensure that the patient is given assistance to inform his legal adviser, and subject to his consent, that his nearest relative or friend is told.

People with Mental Handicap

28.4   It is desirable that no patient should be classified under the Act as mentally impaired or severely mentally impaired in the absence of a formal psychological assessment.

28.5   Key factors in mental impairment and severe mental impairment:

Incomplete or arrested development of mind implies that the determining features prevented the usual maturation of intellectual and social development. It excludes handicaps derived from accident, injury, or illness after development is completed.

Severe or significant impairment of intelligence must be reliably or carefully assessed.

Severe or significant impairment of social functioning should be assessed by recent observations from a number of sources, such as social workers, nurses, and psychologists; evidence should include one or more social functioning assessment tests.

Abnormally aggressive behaviour should mean that the actions are outside the usual range of aggressive behaviour and cause actual damage and/or real distress recently, persistently, or with excessive severity.

Irresponsible conduct implies a disregard of action taken where the results cause actual damage or real distress recently, persistently, or with excessive severity.

Children and Young People under the age of 18 years

29.1   There is no minimum age limit for admission to hospital under the Act.

29.2   a. Young people should be kept as fully informed as possible about their care and treatment; their views and wishes must always be taken into account.
    b. Unless statute specifically overrides, young people should be regarded as having the right to make their own decisions when they have sufficient understanding and intelligence.

29.4   When the care and treatment of somebody under the age of 16 is being considered, the following questions need to be asked (among others). Who is legally responsible for this child, and who has the authority to take decisions for him? What is the capacity of the child to make his own decisions? Where a parent refuses consent to treatment, how sound are the reasons? How necessary is treatment for the child? It is essential to request copies of statutory orders (e.g. wardship, access arrangements).

29.5   *Children under 16.* Parents or guardians may arrange for the admission of children under the age of 16 to hospital as informal patients. Where a doctor concludes, however, that a child under the age of 16 has the capacity to make such a decision for himself, there is no right to admit him to hospital informally, or to keep him there on an informal basis against his will.
    Where a child is willing to be so admitted to hospital, but the parents/guardian object, their views should be accorded serious consideration and given due weight. Recourse to law to stop such an admission could be sought.

29.6   *Young people aged 16–18.* Anyone in this age group who is capable of expressing his own wishes can admit or discharge himself as an informal patient, irrespective of the wishes of his parents or guardian.

29.7   *Consent to medical treatment aged under 16.* If a child has sufficient understanding and intelligence, he can take decisions about his own medical treatment in the same way as an adult. Otherwise the permission of parents/guardians must be sought (save in emergencies). If parents/guardians do not consent to treatment, consideration should be given to both the use of child care legislation and the MHA 1983. In complex cases, wardship may be the preferable course. The same principles apply where the child is in the care of a local authority but, wherever possible, parents should be consulted. Where children are wards of court, then the consent of the High Court must be sought.

29.8   Consent should be sought for each aspect of the child's care and treatment as it arises. Blanket consent forms must not be used.

29.9   Where a child in care is placed in accommodation where liberty is restricted (for example in secure units), application must be made to a juvenile court within 72 hours if the restriction is to last beyond that period (section 21A of the Child Care Act 1980). This provision does not apply to children detained under the MHA 1983. Where the child is a ward of court, the local authority must obtain the permission of the High Court prior to any restriction of liberty.

29.11   Young people's legal rights to confidentiality should be strictly observed.

29.12   Children and young persons should not be placed in adult wards except in an emergency.

29.14   All children and young people in hospital should receive appropriate education.

Appendix 3
Supervision and Aftercare of Conditionally Discharged Restricted Patients (Home Office, DHSS 1987)
Notes for the Guidance of Supervising Psychiatrists

These notes on the supervision and aftercare of restricted patients are produced jointly by the Home Office and the Department of Health from whom a copy can be obtained. This summary is to give readers some idea of the principles involved. Its wording differs from the original in places and important sections have been omitted entirely. It should not be relied upon as a primary source.

I. Introduction

1. The notes are not intended to limit the clinical freedom of the supervising psychiatrist.

2. Any questions arising from the notes, or suggestions for their improvement, should be sent to C3 division, 50, Queen Anne's Gate, London SW1H 9AT.

II. The Restricted Patient Population

3. Restricted patients represent only a tiny percentage of all patients in mental hospitals. There are about 1700 restricted patients detained in hospital. Over half are classified as suffering from mental illness, about a quarter from psychopathic disorder and the remainder from either mental impairment or, most rarely, severe mental impairment. Over 60% have been convicted of offences of violence against the person; a further 12% of sexual offences and 12% of arson. About 1100 are detained in special hospitals.

4. The number of conditionally discharged patients under active supervision in the community is estimated at 600–700.

III. The Role of the Home Office

5. C3 division of the Home Office comprises about 40 officers whose sole concern is to carry out the Home Secretary's responsibilities under the Mental Health Act 1983 and related legislation.

6. Staff in C3 division are ready and willing to discuss the care of any restricted patient with a supervising psychiatrist.

IV. The Purpose of Conditional Discharge

7. The Home Secretary will usually decide to make a restricted patient's discharge from hospital subject to certain conditions. The conditions are usually those of residence at a stated address, supervision by a local social worker or probation officer and psychiatric supervision. Tribunals also are likely to make discharge directions conditional either for the protection of the public or of the patient himself, and to impose similar conditions. If they do not, the Home Office, using powers under section 73(4) of the 1983 Act, usually requires social and psychiatric supervision.

8. The purpose of the formal supervision from conditional discharge is to protect the public from further serious harm in two ways: (1) by assisting the patient's successful reintegration into the community, and (2) by close monitoring of the patient's mental health.

V. Preparation of Supervision and Aftercare Arrangements

9. On admission of a restricted patient to hospital, the responsible medical officer (RMO) will seek not only to treat the patient's mental disorder, but to understand the relationship, if any, between the disorder and the patient's behaviour.

10. Staff in the detaining hospital will begin preparations for a patient's conditional discharge before authority for discharge is sought. These preparations include the patient's personal preparation for life outside the hospital, and the consideration and choice of suitable accommodation, employment or other day-time occupation, a social supervisor, who may be a social worker or a probation officer, and a supervising consultant psychiatrist.

VII. The Role of the Supervising Psychiatrist

18. The supervising psychiatrist is responsible for all matters relating to the mental health of the patient, including the regular assessment of the patient's condition, the monitoring of any necessary medication and the consideration of action in the event of deterioration in the patient's mental state.

20. The supervising psychiatrist should be prepared to be directly involved in the treatment and rehabilitation of the patient and to offer constructive support to the patient's progress in the community, rather than simply checking that the patient is symptom free and 'staying out of trouble'.

21. Outside the medical sphere, C3 division of the Home Office can provide information about an individual's care or advice on any aspect of supervision, including the legal framework.

23. The two most important elements in effective supervision are the development of a close relationship with the patient and the maintenance of good liaison with the social supervisor.

IX. Liaison between the Supervising Psychiatrist and Other Professionals Involved

30. It is recommended that the social supervisor sees the patient at home at least once each week for the first month after discharge reducing to once each fortnight and then once each month as the supervisor judges appropriate.

31. Close liaison between the supervising psychiatrist and social supervisor is essential if supervision is to be effective.

32. The supervising psychiatrist should inform the social supervisor of the nature of any medication, its effects on the patient's condition and behaviour and any possible side-effects. The psychiatrist should also inform the social supervisor of the arrangements to be made for the medication to be given including when, where, and by whom, and any changes in those arrangements.

33. The supervising psychiatrist should send a copy of all reports sent to the Home Office to the social supervisor, who should reciprocate.

35. All conditionally discharged patients should be registered with a general medical practitioner (GP) and arrangements for this should be made before discharge by the discharging hospital. The discharging hospital should inform the GP of the names and addresses of the patient's supervising psychiatrist and social supervisor. The supervising psychiatrist should contact the GP to give him brief details of the patient's background and current status.

36. The work of other clinical personnel, such as psychiatric nurses or psychologists, should be under the general direction of the supervising psychiatrist who should consult with them periodically.

37. If there is a community psychiatric nurse, he ought to be acquainted with the patient's needs and circumstances.

X. Reports to the Home Office

39. The Home Office usually asks for reports of the patient's progress from both supervisors 1 month after conditional discharge and every 3 months thereafter.

40. After a period in the community when a conditionally discharged patient has settled down and is maintaining a steady pattern of life, the supervising psychiatrist may consider it appropriate to recommend longer reporting intervals or even the discontinuance of psychiatric supervision. The Home Office will not agree to reporting intervals of more than 6 months while supervision continues.

XII. Action in the Event of Concern about the Patient's Condition

48. If a supervising psychiatrist is concerned about a patient's mental state or behaviour, the concern should be discussed with other professionals involved, particularly the social supervisor.

49. The supervising psychiatrist may decide to take immediate local action to admit the patient to hospital either with the patient's consent or using the civil powers of the MHA (sections 2, 3 or 4). Whether or not such action is taken, and even if the social supervisor does not share the psychiatrist's concern, the supervising psychiatrist should report to the Home Office at once.

51. A report to the Home Office must always be made in a case in which—
    a. there appears to be an actual or potential risk to the public;
    b. contact with the patient is lost or the patient is unwilling to cooperate with supervision;
    c. the patient's behaviour or condition suggests a need for further inpatient treatment in hospital;
    d. the patient is charged with or convicted of an offence.

52. It is generally inappropriate for a conditionally discharged patient to remain in hospital for more than a short time informally or under civil powers of detention, and the Home Secretary would usually wish to consider the issue of a warrant of recall if the period of inpatient treatment seemed likely to be protracted.

53. In cases where it seems that admission is necessary to protect the patient from possible harm, the supervising psychiatrist may recommend that the patient be formally recalled to hospital. The Home Secretary would normally be prepared to act on such a recommendation.

54. Whether the Home Secretary decides to recall a patient depends largely on the degree of danger which the particular patient might present. There are cases in which recall to hospital for a period of observation can be seen as a necessary step in continuing psychiatric treatment. There are other cases in which antisocial behaviour may be unconnected with mental disorder, so that recall to hospital is inappropriate and the patient may be dealt with by the criminal law.

56. The Home Secretary is obliged to refer the care of a recalled patient to a mental health review tribunal within 1 month of recall.

59. If a patient has committed an offence and a prosecution is pending, and if he is in safe custody and is no danger to himself, the Home Secretary will usually let the law take its course. In that event, the court will be able to decide whether the patient needs a fresh medical disposal, whether some other non-medical disposal is called for, or whether the most appropriate course would be for the patient to be recalled to hospital.

61. If a conditionally discharged patient is convicted of a further offence and the court imposes a sentence of imprisonment, the Home Secretary will often reserve judgment on the patient's status under the MHA 1983 until he nears the end of his prison sentence.

XIII. Length of Supervision and Absolute Discharge

62. Where a conditionally discharged patient is subject to a restriction order of specified duration, then on the date of expiration of the order, he is no longer subject to condition or to recall.

63. Where, as in most cases, the restriction order is of indefinite duration, the Home Secretary normally requires active supervision and reporting to be kept up for at least 5 years after discharge from hospital in serious cases, and for at least 2 years in less serious cases.

66. MHRTs have the power to hear the case of a conditionally discharged patient and either to direct a variation in the conditions attaching to discharge or to direct absolute discharge.

XIV. Mental Health Review Tribunals

68. MHRTs are held in informal conditions. For restricted patients, they are chaired by a judge and also comprise a psychiatrist and a lay member.

69. The supervising psychiatrist will be asked to provide a report.

71. Supervisors will not necessarily be informed of the date of the hearing or invited to appear.

Appendix 4
Ethics Codes

Declaration of Geneva

Adopted by the 2nd General Assembly of the World Medical Association, Geneva, Switzerland, September 1948;

Amended by the 22nd World Medical Assembly, Sydney, Australia, August 1968, *and* the 35th World Medical Assembly, Venice, Italy, October 1983

AT THE TIME OF BEING ADMITTED AS A MEMBER OF THE MEDICAL PROFESSION:

I solemnly pledge myself to consecrate my life to the service of humanity;
I will give to my teachers the respect and gratitude which is their due;
I will practice my profession with conscience and dignity;
the health of my patient will be my first consideration;
I will respect the secrets which are confided in me, even after the patient has died;
I will maintain by all the means in my power, the honor and the noble traditions of the medical profession;
my colleagues will be my brothers;
I will not permit considerations of religion, nationality, race, party politics or social standing to intervene between my duty and my patient;
I will maintain the utmost respect for human life from its beginning even under threat and I will not use my medical knowledge contrary to the laws of humanity;
I make these promises solemnly, freely and upon my honor.

International Code of Medical Ethics

Adopted by the 3rd General Assembly of the World Medical Association, London, England, October 1949;

Amended by the 22nd World Medical Assembly, Sydney, Australia, August 1968, *and* the 35th World Medical Assembly, Venice, Italy, October 1983

Duties of Physicians in General

A physician shall always maintain the highest standards of professional conduct.

A physician shall not permit motives of profit to influence the free and independent exercise of professional judgement on behalf of patients.

A physician shall, in all types of medical practice, be dedicated to providing competent medical service in full technical and moral independence, with compassion and respect for human dignity.

A physician shall deal honestly with patients and colleagues, and strive to expose those physicians deficient in character or competence, or who engage in fraud or deception.

The following practices are deemed to be unethical conduct:
  a. Self advertising by physicians, unless permitted by the laws of the country and the code of ethics of the national medical association.

b. Paying or receiving any fee or any other consideration solely to procure the referral of a patient or for prescribing or referring a patient to any source.

A physician shall respect the rights of patients, of colleagues and of other health professionals, and shall safeguard patient confidences.

A physician shall act only in the patient's interest when providing medical care which might have the effect of weakening the physical and mental condition of the patient.

A physician shall use great caution in divulging discoveries or new techniques or treatment through non-professional channels.

A physician shall certify only that which he has personally verified.

Duties of Physicians to the Sick

A physician shall always bear in mind the obligation of preserving human life.

A physician shall owe his patients complete loyalty and all the resources of his science. Whenever an examination or treatment is beyond the physician's capacity he should summon another physician who has the necessary ability.

A physician shall preserve absolute confidentiality on all he knows about his patient even after the patient has died.

A physician shall give emergency care as a humanitarian duty unless he is assured that others are willing and able to give such care.

Duties of Physicians to Each Other

A physician shall behave towards his colleagues as he would have them behave towards him.

A physician shall not entice patients from his colleagues.

A physician shall observe the principles of the 'Declaration of Geneva' approved by the World Medical Association.

Declaration of Hawaii

As approved by the General Assembly of the **World Psychiatric Association** in Vienna, Austria, on 10th July, 1983

Ever since the dawn of culture, ethics has been an essential part of the healing art. It is the view of the World Psychiatric Association that due to conflicting loyalties and expectations of both physicians and patients in contemporary society and the delicate nature of the therapist-patient relationship, high ethical standards are especially important for those involved in the science and practice of psychiatry as a medical specialty. These guidelines have been delineated in order to promote close adherence to those standards and to prevent misuse of psychiatric concepts, knowledge and technology.

Since the psychiatrist is a member of society as well as a practitioner of medicine, he or she must consider the ethical implications specific to psychiatry as well as the ethical demands on all physicians and the societal responsibility of every man and woman.

Even though ethical behavior is based on the individual psychiatrist's conscience and personal judgement, written guidelines are needed to clarify the profession's ethical implications.

Therefore, the General Assembly of the World Psychiatric Association has approved these ethical guidelines for psychiatrists, having in mind the great differences in cultural backgrounds, and in legal, social and economic conditions which exist in the various countries of the world.

It should be understood that the World Psychiatric Association views these guidelines to be minimal requirements for ethical standards of the psychiatric profession.

1. The aim of psychiatry is to treat mental illness and to promote mental health. To the best of his or her ability, consistent with accepted scientific knowledge and ethical principles, the psychiatrist shall serve the best interests of the patient and be also concerned for the common good and a just allocation of health resources. To fulfil these aims requires continuous research and continual education of health care personnel, patients and the public.
2. Every psychiatrist should offer to the patient the best available therapy to his knowledge and if accepted must treat him or her with the solicitude and respect due to the dignity of all human beings. When the psychiatrist is responsible for treatment given by others he owes them competent supervision and education. Whenever there is a need, or whenever a reasonable request is forthcoming from the patient, the psychiatrist should seek the help of another colleague.
3. The psychiatrist aspires for a therapeutic relationship that is founded on mutual agreement. At its optimum it requires trust, confidentiality, cooperation and mutual responsibility. Such a relationship may not be possible to establish with some patients. In that case, contact should be established with a relative or other person close to the patient. If and when a relationship is established for purposes other than therapeutic, such as in forensic psychiatry, its nature must be thoroughly explained to the person concerned.
4. The psychiatrist should inform the patient of the nature of the condition, therapeutic procedures, including possible alternatives, and of the possible outcome. This information must be offered in a considerate way and the patient must be given the opportunity to choose between appropriate and available methods.
5. No procedure shall be performed nor treatment given against or independent of a patient's own will, unless because of mental illness, the patient cannot form a judgement as to what is in his or her own best interest and without which treatment serious impairment is likely to occur to the patient or others.
6. As soon as the conditions for compulsory treatment no longer apply, the psychiatrist should release the patient from the compulsory nature of the treatment and if further therapy is necessary should obtain voluntary consent. The psychiatrist should inform the patient and/or relatives or meaningful others, of the existence of mechanisms of appeal for the detention and for any other complaints related to his or her well-being.
7. The psychiatrist must never use his professional possibilities to violate the dignity or human rights of any individual or group and should never let inappropriate personal desires, feelings, prejudices or beliefs interfere with the treatment. The psychiatrist must on no account utilize the tools of his profession, once the absence of psychiatric illness has been established. If a patient or some third party demands actions contrary to scientific knowledge or ethical principles the psychiatrist must refuse to cooperate.
8. Whatever the psychiatrist has been told by the patient, or has noted during examination or treatment, must be kept confidential unless the patient relieves the psychiatrist from this obligation, or to prevent serious harm to self or others makes disclosure necessary. In these cases however, the patient should be informed of the breach of confidentiality.
9. To increase and propagate psychiatric knowledge and skill requires participation of the patients. Informed consent must, however, be obtained before presenting a patient to a class and, if possible, also when a case-history is released for scientific publication, whereby all reasonable measures must be taken to preserve the dignity and anonymity of the patient and to safeguard the personal reputation of the subject. The patient's participation must be voluntary, after full information has been given of the aim, procedures, risks and inconveniences of a research project and there must always be a reasonable relationship between calculated risks or inconveniences and the benefit of the study. In clinical research every subject must retain and exert all his rights as a patient. For children and other patients who cannot themselves give informed consent, this should be obtained from the legal next-of-kin. Every patient or research subject is free to withdraw for any reason at any time from any voluntary treatment and from any teaching or research program in which he or she participates. This withdrawal, as well as any

refusal to enter a program, must never influence the psychiatrist's efforts to help the patient or subject.

10. The psychiatrist should stop all therapeutic, teaching or research programs that may evolve contrary to the principles of this Declaration.

Principles of Medical Ethics of the American Medical Association with Annotations Applicable to Psychiatry

Following are each of the AMA Principles of Medical Ethics printed separately along with annotations especially applicable to psychiatry.

Preamble

The medical profession has long subscribed to a body of ethical statements developed primarily for the benefit of the patient. As a member of this profession, a physician must recognize responsibility not only to patients but also to society, to other health professionals, and to self. The following Principles, adopted by the American Medical Association, are not laws but standards of conduct, which define the essentials of honorable behavior for the physician.*

Section 1

A physician shall be dedicated to providing competent medical service with compassion and respect for human dignity.

1. The patient may place his/her trust in his/her psychiatrist knowing that the psychiatrist's ethics and professional responsibilities preclude him/her gratifying his/her own needs by exploiting the patient. This becomes particularly important because of the essentially private, highly personal, and sometimes intensely emotional nature of the relationship established with the psychiatrist.
2. A psychiatrist should not be a party to any type of policy that excludes, segregates or demeans the dignity of any patient because of ethnic origin, race, sex, creed, age, socioeconomic status or sexual orientation.
3. In accord with the requirements of law and accepted medical practice, it is ethical for a physician to submit his/her work to peer review and to the ultimate authority of the medical staff executive body and the hospital administration and its governing body. In case of dispute, the ethical psychiatrist has the following steps available:
   a. Seek appeal from the medical staff decision to a joint conference committee, including members of the medical staff executive committee and the executive committee of the governing board. At this appeal, the ethical psychiatrist could request that outside opinions be considered.
   b. Appeal to the governing body itself.
   c. Appeal to state agencies regulating licensure of hospitals if, in the particular state, they concern themselves with matters of professional competency and quality of care.
   d. Attempt to educate colleagues through development of research projects and data and presentations at professional meetings and in professional journals.
   e. Seek redress in local courts, perhaps through an enjoining injunction against the governing body.
   f. Public education as carried out by an ethical psychiatrist would not utilize appeals based solely upon emotion, and would be presented in a professional way and without any potential exploitation of patients through testimonials.
4. A psychiatrist should not be a participant in a legally authorized execution.

---

* Statements in italics are taken directly from the American Medical Association's Principles of Medical Ethics.

Section 2

A physician shall deal honestly with patients and colleagues, and strive to expose those physicians deficient in character or competence, or who engage in fraud or deception.

1. The requirement that the physician conduct himself/herself with propriety in his/her profession and in all the actions of his/her life is especially important in the case of the psychiatrist because the patient tends to model his/her behavior after that of his/her therapist by identification. Further, the necessary intensity of the therapeutic relationship may tend to activate sexual and other needs and fantasies on the part of both patient and therapist, while weakening the objectivity necessary for control. Sexual activity with a patient is unethical. Sexual involvement with one's former patients generally exploits emotions deriving from treatment and therefore almost always is unethical.
2. The psychiatrist should diligently guard against exploiting information furnished by the patient and should not use the unique position of power afforded him/her by the psychotherapeutic situation to influence the patient in any way not directly relevant to the treatment goals.
3. A psychiatrist who regularly practices outside his/her area of professional competence should be considered unethical. Determination of professional competence should be made by peer review boards or other appropriate bodies.
4. Special consideration should be given to those psychiatrists who, because of mental illness, jeopardize the welfare of their patients and their own reputations and practices. It is ethical, even encouraged, for another psychiatrist to intercede in such situations.
5. Psychiatric services, like all medical services, are dispensed in the context of a contractual arrangement between the patient and the treating physician. The provisions of the contractual arrangement, which are binding on the physician as well as on the patient, should be explicitly established.
6. It is ethical for the psychiatrist to make a charge for a missed appointment when this falls within the terms of the specific contractual agreement with the patient. Charging for a missed appointment or for one not cancelled 24 hours in advance need not, in itself, be considered unethical if a patient is fully advised that the physician will make such a charge. The practice, however, should be resorted to infrequently and always with the utmost consideration for the patient and his/her circumstances.
7. An arrangement in which a psychiatrist provides supervision or administration to other physicians or non-medical persons for a percentage of their fees or gross income is not acceptable; this would constitute fee-splitting. In a team of practitioners, or a multidisciplinary team, it is ethical for the psychiatrist to receive income for administration, research, education or consultation. This should be based upon a mutually agreed upon and set fee or salary, open to renegotiation when a change in the time demand occurs. (*See also* Section 5, Annotations 2, 3 and 4.)
8. When a member has been found to have behaved unethically by the American Psychiatric Association or one of its constituent district branches, there should not be automatic reporting to the local authorities responsible for medical licensure, but the decision to report should be decided upon the merits of the case.

Section 3

A physician shall respect the law and also recognize a responsibility to seek changes in those requirements which are contrary to the best interests of the patient.

1. It would seem self-evident that a psychiatrist who is a law-breaker might be ethically unsuited to practice his/her profession. When such illegal activities bear directly upon his/her practice, this would obviously be the case. However, in other instances, illegal activities such as those concerning the right to protest social injustices might not bear on either the image of the psychiatrist or the ability of the specific psychiatrist to treat his/her patient ethically and well. While no committee or board could offer prior assurance that any illegal activity would not be considered unethical, it is conceivable that an individual could violate a law without being guilty of professionally unethical behavior. Physicians lose no right of citizenship on entry into the profession of medicine.
2. Where not specifically prohibited by local laws governing medical practice, the practice of acupuncture by a psychiatrist is not unethical *per se*. The psychiatrist should have

professional competence in the use of acupuncture. Or, if he/she is supervising the use of acupuncture by non-medical individuals, he/she should provide proper medical supervision. (*See also* Section 5, Annotations 3 and 4.)

Section 4

A physician shall respect the rights of patients, of colleagues and of other health professionals, and shall safeguard patient confidences within the constraints of the law.

1. Psychiatric records, including even the identification of a person as a patient, must be protected with extreme care. Confidentiality is essential to psychiatric treatment. This is based in part on the special nature of psychiatric therapy as well as on the traditional ethical relationship between physician and patient. Growing concern regarding the civil rights of patients and the possible adverse effects of computerization, duplication equipment, and data banks makes the dissemination of confidential information an increasing hazard. Because of the sensitive and private nature of the information with which the psychiatrist deals, he/she must be circumspect in the information that he/she chooses to disclose to others about a patient. The welfare of the patient must be a continuing consideration.

2. A psychiatrist may release confidential information only with the authorization of the patient or under proper legal compulsion. The continuing duty of the psychiatrist to protect the patient includes fully apprising him/her of the connotations of waiving the privilege of privacy. This may become an issue when the patient is being investigated by a government agency, is applying for a position, or is involved in legal action. The same principles apply to the release of information concerning treatment to medical departments of government agencies, business organizations, labor unions, and insurance companies. Information gained in confidence about patients seen in student health services should not be released without the students' explicit permission.

3. Clinical and other materials used in teaching and writing must be adequately disguised in order to preserve the anonymity of the individuals involved.

4. The ethical responsibility of maintaining confidentiality holds equally for the consultations in which the patient may not have been present and in which the consultee was not a physician. In such instances, the physician consultant should alert the consultee to his/her duty of confidentiality.

5. Ethically the psychiatrist may disclose only that information which is relevant to a given situation. He/she should avoid offering speculation as fact. Sensitive information such as an individual's sexual orientation or fantasy material is usually unnecessary.

6. Psychiatrists are often asked to examine individuals for security purposes, to determine suitability for various jobs, and to determine legal competence. The psychiatrist must fully describe the nature and purpose and lack of confidentiality of the examination to the examinee at the beginning of the examination.

7. Careful judgement must be exercised by the psychiatrist in order to include, when appropriate, the parents or guardian in the treatment of a minor. At the same time, the psychiatrist must assure the minor proper confidentiality.

8. Psychiatrists at times may find it necessary, in order to protect the patient or the community from imminent danger, to reveal confidential information disclosed by the patient.

9. When the psychiatrist is ordered by the court to reveal the confidences entrusted to him/her by patients, he/she may comply or he/she may ethically hold the right to dissent within the framework of the law. When the psychiatrist is in doubt, the right of the patient to confidentiality and, by extension, to unimpaired treatment, should be given priority. The psychiatrist should reserve the right to raise the question of adequate need for disclosure. In the event that the necessity for legal disclosure is demonstrated by the court, the psychiatrist may request the right to disclosure of only that information which is relevant to the legal question at hand.

10. With regard for the person's dignity and privacy and with truly informed consent, it is ethical to present a patient to a scientific gathering, if the confidentiality of the presentation is understood and accepted by the audience.

11. It is ethical to present a patient or former patient to a public gathering or to the news

media only if the patient is fully informed of enduring loss of confidentiality, is competent, and consents in writing without coercion.

12. When involved in funded research, the ethical psychiatrist will advise human subjects of the funding source, retain his/her freedom to reveal data and results, and follow all appropriate and current guidelines relative to human subject protection.

13. Ethical considerations in medical practice preclude the psychiatric evaluation of any adult charged with criminal acts prior to access to, or availability of, legal counsel. The only exception is the rendering of care to the person for the sole purpose of medical treatment.

14. Sexual involvement between a faculty member or supervisor and a trainee or student, in those situations in which an abuse of power can occur, often takes advantage of inequalities in the working relationship and may be unethical because: (a) any treatment of a patient being supervised may be deleteriously affected; (b) it may damage the trust relationship between teacher and student; and (c) teachers are important professional role models for their trainees and affect their trainees' future professional behavior.

Section 5

A physician shall continue to study, apply and advance scientific knowledge, make relevant information available to patients, colleagues, and the public, obtain consultation, and use the talents of other health professionals when indicated.

1. Psychiatrists are responsible for their own continuing education and should be mindful of the fact that theirs must be a lifetime of learning.

2. In the practice of his/her specialty, the psychiatrist consults, associates, collaborates or integrates his/her work with that of many professionals, including psychologists, psychometricians, social workers, alcoholism counselors, marriage counselors, public health nurses, etc. Furthermore, the nature of modern psychiatric practice extends his/her contacts to such people as teachers, juvenile and adult probation officers, attorneys, welfare workers, agency volunteers and neighborhood aides. In referring patients for treatment, counseling, or rehabilitation to any of these practitioners, the psychiatrist should ensure that the allied professional or paraprofessional with whom he/she is dealing is a recognized member of his/her own discipline and is competent to carry out the therapeutic task required. The psychiatrist should have the same attitude toward members of the medical profession to whom he/she refers patients. Whenever he/she has reason to doubt the training, skill or ethical qualifications of the allied professional, the psychiatrist should not refer cases to him/her.

3. When the psychiatrist assumes a collaborative or supervisory role with another mental health worker, he/she must expend sufficient time to assure that proper care is given. It is contrary to the interests of the patient and to patient care if he/she allows himself/herself to be used as a figurehead.

4. In relationships between psychiatrists and practising licensed psychologists, the physician should not delegate to the psychologist or, in fact, to any non-medical person any matter requiring the exercise of professional medical judgement.

5. The psychiatrist should agree to the request of a patient for consultation or to such a request from the family of an incompetent or minor patient. The psychiatrist may suggest possible consultants, but the patient or family should be given free choice of the consultant. If the psychiatrist disapproves of the professional qualifications of the consultant or if there is a difference of opinion that the primary therapist cannot resolve, he/she may, after suitable notice, withdraw from the case. If this disagreement occurs within an institution or agency framework, the differences should be resolved by the mediation or arbitration of higher professional authority within the institution or agency.

Section 6

A physician shall, in the provision of appropriate patient care, except in emergencies, be free to choose whom to serve, with whom to associate, and the environment in which to provide medical services.

1. Physicians generally agree that the doctor-patient relationship is such a vital factor in effective treatment of the patient that preservation of optimal conditions for development of a sound working relationship between a doctor and his/her patient should take precedence over all other considerations. Professional courtesy may lead to poor psychiatric

care for physicians and their families because of embarrassment over the lack of a complete give-and-take contract.

2. An ethical psychiatrist may refuse to provide psychiatric treatment to a person who, in the psychiatrist's opinion, cannot be diagnosed as having a mental illness amenable to psychiatric treatment.

Section 7

A physician shall recognize a responsibility to participate in activities contributing to an improved community.

1. Psychiatrists should foster the cooperation of those legitimately concerned with the medical, psychological, social and legal aspects of mental health and illness. Psychiatrists are encouraged to serve society by advising and consulting with the executive, legislative and judiciary branches of the government. A psychiatrist should clarify whether he/she speaks as an individual or as a representative of an organization. Furthermore, psychiatrists should avoid cloaking their public statements with the authority of the profession (e.g., 'Psychiatrists know that . . .').
2. Psychiatrists may interpret and share with the public their expertise in the various psychosocial issues that may affect mental health and illness. Psychiatrists should always be mindful of their separate roles as dedicated citizens and as experts in psychological medicine.
3. On occasion psychiatrists are asked for an opinion about an individual who is in the light of public attention, or who has disclosed information about himself/herself through public media. It is unethical for a psychiatrist to offer a professional opinion unless he/she has conducted an examination and has been granted proper authorization for such a statement.
4. The psychiatrist may permit his/her certification to be used for the involuntary treatment of any person only following his/her personal examination of that person. To do so, he/she must find that the person, because of mental illness, cannot form a judgement as to what is in his/her own best interests and that, without such treatment, substantial impairment is likely to occur to the person or others.

American Psychiatric Association
1989b

World Medical Association Declaration of Helsinki

Recommendations guiding physicians in biomedical research involving human subjects

Adopted by the 18th World Medical Assembly, Helsinki, Finland, June 1964

and amended by the 29th World Medical Assembly, Tokyo, Japan, October 1975; 35th World Medical Assembly, Venice, Italy, October 1983; and the 41st World Medical Assembly, Hong Kong, September 1989

Introduction

It is the mission of the physician to safeguard the health of the people. His or her knowledge and conscience are dedicated to the fulfilment of this mission.

The Declaration of Geneva of the World Medical Association binds the physician with the words, 'The health of my patient will be my first consideration,' and the International Code of Medical Ethics declares that, 'A physician shall act only in the patient's interest when providing medical care which might have the effect of weakening the physical and mental condition of the patient.'

The purpose of biomedical research involving human subjects must be to improve diagnostic, therapeutic and prophylactic procedures and the understanding of the aetiology and pathogenesis of disease.

In current medical practice most diagnostic, therapeutic or prophylactic procedures involve hazards. This applies especially to biomedical research.

Medical progress is based on research which ultimately must rest in part on experimentation involving human subjects.

In the field of biomedical research a fundamental distinction must be recognized between medical research in which the aim is essentially diagnostic or therapeutic for a patient, and medical research, the essential object of which is purely scientific and without implying direct diagnostic or therapeutic value to the person subjected to the research.

Special caution must be exercised in the conduct of research which may affect the environment, and the welfare of animals used for research must be respected.

Because it is essential that the results of laboratory experiments be applied to human beings to further scientific knowledge and to help suffering humanity, the World Medical Association has prepared the following recommendations as a guide to every physician in biomedical research involving human subjects. They should be kept under review in the future. It must be stressed that the standards as drafted are only a guide to physicians all over the world. Physicians are not relieved from criminal, civil and ethical responsibilities under the laws of their own countries.

I. Basic Principles

1. Biomedical research involving human subjects must conform to generally accepted scientific principles and should be based on adequately performed laboratory and animal experimentation and on a thorough knowledge of the scientific literature.

2. The design and performance of each experimental procedure involving human subjects should be clearly formulated in an experimental protocol which should be transmitted for consideration, comment and guidance to a specially appointed committee independent of the investigator and the sponsor provided that this independent committee is in conformity with the laws and regulations of the country in which the research experiment is performed.

3. Biomedical research involving human subjects should be conducted only by scientifically qualified persons and under the supervision of a clinically competent medical person. The responsibility for the human subject must always rest with a medically qualified person and never rest on the subject of the research, even though the subject has given his or her consent.

4. Biomedical research involving human subjects cannot legitimately be carried out unless the importance of the objective is in proportion to the inherent risk to the subject.

5. Every biomedical research project involving human subjects should be preceded by careful assessment of predictable risks in comparison with foreseeable benefits to the subject or to others. Concern for the interests of the subject must always prevail over the interests of science and society.

6. The right of the research subject to safeguard his or her integrity must always be respected. Every precaution should be taken to respect the privacy of the subject and to minimize the impact of the study on the subject's physical and mental integrity and on the personality of the subject.

7. Physicians should abstain from engaging in research projects involving human subjects unless they are satisfied that the hazards involved are believed to be predictable. Physicians should cease any investigation if the hazards are found to outweigh the potential benefits.

8. In publication of the results of his or her research, the physician is obliged to preserve the accuracy of the results. Reports of experimentation not in accordance with the principles laid down in this Declaration should not be accepted for publication.

9. In any research on human beings, each potential subject must be adequately informed of the aims, methods, anticipated benefits and potential hazards of the study and the discomfort it may entail. He or she should be informed that he or she is at liberty to abstain from participation in the study and that he or she is free to withdraw his or her consent to participation at any time. The physician should then obtain the subject's freely-given informed consent, preferably in writing.

10. When obtaining informed consent for the research project the physician should be particularly cautious if the subject is in a dependent relationship to him or her or may consent under duress. In that case the informed consent should be obtained by a physician who is not engaged in the investigation and who is completely independent of this official relationship.

11. In case of legal incompetence, informed consent should be obtained from the legal guardian in accordance with national legislation. Where physical or mental incapacity makes it impossible to obtain informed consent, or when the subject is a minor, permission from the responsible relative replaces that of the subject in accordance with national legislation. Whenever the minor child is in fact able to give a consent, the minor's consent must be obtained in addition to the consent of the minor's legal guardian.
12. The research protocol should always contain a statement of the ethical considerations involved and should indicate that the principles enunciated in the present Declaration are complied with.

II.   Medical Research Combined with Professional Care (Clinical research)

1. In the treatment of the sick person, the physician must be free to use a new diagnostic and therapeutic measure, if in his or her judgement it offers hope of saving life, reestablishing health or alleviating suffering.
2. The potential benefits, hazards, and discomfort of a new method should be weighed against the advantages of the best current diagnostic and therapeutic methods.
3. In any medical study—every patient—including those of a control group, if any—should be assured of the best proven diagnostic and therapeutic method.
4. The refusal of the patient to participate in a study must never interfere with the physician-patient relationship.
5. If the physician considers it essential not to obtain informed consent, the specific reasons for this proposal should be stated in the experimental protocol for transmission to the independent committee (I, 2).
6. The physician can combine medical research with professional care, the objective being the acquisition of new medical knowledge, only to the extent that medical research is justified by its potential diagnostic or therapeutic value for the patient.

III.   Non-therapeutic Biomedical Research Involving Human Subjects
(Non-clinical biomedical research)

1. In the purely scientific application of medical research carried out on a human being, it is the duty of the physician to remain the protector of the life and health of that person on whom biomedical research is being carried out.
2. The subjects should be volunteers—either healthy persons or patients for whom the experimental design is not related to the patient's illness.
3. The investigator or the investigating team should discontinue the research if in his/her or their judgement it may, if continued, be harmful to the individual.
4. In research on man, the interest of science and society should never take precedence over considerations related to the well-being of the subject.

Appendix 5
Mental Health Acts—Terminology

An ugly and unhelpful custom has developed amongst English mental health professionals. A patient detained against his wishes is said to be 'sectioned'. This conjures up a fate far worse than that actually suffered, and imparts very little information. (Would the Northern Ireland equivalent be 'articled'?) 'He is on a section 47' is very little better, because it is rarely followed by a reference to the Act concerned, and in any case is totally incomprehensible to the uninitiated. We therefore recommend that descriptive labels which have at least some meaning and some comparability across UK legislation be adopted as far as possible. A list suggesting names for some arrangements for the UK legislation follows listed against the relevant section and article numbers in that legislation. Some of these names have no official status, are approximate and may be bettered by others. All we are trying to suggest is clearer communication in non-threatening language. An example might be to translate 'he is on section 47' to 'after sentence he was transferred to hospital under the Mental Health Act' or 'he is detained in hospital under section 47 of the Mental Health Act as a sentenced prisoner'. Admittedly, the translations require a few more words, but the increment of meaning and the decrement of stigma are worth the extravagance. For those who cannot bear more than half a dozen words and say things like 'he was sectioned last night', we recommend 'he was detained on an order' or 'we have detained him'.

	MHA 1983 Section	MHA(S) 1984 Section	MH(NI)O 1986 Section
Assessment order	2		4
Treatment order	3		2
Admission order		18	
Emergency order	4	24	
Detention order	5	25	7
Short-term detention order		26	
Guardianship order	7	37	18
Remand for report	35	★	42
Remand for treatment	36	★	43
Hospital order	37	★	44
Interim hospital order	38	★	45
Restriction order	41	★	47
Transfer for sentenced prisoners	47	71	53
Transfer for unsentenced prisoners	48	70	54
Restriction direction	49	72	55
Police order	136	118	130

* *See* table 2.8 (pp. 86–7), these are dealt with by the Criminal Procedure (Scotland) Act 1975.

Appendix 6
Canada

Since the main body of the text went to press the Canadian criminal code has been amended with the most far reaching changes since the 1800s. This has had a profound effect on the laws in Canada governing the mentally disordered offender, and is stimulating at least one province (British Columbia) to produce a new mental health act. Owing to the timing of its production this book has not been able fully to take into account these changes. This appendix is to give the reader some indication of their extent and nature.

For example the new code specifies the criteria for fitness to stand trial. Unfitness means the inability 'to conduct a defence', or instruct counsel to do so, and in particular an inability, on account of mental disorder, to:

1. understand the nature or object of the proceedings;
2. understand the possible outcomes of the proceedings;
3. communicate with counsel.

If an individual is found unfit a disposition order provides the possibilities of absolute or conditional discharge, detention in custody in hospital, or an order specifying treatment for up to 60 days. Those individuals who are detained as 'unfit' are subject to the authority of the Review Board, mentioned below, and to identical procedures as those found 'not criminally responsible' on account of mental disorder.

Section 16 of the Code now reads:

1. No person is criminally responsible for an act or omission committed whilst suffering from a mental disorder that rendered the person incapable of appreciating the nature and quality of the act or omission, or of knowing that it was wrong.
2. Every person is presumed not to suffer from a mental disorder so as to be exempt from criminal responsibility by virtue of sub-section (1) until the contrary is proved on the balance of probabilities.
3. The burden of proof that an accused was suffering from a mental disorder so as to be exempt from the criminal responsibility is on the party that raises the issue.

These changes were not intended to alter the scope of the traditional insanity defence. As in other jurisdictions the meanings of the various key words in the legal definition have been subjected to a long line of judicial interpretations. Under the new changes 'natural imbecility' has been deleted and there appear to be no specific provisions for the mentally handicapped.

The new provisions also allow a judge to order an assessment on one or more of five specific grounds: fitness to stand trial, criminal responsibility, appropriate disposition following a verdict of 'not criminally responsible' or unfitness, whether to make a hospital order (a proposed provision so far not enacted), and in cases of suspected infanticide. The assessment and report must be carried out by a medical practitioner and be completed within thirty, or a maximum of sixty, days. Once an accused has been found unfit to stand trial, or not criminally responsible, the court or a Review Board must decide whether the individual needs to be confined in a hospital and, if so which one and subject to what conditions. To assist with the decisions the court or board may order a further assessment to address dispositional issues, including recommendations for the appropriate management of the patient, including the required level of custody or availability of treatment programmes. Once the disposition is decided the Board must hold a hearing within twelve months and every twelve months thereafter as long as the disposition remains in force. Under the system that existed previously involving warrants issued by the provincial Lieutenant Governor and monitored by a Board that made recommendations to him or her, no system of appeal or judicial review was available. This is now possible.

The Code had already been amended to allow an application by the Crown after a verdict of 'not criminally responsible' to have an accused who has committed an act of serious personal violence to be declared by the court 'a dangerous mentally disordered accused'. The court would seek evidence that the accused was unlikely to be inhibited by normal standards of behaviour restraint, or he has shown a failure to control his sexual impulses and will be likely to cause injury, pain or harm as a result. If this application is allowed, the accused 'not criminally responsible' person may be detained in prison for life. The individual is however subject to the Review Board's annual reviews.

The examples given in ch. 3 can still be read as illustrations of the way in which a particular system, the previous Canadian system, would deal with such a case.

Dr Derek Eaves, of British Columbia, has produced the attached figure to show the routes an accused may take under the new legislation and the possible outcomes. Dr Hucker, Head of the Forensic Division at the Clarke Institute of Psychiatry, 250 College Street, Toronto, Ontario M5T 1R8, Canada, will be able to furnish more details and further updates to interested readers.

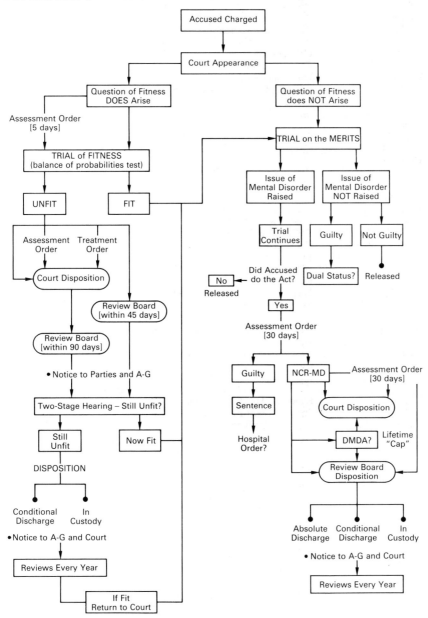

Cases Cited

Bold numbers, in brackets, after the citations indicate the pages in this book which refer to the particular case

References

Bold numbers in brackets after the references indicate the pages which cite the reference.

Please note the following common abbreviations:

APA – American Psychiatric Association
DHSS – Department of Health & Social Security
DOH – Department of Health
HMSO– Her Majesty's Stationery Office
MHAC– Mental Health Act Commission
WHO – World Health Organisation

Some references are cited in the text by one of these common abbreviations, they should be searched for by the full title.

The references are listed in strict alphabetical order so that MacCulloch comes well before McCabe. Alphabetical listing takes precedence over chronological order, so that, for example Jones (1988) appears before Jones (1972), as a result of the alphabetical order of the first author's initials, and Abel et al. (1984a) is separated from Abel et al. (1984b) by Abel et al. (1988) because of the alphabetical listing of the papers using the co-authors names. Papers 'in preparation' are not listed.

Aarvold, C., Hill, Sir D. and Newton, G. P. (1973) *Report on the Review of Procedures for the Discharge and Supervision of Psychiatric Patients subject to Special Restrictions*, HMSO Cmnd 5191: London (**185, 707**)

Abbott, R. J. and Loizou, L. A. (1986) Neuroleptic malignant syndrome. *British Journal of Psychiatry*, **148**, 47–51 (**667**)

Abel, G. G., Becker, J. V. and Cunningham-Rathner, J. (1984a) Complications, consent and cognitions in sex between children and adults. *International Journal of Law and Psychiatry*, 7, 89–103 (**557**)

Abel, G. G., Becker, J. V., Cunningham-Rathner, J., Mittelman, M. and Rouleau, J. L. (1988). Multiple paraphilic diagnoses among sex offenders. *Bulletin of the American Academy of Psychiatry and the Law*, **16**, 153–168 (**538**)

Abel, G. G., Becker, J. V., Cunningham-Rathner, J., Rouleau, J. L., Kaplan, M. and Reich, J. (1984b) *The Treatment of Child Molesters*. (Available from SBC-TM, 722 West 168th Street, Box 17, NY, NY10032) (**557**)

Abel, G. G., Becker, J. V., Murphy, W. D. and Flanagan, B. (1981) Identifying dangerous child molesters. In *Violent Behavior: Social Learning Approaches to Prediction, Management and Treatment* (ed. R. B. Stuart) Brunner/Mazel: New York (**538**)

Abel, G. G., Blanchard, E. B., Barlow, D. H. and Guild, D. (1977) The components of rapists' sexual arousal. *Archives of General Psychiatry*, **34**, 895–903 (**546, 552**)

Abelson, E. S. (1989) *When Ladies Go A-Thieving*, Oxford University Press: Oxford (**572**)

Ablon, S. L. and Goodwin, F. K. (1974) High frequency of dysphoric reactions to tetrahydro-cannabinol among depressed patients. *American Journal of Psychiatry*, **131**, 448–53 (**468**)

Abram, K. M. and Teplin, L. A. (1991) Co-occurring disorders among mentally ill jail detainees. *American Psychologist*, **46**, 1036–45 (**373**)

Abrams, A. (1983) The multiple personality: a legal defence. *American Journal of Clinical Hypnotism*, 25, 225–31 (65)

Ackerknecht, E. H. (1959) *A Short History of Psychiatry*, Hafner Publishing: London (691)

Acres, D. I. (1975) The after-care of special hospital patients. Appendix 3 in the *Report of the Committee on Mentally Abnormal Offenders*, Home Office, DHSS. HMSO Cmnd 6244: London (704, 707)

Adair, L. (1973) Suicide and homicide among alcoholics. *Alcoholism Review*, 12, 10–11 (448)

Adams-Tucker, C. (1982) Proximate effects of sexual abuse in childhood: a report on 28 children. *American Journal of Psychiatry*, 139, 1252–6 (918)

Addad, M., Benezech, M., Bourgeois, M. and Yesevage, J. (1981) Criminal acts among schizophrenics in French Mental Hospitals. *Journal of Nervous and Mental Diseases*, 169, 289–93 (367)

Addonizio, G., Susman, V. L. and Roth, S. D. (1986) Symptoms of neuroleptic malignant syndrome in 82 consecutive inpatients. *American Journal of Psychiatry*, 143, 1587–90 (666)

Adelson, L. (1961) Slaughter of the innocents. *New England Journal of Medicine*, 264 1345–9 (515)

Adler, F. (1977) The interaction between women's emancipation and female criminality: a cross cultural perspective. *International Journal of Criminology and Penology*, 5, 101–12 (604)

Adler, G. (1986) Psychotherapy of the narcissistic personality disorder patient: two contrasting approaches. *American Journal of Psychiatry*, 143, 430–6 (388)

Adler, R. (1985) *Taking Juvenile Justice Seriously*, Scottish Academic Press: Edinburgh (210, 237)

Advisory Committee on Dangerous Pathogens (1990) *HIV—the Causative Agent of AIDS and Related Conditions (second revision)*, Crown Copyright: London (818)

Advisory Council on the Misuse of Drugs (1979) *Report on Drug Users in the Prison System*, Home Office: London (476, 477)

Advisory Council on the Misuse of Drugs (1988) *AIDS and Drug Misuse: Part I*, Department of Health & Social Security: London (479, 480)

Aiken, G. J. M. (1984) Assaults on staff in a locked ward. *Medicine, Science and the Law*, 24, 190–207 (655)

Ainsworth, P. B. and Pease, K. (1987) *Police Work*, British Psychological Society & Methuen; London (733, 740)

Akhtar, S., Crocker, E., Dickey, N., Helfrich, J. and Rheuban, W. (1977) Overt sexual behavior among psychiatric inpatients. *Diseases of the Nervous System*, 38, 359–61 (821)

Akiskal, H. S. (1983) Dysthymic disorder: psychopathology of proposed chronic depressive subtypes. *American Journal of Psychiatry*, 140, 11–20 (366)

Akiskal, H. S., Djenderedjian A. H. and Rosenthal, R. H. (1977) Cyclothymic disorder: validating criteria for inclusion in the bipolar affective group. *American Journal of Psychiatry*, 134, 1227–33 (347, 366)

Akiskal, H. S., Rosenthal, T. L., Haykal, R. F., Lemmi, H., Rosenthal, R. H., and Scott-Strauss, A. (1980). Characterological depressions. *Archives of General Psychiatry*, 37, 777–83 (366)

Alanen, Y. O. (1968) From the mothers of schizophrenic patients to the interactional family dynamics. In *Transmission of Schizophrenia* (ed. D. Rosenthal and S. Kety) Pergamon: Oxford (367)

Albee, G. (1950) Patterns of aggression in psychopathology. *Journal of Consulting and Clinical Psychology*, 14, 465–8 (343)

Allderidge, P. (1974) Criminal insanity: Bethlem to Broadmoor. *Proceedings of the Royal Society of Medicine*, 67, 897–904 (692, 693)

Allderidge, P. (1979) Hospitals, madhouses and asylums: cycles in the care of the insane. *British Journal of Psychiatry*, 134, 321–34 (691)

Allen, H. (1987) *Justice Unbalanced. Gender, Psychiatry and Judicial Decisions*, Open University Press: Milton Keynes (616)

Allen, J. E. (1952) *Inside Broadmoor*, W. H. Allen: London (697)

Allen, N. (1990) *Making Sense of the Children Act 1989. A Guide for the Social and Welfare Services*, Longman: Harlow (239)

Allen, R. P., Safer, D. & Covi, L. (1975) Effects of psychostimulants on aggression. *Journal of Nervous and Mental Disease*, 160, 138–45 (663)

Allodi, F. and Cowgill, G. (1982) Ethical and psychiatric aspects of torture: A Canadian study. *Canadian Journal of Psychiatry*, 27, 98–102 (924)

Alström, C. H. (1950) Epilepsy. *Acta Psychiatrica et Neurologica Scandinavica*, Suppl. 63 **(302)**

Altshuler, K. Z., Abdullah, S. and Rainer, J. D. (1977) Lithium and aggressive behaviour in patients with early total deafness. *Diseases of the Nervous System*, **38**, 521–4 **(664)**

Alves, E. A. (1985) The control of anger in the 'mentally abnormal' offender. In *Current Contents in Clinical Psychology*, (ed. E. Kars) Plenum Press: New York **(676)**

Amark, C. (1951) A study in alcoholism. *Acta Psychiatrica et Neurologica Scandinavica, Suppl. 70* **(445)**

American Bar Association/Institute of Judicial Administration (1977) *Juvenile Justice Standards Project*, Ballinger: Cambridge, Mass. **(219)**

American Bar Association (1985) *American Bar Association, Criminal Justice-Mental Health Standards*, American Bar Association: Washington DC **(640)**

American Law Institute (1962) *Model Penal Code* American Law Insitute: Philadelphia **(142)**

American Medical Association (1981) *Standards for Health Services in Jails*, 2nd edn, American Medical Association: Chicago **(768)**

American Medical Association (1984) Insanity defense in criminal trials and limitations of psychiatric testimony. *Journal of the American Medical Association*, **251**, 2967–81 **(143)**

American Psychiatric Association (1980) *Diagnostic and Statistical Manual of Mental Disorders*, 3rd edn, American Psychiatric Association: Washington DC **(377)**

American Psychiatric Association (1983a) American Psychiatric Association statement on the insanity defense. *American Journal of Psychiatry*, **140**, 681–8 **(153)**

American Psychiatric Association (1983b) *Model State Law on Civil Commitment* **(640)**

American Psychiatric Association (1987a) *Diagnostic and Statistical Manual of Mental Disorders, 3rd edn, revised*, American Psychiatric Association: Washington DC **(284, 374–8, 384–95, 428, 443, 484, 886–8)**

American Psychiatric Association (1987b) Guidelines on confidentiality. *American Journal of Psychiatry*, **144**, 1522–6 **(864)**

American Psychiatric Association (1989a) Position statement on psychiatric services in jails and prisons. *American Journal of Psychiatry*, **146**, 1244 **(766)**

American Psychiatric Association (1989b) *The Principles of Medical Ethics with Annotations especially applicable to psychiatry*. American Psychiatric Assocation: Washington DC **(1018)**

American Psychiatric Association Commission on Psychotherapies (1982) *Psychotherapy Research*, American Psychiatric Association: Washington DC **(686)**

Amir, M. (1967) Alcohol and forcible rape. *British Journal of Addiction*, **62**, 219–32 **(448)**

Amir, M. (1971) *Patterns in Forcible Rape*, University of Chicago Press: Chicago **(543, 899)**

Amnesty International (1984) *Torture in the 80s—Amnesty International Report*, Amnesty International Publications: London **(924)**

Anderson, E. W. (1960) Amnesia. *The Medical Society's Translation*, **76**, 129–42 **(424)**

Anderson, E. W. & Mallinson, W. P. (1941) Psychogenic episodes in the course of major psychoses. *Journal of Mental Science*, **87** 383–96 **(425)**

Anderson, E. W., Trethowan, W. H. and Kenna, J. C. (1959) An experimental investigation of simulation and pseudo-dementia. *Acta Psychiatrica Scandinavica* Suppl. 132, vol. 34 **(419, 425)**

Anderson, R. A., Watson, A. A. and Harland, W. A. (1981) Fire deaths in the Glasgow area. *Medicine, Science and the Law*, **21**, 175–83 **(590)**

Andreasen, M. C. and Noyes, R. (1975) Suicide attempted by self-immolation. *American Journal of Psychiatry*, **132**, 554–6 **(595)**

Andrulonis, P. A., Glueck, B. C., Stroebel, C. F., and Vogel, N. G. (1982) borderline personality subcategories. *Journal of Nervous and Mental Disease*, **170**, 670–9 **(389)**

Angold, A. (1989) Seclusion. *British Journal of Psychiatry*, **154**, 437–44 **(669)**

Aniline, O. (1980) Current advice regarding diagnosis and management of PCP psychosis, (unpublished). University of Southern California: Los Angeles **(468)**

Anisman, H. L. (1978) Neurochemical changes elicited by stress: behavioral correlates. In *Psychopharmacology of Aversively Motivated Behavior* (eds. H. Anisman and G. Bignami) Plenum Press: New York **(932)**

Anisman, H. L., Ritch, M. and Sklar, Y. (1981) Noradrenergic and dopaminergic interactions in escape behavior: analysis of uncontrollable stress effects. *Psychopharmacology*, **74**, 263–8 **(932)**

Antoinette, T., Iyengar, S. and Puig-Antich, J. (1990) Is locked seclusion necessary for children under the age of 14? *American Journal of Psychiatry*, **147**, 1283–9 **(659)**

Appelbaum, P. S. (1986) Competence to be executed: another conundrum for mental health professionals. *Hospital and Community Psychiatry*, **37**, 682–4 **(122)**

Appelbaum, P. S. (1988) The right to refuse treatment with antipsychotic medications: retrospect and prospect. *American Journal of Psychiatry*, **145**, 413–9 **(121)**

Applebaum, P. S. and Roth, L. H. (1981) Clinical issues in the assessment of competency. *American Journal of Psychiatry*, **138**, 1462–7 **(875)**

Appelbaum, P. S. and Roth, L. H. (1984) Involuntary treatment in medicine and psychiatry. *American Journal of Psychiatry*, **141**, 202–5 **(877)**

Appelbaum, P. S., Jackson, A. H. and Shader, R. I. (1983) Psychiatrists' responses to violence: pharmacologic management of psychiatric inpatients. *American Journal of Psychiatry*, **140**, 301–4 **(661)**

Appelbaum, P. S., Zonana, H., Bonnie, R. and Roth, L. H. (1989) Statutory approaches to limiting psychiatrists' liability for their patients' violent acts. *American Journal of Psychiatry*, **146**, 321–8 **(864)**

Arieti, S. and Bemporad, J. R (1974) Rare unclassifiable and collective psychiatric syndromes. In *American Handbook of Psychiatry* (eds. S. Arieti and E. Brody) Basic Books: New York **(425)**

Äsberg, M., Montgomery, S. A., Perris, C., Schalling, D. and Sedvall, G. (1978) The Comprehensive Psychiatric Rating Scale. *Acta Psychiatrica Scandinavica* Suppl. 271, 5–27 **(294, 341)**

Asher, R. (1951) Munchausen's Syndrome. *Lancet* i, 339–41 **(412)**

Asher, R. (1958) 'Malingering'. *Transactions of the Medical Society of London*, **75**, 34–44 **(418)**

Ashley, M. C. (1922) Outcome of 1000 cases paroled from the Middletown State Hospital. *New York State Hospital Quarterly*, **8**, 64–70 **(333)**

Ashton, C. H. (1987) Dangers and medico-legal aspects of benzodiazepines. *Journal of the Medical Defence Union*, **3**, 6–8 **(474)**

Ashton, H. (1984) Benzodiazepine withdrawal: an unfinished story. *British Medical Journal*, **288**, 1135–40 **(474)**

Ashton, J. R. and Donnan, S. (1981) Suicide by burning as an epidemic phenomenon: an analysis of 82 deaths and inquests in England and Wales in 1978–9. *Psychological Medicine*, **11** 735–9 **(595)**

Ashworth, A. (1991) *Principles of Criminal Law*, Clarendon Press: Oxford **(60)**

Asperger, H. (1944) Die 'Autistischen Psychopathen' im Kindesalter. *Archiv für Psychiatries und Nerven Krankheiten*, **117**, 76–136 **(394)**

Asquith, S. (1983) *Children and Justice: Decision making in Children's Hearings and Juvenile Courts*, University Press: Edinburgh **(210, 237)**

Association of County Councils (1984) *Juvenile Courts*, ACC: London **(236)**

Association of Directors of Social Services (1985) *Children Still in Trouble*. Report of an ADSS Study Group. ADSS: Taunton **(236)**

Astrup, C. (1984) Querulent paranoia: a follow-up. *Neuropsychobiology*, **11** 149–54 **(356)**

Atiyah, P. (1983) *Law and Modern Society*, Oxford University Press: Oxford **(178)**

Atkeson, B. J., Calhoun, K. S. Resich, P. A. and Ellis, E. M. (1982) Victims of rape: reported assessment by depressive symptoms. *Journal of Consulting and Clinical Psychology*, **50**, 96–102 **(895, 916)**

Atkinson, J. M. (1989) To tell or not to tell the diagnosis of schizophrenia. *Journal of Medical Ethics*, **15**, 21–4 **(866)**

Aubert, V. (1963) The structure of legal thinking. *Legal Essays* (ed. F. Castberg) Universitets-forlaget: Norway **(827)**

Auerbach, D. B. (1982) The Ganser Syndrome. In *Extraordinary Disorders of Human Behaviour* (eds. C. T. H. Friedmann and R. A. Faguet) Plenum Press: New York **(425, 426)**

Ausubel, D. P. (1961) Personality disorder *is* disease. *American Psychologist*, **16**, 69–74 **(10)**

Averill, J. R. (1983) Studies on anger and aggression: implications for theories of emotion. *American Psychologist*, **38**, 1145–60 **(494)**

Awad, G. A. (1987) The assessment of custody and access disputes in cases of sexual abuse allegations. *Canadian Journal of Psychiatry*, **32**, 539–44 **(943)**

Axelrod, R. (1984) *The Evolution of Co-operation*, Basic Books: New York **(495)**

Ayd, F. (1972) Haloperidol: fifteen years of clinical experience. *Diseases of the Nervous System*, **33**, 459–69 **(661)**

Ayllon, T. and Milan, M. A. (1979) *Correctional Rehabilitation and Management: a Psychological Approach*, Wiley: Chichester **(674)**

Azrin, N. H. and Foxx, R. M. (1971) A rapid method of toilet training for the institutionalised retarded. *Journal of Applied Behaviour Analysis*, **4**, 89–99 **(674)**

Babington, A. (1985) *For the Sake of Example*, Paladin: London (**886**)

Bach-y-Rita, G., Lion, J. R., Climent, C. and Ervin, F. R. (1971) Episodic dyscontrol: a study of 130 violent patients. *American Journal of Psychiatry*, 127, 1473–8 (**288**)

Bach-y-Rita, G., Lion, J. R. and Ervin, E. R. (1970) Pathological intoxication: clinical and electroencephalographic studies. *American Journal of Psychiatry*, 127, 158–163 (**443**)

Bach-y-Rita, G. and Veno, A. (1974) Habitual violence: a profile of 62 men. *American Journal of Psychiatry*, 131, 1015–7 (**334, 809**)

Bachman, J. G., O'Malley, P. M. and Johnston, J. (1978) *Youth in Transition, Vol. 6*, University of Michigan Institute for Social Research: Ann Arbor, MI (**265**)

Baker, A. W. and Duncan, S. P. (1985) Child sexual abuse: a study of prevalence in Great Britain. *Child Abuse and Neglect*, 9, 457–67 (**533, 537, 917**)

Baker, F. M., Perr, I. N. and Yesevage, J. A. (1986) *An Overview of Legal Issues in Geriatric Psychiatry*, American Psychiatric Press: Washington DC (**325**)

Baldessarini, R. J., Cohen, B. M. and Teicher, M. H. (1988) Significance of neuroleptic dose and plasma level in the pharmacological treatment of psychoses. *Archives of General Psychiatry*, 45, 79–91 (**663**)

Baldwin, J. (1976) The social composition of the magistracy. *British Journal of Criminology*, 16, 171–4 (**221**)

Baldwin, J. (1979) Ecological and area studies in Great Britain and the United States. In *Crime and Justice* (eds. N. Morris and M. Tonry) University of Chicago Press: Chicago, Vol. 1, pp. 29–66 (**273**)

Baldwin, J. and Bottoms, A. E. (1976) *The Urban Criminal*, Tavistock: London (**274**)

Baldwin J. and McConville, M. (1979) *Jury Trials*, Clarendon Press: Oxford (**177**)

Baldwin, S. (1983) Nursing models in special hospital settings. *Journal of Advanced Nursing*, 8, 473–6 (**652**)

Balier, C. (1988) *Psychanalyse des comportements violents*, Presses Universitaires Françaises: Paris. (**153**)

Balla, J. E. and Moraitis, S. (1970) Knights in armour: a follow-up study of injuries after legal settlement. *Medical Journal of Australia*, 2, 355–61 (**416**)

Ballenger, J. C. and Post, R. M. (1980) Carbamazepine in manic-depressive illness: a new treatment. *American Journal of Psychiatry*, 137, 782–90 (**666**)

Banay, R. S. (1942) Alcoholism and crime. *Quarterly Journal of Studies in Alcohol*, 2, 686– 716 (**446, 448**)

Banay, R. S. (1944) Pathological reaction to alcohol. 1. Review of the lifetime and original case reports. *Quarterly Journal of Studies on Alcohol*, 4, 580–605 (**443**)

Bancroft, J. (1989) *Human Sexuality and its Problems*, 2nd edn, Churchill Livingstone: Edinburgh (**524**)

Bancroft, J. (1991) The sexuality of sexual offending: the social dimension. *Criminal Behaviour and Mental Health*, 1, 181–92 (**524, 531, 532, 545, 554**)

Bancroft, J., Tennent, G., Loucas, K. and Cass, J. (1974) The control of deviant sexual behaviour with drugs. *British Journal of Psychiatry*, 125, 310–5 (**565**)

Bandura, A. (1973) *Aggression: A Social Learning Analysis*. Prentice-Hall: Englewood Cliffs, NJ (**670, 671**)

Bandura, A. (1983) Psychological mechanisms of aggression. In *Aggression: Theoretical and Experimental Reviews Vol. 1*, (eds. R. G. Geen and E. I. Donnerstein) Academic Press: New York (**494**)

Bandura, A. (1986) *Social Foundations of Thought and Action*, Prentice-Hall: Englewood Cliffs, NJ (**382**)

Banks, A. and Waller, T. A. N. (1988) *Drug Misuse: A Practical Handbook for GPs*, Blackwell Scientific Publications (in association with the Institute for the Study of Drug Dependence): London (**471**)

Barclay, G. C., Vennard, J. and Turner, D. (1991) *A Digest of Information on the Criminal Justice System*, Home Office: London (**803**)

Barker, A. F. (1988) Mentally disordered offenders and the courts. *Justice of the Peace*, 152, 55–7 (**770**)

Barker, J. C. and Miller, M. (1968) Aversion therapy for compulsive gamblers. *Journal of Nervous and Mental Disease*, 146, 285–302 (**488**)

Barlow, D. H. (1977) Assessment of sexual behavior. In *Handbook of Behavioral Assessment* (eds. R. A. Ciminero, K. S. Calhoun and H. E. Adams) Wiley: New York (**555**)

Barlow, D. H. and Agras, W. S. (1973) Fading to increase heterosexual responsiveness in homosexuals. *Journal of Applied Behavior Analysis*, **6**, 855–66 **(561)**

Barlow, G. (1978) Security—a dirty word? *Journal of Adolescence*, **1**, 345–51 **(235)**

Barnes, T. R. E. and Bridges, P. K. (1980) Disturbed behaviour induced by high-dose antipsychotic drugs. *British Medical Journal* **281**, 274–5 **(663)**

Baron, R. A. (1983) Control of human aggression: an optimistic perspective. *Journal of Social and Clinical Psychology*, **1**, 97–119 **(493)**

Bart, P. B. (1981) A study of women who both were raped and avoided rape. *Journal of Social Issues*, **37**, 123–37 **(916, 920)**

Bartholomew, A. A., Milte, K. L. and Galbally, G. (1978) Homosexual necrophilia. *Medicine, Science and the Law*, **18**, 29–35 **(553)**

Barton, R. W. (1959) *Institutional Neurosis*, Wright: Bristol **(796)**

Baruk, H. (1959) Delusions of passion. In *Themes and Variations in European Psychiatry* (eds S. R. Hirsch and M. Shepherd) Wright: Bristol, 1974, pp. 375–83 **(350)**

Basson, J. V. and Woodside, M. L. (1981) Assessment of a secure/intensive care/forensic ward. *Acta Psychiatrica Scandinavica*, **64**, 132–41 **(722)**

Bassuk, E. L. and Gerson, S. (1978) Deinstitutionalisation and mental health services. *Scientific American*, **238**, 45–53 **(693)**

Bateson, G., Jackson, D., Haley, J. and Weahland, J. (1956) Toward a theory of schizophrenia. *Behavioural Science*, **1**, 251–64 **(367)**

Batt, J. C. (1948) Homicidal incidence in the depressive psychoses. *Journal of Mental Science*, **94**, 782–92 **(347)**

Batta, I., McCulloch, J. W. and Smith, N. J. (1975) A study of juvenile delinquency amongst Asians and half-Asians. *British Journal of Criminology*, **15**, 32–42 **(277)**

Baumgartner, A. M., Jones, P. F., Baumgartner, A. W. and Black, T. C. (1979) Radioimmunassay of hair for determining opiate abuse histories. *Journal of Nuclear Medicine*, **20**, 748 **(467)**

Bazelon, D. L. (1969) Introduction. In *The Right to Treatment* (ed. D. S. Burris) Springer: New York **(873)**

Bean, P. T. (1985) Social control and social theory. In *Secure Provision* (ed. L. Gostin) Tavistock: London, pp 288–306 **(798)**

Beardshaw, V. (1981) *Conscientious Objectors at Work*, Social Audit: London **(797)**

Beattie, J. M. (1986) *Crime and the Courts in England 1660–1800*, Clarendon Press: Oxford **(49)**

Beck, A. T., Ward, C. H., Mendelson, M., Mock, J. and Erbaugh, J. (1961) An inventory for measuring depression. *Archives of General Psychiatry*, **4**, 461–571 **(294)**

Beck, A. T., Weissman, A. and Kovacs, M. (1976) Alcoholism, hopelessness and suicidal behaviour. *Journal of Hospital Medicine*, **22**, 366–77 **(445)**

Beck, T. R. (1829) *Elements of Medical Jurisprudence*, Londman Rees: Edinburgh **(417)**

Becker, J. V., Abel, G. G. and Skinner, L. J. (1979) The impact of a sexual assault on the victim's sexual life. *Victimology*, **5**, 229–35 **(916)**

Beebe, G. W. (1975) Follow-up studies of World War II and Korean War prisoners. II: Morbidity, disability and maladjustments. *American Journal of Epidemiology*, **101**, 400–22 **(925)**

Beigel, A., Beeren, M. R. and Harding, T. W. (1984) The paradoxical impact of a commitment statute on prediction of dangerousness. *The American Journal of Psychiatry*, **141**, 373–7 **(146)**

Beigel, A., and Murphy, D. S. (1971) Assessing clinical characteristics of the manic state. *American Journal of Psychiatry*, **128**, 688–94 **(348)**

Bell, A. P., Weinberg, M. S. and Hammersmith, S. K. (1981) *Sexual Preference*, Bloomington: Indiana University Press, Indiana **(535, 540, 919)**

Bell, D. S. and Champion, R. A. (1979) Deviancy, delinquency and drug use. *British Journal of Psychiatry*, **134**, 269–76 **(447)**

Bell, P., Kee, M., Loughrey, G. C., Curran, P. S. and Roddy, R. J. (1988) Post-traumatic stress in Northern Ireland. *Acta Psychiatrica Scandinavica*, **77** 166–9 **(896)**

Bell, S. (1988) *When Salem came to the Boro*, Pan: London **(535, 536)**

Bender, L. and Grugett, A. E. (1952) A follow-up report on children who had atypical sexual experience. *American Journal of Orthopsychiatry*, **22**, 825–37 **(918)**

Benedek, E. (1985) Premenstrual syndrome: a new defence? In *The Psychiatric Complications of Menstruation* (ed J. H. Gold) American Psychiatric Press Inc: Washington DC **(607)**

Benezech, M., Bourgeois, M. and Noel, B. (1974) Les hommes double Y. *Annales de Médecine Psychologique*, **2**, 365–94 **(315)**

Bennet, G. (1970) Bristol floods 1968. Controlled survey of effects on health of local community disaster. *British Medical Journal*, 3 454–8 (**906, 933**)

Bennett, B. (1989) *Education in a special hospital*. University of Nottingham: Nottingham (**703**)

Bennett, T. and Wright, R. (1986) The impact of prescribing on the crimes of opiate users. *British Journal of Addiction*, 81, 265–73 (**475**)

Beresford, D. (1987) *Ten Men Dead*, Grafton Books: London (**759**)

Berg, I., Hullin, R. and McGuire, R. (1979) A randomly controlled trial of two court procedures in truancy. In *Psychology, Law and Legal Processes* (eds. D. P. Farrington, K. Hawkins and S. Lloyd-Bostock) MacMillan: London, pp. 143–51 (**281**)

Bergler, E. (1958) *The Psychology of Gambling*, Harrison: London (**483, 487**)

Berkowitz, L. (1962) *Aggression: A Psychological Analysis*, McGraw-Hill Book Co. Inc: New York (**347**)

Berkowitz, L. (1989) Frustration-aggression hypothesis: examination and reformulation, *Psychological Bulletin*, 106, 59–73 (**493**)

Berlin, F. S. and Meinecke, C. F. (1981) Treatment of sex offenders with antiandrogenic medication: conceptualisation, review of treatment modalities, and preliminary findings. *American Journal of Psychiatry*, 138, 601–7 (**562**)

Berlyne, N. (1972) Confabulation. *British Journal of Psychiatry*, 120, 31–9 (**411**)

Berman, A. and Seigal, A. (1976) Adaptive and learning skills in juvenile delinquents: a neuropsychological analysis. *Journal of Learning Disability*, 9, 583–90 (**289**)

Berner, W. and Karlick-Bolten, E. (1986) *Verlaufsformen der Sexualdelinquenz*, Enke: Stuttgart (**132**)

Berrington, W. P., Liddell, D. W. and Foulds, G. A. (1956) A re-evaluation of the fugue. *Journal of Mental Science*, 102, 281–6 (**295**)

Berrueta-Clement, J. R., Schweinhart, L. J., Barnett, W. S., Epstein, A. S. and Weikart, D. P. (1984) *Changed Lives*, High/Scope: Ypsilanti, MI (**281**)

Berry, M. J. (1986) Evaluating secure units: some methodological difficulties. *Paper presented at the Spring Quarterly Meeting of the Royal College of Psychiatrists*, Manchester, April 1986 (unpublished) (**716**)

Berry, M. J. (1987) Staffing secure units. *Nursing Times*, July 22, 83, No. 29 (**712**)

Betts, P. (1988) Small stature and physical signs. *Journal of Social Welfare Law* 79–81 (**834**)

Beyaert, F. H. L. (1980) The Dutch situation and some problems. *International Journal of Law and Psychiatry*, 14, 231–44 (**153**)

Bieber, S., Pasewark, R., Bosten, K, and Steadman, H. (1988) Predicting criminal recidivism of insanity acquitees. *International Journal of Law and Psychiatry*, 11, 105–12 (**641**)

Binder, R. L. (1979) The use of seclusion on an inpatient crisis intervention unit. *Hospital and Community Psychiatry*, 30, 266–9 (**659**)

Binder, R. and McNeil, D. (1988) Effects of diagnosis and context on dangerousness. *American Journal of Psychiatry*, 145, 728–32 (**349, 641**)

Bion, W. (1957) Differentiation of the psychotic from the non-psychotic personalities. *International Journal of Psychoanalysis*, 38, 266–75 (**679**)

Birrell, A. G. and Birrell, J. H. W. (1968) The maltreatment syndrome in children: a hospital survey. *Medical Journal of Australia*, ii, 1023–9 (**912**)

Birtchnell, J. (1988) Depression and family relationships: a study of young, married women on a London housing estate. *British Journal of Psychiatry*, 157, 758–69 (**367**)

Bjorndal, N., Bjerre, M., Gerlach, J., Kristjansen, P., Magelund, G., Oestrich, I. H. and Waehrens, J. (1980) High dosage haloperidol therapy in chronic schizophrenic patients: a double-blind study of clinical response, side effects, serum haloperidol and serum prolactin. *Psychopharmacology*, 67, 17–23 (**663**)

Black, D. (1981) The extended Munchausen's Syndrome: a family case. *British Journal of Psychiatry*, 138, 446–69 (**422**)

Black, D. and Kaplan, T. (1988) Father kills mother. *British Journal of Psychiatry*, 153, 624–30 (**921**)

Black, D. A. (1982) A 5-year follow up study of male patients discharged from Broadmoor hospital. In *Abnormal Offenders, Delinquency and the Criminal Justice System* (eds. J. Gunn and D. P. Farrington) Wiley: Chichester (**627, 706**)

Black, D. A. (1984) Treatment in maximum security settings. In *Mentally Abnormal Offenders* (ed. M. Craft and A. Craft) Baillière Tindall: London (**703**)

Blackburn, I. M. (1974) The pattern of hostility in affective illness. *British Journal of Psychiatry*, 125, 141–5 (**364**)

Blackburn, R. (1968) Emotionality, extraversion and aggression in paranoid and non-paranoid schizophrenic offenders. *British Journal of Psychiatry*, 115, 301–2 (**363**)

Blackburn, R. (1970) Personality types among abnormal homicides. *Special Hospitals Research Report No. 1*, DHSS: London (**359, 364**)

Blackburn, R. (1974) Personality and classification of psychopathic disorders. *Special Hospitals Research Report No. 10*, DHSS: London (**348**)

Blackburn, R. (1988a) Psychopathy and personality disorder. In *Adult Abnormal Psychology* (eds. E. Miller and P. Cooper) Churchill Livingstone: London (**378**)

Blackburn, R. (1988b) On moral judgments and personality disorders. *British Journal of Psychiatry*, 152, 505–12 (**386**)

Blackler, C. (1968) Primary recidivism in adult men: differences between men on first and second prison sentence. *British Journal of Criminology*, 8, 130–67 (**323**)

Blanchard, E. B. and Abel, G. (1976) An experimental case study of the biofeedback treatment of a rape-induced psychophysiological cardiovascular disorder. *Behavior Therapy*, 7, 113–9 (**938**)

Blanchard, E. B., Kolb, L. C., Pallmeyer, T. P. and Gerardi, R. J. (1983) A psychophysiologic study of post-traumatic stress disorder in Vietnam veterans. *Psychiatric Quarterly*, 54 220–8 (**928**)

Blanchard, R. and Hucker, S. J. (1991) Age, transvestism, bondage and concurrent paraphilic activities in 17 fatal cases of autoerotic asphyxia. *British Journal of Psychiatry*, 159, 371–7 (**552**)

Bleich, A., Siegel, B., Garb, R. and Lever, B. (1986) Post-traumatic stress disorder following combat experience: clinical features and psychopharmacological treatment. *British Journal of Psychiatry*, 149, 365–9 (**936, 937**)

Bleuler, E. (1916) *Textbook of Psychiatry* (trans. A. A. Brill 1924) Macmillan: New York (Reissued by Dover Publication 1951) (**425**)

Bloch, S. and Reddaway, P. (1977) *Russia's Political Hospitals: the Abuse of Psychiatry in the Soviet Union*. Gollancz: London (**859**)

Block, R. (1981) Victim-offender dynamics in violent crime. *The Journal of Criminal Law and Criminology*, 72, 743–61 (**920**)

Bloom, J. D., Williams, M. H., Rogers, J. L. and Barbur, P. (1986) Evaluation and treatment of insanity acquittees in the community. *Bulletin of the American Academy of Psychiatry and the Law*, 14, 231–44 (**143, 144**)

Bluglass, R. (1979) The psychiatric assessment of homicide. *British Journal of Hospital Medicine*, 22, 366–7 (**515**)

Bluglass, R. (1984) *A Guide to the Mental Health Act 1983*, Churchill Livingstone: Edinburgh (**40**)

Bluglass, R. (1985) The development of regional secure units. In *Secure Provision: A Review of Special Services for the Mentally Ill and Mentally Handicapped in England and Wales* (ed. L. Gostin) Tavistock: London (**710**)

Blumstein, A., Cohen, J. and Farrington, D. P. (1988a) Criminal career research: its value for criminology. *Criminology*, 26, 1–35 (**278**)

Blumstein, A., Cohen, J. and Farrington, D. P. (1988b) Longitudinal and criminal career research: further clarifications. *Criminology*, 26, 57–74 (**278**)

Blumstein, A., Cohen, J., Roth, J. and Visher, C. (1986) *Criminal Careers and Career Criminals*, National Academy Press: Washington DC (**641**)

Blunt, L. W. and Stock, H. V. (1985) Guilty but mentally ill: an alternative verdict. *Behavioral Sciences and the Law*, 3, 49–68 (**49, 143, 144**)

Board of Control (1921) *7th Annual Report 1920*, HMSO: London (**317**)

Board of Control (1928) *14th Annual Report 1927*, HMSO: London (**317**)

Board of Control (1939) *25th Annual Report 1938*, HMSO: London (**317**)

Board of Control (1947) *33rd Annual Report 1946*, HMSO: London (**318**)

Bobon, D. and De Bleeker, E. (1990) Zuclopenthixol acetate and haloperidol in acute psychotic patients—a randomised multicentre study. In *New Strategies in the Treatment of Aggressive, Acutely Psychotic Patients* (ed. B. Wistedt) Excerpta Medica: Amsterdam (**663**)

Bochel, D. (1976) *Probation and After-care, its Development in England & Wales*, Scottish Academic Press: Edinburgh & London (**769, 771, 782**)

Bodde, D. (1973) Age, youth and infirmity in the law of Ch'ing China. *University of Pennsylvania Law Review*, 121, 437–41 (**325**)

Bollini, P., Andreani, A., Colombo, F., Bellantuonto, C., Beretta, P., Arduini, A., Galli, T.

and Tognani, G. (1984) High dose neuroleptics: uncontrolled clinical practice confirms controlled clinical trial. *British Journal of Psychiatry*, **144**, 25–7 (**663, 664**)

Bolton, N., Smith, F. V., Heskin, K. J. and Bannister, P. A. (1976) Psychological correlates of long-term imprisonment IV. A longitudinal analysis. *British Journal of Criminology*, **16**, 38–47 (**803**)

Bomio, G. (1990) Auguste Forel et le droit pénal. *Revue Pénale Suisse*, **107**, 87–105 (**139**)

Bond, A. and Lader, M. (1984) The psychopharmacology of aggression. In *Current Themes in Psychiatry Vol. 3* (eds. R. N. Gaind, I. F. Fawzy, B. L. Hudson, R. O. Pasnau) Macmillan Press: London (**660**)

Bond, M. (1989) Referrals to a new regional secure unit—what happens to patients refused admission. *Medicine, Science and the Law*, **29**, 329–32 (**718**)

Bond, M. R. (1984) The psychiatry of closed head injury. In *Closed Head Injury* (ed. D. N. Brooks) Oxford University Press: Oxford (**287**)

Bonhoeffer, K. (1904) Quoted in Berlyne (1972) (**411**)

Bonkalo, A. (1974) Impulsive acts and confusional states during incomplete arousal from sleep: criminological and forensic implications. *Psychiatry Quarterly*, **48**,. 400–9 (**309**)

Boor, M. (1982) The multiple personality epidemic. *Journal of Nervous and Mental Disease*, **170**, 302–4 (**428**)

Boorse, C. (1975) On the distinction between disease and illness. *Philosophy and Public Affairs*, **5**, 49–68 (**7**)

Boorse, C. (1976) What a theory of mental health should be. *Journal of the Theory of Social Behaviour*, **6**, 61–84 (**7**)

Borison, R. L., Diamond, B. L., Sinha, D., Gupta, R. P. and Ajiboye, P. A. (1988) Clozapine withdrawal rebound psychosis. *Psychopharmacological Bulletin*, **24**, 260–3 (**665**)

Bottomley, S. (1987) Mental health and law reform and psychiatric de-institutionalisation: the issues in New South Wales. *International Journal of Law and Psychiatry*, **10**, 369–81 (**726**)

Bottoms, A. E. (1985) Justice for juveniles 75 years on. In *75 years of Law at Sheffield 1909–84* (ed. D. Heath) University Printing Unit: Sheffield (**237**)

Bottoms, A. E. and McWilliams, W. (1979) A non-treatment paradigm for probation practice. *British Journal of Social Work*, **9**, 159–202 (**785**)

Botvin, G. J. and Eng, A. (1982) The efficacy of a multicomponent approach to the prevention of cigarette smoking. *Preventive Medicine*, **11**, 199–211 (**283**)

Bourgeois, M. (1969) Suicide par le feu à la manière de bonzes. *Annales Médico-psychologiques, Revue Psychiatrique*, **127**, 116–26. (**595**)

Bowden, P. (1976) Medical practice: defendants and prisoners. *Journal of Medical Ethics*, **24**, 163–72 (**870**)

Bowden, P. (1978a) A psychiatric clinic in a probation office. *British Journal of Psychiatry*, **133**, 448–51 (**728**)

Bowden, P. (1978b) Men remanded into custody for medical reports: the selection for treatment. Men remanded into custody for medical reports: the outcome of the treatment recommendation. *British Journal of Psychiatry*, **133**, 320–31, 332–8 (**360, 362, 723, 742**)

Bowker, L. H. (1978) *Women, Crime and the Criminal Justice System*, Heath: Lexington, Mass (**603**)

Box, S. and Hale, C. (1983) Liberation and female criminality in England and Wales. *British Journal of Criminology*, **23**, 35–49 (**603**)

Boyd, W. H. and Bolen, D. W. (1970) The compulsive gambler and spouse in group psychotherapy. *International Journal of Group Psychotherapy*, **20**, 77–90 (**488**)

Boyle, C. K. and Allen, M. J. (1983) *Sentencing Law and Practice in Northern Ireland*, SLS Legal Publications: Belfast (**97**)

Boyle, J. (1977) *A Sense of Freedom*, Pan: London (**753**)

Bradford, J. and Balmaceda, R. (1983) 'Shoplifting'—is there a specific psychiatric syndrome? *Canadian Journal of Psychiatry*, **28**, 248–53 (**575**)

Bradford, J. and Smith, S. M. (1979) Amnesia and homicide: the Podola case and a study of thirty cases. *Bulletin of the American Academy of Psychiatry and the Law*, **7**, 219–31 (**291, 292, 293, 297**)

Brahams, D. (1981) Premenstrual syndrome: a disease of the mind? *Lancet*, ii, 1238–40 (**607**)

Brahams, D. (1982) Rejection of premenstrual syndrome as a defence in English law. *Lancet*, i, 1134–5 (**607**)

Brahams, D. (1987) Iatrogenic crime: criminal behaviour in patients receiving drug treatment. *Lancet*, i 874–5 (**64**)

Brahams, D. (1991) Sleepwalking, 'disease of the mind'? *Lancet*, **338**, 375–6 (**308**)

Brakel, S. J., Parry, J. and Weiner, B. A. (1985) *The Mentally Disabled and the Law* 3rd edn, American Bar Foundation: Chicago (**126, 145**)

Brandt, J. and Butters, N. (1986) The alcoholic Wernicke-Korsakoff syndrome and its relationship to long-term alcohol abuse. In *Neuropsychological Assessment of Neuropsychiatric Disorders* (eds. I. Grant and K. M. Adams) Oxford University Press: Oxford (**444**)

Braun, B. (1984) Hypnosis creates multiple personality: myth or reality? *International Journal of Experimental Hypnosis*, **32**, 191–7 (**428**)

Brecher, E. M. (1978) *Treatment Programs for Sex offenders*, US Dept of Justice, Govt Printing Office: Washington DC (**566**)

Breier, A., Albus, M., Pickar, D., Zahn, T. P., Wolkowitz, O. M. and Paul, S. M. (1987) Controllable and uncontrollable stress in humans: alterations in mood and neuroendocrine and psychophysiological function. *American Journal of Psychiatry*, **144**, 1419–25 (**931**)

Brende, J. O. (1982) Electrodermal responses in post-traumatic syndrome: a pilot of study of cerebral hemisphere functioning in Vietnam Veterans. *Journal of Nervous and Mental Diseases*, **170**, 353–61 (**932**)

Brenner, C., Friedman, A. P., Merritt, H. H. and Denny-Brown, D. E. (1944) Post-traumatic headache. *Journal of Neurosurgery*, **1** 379–91 (**907**)

Brennan, J. J. (1964) Mentally ill aggressiveness, popular delusions as reality. *American Journal of Psychiatry*, **120**, 1181–4 (**333**)

Brett, E. A. and Ostroff, R. (1985) Imagery and post-traumatic stress disorder: an overview. *American Journal of Psychiatry*, **142**, 417–24 (**932**)

Brettle, R. P., Bisset, K., Burns, S., Davidson, S. J., Gray, J. M. N., Inglis, J. M., Lees, J. S. and Mok, J. (1987) Human immuno-deficiency virus and drug misuse: the Edinburgh experience. *British Medical Journal*, **295**, 441–24 (**470**)

Brill, H. (1982) Auto theft and the role of big business. *Crime and Social Justice*, **18**, 62–8 (**579**)

Brill, H. and Malzberg, B. (1962) Statistical report based on the arrest records of 5354 male ex-patients released from New York State Mental Hospitals during the period 1946–1948. *Mental Hospital Service Supplement 153*, American Psychiatric Association: Washington DC (**333**)

Brinkley, J. R., Beitman, B. D. and Friedel, R. O. (1979) Low-dose neuroleptic regimens in the treatment of borderline patients. *Archives of General Psychiatry*, **36**, 319–26 (**668**)

British Journal of Psychiatry (1992) Clozapine, the atypical antipsychotic. *British Journal of Psychiatry*, **160**, Suppl 17 (**664**)

British Medical Association (1974) Ethical statement (on Hunger Strikers). *British Medical Journal*, **2**, 52 (**769**)

British Medical Association (1987) *Immunisation against Hepatitis B*, British Medical Association: London (**818**)

British Medical Association and Royal Pharmaceutical Society of Great Britain (continuous) *British National Formulary*—published twice yearly, BMA: London (**xxviii**)

British Medical Association Foundation for AIDS (1988) *HIV Infection and AIDS: Ethical considerations for the Medical Profession*, British Medical Association: London (**875**)

British Medical Journal (1965) Editorial: pathological gambling. **1**. 809 (**482**)

British Medical Journal Legal Correspondent (1974) The law and force feeding. *British Medical Journal*, **2**, 737–8 (**759**)

British Medical Journal Notes and News (1974a) Parliament, artificial feeding of prisoners. *British Medical Journal*, **3**, 267 (**760**)

British Medical Journal Notes and News (1974b) Ethical statement, artificial feeding of prisoners. *British Medical Journal*, **3**, 52 (**760**)

Brittain, R. P. (1970) The sadistic murderer. *Medicine, Science and the Law*, **10**, 198–207 (**390**)

Brodsky, S. L. and West, D. J. (1981) Life-skills treatment of sex-offenders. *Law and Psychology Review*, **6**, 97–168 (**539**)

Brody, S. R. (1976) *The Effectiveness of Sentencing*, Home Office Research Study No. 32, HMSO: London (**280, 784**)

Brody, S. (1977) *Screen Violence and Film Censorship*, Home Office Research Study No. 40, HMSO: London (**496, 497**)

Brongersma, E. (1986) *Loving Boys (vol. 1) A Multidisciplinary Study of Sexual Relations between Adult and Minor Males*, Global Academic: New York (**535**)

Brooks, D. S., Murphy, D., Janota, I. and Lishman, W. A. (1987) Early onset of Huntington's chorea—diagnostic clues. *British Journal of Psychiatry*, **151**, 850–2 (**297**)

Brooks, N. (1984) Cognitive deficits after head injury. In *Closed Head Injury: Psychological, Social and Family Consequences* (ed. N. Brooks) Oxford University Press: Oxford (**287, 296**)

Broughton, R. J. (1968) Sleep disorders: disorders of arousal? *Science*, **159**, 1070–8 (**309**)

Brown, C. R. (1978) The use of benzodiazepines in prison populations. *Journal of Clinical Psychiatry*, **39**, 219–22 (**669**)

Brown, G. W., Birley, J. L. T. and King, J. K. (1972) Influence of family life on the course of schizophrenic disorders: a replication. *British Journal of Psychiatry*, **121**, 241–58 (**367**)

Brown, G. W., Bone, M., Dalison, B. and Wing, J. K. (1966) *Schizophrenia and Social Care*, Oxford University Press: London (**797**)

Brown, G. W. and Harris, T. (1978) *Social Origins of Depression*, Tavistock: London (**366, 367**)

Brown, J. M., Cornish, J. and Swart, G. T. (1986) Suicide and attempted suicide: legal issues. *Canadian Journal of Psychiatry*, **31**, 101–3 (**813**)

Brown, P. and Smith, C. V. (1988) Mental patients' rights: an empirical study of variation across the United States. *International Journal of Law and Psychiatry*, **11**, 157–65 (**663**)

Browne, F. W. A., Cooper, S. J., Wilson, R. and King, D. J. (1988) Serum haloperidol levels and clinical response in chronic, treatment resistant schizophrenic patients. *Journal of Psychopharmacology*, **2**, 94–103 (**663**)

Buchanan, A., Reed, A., Wessely, S., Taylor, P. J., Grubin, D. and Dunn, G. (in press) Precipitants of delusional acts. *British Journal of Psychiatry* (**343**)

Buckle, A. and Farrington, D. (1984) An observational study of shoplifting. *British Journal of Criminology*, **24**, 63–73 (**572**)

Bucknall, P. and Ghodse, H. (1986) *Misuse of Drugs*, The Criminal Law Library, No. 2 and Supplement No. 1 Waterlow: London (**464**)

Buhrich, N. (1977) Transvestism in history. *Journal of Nervous and Mental Disease*, **165**, 64–6 (**550**)

Buhrich, N. (1978) Motivation in cross-dressing in heterosexual transvestism. *Acta Psychiatrica Scandinavica*, **57**, 145–52 (**550**)

Bureau of Justice Statistics (1986) *Capital Punishment 1985*, US Sort Printing Office: Washington DC (**122**)

Bureau of Justice Statistics (1987) *Capital Punishment 1986*, US Sort Printing Office: Washington DC (**122**)

Burges-Watson, I. P., Hoffman, L. and Wilson, G. V. (1988) The neuropsychiatry of post-traumatic stress disorder. *British Journal of Psychiatry*, **152**, 164–73 (**932**)

Burgess, A. W., Hadman, C. R. and McCormack, A. (1987) Abused to abuser—antecedents of socially deviant behaviors. *American Journal of Psychiatry*, **144**, 1431–6 (**367, 672, 918, 922**)

Burgess, A. W., Hartman, C. R., MacCausland, M. P. and Powers, P. (1984) Response patterns in children and adolescents exploited through sex rings and pornography. *American Journal of Psychiatry*, **17**, 315–23 (**528**)

Burgess, A. W. and Holmstrom, L. L. (1974a) Rape Trauma Syndrome. *American Journal of Psychiatry*, **131**, 981–6 (**895, 916**)

Burgess, A. W. and Holmstrom, L. L. (1974b) *Rape: Victims of Crisis*, Brady and Co: Bowie, Maryland (**895, 916**)

Burgess, A. W. and Holmstrom, L. L. (1979) *Rape: Crisis and Recovery*, Brady & Co: Bowie, Maryland (**916**)

Burgoine, E. and Wing, L. (1983) Identical triplets with Asperger's Syndrome. *British Journal of Psychiatry*, **143**, 261–5 (**395**)

Burke, J. D., Borus, J. F., Burns, B. J., Millstein, K. H. and Beasley, M. C. (1982) Changes in children's behaviour after a natural disaster. *American Journal of Psychiatry*, **139**, 1010–4 (**888,892**)

Burnam, M. A., Stein, J. A., Golding, J. M., Sorenson, J. M., Sorenson, S. B., Forsythe, A. B. and Telles, C. A. (1988) Sexual assault and mental disorders in a community population. *Journal of Consulting and Clinical Psychology*, **56**, 843–50 (**538**)

Burney, E. (1985) *Sentencing Young People*, Gower: Aldershot (**234**)

Burns, M. E. (1980) Droperidol in the management of hyperactivity, self-mutilation and aggression in mentally handicapped patients. *Journal of International Medical Research*, **8**, 31–3 (**662**)

Buros, O. K. (1970) *Personality Tests and Reviews*, Gryphon Press: New Jersey (**xxxi**)

Bursik, R. J. and Webb, J. (1982) Community change and patterns of delinquency. *American Journal of Sociology*, **88**, 24–42 (**273**)

Burstein, A. (1982) Treatment of post-traumatic stress disorder with imipramine. *Psychosomatics*, 25, 681–7 **(937)**

Burstein, A. (1989) Post-traumatic stress disorders in victims of motor vehicle accidents. *Hospital and Community Psychiatry*, 40, 295–7 **(887, 908)**

Bursten, B. (1986) Posthospital mandatory outpatient treatment. *American Journal of Psychiatry*, 143, 1255–8 **(726)**

Burt, C. (1923) *The Young Delinquent vol. 1*, University of London Press: London **(427)**

Burt, M. R. (1980) Cultural myths and supports for rape. *Journal of Personality and Social Psychology*, 38, 217–30 **(557)**

Burtch, B. E. (1979) Prison suicides reconsidered. *International Journal of Law and Psychiatry*, 2, 407–13 **(813, 814)**

Burton, J. D. K., Chambers, D. R. and Gill, P. S. (1983) *Coroners' Inquiries: a Guide to Law and Practice*, Kluwer Law: Brentford **(180, 181)**

Burton-Bradley, B. G. (1968) The Amok Syndrome in Papua New Guinea. *Medical Journal of Australia*, 1 252–6 **(432, 433)**

Buss, A. H. and Plomin, R. (1986) The EAS approach to temperament. In *The Study of Temperament: Changes, Continuities and Challenges* (eds. R. Plomin and J. Dunn) Lawrence Elbaum: Hillsdale,180 NJ **(380)**

Busuttil, A. and Wallace, N. W. (1990) Medication in police custody. *Journal of the Royal Society of Medicine*, 83, 566–8 **(733)**

Butler-Sloss, L. J. (1988) *Report of the Inquiry into Child Abuse in Cleveland* 1987. Cmnd. 412 HMSO: London **(240, 535)**

Buttigliere, M., Brause, A. J. and Case, H. W. (1972) Effect of alcohol and drugs on driving behavior. In *Human Factors in Highway Traffic Safety Research* (ed. T. W. Forbes) Wiley: New York **(582)**

Bynum, W. F., Porter, R. and Shepherd, M. (1985a) *The Anatomy of Madness Vol. 1 People and Ideas*, Tavistock: London **(691)**

Bynum, W. F., Porter, R. and Shepherd, M. (1985b) *The Anatomy of Madness Vol. 2 Institutions and Society*, Tavistock: London **(691)**

Bynum, W. F., Porter, R. and Shepherd, M. (1988) *The Anatomy of Madness Vol. 3 The Asylum and its Psychiatry*, Tavistock: London **(691)**

Cadoret, R. J. and Cain, C. (1980) Sex differences in predictors of antisocial behavior in adoptees. *Archives of General Psychiatry*, 37, 1171–5 **(605)**

Caffey, J. (1946) Multiple fractures in the long bones of children suffering from chronic subdural haematoma. *American Journal of Roentgenology*, 56, 163–73 **(911)**

Calabrese, J. R., King, M. A. and Gold, P. W. (1987) Alterations in immunocompetence during stress, bereavement and depression: focus on neuroendocrine regulation. *American Journal of Psychiatry*, 144, 1123–34 **(889, 933)**

Callahan, L., Mayer, C. and Steadman, H. J. (1987) Insanity defense reform in the United States-post-Hinckley. *Mental and Physical Disability Law Reporter*, 11, 54–9 **(142)**

Cameron, D. C. (1969) Non-medical judgment of medical matters. In *The Right to Treatment* (ed. D. S. Burris) Springer: New York **(873)**

Campbell, A. (1981) *Girl Delinquents*, Basil Blackwell: Oxford **(602)**

Campbell, C. (1974) Legal thought and juristic values. *British Journal of Law and Society*, 1, 13–31. **(830)**

Campbell, W., Shepherd, H. and Falconer, R. (1982) The use of seclusion. *Nursing Times*, 27, 1821–5 **(660)**

Cancro, R. and Wilder, R. (1970) A mechanism of sudden death in chlorpromazine therapy. *American Journal of Psychiatry*, 127, 368–71 **(663)**

Caplan, N. S. and Siebert, L. A. (1964) Distribution of juvenile delinquent intelligence test scores over a thirty-four year period. *Journal of Clinical Psychology*, 20, 242–7 **(321)**

Carlen, P. (1983) *Women's Imprisonment. A Study in Social Control*, Routledge and Keegan Paul: London **(614, 621)**

Carlen, P. (1990) *Alternatives to Women's Imprisonment*, Open University Press: Milton Keynes **(623)**

Carlen, P. and Powell, M. (1979) Professionals in the magistrates court. In *Social Work and the Courts* (ed. H. Parker) Edward Arnold: London **(772)**

Carlson, G. A. and Goodwin, F. K. (1973) The stages of mania: a longitudinal analysis of the manic episode. *Archives of General Psychiatry*, 28, 221–8 **(348)**

Carmen, E., Ricker, P. P. and Mills, T. (1984) Victims of violence and psychiatric illness. *American Journal of Psychiatry*, **141**, 378–83 **(916, 917)**

Caroff, S. N. (1980) The neuroleptic malignant syndrome. *Journal of Clinical Psychiatry*, **41**, 79–83 **(667)**

Carr, J. E. and Tan, E. K. (1976) In search of the true amok, amok as viewed within the Malay culture. *American Journal of Psychiatry*, **133**, 1295–9 **(432, 433)**

Carson, D. (1987) *Making the Most of the Court of Protection*, Kings Fund Centre: London **(198)**

Carson, D. (1990a) Take the best and leave the rest. *Health Service Journal*, 22 March p. 428 **(112)**

Carson, D. (1990b) Reports to court, a role in preventing decision error. *Journal of Social Welfare Law*, July 151–63 **(837)**

Carson, D. (1990c) *Professionals and the Courts. A Handbook for Expert Witnesses*. Venture: Birmingham **(856, 869)**

Carter, D. L., Prentky, P., Knight, R. A., Vanderveer, P. and Boucher, R. (1986) Use of pornography in the criminal and developmental histories of sexual offenders. (Unpublished, cited in Murrin and Laws, 1990) **(527)**

Carter, J. (1974) *The Maltreated Child*, Priory Press: London **(504)**

Carvell, A. L. M. and Hart, G. J. (1990) Risk behaviours for HIV infection among drug users in prison. *British Medical Journal*, **300**, 1383–4 **(476)**

Catalan, J., Riccio, M. and Thompson, C. (1989) HIV disease and psychiatric practice. *Psychiatric Bulletin*, **13**, 316–32 **(875)**

Catan, L. (1988) The development of young children in HMP mother and baby units. *Working Papers in Psychology Series*—No. 1, University of Sussex: Falmer **(622)**

Catan, L. (1989) The development of young children in prison mother and baby units. *Research Bulletin No. 26*, Home Office Research and Planning Unit: London **(622)**

Cautela, J. R. (1967) Covert sensitization. *Psychological Reports*, **20**, 459–68 **(673)**

Cautela, J. R. and Wisocki, P. A. (1971) Covert sensitisation for the treatment of sexual deviations. *Psychological Records*, **21**, 37–48 **(560, 673)**

Cawson, P. and Martell, M. (1979) *Children referred to Closed Units*, DHSS Research Report No. 5, HMSO: London **(215, 234)**

Centers for Disease Control (1988) Health status of Vietnam veterans. *Journal of the American Medical Association*, **259**, 2701–19 **(928)**

Chalke, R. (1973) *The General Program for the Development of Psychiatric Services in Federal Corrections Services in Canada*. Solicitor General, Canada **(155)**

Cham, M. K. M. (1982) Outpatient status: beyond the term of commitment. *Pacific Law Journal*, **13** 1189–204 **(726)**

Chamberlin, J. (1985) An ex-patient's response to Soliday. *Journal of Nervous and Mental Disease*, **173**, 288–9 **(660)**

Chambers, G. and Millar, A. (1983) *Investigating Sexual Assaults*, HMSO: Edinburgh **(545)**

Chambers, G. and Millar, A. (1986) *Prosecuting Sexual Assaults*, HMSO: Edinburgh **(545)**

Channon, S. (1982) The resettlement of epileptic offenders. In *Abnormal Offenders, Delinquency and the Criminal Justice System* (Ed. J. Gunn and D. P. Farrington) Wiley: Chichester **(307)**

Chapman, J. and Gates, M. (1978) *The Victimization of Women*, Sage: Beverly Hills **(936)**

Charle, S. (1981) Suicide in the cell blocks. *Corrections Magazine*, August 1981, 6–15 **(814)**

Cheadle, J. and Ditchfield, J. (1982) *Sentenced Mentally Ill Offenders*, Home Office Research and Planning Unit: London **(756)**

Cheung, P. T. K. (1986) Maternal filicide in Hong Kong 1971–85. *Medicine, Science and the Law*, **26**, 185–92 **(612)**

Child Care Law Review Group (1990) *Review of Child Care Law in Scotland (Black Committee Report)*, HMSO: Edinburgh **(250)**

Children and Young Persons Review Group (1979) *Report*, HMSO: Belfast **(210, 219, 239, 249)**

Chiswick, D. (1978) Insanity in bar of trial: a state hospital study. *British Journal of Psychiatry*, **132**, 598–601 **(85)**

Chiswick, D. (1982) The special hospitals: a problem of clinical credibility. *Bulletin of the Royal College of Psychiatrists*, **6**, 130–2 **(698)**

Chiswick, D. (1985) Use and abuse of psychiatric testimony. *British Medical Journal*, **290**, 975–7. **(830)**

Chiswick, D., McIsaac, M. W. and McClintock, F. H. (1984) *Prosecution of the Mentally Disturbed: Dilemmas of Identification and Discretion*. University Press: Aberdeen **(79)**

Chodoff, P. (1983) Paternalism versus autonomy in medicine and psychiatry. *Psychiatric Annals*, 13, 818–20 (**145**)

Christiansen, K. O. (1977) A preliminary study of criminality among twins. In *Biosocial Bases of Criminal Behaviour* (S. A. Mednick and K. O. Christiansen) Gardner Press: New York, pp. 89–108 (**258**)

Christie-Brown, J. R. W. (1983) Paraphilias: sadomasochism, fetishism, transvestism, and transsexuality. *British Journal of Psychiatry*, 143, 227–31 (**529**)

Christopherson, R. J. (1981) Two approaches to the handling of child abuse: a comparison of the English and Dutch systems. *Child Abuse and Neglect*, 5, 869–73 (**559**)

Cienfuegos, A. J. and Monelli, C. (1983) The testimony of political repression as a therapeutic instrument. *American Journal of Orthopsychiatry*, 53, 43–51 (**924**)

Clack, J. (1963) Nursing intervention into the aggressive behaviour of patients. In *Some Clinical Approaches to Psychiatric Nursing* (eds S. F. Burd and M. A. Marshall) Macmillan: New York (**653**)

Claghorn, J., Honigfield, G., Abuzzahab, F. S., Wang, R., Steinbook, R., Tuason, V. and Klerman, G. (1987) The risks and benefits of clozapine versus chlorpromazine. *Journal of Clinical Psychopharmacology*, 7, 377–84 (**665**)

Clare, A. W. (1979) The causes of alcoholism. *British Journal of Hospital Medicine*, 21, 403–11 (**441**)

Clare, A. W. (1983) *Psychiatric and Social Aspects of Premenstrual Complaint*, Psychological Medicine Monograph Supplement No. 4 Cambridge University Press: Cambridge (**606**)

Clare, A. W. (1986) The disease concept in psychiatry. In *Essentials of Postgraduate Psychiatry*, 2nd edn (ed. P. Hill, R. Murray and A272. Thorley) Grune & Stratton: London (**8**)

Clare, A. and Bristow, M. (1987) Drinking drivers: the need for research and rehabilitation. *British Medical Journal*, 295, 1432–3 (**439**)

Clark, J. P. and Wenninger, E. P. (1962) Socio-economic class and area as correlates of illegal behaviour among juveniles. *American Sociological Review*, 27, 826–34 (**272**)

Clarke, R. V. G. (1985) Jack Tizard Memorial Lecture: delinquency, environment and intervention. *Journal of Child Psychology and Psychiatry*, 26, 505–23 (**579**)

Clarke, R., Ekblom, P., Hough, M. and Mayhew, P. (1985) Elderly victims of crime and exposure to risk. *The Howard Journal of Criminal Justice*, 24, 1–9 (**325, 891**)

Clarke, R. V. and Cornish D. B. (1985) Modelling offenders' decisions: a framework for research and policy. In *Crime and Justice* Vol. 6 (eds. M. Tonry and N. Morris) University of Chicago Press: Chicago pp 147–185 (**253**)

Clear, T. and O'Leary, V. (1983) *Controlling the offender in the Community*, Lexington Books: D C Heath & Co., Lexington, Mass. (**789**)

Cleckley. H. (1976) *The Mask of Sanity*, 6th edn. Mosby: St Louis (**383, 385**)

Clifford, B. R. and Bull, R. (1978) *The Psychology of Personal Identification*. Routledge & Keegan Paul: London (**943**)

Clifford, B. R. and Scott, J. (1978) Individual and situational factors in eyewitness testimony. *Journal of Applied Psychology*, 63, 852–9 (**239, 297**)

Cloninger, C. R. (1983) Antisocial behaviour. In *Psychopharmacology* (eds. D. Grahame-Smith, H. Hippius and G. Winokur), Excerpta Medica: Amsterdam (**668**)

Cloninger, C. R., Sigvardsson, S., Bohman, M. and Von Knorring, A. (1982) Predisposition to petty crime in Swedish adoptees. II. Cross-fostering analysis of gene-environment interaction. *Archives of General Psychiatry*, 39, 1242–7 (**259**)

Cloward, R. A. and Ohlin, L. E. (1960) *Delinquency and Opportunity*, Free Press: New York (**278**)

Cobb, J. (1979) Morbid jealousy. *British Journal of Hospital Medicine*, 21, 511–8 (**445**)

Cocozza, J. and Steadman, H. (1976) The failure of psychiatric predictions of dangerousness: clear and convincing evidence. *Rutgers Law Review*, 29, 1084–101 (**628**)

Cohen, A. K. (1955) *Delinquent Boys*, Free Press: Glencoe, Il. (**278**)

Cohen, B. M. and Cooper, M. Z. (1954) A follow-up study of World War II prisoners of war. *Veterans Administration Monograph*, US Government Printing Office: Washington DC (cited in Kluznik et al., 1986) (**925**)

Cohen, J. (1963) *Alcohol and Road Traffic*, British Medical Association: London (**438**)

Cohen, J., Dearnalay, E. J. and Hansel, C. E. M. (1958) The risk taken in driving under the influence of alcohol. *British Medical Journal*, 1, 1438–42 (**442**)

Cohen, L. H. and Freeman, H. (1945) How dangerous to the community are State hospital patients? *Connecticut State Medical Journal*, 9, 697–700 (**333**)

Cohen, L. J. (1988) Providing treatment and support for partners of sexual-assault survivors., *Psychotherapy*, **25** 94–8 **(921)**

Cohen, M., Freedman, N., Engelhardt, D. M. and Margolis, R. A. (1968) Family interaction patterns, drug treatment, and change in social aggression. *Archives of General Psychiatry*, **19**, 50–6 **(663)**

Cohen, M., McEwen, J., Williams, K., Silver, S. and Spodak, M. (1986) *A Base Expectancy Model for Forensic Release Decisions*, Research Management Associates, Inc: Alexandria VA **(641, 643)**

Cohen, M. R., Pickor, D., Dubois, M. and Bunney, W. E. (1982) Stress-induced plasma beta-endorphin immunoreactivity may predict post-operative morphine usage. *Psychiatry Research*, **6**, 7–12 **(932)**

Cohen, S. and Taylor, L. (1981) *Psychological Survival* (2nd ed) Penguin Books: Harmondsworth **(802, 804)**

Coid, J. (1979) Mania à potu: a critical review of pathological intoxication. *Psychological Medicine*, **9**, 709–19 **(62, 443)**

Coid, J. (1982) Alcoholism and violence. *Drug and Alcohol Dependence*, **9**, 1–13 **(449)**

Coid, J. (1983) The epidemiology of abnormal homicide and murder followed by suicide. *Psychological Medicine*, **13**, 855–60 **(512, 817, 932)**

Coid, J. (1986) Alcohol, rape and sexual assault; b) Socio-culture factors in alcohol-related aggression. In *Alcohol and Aggression* (ed. P. F. Brain) London: Croom Helm, pp. 161–183, 184–211 **(448)**

Coid, J. (1988) Mentally abnormal prisoners on remand. I. Rejected or accepted by the NHS? II. Comparison of services provided by Oxford and Wessex regions. *British Medical Journal*, **296**, 1979–82, 1783–4 **(329, 756)**

Coid, J., Robertson, G. and Gunn, J. (1991) A psychiatric study of inmates in Parkhurst Special Unit. In *Managing Difficult Prisoners: The Parkhurst Special Unit*, Home Office Research Study 122, HMSO: London **(755)**

Coid, J. and Strang, J. (1982) Mania secondary to procyclidine (Kemadrin) abuse. *British Journal of Psychiatry*, **141**, 81–4 **(458, 474)**

Coid, J., Allolio, B. and Rees, L. H. (1983) Raised plasma metenkephalin in patients who habitually mutilate themselves. *Lancet*, **ii**, 545–6 **(817)**

Coker, J. B. and Martin, J. P. (1985) *Licensed to Live*, Basil Blackwell: Oxford **(781, 804)**

Cole, K. E., Fisher, G. and Cole, S. S. (1968) Women who kill. *Archives of General Psychiatry*, **19**, 1–8 **(368, 416)**

Collie, J. (1917) *Malingering and Feigned Sickness*, Edward Arnold: London **(418)**

Collins, J. J. (1982) *Drinking and Crime: Perspective on the Relationships between Alcohol Consumption and Criminal Behaviour*, Tavistock Publications: London **(445, 450)**

Collomb, H. (1972) Public health and psychiatry in Africa. In *Biomedical Lectures: AFRO Technical Paper 1*, World Health Organisation: Brazzaville **(119)**

Collomb, H. (1979) De l'ethnopsychiatrie à la psychiatrie sociale. *Canadian Journal of Psychiatry*, **24**, 459–70 **(119)**

Commission on the Review of the National Policy Toward Gambling (1976) *Gambling in America*, US Government Printing Office: Washington DC **(481)**

Commissioners of Prisons (1921) *Report for 1919–20* HMSO: London **(749)**

Commissioners of Prisons (1924) *Report for 1922–3* HMSO: London **(749)**

Congdon, M. H. and Abels, B. S. (1983) *Multiple Personality: Etiology, Diagnosis and Treatment*, Human Sciences: New York **(428)**

Conley, R. R., Schulz, S. C., Baker, R. W., Collins, J. R. and Ball, J. A. (1988) Clozapine efficacy in schizophrenic non-responders. *Psychopharmacology Bulletin*, **24**, 260–3 **(665)**

Conn, L. M. and Lion, J. R. (1984) Pharmacologic approaches to violence. *Psychiatric Clinics of North America*, **7**, 879–86 **(660, 661, 668)**

Connell, P. H. (1958) *Amphetamine Psychosis*, Maudsley Monograph No. 5 Oxford University Press: London **(458, 468, 474)**

Connors, G. J., Maisto, S. A. and Ersner-Hershfield, S. M. (1986) Behavioral treatment of drunk-driving recidivists: short term and long term effects. *Behavioural Psychotherapy*, **14**, 34–45 **(583)**

Connors, K. (1979) The use of published minimum standards to determine when inadequate prison medical care constitutes cruel and unusual punishment. *Suffolk University Law Review*, **13**, 603–14 **(766)**

Constantine, L. L. (1981) The effects of early sexual experience. In *Children and Sex* (eds. L. L. Constantine and F. M. Martinson) Little, Brown: Boston (**535**)

Constantine, L. L. and Martinson, F. M. (eds.) (1981) *Children and Sex: New Findings, New Perspectives*, Little, Brown: Boston (**918**)

Conte, J. R. (1986) Child sexual abuse and the family: a critical analysis. *Journal of Psychotherapy and the Family*, 2, 113–26 (**537**)

Convit, A., Isay, D., Gadioma, R. and Volavka, J. (1988a) Underreporting of physical assaults in schizophrenic inpatients. *Journal of Nervous and Mental Disease*, 176, 507–9 (**643**)

Convit, A., Jaeger, J., Lin, S., Meisner, M. and Volavka, J. (1988b) Predicting assaaultiveness in psychiatric inpatients: A pilot study. *Hospital and Community Psychiatry*, 39, 429–34 (**641**)

Cook, D. A. G., Fox, C. A., Weaver, C. M. and Rooth, F. G. (1991) The Berkley group: ten years' experience of a group for non-violent sex offenders. *British Journal of Psychiatry*, 158, 238–43 (**728**)

Cooke, D. J. (1989) Containing violent prisoners: an analysis of the Barlinnie Special Unit. *British Journal of Criminology*, 29, 129–43 (**753, 808**)

Cooke, D. J. (1991) Treatment as an alternative to prosecution: offenders diverted from treatment. *British Journal of Psychiatry*, 158, 785–91 (**727, 728**)

Cookson, H. M. (1977) A survey of self-injury in a closed prison for women. *British Journal of Criminology*, 17, 332–46 (**617**)

Cooper, J. E., Kendell, R. E., Gurland, B. J., Sharpe, L., Copeland, I. R. M. and Simon, R. (1972) *Psychiatric Diagnosis in New York and London*, Maudsley Monograph No. 20, Oxford University Press: Oxford (**12**)

Cooper, S. J., Brown, F. W. A., McClean, K. J. and King, D. J. (1983) Aggressive behaviour in a psychiatric observation ward. *Acta Psychiatrica Scandinavica*, 68, 386–93 (**808**)

Copas, J. B., and Robin, A. (1982) Suicide in psychiatric inpatients. *British Journal of Psychiatry*, 141, 503–11 (**811, 812**)

Copas, J. B. and Whiteley, J. S. (1976) Predicting success in the treatment of psychopaths *British Journal of Psychiatry*, 129, 888–92 (**688**)

Cope, R. and Ndegwa, D. (1991) Ethnic differences in admission to a regional secure unit. *Journal of Forensic Psychiatry*, 1, 365–8 (**716**)

Corbett, J. A. (1985) Mental retardation: psychiatric aspects. In *Child and Adolescent Psychiatry*, 2nd edn. (ed. M. Rutter and L. Hersov) Blackwell: Oxford (**313**)

Cormier, B. M. and Cooper, I. (1982a) Intergenerational transmission of incest. *Canadian Journal of Psychiatry*, 27, 231–5 (**538**)

Cormier, P. M. and Cooper, I. (1982b) *Incest in Contemporary Society: Legal and Clinical Management*, McGill Forensic Clinic: Montreal (**919**)

Cornish, D. (1978) *Gambling: A Review of the Literature*, Home Office Research Study No. 42, HMSO: London (**481, 482**)

Correctional Services of Canada (1981) *The Prevention of Suicide in Prison*, Communications Branch for Medical and Health Care Services: Ottawa (**814**)

Coser, R. L. (1979) Suicide and relational systems. In *Training in Ambiguity—Learning through Teaching in a Mental Hospital*, Macmillan: London (**813**)

Court, J. H. (1976) Pornography and sex crimes: a re-evaluation in the light of recent trends around the world. *International Journal of Criminology and Penology*, 5, 129–57 (**526**)

Cowie, J., Cowie, V. & Slater, E. (1968) *Delinquency in Girls*, Heinemann: London (**604**)

Cowie, V. (1977) Chromosome abnormalities. In *Child Psychiatry Modern Approaches* (eds M. Rutter & L. Hersov) Blackwell: Oxford (**313**)

Cox, M. (1976) Group psychotherapy in a secure setting. *Proceedings of the Royal Society of Medicine*, 69, 215–20 (**703**)

Cox, M. (1978) *Structuring the Therapeutic Process: Compromise with Chaos*, Pergamon Press: Oxford (reprinted, 1988, Jessica Kingsley: London) (**703**)

Cox, M. (1979) Dynamic psychotherapy with sex offenders. In *Sexual Deviation*, 2nd edn, (ed. I. Rosen) Oxford University Press: Oxford (**703**)

Cox, M. (1982) 'I took a life because I needed one': psychotherapeutic possibilities with the schizophrenic offender-patient. *Psychotherapy and Psychosomatics*, 37, 96–105 (**703**)

Cox, M. (1983) The contribution of dynamic psychotherapy to forensic psychiatry and vice versa. *International Journal of Law and Psychiatry*, 6, 89–99 (**703**)

Cox, M. (1986) The 'holding function' of dynamic psychotherapy in a custodial setting: a review. *Journal of the Royal Society of Medicine*, 79, 162–4 (**684, 685, 703**)

Cox, M. and Theilgaard, A. (1987) *Mutative Metaphors in Psychotherapy*, Tavistock Publications: London (**677, 683, 703**)

Cox, T. (1978) *Stress*, Macmillan: London (**684, 929**)

Coyle, A. G. (1987) The Scottish experience with small units. In *Problems of Long-Term Imprisonment* (eds. A. E. Bottoms and R. Light) Gower: Aldershot (**752**)

Craft, M., Ismail, I. A. Krishnamurti, D., Mathews, J., Regan, A., Seth, R. V. and North, P. M. (1987) Lithium in the treatment of aggression in mentally handicapped patients: a double-blind trial. *British Journal of Psychiatry*, **150**, 685–9 (**662**)

Craig, M. M. and Budd, L. A. (1967) The juvenile offender: recidivism and companions. *Crime and Delinquency*, **13**, 344–51 (**265**)

Craig, M. M. and Glick, S. J. (1968) School behaviour related to later delinquency and non-delinquency. *Criminologica*, **5**, 17–27 (**262, 264**)

Craig, R. J. (1982) Personality characteristics of heroin addicts: review of empirical research 1976–1979. *International Journal of the Addictions*, **17**, 227–48 (**469, 641, 642**)

Craig, T. (1982) An epidemiologic study of problems associated with violence among psychiatric inpatients. *American Journal of Psychiatry*, **139**, 1262–6 (**335, 348**)

Craine, L. S., Henson, C. E., Colliver, J. A. and Maclean, D. G. (1988) Prevalence of a history of sexual abuse among female psychiatric patients in a State hospital system. *Hospital and Community Psychiatry*, **39**, 300–4 (**888, 895, 903**)

Cramer, C. and Harris, S. (1982) *Hostage*, John Clare: London (**927**)

Crammer, J. L. (1983) Inpatients sometimes kill themselves. *Bulletin of the Royal College of Psychiatrists*, **7**, 2–4 (**811**)

Crammer, J. L. (1984) The special characteristics of suicide in hospital inpatients. *British Journal of Psychiatry*, **145**, 460–3 (**812**)

Crancer, A. and Quiring, D. L. (1969) The mentally ill as motor vehicle operators. *American Journal of Psychiatry*, **126**, 807–13 (**582**)

Crawford, D. A. and Allen, J. W. (1979) A social skills training programme with sex offenders. In *Love and Attraction: Proceedings of an International Conference* (eds. M. Cook and G. Wilson) Pergamon: Oxford (**559**)

Crisp, A. H., Hsu, L. K. G. and Harding, B. (1980) The starving hoarder and voracious spender: stealing in anorexia nervosa *Journal of Psychosomatic Research*, **24**, 225–31 (**570**)

Cross, R., Tapper, C. (1985) *Cross on Evidence*, 6th edn, Butterworths: London (**828**)

Cummings, J. L. (1985) Organic delusions: phenomenology, anatomical correlations and review. *British Journal of Psychiatry*, **146** , 184–97 (**325**)

Cupchick, W. and Acherson, J. D. (1983) Shoplifting: an occasional crime of the moral majority. *Bulletin of the American Academy of Psychiatry and the Law*, **11**, 343–54 (**574**)

Currier, R. L. (1981) Juvenile sexuality in global perspective. In *Children and Sex* (eds. L. L. Constantine and F. M. Martinson) Little, Brown: Boston (**528, 918**)

Cutting, J. (1978) A re-appraisal of alcoholic psychosis. *Psychological Medicine*, **8**, 285–95 (**443, 445**)

Cutting, J. (1979) Alcohol dependence and alcohol-related disabilities. In *Recent Advances in Clinical Psychiatry Vol 3* (ed. K. Granville-Grossman) Churchill Livingstone: Edinburgh, pp. 225–49 (**442, 444**)

Cutting, J. and Shepherd, M. (1986) *The Clinical Roots of the Schizophrenic Concept*, Cambridge University Press: Cambridge (**340**)

Dahlstrom, W. G. and Welsh, G. S. (1960) *An MMPI Handbook: A Guide to Use in Clinical Practice and Research*, University of Minnesota Press: Minneapolis (**xxxi**)

Dale, P., Davies, M., Morrison, T. and Wates, J. (1986a) *Dangerous Families*, Tavistock: London (**367, 911, 940**)

Dale, P., Waters, J., Davies, M., Roberts, W. and Morrison, T. (1986b) The towers of silence: creative and destructive issues for therapeutic teams dealing with sexual abuse. *Journal of Family Therapy*, **8**, 1–25 (**941**)

Dalton, K. (1961) Menstruation and crime. (Letter) *British Medical Journal*, ii, 1752–3 (**605**)

Dalton, K. (1975) Paramenstrual baby battering. (Letter) *British Medical Journal*, ii, 279 (**605**)

Dalton, K. (1980) Cyclical criminal acts in premenstrual syndrome. *Lancet*, ii, 1070–1 (**605**)

Daly, M., Wilson, M. and Weyhorst, S. J. (1982) Male sexual jealousy. *Ethology & Sociobiology*, 3 11–27 (**352**)

Daly, R. F. (1969) Neurological abnormalities in XYY males. *Nature*, **221**, 472–3 (**315**)

Daly, R. V. (1983) Samuel Pepys and post-traumatic stress disaster. *British Journal of Psychiatry*, **143**, 64–8 (**886**)

Danadjhiev, S. (1922) *Irresponsibility in our Criminal Law*, Bulgarian Academy of Sciences: Sofia (in Bulgarian) **(134)**

Danadjhiev, S. (1927) *On Affect in the Criminal Law*, Iv. Bozhinov Publishing House: Sofia (in Bulgarian) **(134)**

Daniel, A. E., Harris, P. W. and Husain, S. A. (1981) Differences between mid-life female offenders and those younger than 40. *American Journal of Psychiatry*, **138**, 1225–8 **(601)**

Daniels, D. N., Gilula, M. F. and Ochberg, F. (1970) *Violence and the Struggle for Existence*, Little, Brown: Boston **(490)**

Danto, B. L. (1973) *Jail House Blues*, Orchard Lake: Michigan **(815)**

Darwin, C. (1883) *The Descent of Man, 2nd edn*, John Murray: London **(16, 17)**

D'Atri, D. A., Fitzgerald, E. F., Kasl, S. V. and Ostfeld, A. M. (1981) Crowding in prison: the relationship between changes in housing mode and blood pressure. *Psychosomatic Medicine*, **43**, 95–105 **(802)**

David, A. S. (1990) Insight and psychosis. *British Journal of Psychiatry*, **156**, 798–808 **(12, 398)**

Davidoff, L. and Dowds, L. (1989) *Recent Trends in Crimes of Violence Against the Person in England & Wales*, Research Bulletin No. 27, Home Office Research & Planning Unit, HMSO: London **(913)**

Davidson, A. D. (1979) Air disaster: coping with stress—a programme that worked. *Police Stress* (Spring) 20–2 (cited in Jones, D. R., 1985, *American Journal of Psychiatry*, **142**, 303–7) **(896)**

Davidson, J. Swartz, M., Storck, M., Krishnan, R. R. and Hammett, E. (1985) A diagnostic and family study of post-traumatic stress disorder. *American Journal of Psychiatry*, **142**, 90–3 **(895)**

Davies, L. M. and Drummond, M. F. (1990) The economic burden of schizophrenia. *Psychiatric Bulletin*, **14**, 522–5 **(666)**

Davies, M. (1969) Offence behaviour and the classification of offenders. *British Journal of Criminology*, **9**, 39–50 **(579)**

Davies, W. (1982) Violence in prisons. In *Developments in the Study of Criminal Behaviour Vol. 2* (ed. M. P. Feldman) Wiley: Chichester **(807, 808, 809)**

Davis, D. R. (1980) Report on Norway's Rampton. *Mindout*, December, 1980 **(709)**

Davis, D. R. (1981) *Mindout: News and Notes*—Report leads to closure in Norway. *Mindout*, August, 1981 **(709)**

Davis, G., Boucherat, J. and Watson, D. (1988) Reparation in the service of diversion: the subordination of a good idea. *The Howard Journal of Criminal Justice*, **27**, 127–34 **(944)**

Davis, J. (1962) Suicide by fire. *Journal of Forensic Science*. **7**, 383–7 **(595)**

Day, K. (1988) A hospital-based treatment programme for male mentally handicapped offenders. *British Journal of Psychiatry*, **153**, 635–44 **(720)**

Day, P. R. (1981) *Social work and social control*, Tavistock: London **(778)**

De Clérambault, C. G. (1942) Les psychoses passionelles. In *Oeuvres Psychiatriques*, Presses Universitaires: Paris **(350, 354)**

De Cuyper, H., Van Praag, H. M. and Verstraeten, D. (1985) The effect of milenperone on the aggressive behaviour of psychogeriatric patients. *Neuropsychobiology* **13**, 1–6 **(662)**

Deffenbacher, K. (1988) Eyewitness research: the next ten years. In *Practical Aspects of Memory* (ed. M. Gruneberg, P. Morris and R. Sykes) Vol. 1 Wiley: Chichester **(297)**

De Leon, G. and Schwartz, S. (1984) The therapeutic community: what are the retention rates? *American Journal on Drug and Alcohol Abuse*, **10**, 267–84 **(477)**

Delbrueck, A. (1891) *Die Pathologischen Luge and Die Psychisch Abnormen Schwindler*, Karger: Stuttgart **(412)**

Delgardo, J. M. R. (1969) Offensive-defensive behaviour in free monkeys and chimpanzees induced by radio stimulation of the brain. In *Aggressive Behaviour* (ed. S. Garaltini and E. B. Sigg) Excerpta Medica: Amsterdam **(287)**

Delgado-Escueta, A. V., Mattson, R. H., King, L., Goldensohn, E. L., Spiegel, H., Madsen, J., Crandall, P., Dreifuss, F. and Porter, R. J. (1981) The nature of aggression during epileptic seizures. *New England Journal of Medicine*, **305**, 711–6 **(303)**

Dell, S. (1980) Transfer of special hospital patients to the NHS. *British Journal of Psychiatry*, **136**, 222–34 **(694)**

Dell, S. (1984) *Murder into Manslaughter*, Maudsley Monograph No. 27, Oxford University Press: Oxford **(52, 77, 347, 517)**

Dell, S., Grounds, A., James, K. and Robertson, G. (1991) *Mentally Disordered Remanded Prisoners*. Report to the Home Office **(743)**

Dell, S. and Robertson, G. (1988) *Sentenced to Hospital*, Maudsley Monograph No. 32, Oxford University Press: Oxford (**701, 707**)

Dell, S., Robertson, G. and Parker, E. (1987) Detention in Broadmoor: factors in length of stay. *British Journal of Psychiatry*, 150, 824–7 (**862**)

Delva, N. J. & Letemendia, F. J. J. (1982) Lithium treatment in schizophrenia and schizoaffective disorders. *British Journal of Psychiatry*, 141, 387–400 (**664**)

De Montmollin, M. J., Zimmerman, E., Bernheim, J. and Harding, T. W. (1986) Sociotherapeutic treatment of delinquents in prison. *International Journal of Offender Therapy and Comparative Criominology*, 30, 25–34 (**689**)

Dencker, S. J., Johansson, R., Lundin, L. and Malm, U. (1978) High doses of fluphenazine enanthate in schizophrenia. *Acta Psychiatrica Scandinavica*, 57, 405–14 (**663**)

Denman, G. (1982) *Intensive Intermediate Treatment with Juvenile Offenders*, Lancaster University (**228**)

Denny-Brown, D. (1945) Disability arising from closed head injury. *Journal of the American Medical Association*, 127, 429–36 (**907**)

Dent, H. and Stephenson, G. (1979) An experimental study of the effectiveness of different techniques of questioning child witnesses. *British Journal of Social and Clinical Psychology*, 18, 41–51 (**942**)

Department of Forensic Psychiatry, Institute of Psychiatry (1992) Evidence submitted by the Department of Forensic Psychiatry, Institute of Psychiatry, London University, to Lord Justice Woolf's Enquiry into Prison Disturbances, *Criminal Behaviour and Mental Health*, 2, 43–57 (**811**)

Department of Health (1989a) *An Introduction to the Children Act 1989*, HMSO: London (**705**)

Department of Health (1989b) *Special Hospitals Patient Statistics 1988*, Department of Health: London (**700, 704, 723**)

Department of Health (1990) *Partnership in the Community* Dept. of Health, London (**793**)

Department of Health (1991) *Local Research Ethics Committees*, Department of Health: London (**878**)

Department of Health, Home Office (1992) *Review of Health and Social Services for Mentally Disordered Offenders and Others Requiring Similar Services* (Reed Report) Cmnd 2088, HMSO, London (**696, 723**)

Department of Health and Social Security (1973) *Community Services for Alcoholics*, Circular 21/73 DHSS: London (**453**)

Department of Health and Social Security (1974) *Revised Report of the Working Party on Security in NHS psychiatric hospitals* (The Glancy Report) HMSO: London (**694**)

Department of Health and Social Security (1975) *Regional Secure Unit: Design Guidelines* HMSO: London (**710, 712, 736, 756**)

Department of Health and Social Security (1980) *Report of the Committee of Inquiry into Rampton Hospital*, Cmnd 8073, HMSO: London (**658, 660, 697**)

Department of Health and Social Security (1981) *Offending by Young People: a survey of Recent Trends*, DHSS: London (**215**)

Department of Health and Social Security (1984) *Guidelines for Good Clinical Practice in the Treatment of Drug Misuse. Report of the Medical Working Group on Drug Dependence*, DHSS: London (**476**)

Department of Health and Social Security (1985) *Review of Child Care Law: Report to the Ministers of an Interdepartmental Working Party*, HMSO: London (**240**)

Department of Health and Social Security (1987a) *Mental Health Act 1983, Memorandum on Parts I to VI, VIII and X*, HMSO: London (**26**)

Department of Health and Social Security (1987b) *The Law on Child Care and Family Services*, Cmnd. 62, HMSO: London (**240**)

Department of Health and Social Security (1988a) *Health and Personal Social Services Statistics for England 1987*, HMSO: London (**319**)

Department of Health and Social Security (1988b) *Report of the Committee of Inquiry into the Care and After-care of Miss Sharon Campbell*, Cmnd 440, HMSO, London (**725**)

Department of Health and Social Security and the Welsh Office (1988) *Working Together*, HMSO: London (**505**)

Department of Health and Social Services (1989) *Co-operating to Protect Children*, Department of Health and Social Services: Belfast (**245, 248, 251**)

Department of Health and the Welsh office (1990) *Code of Practice*, HMSO: London (**196, 999**)

Department of the Environment (1976) *Drinking and Driving: A Report of the Departmental Committee*, (Blennerhassett Report) London: HMSO (**114, 439, 582**)

De Pauw, K and Szulecka, T. (1988) Dangerous delusions: violence and the misidentification syndromes. *British Journal of Psychiatry*, **152**, 91–6 (**343**)

Depp, F. C. (1983) Assaults in a public mental hospital. In *Assaults within Psychiatric Facilities*, (eds. J. R. Lion and W. H. Reid) Grune & Stratton: New York (**345**)

De Rubeis, R. J. and Beck, A. T. (1988) Cognitive therapy. In *Handbook of Cognitive-behavioural Therapies* (ed. K. S. Dobson) Hutchinson: London (**675**)

Deutsch, L. H., Bylsma, F. W., Rovner, B. W., Steale, C. and Folstein, M. F. (1991) Psychosis and physical aggression in probable Alzheimer's Disease. *American Journal of Psychiatry*, **148**, 1159–63 (**327**)

Dew, M. A., Bromet, E. J., Schulberg, H. C., Dunn, L. O. and Parkinson, D. K. (1987) Mental health effects of Three Mile Island nuclear reactor restart. *American Journal of Psychiatry*, **144**, 1074–7 (**898**)

Dewhurst, K., Oliver, J. E. and McKnight, A. L. (1970) Sociopsychiatric consequences of Huntington's disease. *British Journal of Psychiatry*, **116**, 255–8 (**312**)

Dickens, C. (1868) *American Notes for General Circulation, 3rd edn. Vol. 1*, Chapman & Hall: London (Republished 1972, Penguin: Harmondsworth) (**800**)

Dickerson, M. G. (1984) *Compulsive Gamblers*, Longman: London (**482, 489**)

Dickson, B. (1989) *The Legal System of Northern Ireland*, SLS Legal Publications: Belfast (**88**)

Dietz, P. E. (1978) Social factors in rapist behaviour. In *Clinical Aspects of the Rapist* (ed R. T. Rada) Grune & Stratton: New York (**543**)

Dietz, P. E. and Rada, R. T. (1982) Battery incidents and batterers in a maximum security hospital. *Archives of General Psychiatry*, **39**, 81–4 (**807, 808**)

Ditchfield, J. (1976) *Police Cautioning in England & Wales*, Home Office Research Study No. 37 HMSO: London (**217**)

Ditton, J. and Speirits, K. (1981) *The Rapid Increase of Heroin-addiction in Glasgow during 1981*, University of Glasgow, Department of Sociology: Glasgow (**475**)

Dix, G. E. (1984) Psychological abnormality and capital sentencing. *International Journal of Law and Psychiatry*, **7**, 249–67 (**121**)

Dobash, R. P., Dobash, R. E. and Guttridge, S. (1986) *The Imprisonment of Women*, Basil Blackwell: Oxford (**617, 619**)

Dobbs, D. and Wilson, W. P. (1960) Observations on persistence of war neurosis. *Diseases of the Nervous System*, **21**, 40–6 (**928**)

Dobson, K. S. and Block, L. (1988) *Handbook of Cognitive Behavioural Therapies* (ed. K. S. Dobson) Hutchinson: London, pp. 3–38 (**675**)

Doek, J. E. (1978) Child abuse in the Netherlands: the medical referee. *Chicago-Kent Law Review*, **54**, 785–826 (**919**)

Dollard, J., Miller, N., Doob, L., Mowrer, O. H. and Sears, R. R. (1939) *Frustration and Aggression*, Yale University Press: New Haven, Conn. (**347, 493**)

Dominik, M. (1970) Pathological jealousy in delusional syndromes. *Acta Medica Poland*, **11**, 267–80 (**351**)

Domovitch, B. E., Berger, P. B. and Wawer, M. J. (1984) Human torture: description and sequelae of 104 cases. *Canadian Family Physician*, **30**, 827–30 (**924**)

Donchev, P. (1983) *Manual of Forensic Psychiatry*, Medicina i Fizkultura: Sofia (in Bulgarian) (**154**)

Donlon, P. T. (1976) High dosage neuroleptic therapy. *International Pharmacopsychiatry*, **11**, 235–45 (**663**)

Donnerstein, E. and Berkowitz, L. (1981) Victim reactions in aggressive-erotic films as a factor in violence against women. *Journal of Personality and Social Psychology*, **41**, 710–24 (**526**)

Doolan, B. (1986) *Principles of Irish Law*, Gill and Macmillan: Dublin (**208**)

Dooley, E. (1990) Prison suicide in England & Wales, 1972–87. *British Journal of Psychiatry*, **156**, 40–45 (**813, 814**)

d'Orbán, P. T. (1969) Habitual drunkenness offenders in Holloway Prison. In *The Drunkenness Offence* (ed. T. Cook, D. Gath and C. Hensman) Pergamon Press: Oxford (**601**)

d'Orbán, P. T. (1970) Heroin dependence and delinquency in women—a study of heroin addicts in Holloway Prison. *British Journal of Addiction*, **65**, 67–78 (**609**)

d'Orbán, P. T. (1971) Social and psychiatric aspects of female crime. *Medicine, Science and the Law*, **11**, 104–16 (**600, 601, 602**)

d'Orbán, P. T. (1972) Baby stealing. *British Medical Journal*, ii, 635–9 (**613**) d'Orbán, P. T. (1973) Female narcotic addicts: a follow-up study of criminal and addiction careers. *British Medical Journal*, **iv**, 345–7 **(609)**

d'Orbán, P. (1974) A follow-up study of female narcotic addicts: variables related to outcome. *British Journal of Psychiatry*, *125*, 28–33 **(475)**

d'Orbán, P. T. (1976) Child stealing: a typology of female offenders. *British Journal of Criminology*, **16** , 275–81 **(613)**

d'Orbán, P. T. (1979) Women who kill their children. *British Journal of Psychiatry*, **134**, 560–71 **(50, 610, 611)**

d'Orbán, P. T. (1981) Premenstrual syndrome: a disease of the mind? (Letter) *Lancet* ii, 1413 **(607)**

d'Orbán, P. T. (1982) Child stealing and pseudocyesis. *British Journal of Psychiatry*, **141**, 196–8 **(613)**

d'Orbán, P. T. (1983) Medicolegal aspects of the premenstrual syndrome. *British Journal of Hospital Medicine*, **30**, 404–9 **(607)**

d'Orbán, P. T. (1985a) Psychiatric aspects of contempt of court among women. *Psychological Medicine*, **15**, 597–607 **(601)**

d'Orbán, P. T. (1985b) *Treatment of Mentally Disordered Women in Holloway Prison*. Submission to Holloway Project Commission (Unpublished) **(620)**

d'Orbán, P. T. (1986) Drugs and alcohol: the psychiatrist as expert witness in court. *British Journal of Addiction*, **81**, 531–9 **(60, 63)**

d'Orbán, P. T. (1989) Steroid induced psychosis. *Lancet*, ii, 694 **(63)**

d'Orbán, P. T. (1990a) Female homicide. *Irish Journal of Psychological Medicine*, 7, 64–70 **(609, 610)**

d'Orbán, P. T. (1990b) A commentary on consecutive filicide. *Journal of Forensic Psychiatry*, 1, 259–65 **(612)**

d'Orbán, P. T. and Dalton, J. (1980) Violent crime and the menstrual cycle. *Psychological Medicine*, **10**, 353–9 **(605)**

d'Orbán, P. T. and Haydn-Smith, P. (1985) Men who steal children. *British Medical Journal*, **290**, 1784. **(613)**

d'Orbán, P. T. and O'Connor, A. (1989) Women who kill their parents. *British Journal of Psychiatry*, **154**, 27–33 **(607)**

Dorian, B. and Garfinkel, P. E. (1987) Stress, immunity and illness—a review. *Psychological Medicine*, **17**, 393–407 **(933)**

Dorner, G. (1988) Neuroendocrine response to estrogen and brain differentiation in heterosexuals, homosexuals and transsexuals. *Archives of Sexual Behavior*, **17**, 57–75 **(540)**

Dorus, E., Dorus, W., Telfer, M. A. and Richardson, C. E. (1976) Height and personality characteristics of 47 XYY males in a sample of tall non-institutionalised males. *British Journal of Psychiatry*, **129**, 564–73 **(314)**

Dostal, T. and Zvolsky, P. (1970) Antiaggressive effect of lithium salts in severe mentally retarded adolescents. *International Pharmacopsychiatry*, 5, 203–7 **(662)**

Douglas, J. W. B., Ross, J. M., Hammond, W. A. and Mulligan, D. G. (1966) Delinquency and social class. *British Journal of Criminology*, 6, 294–302 **(271)**

Downes, D. (1982) The origins and consequences of Dutch penal policy since 1945. *British Journal of Criminology*, **22**, 325–62 **(764)**

Drew, G., Colquhoun, W. and Long, H. (1958) Effect of small doses of alcohol on a skill resembling driving. *British Medical Journal*, 2, 993–9 **(442)**

Drug Indicators Project (1989) *Study of Help Seeking and Service Utilisation by Problem Drug Takers*, Institutes of the Study of Drug Dependence: London **(477)**

Drummond, D. J., Sparr, L. F., Gordon, G. H. (1989) Hospital violence reduction among high risk patients. *Journal of the American Medical Association*, **261**, 2531–4 **(901)**

Du Bow, F. L. and Becker, T. M. (1976) Patterns in victim advocacy. In *Criminal Justice and the Victim* (ed. N. McDonald) Sage: Beverly Hills **(943)**

Dubin, W. R. (1989) The role of fantasies, countertransference and psychological defenses in patient violence. *Hospital and Community Psychiatry*, **40**, 1280–3 **(654)**

Duffy, J. C. and Plant, M. A. (1986) Scotland's liquor licensing changes: an assessment. *British Medical Journal*, **292**, 36–9 **(437)**

Dunbar, J. A., Ogston, S. A., Ritchie, A., Devgun, M. S., Hagart, J. and Martin, B. T. (1985) Are problem drinkers dangerous drivers? An investigation of arrest for drinking and driving, serum gamma-glutamyltranspeptidase activities, blood alcohol concentrations, and road traffic accidents: the Tayside Safe Driving Project. *British Medical Journal*, **290**, 827–30 **(438)**

Dunbar, J. A., Penttila, A. and Pikkarainen, J. (1987a) Drinking and driving; success of random breath testing in Finland. *British Medical Journal*, 295, 101–3 (**439**)

Dunbar, J. A., Penttila, A. and Pikkarainen, J. (1987b) Drinking and driving: choosing the legal limits *British Medical Journal*, 295, 1458–60 (**439**)

Dunlop, A. (1980) *Junior Attendance Centres*, Home Office Research Study No. 60, HMSO; London (**227**)

Dunlop, A. and Frankenburg, C. (1982) The detention of juveniles for grave crimes. *Home Office Research & Planning Unit Research Bulletin* No. 14, 41–4 (**235**)

Dunn, J. and Fahy, T. A. (1987) Section 136 and the Police. *Bulletin of the Royal College of Psychiatrists*, 11, 224–5 (**736, 738**)

Durbin, J. R., Pasework, R. A. and Albers, D. (1977) Criminality and mental illness: a study of arrest rates in a rural state. *American Journal of Psychiatry*, 134, 80–3 (**333**)

Durham, M. L. and La Fond, J. Q. (1985) The empirical consequences and policy implications of broadening the statutory criteria for civil commitment. *Yale Law and Policy Review*, 3, 395–446 (**152**)

Durkheim, E. (1901) 'The Normal and the Pathological' reprinted in *The Sociology of Crime and Delinquency*, 2nd edn. 1970 eds. M. E. Wolfgang, L. Savitz and N. Johnston, Wiley: New York, as an extract from *Les Règles de la méthode sociologique (8th edn)* Alean: Paris, trans. by S. A. Solovey and J. H. Mueller as *The Rules of Sociological Method*, Free Press: Glencoe, Ill (1950) (**569**)

Dye, S. and Isaacs, C. (1991) Intravenous drug misuse among prison inmates: implications for the spread of HIV. *British Medical Journal*, 302, 1506 (**819**)

Dyer, A. R. (1988) *Ethics and Psychiatry: Toward Professional Definition*, American Psychiatric Association Press: Washington DC (**864**)

Dyer, C. (1991) Unfitness to plead. *British Medical Journal*, 303, 11 (**308**)

Dyer, D. (1988) No fault compensation. *British Medical Journal*, 297, 939–40 (**107**)

Eagles, J. M. and Besson, J. A. O. (1986) Scotland's liquor licensing changes. (letter) *British Medical Journal*, 292, 486 (**437**)

Earls, C. M., Bouchard, L. and Laberge, J. (1984) *Étude Descriptive des Délinquants Sexuels Incarcéres dans les Pénitenciers Quebecois.* Cahier de Recherche No. 7 Institute Philippe Pinel: Montreal (**922**)

Eason, R. J. and Grimes, J. A. (1976) Inpatient care of the mentally ill: a statistical study of future provision. *Health Trends*, 8, 2–4 (**693**)

East, W. N. (1927) *An Introduction to Forensic Psychiatry in the Criminal Courts*, Churchill: London (**407, 424**)

East, W. N. (1936) *Medical Aspects of Crime*, Churchill: London (**357**)

East W. N. and Hubert, W. H. de B (1939) *The Psychological Treatment of Crime*, HMSO: London (**749**)

Edlund, M. J., Craig, T. J. and Richardson, M. A. (1985) Informed consent as a form of volunteer bias. *American Journal of Psychiatry*, 142, 624–7 (**879**)

Edwards, D. (1986) Mandatory drug testing in the workplace. *American Bar Association Journal*, 72, 34–5 (**465**)

Edwards, G. (1982) *The Treatment of Drinking Problems*, Grant McIntryre: London (**444**)

Edwards, G. and Gross, M. M. (1976) Alcohol dependence: provisional description of a clinical syndrome. *British Medical Journal*, i, 1058–61 (**441, 470**)

Edwards, G., Hensman, C. and Peto, J. (1971) Drinking problems among recidivist prisoners. *Psychological Medicine*, 1, 388–99 (**441, 446, 449, 455, 456**)

Edwards, G., Kyle, E. and Nicholls, P. (1977) Alcoholics admitted to four hospitals in England. 3: Criminal Records. *Journal of Studies on Alcohol*, 38, 1648–64 (**447**)

Edwards, S. S. M. (1984) *Women on Trial*, Manchester University Press: Manchester (**621**)

Edwards, S. S. M. (1987) Prostitutes: victims of law, social policy and organised crime. In *Gender Crime and Justice* (ed. P. Carlen and A. Worrall) Open University Press: Milton Keynes (**608**)

Eekelaar, J. and Dingwall, R. (1990) *The Reform of Child Care Law. A Practical Guide to the Children's Act 1989*, Tavistock/Routledge: London (**239, 246**)

Eggleston, R. (1983) *Evidence, Proof and Probability*, 2nd edn, Weidenfeld: London (**828**)

Eichelman, B., Wikler, D. and Hartwig, A. (1984) Ethics and psychiatric research: problems and justification. *American Journal of Psychiatry*, 141, 400–5 (**879**)

Eilenberg, M. D. (1961) Remand home boys 1930–1955. *British Journal of Criminology*, 2, 111–31 (**321**)

Ekblom, B. (1970) *Acts of Violence by Patients in Mental Hospitals*, Scandinavian University Books: Almqvist and Wiksells, Uppsala (**334, 807, 895**)

Ellard, J. (1970) The problems of the immigrant. *Proceedings of the Medico-Legal Society of New South Wales*, **4**, 87–98 (**416**)

Ellenberger, H. F. (1970) *The Discovery of the Unconscious*, Basic Books: New York (**427, 430**)

Ellinwood, E. H. (1971) Assault and homicide associated with amphetamines. *American Journal of Psychiatry*, **127**, 1170–5 (**341**)

Ellinwood, E. H. and Petrie, W. M. (1976) Psychiatric syndromes induced by non-medical use of drugs. In *Research Advances in Alcohol and Drug Problems 3*. (ed. R. J. Gibbons, et al.) John Wiley: New York (**458**)

Elliott, D. S., Huizinga, D. and Ageton, S. (1985) *Explaining Delinquency and Drug Use*, Sage: Beverly Hills, CA (**254, 267, 278**)

Elliott, D. S., Huizinga, D. and Menard, S. (1989) *Multiple Problem Youth*, Springer-Verlag: New York (**254, 256**)

Elliott, D. S. and Menard, S. (1988) *Delinquent Behavior and Delinquent Peers: Temporal and Developmental Patterns*. Unpublished manuscript (**267**)

Elliott, F. A. (1977) Propranolol for the control of belligerent behaviour following acute brain damage. *Annals of Neurology*, **1**, 489–91 (**662**)

Ellis, B. E. (1991) *American Psycho*, Vintage Books: New York (**520**)

Ellis D. P. and Austin, P. (1971) Menstruation and aggressive behavior in a correctional center for women. *Journal of Criminal Law, Criminology and Police Science*, **62**, 888–95 (**605**)

Ellis, E. M. (1983) A review of empirical rape research: victim reactions and response to treatment. *Clinical Psychology Review*, **3**, 473–90 (**896, 916**)

Ellis, E. M., Atkeson, B. and Calhoun, K. (1981) An assessment of longterm reactions to rape. *Journal of Abormal Psychology*, **90**, 263–6 (**916**)

Elmer, E. (1977) *Fragile Families, Troubled Children*, University of Pittsburg Press: Pittsburg (**900**)

Elmer, E. and Gregg, G. D. (1967) Development characteristics of abused children. *Pediatrics*, **40**, 596–602 (**894**)

Elton, P. J. (1987) Mothers and babies in prison. *Lancet*, **ii**, 501–2 (**622**)

Emmins, C. (1986) Unfitness to plead: thoughts prompted by Glen Pearson's Case. *Criminal Law Review*, 604–18 (**45**)

Enoch, M. D. and Trethowan, W. H. (1979) *Some Uncommon Psychiatric Syndromes*, 2nd edn, Wright: Bristol (**353, 417, 422, 426**)

Enos, W. F., Conrath, T. B. and Byer, J. C. (1986) Forensic examination of the sexually abused child. *Paediatrics*, **78**, 385–98 (**535**)

Epps, P. (1962) Women shoplifters in Holloway Prison. In *Shoplifting* (eds. T. C. N. Gibbens and J. Prince) Institute for the Study and Treatment of Delinquency: London (**605**)

Epstein, L. J., Mills, C. and Simon, A. (1970) Antisocial behavior of the elderly. *Comprehensive Psychiatry*, **ii**, 36–42 (**326**)

Esquirol, J. E. D. (1838) *Des Maladies Mentales*, Baillière: Paris (reprinted by Armo Press: New York, 1976) (**353**)

Estroff, T. W. (1987) Medical and biological consequences of cocaine abuse. In *Cocaine: A Clinician's Handbook* (eds. A. M. Washton, and M. S. Gold) Wiley: Chichester (**471**)

Evans, A. C. and Raistrick, D. (1987a) Phenomenology of intoxication with toluene-based adhesives and butane gas. *British Journal of Psychiatry*, **150**, 769–73 (**474**)

Evans, A. C. and Raistrick, D. (1987b) Patterns of use and related harm with toluene-based adhesives and butane gas. *British Journal of Psychiatry*, **150**, 773–6 (**474**)

Evans, K. (1983) *Advocacy at the Bar*, Financial Training Publications: London (**827**)

Evans, P. (1986) Forgotten victims of murder. *The Times*, October 20 1986 (**921**)

Evans, R. I., Rozelle, R. M., Maxwell, S. E., Raines, B. E., Dill, C. A., Guthrie, T. J., Henderson A. H. and Hill, P. C. (1981) Social modelling films to deter smoking in adolescents: results of a three-year field investigation. *Journal of Applied Psychology*, **66**, 399–414 (**283**)

Evanson, R. C., Wood, J. B., Nuttall, E. A. and Cho, D. W. (1982) Suicide rates among public health patients. *Acta Psychiatrica Scandinavica*, **66**, 254–64 (**811, 812**)

Evershed, S. (1987) Special Unit C Wing HMP Parkhurst. In *Problems of Long-Term Imprisonment* (ed. A. E. Bottoms and R. Light) Gower: Aldershot (**755**)

Eynont, G. and Reckless, W. C. (1961) Companionship at delinquency onset. *British Journal of Criminology*, **2**, 162–170 (**266**)

Eysenck, H. J. (1977) *Crime and Personality*, 3rd edn, Routledge & Kegan Paul: London (**261**)

Eysenck, H. J. and Eysenck, S. B. G. (1964) *Manual of Eysenck Personality Inventory*, University of London Press: London (**xii**)

Eysenck, S. B. G. and Eysenck, H. J. (1973) The personality of female prisoners. *British Journal of Psychiatry*, **123**, 693–8 (**616**)

Fahy, T., Bermingham, D. and Dunn, J. (1987) Police admissions to mental hospitals: a challenge to community psychiatry? *Medicine, Science and the Law*, **27**, 263–8 (**369, 735**)

Fahy, T. and Dunn, J. (1987) Where section 136 fails? *Police Review*, **95**, 1580–1 (**171**)

Falconer, M. A. (1973) Reversibility by temporal lobe resection of the behavioural abnormalities of temporal lobe epilepsy. *New England Journal of Medicine*, **289**, 451–5 (**301**)

Falconer, M. A. and Taylor, D. C. (1970) Temporal lobe epilepsy: clinical features, pathology, diagnosis and treatment. In *Modern Trends in Psychological Medicine Vol. 2* (ed. J. H. Price) Butterworth: London (**301**)

Faller, K. C. (1984) Is the child victim of sexual abuse telling the truth? *Child Abuse and Neglect*, **8**, 473–81 (**942**)

Falloon, I. R. H. and Talbot, R. E. (1981) Persistent auditory hallucinations: coping mechanisms and implications for management. *Psychological Medicine*, **11**, 329–39 (**345**)

Famularo, R., Kincherff, R. and Fenton, T. (1988) Propranolol treatment for childhood post-traumatic stress disorder, acute type—a pilot study. *American Journal of the Diseases of Childhood*, **142**, 1244–7 (**937**)

Farrell, M. and Strang, J. (1991) Drugs, HIV and prison. *British Medical Journal*, **302**, 1477–8 (**820**)

Farrington, D. P. (1972) Delinquency begins at home. *New Society*, **21**, 495–7 (**268**)

Farrington, D. P. (1973) Self-reports of deviant behaviour: predictive and stable? *Journal of Criminal Law and Criminology*, **64**, 99–110 (**253**)

Farrington, D. P. (1977) The effects of public labelling. *British Journal of Criminology*, **17**, 112–25 (**279**)

Farrington, D. P. (1978) The family backgrounds of aggressive youths. In *Aggression and Antisocial Behaviour in Childhood and Adolescence* (eds. L. Hersov, M. Berger and D. Straffer) Pergamon: Oxford, pp. 73–93 (**263**)

Farrington, D. P. (1979) Environmental stress, delinquent behaviour, and convictions. In *Stress and Anxiety, vol. 6* (eds. I. G. Sarason and C. D. Spielberger) Hemisphere: Washington DC, pp. 93–107 (**263, 264**)

Farrington, D. P. (1981) The prevalence of convictions. *British Journal of Criminology*, **21**, 173–5 (**604**)

Farrington, D. P. (1983) Randomized experiments on crime and justice. In *Crime and Justice* vol. 4 (eds. M. Tonry and N. Morris) University of Chicago Press: Chicago, pp. 257–308 (**280**)

Farrington, D. P. (1984) England and Wales. In *Western Systems of Juvenile Justice* (ed. M. Klein) Sage: London (**222**)

Farrington, D. P. (1986a) Age and crime. In *Crime and Justice* vol. 7 (eds. M. Tonry and N. Morris) University of Chicago Press: Chicago, pp. 189–250 (**256, 257**)

Farrington, D. P. (1986b) Stepping stones to adult criminal careers. In *Development of Antisocial and Prosocial Behaviour* (eds. D. Olweus, J. Block and M. R. Yarrow) Academic Press: New York, pp. 359–84 (**262, 263, 264, 267, 272, 278**)

Farrington, D. P. (1988a) Advancing knowledge about delinquency and crime: the need for a coordinated programme of longitudinal research. *Behavioral Sciences and the Law*, **6**, 307–31 (**253, 256, 285**)

Farrington, D. P. (1988b) Studying changes within individuals: the causes of offending. In *Studies of Psychosocial Risk* (ed. M. Rutter) Cambridge University Press: Cambridge, pp. 158–83 (**268**)

Farrington, D. P. (1989a) *Childhood Origins of Adult Social Failure and Antisocial Behaviour*. Paper given at meeting on 'Research and Practice in Forensic Psychiatry', Royal Society of Medicine, Section of Psychiatry: London (**272**)

Farrington, D. P. (1989b) Self-reported and official offending from adolescence to adulthood. In *Cross-national Research in Self-reported Crime and Delinquency* (ed. M. W. Klein) Kluwer: Dordrecht, Netherlands, pp. 399–423 (**253, 256, 257**)

Farrington, D. P. (1990a) Childhood aggression and adult violence: early precursors and later life outcomes. In *The Development and Treatment of Childhood Aggression* (eds. D. J. Pepler and K. H. Rubin) Lawrence Erlbaum: Hillsdale, NJ (**264**)

Farrington, D. P. (1990b) Implications of criminal career research for the prevention of offending. *Journal of Adolescence* 13 (**280**)

Farrington, D. P. (1991) Childhood aggression and adult violence early precursors and later life outcomes. In *The Development and Treatment of Childhood Aggression* (eds. D. J. Pepler & K. H. Rubin) Erlbaun: Hillsdale, NJ (**252**)

Farrington, D. and Bennett, T. (1981) Police cautioning of juveniles in London. *British Journal of Criminology*, **21**, 123–35 (**217**)

Farrington, D. P., Biron, L. and LeBlanc, M. (1982) Personality and delinquency in London and Montreal. In *Abnormal Offenders, Delinquency and the Criminal Justice System* (eds. J. Gunn and D. P. Farrington) Wiley: Chichester, pp. 153–201 (**262**)

Farrington, D. P., Gallagher, B., Morley, L., St Ledger, R. J. and West, D. J. (1986) Unemployment, school leaving, and crime. *British Journal of Criminology*, **26**, 335–56 (**272**)

Farrington, D. P., Gallagher, B., Morley, L., St Ledger, R. J. and West, D. J. (1988a) A 24-yr follow-up of men from vulnerable backgrounds. In *The Abandonment of Delinquent Behaviour* (eds. R. L. Jenkins and W. K. Brown) Praeger: New York, pp. 155–173 (**268**)

Farrington, D. P., Gallagher, B., Morley, L., St Ledger, R. J. and West, D. J. (1988b) Are there any successful men from criminogenic backgrounds? *Psychiatry* **51**, 116–130 (**268**)

Farrington, D. P., Loeber, R., Elliott, D. S., Hawkins, J. D. Kandel, D. B., Klein, M. W., McCord, J., Rowe, D. C. and Tremblay, R. E. (1990) Advancing knowledge about the onset of delinquency and crime. In *Advances in Clinical Child Psychology* (eds. B. B. Lahoy and A. E. Kazdin) vol. 13 Plenum: New York, pp. 283–342 (**278**)

Farrington, D. P., Loeber, R. and Van Kammen, W. B. (1990) Long-term criminal outcomes of hyperactivity-impulsivity-attention deficit and conduct problems in childhood. In *Straight and Devious Pathways from Childhood to Adulthood* (eds. L. N. Robins and M. Rutter) Cambridge University Press: Cambridge (**262**)

Farrington, D. P. Ohlin, L. E. and Wilson, J. Q. (1986) *Understanding and Controlling Crime*, Springer-Verlag: New York (**280, 285**)

Farrington, D. P. and West, D. J. (1990) The Cambridge study in delinquent development: a long-term follow-up of 411 London males. In *Criminality: Personality, Behaviour, Life History* (eds. H. J. Kerner and G. Kaiser) Springer-Verlag: Heidelberg (**256, 257, 284**)

Faulk, M. (1974) Men who assault their wives. *Medicine, Science and the Law*, **2**, 180–3 (**510**)

Faulk, M. (1976) A psychiatric study of men serving a sentence in Winchester prison. *Medicine, Science and the Law*, **16**, 244–51 (**334, 616, 813**)

Faulk, M. (1988) *Basic Forensic Psychiatry*, Blackwell: Oxford (**818**)

Faulk, M. and Taylor, J. C. (1986) Psychiatric interim regional secure unit: seven years experience. *Medicine, Science and the Law*, **26**, 17–22 (**714**)

Fazey, C. S. J. (1988) The evaluation of Liverpool Drug Dependency Clinic: The first two years 1985–87. *Research, Evaluation and Data Analysis*, private circulation (**472**)

Federal Bureau of Investigation (1988) *Age-specific Arrest Rates and Race-specific Arrest Rates for Selected Offences 1965–1986*, US Department of Justice: Washington DC (**256, 275**)

Feighner, J. P., Aden, G. C. and Fabre, L. F. (1983) Comparison of alprazolam, imipramine and placebo in the treatment of depression. *Journal of the American Medical Association*, 249, 3057–64 (**937**)

Feinberg, G. (1984) White haired offenders: an emergent social problem. In *Elderly Criminals* (ed. W. Wilbanks and P. K. H. Kim) University Press of America: Lanham, MD (**326**)

Feinberg, G., Glugover, S. and Zwetchkerbaum, I. (1984) The Broward senior intervention and education program: a pilot program. In *Elderly Criminals* (eds. E. S. Newman, D. J. Newman, and M. L. Gewirtz) Oelgeschlager, Gunn & Hain: Cambridge, Mass. (**328**)

Feldbrugge, J. T. T. M. (1986) *Commitment to the Committed: Treatment as Interaction in a Forensic Mental Hospital*, Swets & Zeitlinger: Lisse, BV Amsterdam (**689**)

Feldman, P. (1989) Applying psychology to the reduction of juvenile offending and offences. In *Clinical Approaches to Working with Offenders* (eds C. Hollin and K. Howells) British Psychological Society: Leicester (**290**)

Feldman, R. A., Caplinger, T. E., and Wodarski, J. S. (1983) *The St Louis Conundrum*, Prentice-Hall: Englewood Cliffs, NJ (**283**)

Fennell, P. (1986) Law and psychiatry: the legal constitution of the psychiatric system. *Journal of Law and Psychiatry*, **13**, 35–65. (**826**)

Fenton, G. W. (1972) Epilepsy and automatism. *British Journal of Hospital Medicine*, 7, 57–64 (**296**)

Fenton, G. W. (1975) Clinical disorder of sleep. *British Journal of Hospital Medicine*, **14**, 120–45 (**308**)

Fenton, G. W. (1984) Epilepsy, mental abnormality and criminal behaviour. In *Mentally Abnormal Offenders* (eds. M. Craft and A. Craft) Ballière Tindall: London (**662**)

Fenton, G. W. (1986) Epilepsy and hysteria. *British Journal of Psychiatry*, **149**, 28–37 (**423**)

Fenton, G. W., Tennent, T. G., Fenwick, P. B. C. and Rattray, N. (1974) The EEG in antisocial behaviour: a study of posterior temporal slow activity in special hospital patients. *Psychological Medicine*, **4**, 181–6 (**288**)

Fenwick, P. (1986) Aggression and epilepsy. In *Aspects of Epilepsy and Psychiatry* (eds. M. R. Trimble and T. G. Bolwig) Wiley: Chichester (**314**)

Fenwick, P. (1987) Somnambulism and the law: a review. *Behavioral Sciences & the Law*, 5, 343–7 (**310**)

Fenwick, P. (1988) Epilepsy and the law. In *Recent Advances in Epilepsy* (eds. T. A. Pedley and B. S. Meldrum) Churchill Livingstone: Edinburgh (**586**)

Fenwick, P. (1989) Automation and the law. *Lancet*, **ii**, 753–4 (**308**)

Fenwick, P. and Fenwick, E. (1985) *Epilepsy and the Law*, Royal Society of Medicine: London (**58**)

Fergusson, D. M. and Horwood, L. J. (1987) Vulnerability to life events exposure. *Psychological Medicine*, 17, 739–49 (**887**)

Fernald, M. R., Hayes, M. H., Dawley, A. and Ruml, B. (1920) *A Study of Women Delinquents in New York State*, Century: New York (**614**)

Fernando, S., and Storm, V. (1984) Suicide among psychiatric patients in a district general hospital. *Psychological Medicine*, **14**, 661–72 (**812**)

Figley, C. (1978) *Stress Disorders among Vietnam Veterans. Theory, Research and Treatment Implications*, Bruner Mazal: New York (**896**)

Finch, J. D. (1984) *Aspects of Law Affecting the Paramedical Professions*, Faber & Faber: London (**734**)

Fingarette, H. (1969) *Self Deception*, Routledge & Kegan Paul: London (**409**)

Fingarette, H. and Hasse, A. F. (1979) *Mental Disabilities and Criminal Responsibility*, University of California Press: Berkley CA (**60, 62**)

Finkel, N. J. and Handel, S. F. (1989) How jurors construe 'insanity'. *Law and Human Behavior*, **13**, 41–59 (**55**)

Finkelhor, D. (1979) *Sexually Victimised Children*, Free Press: New York (**917, 918**)

Finkelhor, D. (1984) *Child Sexual Abuse: New Theory and Research*, Free Press: London (**537, 557**)

Finkelhor, D. (1986) *A Sourcebook on Child Sexual Abuse*, Sage: Beverly Hills CA (**533**)

Finkelhor, D. and Browne, A. (1986) The traumatic impact of child sexual abuse. *American Journal of Orthopsychiatry*, **55**, 530–41 (**528**)

Finn, P (1985) Decriminalisation of public drunkenness: response of the health care system. *Journal of Studies on Alcohol*, **46**, 7–23 (**453**)

Fisher, C., Kahn, E., Edwards, A. and Davis, D. M. (1973) A psychophysiological study of nightmares and night terrors. *Journal of Nervous & Mental Disease*, **157**, 75–98 (**310**)

Fisher, H. A. P. (1977) *Report of an Inquiry by the Hon. Sir Henry Fisher into the Circumstances leading to the Trial of Three Persons on Charges arising out of the Death of Maxwell Confait and the Fire at 27 Doggett Road, London SE5*, House of Commons, HMSO: London (**739**)

Fitton, A. and Heel, R. C. (1990) Clozapine—a review of its pharmacological properties and therapeutic use in schizophrenia. *Drugs*, **40**, 722–47 (**664**)

Flaherty, J. A. and Lahmeyer, H. W. (1978) Laryngeal-pharyngeal dystonia as a possible cause of asphyxia and haloperidol treatment. *American Journal of Psychiatry*, **135**, 1414–5 (**664**)

Flemenbaum, A. (1976) Pavor nocturnus: a complication of single daily tricyclic or neuroleptic dosage. *American Journal of Psychiatry*, **133**, 570–2 (**310**)

Fleszar-Szumigajowa, J (1969) The perpetrators of arson in forensic-psychiatric material. *Polish Medical Journal*, **vii**, 212–9 (**595**)

Flor-Henry, P. (1987) Cerebral aspects of sexual deviation. In *Variant Sexuality: Research and Theory* (ed. G. D. Wilson) Johns Hopkins University Press: Baltimore (**523**)

Floud, J. and Young, W. (1981) *Dangerousness and Criminal Justice*, Heinemann: London (**639**)

Folkard, M. S., Fowles, A. J., McWilliams, B. C., McWilliams, W., Smith, D. D., Smith, D. E. and Walmsley, G. R. (1974) *Intensive Matched Probation and After-care Treatment, vol. I: The Design of the Probation Experiment and an Interim Evaluation*, Home Office Research Study No. 24, HMSO: London (**785**)

Folkard, M. S., Smith, D. E. and Smith, D. D. (1976) *Intensive Matched Probation and After-Care Treatment Vol. II: The Results of the Experiment*, Home Office Research Study No. 36, HMSO: London (**785**)

Fonagy, P., Steele, H. and Steele, M. (1991) Maternal representations of attachment during pregnancy and subsequent infant-mother attachments at one year of age. *Child Development*, **62**, 891–905 (**381**)

Fontana, V. J. (1976) *Somewhere a Child is Crying*, Macmillan: New York (**910**)

Ford, C. S. and Beach, F. A. (1952) *Patterns of Sexual Behaviour*, Eyre & Spottiswoode: London (**918**)

Ford, C. V., King, B. H. and Hollender, M. H. (1988) Lies and liars: psychiatric aspects of prevarication. *American Journal of Psychiatry*, **145**, 554–62 (**408**)

Forman, B. (1980) Cognitive modification of obsessive thinking in a rape victim: a preliminary study. *Psychological Reports*, **47**, 819–22 (**938**)

Forssman, H. and Hambert, G. (1966) Chromosomes and antisocial behaviour. (Letter) *Lancet*, ii, 282 (**314**)

Fottrell, E. (1980) A study of violent behaviour among patients in psychiatric hospitals. *British Journal of Psychiatry*, **136**, 216–21 (**618, 806, 807**)

Foucault, M. (1967) *Madness and Civilisation—A History of Insanity in the Age of Reason*, Tavistock: London (**796**)

Foulds, G. A. (1971) Personality deviance and personal symptomatology. *Psychological Medicine*, **1**, 222–33 (**376**)

Foville, A. (1882) Folie à double forme (Alternating insanity). *Brain*, **5**, 289–323 (**349**)

Fowles, M. W. (1978) *Sexual Offenders in Rampton*. Special Hospitals Research Report, No. 14 DHSS: London (**323**)

Foxx, R. M. and Bechtel, D. R. (1982) Overcorrection. In *Progress in Behavior Modification*, vol. 13 (eds. M. Hersen, R. M. Eisler and P. M. Miller) Academic Press: New York (**674**)

Foy, D., Sipprelle, R. C., and Rueger, D. B. (1984) Aetiology of post-traumatic stress disorders in Vietnam veterans: analysis of premilitary, military and combat exposure influences. *Journal of Consulting and Clinical Psychology*, **52**, 79–87 (**895, 897**)

Frances, A. (1982) Categorical and dimensional systems of personality diagnosis: a comparison. *Comprehensive Psychiatry*, **23**, 516–27 (**378**)

Franchini, A., Canepa, G. and Giaretta, R. (1984) Formation et choix des médecins-légistes experts en Italie. *Reveue International de Criminologie et Police Technique*, **37**, 354–62 (**156**)

Frank, E., Turner, S. M. and Stewart, B. D. (1980) Initial response to rape: the impact of factors within the rape situation. *Journal of Behavioral Assessment*, **2**, 39–53 (**897**)

Frank, E., Turner, S. M., Stewart, B. D., Jacob, M. and West, D. (1981) Past psychiatric symptoms and the response to sexual assault. *Comprehensive Psychiatry*, **22**, 479–87 (**895**)

Frank, R. T. (1931) The hormonal causes of premenstrual tension. *Archives of Neurology and Psychiatry*, **26**, 1053–7 (**605**)

Frazier, S. H. (1974) Murder—single and multiple. In *Aggression Res. Pub. ARNMD vol. 52*, The Association for Research in Nervous and Mental Disease: Washington DC (**520**)

Freeman, M. D. A. (1979) *Violence in the Home*, Gower: London (**511**)

French, A. P. and Schechmeister, B. R. (1983) The multiple personality syndrome and criminal defense. *Bulletin of the American Academy of Psychiatry and the Law*, **11**, 17–25 (**66, 429**)

Freud, S. (1905a) Three essays on the theory of sexuality. In *The Complete Psychological Works of Sigmund Freud* (Standard edn. vol. 7) Hogarth Press (1953), London (**523**)

Freud, S. (1905b) Fragment of an analysis of a case of hysteria. In *The Complete Psychological Works of Sigmund Freud, vol. 7* Hogarth Press (1953): London (**678**)

Freud, S. (1908) Character and anal eroticism. In *On Sexuality, Three Essays on the Theory of Sexuality and other works by S. Freud*, Pelican Freud Library, vol. 7 (ed. A. Richards) Penguin (1977): Harmondsworth (**392**)

Freud, S. (1913) *Totem and Taboo* (trans. J. Strachey) Routledge & Kegan Paul (1960): London (**536**)

Freud, S. (1917) Mourning and melancholia. In *Collected Papers*, vol. IV, Hogarth Press (1934): London (**516**)

Freud, S. (1920) *Beyond the Pleasure Principle* (trans. C. J. M. Hubbach) International Psycho-analytical Library, Hogarth Press (1922): London (**16, 492**)

Freud, S. (1928) Dostoevski and parricide. In *Collected Papers*, 5. (ed J. Strachey) Basic Books (1959): New York (**482**)

Freud, S. (1929) *Civilisation and its Discontents*, International Psycho-analytic Library, Hogarth Press (1963): London **(594)**

Freudenberger, H. J. (1974) Staff burnout. *Journal of Social Issues*, **30**, 159–65 **(935, 941)**

Freund, K. (1980) Therapeutic sex drive reduction. *Acta Psychiatrica Scandinavica*, **62**, Suppl. 287 **(562)**

Freund, K., Scher, H. and Hucker, S. (1983) The courtship disorders. *Archives of Sexual Behavior*, **12**, 369–79 **(549)**

Freund, K., Scher, H. and Hucker, S. (1984) The courtship disorders: a further investigation. *Archives of Sexual Behavior*, **13**, 133–9 **(549)**

Friedman, M. J. (1981) Post-Vietnam syndrome: recognition and management. *Psychosomatics*, **22**, 931–4 3 **(937)**

Friedman, M. J. (1988) Toward rational pharmacotherapy for post-traumatic stress disorder: an interim report. *American Journal of Psychiatry*, **145**, 281–92 **(889, 932, 936, 937)**

Friedmann, C. T. H. (1982) The so-called hystero-psychoses. In *Extraordinary Disorders of Human Behavior* (ed. C. T. H. Friedman and R. A. Faguet) Plenum Press: New York **(433)**

Fritz, G. S., Stoll, K. and Wagner, N. N. (1981) A comparison of males and females who were sexually molested as children. *Journal of Sex and Marital Therapy*, **7**, 154–9 **(919)**

Fromm, E. (1973) *The Anatomy of Human Destructiveness*, Holt, Rinehard & Winston: New York (Penguin, 1977: Harmondsworth) **(16, 17, 392)**

Fromm-Reichmann, F. (1948) Notes on the development of treatment of schizophrenia by psychoanalytic psychotherapy. *Psychiatry*, **11**, 263–73 **(367)**

Fry, M. (1951) *Arms of the Law*, Gollancz: London **(105)**

Fry, M. (1959) Justice for Victims. *Journal of Public Law*, **8**, 191–4 **(105)**

Fulford, K. W. M. (1989) *Moral Theory & Medical Practice*, Cambridge University Press: Cambridge **(6, 7)**

Funayama, M. and Sagisaka, K. (1988) Consecutive infanticides in Japan. *American Journal of Forensic Medicine and Pathology*, **9**, 9–11 **(612)**

Furniss, T., Bingley-Miller, L. and Bentovim, A. (1984) Child sexual abuse: a therapeutic approach to an under-reported problem. *Archives of Disease in Childhood*, **59**, 865–70 **(559)**

Gagné, P. (1989) More laws for better medicine? *American Journal of Psychiatry*, **146**, 819–20 **(865)**

Gagnon, J. H. (1965) Female child victims of sex offences. *Social Problems*, **13**, 176–92 **(914, 917, 918)**

Galaway, B. (1984) Victim participation in the penal-corrective process. *Victimology*, **10**, 617–30 **(944)**

Gallwey, P. L. G., (1985) The psychodynamics of borderline personality. In *Aggression and Dangerousness* (eds. D. Farrington and J. Gunn) Wiley: Chichester **(389)**

Gan, S. and Pullen, G. P. (1984) The Unicentre: an activity centre for the mentally ill. The first two years. *The British Journal of Occupational Therapy*, **47**, 216–8 **(704)**

Ganser, S. J. M. (1898) Über einen Eigenartigen Hysterischen Dammerzustand. *Archiv für Psychiatrie und nervenkrankheiten*, **30**, 633–40 (trans. C. E. Schoser in *British Journal of Criminology* (1965) **5**, 120–6) **(425)**

Garb, R., Kutz, I., Bleich, A. and Solomon, Z. (1987) Varieties of combat stress reaction: an immunological metaphor. *British Journal of Psychiatry*, **151**, 248–51 **(931)**

Garrett, C. J. (1985) Effects of residential treatment on adjudicated delinquents: a meta-analysis. *Journal of Research on Crime and Delinquency*, **22**, 287–308 **(675)**

Gath, D. (1978) *Secure Psychiatric Facilities in the Oxford Region*, Oxford Regional Health Authority: Oxford **(719)**

Gath, D. and Orly, J. (1976) *Survey of the Need for Secure Psychiatric Facilities in the Oxford Region*, Oxford Regional Health Authority: Oxford **(719)**

Gathercole, C. E., Craft, M. J., McDougall, J., Barnes, H. M. and Peck, D. F. (1968) A review of 100 discharges from a special hospital. *British Journal of Criminology*, **87**, 419–24 **(707)**

Gauthier, J. and Pellerin, D. (1982) Management of compulsive shoplifting through covert sensitisation. *Journal of Behavior Therapy and Experimental Psychiatry*, **13**, 73–5 **(578)**

Gauthier, J. and Pye, C. (1979) Graduated self-exposure in the management of grief. *Behavior Analysis and Modification*, **3**, 202–8 **(938)**

Gay, M. J., Holman, C. and Thomas, M. S. (1975) Helping the victims. *International Journal of Offender Therapy and Comparative Criminology*, **19**, 263–69 **(934)**

Gayford, J. J. (1975a) Battered wives. *Medicine, Science and the Law*, 15, 237–45 (**352, 449, 894, 913, 921**)

Gayford, J. (1975b) Wife battering: a preliminary survey of 100 cases. *British Medical Journal*, i, 194–7 (**449, 509, 894, 913**)

Gayford, J. (1978) Battered wives. In *Violence and the Family* (ed. J. P. Martin) Wiley: Chichester (**509**)

Gearing, M., Heckel, R. and Matthey, W. (1980) The screening and referral of mentally disordered inmates in a state correctional system. *Professional Psychology*, 11, 849–54 (**757**)

Gebhard, P. H., Gagnon, J. H., Pomeroy, W. B. and Christenson, C. V. (1965) *Sex Offenders*, Heinneman: London (**543, 548**)

Gee, D. J. and Mason, J. K. (1990) *The Courts and the Doctor*, Oxford University Press: Oxford (**856**)

Gelder, M., Gath, D. and Mayou, R. (1989) *Oxford Textbook of Psychiatry, 2nd edn*, Oxford University Press: Oxford (**11**)

Geller, J. and Bertsch, G. (1985) Fire setting behavior in the histories of a state hospital population. *American Journal of Psychiatry*, 142, 464–8 (**590**)

Gelsthorpe, L. and Morris, A. (1983) Attendance centres: policy and practice. *Howard Journal*, 22, 101–18 (**227**)

Gelsthorpe, L. and Tutt, N. (1986) The Attendance Centre Order. *Criminal Law Review*, March, 146–53 (**227**)

Genders, E. and Player, E. (1986) Women's imprisonment. The effects of youth custody. *British Journal of Criminology*, 26, 357–71 (**618**)

Genders, E. and Player, E. (1987) Women in prison: the treatment, the control and the experience. In *Gender, Crime and Justice* (ed. P. Carlen and A. Worrall) Open University Press: Milton Keynes (**621**)

Genders, E. and Player E. (1989) *Grendon. A Study of a Therapeutic Community within the Prison System* (unpublished) Report to Home Office (**751**)

Gendreau, P. and Ross, R. R. (1979) Effective correctional treatment: bibliotherapy for cynics. *Crime and Delinquency*, 25, 463–89 (**282**)

Gendreau, P. and Ross, R. R. (1984) Correctional treatment: some recommendations for effective intervention. *Juvenile and Family Court Journal*, Winter, 31–9 (**290**)

Gendreau, P. and Ross, R. R. (1987) Revivification of rehabilitation: evidence from the 1980s. *Justice Quarterly*, 4, 349–407 (**282**)

General Medical Council (1987) *Professional Conduct and Discipline: Fitness to Practise*, General Medical Council: London (**200, 863**)

General Medical Council (1988) *HIV Infection and AIDS: The Ethical Considerations*, General Medical Council: London (**875**)

Gerber, P. (1984) Psychiatry in the dock—a lawyer's afterthoughts. In *Mentally Abnormal Offenders* (ed. M. & A. Craft) Baillière Tindall: London (**855**)

Ghodse, A. H. (1987) Cannabis psychosis. *British Journal of Addiction*, 81, 473–8 (**458, 468**)

Ghodse, A. H. (1989) *Drugs and Addictive Behaviour*, Oxford: Blackwell (**465**)

Ghodse, A. H., Bewley, T. H., Kearney, M. K. and Smith, S. E. (1986) Mydriatic response to topical naloxone in opiate abusers. *British Journal of Psychiatry*, 148, 44–6 (**468**)

Giallombardo, R. (1966) *Society of Women: A Study of Women's Prison*, Wiley: New York (**618**)

Giaretto, H. (1982) A comprehensive child sexual abuse program. *Child Abuse and Neglect*, 6, 263–78 (**940**)

Gibbens, T. C. N. (1958a) Sane and insane homicide. *Journal of Criminal Law, Criminology and Police Science*, 49, 110–5 (**338, 352, 447**)

Gibbens, T. C. N. (1958b) Car thieves. *British Journal of Delinquency*, 8, 257–65 (**579**)

Gibbens, T. C. N. (1963) *Psychiatric Studies of Borstal Lads*, Maudsley Monograph No. 11, Oxford University Press: London (**323**)

Gibbens, T. C. N. (1970) Hooliganism and vandalism. *The Medico-Legal Journal*, 38, 122–34 (**587**)

Gibbens, T. C. N. (1971) Female offenders. *British Journal of Hospital Medicine*, 6, 279–86 (**295, 608**)

Gibbens, T. C. N. (1974) Preparing psychiatric reports. *British Journal of Hospital Medicine*, 12, 278–84 (**837**)

Gibbons, T. C. N. (1978) Mental illness, personality and behaviour disorders. In *Medical Aspects of Fitness to Drive*, 3rd edn. (ed. A. Raffle) Medical Commission on Accident Prevention: London (**113**)

Gibbens, T. C. N. (1983) Medicolegal aspects. In *Handbook of Psychiatry. Vol. 1. General Psychopathology* (eds. M. Shepherd and O. L. Zangwill) Cambridge University Press: Cambridge (**309**)

Gibbens, T. C. N. and Ahrenfeldt, R. J. H. (1966) *Cultural Factors in Delinquency*, Tavistock Publications: London (**601, 604**)

Gibbens, T. C. N., Goodman, N., Dell, S. and Prince, J. (1971a) *A Medical Survey of Women received into Holloway Prison during 1967* (unpublished) (**601, 614, 619, 621**)

Gibbens, T. C. N., Palmer, C. and Prince, J. (1971b) Mental health aspects of shoplifting. *British Medical Journal*, iii, 612–5 (**574**)

Gibbens, T. C. N. and Prince, J. (1962) *Shoplifting*, Institute for the Study and Treatment of Delinquency: London (**572, 601**)

Gibbens, T. C. N. and Prince, J. (1963) *Child Victims of Sex Offences*, Institute for the Study and Treatment of Delinquency: London (**918**)

Gibbens, T. C. N. and Robertson, G. (1983) 1. A survey of the criminal careers of hospital order patients, 2. A survey of the criminal careers of restriction order patients. *British Journal of Psychiatry*, **143** 362–9, 370–5 (**360, 363**)

Gibbens, T. C. N. and Silberman, M. (1970) Alcoholism among prisoners. *Psychological Medicine*, **1**, 73–8 (**446, 448, 451**)

Gibbens, T. C. N., Soothill, K. L. and Pope, P. (1977a) *Medical Remands in the Criminal Courts*, Maudsley Monograph No. 25, Oxford University Press: Oxford (**543, 728, 742, 743**)

Gibbens, T. C. N., Soothill, K. L. and Way, C. K. (1978) Sibling and parent-child incest offenders. *British Journal of Criminology*, **18**, 40–52 (**538**)

Gibbens, T. C. N., Soothill, K. L. and Way, C. (1981) Psychiatric treatment on probation. *British Journal of Criminology*, **21**, 4, 324–34 (**784**)

Gibbens, T. C. N., Way, C. and Soothill, K. L. (1977b) Behavioural types of rape. *British Journal of Psychiatry*, **130**, 32–42 (**546**)

Gibbs, C. (1971) The effect of the imprisonment of women upon their children. *British Journal of Criminology*, **11**, 113–30 (**622**)

Gibson, D. (1978) *Down's Syndrome: the Psychology of Mongolism*, Cambridge University Press: Cambridge (**313**)

Gibson, E. (1975) *Homicide in England & Wales 1967–1971*, Home Office Research Study No. 31, HMSO: London (**512, 516, 609, 610**)

Gibson, E. and Klein, S. (1969) *Murder 1957–1968*, Home Office Research Study No. 3 HMSO: London (**512**)

Gibson, H. B. and West, D. J. (1970) Social and intellectual handicaps as precursors of early delinquency. *British Journal of Criminology*, **10**, 21–32 (**332**)

Gil, D. G. (1968) Incidence of child abuse and demographic characteristics of persons involved. In *The Battered Child* (eds. R. E. Helfer and C. H. Kempe) University of Chicago Press: Chicago (**502**)

Gil, D. G. (1969) Physical abuse of children: findings and implications of a nationwide survey. *Pediatrics*, **44**, 857–64 (**912**)

Gillett, G. (1986) Multiple personality and the concept of a person. *New Ideas in Psychology*, **4**, 173–84 (**430**)

Gillies, H. (1965) Murder in the west of Scotland. *British Journal of Psychiatry*, **111**, 1087–94 (**346, 363**)

Gillies, H. (1976) Homicide in the west of Scotland. *British Journal of Psychiatry*, **128**, 105–27 (**448, 609, 610**)

Gillin, J. C. and Ochberg, F. M. (1970) Firearms control and violence. In *Violence and the Struggle for Existence* (eds. D. N. Daniels, M. F. Gilula and F. M. Ochberg) Little, Brown: Boston (**499**)

Gimlette, J. D. (1901) Notes on a case of amok. *Journal of Tropical Medicine and Hygiene*, **4**, 195–9 (**432**)

Giovannoni, J. M. and Gurel, L. (1967) Socially disruptive behaviour of ex-mental patients. *Archives of General Psychiatry*, **7**, 146–53 (**333**)

Gise, L. H. and Paddison, P. (1988) Rape, sexual abuse and its victims. *Psychiatric Clinics of North America*, **11**, 629–47 (**916**)

Gittelman, R., Mannuzza, S., Shenker, R. and Bonagura, N. (1985) Hyperactive boys almost grown up. *Archives of General Psychiatry*, **42**, 937–47 (**262**)

Gittleson, N. L., Encott, S. E. and Mehlan, B. M. (1978) Victims of indecent exposure. *British Journal of Psychiatry*, **132**, 61–6 (**914, 921**)

Gladue, B. A., Green, R. and Hellman, R. E. (1984) Neuroendocrine response to estrogen and sexual orientation. *Science* 225, 1496–9 (523)

Glanz, A. and Taylor, C. (1987) Findings of a national survey of the role of general practitioners in the treatment of opiate misuse. In *Drug Use and Misuse: A Reader* (eds. T. Heller, M. Gott and C. Jeffrey) Wiley: Chichester (478)

Glatt, M. M. (1964) Alcoholism in impaired and drunken driving. *Lancet*, i, 62 (438)

Glatt, M. M. (1977) A therapeutic community for dependent individuals (addicts) in prison. In *Drug Dependence* (ed. M. M. Glatt) MTP: Lancs. (476)

Glatt, M. M. (1982) *Alcoholism*, Hodder & Stoughton: Sevenoaks (63)

Glatt, M. M. (1985) The Wormwood Scrubs Annex: reflections on the working and functioning of an addict's therapeutic community within a prison. In *Prison Medicine: Ideas of Health Care in Penal Establishments*, Prison Reform Trust: London (476)

Glueck, B. (1918) A study of 608 admissions to Sing Sing Prison. *Mental Hygiene*, 2, 85–151 (334)

Glueck, S. and Glueck, E. (1934) *Five Hundred Delinquent Women*, Knopf: New York (614)

Glueck, S. and Glueck, E. T. (1950) *Unravelling Juvenile Delinquency*, Harvard University Press: Cambridge, Mass. (254)

Glueck, S. and Glueck, E. T. (1968) *Delinquents and Non-delinquents in Perspective*, Harvard University Press: Cambridge, Mass. (254)

Goetting, A. (1983) The elderly in prison: issues and perspectives. *Journal of Research in Crime and Delinquency*, 20, 291–309 (328)

Goffman, E. (1961) *Asylums*, Anchor Books, reprinted Penguin Books (1968): Harmondsworth (795)

Goh, S. E., Salmons, P. E. and Whittington, R. M. (1989) Hospital suicides: are there preventable factors? *British Journal of Psychiatry*, 154, 247–9 (812)

Gold, M. and Mann, D. W. (1984) *Expelled to a Friendlier Place* University of Michigan Press: Ann Arbor, MI (269)

Gold, M. and Reimer, D. J. (1975) Changing patterns of delinquent behaviour among Americans, 13 through 16 years old: 1967–72. *Crime and Delinquency Literature*, 7, 483–517 (272)

Gold, M. and Williams, J. R. (1969) National study of the aftermath of apprehension. *Prospectus*, 3, 3–12 (279)

Goldberg, D. P. (1972) *The Detection of Psychiatric Illness by Questionnaire*, Maudsley Monograph, No. 21, Oxford University Press: London (905)

Goldberg, E. M. and Morrison, S. L. (1963) Schizophrenia and social class. *British Journal of Psychiatry*, 109, 785–802 (368)

Goldberg, E. M. and Stanley, S. J. (1985) Task centred case-work in a probation setting. In *Problem, Tasks and Outcomes* (eds E. M. Goldberg, J. Gibbons & I. Sinclair) Allen & Unwin: London (778)

Golden, D. (1984) Elderly offenders in jail. In *Elderly Criminals* (ed. E. S. Newman, D. J. Newman and M. L. Gewirtz) Oelgeschlager, Gunn, & Hain: Cambridge, Mass. (327)

Goldfeld, A. E., Mollica, R. F., Pesavento, B. H. and Faraone, S. V. (1988) The physical and psychological sequelae of torture. Symptomatology and diagnosis. *Journal of the American Medical Association*, 259, 2725–9 (924)

Goldstein, J., Freud, A. and Solnit, A. J. (1979) *Before the Best Interests of the Child*, Free Press: New York (919)

Goldstein, M. J., Kant, H. S. and Hartman, J. J. (1973) *Pornography and Sexual Deviance*, University of California Press: Los Angeles (526, 535)

Goldstein, P. J. (1979) *Prostitution and Drugs*, Heath: Lexington, Mass (608, 609)

Goldstone, J. (1982) A fresh look at Community Service Orders. *The Magistrate*, 38, May (786)

Good, M. I. (1978) Primary affective disorder, aggression and criminality. *Archives of General Psychiatry*, 35, 954–60 (347, 348)

Goodwin, D. W. (1973) Alcohol in suicide and homicide. *Quarterly Journal of Studies in Alcohol*, 34, 144–56 (515)

Goodwin, D., Alderson, P. and Rosenthal, R. (1971) Clinical significance of hallucinations in psychiatric disorders. *Archives of General Psychiatry*, 24, 76–80 (344)

Goodwin, D. W., Crane, J. B. and Guze, S. E. (1969) Phenomenological aspects of the alcoholic 'blackout'. *British Journal of Psychiatry*, 115, 1033–8 (293, 443)

Goodwin, J. (1981) Suicide attempts in sexual abuse victims and their mothers. *Child Abuse and Neglect*, 5, 217–21 (918)

Gooren, L., Fliers, E. and Courtney, K. (1990) Biological determinants of sexual orientation *Annual Review of Sex Research*, 1, 175–96 **(523)**

Goorney, A. B. (1968) The treatment of a compulsive horse race gambler by aversion therapy. *British Journal of Psychiatry*, 114, 329–33 **(488)**

Gordon, G. H. (1978) *The Criminal Law of Scotland*, 2nd edn, Green: Edinburgh **(88)**

Gordon, R. and Verdun-Jones, S. N. (1983) The right to refuse treatment: Commonwealth developments and issues. *International Journal of Law and Psychiatry*, 6, 57–73 **(124)**

Gordon, R. A. (1976) Prevalence: the rare datum in delinquency measurement and its implications for the theory of delinquency. In *The Juvenile Justice System* (ed. M. W. Klein) Sage: Beverley Hills, CA **(277)**

Gordon, R. A. (1987) SES versus IQ in the race-IQ-delinquency model. *International Journal of Sociology and Social Policy*, 7, 30–96 **(277)**

Gosselin, C. and Wilson, G. (1980) *Sexual Variations*, Faber: London **(551)**

Gosselin, C. and Wilson, G. (1984) Fetishism, sadomasochism and related behaviours. In *The Psychology of Sexual Diversity* (ed. K. Howells) Blackwell: Oxford **(531)**

Gossop, M. (1978) Drug dependence, crime and personality among female addicts. *Drug and Alcohol Dependence*, 3, 359–64 **(477)**

Gossop, M., Bradley, B. and Phillips, G. T. (1987) An investigation of withdrawal symptoms shown by opiate addicts during and subsequent to a 21-day inpatient methadone detoxification procedure. *Addictive Behaviours*, 12, 1–6 **(459)**

Gossop, M. and Eiser, J. R. (1979) Hooked or sick: addicts' perceptions of their addiction. *Addictive Behaviours*, 4, 185–91 **(469)**

Gostin, L. (1983a) *The Court of Protection*, MIND: London **(197)**

Gostin, L. (1983b) The ideology of entitlement: the application of contemporary legal approaches to psychiatry. *Mental Illness: Changes and Trends* (ed. P. Bean) Wiley: Chichester **(829)**

Gostin, L. (1985) Human rights in mental health. In *Psychiatry, Human Rights and the Law* (eds. M. Roth and R. Bluglass) Cambridge University Press: Cambridge **(798)**

Gottfredson, D. C. (1987) Examining the potential of delinquency prevention through alternative education. *Today's Delinquent*, 6, 87–100 **(269)**

Gottfredson, M. R. (1984) *Victims of Crime: The Dimensions of Risk*, Home Office Research Study No. 81, HMSO London **(893, 899)**

Goyer, P. F. and Eddleman, H. C. (1984) Same sex rape of non-incarcerated men. *American Journal of Psychiatry*, 141, 576–9 **(917)**

Graham, J. (1988) *Amusement machines: Dependency and Delinquency*, Home Office Research Study No. 101, HMSO: London **(482, 489)**

Graham, P. and Rutter, M. (1968) Organic brain dysfunction and child psychiatric disorder. *British Medical Journal*, iii, 695–700 **(305)**

Grassian, S. (1983) Psychopathological effects of solitary confinement. *American Journal of Psychiatry*, 140, 1450–4 **(654, 659)**

Gratz, W. (1986) *Die praxis der Unterbringung Zurechnungsfähiger Geistig Abnormer Rechtsbrecher*, Orac: Wien **(132)**

Greaves, G. B. (1980) Multiple personality 165 years after Mary Reynolds. *Journal of Nervous and Mental Diseases*, 168, 577–96 **(428)**

Green, A. H. (1978) Self-destructive behavior in battered children. *American Journal of Psychiatry*, 135, 579–82 **(913)**

Green, B. L., Grace, M. C. and Green, G. G. (1985) Identifying survivors at risk: long-term impairment following the Beverly Hills Supper Club fire. *Journal of Consulting and Clinical Psychology*, 53, 672–8 **(897)**

Green, C. M. and Manohar, S. V. (1990) Neonaticide and hysterical denial of pregnancy. *British Journal of Psychiatry*, 156, 121–3 **(611)**

Green, R. (1987) *The 'Sissy Boy Syndrome' and the Development of Homosexuality*, Yale University Press: New Haven **(540)**

Greenberg, D. (1983) Age and crime. In *Encyclopedia of Crime and Justice* (ed. S. H. Kadish) Macmillan: New York **(325)**

Greenberg, D. and Rankin, H. (1982) Compulsive gamblers in treatment. *British Journal of Psychiatry*, 140, 364–6 **(487)**

Greenblatt, M., Grosser, G. H. and Wechsler, H. (1964) Differential response of hospitalised depressed patients to somatic therapy. *American Journal of Psychiatry*, 120, 935–43 **(937)**

Greenblatt, M., York, R. H., Brown, E. L. and Hyde, R. W. (1955) *From Custodial to Therapeutic Patient care in Mental Hospitals*, Russell Sage Foundation: New York (655)

Greendyke, R. M. and Kanter, D. R. (1986) Therapeutic effects of pindolol on behavioural disturbances associated with organic brain disease: a double-blind study. *Journal of Clinical Psychiatry*, 47, 423–6 (662)

Greendyke, R. M., Kanter, D. R., Schuster, D. B., Verstreate, S. and Wooton, J. (1986) Propranolol treatment of assaultive patients with organic brain disease. *Journal of Nervous & Mental Disease*, 174, 290–4 (662)

Greendyke, R. M., Schuster, D. B., and Wooton, J. A. (1984) Propranolol in the treatment of assaultive patients with organic brain disease. *Journal of Clinical Psychopharmacology*, 4, 282–5 (662)

Greyson, B. (1985) A typology of near-death experiences. *American Journal of Psychiatry*, 142, 967–9 (932)

Griew, E. (1988) The future of diminished responsibility. *Criminal Law Review*, 75–87 (51)

Griffith, J. D., Cavanaugh, J., Held, J. and Oates, J. A. (1972) Dextroamphetamines. *Archives of General Psychiatry*, 26, 97–100 (458)

Griffith, R. W. and Saameli, K. (1975) Clozapine and agranulocytosis. (Letter) *Lancet*, ii 657 (665)

Griffiths, A. W. (1971) Prisoners of XYY constitution: psychological aspects. *British Journal of Psychiatry*, 119, 193–4 (314)

Grimes, R. and Horgan, P. (1988) *Introduction to Law in the Republic of Ireland*, Wolfhound Press: Dublin (208)

Groeneveld, L. P., Short, J. F. and Thoits, P. (1979) *Design of a Study to Assess the Impact of Income Maintenance on Delinquency*. Final Report to the National Institute of Juvenile Justice and Delinquency Prevention: Washington DC (284)

Grohmann, R., Rutho, E., Sassin, N. and Schmidt, L. G. (1989) Adverse effects of clozapine. *Psychopharmacology*, 99, 101–104 (665)

Grossman, K., Fremmer-Bombik, E., Rudolph, J. and Grossman, K. E. (1989) Maternal attachment representation as related to patterns of infant-mother attachment and maternal care during the first year. In *Relationships with Families* (eds. R. A. Hinde and J. Stevenson-Hinde) Oxford University Press: Oxford (381)

Groth, A. N. and Birnbaum, J. (1979) *Men who Rape: the Psychology of the Offender*, Plenum Press: New York (542, 547, 918)

Groth, A. N. and Burgess, A. W. (1980) Male rape: offenders and victims. *American Journal of Psychiatry*, 137, 806–10 (547, 892, 916)

Groth, A. N., Burgess, A. W. and Holstrom, L. L. (1977) Rape, power, anger, and sexuality. *American Journal of Psychiatry*, 134, 1239–43 (915)

Grounds, A. T. (1985) The psychiatrist in court. *British Journal of Hospital Medicine*, 33, 55–8 (837)

Grounds, A. T. (1986) Psychiatry and patients' rights. *British Journal of Hospital Medicine*, 36, 147–8 (798)

Grounds, A. T. (1987) Detention of 'psychopathic disorder' patients in special hospitals— critical issues. *British Journal of Psychiatry*, 151, 474–8 (402)

Grounds, A. (1991) The transfer of sentenced prisoners to hospital 1960–83: a study in one special hospital. *British Journal of Criminology*, 31, 54–71 (757, 758)

Grounds, A. T., Quayle, M. T., France, J., Brett, T., Cox, M. and Hamilton, J. R. (1987) A unit for 'psychopathic disorder' patients in Broadmoor Hospital. *Medicine, Science and the Law*, 27, 21–31 (558, 703)

Group for the Advancement of Psychiatry (1960) *Confidentiality and Privileged Communications in the Practise of Psychiatry Report 45*, Group for the Advancement of Psychiatry: New York (863)

Grubin, D. H. and Gunn, J. (1990) *The Imprisoned Rapist and Rape*, Department of Forensic Psychiatry, Institute of Psychiatry, London (private circulation) (537, 543, 544)

Grubin, D. H. and Kennedy, H. G. (1991) The classification of sexual offenders. *Criminal Behaviour and Mental Health*, 1, 123–9 (532)

Grubin, D. H. (1991a) Unfit to plead in England and Wales 1976–1988: a survey. *British Journal of Psychiatry*, 158, 540–8 (45)

Grubin, D. H. (1991b) Regaining fitness: patients found unfit to plead who return for trial. *Journal of Forensic Psychiatry*, 2, 139–84 (45)

Grubin, D. H. (1991c) Unfit to plead, unfit for discharge. *Criminal Behaviour & Mental Health*, **1**, 282–94 **(45)**

Grunberg, F., Klinger, B. I. and Grumet, B. (1977) Homicide and de-institutionalisation of the mentally ill. *American Journal of Psychiatry*, **134**, 685–7 **(333)**

Grunberg, F., Klinger, B. I. and Grumet, B. (1978) Homicide and community-based psychiatry. *Journal of Nervous and Mental Disease*, **166**, 868–74 **(333)**

Gruneberg, M., Morris, P. and Sykes, R. (1988) *Practical Aspects of Memory*, Wiley: Chichester **(291)**

Gudden, H. (1905) Die Physiologische und Pathologische Schlaftrunkenheit. *Archiv für Psychiatrie und Nervenkrankheiten*, **40**, 989–1015 **(309)**

Gudjonsson, G. H. (1982) The nature of shoplifting in Iceland. *Forensic Science International*, **19**, 209–16 **(577)**

Gudjonsson, G. H. (1984a) A new scale of interrogative suggestibility. *Personality and Individual Differences*, **5**, 803–14 **(740)**

Gudjonsson, G. H. (1984b) Interrogative suggestibility: comparison between 'false confessors' and 'deniers' in criminal trials. *Medicine, Science and the Law*, **24**, 56–60 **(740)**

Gudjonsson, G. H. (1987a) The significance of depression in the mechanisms of 'compulsive' shoplifting. *Medicine, Science and the Law*, **27**, 171–6 **(576, 578)**

Gudjonsson, G. H. (1987b) A parallel form of the Gudjonsson Suggestibility Scale. *British Journal of Clinical Psychology*, **26**, 215–21 **(576, 845)**

Gudjonsson, G. H. (1988a) Causes of compulsive shoplifting. *British Journal of Hospital Medicine*, **40**, 169 **(576)**

Gudjonsson, G. H. (1988b) Interrogative suggestibility: its relationship with assertiveness, social-evaluative anxiety, state anxiety and method of coping. British Journal of Clinical Psychology, **27**, 159–66 **(845)**

Gudjonsson, G. H. (1989) Compliance in an interrogative situation: a new scale. *Personality and Individual Differences*, **10**, 535–40 **(845)**

Gudjonsson, G. H., and Clark, N. K. (1986) Suggestibility in police interrogation: a social psychological model. *Social Behaviour*, **1**, 83–104 **(845)**

Gudjonsson, G. H. and Drinkwater, J. (1986) Intervention techniques for violent behaviour. In *Clinical Approaches to Criminal Behaviour (Issues in Criminological & Legal Psychology No. 9)* (eds. C. Hollin and K. Howells), British Psychological Society: Leicester **(671, 673)**

Gudjonsson, G. H. and Gunn, J. (1982) The competence and reliability of a witness in the criminal court: a case report. *British Journal of Psychiatry*, **141**, 624–7 **(844)**

Gudjonsson, G. H. and MacKeith, J. A. C. (1982) False confessions. Psychological effects of interrogation. In *Reconstructing the Past. The role of Psychologists in Criminal Trials* (ed. A. Trankell) P. A. Norstedt and Sovers Forlag: Stockholm **(739)**

Gudjonsson, G. H. and MacKeith, J. (1983a) A specific recognition deficit in a case of homicide. *Medicine, Science and the Law*, **23**, 37–40 **(297)**

Gudjonsson, G. H. and MacKeith, J. A. C. (1983b) A regional interim secure unit at the Bethlem Royal Hospital: the first fourteen months. *Medicine, Science and the Law*, **23**, 209–19 **(714, 715)**

Gudjonsson, G. H. and MacKeith, J. (1988) Retracted confessions: legal, psychological, and psychiatric aspects. *Medicine, Science and the Law*, **28**, 187–94 **(844, 845)**

Gudjonsson, G. H. and Petursson, H. (1982) Some criminological and psychiatric aspects of homicide in Iceland. *Medicine, Science and the Law*, **22**, 91–8 **(448)**

Gudjonsson, G. H. and Petursson, H. (1986) Changing characteristics of homicide in Iceland. *Medicine, Science and the Law*, **26**, 299–303 **(512)**

Gudjonsson, G. H., Petursson, H., Skulason, S. and Sigurdardottir, H. (1989) Psychiatric evidence: a study of psychological issues. *Acta Psychiatrica Scandinavica*, **80**, 165–9 **(529)**

Gudjonsson, G. H. and Taylor, P. J. (1985) Cognitive deficit in a case of retrograde amnesia. *British Journal of Psychiatry*, **147**, 715–8 **(297, 444)**

Gudmundsson, G. (1966) Epilepsy in Iceland. *Acta Neurologica Scandinavica*, **43**, Supp. 25 **(302)**

Gunderson, J. G., Frank, A. F., Katz, H. M., Vannicelli, M. L., Frosch, J. P. and Knapp, P. H. (1984) Effects of psychotherapy in schizophrenia: II. Comparative outcome of two forms of treatment. *Schizophrenia Bulletin*, **10**, 564–98 **(687)**

Gunn, J. (1973) *Violence in Human Society*, David & Charles: Newton Abbot **(490)**

Gunn, J. (1976) Management of the mentally abnormal offender: integrated or parallel. *Proceedings of the Royal Society of Medicine*, **70**, 877–80 **(694, 721, 727)**

Gunn, J. (1977) *Epileptics in Prison*, Academic Press: London (**299, 301, 302, 303, 304, 307, 514**)

Gunn, J. (1978) Epileptic homicide: a case report. *British Journal of Psychiatry* **132**, 510–3 (**304**)

Gunn, J. (1981) Medico-legal aspects of epilepsy. In *Epilepsy and Psychiatry*, (eds. E. H. Reynolds and M. Trimble) Churchill Livingstone: Edinburgh (**300**)

Gunn, J. (1982) Postgraduate education in forensic psychiatry. *Association of University Teachers of Psychiatry Newsletter*, December 6–18 AUTP (private circulation) (**2**)

Gunn, J. (1983) Sociopathic (psychopathic) personality in the adult. In *The Neuroses and Personality Disorders* (eds. G. F. M. Russell and L. Hersov) *Handbook of Psychiatry, vol. 4*, Cambridge University Press: Cambridge (**401**)

Gunn, J. (1985a) Psychiatry and the Prison Medical Service. In *Secure Provision* (ed. L. Gostin) Tavistock: London (**741, 766**)

Gunn, J. (1985b) What is the origin of the term Stockholm Syndrome? *British Medical Journal*, **291**, 1629 (**927**)

Gunn, J. (1986a) Education and forensic psychiatry. *Canadian Journal of Psychiatry*, **31**, 273–9 (**2, 4, 730**)

Gunn, J. (1986b) The violent patient. *Medicine North America*, **37**, 5485–9 (**808**)

Gunn, J. (1988) Personality disorder: a clinical suggestion. In *Personality Disorders* (ed. P. Tyrer) Wright: London (**379**)

Gunn, J. (1990) *La Paquerette Sociotherapeutic Centre at Champ-Dollon Prison* (unpublished report to the Institut Universitaire de Médecine Légale, Genève) (**754**)

Gunn, J. (1991a) The trials of psychiatry: insanity in the twentieth century. In *The Mentally Disordered Offender* (ed. K. Herbst and J. Gunn) Butterworth-Heinemann: Oxford (**18, 880**)

Gunn, J. (1991b) Epilepsy and the law. In *Advances in Neurology*, vol. 55. Neurobehavioral Problems in Epilepsy (ed. D. B. Smith, D. M. Treiman and M. R. Trimble) Raven: New York (**300, 334, 609, 617**)

Gunn, J. (1991c) The Effra Trust, past, present and future. In *Annual Report of the Effra Trust 1990/91*, Effra Trust: London (**307**)

Gunn, J. (1991d) Human violence. A biological perspective. *Criminal Behaviour & Mental Health*, **1**, 34–54 (**392, 490, 502, 824**)

Gunn, J. and Fenton, G. (1971) Epilepsy, automatism and crime, *Lancet*, **i**, 173–6 (**303, 514**)

Gunn, J. and Gudjonsson, G. (1988) Using the psychological stress evaluator in conditions of extreme stress. *Psychological Medicine*, **18**, 235–8 (**738**)

Gunn, J., Maden, A. and Swinton, M. (1991a) Treatment needs of prisoners with psychiatric disorders. *British Medical Journal*, **303**, 338–40 (**616, 746, 862**)

Gunn, J., Maden, A. and Swinton, M. (1991b) *Mentally Disordered Prisoners*, Home Office: London (**290, 302, 334, 616, 745, 811, 862**)

Gunn, J. and Robertson, G. (1976a) Drawing a criminal profile. *British Journal of Criminology*, **16**, 156–60 (**339, 342**)

Gunn, J. and Robertson G. (1976b) Psychopathic personality: a conceptual problem. *Psychological Medicine*, **6**, 631–4 (**386**)

Gunn, J. and Robertson, G. (1982) An evaluation of Grendon prison. In *Abnormal Offenders, Delinquency and the Criminal Justice System* (eds. J. Gunn and D. P. Farrington) Wiley: Chichester (**750**)

Gunn, J., Robertson, G., Dell, S. and Way, C. (1978) *Psychiatric Aspects of Imprisonment*, Academic Press: London (**334, 400, 455, 616, 655, 688, 741, 745, 747, 749, 750, 808, 811, 813, 818**)

Gunter, B. and McAleer, J. L. (1990) *Children and Television: the One-Eyed Monster?* Routledge: London (**496, 498**)

Gutheil, T. G. (1984) Review of individual quantative studies. In *The Psychiatric Uses of Seclusion and Restraint* (ed. K. Tardiff) American Psychiatric Press: Washington DC (**660**)

Guttman, E. (1946) Late effects of closed head injuries: psychiatric observations. *Journal of Mental Science*, **92**, 1–18 (**907**)

Guze, S. B. (1976) *Criminality and Psychiatric Disorders*, Oxford University Press: New York (**321, 334, 447, 615**)

Guze, S. B., Woodruff, R. A. and Clayton, P. J. (1974) Psychiatric disorders and criminality. *Journal of American Medical Association*, **227**, 641–2 (**447**)

Haber-Schaim, N., Solomon, Z., Bleich, A. and Kottler, M. (1988) Letter on the prevalence of post-traumatic stress disorder. *New England Journal of Medicine*, **318**, 1691 (**905**)

Häfner, H. and Böker, W. (1973) *Crimes of Violence by Mentally Abnormal Offenders* (trans. H.

Marshall) Cambridge University Press (1982) (**290, 334–348** *passim*, **357, 358, 360, 368, 370, 513**)

Hakola, H. P. A. and Laulumaa, V. A. (1982) Carbamazepine in treatment of violent schizophrenics, (letter) *Lancet*, **1**, 1358 (**664**)

Hall, A. and Harris, R. J. (1988) The development of a multi-disciplinary approach to the assessment and management of child sexual abuse in an inner city health district. *Health Trends*, **20**, 39–43 (**919, 940**)

Hall, B. D. and Smith, D. W. (1972) Prader-Willi syndrome: resumé of 32 cases. *Journal of Pediatrics*, **81**, 286–93 (**313**)

Hall, R. C. W. and Zisook, S. (1981) Paradoxical reactions to benzodiazepines. *British Journal of Clinical Pharmacology*, **11**, Supp. 1, 99s–104s (**474, 669**)

Hallam, I. and Rachman, S. (1976) Current status of aversion therapy. In *Progress in Behavior Modification* vol. 2 (eds. M. Hersen, R. M. Eisler and P. M. Miller) Academic Press: New York (**672**)

Halleck, S. L. (1966) A critique of current psychiatric roles in the legal process. *Wisconsin Law Review*, 379, 370–401 (**757**)

Halleck, S. L. (1986) *The Mentally Disordered Offender*, Government Printing Office: Washington DC (**145, 641**)

Haller, E. and Binder, R. L. (1990) Clozapine and seizures. *American Journal of Psychiatry*, **147**, 1069–71 (**665**)

Halloran, J. D., Brown, R. L. and Chaney, D. C. (1970) *Television and Delinquency*, Leicester University Press: Leicester (**498**)

Hamberger, L. K. and Hastings, J. (1988) Characteristics of male spouse abusers consistent with personality disorder. *Hospital and Community Psychiatry*, **39**, 763–70 (**509**)

Hamilton, J. R. (1985) The special hospitals. In *Secure Provision* (ed. L. Gostin) Tavistock Publications: London (**704**)

Hamilton, J. R. (1986) Code of Practice for the Mental Health Act 1983 (Editorial). *British Medical Journal*, **292**, 1219–20 (**196**)

Hamilton, J. R., Griffith, A., Ritson, B. and Aitken, R. C. B. (1978) *Detoxification of Habitual Drunken Offenders*, Scottish Health Services Studies No. 39, Scottish Home & Health Department: Edinburgh (**453**)

Hammersley, R., Forsyth, A., Morrison, V., & Davies, J. B. (1990) The relationship between crime and opioid use. *British Journal of Addictions* 84, 1029–44 (**472**)

Hampshire, S. (1989) *Innocence and Experience*, Allen Lane Press: London (**16**)

Hands, J., Herbert, V. and Tennent, G. (1974) Menstruation and behaviour in a special hospital. *Medicine, Science and the Law*, **14**, 32–5 (**605**)

Harding, C. M., McCormick, R. V., Strauss, J. S., Ashikaga, T. and Brooks, G. W. (1989) Computerised life chart methods to map domains of function and illustrate patterns of interactions in the long-term course trajectories of patients who once met the criteria for DSM–III schizophrenia. *British Journal of Psychiatry*, **155** (Supp. 5) 100–6 (**120, 358**)

Harding, L. (1985) *Born a Number*, MIND: London (**697**)

Harding, T. W. (1987) AIDS in prison. *Lancet*, ii, 1260–3 (**819, 820**)

Harding, T. W. (1989a) The application of the European Convention of Human Rights to the field of psychiatry. *International Journal of Law and Psychiatry*, **12**, 245–62 (**146**)

Harding, T. W. (1989b) Prevention of torture and inhuman or degrading treatment: medical implications of a new European convention. *Lancet* i, 1191–3 (**860**)

Harding, T. W. (1991) Ethical issues in the delivery of mental health services: abuses in Japan. In *Psychiatric Ethics, 2nd edn* (eds. S. Bloch and P. Chodoff) Oxford University Press: Oxford (**859, 860**)

Harding, T. W. and Curran, W. J. (1979) Mental health legislation and its relationship to program development. *Harvard Journal on Legislation*, **16**, 19–57 (**145**)

Harding, T. W., and Montandon, C. (1982) Does dangerousness travel well. In *Dangerousness: Psychiatric Assessment and Management* (eds. J. R. Hamilton and H. Freeman) Gaskell: London (**626**)

Hardt, R. H. and Peterson, S. J. (1968) Arrests of self and friends as indicators of delinquency involvement. *Journal of Research in Crime and Delinquency*, 5, 44–51 (**267**)

Hare, E. H. (1962) Masturbatory insanity: the history of an idea. *Journal of Mental Science*, **108**, 2–25 (**529**)

Hare, R. D. (1986) Twenty years of experience with the Cleckley psychopath. In *Unmasking the Psychopath* (eds. W. H. Reid, D. Dorr, J. I. Walker and J. W. Bonner) Norton: New York (385)

Harford, R. J., Ungerer, J. C. and Kinsella, J. K. (1976) Effects of legal pressure on prognosis for treatment of drug dependence. *American Journal of Psychiatry*, 133, 1399–404 (477)

Harlow, H. F. and Harlow, M. K. (1962) The effect of rearing conditions on behaviour. *Bulletin of the Menninger Clinic*, 26, 213–24 (505, 913)

Harlow, H. F. and Harlow, M. K. (1969) Effects of various mother-infant relationships on rhesus monkey behaviors. In *Determinants of Infant Behaviour*, vol. VI (ed. B. M. Foss) Methuen: London (913)

Harmon, R. B., Rosner, R., and Wielderlight, M. (1985) Women and arson; a demographic study. *Journal of Forensic Science*, 30, 467–77 (590)

Harrer, G. and Kofler-Westergren, B. (1986) Depression and criminality. *Psychopathology*, 19, supp. 2, 215–19 (347)

Harris, A. (1959) Sensory deprivation and schizophrenia. *Journal of Mental Sciences*, 105, 235–7 (659)

Harris, I. D. (1978) Assassins. In *Violence* (eds. I. L. Kurtash, S. Kurtash and L. B. Schlesinger) Josey-Bass: San Francisco (518)

Harrison, F. (1987) *Brady and Hindley*, Grafton: London (391)

Hart, H. L. A. (1963) Preface. In *The Idea of Justice and the Problem of Argument* (C. Perelman) Routledge: London (829)

Hart, H. L. A. (1968) *Punishment and Responsibility*, Clarendon Press: Oxford (41, 64)

Hart, H. L. A. and Honore, A. M. (1983) *Causation of the Law*, 2nd edn, Oxford University Press: Oxford (828)

Harter, S., Alexander, P. C. and Neimeyer, R. A. (1988) Long-term effects of incestuous child abuse in college women: social adjustment, social cognition, and family characteristics. *Journal of Consulting and Clinical Psychology*, 56, 6–8 (367, 917, 919)

Hartmann, E. (1983) Two case reports: night terrors with sleepwalking—a potentially lethal disorder. *Journal of Nervous & Mental Disease*, 171, 503–5 (310, 311)

Hartmann, E., Greenwald, D. and Brune, P. (1982) Night terrors—sleep walking: personality characteristics. *Sleep Research*, 11, 121 (310)

Hartmann, H., Kris, E. and Lowenstein, R. (1949) Notes on the theory of aggression. In *The Psychoanalytic Study of the Child*, vol. 3 (ed. A. Freud) International Universities Press: New York (492)

Hartnoll, R. L., Mitcheson, M. C., Battersby, A., Brown, G., Ellis, M., Fleming, P. and Hedley, N. (1980) Evaluation of heroin maintenance in controlled trial. *Archives of General Psychiatry*, 37, 877–84 (475)

Hartshorne, H. and May, M. A. (1928) *Studies in Deceit*, Macmillan: New York (408, 569)

Hartstone, E., Steadman, H. J., Robbins, P. C. and Monahan, J. (1984) Identifying and treating the mentally disordered prison inmate. In *Mental Health and Criminal Justice* (ed. L. Teplin) Sage: Beverley Hills (757)

Haslam, J. (1817) *Medical Jurisprudences, as it relates to Insanity according to the Law of England*, J. Hunter: London (407)

Hathaway, S. R. and MacKinley, J. C. (1940) A multiphasic personality schedule (Minnesota). Construction of the Schedule. *Journal of Psychology*, 10, 249–54 (xxxi)

Hauser, A. W. and Kurland, L. T. (1975) The epidemiology of epilepsy in Rochester, Minnesota, 1935 through 1967. *Epilepsia*, 16, 1–66 (301)

Hawkins, J. D. and Lishner, D. M. (1987) Schooling and delinquency. In *Handbook on Crime and Delinquency Prevention* (ed. E. H. Johnson) Greenwood Press: Westport, CT (270)

Hawkins, J. D. and Weis, J. D. (1985) The social development model: an integrated approach to delinquency prevention. *Journal of Primary Prevention*, 6, 73–97 (278)

Haxby, D. (1978) *Probation, A Changing Service*, Constable: London (787)

Haydn-Smith, P., Marks, I., Buchaya, H., Repper, D. (1987) Behavioural treatment of life-threatening masochistic asphyxiation: a case study. *British Journal of Psychiatry*, 150, 518–9 (553)

Hayes, L. M. (1983) And darkness closes in . . . A national study of jail suicides. *Criminal Justice and Behavior*, 10, 461–84 (813)

Hays, J. R., Roberts, T. K. and Solway, K. S. (1981) *Violence and the Violent Individual*, Spectrum: New York (490)

Hazelwood, R. R., Dietz, P. E., and Burgess, A. W. (1983) *Auto-erotic Fatalities*, Heath: Lexington, Mass. (553)

Health Services Advisory Committee (1987) *Violence to Staff in the Health Services*, Health and Safety Commission HMSO: London (**807**)

Healy, W. and Healy, M. (1915) *Pathological Lying, Accusation and Swindling*, Heinemann: London (**412**)

Hearst, H., Newman, T. B. and Hulley, S. B. (1986) Delayed effects of military draft on mortality. *New England Journal of Medicine*, **314**, 620–24 (**902, 904, 905, 928**)

Heath, J. (1963) *Eighteenth Century Penal Theory*, Oxford University Press: Oxford (**795**)

Heather, N. (1977) Personal illness in 'lifers' and the effects of long-term indeterminate sentences. *British Journal of Criminology*, **17**, 378–86 (**761, 809**)

Heather, N. (1981a) Relationship between delinquency and drunkenness among Scottish young offenders. *British Journal of Alcohol and Alcoholism*, **16**, 50–61 (**450**)

Heather, N. (1981b) Alcohol dependence and problem drinking in Scottish young offenders. *British Journal of Alcohol & Alcoholism*, **17**, 145–54 (**450**)

Hebenstreit, G. (1990) Clinical experience with zuclopenthixol acetate and co-injection with zuclopenthixol actetate and zuclopenthixol decanoate. In *New Strategies in the Treatment of Aggressive, Acutely Psychotic Patients* (ed. B. Wistedt) Excerpta Medica: Amsterdam (**663**)

Heidensohn, F. (1985) *Women and Crime*, Macmillan: London (**603**)

Heilbrun, K. S. (1987) The assessment of competency for execution: an overview. *Behavioral Sciences and the Law*, 5, 383–96 (**122**)

Hellerstein, D., Frosch, W. and Koeningsberg, H. W. (1987) The clinical significance of command hallucinations. *American Journal of Psychiatry*, **144**, 219–21 (**344, 420**)

Hellman, L. (1988) An open and closed case: SETRHA medium secure units. *The Architects' Journal* (8 June), 35–55 (**712**)

Helmchen, H. and Henn, F. A. (1987) *Biological Perspectives of Schizophrenia*, Wiley: Chichester (**290**)

Helzer, J. E., Robins, L. N. and McEvoy, L. (1987) Post-traumatic stress disorder in the general population. *New England Journal of Medicine*, **318**, 1630–4 (**904, 905, 914, 928**)

Hennigam, K. M., Rosario, M. L., Cook, T. D., Wharton, J. D. and Calder, B. J. (1982) Impact of the introduction of television on crime in the United States: empirical findings and theoretical implications. *Journal of Personality and Social Psychology*, **42**, 461–77 (**498**)

Henriksen, B., Juul-Jensen, P. and Lund, M. (1970) The mortality of epileptics. In *Life Assurance Medicine: Proceedings of the 10th International Conference of Life Assurance Medicine* (ed. R. D. C. Brackenridge) Pitman: London (**301**)

Her Majesty's Chief Inspector of Prisons for England and Wales (1984) *Suicides in Prisons* HMSO: London (**814**)

Her Majesty's Chief Inspector of Prisons for England and Wales (1990) *Report of a Review of Suicide and Self-harm in Prison Service Establishments in England & Wales* Cmnd.1383, HMSO: London (**813, 814, 815**)

Her Majesty's Chief Inspector of Fire Services for England and Wales (1990) *Report for 1989*, Cmnd. 1146 Home Office, HMSO: London (**814**)

Herdt, G. H. (1984) *Ritualised Homosexuality in Melanesia*, University of California Press: Berkley (**528**)

Herjanic, M., Henn, F. A. and Vanderpearl, R. H. (1977) Forensic psychiatry: female offenders. *American Journal of Psychiatry*, **134**, 556–8 (**348**)

Herman, J. (1981) Father/daughter incest. *Professional Psychology*, **12**, 76–80 (**918**)

Herman, J. and Hirschman, L. (1981) Families at risk for father/daughter incest. *American Journal of Psychiatry*, **138**, 967–70 (**918**)

Herman, J. L. and Schatzow, E. (1987) Recovery and verification of memories of childhood sexual trauma. *Psychoanalytic Psychology*, **4**, 1–14 (**917**)

Herner, B., Shedby, B. and Ysander, L. (1966) Sudden illness as a cause of motor vehicle accidents. *British Journal of Industrial Medicine*, **23**, 37–41 (**583**)

Herrera, J. M., Costa, J., Sramet, J. and Heh, C. (1988) Clozapine in refractory schizophrenia. *Schizophrenia Research*, **1**, 305–6 (**665**)

Heston, L. L. and Shields, J. (1968) Homosexuality in twins. *Archives of General Psychiatry*, **18**, 149–60 (**523**)

Higgins, J. (1981) Four years' experience of an interim secure unit. *British Medical Journal*, **282**, 889–93 (**714, 715, 718**)

Hilberman, E. and Manson, M. (1977) Sixty battered women. *Victimology*, 2, 460–71 (**352**)

Hilgard, E. (1977) *Divided Consciousness: Multiple Controls in Human Thought and Action*, Wiley: New York (**427**)

Hill, D. (1982) Public attitudes to mentally abnormal offenders. In Abnormal Offenders, Delinquency and the Criminal Justice System (eds. J. Gunn and D. P. Farrington) Wiley: Chichester (**873, 881**)

Hill, D. and Watterson, D. (1942) Electroencephalographic studies of psychopathic personalities. *Journal of Neurology and Psychiatry*, 5, 47–65 (**288**)

Hill, J. (1984) Child Development. In *The Scientific Principles of Psychopathology* (ed. P. McGuffin, M. Shanks and R. Hodgson) Academic Press: London (**380**)

Hillman, R. G. (1981) The psychopathology of being held hostage. *American Journal of Psychiatry*, **138**, 1193–7 (**927**)

Hinde, R. A. (1979) *Towards Understanding Relationships*, Academic Press: London (**381**)

Hinde, R. S. E. (1951) *The British Penal System 1773–1950*, Duckworth: London (**795**)

Hindelang, M. J. (1976) With a little help from their friends: group participation in reported delinquent behaviour. *British Journal of Criminology*, **16**, 109–25 (**266**)

Hindelang, M. J. (1981) Variations in sex-race-age-specific incidence rates of offending. *American Sociological Review*, **46**, 461–74 (**275**)

Hindelang, M. J., Hirschi, T. and Weis, J. G. (1981) *Measuring Delinquency*, Sage: Beverly Hills, CA (**271, 275, 276**)

Hirsch, S. R. and Leff, J. P. (1975) *Abnormalities in Parents of Schizophrenics*, Oxford University Press: Oxford (**367**)

Hirschi, T. (1969) *Causes of Delinquency*, University of California Press: Berkeley, CA (**267, 272, 278**)

Hirschi, T. and Gottfredson, M. (1983) Age and the explanation of crime. *American Journal of Sociology*, **89**, 552–84 (**257**)

Hoche, D. O. (1929) Die Unfalneuroses. In *Arbeit und Gesundheit* (ed. P. Martinek), **13**, 55–71. Publication of the German Ministry of Labour (cited in Krystal and Niederland, 1968) (**926**)

Hodges, J. and Tizard, B. (1989) Social and family relationships of ex-institutional adolescents. *Journal of Child Psychology and Psychiatry*, **30**, 77–97 (**381**)

Hodgkinson, T. (1990) *Expert Evidence, Law and Practice*, Sweet & Maxwell: London (**828**)

Hoenig, J. and Kenna, J. C. (1979) EEG abnormalities and transsexualism. *British Journal of Psychiatry*, **134**, 293–300 (**523**)

Hoff, H. (1965) Prevention of suicide among prisoners (trans. W. Heuss). In *Jailhouse Blues* (ed. B. L. Danto) Epic Publications (1973): Orchard Lake, MI (**815**)

Hogben, G. L. and Cornfeld, R. B. (1981) Treatment of traumatic war neurosis with phenelzine. *Archives of General Psychiatry*, **38**, 440–5 (**937**)

Hoggett, B. (1985) Legal aspects of secure provision. In *Secure Provision* (ed. L. Gostin) Tavistock: London, pp. 236–262 (**798**)

Hoggett, B. (1990a) *Mental Health Law, 3rd edn*, Sweet & Maxwell: London (**25, 108, 110, 111**)

Hoggett, B. (1990b) *Mentally Incapacitated Adults and Decision-making*. Paper read at one day workshop on guardianship laws, Kings Fund Centre, March 12 1990 (unpublished) (**112**)

Hogh, F. and Wolf, P. (1983) Violent crime in a birth cohort: Copenhagen 1953–1977. In *Prospective Studies of Crime and Delinquency* (eds. K. T. Van Dusen and S. A. Mednick) Kluwer-Nijhoff: Boston (**271**)

Hoiberg, A. and McCaughey, B. G. (1984) The traumatic after-effects of collision at sea. *American Journal of Psychiatry*, **141**, 70–3 (**897, 898**)

Holden, A. (1974) *The St Albans Poisoner*. Hodder & Stoughton: London (**391, 517, 710**)

Hollender M., Brown, W. and Roback, H. (1977) Genital exhibitionism in women. *American Journal of Psychiatry*, **134**, 436–8 (**548**)

Hollender, M. H. and Callahan, A. S. (1975) Erotomania or De Clerambault's syndrome. *Archives of General Psychiatry*, **32**, 1574–6 (**353, 354**)

Holley, H. L. and Arboleda-Florez, J. (1988) Criminalisation of the mentally ill: part I, Police perceptions; part II, Initial detention. *Canadian Journal of Psychiatry*, **33**, 81–95 (**329**)

Hollin, C. R. (1983) Young offenders and alcohol: a survey of the drinking behaviour of a Borstal population. *Journal of Adolescence*, **6**, 161–74 (**451**)

Hollister, L. E. and Kim, D. Y. (1982) Intensive treatment with haloperidol of treatment-resistant chronic schizophrenic patients. *American Journal of Psychiatry*, **139**, 1466–8 (**663**)

Holmstrom, L. L. and Burgess, A. W. (1980) Sexual behavior of assailants during reported rapes. *Archives of Sexual Behavior*, **16**, 107–24 (**524**)

Home Office (1932) *Report of the Departmental Committee on Persistent offenders*, Cmnd. 4090, HMSO: London (**749**)

Home Office (1946) *Report of Committee on the Care of Children*, HMSO: London (**212**)

Home Office (1953) *Report of the Committee on Discharged Prisoners' Aid Societies* (Maxwell Report) HMSO: London (775)

Home Office (1960) *Report of the Committee on Children and Young Persons*, Cmnd. 1191, HMSO: London (212)

Home Office (1961) *Compensation for Victims of Crimes of Violence*, Cmnd. 645, HMSO: London (105)

Home Office (1963) *The Organisation of After-Care: Report of the Advisory Council on the Treatment of Offenders*, HMSO: London (775)

Home Office (1964) *Report of the Working Party on the Organisation of the Prison Medical Service* (The Gwynne Report), HMSO: London (710)

Home Office (1965) *Child, Family and Young Offender*, Cmnd.2742, HMSO: London (213)

Home Office (1968) *Children in Trouble*, Cmnd.3601, HMSO: London (213)

Home Office (1971a) *Criminal Statistics England & Wales 1970*, Cmnd.4708, HMSO: London (227)

Home Office (1971b) *Habitual Drunken Offenders: Report of a Working Party*, HMSO: London (452, 455)

Home Office (1971c) *Report of the Committee on Death Certification and Coroners*, Cmnd.4810 HMSO: London (180)

Home Office (1974) *Working Party on Vagrancy and Street Offences* Working Paper, HMSO: London (608)

Home Office (1977) *Report of the Work of the Prison Department 1976*, Cmnd.6877, HMSO: London (321)

Home Office (1978a) *Review of the Criminal Injuries Compensation Scheme: Report of an Interdepartmental Working Party*, HMSO: London (105)

Home Office (1978b) *Report on the Work of the Prison Department 1977*, Cmnd.7290, HMSO: London (321)

Home Office (1978c) *A Survey of the South East Prison Population*, Research Bulletin No. 5, HMSO: London (814)

Home Office (1979) *Report on the Work of Prison Department 1978*, Cmnd.7619, HMSO: London (321)

Home Office (1980a) *Report on the Work of the Prison Department 1979* Cmnd.7965, HMSO: London (321)

Home Office (1980b) *Criminal Statistics—England & Wales 1979*, Cmnd.8098, HMSO: London (326, 589, 590)

Home Office (1981) *Report on the Work of the Prison Department 1980*, Cmnd.8228, HMSO: London (321)

Home Office (1982) *Report on the Work of the Prison Department 1981*, Cmnd.8543, HMSO: London (321, 766)

Home Office (1983) *Report on the Work of the Prison Department 1982*, Cmnd.9057, HMSO: London (321)

Home Office (1984a) *Managing the Long-Term Prison System. The Report of the Control Review Committee*, HMSO: London (754, 803)

Home Office (1984b) *Probation Statistics: England & Wales 1982*, HMSO: London (786, 787)

Home Office (1984c) *Throughcare and Supervision of Life Sentence Prisoners*, Home Office Circular No. 55/1984, Prison Department Circular Instruction No. 37/1984 (761, 779)

Home Office (1985a) *Criminal Statistics England and Wales 1984*, Cmnd. 9621, HMSO: London (50)

Home Office (1985b) *Criminal Convictions of Persons first notified as Narcotic Drug Addicts in 1971–81*, Statistical Bulletin, Issue 19/85 HMSO: London (473)

Home Office (1985c) *Holloway Project Committee Report*, HM Prison Service, Home Office: London (619, 620)

Home Office (1985d) *First Report of the Advisory Committee on the Therapeutic Regime at Grendon*, Prison Department, HMSO: London (751)

Home Office (1985e) *Police and Criminal Evidence Act 1984 (S.66) codes of Practice*, HMSO: London (844)

Home Office (1986a) *Criminal Statistics England & Wales 1985*, Cmnd.10, HMSO: London (229)

Home Office (1986b) *Report on the Work of the Prison Department 1985/86*, Cmnd.11, HMSO: London (617, 621)

Home Office (1986c) *Report of the Working Group on Suicide Prevention*, London: HMSO **(813, 814)**

Home Office (1987a) *Criminal Statistics England & Wales 1986, Supplementary Vol. 1&2*, HMSO: London **(233, 326, 436, 437, 600, 601, 610)**

Home Office (1987b) *Criminal Statistics—England & Wales 1986*, Cmnd.233, HMSO: London **(454, 599, 600, 601, 608, 613, 617)**

Home Office (1987c) *Prison Statistics England & Wales 1986*, Cmnd.210, HMSO: London **(614)**

Home Office (1987d) *Criminal Statistics England & Wales 1986*, Supplementary Vol. 4 HMSO: London **(600)**

Home Office (1987e) *Special Units for Long-Term Prisoners: Regimes, Management and Research. A Report by the Research & Advisory Group on the Long-Term Prison System*, HMSO: London **(755)**

Home Office (1988a) *Criminal Statistics. England and Wales 1987*, Cmnd.498, HMSO: London **(256, 472, 578, 579, 585)**

Home Office (1988b) *Statistics of the Misuse of Drugs, United Kingdom 1987* Supplementary Tables. HMSO: London **(585)**

Home Office (1988c) *Policy Statement on Throughcare of Drug Misusers in the Prison System*, Prison Department, Home Office: London **(476)**

Home Office (1988d) *Standing Conference on Crime Prevention. Report of the Working Group on Car Crimes*, HMSO: London **(579)**

Home Office (1988e) *Life Sentence: Your Questions Answered*, HMSO: London **(761, 766)**

Home Office (1989a) *Judicial Statistics 1988*, HMSO: London **(221, 225, 226, 227, 229, 231)**

Home Office (1989b) *Criminal Statistics England & Wales 1988*, Cmnd.847, HMSO: London **(567, 568, 585)**

Home Office (1989c) *Prison Statistics England & Wales 1988*, HMSO: London **(614, 747)**

Home Office (1990a) *Crime, Justice and Protecting the Public*, HMSO: London **(225, 226, 229, 704, 771)**

Home Office (1990b) *Report on an Efficiency Scrutiny of the Prison Medical Service Vol.1* (unpublished) **(741)**

Home Office (1990c) *A Digest of Information on the Criminal Justice System: Crime and Justice in England & Wales* (eds. G. C. Barcley, J. Vennard and D. Turner) Home Office: London **(763)**

Home Office (1990d) *Probation Statistics England & Wales 1989*, Home Office: London **(770, 775, 783)**

Home Office (1990e) *Criminal Statistics England & Wales 1989*, Cmnd.1322, HMSO: London **(770)**

Home Office (1991) *Prison Statistics 1989*, HMSO: London **(770)**

Home Office (1992) *Criminal Justice Act 1991. A Quick Reference Guide for the Probation Service* Probation Service Division of the Home Office, London (copies to be obtained from NACRO, 169 Clapham Road, London SW9 0PU) **(1, 710)**

Home Office, Department of Health and Social Security (1974) *Interim Report of the Committee on Mentally Abnormal Offenders*, Cmnd.5698, HMSO: London **(769)**

Home Office, Department of Health and Social Security (1975) *Report of the Committee on Mentally Abnormal Offenders* (The Butler Report), Cmnd.6244, HMSO: London **(1, 61, 386, 440, 655, 694, 710, 756)**

Home Office, Department of Health and Social Security (1980) *Young Offenders*, Cmnd.8045, HMSO: London **(218)**

Home Office, Department of Health and Social Security (1987) *Mentally Disordered Offenders in the Prison System—Report of the Interdepartmental Working Group*, Home Office/DHSS: London **(756)**

Home Office, Department of Health, Welsh Office (1992) *National Standards for the Supervision of offenders in the Communities* Probation Services Division of the Home Office, London **(769, 1014)**

Home Office, Lord Chancellor's Office (1961) *Report of the Interdepartmental Committee on the Business of the Criminal Courts*, Cmnd.1289, HMSO: London **(69)**

Home Office, Scottish Home Department (1962) *Report of the Departmental Committee on the Probation Service*, Cmnd.1650, HMSO: London **(771)**

Home Office Statistical Bulletin (1989) *Crime Statistics for the Metropolitan Police District by Ethnic Group. 1987: Victims, Suspects and those Arrested*, Home Office Statistical Department: London **(275)**

Home Office, Welsh office, Department of Health and Social Security, Department of Education and Science (1976) *Children and Young Persons Act 1969: Observations on the Eleventh Report from the Expenditure Committee*, Cmnd.6494, HMSO: London

Homer, A. C. and Gilleard, C. (1990). Abuse of elderly people by their carers. *British Medical Journal*, 301, 1359–62 **(911)**

Hook, E. B. (1973) Behavioral implications of the human XYY genotype. *Science*, 179, 139–50 **(314)**

Hopwood, J. S. and Snell, H. K. (1933) Amnesia in relation to crime. *Journal of Mental Science*, 79, 27–41 **(292–297 passim, 309, 424)**

Horowitz, M. J. (1976) *Stress Response Syndromes*, Jason Aronson: New York **(903, 931)**

Horowitz, M. J. and Wilner, N. (1976) Field studies on the impact of life events. In *Stress Response Syndromes* (ed. M. J. Horowitz) Jason Aronson: New York **(889, 933)**

Hough, M. and Mayhew, P. (1983) *The British Crime Survey: First Report*, Home Office Research Study No. 76, HMSO: London **(325, 891, 892, 893, 904, 906)**

Hough, M. and Mayhew, P. (1985) *Taking Account of Crime: Key Findings from the Second British Crime Survey*, Home Office Research Study No. 85, HMSO: London **(936)**

House of Commons (1968) *Second Report from the Estimates Committee, Session 1967–68, The Special Hospitals and the State Hospital*, HMSO: London **(697)**

House of Commons (1972) Written answers. *House of Commons Official Report (Hansard)* June 29, cols 1673–85 **(710)**

House of Commons (1975a) *Eleventh Report from the Expenditure Committee: Children and Young Persons Act 1969*, HMSO: London **(218)**

House of Commons (1975b) *Report from the Select Committee on Violence in Marriage Vol. 2 Report, Minutes of Evidence, & Appendices* (HC553–11), HMSO: London **(508, 511, 911)**

House of Commons (1984) *Second Report from the House of Commons Social Services Committee on Children in Care* (HC360), HMSO: London **(240)**

House of Commons (1986a) *Special Reports from the Select Committee on the Armed Forces Bill, session 1985–6* (HC170), HMSO: London **(116)**

House of Commons (1986b) Adjournment debate. *House of Commons Official Report (Hansard)*, 21 March **(455, 716, 741, 800)**

House of Commons (1986c) *Third Report from the Social Services Committee, Session 1985–6 Prison Medical Service*, HMSO: London **(455, 622, 802)**

House of Commons (1989) *Crack: the Threat of Hard Drugs in the Next Decade. Interim Report from the Home Affairs Committee*, HMSO: London **(474)**

Howard League (1985) *Unlawful Sex: Offences, Victims and Offenders in the Criminal Justice System of England and Wales*, Waterlow: London **(531, 551, 566)**

Howard, C. and d'Orbán, P. T. (1987) Violence in sleep: medico-legal issues and two case reports. *Psychological Medicine*, 17, 915–25 **(309, 310, 311)**

Howells, K. (1981) Adult sexual interest in children: considerations relevant to the aetiology. In *Adult Sexual Interest in Children* (eds. M. Cook and K. Howells) Academic Press: London **(533)**

Howells, K. (1987) The management of angry aggression. A cognitive-behavioural approach. In *Developments in Cognitive Psychotherapy* (eds. W. Dryden and P. Trower) Lawrence Erlbaum: London **(676)**

Howitt, D. and Cumberbatch, G. (1990) *Pornography: Impacts and Influences*. Home Office: London **(527)**

Huapaya, L. V. (1979) Seven cases of somnambulism induced by drugs. *American Journal of Psychiatry*, 136, 985–6 **(310)**

Hucker, S., Arnup, J., Busse, E. W., Gunn, J., Richardson, H., Smale, S. and Webster, C. D. (1986) *Oak Ridge: A Review and an Alternative*, Ontario Ministry of Health: Toronto (unpublished—private circulation) **(801)**

Hucker, S. J., Webster, C. D., and Ben-Aron, M. H. (1981) *Mental Disorder and Criminal Responsibility*, Butterworths: Toronto **(135)**

Huessy, H. R., and Howell, D. C. (1985) Relationships between adult and childhood behaviour disorders. *Psychiatric Journal of the University of Ottawa*, 10, 114–9 **(262)**

Huff, G. and Collinson, F. (1987) Young offenders, gambling and video game playing. *British Journal of Criminology*, 27, 401–10 **(489)**

Hughes, H. M. (1988) Psychological and behavioral correlates of family violence in child witnesses and victims. *American Journal of Orthopsychiatry*, 58, 77–90 **(914)**

Huizinga, D. and Elliott, D. S. (1986) Reassessing the reliability and validity of self-report measures. *Journal of Quantitative Criminology*, **2**, 293–327 **(253,276)**

Huizinga, D. and Elliott, D. S. (1987) Juvenile offenders: prevalence, offender incidence and arrest rates by race. *Crime and Delinquency*, **33**, 206–23 **(276)**

Humphreys, M. S., Johnstone, E. C., Macmillan, J. F. and Taylor, P. J. (1992) Dangerous behaviour preceding first admissions for schizophrenia. *British Journal of Psychiatry*, 161: 501–5 **(342, 357)**

Hunt, A. and Dennis, J. (1987) Psychiatric disorder among children with tuberous sclerosis. *Development Medicine and Child Neurology*, **29**, 190–8 **(314)**

Hunter, R. and MacAlpine, I. (1963) *Three Hundred Years of Psychiatry*, Oxford University Press: London **(353, 657)**

Hurley, W. and Monohan, T. M. (1969) Arson: the criminal and the crime. *British Journal of Criminology*, **9**, 4–21 **(594)**

Hurwitz, S. and Christiansen, K. O. (1983) *Criminology*, George Allen & Unwin: London **(600, 604)**

Ingham, J. (1975) What sort of security do we need? *New Psychiatry*, **2**, 12–14 **(712)**

Ingleby, D. (1981) Understanding mental illness, *Critical Psychiatry* (ed. D. Ingleby) Penguin: Harmondsworth **(827)**

Inner London Probation Service (1988) *Review of Through-care*, Inner London Probation Service: London **(776)**

Institute for the study of Drug Dependence (1982) Cannabis, law and enforcement. *Drug Link*, **17**, 21, Institute for the Study of Drug Dependence: London **(465)**

Institute for the Study of Drug Dependence (1984) *Drug Abuse Briefing, 2nd ed*, Institute for the Study of Drug Dependence: London **(465)**

Irving, B. and Hilgendorf, L. (1980) *Police Interrogation Research Study No. 1. The Psychological Approach*, Royal Commission on Criminal Procedure, HMSO: London **(739)**

Irwin, W. G., McClelland, R. J., Stout, R. W. and Stchedroff, M. (1988) Multidisciplinary teaching in a formal ethics course for clinical students. *Journal of Medical Ethics*, **14**, 125–8 **(884)**

Itil, T. M. and Wadud, A. (1975) Treatment of human aggression with major tranquillisers, anti-depressants, and newer psychotropic drugs. *Journal of Nervous and Mental Disease*, **160**, 83–99 **(663)**

Itoh, H., Ohtsuka, N., Ogita, K., Yogi, G., Mivra, S. and Koga, Y. (1977) Malignant neuroleptic syndrome. Its present status in Japan and clinical problems. *Folia Psychiatrica et Neurologica Japonica*, **31**, 565–76 **(667)**

Jackson, G. (1973) *People's Prison*, Faber & Faber: London **(927)**

Jacobs, P. A., Brunton, M., Melville, M. M., Brittain, R. P. and McClemont, W. F. (1965) Aggressive behaviour, mental subnormality and the XYY male. (letter) *Nature*, **208**, 1351–2 **(314)**

Jacobson, A. and Richardson, B. (1987) Assault experiences of 100 psychiatric inpatients— evidence of the need for routine enquiry. *American Journal of Psychiatry*, **144**, 908–12 **(903)**

Jacobson, G. F. (1979) Crisis-oriented therapy. *Psychiatric Clinics of North America*, **2**, 39–54 **(935)**

Jacobson, R., Jackson, M. and Berelowitz, M. (1985) Self-incineration: a controlled comparison of inpatient suicide attempts. *Psychological Medicine*, **16**, 107–16 **(596)**

Jaffe, J. H. (1980) Drug addiction and drug abuse. In *The Pharmacological Basis of Therapeutics* 6th edn. (eds. A. G. Gilman, L. S. Goodman, and A. Gilman) Macmillan: New York **(458)**

James, I. P. (1976) A case of shoplifting in the eighteenth century. *Prison Medical Journal*, No.17, 28–30 **(574)**

James, J. (1976) Motivation for entrance into prostitution. In *The Female Offender* (ed. L. Crites) Heath: Lexington, Nass. **(608)**

James, J. and Meyerding, J. (1977) Early sexual experience and prostitution. *American Journal of Psychiatry*, **134**, 1381–5 **(918)**

James, J. F., Gregory, D., Jones, R. K. and Rundell, O. H. (1980) Psychiatric morbidity in prisons. *Hospital and Community Psychiatry*, **31**, 674–7 **(334)**

James, W. (1890) *The Principles of Psychology* (two volumes) Macmillan: London **(427, 430)**

Jamieson, K. M. and Flanagan, T. J. (1987) *Sourcebook of Criminal Justice Statistics 1986*, Bureau of Justice Statistics: Washington DC **(276)**

Janerich, D. T., Stark, A. D., Greenwald, P., Burnett, W. S., Jacobson, H. I. and McCusker,

J. (1981) Increased leukaemia, lymphoma and spontaneous abortion in western New York following a flood disaster. *Public Health Reports*, 96, 350–4 (**906, 933**)

Janowsky, D., Leff, M. and Epstein, R. (1970) Playing the manic game: interpersonal manoevres of the acutely manic patient. *Archives of General Psychiatry*, 22, 252–61 (**349**)

Janson, C. G. (1983) Delinquency among metropolitan boys: a progress report. In *Prospective Studies of Crime and Delinquency* (eds. K. T. Van Dusen and S. A. Mednick) Kluwer-Nijhoff: Boston (**271**)

Janson, C. G. (1984) *Project Metropolitan: A presentation and progress report*, University of Stockholm Department of Sociology: Stockholm (**254**)

Jarvis, G. and Parker, H. (1989) Young heroin users and crime: how do the new users finance their habits? *British Journal of Criminology*, 29, 175–85 (**473**)

Jarvis, G. and Parker, H. (1990) Does medical treatment reduce crime amongst young heroin users? *The Research Bulletin*, 28, 29–32 Home Office Research & Statistics Department: London (**473**)

Jaspers, K. (1910) Eifersuchtswahm. Zeitschrift für die Gesamte. Neurologie und Psychiatrie, 1, 567–637 (**351**)

Jaspers, K. (1946) *Allgemeine Psychopathologie* (trans. J. Hoenig and M. W. Hamilton as *General Psychopathology*, 7th edn) Manchester University Press (1963): Manchester (**352, 407**)

Jellinek, E. M. (1960) *The Disease Concept of Alcoholism*, Hillhouse Press: New Haven, CT (**440**)

Jenkins, R., Smeeton, N. and Shepherd, M. (1988) Classification of mental disorder in primary care. *Psychological Medicine*, Monograph Supplement 12 (**7**)

Jensen, G. F. (1976) Race, achievement and delinquency: a further look at delinquency in a birth cohort. *American Journal of Sociology*, 82, 379–87 (**260**)

Jessen, J. L. and Roosenburg, A. M. (1971) Treatment results at the Dr Henri van der Hoeven Clinic, Utrecht, The Netherlands. *Excerpta Medica Psychiatry International Congress, Series No. 274* (**688**)

Johnson, B. A. (1990) Psychopharmacological effects of cannabis. *British Journal of Hospital Medicine*, 43, 114–22 (**468**)

Johnson, E. H. (1973) Felon self-mutilation: correlates of stress in prison. In *Jail House Blues* (ed. B. L. Danto) Epic: Orchard Lake, MI (**817**)

Johnstone, E. C., Crow, T. J., Johnson, A. L. and Macmillan, J. F. (1986) The Northwick Park study of first episodes of schizophrenia. *British Journal of Psychiatry*, 148, 115–43 (**331, 357, 805**)

Joint Committee on Higher Psychiatric Training (1990) *Handbook* JCHPT, Royal College of Psychiatrists: London (**4, 730**)

Jones, D. P. H. and McGraw, J. M. (1987) Reliable and fictitious accounts of sexual abuse to children. *Journal of Interpersonal Violence*, 2, 27–45 (**942**)

Jones, D. R. (1985) Secondary disaster victims: the emotional effects of recovering and identifying human remains. *American Journal of Psychiatry*, 142, 303–7 (**896, 941**)

Jones, E. (1986) *Development of Work with Young People at Risk and in Trouble*, National Youth Bureau: Leicester (**228**)

Jones, G. R. N. (1990) Judicial electrocution and the prison doctor. *The Lancet*, 335, 713–4 (**883**)

Jones, H. G. and Berry, M. J. (1985) Regional secure units: the emerging picture. In *Current Issues in Clinical Psychology* (ed. C. Edward) Plenum Press: London (**711**)

Jones, I. H. (1988) *An Animal Model of Self-injury*, Paper presented at RANZCP Congress, Hobart 1985 (**817**)

Jones, I. H. and Frei, D. (1977) Provoked anxiety as a treatment of exhibitionism. *British Journal of Psychiatry*, 131, 295–300 (**561**)

Jones, K. (1972) *A History of the Mental Health Services*, Routledge & Kegan Paul: London (**691**)

Jones, K. and Fowles, A. J. (1984) *Ideas on Institutions*, Routledge & Kegan Paul: London (**794, 796**)

Jones, M. (1956) The concept of a therapeutic community. *American Journal of Psychiatry*, 112, 647–50 (**686**)

Joseph, P. L. A. (1990a) A psychiatric clinic for the single homeless in a primary care setting in inner London. *Psychiatric Bulletin*, 14, 270–1 (**728**)

Joseph, P. L. A. (1990b) Mentally disordered homeless offenders—diversion from custody. *Health Trends*, 22, 51–3 (**728**)

Jung, R. S. and Jason, L. A. (1988) Firearm violence and the efforts of gun control legislation. *American Journal of Community Psychology*, **16**, 515–24 (**901**)

Junginger, J. (1990) Predicting compliance with command hallucinations. *American Journal of Psychiatry*, **147**, 245–7 (**345**)

Jus, A., Villeneuve, A., Gautier, J., Pires, A., Cote, J. M., Jus, K., Villeneuve, R. and Perron, D. (1973) Some remarks on the influence of lithium carbonate on patients with temporal epilepsy. *International journal of Clinical Pharmacology, Therapy and Toxicology*, **7**, 67–74 (**662**)

Juul-Jensen, P. (1964) Epilepsy, a clinical and social analysis of 1020 adult patients with epileptic seizures. *Acta Neurologica Scandinavica*, **40**, Supp. 5 (**302**)

Kafry, D. (1980) Playing with matches: children and fire. In *Fires and Human Behaviour* (ed. D. Canter) Wiley: New York (**589**)

Kales, A., Soldatos, C. R., Caldwell, A. B., Dales, J. D., Humphrey, F. J., Charney, D. S. and Schweitzer, P. K. (1980a) Somnabulism. *Archives of General Psychiatry*, **37**, 1406–10 (**310**)

Kales, J. D., Kales, A., Soldatos, C. R., Caldwell, A. B., Charney, D. S. and Martin, E. D. (1980b) Night terrors. *Archives of General Psychiatry*, **37**, 1413–7 (**310**)

Kalina, R. K. (1964) Diazepam: its role in a prison setting. *Diseases of the Nervous System*, **25**, 101–7 (**669**)

Kalk, W. J. and Veriava, Y. (1991) Hospital management of voluntary total fasting among political prisoners. *Lancet*, **337**, 660–2 (**759**)

Kammerer, T. H., Singer, L. and Michel, D. (1967) Les incendiaries. Etude criminologique et psychologique de 72 cas. *Annales Médico-Psychologique*, **125**, 687–716 (**590**)

Kandel, E., Mednick, S. A., Kirkegaard-Sorenson, L., Hutchings, B., Knop, J., Rosenberg, R. and Schulsinger, F. (1988) IQ as a protective factor for subjects at high risk for antisocial behaviour. *Journal of Consulting and Clinical Psychology*, **56**, 224–6 (**261**)

Kane, J., Honigfield, G., Singer, J., Mertzer, H. and the Clozaril Collaborative Study Group (1988) Clozapine for the treatment-resistant schizophrenic. *Archives of General Psychiatry*, **45**, 789–96 (**665**)

Kanin, E. J. (1982) Female rape fantasies: a victimisation study. *Victimology*, **7**, 114–21 (**530**)

Kanin, E. J. (1985) Date rapists: differential sexual socialisation and relative deprivation. *Archives of Sexual Behavior*, **16**, 107–24 (**545**)

Kanzer, M. (1939) Amnesia: a statistical study. *American Journal of Psychiatry*, **96**, 711–6 (**295**)

Kaplun, M. S. W. and Reich, R. (1976) The murdered child and his killers. *American Journal of Psychiatry*, **133**, 809–13 (**516**)

Kardiner, A. (1941) *The Traumatic Neurosis of War*, Hoeber: New York (**932**)

Karpman, B. (1948) The myth of the psychopathic personality. *American Journal of Psychiatry*, **104**, 523–34 (**385**)

Kassin, S. M., and Wrightsman, L. S. (1985) Confession evidence. In *The Psychology of Evidence and Trial Procedure* (ed. S. Kassin and L. Wrightsman) Sage Publications: London, pp. 67–84 (**844**)

Kastrup, M. (1988) Psychiatry and the death penalty. *Journal of Medical Ethics*, **14**, 179–83 (**883**)

Katz, S. and Mazur, M. A. (1979) *Understanding the Rape Victim: A Synthesis of Research*, Wiley: New York (**545, 902**)

Kaufman, A., Divasto, P., Jackson, R., Voorhees, D. and Christy, D. (1980) Male rape victims: non-institutionalised sexual assault. *American Journal of Psychiatry*, **137**, 221–3 (**547, 916, 917**)

Kavanagh, G. (1985) *Coroners' Rules and Statues*, Sweet & Maxwell: London (**180**)

Kay, D. W. K. and Bergmann, K. (1980) Epidemiology of mental disorders among the aged in the community. In *Handbook of Mental Health & Aging* (eds. J. F. Birren and R. B. Sloane) Prentice Hall: Englewood Cliffs, NJ (**327**)

Kay, L. (1987) *Aramah* and the street value of drugs. *Criminal Law Review*, 814–20 (**464**)

Kazdin, A. E. (1978) *History of Behavior Modification: Experimental Foundations of Contemporary Research*, University Park Press: Baltimore, MD (**675**)

Keane, T. M., Caddell, J. M. and Taylor, K. L. (1988) Mississippi Scale for combat related post-traumatic stress disorder: three studies in reliability and validity. *Journal of Consulting and Clinical Psychology*, **56**, 85–90 (**888**)

Keane, T. M. and Penk, W. E. (1988) The prevalence of post-traumatic stress disorder. *New England Journal of Medicine*, **318**, 1690–1 (**905**)

Keane, T. M., Wolf, J. and Taylor, K. L. (1987) Post-traumatic stress disorder: evidence for diagnostic validity and methods of psychological assessment. *Journal of Clinical Psychology*, **43**, 32–43 (**889**)

Kellam, A. M. P. (1987) The neuroleptic malignant syndrome, so-called. A survey of the world literature. *British Journal of Psychiatry*, **150**, 752–9 (**667**)

Kelleher, M. J. and Copeland, J. R. M. (1972) Compulsory psychiatric admission by the police. *Medicine, Science and the Law*, **12**, 220–4 (**735**)

Keller, O. J. and Vedder, C. B. (1968) The crimes that old people commit. *The Gerontologist*, **8**, 43–50 (**326**)

Kelly, R. (1975) The post-traumatic syndrome: an iatrogenic disease. *Forensic Science*, **6**, 17–24 (**907, 934**)

Kelly, R. (1981) The post-traumatic syndrome. *Journal of the Royal Society of Medicine*, **74**, 242–4 (**416**)

Kelly, R. and Smith, B. N. (1981) Post-traumatic syndrome: another myth discredited. *Journal of the Royal Society of Medicine*, **74**, 275–82 (**907**)

Kempe, C. H. (1971) Pediatric implications of the battered baby syndrome. *Archives of Disease in Childhood*, **46**, 28–37 (**911**)

Kempe, C. H. and Helfer, R. E. (1972) *Helping the Battered Child and his Family*, Lippincott: Philadelphia (**507**)

Kempe, R. S. and Kempe, C. H. (1978) *Child Abuse*, Fontana: London (**503, 912, 917**)

Kempe, C. H., Silverman, F. N., Steele, B. S., Droegemueller, W. and Silver, H. K. (1962) The battered child syndrome. *Journal of the American Medical Association*, **181**, 17–24 (**305**)

Kendell, R. E. (1970) Relationship between aggression and depression. *Archives of General Psychiatry*, **22**, 308–18 (**347**)

Kendell, R. E. (1973) Psychiatric diagnoses: a study of how they are made. *British Journal of Psychiatry*, **122**, 437–45 (**5**)

Kendell, R. E. (1975) *The Role of Diagnosis in Psychiatry*, Blackwell Scientific: Oxford (**379, 384**)

Kendler, K. S. (1985) Diagnostic approaches to schizotypal personality disorder: a historical perspective. *Schizophrenia Bulletin*, **11**, 538–53 (**365**)

Kennedy, A. and Neville, J. (1957) Sudden loss of memory. *British Medical Journal*, **2**, 428–33 (**424**)

Kennedy, D. H., Nair, G., Elliott, L. and Ditton, J. (1991) Drug misuse and sharing of needles in Scottish prisons. *British Medical Journal*, **302**, 1507 (**819**)

Kennedy, F. (1946) The mind of the injured worker, its effect on disability periods. *Compensation Medicine*, **1**, 19–24 (**415**)

Kennedy, H. and Grubin, D. (1992) Patterns of denial in sex offenders. *Psychological Medicine*, **22**, 191–6 (**557**)

Kenny, A. (1983) The expert in court. *Law Quarterly Review*, **99**, 197–216. (**830**)

Kenny, P. J. (1982) Confidentiality: the confusion continues. *Journal of Medical Ethics*, **8**, 9–11 (**863**)

Kernberg, O. (1975) *Borderline Conditions and Pathological Narcissism*, Aronson: New York (**375, 389**)

Kerr, W. C. (1976) Lithium salts in the management of a child batterer. *Medical Journal of Australia*, **2**, 414–5 (**668**)

Ketai, R., Matthews, J. and Mozdzen, J. J. (1979) Sudden death in a patient taking haloperidol. *American Journal of Psychiatry*, **136**, 112–3 (**664**)

Keutzer, C. S. (1972) Kleptomania: a direct approach to treatment. *British Journal of Medical Psychology*, **45**, 59–63 (**578**)

Khan, K. (1987) *Psychiatric Morbidity amongst ex Far-East Prisoners of War more than Thirty Years after Repatriation*, Ph.D Thesis (unpublished) University of Liverpool (**925**)

Kierkegaard, S. (1845) *Stages of Life's Way* (trans W. Lowrie) Oxford University Press (1945): London (**409**)

Kilpatrick, D. G., Best, C. L. and Averonen, L. J. (1984) Mental health consequences of criminal victimization: a random community survey. Presented at *The American Psychological Association Annual Convention*, Toronto, Canada, August 1984 (**894, 895**)

Kilpatrick, D. G., Miller, W. C. and Williams, A. V. (1972) Locus of control and adjustment to long-term hemodialysis. *The Proceedings 80th Annual Convention of the American Psychiatric Association*, 727–8 (**931**)

Kilpatrick, D. G., Resick, P. A. and Veronen, I. J. (1981) Effects of a rape experience: a longitudinal study. *Journal of Social Issues*, **37**, 105–22 (**902, 916**)

Kilpatrick, D. G., Veronen, L. J. and Best, C. L. (1985) Factors predicting psychological distress among rape victims. in *Trauma and its Wake* (ed. C. R. Figley) Brunner/Mazel: New York (**916**)

Kilroy-Silk, R. (1982) Too little too late. *Nursing Times*, July 20, 11–12 (**711**)

King, B. H. and Ford, C. V. (1988) Pseudologia fantastica. *Acta Psychiatrica Scandinavica*, **77**, 1–6 (**412**)

Kinney, L. and Kramer, M. (1985) Sleep and sleep responsivity in disturbed dreamers. *Sleep Research*, **14**, 140 (**889**)

Kinsey, A. C. Pomeroy, W. B. and Martin, C. E. (1948) *Sexual Behavior in the Human Male*, Saunders: Philadelphia (**551**)

Kinsey, A. C., Pomeroy, W. B., Martin, C. E. and Gebhard, P. H. (1953) *Sexual Behavior in the Human Female*, Saunders: Philadelphia (**537, 551**)

Kinston, W. and Rosser, R. (1974) Disaster: effects on mental and physical state. *Journal of Psychosomatic Research*, **18**, 437–56 (**922, 923**)

Kitchner, I. and Greenstein, R. (1985) Low dose lithium carbonate in the treatment of post-traumatic stress disorder: a brief communication. *Military Medicine*, **150**, 378–81 (**937**)

Klajner-Diamond, H., Wehrspann, W. and Steinhauer, P. (1987) Assessing the credibility of young children's allegations of sexual abuse: clinical issues. *Canadian Journal of Psychiatry*, **32**, 610–4 (**943**)

Klama, J. (1988) *Aggression*, Longman Scientific & Technical: Harlow (**490, 494**)

Klassen, D. and O'Connor, W. (1985) *Predicting Violence among Ex-mental Patients: Preliminary Research Results*. Presented at the Annual Meeting of the American Society of Criminology (unpublished) (**643**)

Klassen, D. and O'Connor, W. (1987) *Predicting Violence in Mental Patients: Cross-validation of an Actuarial Scale*. Presented at the Annual Meeting of the American Public Health Association. (**643**)

Klassen, D. and O'Connor, W. (1988) A prospective study of predictors of violence in adult male mental patients. *Law & Human Behavior*, **11**, 143–58 (**641, 643, 644**)

Klein, E., Bental, E., Lerer, B. and Belmaker, R. H. (1984) Carbamazepine and haloperidol v placebo and haloperidol in excited psychoses. *Archives of General Psychiatry*, **41**, 165–70 (**664**)

Klein, M. (1946) Notes on some schizoid mechanisms. *International Journal of Psychoanalysis*, **27**, 99–110 (**678, 679**)

Klein, M. (1952) The origins of transference. *International Journal of Psychoanalysis*, **33**, 433–8 (**678**)

Klein, M. (1985) *Western Systems of Juvenile Justice*. Sage: Beverley Hills, CA (**210, 216, 217**)

Kligman, D. and Goldberg, D. A. (1975) Temporal lobe epilepsy and aggression. *Journal of Nervous and Mental Disease*, **160**, 324–41 (**288**)

Kluznik, J. C., Speed, N., Van Valkenburg, C. and Magraw, R. (1986) Forty-year follow-up of United States prisoners of war. *American Journal of Psychiatry*, **143**, 1443–6 (**924, 925**)

Knapman, P. and Powers, M. (1985) *The Law and Practice on Coroners*, Barry Rose: London (**180**)

Knesper, D. L. (1978) Psychiatric manpower for state mental hospitals. A continuing dilemma. *Archives of General Psychiatry*, **35**, 19–24 (**799, 802**)

Knight, R. A. and Prentky, R. A. (1989) Classifying sexual offenders: the development and corroboration of taxonomic models. In *Handbook of Sexual Assault* (eds. W. Marsh, R. Laws and H. Barbaree) Plenum: New York (**544**)

Knopp, F. H. (1984) *Retraining Adult Sex Offenders. Methods and Models* (revised 3rd printing), Safer Society: Orwell, VT. (**566**)

Knox, S. J. (1968) Epileptic automatism and violence. *Medicine, Science and the Law*, **8**, 96–104 (**296, 302**)

Kohlberg, L. (1976) Moral stages and moralisation. In *Moral Development and Behaviour* (ed. T. Lickona) Holt, Rinehart and Winston: New York (**260**)

Kolb, L. C. (1986) A theoretical model for planning treatment of post-traumatic stress disorders of combat. *Current Psychiatric Therapy*, **23**, 119–26 Grune & Stratton: New York (**937**)

Kolb, L. C. (1987) A neuropsychological hypothesis explaining post-traumatic stress disorders. *American Journal of Psychiatry*, **144**, 989–95 (**930, 932**)

Kolb, L. C. (1989) Chronic post-traumatic stress disorder: implications of recent epidemiological and neuropsychological studies. *Psychological Medicine*, **19**, 821–4 (**896, 928, 936**)

Kolb, L. C., Burris, B. C. and Griffiths, S. (1984) Propranolol and clonidine in treatment of the chronic post-traumatic stress disorders of war. In *Post-Traumatic Stress Disorder: Psychological and Biological Sequelae* (ed. B. A. van der Kolk) American Psychiatric Press: New York **(937)**

Kolvin, I., Miller, F. J. W., Fleeting, M. and Kolvin, P. A. (1988) Social and parenting factors affecting criminal-offence rates: findings from the Newcastle Thousand Family Study (1947–1980). *British Journal of Psychiatry*, **152**, 80–90 **(271)**

Kopelman, M. D. (1987a) Crime and amnesia: a review. *Behavioral Sciences and the Law*, **5**, 323–42 **(46, 291–298 passim 443)**

Kopelman, M. D. (1987b) Amnesia: organic and psychogenic. *British Journal of Psychiatry*, **150**, 428–42 **(292–298 passim, 444)**

Kopelman, M. D. (1987c) Two types of confabulation. *Journal of Neurology, Neurosurgery and Psychiatry*, **50**, 1482–7 **(411)**

Kosky, R. and Silburn, S. (1984) Children who light fires: a comparison between firesetters and non-firesetters referred to a child psychiatric outpatient service. *Australian and New Zealand Journal of Psychiatry*, **18**, 251–5 **(587)**

Koson, D. F. and Dvoskin, J. (1982) Arson: a diagnostic study. *Bulletin of American Academy of Psychiatry & Law*, **10**, 19–49 **(590, 591)**

Kozol, H. L., Boucher, R. J. and Garofalo, R. F. (1972) The diagnosis and treatment and dangerousness. *Crime and Delinquency*, **18**, 371–92 **(132, 644)**

Kraepelin, E. (1896) *Psychiatrie Ein Lehrbuch für Studierende und Aerzte* (Reprinted by Arno Press, 1976): New York **(384, 412, 425)**

Krafft-Ebing, R. von (1886) *Textbook of Insanity* (trans. C. G. Chaddock) S. A. Davis (1905): Philadelphia **(351, 352, 353, 355, 412)**

Krag-Olsen, B., Brask, B. H., Jacobsen, P. and Nielsen, J. (1981) Is there an increased risk of psychoses in patients with ring 18 and deletion long arm 18. In *Human Behaviour and Genetics* (eds. W. Schmid and J. Nielsen) Elsevier/North Holland Biomedical Press: Amsterdam **(365)**

Krakowski, M., Jaeger, J. and Volavka, J. (1988) Violence and Psychopathology: a longitudinal study. *Comprehensive Psychiatry*, **29**, 174–81 **(359, 644, 805)**

Krakowski, M., Volavka, J. and Brizer, D. (1986) Psychopathology and violence: a review of the literature. *Comprehensive Psychiatry*, **27**, 131–48 **(642, 643)**

Kramlinger, K. G. and Post, R. M. (1989a) Adding lithium carbonate to carbamazepine: antimanic efficacy in treatment-resistant mania. *Acta Psychiatrica Scandinavica*, **79**, 378–85 **(666)**

Kramlinger, K. G. and Post, R. M. (1989b) The addition of lithium to carbamazepine: antidepressant efficacy in treatment-resistant depression. *Archives of General Psychiatry*, **46**, 794–800 **(666)**

Kramlinger, K. G. and Post, R. M. (1990) Addition of lithium carbonate to carbamazepine: hematological and thyroid effects. *American Journal of Psychiatry*, **147**, 615–20 **(666)**

Kraus, J. (1974) A comparison of corrective effect of probation and detention on male juvenile offenders. *British Journal of Criminology*, **14**, 49–62 **(580)**

Kretschmer, E. (1930) *A Textbook of Medical Psychology* (trans. E. B. Strauss) Oxford University Press (1934): London **(354)**

Kroll, J. and Mackenzie, T. B. (1983) When psychiatrists are liable: risk management and violent patients. *Hospital and Community Psychiatry*, **34**, 29–37 **(338)**

Krueger, D. W. (1978) Symptom passing in a transvestite father and three sons. *American Journal of Psychiatry*, **135**, 739–42 **(550)**

Krynicki, V. E. (1978) Cerebral dysfunction in repetitively assaultive adolescents. *Journal of Nervous and Mental Disease*, **166**, 59–67 **(288, 289)**

Krystal, H. (1968) *Massive Psychic Trauma*, International Universities Press: New York **(903, 939)**

Krystal, H. and Niederland, W. G. (1968) Clinical observations on the survivor syndrome. In *Massive Psychic Trauma* (ed. H. Krystal) International Universities Press: New York **(897, 925, 926)**

Kuehn, L. L. (1974) Looking down a gun barrel: person perception and violent crime. *Perceptual and Motor Skills*, **39**, 1159–64 **(293, 297)**

Kulka, R. A., Schlenger, W. E., Fairbank, J. A., Hough, R. L., Jordan, B. K., Marmer, C. R. and Weiss, D. S. (1988) *National Vietnam Veterans Readjustment Study. Description, Current Status, and Initial PTSD Prevalence Estimates*, Research Triangle Institute: Research Triangle

Park, North Carolina (cited Friedman, M. J. 1989 Post-traumatic stress disorder. *Current Opinion in Psychiatry*, 2, 230–4, and Kolb, 1989) (**905, 928**)

Kutash, I. L., Kutash, S. B. and Schlesinger, L. B. (1978) *Violence*, Jossey-Bass: San Francisco (**490**)

Kutchinsky, B. (1973) The effect of easy availability of pornography on the incidence of sex crimes: the Danish experience. *Journal of Social Issues* 29, 163–81 (**526**)

Lader, M. (1977) *Psychiatry on Trial*, Penguin: Harmondsworth (**859**)

La Fave, W. R. and Scott, A. W. (1972) *Handbook of Criminal Law*, West: New York (**353**)

La Fontaine, J. S. (1987) A sociological study of cases of child sexual abuse in Britain. *Economic and Social Research Council Report No. G0023 2244*, Economic and Social Research Council: London (**537**)

Lagache, D. (1947) *La Jalousie Amoureuse*, Presses Universitaires de France: Paris (**352**)

Lagos, J. M., Perlmutter, K. and Saexinger, H. (1977) Fear of the mentally ill: empirical support for the common man's response. *American Journal of Psychiatry*, **134**, 1134–7 (**331, 805**)

Lancet (1958) Stress and mental illness. *Lancet*, ii, 205–8 (**929**)

Lancet (1971) Editorial: Violent parents. *Lancet*, ii, 1017–8 (**911**)

Lancet (1976) Editorial: Who's for the locked ward? *Lancet*, i, 461 (**711**)

Lancet (1978) Editorial: Factitious hypoglycaemia. *Lancet*, i, 1293 (**296**)

Lancet (1980) Editorial: Close Rampton? *Lancet*, ii, 1171–2 (**697, 799**)

Lancet (1981) Editorial: Alcoholic brain damage. *Lancet*, i, 477–8 (**441**)

Lancet (1987) Editorial: Screening for drugs of abuse. *Lancet*, i, 365–6 (**467**)

Lancet (1991) A European committee looks at degrading treatment in custody. *Lancet*, 338, 1559–60 (**154**)

Lancet Correspondent (1987) The management of mental illness: forgotten millions. *Lancet*, i, 678–9 (**859**)

Landau, S., (1981) Juveliles and the police. *British Journal of Criminology*, 21, 27–46 (**276**)

Landes, R. (1938) *The Ojibwa Woman*, Norton: New York (**433**)

Landis, V. (1956) Experiences of 500 children with adult sexual deviants. *Psychiatric Quarterly Supplement*, **30**, 91–109 (**917**)

Langevin, R. (1983) *Sexual Strands. Understanding and treating sexual anomalies in man*, Faber: London (**555, 556**)

Langevin, R., Paitich, B., Orchard, B., Handy, L. and Russer, A. (1982) Diagnosis of killers seen for psychiatric assessment. *Acta Psychiatrica Scandinavica*, **66**, 216–28 (**329**)

Langfeldt, G. (1961) The erotic jealousy syndrome: a clinical study. *Acta Psychiatrica Scandinavica*, Suppl. 151 (**352**)

Langley, G. E. and Bayatti, N. N. (1984) Suicides in Exe Vale Hospital 1972–1981. *British Journal of Psychiatry*, **145**, 463–7 (**813**)

Langton, J. and Torpy, D. (1988) Confidentiality and a 'future' sadistic sex offender. *Medicine, Science and the Law*, **28**, 195–9 (**865**)

Lanyon, R. I. (1991) Theories of sex offending. In *Clinical Approaches to Sex Offenders and their Victims* (ed. C. R. Hollin and K. Howells) Wiley: Chichester (**532**)

Lanza, M. L. (1983) The reactions of nursing staff to physical assault by a patient. *Hospital and Community Psychiatry*, **34**, 44–7 (**931**)

Lanzkron, J. (1963) Murder and insanity. A survey. *American Journal of Psychiatry*, **119**, 754–8 (**346, 365**)

Laudenslager, M. L., Ryan, S. H., Drugan, R. C., Hyson, R. L. and Maier, S. F. (1983) Coping and immunosuppression: inescapable but not escapable shock suppresses lymphocyte proliferation. *Science*, 221, 568 (**931, 933**)

Laurance, B. M. (1967) Hypotonia, mental retardation, obesity and cryptorchidism associated with dwarfism and diabetes in children. *Archives of Diseases in Childhood*, **42**, 126–39 (**313**)

Law Commission (1987) *Family Law: Review of Child Law: Wards of Court, Working Paper No. 101*, HMSO: London (**240**)

Law Commission (1988) *Family Law: Review of Child Law: Guardianship and Custody. Law Commission Paper No. 172*, HMSO: London (**240**)

Law Commission (1990) *Mentally Incapacitated Adults and Decision Making: an Overview* Consultation Paper No. 19, HMSO: London (**32**)

Laws, D. R. (1984) The assessment of dangerous sexual behavior in males. *Medicine and Law*, 3, 127–40 (**556, 561**)

Lawton, Lord Justice (1979) Mercy killing: the judicial dilemma. *Journal of the Royal Society of Medicine*, 72, 460–1 (517)

Lazarus, A. A. (1968) A case of pseudo-necrophilia treated by behaviour therapy. *Journal of Clinical Psychology*, 24, 113–5 (554)

Leary, T. (1957) *Interpersonal Diagnosis of Personality*, Ronald Press: New York (378, 392, 394)

LeBlanc, M. and Frechette, M. (1989) *Male Criminal Activity from Childhood through Youth*, Springer-Verlag: New York (254)

Ledbetter, D. H., Riccardi, V. M., Airhart, S. D., Strobel, R. J., Keenan, B. S. and Crawford, J. D. (1981) Chromosome abnormalities and the Prader-Willi syndrome: a follow-up report of 40 cases. *American Journal of Human Genetics*, 34, 278–85 (313)

Lee, A. (1980) A philosophy of care for the disturbed violent patient in a special hospital. *Nursing Times*, 76, 2048–51 (654)

Lee, C. L. and Bates, J. F. (1985) Mother-child interaction at age two years and perceived difficult temperament. *Child Development*, 56, 1314–25 (380)

Lee, M. and Prentice, N. M. (1988) Interrelations of empathy, cognition, and moral reasoning with dimensions of juvenile delinquency. *Journal of Abnormal Child Psychology*, 16, 127–39 (260)

Leff, J. P., Kuipers, L., Berkowitz, R., Eberlein-Vries, R. and Sturgeon, D. (1982) A controlled trial of social intervention in the families of schizophrenic patients. *British Journal of Psychiatry*, 141, 121–34 (367)

Lehman, A. F. and Linn, L. S. (1984) Crimes against discharged mental patients in Board-and-Care Homes. *American Journal of Psychiatry*, 141, 271–4 (895)

Leiba, P. A. (1980) Management of violent patients. *Nursing Times*, 76, 101–4 (654)

Leicester, J. (1982) Temper tantrums, epilepsy and episodic dyscontrol. *British Journal of Psychiatry*, 141, 262–6 (662)

Leigh, D. (1961) *The Historical Development of British Psychiatry, Vol. 1*, Pergamon: Oxford (385, 691)

Leitch, A. (1948) Notes on amnesia in crime for the general practitioner. *Medical Press*, 219, 459–63 (292, 297)

Lemert, E. M. (1972) *Human Deviance, Social Problems and Social Control*, 2nd edn, Prentice-Hall: NJ (278)

Leopold, R. L. and Dillon, H. (1963) Psycho-anatomy of a disaster: a longterm study of post-traumatic neuroses in survivors of a marine explosion. *American Journal of Psychiatry*, 119, 913–21 (923)

Lerer, B., Ebstein, R. P., Shestatsky, M., Shemash, Z. and Greenberg, D. (1987) Cyclic AMP signal transduction in post-traumatic stress disorder. *American Journal of Psychiatry*, 144, 1324–7 (932)

Lerner, S. E. and Burns, R. S. (1978) Phencyclide use among youth: history, epidemiology and acute and chronic use In *Phencyclidine (PCP) Abuse: an Appraisal* (eds. R. C. Petersen and R. C. Stillman) National Institute for Drug Abuse: Washington DC (458)

Lesch, M. and Nyham, W. L. (1964) A familial disorder of uric acid metabolism and central nervous system function. *American Journal of Medicine* 36, 561–70 (313)

Lesieur, H. R. and Blume, S. B. (1987) The South Oaks Gambling Screen: a new instrument for the identification of pathological gamblers. *American Journal of Psychiatry*, 144, 1184–8 (482, 484)

Lester, A. and Taylor, P. J. (1989) '*H' Wing, HM Prison Durham*, Women in Prison: London (unpublished) (621)

Lester, D. (1982) Suicide and homicide in US prisons. *American Journal of Psychiatry*, 139, 1527–8 (813)

Levenson, J. L. (1985) Neuroleptic malignant syndrome. *American Journal of Psychiatry*, 142, 1137–45 (667)

Levine, J. M., Kramer, G. G. and Levine, E. N. (1975) Effects of alcohol on human performance: an integration of research findings based on abilities classification. *Journal of Applied Psychology*, 60, 285–93 (583)

Levy, C. J. (1988) Agent orange exposure and post-traumatic stress disorder. *The Journal of Nervous and Mental Disease*, 176, 242–5 (929)

Lewis, A. J. (1934) The psychopathology of insight. *British Journal of Medical Psychology*, 14, 322–48 (11, 12)

Lewis, A. J. (1942) Discussion on differential diagnosis and treatment of post-contusional states. *Proceedings of the Royal Society of Medicine*, 35, 607–14 (415)

Lewis, A. J. (1947). The education of psychiatrists, *Lancet*, **ii**, 79–83 **(4)**

Lewis, A. J. (1955) British psychiatry in the first half of the 19th century: Philippe Pinel and the English. *Proceedings of the Royal Society of Medicine*, **48**, 581–6 **(691)**

Lewis, A.J. (1974) Psychopathic personality a most elusive category. *Psychological Medicine*, **4**, 133–40 **(375, 386)**

Lewis, D. O. and Balla, D. (1975) 'Sociopathy' and its synonyms: inappropriate diagnoses in child psychiatry. *American Journal of Psychiatry*, **132**, 720–2 **(386)**

Lewis, D. O., Pincus, J. H., Bard, B., Richardson, E., Prichep, L. S., Feldman, M. and Yeager, C. (1988) Neuropsychiatric, pseudoeducational, and family characteristics of 14 juveniles condemned to death in the United States. *American Journal of Psychiatry*, **145**, 584–9 **(862, 883)**

Lewis, D. O., Pincus, J. H. and Feldman, M. (1986) Psychiatric, neurological and psychoeducational characteristics of 15 death row inmates in the United States. *American Journal of Psychiatry*, **143**, 838–45 **(883)**

Lewis, M. and Sarrel, P. M. (1969) Some psychological aspects of seduction, incest and rape in childhood. *Journal of the American Academy of Child Psychiatry*, **19**, 342–53 **(918)**

Lewis, N. D. G. and Yarnell, H. (1951) Pathological fire-setting. *Nervous & Mental Disease Monographs*, No. 82, Journal of Nervous & Mental Disease Publishing: New York **(588, 592, 593, 595)**

Lewis, P. (1980) *Psychiatric Probation Orders*, Institute of Criminology: Cambridge **(71)**

Lidz, C., Meisel, A., Zerubavel, E., Carter, M., Sestak, R. M. and Roth, L. H. (1984) *Informed Consent, a Study of Decision-making in Psychiatry*, Guilford Press: New York **(876)**

Liebert, R. M. and Sprafkin, J. (1988) *The Early Window*, 3rd edn, Pergamon: New York **(496, 498)**

Light, R. (1988) Public drunkenness: the failure of reform. *British Medical Journal*, **296**, 833–5 **(454)**

Lindelius, R. and Salum, I. (1975) Alcoholism and crime: a comparative study of three groups of alcoholics. *Journal of Studies in Alcohol*, **36**, 1452–8 **(446, 515)**

Lindemann, E. (1944) Symptomatology and management of acute grief. *American Journal of Psychiatry*, **101**, 141–8 **(889, 923, 934)**

Linden, R. D., Pope, H. G., and Jonas, J. M. (1986) Pathological gambling and major affective disorder: preliminary findings. *Journal of Clinical Psychiatry*, **47**, 201–3 **(485)**

Lindqvist, P. and Allebeck, P. (1990a) Schizophrenia and crime. A longitudinal follow-up of 644 schizophrenics in Stockholm. *British Journal of Psychiatry*, **157**, 345–50 **(331)**

Lindqvist, P. and Allebeck, P. (1990b) Schizophrenia and assaultive behaviour: the role of drug and alcohol abuse. *Acta Psychiatrica Scandinavica*, **82**, 191–5 **(373)**

Linton, R. (1956) *Culture and Mental Disorders*, Thomas: Springfield, IL **(432)**

Lion, J. R. (1975) Developing a violence clinic. In *Violence and Victims* (ed. S. A. Pasternack) Spectrum: New York **(727)**

Lion, J. R., Bach-y-Rita, G. and Ervin, F. R. (1969) Violent patients in the emergency room. *American Journal of Psychiatry*, **25**, 120–5 **(727)**

Lion, J. R., Hill, J. and Madden, D. J. (1975) Lithium carbonate and aggression: a case report. *Diseases of the Nervous System*, **36**, 97–8 **(662, 727)**

Lion, J. R., Snyder, W. and Merrill, G. L. (1981) Under-reporting of assaults on staff in a state hospital. *Hospital and Community Psychiatry*, **33**, 497–8 **(657, 806, 807)**

Lion, J. R. and Soloff, P. H. (1984) Implementation of seclusion and restraint. In *The Psychiatric Uses of Seclusion and Restraint* (ed. K. Tardiff) American Psychiatric Press: Washington DC **(657)**

Lipkin, J. O., Blank, A. S., Parson, E. R. and Smith, J., (1982) Vietnam veterans and post-traumatic stress disorder. *Hospital and Community Psychiatry*, **33**, 908–12 **(904)**

Lipton, D., Martinson, R. and Wilks, J. (1975) *The Effectiveness of Correctional Treatment: A survey of Treatment Evaluation Studies*, Praeger: New York **(784)**

Lishman, W. A. (1968) Brain damage in relation to psychiatric disability after head injury. *British Journal of Psychiatry*, **114**, 373–410 **(286, 296, 415)**

Lishman, W. A. (1987) *Organic Psychiatry*, 2nd edn, Blackwell: Oxford **(299, *passim*, 424, 425, 441, 907)**

Lissner, A. R., Gilmore, J. and Pomp, K. F. (1976) The dilemmas of co-ordinating treatment with criminal justice. *American Journal on Drug and Alcohol Abuse*, **3**, 621–8 **(477)**

Livesley, W. J., (1986) Trait and behavioral prototypes of personality disorder. *American Journal of Psychiatry*, **143**, 728–32 **(377)**

Lloyd, C. and Walmsley, R. (1989) Changes in rape offences and sentencing. *Home Office Research Study* No. 105, HMSO: London **(542, 543)**

Lloyd, R. J. and Williamson, S. (1968) *Born to Trouble: Portrait of a Psychopath*, Faber: London **(404, 818)**

Lock, S. (1984) A question of confidence. *British Medical Journal*, **288**, 23–5 **(863)**

Lock, S. (1990) Monitoring research ethical committees. *British Medical Journal*, **300**, 61–2 **(878)**

Loeber, R. (1987) Behavioural precursors and accelerators of delinquency. In *Explaining Criminal Behaviour* (eds. W. Buikhuisen and S. A. Mednick) Brill: Leiden **(262)**

Loeber, R. and Dishion, T. (1983) Early predictors of male delinquency: review. *Psychological Bulletin*, **94**, 68–99 **(259)**

Loeber, R. and Stouthamer-Loeber, M. (1986) Family factors as correlates and predictors of juvenile conduct problems and delinquency. In *Crime and Justice*, vol. 7 (eds. M. Tonry and N. Morris) University of Chicago Press: Chicago **(263)**

Loeber, R. and Southamer-Loeber, M. (1987) Prediction. In *Handbook of Juvenile Delinquency* (ed. H. C. Quay) Wiley: New York **(259)**

Loftus, E. F. (1979) *Eyewitness Testimony*, Harvard University Press: Cambridge, Mass. **(291)**

Lombroso, C. (1874) *L'uomo Delinquente*, Bocca: Torino **(290)**

London Borough of Brent (1985) *A Child in Trust. The Report of the Panel of Inquiry into the Circumstances Surrounding the Death of Jasmine Beck* (Chairman: Mr Louis Blom-Cooper). London Borough of Brent: London **(240)**

London, W. P. and Taylor, B. M. (1982) Bipolar disorders in a forensic setting. *Comprehensive Psychiatry*, **23**, 33–7 **(348)**

Lorenz, K. (1966) *On Aggression*, Methuen: London **(491)**

Lucas, C. J., Sainsbury, P. and Collins, J. G. (1962) A social and clinical study of delusions in schizophrenia. *Journal of Mental Science*, **108**, 747–58 **(336)**

Luchins, D. J. (1983) Psychopathology and cerebral asymmetries detected by computed tomography. In *Laterality and Psychopathology* (eds. P. Flor-Henry and J. Gruzelier) Elsevier Science Publishers: Amsterdam **(289)**

Ludwig, A. M., Brandsma, J. M., Wilbur, C. B., Benfeldt, F. and Jameson, D. G. (1972) The objective study of multiple personality, or are four heads better than one? *Archives of General Psychiatry*, **26**, 772–7 **(428, 429)**

Luisada, R. V. and Brown, B. I. (1976) Clinical management of phencyclidine psychosis. *Clinical Toxicology*, **9**, 539–45 **(459)**

Lukianowicz, N. (1972) Incest I. Paternal incest, II. Other types of incest. *British Journal of Psychiatry*, **120**, 301–13 **(918)**

Lund, J. (1988) Retspsykiatriske patienter. *Ugeskr Lager*, **150**, 1209–12 **(138)**

Lund, V. (1985) The Danish experience: one model of psychiatric testimony to courts of law. In *Psychiatry, Human Rights and the Law* (eds. M. Roth and R. Bluglass) Cambridge University Press: Cambridge **(156)**

Lundman, R. J. (1984) *Prevention and Control of Juvenile Delinquency*, Oxford University Press: Oxford **(671)**

Lynch, B. E. and Bradford, J. M. W. (1980) Amnesia—its detection by psychophysiological measures. *Bulletin of the American Academy of Psychiatry and the Law*, **8**, 288–97 **(292, 293)**

Lynch, D. M., Eliatamby, C. L. S. and Anderson, A. A. (1985) Pipothiazine palmitate in the management of aggressive mentally handicapped patients. *British Journal of Psychiatry*, **146**, 525–9 **(662)**

Lynch, M. A. (1975) Ill-health and child abuse. *Lancet*, **ii**, 317–9 **(894, 919)**

MacAndrew, C. and Edgerton, R. B. (1969) *Drunken Comportment: A Social Explanation*, Thomas Nelson: London **(450)**

Macara, A. W. (1984) Confidentiality—a decrepit concept? *Journal of Royal Society of Medicine*, **77**, 577–84 **(863)**

Maccoby, E. E. and Jacklin, C. N. (1980) Psychological sex differences. In *Scientific Foundations of Developmental Psychiatry* (ed. M. Rutter) Heinemann Medical: London **(602)**

MacCulloch, M. J. and Waddington, J. L. (1981) Neuroendocrine mechanisms and the aetiology of male and female homosexuality. *British Journal of Psychiatry*, **139**, 341–5 **(540)**

Macdonald, J. M. (1961) *The Murderer and his Victim*, Thomas: Springfield, IL **(514)**

Macdonald, J. M. (1963) The Threat to kill. *American Journal of Psychiatry*, **120**, 125–30 **(341)**

Macdonald, J. M. (1964) Suicide and homicide by automobile. *American Journal of Psychiatry*, **121**, 366–70 **(584)**

Macdonald, J. M. (1968) *Homicidal Threats*, Thomas: Springfield, IL. **(520)**

Macdonald, J. M. (1969) *Psychiatry and the Criminal*, Thomas: Springfield, IL **(303)**

Macdonald, J. M. (1971) *Rape Offenders and their Victims*, Thomas: Springfield, IL **(899)**

Macdonald, J. M. (1977) *Bombers and Firesetters*, Thomas: Springfield, IL. **(595)**

MacFarlane, A. B. (1985) Medical evidence in the Court of Protection. *Bulletin of the Royal College of Psychiatrists*, **9**, 26–8 **(199)**

Mackay, C. (1869) *Memoirs of Extraordinary Popular Delusions and the Madness of Crowds*, Routledge: London **(16)**

Mackay, R. D. (1983) The automatism defence—what price rejection? *Northern Ireland Legal Quarterly*, **34**, 82–94 **(432)**

MacKeith, R. (1975) Speculations on some possible long-term effects. In *Concerning Child Abuse* (ed. A. H. Franklin) Churchill Livingstone: Edinburgh **(912)**

MacKinnon, F. (1937) *Grand Larceny—being the Trial of Jane Leigh-Perrot*, Oxford University Press: London **(574)**

MacMillan, J. F., Gold, A., Crow, T. J., Johnston, A. L. and Johnstone, E. C. (1986) Expressed emotion and relapse. *British Journal of Psychiatry*, **148**, 133–43 **(367)**

MacVicar, K. (1979) Psychotherapeutic issues in the treatment of sexually abused girls. *Journal of the American Academy of Child Psychiatry*, **19**, 243–53 **(918)**

Maden, A., Swinton, M. and Gunn, J. (1990) Women in prison and use of illicit drugs before arrest. *British Medical Journal*, **301**, 1133 **(476, 609, 615)**

Maden, A., Swinton, M. and Gunn, J. (1991) Drug dependence in prisons. *British Medical Journal*, **302**, 880 **(476, 489, 820)**

Maden, A., Swinton, M. and Gunn, J. (1992) Gambling in young offenders. *Criminal Behaviour and Mental Health*, **2**, 300–8 **(489)**

Magnusson, D. (1988) *Individual Development from an Interactional Perspective*. Erlbaum: Hillsdale, NJ **(256)**

Magnusson, D., Stattin, H. and Duner, A. (1983) Aggression and criminality in a longitudinal perspective. In *Prospective Studies of Crime and Delinquency* (eds. K. T. Van Dusen and S. A. Mednick) Kluwer-Nijhoff: Boston **(271)**

Maguire, M. and Bennett, T. (1982) *Burglary in a Dwelling*, Heinemann: London **(892, 901, 908)**

Maier, G. J. (1990) Psychopathic disorders: beyond counter-transference. *Current Opinion in Psychiatry*, **3**, 766–9 **(654)**

Maier, S. F. and Seligman, M. E. P. (1976) Learned helplessness: theory and evidence. *Journal of Experimental Psychiatry*, **105**, 3–46 **(930)**

Main, M., Kaplan, N. and Cassidy, J. (1985) Security in infancy, childhood and adulthood: a move towards the level of representation. In *Growing Points in Attachment Theory and Research. Monographs of the Society for Research in Child Development* 50 (Serial No. 209), 66–104 **(381, 382)**

Main, M. and Weston, D. (1981) The quality of toddlers' relationship to mother and father. *Child Development*, **52**, 932–40 **(381)**

Mair, G. (1988) *Probation Day Centres*, Home Office Research Study No. 123, HMSO: London **(788)**

Mairet, A. (1908) *La Jalousie: Etude Psycho-Physiologique Clinique et Médico-Légale*. Montpellier: Paris **(351)**

Maisch, H. (1973) *Incest*, Andre Deutsch: London **(536)**

Maitland, P. and Woodward, R. (1983) *Research into the Perceptions of Hostel Residents*. Inner London Probation Service: London **(777, 778)**

Malamuth, M. R. (1981) Rape proclivity. *Journal of Social Issues*, **37**, 138–57 **(545)**

Malamuth, M. R. and Check, J. V. P. (1981) The effects of mass media exposure on acceptance of violence against women: a field experiment. *Journal of Research in Personality*, **15**, 436–46 **(526)**

Malamuth, N. M. and Donnerstein, E. (1982) The effects of aggressive and pornographic mass media stimuli. In *Advances in Experimental Social Psychology, Vol. 15* (ed. L. Berkowitz) Academic Press: New York **(545)**

Maletzky, B. M. (1973) The episodic dyscontrol system. *Diseases of the Nervous System*, **34**, 178–85 **(288, 663)**

Maletzky, B. M. (1976) The diagnosis of pathological intoxication. *Quarterly Journal of Studies on Alcohol*, **37**, 1215–28 **(63, 443)**

Maletzky, B. M. (1991) *Treating the Sexual Offender*, Sage: Newbury Park **(560, 671, 673)**

Maletzky, B. M. and Klotter, J. (1974) Episodic dyscontrol: a controlled replication. *Diseases of the Nervous System*, 35, 175–9 **(663)**

Malseed, R. T. and Goldstein, F. J. (1979) Enhancement of morphine analgesic by tricyclic antidepressants. *Neuropharmacology*, 18, 827–9 **(937)**

Mandaraka-Sheppard, A. (1986) *The Dynamics of Aggression in Women's Prisons in England*, Gower: London **(618, 621, 762)**

Mandlebrote, B. (1958) An experiment in the rapid conversion of a closed mental hospital into an open door hospital. *Mental Hygiene*, 42, 3–16 **(652)**

Mann, R. D. (1989) No fault compensation. *Journal of the Royal Society of Medicine*, 82, 249–50 **(107)**

Mann, T. (1924) Die Zauberberg *(The Magic Mountain)* (trans. H. T. Lowe-Porter) Penguin (1960): Aylesbury **(796)**

Mannheim, H. (1965) *Comparative Criminology*, Routledge & Kegan Paul: London **(601)**

Marcus, B. (1955) Intelligence, criminality and the expectation of recidivism. *British Journal of Delinquency*, 6, 147–51 **(323)**

Mark, V. H. and Ervin, P. R. (1970) *Violence and the Brain*, Harper & Row: New York **(288, 491)**

Markowe, H. L. J. (1988) The frequency of child sexual abuse in the UK. *Health Trends*, 20, 2–6 **(917)**

Marks, B. and Rose, F. C. (1965) *Hypolglycaemia*, Blackwell: Oxford **(443)**

Marmar, C. R., Horowitz, M. J. and Kaltreider, N. B. (1988) A controlled trial of brief psychotherapy and mutual-help group treatment of conjugal bereavement. *American Journal of Psychiatry*, 145, 203–9 **(939)**

Marquis, J. N. (1990) Orgasmic reconditioning: changing sexual object choice through controlling masturbation fantasies. *Journal of Behavior Therapy and Experimental Psychiatry*, 1, 263–71 **(561)**

Marsden, D. (1978) Sociological perspectives on family violence. In *Violence and the Family* (ed. J. P. Martin) Wiley: Chichester **(511)**

Marshall, T. F. and Walpole, M. E. (1985) *Bringing People Together: Mediation and Reparation Projects in Great Britain* Paper No. 33, Home Office Research & Planning Unit: London **(944)**

Marshall, W. L. and Barbaree, H. E. (1978) The reduction of sexual arousal. Satiation treatment for aggressors. *Criminal Justice and Behavior*, 5, 294–303 **(561)**

Marshall, W. L. Barbaree, H. E. and Christophe, D. (1986) Sexual offenders against female children: sexual preferences for age of victims and type of behavior. *Canadian Journal of Behavioral Science*, 18, 391–402 **(538)**

Marshall, W. L. and Eccles, A. (1991) Issues in clinical practice with sex-offenders. *Journal of Interpersonal Violence*, 6, 68–93 **(556)**

Martin, E. (1984) Comparison of medical care in prison and in general practice. *British Medical Journal*, 289, 967–9 **(742)**

Martin, E., Colebrook, M. and Gray, A. (1984) Health of prisoners admitted to and discharged from Bedford Prison. *British Medical Journal*, 289, 985–7 **(742)**

Martin, F., Fox, S. J. and Murray, K. (1981) *Children Out of Court*, Scottish Academic Press: Edinburgh **(237)**

Martin, J. P. (1978) *Violence in the Family*, Wiley: Chichester **(367, 736, 911)**

Martin, J. P. (1984) *Hospitals in Trouble*, Blackwell: Oxford **(742, 797)**

Martinson, R. M. (1974) What works? Questions and answers about prison reform. *The Public Interest*, 35, 22–54 **(280)**

Mason, K. H., Ryan, A. B. and Bennett, M. R. (1988) *Report of the Committee of Enquiry into Proceedings in Certain Psychiatric Hospitals in Relation to Admission, Discharge, or Release on Leave of Certain Classes of Patients* (The Mason Report) New Zealand Ministry of Health: Wellington **(709)**

Masserman, J. H. (1953) Faith and delusion in psychotherapy. *American Journal of Psychiatry*, 110, 324–34 **(683, 890)**

Masters, B., (1985) *Killing for company* Cape: London **(54, 391, 393, 520, 553)**

Masters, R., Friedman, L. N. and Getwel, G. (1988) Helping families of homicide victims: a multidimensional approach. *Journal of Traumatic Stress*, 1, 109–25 **(921)**

Mattes, J. A. (1985) Metoprolol for intermittent explosive disorder. *American Journal of Psychiatry*, 142, 1108–9 **(662)**

Matthews, J. (1983) *Forgotten Victims: How Prison Affects the Family*. National Association for the Care and Resettlement of Offenders: London **(922)**

Matthews, P. and Foreman, J. C. (1986) *Jervis on the Office and Duties of Coroners*, Sweet & Maxwell: London (**180**)

Mattson, M. R. and Sacks, M. H. (1978) Seclusion: uses and complications. *American Journal of Psychiatry*, **135**, 1210–3 (**658, 659**)

Matza, D. (1964) *Delinquency and Drift*, Wiley: New York (**798**)

Maudsley, H. (1867) *The Physiology and Pathology of Mind*, Macmillan: London (**417**)

Maudsley, H. (1876) *Responsibility in Mental Disease 3rd edn*, King: London (**288**)

Mawby, R. I. (1984) Bystander responses to victims of crime: is the good samaritan alive and well? *Victimology*, **10**, 461–75 (**933**)

Mawby, R. I. and Gill, M. L. (1987) *Crime Victims: Needs, Services and the Voluntary Sector*, Tavistock: London (**106, 936, 941, 944, 1030**)

Mawby, R. I., McCulloch, J. W. and Batta, I. D. (1979) Crime amongst Asian juveniles in Bradford. *International Journal of the Sociology of Law*, **7**, 297–306 (**276, 277**)

Mawson, D. (1983) Psychopaths in special hospitals. *Bulletin of the Royal College of Psychiatrists*, **7**, 178–81 (**402**)

Mawson, D. (1985) Delusions of poisoning. *Medicine, Science and the Law*, **25**, 279–87 (**342, 344**)

Mawson, D., Grounds, A. and Tantum, D. (1985) Violence and Asperger's syndrome: a case study. *British Journal of Psychiatry*, **147**, 566–9 (**396**)

Mawson, D., Marks, I. M., Ramir, L. and Stern, R. S. (1981) Guided mourning for morbid grief: a controlled study. *British Journal of Psychiatry*, **138**, 185–93 (**938**)

May, M. (1978) Violence in the family: an historical perspective. In *Violence in the Family* (ed. J. P. Martin) Wiley: Chichester (**501**)

May, P. R. A. (1968) *Treatment of Schizophrenia*, Science House: New York (**655**)

May, P. R. A. and Ebaugh, F. G. (1953) Pathological intoxication, alcoholic hallucinosis, and other reactions to alcohol: a clinical study. *Quarterly Journal of Studies on Alcohol*, **14**, 200–27 (**443**)

Mayer, R. E. and Treat, J. R. (1977) Psychological, social and cognitive characteristics of high risk drivers: a pilot study. *Accident Analysis and Prevention*, **9**, 1–8 (**581**)

Mayhew, P., Elliott, D. and Dowds, L. (1989) *The 1988 British Crime Survey*, Home Office Research Study No.111, HMSO: London (**567**)

McCabe, S. and Treitel, P. (1984) *Juvenile Justice in the United Kingdom, Comparisons and Suggestions for Change*. New Approaches to Juvenile Crime: London (**236**)

McClelland, H. A., Farquharson, R. G., Leyburn, P., Furness, J. A. and Schiff, A. A. (1976) Very high dose fluphenzine decanoate. *Archives of General Psychiatry*, **33**, 1435–9 (**663**)

McClintock, F. H. (1963) *Crimes of Violence*, Cambridge Studies in Criminology Vol. XVIII, Macmillan: London (**369, 500**)

McClintock, F. H. (1978) Criminological aspects of family violence. In *Violence in the Family* (ed. J. P. Martin) Wiley: Chichester (**449, 911, 912**)

McClintock, F. H. and Avison, N. H. (1968) *Crime in England & Wales*, Heinemann: London (**569**)

McClure G. M. G. (1987) Suicide in England & Wales 1975–1984 *British Journal of Psychiatry*, **150**, 309–14 (**813**)

McConaghy, N., Armstrong, M. S., Blaszcynski, A. and Allcock, C. (1983) Controlled comparison of aversive therapy and imaginal desensitisation in compulsive gambling. *British Journal of Psychiatry*, **142**, 366–72 (**488**)

McConville, S. (1981) *A History of English Prison Administration Vol. 1 1750–1877*, Routledge & Kegan Paul: London (**795**)

McCord, J. (1977) A comparative study of two generations of native Americans. In *Theory in criminology* (ed. R. F. Meier) Sage: Beverly Hills, CA, pp. 83–92 (**264**)

McCord, J. (1978) A thirty-year follow-up of treatment effects. *American Psychologist*, **33**, 284–9 (**254, 689, 776**)

McCord, J. (1979) Some child-rearing antecedents of criminal behavior in adult men. *Journal of Personality and Social Psychology*, **37**, 1477–86 (**263**)

McCord, J. (1982) A longitudinal view of the relationship between paternal absence and crime. In *Abnormal Offenders, Delinquency and the Criminal Justice System* (eds. J. Gunn and D. P. Farrington) Wiley: Chichester (**263**)

McCord, J. (1988) Parental behavior in the cycle of aggression. *Psychiatry*, **51**, 14–23 (**254**)

McCord, W. and Sanchez, J. (1982) The Wiltwyck-Lyman project: a twenty-five year follow-up study of milieu therapy. In *The Psychopath and Milieu Therapy* (ed. W. N. M. McCord) Academic Press: New York **(689)**

McCormick, R. A., Russo, A. M., Ramiriz, L. F. and Taber, J. I. (1984) Affective disorders among pathological gamblers seeking treatment. *American Journal of Psychiatry*, 141, 215–8 **(484)**

McCreadie, R. G., Flanagan, W. L., McKnight, J. and Jorgensen, A. (1979) High dose flupenthixol decanoate in chronic schizophrenia. *British Journal of Psychiatry*, 135, 175–9 **(663)**

McCreadie, R. G. and MacDonald, I. M. (1977) High dosage haloperidol in chronic schizophrenia. *British Journal of Psychiatry*, 131, 310–6 **(663)**

McCreadie, R. G. and Phillips, K. (1988) The Nithsdale Schizophrenia Survey: VII. Does relatives' high expressed emotion predict relapse? *British Journal of Psychiatry*, 152, 477–81 **(367)**

McFall, M. E., McKay, P. W. and Donovan, D. M. (1991) Combat-related PTSD and psychosocial adjustment problems among substance-abusing veterans. *Journal of Nervous and Mental Disease*, 179, 33–8 **(929)**

McFarland, R. A., Tune, G. S. and Welford, A. T. (1964) On driving of automobiles by older people. *Journal of Gerontology*, 19, 190–7 **(584)**

McFarlane, A. C. (1987) Life events and psychiatric disorder: the role of a natural disaster. *British Journal of Psychiatry*, 151, 362–7 **(902)**

McFarlane, A. C. (1988a) The aetiology of post-traumatic stress disorders following a natural disaster. *British Journal of Psychiatry*, 152, 116–21 **(893–897 passim 905)**

McFarlane, A. C. (1988b) The longitudinal cause of post-traumatic morbidity. The range of outcomes and their predictors. *Journal of Nervous and Mental Disease*, 176, 30–9 **(895, 896, 905)**

McFarlane, A. C., Policansky, S. K. and Irwin, C. (1987) A longitudinal study of the psychological morbidity in children, due to a natural disaster. *Psychological Medicine*, 17, 727–38 **(891, 923)**

McGarry, A. L. (1965) Competency for trial and due process via the state hospital. *American Journal of Psychiatry*, 122, 623–30 **(176)**

McGillis, D. and Smith, P. (1983) *Compensating Victims of Crime: An Analysis of American Programs*, National Institute of Justice: Washington DC **(105)**

McGlashan, T. (1986) The prediction of outcome in chronic schizophrenia. IV. The Chestnut Lodge follow-up study. *Archives of General Psychiatry*, 43, 167–76 **(335)**

McGovern, D. and Cope, R. (1987) The compulsory detention of males of different ethnic groups, with special reference to offender patients. *British Journal of Psychiatry*, 150, 505–12 **(370)**

McHale, J. V. (1991) Confidentiality and the examining psychiatrist. *Psychiatric Bulletin*, 15, 160 **(869)**

McKellar, P. (1979) *Mindsplit*, Dent: London **(427, 429)**

McKenna, P. J. (1984) Disorders with overvalued ideas. *British Journal of Psychiatry*, 145, 579–85 **(356)**

McKerracher, D. W., Street, D. R. K. and Segal, L. J. (1966) Behaviour problems presented by male and female subnormal offenders. *British Journal of Psychiatry*, 112, 891–7 **(618)**

McKnight, C. K., Mohr, J. W., Quinsey, R. E. and Erochko, J. (1966) Mental illness and homicide. *Canadian Psychiatric Association Journal*, 11, 91–8 **(339)**

McLaren, S., Browne, F. W. A. and Taylor, P. J. (1990) A study of psychotropic medication given 'as required' in a regional secure unit. *British Journal of Psychiatry*, 156, 732–5 **(661)**

McMurran, M. (1989) Services for prisoners who drink. *Prison Service Journal*, 75, 5–6 **(455)**

McMurran, M. and Baldwin, S. (1989) Services for prisoners with alcohol-related problems: a survey of UK prisons. *British Journal of Addiction*, 84, 1053–8 **(455)**

McMurry, L. (1970) Emotional stress and driving performance: the effects of divorce. *Behavioral Research in Highway Safety*, 1, 100–14 **(582)**

McNee, M. P., Egli, D. S. Marshall, R. S., Schnelle, J. F. and Risley, T. R. (1976) Shoplifting prevention: providing information through signs. *Journal of Applied Behavior Analysis*, 9, 399–405 **(577)**

McNiel, D. E. and Binder, R. L. (1987) Predictive validity of judgments of dangerousness in emergency civil commitment. *American Journal of Psychiatry*, 144, 197–200 **(644)**

McNiel, D., Binder, R. and Greenfield, T. (1988) Predictors of violence in civilly committed acute psychiatric patients. *American Journal of Psychiatry*, 145, 965–70 **(641)**

McWilliams, W. (1986) The English probation system and the diagnostic ideal. *The Howard Journal of Criminal Justice*, 25, 241–60 (**771**)

Mead, M. (1935) *Sex and Temperament in Three Primitive Societies*, Gollancz: London (**528**)

Meadow, R. (1977) Munchausen syndrome by proxy. *Lancet*, ii, 343–5 (**422, 912**)

Meadow, R. (1982) Munchausen syndrome by proxy. *Archives of Disease in Childhood*, 57, 92–8 (**422, 912**)

Meadow, R. (1989) Munchausen syndrome by proxy. *British Medical Journal* 299, 248–50 (**422, 912**)

Mechanic D. (1962) The concept of illness behavior. *Journal of Chronic Diseases*, 15, 189–94 (**414**)

Mechanic, D. (1986) The concept of illness behaviour: culture, situation and personal predisposition. *Psychological Medicine*, 16, 1–7 (**414**)

Medical Research Council (1965) Clinical trial of the treatment of depressive illness. *British Medical Journal*, 1, 881–6 (**935**)

Medical Working Group on Drug Dependence (1984) *Guidelines of Good Clinical Practice in the Treatment of Drug Misuse*, Department of Health & Social Security: London (**476**)

Medlicott, R. W. (1968) Fifty thieves. *New Zealand Medical Journal*, 428, 183–8 (**570**)

Mednick, S., Brennan, P. and Kandel, E. (1988) Predisposition to violence. *Aggressive Behavior*, 14, 25–33 (**642**)

Mednick, S. A. and Christiansen, K. O. (1977) *Biosocial Bases of Criminal Behaviour*, Gardner Press: New York (**254**)

Mednick, S. A., Gabrielli, W. F. and Hutchings, B. (1983) Genetic influences on criminal behavior: evidence from an adoption cohort. In *Prospective Studies of Crime and Delinquency* (eds. K. T. Van Dusen and S. A. Mednick) Kluwer-Nijhoff: Boston (**258**)

Meehan, E. and MacRae, K. (1986) Legal implications of pre-menstrual syndrome: a Canadian perspective. *Canadian Medical Association Journal*, 135, 601–7 (**608**)

Megargee, E. I. (1966) Undercontrolled and overcontrolled personality types in extreme antisocial aggression. *Psychological Monographs*, 80, No. 611 (**359, 363, 529**)

Mehl, M. and Cromwell, R. (1969) The effect of brief sensory deprivation and sensory stimulation on the cognitive functioning of chronic schizophrenics. *Journal of Nervous & Mental Disease*, 148, 586–96 (**659**)

Meichenbaum, D. (1975) A self-instructional approach to stress management: a proposal for stress inoculation training. In *Stress and Anxiety, vol. 2* (eds. C. Speilberger and I. Sarason) Wiley: New York (**676**)

Meichenbaum, D. (1985) *Stress Inoculation Training*, Pergamon Press: Oxford (**931, 938, 939**)

Melella, J. T., Sheldon, T. and Cullen, K. (1989) Legal and ethical issues in the use of antiandrogens in treating sex offenders. *Bulletin of the American Academy of Psychiatry and the Law*, 17, 223–32 (**563**)

Mellor, C. S. (1970) First rank symptoms of schizophrenia. *British Journal of Psychiatry*, 117, 15–23 (**336**)

Mellsop, G., Varghese, F., Joshua, S. and Hicks, A. (1982) The reliability of Axis II of DSM–III. *American Journal of Psychiatry*, 139, 1360–1 (**377**)

Melville, H. (1924) Billy Budd, Sailor. Reprinted in *Billy Budd, Sailor and Other Stories*, Penguin (1967): Harmondsworth (**1**)

Melville, J. (1978) A note on Men's Aid. In *Violence and the Family* (ed. J. P. Martin) Wiley: Chichester (**510**)

Menczer, L. F. (1968) The Hartford disaster exercise. *New England Journal of Medicine*, 278, 822–4 (**922**)

Mendelson, E. F. (1988) A community treatment service for sex offenders. *Bulletin of the Royal College of Psychiatrists*, 12, 416–9 (**727**)

Mendelson, G. (1984) Follow-up studies of personal injury litigants. *International Journal of Law & Psychiatry*, 7, 179–88 (**416**)

Mental Health Act Commission (1985) *The First Biennial Report of the Mental Health Act Commission 1983–85*, HMSO: London (**195, 698**)

Mental Health Act Commission (1986) *Second Biennial Report 1985–7*, HMSO: London (**40**)

Mental Health Act Commission (1987) *Third Biennial Report 1987–9*, HMSO: London (**33, 37, 110, 698**)

Mental Welfare Commission for Scotland (1989) *Report of the Mental Welfare Commission for Scotland 1988*, HMSO: Edinburgh (**205, 698**)

Menzies, I. E. P. (1960) A case study in functioning of social systems as a defence against anxiety. *Human Relations*, **13**, 95–121 (**798**)

Menzies, R. J., Webster, C. D., and Sepejak, D. S. (1985) Hitting the forensic sound barrier: predictions of dangerousness in a pretrial psychiatric clinic. In *Dangerousness* (eds. C. D. Webster, M. H. Ben-Aron and S. J. Hucker) Cambridge University Press: Cambridge (**644**)

Mersey Regional Health Authority (1987) *Internal Enquiry into the Regional Secure Unit—Rainhill Hospital, Summary Report*, Mersey RHA: Liverpool (**718**)

Messinger, E. and Apfelberg, B. (1961) A quarter century of court psychiatry. *Crime and Delinquency*, **7**, 343–62 (**321**)

Meth, J. M. (1974) Exotic psychiatric syndromes. In *American Handbook of Psychiatry* (ed. S. Arieti) Basic Books: New York (**433**)

Mezey, G. (1991) Treatment in the community. *Criminal Behaviour & Mental Health*, **1**, 169–72 (**728**)

Mezey, G. and King, M. (1989) The effects of sexual assault on men: a survey of twenty-two victims. *Psychological Medicine*, **19**, 205–9 (**892, 916, 917**)

Mezey, G. C. and Taylor, P. J. (1988) Psychological reactions of women who have been raped: a descriptive and comparative study. *British Journal of Psychiatry*, **152**, 330–9 (**894, 899, 901, 902, 904, 916, 941**)

Michelson, L. (1987) Cognitive-behavioral strategies in the prevention and treatment of antisocial disorders in children and adolescents. In *Prevention of Delinquent Behaviour* (eds. J. D. Burchard and S. N. Burchard) Sage: Beverly Hills, CA (**281**)

Midgley, M. (1984) *Wickedness*, Routledge & Kegan Paul: London (**15**)

Miers, D. (1978) *Responses to Victimisation*, Professional Books: Abingdon (**105**)

Miers, D. (1980) Victim compensation as a labelling process. *Victimology*, **1**, 3–16 (**106**)

Milgram, R. M. and Milgram, N. A. (1976) The effect of the Yom Kippur War on anxiety level in Israeli children. *Journal of Psychology*, **94**, 107–13 (**888, 892**)

Miller, F. J. W., Court, S. D., Knox, E. G. and Brandon, S. (1974) *The School Years in Newcastle upon Tyne*. Oxford University Press: Oxford (**254**)

Miller, F. J. W., Court, S. D., Walton, W. S. and Knox, E. G. (1960) *Growing up in Newcastle upon Tyne*, Oxford University Press: Oxford (**305**)

Miller, F. J. W., Kolvin, I. and Fells, H. (1985) Becoming deprived: a cross-generation study based upon the Newcastle upon Tyne 1000 family survey. In *Longitudinal Studies in Child Psychology and Psychiatry* (ed. A. R. Nicol) Wiley: Chichester (**254**)

Miller, G. R. and Burgoon, J. K. (1982) Factors affecting assessments of witness credibility. In *The Psychology of the Courtroom* (ed. N. L. Kerr and R. M. Bray) Academic Press: New York (**856**)

Miller, H. (1961) Accident neurosis. *British Medical Journal*, **1**, 919–22; 992–8 (**416, 906**)

Miller, H. (1966) Mental after-effects of head injury. *Proceedings of Royal Society of Medicine*, **59**, 257–61 (**416**)

Miller, H. (1969) Problems of medicolegal practice. In *The Late Effects of Head Injury* (ed. A. E. Walker, W. F. Caveness and M. Critchley) Thomas: Springfield, IL (**907**)

Miller, H. and Cartlidge, N. (1972) Simulation and malingering after injuries to the brain and spinal cord. *Lancet*, **i**, 580–5 (**418**)

Miller, L. (1987) Neuropsychology of the aggressive psychopath: an integrated review. *Aggressive Behavior*, **13**, 119–40 (**290**)

Miller, W. B. (1975) *Violence by Youth Gangs and Youth Groups as a Crime problem in Major American Cities*, National Institute of Juvenile Justice and Delinquency Prevention: Washington, DC (**266**)

Millham, S., Bullock, R. and Hosie, R. (1978) *Locking up Children*, Saxon House: Farnborough (**215, 234**)

Millon, T. (1981) *Disorders of Personality DSM-III: Axis II*, Wiley: New York (**375**)

Milstein, V. (1988) EEG topography in patients with aggressive violent behaviour. In *Biological Contributions to Crime Causation* (eds. T. E. Moffitt and S. A. Mednick) Martinus Nijhoff: Dordrecht (**288**)

Ministry of Health (1926) *Report of the Departmental Committee on Morphine and Heroin Addiction*, HMSO: London (**460**)

Ministry of Health (1961) *Special Hospitals: Report of a Working Party* (The Emery Report), HMSO: London (**461, 694, 710**)

Ministry of Health and Department of Health for Scotland (1961) *Drug Addiction: Report of the Interdepartmental Committee*, HMSO: London (**461**)

Ministry of Health and Department of Health for Scotland (1965) *Drug Addiction: the Second Report of the Interdepartmental Committee*, HMSO: London (461)

Mlele, T. J. J. and Wiley, Y. V. (1986) Clopenthixol decanoate in the management of aggressive mentally handicapped patients. *British Journal of Psychiatry*, 149, 373–76 (662)

Moberg, D. O. (1953) Old Age and crime. *Journal of Criminal Law, Criminology and Police Science*, 43, 764–76 (326)

Modan, B., Nissekorn, I. and Lewkowski (1970) Comparative epidemiological aspects of suicide and attempted suicide in Israel. *American Journal of Epidemiology*, 91, 383–91 (595)

Modestin, J., Krapf, R. and Boker, W. (1981) A fatality during haloperidol treatment: mechanism of sudden death. *American Journal of Psychiatry*, 138, 1616–7 (664)

Modestin, J., Toffler, G., Pia, M. and Greub, E. (1983) Haloperidol in acute schizophrenic inpatients. *Pharmacopsychiatry*, 16, 121–6 (663)

Moffitt, T. E. (1989) The neuropsychology of juvenile delinquency: a critical review of research and theory. In *Crime and Justice* vol 12 (eds. M. Tonry and N. Morris) University of Chicago Press: Chicago (261)

Moffitt, T. E. and Silva, P. A. (1988a) IQ and delinquency: a direct test of the differential detection hypothesis. *Journal of Abnormal Psychology*, 97, 330–3 (255, 260)

Moffitt, T. E. and Silva, P. A. (1988b) Neuropsychological deficit and self-reported delinquency in an unselected birth cohort. *Journal of the American Academy of Child & Adolescent Psychiatry*, 27, 233–40 (255, 271)

Moffitt, T. E. and Silva, P. A. (1988c) Self-reported delinquency: results from an instrument for New Zealand. *Australian and New Zealand Journal of Criminology*, 21, 227–240 (255, 271)

Mohr, J. W., Turner, R. E. and Jerry, M. B. (1964) *Pedophilia and Exhibitionism*, University of Toronto Press: Toronto (547)

Mollica, R. F., Wyshak, G. and Lavelle, J. (1987) The psychosocial impact of war trauma and torture on South-east Asian refugees. *American Journal of Psychiatry*, 144, 1567–72 (892, 926)

Mollica, R. F., Wyshak, G., Lavelle, J., Truong, T., Tor, S. and Yang, T. (1990) Assessing symptom change in South-east Asian refugee survivors of mass violence and torture. *American Journal of Psychiatry*, 147, 83–8 (893, 926)

Molnar, G., Keitner, L. and Harwood, B. T. (1984) A comparison of partner and solo arsonists. *Journal of Forensic Science*, 29, 574–83 (591)

Monahan, J. (1977) Strategies for an empirical analysis of the prediction of violence in emergency civil commitment. *Law and Human Behavior*, 1, 363–71 (644)

Monahan, J. (1978) Prediction research and the emergency commitment of dangerous mentally ill persons: a reconsideration. *American Journal of Psychiatry*, 135, 198–201 (626)

Monahan, J. (1981) *The Clinical Prediction of Violent Behavior*, Government Printing Office, Washington DC & National Institute of Mental Health: Rockville MD (121, 627, 628)

Monahan, J. (1984) The prediction of violent behavior: toward a second generation of theory and policy. *American Journal of Psychiatry*, 141, 10–5 (641)

Monahan, J. (1988) Risk assessment of violence among the mentally disordered: generating useful knowledge. *International Journal of Law and Psychiatry*, 11, 249–57 (641)

Monahan, J., Caldeira, C. and Lander, H. D. F. (1979) Police and the mentally ill: a comparison of committed and arrested persons. *International Journal of Law and Psychiatry*, 2, 509–18 (330)

Monahan, J., Davis, S. K., Hartstone, E. and Steadman, H. J. (1983) Prisoners transferred to mental hospitals. In *Mentally Disordered Offenders: Perspectives from Law and Social Sciences* (eds. J. Monahan and H. J. Steadman) Plenum Press: New York (757)

Monahan, J. and Klassen, D. (1982) situational approaches to understanding and predicting individual violent behavior. In *Criminal Violence* (eds. M. Wolfgang and N. Weiner) Sage: Beverly Hills CA, pp. 292–319 (643)

Monahan, J. and Steadman, H. (1983) Crime and mental disorder: an epidemiological approach. In *Crime and Justice: An Annual Review of Research, vol. 3* (eds. N. Morris and M. Tonry) University of Chicago Press: Chicago, pp. 145–189 (330, 642)

Money, J. & Ehrhardt, A. (1972) *Man and Woman, Boy and Girl*, Johns Hopkins University Press: Baltimore MD. (528)

Monroe, R. R. (1970) *Episodic Behavioral Disorders*, Harvard University Press: Massachusetts (662)

Monroe, R. R. (1975) Anticonvulsants in the treatment of aggression. *Journal of Nervous and Mental Disease*, 160, 119–26 (663)

Monroe, R. R., Paskewitz, D. A., Balin, G. U., Lion, J. R. and Rubin, J. S. (1978) Response to anticonvulsant medication. In *Brain Dysfunction in Aggressive Criminals* (ed. R. R. Monroe) Lexington Books: Lexington, Mass. **(288)**

Montandon, C. and Harding, T. W. (1984) The reliability of dangerousness assessments: a decision-making exercise. *British Journal of Psychiatry*, **144**, 149–55 **(119, 132)**

Montmollin, M–J de, Zimmerman, E., Bernheim, J. and Harding, J. W. (1986) Sociotherapeutic treatment of delinquents in prison. *International Journal of Offender Therapy and Comparative Criminology*, **30**, 25–34 **(754)**

Moodley, P. and Thornicroft, G. (1988) Ethnic group and compulsory detention. *Medicine, Science and the Law*, **28**, 324–8 **(360, 369)**

Moore, M. (1984) *Law and Psychiatry*, Cambridge University Press: Cambridge **(831)**

Moore, M. T. and Book, M. H. (1970) Sudden death in phenothiazine therapy. *Psychiatric Quarterly*, **44**, 389–402 **(664)**

Moore, R. H. (1984) Shoplifting in middle America: patterns and motivational correlates. *International Journal of Offender Therapy and Comparative Criminology*, **28**, 53–64 **(578)**

Moran, E. (1970) Pathological gambling. *British Journal of Hospital Medicine*, **3**, 59–70 **(483, 484)**

Morand, C., Young, S. N. and Ervin, F. R. (1983) Clinical response of aggressive schizophrenics to oral tryptophan. *Biological Psychiatry*, **18**, 575–8 **(664)**

Morash, M. (1983) Gangs, groups and delinquency. *British Journal of Criminology*, **23**, 309–31 **(266)**

Morash, M. and Rucker, L. (1989) An exploratory study of the connection of mother's age at childbearing to her children's delinquency in four data sets. *Crime and Delinquency*, **35**, 45–93 **(263)**

Morgan, H. G. and Priest, P. (1984) Assessment of suicide risk in psychiatric inpatients. *British Journal of Psychiatry*, **145**, 460–3 **(812)**

Morgan, J. R. (1990) Clinical Management. In *Substance Abuse and Dependence* (eds. H. Ghodse and D. Maxwell) Macmillan Press: Basingstoke **(465)**

Morgan, R. and Rogers, J. (1971) Some results of the policy of integrating men and women in a mental hospital. *Social Psychiatry*, **6**, 113–6 **(822)**

Morris, A. (1978a) Revolution in the Juvenile Court. *Criminal Law Review*, Sept. 529–39 **(211)**

Morris, A. (1978b) Diversion of juvenile offenders from the criminal justice system. In *Alternative Strategies for Coping with Crime* (ed. N. Tutt) Blackwell: Oxford **(217)**

Morris, A. (1987) *Women, Crime and Criminal Justice*, Blackwell: Oxford **(602, 603, 604, 621, 622)**

Morris, A. and Giller, H. (1977) The juvenile court—the client's perspective. *Criminal Law Review*, 198–205 **(238)**

Morris, A. and Giller, H. (1983) *Providing Criminal Justice for Children*, Edward Arnold: London **(211)**

Morris, A., Giller, H., Szwed, E. and Geach, H. (1980) *Justice for Children*, Macmillan: London **(211, 219)**

Morris, A. and McIsaac, M. (1978) *Juvenile Justice?* Heinemann: London **(210, 237)**

Morris, J. (1974) *Conundrum*, Faber: London **(551)**

Morris, N. and Hawkins, G. (1970) *The Honest Politician's Guide to Crime Control*, University of Chicago Press: Chicago **(500)**

Morris, P. (1965) *Prisoners and their Families*, Allen & Unwin: London **(922)**

Morris, P. and Beverley F. (1992) *On Licence: a Study of Parole* Wiley, Chichester **(777)**

Morris, T. and Blom-Cooper, L. (1964) *A Calender of Murder*, Michael Joseph: London **(513)**

Morris, T. and Morris, P. (1963) *Pentonville: A Sociological Study of an English Prison*, Routledge & Kegan Paul: London **(548, 802)**

Morrison, S. D., Erwin, C. W., Gianturco, D. T. and Gerber, C. J. (1973) Effect of lithium in combative behavior in humans. *Diseases of the Nervous System*, **34**, 186–9 **(662)**

Morse, C. W., Sahler, J. Z. and Friedman, S. B. (1970) A three-year follow-up study of abused and neglected children. *American Journal of Diseases of Children*, **120**, 439–46 **(913)**

Morse, S. J. (1984) Undiminished confusion in diminished capacity. *The Journal of Criminal Law and Criminology*, **75**, 1–55 **(144)**

Morton, J. H., Additon, H., Addison, R. G., Hunt, L. and Sullivan, J. J. (1953) A clinical study of premenstrual tension. *American Journal of Obstetrics and Gynaecology*, **65**, 1182–91 **(605)**

Moser, J. (1985) *Alcohol Policies in National Health and Development Planning*. WHO Offset Publication No. 89, World Health Organisation: Geneva **(435)**

Mossman, D. (1987) Assessing and restoring competency to be executed: should psychiatrists participate? *Behavioral Sciences and the Law*, 5, 397–410 (122, 882)

Mott, J. (1972) The psychological basis of drug dependence: the intellectual and personality characteristics of opiate users. *British Journal of Addiction*, 67, 89–99 (469)

Mount, F. (1984) The flourishing art of lying. *The Times*, 30 April (418)

Mowat, R. R. (1966) *Morbid Jealousy and Murder*, Tavistock Publications: London (342, 344, 352, 357)

Moxon, D. (1988) *Sentencing Practice in the Crown Court*, Home Office Research Study No. 103, HMSO: London (276)

Moyer, K. E. (1981) Biological substrates of aggression and implications for control. In *The Biology of Aggression* (eds. P. F. Brain and D. Benton) Sijthoff & Noordhoff: Alphen aan der Rija (491)

Mozdziera, G. J., Macchitelli, F. J., Planek, T. W. and Lottman (1975) Personality and temperament differences between alcoholics with high and low records of traffic accident and violations. *Journal of Studies on Alcohol*, 36, 395–9 (582)

Mrazek, P. B., Lynch, M. A. and Bentovim, A. (1983) Sexual abuse of children in the United Kingdom. *Child Abuse and Neglect*, 7, 147–53 (919)

Mueller, C. W. and Parcel, T. L. (1981) Measures of socio-economic status: alternatives and recommendations. *Child Development*, 52, 13–30 (270)

Mueser, K. T. and Butler, R. W. (1987) Auditory hallucinations in combat-related chronic post-traumatic stress disorder. *American Journal of Psychiatry*, 144, 299–302 (932)

Mullen, P. E. (1985) The mental state and states of mind. In *Essentials of Postgraduate Psychiatry*, 2nd edn. (eds. P. Hill, R. Murray and A. Thorley) Grune & Stratton: London (352)

Mullen, P. E. (1990) The long-term influence of sexual assault on the mental health of victims. *Journal of Forensic Psychiatry*, 1, 13–34 (3)

Mullen, P. E. and Maack, L. H. (1985) Jealousy, pathological jealousy and aggression. In *Aggression and Dangerousness* (eds. D. P. Farrington and J. Gunn) Wiley: Chichester (337, 252)

Mullen, P. E., Romans-Clarkson, S. E., Walton, V. A. and Herbison, G. P. (1988) Impact of sexual and physical abuse on women's mental health. *Lancet*, i, 841–5 (367, 537, 538, 903, 914)

Mulvey, E., Blumstein, A. and Cohen, J. (1986) Reframing the research question of mental patient criminality. *International Journal of Law and Psychiatry*, 9, 57–65 (642)

Mulvey, E. P., Gelber, J. L. and Roth, L. H. (1987) The promise and peril of involuntary outpatient commitment. *American Psychologist*, 42, 571–84 (726)

Mulvey, E. P. and Haugaard, J. L. (1986) *Report of the Surgeon General's Workshop on Pornography and Public Health*, US Department of Health & Human Services: Washington DC (527, 642)

Mulvey, E. and Lidz, C. (1984) Clinical considerations in the prediction of dangerousness in mental patients. *Clinical Psychology Review*, 4, 379–401 (643)

Murphy, W. D., Haynes, M. R. and Worley, P. J. (1991) Assessment of adult sexual interest. In *Clinical Approaches to Sex Offenders and Their Victims* (ed. C. R. Hollin and K. Howells) Wiley: Chichester (556)

Murray, D. M., Leupker, R. V., Johnson, C. A. and Mittelmark, M. B. (1984) The prevention of cigarette smoking in children: a comparison of four strategies. *Journal of Applied Social Psychology*, 14, 274–88 (283)

Murray, R. (1986) Alcoholism. In *Essentials of Postgraduate Psychiatry*, 2nd edn (eds. P. Hill, R. Murray and A. Thorley) Grune & Stratton: London (444)

Murrin, M. R. and Laws, D. R. (1990) The influence of pornography on sexual crimes. In *Handbook of Sexual Assault* (eds. W. Marshal, D. R. Laws and H. Barbaree) Plenum: New York (527)

Musto, D. F. (1973) *The American Disease—Origins of Narcotic Control*, Yale University Press: London (461)

Musto, D. F. (1991) A historical perspective. In *Psychiatric Ethics*, 2nd edn (ed. S. Bloch, and P. Chodoff) Oxford University Press: Oxford (858, 859)

Nachshon, I. (1988) Hemisphere function in violent offenders. In *Biological Contributions to Crime Causation* (eds. T. E. Moffitt and S. A. Mednick) Martinus Nijhoff Publishers: Dordrecht/Boston (290)

Nadelson, C. C., Norman, M. T., Zackson, H. and Gornick, J. (1982) A follow-up study of rape victims. *American Journal of Psychiatry*, **139**, 1266–70 (**902, 916**)

Nadler, L. B. (1985) The epidemiology of pathological gambling: critique of existing research and alternative strategies. *Journal of Gambling Behavior*, **1**, 35–70 (**482**)

Nagler, N. (1984) Forfeiture of the proceeds of drug trafficking. *Bulletin on Narcotics*, **36**, 21–30 (**464**)

Naismith, L. J. and Coldwell, J. B. (1990) A comparison of male admissions to a special hospital 1970–71 and 1987–88. *Medicine, Science and the Law*, **30**, 301–8 (**700**)

Napley, D. (1983) *The Technique of Persuasion*, 3rd edn, Sweet & Maxwell: London (**827**)

Nash, C. L. and West, D. J. (1985) Sexual molestation of young girls: a retrospective survey. In *Sexual Victimisation* (ed. D. J. West) Gower: Aldershot (**918, 931**)

National Association for the Care and Resettlement of Offenders (1985) *Submission to the Special Committee on the Future of Holloway Prison*, April 1985 (unpublished report) (**614**)

National Association for the Care and Resettlement of Offenders (1989a) *Replacing Custody*, National Association for the Care and Resettlement of Offenders: London (**237**)

National Association for the Care and Resettlement of Offenders (1989b) *Briefing No. 64 'Vandalism'*, National Association for the Care and Resettlement of Offenders: London (**587**)

National Association for the Care and Resettlement of Offenders (1990a) *Criteria for Custody*, Briefing Paper National Association for the Care & Resettlement of Offenders: London (**234**)

National Association for the Care and Resettlement of Offenders (1990b) *Briefing No. 61 'Shoplifting'*, National Association for the Care & Resettlement of Offenders: London (**572**)

National Association for the Care and Resettlement of offenders (1991) *The Cost of Penal Measures*, Briefing Paper No. 23, National Association for the Care and Resettlement of Offenders: London (**566**)

National Audit Office (1987) *Community Care Developments*, HMSO: London (**325, 694**)

National Center for State Courts (1986) Guidelines for the involuntary commitment. *Mental and Physical Disability Law Reporter*, **10**, 409–514 (**153, 646**)

National Commission on the Causes and Prevention of Violence (1969) *Final Report to Establish Justice, to Ensure Domestic Tranquility*, Government Printing Office: Washington DC (**497**)

National Health Service Health Advisory Service, DHSS Social Services Inspectorate (1988) *Report on Services provided by Broadmoor Hospital*, Department of Health & Social Security: London (**697, 698, 800**)

National Institute of Mental Health (1986) *Directory of Programs and Facilities for Mentally Disordered Offenders*, US Department of Health & Human Services: Rockville, MD (**157**)

National Society for the Prevention of Cruelty to Children (1969) *Annual Report*, NSPCC: London (**912**)

National Society for the Prevention of Cruelty to Children (1989) *Annual Report*, NSPCC: London (**912**)

Negrete, J. C., Werner, P. K., Douglas, D. E. and Bruce Smith, W. (1986) Cannabis affects (sic) the severity of schizophrenic symptoms: results of a clinical survey. *Psychological Medicine*, **16**, 515–20 (**468**)

Newburn, T. (1988) *The Use of Enforcement of Compensation Orders in Magistrates' Courts*, Home Office Research Study No. 102, HMSO: London (**106**)

Newburn, T. (1989) *The Settlement of Claims at the Criminal Injuries Compensation Board*, Home Office Research Study No. 112, HMSO: London (**106**)

Newman, E. s. and Newman, D. J. (1984) Public policy implications of elderly crime. In *Elderly Criminals* (eds. E. S. Newman, D. J. Newman and M. L. Gewirtz) Oelgeschlager, Gunn & Hain: Cambridge, Mass. (**328**)

Newman, J. C. (1976) Children of disaster: clinical observations at Buffalo Creek. *American Journal of Psychiatry*, **133**, 306–12 (**923**)

Nicholls, M. (1988) Mental patients and the official solicitor. *Medicine, Science and the Law*, **28**, 14–5 (**200**)

Nicholson, C. G. B. (1981) *The Law and Practice of Sentencing in Scotland*, Green: Edinburgh (**88**)

Nicholson, R. H. (1986) *Medical Research with Children*, Oxford University Press: Oxford (**867, 879**)

Nietzche, F. (1886) *Beyond Good and Evil* (trans. W. Kaufman) Roman House (1968): New York (**407**)

Nitsche, P. and Williams, K. (1913) The history of prison psychoses. *Nervous and Mental Disease Monograph Series No. 13* Journal of Nervous and Mental Disease Publishing Co: New York **(659)**

Noel, B. and Revil, D. (1974) Some personality perspectives of XYY individuals taken from the general population. *Journal of Sexual Research*, **10**, 219–25 **(314, 315)**

Noel, B., Dupont, J. P., Revil, D., Dussuyer, I. and Quack, B. (1974) The XYY syndrome: reality or myth? *Clinical Genetics*, **5**, 387–94 **(315)**

Nolan, B. S. (1984) Functional evaluation of the elderly in guardianship proceedings. *Law, Medicine and Health Care*, **12**, 210–18 **(325)**

Nordwind, B. L. (1982) Developing an enforceable 'right to treatment' theory for the chronically, mentally disabled in the community. *Schizophrenia Bulletin*, **8**, 642–51 **(873)**

Norris, J. and Feldman-Summers, S. (1981) Factors related to the psychological impacts of rape on the victim. *Journal of Abnormal Psychology*, **90**, 562–7 **(897)**

Norris, M. (1984) *Integration of Special Hospital Patients into the Community*, Gower: Aldershot, and Brookfield, Vt **(183, 771, 778)**

Norton, K. (1992) Personality disordered individuals: the Henderson Hospital model of treatment, *Criminal Behaviour and Mental Health* 2, 180–91 **(399)**

Novaco, R. W. (1975) *Anger Control: the Development and Evaluation of an Experimental Treatment*, Heath: Lexington, Mass. **(676)**

Novaco, R. W. (1976) The functions and regulation of the arousal of anger. *American Journal of Psychiatry*, **133**, 1124–8 **(675)**

Novaco, R. W. (1978) Anger and coping with stress. In *Cognitive Behavior Therapy* (eds. J. P. Foreyt and D. P. Rashjen) Penguin: New York **(676)**

Novaco, R. W. (1986) Anger as a clinical and social problem. In *Advances in the Study of Aggression, vol. 2* (eds. R. Blanchard and D. Blanchard) Academic Press: New York **(642)**

Novaco, R. W. and Welsh, W. N. (1989) Anger disturbances: cognitive mediation and clinical prescriptions. In *Clinical Approaches to Violence* (ed. K. Howells and C. R. Hollin) Wiley: Chichester **(675)**

Noyes, R. (1985) Motor vehicle accidents related to psychiatric impairment. *Psychomatics*, **26**, 569–80 **(583, 585)**

Nurcombe, B. (1986) The child as witness: competency and credibility. *Journal of the American Academy of Child Psychiatry*, **25**, 473–80 **(942)**

Nylander, I. (1979) A 20-year prospective follow-up study of 2164 cases at the child guidance clinics in Stockholm. *Acta Paediatrica Scandinavica*, Suppl 276 **(262)**

Ochberg, F. M. & Gunn, J. (1980) The psychiatrist and the policeman. *Psychiatric Annals*, **10**, 5, 31–45 **(871)**

O'Connell, B. A. (1960) Amnesia and homicide. *British Journal of Delinquency*, **10**, 262–76 **(46, 66, 292–297 passim)**

O'Connell, B. A. (1963) Matricide. *Lancet*, i, 1083–4 **(515)**

O'Connor, A. (1987) Female sex offenders. *British Journal of Psychiatry*, **150**, 615–20 **(537, 600)**

O'Connor, A. and Johnson-Sabine, E. (1988) Hunger strikers. *Medicine, Science and the Law*, **28**, 62–4 **(759)**

O'Connor, A. (1990) Male prison transfers to the Central Mental Hospital, a special hospital (1983–88). *Irish Journal of Psychological Medicine*, **7**, 118–20 **(763)**

O'Connor, M. & Baker, H. W. G. (1983) Depo-medroxy progesterone acetate as an adjunctive treatment in three aggressive schizophrenic patients. *Acta Psychiatrica Scandinavica*, **67**, 399–403 **(664)**

Ødegaard, J. (1968) Interaksjoner Mellom patnerne ved de patologiske ajalusireaksjoner. *Nordisk Psykiatrisk Tidsskrift*, **22**, 314–9 **(352)**

O'Dwyer, T., Wilson, J. and Carlen, P. (1987) Women's imprisonment in England, Wales & Scotland: recurring issues. In *Gender, Crime and Justice* (eds. P. Carlen and A. Worrall) Open University Press: Milton Keynes **(614)**

Offen, L. and Taylor, P. J. (1985) Violence and resources: factors determining admission to an interim secure unit. *Medicine, Science and the Law*, **25**, 165–71 **(714, 715)**

Office of Law Reform and Department of Health and Social Services (1989) *Proposed Changes to Some Aspects of the Law Relating to Children in N. Ireland Consultation Paper*, Department of Health and Social Services: Belfast **(251)**

Office of Population Censuses and Surveys (1985) *Drinking and Attitudes to Licensing in Scotland*, Government Statistical Service: London **(437)**

Offord, D. R. (1974) School performance of adult schizophrenics, their siblings and age mates. *British Journal of Psychiatry*, **125**, 12–19 **(362)**

Ogden, M., Wright, M. and Crowther, W. (1989) Report of an arbitration concerning the claims of ten passengers who survived the capsize of the 'Herald of Free Enterprise'. *The Personal and Medical Injuries Law Letter*, **5**, 37–9 **(104)**

O'Gorman, G. (1979) Abnormalities of movement. In *Psychiatric Illness and Mental Handicap* (eds. F. E. James and R. P. Snaith) Gaskell Press: London **(590)**

O'Hagan, F. J. (1976) Gang characteristics: an empirical study. *Journal of Child Psychology and Psychiatry*, **17**, 305–14 **(266)**

Oleck, H. L. (1953) Legal aspects of premenstrual tension. *International Record of Medicine and General Practice Clinics*, **166**, 492–501 **(607)**

Oliver, J. E. and Cox, J. (1973) A family kindred with ill-used children: the burden on the community. *British Journal of Psychiatry*, **123**, 81–90 **(922)**

Oliver, J. E., Cox, J., Taylor, A. and Baldwin, J. A. (1974) *Severely Ill-Treated Young Children in North-East Wiltshire*. Oxford University Unit of Clinical Epidemiology Research Report No. 4 **(912, 913)**

Opie, I. and Opie, P. (1983) *The Oxford Book of Narrative Verse*, Oxford University Press: Oxford **(xvii)**

Orford, J. (1978) The future of alcoholism: a commentary on the Rand Report. *Psychological Medicine*, **8**, 5–8 **(441)**

Orford, J. and Wawman, T. (1986) *Alcohol Detoxification Services. A Review*, Addictions and Homelessness Research Liaison Group, Department of Health and Social Security: London **(453)**

Osborn, S. G. (1980) Moving home, leaving London, and delinquent trends. *British Journal of Criminology*, **20**, 54–61 **(274)**

Osborne, L. W. and Martin, C. M. (1989) The importance of listening to medical students' experiences when teaching medical ethics. *Journal of Medical Ethics*, **15**, 35–8 **(884)**

O'Siochain, P. A. (1981) *The Criminal Law of Ireland*, Dublin Foilsiuchain Dli (Dublin Law Publications): Dublin **(208)**

Oswald, I. and Evans, J. (1985) On serious violence during sleepwalking. *British Journal of Psychiatry*, **147**, 688–91 **(88, 309, 310)**

Ota, Y. (1969) Psychiatric studies on civilian head injuries. In *The Late Effects of Head Injury* (eds. A. E. Walker, W. F. Caveness and M. Critchley) Thomas: Springfield, IL **(907)**

Ouston, J. (1984) Delinquency, family background and educational attainment. *British Journal of Criminology*, **24**, 2–26 **(271, 275, 277, 604)**

Overall, G. E. and Gorham, D. R. (1962) The Brief Psychiatric Rating Scale. *Psychological Reports*, **10**, 799–812 **(344)**

Pailthorpe, G. W. (1932) *What we put in Prison and in Preventive and Rescue Homes*, Williams & Norgate: London **(614)**

Palmer, T. B. (1973) Matching client and worker in corrections. *Social Work*, **18**, 95–103 **(400)**

Palmer, T. B. (1975) Martinson revisited. *Journal of Research in Crime and Delinquency*, **12**, 133–92 **(784)**

Panter, B. M. (1977) Lithium in the treatment of a child abuser. *American Journal of Psychiatry*, **134**, 1436–7 **(668)**

Parker, A. (1970) *The Frying Pan*, Hutchinson: London **(802)**

Parker, E. (1985) The development of secure provision. In *Secure Provision* (ed. L. Gostin) Tavistock: London **(696, 794)**

Parker, E. and Tennent, G. (1979) The 1959 Mental Health Act and mentally abnormal offenders. *Medicine, Science and the Law*, **19**, 29–8 **(711, 756)**

Parker, H., Casburn, M. and Turnbull, D. (1981) *Receiving Juvenile Justice*, Blackwell: Oxford **(221)**

Parker, H. and Newcombe, R. (1987) Heroin use and acquisitive crime in an English community. *The British Journal of Sociology*, **38**, 331–50 **(473)**

Parker, H., Newcombe, R. and Bakx, K. (1987) The new heroin users: prevalence and characteristics in Wirral, Merseyside. *British Journal of Addiction*, **82**, 147–57 **(473, 475)**

Parker, H., Jarvis, G. and Sumner, M. (1987) Under new orders: the redefinition of social work with young offenders. *British Journal of Social Work*, **17**, 21–43 **(234)**

Parker, J. G. and Asher, S. R. (1987) Peer relations and later personal adjustment: are low accepted children at risk? *Psychological Bulletin*, **102**, 357–89 **(267)**

Parker, N. (1988) *Malingering*. Lecture given to Anglo-Australian Bicentennial Meeting on Forensic Psychiatry (unpublished) **(418)**

Parkes, C. M. (1965) Bereavement and mental illness. Part 2: A classification of bereavement reactions. *British Journal of Medical Psychology*, **38**, 13–26 **(891)**

Parkes, C. M. (1972) *Bereavement: Studies of Grief in Adult Life*. Penguin Books: Harmondsworth **(890)**

Parlee, M. B. (1973) The premenstrual syndrome. *Psychological Bulletin*, **80**, 454–65 **(606)**

Parliamentary All-Party Penal Affairs Group (1981) *Young Offenders—a Strategy for the Future*, Barry Rose: Chichester **(220)**

Parole Release Scheme (1988) *A Guide to the Prison System for Residential Drug Projects*, Parole Release Scheme: London **(478)**

Parrott, J., Strathdee, G. and Brown, P. (1988) Patient access to psychiatric records: the patient's view. *Journal of the Royal Society of Medicine*, **81**, 520–2 **(650, 866)**

Parry, M. H. (1968) *Aggression on the Road*, London: Tavistock **(584)**

Parry-Jones, W. L. (1971) *The Trade in Lunacy: a Study of Private Madness in England in the Eighteenth and Nineteenth Centuries*, Routledge & Kegan Paul: London **(691)**

Parsons, T. (1951) *The Social System*, Free Press of Glencoe: New York **(6, 414)**

Parwatikar, S. D., Holcomb, W. R. and Meninger, K. A. (1985) The detection of malingered amnesia in accused murderers. *Bulletin of the American Academy of Psychiatry and the Law*, **13**, 97–103 **(293, 294, 295)**

Pasewark, R. A. (1981) Insanity plea: a review of the research literature. *The Journal of Psychiatry and Law*, **9**, 357–401 **(144)**

Pasewark, R. A. and McGinley, H. (1985) Insanity plea: national survey of frequency and success. *The Journal of Psychiatry and Law*, **13**, 101–8 **(144)**

Pasmanik, D. S. (1899) Forensic psychopathology (Sadena psihopatologija) *Legal Review (Juridicheski pregled)*, Plovdiv, VII, 3, 5, 6, 8 (in Bulgarian) **(154)**

Paton, A. (1985) The politics of alcohol. *British Medical Journal*, **290**, 1–2 **(435)**

Patrick, V. and Patrick, W. K. (1981) Cyclone 1978 in Sri Lanka—the mental health trail. *British Journal of Psychiatry*, **138**, 210–6 **(897, 902, 905, 923)**

Patterson, G. R. (1979) A performance theory for coercive family interaction. In *Social Interaction: Methods, Analysis and Illustration* (ed. R. Cairns) Erlbaum: Hillsdale, NJ **(493)**

Patterson, G. R. (1982) *A Social Learning Approach*, vol. 3 *Coercive Family Process*, Castalia Publishing: Eugene, OR **(288, 380)**

Paty, J. and Benejech, M. (1978) EEG studies in male polygonosmic psychopaths (47 XYY and 47 XXY). *British Journal of Psychiatry*, **133**, 285–6 **(315)**

Paul, D. M. (1986) 'What really did happen to Baby Jane?' The medical aspects of the investigation of alleged sexual abuse of children. *Medicine, Science and the Law*, **26**, 85–102 **(535)**

Paul, G. L. and Lentz, R. J. (1977) *Psychosocial Treatment of Chronic Mental Patients*, Harvard University Press: Cambridge, Mass. **(650, 652, 655)**

Pavlov, I. P., (1923) *Lectures on Conditioned Reflexes* Vol 1 (trans. W. Horsley) Gautt International Publishers (1928): New York **(670)**

Paykel, E. S. (1974) Life stress and psychiatric disorder; applications of the clinical approach. In *Stressful Life Events: Their Nature and Effect* (eds. B. S. Dohrerwend and B. P. Dohrerwend) Wiley: New York **(887)**

Pearce, I. and Wareham, A. (1977) The questionable relevance of research into social enquiry reports. *Howard Journal*, **16**, 97–108 **(772)**

Pearson, F. S. and Weiner, N. A. (1985) Toward an integration of criminological theories. *Journal of Criminal Law and Criminology*, **76**, 116–50 **(278)**

Pease, K. (1981) *Community Service Orders: a First Decade of Promise*, Howard League for Penal Reform: London **(786)**

Peay, J. (1988) Offenders suffering from psychopathic disorder. The rise and demise of a consultative document. *British Journal of Criminology*, **28**, 67–81 **(403, 852)**

Peay, J. (1989) *Tribunals on Trial*, Clarendon Press: Oxford **(193)**

Peele, R. and Von Loetzen, I. (1973) Phenothiazine deaths: a critical review. *American Journal of Psychiatry*, **130**, 306–8 **(664)**

Peet, M., Bethell, M. S., Coates, A., Khamnee, A. K., Hall, P., Cooper, S. J., King, D. J. and Yates, R. A. (1981a) Propranolol in schizophrenia: I. comparison of propranolol, chlorpromazine and placebo. *British Journal of Psychiatry*, **139**, 105–11 **(662, 664)**

Peet, M., Middelmiss, D. N. and Yates, R. A. (1981b) Propranolol in schizophrenia II. Clinical and biochemical aspects of combining propranolol with chlorpromazine. *British Journal of Psychiatry*, **139**, 112–7 **(664)**

Penk, W. E., Woodward, W. A., Robinowitz, R. and Oarr, W. C. (1981) An MMPI comparison of polydrug and heroin abusers. *Journal of Abnormal Psychology*, **89**, 299–302 **(470)**

Pennebaker, J. W., Kiecolt-Glazer, J. K. and Glaser, R. (1988) Disclosures of traumas and immune function: health implications for psychotherapy. *Journal of Consulting and Clinical Psychology*, **56**, 239–45 **(935)**

Penrose, L. S. (1939) Mental disease and crime: outcome of a comparative study of European statistics. *British Journal of Medical Psychology*, **18**, 1–15 **(332)**

Peplau, H. E. (1952) *Interpersonal Relations in Nursing*, Putnams & Sons: New York **(653)**

Percival, T. (1803) *Medical Ethics or a Code of Institutes and Precepts adapted to the Professional Conduct of Physicians and Surgeons*, S. Russell: Manchester (reprinted, 1985, Classics of Medicine Library: Birmingham, AL.) **(958)**

Perelman, C. (1963) *The Idea of Justice and the Problem of Argument*, Routledge: London **(829)**

Perkins, D. (1991) Clinical work with sex offenders in secure settings. In *Clinical Approaches to Sex Offenders and their Victims* (eds. C. R. Hollin and K. Howells) Wiley: Chichester **(558)**

Perkins, R. M. (1969) *Criminal Law*, Foundation Press: New York **(353)**

Perr, I. (1979) Comments on arson. *Journal of Forensic Science*, **24**, 885–9 **(589)**

Peters, R., Miller, K. S., Schmidt, W., and Meeters, D. (1987) The effects of statutory change on the civil commitment of the mentally ill. *Law and Human Behavior*, **11**, 73–99 **(153)**

Petrella, R. C., Benedek, E. P., Bank, S. C. and Packer, I. K. (1985) Examining the application of the guilty but mentally ill verdict in Michigan. *Hospital and Community Psychiatry*, **36**, 254–9 **(143)**

Petrie, K., Chamberlain, K. and Clarke, D. (1988) Psychological preditors of future suicidal behavior in hospitalized suicide attempters. *British Journal of Clinical Psychology*, **27**, 247–57 **(813)**

Petursson, H. and Gudjonsson, G. H. (1981) Psychiatric aspects of homicide. *Acta Psychiatrica Scandinavica*, **64**, 363–72 **(332, 512)**

Pfohl, B., Coryell, W., Zimmerman, M. and Stangl, D. (1986) DSM–III personality disorders: diagnostic overlap and internal consistency of individual DSM–III criteria. *Comprehensive Psychiatry*, **27**, 21–34 **(378)**

Phemister, J. C. (1961) Epilepsy and car driving. *Lancet*, **i**, 1276–7 **(583)**

Phillips, D. J. (1977) Motor vehicle fatalities increase just after publicised suicide stories. *Science*, **196**, 1464–5 **(582)**

Phillips, G. T., Gossop, M. and Bradley, B. (1986) The influence of psychological factors on the opiate withdrawal syndrome. *British Journal of Psychiatry*, **149**, 235–8 **(470)**

Phillips, G. T., Gossop, M. R., Edwards, G., Sutherland, G., Taylor, C. and Strang, J. (1987) The application of the SODQ to the measurement of the severity of opiate dependence in a British sample. *British Journal of Addictions*, **82** , 691–9 **(470)**

Phillips, M. (1983) Some trends and issues in the delivery of forensic psychiatry services in Canada. In *Basic Forensic Psychiatry* (eds. S. J. Hucker and R. E. Turner) Clarke Institute of Psychiatry & Department of Justice: Toronto **(155)**

Phillips, M. (1986) *A Study of Suicides and Attempted Suicides at HMP Brixton 1973–1990*, DPS Report, Series 1, No. 24 Prison Department, Home Office: London **(814)**

Philpotts, G. J. D. and Lancucki, L. B. (1979) Previous convictions, sentence and reconviction. *Home Office Research Study No. 53*, HMSO: London **(785)**

Pickering, G. (1962) Postgraduate medical education: the present opportunity and the immediate need. *British Medical Journal*, **i**, 421–5 **(4)**

Pillard, R. C. (1970) Marijuana. *New England Journal of Medicine*, **283**, 292–4 **(468)**

Pilowsky, I. (1969) Abnormal illness behaviour. *British Journal of Medical Psychology*, **42**, 347–51 **(414)**

Pithers, W. D. (1990) Relapse prevention with sexual aggressors. In *Handbook of Sexual Assault. Illness, Theories and Treatment of the Offender* (eds. W. C. Marshall, D. R. Laws and H. E. Barakee) Plenum Press: New York **(558)**

Pitman, R. K., Orr, S. P., Forque, D. F., De Jong, J. B. and Claiborn, J. M. (1987) Psychophysiologic assessment of post-traumatic stress disorder imagery in Vietnam combat veterans. *Archives of General Psychiatry*, **44**, 970–5 **(889)**

Pizzey, E. (1974) *Scream Quietly or the Neighbours will Hear*, Penguin: Harmondsworth **(509)**

Pizzey, E. and Shapiro, J. (1982) *Prone to Violence*, Hamlyn Paperbacks: Middlesex **(911, 920)**

Planansky, K. and Johnston, R. (1977) Homicidal aggression in schizophrenic men. *Acta Psychiatrica Scandinavica*, 55, 65–73 (**336, 338, 349, 368**)

Podolsky, E. (1964) The manic murderer. *Corrective Psychiatry and Journal of Social Therapy*, 10, 213–7 (**348**)

Pokorny, A. D. (1965) Human violence: a comparison of homicide, aggravated assault, suicide and attempted suicide. *Journal of Criminal Law, Criminology and Political Science*, 56, 488–97 (**363**)

Polakoff, S. A., Sorgi, P. J. and Ratey, J. J. (1986) The treatment of impulsive and aggressive behaviour with nadolol. *Journal of Clinical Psychopharmacology*, 6, 125–6 (**662**)

Pollack, J. M. (1979) Obsessive-compulsive personality: a review. *Psychological Bulletin*, 86, 225–41 (**378**)

Pollack, S. (1980) Psychiatry and the administration of justice. In *Modern Legal Medicine, Psychiatry and Forensic Science* (eds. W. J. Curran, A. L. McGarry and C. S. Petty) T. A. Davis: Philadelphia (**882**)

Pollak, O. (1950) *The Criminality of Women*, University of Pennsylvania Press: New York (**601–605 passim**)

Pollock, F. and Maitland, F. W. (1968) *The History of English Law, vol. 1*, 2nd edn, Cambridge University Press: Cambridge (**23**)

Pollock, H. M. (1938) Is the paroled patient a menace to the community? *Psychiatric Quarterly*, 12, 236–44 (**333**)

Pomeroy, V. C. and Ricketts, B. (1985) Long-term attendance in the psychiatric outpatient department for non-psychotic illness. *British Journal of Psychiatry*, 147, 508–16 (**861**)

Pompi, K. F. and Resnick, J. (1987) Retention of court referred adolescents and young adults in the therapeutic community. *American Journal on Drug and Alcohol Abuse*, 13, 309–25 (**477**)

Pond, D. A. and Bidwell, B. H. (1960) A survey of epilepsy in fourteen general practices, II. Social and psychological aspects. *Epilepsia*, 1, 285–99 (**300, 583**)

Pond, D. A. and Espir, M. (1971) Epilepsy. In *Medical Aspects of Fitness to Drive* (ed. A. Raffle) Royal College of Surgeons, Medical Commission on Accident Prevention: London (**583**)

Porter, R. (1991) History of psychiatry in Britain. *History of Psychiatry*, 2, 271–9 (**691**)

Posen, I. (1979) *A Survey of Women in Holloway with Children under Five*, Psychology Unit, Holloway Prison: London (unpublished) (**622**)

Post, R. M., Uhde, T. W., Roy-Byrne, P. P. and Joffee, R. T. (1986) Antidepressant effects of carbamazepine. *American Journal of Psychiatry*, 143, 29–34 (**666**)

Powell, G. E., Gudjonsson, G. H. and Mullen, P. (1983) Application of the guilty-knowledge technique in a case of pseudologia fantastica. *Personality and Individual Differences*, 4, 141–6 (**413**)

Power, M. J., Alderson, M. R., Phillipson, C. M., Shoenberg, E., and Morris, J. N. (1967) Delinquent Schools? *New Society*, 10, 542–3 (**268**)

Power, M. J., Benn, R. T. and Morris, J. N. (1972) Neighbourhood, school and juveniles before the courts. *British Journal of Criminology*, 12, 111–32 (**273**)

Prentky, R. (1985) The neurochemistry and neuroendrocrinology of sexual aggression. In *Aggression and Dangerousness* (eds. D. P. Farrington and J. Gunn) Wiley: Chichester (**523, 602**)

Prentky, R. A., Knight, R. A., Sims-Knight, J. E., Straus, H., Rokous, R. and Cerce, D. (1989) Developmental antecedents of sexual aggression. *Development and Psychopathology*, 1, 153–69 (**538**)

President's Commission (1967) *Task Force Report: Juvenile Delinquency and Youth Crime*, US Government Printing Office: Washington DC (**219**)

Prewer, R. R. (1959) Some observations on window-smashing. *British Journal of Delinquency*, 10, 104–13 (**587**)

Price, W. H. and Whatmore, P. B. (1967) Behaviour disorders and pattern of crime among XYY males identified at a maximum security hospital. *British Medical Journal*, 1, 533–6 (**314**)

Priestley, P. (1989) *Jail Journeys: The English Prison Experience 1918–1990*, Routledge & Kegan Paul: London (**802**)

Prigatano, G. P. (1987) Psychiatric aspects of head injury: problem areas and suggested guidelines for research. In *Neurobehavioral Recovery of Head Injury* (eds. H. S. Levin, J. Grafman and H. M. Eisenberg) Oxford University Press: New York (**287**)

Primrose, D. A. (1984) Changing sociological and clinical patterns in mental handicap. *British Journal of Psychiatry*, **1441**, 1–8 (318)

Prince, J. (1980) Shoplifting. *The Police Surgeon*, **17**, 31–6 (577)

Prince, M. (1906) *The Dissociation of Personality*, Longmans Green: London (427, 429)

Prins, H. (1980) *Offenders, Deviants or Patients?* Tavistock: London (323)

Prins, H., Tennent, G. and Trick, K. (1985) Motives for arson (fire raising). *Medicine, Science and the Law*, **25**, 275–8 (588)

Prison Reform Trust (1991) HIV and AIDS, and prisons. *Update*, Prison Reform Trust: London (821)

Prochaska, J. O. and DiClemente, C. C. (1983) Stages and processes of self-change of smoking: toward an integrative model of change. *Journal of Consulting and Clinical Psychology*, **51**, 390–5 (477)

Prochaska, J. O. and DiClemente, C. C. (1986) Towards a comprehensive model of change. In *Treating Addictive Behaviors* (eds. W. E. C. Miller and N. Heather) Plenum Press: New York (477)

Prudhomme, C. (1941) Epilepsy and suicide. *Journal of Nervous and Mental Disease*, **94**, 722–31 (310)

Psarska, A. D. (1970) Jealousy factors in homicide in forensic material. *Polish Medical Journal*, **9**, 1504–10 (352)

Pulkkinen, L. (1988) Delinquent development: theoretical and empirical considerations. In *Studies of Psychosocial Risk* (ed. M. Rutter) Cambridge University Press: Cambridge, pp. 184–99 (255)

Quayle, M. T. (1989) *Group Therapy for Personality Disordered Offenders*. Paper presented at annual conference of special hospital psychologists—unpublished—cited in Perkins, 1991 (559)

Quinn, J. T., Harbison, J. J. M. and McAllister, H. (1970) An attempt to shape human penile responses. *Behavior Research and Therapy*, **8**, 213–6 (561)

Quinsey, V. L. (1984) Sexual aggression: studies of offenders against women. In *Law and Mental Health: International Perspectives, vol. 1* (ed. D. Weisstub) Pergamon: New York (543)

Quinsey, V. L. (1986) Men who have sex with children. In *Law and Mental Health, vol. 2* (ed. D. Weisstub) Pergamon: Oxford (532, 533, 534)

Quinsey, V. L., Chaplin, T. C. and Carrigan, W. F. (1979) Sexual preferences amongst incestuous and non-incestuous child molesters. *Behavior Therapy*, **10**, 562–5 (538)

Quinsey, V. L., Chaplin, T. C. and Varney, G. A. (1981) A comparison of rapists and non-sex offenders' sexual preferences for mutually consenting sex, rape, and physical abuse. *Behavioral Assessment*, **3**, 127–35 (545)

Quinsey, V. and Maguire, A. (1986) Maximum security psychiatry patients: actuarial and clinical prediction of dangerousness. *Journal of Interpersonal Violence*, **1**, 143–71 (554, 644)

Quinton, D., Rutter, M. and Liddle, C. (1984) Institutional rearing, parenting difficulties and marital support. *Psychological Medicine*, **14**, 107–24 (382)

Quitkin, F., Rifkin, A. and Klein, D. F. (1975) Very high dosage v. standard dosage fluphenazine in schizophrenia. *Archives of General Psychiatry*, **32**, 1276–81 (663)

Rachlin, S. (1974) With liberty and psychosis for all. *Psychiatric Quarterly*, **48**, 410–9 (873)

Radbill, S. X. (1968) A history of child abuse and infanticide. In *The Battered Child* (eds. R. E. Helfer and C. H. Kempe) University of Chicago Press: Chicago (501)

Radelet, M. L. and Barnard, G. W. (1986) Ethics and the psychiatric determination of competency to be executed. *Bulletin of the American Academy of Psychiatry and the Law*, **14**, 37–53 (122)

Radelet, M. L. and Barnard, G. W. (1988) Treating those found incompetent for execution: ethical chaos with only one solution. *Bulletin of the American Academy of Psychiatry and the Law*, **16**, 297–308 (122)

Raffle, P. A. B. (1970) The occupational physician as community physician. *Proceedings of the Royal Society of Medicine*, **63**, 731–9 (583)

Raffle, P. A. B. (1985) *Medical Aspects of Fitness to Drive, 4th edn*, Medical Commission on Accident Prevention: London (115, 586)

Ramirez, L. F. (1988) Plasma cortisol and depression in pathological gamblers. *British Journal of Psychiatry*, **153**, 684–6 (485)

Ramsey, R. W. (1977) Behavioral approaches to bereavement. *Behavior Research and Therapy*, **15**, 131–5 (938)

Randell, J. (1970) Transvestism and trans-sexualism. *British Journal of Hospital Medicine*, **3**, 211–3 (**550, 551**)

Rapoport, R., (1960) *Community as Doctor*, Tavistock: London (**686**)

Rappeport, J. R. and Lasson, G. (1965) Dangerousness—arrest rate comparisons of discharged mental patients and the general population. *American Journal of Psychiatry*, **121**, 776–83 (**333**)

Rasch, W. (1981) The effects of indeterminate detention: a study of men sentenced to life imprisonment. *International Journal of Law & Psychiatry*, **4**, 417–31 (**761**)

Raskin, D. E. and Sullivan, K. E. (1974) Erotomania. *American Journal of Psychiatry*, **131**, 1033–5 (**353**)

Rasmussen, O. V. and Lunde, I. (1980) Evaluation of investigation of 200 torture victims. *Danish Medical Bulletin*, **27**, 241–3 (**924**)

Raspe, R. E. (1786) *The Surprising Adventures of Baron Munchausen* (ed. F. J. H. Darton) Navarre Society 1930: London (**422**)

Ratcliff, R. A. W. (1988) The progress of 'state' (i.e. 'restricted') patients after transfer or discharge from the State Hospital at Carstairs, from 1.1.78 to 1.1.88. *Health Bulletin*, **46**, 200–4 (**709**)

Ratcliffe, S. G., Stewart, A. L., Melville, M. M., Jacobs, P. A. and Keay, A. J. (1970) Chromosome studies on 3500 newborn male infants. *Lancet*, **i**, 121–2 (**314**)

Ray, I. (1838) *A Treatise on the Medical Jurisprudence of Insanity* (Ch.XV Simulated Insanity) Reprinted (1962) Harvard University Press: Cambridge, Mass. (**407, 418**)

Reason, J. and Lucas, D. (1984) Absent mindedness in shops: its incidence, correlates and consequences. *British Journal of Clinical Psychology*, **23**, 121–31 (**575**)

Reeve, A. (1983) *Notes from a Waiting Room*, Heretic Books: London (**697**)

Regier, D. A., Boyd, J. H., Burke, J. D., Rae, D. S., Myers, J. K., Kramer, M., Robins, L. N., George, L. K., Karno, M. and Locke, B. Z. (1988) One month prevalence of mental disorders in the United States. *Archives of General Psychiatry*, **45**, 977–86 (**616**)

Regier, D. A., Myers, J. K. and Kraner, M. (1984) The Epidemiologic Catchment Area program. *Archives of General Psychiatry*, **41**, 934–41 (**332**)

Reid, A., Lea, J. and Wallace, D. (1982) Rehabilitation on Elton Ward, an Interim Secure Unit: a description after four and a half years. *Nursing Times*, **78**, 20–32 (**715**)

Reid, I. (1982) The development and maintenance of a behavioural regime in a secure youth treatment centre. In *The Prevention and Control of Offending* (ed. P. Feldman) Wiley: Chichester (**235, 236, 714**)

Reid, W. H. (1985) The antisocial personality: a review. *Hospital and Community Psychiatry*, **36**, 831–7 (**654, 685**)

Reiss, A. J. (1986) Why are communities important in understanding crime? In *Communities and Crime* (eds. A. J. Reiss and M. Tonry) University of Chicago Press: Chicago, (**274**)

Reiss, A. J. (1988) Co-offending and criminal careers. In *Crime and Justice vol. 10* (eds. M. Tonry and N. Morris) University of Chicago Press: Chicago (**265, 268**)

Reiss, A. J., and Farrington, D. P. (1991) Advancing knowledge about co-offending: results from a prospective longitudinal survey of London males. *Journal of Criminal Law and Criminology*, **82**, 360–95 (**265**)

Reitman, B. and Cleveland, S. (1964) Changes in body image following sensory deprivation in schizophrenia and control groups. *Journal of Abnormal and Social Psychology*, **68**, 168–76 (**659**)

Remschmidt, H., Hohner, G., Merschmann, W. and Walter, R. (1977) Epidemiology of delinquent behaviour in children. In *Epidemiological Approaches to Child Psychiatry* (ed. P. J. Graham) Academic Press: London (**271**)

Research and Advisory Group on the Long-Term Prison System (1987) *Special Units for Long-Term Prisoners: Regimes, Management and Research*, HMSO: London (**807**)

Resnick, M. and Burton, B. T. (1984) Droperidol vs. haloperidol in the initial management of acutely agitated patients. *Journal of Clinical Psychiatry*, **45**, 298–9 (**661**)

Resnick, P. J. (1969) Child murder by parents: a psychiatric review of filicide. *American Journal of Psychiatry*, **126**, 325–34 (**610**)

Resnick, P. J. (1970) Murder of the newborn: a psychiatric review of neonaticide. *American Journal of Psychiatry*, **126**, 1414–20 (**610, 611**)

Ressler, R., Burgess, A. W. and Douglas, J. (1983) Rape and rape murder: one offender and twelve victims. *American Journal of Psychiatry*, **140**, 36–40 (**915**)

Revicki, D. A., Luce, B. R., Weschler, J. M., Brown, R. E. and Adler, M. A. (1990) Cost-effectiveness of clozapine for treatment-resistant schizophrenic patients. *Hospital and Community Psychiatry*, **41**, 850–4 (**666**)

Reynolds, A. (1991) *Tightrope*, Sidgwick & Jackson: London **(607)**

Riccio, M. L. and Thompson C. (1987) AIDS and dementia. *British Journal of Hospital Medicine*, 38, 11 **(470)**

Rich, J. (1956) Types of stealing. *Lancet* i, 496–8 **(570)**

Richards, B. (1978) The experience of long-term imprisonment. *British Journal of Criminology*, 18, 162–9 **(804)**

Richman, J. (1987) Legal aid at work. *The Magistrate*, 43, 123–4 **(174)**

Richman, J. and Draycott, A. T. (1988) *Stone's Justices' Manual. 1988. One hundred and twentieth edition*, Butterworth: London **(171)**

Rifkin, A., Quitkin, F., Carillo, C. and Klein, D. F. (1971) Very high dosage fluphenazine for non-chronic treatment-refractory patients. *Archives of General Psychiatry*, 25, 398–403 **(663)**

Rifkin, A., Quitkin, F., Carillo, C., Blumberg, A. G. and Klein, D. F. (1972) Lithium carbonate in emotionally unstable character disorder. *Archives of General Psychiatry*, 27, 519–23 **(366, 668)**

Rimon, R., Averbuch, I., Rozick, P., Fijman-Danilovich, L., Kara, T., Dasberg, H., Ebstein, R. and Belmaker, R. H. (1981) Serum and CSF levels of haloperidol by radioimmunoassay and radiorecepter assay during high-dose therapy of resistant schizophrenic patients. *Psychopharmacology*, 73, 197–9 **(663)**

Rinella, V. J. (1976) Rehabilitation or bust: the impact of criminal justice system referrals on the treatment of drug addicts and alcoholics in a therapeutic community (Eagleville's experience). *American Journal of Drug and Alcohol Abuse*, 3, 53–8 **(477)**

Ritchie, S. (1985) *Report to the Secretary of State for Social Services concerning the Death of Mr Michael Martin at Broadmoor Hospital on 6th July 1984* (private circulation) **(799)**

Rix, G. (1988) Nursing the violent patient. In *Using Nursing Models* (ed. B . Collister) Hodder & Stoughton: London **(653)**

Rix, G. and Seymour, D. (1988) Violent incidents on a regional secure unit. *Journal of Advanced Nursing*, 13, 746–51 **(807)**

Robbins, D. M., Beck, J. C., Preis, R., Jacobs, D. and Smith, C. (1983) Learning disability and neuropsychological impairment in adjudicated, unincarcerated male delinquents. *Journal of American Academy of Child Psychiatry*, 2, 40–6 **(289)**

Robertson, G. (1981) The extent and pattern of crime amongst mentally handicapped offenders. *Apex, Journal of British Institute of Mental Handicap*, 9, 100–3 **(319, 320, 324)**

Robertson, G. (1982) The 1959 Mental Health Act of England & Wales: changes in the use of its criminal provisions. In *Abnormal Offenders, Delinquency and the Criminal Justice System* (eds. J. Gunn and D. Farington) Wiley: Chichester **(861)**

Robertson, G. (1987) Mentally abnormal offenders: manner of death. *British Medical Journal*, 295, 632–4 **(397)**

Robertson, G. (1988) Arrest patterns among mentally disordered offenders. *British Journal of Psychiatry*, 153, 313–6 **(332)**

Robertson, G. (1989) Treatment for offender patients: how should success be measured? *Medicine, Science and the Law*, 29, 303–7 **(688)**

Robertson, G. and Gibbens, T. C. N. (1980) Transfers from prisons to local psychiatric hospitals under section 72 of the 1959 Mental Health Act. *British Medical Journal*, 280, 1263–6 **(756)**

Robertson, G. and Gunn, J. (1987) A ten year follow-up of men discharged from Grendon prison. *British Journal of Psychiatry*, 151, 674–8 **(290, 689, 690, 750, 776)**

Robertson, G. and Taylor, P. J. (1985) a. Some cognitive correlates of schizophrenic illnesses. *Psychological Medicine*, 15, 81–98. b. Some cognitive correlates of affective disorders. *Psychological Medicine*, 15, 297–309 **(290, 338)**

Robertson, G., Taylor, P. J. and Gunn, J. (1987) Does violence have cognitive correlates? *British Journal of Psychiatry*, 151, 63–8 **(323)**

Robertson, R. G., Bankier, R. G. and Schwartz, L. (1987) The female offender: a Canadian study. *Canadian Journal of Psychiatry*, 32, 749–55 **(615)**

Robins, L. N. (1966) *Deviant Children Grown Up*, Williams and Wilkins: Baltimore **(255, 383)**

Robins, L. N. (1978) Sturdy predictors of adult antisocial behaviour: replications from longitudinal studies. *Psychological Medicine*, 8, 611–22 **(263, 271, 284, 383)**

Robins, L. N., and Ratcliff, K. S. (1980) Childhood conduct disorders and later arrest. In *The Social Consequences of Psychiatric Illness* (eds. L. N. Robins, P. J. Clayton and J. K. Wing) Brunner/Mazel: New York **(262)**

Robins, L. N., West, P. J. and Herjanic, B. L. (1975) Arrests and delinquency in two generations: a study of black urban families and their children. *Journal of Child Psychology and Psychiatry*, **16**, 125–40 (**264**)

Robins, L. N., Helzer, J. C., Croughan, J., Williams, J. B. W. and Spitzer, R. L. (1979) *The National Institute of Mental Health Diagnostic Interview Schedule*, NIMH: Rockville, MD (**255**)

Roff, J. D. and Wirt, R. D. (1984) Childhood aggression and social adjustment as antecedents of delinquency. *Journal of Abnormal Child Psychology*, **12**, 111–26 (**267, 270**)

Rofman, E. S., Askinazi, C. and Fant, E. (1980) The prediction of dangerous behavior in emergency civil commitment. *American Journal of Psychiatry*, **137**, 1061–4 (**338, 804**)

Rogers, A. and Faulkner, A. (1987) *A Place of Safety*, MIND: London (**736**)

Rogers, C. R. (1961) *On Becoming a Person*, Houghton Mifflin Company: Boston (**8**)

Rogers, J. L., Bloom, J. D. and Manson, S. M. (1984) Insanity defenses: contested or conceded? *American Journal of Psychiatry*, **141**, 885–8 (**144**)

Rogers, R., Nussbaum, D. and Gillis, R. (1988) Command hallucinations and criminality: a clinical quandary. *Bulletin of the American Academy of Psychiatry and the Law*, **16**, 251–8 (**344, 345**)

Ron, M. A. (1983) The alcoholic brain: CT scan and psychological findings. *Psychological Medicine, Monograph, Suppl. 3*, Cambridge University Press: Cambridge (**62, 294, 443, 444**)

Ron, M. A. (1986) Volatile substance abuse: a review of possible long-term neurological, intellectual and psychiatric sequelae. *British Journal of Psychiatry*, **148**, 235–46 (**471**)

Rooth, F. G. (1971) Indecent exposure and exhibitionism. *British Journal of Hospital Medicine*, **5**, 521–34 (**448, 548**)

Rooth, F. G. (1973) Exhibitionism, sexual violence and paedophilia. *British Journal of Psychiatry*, **122**, 705–10 (**548**)

Roper, W. F. (1950) A comparative survey of the Wakefield prison population in 1948. Part 1. *British Journal of Delinquency*, **1**, 15–28 (**322**)

Roper, W. F. (1951) A comparative survey of the Wakefield prison population in 1948 and 1949. Part 2. *British Journal of Delinquency*, **1**, 243–70 (**322**)

Roscoe, J. (1988) *Prediction of Inpatient Violence from Prior Violent Behaviour* (unpublished) (**805**)

Rose, N. (1985) Unreasonable rights: mental illness and the limits of law. *Journal of Law and Society*, **12**, 199–219 (**798**)

Rose, N. (1986) Law, rights and psychiatry, *The Power of Psychiatry* (eds. P. Miller and N. Rose) Polity Press: Cambridge (**797, 798, 831**)

Rosenfeld, A. A. (1979) Incidence of a history of incest among 18 female psychiatric patients. *American Journal of Psychiatry*, **136**, 791–5 (**931**)

Rosenfeld, H. (1952) Transference-phenomena and transference-analysis in an acute catatonic schizophrenic patient. *International Journal of Psychoanalysis*, **33**, 457–64 (**679**)

Rosenfield, I. (1988) *The Invention of Memory*, Basic Books: New York (**411**)

Rosenhan, D. L. (1973) On being sane in insane places. *Science*, **179**, 250–8 (**419**)

Ross, C. F. J. (1971) Comparison of hospital and prison alcoholics. *British Journal of Psychiatry*, **118**, 75–8 (**456**)

Ross, R. J., Ball, W. A., Sullivan, K. A. and Caroff, S. N. (1989) Sleep disturbance as the hallmark of post-traumatic stress disorder. *American Journal of Psychiatry*, **146**, 697–707 (**932**)

Ross, R. R. and Fabiano, E. A. (1985) *Time to Think. A Cognitive Model of Delinquency Prevention and Offending Rehabilitation*, Institute of Social Services & Arts: Johnson City, NJ (**675**)

Ross, R. R., Fabiano, E. A. and Ewles, C. D. (1988) Reasoning and rehabilitation. *International Journal of Offender Therapy and Comparative Criminology*, **32**, 29–35 (**281**)

Ross, R. R. and Ross, B. D. (1988) Delinquency prevention through cognitive training. *New Education*, **10**, 70–5 (**281**)

Rossi, A., Jacobs, M., Monteleone, M., Olsen, R., Surber, R., Winkler, E. and Wommack, A. (1986) Characteristics of psychiatric patients who engage in assaultive or other fear-inducing behaviors. *Journal of Nervous and Mental Disease*, **174**, 154–60 (**349, 642**)

Rossi, P. H., Berk, R. A. and Lenihan, K. J. (1980) *Money, Work and Crime*, Academic Press: New York (**284**)

Roth, L. (1979) A commitment law for patients, doctors, and lawyers. *American Journal of Psychiatry*, **136**, 1121–7 (**640**)

Roth, L. (1980) Correctional psychiatry. In *Modern Legal Medicine, Psychiatry and Forensic Science* (eds. W. J. Curran, A. L. McGarry and C. S. Petty) Davis: Philadelphia **(766, 768)**

Roth, L. (1985) *Clinical Treatment of the Violent Person*, US Department of Health and Human Services: Rockville, MD **(635)**

Roth, L. R. and Ervin, F. R. (1971) Psychiatric care of federal prisoners, psychiatric disorders and criminal recidivism. *American Journal of Psychiatry*, 128, 424–30 **(334)**

Roth, L. H., Lidz, C. W., Meisel, A., Soloff, P. H., Kaufmann, K., Spiker, D. G. and Foster, F. G. (1982) Competency to decide about treatment or research—an overview of some empirical data. *International Journal of Law and Psychiatry*, 5 , 29–50 **(877)**

Roth, M. (1968) Cerebral disease and mental disorders of old age as causes of antisocial behaviour. In *The Mentally Abnormal Offender* (eds. A. V. S. de Reuck and R. Porter) Churchill: London **(327)**

Roth, S., Dye, E. and Lebowitz, L. (1988) Group therapy for sexual assault victims. *Psychotherapy*, 25, 82–93 **(939)**

Rothenberg, A. (1971) On anger. *American Journal of Psychiatry*, 128, 454–60 **(675)**

Rothenberg, M. (1975) Effect of television violence on children and youth *Journal of American Medical Association* 234: 1043–6 **(496, 497)**

Rothstein, D. A. (1964) Presidential assassination syndrome. *Archives of General Psychiatry*, 11, 245–54 **(518)**

Rotter, J. B. (1966) Generalised expectancies for internal versus external control of reinforcement. *Psychological Monographs* Vol. 80, No. 1 **(930)**

Rounsaville, B. J. (1978) Battered wives: barriers to identification and treatment. *American Journal of Orthopsychiatry*, 48, 487–94 **(902)**

Rounsaville, B. J., Rosenberger, P., Wilber, C., Weissman, M. N. and Kleber, H. D. (1980) A comparison of the SAD/RDC and the DSM–III. *Journal of Nervous and Mental Disease*, 168, 90–7 **(470)**

Rounsaville, B. J., Weismann, M. M., Wilber, C. H. and Kleber, H. (1982) Pathways to opiate addiction: an evaluation of different antecedents. *British Journal of Psychiatry*, 141, 437–46 **(471)**

Rowe, D. C. (1987) Resolving the person-situation debate: invitation to an interdisciplinary dialogue. *American Psychologist*, 42, 218–27 **(258)**

Rowe, D. C. and Osgood, D. W. (1984) Heredity and sociological theories of delinquency: a reconsideration. *American Sociological Review*, 49, 526–40 **(258)**

Rowlands, M. W. D. (1988) Psychiatric and legal aspects of persistent litigation. *British Journal of Psychiatry*, 153, 317–23 **(355, 356)**

Roy, A. (1977) Hysterical fits previously diagnosed as epilepsy. *Psychological Medicine*, 7, 271–3 **(423)**

Roy, A. (1985) Suicide and psychiatric patients. *Psychiatric Clinics of North America*, 8, 227–41 **(812)**

Roy, A., Adinoff, B., Roehrich, L., Lamparski, D., Custor, R., Lorenz, V., Barbaccia, M., Guidotti, A., Costa, E. and Lkinnoila, M. (1988) Pathological gambling. *Archives of General Psychiatry*, 45, 369–73 **(485)**

Royal College of Physicians (1990a) *Compensation for adverse consequences of medical intervention*. Royal College of Physicians of London **(107)**

Royal College of Physicians (1990b) *The Prison Medical Service in England and Wales*, A Report of a Working party of the Royal College of Physicians to the Chief Medical Officer 1989. Dmd.8255369, HMSO: London **(741)**

Royal College of Psychiatrists (1977) Evidence to the Select Committee on Violence in the Family. In *First Report from the Select Committee on Violence in the Family Session 1976–7 Vol. II Evidence*, House of Commons, HMSO: London **(503)**

Royal College of Psychiatrists (1980) *Secure Facilities for Psychiatric Patients: A Comprehensive Policy*, Royal College of Psychiatrists: London **(694)**

Royal College of Psychiatrists (1982) Locking up patients by themselves. *Bulletin of the Royal College of Psychiatrists*, 6, 199–200 **(658)**

Royal College of Psychiatrists (1983) Medical visitors and the Court of Protection. *Bulletin of the Royal College of Psychiatrists*, 7, 34–5 **(199)**

Royal College of Psychiatrists (1986) *Alcohol: our Favourite Drug*, Tavistock: London **(436)**

Royal College of Psychiatrists (1987) *Community Treatment Orders: A Discussion Document*, Royal College of Psychiatrists: London **(726)**

Royal College of Psychiatrists (1990a) The seclusion of psychiatric patients. *Psychiatric Bulletin*, 14, 754–6 (658)

Royal College of Psychiatrists (1990b) Position statement on confidentiality. *Psychiatric Bulletin*, 14, 97–109 (864)

Royal College of Psychiatrists (1991) *Good Medical Practice in the Aftercare of Potentially Violent and Vulnerable Patients Discharged from Inpatient Psychiatric Treatment*, Royal College of Psychiatrists: London (107, 725)

Royal Commission on Assizes and Quarter Sessions, 1966–9 (1969) *Report*, Cmnd.4153, HMSO: London (169)

Royal Commission on Capital Punishment (1953) *Report 1949–1953*, Cmnd.8932, HMSO: London (760)

Royal Commission on Civil Liability and Compensation for Personal Injury (1978) *Report, Vol. 1*, Cmnd.7054–1, HMSO: London (173)

Royal Commission on Criminal Procedure (1981) *Report*, Cmnd. 8092, HMSO: London (172, 739)

Royal Commission on Gambling (1978) *Final Report of the Royal Commission on Gambling* (Rothschild), Cmnd.7200, HMSO: London (481)

Royal Commission on the Police (1962) *Final Report*, Cmnd.1728, HMSO: London (171)

Rubenstein, D. (1984) The elderly in prison: A review of the literature. In *Elderly Criminals* (eds. E. S. Newman, D. J. Newman and M. L. Gerwitz) Oelgeschlager, Gunn, and Hain: Cambridge, Mass. (328)

Rubenstein, E. A. (1974) The TV violence report: what's next? *Journal of Communication*, (Winter) p. 85 (497)

Ruch, L., Chandler, S. and Hunter, R. (1980) Life change and rape impact. *Journal of Health and Social Behaviors*, 21, 248–60 (894)

Rudden, M., Gilmore, M. and Frances, A. (1982) Delusions: when to confront the facts of life. *American Journal of Psychiatry*, 139, 929–32 (337)

Rudden, M., Sweeney, J. and Allen, F. (1990) Diagnosis and clinical course of erotomanic and other delusional patients. *American Journal of Psychiatry*, 147, 625–8 (353, 354)

Runyan, D. K., Everson, M. D., Edelsohn, G. A., Hunter, W. M., Coulter, M. L. and Hill, C. (1988) Impact of legal intervention on sexually abused children. *Journal of Paediatrics*, 113, 647–53 (919)

Russell, D. E. H. (1986) *The Secret Trauma: Incest in the Lives of Girls and Women*. Basic Books: New York (917)

Russell, W. R. and Nathan, P. W. (1946) Traumatic amnesia. *Brain*, 69, 280–300 (296)

Rutherford, A. (1986a) *Growing out of Crime*, Penguin: Harmondsworth (228)

Rutherford, A. (1986b) *Prisons and the Process of Justice*, Oxford University Press: Oxford (802)

Rutherford, W. and Fee, C. R. A. (1988) No fault compensation. *British Medical Journal*, 297, 1405 (letter) (107)

Rutter, M. (1980) *Scientific Foundations of Developmental Psychiatry*, Heinemann: London (380)

Rutter, M. (1981a) The city and the child. *American Journal of Orthopsychiatry*, 51, 610–25 (274)

Rutter, M. (1981b) Isle of Wight and Inner London studies. In *Prospective Longitudinal Research* (eds. S. A. Mednick and E. E. Baert) Oxford University Press: Oxford (255)

Rutter, M. (1985) Infantile autism and other pervasive developmental disorders. In *Child and Adolescent Psychiatry. Modern Approaches* (eds. M. Rutter and L. Hersov) Blackwell Scientific: Oxford (383)

Rutter, M. (1987) Temperament, personality and personality disorder. *British Journal of Psychiatry*, 150, 443–58 (373, 381)

Rutter, M., Cox, A., Tupling, C., Berger, M. and Yule, W. (1975a) Attainment and adjustment in two geographical areas: I. The prevalence of psychiatric disorder. *British Journal of Psychiatry*, 126, 493–509 (273)

Rutter, M. and Giller, H. (1983) *Juvenile Delinquency. Trends and Perspectives*, Penguin: London (291, 222, 253, 451, 604)

Rutter, M. and Madge, N. (1976) *Cycles of Disadvantage*, Heinemann: London (921)

Rutter, M., Maughan, B., Mortimore, P. and Ouston, J. (1979) *Fifteen Thousand Hours*. Open Books: London (269)

Rutter, M., Quinton, D. and Hill, J. (1990) Adult outcome of institute reared children: males and females compared. In *Straight and Dubious Partnerships from Childhood to Adulthood* (eds. L. Robins and M. Rutter) Cambridge University Press: New York **(382)**

Rutter, M., Yule, B., Morton, J. and Bagley, C. (1975b) Children of West Indian immigrants: III. Home circumstances and family patterns. *Journal of Child Psychology and Psychiatry*, **16**, 105–23 **(277)**

Rutter, M., Yule, B., Quinton, D., Rowlands, O., Yule, W. and Berger, M. (1975c) Attainment and adjustment in two geographical areas: III. Some factors accounting for area differences. *British Journal of Psychiatry*, **126**, 520–33 **(273)**

Rycroft, C. (1968) *A Critical Dictionary of Psychoanalysis*, Nelson: London **(679)**

Sacks, M. H., Carpenter, W. T. and Strauss, J. S. (1974) Recovery from delusions. *Archives of General Psychiatry*, **30**, 117–20 **(337)**

Sadoff, R. L. (1988) Ethical issues in forensic psychiatry. *Psychiatric Annals*, **18**, 320–3 **(881)**

Sagarin, E. (1976) Prison homosexuality and its effect on post-prison sexual behaviour. *Psychiatry*, **39**, 245–57 **(547, 916, 922)**

Saghir, M. T. and Robins, E. (1973) *Male and Female Homosexuality. A Comprehensive Investigation*, Williams and Wilkins: Baltimore **(540)**

Sakuta, T. and Saito, S. (1981) A socio-medical study of 71 cases of infanticide in Japan. *Keio Journal of Medicine*, **30**, 155–68 **(612)**

Salter, A. C. (1988) *Treating Child Sex Offenders and Victims; A Practical Guide*, Sage: London **(557)**

Sampson, G. A. (1987) Premenstrual syndrome: characterisation, therapies and the law. In *Premenstrual Syndrome. Ethical and Legal Issues in a Biomedical Perspective* (eds. B. E. Ginsburg and B. F. Carter) Plenum Press: New York **(607)**

Samuels, A. (1973) Criminal Injuries Compensation Board. *Criminal Law Review*, 418–31 **(105)**

Samuels, A. (1986) Non-crown prosecutions by non-police agencies and by private individuals. *Criminal Law Review*, 33–44 **(172, 173)**

Sanday, P. R. (1981) The socio-cultural context of rape: a cross-cultural study. *Journal of Social Issues*, **37**, 5–27 **(528, 545)**

Sandberg, A. A., Koepf, G. F., Ishihara, T. and Hauschka, T. S. (1961) An XYY human male. *Lancet*, ii, 588–9 **(314)**

Sanders, A. (1986) An independent Crown Prosecution Service? *Criminal Law Review*, 16–27 **(172)**

Sandfort, T. (1987) *Boys on their Contacts with Men*, Global Academic: Elmhurst, NY **(535)**

Sansone, J. (1980) Retention patterns in the therapeutic community for the treatment of drug abuse. *International Journal of the Addictions*, **15**, 711–36 **(477)**

Sapira, J. O. and Cherubin, C. E. (1975) Drug abuse: a guide to the clinician *Excerpta Medica*, Amsterdam 365–83, pp. 216–8 **(471)**

Sapsford, R. J., (1978) Life-sentence prisoners: psychological changes during sentence. *British Journal of Criminology*, **18**, 128–45 **(803)**

Sapsford, R. J. (1983) *Life Sentenced Prisoners—Reaction, Response and Change*. Open University Press: Milton Keynes **(761, 809)**

Sapsford, R. J. and Fairhead, S. (1980) Reconviction, alcohol and mental disorder. *British Journal of Criminology*, **20**, 157–65 **(451)**

Sargant, W. (1957) *Battle for the Mind*, Heinemann: London **(927)**

Sarri, R. (1983) Paradigms and pitfalls in juvenile justice diversion. In *Providing Criminal Justice for Children* (eds. A. Miller and H. Giller) Edward Arnold: London **(217)**

Sartre, J. P. (1953) *Being and Nothingness* (trans H. Barnes) Washington Square Press (1963): New York **(409)**

Satterfield, J. H. (1987) Childhood diagnostic and neurophysiological predictors of teenage arrest rates: an 8-year prospective study. In *The Causes of Crime* (eds. S. A. Mednick, T. E. Moffitt and S. A. Stack) Cambridge University Press: Cambridge **(262)**

Savage, G. H. (1892) Jealousy as a symptom of insanity. In *A Dictionary of Psychological Medicine* (ed. D. Hack Tuke) Churchill: London **(354)**

Savage, H. and McKague, C. (1987) *Mental Health Law in Canada*, Butterworths: Toronto **(124, 126)**

Scadding, J. G. (1967) Diagnosis: the clinician and the computer. *Lancet* ii, 877–82 **(9)**

Scadding, J. G. (1990) The semantic problems of psychiatry. *Psychological Medicine*, **20**, 243–8 **(7, 9)**

Scarlett, J. A., Mako, M. E., Rubenstein, A. H., Blix, P. M., Goldman, J., Horowitz, D. L.,

Tager, H., Jaspan, J. B., Stjemholm, M. R. and Olefsky, J. M. (1977) Factitious hypoglycaemia. *New England Journal of Medicine*, 297, 1029–32 (**296**)

Schachter, M. (1977) Érotomanie ou conviction délirante d'être aimé. Contribution à la psychopathologie de la vie amoureuse. *Annales Médico-psychologiques*, Paris, 135, 729–48 (**354**)

Schacter, D. L. (1986) Amnesia and crime: how much do we really know? *American Psychologist*, 41, 286–95 (**295, 297, 424, 444**)

Schafer, S. (1960) *Restitution to Victims of Crime*, Stevens & Sons: London (**941**)

Scheiffer, C., Derbyshire, L. and Martin, J. (1968) Clinical change in jail referred mental patients. *Archives of General Psychiatry*, 18, 42–6 (**370**)

Schenck, C. H., Bundlie, S. R., Ettinger, M. G. and Mahowald, M. W. (1986) Chronic behavioural disorders of human REM sleep: a new category of parasomnia. *Sleep*, 9, 293–308 (**310**)

Schenck, C. H., Bundlie, S. R., Patterson, A. L. and Mahowald, M. W. (1987) Rapid eye-movement sleep behavior disorder. *Journal of American Medical Association*, 257, 1786–9 (**310, 311**)

Schiff, H. B., Sabin, T. D., Geller, A., Alexander, L. and Mark, V. (1982) Lithium in aggressive behaviour. *American Journal of Psychiatry*, 139, 1346–8 (**662**)

Schiffer, M. (1978) *Mental Disorder and the Criminal Trial Process*, Butterworths: Toronto (**126**)

Schildkraut, J. J. and Kety, S. S. (1967) Biogenic crisis and emotion. *Science*, 156, 21–30 (**932**)

Schinzel, A. (1981) Particular behavioural symptomatology in patients with rarer autosomal chromosome aberrations. In *Human Behaviour and Genetics* (eds. W. Schmid and J. Nielsen) Elsevier: Amsterdam (**365**)

Schipkowensky, N. (1938) *Schizophrenie und Mord*, Springer: Berlin (**154**)

Schipkowensky, N. (1963) Epilepsie und Zurechnungsfähigkeit. *Monatschriften Kriminologie Strafrechtsreferent*, 4, 241–50 (**154**)

Schipkowensky, N. (1968) Affective disorders: cyclophrenia and murder. *The Mentally Abnormal Offender* (eds. A. V. S. de Reuck and R. Porter) CIBA, Churchill: London (**335, 348**)

Schipkowensky, N. (1975) Todtung und Psychose. In *Handwörterbuch der Kriminologie*, bd. 3, (ed. W. de Gryuter) Berlin–New York (**154**)

Schlossman, S. and Sedlak, M. (1983) The Chicago Area Project revisited. *Crime and Delinquency*, 29, 398–462 (**284**)

Schmauss, M., Wolff, R., Erfurth, A. and Ruther, E. (1989) Tolerability of long-term clozapine treatment. *Psychopharmacology*, 99, s105–8 (**666**)

Schmidt, G. (1943) Die Verbrechen in der Schlaftrunkenheit. *Zeitschrift für die Gesamte Neurologie und Psychiatrie*, 176, 208–54 (**309**)

Schmidt, R. P. and Wilder, B. J. (1988) Epilepsy and the law. In *Recent Advances in Epilepsy* (eds. T. A. Pedler and B. S. Meldrum) Churchill-Livingstone: Edinburgh (**586**)

Schneider, A. L. and Schneider, P. R. (1981) Victim assistance programs. In *Perspectives on Crime Victims* (eds. B. Galaway and J. Hudson) Molsby: St Louis (**943**)

Schneider, K. (1950) *Psychopathic Personalities*, 9th edn (English translation 1958) Cassell: London (**384**)

Schneider, K. (1959) *Clinical Psychopathology* (trans. M. W. Hamilton, and E. W. Anderson) Grune & Stratton: New York (**413**)

Schottenfeld, R. S. and Cullen, M. R. (1985) Occupation—induced post-traumatic stress disorders. *American Journal of Psychiatry*, 142, 198–202 (**897**)

Schreiber, F. R. (1984) *The Shoemaker*, Penguin: Harmondsworth (**391**)

Schuman, D. C. (1986) False allegations of physical and sexual abuse. *Bulletin of the Academy of Psychiatry and the Law*, 14, 5–21 (**535**)

Schwab, P. J. and Lahmeyer, C. B. (1979) The use of seclusion on a general hospital psychiatric unit. *Journal of Clinical Psychiatry*, 40, 228–31 (**659**)

Schwartz, R. A. and Schwartz, I. K. (1976) Are personality disorders diseases? *Diseases of the Nervous System*, 37, 613–7 (**9**)

Schweinhart, L. J. and Weikart, D. P. (1980) *Young Children Grow Up*, High/Scope: Ypsilanti, MI (**281**)

Scodel, A. (1964) Inspirational group therapy. *American Journal of Psychotherapy*, 18, 115–25 (**488**)

Scoles, P. and Fine, E. W. (1977) Short-term effects of an education programme for drinking drivers. *Journal of Studies on Alcohol*, 38, 633–7 (**583**)

Scott, D. (1978) The problems of malicious fire-raising. *British Journal of Hospital Medicine*, **19**, 259–63 (**588, 593**)

Scott, P. D. (1953) Psychiatric reports for magistrates' courts. *British Journal of Delinquency*, **4**, 87–7 (**837**)

Scott, P. D. (1965) Commentary. *British Journal of Criminology*, **5**, 127–31 (**426**)

Scott, P. D. (1968) Offenders, drunkenness and murder. *British Journal of Addiction*, **63**, 221–6 (**440, 448**)

Scott, P. D. (1973) Parents who kill children. *Medicine, Science and the Law*, **13**, 120–6 (**506, 610**)

Scottish Child Law Centre (1990) *Review of Child Care Law in Scotland, Briefing Notes* , Scottish Child Law Centre: Glasgow (**250**)

Scottish Home and Health Department (1985) *Report of the Review of Suicide Precautions at HM Detention Centre and HM Young Offenders Institution, Glenochil*, HMSO: Edinburgh (**816**)

Scottish Home and Health Department (1989) *Parole and Related Issues in Scotland: Report of the Review Committee*, Cm.598, HMSO: Edinburgh (**205**)

Seager, C. P. (1970) Treatment of compulsive gamblers by electrical aversion. *British Journal of Psychiatry*, **17**, 545–53 (**485, 488**)

Sechrest, L., White, S. O., and Brown, E. D. (1979) *The Rehabilitation of Criminal Offenders: Problems and Prospects*, National Academy of Sciences: Washington DC (**280**)

Seeman, M. V. (1978) Delusional loving. *Archives of General Psychiatry*, **35**, 1265–7 (**354**)

Seemanova, E. (1971) A study of children of incestuous mates. *Human Heredity*, **21**, 108–28 (**919**)

Segal, S. (1989) Civil commitment standards and patient mix in England/Wales, Italy and the United States. *American Journal of Psychiatry*, **146**, 187–93 (**146**)

Segal, S., Watson, M., Goldfinger, S. and Averbuck, D. (1988) Civil commitment in the psychiatric emergency room. II: Mental disorder indicators and three dangerousness criteria. *Archives of General Psychiatry*, **45**, 753–8 (**642**)

Seighart, P. (1982) Professional ethics—for whose benefit? *Journal of Medical Ethics*, **8**, 25–32 (**863**)

Seligman, M. and Maier, S. (1967) Failure to escape traumatic shock. *Journal of Experimental Physiology*, **74**, 1–9 (**893, 930**)

Selzer, W. (1963) Alcoholism, mental illness and the drunken driver. *American Journal of Psychiatry*, **120**, 326–31 (**438**)

Sensky, T., Hughes, T. and Hirsch, S. (1991) Compulsory psychiatric treatment in the community (I&II). *British Journal of Psychiatry*, **158**, 792–804 (**725**)

Serber, M. and Keith, C. G. (1974) The Atascadero Project: model of a sexual retraining program for incarcerated homosexual paedophiles. *Journal of Homosexuality*, **1**, 87–97 (**552**)

Sergeant, H. (1986) Should psychiatric patients be granted access to their hospital records? *The Lancet*, **ii** , 1322–5 (**866**)

Shader, R. I., Jackson, A. H., Harmatz, J. S. and Appelbaum, P. S. (1977) Patterns of violent behavior among schizophrenic inpatients. *Diseases of the Nervous System*, **38**, 13–6 (**338, 358**)

Shah, A., Holmes, N. and Wing, L. (1982) Prevalence of autism and related conditions in adults in a mental handicap hospital. *Applied Research in Mental Retardation*, **3**, 303–17 (**314**)

Shannon, L. W. (1988) *Criminal Career Continuity*, Human Sciences Press: New York (**272**)

Shapiro, A. (1968) Delinquent and disturbed behaviour within the field of mental deficiency. In *The Mentally Abnormal Offender* (eds. A. V. S. de Reuck and R. Porter) Ciba, Churchill: London (**323**)

Shapland, J., Willmore, J. and Duff, P. (1985) *Victims in the Criminal Justice System*, Gower: Aldershot (**106, 890, 893, 899, 909, 920, 921, 933, 941**)

Shapland, J. (1978) Self-reported delinquency in boys aged 11–14. *British Journal of Criminology*, **18**, 255–66 (**266**)

Sharrock, R. and Cresswell, M. (1989) Pseudologia fantastica: a case study of a man charged with murder. *Medicine Science and the Law*, **29**, 323–8 (**413**)

Shaw, D. M., Churchill, C. M., Noyes, R. and Loeffer Holz, P. L. (1987) Criminal behavior and post-traumatic stress disorder in Vietnam veterans. *Comprehensive Psychiatry*, **28**, 403–11 (**928**)

Shaw, R. (1987) *Children of Imprisoned Fathers*, Hodder & Stoughton: London (**804**)

Shaw, C. R. and McKay, H. D. (1969) *Juvenile Delinquency and Urban Areas* (rev. edn.) University of Chicago Press: Chicago (**273, 284**)

Shaw, S. (1980) *Paying the Penalty: An analysis of the Cost of Penal Sanctions*, National Association for the Care and Resettlement of Offenders: London **(788)**

Sheard, M. H. (1975) Lithium in the treatment of aggression. *Journal of Nervous and Mental Disease*, **160**, 108–18 **(668)**

Sheard, M. H. (1983) Psychopharmacology of aggression. In *Psychopharmacology* (eds. D. Grahame-Smith, H. Hippius and G. Winokur) Excerpta Medica: Amsterdam **(660, 668)**

Sheard, M. H. (1984) Clinical pharmacology of aggressive behavior. *Clinical Neuropharmacology*, **7**, 173–83 **(664)**

Sheard, M. H., Marini, J. L., Bridges, C. I. and Wagner, E. (1976) The effect of lithium on impulsive aggressive behavior in man. *American Journal of Psychiatry*, **133**, 1409–13 **(366, 668)**

Shepherd, M. (1961) Morbid jealousy: some clinical and social aspects of a psychiatric symptom. *Journal of Mental Science*, **107**, 687–753 **(351, 352, 445)**

Sheridan, M. (1960) *The Developmental Progress of Infants and Young Children*, DHSS Report on Public Health and Medical Subjects, No. 102, HMSO: London **(246)**

Sherrington, R., Brynjolfsson, J., Petursson, H., Potter, M., Dudleston, K., Barraclough, B., Wasmuth, J., Dobbs, M. and Gurling, H., (1988) Localisation of a susceptibility locus for schizophrenia on chromosome 5. *Nature*, **336**, 164–7 **(365)**

Shestatsky, M., Greenberg, D. and Lever, B. (1988) A controlled trial of phenelzine in post-traumatic stress disorder. *Psychiatry Research*, **24**, 149–55 **(937)**

Shichor, D. (1984) The extent and nature of lawbreaking by the elderly: a review of arrest statistics. In *Elderly Criminals* (eds. E. S. Newman, D. J. Newman, M. L. Gewirtz & Associates) Oelgeschlager, Gunn & Hain: Cambridge, Mass. **(326)**

Shields, J. (1962) *Monozygotic Twins Brought up Apart and Brought up Together*, Oxford University Press: London **(258)**

Shinar, D. (1978) *Psychology on the Road: the Human Factor in Traffic Safety*, Wiley: New York **(582)**

Shore, D. (1979) Self-mutilation and schizophrenia. *Comprehensive Psychiatry*, **20**, 384–7 **(817)**

Shore, D., Anderson, D. J. and Cutler, N. R. (1978) Prediction of self-mutilation in hospitalised schizophrenics. *American Journal of Psychiatry*, **135**, 406–7 **(817)**

Shore, D., Filson, R. and Johnson, W. E. (1988) Violent crime arrests and paranoid schizophrenia: the White House case studies. *Schizophrenia Bulletin*, **14**, 279–81 **(342)**

Shore, D., Filson, R., Johnson, W. E., Rae, D. S., Muehrer, P., Kelley, D. J., Davis, T. S., Waldman, I. N. and Wyatt, R. J. (1989) Murder and assault arrests of White House cases: clinical and demographic correlates of violence subsequent to civil commitment. *American Journal of Psychiatry*, **146**, 645–51 **(342)**

Short, J. F. and Nye, F. I. (1957) Reported behavior as a criterion of deviant behaviour. *Social Problems*, **5**, 207–13 **(271)**

Short, J. F. and Strodtbeck, F. L. (1965) *Group Process and Gang Delinquency*, University of Chicago Press: Chicago **(266)**

Shrestha, K., Rees, D. W., Rix, K. J. B., Hore, B. D. and Faragjer, E. B. (1985) Sexual jealousy in alcoholics. *Acta Psychiatrica Scandinavica*, **72**, 283–90 **(352)**

Shupe, L. M. (1954) Alcohol and crime: a study of the urine concentration found in 882 persons arrested during or immediately after the commission of a felony. *Journal of Criminal Law and Criminology*, **44**, 661–4 **(443, 448)**

Siegel, H. A. (1985) The intervention approach to drunk driver re-habilitation Part II. Evaluation. *The International Journal of Addictions*, **20**, 675–89 **(439)**

Sifneos, P. (1967) Two different kinds of psychotherapy of short duration. *American Journal of Psychiatry*, **123**, 1069–74 **(934)**

Sigal, J. J., Dinicola, V. F. and Buonvino, M. (1988) Grandchildren of survivors: can negative effects of prolonged exposure to excessive stress be observed two generations later? *Canadian Journal of Psychiatry*, **33**, 207–12 **(903, 922)**

Silber, E., Perry, S. E. and Bloch, D. A. (1957) Patterns of parent-child interaction in a disaster. *Psychiatry*, **21**, 159–67 **(891)**

Silbert, M. H. and Pines, A. M. (1982) Victimisation of street prostitutes. *Victimology*, **7**, 122–33 **(918)**

Simcha-Fagan, O. and Schwartz, J. E. (1986) Neighbourhood and delinquency: an assessment of contextual effects. *Criminology*, **24**, 667–703 **(273)**

Simon, F. H. (1971) *Prediction Methods in Criminology*, Home Office, HMSO: London **(627)**

Simon, R. J. (1975) *Women and Crime*, Heath: Lexington, Mass. **(604)**

Simpson, M. A. (1976) Self-mutilation. *British Journal of Hospital Medicine*, 16, 430–8 (817)
Sims, A. C. P. and Symonds, R. L. (1975) Psychiatric referrals from the police. *British Journal of Psychiatry*, 127, 171–8 (368–9,735)
Sinclair, I. and Clarke, R. (1981) Cross-institutional designs. In *Evaluative Research in Social Care* (eds. E. M. Goldberg and N. Connolly) Heinemann Educational: London (788)
Singhal, R. L. and Telner, J. I. (1983) Psychopharmacological aspects of aggression in animals and man. *Psychiatric Journal of the University of Ottawa*, 8, 145–53 (660)
Skegg, D. C. G., Doll, R. and Perry, J. (1977) Use of medicines in general practice. *British Medical Journal*, 1, 1561–3 (621)
Skinner, B. F. (1938) *The Behavior of Organisms*, Appleton Century Crofts: New York (670)
Skinner, B. F. (1953) *Science and Human Behavior*, Macmillan: New York (670)
Skinner, B. F. and Lindsley, O. R. (1954) *Studies in Behavior Therapy*, Status Reports II and III, Office of Naval Research, Contract N5 Ori–7662, USA (669)
Skyrme, T. (1983) *The Changing Image of the Magistracy*, Macmillan: London (174)
Sloan, J. H., Kellerman, A. L., Reay, D. T., Ferris, J. A., Koepseli, T., Rivara, F. P., Rice, C., Gray, L. and Logerfo, J. (1988) Hand-gun regulations, crime, assaults and homicide: a tale of two cities. *New England Journal of Medicine*, 319, 1256–61 (901)
Slobogin, C. (1985) The guilty but mentally ill verdict: an idea whose time should not have come. *George Washington Law Review* 53, 494–527 (143)
Slovic, P. (1987) Perception of risk. *Science*, 236, 280–5 (625)
Slovic, P. (1989) *The Perception and Management of Therapeutic Risk CMR Annual Lecture 1989*, Centre for Medicines Research: Carshalton (625)
Smart, C. (1976) *Women, Crime and Criminology*, Routledge & Kegan Paul: London (602)
Smart, R. G. and Schmidt, W. (1969) Physiological impairment and personality factors in traffic accidents of alcoholics. *Quarterly Journal of Studies on Alcohol*, 30, 440–5 (582)
Smego, R. A. and Durack, D. T. (1982) The neuroleptic malignant syndrome. *Archives of Internal Medicine*, 142, 1183–5 (667)
Smith, D. (1985) *Police and People in London* (4 vols), Policy Study Institution: London (171)
Smith, J. C. and Hogan, B. (1986) *Criminal Law, Cases and Materials*, 3rd edn, Butterworths: London (57)
Smith, J. C. and Hogan, B. (1988) *Criminal Law*, 6th edn, Butterworths: London (41, 56, 106, 353, 541, 581, 848)
Smith, K. and Keenan, D. (1982) *English Law*, 7th edn, Pitman: London (167, 174)
Smith, L. J. F. (1989) *Domestic Violence: An Overview of the Literature*, Home Office Research Study No. 107, HMSO: London (502)
Smith, M. Hamblin (1922) *The Psychology of the Criminal*, Methuen: London (749)
Smith, M. Hamblin (1934) *Prisons and a Changing Civilisation*, John Lane: London (749)
Smith, R. (1981) *Trial by Medicine*, University Press: Edinburgh (49, 53, 55, 605)
Smith, R. (1984) *Prison Health Care*, British Medical Association: London (620, 689, 741, 764, 802)
Smith, R. (1988) Seizing the initiative on compensation *British Medical Journal* 246, 1487–8 (106)
Smith, R. (1991) Taken from this place and hanged by the neck. . . . *British Medical Journal*, 302, 64–5 (814)
Smith, R. C., Parker, E. S. and Noble, P.S. (1975) Alcohol's effect on some formal aspects of verbal social communication. *Archives of General Psychiatry*, 32, 1394–402 (442)
Smith, S. M. and Hanson, R. (1974) 134 battered children: a medical and psychological study. *British Medical Journal*, 3, 666–70 (502)
Smith, S. M., Hanson, R. and Noble, S. (1973) Parents of battered babies: a controlled study. *British Medical Journal*, 4, 388–91 (288)
Smith, S. M., Honigsberger, L. and Smith, C. A. (1973) EEG and personality factors in child batterers. *The Tunbridge Wells Study Group on Non-Accidental Injury to Children*, Spastics Society: London (504)
Smith, S. M. and Kunjukrishnan, R. (1986) Medicolegal aspects of mental retardation. *Psychiatric Clinics of North America*, 9, 699–712 (317)
Snowdon, J., Solomons, R. and Druce, H. (1978) Feigned bereavement: twelve cases. *British Journal of Psychiatry*, 133, 15–9 (412)
Snowden, P. R. (1985) A survey of the regional secure unit programme. *British Journal of Psychiatry*, 147, 499–507 (711)

Snowden, P. R. (1986) Forensic psychiatry services and regional secure units in England & Wales: an overview. *Criminal Law Review*, 790–9 **(710)**

Socarides, C. (1978) *Homosexuality*, Jason Aronson: New York **(540)**

Social Information Systems (1986) *Custody Controlled*, Social Information Services: Manchester **(228)**

Soliday, S. M. (1985) A comparison of patient and staff attitudes towards seclusion. *Journal of Nervous and Mental Disease*, 172, 282–6 **(660)**

Soloff, P. H. (1984) Historical notes on seclusion and restraint. In *The Psychiatric Uses of Seclusion and Restraint* (ed. K. Tardiff) American Psychiatric Press: Washington DC **(656)**

Soloff, P. H. and Turner, S. M. (1981) Patterns of seclusion: a prospective study. *Journal of Nervous and Mental Disease*, 169, 37–44 **(659)**

Solomon, G. S. and Ray, J. B. (1984) Irrational beliefs of shoplifters. *Journal of Clinical Psychology*, **40**, 1075–9 **(577,578)**

Solomon, Z., Kotler, M. and Mikulincer, M. (1988) Combat related post-traumatic stress disorder among second-generation holocaust survivors: preliminary findings. *American Journal of Psychiatry*, 145, 865–8 **(893,903)**

Solursh, L. (1988) Combat addiction: post-traumatic stress disorder re-explored. *Psychiatric Journal of the University of Ottawa*, 13, 17–20 **(929)**

Somers, A. R. (1976) Violence, television and the health of American youth. *New England Journal of Medicine*, 294, 811–7 **(497)**

Somerville, J. G. (1969) A study of the preventive aspects of police work with juveniles III. Police cautioning—a close up study. *Criminal Law Review*, 472–84 **(225)**

Soothill, K. L., Adserballe, H., Bernheim, J., Dasananjali, T., Harding, T. W., Thomaz, T., Reinhold, F. and Ghali, H. (1983) Psychiatric reports requested by the courts in six countries. *Medicine, Science and the Law*, 23, 4, 231–41 **(119)**

Soothill, K. L., Harding, T. W., Adserballe, H., Bernheim, J., Erne, S., Magdi, S., Panpreecha, C. and Reinhold, F. (1981) Compulsory admissions to mental hospital in six countries. *International Journal of Law and Psychiatry*, 4, 327–44 **(119)**

Soothill, K. L., Jack, A. and Gibbens, T. C. N. (1976) Rape: a 22-year cohort study. *Medicine, Science and the Law*, 16, 62–9 **(546)**

Soothill, K. L., Jack, A. and Gibbens, T. C. N. (1980) Rape acquittals. *Modern Law Review*, **43**, 159–72 **(543)**

Soothill, K. L. and Pope, P. J. (1973) Arson: a twenty-year cohort study. *Medicine, Science & the Law*, 13 , 127–38 **(591)**

Sorgi, P. J., Ratey, J. J. and Polakoff, S. (1986) B-adrenergic blockers for the control of aggressive behaviors in patients with chronic schizophrenia. *American Journal of Psychiatry*, 143, 775–6 **(664)**

Soskis, D. A. (1978) Schizophrenic and medical inpatients as informed drug consumers. *Archives of General Psychiatry*, 35, 645–7 **(866)**

Sours, J. A., Frumpkin, P. and Indermill, R. R. (1963) Somnambulism. *Archives of General Psychiatry*, 9, 400–13 **(310)**

Special Hospitals Service Authority (1992) *Special Hospitals Patient Statistics 1991*, SHSA: London **(723)**

Speed, D. (1973) Discussion: violence in prisoners and patients. In *Medical Care of Prisoners and Detainees*. CIBA Foundation Symposium No. 16, Elsevier: Amsterdam **(809)**

Speed, N., Engdahl, B., Schwartz, J. and Eberly, R. (1989) Post-traumatic stress disorder as the consequence of the POW experience. *Journal of Nervous and Mental Disease*, 177, 147–53 **(897, 903)**

Spellacy, F. (1978) Neuropsychological discrimination between violent and non-violent men. *Journal of Clinical Psychology*, 34, 49–52 **(289)**

Spencer, D. A. (1989) The evolution of mental handicap services in the Yorkshire Region and the Association of Yorkshire Regional Consultants in Mental Handicap. *Psychiatric Bulletin*, 13, 368–70 **(720)**

Spengler, A. (1977) Manifest sadomasochism in males. Results of an empirical study. *Archives of Sexual Behavior*, 6, 441–56 **(551)**

Spiegel, D. (1984) Multiple personality as a post-traumatic stress disorder. *Psychiatric Clinics of North America*, 7, 101–10 **(428)**

Spiegel, D., Hunt, T. and Dondershine, H. E. (1988) Dissociation and hypnotisability in post-traumatic stress disorder. *American Journal of Psychiatry*, 145, 301–5 **(890, 932)**

Spinoza, B. (1677) *Ethics*, Dent (1948): London **(352)**

Spitzer, R. L. (1975) On pseudoscience in science, logic in remission and psychiatric diagnosis: a critique of Rosenhan's 'On being sane in insane places'. *Journal of Abnormal Psychology*, **84**, 442–52 **(419)**

Spitzer, R. L. and Endicott, J. (1978) Research diagnostic criteria. *Archives of General Psychiatry*, **35**, 773–82 **(xv)**

Spitzer, R. L. and Williams, J. B. W. (1987) Introduction. *Diagnostic and Statistical Manual of Mental Disorders*, 3rd edn. (rev), American Psychiatric Association: Washington DC **(8)**

Spivack, G. (1983) *High Risk Early Behaviors Indicating Vulnerability to Delinquency in the Community and School*, National Institute of Juvenile Justice and Delinquency Prevention: Washington DC **(262)**

Spores, J. C. (1988) *Running Amok, an Historical Enquiry*, S. E. Asia Series No. 82, Ohio University: Athens, Ohio **(432, 433)**

Spreen, O. (1981) The relationship between learning disability, neurological impairment, and delinquency. *Journal of Nervous and Mental Disease*, **169**, 791–9 **(289)**

Sprei, J. and Goodwin, R. A. (1983) Group treatment of sexual assault survivors. *Journal for Specialists in Group Work*, **8**, 39–46 **(939)**

Spry, W. B. and Craft, M. (1984) The function of a forensic assessment and rehabilitation unit. In *Mentally Abnormal Offenders* (eds. M. Craft and A. Craft) Baillière Tindall: London **(324)**

Sroufe, L. A. (1986) Bowlby's contribution to psychoanalytic theory and developmental psychology: attachment, separation, loss. *Journal of Child Psychology & Psychiatry*, **27**, 841–9 **(381)**

Stafford-Clark, D. and Taylor, F. H. (1949) Clinical and electroencephalographic studies of prisoners charged with murder. *Journal of Neurology, Neurosurgery and Psychiatry*, **12**, 325–30 **(288)**

Stalstrom, O. H. (1980) Querulous paranoia: diagnosis and dissent. *Australian and New Zealand Journal of Psychiatry*. **14**, 145–50 **(356)**

Stanko, E., (1990) *Everyday Violence*, Pandora: London **(910, 920)**

Stanley, B. (1983) Senile dementia and informed consent. *Behavioral Sciences and the Law*, **1**, 57–74 **(352)**

Stanley, S. and Baginsky, M. (1984) *Alternatives to Prison*, Peter Owen: London **(777, 785, 789)**

Stannard, J. E. (1984) *Northern Ireland Supplement to Smith & Hogan Criminal Law*, SLS Legal Publications (NI): Belfast **(97)**

Stanton, A. H., Gunderson, J. G., Knapp, P. H., Frank, A. F., Vannicelli Schnitzer, R. and Rosenthal, R. (1984) Effects of psychotherapy in schizophrenia 1. Design and implementation of a controlled study. *Schizophrenia Bulletin*, **10**, 520–63 **(687)**

Stattin, H., Magnusson, D. and Reichel, H. (1986) *Criminality from Childhood to Adulthood*, University of Stockholm Department of Psychology: Stockholm **(254)**

Steadman, H. (1982) A situational approach to violence. *International Journal of Law and Psychiatry*, **5**, 171–86 **(629)**

Steadman, H. J. (1985) Empirical research on the insanity defense. *Annals of the American Academy of Political and Social Science*, **477**, 58–71 **(144, 805–6)**

Steadman, H. and Cocozza, J. (1974) *Careers of the Criminally Insane*, Lexington Books: Lexington, Mass. **(626, 628, 644, 645)**

Steadman, H. J., Cocozza, J. J. and Melick, M. E. (1978) Explaianing the increased arrest rate among mental patients: the changing clientele of State hospitals. *American Journal of Psychiatry*, **135**, 816–20 **(333)**

Steadman, H. and Keveles, C. (1972) The community adjustment and criminal activity of the Baxstrom patients: 1966–70. *American Journal of Psychiatry*, **129**, 304–10 **(626)**

Steadman, H., McCarty, D. W. and Morrissey, J. P. (1989) *The Mentally Ill in Jail*, The Guildford Press: New York **(767, 768)**

Steadman, H. J., Monahan, J., Duffee, B., Hartstone, E. and Robbins, P. C. (1984) The impact of state mental hospital de-institutionalisation on United States prison populations 1968–1978. *Journal of Criminal Law and Criminology*, **75**, 474–50 **(333)**

Steadman, H. and Ribner, S. (1982) Life stress and violence among ex-mental patients. *Social Science in Medicine*, **16**, 1641–7 **(643)**

Steadman, H. J., Rosenstein, M. J. MacAskill, R. L. and Manderscheid, R. W. (1988) A profile of mentally disordered offenders admitted to inpatient psychiatric services in the United States. *Law & Human Behavior*, **12**, 91–9 **(157)**

Steele, B. F. and Pollock, C. B. (1968) A psychiatric study of parents who abused infants and small children. In *The Battered Child* (eds. R. E. Helfer and C. H. Kempe) University of Chicago Press: Chicago **(503)**

Stein, P. (1984) *Legal Institutions: the Development of Dispute Settlement*, Butterworths: London **(168)**

Stengel, E. (1941) On the aetiology of the fugue state. *Journal of Mental Science*, **87**, 572–99 **(295, 427, 430)**

Stern, A. (1938) Psychoanalytic investigation of and therapy in the borderline group of neuroses. *Psychiatric Quarterly*, **7**, 467–89 **(388)**

Stern, E. S. (1948) The Medea complex: mother's homicidal wishes to her child. *Journal of Mental Science*, **94**, 321–31 **(611)**

Stern, G. M. (1976) From chaos to responsibility. *American Journal of Psychiatry*, **133**, 300–1 **(102, 922)**

Stern, V. (1989) *Bricks of Shame*, 2nd edn, Penguin: Harmondsworth **(802, 803)**

Stevens, E. (1981) *Civil and Criminal Procedure in a Nutshell*, Sweet & Maxwell: London **(179)**

Stevens, P. and Willis, C. F. (1979) *Race, Crime and Arrests*, Home Office Research Study No. 58, Home Office, HMSO: London **(369)**

Stewart, G. and Tutt, N. (1987) *Children in Custody*, Avebury: Aldershot **(215, 233)**

Stocking, B. (1985) *Initiative and Inertia*, Nuffield Hospital Trust: London **(711)**

Stockwell, T., Hodgson, R. J., Edwards, G., Taylor, C. and Rankin, H. (1979) The development of a questionnaire to measure severity of alcohol dependence. *British Journal of Addiction*, **74**, 79–87 **(470)**

Stone, A. A. (1982) Psychiatric abuse and legal reform. *International Journal of Law and Psychiatry*, **5**, 9–27 **(830)**

Stone, C. (1988) *Bail Information for the Crown Prosecution Service*, Association of Chief Officers of Probation, Wakefield, W. Yorks (England) & The Vera Institute: New York **(773)**

Stone, C. (1989) *Public Interest Case Assessments*, Vera Institute: New York. **(774)**

Stone, N. (1985) Prison based work. In *Working with Offenders* (eds. H. Walker and B. Beaumont) Macmillan: Basingstoke **(775)**

Stone, W. E. (1984) Jail suicide. *Corrections Today*, **46**, 84–7 **(813)**

Strachey, J. (1934) The nature of the therapeutic action of psychoanalysis. *International Journal of Psychoanalysis*, **15**, 127–59 **(678)**

Strang, J. (1988) Changing injecting practices: blunting the needle habit. *British Journal of Addiction*, **83**, 237–9 **(479)**

Strang, J. (1989) 'The British System': past, present and future. *International Review of Psychiatry*, **1**, 109–20 **(461)**

Strang, J. (1990) Heroin and cocaine: new technologies, new problems. In *Addiction Controversies* (ed. D. M. Warburton) Harwood Academic Publishers: Reading **(460)**

Strang, J., Heathcote, S. and Watson, P. (1987) Habit moderation in injecting drug addicts. *Health Trends*, **19**, 16–8 **(479)**

Strang, J. and Yates, R. (1984) *Non-voluntary Treatment of Drug-takers—Some Preliminary Findings*, Proceedings of the Pompidou Group of the Council of Europe: Strasbourg **(477)**

Stringer, A. Y. and Josef, N. C. (1983) Methylphenidate in the treatment of aggression in two patients with antisocial personality disorder. *American Journal of Psychiatry*, **140**, 1365–6 **(663)**

Stromberg, C. D. and Stone, A. A. (1983) A model state law on civil commitment of the mentally ill. *Harvard Journal on Legislation*, **20**, 275–396 **(145)**

Stumphauzer, J. S. (1986) *Helping Delinquents Change: A Treatment Manual of Social Learning Approaches*, Haworth Press: New York **(670, 671, 674)**

Sturgess, J. and Heal, K. (1977) Non-accidental injury to children under the age of 17. *First Report from the Select Committee on Violence in the Family Session 1976–7 Vol. II Evidence*, House of Commons, HMSO: London **(504)**

Sturup, G. K. (1968) *Treating the 'Untreatable'*, The Johns Hopkins Press: Baltimore **(137)**

Stutman, R. K. and Bliss, E. L. (1985) Post-traumatic stress disorder, hypnotizability, and imagery. *American Journal of Psychiatry*, **142**, 741–3 **(932)**

Suarez, J. M. (1972) Psychiatry and the criminal law system. *American Journal of Psychiatry*, **129**, 293–7 **(766)**

Subhan, Z. (1984) Benzodiazepines and memory. *Psychiatry in Practice*, **3**, 15–20 **(63)**

Suedfeld, P. and Roy, C. (1975) Using social isolation to control the behavior of disruptive inmates. *International Journal of Offender Therapy and Comparative Criminology*, **19**, 90–9 **(659)**

Sugar, M. (1989) Children in a disaster: an overview. *Child Psychiatry & Human Development*, **19**, 163–79 **(891)**

Sunday Times Insight Team (1980) *Siege!*, Hamlyn: London **(927)**

Sutherland, E. H. and Cressey, D. R. (1974) *Criminology*, 9th edn, Lippincott: Philadelphia **(278)**

Sutherland, G., Edwards, G., Taylor, C., Phillips, G., Gossop, M. and Brady, R. (1986) The measurement of opiate dependence. *British Journal of Addictions*, **81**, 485–94 **(470)**

Sutherland, S. and Scherl, D. (1970) Patterns of response among victims of rape. *American Journal of Orthopsychiatry*, **40**, 503–11 **(902, 916)**

Svendsen, B. B. (1977) Present status of forensic psychiatry in Denmark. *Acta Psychiatrica Scandinavica*, **55**, 176–80 **(136)**

Sveri, K. (1965) Group activity. In *Scandinavian Studies in Criminology*, vol. 1 (ed. K. O. Christiansen) Tavistock: London **(265)**

Swanson, J. W., Holzer, C. E., Ganju, V. K. and Jonjo, R. T. (1990) Violence and psychiatric disorder in the community: evidence from the Epidemiologic Catchment Area surveys. *Hospital and Community Psychiatry*, **41**, 761–70 **(332, 335)**

Sweet, W. H., Ervin, F. and Mark, V. H. (1969) The relationship of violent behaviour to focal cerebral disease. In *Aggressive Behaviour* (eds. S. Garattini and E. B. Sigg) Excerpta Medica: Amsterdam, pp. 336–52 **(286)**

Symonds, M. (1975) Victims of violence: psychological effects and after-effects. *American Journal of Psychoanalysis*, **35**, 19–26 **(890, 896)**

Szasz, T. (1962) *The Myth of Mental Illness*, Harper & Row: New York **(6, 10)**

Szmukler, G., Bird, A. S. and Button, E. J. (1981) Compulsory admissions in a London Borough: 1. Social and clinical features and a follow-up. *Psychological Medicine*, **11**, 617–36 **(360, 369, 335)**

Taber, J. I., McCormick, R. A. and Ramirez, L. F. (1987a) The prevalence and impact of major life stressors among pathological gamblers. *International Journal of Addictions*, **22**, 71–9 **(483, 484)**

Taber, J. I., McCormick, R. A., Russo, A. M., Adkins, B. J. and Ramirez, L. F. (1987b) Follow-up of pathological gamblers after treatment. *American Journal of Psychiatry*, **144**, 757–61 **(486)**

Talbot, E. S. (1898) A study of the stigmata of degeneracy among the American criminal youth. *Journal of the American Medical Association*, **30**, 849–56 **(290)**

Tamerin, J. S., Weiner, S., Poppen, R., Steinglass, P. and Mendelson, J. H. (1971) Alcohol and memory: amnesia and short-term memory function during experimentally induced intoxication. *American Journal of Psychiatry*, **127**, 659–64 **(443)**

Tancredi, L. and Volkow, N. (1988) Neural substrates of violent behavior: implications for law and public policy. *International Journal of Law and Psychiatry*, **11**, 13–49 **(642)**

Tanay, E. (1969) Psychiatric study of homicide. *American Journal of Psychiatry*, **125**, 252–8 **(291)**

Tardiff, K. (1983a) A survey of drugs used in the management of assaultive inpatients. *Bulletin of the American Academy of Psychiatry and the Law*, **11**, 215–22 **(663)**

Tardiff, K. (1983b) A survey of assault by chronic patients in a state hospital system. In *Assaults within Psychiatric Facilities* (eds. J. R. Lion and W. H. Reid) Grune & Stratton: New York **(806)**

Tardiff, K. and Sweillam, A. (1980) Assault, suicide and mental illness. *Archives of General Psychiatry*, **37**, 164–9 **(331, 338, 370, 805, 806)**

Tardiff, K. and Sweillam, A. (1982) Assaultive behavior among chronic inpatients. *American Journal of Psychiatry*, **139**, 212–5 **(641)**

Tarnopolsky A. and Berelowitz M. (1987) Borderline personality. *British Journal of Psychiatry*, **151**, 724–34 **(389)**

Tarrier, N., Barrowclough, C., Porceddu, K. and Watts, S. (1988) The assessment of psychophysiological reactivity to the expressed emotion of the relatives of schizophrenic patients. *British Journal of Psychiatry*, **152**, 618–24 **(367)**

Tarsh, M. J. (1986) On serious violence during sleepwalking (letter). *British Journal of Psychiatry*, **148**, 476 **(309, 30, 311)**

Tarsh, M. J. and Royston, C. (1985) A follow-up study of accident neurosis. *British Journal of Psychiatry*, **146**, 178–25 **(416)**

Tarter, R. E. and Schneider, D. U. (1976) Blackouts—relationship with memory capacity and alcoholism history. *Archives of General Psychiatry*, **33**, 1492–6 **(443)**

Taylor, D. C. (1969a) Some psychiatric aspects of epilepsy. In *Current Problems in Neuropsychiatry* (ed. R. N. Herrington) British Journal of Psychiatry Special Publication No. 4, Royal Medico-Psychological Association: London **(300)**

Taylor, D. C. (1969b) Sexual behavior and temporal lobe epilepsy. *Archives of Neurology*, 27, 510–6 **(304)**

Taylor, F. Kraupl (1979) *Psychopathology, its Causes and Symptoms*, rev. edn., Quatermaine: Sunbury-on-Thames **(337, 354, 413)**

Taylor, L., Lacey, R. and Bracken, D. (1980) *In Whose Best Interests?* Cobden Trust/MIND: London **(211, 219)**

Taylor, P. J. (1981) Cerebral disorder in violence and psychosis. *Proceedings of IIIrd World Congress of Biological Psychiatry* (eds. C. Perris, G. Struwe and B. Janssen) Elsevier: North Holland **(341, 359)**

Taylor, P. J. (1982) Schizophrenia and violence. In *Abnormal Offenders, Delinquency and the Criminal Justice System* (eds. J. Gunn and D. P. Farrington) Wiley: Chichester **(642)**

Taylor, P. J. (1983) Consent, competency and ECT: a psychiatrist's view. *Journal of Medical Ethics*, 9, 146–51 **(349, 877)**

Taylor, P. J. (1985a) Epilepsy and insanity. In *Epilepsy and the Law* (eds. P. Fenwick and E. Fenwick) Royal Society of Medicine: London **(58)**

Taylor, P. J. (1985b) Motives for offending among violent and psychotic men. *British Journal of Psychiatry*, 147, 491–8 **(336, 340, 346, 352, 365)**

Taylor, P. J. (1986) Psychiatric disorder in London's life-sentenced prisoners. *British Journal of Criminology*, 26, 63–78 **(448, 751, 761, 782, 803, 809, 862)**

Taylor, P. J. (1987) Social implications of psychosis. *British Medical Bulletin*, 43, 718–40 **(359, 751)**

Taylor, P. J. (1988a) Reading about forensic psychiatry. *British Journal of Psychiatry*, 153, 271–8 **(641)**

Taylor, P. J. (1988b) *Birth Place, Offending and Mental Disorder and Custodial Remand* Presentation to the Royal College of Psychiatrists, Forensic Psychiatry Specialist Section Conference, Stratford-upon-Avon (unpublished) **(370, 751)**

Taylor, P. J. (1990) Schizophrenia and ECT: a case for a change in prescription? In *Dilemmas and Difficulties in the Management of Psychiatric Patients*, (eds. K. Hawton and P. Cowan) Oxford University Press: Oxford **(664)**

Taylor, P. J. (1993) Schizophrenia and crime: distinctive patterns in association. In *Crime and Mental Disorder* (ed. S. Hodgins) Sage: Beverley Hills, CA. **(341, 358, 360, 362, 368, 371)**

Taylor, P. J., Dalton, R. and Fleminger, J. J. (1982) Handedness and schizophrenic symptoms. *British Journal of Medical Psychology*, 55, 287–91 **(336)**

Taylor, P. J., Garety, P., Buchanan, A., Reed, A., Wessely, S., Ray, K., Dunn, G. and Grubin, D. (in press) Delusions and violence. In *Violence and Mental Disorder: Developments in Risk Assessment* (eds. J. Monahan and H. Steadman) Chicago University Press: Chicago **(12, 343)**

Taylor, P. J. and Gunn, J. C. (1984) Violence and psychosis. *British Medical Journal*, 288, 1945–9; 289, 9–12 **(334, 336, 347, 362, 444, 447, 456, 743, 744, 862)**

Taylor, P. J. and Kopelman, M. (1984) Amnesia for criminal offences. *Psychological Medicine*, 14, 581–8 **(46, 292–298 passim, 424)**

Taylor, P. J., Mahendra, B. and Gunn, J. (1983) Erotomania in males. *Psychological Medicine*, 13, 645–50 **(354)**

Taylor, P. J. and Parrott, J. M. (1988) Elderly offenders: a study of age-related factors among custodially remanded prisoners. *British Journal of Psychiatry*, 152, 340–6 **(326, 327, 328, 601)**

Taylor, R. L. and Weisz, A. E. (1970) American presidential assassination. In *Violence and the Struggle for Existence* (eds. D. N. Daniels, M. F. Gilula and F. M. Ochberg) Little, Brown: Boston **(518)**

Taylor, W. and Martin, M. (1964) Multiple personality. *Journal of Abnormal Social Psychology*, 39, 281–300 **(429)**

Telch, M. J., Killen, J. D., McAllister, A. L., Perry, C. L. and Maccoby, N. (1982) Long-term follow-up of a pilot project on smoking prevention with adolescents. *Journal of Behavioural Medicine*, 5, 1–8 **(283)**

Tennant, C., Bebbington, P. and Hurry, J. (1980) Parental death in childhood and risk of adult depressive disorders: a review: *Psychological Medicine*, 10, 289–99 **(367)**

Tennant, C., Bebbington, P. and Hurry, J. (1982) Social experiences in childhood and adult psychiatric morbidity: a multiple regression analysis. *Psychological Medicine*, 12, 321–7 **(367)**

Tennant, C., Goulston, K. and Dent, O. (1986) Clinical psychiatric illness in prisoners of war of the Japanese: forty years after release. *Psychological Medicine*, 16, 833–9 (**897**)

Tennenbaum, D. J. (1977) Personality and criminality: a summary and implications of the literature. *Journal of Criminal Justice*, 5, 225–35 (**261**)

Tennent, G., Loucas, K., Fenton, G. and Fenwick, P. (1974) Male admissions to Broadmoor Hospital. *British Journal of Psychiatry*, 125, 44–50 (**700**)

Tennent, T. G., McQuaid, A., Loughnane, T. and Hands, A. J. (1971) Female arsonists. *British Journal of Psychiatry*, 119, 497–502 (**590**)

Tennent, G. and Way, C. (1984) The English special hospitals—12–17 year follow up study: a comparison of violent and non-violent re-offenders and non-offenders. *Medicine, Science and the Law*, 24, 81–91 (**707**)

Teoh, J. I. (1972) The changing psychopathology of amok. *Psychiatry*, 35, 345–50 (**434**)

Teplin, L. A. (1985) The criminality of the mentally ill: a dangerous misconception. *American Journal of Psychiatry*, 142, 593–9 (**171, 330**)

Terr, L. C. (1981) Psychic trauma in children: observations following the Chowchilla school bus kidnapping. *American Journal of Psychiatry*, 138, 14–9 (**891**)

Terr, L. C. (1983a) Child snatching: a new epidemic of an ancient malady. *Journal of Pediatrics*, 103, 141–55 (**612**)

Terr, L. C. (1983b) Chowchilla revisited: the effects of psychic trauma four years after a school bus kidnapping. *American Journal of Psychiatry*, 140, 1543–50 (**892, 928, 930**)

Terr, L. C. (1988) Anatomically correct dolls: should they be used as the basis for expert testimony?—Negative. *Journal of the American Academy of Child and Adolescent Psychiatry*, 27, 255–7 (**942**)

Terr, L. C. (1991) Childhood traumas: an outline and overview. *American Journal of Psychiatry*, 148, 10–20 (**891**)

Theilgaard, A. (1984) A psychological study of the personalities of XYY and XXY men. *Acta Psychiatrica Scandinavica Supplementum*, 315, vol. 69 (**315**)

Thigpen, C. and Cleckley, H. A. (1957) *The Three Faces of Eve*, McGraw Hill: New York (**428**)

Thomas, A. and Chess, S. (1984) Genesis and evolution of behavioral disorders: from infancy to early adult life *American Journal of Psychiatry*, 141, 1–9 (**380**)

Thomas, D. A. (1979) *Principles of Sentencing*, 2nd edn, Heinemann: London (**67, 68, 70, 75, 76, 105, 402, 403, 744, 761**)

Thompson, P. (1972) *Bound for Broadmoor*, Hodder & Stoughton: London (**697**)

Thompson, P. (1986) The use of seclusion in hospitals in the Newcastle area. *British Journal of Psychiatry*, 149, 471–4 (**659, 660**)

Thorley, A. (1983) Managing the opiate drug taker—the general practitioner's role. *Medicine in Practice*, 666–73 (**471**)

Thornberry, T. P. (1973) Race, socio-economic status, and sentencing in the juvenile justice system. *Journal of Criminal Law and Criminology*, 64, 90–8 (**276**)

Thornberry, T. P. and Farnworth, M. (1982) Social correlates of criminal involvement: further evidence on the relationship between social status and criminal behavior. *American Sociological Review*, 47, 505–18 (**270, 271**)

Thornberry, T. and Jacoby, J. (1979) *The Criminally Insane: A Community Follow-up of Mentally Ill Offenders*, University of Chicago Press: Chicago (**644**)

Thorndike, E. L. (1911) *Animal Intelligence: Experimental Studies*, Macmillan: New York (**670**)

Thorneloe, W. F. and Crews, E. L. (1981) Manic depressive illness concomitant with antisocial personality disorder: six case reports and review of the literature. *Journal of Clinical Psychiatry*, 42, 5–9 (**347**)

Thornton, D. M. (1987) Moral development theory. In *Applying Psychology to Imprisonment* (eds. B. J. McGurk, D. M. Thornton and M. Williams) HMSO: London (**260**)

Thorpe, D., Smith, D., Green, C. and Paley, J. (1980) *Out of Care*, Allen & Unwin: London (**217, 228**)

Tildesley, W. and Bullock, W. (1983) Curfew orders: the arguments for *Probation Journal*, 10, 10–11 (**229**)

Tillmann, W. A. and Hobbs, G. E. (1949) The accident prone automobile driver. *American Journal of Psychiatry*, 106, 321–31 (**581, 584**)

Tippell, S. (1989) Drug users and the prison system. In *Drugs and British Society: Responses to a Social Problem in the 1980s* (ed. S. MacGregor) Routledge: London (**476**)

Todd, J. and Dewhurst, K. (1955) The Othello syndrome: a study of the psychopathology of sexual jealousy. *Journal of Nervous and Mental Diseases*, 122, 367–74 (**351**)

Tong, J. E. and Mackay, G. W. (1959) A statistical follow-up of mental defectives of dangerous or violent propensities. *British Journal of Delinquency*, **9**, 275–84 **(707)**

Topp, D. (1973) Fire as a symbol and as a weapon of death. *Medicine, Science and the Law*, **13**, 79–86 **(596)**

Topp, D. O. (1979) Suicide in prison. *British Journal of Psychiatry*, **134**, 24–7 **(813)**

Totsuka, E., Mitsuishi, T. and Kitamura, Y. (1986) Mental health and human rights: illegal detention in Japan. In *Psychiatry, Law and Ethics* (eds. A. Carni, S. Schneider and A. Hafez) Springer–Verlag: Berlin **(859)**

Tournier, P. (1983) *Report on Prison Demography in the Member States of the Council of Europe*. Paper prepared for the Sixth Conference of Directors of Prison Administrations, Council of Europe: Strasbourg **(813)**

Trace, M. (1988) Why not work in prison? *Drug Link*, **3**, 6–8 **(478)**

Tracy, P. E., Wolfgang, M. E. and Figlio, R. M. (1985) *Delinquency in Two Birth Cohorts*. National Institute of Juvenile Justice and Delinquency Prevention: Washington DC **(275)**

Trades Union Congress (1987) *Women and Prison. A TUC Report*, Trades Union Congress: London **(622)**

Trasler, G. B. (1962) *The Explanation of Criminality*, Routledge & Kegan Paul: London **(265, 278)**

Treasaden, I. H. (1985) Current practice in regional interim secure units. In *Secure Provision* (ed. L. Gostin) Tavistock: London **(717)**

Treasaden, I. H. and Shepherd, D. (1983) *Evaluation of the Lyndhurst Interim Secure Unit, Knowle Hospital*, (unpublished) **(714, 715)**

Treffert, D. (1978) Marijuana use in schizophrenia: a clear hazard. *American Journal of Psychiatry*, **135**, 1213–5 **(468)**

Treiman, D. M. (1986) Epilepsy and violence: medical and legal issues. *Epilepsia*, 27, Suppl. 2 S77–S103 **(303)**

Treiman, D. M. and Delgado-Escueta, A. V. (1983) Violence and epilepsy: a critical review. In *Recent Advances in Epilepsy* vol. 1 (eds. T. A. Pedley & B. S. Meldrum) Churchill–Livingstone: London **(303)**

Trotter, T. (1788) Ebrietate ejusque effectibus in corporis humanun complectens. *MD Thesis* University of Edinburgh (unpublished) **(452)**

Tsai, M. and Wagner, M. (1978) Therapy groups for women, sexually molested as children. *Archives of Sexual Behavior*, **7**, 417–27 **(919)**

Tscholakov, K. (1947) *Basic Concepts in Forensic Psychopathology (Responsibility, Irresponsibility, Diminished Responsibility)*, Hudozhnick: Sofia (in Bulgarian) **(134)**

Tuke, D. Hack (1892) *A Dictionary of Psychological Medicine*, Churchill: London **(417)**

Tunks, E. R. and Dermer, S. W. (1977) Carbamazepine in the dyscontrol syndrome associated with limbic system dysfunction. *Journal of Nervous and Mental Disease*, **164**, 56–63 **(663)**

Tupin, J. P., Smith, D. B., Clanon, T. L., Kim, L. I., Nugent, A. and Groupe, A. (1973) The long-term use of lithium in aggressive prisoners. *Comprehensive Psychiatry*, **14**, 311–7 **(662)**

Turner, T. H. and Tofler, D. S. (1986) Indicators of psychiatric disorder among women admitted to prison. *British Medical Journal*, **292**, 651–3 **(615)**

Tutt, N. (1971) The subnormal offender. *British Journal of Mental Subnormality*, **17**, 42–7 **(320, 323)**

Tutt, N. (1981) A decade of policy. *British Journal of Criminology*, **21**, 246–56 **(218)**

Tutt, N. (1985) Attendance centres—should the police role be extended? In *Periodic Restriction of Liberty* (eds. R. Shaw and R. Hutchinson) Cropwood Conference Series No. 17, University of Cambridge, Institute of Criminology: Cambridge **(227)**

Tutt, N. and Giller, H. (1987) 'Manifesto for Mangement'; the elimination of custody. *Justice of the Peace*, **28**, 200–2 **(216)**

Tyhurst, J. S. (1951) Individual reactions to community disaster. The natural history of psychiatric phenomena. *American Journal of Psychiatry*, **107**, 764–9 **(896)**

Tyrer, P. (1988) Synthesis and prospectus. In *Personality Disorders, Diagnosis, Management and Course* (ed. P. Tyrer) Wright: London **(374)**

Tyrer, P. and Alexander, J. (1979) Classification of personality disorder. *British Journal of Psychiatry*, **135**, 163–7 **(378)**

UK Health Departments (1990) *Guidance for Clinical Health Care Workers: Protection Against Infection with HIV and Hepatitis Viruses*, HMSO: London **(818)**

Undeutsch, V. (1982) Statement reality analysis. In *Reconstructing the Past: The Role of Psychologists in Criminal Trials* (ed. A. Trankell) Norstedt & Soners: Stockholm **(942)**

United Nations Economic and Social Council (1988) *Report of the Sessional Working Group on the Question of Persons Detained on the Grounds of Mental Ill Health* (Chairman Mrs C. Palley), Commission on Human Rights E/CN4/Sub.2/1988/22, Strasbourg **(146)**

US Delegation to Assess Recent Changes in Soviet Psychiatry (1989) Report. *Schizophrenia Bulletin NIMH* Supplement to Vol. 15, No. 4 **(859)**

US Public Health Service (1972) *Surgeon General's Scientific Advisory Committee on Television and Social Behavior: Television and Growing Up. The Impact of Televised Violence: Report to the Surgeon General*, Government Printing Office: Washington DC **(496, 497)**

Vaillant, G. E. (1983) *The Natural History of Alcoholism*, Harvard University Press: Cambridge, MASS **(254)**

Vaillant, G. E. and Milofsky, M. S. (1982) Natural history of male alcoholism. IV Paths to recovery. *Archives of General Psychiatry*, **39**, 127–33 **(441)**

Valenstein, E. S. (1976) Brain stimulation and the origin of violent behaviour. In *Issues in Brain/Behaviour Control* (eds. W. L. Smith and A. Kling) Spectrum: New York **(496)**

Valente, D., Cassini, M., Pigliapochi, M. and Vansetti, G. (1981) Hair as the sample in assessing morphine and cocaine addiction. *Clinical Chemistry*, **27**, 1952–3 (letter) **(468)**

Valzelli, L. (1981) Psychopharmacology of aggression: an overview. *International Pharmacopsychiatry*, **16**, 39–48 **(660)**

van der Kolk, B. A. (1983) Psychopharmacological issues in post-traumatic stress disorder. *Hospital and Community Psychiatry*, **34**, 683–91 **(937)**

van der Kolk, B. A. and Greenberg, M. S. (1987) The psychobiology of the trauma response: hyperarousal, constitution, and addiction to traumatic response. In *Psychological Trauma* (ed. B. A. van der Kolk) American Psychiatric Press: Washington DC **(937)**

van der Kolk, B., Greenberg, M., Boyd, H. and Krystal, J. (1985) Inescapable shock, neurotransmitters and addiction to trauma: toward a psychobiology of post-traumatic stress. *Biological Psychiatry*, **20**, 314–25 **(889, 930, 932)**

van Dusen, K. T., Mednick, S. A., Gabrielli, W. F. and Hutchings, B. (1983) Social class and crime in an adoption cohort. *Journal of Criminal Law and Criminology*, **74**, 249–69 **(271)**

van Krevelen, D. A. (1971) Early infantile autism and autistic psychopathy. *Journal of Autism and Childhood Schizophrenia*, **1**, 82–6 **(394)**

van Loon, F. G. H. (1927) Amok and latah. *Journal of Abnormal Social Psychology*, **21**, 434–44 **(433)**

van Praag, H. M. (1986) Affective disorders and aggression disorders: evidence for a common biological mechanism. *Suicide and Life-Threatening Behavior*, **16**, 103–32 **(666)**

van Putten, T. (1973) Milieu therapy: contraindications? *Archives of General Psychiatry*, **29**, 640–3 **(655)**

van Putten, T. and Emory, W. H. (1973) Traumatic neuroses in Vietnam returnees. *Archives of General Psychiatry*, **29**, 695–8 **(932)**

van Putten, T., Mutalipassi, L. R. and Malkin, M. D. (1974) Phenothiazine-induced decompensation. *Archives of General Psychiatry*, **30**, 102–5 **(663)**

van Putten, T. and Sanders, D. G. (1975) Lithium in treatment failures. *Journal of Nervous & Mental Disease*, **161**, 255–64 **(664)**

Vandersall, T. A. and Wiener, J. M. (1970) Children who set fires. *Archives of General Psychiatry*, **22**, 63–71 **(596)**

Vaughn, C. E. and Leff, J. P. (1976) The influence of family and social factors on the course of psychiatric illnesses. *British Journal of Psychiatry*, **129**, 125–37 **(367)**

Vauhkonen, K. (1968) On the pathogenesis of morbid jealousy. *Acta Psychiatrica Scandinavica*, Suppl. 202 **(352)**

Veronen, L. J. and Kilpatrick, D. G. (1983) Stress management for rape victims. In *Stress Reduction and Prevention* (eds. D. Meichenbaum and M. Jarenko) Plenum Press: New York **(938, 939)**

Vestergaard, J. (1984) The Danish Mental Health Act of 1938: 'progressive' psychiatric paternalism revised. *International Journal of Law and Psychiatry*, **7**, 441–53 **(151)**

Victor, M. (1966) Treatment of alcoholic intoxication and the withdrawal syndrome. *Psychosomatic Medicine*, **28**, 636–50 **(444)**

Victor, R. G. and Krug, C. M. (1967) 'Paradoxical intention' in the treatment of compulsive gambling. *American Journal of Psychotherapy*, **21**, 808–14 **(487)**

Vingilis, E. (1981) A literature review of the young drinking offender. Is he a problem drinker? *British Journal of Addiction*, **76**, 27–46 **(452)**

Virkkunen, M. (1974) a. Observation on violence in schizophrenia; b. on arson committed by schizophrenics. *Acta Psychiatrica Scandinavica*, **50**, 145–60 (**336, 370**)

Visher, C. A. and Roth, J. A. (1986) Participation in criminal careers. In *Criminal Careers and 'Career Criminals'*, vol. 1 (eds. A. Blumstein, J. Cohen, J. A. Roth and C. A. Visher) National Academy Press: Washington DC (**275**)

Visintainer, M. A., Volpicelli, J. R. and Seligman, M. E. P. (1982) Tumor rejection in rats after inescapable or escapable shock. *Science*, **216**, 437–9 (**933**)

Volberg, R. A. and Steadman, H. J. (1988) Refining prevalence estimates of pathological gambling. *American Journal of Psychiatry*, **145**, 502–5 (**482, 485**)

Volkow, N. D. and Tancredi, L. (1987) Neural substrates for violent behaviour. *British Journal of Psychiatry*, **151**, 668–73 (**289**)

Voss, H. L. (1966) Socio-economic status and reported delinquent behaviour. *Social Problems*, **13**, 314–24 (**277**)

Voss, H. L. and Hepburn, J. R. (1968) Patterns in criminal homicide in Chicago. *Journal of Criminal Law, Criminology and Police Science*, **59**, 499–508 (**920**)

Wadeson, H. and Carpenter, W. T. (1976) Impact of the seclusion room experience. *Journal of Nervous and Mental Disease*, **163**, 318–28 (**660**)

Wadsworth, M. (1979) *Roots of Delinquency*, Martin Robertson: London (**254, 264, 271**)

Wagstaff, G. F. (1982) Hypnosis and witness recall: discussion paper. *Journal of the Royal Society of Medicine*, **75**, 793–8 (**943**)

Wahl, C. W. (1956) Some antecedent factors in the family histories of 568 male schizophrenics of the United States Navy. *American Journal of Psychiatry*, **113**, 201–10 (**366**)

Wald, M. S. (1982) State intervention on behalf of endangered children—a proposed legal response. *Child Abuse and Neglect*, **6**, 3–45 (**919**)

Walker, D. M. (1980) *The Oxford Companion to Law*, Clarendon: Oxford (**22**)

Walker, N. (1965) *Crime and Punishment in Britain*, Edinburgh University Press: Edinburgh (**616**)

Walker, N. (1968) *Crime and Insanity in England*, vol. 1: *The Historical Perspective*, Edinburgh University Press: Edinburgh (**45, 48, 49, 50, 51, 60, 309, 317**)

Walker, N. (1977) *Behaviour and Misbehaviour: Explanations and Non-Explanations*, Blackwell: Oxford (**602**)

Walker, N. (1985) *Sentencing, Theory, Law and Practice*, Butterworths: London (**67, 75, 76, 174**)

Walker, N. (1987) The unwanted effects of long-term imprisonment. In *Problems of Long-Term Imprisonment* (eds. A. C. Bottoms and R. Wright) Gower: Aldershot (**803**)

Walker, N., Farrington, D. P. and Tucker, G. (1981) Reconviction rates of adult males after different sentences. *British Journal of Criminology*, **21**, 357–60 (**785**)

Walker, N. and McCabe, S. (1973) *Crime and Insanity in England*, Vol. 2: *New Solutions and New Problems*, Edinburgh University Press: Edinburgh (**317–324 passim, 357, 358, 360, 756**)

Walker, P. N. (1972) *Punishment, an Illustrated History*, David & Charles: Newton Abbott (**795**)

Wallace, A. (1986) *Homicide—The Social Reality*, Bureau of Crime Statistics and Research, Attorney General's Department, Sydney: New South Wales (**612**)

Wallace, A. F. C. (1956) Tornado in Worcester: an exploratory study of individual and community behavior in an extreme situation. *Disaster Study No. 3*, National Academy of Sciences, National Research Council: Washington DC (cited in Weil, 1973) (**923**)

Wallach, A. and Rubin, L. (1972) The premenstrual syndrome and criminal responsibility. *UCLA Law Review*, **19**, 209–312 (**607**)

Wallach, M. A., Kogan, N. and Bem, D. J. (1964) Group influence on individual risk taking. *Journal of Abnormal and Social Psychology*, **68**, 263–74 (**579**)

Waller, I. and Okihiro, N. (1978) *Burglary: The Victim and the Public*, University of Toronto Press: Toronto (**908**)

Waller, J. A. (1965) Chronic medical conditions and traffic safety. *New England Journal of Medicine*, **273**, 1413–20 (**582**)

Waller, J. A. (1967) Cardiovascular disease, aging and traffic accidents. *Journal of Chronic Disease*, **20**, 615–20 (**584**)

Waller, J. A. (1973) *Medical Impairment to Driving*, Thomas: Springfield, IL. (**582**)

Wallis, C. P. and Maliphant, R. (1967) Delinquent areas in the county of London: ecological factors. *British Journal of Criminology*, **7**, 250–84 (**273**)

Walmsley, R. (1986) *Personal Violence*, Home Office Research Study No. 89, HMSO: London **(499, 501, 808)**

Walmsley, R. and White, K. (1979) *Sexual Offences, Consent and Sentencing*, Home Office Research Study No. 54, HMSO: London **(532, 540)**

Ward, B. A. (1986) Competency for execution: problems in law and psychiatry. *Florida State University Law Review*, **14**, 35–107 **(122)**

Ward, D. A. and Kassebaum, G. G. (1966) *Women's Prisons*, Weidenfeld & Nicholson: London **(618)**

Ward, M. E., Saklad, S. R. and Ereshefsky, L. (1986) Lorazepam for the treatment of psychotic agitation. *American Journal of Psychiatry*, **143**, 1195–6 **(661)**

'Warmark' (1931) *Guilty but Insane: A Broadmoor Autobiography*, Chapman & Hall: London **(697)**

Warner, R. (1978) The diagnosis of anti-social and hysterical personality disorders. *Journal of Nervous and Mental Disease*, **166**, 839–45 **(378)**

Warren, M. Q. (1969) The case for differential treatment of delinquents. *Annals of the American Academy of Political and Social Science*, **381**, 47–59 **(400)**

Washbrook, R. A. H. (1977) Alcoholism versus crime in Birmingham, England. *International Journal of Offender Therapy and Comparative Criminology*, **21**, 166–73 **(443, 447)**

Wasik, M. (1982) Cumulative provocation and domestic killings. *Criminal Law Review*, 29–38 **(353)**

Watkins, L. (1976) *The Sleepwalk Killers*, Everest Books: London **(309)**

Watson, C. G., Kucala, T., Manifold, V., Vassar, P. and Juba, M. (1988) Differences between post-traumatic stress disorder patients with delayed and undelayed onsets. *Journal of Nervous & Mental Disease*, **176**, 568–72 **(902)**

Watson, J. B. (1913) Psychology as the behaviorist views it. *Psychological Review*, **20**, 158–77 **(670)**

Watson, J. B. (1924) *Behaviorism*, Norton: New York **(670)**

Watson, J. B. and Raynor, R. (1920) Conditioned emotional reactions. *Journal of Experimental Psychology*, **3**, 1–14 **(670)**

Watson, J. M. (1977) Glue sniffing in profile. *The Practitioner*, **218**, 255–9 **(466)**

Watson, J. M. (1986) *Solvent Abuse: The Adolescent Epidemic*, Croom Helm: London **(466)**

Watts, F. N. and Sharrock, R. (1985) Concentration problems in depression. *Psychological Medicine*, **15**, 317–26 **(582)**

Waxman, D. (1983) Use of hypnosis in criminology: discussion paper. *Journal of the Royal Society of Medicine*, **76**, 480–4 **(943)**

Weaver, S. M., Armstrong, N. E., Broome, A. K. and Stewart, L. (1978a) Behavioural principles applied to a security ward. *Nursing Times*, **5**, 22–4 **(651, 656)**

Weaver, S. M., Broome, A. K. and Kat, B. J. B. (1978b) Some patterns of disturbed behaviour in a closed ward environment. *Journal of Advanced Nursing*, **3**, 251–63 **(651, 656)**

Webb, D. and Harris, R. (1984) Social workers and the supervision order: a case of occupational uncertainty. *British Journal of Social Work*, **14**, 579–99 **(228)**

Wehrspann, W. H., Steinhauer, P. D. and Klajner-Diamond, H. (1987) Criteria and methodology for assessing credibility of sexual abuse allegations. *Canadian Journal of Psychiatry*, **32**, 615–23 **(942)**

Weil, R. J. (1973) Psychiatric aspects of disaster. In *World Biennial of Psychiatry and Psychotherapy*, vol. 2 (ed. S. Arienti) Basic Books: New York **(890)**

Weiner, B. A. (1985) The insanity defense: historical development and present state. *Behavioral Sciences and the Law*, **3**, 3–36 **(49, 278)**

Weiner, H. and Braiman, A. (1955) The Ganser Syndrome. *American Journal of Psychiatry*, **111**, 767–74 **(425, 426)**

Weiner, I. B. (1980) Psychopathology in adolescence. In *Handbook of Adolescent Psychology* (ed. J. Adelson) Wiley: New York **(580)**

Weinstock, R. (1988a) Confidentiality and the new duty to protect: the therapist's dilemma. *Hospital and Community Psychiatry*, **39**, 607–9 **(880)**

Weinstock, R. (1988b) Controversial ethical issues in forensic psychiatry: a survey. *Journal of Forensic Science*, **33**, 176–86 **(865)**

Weisaeth, L. (1989) Individual and organisational responses to disaster. Presented to VIII World Congress of Psychiatry, Athens. *Excerpta Medica International Congress Series*, 899 P706 No. 2743: Amsterdam **(898)**

Weiss, G. and Hechtman, L. T. (1986) *Hyperactive Children Grown Up*, Guilford Press: New York **(262)**

Weiss, J., Rogers, E., Darwin, M. R. and Dutton, C. E. (1955) A study of girl sex victims. *Psychiatric Quarterly*, **29**, 1–27 **(918)**

Weiss, J. W. A., Lamberti, J. W. and Blackman, N. (1960) The sudden murderer. *Archives of General Psychiatry*, **2**, 669–78 **(363)**

Weleminsky, J. and Birley, J. (1990) Mental Health Act 1983. Correspondence between the President and the Director of the National Schizophrenia Fellowship. *Psychiatric Bulletin*, **14**, 235–6 **(31)**

Wells, G. L. and Loftus, E. F. (1984) *Eyewitness Testimony: Psychological Perspectives*, Cambridge University Press: Cambridge **(291)**

Werner, E. E. (1987) Vulnerability and resiliency in children at risk for delinquency: a longitudinal study from birth to young adulthood. In *Prevention of Delinquent Behavior* (eds. J. D. Burchard and S. N. Burchard) Sage: Beverley Hills, CA, **(255)**

Werner, E. E. and Smith, R. A. (1982) *Vulnerable but Invincible*, McGraw-Hill: New York **(255)**

Werner, P. D., Rose, T. and Yesavage, J. (1983) Reliability, accuracy, and decision-making strategy in clinical predictions of imminent dangerousness. *Journal of Consulting and Clinical Psychology*, **51**, 815–25 **(644, 804)**

Werner, P. D., Rose, T. L., Yesavage, J. A. and Seeman, K. (1984) Psychiatrists' judgements of dangerousness in patients on an acute care unit. *American Journal of Psychiatry*, **141**, 263–6 **(344)**

Wessely, S. and Taylor, P. J. (1991) Madness and crime: criminology versus psychiatry. *Criminal Behaviour and Mental Health*, **1**, 193–228 **(332)**

Wessely, S., Buchanan, A., Reed, A., Taylor, P. J., Garety, P. and Everitt, B. (in press) Acting on delusions. *British Journal of Psychiatry* **(341, 343)**

West, D. J. (1965) *Murder Followed by Suicide*, Heinemann: London **(347, 363, 516)**

West, D. J. (1968) A note on murders in Manhattan. *Medicine, Science and the Law*, **8**, 249–55 **(363, 899)**

West, D. J. (1969) *Present Conduct and Future Delinquency*, Heinemann: London **(322)**

West, D. J. (1982) *Delinquency: Its Roots, Careers and Prospects*, Heinemann: London **(265, 450, 451)**

West, D. J. (1985) (ed.) *Sexual Victimisation*, Gower: Aldershot **(533)**

West, D. J. and Farrington, D. P. (1973) *Who Becomes Delinquent?* Heinemann: London **(255, 259, 264, 267, 272, 322)**

West, D. J. and Farrington, D. P. (1977) *The Delinquent Way of Life*, Heinemann: London **(255, 263, 264, 266, 267, 322, 489)**

West, D. J., Roy, C., and Nichols, F. L. (1978) *Understanding Sexual Attacks*, Heinemann: London **(552)**

West, D. J., and Walk, A. (1977) *Daniel McNaughton, his Trial and the Aftermath*, Gaskell Books: London **(48)**

Westermeyer, J. (1973) On the epidemicity of amok violence. *Archives of General Psychiatry*, **28**, 873–6 **(433)**

Westermeyer, J. (1982) Amok. In *Extraordinary Disorders of Human Behavior*. (eds. C. T. H. Friedmann and R. A. Fauget) Plenum Press: New York **(432, 434)**

Westmore, B. (1988) The law and the mentally ill person: Britain, Australia and other international comparisons. *Current Opinion in Psychiatry*, **1**, 700–4 **(726)**

Weston, W. R. (1987) *Jarvis's Probation Officers' Manual*, Butterworth: London **(184, 776)**

Wettstein, R. M. (1989) Involuntary administration of psychotropic drugs: the case against requiring prior court review. *Hospital Law Newsletter*, **6**, 3–7 **(153)**

Wettstein, R. M. and Mulvey, E. P. (1988) Disposition of insanity acquittees in Illinois. *Bulletin of the American Academy of Psychiatry and the Law* **16**, 11–24 **(144)**

Wexler, H. K. and De Leon, G. (1977) The therapeutic community: multivariate prediction of retention. *American Journal of Drug and Alcohol Abuse*, **4**, 145–51 **(477)**

Whatmore, P. (1987) Barlinnie Special Unit: an insider's view. In *Problems of Long-Term Imprisonment* (eds. A. Bottoms and R. Wright) Gower: Aldershot **(752, 753)**

Whitam, F. L. and Mathy, R. M. (1986) *Male Homosexuality in Four Societies*, Praeger: New York **(540)**

White, G. L. and Mullen, P. E. *Jealousy, Theory, Research and Clinical Strategies*, Guildford Press: New York **(351)**

White, R., Carr, P. and Lowe, N. (1990) *A Guide to the Children Act 1989*, HMSO: London **(239)**

White, R. A. C. (1985) *The Administration of Justice*, Blackwell: Oxford **(168, 170, 173, 174, 178, 179)**

White, S. (1991) Insanity defences and magistrates courts *Criminal Law Review* 501–9 **(59)**

Whitehurst, R. N. (1971) Violently jealous husbands. *Sexual Behaviour*, **1**, 32–47 **(352)**

Whiteley, J. S. (1970) The response of psychopaths to a therapeutic community. *British Journal of Psychiatry*, **116**, 517–29 **(688)**

Whiteley, J. S. (1986) Sociotherapy and psychotherapy in the treatment of personality disorder: discussion paper. *Journal of the Royal Society of Medicine*, **79**, 721–5 **(685, 686)**

Whitlock, F. A. (1963) *Criminal Responsibility and Mental Illness*, Butterworth: London **(44, 60)**

Whitlock, F. A. (1967) The Ganser Syndrome. *British Journal of Psychiatry*, **113**, 19–29 **(426)**

Whitlock, F. A. (1981) Some observations on the meaning of confabulation. *British Journal of Medical Psychology*, **54**, 213–8 **(411)**

Whitman, S., Coleman, T., Berg, B., King, L. and Desai, B. (1980) Epidemiological insights into the socioeconomic correlates of epilepsy. In *A Multidisciplinary Handbook of Epilepsy* (ed. B. P. Herman) Thomas: Springfield, IL **(301, 514)**

Whitman, S., Coleman, T. E., Patmon, C., Desai, B. T., Cohen, R. and King, L. N. (1984) Epilepsy in prison: elevated prevalence and no relationship to violence. *Neurology*, **34**, 775–82 **(301, 514)**

Widiger, T. A. and Frances A. (1985) The DSM–III personality disorders: perspectives from psychology. *Archives of General Psychiatry*, **42**, 615–23 **(377, 378)**

Wiepert, G. D., d'Orbán, P. T. and Bewley, T. H. (1979) Delinquency by opiate addicts treated at two London clinics. *British Journal of Psychiatry*, **134**, 14–23 **(609)**

Wiersma, A. D., Giel, R., de Jong, A. and Slooff, C. J. (1983) Social class and schizophrenia in a Dutch cohort. *Psychological Medicine*, **13**, 141–50 **(368)**

Wikstrom, P. O. (1987) *Patterns of Crime in a Birth Cohort*, University of Stockholm Department of Sociology: Stockholm **(254)**

Wilkey, I., Pearn, J., Petrie, G. and Nixon, J. (1982) Neonaticide, infanticide and child homicide. *Medicine, Science and the Law*, **22**, 31–4 **(612)**

Wilkins, A. J. (1985) Attempted infanticide. *British Journal of Psychiatry*, **146**, 206–8 **(50)**

Wilkins, J. and Coid, J. (1991) Self-mutilation in female remanded prisoners. 1. An indication of severe psychopathology. *Criminal Behaviour & Mental Health*, **1**, 247–67 **(617)**

Wilkinson, C. B. (1983) Aftermath of a disaster. The collapse of the Hyatt Regency Hotel Skywalks. *American Journal of Psychiatry*, **140**, 1134–9 **(923)**

Williams, A. (1976) The design of security units, engineering considerations. *Hospital Engineering*, 6–14 **(712)**

Williams, D. (1969) Neural factors related to habitual aggression. *Brain*, **92**, 503–20 **(288)**

Williams, E. and Holmes, K. A. (1981) *The Second Assault: Rape and Public Attitudes*, Greenwood Press: Westpoint, Conn. **(916)**

Williams, G. L. (1965) *The Mental Element in Crime*, Hebrew University: Jerusalem **(65)**

Williams, G. L. (1978) *Textbook of Criminal Law*, Stevens & Sons: London **(353)**

Williams, J. E. H. (1970) *The English Penal System in Transition*, Butterworth: London **(795)**

Williams, J. R. and Gold, M. (1972) From delinquent behavior to official delinquency. *Social Problems*, **20**, 209–29 **(271, 276)**

Williams, K. (1983) *Community Resources for Victims of Crime*, Home Office Research and Planning Unit Paper 14, Home Office: London **(936)**

Williamson, S., Hare, R. and Wong, S. (1987) Violence: criminal psychopaths and their victims. *Canadian Journal of Behavioral Science*, **19**, 454–62 **(642)**

Wilmanns, K. (1940) Über Morde in Prodromalstadium der Schizophrenie. *Zeit Neurologie*, **170**, 583–662 **(346, 357)**

Wilson, G., Rupp, C. and Wilson, W. W. (1950) Amnesia. *American Journal of Psychiatry*, **106**, 481–5 **(295)**

Wilson, G. D. (1978) *The Secrets of Sexual Fantasy*, Dent: London **(555)**

Wilson, G. D. (1987) An ethological approach to sexual deviation. In *Variant Sexuality: Research and Theory* (ed. G. D. Wilson) Johns Hopkins University Press: Baltimore **(523)**

Wilson, J. P. and Zigelbaum, S. D. (1983) The Vietnam veteran on trial: the relation of post-traumatic stress disorder to criminal behavior. *Behavioral Sciences and the Law*, **1**, 69–83 **(929)**

Wilson, J. Q. and Herrnstein, R. J. (1985) *Crime and Human Nature*, Simon & Schuster: New York (**253, 258, 259, 268, 277**)

Wilson, P. (1973) *Children Who Kill*, Michael Joseph: London (**517**)

Wilson, R. (1980) Who will care for the mad and bad? *Corrections Magazine*, **6**, 5–17 (**766**)

Wing, J. K. (1962) Institutionalism in mental hospitals. *British Journal of Social and Clinical Psychology*, **1**, 38–51 (**796**)

Wing, J. K. (1978) *Reasoning about Madness*, Oxford University Press: Oxford (**9**)

Wing, J. K. (1990) The functions of asylum. *British Journal of Psychiatry*, **157**, 822–7 (**797**)

Wing, J. K. and Brown, G. W. (1970) *Institutions and Schizophrenia*, Cambridge University Press: Cambridge (**654, 796–7**)

Wing, J. K., Cooper, J. E. and Sartorius, N. (1974) *The Measurement and Classification of Psychiatric Symptoms*, Cambridge University Press: Cambridge (**341**)

Wing, L. (1981) Asperger's Syndrome: a clinical account. *Psychological Medicine*, **11**, 115–29 (**314, 395**)

Winnicott, D. W. (1965) *The Maturational Processes and the Facilitating Environment*, Hogarth Press: London (**685**)

Winokur, G. (1972) Depression spectrum disease: description and family study. *Comprehensive Psychiatry*, **13**, 3–8 (**366**)

Winokur, G., Reich, T. and Rimmer, J. (1970) Alcoholism III: diagnosis and familial psychiatric illness in 259 alcoholic probands. *Archives of General Psychiatry*, **23**, 104–111 (**366, 484**)

Winokur, G., Rimmer, J. and Reich, T. (1971) Alcoholism IV: Is there more than one type of alcoholism? *British Journal of Psychiatry*, **118**, 525–31 (**445**)

Witkin, H. A., Sarnoff, A. M., Schulringer, F., Bakkestrom, E., Christiansen, K. D., Goodenough, D. R., Hirschhorn, K., Lundsteen, C., Owen, D., Philip, J., Rubin, D. B. and Stocking, M. (1976) Criminality in XYY and XXY men. *Science*, **193**, 547–55 (**315**)

Wolf, A. S. (1980) Homicide and blackouts in Alaskan natives. *Journal of Studies on Alcohol*, **41**, 456–62 (**63, 443**)

Wolf, M. S. (1977) A review of literature of milieu therapy. *Journal of Psychiatric Nursing*, **15**, 7–12 (**656**)

Wolf, S. and Ripley, H. S. (1947) Reactions among allied prisoners of war subjected to three years of imprisonment and torture by the Japanese. *American Journal of Psychiatry*, **104**, 180–93 (**925**)

Wolff, S. (1984a) Schizoid personality. In *Mental Retardation and Developmental Disabilities*, vol. 13 (ed. J. Wortis) Plenum Publishing: New York (**395**)

Wolff, S. (1984b) personal communication (**396**)

Wolff, S. (1985) Non-delinquent disturbances of conduct. In *Child and Adolescent Psychiatry— Modern Approaches*, 2nd edn (eds. M. Rutter and L. Hersov) Blackwell: Oxford (**570**)

Wolfgang, M. E. (1958a) *Patterns of Criminal Homicide*, University of Pennsylvania Press: Philadelphia (**339, 512, 609, 919**)

Wolfgang, M. E. (1958b) An analysis of homicide-suicide. *Journal of Clinical and Experimental Psychopathology*, **19**, 208–18 (**516**)

Wolfgang, M. E. (1980) Some new findings from the longitudinal study of crime. *Australian Journal of Forensic Sciences*, **13**, 12–29 (**257**)

Wolfgang, M. E., Figlio, R. M. and Sellin, T. (1972) *Delinquency in a Birth Cohort*, University of Chicago Press: Chicago (**255, 259, 275**)

Wolfgang, M. E. and Strohm, R. B. (1956) The relationship between alcohol and criminal homicide. *Quarterly Journal of Studies in Alcohol*, **17**, 411–25 (**447, 514**)

Wolfgang, M. E., Thornberry, T. P. and Figlio, R. M. (1987) *From Boy to Man, from Delinquency to Crime*. University of Chicago Press: Chicago (**255, 256, 257, 275**)

Wolkind, S. (1988) Emotional signs. *The Journal of Social Welfare* 82–7 (**834**)

Wolpe, J. (1973) *The Practice of Behavior Therapy*, Pergamon Press: Oxford (**669**)

Woodside, M. (1962) Instability in women prisoners. *Lancet*, **ii**, 928–30 (**614**)

Woodside, M., Harrow, A., Basson, J. V. and Affleck, J. W. (1976) Experiment in managing sociopathic behaviour disorders. *British Medical Journal*, **2**, 1056–9 (**722**)

Woodward, M. (1955) The role of low intelligence in delinquency. *British Journal of Delinquency*, **5**, 281–303 (**321**)

Woody, G. E., Luborsky, L., McLellan, A. T., O'Brien, C. P., Beck, A. T., Blaine, J., Herman, I. and Hole, A. (1983) Psychotherapy for opiate addicts: does it help? *Archives of General Psychiatry*, **40**, 639–45 (**469**)

Woolf, Lord Justice, and Tumim, S. (1991) *Prison Disturbances, April 1990* Cmnd.1456, HMSO: London **(809, 820)**

Woolley, P. V. and Evans, W. A. (1955) Significance of skeletal lesions in infants resembling those of traumatic origin. *Journal of the American Medical Association*, **158**, 539–43 **(911)**

World Health Organisation (1975) *Health Aspects of Avoidable Maltreatment of Prisoners and Detainees. Evidence presented to the Fifth United Nations Congress on the Prevention of Crime and Treatment of Offenders*, World Health Organisation: Geneva **(119, 872)**

World Health Organisation (1977) *Forensic Psychiatry. Report of a Working Group, Sienna 1975* WHO: Copenhagen **(120)**

World Health Organisation (1978) *Mental Disorders: Glossary and Guide to their Classification in Accordance with the Ninth Revision of the International Classification of Diseases*, WHO: Geneva **(484, 694, 745)**

World Health Organisation (1987a) Consultation on prevention and control of AIDS in prison. *Lancet*, **ii**, 1263–4 **(479)**

World Health Organisation (1987b) *Report of the Meeting on Criteria for HIV Screening Programmes*, WHO: Geneva **(479, 875)**

World Health Organisation (1992) *The classification of Mental and Behavioural Disorders, ICD 10*, WHO: Geneva **(387)**

World Health Organisation Expert Committee on Mental Health (1975) *Organisation of Mental Health Services in Developing Countries: Technical Report Series 564*, WHO: Geneva **(119)**

World Health Organisation Working Party (1978) *The Future of Mental Hospitals*, WHO: Copenhagen **(362)**

World Psychiatric Association Team (1991) *Report of the Visit to the Soviet Union* (private circulation) **(859)**

Wright, M. (1984) The impact of victim/offender mediation on the assumptions and procedures of criminal justice. *Victimology*, **10**, 631–45 **(944)**

Wright, S. G. (1986) *Building and Using a Model of Nursing*, Edward Arnold: London **(652)**

Wulach, J. S. (1983) Mania and crime: a study of 100 manic defendants. *Bulletin of the American Academy of Psychiatry and the Law*, **11**, 69–75 **(348)**

Wyatt, G. E. (1985) The sexual abuse of Afro-American and White American women in childhood. *Child Abuse and Neglect*, **9**, 507–19 **(917)**

Yap, P. M. (1969) The culture bound reactive syndromes. In *Mental Health Research in Asia and the Pacific* (eds. W. Candill and T-y Lin) East-West Center Press: Honolulu **(432)**

Yarnell, H. (1940) Firesetting in children. *American Journal of Orthopsychiatry*, **10**, 272–86 **(589, 590, 596)**

Yassa, R. and Dupont, D. (1983) Carbamazepine in the treatment of aggressive behaviour in schizophrenic patients: a case report. *Canadian Journal of Psychiatry*, **28**, 566–8 **(664)**

Yates, A. (1982) children eroticised by incest. *American Journal of Psychiatry*, **139**, 482–5 **(918)**

Yates, A. (1988) Anatomically correct dolls: should they be used as the basis for expert testimony?—Affirmation. *Journal of the American Academy of Child and Adolescent Psychiatry*, **27**, 254–5 **(942)**

Yates, R. (1981) *Out from the Shadows—Report of Ten years of the Life Line Project*, National Association for the Care and Rehabilitation of Offenders: London **(477)**

Yates, R. (1985) Addiction: an everyday 'disease'. In *Approaches to Addiction* (eds. J. Lishman, and G. Horobin) Kogan-Page: London **(456)**

Yellowlees, D. (1878) Homicide by a somnambulist. *Journal of Mental Sciences*, **24**, 451–8 **(309)**

Yeudall, L. T., Fromm-Auch, D. and Davies, P. (1982) Neuropsychological impairment of persistent delinquency. *Journal of Nervous and Mental Disease*, **170**, 257–65 **(289)**

Yorkston, N. J., Zaki, S. A., Pitcher, D. R., Gruzelier, J. H., Hollander, D. and Sergeant, H. G. S. (1977) Propranolol as an adjunct to the treatment of schizophrenia. *Lancet*, **ii**, 575–8 **(664)**

Young, T., Lawson, G. and Gacono, C. (1987) Clinical aspects of phencyclidine (PCP). *International Journal of Addictions*, **22**, 1–15 **(474)**

Yudofsky, S., Williams, D. and Gorman, J. (1981) Propranolol in the treatment of rage and violent behavior in patients with chronic brain syndromes. *American Journal of Psychiatry*, **138**, 218–20 **(662)**

Yuille, J. C. (1987) *The Effects of Alcohol and Marijuana on Eyewitness Recall*. Paper presented at Conference on Practical Aspects of Memory, Swansea: UK (unpublished) **(297)**

Yuille, J. C. and Cutshall, J. L. (1986) A case study of eye-witness memory of a crime. *Journal of Applied Psychology*, **71**, 291–301 **(293, 297)**

Zacune, J. and Hensman, C. (1971) *Drugs, Alcohol and Tobacco in Britain*, Heinemann: London (**448**)

Zang K. D., and Leyking, B. (1981) *Der XYY Mann*, Thieme: Stuttgart (**314**)

Zarifian, E., Scatton, B., Bianchetti, G., Cuche, H., Loo, H. and Morselli, P. L. (1982) High doses of haloperidol in schizophrenia. *Archives of General Psychiatry*, **39**, 212–5 (**663**)

Zborowski, M. (1952) Cultural components in response to pain. *Journal of Social Issues*, **8**, 16–30 (**892**)

Zeeman, E. C., Hall, C. S., Harrison, P. J., Marriage, G. H. and Shapland, P. H. (1976) A model for institutional disturbances. *British Journal of Mathematical and Statistical Psychology*, **29**, 66–80 (**808**)

Zeiss, R. A. and Dickman, H. R. (1989) PTSD 40 years later: incidence and person-situation correlates in former POWs. *Journal of Clinical Psychology*, **45**, 80–7 (**903**)

Ziegenhagen, E. A. (1976) The recidivist victim of violent crime. *Victimology*, **1**, 538–50 (**900**)

Zillman, D. (1979) *Hostility and Aggression*, Erlbaum: Hillsdale (**494**)

Zimring, F. E. (1981) Kids, groups and crime: some implications of a well-known secret. *Journal of Criminal Law and Criminology*, **72**, 867–85 (**265**)

Zitrin, H., Hardesty, A. S. and Burdock, E. T. (1976) Crime and violence among mental patients. *American Journal of Psychiatry*, **133**, 142–9 (**333**)

Index